American Historic Inns™

Bed & Breakfasts
and
Country Inns

by Deborah Edwards Sakach

Published by

PO Box 669
Dana Point
California
92629-0669

Bed & Breakfasts and Country Inns

FRONT COVER:

Grand Victorian B&B Inn, Bellaire Michigan.
Photo by Don Rutt

BACK COVER:

The Keeper's House, Isle Au Haut, Maine
The White Oak Inn, Danville, Ohio
Scofield House B&B, Sturgeon Bay, Wis.
Photos by American Historic Inns
La Grande Maison, Broussard, La.
Photo by Allen Breaux
L'Auberge Provencale, White Post, Va.
Photo by Esther and Frank Schmidt

COVER DESIGN:
David Sakach

OPERATIONS MANAGER:
Sandy Imre

DATABASE ASSISTANTS:
Julie Mayer, Alex Murashko, Joyce Roll

EDITORIAL ASSISTANTS:
Tiffany Crosswy, Carol O'Connell, Lucy Poshek, Joshua Prizer, Stephen Sakach

PROGRAMMING AND CARTOGRAPHY:
Tim Sakach

DIGITAL SCANNING:
Andrew Lithgoe, James Lin

Publisher's Cataloging in Publication Data

Sakach, Deborah Edwards
American Historic Inns, Inc.
Bed & Breakfasts and Country Inns

1. Bed & Breakfast Accommodations - United States, Directories, Guide Books.
2. Travel - Bed & Breakfast Inns, Directories, Guide Books.
3. Bed & Breakfast Accommodations - Historic Inns, Directories, Guide Books.
4. Hotel Accommodations - Bed & Breakfast Inns, Directories, Guide Books.
5. Hotel Accommodations - United States, Directories, Guide Books.
I. Title. II. Author. III Bed & Breakfast, Bed & Breakfasts and Country Inns.

American Historic Inns is a trademark of American Historic Inns, Inc.

ISBN: 1-888050-01-2
Softcover
Printed in the United States of America.
10 9 8 7 6 5 4 3 2 1

Table Of Contents

How To Make A Reservation

1. **You must make ADVANCE reservations.** The FREE night offer is only valid by making reservations in advance directly with the participating lodging establishment AND when you identify yourself as having a Certificate from this guide.

2. **You must identify yourself FIRST as holding a Certificate from this guide, or the innkeeper is not obligated to honor the Certificate.**

3. All FREE nights are subject to availability. In some cases this may mean that the lodging establishment has rooms but is projecting that those rooms will be filled with full-fare customers. Most hotels consider they are at full occupancy when they are about 80% filled, and then cut off all reduced-fare programs at that time. Smaller properties such as Bed & Breakfast homes and Inns may use different formulas. Some set aside a specific number of rooms or suites for Certificate holders and then will not accept any more reservations for the promotion after those rooms are filled. Others will accept Certificate holders at the last minute when they project that they will have rooms available.

4. Try to obtain a confirmation number, confirmation letter or the name of the person taking your reservation.

5. If you have children or pets coming with you, or if you smoke, be sure to tell the innkeeper in advance. Most Bed & Breakfasts and Country Inns are non-smoking. Accommodations for children or pets may be limited or non-existent.

6. Understand the cancellation policy. A number of Bed & Breakfasts and Country Inns require a two-week or more notice of cancellation in order to refund your deposit. You should find out what the policy is at the same time you make your reservations.

7. **All holidays are excluded.** There may be other periods of time that are excluded as well.

8. This is a two-night minimum program and the two nights MUST BE CONSECUTIVE, i.e. "Monday and Tuesday," or "Sunday and Monday." You can stay longer, of course. Please read each inn's specific restrictions.

9. Always find out what meals, if any, are included in the rates and whether you will have to pay for meals. Not every establishment participating in this program provides a free breakfast.

10. Some locales require that bed tax be collected, even on FREE nights. If you have a question, check with the innkeeper, chamber of commerce or city hall serving the area in which you wish to stay.

11. For more information, request a brochure from participating Inns before you make your reservation.

12. Don't forget to take this book with the Certificate along with you.

The FREE night is given to you directly from the innkeeper in the hope that you or your friends will return and share your discovery with others. **The inns are not reimbursed by American Historic Inns, Inc.**

AMERICAN HISTORIC **INNS**
INCORPORATED

Certificate

∞ *redeemable for* ∞

One Free Night at a Bed & Breakfast or Country Inn

∞ ∞ ∞ ∞ ∞ ∞ ∞ ∞

Compliments of American Historic Inns, Inc. and participating Bed & Breakfasts and Country Inns.

This certificate entitles the bearer
to one free night at any one of the more
than 1,600 Bed & Breakfasts and Country Inns
included in this book when the bearer buys the
first night at the regular rate.
See back for requirements.

VOID IF DETACHED FROM BOOK OR ALTERED

AMERICAN HISTORIC INNS
INCORPORATED

This section should be completed by the innkeeper when the certificate is redeemed.
MAIL COMPLETED CERTIFICATE TO:
AMERICAN HISTORIC INNS, INC.
PO BOX 669, DANA POINT, CA 92629-0669

_____
Name of Guest

_____
Guest Home Address

_____
Guest City/State/Zip

_____
Guest Home Phone

_____
Name of Bed & Breakfast/Inn

_____
Signature of Innkeeper

৪০ ৪০ ৪০ ৪০ ৪০ ৪০ ৪০ ৪০

Certificate is good for one (1) free consecutive night when you purchase the first night at the regular rate. Offer not valid at all times. Contact inn in advance for availability, rates, reservations, meal plans, cancellation policies and other requirements. Offer valid only at participating inns featured in this Bed & Breakfast Guide. Not valid during holidays. Minimum 2-night stay. Certificate is for no more than two people and no more than one room. Other restrictions may apply. Bed tax, sales tax and gratuities not included. American Historic Inns, Inc. is not responsible for any changes in individual inn operation or policy. By use of this certificate, consumer agrees to release American Historic Inns, Inc. from any liability in connection with their travel to and stay at any participating Inn. This certificate may not be reproduced and cannot be used in conjunction with any other promotional offers. Certificate must be redeemed at participating inn by December 31, 1998. Void where prohibited.

Certificate Expires December 31, 1998

VOID IF DETACHED FROM BOOK OR ALTERED

How To Use This Book

You hold in your hands a delightful selection of America's best Bed & Breakfasts and Country Inns. The innkeeper of each property has generously agreed to participate in our FREE night program. **They are not reimbursed for the second night, but make it available to you in the hope that you will return to their inn or tell others about your stay.**

Most knowledgeable innkeepers enjoy sharing regional attractions, local folklore, history, and pointing out favorite restaurants and other special features of their areas. They have invested much of themselves in creating an experience for you to long remember. Many have personally renovated historic buildings, saving them from deterioration and often, the bulldozer. Others have infused their inns with a unique style and personality to enliven your experience with a warm and elegant environment. Your innkeepers are a tremendous resource. Treat them kindly and you will be well rewarded.

Accommodations

You'll find Bed & Breakfasts and Country Inns in converted schoolhouses, stone castles, lighthouses, 18th-century farmhouses, Queen Anne Victorians, adobe lodges and more.

Many are listed in the National Register of Historic Places and have preserved the stories and memorabilia from their participation in historical events such as the Revolutionary or Civil wars.

The majority of inns included in this book were built in the 17th, 18th and 19th centuries. We have stated the date each building was constructed at the beginning of each description.

No inn paid to be featured in this guidebook. All costs for the production of the book have been absorbed by American Historic Inns. The selection of inns for this guidebook was made as carefully as possible from among the many that wanted to be included. American Historic Inns, as publishers, produced and financed the project. Inns did not pay advertising fees to be in the book.

They did, however, agree to honor the certificate for the free night when the first night is purchased. We hope you enjoy the choices we made and we encourage you to suggest new inns that you discover.

A Variety of Inns

A COUNTRY INN generally serves both breakfast and dinner and may have a restaurant associated with it. Many have been in operation for years; some, since the 18th century as you will note in our "Inns of Interest" section. Although primarily found on the East Coast, a few Country Inns are in other regions of the nation.

A BED & BREAKFAST facility's primary focus is lodging. It can have from three to 20 rooms or more. The innkeepers usually live on the premises. Breakfast is the only meal served and can be a full-course, gourmet breakfast or a simple buffet. Many B&B owners pride themselves on their culinary skills.

As with Country Inns, many B&Bs specialize in providing historic, romantic or gracious atmospheres with amenities such as canopied beds, fireplaces, spa tubs, afternoon tea in the library and scenic views.

Some give great attention to recapturing a specific historic period, such as the Victorian or Colonial eras. Many display antiques and other furnishings from family collections.

A HOMESTAY is a room available in a private home. It may be an elegant stone mansion in the best part of town or a charming country farm. Homestays have one to three guest rooms. Because homestays are often operated as a hobby-type business and open and close frequently, only a very few unique properties are included in this publication.

Baths

Not all Bed & Breakfasts and Country Inns provide a private bath for each guest room. We have included the number of rooms and the number of private baths in each facility. If you must have a private bath, make sure the room reserved for you provides this.

Beds

K, Q, D, T, indicates King, Queen, Double or Twin beds available at the inn.

Credit cards/Payments

MC	MasterCard
VISA	Visa
DC	Diner's Club
CB	Carte Blanche
AX	American Express
DS	Discover
TC	Traveler's checks
PC	Personal checks

Meals

Breakfasts/Teas

Continental breakfast: Coffee, juice, toast or pastry.

Continental-plus breakfast: A continental breakfast plus a variety of breads, cheeses and fruit.

Full breakfast: Coffee, juice, breads, fruit and an entree.

Gourmet breakfast: May be an elegant four-course candlelight offering or especially creative cuisine.

Teas: Usually served in the late afternoon with cookies, crackers or other in-between-meal offerings.

Meal Plans

AP: American Plan. All three meals may be included in the price of the room. Check to see if the rate quoted is for two people or per person.

MAP: Modified American Plan. Breakfast and dinner may be included in the price of the room.

EP: European Plan. No meals are included. We have listed only a few historic hotels that operate on an EP plan.

Always find out what meals, if any, are included in the rates. Not every establishment participating in this program provides breakfast, although most do. Inns offering the second night free may or may not include a complimentary lunch or dinner with the second night. Occasionally an innkeeper has indicated MAP and AP when she or he actually means that both programs are available and you must specify which program you are interested in.

Please do not assume meals are included in the rates featured in the book.

Rates

Rates are usually listed in ranges, i.e., $45-$105. The LOWEST rate is almost always available during off-peak periods and may apply only to the least expensive room. Rates always are subject to change and are not guaranteed. You always should confirm the rates when making the reservations. Rates for Canadian listings usually are listed in Canadian dollars. Rates are quoted for double occupancy for two people.

Breakfast and other meals MAY or MAY NOT be included in the rates and may not be included in the discount.

Smoking

The majority of Country Inns and B&Bs in historic buildings prohibit smoking; therefore, if you are a smoker we advise you to call and specifically check with each inn to see if and how they accommodate smokers.

Rooms

Under some listings, you will note that suites are available. We typically assume that suites include a private bath.

Additionally, under some listings, you will note a reference to cottages. A cottage may be a rustic cabin tucked in the woods, a seaside cottage or a private apartment-style accommodation.

Fireplaces

When fireplaces are mentioned in the listing they may be in guest rooms or in common areas. A few have fireplaces that are non-working because of city lodging requirements. Please verify this if you are looking forward to an intimate, fireside chat in your room.

State maps

The state maps have been designed to help travelers find an inn's location quickly and easily. Each city shown on the maps contains one or more inns.

As you browse through the guide, you will notice coordinates next to each city name, i.e. C3. The coordinates designate the location of inns on the state map.

Media coverage

Some inns have provided us with copies of magazine or newspaper articles written by travel writers about their establishments and we have indicated that in the listing. Articles written about the inns may be available either from the source as a reprint, through libraries or from the inn itself.

Comments from guests

Over the years, we have collected reams of guest comments about thousands of inns. Our files are filled with these documented comments. At the end of some descriptions, we have included a guest comment received about that inn.

Inspections

This book contains descriptions of more than 1,600 inns. Each year we travel across the country visiting hundreds of inns. Since 1981, we have had a happy, informal team of Inn travelers and prospective innkeepers who report to us about new Bed & Breakfast discoveries and repeat visits to favorite inns.

Although our staff usually sees hundreds of inns each year, inspecting inns is not the major focus of our travels. We visit as many as possible, photograph them and meet the innkeepers. Some inns are grand mansions filled with classic, museum-quality antiques. Others are rustic, such as reassembled log cabins or renovated barns or stables. We have enjoyed them all and cherish our memories of each establishment, pristine or rustic. Only rarely have we come across a truly disappointing inn poorly kept or poorly managed. This type of business usually does not survive because an inn's success depends upon repeat guests and enthusiastic word-of-mouth referrals from satisfied guests. We do not promote these types of establishments.

Traveler or tourist

Travel is an adventure into the unknown, full of surprises and rewards. A seasoned "traveler" learns that even after elaborate preparations and careful planning, travel provides the new and unexpected. The traveler learns to live with uncertainty and considers it part of the adventure.

To the "tourist," whether "accidental" or otherwise, new experiences are disconcerting. Tourists want no surprises. They expect things to be exactly as they had envisioned them. To tourists we recommend staying in a hotel or motel chain where the same formula is followed from one locale to another.

We have found that inngoers are travelers at heart. They relish the differences found at these unique Bed &

Breakfasts and Country Inns. This is the magic that makes traveling from Inn to Inn the delightful experience it is.

Minimum stays

Many inns require a two-night minimum stay on weekends. A three-night stay often is required during holiday periods.

Cancellations

Cancellation policies are individual for each Bed & Breakfast. It is not unusual to see 7- to 14-day cancellation periods or more. Please verify the inn's policy when making your reservation.

What if the Inn is full?

Ask the innkeeper for recommendations. They may know of an Inn that has opened recently or one nearby but off the beaten path. Call the local Chamber of Commerce in the town you hope to visit. They also may know of inns that have opened recently. Please let us know of any new discoveries you make.

We want to hear from you!

We've always enjoyed hearing from our readers and have carefully cataloged all letters and recommendations. If you wish to participate in evaluating your inn experiences, use the **Inn Evaluation Form** in the back of this book. You might want to make copies of this form prior to departing on your journey.

We hope you will enjoy this book so much that you will want to keep an extra copy or two on hand to offer to friends. Many readers have called to purchase our Free Night Certificate book for hostess gifts, birthday presents, or for seasonal celebrations. It's a great way to introduce your friends to America's enchanting Country Inns and Bed & Breakfasts.

Alabama

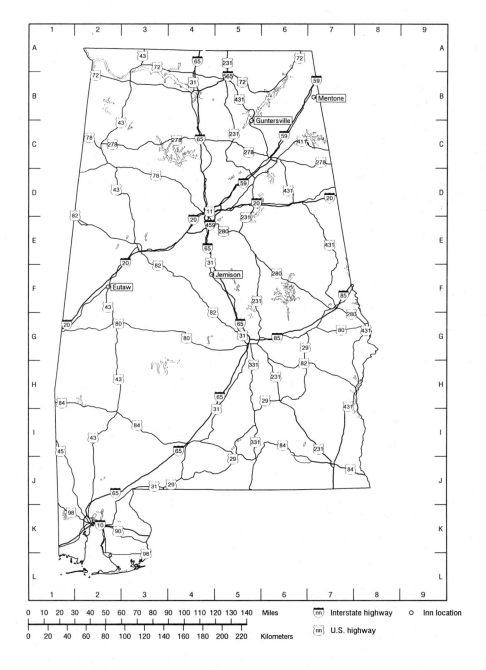

	Miles
0 10 20 30 40 50 60 70 80 90 100 110 120 130 140	
0 20 40 60 80 100 120 140 160 180 200 220	Kilometers

(nn) Interstate highway   ○ Inn location

(nn) U.S. highway

Eutaw
F2

Kirkwood Plantation
111 Kirkwood Dr
Eutaw, AL 35462-1101
(205)372-9009

Located on more than eight acres of green lawns, pecan trees and azaleas, this is a stately antebellum Greek Revival plantation house. There are eight Ionic columns on the front and side of the house and inside, Italian Carrara marble mantels adorn the fireplaces. Massive mirrors and a Waterford crystal chandelier add to the elegance of the inn's furnishings, most of which are original to the house. The innkeeper gives tours of the plantation along with a mini history lesson on the Civil War and its influence on Kirkwood Plantation.

Innkeeper(s): Mary Swayze. $75. 4 rooms. Breakfast included in rates. Type of meal: full breakfast. Air conditioning in room.

Certificate may be used: Based upon availability.

Guntersville
C5

Lake Guntersville B&B
2204 Scott St
Guntersville, AL 35976-1120
(205)505-0133 Fax:(205)505-0133

Circa 1910. It's just a short walk from this bed & breakfast to Alabama's largest lake where guests can enjoy fishing, boating and more than 900 miles of shoreline. The early 20th-century home is decorated with a variety of antiques. There are lake views from several rooms, and if weather permits, breakfast is served on the veranda where guests can enjoy the scenery. The veranda also offers wicker chairs and a hammock for those who wish to relax.

Innkeeper(s): Carol Dravis. $60-95. MC VISA AX PC TC. 8 rooms. 4 suites. 1 conference room. Breakfast and evening snack included in rates. Types of meals: gourmet breakfast and early coffee/tea. Catering service and room service available. Beds: KQDT. Air conditioning, ceiling fan and TV in room. Fax and pet boarding on premises. Handicap access. Antiques, fishing, parks, shopping, sporting events, golf, theater and watersports nearby.

Publicity: *Huntsville Times, Sun Herald, Mobile Press, Advertiser Gleam.*

Certificate may be used: Sunday through Wednesday nights, November through March, subject to certificate holder rooms being available.

Jemison
F4

The Jemison Inn
212 Hwy 191
Jemison, AL 35085
(205)688-2055

Circa 1930. Heirloom quality antiques fill this gabled brick house. A Victorian decor predominates. Casseroles, sausage, cheese grits and muffins comprise the inn's hearty breakfast.

Innkeeper(s): Nancy Ruzicka. $55-60. MC VISA AX DC CB DS. 3 rooms, 1 with PB, 1 with FP. Breakfast and afternoon tea included in rates. Type of meal: full breakfast. Picnic lunch available. Beds: T.

Location: Midway between Birmingham and Montgomery in the heart of horse country.

"I've never had a better breakfast anywhere."

Certificate may be used: January through December, Sunday through Thursday.

Mentone
B7

Mentone Inn
Hwy 117, PO Box 290
Mentone, AL 35984
(205)634-4836 (800)455-7470

Circa 1927. Mentone is a refreshing stop for those in search of the cool breezes and natural air conditioning of the mountains. Here antique treasures mingle with modern-day conveniences. A sun deck and spa complete the experience. Sequoyah Caverns, Little River Canyon and DeSoto Falls are moments away.

Innkeeper(s): Frances & Karl Waller. $60-125. MC VISA AX TC. 12 rooms, 11 with PB. Breakfast and afternoon tea included in rates. Types of meals: full breakfast and early coffee/tea. Restaurant on premises. Beds: QT. Air conditioning and ceiling fan in room. Cable TV, VCR and spa on premises. Antiques, parks, downhill skiing and watersports nearby.

Location: On Lookout Mountain in northeast Alabama.

Publicity: *Birmingham News.*

Certificate may be used: April 1-Aug. 31 (Monday-Thursday); Sept. 1-Oct. 31 (subject to availability); Dec. 1-March 31 (Sunday-Saturday).

Alaska

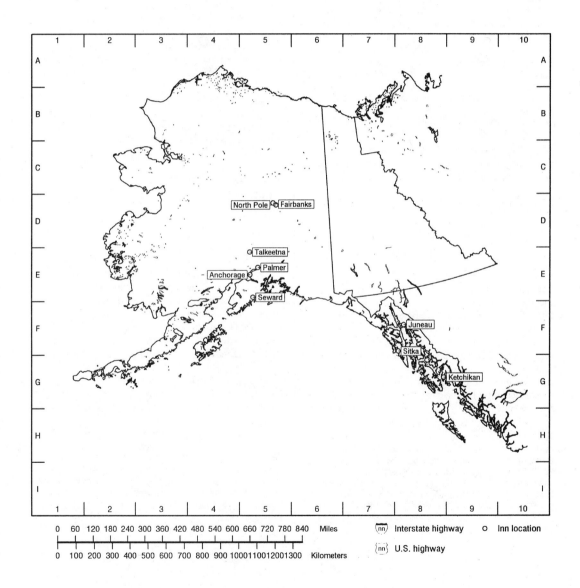

0 60 120 180 240 300 360 420 480 540 600 660 720 780 840 Miles

0 100 200 300 400 500 600 700 800 900 1000 1100 1200 1300 Kilometers

(nn) Interstate highway   o Inn location

{nn} U.S. highway

Anchorage   E5

Elderberry B&B
8340 Elderberry St
Anchorage, AK 99502-4245
(907)243-6968 Fax:(907)243-6968
E-mail: Compuserve 103260,3221

Circa 1974. This homestay bed & breakfast is located in a quiet Anchorage residential neighborhood and offers three homey rooms with comfortable furnishings. It's not unusual to see moose walking around the neighborhood. The home is close to the airport, as well as shops and restaurants.

Innkeeper(s): Norm & Linda Seitz. $50-80. MC VISA PC TC. 3 rooms, 2 with PB. Breakfast included in rates. Types of meals: continental breakfast, continental-plus breakfast, full breakfast and early coffee/tea. Beds: QDT. VCR in room. Cable TV, fax and copier on premises. Fishing, parks, shopping, downhill skiing, cross-country skiing, theater and watersports nearby.

"A friendly face, a lovely breakfast, and a good bed made our stay in your wonderful state more enjoyable."

Certificate may be used: Sept. 15-May 15, Sunday-Thursday.

Glacier Bear B&B
4814 Malibu Rd
Anchorage, AK 99517-3274
(907)243-8818 Fax:(907)248-4532
E-mail: 76602.505@compuserve.com

Circa 1986. This cedar-sided contemporary home is located just a mile and a half from the world's largest float plane lake. The B&B is decorated with a mix of Oriental and Victorian pieces. One bedroom includes a pencil canopy bed, while another offers an antique king bed and a fireplace. The landscaped grounds include an eight-person spa surrounded by ferns, trees and wild berry bushes. The innkeepers offer both a hearty full breakfast or continental fare. Freshly ground coffee, tea, soft drinks and freshly baked cookies are available throughout the day. The innkeepers provide a courtesy van to and from the airport.

Innkeeper(s): Marge Brown & Georgia Taton. $59-95. MC VISA AX DS PC TC. 5 rooms, 3 with PB, 1 with FP. Breakfast included in rates. Types of meals: full breakfast, gourmet breakfast and early coffee/tea. Evening snack available. Beds: KQT. Cable TV, VCR, fax, spa, bicycles and library on premises. Antiques, fishing, parks, shopping, downhill skiing, cross-country skiing, sporting events and watersports nearby.

Certificate may be used: Oct. 1-April 1.

North Country Castle B&B
PO Box 111876, 14600 Joanne Circle
Anchorage, AK 99511
(907)345-7296 Fax:(907)345-7296

Circa 1986. While this modern, Victorian cottage-style home is not actually a castle, guests are treated like royalty. The innkeepers offer two rooms with mountain views, and the Turnagain View Suite, which features a fireplace, double Jacuzzi and private deck. The home, which is surrounded by woods, rests in the foothills of the Chugach Mountains. The innkeepers serve a hearty, traditional breakfast with muffins, French toast, egg dishes, fresh fruit, juice and reindeer sausage.

Innkeeper(s): Cindy & Wray Kinard. $74-134. PC TC. 3 rooms, 1 with FP. 1 suite. Breakfast included in rates. Types of meals: continental breakfast, continental-plus breakfast, full breakfast and gourmet breakfast. Beds: QT. Turndown service in room. Fax, copier and library on premises. Fishing, parks, shopping, downhill skiing, cross-country skiing, sporting events and theater nearby.

Certificate may be used: Oct, 10-Nov. 10, March 10-April 10, seven days a week

The Oscar Gill House
1344 W 10th Ave
Anchorage, AK 99501-3245
(907)258-1717 Fax:(907)258-6613

Circa 1913. This clapboard, Craftsman-style home was built in Knik, Alaska, but later disassembled and moved to Anchorage in 1916. The home is the city's oldest, and the innkeepers have kept the decor simple and comfortable, with antiques here and there, as well as vintage furnishings from the '30s and '40s. Down comforters and bathrooms stocked with toiletries are a few of the special touches guests will find. Breakfasts are served up in the cheery dining room, which features panoramic photos of Anchorage and the home in its original location. Innkeeper Susan Lutz prepares a variety of entrees for the morning meal, including items such as sourdough French toast or Mexican egg casseroles accompanied by freshly ground coffee, a selection of teas and homemade hot chocolate.

Innkeeper(s): Mark & Susan Lutz. $75-95. MC VISA AX PC. 3 rooms, 1 with PB. Breakfast included in rates. Type of meal: full breakfast. Beds: QDT. Fax, bicycles and child care on premises. Fishing, parks, downhill skiing, cross-country skiing, sporting events and theater nearby.

Certificate may be used: Jan. 2-April 1, Oct. 1 through Nov. 22, Nov. 28 through Dec. 22.

Fairbanks   D5

Chena River B&B
1001 Dolly Varden Dr
Fairbanks, AK 99709-3229
(907)479-2532
Located on 10 acres along the Chena River, this inn offers spectacular views of the Northern Lights. Two of the rooms feature views of the river, woodlands and flower garden. (In the winter, moose are frequent visitors to the garden where they nibble its remnants.) The inn features hardwood floors, Oriental rugs and an enormous collection of books, many about Alaska. The innkeeper is a native Alaskan and has extensive knowledge about his home state. Breakfast features sourdough pancakes, bacon, sausage, eggs and fresh fruit salad. Guests are welcome to use the kitchen for snacks. Fairbanks is four miles. University museum, Riverboat Discovery and historic Chena Pump House are close-by.
Innkeeper(s): Steve Mease. $40-100. 5 rooms, 1 with PB. Breakfast included in rates. Type of meal: full breakfast. Beds: QDT.
Publicity: *Washington Post, Northwest Living.*
"Felt just like home, but the food was better."
Certificate may be used: September through May.

Juneau   F8

Pearson's Pond Luxury Inn & Gardens
4541 Sawa Cir
Juneau, AK 99801-8723
(907)789-3772 Fax:(907)789-6722
E-mail: pearsons.pond@juneau.com
Circa 1985. From this award-winning B&B resort, guests can view glaciers, visit museums and chance their luck at gold-panning streams, or simply soak in a hot tub surrounded by a lush forest and nestled next to a picturesque duck pond. Blueberries hang over the private decks of the guest rooms. A full, self-serve breakfast is provided each morning in the kitchenettes. Nearby trails offer excellent hiking, and the Mendenhall Glacier is within walking distance. The sportsminded will enjoy river rafting or angling for world-class halibut and salmon.
Innkeeper(s): Steve & Diane Pearson. $79-169. MC VISA AX DC CB PC TC. 3 rooms with PB, 2 with FP. 2 suites. Breakfast, afternoon tea and evening snack included in rates. Types of meals: continental-plus breakfast and early coffee/tea. Beds: Q. TV and VCR in room. Fax, copier, spa, bicycles and library on premises. Antiques, fishing, parks, shopping, downhill skiing, cross-country skiing, theater and watersports nearby.
Location: Three miles to airport and ferry terminal.

Publicity: *Good Housekeeping, Cross Country, Skier and Senior Voice.*
"A definite 10!"
Certificate may be used: October through April.

Ketchikan   G8

D & W's "Almost Home" B&B
412 D 1 Loop Rd N
Ketchikan, AK 99901-9202
(907)225-3273 (800)987-5337 Fax:(907)247-5337
E-mail: krs@ktn.net
Circa 1981. These rural B&B accommodations, located a few minutes' drive north of Ketchikan, provide guests with a completely outfitted two-bedroom apartment that sleeps six. A special welcome is extended to fishing parties. Ketchikan is known for its excellent salmon and halibut fishing and offers several fishing derbies each summer. A gas barbecue grill on the deck outside your room comes in handy for the catch of the day.
Innkeeper(s): Darrell & Wanda Vandergriff. $75. MC VISA AX DS PC TC. 3 cottages. Breakfast included in rates. Type of meal: continental-plus breakfast. Beds: KDT. TV in room. Fax on premises. Fishing, parks, shopping, theater and watersports nearby.
Certificate may be used: Oct. 1-March 31.

North Pole   D5

Birch Tree B&B
3104 Dyke Rd
North Pole, AK 99705-6801
(907)488-4667 Fax:(907)488-4667
Few people can boast that they've weathered the rugged North Pole country. At this modern-style B&B, however, visitors can enjoy the wilderness of Alaska in pleasant, inviting surroundings. The innkeepers offer four individually decorated rooms, one includes a hide-a-bed and separate dressing area. The den offers plenty of amenities, including a fireplace, books about Alaska and a pool table. Guests are invited to use the inn's barbecue grill and picnic table. The stunning Northern Lights often are visible from the home, and it's not unusual to see a moose or two roaming the grounds.
Innkeeper(s): Pat Albrecht. $45-70. MC VISA. 4 rooms. Breakfast included in rates. Type of meal: full breakfast.
Certificate may be used: October-April (anytime).

Palmer E5

Colony Inn
325 E Elmwood
Palmer, AK 99645
(907)745-3330 Fax:(907)746-3330

Circa 1935. Historic buildings are few and far between in Alaska, and this inn is one of them. The structure was built to house teachers and nurses in the days when President Roosevelt was sending settlers to Alaska to establish farms. When innkeeper Janet Kincaid purchased it, the inn had been empty for some time. She restored the place, including the wood walls, which now create a cozy ambiance in the common areas. The 12 guest rooms are nicely appointed, and 10 include a whirlpool tub. Meals are not included, but the inn's restaurant offers breakfast and lunch. The inn is listed in the National Register.

Innkeeper(s): Janet Kincaid. $80-100. MC VISA AX DS PC TC. 12 rooms with PB. Types of meals: full breakfast and early coffee/tea. Lunch available. Restaurant on premises. Beds: DT. TV and VCR in room. Library on premises. Handicap access. Antiques, fishing, parks, shopping, downhill skiing, cross-country skiing and golf nearby.

"Love the antiques and history."

Certificate may be used: Oct. 1-May 1.

Seward E5

"The Farm" B&B
PO Box 305
Seward, AK 99664-0305
(907)224-5691 Fax:(907)224-2300

Circa 1906. This country home is located on 20 acres of farmlike setting with plenty of fields to enjoy. Rooms are spacious and comfortable, one includes a canopied waterbed. The innkeepers offer sleeping cottages and a three-room bungalow as well. Guests may use the laundry facilities. The home is three miles outside of Seward.

$45-85. MC VISA. 11 rooms, 7 with PB. 2 suites. Breakfast included in rates. Type of meal: continental-plus breakfast. Beds: KQT. TV in room. VCR and fax on premises. Handicap access. Fishing, parks, shopping, cross-country skiing and watersports nearby.

Certificate may be used: September-May.

Sitka F8

Alaska Ocean View B&B
1101 Edgecumbe Dr
Sitka, AK 99835-7122
(907)747-8310 Fax:(907)747-8310

Circa 1986. This Alaska-style all-cedar home is located in a quiet neighborhood just one block from the seashore and the Tongass National Forest. Witness the spectacular Alaska sunsets over Sitka Sound and surrounding islands. On clear days, view Mt. Edgecumbe, which is an extinct volcano located on Kruzoff Island and looks like Mt. Fuji. Binoculars are kept handy for guests who take a special treat in viewing whales and eagles.

Innkeeper(s): Carole & Bill Denkinger. $79-139. MC VISA AX PC TC. 3 rooms with PB. 2 suites. 1 conference room. Breakfast, afternoon tea and evening snack included in rates. Types of meals: continental-plus breakfast, full breakfast, gourmet breakfast and early coffee/tea. Beds: KQDT. Turndown service, ceiling fan, TV and VCR in room. Fax, copier, spa and library on premises. Antiques, fishing, parks, shopping, theater and watersports nearby.

Certificate may be used: January, February, March and October, November, December.

Arizona

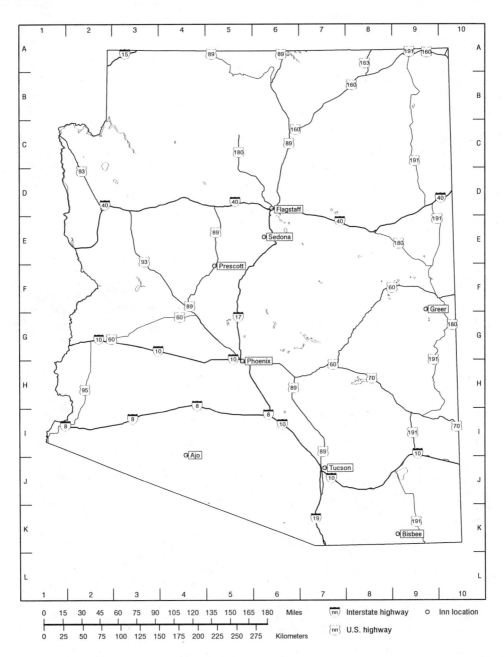

	Miles
0 15 30 45 60 75 90 105 120 135 150 165 180	Miles
0 25 50 75 100 125 150 175 200 225 250 275	Kilometers

(nn) Interstate highway   ○ Inn location

(nn) U.S. highway

Ajo I4

The Mine Manager's House Inn B&B

1 W Greenway Dr
Ajo, AZ 85321-2713
(520)387-6505 Fax:(520)387-6508

Circa 1919. Overlooking the Southwestern Arizona desert and a mile-wide copper mine pit, the Mine Manager's is a large Craftsman home situated on three acres. Built by the local copper mining industry, it has 10-inch-thick walls. A library, coin laundry and gift shop are on the premises. The Greenway Suite features a marble tub and shower, and one other suite has two queen-size beds. A full breakfast is served in the formal dining room.
Innkeeper(s): Jean & Micheline Fournier. $69-105. MC VISA TC. 5 rooms with PB. 3 suites. Breakfast and evening snack included in rates. Type of meal: full breakfast. Beds: QT. Air conditioning and ceiling fan in room. Cable TV, VCR, fax and spa on premises. Handicap access. Parks and shopping nearby.
Publicity: *Arizona Daily Star, Tucson Citizen, Catalina-Oracle, Arizona Sun, Arizona Highways-Sunset.*

"The hospitality is what makes this place so inviting! A palace at the top of the hill with service to match."
Certificate may be used: May to July and September to Nov. 15.

Bisbee K9

Bisbee Grand Hotel, A B&B Inn

61 Main Street, Box 825
Bisbee, AZ 85603
(520)432-5900 (800)421-1909

Circa 1906. This National Register treasure is a stunning example of an elegant turn-of-the-century hotel. The hotel originally served as a stop for mining executives, and it was restored back to its Old West Glory in the 1980s. Each of the rooms is decorated with Victorian furnishings and wallcoverings. The suites offer special items such as clawfoot tubs, an antique Chinese wedding bed, a fountain or four-poster bed. The Grand Western Salon boasts the back bar fixture from the Pony Saloon in Tombstone. After a full

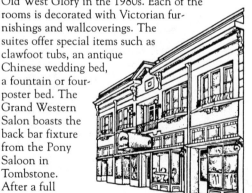

breakfast, enjoy a day touring the Bisbee area, which includes mine tours, museums, shops, antiquing and a host of outdoor activities.
Innkeeper(s): Bill Thomas. $53-110. MC VISA AX DS. 11 rooms. Breakfast included in rates. Type of meal: full breakfast.
Certificate may be used: Excludes weekends and holidays. Two-week advanced reservation required.

Flagstaff D6

Inn at Four Ten

410 N Leroux St
Flagstaff, AZ 86001-4502
(520)774-0088 (800)774-2008 Fax:(520)774-6354

Circa 1894. This inn was once the stately family residence of a wealthy banker, businessman and cattle rancher. Today, guests enjoy hospitality, outstanding cuisine and a wonderful home base from which to enjoy Northern Arizona. Each of the guest rooms is individually decorated in a unique style. Seven of the guest rooms include a fireplace, and some offer an oversized Jacuzzi tub. Award-winning recipes are

featured during the gourmet breakfasts, and afternoon cookies and tea are served in the dining room. A two-block walk takes guests to shops, galleries and restaurants in historic downtown Flagstaff. The Grand Canyon, Sedona, Native American sites and the San Francisco Peaks are nearby.
Innkeeper(s): Howard & Sally Krueger. $100-175. MC VISA PC TC. 9 rooms with PB, 7 with FP. 4 suites. Breakfast and evening snack included in rates. Type of meal: gourmet breakfast. Beds: KQT. Air conditioning and ceiling fan in room. Library on premises. Handicap access. Antiques, parks, shopping, downhill skiing, cross-country skiing and theater nearby.
Publicity: *Westways, Arizona Daily Sun, Mountain Living, Mountain Morning.*

"It was a joy to discover that the inn embodied the finest qualities of what make a bed and breakfast our first choice when staying out of town."
Certificate may be used: Sunday-Thursday. November-February, excluding holidays.

Greer
F9

White Mountain Lodge

PO Box 143
Greer, AZ 85927-0143
(520)735-7568 Fax:(520)735-7498

Circa 1892. This 19th-century lodge affords views of Greer meadow and the Little Colorado River. The guest rooms are individually decorated in a Southwestern or country style. The common rooms are decorated with period antiques, Southwestern

art and Mission-style furnishings. The Lodge's living room is an ideal place to relax with its stone fireplace. While dining on the hearty breakfasts, guests not only are treated to entrees that range from traditional country fare to the more gourmet, they also enjoy a view from the picture window. The cookie jar is always filled with homemade goodies and hot drinks are available throughout the day. Small pets are allowed, although certain restrictions apply. The inn is near excellent hiking trails.

Innkeeper(s): Charles & Mary Bast. $65-95. MC VISA AX DC DS PC TC. 7 rooms with PB. 3 cottages. Breakfast and evening snack included in rates. Types of meals: full breakfast and early coffee/tea. Beds: KQDT. Cable TV, VCR, fax, copier and library on premises. Antiques, fishing, shopping, downhill skiing and cross-country skiing nearby.

Certificate may be used: Sunday-Thursday (no holidays).

Phoenix
H5

Maricopa Manor

15 W Pasadena Ave
Phoenix, AZ 85013
(602)274-6302 (800)292-6403 Fax:(602)266-3904
E-mail: mmanor@getnet.com

Circa 1928. The secluded Maricopa Manor stands amid palm trees on an acre of land. The Spanish-style house features four graceful columns in the entry hall, an elegant living room with a marble mantel and a music room. The spacious suites are decorated with satins, lace, antiques and leather-bound books. Guests may relax on the deck, on the patio, by the pool or in the gazebo spa.

Innkeeper(s): Mary Ellen & Paul Kelley. $79-179. MC VISA AX DS PC TC. 5 suites, 2 with FP. Breakfast included in rates. Type of meal: continental-plus breakfast. Beds: KQ. Air conditioning, ceiling fan and TV in room. VCR, fax, copier, spa and swimming on premises. Handicap access. Antiques, parks, shopping, sporting events and theater nearby.

Location: North central Phoenix near museums, theaters.

Publicity: *Arizona Business Journal, Country Inns, AAA Westways, San Francisco Chronicle, Focus, Sombrero.*

"I've stayed 200+ nights at B&Bs around the world, yet have never before experienced the warmth and sincere friendliness of Maricopa Manor."

Certificate may be used: June 1-Aug. 31.

Prescott
F5

Briar Wreath Inn

232 S Arizona Ave
Prescott, AZ 86303-4404
(520)778-6048 Fax:(520)778-0039
E-mail: bwreath@primenet.com

Circa 1904. This Craftsman-style bed & breakfast exudes warmth and charm. Rooms are cozy, decorated in French-country style. The historic home still maintains many original features, including the hardwood floors and beamed ceilings. Guest chambers feature beds topped with Waverly prints and coordinating prints decorate the windows. Breakfasts are served in a dining room with a window seat lining one of the walls. The gourmet meal includes items such as eggs Benedict, fresh fruit with granola and homemade muffins. The innkeepers cater a variety of events, from weddings to special teas. As well, murder-mystery dinners, cooking classes and business meetings often take place at the B&B. Historic sites and outdoor activities abound in the area.

Innkeeper(s): Richard & Greta Varish. $100. AP. AX PC TC. 3 rooms with PB. 1 suite. 1 conference room. Breakfast, afternoon tea, evening snack and picnic lunch included in rates. Types of meals: continental breakfast, continental-plus breakfast, full breakfast, gourmet breakfast and early coffee/tea. Dinner, lunch, gourmet lunch, banquet service, catering service, catered breakfast and room service available. Beds: Q. Air conditioning, turndown service, ceiling fan and TV in room. VCR, fax, copier and library on premises. Antiques, fishing, parks, shopping, downhill skiing, sporting events, golf, theater and watersports nearby.

Publicity: *Country Inns, Country Register, Courier.*

Certificate may be used: Jan. 30-Dec. 1, Sunday-Thursday.

Juniper Well Ranch

PO Box 11083
Prescott, AZ 86304-1083
(520)442-3415

Circa 1991. A working horse ranch sits on the front 15 acres of this 50-acre, wooded property, which is surrounded by the Prescott National Forest. Guests are welcome to feed the horses, and children have been known to take a ride on a tractor with innkeeper David Bonham. Two log cabins and the ranch house sit farther back on the land where families can enjoy nature, "unlimited" hiking and seclusion. A summer house, which can be reserved by guests staying at the ranch, has no walls, a sloping roof with skylight, and an eight-foot hot tub. Guest pets, including horses, are welcome on an individual basis.

Innkeeper(s): David Bonham. $105. MC VISA AX DS PC TC. 3 cottages with PB, 3 with FP. Breakfast included in rates. Type of meal: full breakfast. Beds: QDT. Ceiling fan in room. Spa on premises. Handicap access. Antiques, fishing, parks, shopping, cross-country skiing and theater nearby.

Certificate may be used: Sunday through Thursday.

Mount Vernon Inn

204 N Mount Vernon Ave
Prescott, AZ 86301-3108
(520)778-0886 Fax:(520)778-7305
E-mail: mtvrnon@primenet.com

Circa 1900. This inn, listed in the National Register, is known as one of Mt. Vernon's "Victorian treasures." Among its architectural features are gables, an enchanting turret and a Greek Revival porch. In addition to the four spacious guest rooms in the main house, there are three country cottages available. The inn is located in the Mt. Vernon Historic District and is just a few blocks from town square.

Innkeeper(s): Michele & Jerry Neumann. $90-120. MC VISA DS TC. 4 rooms with PB. 3 cottages. Breakfast included in rates. Beds: QDT. Ceiling fan in room. Cable TV, fax and library on premises. Handicap access. Antiques, parks, shopping and theater nearby.

Certificate may be used: Nov. 1-March 31. Sunday through Thursday only. Exclude holidays.

Pleasant Street Inn

142 S Pleasant St
Prescott, AZ 86303-3811
(520)445-4774

Pleasant Street Inn was moved to its present site, in the heart of historic Prescott, in an effort to save the home from demolition. Rooms at this quaint, Victorian inn are decorated with a touch of whimsy with floral prints and chintz fabrics. The PineView Suite boasts a sitting room and fireplace. Another suite includes a sitting room and private, covered deck. Guests are treated to a full breakfast, and afternoon hors d'oeuvres and refreshments are served. Prescott, which served twice as the state capital, offers a variety of museums and art galleries to explore, as well as the historic Court House Square. Nearby Prescott National Forest is a perfect place to enjoy hiking, climbing and other outdoor activities.

Innkeeper(s): Jean Urban. $80-120. MC VISA DS. 4 rooms. Breakfast included in rates. Type of meal: full breakfast.

Certificate may be used: Nov. 1-April 30, Sunday through Thursday.

Prescott Pines Inn

901 White Spar Rd
Prescott, AZ 86303-7231
(520)445-7270 (800)541-5374 Fax:(520)778-3665

Circa 1934. A white picket fence beckons guests to the veranda of this comfortably elegant country Victorian inn, originally the Haymore Dairy. There are masses of fragrant pink roses, lavenders and delphiniums, and stately ponderosa pines tower above the inn's four renovated cottages, which were once shelter for farmhands. The acre of grounds

includes a garden fountain and romantic tree swing.

Innkeeper(s): Gary May & Karen Mink. $65-249. EP. MC VISA PC. 13 rooms with PB, 3 with FP. 3 cottages. Breakfast included in rates. Types of meals: full breakfast and early coffee/tea. Beds: KQ. Air conditioning, ceiling fan and TV in room. Fax and copier on premises. Antiques, parks, shopping and theater nearby.

Location: One-and-a-third miles south of Courthouse Plaza & historic Whiskey Row.

Publicity: *Sunset, Arizona Republic News, Arizona Highways.*

"The ONLY place to stay in Prescott! Tremendous attention to detail."

Certificate may be used: Sunday-Thursday (except holidays); Oct. 15-May 15.

Victorian Inn of Prescott B&B

246 S Cortez St
Prescott, AZ 86303-3939
(520)778-2642 (800)704-2642

Circa 1893. The blue- and white-trimmed Victorian home with its tower and bay windows is a popular landmark of Prescott and is located one block from the historic town square. When it was constructed in the late 19th century, all the materials had to be brought in by train from the East Coast. Mauve and raspberry colors dominate the interior, which has been restored with many original fixtures. A favorite among the second-floor guest quarters is the spacious Victoriana Suite. Breakfast is a gourmet sit-down affair served on elegant china and linens.

Innkeeper(s): Tamia Thunstedt. $90-145. MC VISA AX DS. 4 rooms, 1 with PB, 1 with FP. 1 suite. Breakfast included in rates. Types of meals: full breakfast and early coffee/tea. Beds: Q. Ceiling fan in room. Antiques, fishing, parks, shopping, sporting events and theater nearby.
Publicity: *Arizona Republic, Arizona Highways, Sunset, Home and Gardens.*

Certificate may be used: Monday through Thursday nights.

Sedona
E6

Territorial House, An Old West B&B

65 Piki Dr
Sedona, AZ 86336-4345
(520)204-2737 (800)801-2737 Fax:(520)204-2230

Circa 1970. This red rock and cedar two-story ranch home, nestled in the serene setting of Juniper and Cottonwood, is a nature lover's delight. Guests can see families of quail march through the landscape of cacti, plants and red rock or at night hear the call of coyotes. The territorial decor includes Charles Russell prints collected from taverns throughout the Southwest. More than 40 western movies were filmed in Sedona.

Innkeeper(s): John & Linda Steele. $95-155. MC VISA AX. 4 rooms with PB, 1 with FP. 1 suite. Breakfast and evening snack included in rates. Type of meal: full breakfast. Beds: KQ. Air conditioning in room. Cable TV, VCR, spa and bicycles on premises. Antiques, fishing, parks, shopping, downhill skiing, theater and watersports nearby.
Certificate may be used: July-August, December-January. Sunday-Thursday. No holidays.

Tucson
J7

Casa Alegre B&B

316 E Speedway Blvd
Tucson, AZ 85705-7429
(520)628-1800 (800)628-5654 Fax:(520)792-1880

Circa 1915. Innkeeper Phyllis Florek decorated the interior of this Craftsman-style home with artifacts reflecting the history of Tucson, including Native American pieces and antique mining tools. Wake to the aroma of fresh coffee and join other guests as you enjoy fresh muffins, fruit and other breakfast

treats, such as succulent cheese pancakes with raspberry preserves. The Arizona sitting room opens onto serene gardens, a pool and a Jacuzzi. An abundance of shopping and sightseeing is found nearby.

Innkeeper(s): Phyllis Florek. $60-105. MC VISA DS PC TC. 5 rooms with PB, 1 with FP. 1 conference room. Breakfast included in rates. Types of meals: full breakfast and gourmet breakfast. Beds: QT. Ceiling fan in room. VCR, fax, spa and swimming on premises. Antiques, parks, shopping, sporting events and theater nearby.
Location: West University Historic District.
Publicity: *Arizona Times, Arizona Daily Star, Tucson Weekly.*

"An oasis of comfort in Central Tucson."
Certificate may be used: June through September.

The Congenial Quail

4267 North Fourth Ave
Tucson, AZ 85705-1701
(520)887-9487 (800)895-2047

Circa 1940. At this bed & breakfast, guests can enjoy a soak in the hot tub, rest in a hammock or stroll around the three-acre grounds and watch the sun set. The home features Mexican tile floors and Southwestern decor. Each of the guest quarters is decorated with a different theme in mind. The innkeepers offer bedrooms in the main house, as well as a cottage. Breakfasts feature spicy items such as a Southwestern-style frittata. The Tucson area offers historic sites, shopping and many other unique attractions.

Innkeeper(s): Laurie & Bob Haskett. $60-110. MC VISA PC TC. 4 rooms, 2 with PB. 1 cottage. Breakfast and evening snack included in rates. Types of meals: gourmet breakfast and early coffee/tea. Picnic lunch, lunch and gourmet lunch available. Beds: QDT. Air conditioning, turndown service and ceiling fan in room. VCR, spa and library on premises. Handicap access. Antiques, parks, shopping, sporting events, golf and theater nearby.

Certificate may be used: April through September (regular published prices).

Jeremiah Inn
10921 E Snyder Rd
Tucson, AZ 85749-9066
(520)749-3072

Circa 1995. The Catalina Mountains serve as a backdrop for this modern Santa Fe-style home. There are three guest rooms, two offer a sitting area, and all are decorated in Southwestern style. Each room has a private entrance, and there is a refrigerator for guest use. Breakfast at the inn is an event. The menu might include a lavish selection of fresh fruit, a Southwestern-style potato sauté and homemade cinnamon toast. Guests enjoy use of a pool and a spa. Guests can spend the day hiking, golfing, shopping or exploring the scenic area on horseback. Innkeeper(s): Bob & Beth Miner. $70-100. MC VISA PC TC. 3 rooms with PB. Breakfast included in rates. Types of meals: full breakfast and early coffee/tea. Beds: Q. Air conditioning, ceiling fan and VCR in room. Spa and swimming on premises. Antiques, parks, golf and theater nearby.

"Next time we'll go for a different room. We want to try them all."

Certificate may be used: May 15-Nov. 15.

The Suncatcher
105 N Avenida Javalina
Tucson, AZ 85748-8928
(520)885-0883 (800)835-8012

Circa 1991. From the picture window in your opulent guest room, you'll enjoy views of mountains and desert scenery. The bedchambers include beautiful furnishings, such as a bed draped in a luxurious canopy. A fireplace or double Jacuzzi tub are options. Guests enjoy use of a pool, tennis facilities and an athletic club, as well as the inn's four acres. All of Tucson's sites and shops are nearby. Innkeeper(s): Shirley Ranierei Martorana. $80-165. MC VISA AX DC DS PC TC. 4 rooms with PB. Breakfast and afternoon tea included in rates. Type of meal: full breakfast. Beds: Q. VCR, fax, copier, spa, swimming and library on premises. Shopping, downhill skiing and golf nearby.

Certificate may be used: June 1-Sept. 15, Sunday-Sunday.

Arkansas

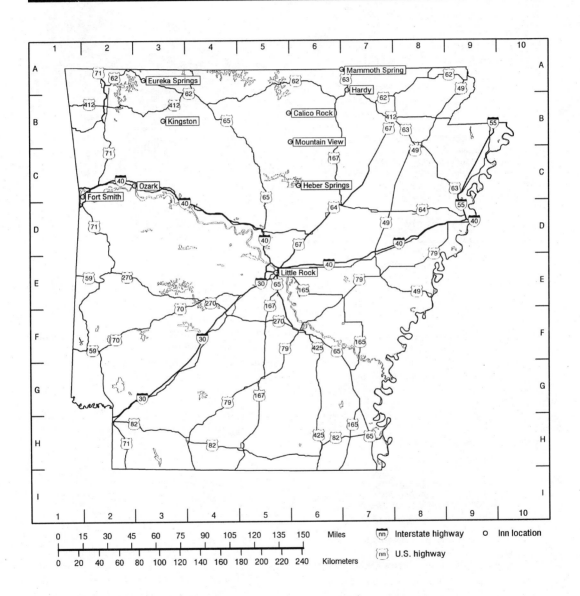

0 15 30 45 60 75 90 105 120 135 150   Miles

0 20 40 60 80 100 120 140 160 180 200 220 240   Kilometers

(nn) Interstate highway   o Inn location

(nn) U.S. highway

Calico Rock B5

Forest Home Lodge & Happy Lonesome Log Cabin
HC 61, Box 72
Calico Rock, AR 72519
(870)297-8764
E-mail: hlcabins@centuryinter.net

Circa 1988. The two rustic log cabins are located on a wooded, 194-acre property. The interiors are simple and comfortable and include a sleeping loft, small kitchen and wood stove. Continental fare is placed in the kitchenette so that guests may enjoy a light breakfast at their leisure. Calico Rock is an interesting historic town, and there are plenty of old buildings and homes to explore.

Innkeeper(s): Carolyn & Christian J. Eck. $63. MC VISA DS PC TC. 4 rooms, 2 with PB. 2 cabins. Breakfast included in rates. Type of meal: continental-plus breakfast. Beds: D. Air conditioning and ceiling fan in room. Amusement parks, antiques, fishing, parks, shopping, golf, theater and watersports nearby.

Certificate may be used: Sunday-Thursday.

Eureka Springs A3

Arsenic & Old Lace B&B Inn
60 Hillside Ave
Eureka Springs, AR 72632-3133
(501)253-5454 (800)243-5223 Fax:(501)253-2246
E-mail: arseniclace@prodigy.net

Circa 1992. This bed & breakfast is a meticulous reproduction of Queen Anne Victorian style, and it offers five guest rooms decorated with antique Victorian furnishings. Popular with honeymooners, the three upper-level guest rooms offer whirlpool tubs, balconies and fireplaces. One ground-floor room also has a whirlpool tub. The inn's gardens complement its attractive exterior, which includes a wraparound veranda and stone wall. Its location in the historic district makes it an excellent starting point for a sightseeing stroll or shopping.

Innkeeper(s): Gary & Phyllis Jones. $106-160. MC VISA AX DS PC TC. 5 rooms with PB, 3 with FP. 2 suites. Breakfast and evening snack included in rates. Type of meal: gourmet breakfast. Beds: KQT. Air conditioning, ceiling fan, TV and VCR in room. Fax, copier and library on premises. Handicap access. Antiques, fishing, parks, shopping, golf, theater and watersports nearby.

Publicity: *Houston Chronicle, Kiplinger's Personal Finance Magazine.*

"It was well worth the 1,000 miles we traveled to share your home for a short while...thanks for a 4-star vacation."

Certificate may be used: Jan. 20-Sept. 30, Sunday through Thursday only. November-December, Sunday through Thursday only.

Bridgeford House
263 Spring St
Eureka Springs, AR 72632-3154
(501)253-7853 Fax:(501)253-5497

Circa 1884. This peach-colored Victorian delight is nestled in the heart of the Eureka Springs Historic District. Rooms feature antiques and are decorated in a wonderfully charming

Victorian style with private entrances. Guests will enjoy the fresh, hot coffee and selection of teas in their suites, and the large gourmet breakfast is the perfect way to start the day. Enjoy the horse-drawn carriage rides down Eureka Springs' famed boulevard with its stately homes.

Innkeeper(s): Denise McDonald. $85-105. MC VISA. 4 rooms, 3 with PB. 1 suite. Breakfast and afternoon tea included in rates. Types of meals: full breakfast, gourmet breakfast and early coffee/tea. Evening snack and room service available. Beds: QT. Air conditioning, ceiling fan and TV in room. VCR on premises. Antiques, fishing, shopping, theater and watersports nearby.

Location: North one mile on 62B in Eureka Springs Historic District.

Publicity: *Times Echo Flashlight, Arkansas National Tour Guide.*

"You have created an enchanting respite for weary people."

Certificate may be used: Jan. 1-Oct. 1; Nov. 1-Dec. 31, Sunday-Thursday.

Candlestick Cottage
6 Douglas St
Eureka Springs, AR 72632-3416
(501)253-6813 (800)835-5184
E-mail: candleci@ipa.net

Circa 1888. Woods and foliage surround this scenic country home, nestled just a few blocks from Eureka Springs historic district. Guests are sure to discover a variety of wildlife strolling by the home, including an occasional deer. Breakfasts are served on the tree-top porch, which overlooks a waterfall and fish pond. The morning meal begins with freshly baked muffins and fresh fruit, followed by an entree. Innkeepers Bill and Patsy Brooks will prepare a basket of sparkling grape juice and wine glasses for those celebrating a special occasion. Guest rooms are decorated in Victorian style, and some include two-person Jacuzzis.

Innkeeper(s): Bill & Patsy Brooks. $65-109. MC VISA DS TC. 6 rooms with PB. Breakfast included in rates. Type of meal: full breakfast. Beds: QF. Air conditioning and TV in room. Antiques, fishing, parks and shopping nearby.

Certificate may be used: Jan. 1-March 31, Sunday-Thursday.

Crescent Cottage Inn

211 Spring St
Eureka Springs, AR 72632-3153
(501)253-6022 (800)223-3246 Fax:(501)253-6234
E-mail: raphael@ipa.net

Circa 1881. This Victorian inn was home to the first governor of Arkansas after the Civil War. Two long verandas overlook a breathtaking valley and two mountain ranges. The home is graced by a beautiful tower, spindlework and coffered ceilings. A

huge arch joins the dining and living rooms, which, like the rest of the inn, are filled with antiques. Four of the guest rooms feature whirlpool spas, and two have a fireplace. The inn is situated on the quiet, residential end of the historic loop. A five-minute walk into town takes guests past limestone cliffs, tall maple trees, gardens and refreshing springs. Try a ride on the steam engine train that departs nearby.

Innkeeper(s): Ralph & Phyllis Becker. $93-130. MC VISA DS PC TC. 4 rooms with PB, 2 with FP. 1 suite. Breakfast included in rates. Types of meals: full breakfast and early coffee/tea. Beds: Q. Air conditioning, ceiling fan, TV and VCR in room. Fax and copier on premises. Amusement parks, antiques, fishing, parks, shopping, sporting events, golf, theater and watersports nearby.

Publicity: *Country Homes, Country Inns, Minneapolis Tribune, Fort Lauderdale News, America's Painted Ladies.*

"You gave us a piece of heaven. We will never forget, what we dreamed of."

Certificate may be used: January-February (except Valentine's Day) to March 15.

Dairy Hollow House

515 Spring St
Eureka Springs, AR 72632-3032
(501)253-7444 (800)562-8650 Fax:(501)253-7223
E-mail: frontdesk@dairyhollow.com

Circa 1888. Dairy Hollow House, the first of Eureka Springs' bed & breakfast inns, consists of a restored Ozark vernacular farmhouse and a 1940s bungalow-style cottage, both in a national historic

district. Stenciled walls set off a collection of Eastlake Victorian furnishings. Outstanding "Nouveau 'zarks" cuisine is available by reservation on six special-occasion dinners a year. Innkeeper Crescent Dragonwagon is the author of more than 40 children's books and cookbooks, including the award-winning Dairy Hollow House Cookbook and the new Soup and Bread Cookbook, and was called upon to cater President Clinton's inaugural brunch in Washington, D.C.

Innkeeper(s): Ned Shank & Crescent Dragonwagon. $135-205. MC VISA AX DC CB DS PC TC. 6 rooms with PB, 6 with FP. 3 suites. 1 conference room. Breakfast and evening snack included in rates. Types of meals: full breakfast and early coffee/tea. Restaurant on premises. Beds: KQD. Air conditioning in room. Fax, copier and spa on premises. Amusement parks, antiques, fishing, parks, shopping, theater and watersports nearby.

Location: At the junction of Spring & Dairy Hollow Road.

Publicity: *Innsider, Christian Science Monitor, Los Angeles Times, Gourmet, Southern Living, Bon Appetit, Country, Country Living, Conde Nast Traveler.*

"The height of unpretentious luxury."

Certificate may be used: Sunday-Thursday, February, March, November, December excluding any major holidays or inn special events.

Evening Shade Inn

Hwy 62E, Rt 1, Box 446
Eureka Springs, AR 72632
(501)253-6264 (800)992-1224
E-mail: eveshade@ipa.net

Circa 1992. This bed & breakfast is set on a private, 10 acres, yet it's a stop on the village's trolley route. Guests choose from spacious rooms in the main house or a private honeymoon cottage. Each room has a Jacuzzi tub, as well as a TV and VCR. Each evening, the innkeepers will pamper you with champagne. In the mornings, a continental-plus breakfast is delivered to your door. Guests in the cottage enjoy the added amenity of a wood-burning fireplace.

Innkeeper(s): Ed & Shirley Nussbaum. $115-150. MC VISA AX DS PC TC. 5 rooms with PB, 2 with FP. 1 cottage. Breakfast included in rates. Type of meal: continental-plus breakfast. Beds: K. Air conditioning, turn-down service, ceiling fan, TV and VCR in room. Fax and copier on premises. Amusement parks, antiques, fishing, parks, shopping, golf and watersports nearby.

Certificate may be used: January-September and November-December, Monday through Thursday except holidays and special events. Advance notice of this offer required.

Heart of The Hills Inn

5 Summit
Eureka Springs, AR 72632
(501)253-7468 (800)253-7468

Circa 1883. Two suites and a Victorian cottage comprise this antique-furnished homestead located just four blocks from downtown. Suites have been restored and decorating in an 1880s style. The cottage is located beside the inn and is decorated in

Victorian-country style. The cottage also offers a private deck that overlooks the garden. The village trolley stops at the inn, but the inn is within walking distance of town.

Innkeeper(s): James & Kathy Vanzandt. $95-125. MC VISA AX PC TC. 3 rooms with PB. 2 suites. 1 cottage. Breakfast and evening snack included in rates. Types of meals: gourmet breakfast and early coffee/tea. Beds: KD. Air conditioning, turndown service, ceiling fan and TV in room. Spa and library on premises. Handicap access. Antiques, fishing, shopping, golf, theater and watersports nearby.

Location: On the historic loop.

Publicity: *Carroll County Tribune's Peddler.*

"The decor and atmosphere of your inn was breathtak-

ing; we were able to relax and not want for a thing."

Certificate may be used: November through September, Sunday through Thursday (may call at last minute).

The Heartstone Inn & Cottages

35 King's Hwy
Eureka Springs, AR 72632-3534
(501)253-8916 (800)494-4921 Fax:(501)253-6821

Circa 1903. Described as a "pink and white confection," this handsomely restored Victorian with its wraparound verandas is located in the historic district. The award-winning inn is filled with antiques

and artwork from the innkeeper's native England. Live music is featured: in May a fine arts festival and in September, a jazz festival. Afternoon refreshments are available on the sunny deck overlooking a wooded ravine. Pink roses line the picket fence surrounding the inviting garden.

Innkeeper(s): Iris & Bill Simantel. $65-120. MC VISA AX DS PC TC. 12 rooms with PB, 1 with FP. 3 suites. 2 cottages. Breakfast included in rates. Type of meal: gourmet breakfast. Beds: KQ. Air conditioning, ceiling fan and TV in room. Fax and spa on premises. Amusement parks, antiques, fishing, parks, shopping, theater and watersports nearby.

Location: Northwest Arkansas, Ozarks.

Publicity: *Innsider, Arkansas Times, New York Times, Arkansas Gazette, Southern Living, Country Home, Country Inns.*

"Extraordinary! Best breakfasts anywhere!"

Certificate may be used: Sunday through Wednesday arrivals during November through April. Other times, last minute only.

Pond Mountain Lodge & Resort

Rt 1, Box 50
Eureka Springs, AR 72632
(501)253-5877 (800)583-8043

Circa 1954. There's no shortage of activities for guests to enjoy at this lodge. Guests can fish at the two ponds, enjoy horseback riding, use the swimming pool, shoot pool in the game room or hike along trails within the 150 acres. There are seven guest rooms, each individually decorated with contemporary, comfortable furnishings. Four rooms include a fireplace, and several have a Jacuzzi tub. There also is a two-bedroom cabin with a Jacuzzi and a wood stove.

Innkeeper(s): Judy Jones. $68-140. MC VISA DS PC TC. 8 rooms, 7 with PB, 4 with FP. 5 suites. 1 cabin. Breakfast included in rates. Types of meals: continental breakfast, full breakfast, gourmet breakfast and early coffee/tea. Picnic lunch, banquet service, catering service and catered breakfast available. Beds: KQD. Air conditioning, ceiling fan and VCR in room. Swimming, stables and library on premises. Handicap access. Antiques, fishing, shopping, sporting events, golf, theater and watersports nearby.

Publicity: *Eureka Springs Times-Echo.*

Certificate may be used: Sunday-Thursday; November, December (except Dec. 25-31), February, March.

Sunnyside Inn
5 Ridgeway Ave
Eureka Springs, AR 72632-3024
(501)253-6638

Circa 1883. Beautifully renovated, this National Register Queen Anne Victorian is located three blocks from town. Traditional Victorian decor is especially outstanding in the Rose Room with a carved, high oak bed and original rose stained-glass windows. The Honeymoon Suite features an Abe Lincoln-era carved walnut bed with matching bureau.

Innkeeper(s): Gladys R. Foris. $69-119. TC. 7 rooms with PB. 1 conference room. Breakfast included in rates. Type of meal: continental breakfast. Beds: Q. Air conditioning in room. Cable TV and VCR on premises. Antiques, fishing, parks, shopping and theater nearby.

"The best weekend of our lives."

Certificate may be used: April 1 to Oct. 1, Monday-Thursday.

Taylor-Page Inn
33 Benton St
Eureka Springs, AR 72632-3501
(501)253-7315

Within easy walking distance of downtown restaurants, shopping and trolley, this turn-of-the-century Square salt-box inn features Victorian and country decor in its three suites and rooms. Guests often enjoy relaxing in the inn's two sitting rooms. The suites offer ceiling fans, full kitchens and sundecks. The inn offers convenient access to antiquing, fishing, museums and parks.

Innkeeper(s): Jeanne Taylor. $60-80. MC VISA. 3 suites. Breakfast included in rates. Type of meal: continental breakfast. Air conditioning, ceiling fan and TV in room. Antiques and shopping nearby.

Certificate may be used: January-March, anytime. April through December, Monday through Thursday.

Fort Smith
C2

Beland Manor Inn B&B
1320 S Albert Pike Ave
Fort Smith, AR 72903-2416
(501)782-3300 (800)334-5052

Circa 1950. Magnolia trees and pink and white azaleas surround this Colonial Revival mansion. Expansive lawns, hundreds of impatiens, a rose garden and patio adjoining a back garden gazebo, make the inn a popular setting for romantic weddings. Furnishings incorporate traditional pieces and antiques. A king-size, four-poster rice bed makes the Bridal Suite the option of choice. Best of all is the three-course Sunday breakfast, often featuring Eggs Benedict with strawberry crepes for dessert.

Innkeeper(s): Mike & Suzy Smith. $65-110. MAP. MC VISA AX DS. 6 rooms, 5 with PB. 1 suite. 1 conference room. Breakfast included in rates. Types of meals: gourmet breakfast and early coffee/tea. Dinner, evening snack, picnic lunch and banquet service available. Beds: KQTD. Air conditioning, ceiling fan and TV in room. VCR, fax and bicycles on premises. Handicap access. Antiques, parks, shopping and theater nearby.

Certificate may be used: September, November, December, January, February and March (excluding holidays).

Thomas Quinn Guest House
815 N B St
Fort Smith, AR 72901-2129
(501)782-0499

Circa 1863. Nine suites with kitchenettes are available at this inn, which in 1916 added a second story and stately columns to its original structure. Located on the perimeter of Fort Smith's historic district, it is close to the art center, historic sites, museums and restaurants. Several state parks are within easy driving distance. Early morning coffee and tea are served.

Innkeeper(s): Michael & Melody Conley. $59-79. EP. MC VISA AX DC CB DS TC. 9 suites. Type of meal: early coffee/tea. Beds: F. Air conditioning, TV and VCR in room. Amusement parks, antiques, fishing, parks, shopping and watersports nearby.

Certificate may be used: All year.

Hardy
A7

Hideaway Inn
RR 1 Box 199
Hardy, AR 72542-4770
(870)966-4770 (888)966-4770

Circa 1980. For those seeking solitude, this contemporary home is an ideal place to hide away, surrounded by more than 370 acres of Ozark wilderness. There are walking trails, a private fishing pond, swimming pool and playground area on the premises for guests to enjoy. There are three guest rooms in the house, and for those needing even more privacy, the innkeeper offers a private log cabin with two bedrooms, two bathrooms and a room that serves as a living, dining and kitchen area. The gourmet breakfasts include such items as homemade granola, freshly baked breakfasts and peach upside-down French toast. For those celebrating a special occasion, the innkeeper can create unique packages.

Innkeeper(s): Julia Baldridge. $55-125. MC VISA AX DS PC TC. 5 rooms, 3 with PB. 1 cabin. Breakfast and evening snack included in rates. Types of meals: continental breakfast, full breakfast, gourmet breakfast and early coffee/tea. Beds: Q. Ceiling fan in room. VCR and swimming on premises. Antiques, fishing, parks, shopping, theater and watersports nearby.

"This is a great place to look at the stars without the interference of the city lights."

Certificate may be used: Jan. 1-Dec. 31, Sunday-Thursday.

The Olde Stonehouse B&B Inn
511 Main St
Hardy, AR 72542-9034
(501)856-2983 (800)514-2983 Fax:(501)856-4036
E-mail: oldestonehouse@centuryinter.net

Circa 1928. The stone fireplace gracing the comfortable living room of this former banker's home is set with fossils and unusual stones, including an Arkansas diamond. Lace tablecloths, china and sil-

ver make breakfast a special occasion. Each room is decorated to keep the authentic feel of the Roaring '20s. The bedrooms have antiques and ceiling fans. Aunt Jenny's room boasts a clawfoot tub and a white iron bed, while Aunt Bette's room is filled with Victorian-era furniture. Spring River is only one block away and offers canoeing, boating and fishing. Old Hardy Town caters to antique and craft lovers. The innkeepers offer "Secret Suites," located in a nearby historic home. These romantic suites offer

plenty of amenities. Breakfasts in a basket are delivered to the door each morning. The home is listed in the National Register. Murder-mystery weekends and fly-fishing school and guide are available.

Innkeeper(s): Peggy Volland. $69-99. MC VISA AX DS PC TC. 9 rooms with PB, 2 with FP. 2 suites. Breakfast and evening snack included in rates. Types of meals: full breakfast and early coffee/tea. Picnic lunch available. Beds: QDT. Air conditioning, ceiling fan and VCR in room. Fax, copier, bicycles and library on premises. Antiques, fishing, parks, shopping, theater and watersports nearby.

Location: In a historic railroad town.

Publicity: *Memphis Commercial Appeal, Jonesboro Sun, Vacations.*

"For many years we had heard about 'Southern Hospitality' but never thought it could be this good. It was the best!"

Certificate may be used: November-April, anytime except special events. May-October, Sunday-Thursday.

Heber Springs   C6

The Anderson House Inn
201 E Main St
Heber Springs, AR 72543-3116
(501)362-5266 (800)264-5279 Fax:(501)362-2326
E-mail: jhildebr@cswnet.com

Circa 1880. The original section of this welcoming two-story inn was built by one of Heber Springs' founding citizens. The main structure of the inn was built to house a theater, and the home also has enjoyed use as a schoolhouse, doctor's clinic and, when the second story was added, a hotel. Rooms are decorated in a cozy, country motif with bright

colors and floral prints. Many of the antiques that fill each room are available for purchase. Historic Spring Park is just across the street offering pleasant scenery for the inn's guests as well as a variety of activities.

Innkeeper(s): Jim & Susan Hildebrand. $75-108. MC VISA AX DS PC TC. 16 rooms with PB, 1 with FP. 2 conference rooms. Breakfast included in rates. Types of meals: full breakfast and early coffee/tea. Banquet service available. Beds: QDT. Air conditioning and ceiling fan in room. Cable TV, VCR, fax and library on premises. Antiques, fishing, parks, shopping and watersports nearby.

Certificate may be used: Jan. 15 to Oct. 1, Sunday-Thursday.

Kingston
B3

Fool's Cove Ranch B&B
HCR 30 Box 198
Kingston, AR 72742-9608
(501)665-2986 Fax:(501)665-2372
E-mail: klobster@nwark.com

Circa 1979. Situated in the Ozarks' Boston Mountain range, this 6,000-square-foot farmhouse, part of a family farm, offers 160 acres of field, meadow and forest.
Guests who have had their horses test negative on a Coggins test may bring them along and utilize the farm's corrals.
Guests may angle for bass or catfish in the pond. Favorite gathering spots are the roomy parlor and the outdoor hot tub. Area attractions include the Buffalo River, Dogpatch USA and several fine fishing spots.
Innkeeper(s): Mary Jo & Bill Sullivan. $55-75. MC VISA AX DC CB DS PC TC. 4 rooms, 1 with PB. Breakfast included in rates. Types of meals: full breakfast and early coffee/tea. Evening snack available. Beds: QD. Air conditioning, turndown service and ceiling fan in room. Cable TV, VCR, fax, copier, spa, library and pet boarding on premises. Handicap access. Amusement parks, antiques, fishing, parks, shopping, sporting events, theater and watersports nearby.

Certificate may be used: Any day open, subject to availability.

Little Rock
E5

The Empress of Little Rock
2120 Louisiana St
Little Rock, AR 72206-1522
(501)374-7966 Fax:(501)375-4537

Circa 1888. Day lilies, peonies and iris accent the old-fashioned garden of this elaborate, three-story Queen Anne Victorian. A grand center hall opens to a double staircase, lit by a stained-glass skylight. The 7,500 square feet include a sitting room at the top of the tower. The original owner kept a private poker game going here and the stained-glass windows allowed him to keep an eye out for local authorities, who might close down his gambling activities. The Hornibrook Room features a magnificent Renaissance Revival bedroom set with a high canopy. The Tower bedroom has an Austrian walnut bed. Gourmet breakfasts are served in the dining room.
Innkeeper(s): Sharon Welch-Blair. $90-140. MC VISA AX. 5 rooms. 1 suite. Breakfast included in rates. Types of meals: continental breakfast, full breakfast and early coffee/tea. Air conditioning, ceiling fan and TV in

room. Antiques, shopping, sporting events and theater nearby.
Certificate may be used: May 1-May 1, excluding mystery weekends, football weekends and holidays. Selected rooms only.

Hotze House
1619 Louisiana St
Little Rock, AR 72216
(501)376-6563

Circa 1900. Upon its completion, this grand Neoclassical mansion was noted as one of the state's finest homes. Opulent restored woodwork, a fireplace and a staircase carved from a South American mahogany tree grace the impressive front entrance. The home is filled with elegant, period pieces and traditional furnishings. Four of the guest rooms include fireplaces, and despite the turn-of-the-century authenticity, modern amenities of television, telephone and climate control are in each room. The innkeepers strive to make their National Register inn a place for both business travelers and those in search of romance or relaxation. Delectables such as frittatas, poached pears and Belgian waffles are served each morning either in the dining room or conservatory. The innkeepers keep a snack area stocked with hot water, soft drinks, beer, wine, cheese, fruit and the like.
Innkeeper(s): Peggy Tooker, Suzanne & Steve Gates. $80-100. MC VISA AX DC DS PC TC. 4 rooms with PB, 4 with FP. 2 conference rooms. Breakfast included in rates. Types of meals: full breakfast and early coffee/tea. Beds: KQ. Air conditioning, turndown service, ceiling fan and TV in room. VCR, fax, copier and library on premises. Amusement parks, antiques, parks, shopping, sporting events and theater nearby.

Certificate may be used: Anytime, based on availability.

Mammoth Spring
A7

Roseland Inn B&B
570 Bethel, PO Box 4
Mammoth Spring, AR 72554
(501)625-3378

Tucked away in a picturesque country town, this Colonial Revival home is just a stone's throw from one of the world's largest natural springs. Innkeeper Jean Pace, a former Mammoth Spring mayor, has decorated her National Register inn with antiques, collectibles and bright flower arrangements. With its reception hall, large front porch and gazebo, the home has served as a site for parties and weddings. Spring River and Mammoth Spring State Park are nearby, and Jean will refrigerate your daily catch.
Innkeeper(s): Jean Pace. $35-40. 4 rooms. Breakfast included in rates. Type of meal: full breakfast.

Certificate may be used: Year-round, Monday-Thursday, excluding weekends.

Mountain View   B6

Ozark Country Inn

PO Box 1201
Mountain View, AR 72560-1201
(501)269-8699 (800)379-8699

Circa 1906. This historic two-story Federal-style inn is located within a block of Courthouse Square and downtown eateries and shops. A full breakfast is served at 8 a.m. before guests head out to explore the many attractions offered in the surrounding area, including Blanchard Springs Caverns and the Ozark Folk Center.

Innkeeper(s): G.W. & Glenna Northern. $55-65. MC VISA. 6 rooms with PB. Breakfast included in rates. Type of meal: full breakfast. Beds: QDT. Air conditioning and TV in room. VCR on premises. Antiques, fishing, shopping and watersports nearby.

Certificate may be used: March 1-Dec. 1, Sunday through Thursday.

Wildflower B&B

100 Washington St, PO Box 72
Mountain View, AR 72560
(501)269-4383 (800)591-4879

Circa 1918. The inn's wraparound porches are a gathering place for local musicians who often play old-time music. If you sit long enough, you're likely to see an impromptu hootenanny in the Courthouse Square across the street. Since there are no priceless antiques, children are welcome.

Innkeeper(s): Andrea Budy. $42-71. MC VISA AX DS. 8 rooms, 6 with PB. 3 suites. Breakfast included in rates. Types of meals: continental-plus breakfast and early coffee/tea. Beds: DT. Air conditioning, turn-down service and ceiling fan in room. Antiques, fishing, parks, shopping, sporting events, theater and watersports nearby.

Location: In the Ozarks.

Publicity: *New York Times, Dan Rather & CBS, Midwest Living, National Geographic Traveler, Travel Holiday.*

"It's the kind of place you'll look forward to returning to."

Certificate may be used: Sunday through Thursday nights only, excluding special events.

Ozark   C3

1887 Inn B&B

100 E Commercial St
Ozark, AR 72949-3210
(501)667-1121

Circa 1885. At the foot of the Ozarks, this Queen Anne Victorian inn has been lovingly restored to its natural beauty. The inn's accommodations include a Honeymoon/Anniversary Suite, an intimate spot for a romantic candlelight dinner arranged by the innkeeper. Desks, fireplaces and queen beds can be found in the rooms. The decor features antique Victorian and country furnishings. Receptions, special events and weddings are popular here. Less than two blocks away is the Arkansas River.

Innkeeper(s): Karen Britting. $50-60. MC VISA. 4 rooms. 1 suite. Breakfast included in rates. Types of meals: full breakfast and early coffee/tea. Dinner, evening snack, picnic lunch, lunch, gourmet lunch, banquet service, catering service, catered breakfast and room service available. Air conditioning, turndown service and ceiling fan in room. Cable TV and VCR on premises. Antiques and shopping nearby.

Certificate may be used: Anytime based on availability.

California

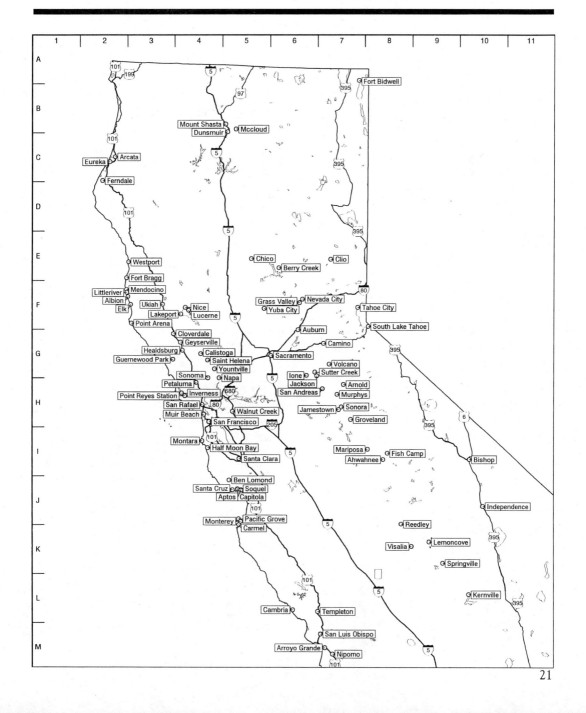

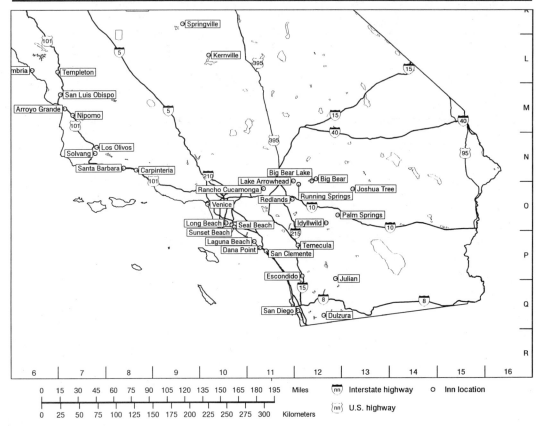

	Miles		
0 15 30 45 60 75 90 105 120 135 150 165 180 195		(nn) Interstate highway	o Inn location
0 25 50 75 100 125 150 175 200 225 250 275 300	Kilometers	(nn) U.S. highway	

Ahwahnee   I8

Apple Blossom Inn B&B
44606 Silver Spur Tr
Ahwahnee, CA 93601
(209)642-2001
E-mail: lhays@sierranet.net.

Circa 1991. A bountiful organic apple orchard surrounds this inn, an attractive country cottage a
short distance from Yosemite National Park. Visitors
choose either the Red Delicious Room, with its two
double beds and private entrance, or the Granny
Smith Room, with queen bed and private balcony.
Both rooms feature ceiling fans, private bath and
sitting areas. Guests enjoy the inn's woodburning
stove and the spa overlooking the woods.
Innkeeper(s): Lance, Lynn & Jenny Hays. $55-130. MC VISA AX DS
TC. 3 rooms, 2 with PB. Breakfast, afternoon tea and evening snack
included in rates. Types of meals: full breakfast and early coffee/tea.
Beds: QD. Air conditioning, turndown service, ceiling fan and VCR in
room. Spa on premises. Antiques, fishing, parks, shopping, downhill
skiing, cross-country skiing, theater and watersports nearby.
Certificate may be used: Oct. 15-March 30, Sunday-Thursday

Albion   F3

Albion Ridge Huckleberry House
29381 Albion Ridge Rd
Albion, CA 95410-9701
(707)937-2374 (800)482-5532 Fax:(707)937-1644
Circa 1995. Acres of Redwood and huckleberry
bushes surround this romantic hideaway tucked just
off the Mendocino coast. The grounds offer a pond
stocked with rainbow trout. The suites include fireplaces and private decks, and the tower room affords
a view of the pond. Three guest rooms include the
amenities of coffee, tea and a refrigerator stocked
with drinks. In the evening, gaze at the stars or grab
a movie from the house library. The innkeepers also
offer a secluded cottage.
Innkeeper(s): Jon & Sally Geller. $100-150. MC VISA PC. 4 rooms, 3
with FP. 2 suites. 1 cottage. Breakfast included in rates. Types of meals:
full breakfast, gourmet breakfast and early coffee/tea. Beds: Q. VCR in
room. Fax on premises. Antiques, fishing, parks, shopping, theater and
watersports nearby.
Certificate may be used: Dec. 1-14, Jan. 8-April 11, midweek
(Sunday-Thursday).

Aptos   J5

Apple Lane Inn
6265 Soquel Dr
Aptos, CA 95003-3117
(408)475-6868 (800)649-8988 Fax:(408)464-5790
Circa 1870. Ancient apple trees border the lane that leads to this Victorian farmhouse set on two acres of gardens and fields. Built by the Porter

brothers, founding fathers of Aptos, the inn is decorated with Victorian wallpapers and hardwood floors. The original wine cellar still exists, as well as the old barn and apple-drying shed used for storage after harvesting the orchard. Miles of beaches are within walking distance. The innkeepers were married at the inn and later purchased it.
Innkeeper(s): Doug & Diana Groom. $95-150. 5 rooms with PB. 2 suites. Breakfast included in rates. Types of meals: full breakfast, gourmet breakfast and early coffee/tea. Afternoon tea and evening snack available. Beds: QDT. Turndown service in room. Cable TV, fax, copier, library and pet boarding on premises. Handicap access. Antiques, parks, shopping, sporting events, theater and watersports nearby.
Location: One mile from the beach, five minutes south of Santa Cruz.
Publicity: *Santa Barbara Times, 1001 Decorating Ideas, New York Times.*

"Our room was spotless and beautifully decorated."
Certificate may be used: All year, Sunday-Thursday except holidays.

Bayview Hotel
8041 Soquel Dr
Aptos, CA 95003-3928
(408)688-8654 (800)422-9843 Fax:(408)688-5128
E-mail: pobrien@bluespruce.com
Circa 1878. This Victorian hotel is the oldest operating inn on the Monterey Coast. Each of the rooms is decorated with local art, antiques, fireplaces and sitting areas. The inn is just half a mile from beautiful beaches, and a redwood forest is nearby. This inn is

an ideal spot for those seeking relaxation or those on a coastal trip. Monterey and San Jose are less than an hour from the hotel, and San Francisco is 90 miles north. Hearty breakfasts are served in the inn's dining room, and there is also has an on-site restaurant.
Innkeeper(s): Gwen Burkhard. $90-150. MC VISA AX TC. 11 rooms with PB, 2 with FP. 1 suite. 1 conference room. Breakfast included in rates. Types of meals: gourmet breakfast and early coffee/tea. Afternoon tea available. Restaurant on premises. Beds: KQD. Turndown service, TV and VCR in room. Fax and copier on premises. Amusement parks, antiques, parks, shopping and watersports nearby.
Location: Santa Cruz County.
Publicity: *Mid-County Post, Santa Cruz Sentinel.*

"Thank you so much for all of your tender loving care and great hospitality."
Certificate may be used: Sunday-Thursday nights, all year.

Mangels House
570 Aptos Creek Rd, PO Box 302
Aptos, CA 95001
(408)688-7982
Circa 1886. Claus Mangels made his fortune in sugar beets and built this house in the style of a Southern mansion. The inn, with its encircling veranda, stands on four acres of lawns and orchards. It is bounded by the Forest of Nisene Marks, 10,000 acres of redwood trees, creeks and trails. Monterey Bay is three-quarters of a mile away.
Innkeeper(s): Jacqueline Fisher. $105-145. MC VISA AX. 6 rooms with PB, 1 with FP. 1 conference room. Breakfast included in rates. Types of meals: full breakfast and early coffee/tea. Evening snack available. Beds: KQT. Amusement parks, antiques, fishing, shopping, sporting events, theater and watersports nearby.
Location: Central Coast.
Publicity: *Inn Serv, Innviews.*

"Compliments on the lovely atmosphere. We look forward to sharing our discovery with friends and returning with them."
Certificate may be used: All year, Sunday-Thursday, holiday weekends excepted, closed over Christmas

Arcata   C2

Hotel Arcata
708 9th St
Arcata, CA 95521-6206
(707)826-0217 (800)344-1221 Fax:(707)826-1737
Circa 1915. This historic landmark hotel is a fine example of Beaux Arts-style architecture. Several rooms overlook Arcata's downtown plaza, which is just

across the way. A variety of rooms are available, each decorated in turn-of-the-century style. All rooms include pedestal sinks and clawfoot tubs. The hotel offers a full-service, renown Japanese restaurant, offering excellent cuisine, and there are many other fine restaurants within walking distance. Guests also enjoy free use of a nearby health club. The starting point of Arcata's architectural homes tour is within walking distance of the hotel.
Innkeeper(s): Virgil Moorehead. $90-142. MC VISA AX DC CB DS TC. 31 rooms with PB. 7 suites. 1 conference room. Breakfast included in rates. Type of meal: continental breakfast. Dinner, lunch, banquet service, catering service and room service available. Restaurant on premises. Beds: KQT. TV in room. Fax and copier on premises. Handicap access. Antiques, fishing, parks, shopping, sporting events, theater and watersports nearby.
Certificate may be used: Subject to availability.

Arnold   H7

Lodge at Manuel Mill B&B
PO Box 998
Arnold, CA 95223-0998
(209)795-2622

Circa 1950. Overlooking a three-acre lake that comes right up to the wraparound deck, this log lodge was once the site of a 19th-century lumber mill. Some structures on the property are a century old. The 43 acres of woods include sugar cone pines with 18-inch cones, dogwood and wild blackberries, and traces of the mill's gauge rail system. Sounds of the 24-foot waterfall that cascades over rocks may be heard from the rooms that open to the deck. The Lottie Crabtree Room, named for a spirited performer in the Gold Rush days, is a peaceful, cozy retreat. The Mr. Manuel Room basks in 19th-century ambiance with an oak canopy bed and Victorian decor. The innkeepers prepare a hearty breakfast and present guests with a bottle of wine upon arrival. Martha Stewart-type weddings are popular here. Calaveras Big Trees State Park, known for its giant sequoias, is nearby.
Innkeeper(s): Linda Johnson. $100-135. MC VISA. 5 rooms with PB. 1 suite. Breakfast included in rates. Type of meal: full breakfast. Picnic lunch and catering service available. Beds: KQD. Swimming on premises. Fishing, downhill skiing, cross-country skiing and watersports nearby.
Certificate may be used: Sunday-Thursday, November-April.

Arroyo Grande   M7

Crystal Rose Inn
789 Valley Rd
Arroyo Grande, CA 93420-4417
(805)481-1854 (800)767-3466 Fax:(805)481-9541

Circa 1890. Once the homestead for a large walnut farm, this picturesque Victorian inn features an acre

and a half of gardens. The inn is decorated with period pieces and reproductions. The gardens are a favorite setting for weddings. Guests are pampered with afternoon tea, evening wine and hors d'oeuvres and full, gourmet breakfast. The inn also houses The Hunt Club, a restaurant serving lunch, dinner and Sunday brunch.
Innkeeper(s): Bonnie Royster. $90-180. MAP. MC VISA AX DS. 8 rooms, 5 with PB. 3 suites. 1 conference room. Breakfast, afternoon tea and evening snack included in rates. Type of meal: full breakfast. Dinner, picnic lunch, lunch, catering service and room service available. Restaurant on premises. Beds: KQDT. Handicap access. Antiques, fishing, theater and watersports nearby.
Location: Halfway between Los Angeles & San Francisco off Hwy 101.
Publicity: *Los Angeles Times, Daughters of Painted Ladies, Travel, Five Cities Times-Press Recorder, Santa Maria Times, Telegram Tribune, Travel & Leisure.*

"What a wonderful magical experience we had at the Crystal Rose. We chose the beautiful Queen Elizabeth room with the enchanted tower. Our romantic interlude was just perfect."
Certificate may be used: Sunday through Thursday of any week.

Auburn   G6

Lincoln House B&B
191 Lincoln Way
Auburn, CA 95603-4415
(916)885-8880

Circa 1933. In the heart of California's gold country, travelers will find the Lincoln House, a captivating Bungalow home. The romantic Shenandoah Room offers a queen-size bed and a view of the inn's koi fish pond. A petrified wood fireplace beautifully complements the Southwest theme of the sitting room, and the dining room boasts a view of the Sierra Nevada mountains. When they are not exploring historic Old Town Auburn, guests may take a dip in the inn's swimming pool or relax on its covered porch.
Innkeeper(s): Leslie & Stan Fronczak. $69-85. MC VISA TC. 3 rooms with PB. 1 suite. Breakfast, afternoon tea and evening snack included in rates. Types of meals: full breakfast, gourmet breakfast and early coffee/tea. Beds: KQT. Air conditioning in room. Spa, swimming and library on premises. Antiques, fishing, parks, shopping, downhill skiing, cross-country skiing, sporting events, theater and watersports nearby.
Certificate may be used: May-October, Sunday through Thursday; October-May, every day except holidays.

Ben Lomond
J5

Fairview Manor
245 Fairview Ave
Ben Lomond, CA 95005-9347
(408)336-3355 (800)553-8840

Circa 1924. More than two acres of woods and foliage shroud this home, offering a private, tranquil setting for guests to enjoy. Follow the paths that wind through the grounds and you'll find lily ponds and the San Lorenzo River. The home rests on the former site of the Ben Lomond Hotel, which was destroyed by fire in 1906. A prominent San Francisco attorney chose this spot to build his summer home, and the manor stayed in the family until the 1980s when the current innkeepers purchased it. The cozy guest rooms are decorated with antiques.
Innkeeper(s): Nancy Glasson. $109-119. MC VISA. 7 rooms, 5 with PB. 1 conference room. Breakfast and evening snack included in rates. Type of meal: full breakfast. Beds: KQ. Handicap access. Antiques, fishing, parks, shopping and watersports nearby.

Certificate may be used: Sunday through Thursday, year-round.

Berry Creek
E6

Lake Oroville Bed and Breakfast
240 Sunday Dr
Berry Creek, CA 95916-9640
(916)589-0700 (800)455-5253 Fax:(916)589-5313

Circa 1970. Situated in the quiet foothills above Lake Oroville, this country inn features panoramic views from the private porches that extend from each

guest room. Two favorite rooms are the Rose Petal Room and the Victorian Room, both with lake views and whirlpool tubs. The inn's 40 acres are studded with oak and pine trees. Deer and songbirds abound.
Innkeeper(s): Cheryl & Ron Damberger. $75-135. MC VISA AX DS PC TC. 6 rooms with PB. 1 conference room. Breakfast included in rates. Types of meals: full breakfast and early coffee/tea. Banquet service available. Beds: KQ. Air conditioning, turndown service, ceiling fan, TV and VCR in room. Fax, copier, spa, library, pet boarding and child care on premises. Handicap access. Antiques, fishing, parks, shopping, golf, theater and watersports nearby.
Location: Twenty minutes out of Oroville in the foothills above the lake.
Publicity: *Oroville Mercury-Register, Chronicle, San Joe Mercury.*

Certificate may be used: Sunday-Thursday (except holidays). All year.

Big Bear
N12

Gold Mountain Manor Historic B&B
1117 Anita, PO Box 2027
Big Bear, CA 92314
(909)585-6997 (800)509-2604 Fax:(909)585-0327
E-mail: goldmtn@bigbear.com

Circa 1928. This spectacular log mansion was once a hideaway for the rich and famous. Eight fireplaces provide a roaring fire in each room in fall and winter. The Lucky Baldwin Room offers a hearth made from stones of gold gathered in the famous Lucky Baldwin mine nearby. In the Clark Gable room is the fireplace Gable and Carole Lombard enjoyed on their  honeymoon. Gourmet country breakfasts and afternoon hors d'oeuvres are served. In addition to the guest rooms, there are three cabins.
Innkeeper(s): Robert Angilella & Jose Tapia. $125-190. MC VISA DS. 6 rooms with PB, 6 with FP. 2 suites. 3 cottages. 1 conference room. Afternoon tea and evening snack included in rates. Types of meals: full breakfast, gourmet breakfast and early coffee/tea. Beds: Q. Ceiling fan in room. Cable TV, VCR, fax, spa, bicycles and library on premises. Fishing, parks, downhill skiing, cross-country skiing, sporting events and watersports nearby.
Location: Two hours northeast of Los Angeles and Orange counties.
Publicity: *Fifty Most Romantic Places, Kenny G holiday album cover.*

"A majestic experience! In this magnificent house, history comes alive!"

Certificate may be used: January through Dec. 20, Monday through Thursday, non-holidays

Big Bear Lake
N12

Eagle's Nest B&B
41675 Big Bear Blvd, Box 1003
Big Bear Lake, CA 92315
(909)866-6465 Fax:(909)866-6025
E-mail: enbb@bigbear.com

Circa 1983. Named for the more than 50 American bald eagles that nest in and around Big Bear, this lodgepole pine inn features a river rock fireplace in the parlor. Antiques, bronzed eagles and baskets of flowers provide a warm mountain setting. Surrounded by tall pine trees, the property also includes several cottage suites.

Innkeeper(s): Diane & Don Johnson. $75-170. MC VISA AX PC. 10 rooms, 5 with PB, 5 with FP. 5 suites. 5 cottages. Breakfast, afternoon tea and evening snack included in rates. Types of meals: full breakfast and early coffee/tea. Beds: Q. Ceiling fan and TV in room. VCR and fax on premises. Antiques, fishing, parks, shopping, downhill skiing, cross-country skiing, golf, theater and watersports nearby.

Publicity: *Los Angeles Times, Sun Living, AM Los Angeles.*

"Each breakfast was delicious and beautiful. A lot of thought and care is obvious in everything you do."

Certificate may be used: Anytime except holidays, subject to availability.

Truffles, A Special Place
PO Box 130649
Big Bear Lake, CA 92315-8972
(909)585-2772

Romance abounds at this mountain inn, which is decorated in a whimsical, English-country style. Rooms include four-poster or antique beds topped with luxurious feather mattresses. The Queen's Legacy room includes a soaking tub, while the Lady Rose offers a cozy alcove sitting area. Other rooms include special features such as a Palladian window or iron bed decorated with cherubs. Ever true to the inn's name, a truffle is placed on each pillow during the nightly turndown service. Those celebrating special occasions might find flowers or champagne in their rooms. The innkeepers deliver morning coffee or tea to their guests, and serve a lavish breakfast, afternoon tea and desserts in the evenings.

Innkeeper(s): Marilyn Kane. $110-140. MC VISA. 5 rooms. Breakfast included in rates. Type of meal: full breakfast.

Certificate may be used: March through June, September and October, Sunday through Thursday.

Wainwright Inn B&B
PO Box 130406
Big Bear Lake, CA 92315-8962
(909)585-6914

Circa 1981. This Tudor-style B&B is located in a quiet, tree-filled residential area adjacent to Bear Mountain ski resort and golf course. The most popular accommodation is the Honeymoon Hideaway, with whirlpool for two, sleigh bed, fireplace, wet bar and private entrance. Canopy beds and English country antiques are found throughout the inn. Afternoon tea is served in the solarium and there's a massive brick fireplace in the Great Room.

Innkeeper(s): Sharon Berton. $95-175. AP. MC VISA AX DC CB. 4 rooms, 2 with PB, 1 with FP. 1 suite. 1 conference room. Breakfast included in rates. Types of meals: full breakfast and early coffee/tea. Picnic lunch available. Beds: Q. Turndown service in room. Cable TV, VCR, spa and bicycles on premises. Antiques, fishing, parks, shopping, downhill skiing, cross-country skiing and theater nearby.

Location: Adjacent to Bear Mountain Ski Resort.

Publicity: *Los Angeles Times, Gourmet Getaway.*

Certificate may be used: Weekdays anytime except Dec. 15-Jan. 15. Seven days a week April 1-June 15.

Bishop

The Matlick House
1313 Rowan Ln
Bishop, CA 93514-1937
(619)873-3133 (800)898-3133

Circa 1906. This gray and pink home with a double veranda was built by Alan Matlick, one of the area's pioneers. The spacious parlor features a clawfoot settee with massive curved arms, antique reclin-

er, European burled-wood armoire and original cherry-wood fireplace. Rooms boast special pieces such as the white iron bed, Eastlake chair and quilted settee in the Lenna room. Guests will enjoy the home's views of both the Sierra Nevadas and the White Mountains. A hearty American breakfast with eggs, bacon and homemade biscuits is served in the dining room. The Eastern Sierras provide a wealth of activities, year-round catch-and-release fly fishing is within 20 minutes from the home.

Innkeeper(s): Ray & Barbara Showalter. $79-89. MC VISA AX DS TC. 5 rooms with PB. Breakfast and evening snack included in rates. Types of meals: continental-plus breakfast, full breakfast and early coffee/tea. Picnic lunch, lunch and catering service available. Beds: QT. Air conditioning and ceiling fan in room. Cable TV, VCR and fax on premises. Antiques, fishing, parks, shopping, downhill skiing and cross-country skiing nearby.

Publicity: *Inyo Register, Sunset.*

"Like sleeping on a nice pink cloud after our Rock Creek Horse drive."

Certificate may be used: Anytime except last two weeks of May (Mule Days).

Calistoga

Foothill House
3037 Foothill Blvd
Calistoga, CA 94515-1225
(707)942-6933 (800)942-6933 Fax:(707)942-5692

Circa 1892. This country farmhouse overlooks the western foothills of Mount St. Helena. Graceful old California oaks and pockets of flowers greet guests.

Each room features country antiques, a four-poster bed, a fireplace and a small refrigerator. Breakfast is served in the sun room or is delivered personally to your room in a basket. Three rooms offer private Jacuzzi tubs.

Innkeeper(s): Doris & Gus Beckert. $135-275. MC VISA AX DS PC TC. 4 suites, 4 with FP. Breakfast and evening snack included in rates. Types of meals: full breakfast, gourmet breakfast and early coffee/tea. Beds: KQT. Air conditioning, turndown service, ceiling fan, TV and VCR in room. Fax, copier and library on premises. Amusement parks, antiques, fishing, parks, shopping and watersports nearby.

Location: Napa Valley.

Publicity: *Herald Examiner, Baltimore Sun, Sunset, S.F. Examiner.*

"Gourmet treats served in front of an open fire. Hospitality never for a moment flagged."

Certificate may be used: December-January, Sunday through Thursday, holidays excluded.

Cambria   L6

The J. Patrick House
2990 Burton Dr
Cambria, CA 93428-4002
(805)927-3812 (800)341-5258
E-mail: jph@jpatrickhouse.com

Circa 1983. This charming log cabin bed & breakfast is nestled in the woods overlooking Cambria's east village. The picturesque grounds include a garden area that separates the main house from the redwood cabin, where all but one of the guest rooms are located. Each of the guest rooms includes a wood-burning fireplace. Rooms are decorated in a romantic style with hand-stitched quilts and feather-filled duvet covers atop the beds. Wine and hors d'oeuvres are served each evening in the main house's fireplaced living room. Fresh fruits, homemade granola and freshly baked breads and muffins are among the fare during the morning meal. Be sure to request one of the innkeeper's "killer" chocolate chip cookies.

Innkeeper(s): Barbara & Mel Schwimmer. $115-180. MC VISA DS PC TC. 8 rooms, 7 with PB, 8 with FP. 1 suite. Breakfast and evening snack included in rates. Types of meals: continental-plus breakfast and early coffee/tea. Beds: KQ. Fax and copier on premises. Antiques, fishing, parks, shopping, golf, theater and watersports nearby.

Publicity: *Los Angeles Times, Country Living.*

Certificate may be used: Sunday-Thursday, excludes August, excludes last two weeks in December and last two weeks in November, excludes holiday periods.

Olallieberry Inn
2476 Main St
Cambria, CA 93428-3406
(805)927-3222 Fax:(805)927-0202

Circa 1873. This restored Greek Revival home features rooms decorated with fabrics and wall coverings and furnished with period antiques. Six of the guest rooms feature fireplaces. Butterfly and herb gardens and a 110-year-old redwood grace the front yard. The cheery gathering room boasts a view of the Santa Rosa Creek. Full breakfast with fresh breads, fruits and a special entree start off the day, and wine and hors d'oeuvres are served in the afternoon. The inn is within walking distance to restaurants and shops.

Innkeeper(s): Peter & Carol Ann Irsfeld. $90-175. MC VISA TC. 9 rooms with PB, 6 with FP. 1 suite. Breakfast and evening snack included in rates. Types of meals: full breakfast, gourmet breakfast and early coffee/tea. Beds: KQ. Fax on premises. Handicap access. Antiques, fishing, shopping and watersports nearby.

Location: Central coast wine country.

Publicity: *Los Angeles Times, Elmer Dills Radio Show.*

"Our retreat turned into relaxation, romance and pure Victorian delight."

Certificate may be used: Sunday-Thursday, except May 1-Oct. 31 and holidays.

The Squibb House
4063 Burton Dr
Cambria, CA 93428-3001
(805)927-9600

Circa 1877. A picket fence and large garden surround this Victorian inn with its Italianate and Gothic Revival architecture. Guests may relax in the main parlor, stroll the gardens or sit and rock on the porch. The home was built by a Civil War veteran and young school teacher. The downstairs once was used as a classroom while an addition was being made in the town's school. Each guest room has a firestove.

Innkeeper(s): Martha Carolyn. $95-140. MC VISA PC TC. 5 rooms with PB, 5 with FP. Breakfast included in rates. Types of meals: continental breakfast and continental-plus breakfast. Beds: Q. Antiques, fishing, parks, shopping, golf and theater nearby. Publicity: *Cambrian.*

Certificate may be used: Sunday-Thursday only, November-March, not valid during holiday weeks.

Camino   G7

The Camino Hotel-Seven Mile House
4103 Carson Rd, PO Box 1197
Camino, CA 95709
(916)644-7740 (800)200-7740 Fax:(916)644-7740

Circa 1888. Once a barracks for the area's loggers, this inn now caters to visitors in the state's famed gold country. Just east of Placerville, historic Camino is on the Old Carson Wagon Trail. Nine guest rooms are available, including the E.J. Barrett Room, a favorite with honeymooners. Other rooms feature names such as Pony Express, Stage Stop and Wagon Train. The family-oriented inn welcomes children, and a local park offers a handy site for their recreational needs. Popular area activities include antiquing, hot air ballooning and wine tasting.

Innkeeper(s): Paula Norbert & John Eddy. $65-95. AP. MC VISA AX DS PC TC. 9 rooms, 3 with PB. 1 conference room. Breakfast and evening snack included in rates. Types of meals: full breakfast and early coffee/tea. Afternoon tea, picnic lunch and banquet service available. Beds: QDT. Turndown service and ceiling fan in room. Fax, copier and library on premises. Antiques, fishing, parks, shopping, downhill skiing, cross-country skiing, theater and watersports nearby.

Location: In the Apple Hill area of California's Gold Country.

Certificate may be used: Year-round except Friday, Saturday, Sunday in September, October, November.

Capitola-By-The-Sea   J5

Inn at Depot Hill
250 Monterey Ave
Capitola-By-The-Sea, CA 95010-3358
(408)462-3376 (800)572-2632 Fax:(408)462-3697

Circa 1901. Once a railroad depot, this inn offers rooms with themes to represent different parts of the world: a chic auberge in St. Tropez, a romantic hideaway in Paris, an Italian coastal villa, a summer home on the coast of Holland, and a traditional English garden room. Five rooms have garden patios boasting hot tubs. The rooms have many amenities, including a fireplace, white marble bathrooms and featherbeds. Guests are greeted with fresh flowers in their room.

Innkeeper(s): Suzie Lankes & Dan Floyd. $165-250. MC VISA AX TC. 12 rooms with PB, 8 with FP. 4 suites. 1 conference room. Breakfast and evening snack included in rates. Beds: KQT. Turndown service, TV and VCR in room. Fax and spa on premises. Handicap access. Amusement parks, antiques, fishing, parks, shopping, golf, theater and watersports nearby.

Publicity: *Country Inn, Santa Cruz Sentinel, McCalls, Choices & Vacation, San Jose Mercury News, Fresno & Sacramento Bee, San Francisco Focus, American Airline Flight, SF Examiner and Sunset.*

"The highlight of our honeymoon. Five stars in our book!"

Certificate may be used: Monday-Thursday, November through April. Excludes holidays and special events.

Carmel   J5

Cobblestone Inn
PO Box 3185
Carmel, CA 93921-3185
(408)625-5222 (800)833-8836 Fax:(408)625-0478

An exterior of wood and cobblestone gathered from the Carmel River provide a friendly facade for visi-

tors to this bed & breakfast located two blocks from the heart of Carmel. Each guest room has its own cobblestone fireplace. The inn's English country decor is enhanced with quilts, a colorful antique carousel horse and other early American antiques. In addition to breakfast and afternoon tea, evening wine and hors d'oeuvres are served. Guests can borrow one of the inn's bicycles to explore the area. The beach and shopping are nearby. Cobblestone is one of the Four Sisters Inns.

Innkeeper(s): Suzi Russo. $95-180. 24 rooms with PB, 24 with FP. Breakfast and afternoon tea included in rates. Types of meals: gourmet breakfast and early coffee/tea. Picnic lunch available. Fax and copier on premises.

Publicity: *Country Inns, Honeymoons.*

Certificate may be used: December & January; Sunday-Thursday, holidays & special events excluded, subject to availability.

The Stonehouse Inn
PO Box 2517, 8th Below Monte Verde
Carmel, CA 93921-2517
(408)624-4569 (800)748-6618

Circa 1906. This quaint Carmel country house boasts a stone exterior, made from beach rocks collected and hand shaped by local Indians at the turn of the century. The original owner, "Nana" Foster,

was hostess to notable artists and writers from the San Francisco area, including Sinclair Lewis, Jack London and Lotta Crabtree. The romantic Jack London room features a dramatic gabled ceiling, a brass bed and a stunning view of the ocean. Conveniently located, the inn is a short walk from Carmel Beach and two blocks from the village.

Innkeeper(s): Kevin Navailles. $89-199. MC VISA AX. 6 rooms, 2 with PB. Breakfast included in rates. Type of meal: full breakfast. Beds: KQDT. Fishing, parks, shopping, theater and watersports nearby.

Location: Two blocks to downtown, 4 blocks to beach.

Publicity: *Travel & Leisure, Country Living.*

"First time stay at a B&B — GREAT!"

Certificate may be used: Nov. 1 through May 31, Sunday through Thursday, except special events such as Thanksgiving, Christmas, New Year, AT&T Golf Tournament.

Carpinteria   N8

Prufrock's Garden Inn
600 Linden Ave
Carpinteria, CA 93013-2040
(805)566-9696 (888)778-3765 Fax:(805)566-9696
Circa 1904. A white picket fence surrounds this California-style cottage, which is just a few blocks from the beach. Five generations of the home's original family lived in this cozy inn. The bedrooms offer private sitting areas. Relax on the porch or stroll through the lush gardens. Carpinteria offers several antique shops and an open-air farmers' market.
Innkeeper(s): Judy & Jon Halversen. $99-199. MC VISA DS PC TC. 7 rooms, 5 with PB. Breakfast, afternoon tea and evening snack included in rates. Types of meals: full breakfast and early coffee/tea. Beds: Q. Turndown service and VCR in room. Bicycles on premises. Antiques, fishing, parks, shopping, sporting events, theater and watersports nearby.
Certificate may be used: Oct. 1-June 30, Sunday-Thursday.

Chico   E5

The Esplanade B&B
620 The Esplanade
Chico, CA 95926
(916)345-8084
Circa 1914. Each of the rooms at this comfortable bed & breakfast is named for someone special in innkeeper Lois Kloss' life. One room includes a Jacuzzi tub and stained-glass window. Others feature poster beds piled high with feather pillows. Lois serves a buffet-style breakfast in the morning, and treats guests to a glass of wine in the afternoons. The home is within walking distance from the university, downtown Chico and the Chico Museum.
Innkeeper(s): Lois I. Kloss. $45-65. MC VISA TC. 6 rooms with PB. Breakfast, afternoon tea and evening snack included in rates. Types of meals: full breakfast and early coffee/tea. Room service available. Beds: QDT. Air conditioning, ceiling fan and TV in room. Fax on premises. Amusement parks, antiques, fishing, parks, shopping, downhill skiing, cross-country skiing, sporting events, theater and watersports nearby.
Certificate may be used: All year, Sunday through Thursday.

Music Express Inn
1091 El Monte Ave
Chico, CA 95928-9153
(530)345-8376 Fax:(530)893-8521
E-mail: icobeen@aol.com
Circa 1977. Music-lovers will delight in this inn's warmth and charm. Nine air-conditioned guest rooms, all with private bath and cable TV, provide country-style comfort to those visiting the college town of Chico. Guests will awake to the smell of homemade bread or rolls. Visitors are welcome to tickle the ivories of the inn's Steinway grand piano. The innkeeper, a music teacher, is adept at many instruments and plays mandolin in a local band. The inn's library also lures many guests, and those who explore the surrounding area will find plenty of opportunities for antiquing and fishing.
Innkeeper(s): Barney & Irene Cobeen. $55-85. MC VISA AX DS PC TC. 9 rooms with PB. 1 suite. 1 cottage. 2 conference rooms. Breakfast included in rates. Type of meal: full breakfast. Beds: KQDT. Air conditioning, ceiling fan, TV and VCR in room. Fax, copier and library on premises. Handicap access. Antiques, fishing, parks, shopping, sporting events, theater and watersports nearby.
Certificate may be used: All year, Sunday-Thursday.

Clio   E7

White Sulphur Springs Ranch
PO Box 136
Clio, CA 96106-0136
(916)836-2387 (800)854-1797 Fax:(916)836-2387
Circa 1857. Originally built by partners in the Jamison mine, this stage coach stop serviced the Truckee to Quincy stage. The inn has passed from relative to relative to friend and has not been sold since 1867 when it was purchased by George McLear. Elegantly restored, the rooms still retain many of the original furnishings, now embellished with colorful wallpapers and fabrics. The Marble Room features a moss green velvet fainting couch, marble-topped antiques and a splendid view of the Mohawk Valley. Breakfast is served in the dining room. Mineral waters from five 85-degree springs fill the inn's swimming pool.
Innkeeper(s): Don & Karen Miller, Tom & Linda Vanella. $85-140. MC VISA DS TC. 9 rooms, 3 with PB. 2 conference rooms. Breakfast and afternoon tea included in rates. Types of meals: full breakfast and early coffee/tea. Picnic lunch available. Beds: KQD. Air conditioning in room. Cable TV, VCR, fax and copier on premises. Handicap access. Antiques, fishing, parks, shopping, downhill skiing, cross-country skiing and watersports nearby.
Publicity: *Sacramento Union, Plumas-Sierra.*
"White Sulphur Springs is alive with its past and its present."
Certificate may be used: Monday-Thursday, year-round, no holidays.

Cloverdale   G3

The Shelford House
29955 River Rd
Cloverdale, CA 95425-3523
(707)894-5956 (800)833-6479 Fax:(707)894-8621
E-mail: email@shelford.com

Circa 1885. Shelford House is a charming yellow
Queen Anne Victorian with lilac trim. The two-acre
grounds are lush and fragrant, and include a small
swimming pool. Guests enjoy views of surrounding
vineyards, and there are more than 150 wineries to
visit. The interior of the home is done in period
style, with clawfoot tubs and antiques. In the
evenings, the innkeepers offer wine to their guests,
and in the mornings, entrees such as almond French
toast are accompanied by chicken-apple sausage and
strawberry parfaits. For an additional fee, guests can
enjoy a tour of the area in an antique car.
Innkeeper(s): Bill & Lou Ann Brennock. $90-135. AP. MC VISA AX DS
PC. 6 rooms with PB. Breakfast and evening snack included in rates.
Types of meals: full breakfast, gourmet breakfast and early coffee/tea.
Beds: KQ. Air conditioning and ceiling fan in room. Fax, copier, spa,
swimming, stables and bicycles on premises. Antiques, fishing, parks
and watersports nearby.

Publicity: *Inland Empire Business Journal.*

"We just love your beautiful location."

Certificate may be used: Dec. 1-April 30, Sunday through Thursday.

Dana Point   P11

Blue Lantern Inn
34343 Street of The Blue Lantern
Dana Point, CA 92629
(714)661-1304 (800)950-1236 Fax:(714)496-1483

Circa 1990. The four-diamond inn is situated high
on a blufftop overlooking a stunning coastline and
the blue waters of Dana Point harbor with its pleasure craft, fishing boats and the tall ship, Pilgrim.
Each guest room features both a fireplace and a
whirlpool tub and many offer private sundecks.
Afternoon tea, evening turndown service and bicycles are just a few of the amenities available. In the
evening, wine and hors d'oeuvres are served. Shops,
restaurants and beaches are nearby, and popular
Laguna Beach is just a few miles to the north. Blue
Lantern is one of the Four Sisters Inns.
Innkeeper(s): Lin McMahon. $135-350. MC VISA AX TC. 29 rooms
with PB, 29 with FP. 3 conference rooms. Breakfast and afternoon tea
included in rates. Type of meal: gourmet breakfast. Picnic lunch available. Beds: KQD. Turndown service in room. Fax and bicycles on
premises. Handicap access. Amusement parks, antiques, fishing,
parks, shopping and watersports nearby.

Location: Overlooking yacht harbor near Laguna Beach.

Publicity: *Los Angeles Magazine, Glamour, Oregonian, Orange County
Register.*

Certificate may be used: Sunday-Thursday, holidays & events excluded, September-May 31, subject to availability.

Dulzura   Q12

Brookside Farm
1373 Marron Valley Rd
Dulzura, CA 91917-2113
(619)468-3043

Circa 1929. Ancient oaks shade terraces leading
from the farmhouse to a murmuring brook. Behind a
nearby stone barn, there is a grape arbor and
beneath it, a spa. Each
room in the inn and
its cottage is fur-
nished with vintage
pieces and hand-
made quilts.
Adventurous hik-
ers can explore mines
nearby, which date
from the gold rush of 1908.
Innkeeper Edd Guishard is a former
award-winning restaurant owner.
Innkeeper(s): Sally or Edd Guishard. $75-115. MC VISA AX DC CB DS.
11 rooms with PB, 4 with FP. 2 suites. 1 conference room. Breakfast
and dinner included in rates. Type of meal: full breakfast. Beds: Q.
Handicap access.

Location: Thirty-five minutes southeast of San Diego.

Publicity: *California, San Diego Home & Garden.*

*"Our stay at the farm was the most relaxing weekend
we've had in a year."*

Certificate may be used: Sunday-Thursday. Dinner not included.

Dunsmuir   B5

Dunsmuir Inn
5423 Dunsmuir Ave
Dunsmuir, CA 96025-2011
(916)235-4543 (888)386-7684 Fax:(916)235-4154

Circa 1925. Set in the Sacramento River Valley,
this country-style inn may serve as a base for an
assortment of outdoor activities. At the end of the
day, guests can enjoy an old-fashioned soda or ice
cream cone. Fishing, available in the crystal-clear
waters of the Upper Sacramento River, is within
walking distance. The innkeepers can suggest hiking
trails and driving tours to mountain lakes, waterfalls, the Castle Crags State Park and Mt. Shasta.
Innkeeper(s): Jerry & Julie Iskra. $60-70. MC VISA AX DC CB DS PC
TC. 5 rooms, 4 with PB. 1 suite. Breakfast included in rates. Types of
meals: full breakfast and early coffee/tea. Evening snack and picnic

lunch available. Restaurant on premises. Beds: KDT. Air conditioning, turndown service and ceiling fan in room. Cable TV, VCR and fax on premises. Antiques, fishing, parks, downhill skiing, cross-country skiing and watersports nearby.

Location: Sacramento River Valley, Shasta Cascade.

Certificate may be used: January-April, October-December.

Elk   F3

Elk Cove Inn
6300 S Hwy 1, PO Box 367
Elk, CA 95432

(707)877-3321 (800)275-2967 Fax:(707)877-1808

Circa 1883. This mansard-style Victorian home was built as a guest house for lumber baron L. E. White. Operated as a full-service country inn for more than 27 years, Elk Cove Inn commands a majestic view from atop a scenic bluff. Four cabins and an addition to the house feature four new suites with large bay windows, skylights and Victorian fireplaces. Most rooms have an ocean view. Antiques, hand-embroidered linens and down comforters add to the amenities. Below the inn is an expansive driftwood-strewn beach. Gourmet breakfasts are served in the ocean-view dining rooms. Guests can enjoy cocktails or cappucinos in the ocean-front bar. Coffee makers with fresh ground coffee, teas, cider and hot chocolate are available in the rooms.

Innkeeper(s): Elaine Bryant & Jim Carr. $108-298. MC VISA AX PC. 15 rooms with PB, 7 with FP. 4 suites. 4 cottages. 1 conference room. Breakfast included in rates. Type of meal: gourmet breakfast. Beds: KQ. VCR and fax on premises. Handicap access. Antiques, fishing, parks, shopping, theater and watersports nearby.

Location: 15 miles south of Mendocino.

"Quiet, peaceful, romantic, spiritual. This room, the inn, and the food are all what the doctor ordered."

Certificate may be used: Nov. 2-March 31, Monday-Thursday, (holiday weeks excepted) limited room availability.

Escondido   P12

Zosa Gardens B&B
9381 W Lilac Rd
Escondido, CA 92026

(760)723-9093 (800)771-8361 Fax:(760)723-3460

E-mail: zosa_bb@ramonamall.com

Circa 1940. Escondido, located in northern San Diego County, is the setting for this Spanish Hacienda. The home rests on 22 well-landscaped acres atop a bluff in the Monserate Mountains. Rooms bear flowery themes. Angel-lovers should try the Angel Room. The Master Suite includes a fireplace. The innkeeper is an accomplished chef, and

her cuisine has been featured on the TV Food Network, as well as in Bon Appetit. She serves a full customized breakfast for her guests. In the evenings, gourmet tidbits are served with a selection of local wines. Guests are free to enjoy the grounds. There is an outside grill and billiards, and massages are available. Golf courses, restaurants and other sites are just minutes away.

Innkeeper(s): Ted & Connie Vlasis. $80-195. MC VISA AX DC CB DS PC TC. 11 rooms, 8 with PB, 1 with FP. 3 suites. 1 cabin. Breakfast and evening snack included in rates. Types of meals: full breakfast, gourmet breakfast and early coffee/tea. Catering service, catered breakfast and room service available. Beds: KQD. Air conditioning, turndown service and TV in room. VCR, fax, copier, spa, swimming and tennis on premises. Handicap access. Amusement parks, antiques, fishing, parks, shopping, sporting events, golf, theater and watersports nearby.

Certificate may be used: Jan. 15-April 15, Sunday-Friday; June 1-July 30, Sunday-Friday.

Eureka   C2

Abigail's "Elegant Victoian Mansion" B&B Lodging Accommodations
1406 C St
Eureka, CA 95501-1765

(707)444-3144 Fax:(707)442-5594

Circa 1888. One of Eureka's leading lumber barons built this picturesque home, a National Historic Landmark, from 1,000-year-old virgin redwood. Original wallpapers, wool carpets and antique light fixtures create a wonderfully authentic Victorian ambiance. A tuxedoed butler and your hosts, decked in period attire, greet guests upon arrival. Croquet fields and Victorian gardens surround the inn. The hosts can arrange horse-drawn rides or boat cruises. Old-fashioned ice cream sodas are served, and to top it all off, each morning guests partake in a multi-course, French gourmet breakfast feast. The beds in the well-appointed guest quarters are topped with custom-made mattresses. There is a video library of vintage silent films. The inn has been host to many historic personalities, including actresses Lillie Langtry and Sarah Bernhardt, and many senators and representatives.

Innkeeper(s): Doug & Lily Vieyra. $95-185. MC VISA. 4 rooms, 2 with PB. 1 suite. 1 conference room. Breakfast, afternoon tea and evening snack included in rates. Types of meals: gourmet breakfast and early coffee/tea. Beds: Q. Air conditioning and turndown service in room. TV, VCR, fax, copier, sauna, bicycles and library on premises. Amusement parks, antiques, fishing, parks, shopping, sporting events, theater and watersports.

"A magnificent masterpiece, both in architecture and service. Four-star service and regal opulence."

Certificate may be used: Van Gogh Room only, during the months of January, February, during midweek (Monday-Thursday). Excluding holidays and local special events. Subject to availability no earlier than two days prior to reservation date. Not good with any other discount.

A Weaver's Inn

1440 B St
Eureka, CA 95501-2215
(707)443-8119 (800)992-8119 Fax:(707)443-7923
E-mail: weavrinn@humboldt1.com

Circa 1883. The stately Queen Anne Colonial Revival house features a spacious fenced garden, parlor and gracious dining room. All four guest rooms are furnished with down comforters, fresh flowers from the garden and are decorated to reflect the genteel elegance of the Victorian era. The Pamela Suite has a sitting room and fireplace, while the Marcia Room includes a window seat. The full breakfast often features home-grown treats from the garden. Honeymooners can enjoy breakfast in their room.

Innkeeper(s): Lea L. & Lee Montgomery, Shoshana McAvoy. $65-110. MC VISA AX DC DS. 1 suite. Breakfast included in rates. Type of meal: full breakfast. Afternoon tea available. Beds: KQDT.

Location: In the historical Victorian seaport of Eureka, in the heart of the Redwoods.

"It's a charming inn, warm ambiance and very gracious hosts!"

Certificate may be used: Anytime, subject to availability.

The Carter House Victorians

301 L St
Eureka, CA 95501
(707)444-8062 (800)404-1390 Fax:(707)444-8067
E-mail: carter52@humboldt1.com

Circa 1884. The Carters found a pattern book in an antique shop and built this inn according to the architectural plans for an 1890 San Francisco Victorian. (The architect, Joseph Newsom, also designed the Carson House across the street.) Three open parlors with bay windows and marble fireplaces provide an elegant backdrop for relaxing. Guests are free to visit the

kitchen in quest of coffee and views of the bay. The inn is famous for its three-course breakfast, including an Apple Almond Tart featured in Gourmet magazine.

Innkeeper(s): Mark & Christi Carter. $95-275. MAP, AP, EP. MC VISA AX DC CB DS PC TC. 31 rooms with PB, 15 with FP. 15 suites. 1 cottage. 2 conference rooms. Breakfast and afternoon tea included in rates. Types of meals: continental breakfast, continental-plus breakfast, full breakfast, gourmet breakfast and early coffee/tea. Dinner, evening snack and room service available. Restaurant on premises. Beds: KQDT. Air conditioning, turndown service, TV and VCR in room. Fax, copier and spa on premises. Handicap access. Antiques, fishing, parks, shopping, sporting events, theater and watersports nearby.

Location: Corner of Third & L streets in Old Town.

Publicity: *Sunset, U.S. News & World Report, Country Home, Country Living, Bon Appetit, San Francisco Focus, Northwest Palate, Gourmet, Art Culinare, San Francisco Chronicle.*

"We've traveled extensively throughout the U.S. and stayed in the finest hotels. You've got them all beat!!"

Certificate may be used: Jan. 15-May 10 upon availability excluding suites.

The Daly Inn

1125 H St
Eureka, CA 95501-1844
(707)445-3638 (800)321-9656 Fax:(707)444-3636

Circa 1905. This 6,000-square-foot Colonial Revival mansion is located in the historic section of Eureka. Enjoy the Belgian antique bedstead, fireplace and view of fish pond and garden from Annie Murphy's Room, or try the former nursery, Miss Martha's Room,  with bleached pine antiques from Holland. Breakfast is served fireside in the inn's formal dining room or in the breakfast parlor or garden patio. In the evenings, wine and cheese is served.

Innkeeper(s): Sue & Gene Clinesmith. $80-150. MC VISA AX DS PC TC. 5 rooms, 3 with PB, 1 with FP. 2 suites. Breakfast and evening snack included in rates. Types of meals: gourmet breakfast and early coffee/tea. Beds: QT. Turndown service in room. Cable TV, VCR, fax, copier and library on premises. Antiques, fishing, parks, shopping, sporting events and theater nearby.

Location: California's north coast.

"A genuine delight."

Certificate may be used: Nov. 1-May 1. Holidays & special event weekends excluded.

Ferndale

Gingerbread Mansion Inn

PO Box 40, 400 Berding St
Ferndale, CA 95536-1380
(707)786-4000 (800)952-4136 Fax:(707)786-4381
E-mail: kenn@humboldt1.com

Circa 1899. Built for Dr. H.J. Ring, the Gingerbread Mansion is now the most photographed of Northern California's inns. Near Eureka, it is in the fairy-tale Victorian village of Ferndale (a California Historical

Landmark). Outside the inn are formal English gardens. Gingerbread Mansion is a unique combination of Queen Anne and Eastlake styles with elaborate gingerbread trim. Inside are spacious and elegant rooms including two suites with "his" and "her" bathtubs. There are four parlors.

Innkeeper(s): Ken Torbert. $120-350. MC VISA AX PC TC. 10 rooms with PB, 5 with FP. 5 suites. Breakfast and afternoon tea included in rates. Types of meals: full breakfast and early coffee/tea. Beds: KQT. Turndown service in room. Library on premises. Antiques, fishing, parks, shopping and theater nearby.

Location: Five miles west off Hwy 101; 30 minutes south of Eureka.

Publicity: *Travel Holiday, Country Inns, Los Angeles Times, Sunset.*

"Absolutely the most charming, friendly and delightful place we have ever stayed."

Certificate may be used: Nov. 1-April 30, Sunday-Thursday, excluding holiday or special event periods.

Fish Camp   I8

Karen's B&B Yosemite Inn
PO Box 8
Fish Camp, CA 93623-0008
(209)683-4550

Circa 1988. This contemporary country house enjoys a setting of pine, oak and cedar trees at 5,000 feet. The Rose Room features wicker furniture and a rose motif on quilts and pillows. There's a porch to relax on and in the evening guests enjoy watching raccoons come by for their evening snacks. Cottage-fried potatoes and fresh-baked muffins are a sample of the country breakfast. It's a three-minute drive to the southern gate of Yosemite National Park.

Innkeeper(s): Karen Bergh. $90. 3 rooms. Breakfast included in rates. Type of meal: full breakfast. Parks nearby.

Location: One mile south of Yosemite National Park.

Publicity: *Contra Costa Times.*

Certificate may be used: Oct. 15-Dec. 15, Jan. 1-March 31, void all holidays.

Fort Bidwell   A7

Fort Bidwell Hotel & Restaurant
Main & Garrison Sts
Fort Bidwell, CA 96101
(916)279-2050 (888)604-6835

Circa 1906. This turn-of-the-century hotel offers comfortable and reasonably priced accommodations in a historic setting. Guest rooms are done in country style, with furnishings such as an iron bed with a soft floral comforter. As is the custom in many European hotels and inns, the baths are shared. Meals are not included in the rates, but the hotel's restaurant serves breakfast, lunch and dinner. There are plenty of outdoor activities to enjoy in the Fort Bidwell area, and there are many local events, from rodeos to summer theater.

Innkeeper(s): Charles & Tracy Massie. $45-55. MC VISA AX PC TC. 7 rooms. Types of meals: full breakfast and early coffee/tea. Dinner, evening snack, picnic lunch, lunch, banquet service and catering service available. Restaurant on premises. Beds: QD. Ceiling fan in room. VCR on premises. Handicap access. Antiques, fishing, parks, shopping, downhill skiing, cross-country skiing, golf and theater nearby.

Certificate may be used: Anytime, based on room availability.

Fort Bragg   E2

Avalon House
561 Stewart St
Fort Bragg, CA 95437-3226
(707)964-5555 (800)964-5556

Circa 1905. This redwood California Craftsman house was extensively remodeled in 1988 and furnished with a mixture of antiques and willow furniture. Some rooms feature fireplaces, whirlpool tubs, or ocean views and decks. The inn is in a quiet residential area, three blocks from the Pacific Ocean, one block west of Hwy. 1, and two blocks from the Skunk Train depot.

Innkeeper(s): Anne Sorrells. $70-140. MC VISA AX DS PC TC. 6 rooms with PB, 4 with FP. Breakfast included in rates. Types of meals: full breakfast and early coffee/tea. Beds: QD. Cable TV and VCR on premises. Antiques, fishing, parks, shopping, theater and watersports nearby.

Location: 150 miles northwest of San Francisco.

Publicity: *Advocate News.*

"Elegant, private and extremely comfortable. We will never stay in a motel again."

Certificate may be used: Nov. 1-March 31, Sunday through Thursday, excluding holiday and special event periods.

Glass Beach B&B

726 N Main St
Fort Bragg, CA 95437-3017

(707)964-6774

Circa 1920. Each of the guest rooms at this Craftsman-style home is decorated in a different theme and named to reflect the decor. The Malaysian and Oriental Jade rooms reflect Asian artistry, while the Forget-Me-Not and Wild Flower rooms are bright, feminine rooms with walls decked in floral prints. Antiques are found throughout the home and the back cottage, which includes three of the inn's nine guest rooms. The inn also offers a hot tub for guest use. Breakfasts are served in the inn's dining room, but guests are free to fix up a tray and enjoy the meal in the privacy of their own room.
Innkeeper(s): Nancy Cardenas. $50-125. MC VISA DS TC. 9 rooms with PB, 4 with FP. 1 suite. Breakfast included in rates. Type of meal: full breakfast. Afternoon tea available. Beds: Q. TV in room. Handicap access. Antiques, fishing, parks, shopping, theater and watersports nearby.

Certificate may be used: Oct. 1-June 30, Sunday through Thursday, holiday periods excluded.

Grey Whale Inn

615 N Main St
Fort Bragg, CA 95437-3240

(707)964-0640 (800)382-7244 Fax:(707)964-4408

E-mail: gwhale@mcn.org

Circa 1915. As the name implies, whales can be seen from many of the inn's vantage points during the creatures' migration season along the West Coast. The stately four-story redwood inn features airy and spacious guest rooms with ocean views. Some rooms include a fireplace, whirlpool tub for two or private deck. Near the heart of downtown Fort Bragg, it's an easy walk to the Skunk Train, shops, galleries, a microbrewery and restaurants. There is also a fireside lounge, TV-VCR room and a recreation area with pool table.
Innkeeper(s): John & Colette Bailey. $90-180. MC VISA AX DS PC TC. 14 rooms with PB, 3 with FP. 2 conference rooms. Breakfast included in rates. Type of meal: full breakfast. Beds: KQDT. TV in room. VCR, fax, copier and library on premises. Handicap access. Antiques, fishing, parks, shopping, theater and watersports nearby.

Location: Almost in the heart of downtown Fort Bragg on the Mendocino Coast Highway.
Publicity: *Inn Times, San Francisco Examiner, Travel, Fort Bragg Advocate News, Mendocino Beacon, Los Angeles Times, Sunset.*

"We are going to return each year until we have tried each room. Sunrise room is excellent in the morning or evening."
Certificate may be used: October through June, Monday through Thursday.

Pudding Creek Inn

700 N Main St
Fort Bragg, CA 95437-3017

(707)964-9529 (800)227-9529 Fax:(707)961-0282

Circa 1884. Originally constructed by a Russian count, the inn comprises two picturesque Victorian homes connected by an enclosed garden. There are mounds of begonias, fuchsias and ferns. The Count's Room, in seafoam green and cranberry accents, features inlaid redwood paneling, a stone fireplace and a brass bed. There is a TV/recreation room for guest use. A full buffet breakfast is provided and you can reserve ahead for a picnic lunch.  (Guests on a long coastal tour will appreciate the laundry service made available.)
Innkeeper(s): Carole Anloff. $65-125. MC VISA AX DS. 10 rooms with PB, 2 with FP. Breakfast and afternoon tea included in rates. Type of meal: full breakfast. Evening snack and picnic lunch available. Beds: KQDT. Fax on premises. Antiques, fishing and theater nearby.
Location: Corner of Bush and North Main.
Publicity: *Evening Outlook.*

"Best stop on our trip!"
Certificate may be used: November-June, midweek Sunday-Thursday only, no holidays.

The Rendezvous Inn & Restaurant

647 N Main St
Fort Bragg, CA 95437-3219

(707)964-8142 (800)491-8142

Circa 1908. This turn-of-the-century inn offers visitors the convenience of lodging and dining. Six large guest rooms, all with private bath and queen beds, are designed with relaxation in mind, meaning television and phones are found elsewhere in the inn. Guests are encouraged to join others in the comfortable parlor for a glass of wine or beer, to watch TV, relax or socialize. Within walking distance are the Guest House Museum, Skunk Train and Glass and Pudding Creek beaches.

Innkeeper(s): Janice & Kim Badenhop. $75-110. MC VISA DS. 6 rooms. 2 suites. Breakfast included in rates. Types of meals: continental-plus breakfast and early coffee/tea. Dinner, lunch, banquet service and catering service available.

Certificate may be used: Sunday through Thursday, mid-September through mid-May. Holidays excluded.

Geyserville   G4

Hope-Merrill House
21253 Geyserville Ave
Geyserville, CA 95441-9637

(707)857-3356 (800)825-4233 Fax:(707)857-4673

Circa 1885. The Hope-Merrill House is a classic example of the Eastlake Stick style that was so popular during Victorian times. Built entirely from redwood, the house features original wainscoting and silk-screened wallcoverings. A swimming pool, vineyard and gazebo are favorite spots for guests to relax. The Hope-Bosworth House, on the same street, was built in the Queen Anne style by an early Geyserville pioneer who lived in the home until the 1960s. The front picket fence is covered with roses. Period details include oak woodwork, sliding doors, polished fir floors and antique light fixtures.

Innkeeper(s): Cosette & Ron Scheiber. $95-164. MC VISA AX PC TC. 12 rooms with PB, 3 with FP. 1 suite. Breakfast included in rates. Types of meals: full breakfast, gourmet breakfast and early coffee/tea. Picnic lunch available. Beds: Q. Ceiling fan in room. Fax and copier on premises. Antiques, parks, shopping and watersports nearby.

Publicity: *San Diego Union, Country Homes, Sunset, Sacramento Union, Los Angeles Times.*

Certificate may be used: Sunday through Thursday. Holidays excluded.

Grass Valley   F6

Murphy's Inn
318 Neal St
Grass Valley, CA 95945-6702

(916)273-6873 (800)895-2488 Fax:(916)273-5157

Circa 1866. The Gold Rush turned this home's builder into a wealthy man, and he built this Victorian for his new bride. The home is decorated by century-old ivy, and the grounds include a 140-year-old giant sequoia. Guests can choose from rooms with fireplaces or a skylight, and all rooms are decorated with antiques. One suite is located in a separate house and includes a kitchen and living room. The Victorian is located in a Grass Valley historic district and is within walking distance to many local attractions.

Innkeeper(s): Ted & Nancy Daus. $95-145. MC VISA AX PC. 8 rooms with PB, 4 with FP. 3 suites. 1 conference room. Breakfast included in rates. Types of meals: full breakfast, gourmet breakfast and early coffee/tea. Beds: KQHIDEBEDS. Air conditioning, ceiling fan, TV and VCR in room. Fax and library on premises. Antiques, fishing, parks, shopping, downhill skiing, cross-country skiing, golf, theater and watersports nearby.

Certificate may be used: Jan. 1-April 1.

Groveland   H7

The Groveland Hotel
18767 Main St, PO Box 481
Groveland, CA 95321

(209)962-4000 (800)273-3314 Fax:(209)962-6674
E-mail: peggy@groveland.com

Circa 1849. Located 23 miles from Yosemite National Park, the newly restored hotel features both an 1849 adobe building with 18-inch-thick walls constructed during the Gold Rush and a 1914 building erected to house workers for the Hetch

Hetchy Dam. Both feature two-story balconies. There is a Victorian parlor, a gourmet restaurant and a Western saloon. Guest rooms feature European antiques, down comforters and in-room coffee. The feeling is one of casual elegance.

Innkeeper(s): Peggy A. & Grover C. Mosley. $95-175. MC VISA AX DC CB DS PC TC. 17 rooms with PB, 3 with FP. 3 suites. 1 conference room. Breakfast included in rates. Types of meals: continental-plus breakfast and early coffee/tea. Picnic lunch, banquet service, catering service and room service available. Restaurant on premises. Beds: QT. Air conditioning and ceiling fan in room. Cable TV, VCR, fax, copier, computer, library, pet boarding and child care on premises. Handicap access. Antiques, fishing, parks, shopping, downhill skiing, cross-country skiing, golf and watersports nearby.

Publicity: *Sonora Union Democrat, Peninsula, Sunset, Stockton Record, Country Inns.*

"Hospitality is outstanding."

Certificate may be used: Oct. 15-April 15, Sunday through Thursday, excluding holidays.

Guernewood Park G3

Fern Grove Inn
16650 River Rd
Guernewood Park, CA 95446-9678
(707)869-9083 (800)347-9083 Fax:(707)869-2948
Clustered in a village-like atmosphere, these crafts-man cottages have romantic fireplaces, private entrances and are decorated with freshly cut flowers. Your day starts with a steaming cup of and a leisure-ly buffet breakfast featuring renowned homemade muffins and pastries served in the relaxed atmos-phere of the Common Room. The morning newspa-pers, soft classical music, warming fire and good conversation will stimulate your spirits. Innkeepers will provide you with concierge service throughout your stay.
Innkeeper(s): Dennis Ekstrom. $89-199. MC VISA AX DS. 17 rooms. 11 suites. Breakfast included in rates. Type of meal: continental-plus breakfast. Evening snack and picnic lunch available.
Certificate may be used: May 1-Oct. 31, Sunday-Thursday; Nov. 1-April 30, anyday; excludes holidays and special events.

Half Moon Bay I4

Old Thyme Inn
779 Main St
Half Moon Bay, CA 94019-1924
(415)726-1616 Fax:(415)726-6394
E-mail: oldthyme@coastside.net
Circa 1899. Located on the historic Main Street of Old Town, this Queen Anne Victorian has a flower and herb garden surrounding it. Seven rooms are named after various herbs that are found in the gar-den. Guests receive a complimentary book on herbs with each reservation. Most of the rooms have whirlpool baths and/or fireplaces. Resident teddy bears help keep guests in good company. The inn is

within walking distance to beaches, restaurants, shops and art galleries.
Innkeeper(s): George & Maria Dempsey. $85-220. MC VISA PC. 7 rooms with PB, 4 with FP. 1 suite. 1 conference room. Breakfast includ-ed in rates. Beds: Q. TV and VCR in room. Fax, computer and spa on premises. Antiques, fishing, parks, shopping, sporting events, theater and watersports nearby.
Location: Five minutes from ocean.
Publicity: *California Weekends, Los Angeles, San Mateo Times, San Jose Mercury News, Herb Companion, San Francisco Examiner.*
"Furnishings, rooms and garden were absolutely won-derful. Delicious breakfast and great coffee .... loved the peaceful neighborhood."
Certificate may be used: November-April, Monday-Thursday.

Healdsburg G4

Madrona Manor, A Country Inn
PO Box 818
Healdsburg, CA 95448-0818
(707)433-4231 (800)258-4003 Fax:(707)433-0703
Circa 1881. The inn is comprised of four historic structures in a national historic district. Surrounded by eight acres of manicured lawns and terraced flower and vegetable gardens, the stately mansion was built for John Paxton, a San Francisco business-man. Embellished with turrets, bay windows, porch-es, and a mansard roof, it provides a breathtaking view of surrounding vineyards. Elegant antique fur-nishings and a noteworthy restaurant add to the genuine country inn atmosphere. The Gothic-style Carriage House offers more casual lodging.
Innkeeper(s): John & Carol Muir. $155-250. MC VISA AX DC CB DS PC TC. 21 rooms with PB, 17 with FP. 3 suites. 1 cottage. 2 conference rooms. Breakfast included in rates. Type of meal: gourmet breakfast. Dinner and picnic lunch available. Restaurant on premises. Beds: KQDT. Air conditioning in room. Fax, copier, computer and swimming on premises. Handicap access. Antiques, fishing, parks, shopping, sport-ing events, theater and watersports nearby.
Location: In the heart of the wine country, Sonoma County.
Publicity: *Gourmet, Woman's Day Home Decorating Ideas, Travel & Leisure, US News, Diversions, Money, Good Housekeeping.*
"Our fourth visit and better every time."
Certificate may be used: Sunday through Thursday, all year.

Idyllwild O12

The Pine Cove Inn
23481 Hwy 243, PO Box 2181
Idyllwild, CA 92549
(909)659-5033 (888)659-5033 Fax:(909)659-5034
Circa 1935. These rustic, A-frame cottages offer a variety of amenities in a natural, mountain setting. Refrigerators and microwaves have been placed in

each unit, several of which include a wood-burning fireplace. One unit has a full kitchen. A full breakfast is served in a separate lodge which dates back to 1935. The village of Idyllwild is three miles down the road, and the surrounding country offers a variety of activities.

Innkeeper(s): Bob & Michelle Bollmann. $70-100. MC VISA AX PC TC. 10 rooms with PB, 6 with FP. 3 suites. 1 conference room. Breakfast included in rates. Type of meal: full breakfast. Beds: QT. Ceiling fan in room. Cable TV, VCR and fax on premises. Antiques, fishing, parks, shopping, cross-country skiing and theater nearby.

Certificate may be used: Sunday through Thursday only, any dates except Dec. 15 through Jan. 4.

Independence   J10

Winnedumah Inn
211 N Edwards St
Independence, CA 93526
(760)878-2040 Fax:(760)878-2833
E-mail: winnedumah@mail.telis.org

Circa 1927. This old hotel was built in a Spanish Colonial style with arches, stucco and a front portico. Its location is at the foot of the Eastern Sierras in Owens Valley. Independence offers a trout-filled steam, majestic scenery and nearby hiking and fishing. The inn's restaurant will provide box lunches for these excursions.

Innkeeper(s): Edie McGee & Sydney Slome. $45-70. MC VISA TC. 24 rooms, 14 with PB. Breakfast included in rates. Types of meals: continental breakfast and continental-plus breakfast. Dinner, picnic lunch and catering service available. Restaurant on premises. Beds: QDT. Cable TV, VCR, fax, copier and bicycles on premises. Antiques, fishing, cross-country skiing and watersports nearby.

Publicity: Los Angeles Times.

Certificate may be used: Nov. 1-June 30.

Inverness   H4

Golden Hinde Inn & Marina
12938 Sir Francis Drake, PO Box 295
Inverness, CA 94937
(415)669-1389 (800)339-9398 Fax:(415)669-1128

Circa 1962. Many of the guest rooms at Golden Hinde offer views of Tomales Bay, and 18 also have a fireplace. Midweek guests enjoy continental breakfast service, and there is a restaurant on the premises. Fresh seafood and oysters are a specialty. The inn is located on the Point Reyes National Seashore, and plenty of outdoor activities are nearby.

Innkeeper(s): Jeanne & Craig Schuller. $67-129. MC VISA AX TC. 35 rooms with PB, 18 with FP. 2 suites. Type of meal: continental breakfast. Restaurant on premises. Beds: KQDT. TV in room. Fax, copier, swimming and library on premises. Antiques, fishing, parks, shopping, golf and watersports nearby.

Certificate may be used: Nov. 1-March 31, Sunday-Thursday, non-holiday.

Hotel Inverness
25 Park Ave, Box 780
Inverness, CA 94937
(415)669-7393 Fax:(415)669-1702
E-mail: desk@hotelinverness.com

Circa 1906. Guests rave about the outdoor breakfasts served in the garden or on the deck. Situated on the edge of a coastal village, Hotel Inverness overlooks Tomales Bay and is a short distance from Point Reyes National Seashore. The garden lawn accommodates picnics, lounging or croquet. Boasting one of the best bird-watching areas in the west, the inn has a park-like setting where one can relax and admire the surrounding wooded area. This great natural area reminds many of Yosemite National Park.

Innkeeper(s): Susan & Tom Simms. $100-175. MC VISA AX PC TC. 5 rooms with PB. Breakfast included in rates. Type of meal: continental-plus breakfast. Beds: Q. Fax on premises. Parks and watersports nearby.

Publicity: Los Angeles Times.

Certificate may be used: Dec. 1-March 31, Monday-Thursday.

Rosemary Cottage
PO Box 273
Inverness, CA 94937-0273
(415)663-9338 (800)808-9338

Circa 1986. From the windows in this secluded cottage, guests can enjoy views of a wooded canyon and hillside in the Point Reyes National Seashore park. The cottage is a cozy, self-contained unit with a well-equipped kitchen, bedroom, library and a living room with a wood-burning stove. The decor is French country, highlighting the wood beams, red oak floors and terra cotta tiles. There is a hot tub in the garden.

Innkeeper(s): Suzanne Storch. $150-170. PC TC. 3 cottages with PB, 3 with FP. Breakfast included in rates. Type of meal: full breakfast. Beds: QT. Spa on premises. Antiques, fishing, parks, shopping and watersports nearby.

Certificate may be used: Sunday through Thursday, January-June, October through December, excluding holiday weeks.

Sandy Cove Inn
12990 Sir Francis Drake Blvd
Inverness, CA 94937
(415)669-2683 (800)759-2683 Fax:(415)669-7511
E-mail: innkeeper@sandycove.com

Circa 1986. This romantic country inn is secluded on five acres adjacent to the Point Reyes National Seashore. Guests can watch the sun set over the Pacific and take a moonlit stroll along the beach. There are just three guest rooms, providing plenty of privacy. Each is warmed by a woodstove, and the decor is contemporary and elegant. The gourmet breakfasts, which are served at intimate tables in the solarium, feature local and organic products. A meal might feature lemon pancakes with savory chicken sausage and fresh fruit. If you wish, breakfast can be enjoyed in the privacy of your room. Tomales Bay is within walking distance.

Innkeeper(s): Gerry & Kathy Coles. $125-250. MC VISA AX DC DS PC TC. 3 suites, 3 with FP. Breakfast and evening snack included in rates. Types of meals: continental breakfast, continental-plus breakfast, full breakfast, gourmet breakfast and early coffee/tea. Room service available. Beds: Q. Air conditioning and turndown service in room. Fax, swimming, stables and library on premises. Antiques, fishing, parks, shopping, golf, theater and watersports nearby.

Certificate may be used: Nov. 1-Jan. 31, Sunday-Thursday (non-holiday, 14-day advanced booking, space available).

Ione
G6

The Heirloom
214 Shakeley Ln, PO Box 322
Ione, CA 95640-9572
(209)274-4468 (888)628-7896

Circa 1863. A two-story Colonial with columns, balconies and a private English garden, the antebellum Heirloom is true to its name. It has many family heirlooms and a square grand piano once owned by Lola Montez. The building was dedicated by the Native Sons of the Golden West as a historic site.

Innkeeper(s): Melisande Hubbs & Patricia Cross. $65-102. MC VISA AX PC TC. 6 rooms, 4 with PB, 3 with FP. 2 cottages. Breakfast and afternoon tea included in rates. Types of meals: full breakfast, gourmet breakfast and early coffee/tea. Room service available. Beds: KQDT. Air conditioning in room. Library on premises. Antiques, fishing, parks, shopping, golf, theater and watersports nearby.

Location: California Gold Country - halfway between Yosemite and Lake Tahoe.

Publicity: *San Francisco Chronicle, Country Living.*

"Hospitality was amazing. Truly we've never had such a great time."

Certificate may be used: Sunday through Thursday, holidays excluded.

Jackson
G6

Court Street Inn
215 Court St
Jackson, CA 95642-2309
(209)223-0416 (800)200-0416 Fax:(209)223-5429
E-mail: ct_st_inn@msn.com

Circa 1872. This cheery yellow and white Victorian-era house is accentuated with a porch stretching across the entire front and decorated with white wicker furniture. Behind the house, a two-story brick structure that once served as a museum for Indian artifacts now houses guests. Afternoon refreshments are served in the dining room under an embossed, carved tin ceiling. Guests relax in front of a marble fireplace in the parlor topped by a gilded mirror. Guest rooms are decorated in antiques. Downtown is only two blocks away.

Innkeeper(s): Dave & Nancy Butow. $95-195. MC VISA AX DS PC TC. 7 rooms with PB, 4 with FP. 1 suite. 1 cottage. Breakfast and afternoon tea included in rates. Types of meals: full breakfast and early coffee/tea. Beds: KQD. Air conditioning, ceiling fan and TV in room. VCR, fax, copier and spa on premises. Antiques, fishing, parks, shopping, downhill skiing, cross-country skiing, theater and watersports nearby.

Location: In the center of the Gold Rush Highway 49 & Highway 88.

Publicity: *Amador Dispatch, Sunset, Vacations.*

"Thank you for creating such a warm, relaxing atmosphere. We enjoyed our stay very much and we'll recommend your hospitality."

Certificate may be used: Sunday through Thursday - holiday periods excluded January to December.

Gate House Inn
1330 Jackson Gate Rd
Jackson, CA 95642-9539
(209)223-3500 (800)841-1072 Fax:(209)223-1299
E-mail: info@gatehouseinn.com

Circa 1902. This striking Victorian inn is listed in the National Register of Historic Places. Set on a hillside amid lovely gardens, the inn is within walking distance of a state historic park and several notable eateries. The inn's country setting, comfortable porches and swimming pool offer many opportunities for relaxation. Accommodations include three

rooms, a suite and a romantic cottage with wood stove and whirlpool tub. All of the guest rooms feature queen beds and elegant furnishings. Nearby are several lakes, wineries and golf courses.

Innkeeper(s): Keith & Gail Sweet. $81-135. MC VISA AX CB DS PC TC. 5 rooms with PB, 3 with FP. 1 suite. 1 cottage. Breakfast included in rates. Types of meals: full breakfast and early coffee/tea. Afternoon tea available. Beds: Q. Air conditioning and ceiling fan in room. Fax, copier and swimming on premises. Antiques, fishing, parks, shopping, downhill skiing, cross-country skiing, theater and watersports nearby.

"Most gracious, warm hospitality."

Certificate may be used: Sunday-Thursday, holidays excluded. Weekends January only.

Wedgewood Inn

11941 Narcissus Rd
Jackson, CA 95642-9600
(209)296-4300 (800)933-4393 Fax:(209)296-4301
E-mail: vic@wedgewoodinn.com

Circa 1987. Located in the heart of Sierra gold country on a secluded, five acres, this Victorian replica is crammed full of sentimental family heirlooms and  antiques. Each room has been designed with careful attention to detail. A baby grand piano rests in the parlor. The carriage house is a separate cottage with its own private entrance. It boasts four generations of family heirlooms, a carved canopy bed, a wood-burning stove and a two-person Jacuzzi tub. The innkeepers' 1921 Model-T, "Henry," is located in its own special showroom. Gourmet breakfasts are served on bone china and include specialties such as cheese-filled blintzes, fruit and baked goods. Breakfast is available in selected guest rooms by request.

Innkeeper(s): Vic & Jeannine Beltz. $100-165. MC VISA AX DS PC TC. 6 rooms, 5 with PB. 1 suite. Breakfast and afternoon tea included in rates. Types of meals: gourmet breakfast and early coffee/tea. Beds: Q. Air conditioning, turndown service and ceiling fan in room. Fax and copier on premises. Antiques, fishing, shopping, downhill skiing, cross-country skiing, golf and theater nearby.

Certificate may be used: Sunday through Thursday inclusive, no holiday weekends. Selected rooms, subject to availability.

Jamestown

The Historic National Hotel B&B

77 Main St, PO Box 502
Jamestown, CA 95327
(209)984-3446 (800)894-3446 Fax:(209)984-5620
E-mail: national@sonnet.com

Circa 1859. One of the 10 oldest continuously operating hotels in California, the inn maintains its original redwood bar where thousands of dollars in gold dust were spent. Electricity and plumbing were added for the first time when the inn was restored a few years ago. It is decorated with Gold Rush period antiques, brass beds and handmade quilts. The restaurant is considered to be one of the finest in the Mother Lode.

Innkeeper(s): Pamela & Stephen Willey. $80-120. MC VISA AX DC CB DS PC TC. 9 rooms with PB. 1 conference room. Breakfast included in rates. Types of meals: continental-plus breakfast and early coffee/tea. Dinner, evening snack, picnic lunch, lunch, gourmet lunch, banquet service and catering service available. Restaurant on premises. Beds: QT. Air conditioning and TV in room. VCR and fax on premises. Antiques, fishing, parks, downhill skiing, cross-country skiing, theater and watersports nearby. Location: Center of town.

Publicity: *Bon Appetit, California Magazine, Focus, San Francisco Magazine, Gourmet, Sunset Magazine*

"Couldn't ask for a more comfortable or peaceful surrounding for resting!"

Certificate may be used: Sunday through Thursday nights, holiday periods excluded. Based upon space availability.

Joshua Tree

Joshua Tree Inn

61259 29 Palms Hwy, PO Box 340
Joshua Tree, CA 92252-0340
(760)366-1188 (800)366-1444 Fax:(760)366-3805

Circa 1940. The hacienda-style inn was once a '50s motel. It now offers Victorian-style rooms with king-size beds. Antiques and Old West memorabilia add to the decor. The inn is one mile from the gateway to the 467,000-acre Joshua Tree National Monument.

Innkeeper(s): Dr. Daniel & Evelyn Shirbroun. $65-175. MAP. MC VISA AX DC CB DS TC. 10 rooms with PB. 2 suites. 1 conference room. Breakfast, afternoon tea, dinner and picnic lunch included in rates. Types of  meals: full breakfast, gourmet breakfast and early coffee/tea. Lunch, gourmet lunch and room service available. Beds: KQTD. Air conditioning, ceiling fan and TV in room. VCR, fax, copier, spa and swimming on premises. Antiques, parks, shopping, golf and theater nearby.

Publicity: *Los Angeles Times, Press Enterprise.*

"Quiet, clean and charming."

Certificate may be used: Sunday thru Friday during non-holiday periods.

Julian

Julian Gold Rush Hotel

2032 Main St, PO Box 1856
Julian, CA 92036
(760)765-0201 (800)734-5854

Circa 1897. The dream of a former slave and his wife lives today in this sole surviving hotel in Southern California's "Mother Lode of Gold Mining." This Victorian charmer is listed in the National Register of Historic Places and is a desig-

nated State of California Point of Historic Interest (#SDI-09). Guests enjoy the feeling of a visit to Grandma's and a tradition of genteel hospitality.
Innkeeper(s): Steve & Gig Ballinger. $72-160. MC VISA AX PC TC. 14 rooms with PB, 1 with FP. 1 suite. 2 cottages. 1 conference room. Breakfast and afternoon tea included in rates. Type of meal: full breakfast. Beds: QDT. Antiques, fishing, parks and theater nearby.
Location: Center of town.
Publicity: *San Diego Union, PSA.*

"Any thoughts you have about the 20th century will leave you when you walk into the lobby of this grand hotel- Westways Magazine"

Certificate may be used: Monday through Thursday, excluding holidays and weekends, shared baths only.

Julian White House

3014 Blue Jay Dr, PO Box 824
Julian, CA 92036-9208
(619)765-1764 (800)948-4687

Circa 1979. Towering white pillars greet this inn's guests, who may feel they have traveled back in time to a Southern plantation. The attractive Colonial-style inn offers four luxurious guest rooms, including the Honeymoon Suite. The French Quarter Room features a New Orleans theme and Mardi Gras memorabilia, and the popular East Room boasts a goose down mattress and Laura Ashley linens on a queen-size Victorian-style brass bed. Guests often enjoy an evening at the Pine Hills Dinner Theatre, an easy walk from the inn.
Innkeeper(s): Mary & Alan Marvin. $90-135. MC VISA PC TC. 4 rooms with PB. 1 suite. Breakfast and evening snack included in rates. Types

of meals: full breakfast and early coffee/tea. Beds: Q. Air conditioning and ceiling fan in room. Library on premises. Antiques, fishing, parks, cross-country skiing, theater and watersports nearby.
Publicity: *San Diego Home/Garden, San Diego Union Tribune, HGTV, Elmer Dills KABC-TV, KABC Talk radio.*

Certificate may be used: Monday-Thursday, except Easter, Thanksgiving and Christmas weeks.

Orchard Hill Country Inn

2502 Washington St, PO Box 425
Julian, CA 92036-0425
(619)765-1700 Fax:(619)765-0290

Circa 1923. This charming Craftsman-style inn is a perfect country getaway for those seeking solace from the city lights. There are three cottages dating back to 1923, and the newer lodge was built as a companion to the original building. Expansive, individually appointed guest suites offer amenities such as fireplaces, whirlpool tubs, hand-knitted afghans

and down comforters all surrounded by warm, country decor. Gourmet coffee, tea and cocoas also are provided in each suite, as are wet bars. The innkeepers also offer more than 100 games to help pass the time. Guests can enjoy a breakfast of fruits, muffins and a special egg dish in the dining room. Wine and hors d'oeuvres are provided each afternoon. The expansive grounds boast a variety of gardens highlighting native plants and flowers.
Innkeeper(s): Darrell & Pat Straube. $140-195. MC VISA AX PC TC. 22 rooms with PB, 11 with FP. 2 conference rooms. Breakfast and evening snack included in rates. Types of meals: full breakfast and early coffee/tea. Dinner, picnic lunch, lunch, gourmet lunch, banquet service and catering service available. Beds: KQ. Air conditioning, ceiling fan, TV and VCR in room. Fax and copier on premises. Handicap access. Antiques, fishing, parks, shopping and theater nearby.
Publicity: *San Diego Union Tribune, Los Angeles Times, Orange County Register, Orange Coast, San Francisco Chronicle, San Bernadino Sun, Oceanside Blade-Citizen.*

"The quality of the rooms, service and food were beyond our expectations."

Certificate may be used: January (excluding two weeks when closed) - December, Monday through Thursday, excluding holidays.

Random Oaks Ranch

3742 Pine Hills Rd, PO Box 454
Julian, CA 92036
(619)765-1094 (800)262-4344

Circa 1987. Guests at this inn, which doubles as a thoroughbred horse ranch, choose from two elegant cottages. The English Squire Cottage features a marble fireplace, Queen Anne furniture and a half-canopy queen bed. The Victorian Garden Cottage offers a custom-manteled fireplace, Victorian cherry bed and sliding French doors. Both cottages sport private decks with spas, wet bars, microwave ovens and small refrigerators. Breakfast is served in the privacy of the cottages. The charming town of Julian is just two miles from the inn.
Innkeeper(s): Shari Foust-Helsel. $120-160. MC VISA. 2 cottages with PB. Breakfast included in rates. Types of meals: continental breakfast and full breakfast. Beds: Q. Antiques, shopping and theater nearby.

Certificate may be used: Monday-Thursday, Jan. 2-Dec. 20 (holidays excluded).

Rockin' A B&B

1531 Orchard Ln
Julian, CA 92036-9607
(619)765-2820

Circa 1981. This contemporary woodsided ranch inn found in the countryside outside Julian offers a relaxing getaway for city folk. The inn boasts a private bass fishing facility and guests also visit the farm animals found on the grounds. The three guest rooms have private baths, and amenities include ceiling fans, a fireplace, spa and turndown service. The inn is a very popular anniversary and honeymoon destination. Visitors enjoy a full breakfast and evening snack and will find Julian a fun place to explore in their spare time.
Innkeeper(s): Gil & Dottie Archambeau. $89-145. MC VISA. 3 rooms with PB, 3 with FP. 1 suite. Breakfast and evening snack included in rates. Type of meal: full breakfast. Beds: QD. Turndown service and ceiling fan in room. VCR and spa on premises. Antiques, fishing, parks, shopping, cross-country skiing and theater nearby.

Certificate may be used: Sunday through Thursday excluding holidays.

Kernville   L10

Kern River Inn B&B

119 Kern River Dr
Kernville, CA 93238
(760)376-6750 (800)986-4382 Fax:(760)376-6643
E-mail: kribb@kernvalley.com

Circa 1991. Located across from Riverside Park and the Kern River, this country-style inn boasts a wrap-around porch with views and sounds of the river. The Whiskey Flat, Whitewater and Piute rooms

include fireplaces. The Big Blue and Greenhorn rooms offer whirlpool tubs. All rooms afford river views. Breakfasts includes the inn's renowned giant home-baked cinnamon rolls, egg and cheese dishes or sweetheart waffles.
Innkeeper(s): Jack & Carita Prestwich. $79-99. MC VISA AX PC TC. 6 rooms with PB, 3 with FP. Breakfast and afternoon tea included in rates. Types of meals: full breakfast and early coffee/tea. Beds: KQ. Ceiling fan in room. Cable TV, VCR, fax and library on premises. Handicap access. Antiques, fishing, parks, shopping, downhill skiing, cross-country skiing, golf and watersports nearby.
Location: In the southern Sierra Nevada Mountains.
Publicity: *Kern Valley Sun, Los Angeles Times, Valley News, Westways*
"For us, your place is the greatest. So romantic."
Certificate may be used: Nov. 1-March 31, Sunday-Thursday.

Laguna Beach   P11

Carriage House

1322 Catalina
Laguna Beach, CA 92651-3153
(714)494-8945

Circa 1920. A Laguna Beach historical landmark, this inn has a Cape Cod clapboard exterior. It housed an art gallery and a bakery before it was converted into apartments with large rooms and kitchens. Now as a cozy inn, each room has a private parlor. Outside, the courtyard fountain is shaded by a large carrotwood tree with hanging moss.
Innkeeper(s): Dee & Thom Taylor. $95-150. PC TC. 6 suites. Breakfast and evening snack included in rates. Type of meal: continental-plus breakfast. Beds: KQDT. TV in room. Antiques, fishing, parks, shopping, theater and watersports nearby.
Location: Two & one-half blocks from the ocean.
Publicity: *Glamour, L.A Times, Orange County Register, Sunset.*
"A true home away from home with all the extra touches added in. Reminds me of New Orleans."
Certificate may be used: Sunday through Thursday, September to June (as available).

Eiler's Inn
741 S Coast Hwy
Laguna Beach, CA 92651-2722
(714)494-3004 Fax:(714)497-2215

Circa 1940. This New Orleans-style inn surrounds a lush courtyard and fountain. The rooms are decorated with antiques and wallpapers. Wine and cheese is served during the evening in front of the fireplace. Named after Eiler Larsen, famous town greeter of Laguna, the inn is just a stone's throw from the beach on the ocean side of Pacific Coast Highway.

Innkeeper(s): Henk & Annette Wirtz. $100-175. MC VISA AX. 12 rooms with PB, 1 with FP. 1 suite. Breakfast included in rates. Type of meal: continental-plus breakfast. Afternoon tea available. Beds: KQD. Amusement parks, antiques, fishing, shopping and theater nearby.

Location: In the heart of the village.

Publicity: *New York Times, Los Angeles Times, California Magazine, Home & Garden.*

"*Who could find a paradise more relaxing than an old-fashioned bed and breakfast with Mozart and Vivaldi, a charming fountain, wonderful fresh-baked bread, ocean air, and Henk's conversational wit?*"

Certificate may be used: October-May, Sunday-Thursday.

Lake Arrowhead N11

Bracken Fern Manor
815 Arrowhead Villas Rd, PO Box 100
Lake Arrowhead, CA 92352
(909)337-8557 Fax:(909)337-3323

Circa 1929. Opened during the height of the '20s as Lake Arrowhead's first membership resort, this country inn provided refuge to Silver Screen heroines, the wealthy and the prominent. Old letters from the Gibson Girls found in the attic bespoke of elegant parties, dapper gentlemen, the Depression, Prohibition and homesick hearts. Each room is furnished with antiques collected from a lifetime of international travel. The Crestline Historical Society has its own museum and curator and a map of historical sites you can visit.

Innkeeper(s): Cheryl Weaver. $65-228. MC VISA. 10 rooms, 9 with PB. 3 suites. Breakfast included in rates. Types of meals: full breakfast and early coffee/tea. Afternoon tea available. Beds: KQDT. Cable TV and VCR on premises. Antiques, fishing, shopping, downhill skiing, cross-country skiing, theater and watersports nearby.

Publicity: *Mountain Shopper & Historic B&B, The Press Enterprise, Sun, Lava.*

"*My husband brought me here for my 25th birthday and it was everything I hoped it would be - peaceful, romantic and so relaxing .... Thank you for the wonderful memories I will hold close to my heart always.*"

Certificate may be used: Jan. 2-March 31, anytime, except holidays. April-Dec., Monday through Thursday, excluding holidays.

Lakeport F4

Forbestown B&B Inn
825 N Forbes St
Lakeport, CA 95453
(707)263-7858 Fax:(707)263-7878

Circa 1863. Located in the downtown area, this early California farmhouse is two blocks from the lake. Wisteria drape the front porch, overlooking

the inn's yard. The dining room, where gourmet breakfasts are served, has a wall of French windows looking out to the back garden with a tall redwood tree and handsome flagstone swimming pool. Clear Lake is fed by rain and underground sulfur and soda springs. The area has been acknowledged as having the cleanest air in California.

Innkeeper(s): Jack & Nancy Dunne. $65-150. MC VISA AX PC TC. 4 rooms, 1 with PB. 1 cottage. Breakfast, afternoon tea and evening snack included in rates. Types of meals: full breakfast, gourmet breakfast and early coffee/tea. Catered breakfast available. Beds: KQ. Turndown service and ceiling fan in room. Cable TV, VCR, fax, copier, spa, swimming and library on premises. Antiques, fishing, parks, shopping and watersports nearby.

Certificate may be used: Sunday through Thursday, year-round.

Lemon Cove K9

Mesa Verde Plantation B&B
33038 Sierra Dr
Lemon Cove, CA 93244-1700
(209)597-2555 (800)240-1466 Fax:(209)597-2551
E-mail: mvpbb@psnw.com

Circa 1908. The history of orange production is deeply entwined in the roots of California, and this home is located on what once was an orange plantation. The original 1908 house burned in the 1960s, but the current home was built on its foundation. In keeping with the home's plantation past, the innkeepers decorated the place with a "Gone With the Wind," theme. The comfortable, country guest rooms sport names such as the Scarlett O'Hara, the

Belle Watling, and of course, the Rhett Butler. A hot tub is located in the orchard, and there also is a heated swimming pool.

Innkeeper(s): Scott & Marie Munger. $70-125. MC VISA AX DC DS PC TC. 8 rooms, 6 with PB, 2 with FP. 1 suite. Breakfast and evening snack included in rates. Types of meals: full breakfast, gourmet breakfast and early coffee/tea. Beds: KQD. Air conditioning, ceiling fan, TV and VCR in room. Fax, spa and swimming on premises. Antiques, fishing, parks, shopping, cross-country skiing, sporting events, golf, watersports nearby.

Publicity: *Exeter Sun, Kaweah Commonwealth.*

"Scarlett O'Hara would be proud to live on this lovely plantation."

Certificate may be used: Sept. 8-May 21, Sunday-Friday, excluding holidays and special local events.

Little River   F2

The Victorian Farmhouse
7001 N Hwy 1
Little River, CA 95456
(707)937-0697 (800)264-4723

Circa 1877. Built as a private residence, this Victorian farmhouse is located on two-and-a-half acres in Little River. Two miles south of the historic village of Mendocino, the inn offers a relaxed country setting with deer, quail, flower gardens, an apple orchard and a running creek (School House Creek). Several of the cottages are enhanced by an ocean view. A short walk will take you to the shoreline.

Innkeeper(s): Carole Molnar. $85-175. MC VISA AX DS. 11 rooms with PB. Breakfast and afternoon tea included in rates. Type of meal: full breakfast. Beds: KQT. Antiques, fishing, parks, shopping, theater and watersports nearby.

"This morning when we woke up at home we really missed having George deliver breakfast. You have a lovely inn and you do a super job."

Certificate may be used: Oct. 1-June 30, Sunday-Thursday.

Long Beach   O10

The Turret House Victorian B&B
556 Chestnut Ave
Long Beach, CA 90802
(562)983-9812 (888)488-7798 Fax:(562)437-4082

Circa 1906. This Queen Anne Victorian does, of course, display a turret as one of its delightful architectural features. The home, located in a Long Beach historic district, remained in the same family until it was purchased by the current owners. The decor is elegant and romantic. Fine linens top the beds and the wallpapers and furnishings are all coordinated with similar prints and colors. Each room has a clawfoot tub, and bubble bath is provid-

ed for a relaxing soak. The breakfasts are an imaginative gourmet treat. Guests might partake of a menu with a granola parfait, followed by cranberry scones and spinach parasol pie. There are two Victorian parlors to enjoy, and a proper afternoon tea is served with succulent treats such as a mocha cheesecake or rich peanut butter pie. Long Beach offers plenty of shops and restaurants, and the city is well situated for those enjoying the many attractions in Southern California.

Innkeeper(s): Lisa Zucker. $90-125. MC VISA DS PC TC. 5 rooms with PB. Breakfast and afternoon tea included in rates. Types of meals: full breakfast, gourmet breakfast and early coffee/tea. Picnic lunch available. Beds: KQT. Air conditioning and ceiling fan in room. Cable TV, VCR and fax on premises. Antiques, fishing, parks, shopping, sporting events, golf, theater and watersports nearby.

Publicity: *Los Angeles Times, Signal Hill Paper.*

Certificate may be used: Jan. 10-Nov. 30, Sunday-Thursday, excluding major holidays, other packages and special events.

Los Olivos   N7

Los Olivos Grand Hotel
2860 Grand Ave
Los Olivos, CA 93441
(805)688-7788 (800)446-2455 Fax:(805)688-1942

Circa 1985. This four-star, four-diamond inn is ideally located in the Santa Ynez Valley, with its picturesque vineyards and rolling hills. Each guest room is decorated with the artwork of a different western or classic impressionist artist. There are fireplaces in all rooms, and many also offer Jacuzzi tubs. Down comforters, room service, laundry service and in-room mini refrigerators are among the many amenities, and the hotel offers plenty of items to help business travelers. A full breakfast and afternoon tea are served daily, and on the weekends, brunch is served. The hotel's Remington Restaurant features an extensive dinner menu. Cocktails are available at Le Saloon, located in the lounge. There is a heated swimming pool and Jacuzzi on the premises, and guests enjoy complimentary use of bicycles for touring the countryside. Los Olivos is one of the Four Sisters Inns.

Innkeeper(s): Ken Mortensen. $160-325. MC VISA AX. 21 rooms with PB, 21 with FP. 1 suite. 3 conference rooms. Breakfast and afternoon tea included in rates. Types of meals: full breakfast and gourmet breakfast. Picnic lunch, lunch and room service available. Restaurant on premises. Beds: KQ. Air conditioning and turndown service in room. Fax, copier, spa, swimming and bicycles on premises. Antiques, fishing, parks, shopping and watersports nearby.

Certificate may be used: January-December, Sunday-Thursday only - holidays & special events not included, subject to availability. Not including blackout dates

Lucerne   F4

Kristalberg B&B
PO Box 1629
Lucerne, CA 95458-1629
(707)274-8009

This country B&B affords a panoramic view of Clear Lake and surrounding mountain areas. Each of the guest rooms is furnished and decorated in a different period style. The master suite offers French Provencal design, other rooms feature 18th-century motifs. The parlor is decked in 18th-century Italian influences, while the dining area is pure Americana. The expansive breakfast is served in the home's formal dining room. German and Spanish are spoken at the B&B.

Innkeeper(s): Merv Myers. $55-150. MC VISA AX DS. 3 rooms. Breakfast included in rates. Type of meal: full breakfast.

Certificate may be used: November through March and weekdays (Sunday-Friday) April-October.

Mariposa   I8

Rockwood Gardens
5155 Tip Top Rd
Mariposa, CA 95338-9003
(209)742-6817 (800)859-8862 Fax:(209)742-7400

Circa 1989. Nestled among the pines in the Sierra foothills, this contemporary Prairie-style inn was designed and built to complement the natural beauty found nearby. A creek, oaks, pond and wildflower meadow all are part of the inn's setting. Guests often use the inn as headquarters when exploring the many wonders of Yosemite National Park. Visitors select from the Rose, Duck and Manzanita rooms. Stroll the grounds and relish the fine view of evening stars.

Innkeeper(s): Gerald & Mary Ann Fuller. $65-95. TC. 3 rooms, 1 with FP. 1 suite. 1 conference room. Breakfast included in rates. Type of meal: continental-plus breakfast. Picnic lunch available. Beds: KQD. Air conditioning, ceiling fan and VCR in room. Cable TV, fax and copier on premises. Antiques, fishing, parks, shopping, downhill skiing, cross-country skiing and watersports nearby.

Certificate may be used: Jan. 2-April 15 & Oct. 1-Dec. 2, every day.

McCloud   B5

McCloud Hotel B&B
408 Main St, PO Box 730
McCloud, CA 96057-0730
(916)964-2822 (800)964-2823 Fax:(916)964-2844
E-mail: mchotel@telis.org

Circa 1915. Having once provided housing for mill workers and teachers, this inn is a nationally registered historic landmark. Guests may listen to music

from the past in the lobby, which is furnished with an original registration desk, overstuffed honest chairs and '30s style sofas. Board games, books and puzzles also can be found in the lobby. Guest rooms feature coordinated decorator fabrics and antique vanities and trunks.

Innkeeper(s): Marilyn & Lee Ogden. $68-130. MC VISA. 18 rooms with PB. 4 suites. 1 conference room. Breakfast and afternoon tea included in rates. Types of meals: full breakfast and early coffee/tea. Room service available. Beds: QT. Ceiling fan in room. Cable TV, fax and copier on premises. Handicap access. Fishing, shopping, downhill skiing, cross-country skiing and watersports nearby.

Publicity: *Sunset, PBS California Gold, Redding Searchlight, Mount Shasta Herald.*

Certificate may be used: From Oct. 1-May 1, Monday through Thursday only. No holidays.

Mendocino   F2

John Dougherty House
571 Ukiah St, PO Box 817
Mendocino, CA 95460
(707)937-5266 (800)486-2104
E-mail: jdhbmw@mcn.org

Circa 1867. Early American furnishings and country-style stenciling provide the decor at this welcoming inn. Four rooms have outstanding water views, including the Captain's Room. The water tower room has an 18-foot ceiling and wood-burning stove. The inn's grounds sparkle with an array of beautiful flowers. The inn has been featured on the cover of Country Homes.

Innkeeper(s): David & Marion Wells. $95-205. MC VISA DS PC TC. 6 rooms with PB, 6 with FP. 3 suites. Breakfast included in rates. Types of meals: gourmet breakfast and early coffee/tea. Beds: Q. TV in room. Antiques, fishing, parks, shopping, theater and watersports nearby.

Location: Historic District.

Publicity: *Mendocino Beacon, Country Home, Los Angeles Times, San Francisco Times/Tribune.*

Certificate may be used: Dec. 1-March 31, Sunday to Thursday, no holiday weeks.

Montara
I4

The Goose & Turrets B&B
835 George St, PO Box 937
Montara, CA 94037-0937
(415)728-5451 Fax:(415)728-0141
E-mail: rhmgt@montara.com

Circa 1908. In the peaceful setting of horse ranches, strawflower farms and an art colony, this Italian villa features beautiful gardens surrounded by a 20-foot-high cypress hedge. The gardens include an orchard, vegetable garden, herb garden, rose garden, fountains, a hammock, swing and plenty of spots to

enjoy the surroundings. The large dining and living room areas are filled with art, collectibles and classical music plays during afternoon tea. Among its many previous uses, the Goose & Turrets once served as Montara's first post office, the town hall, a Sunday school and a grocery store.

Innkeeper(s): Raymond & Emily Hoche-Mong. $85-120. MC VISA AX DC DS PC TC. 5 rooms with PB, 3 with FP. Breakfast and afternoon tea included in rates. Beds: KQDT. Turndown service in room. Library on premises. Antiques, fishing, parks and watersports nearby.

Location: One-half mile from the Pacific Ocean, 20 minutes from San Francisco airport.

Publicity: *San Jose Mercury News, Half Moon Bay Review, Peninsula Times Tribune, San Mateo Times, Los Angeles Times, Tri-Valley Herald, Contra Costa Times.*

"*Lots of special touches. Great Southern hospitality — we'll be back.*"

Certificate may be used: All year, Monday-Thursday.

Monterey
J5

The Jabberwock
598 Laine St
Monterey, CA 93940-1312
(408)372-4777 (888)428-7253 Fax:(408)655-2946

Circa 1911. Set in a half-acre of gardens, this Craftsman-style inn provides a fabulous view of Monterey Bay with its famous barking seals. When you're ready to settle in for the evening, you'll find huge Victorian beds complete with lace-edged sheets and goose-down comforters. In the late afternoon, hors d'oeuvres and aperitifs are served in an enclosed sun porch. After dinner, guests are tucked into bed with homemade chocolate chip cookies

and milk. To help guests avoid long lines, the innkeepers have tickets available for the popular and nearby Monterey Bay Aquarium.

Innkeeper(s): Joan & John Kiliany. $105-190. MC VISA. 7 rooms, 5 with PB, 3 with FP. Types of meals: gourmet breakfast and early coffee/tea. Beds: KQ. Fax and copier on premises. Antiques, fishing, parks, shopping, theater and watersports nearby.

Location: Four blocks above Cannery Row, the beach and Monterey Bay Aquarium.

Publicity: *Sunset, Travel & Leisure, Sacramento Bee, San Francisco Examiner, Los Angeles Times, Country Inns, San Francisco Chronicle, Diablo, Elmer Dill's KABC-Los Angeles TV.*

"*Words are not enough to describe the ease and tranquility of the atmosphere of the home, rooms, owners and staff at the Jabberwock.*"

Certificate may be used: November through April, Sunday-Thursday.

Mount Shasta
B5

Mount Shasta Ranch B&B
1008 W.A. Barr Rd
Mount Shasta, CA 96067-9465
(916)926-3870 Fax:(916)926-6882
E-mail: alpinere@snowcrest.net

Circa 1923. This large two-story ranch house offers a full view of Mt. Shasta from its 60-foot-long redwood porch. Spaciousness abounds from the 1,500-square-foot living room with a massive rock fireplace to the large suites with private bathrooms that include large tubs and roomy showers. A full country breakfast may offer cream cheese-stuffed French toast or fresh, wild blackberry crepes. Just minutes away, Lake Siskiyou boasts superb fishing, sailing, swimming, and 18 hole golf course with public tennis courts.

Innkeeper(s): Bill & Mary Larsen. $50-95. MC VISA AX DS PC TC. 9 rooms, 4 with PB. 1 cottage. 1 conference room. Breakfast included in rates. Types of meals: full breakfast and early coffee/tea. Afternoon tea available. Beds: Q. Air conditioning, ceiling fan and TV in room. VCR, fax, copier, spa and library on premises. Antiques, fishing, parks, shopping, downhill skiing, cross-country skiing and watersports nearby.

Certificate may be used: Anytime.

Murphys   H7

Trade Carriage House
230 Big Trees Rd
Murphys, CA 95247-2429
(209)728-3909 (800)800-3408 Fax:(209)728-3408
E-mail: sales@realtyworld-murphys.com

Circa 1930. This little cottage is surrounded by a white picket fence. The structure was built in Stockton and was later moved to Murphys, a historic California town. There are two bedrooms, furnished with a few antiques and some wicker pieces. There is no meal service, but the cottage does have a kitchen. Shops, restaurants and other local sites are within walking distance.

Innkeeper(s): Cynthia Trade. $113. PC TC. 1 cottage. Beds: QD. Air conditioning and TV in room. Antiques, fishing, parks, shopping, downhill skiing, cross-country skiing, golf, theater and watersports nearby.

Certificate may be used: January to June, September to December, Sunday through Thursday.

Napa   H4

1801 Inn
1801 First St
Napa, CA 94581
(707)224-3739 (800)518-0146 Fax:(707)224-3932
E-mail: the1801inn@aol.com

Circa 1903. The innkeepers at this Queen Anne Victorian have created a setting perfect for romance. The guest rooms feature Victorian decor, Oriental rugs top the hardwood floors, and beds are dressed with fine linens and soft comforters. Each guest bathroom has a large soaking tub, and each bedchamber has a fireplace. The turn-of-the-century inn is located in Old Town Napa and is close to the multitude of wineries in the valley, as well as antique shops and restaurants.

Innkeeper(s): Linda & Chris Craiker. $125-169. MC VISA DS. 5 rooms with PB, 5 with FP. Breakfast and evening snack included in rates. Types of meals: full breakfast and gourmet breakfast. Beds: K. Air conditioning and ceiling fan in room. Cable TV, VCR and fax on premises.

Publicity: *Sacramento Bee.*

Certificate may be used: Jan. 5-April 30, Sunday-Thursday.

Beazley House
1910 1st St
Napa, CA 94559-2351
(707)257-1649 (800)559-1649 Fax:(707)257-1518
E-mail: jbeazley@napanet.net

Circa 1902. Nestled in green lawns and gardens, this graceful shingled mansion is frosted with white trim on its bays and balustrades. Stained-glass windows and polished-wood floors set the atmosphere in the parlor. There are six rooms in the main house

and the carriage house features five more, many with fireplaces and whirlpool tubs. The venerable Beazley House was Napa's first bed & breakfast inn.

Innkeeper(s): Carol & Jim Beazley. $105-225. MC VISA. 11 rooms with PB, 6 with FP. 5 suites. Breakfast and afternoon tea included in rates. Types of meals: full breakfast and early coffee/tea. Beds: KQDT. Air conditioning and ceiling fan in room. Fax on premises. Handicap access. Antiques, fishing, parks and shopping nearby.

Location: In the historic neighborhood of Old Town Napa, at the south end of Napa Valley.

Publicity: *Los Angeles Times, USA Today, Yellow Brick Road, Emergo, Sacramento Bee.*

"There's a sense of peace & tranquility that hovers over this house, sprinkling magical dream dust & kindness."

Certificate may be used: Dec. 1-23, Sunday-Thursday and Jan. 2-30, Sunday-Thursday.

Belle Epoque
1386 Calistoga Ave
Napa, CA 94559-2552
(707)257-2161 (800)238-8070 Fax:(707)226-6314

Circa 1893. This Queen Anne Victorian has a wine cellar and tasting room where guests can casually sip Napa Valley wines. The inn, which is one of the most unique architectural structures found in the wine country, is located in the heart of Napa's Calistoga Historic District. Beautiful original stained-glass windows include a window from an old church. A selection of fine restaurants and shops are within easy walking distance, as well as the riverfront, city parks and the Wine Train Depot. The train, which serves all meals, takes you just beyond St. Helena and back.

Innkeeper(s): Georgia Jump. $100-195. MC VISA AX DS PC TC. 6 rooms with PB, 2 with FP. 1 suite. 1 conference room. Breakfast and evening snack included in rates. Types of meals: gourmet breakfast and early coffee/tea. Beds: KQT. Air conditioning, ceiling fan and TV in room. VCR, fax, copier and spa on premises. Amusement parks, antiques, parks, shopping, sporting events, golf and theater nearby.

"At first I was a bit leery, how can a B&B get consistent rave reviews? After staying here two nights, I am now a believer!"

Certificate may be used: Dec. 1-23, Jan. 1-March 15, Monday-Thursday, holidays excluded.

Blue Violet Mansion

443 Brown St
Napa, CA 94559-3349

(707)253-2583 (800)959-2583 Fax:(707)257-8205

Circa 1886. English lampposts, a Victorian gazebo, and a rose garden welcome guests to this blue and white Queen Anne Victorian. Listed in the National Register, the house originally was built for a tannery executive. There are three-story bays, and from the balconies guests often view hot air bal-

loons in the early morning. Eight rooms feature two-person spas and 11 have fireplaces. A full breakfast is served in the dining room. The innkeepers offer room service by request, as well as a massage service. In the evenings, desserts are presented. Nearby is the wine train and restaurants.

Innkeeper(s): Kathy & Bob Morris. $145-285. MC VISA AX DC DS PC TC. 14 rooms with PB, 11 with FP. 3 suites. 1 conference room. Breakfast and evening snack included in rates. Type of meal: full breakfast. Dinner, picnic lunch, banquet service, catering service and room service available. Restaurant on premises. Beds: KQ. Air conditioning, turndown service and ceiling fan in room. Cable TV, VCR, fax, copier, spa and swimming on premises. Handicap access. Amusement parks, antiques, fishing, parks, shopping, theater and watersports nearby.

Certificate may be used: Monday through Wednesday, November through March. Christmas week, holidays and special events excluded. Deluxe rooms only: $185-225.

The Hennessey House B&B

1727 Main St
Napa, CA 94559-1844

(707)226-3774 Fax:(707)226-2975

Circa 1889. This gracious Queen Anne Eastlake Victorian was once home to Dr. Edwin Hennessey, a Napa County physician. Pristinely renovated, the inn features stained-glass windows and a curving wraparound porch. A handsome hand-painted, stamped-tin ceiling graces the dining room. All rooms are furnished in antiques. The four guest rooms in the carriage house boast whirlpool baths, fireplaces or patios.

Innkeeper(s): Andrea LaMar. $85-160. MC VISA AX DS. 10 rooms with PB, 4 with FP. Breakfast included in rates. Type of meal: full breakfast. Beds: KQT. Air conditioning, ceiling fan and TV in room. Fax, spa and sauna on premises. Antiques and shopping nearby.

Location: One hour from San Francisco.

Publicity: *AM-PM Magazine.*

"Thank you for making our stay very pleasant."

Certificate may be used: November-June, Sunday-Thursday, non-holiday. Carriage House rooms only in winter months.

Old World Inn

1301 Jefferson St
Napa, CA 94559-2412

(707)257-0112

Circa 1906. The decor in this exquisite bed & breakfast is second to none. In 1981, Macy's sought out the inn to showcase a new line of fabrics inspired by Scandinavian artist Carl Larrson. Each romantic room is adorned in bright, welcoming colors and includes special features such as canopy beds and clawfoot tubs. The Garden Room boasts three skylights, and the Anne Room is a must for honeymoons and romantic retreats. The walls and ceilings are painted in a warm peach and blue, bows are stenciled around the perimeter of the room. A decorated canopy starts at the ceiling in the center of the bed and falls downward producing a curtain-like

effect. A buffet breakfast is served each morning and a delicious afternoon tea and wine and cheese social will curb your appetite until dinner. After sampling one of Napa's gourmet eateries, return to the inn where a selection of desserts await you.

Innkeeper(s): Sam Van Hoeve. $115-150. MC VISA AX DS PC TC. 8 rooms with PB. Breakfast and afternoon tea included in rates. Beds: KQ. Spa and bicycles on premises. Antiques nearby.

Publicity: *Napa Valley Traveller.*

"Excellent is an understatement. We'll return."

Certificate may be used: Sunday - Thursday, November through May.

Stahlecker House B&B Country Inn & Garden

1042 Easum Dr
Napa, CA 94558-5525
(707)257-1588 (800)799-1588 Fax:(707)224-7429

Circa 1947. This country inn is situated on the banks of tree-lined Napa Creek. The acre and a half of grounds feature rose and orchard gardens, fountains and manicured lawns. Guests often relax on the sun deck. There is an antique refrigerator stocked with soft drinks and lemonade. Full, gourmet breakfasts are served by candlelight in the glass-wrapped dining room. In the evenings, coffee, tea and freshly made chocolate chip cookies are served. The Napa Wine Train station is five minutes away. Wineries, restaurants, antique shops, bike paths and hiking all are nearby.

Innkeeper(s): Ron & Ethel Stahlecker. $95-185. MC VISA AX TC. 4 rooms with PB, 4 with FP. 1 suite. Breakfast and evening snack included in rates. Types of meals: full breakfast, gourmet breakfast and early coffee/tea. Afternoon tea available. Beds: QT. Air conditioning and turndown service in room. Library on premises. Antiques, fishing, parks, shopping, theater and watersports nearby.

Publicity: *Napa Valley Traveler.*

"Friendly hosts and beautiful gardens."

Certificate may be used: Feb. 28 to July 31, Oct. 1 to Dec. 20, Monday to Thursday (not Friday, Saturday or Sunday)

Nevada City   F6

Emma Nevada House

528 E Broad St
Nevada City, CA 95959-2213
(916)265-4415 (800)916-3662 Fax:(916)265-4416
E-mail: emmanev@oro.net

Circa 1856. What is considered the childhood home of 19th-century opera star Emma Nevada now serves as an attractive Queen Anne Victorian inn. English roses line the white picket fence in front, and the forest-like back garden has a small stream with benches. The Empress' Chamber is the most romantic room with ivory Italian linens atop a French antique bed, a bay window and a massive French armoire. Some rooms have whirlpool baths. Guests enjoy relaxing in the hexagonal sunroom and on the inn's wraparound porches. Empire Mine State Historic Park is nearby.

Innkeeper(s): Ruth Ann Riese. $90-150. MC VISA AX DC PC TC. 6 rooms with PB, 1 with FP. Breakfast and afternoon tea included in rates. Types of meals: full breakfast and early coffee/tea. Beds: Q. Air conditioning in room. Fax and library on premises. Antiques, fishing, parks, shopping, downhill skiing, theater and watersports nearby.

Publicity: *Country Inns, Los Angeles Times, San Jose Mercury News.*

"A delightful experience: such airiness and hospitality in the midst of so much history. We were fascinated by the detail and the faithfulness of the restoration. This house is a quiet solace for city-weary travelers. There's a grace here."

Certificate may be used: From Jan. 2 to Sept. 30, Sunday-Thursday, holidays excluded.

The Parsonage B&B

427 Broad St
Nevada City, CA 95959-2407
(916)265-9478 Fax:(916)265-8147

Circa 1865. Guests in search of California history would do well to stop in Nevada City and at the Parsonage. The Gold Rush town is a registered National Monument, and the home is one of the older homes in the state, dating to the 1860s. Innkeeper Deborah Dane's family has been in California since Gold Rush days, and the home features many heirlooms. Although used to house

Methodist ministers for 80 years, the home was in a quite ungodly state by the time Deborah found it. She painstakingly restored the gem and filled it with beautiful antiques and delightful, elegant decor. Special furnishings, knickknacks and artwork are located throughout, including an amazing carved mahogany bed the Dane family brought along the Oregon Trail. In addition to her flair for restoration and decorating, Deborah is a dietitian and Cordon Bleu graduate, so be prepared for a gourmet breakfast that's as healthy as it is delicious.

Innkeeper(s): Pam Ashton & Deborah Dane. $70-135. MC VISA PC TC. 6 rooms with PB, 1 with FP. 1 cottage. 1 conference room. Breakfast included in rates. Types of meals: continental-plus breakfast, full breakfast and early coffee/tea. Restaurant on premises. Beds: QT. Air conditioning, ceiling fan and TV in room. Fax, copier and library on premises. Antiques, fishing, shopping, downhill skiing, cross-country skiing, golf, theater and watersports nearby.

Publicity: *Country Inns*

Certificate may be used: Jan. 1-Easter week, Sunday-Friday; Easter week-Dec. 1, Sunday-Thursday, subject to availability.

The Red Castle Inn Historic Lodgings
109 Prospect St
Nevada City, CA 95959-2831
(916)265-5135 (800)761-4766

Circa 1860. The Smithsonian has lauded the restoration of this four-story brick Gothic Revival known as "The Castle" by townsfolk. Its roof is laced with wooden icicles and the balconies are adorned with gingerbread. Within, there are intricate moldings, antiques, Victorian wallpapers, canopy beds and decorative woodstoves. Verandas provide views of the historic city through cedar, chestnut and walnut trees, and of terraced gardens with a fountain pond.

Innkeeper(s): Conley & Mary Louise Weaver. $100-135. MC VISA PC TC. 7 rooms, 4 with PB. 3 suites. Breakfast and afternoon tea included in rates. Types of meals: gourmet breakfast and early coffee/tea. Catering service available. Beds: QD. Air conditioning and turndown service in room. Library on premises. Antiques, fishing, parks, shopping, downhill skiing, cross-country skiing, theater and watersports nearby.

Location: Within the Nevada City historic district overlooking the town.

Publicity: *Sunset, Gourmet, Northern California Home and Garden, Sacramento Bee, Los Angeles Times, Travel Holiday, Victorian Homes, Innsider, U.S. News and World Report, USAir, McCalls, New York Times, Brides, San Francisco Focus, Motorland.*

"The Red Castle Inn would top my list of places to stay. Nothing else quite compares with it-Gourmet."

Certificate may be used: Sunday through Thursday, April 1-Aug. 31 except Easter week and town special events; Sunday through Friday, Jan. 1-March 31 except town special events.

Nice
F4

Featherbed Railroad Company B&B
2870 Lakeshore Blvd, PO Box 4016
Nice, CA 95464
(707)274-4434

Circa 1940. Located on five acres on Clear Lake, this unusual inn features guest rooms in nine luxuriously renovated, painted, and papered cabooses. Each has its own featherbed and private bath, most have Jacuzzi tubs for two. The Southern Pacific cabooses have a bay window alcove, while those from the Santa Fe feature small cupolas. Bicycles, canopied patio boats and jet skis are available for rent.

Innkeeper(s): Lorraine Bassignani. $90-140. MC VISA AX DS. 9 rooms, 5 with PB. Breakfast included in rates. Type of meal: full breakfast. Beds: QDT. Spa on premises.

Publicity: *Santa Rosa Press Democrat, Fairfield Daily Republic.*

Certificate may be used: Sunday-Thursday, Oct. 15-April 15.

Nipomo
M7

The Kaleidoscope Inn
130 E Dana St
Nipomo, CA 93444-1297
(805)929-5444

Circa 1887. The sunlight that streams through the stained-glass windows of this charming Victorian creates a kaleidoscope effect and thus the name.

The inn is surrounded by gardens. Each romantic guest room is decorated with antiques and the library offers a fireplace. Fresh flowers add a special touch. Breakfast is either served in the dining room, in the gardens, or in your room. L.A. Times readers voted the inn as one of the best lodging spots for under $100 per night.

Innkeeper(s): Patty & Bill Linane. $90. MC VISA AX. 3 rooms with PB. 1 conference room. Breakfast included in rates. Types of meals: full breakfast, gourmet breakfast and early coffee/tea. Room service available. Beds: KQ. Turndown service and ceiling fan in room. Cable TV, VCR and library on premises. Antiques, fishing, parks, shopping, theater and watersports nearby.

Location: Twenty miles south of San Luis Obispo, near Pismo Beach.

Publicity: *Santa Maria Times, Los Angeles Times, Country.*

"Beautiful room, chocolates, fresh flowers, peaceful night's rest, great breakfast."

Certificate may be used: Jan. 1-July 1, Nov. 1-Dec. 30, any time of week.

Pacific Grove   J5

Gatehouse Inn
225 Central Ave
Pacific Grove, CA 93950-3017
(408)649-8436 (800)753-1881 Fax:(408)648-8044

Circa 1884. This Italianate Victorian seaside inn is just a block from the ocean and Monterey Bay. The inn is decorated with Victorian and 20th-century antiques and touches of Art Deco. Guest rooms feature fireplaces, clawfoot tubs and down comforters. Some rooms have ocean views. The dining room boasts opulent Bradbury & Bradbury Victorian wallpapers as do some of the guest rooms. Afternoon hors d'oeuvres, wine and tea are served. The refrigerator is stocked for snacking.

Innkeeper(s): Lois Deford. $110-150. MC VISA AX DS PC TC. 9 rooms with PB, 5 with FP. Breakfast, afternoon tea and evening snack included in rates. Types of meals: full breakfast, gourmet breakfast and early coffee/tea. Beds: KQT. Turndown service in room. Fax, copier and bicycles on premises. Handicap access. Antiques, fishing, parks, shopping, theater and watersports nearby.

Location: One block from the ocean.

Publicity: *San Francisco Chronicle, Monterey Herald, Time, Newsweek, Inland Empire, Bon Appetit.*

"Thank you for spoiling us."

Certificate may be used: Jan. 1-April 30, Sunday-Thursday.

Gosby House Inn
643 Lighthouse Ave
Pacific Grove, CA 93950-2643
(408)375-1287 (800)527-8828 Fax:(408)655-9621

Circa 1887. Built as an upscale Victorian inn for those visiting the old Methodist retreat, this sunny yellow mansion features an abundance of gables, turrets and bays. During renovation the innkeeper slept in all the rooms to determine just what antiques were needed and how the beds should be situated. Eleven of the romantic rooms include fireplaces and many offer canopy beds. The Carriage House rooms include fireplaces, decks and spa tubs. Gosby House, which has been open to guests for more than a century, is in the National Register. Gosby House is one of the Four Sisters Inns. The Monterey Bay Aquarium is nearby.

Innkeeper(s): Tess Arthur. $90-160. MC VISA AX TC. 22 rooms, 20 with PB, 11 with FP. Breakfast and afternoon tea included in rates. Types of meals: gourmet breakfast and early coffee/tea. Picnic lunch available. Beds: KQD. Turndown service in room. Fax, copier and bicycles on premises. Handicap access. Antiques and shopping nearby.

Location: Six blocks from Monterey Bay.

Publicity: *San Francisco Chronicle, Oregonian, Los Angeles Times, Travel & Leisure.*

Certificate may be used: November-March, Sunday-Thursday excluding holidays & special events, subject to availability

Green Gables Inn
104 5th St
Pacific Grove, CA 93950-2903
(408)375-2095 (800)722-1774 Fax:(408)375-5437

Circa 1888. This half-timbered Queen Anne Victorian appears as a fantasy of gables overlooking spectacular Monterey Bay. The parlor has stained-glass panels framing the fireplace and bay windows

looking out to the sea. A favorite focal point is an antique carousel horse. Most of the guest rooms have panoramic views of the ocean, fireplaces, gleaming woodwork, soft quilts and teddy bears. Across the street is the Monterey Bay paved ocean-front cycling path. (Mountain bikes may be borrowed from the inn.) Green Gables is one of the Four Sisters Inns.

Innkeeper(s): Emily Frew. $110-180. MC VISA AX TC. 11 rooms, 7 with PB, 7 with FP. 1 suite. Breakfast and afternoon tea included in rates. Type of meal: gourmet breakfast. Picnic lunch available. Beds: KQD. Turndown service in room. Fax, copier and bicycles on premises. Handicap access. Antiques, shopping and theater nearby.

Location: On Monterey Bay four blocks from Monterey Bay Aquarium.

Publicity: *Travel & Leisure, Country Living.*

Certificate may be used: December; January (excluding February-November) Sunday-Thursday no holidays, special events, subject to availability

Old St. Angela Inn
321 Central Ave
Pacific Grove, CA 93950-2934
(408)372-3246 (800)748-6306 Fax:(408)372-8560

Circa 1910. Formerly a convent, this Cape-style inn has been restored and includes a glass solarium where breakfast is served. The ocean is a block away and it's just a short walk to the aquarium or fisherman's wharf.

Innkeeper(s): Lewis Shaefer & Susan Kuslis. $90-115. MC VISA DS PC TC. 8 rooms, 5 with PB. Breakfast, afternoon tea and evening snack included in rates. Types of meals: full breakfast, gourmet breakfast and early coffee/tea. Beds: QDT. Fax and spa on premises. Antiques, fishing, parks, shopping, theater and watersports nearby.

"Outstanding inn and outstanding hospitality."

Certificate may be used: Nov. 1-30, Jan. 1-April 30, Sunday-Thursday.

Casa Cody Country Inn
175 S Cahuilla Rd
Palm Springs, CA 92262-6331
(760)320-9346 (800)231-2639 Fax:(760)325-8610

Circa 1920. Casa Cody, built by a relative of Wild Bill Cody and situated in the heart of Palm Springs, is the town's oldest continuously operating inn. The San Jacinto Mountains provide a scenic background for the tree-shaded spa, the pink and purple bougainvillaea and the blue waters of the inn's two swimming pools. Each suite has a small kitchen and features red and turquoise Southwestern decor. Several have wood-burning fireplaces. There are

Mexican pavers, French doors and private patios. The area offers many activities, including museums, a heritage center, boutiques, a botanical garden, horseback riding and golf.

Innkeeper(s): Elissa Goforth. $49-199. MC VISA AX DC CB DS PC TC. 23 rooms, 24 with PB, 10 with FP. 8 suites. 2 cottages. Breakfast included in rates. Type of meal: continental-plus breakfast. Beds: KQT. Air conditioning, ceiling fan and TV in room. Fax, copier, spa, swimming and library on premises. Antiques and theater nearby.

Publicity: *New York Times, Washington Post, Los Angeles Times, San Diego Union Tribune, Seattle Times, Portland Oregonian, Los Angeles, San Diego Magazine, Pacific Northwest Magazine, Sunset, Westways, Alaska Airlines Magazine*

"Outstanding ambiance, friendly relaxed atmosphere."

Certificate may be used: Sunday through Thursday except February, March and April and holidays.

Ingleside Inn
200 W Ramon Rd
Palm Springs, CA 92264-7385
(760)325-0046 (800)772-6655 Fax:(760)325-0710
E-mail: ingleside@earthlink.net

Circa 1925. This posh, intimate hotel has been hosting the rich and famous since the 1930s when it was converted from a private estate into a luxurious hostelry. Among its notable guests are Greta Garbo, Greer Garson, President Ford, Marlon Brando, Goldie Hawn, John Travolta and many more. Each of the inn's suites and rooms is individually decorated. The spacious accommodations include amenities such as whirlpool tubs, steam rooms, sitting rooms, private porches and refrigerators stocked with drinks and snacks. Guests can enjoy the mountainous scenery while relaxing by the Olympic-size pool or in the Jacuzzi. Ingleside guests also receive special tee times at several local golf courses. The inn's restaurant, Melvyn's, is a multiple award winner. The two dining rooms are romantic in decor and the menu selection is vast, featuring everything from chateaubriand to shrimp scampi. Lunch and a gourmet Sunday brunch also are served. The inn is a Palm Springs historic site.

Innkeeper(s): Robert Timperio & Armida Pedrin. $72-385. MC VISA AX DC DS PC TC. 30 rooms with PB, 15 with FP. 10 suites. 2 conference rooms. Breakfast included in rates. Types of meals: continental breakfast, continental-plus breakfast, full breakfast and gourmet breakfast. Afternoon tea, dinner, evening snack, picnic lunch, lunch, gourmet lunch, banquet service, catering service, catered breakfast and room service available. Restaurant on premises. Beds: KQDT. Air conditioning, turndown service and TV in room. Fax, copier, spa, swimming and sauna on premises. Handicap access. Amusement parks, parks, shopping, golf and theater nearby.

Publicity: *USA Today, Los Angeles Times, Time, Bon Appetit, Cosmopolitan, Chicago Tribune, New York Times, San Francisco Coronicle, Detroit News.*

Certificate may be used: Sunday-Thursday, July and August.

Sakura, Japanese B&B
1677 N Via Miraleste at Vista Chino
Palm Springs, CA 92262
(619)327-0705 (800)200-0705 Fax:(619)327-6847

Circa 1945. An authentic Japanese experience awaits guests of this private home, distinctively decorated with Japanese artwork and antique kimonos. Guests are encouraged to leave their shoes at the door, grab kimonos and slippers and discover what real relaxation is all about. Guests may choose either American or Japanese breakfasts, and Japanese or vegetarian dinners also are available. The Palm Springs area is home to more than 70 golf courses and many fine shops. During the summer months, the innkeepers conduct tours in Japan.

Innkeeper(s): George & Fumiko Cebra. $45-75. 3 rooms, 2 with PB. 1 suite. Breakfast included in rates. Types of meals: full breakfast and early coffee/tea. Afternoon tea, dinner and picnic lunch available. Beds: Q. Air conditioning and TV in room. VCR, fax, spa and child care on premises. Amusement parks, antiques, fishing, parks, shopping, cross-country skiing, sporting events, theater and watersports nearby.

Certificate may be used: All year, Sunday through Thursday.

Petaluma
H4

Cavanagh Inn
10 Keller St
Petaluma, CA 94952-2939
(707)765-4657 (888)765-4658 Fax:(707)769-0466

Circa 1902. Embrace turn-of-the-century California at this picturesque Georgian Revival manor. The garden is filled with beautiful flowers, plants and fruit trees. Innkeeper Jeanne Farris is an award-winning chef and prepares the mouthwatering breakfasts. A typical meal might start off with butterscotch pears and fresh muffins with honey butter. This starter would be followed by an entree, perhaps eggs served with rosemary potatoes. The innkeepers also serve wine at 5:30 p.m. The parlor and library, which boasts heart-of-redwood panelled walls, is an ideal place to relax. Cavanagh Inn is located at the edge of Petaluma's historic district, and close to shops and the riverfront, including the Petaluma Queen Riverboat.

Innkeeper(s): Ray & Jeanne Farris. $70-125. MC VISA AX PC. 7 rooms, 5 with PB. 1 conference room. Breakfast included in rates. Type of meal: gourmet breakfast. Evening snack available. Beds: KQDT. Turndown service in room. Cable TV, VCR, fax and library on premises. Antiques, parks, shopping and theater nearby.

Publicity: *Argus-Courier.*

"This is our first B&B. . .sort of like learning to drive with a Rolls-Royce!"

Certificate may be used: All year, Sunday-Thursday

Point Arena
F3

Coast Guard House
695 Arena Cove
Point Arena, CA 95468
(707)882-2442 Fax:(707)882-2442

This National Register, Cape Cod-style home was built by the Lifesaving Service and later was used by the U.S. Coast Guard. The innkeepers have kept and preserved many of the lifeboats that were used throughout the home's 50-year service as a Coast Guard station. A collection of photographs and memorabilia also is displayed. Guest rooms are decorated in Arts and Crafts or Art Deco style, many afford ocean or canyon views. The Boathouse, a

replica of the ground's original boathouse, is a romantic cabin with a woodburning stove, private patio and spa with an ocean view. The Point Arena Lighthouse and Museum, as well as many shops and restaurants are just a few miles away.
Innkeeper(s): Mia & Kevin Gallagher. $75-175. MC VISA DC CB. 6 rooms. Breakfast included in rates. Type of meal: continental breakfast.
Certificate may be used: Monday-Thursday, November through April, holidays excluded.

Point Reyes Station H4

Carriage House
325 Mesa Rd, PO Box 1239
Point Reyes Station, CA 94956
(415)663-8627 Fax:(415)663-8431
Circa 1960. This recently remodeled home boasts a view of Inverness Ridge. One guest room and two suites are furnished in antiques and folk art with a private parlor, television, VCR and a fireplace. Children are welcome and cribs and daybeds are available. Point Reyes National Seashore has 100 miles of trails for cycling, hiking or horseback riding. Breakfast items such as freshly squeezed juice, muffins and breads are stocked in your room, so guests may enjoy it at leisure.
Innkeeper(s): Felicity Kirsch. $110-160. 1 room, 2 with PB, 2 with FP. 2 suites. Breakfast included in rates. Type of meal: continental-plus breakfast. Beds: QT. TV and VCR in room. Bicycles and child care on premises. Antiques, fishing, parks and shopping nearby.
Location: Near Point Reyes National Seashore & Tomales Bay State Park.
"What a rejuvenating getaway. We loved it. The smells, sounds and scenery were wonderful."
Certificate may be used: Sunday-Thursday, no holiday weeks

The Tree House
PO Box 1075
Point Reyes Station, CA 94956-1075
(415)663-8720
Circa 1970. This homestay offers an outstanding view of Point Reyes Station from the deck and some of the guest rooms. The King's Room features a king-size waterbed while Queen Quarter boasts its own fireplace. A hot tub is tucked away in a cozy spot of the garden.
Innkeeper(s): Lisa Patsel. $90-110. 3 rooms with PB, 2 with FP. 1 suite. Breakfast included in rates. Type of meal: continental-plus breakfast. Ceiling fan and VCR in room. Spa and pet boarding on premises. Antiques, parks and shopping nearby.
Certificate may be used: Sunday through Thursday.

Rancho Cucamonga O11

Christmas House B&B
9240 Archibald Ave
Rancho Cucamonga, CA 91730-5236
(909)980-6450
Circa 1904. This Queen Anne Victorian has been renovated in period elegance, emphasizing its intricate wood carvings and red and green stained-glass windows. Once surrounded by 80 acres of citrus groves and vineyards, the home, with its wide, sweeping veranda, is still a favorite place for taking in the beautiful lawns and palm trees. The elegant atmosphere attracts the business traveler, romance-seeker and vacationer.
Innkeeper(s): Janice Ilsley. $85-185. MC VISA AX DS. 6 rooms, 4 with PB, 3 with FP. 1 suite. 1 conference room. Breakfast included in rates. Types of meals: full breakfast, gourmet breakfast and early coffee/tea. Beds: QD. Air conditioning, ceiling fan and VCR in room. Spa on premises. Antiques, fishing, shopping, downhill skiing, sporting events and theater nearby.
Location: East of downtown Los Angeles, three miles from Ontario Airport.
Publicity: *Country Inns, Los Angeles Times, Elan.*
"Coming to Christmas House is like stepping through a magic door into an enchanted land. Many words come to mind — warmth, serenity, peacefulness."
Certificate may be used: Any night except Saturday night.

Redlands O11

Morey Mansion
190 Terracina Blvd
Redlands, CA 92373-4846
(909)793-7970 Fax:(909)793-7870
The exquisite exterior of this fanciful Victorian is like a fairy tale manor with its gingerbread trim and unique onion dome. David Morey, a shipbuilder and cabinet maker built the home for his wife, Sarah, using a variety of architectural styles. David also carved much of the ornate woodwork. The home has been featured in several movies and commercials. The current owner is an antique dealer and has filled the home with museum-quality pieces. Each room is dramatic, boasting many one-of-a-kind pieces. Carole Lombard once stayed in the home, and one of the rooms is named for her.
Innkeeper(s): Dolly Wimer. $109-185. MC VISA AX DC CB DS. 5 rooms. Breakfast included in rates. Type of meal: continental-plus breakfast.
Certificate may be used: Sunday through Thursday (Saturday and Sunday okay-Thursday and Friday okay).

Reedley J8

The Fairweather Inn B&B
259 S Reed Ave
Reedley, CA 93654-2845
(209)638-1918

Circa 1914. This Craftsman-style inn is situated on the bluffs of the Kings River, a half-hour's drive from Sequoia and Kings Canyon national parks. After a restful night in one of the inn's four guest rooms, all with queen beds, visitors will enjoy their gourmet breakfast in the dining room. The antique-filled inn is within walking distance of downtown restaurants and shops, and Reedley also offers a beautiful golf course near the river. Fresno and Visalia are 20 minutes away.
Innkeeper(s): Violet Demyan. $75-85. MC VISA AX. 4 rooms, 2 with PB. 1 suite. Breakfast included in rates. Type of meal: full breakfast. Beds: Q. Air conditioning in room. Antiques, fishing, downhill skiing, sporting events and watersports nearby.

"The Fairweather Inn is like an 'Oasis in the Desert'."

Certificate may be used: Sunday through Thursday.

Running Springs O12

Spring Oaks B&B
PO Box 2918
Running Springs, CA 92382-2918
(909)867-7797 (800)867-9636

Circa 1953. From the hot tub at this B&B guests can see for 100 miles. Aside from viewing far-reaching mountains, guests at this mountain home enjoy cozy bedchambers decorated with country furnishings. Each room is different. One features a white iron bed topped with a quilt, a Victorian dollhouse and a wicker rocking chair. The innkeepers offer a variety of specials, including inn-to-inn hiking trips and massage therapy. Breakfasts are healthy and made from organic ingredients.
Innkeeper(s): Bill & Laura Florian. $95. MC VISA PC. 3 rooms, 1 with PB. Breakfast and afternoon tea included in rates. Type of meal: full breakfast. Beds: Q. Ceiling fan in room. Spa on premises. Amusement parks, antiques, fishing, parks, shopping, downhill skiing, cross-country skiing, theater and watersports nearby.

Certificate may be used: When available, subject to availability.

Sacramento G6

Amber House
1315 22nd St
Sacramento, CA 95816-5717
(916)552-6525 (800)755-6526 Fax:(916)552-6529

Circa 1905. This Craftsman-style bungalow on the city's Historic Preservation Register is in a neighborhood of fine old homes eight blocks from the capi-

tol. Each room is named for a famous poet and features stained glass, English antiques, selected volumes of poetry and fresh flowers. Ask for the Lord Byron Room where you can soak by candlelight in the whirlpool tub or enjoy one of the new rooms with marble baths and Jacuzzi tubs in the adjacent 1913 Mediterranean mansion.
Innkeeper(s): Michael & Jane Richardson. $99-249. MC VISA AX DC CB DS PC TC. 9 rooms with PB, 1 with FP. 1 suite. 1 conference room. Breakfast included in rates. Type of meal: early coffee/tea. Gourmet lunch and catering service available. Beds: KQ. Air conditioning, turn-down service, TV and VCR in room. Fax, bicycles and library on premises. Antiques, fishing, parks, shopping, downhill skiing, cross-country skiing, theater and watersports nearby.

Location: Eight blocks to the east of the State Capitol.

Publicity: *Travel & Leisure, Village Crier.*

"Your cordial hospitality, the relaxing atmosphere and delicious breakfast made our brief business/pleasure trip so much more enjoyable."

Certificate may be used: All year except holidays, subject to availability.

Saint Helena G4

Deer Run Inn
PO Box 311 3995 Spring Mountain Rd
Saint Helena, CA 94574-0311
(707)963-3794 (800)843-3408 Fax:(707)963-9026

Circa 1929. This secluded mountain home is located on four forested acres just up the road from the house used for the television show "Falcon Crest." A fir-tree-shaded deck provides a quiet spot for breakfast while watching birds and deer pass by. Your host, Tom, was born on Spring Mountain and knows the winery area well. There is a watercolorist in residence.
Innkeeper(s): Tom & Carol Wilson. $125-155. MC VISA AX PC TC. 4 rooms with PB, 3 with FP. 1 suite. 1 cottage. Breakfast included in rates. Types of meals: gourmet breakfast and early coffee/tea. Beds: KQ. Air conditioning and ceiling fan in room. Fax, copier and swimming on premises. Amusement parks, antiques, fishing, parks, shopping, sporting events, theater and watersports nearby.

Location: Napa Valley.

Publicity: *Forbes, Chicago Tribune, Napa Record.*

"The perfect honeymoon spot! We loved it!"

Certificate may be used: Dec. 1-March 1, Sunday-Thursday only, Carriage Room and cottage only.

Spanish Villa
474 Glass Mountain Rd
Saint Helena, CA 94574-9669
(707)963-7483

Circa 1981. This contemporary Mission-style Spanish villa is nestled in a wooded valley in the Napa wine country, three miles from town. Tiffany lamp replicas are found throughout the inn, including the guest rooms. A large sitting room and fireplace are favorite gathering spots. The quiet, country roads found in the area are popular for biking, jogging or walking. Don't miss the chance to visit nearby Calistoga, with its hang gliding and famous mud baths.

Innkeeper(s): Roy & Barbie Bissember. $115-175. 3 rooms with PB. Breakfast included in rates. Types of meals: continental breakfast and early coffee/tea. Beds: K. Cable TV and VCR on premises. Amusement parks, antiques, fishing, parks, shopping, theater and watersports nearby.

Certificate may be used: Sunday-Thursday.

San Andreas   H7

Robin's Nest
PO Box 1408
San Andreas, CA 95249-1408
(209)754-1076 (888)214-9202 Fax:(209)754-3975

Circa 1895. Expect to be pampered from the moment you walk through the door at this three-story Queen Anne Victorian. Guests are greeted with homemade goodies upon arrival, and treated to an elegant, gourmet breakfast. The late 19th-century gem includes many fine architectural features, including eight-foot round windows, 12-foot ceilings on the first floor and gabled ceilings with roof windows on the second floor. Antiques deco-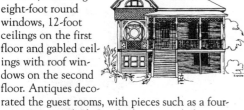rated the guest rooms, with pieces such as a four-poster, step-up bed. One bathroom includes an original seven-foot bathtub. The grounds boast century-old fruit trees, grapevines, a brick well, windmill and the more modern addition of a redwood spa.

Innkeeper(s): Karen & Bill Konietany. $55-105. 9 rooms, 7 with PB. 5 suites. Breakfast included in rates. Type of meal: full breakfast. Beds: QDT. Antiques, fishing, downhill skiing, cross-country skiing, theater and watersports nearby.

Publicity: *Stockton Record, In Flight, Westways.*

"An excellent job of making guests feel at home."

Certificate may be used: Anytime except holidays and Saturdays.

San Clemente   P11

Casa De Flores B&B
184 Ave La Cuesta
San Clemente, CA 92672
(714)498-1344

Circa 1974. Located a mile from the Pacific, you can enjoy a 180-degree view of the ocean, harbor and hills from this home. In a residential area, it was designed by your hostess. The Private Patio room offers sky-lights, a private spa and an ocean view. More than 1,000 orchid plants are grown on the grounds. Grab a sand chair and towel and head for your own stretch of the five miles of San Clemente beaches. Whale watching and fishing charters are available at the Dana Point Harbor, 10 minutes away.

Innkeeper(s): Marilee Arsenault. $75-100. PC. 2 suites, 1 with FP. Breakfast included in rates. Type of meal: gourmet breakfast. Beds: K. TV and VCR in room. Library on premises. Amusement parks, antiques, fishing, parks, shopping and watersports nearby.

Location: South of the Dana Point Harbor.

Certificate may be used: Sunday through Thursday except holidays.

San Diego   Q12

Heritage Park Inn
2470 Heritage Park Row
San Diego, CA 92110-2803
(619)299-6832 (800)995-2470 Fax:(619)299-9465

Circa 1889. Situated on a seven-acre Victorian park in the heart of Old Town, this inn is two of seven preserved classic structures. The main house offers a variety of beautifully appointed guest rooms, decked in traditional Victorian furnishings and decor. The opulent Manor Suite includes two bedrooms, a Jacuzzi tub and sitting room. Several rooms offer ocean views, and guest also can see the nightly fireworks show at nearby Sea World. A collection of classic movies is available, and a different movie is shown each night in the inn's parlor. Guests are treated to a light afternoon tea, and breakfast is served on fine china on candlelit tables. The home is within walking distance to the many sites, shops and restaurants in the historic Old Town. A small antique shop and Victorian toy store also are located next to the inn.

Innkeeper(s): Nancy & Charles Helsper. $90-225. MAP. MC VISA TC. 10 rooms with PB. 1 suite. 1 conference room. Breakfast and afternoon tea included in rates. Types of meals: gourmet breakfast and early coffee/tea. Picnic lunch and catering service available. Beds: KQT. Turndown service and ceiling fan in room. VCR, fax and copier on premises. Amusement parks, antiques, fishing, parks, shopping, sporting events, theater and watersports nearby.

Location: In historic Old Town.

Publicity: *L.A. Herald Examiner, Innsider, Los Angeles Times, Orange County Register, San Diego Union, In-Flight, Glamour, Country Inns.*

"A beautiful step back in time. Peaceful and gracious."

Certificate may be used: Call innkeeper for dates. Based on availability.

San Francisco   H4

Archbishop's Mansion

1000 Fulton St (at Steiner)
San Francisco, CA 94117-1608
(415)563-7872 (800)543-5820 Fax:(415)885-3193

Circa 1904. This French Empire-style manor was built for the Archbishop of San Francisco. It is designated as a San Francisco historic landmark. The grand stairway features redwood paneling, Corinthian columns and a stained-glass dome. The parlor has a hand-painted ceiling. Each of the guest rooms is named for an opera. Rooms have antiques, Victorian window treatments and embroidered linens. Breakfast is delivered to your guest quarters or served in the dining room.
Innkeeper(s): Rick Janvier. $129-385. MC VISA AX DC. 15 rooms with PB, 11 with FP. 5 suites. Breakfast included in rates. Types of meals: continental-plus breakfast and early coffee/tea. Beds: KQD. Turndown service, TV and VCR in room. Fax and copier on premises. Parks nearby.

Publicity: *Travel-Holiday, Travel & Leisure.*

"The ultimate, romantic honeymoon spot."

Certificate may be used: Nov. 15-April 15, Sunday-Thursday, holidays excluded.

Dockside Boat & Bed

Pier 39, Jack London Square In Oakl
San Francisco, CA 94133
(510)444-5858 (800)436-2574 Fax:(510)444-0420

Enjoy views of San Francisco's skyline at this unique bed & breakfast, which offers dockside lodging aboard private motor or sailing yachts. The 14 private yachts vary in size from a 35-foot vessel to a 60-foot yacht. Each boat includes staterooms, galleys, bathrooms and living/dining areas. A continental breakfast is served each morning. Private charters and catered, candlelight dinners can be arranged. The yachts are docked at Pier 39 in San Francisco and Jack London Square in Oakland. Both locations are convenient to restaurants, shops and other attractions.
Innkeeper(s): Rob & Mollie Harris. $95-275. MC VISA AX DS TC. Breakfast included in rates. Type of meal: continental breakfast. Picnic lunch and catering service available. Beds: QDT. VCR in room. Fax and copier on premises. Antiques, fishing, parks, shopping, sporting events, theater and watersports nearby.

Location: On San Francisco Bay.

Publicity: *People, San Jose Mercury News, San Francisco Chronicle, Portland Oregonian, Denver Post, Washington Post.*

Certificate may be used: Sunday through Thursday evenings (maximum 6 nights per year), Nov. 1-March 30.

Petite Auberge

863 Bush St
San Francisco, CA 94108-3312
(415)928-6000 (800)365-3004 Fax:(415)775-5717

Circa 1917. This five-story hotel features an ornate baroque design with curved bay windows. Now transformed to a French country inn, there are antiques, fresh flowers and country accessories. Most rooms also have working fireplaces. It's a short walk to the Powell Street cable car. In the evenings, wine and hors d'oeuvres are served. Petite Auberge is one of the Four Sisters Inns.

Innkeeper(s): Brian Larsen. $110-225. MC VISA AX TC. 26 rooms with PB, 17 with FP. 1 suite. Breakfast and afternoon tea included in rates. Types of meals: gourmet breakfast and early coffee/tea. Picnic lunch available. Beds: KQ. Turndown service in room. Fax and copier on premises. Handicap access. Antiques, parks, shopping, sporting events and theater nearby.

Location: Two-and-a-half blocks from Union Square.

Publicity: *Travel & Leisure, Oregonian, Los Angeles Times, Brides.*

"Breakfast was great, and even better in bed!"

Certificate may be used: November-March Sunday-Thursday. Holidays & special events excluded, subject to availability

Victorian Inn on The Park

301 Lyon St
San Francisco, CA 94117-2108
(415)931-1830 (800)435-1967 Fax:(415)931-1830
E-mail: vicinn@aol.com

Circa 1897. This grand three-story Queen Anne inn, built by William Curlett, has an open belvedere turret with a teahouse roof and Victorian railings.

Silk-screened wall-papers, created especially for the inn, are accentuated by intricate mahogany and redwood paneling. The opulent Belvedere Suite features French doors opening to a Roman tub for two. Overlooking Golden Gate Park, the inn is 10 minutes from downtown.

Innkeeper(s): Lisa & William Benau. $99-169. MC VISA AX DC CB DS PC TC. 12 rooms with PB, 3 with FP. 2 suites. Breakfast included in rates. Types of meals: continental-plus breakfast and early coffee/tea. Beds: QT. Cable TV, fax, library and child care on premises. Antiques, parks, sporting events and theater nearby.

Location: Adjacent to Golden Gate Park.

Publicity: *Innsider, Country Inns, Good Housekeeping, New York Times, Good Morning America, Country Inns USA, Great Country Inns of America.*

"The excitement you have about your building comes from the care you have taken in restoring and maintaining your historic structure."

Certificate may be used: Both nights must be Sunday through Thursday. Holidays excluded, May 1-31 excluded, Aug. 1-31 excluded.

White Swan Inn

845 Bush St
San Francisco, CA 94108-3300
(415)775-1755 (800)999-9570 Fax:(415)775-5717

Circa 1915. This four-story inn is near Union Square and the Powell Street cable car. Beveled-glass doors open to a reception area with granite floors, an antique carousel horse and English artwork. Bay windows and a rear deck contribute to the feeling of an English garden inn. The guest rooms are decorated with bold English wallpapers and prints. All rooms have fireplaces. Turndown service and complimentary newspapers are included, and in the evenings, wine and hors d'oeuvres are served. White Swan is a Four Sisters Inns.

Innkeeper(s): Brian Larsen. $150-250. MC VISA AX TC. 26 rooms with PB, 26 with FP. 3 suites. 1 conference room. Breakfast and afternoon tea included in rates. Types of meals: gourmet breakfast and early coffee/tea. Picnic lunch available. Beds: KQT. Turndown service in room. Fax and copier on premises. Antiques, parks, shopping, sporting events and theater nearby.

Location: In the heart of downtown.

Publicity: *Travel & Leisure, Victoria, Wine Spectator.*

"Wonderfully accommodating. Absolutely perfect."

Certificate may be used: November-March, Sunday-Thursday. Holidays, special events excluded, subject to availability

San Luis Obispo M7

Garden Street Inn

1212 Garden St
San Luis Obispo, CA 93401-3962
(805)545-9802 Fax:(805)545-9403

Circa 1887. Innkeepers Dan and Kathy Smith restored this elegant home, paying meticulous attention to detail. Each room has a special theme. The Field of Dreams room, dedicated to Kathy Smith's father, includes memorabilia from his sports reporting days, toy figures from various baseball teams and framed pictures of antique baseball cards. The Cocoon room displays dozens of beautiful butterfly knickknacks. Situated downtown, the inn is within

walking distance of shops and restaurants and the San Luis Obispo Mission. Pismo Beach and Hearst Castle are also nearby attractions.

Innkeeper(s): Kathy & Dan Smith. $90-160. MC VISA AX. 13 rooms with PB, 5 with FP. 4 suites. 2 conference rooms. Breakfast and afternoon tea included in rates. Types of meals: full breakfast, gourmet breakfast and early coffee/tea. Beds: KQ. Air conditioning and turndown service in room. Fax on premises. Handicap access. Antiques, fishing, parks, shopping, sporting events, theater and watersports nearby.

Publicity: *Times-Press-Recorder, Telegram-Tribune, San Francisco Chronicle, Los Angeles Times, Orange County Register, Los Angeles Daily News.*

"We appreciate your warmth and care."

Certificate may be used: Sunday-Thursday; suites only; October-May.

San Luis Obispo (Arroyo Grande)　　M7

Arroyo Village Inn
407 El Camino Real
San Luis Obispo
(Arroyo Grande), CA 93420
(805)543-9075 (800)563-7762

Circa 1984. The travel section of the Los Angeles Times has featured many rare reviews of this award-winning inn, a replica of an English country inn.

The decor, highlighted by Laura Ashley prints and antiques, is welcoming and nostalgic. Skylights, window seats and balconies combine with country wreaths, baskets and candles to create a romantic ambiance. Rooms are decorated in garden themes, with names such as Forget-Me-Not, Potpourri Loft and Spring Bouquet. The gourmet breakfasts feature such items as frittatas, Mexican quiche, Swedish crepes, a variety of breads and bagels, as well as fresh fruits and specialty coffees and teas. After a memorable morning meal, guests head out for a day of activity. Among the many nearby attractions are Hearst Castle, wineries, mineral spas, beautiful beaches and horseback riding.

Innkeeper(s): Gina Glass. $80-195. MC VISA AX DS. 7 suites. Breakfast and evening snack included in rates. Types of meals: gourmet breakfast and early coffee/tea. Beds: KQ. Air conditioning in room. Cable TV and

fax on premises.

Location: Half-way between Los Angeles and San Francisco on California's central coast.

"Absolutely all the essentials of a great inn."

Certificate may be used: Sunday-Thursday on $145 and up suites, year-round, Friday & Saturday as available September-June, holidays excluded.

San Rafael　　H4

Casa Soldavini
531 C St
San Rafael, CA 94901-3809
(415)454-3140 Fax:(415)461-3965

The first Italian settlers in San Rafael built this home. Their grandchildren now own it and proudly hang pictures of their family. Grandfather Joseph, a wine maker, planned and planted what are now the lush gardens surrounding the home. The many Italian antiques throughout the house complement the Italian-style decor. A homemade breakfast is included, and snacks and beverages are served throughout the day.

Innkeeper(s): Linda Soldavini Cassidy. $60-95. 3 rooms. Breakfast included in rates. Type of meal: continental-plus breakfast.

Certificate may be used: Anytime.

Santa Barbara　　N8

Blue Dolphin Inn
420 W Montecito St
Santa Barbara, CA 93101
(805)965-2333 Fax:(805)962-4907

Circa 1870. It's a short walk to the beach and harbor from this Victorian inn, which offers accommodations in the main house and adjacent carriage house. Guest rooms are decorated in period style with antiques. Brass beds, tapestry pillows, and fluffy

comforters add a romantic touch. Several rooms include fireplaces, Jacuzzi tubs or private balconies and terraces. Fresh fruit salads, croissants, home-made breads and quiche highlight the breakfast fare. With prior notice and for an extra cost, the innkeepers can arrange in-room gourmet dinners.
Innkeeper(s): Byria O'Hayon-Crosby. $65-185. EP. MC VISA AX DC DS PC TC. 9 rooms with PB, 6 with FP. 3 suites. Breakfast and afternoon tea included in rates. Types of meals: gourmet breakfast and early coffee/tea. Picnic lunch and room service available. Beds: KQT. Ceiling fan, TV and VCR in room. Fax and library on premises. Handicap access. Antiques, fishing, parks, shopping, sporting events, theater and watersports nearby.

Certificate may be used: At full tariff Sunday through Thursday, non-holiday periods, Oct. 15 through May 15. No other discounts apply.

Cheshire Cat Inn
36 W Valerio St
Santa Barbara, CA 93101-2524
(805)569-1610 Fax:(805)682-1876

Circa 1894. The Eberle family built two graceful houses side by side, one a Queen Anne, the other a Colonial Revival. President McKinley was entertained here on a visit to Santa Barbara. There is a pagoda-like porch, a square and a curved bay, rose gardens, grassy lawns and a gazebo. Laura Ashley wallpapers and furnishings are featured. Outside, guests will enjoy English flower gardens, an outdoor Jacuzzi, a new deck with sitting areas and fountains.
Innkeeper(s): Christine Dunstan. $140-300. MC VISA PC TC. 17 rooms with PB. 7 suites. 1 conference room. Breakfast included in rates. Type of meal: full breakfast. Room service available. Beds: KQT. Ceiling fan and TV in room. Spa on premises. Amusement parks, antiques, fishing, shopping, sporting events, theater and watersports nearby.
Location: Downtown.
Publicity: *Two on the Town, KABC, Los Angeles Times, Santa Barbara, American In Flight, Elmer Dills Recommends.*

"Romantic and quaint."

Certificate may be used: October through May, Sunday through Thursday, excluding public holidays.

Glenborough Inn
1327 Bath St
Santa Barbara, CA 93101-3623
(805)966-0589 (800)962-0589 Fax:(805)564-8610
E-mail: glenboro@silcom.com

Circa 1906. This Craftsman-style inn recreates a turn-of-the-century atmosphere in the Main house and White house. There is also an 1880s cottage reminiscent of the Victorian era. Inside are antiques, rich wood trim and elegant fireplace suites with canopy beds. There's always plenty of hospitality and an open invitation to the secluded garden hot tub. Breakfast is homemade and has been written up in "Bon Appetit" and "Chocolatier."
Innkeeper(s): Michael Diaz & Steve Ryan. $100-250. MC VISA AX DC CB DS PC TC. 11 rooms with PB, 6 with FP. 4 suites. 1 cottage. Breakfast included in rates. Types of meals: continental breakfast, full

breakfast, gourmet breakfast and early coffee/tea. Dinner, picnic lunch and gourmet lunch available. Beds: KQD. Ceiling fan in room. Fax and spa on premises. Antiques, fishing, parks, shopping, sporting events, theater and watersports nearby.
Publicity: *Houston Post, Los Angeles Times, Horizon, Los Angeles, Pasadena Choice.*

"A delightful, elegant and charming suite."

Certificate may be used: October-June, Sunday-Thursday, except holidays.

Hotel Santa Barbara
533 State St
Santa Barbara, CA 93101
(805)965-4574 (888)259-7700 Fax:(805)962-2412
E-mail: sb@aol.com

Circa 1926. This historic hotel appears much like a little European hotel, featuring Spanish-style architecture. The hotel is located in a Santa Barbara historic district and is just five blocks from the ocean. The decor is elegant, done in Mediterranean style. Many amenities are included in the rates, such as in-room coffee makers, turn-down service, continental-plus breakfast, evening snacks and privileges at a pool and athletic club. Shops and restaurants are within walking distance, and UCSB is 15 minutes away.
Innkeeper(s): Joel Jacks. $99-275. MC VISA AX DC DS TC. 75 rooms, 65 with PB. 10 suites. 2 conference rooms. Breakfast and evening snack included in rates. Types of meals: continental-plus breakfast and early coffee/tea. Beds: KQ. Air conditioning and turndown service in room. VCR, fax, copier and library on premises. Antiques, fishing, parks, shopping, golf, theater and watersports nearby.

Certificate may be used: Dec. 1-March 1, Sunday-Friday.

The Mary May Inn
111 W Valerio St
Santa Barbara, CA 93101-2912
(805)569-3398

Circa 1880. This Victorian is a local and state historical site, and it features many romantic touches. Some guest rooms offer Jacuzzi tubs, some have a fireplace. A few are lit by chandeliers, and each room is different. Open the double doors from the spacious bedchamber in the Brooke Marie room and you'll find a sitting room and bath with a clawfoot tub. The Thimbleberry includes a private entrance, which guests access via a little garden trail. Mexican and Italian influences are prevalent in the breakfast fare. Guests can walk to many Santa Barbara sites from the inn, including the mission, an art museum and shopping.
Innkeeper(s): Kathleen Pohring & Mark Cronin. $125-175. MC VISA AX TC. 12 rooms with PB, 4 with FP. Breakfast, afternoon tea and evening

snack included in rates. Types of meals: full breakfast and early coffee/tea. Beds: Q. Air conditioning and TV in room. Antiques, fishing, parks, shopping, sporting events, golf, theater and watersports nearby.

Publicity: *Santa Barbara News Press.*

Certificate may be used: Sept. 10-Dec. 10, Sunday-Thursday; Jan. 2-May 20, Sunday-Thursday.

The Old Yacht Club Inn

431 Corona Del Mar
Santa Barbara, CA 93103-3601
(805)962-1277 (800)676-1676 Fax:(805)962-3989

Circa 1912. This California Craftsman house was the home of the Santa Barbara Yacht Club during the Roaring '20s. It was opened as Santa Barbara's first B&B and has become renowned for its gourmet food and superb hospitality. Innkeeper Nancy Donaldson is the author of The Old Yacht Club Inn Cookbook.

Innkeeper(s): Nancy Donaldson. $140-185. MC VISA AX DS. 10 rooms with PB. 1 conference room. Breakfast included in rates. Types of meals: full breakfast, gourmet breakfast and early coffee/tea. Dinner available. Beds: KQ. Cable TV, fax, copier and bicycles on premises. Antiques, fishing, shopping, sporting events, theater and watersports nearby.

Location: East Beach.

Publicity: *Los Angeles, Valley.*

"Donaldson is one of Santa Barbara's better-kept culinary secrets."

Certificate may be used: November, December, January, February, Monday-Thursday only. Reservations taken only within two weeks of date requested.

Secret Garden Inn and Cottages

1908 Bath St
Santa Barbara, CA 93101-2813
(805)687-2300 (800)676-1622 Fax:(805)687-4576

Circa 1908. The main house and adjacent cottages surround the gardens and are decorated in American and English-Country style. The Hummingbird is a large cottage guest room with a queen-size white iron bed and a private deck with a hot tub for your exclusive use. The three suites have private outdoor hot tubs. Wine and light hors d'oeuvres are served in the late afternoon, and hot apple cider is served each evening.

Innkeeper(s): Jack Greenwald, Christine Dunstan. $115-225. MC VISA AX PC TC. 11 rooms, 10 with PB, 1 with FP. 3 suites. 4 cottages. Breakfast, afternoon tea and evening snack included in rates. Types of meals: full breakfast and early coffee/tea. Beds: KQ. Cable TV, fax, copier and bicycles on premises. Antiques, fishing, shopping, theater and watersports nearby.

Location: Quiet residential area near town and the beach.

Publicity: *Los Angeles Times, Santa Barbara, Independent*

"A romantic little getaway retreat that neither of us will be able to forget. It was far from what we expected to find."

Certificate may be used: All year

The Upham Hotel & Garden Cottages

1404 De La Vina St
Santa Barbara, CA 93101-3027
(805)962-0058 (800)727-0876 Fax:(805)963-2825

Circa 1871. Antiques and period furnishings decorate each of the inn's guest rooms and suites. The inn is the oldest continuously operating hostelry in Southern California. Situated on an acre of gardens in the center of downtown, it's within easy walking distance of restaurants, shops, art galleries and

museums. The staff is happy to assist guests in discovering Santa Barbara's varied attractions. Garden cottage units feature porches or secluded patios and several have gas fireplaces.

Innkeeper(s): Jan Martin Winn. $125-360. MC VISA AX DC CB DS TC. 50 rooms with PB, 8 with FP. 4 suites. 4 cottages. 4 conference rooms. Breakfast and evening snack included in rates. Types of meals: continental-plus breakfast and early coffee/tea. Banquet service available. Restaurant on premises. Beds: KQD. Ceiling fan and TV in room. VCR, fax and copier on premises. Antiques, fishing, parks, shopping, sporting events, theater and watersports nearby.

Publicity: *Los Angeles Times, Santa Barbara, Westways, Santa Barbara News-Press.*

"Your hotel is truly a charm. Between the cozy gardens and the exquisitely comfortable appointments, The Upham is charm itself."

Certificate may be used: Sunday - Thursday nights, Jan. 2-Dec. 30.

Santa Clara   I5

Madison Street Inn

1390 Madison St
Santa Clara, CA 95050-4759
(408)249-5541 (800)491-5541
Fax:(408)249-6676
E-mail: madstinn@aol.com

Circa 1890. This Queen Anne Victorian inn still boasts its original doors and locks, and "No Peddlers or Agents" is engraved in the cement of

the original carriageway. Guests, however, always receive a warm and gracious welcome to high-ceilinged rooms furnished in antiques, Oriental rugs and Victorian wallpaper.

Innkeeper(s): Theresa & Ralph Wigginton. $60-85. MC VISA AX DC DS PC TC. 6 rooms, 4 with PB. Breakfast, afternoon tea and evening snack included in rates. Types of meals: continental breakfast, continental-plus breakfast, full breakfast, gourmet breakfast and early coffee/tea. Picnic lunch, gourmet lunch, banquet service, catering service and catered breakfast available. Beds: QD. Ceiling fan in room. Cable TV, VCR, fax, spa, swimming and bicycles on premises. Amusement parks, antiques, parks, sporting events, theater and watersports nearby.

Location: Ten minutes from San Jose airport.

Publicity: *Discovery.*

"We spend many nights in hotels that look and feel exactly alike whether they are in Houston or Boston. Your inn was delightful. It was wonderful to bask in your warm and gracious hospitality."

Certificate may be used: Anytime.

Santa Cruz J5

The Darling House-
A B&B Inn By The Sea
314 W Cliff Dr
Santa Cruz, CA 95060-6145
(408)458-1958

Circa 1910. It's difficult to pick a room at this oceanside mansion. The Pacific Ocean Room features a fireplace and a wonderful ocean view. The Chinese Room might suit you with its silk-draped, hand-carved rosewood canopy wedding bed. Elegant oak, ebony, and walnut woodwork is enhanced by the antique decor of Tiffanys and Chippendales. Roses, beveled glass and libraries add to the atmosphere. Beyond the ocean-view veranda are landscaped gardens. Guests often walk to the wharf for dinner.

Innkeeper(s): Karen Darling. $125-150. MC VISA AX DS. 5 rooms. 1 conference room. Breakfast included in rates. Type of meal: continental breakfast. Beds: KQDT. Turndown service in room. Spa on premises. Amusement parks, antiques, fishing, shopping, sporting events and theater nearby.

Location: A stone's throw from the Pacific Ocean.

Publicity: *Modern Maturity, Pacific.*

"So pretty, so sorry to leave."

Certificate may be used: November-April, Sunday-Thursday, holidays excluded

Seal Beach O10

The Seal Beach Inn & Gardens
212 5th St
Seal Beach, CA 90740-6115
(562)493-2416 (800)433-3292 Fax:(562)799-0483

Circa 1923. This historic Southern California inn has lush gardens and the look of an oceanside estate. It's a short walk to the Seal Beach pier, shops and restaurants. Major attractions in Orange County and the Los Angeles area are within short driving distances. Business travelers can plan meetings in rooms where 24 people can sit comfortably. The inn has a Mediterranean villa ambiance, and no two rooms are alike.

Innkeeper(s): Marjorie B. & Harty Schmaehl. $125-275. AP. MC VISA AX DC CB DS TC. 23 rooms with PB, 4 with FP. 11 suites. Breakfast and evening snack included in rates. Types of meals: full breakfast and early coffee/tea. Afternoon tea available. Beds: KQ. Turndown service in room. Fax and copier on premises. Amusement parks, antiques, fishing, parks, shopping, sporting events, golf, theater and watersports nearby.

Location: 300 yards from the ocean, five minutes from Long Beach.

Publicity: *Brides, Country Inns, Glamour, Country, Long Beach Press Telegram, Orange County Register, Los Angeles Times, Country Living, Sunset.*

"The closest thing to Europe since I left there. Delights the senses and restores the soul."

Certificate may be used: Sunday through Thursday, Thursday as second night. October to April, space available. Offer includes any King suite.

Solvang
N7

Storybook Inn B&B
409 1st St
Solvang, CA 93463-2713
(805)688-1703 (800)786-7925 Fax:(805)688-0953

Circa 1993. Solvang, a historic California town steeped in Danish history, is the location for this European-style Tudor inn. Innkeeper Angela Bomba is an interior designer and has decorated each bedchamber in a whimsical, European style. Each of the rooms is named for a Hans Christian Andersen fairy tale. The "Ugly Duckling" room appears as more of a swan, with an antique armoire and pine bed. Other rooms have names such as "The Steadfast Tin Soldier" or "The Princess and the Pea." Antiques collected from Angela's world travels, as well as sleigh, canopy or poster beds, fill the guest rooms. The continental breakfast features European-style coffee and items such as croissants, Danish cheese and apple-cinnamon strudel.

Innkeeper(s): Angela Bomba. $75-195. MC VISA AX DC DS PC TC. 9 rooms, 7 with PB, 8 with FP. 2 suites. Breakfast included in rates. Type of meal: continental-plus breakfast. Dinner and lunch available. Restaurant on premises. Beds: Q. Air conditioning, TV and VCR in room. Fax on premises. Handicap access. Antiques, shopping, golf and theater nearby.

Publicity: *Wine Country Review*

Certificate may be used: Jan. 1-Nov. 10, Sunday-Thursday excluding suites.

Sonoma
H4

The Hidden Oak
214 E Napa St
Sonoma, CA 95476-6721
(707)996-9863
E-mail: hidenoak@pacbell.net

Circa 1913. This shingled California craftsman bungalow features a gabled roof and front porch with stone pillars. Located a block and a half from the historic Sonoma Plaza, the inn once served as the rectory for the Episcopal Church. Rooms are furnished with antiques and wicker. Nearby wineries may be toured by hopping on one of innkeeper's bicycles.

Innkeeper(s): Erin & Kurt Heeley. $95-210. MC VISA AX DS PC TC. 4 rooms, 3 with PB, 1 with FP. 1 suite. Breakfast and afternoon tea included in rates. Types of meals: full breakfast and early coffee/tea. Beds: KQ. Ceiling fan, TV and VCR in room. Bicycles on premises. Antiques, fishing, parks, shopping, sporting events and golf nearby.

"The room was delightful and breakfast was excellent."

Certificate may be used: Nov. 1-Feb. 28, anytime, except President's Holiday. Good for free night in the French Lilac Room with purchase of first night in same room.

Starwae Inn
21490 Broadway
Sonoma, CA 95476-8204
(707)938-1374 (800)793-4792 Fax:(707)935-1159

Circa 1930. There are two cottages at this inn, divided somewhat like a duplex. Each side of the cottages has a suite with a separate entrance, bathroom and bedroom. The innkeepers, both local artists live on the property and their studios are on the grounds as well. The cottages feature original artwork and pottery, and guest rooms also feature some furnishings handcrafted by one of the innkeepers. Individual quiche, fresh fruit and scones are among the treats served for breakfast.

Innkeeper(s): John Curry & Janice Crow. $125-185. EP. MC VISA TC. 4 suites. 2 cottages. 1 conference room. Breakfast included in rates. Type of meal: continental-plus breakfast. Beds: QD. Air conditioning and TV in room. Fax, copier and bicycles on premises. Antiques, fishing, parks, shopping and theater nearby.

Certificate may be used: Nov. 1 to March 1, Sunday through Thursday, holidays excluded.

Sonora
H7

Hammons House Inn B&B
22963 Robertson Ranch Rd
Sonora, CA 95370-9555
(209)532-7921 Fax:(209)586-4935
E-mail: hammons@hammonshouseinn.com

Circa 1983. This bed & breakfast is secluded on seven wooded acres from which guests can enjoy a view of the mountains and foothills. There are rooms and a suite in the main house and a private cottage. The suite includes a double Jacuzzi tub. The cottage includes a sleeping loft, kitchenette, bathroom and fireplace. The decor in all accommodations is contemporary in style and comfortable. There is a pool and deck for guests to enjoy. Wineries, outdoor activities and two historic state parks are nearby.

Innkeeper(s): Linda Hammons. $86-140. MC VISA AX DS PC TC. 4 rooms, 3 with PB, 2 with FP. 1 suite. 1 cottage. Breakfast and evening snack included in rates. Types of meals: full breakfast, gourmet breakfast and early coffee/tea. Afternoon tea and banquet service available. Beds: KQ. Turndown service, ceiling fan and VCR in room. Fax, copier, swimming and library on premises. Antiques, fishing, parks, shopping, downhill skiing, cross-country skiing, golf, theater and watersports nearby.

Certificate may be used: Jan. 2-Dec. 20, Sunday-Thursday, no holidays.

Lavender Hill B&B

683 S Barretta St
Sonora, CA 95370-5132
(209)532-9024 (800)446-1333
E-mail: lavender@sonnet.com

Circa 1900. In the historic Gold Rush town of
Sonora is this Queen Anne Victorian inn. Its four
guest rooms include the Lavender Room, which has
a mini-suite with desk, sitting area and clawfoot tub
and shower. After a busy day fishing, biking, river
rafting or exploring nearby Yosemite National Park,
guests may relax in the antique-filled parlor or the
sitting room. Admiring the inn's gardens from the
wraparound porch is also a favorite activity. Be sure
to ask about dinner theater packages.

Innkeeper(s): Charlie & Jean Marinelli. $75-95. MC VISA AX PC TC. 4
rooms with PB. 1 suite. Breakfast included in rates. Types of meals: full
breakfast and early coffee/tea. Beds: KQ. Air conditioning and ceiling
fan in room. Cable TV and library on premises. Antiques, fishing, parks,
shopping, downhill skiing, cross-country skiing, golf, theater and watersports nearby.

Certificate may be used: Jan. 1 to March 31, Sunday - Thursday.

Soquel   J5

Blue Spruce Inn

2815 S Main St
Soquel, CA 95073-2412
(408)464-1137 (800)559-1137 Fax:(408)475-0608
E-mail: pobrien@bluespruce.com

Circa 1875. Near the north coast of Monterey Bay,
this old farmhouse has been freshly renovated and
refitted with luxurious touches. The Seascape is a
favorite room with its private entrance, wicker furnishings and bow-shaped Jacuzzi for two. The

Carriage House offers skylights above the bed, while
a heart decor dominates Two Hearts. Local art,
Amish quilts and featherbeds are featured throughout. Brunch enchiladas are the inn's speciality.
Santa Cruz is four miles away.

Innkeeper(s): Patricia & Tom O'Brien. $85-150. MC VISA AX PC TC. 6
rooms with PB, 5 with FP. 1 conference room. Breakfast and evening
snack included in rates. Types of meals: full breakfast, gourmet breakfast and early coffee/tea. Beds: QT. Turndown service, TV and VCR in
room. Fax and library on premises. Amusement parks, antiques, fishing, parks, shopping, theater and watersports nearby.

Location: At the edge of Soquel Village, mid-Santa Cruz County, north
shore of the Monterey Bay.

Publicity: *Village View.*

*"You offer such graciousness to your guests and a true
sense of welcome."*

Certificate may be used: Monday-Thursday, all year, subject to
availability.

South Lake Tahoe   F8

The Inn at Heavenly

1261 Ski Run Blvd
South Lake Tahoe, CA 96150
(916)544-4244 (800)692-2246 Fax:(916)544-5213
E-mail: mycabin@sierra.net

This inn is just half a mile from the Heavenly
Valley ski area. Guests will find the log cabin exteri-
or and interior pine walls and rock fireplaces cozy
and inviting. Bedchambers offer plenty of amenities,
including in-room coffee makers, refrigerators,
microwaves and cable TVs. Some rooms offer
VCRs. Guests can reserve to spend an hour in the
hot tub and steam bath. A free shuttle goes to casinos and the ski area.

Innkeeper(s): Sue Ogden & Paul Gardner. $75-165. MC VISA AX PC TC.
14 rooms with PB, 7 with FP. 7 suites. 2 cottages. 1 conference room.
Breakfast, afternoon tea and evening snack included in rates. Types of
meals: continental-plus breakfast and early coffee/tea. Banquet service
and catering service available. Beds: KQD. Ceiling fan, TV and VCR in
room. Fax, copier, spa, sauna, bicycles and library on premises.
Amusement parks, fishing, parks, shopping, downhill skiing, cross-
country skiing, theater and watersports nearby.

Certificate may be used: Jan. 5 to Dec. 18, Sunday-Thursday, excluding holiday periods.

Springville   K9

Annie's B&B

33024 Globe Dr
Springville, CA 93265-9718
(209)539-3827 Fax:(209)539-2179

Circa 1903. Innkeepers Annie and John Bozanich
nicknamed their country-style bed & breakfast "Hog
Heaven," in honor of their bountiful sow, Blossom,
and more petite potbellied pig, Boo. The five-acre
grounds boast wonderful views of the Sierra
Nevadas. The grounds also include John's custom
saddle shop. In keeping with the swine theme,

Annie has named one guest quarter Sows Room and another the Boars Room. The third room was named in honor of Annie's grandmother, Ode. Ode's Room features her grandmother's bedroom set and a bedspread crocheted by Ode. This room is located in the back house and has its own private entrance. Annie prepares the multitude of home-baked treats on an antique, woodburning cookstove. In addition to the ample breakfast, afternoon refreshments are served.

Innkeeper(s): Ann & John Bozanich. $75-85. MC VISA AX DC TC. 3 rooms with PB. Breakfast, afternoon tea and evening snack included in rates. Types of meals: full breakfast and early coffee/tea. Dinner available. Beds: DT. Ceiling fan in room. Cable TV, VCR and spa on premises. Antiques, fishing, parks, shopping, cross-country skiing, theater and watersports nearby.

Certificate may be used: Sunday-Thursday only, no holidays or special events days.

Sunset Beach   O10

Harbour Inn
PO Box 1439
Sunset Beach, CA 90742-1439
(310)592-4770 (800)596-4770 Fax:(310)592-3547

Circa 1989. This waterside inn offers relaxing accommodations in a setting convenient to the beach (it's just a block away) and many of Southern California's popular attractions. Situated midway between Huntington Beach and Long Beach, the inn is close to Disneyland, Knott's Berry Farm and many fine restaurants and shops. The simple, comfortable rooms are decorated in cheerful floral prints, and many afford ocean or harbor views. An expanded continental breakfast is served each morning, offering a variety of cereals, pastries, bagels and homemade breads.

Innkeeper(s): Joyce & Marion Dooley. $69-109. MC VISA AX DC CB DS TC. 25 rooms, 17 with PB. 8 suites. 1 conference room. Type of meal: continental-plus breakfast. Catering service and room service available. Beds: KQ. Air conditioning, TV and VCR in room. Fax and copier on premises. Handicap access. Amusement parks, antiques, fishing, parks, sporting events, theater and watersports nearby.

Certificate may be used: Oct. 1 to May 15, Sunday-Friday, holidays and special events excluded.

Sutter Creek   G6

Grey Gables B&B Inn
161 Hanford St, PO Box 1687
Sutter Creek, CA 95685-1687
(209)267-1039 (800)473-9422 Fax:(209)267-0998

Circa 1897. The innkeepers of this Victorian home offer poetic accommodations both in the delightful decor and by the names of their guest rooms. The

Keats, Bronte and Tennyson rooms afford garden views, while the Byron and Browning rooms include clawfoot tubs. The Victorian Suite, which encompasses the top floor, affords views of the garden, as well as a historic churchyard. All of the guest rooms boast fireplaces. Stroll down brick pathways through the terraced garden or relax in the parlor. A proper English tea is served with cakes and scones. Hors d'oeuvres and libations are served in the evenings.

Innkeeper(s): Roger & Susan Garlick. $90-140. MC VISA DS PC TC. 8 rooms with PB, 8 with FP. Breakfast, afternoon tea and evening snack included in rates. Types of meals: gourmet breakfast and early coffee/tea. Beds: KQT. Air conditioning and ceiling fan in room. Fax and copier on premises. Handicap access. Antiques, fishing, parks, shopping, downhill skiing, cross-country skiing, theater and watersports nearby.

Certificate may be used: Year-round, Sunday-Thursday, holidays excluded.

The Hanford House
61 Hanford St, Hwy 49
Sutter Creek, CA 95685
(209)267-0747 (800)871-5839 Fax:(209)267-1825
E-mail: bobkat@hanfordhouse.com

Circa 1929. When Karen and Bob Tierno purchased this unique Gold Country inn, they were determined to maintain the former innkeepers' standards for hospitality. Karen and Bob went a step further and added many new amenities for their guests, including a conference room, fax machine and providing computer access. While these touches are perfect for the business traveler, the inn is still a place to relax. The inn offers a shaded outdoor patio, charming parlor and a roof-top sundeck. Guests are greeted with freshly baked cookies upon check-in, treated to a homemade breakfast each morning and invited to partake in afternoon refreshments. Wineries, antiquing and historic sites are nearby.

Innkeeper(s): Bob & Karen Tierno. $69-149. MC VISA DS PC TC. 10 rooms with PB, 5 with FP. 3 suites. 1 conference room. Breakfast, afternoon tea and evening snack included in rates. Types of meals: gourmet breakfast and early coffee/tea. Beds: KQ. Air conditioning and ceiling fan in room. Cable TV, VCR and fax on premises. Handicap access. Antiques, fishing, shopping, downhill skiing, cross-country skiing, golf, theater and watersports nearby.

Certificate may be used: Sunday-Thursday, excluding holidays, all year.

Tahoe City   F7

Mayfield House
236 Grove St, PO Box 5999
Tahoe City, CA 96145

(916)583-1001

Circa 1932. Norman Mayfield, Lake Tahoe's pioneer contractor, built this house of wood and stone, and Julia Morgan, architect of Hearst Castle, was a frequent guest. Dark-stained pine paneling, a beamed ceiling, and a large stone fireplace make an inviting living room. Many rooms have views of mountains, woods, or the golf course.

Innkeeper(s): Cynthia & Bruce Knauss. $85-150. MC VISA AX. 6 rooms, 3 with PB. Breakfast included in rates. Types of meals: full breakfast and early coffee/tea. Evening snack available. Beds: KQD. Cable TV on premises. Fishing, parks, shopping, downhill skiing, cross-country skiing and watersports nearby.

Location: Downtown off Highway 28.

Publicity: *Sierra Heritage, Tahoe Today, San Francisco Chronicle.*

"The place is charming beyond words, complete with down comforters and wine upon checking in. The breakfast is superb."

Certificate may be used: Jan. 5-June 30, Sunday-Thursday, Oct. 1-Nov. 22, Sunday-Thursday.

Templeton   L6

Country House Inn
91 S Main St
Templeton, CA 93465-8701

(805)434-1598 (800)362-6032

Circa 1886. This Victorian home, built by the founder of Templeton, is located in rural wine country. Ancient oak trees shade the grounds. The inn was designated as a historic site in San Luis Obispo County.

Innkeeper(s): Dianne Garth. $95-105. MC VISA DS PC. 5 rooms with PB, 1 with FP. 1 suite. Breakfast included in rates. Types of meals: gourmet breakfast and early coffee/tea. Afternoon tea available. Beds: KQ. Ceiling fan in room. Antiques, fishing, parks, shopping, theater and watersports nearby.

Location: Twenty miles north of San Luis Obispo on Hwy 101.

"A feast for all the senses, an esthetic delight."

Certificate may be used: April-September, Sunday-Thursday; October-March, Sunday-Saturday.

Ukiah   F3

Vichy Hot Springs Resort & Inn
2605 Vichy Springs Rd
Ukiah, CA 95482-3507

(707)462-9515 Fax:(707)462-9516

E-mail: vichy@pacific.net

Circa 1854. This famous spa once attracted guests such as Jack London, Mark Twain and Teddy Roosevelt. Seventeen rooms and three redwood cottages have been renovated for bed & breakfast, while the 1860s naturally warm and sparkling mineral baths remain unchanged. A hot spa and Olympic-size pool await your arrival. A magical waterfall is a 30-minute walk along a year-round stream.

Innkeeper(s): Gilbert & Marjorie Ashoff. $95-185. MC VISA AX DC CB DS PC TC. 17 rooms with PB, 3 with FP. 3 cottages. 2 conference rooms. Breakfast included in rates. Type of meal: full breakfast. Catering service available. Beds: QT. Air conditioning in room. Fax, copier, computer, spa and swimming on premises. Handicap access. Antiques, fishing, parks, shopping, theater and watersports nearby.

Location: Two hours north of San Francisco and three miles east of US Hwy 101 in Ukiah, Mendocino County.

Publicity: *Sunset, Sacramento Bee, San Jose Mercury News, Gulliver (Japan), Oregonian, Contra Costa Times, New York Times, San Francisco Chronicle, San Francisco Examiner, Adventure West.*

"Very beautiful grounds and comfortable accommodations. Thanks for your gracious hospitality and especially the opportunity to meet such good friends....and the water's great!- Attorney General State of California, Dan Lungren. Great place! Good for Presidents and everyone else.- Ex-Governor California, Jerry Brown."

Certificate may be used: Sunday-Thursday (May-October), Sunday-Friday (November-April), no holidays, rooms only.

Venice   O10

Venice Beach House
15 30th Ave
Venice, CA 90291-0043

(310)823-1966 Fax:(310)823-1842

Circa 1911. This California Craftsman house was the summer home of relatives Warren Wilson and Abbot Kinney and their families. Wilson founded the Los Angeles Daily News, and Kinney founded the town of Venice, a popular L.A. hot spot for those in search of surf, sand, shopping, food or people watching. The home has been fully restored to its original state. Guest rooms are individually decorated. James Peasgood's Room is especially sweet and spacious for guests in search of romance. It offers a king-size bed, balcony and a double Jacuzzi tub. The Pier Suite is another idyllic choice, offering a partial ocean view, a fireplace and sitting room.

Innkeeper(s): Elayne Alexander. $85-165. MC VISA AX PC TC. 9 rooms, 5 with PB, 1 with FP. 2 suites. Breakfast and afternoon tea included in rates. Type of meal: continental breakfast. Beds: KQDT. TV in room. Fax and library on premises. Amusement parks, antiques, fishing, parks, shopping, sporting events, theater and watersports nearby.

Location: One-quarter block from the famous Venice beach boardwalk, bordering Marina del Rey.

Publicity: *Independent Journal, Sunset, Daily News, Herald Examiner, The Outlook, The Travel Channel, The Argonaut.*

"To stay at the Venice Beach House is to stay with a friendly family - a 'home away from home' (except the breakfasts are a lot better!). We've stayed in four different rooms, each better than the last."

Certificate may be used: September-April, whole week.

Visalia   K8

Ben Maddox House B&B
601 N Encina St
Visalia, CA 93291-3603
(209)739-0721 (800)401-9800 Fax:(209)625-0420

Circa 1876. Just 40 minutes away from Sequoia National Park sits this late-19th-century home, constructed completely of gorgeous Sequoia redwood. The parlor, dining room and bedrooms remain in their original state. The house has been tastefully furnished with antiques from the late 1800s to the early 20th century. "Big Bertha," a coal-burning furnace that has been converted to gas, heats the home from her spot in the basement, so no fireplaces are necessary. Breakfast menu choices include fresh fruit, a selection of homemade breads, eggs and meat. The meal, served either in the historic dining room or on the deck, is surrounded by flowers, antique china and goldware.

Innkeeper(s): Diane & Al Muro. $75-85. MC VISA AX DS. 4 rooms with PB. Breakfast and evening snack included in rates. Types of meals: full breakfast and early coffee/tea. Beds: KQ. Air conditioning and TV in room. Spa, swimming and bicycles on premises. Antiques, fishing, parks, shopping, cross-country skiing, sporting events, theater and watersports nearby.

Publicity: *Southland, Fresno Bee*

"Just a very gracious and delightful place and excellent breakfast, also comfortable and a warm and friendly hostess, a delightful experience in all."

Certificate may be used: March 1-Jan. 31, Sunday-Friday.

Volcano   G7

St. George Hotel
16104 Pine Grove, PO Box 9
Volcano, CA 95689-0009
(209)296-4458 Fax:(209)296-4458

Circa 1862. This handsome old three-story hotel in the National Register features a double-tiered wrap-around porch. There is a dining room, full bar and lounge area with fireplace. It is situated on one acre of lawns. An annex built in 1961 provides rooms with private baths. Volcano is a Mother Lode town that has been untouched by supermarkets and modern motels and remains much as it was during the Gold Rush. Modified American Plan (breakfast and dinner) available.

Innkeeper(s): Marlene & Chuck Inman. $71-94. MAP. MC VISA AX PC TC. 20 rooms, 6 with PB. 1 conference room. Breakfast included in rates. Type of meal: full breakfast. Dinner available. Beds: QDT. Fax and copier on premises. Antiques, fishing, parks, shopping, downhill skiing, cross-country skiing, theater and watersports nearby.

Location: Sixty-one miles from Sacramento.

"What is so precious about the hotel is its combination of graciousness and simplicity."

Certificate may be used: Wednesday-Friday, except January and half of February, and subject to availability.

Walnut Creek   H5

The Secret Garden Mansion
1056 Hacienda Dr
Walnut Creek, CA 94598-4740
(510)945-3600 (800)477-7898 Fax:(510)945-3608

Secluded acres with garden paths, fountains and a gazebo surround this Victorian hideaway. Guests are pampered with flowers, fluffy robes, bath salts and rooms scented with potpourri. Heart-shaped chocolates and poetry books restored many weary guests' tired spirits. The grounds were part of an old Spanish land grant, and the home was built by an early Walnut Creek settler. The old-fashioned chandeliers and antiques add to the historical charm. The Juliet Suite includes a balcony with a garden view. Another room offers a Jacuzzi tub, and still others include fireplaces, four-poster beds and canopies.

Innkeeper(s): Sharyn McCoy. $135-300. MC VISA AX DS. 7 rooms with PB, 2 with FP. 2 suites. 1 conference room. Breakfast included in rates. Type of meal: continental-plus breakfast. Beds: KQ.

Certificate may be used: January through December, Sunday through Thursday (no Fridays or Saturdays).

Westport
E3

Howard Creek Ranch
40501 N Hwy One, PO Box 121
Westport, CA 95488

(707)964-6725 Fax:(707)964-1603

Circa 1871. First settled as a land grant of thousands of acres, Howard Creek Ranch is now a 40-acre farm with sweeping views of the Pacific Ocean, sandy beaches and rolling mountains. A 75-foot bridge spans a creek that flows past barns and outbuildings to the beach 200 yards away. The farmhouse is surrounded by green lawns, an award-winning flower garden, and grazing cows and horses. This rustic rural location offers antiques, a hot tub and sauna.

Innkeeper(s): Charles & Sally Grigg. $55-145. MC VISA AX. 11 rooms, 9 with PB, 5 with FP. 3 suites. Breakfast included in rates. Types of meals: gourmet breakfast and early coffee/tea. Beds: KQD. Ceiling fan in room. Fax, spa, swimming, sauna and library on premises. Antiques, fishing, parks, shopping and theater nearby.

Location: Mendocino Coast on the ocean.

Publicity: *California, Country, Vacations, Forbes.*

"Of the dozen or so inns on the West Coast we have visited, this is easily the most enchanting one."

Certificate may be used: Oct. 15-May 15, Sunday-Thursday, excluding holiday periods.

Yountville
G4

Bordeaux House
6600 Washington St
Yountville, CA 94599-1301

(707)944-2855 (800)677-6370

Circa 1980. Surrounded by some of California's most famous vineyards, this inn offers a variety of guest rooms, each appointed with modern-style decor and a woodburning fireplace. A majestic pine tree and unique, brick spiral staircase designate the front of this inn, which is set on nearly one acre of landscaped grounds. Guests are pampered with an afternoon tea. Aside from the famed wineries, the area is full of antique shops, galleries and boutiques to explore.

Innkeeper(s): Jean Lunney. $95-135. MC VISA TC. 7 rooms with PB, 6 with FP. 1 conference room. Breakfast and afternoon tea included in rates. Type of meal: continental-plus breakfast. Beds: QT. Air conditioning and TV in room. Antiques, parks, shopping and theater nearby.

Certificate may be used: November-April, Sunday through Thursday.

Maison Fleurie
6529 Yount St
Yountville, CA 94599-1278

(707)944-2056 (800)788-0369 Fax:(707)944-9342

Circa 1894. Vines cover the two-foot thick brick walls of the Bakery, the Carriage House and the Main House of this French country inn. One of the Four Sisters Inns, it is reminiscent of a bucolic setting in Provence. Rooms are decorated in a warm, romantic style, some with vineyard and garden views. Rooms in the Old Bakery have fireplaces. A pool and outdoor spa are available and you may borrow bicycles for wandering the countryside. In the evenings, wine and hors d'oeuvres are served. Yountville, just north of Napa, offers close access to the multitude of wineries and vineyards in the valley.

Innkeeper(s): Roger Asbill. $110-230. MC VISA AX TC. 13 rooms with PB, 7 with FP. Breakfast and afternoon tea included in rates. Type of meal: gourmet breakfast. Beds: KQD. Turndown service in room. Fax, spa and bicycles on premises. Handicap access. Antiques nearby.

"Peaceful surroundings, friendly staff."

Certificate may be used: November-March, Sunday-Thursday holidays, special events excluded, subject to availability

Yuba City
F5

Harkey House B&B
212 C St
Yuba City, CA 95991-5014

(916)674-1942

Circa 1875. An essence of romance fills this Victorian Gothic house set in a historic neighborhood. Every inch of the home has been given a special touch, from the knickknacks and photos in the sitting room to the quilts and furnishings in the guest quarters. The Harkey Suite features a brass bed with a down comforter and extras such as an adjoining library room and a pellet-burning stove. Breakfasts of muffins, fresh fruit, juice and freshly ground coffee are served in a glass-paned dining room or on the patio.

Innkeeper(s): Bob & Lee Jones. $75-100. MC VISA AX DS PC TC. 4 rooms with PB, 2 with FP. 1 suite. 1 conference room. Breakfast included in rates. Types of meals: full breakfast and early coffee/tea. Beds: Q. Air conditioning, turndown service, ceiling fan and TV in room. VCR, spa and library on premises. Antiques, fishing, parks, shopping, theater and watersports nearby.

Publicity: *Country Magazine.*

"This place is simply marvelous...the most comfortable bed in travel."

Certificate may be used: Sunday through Saturday.

Colorado

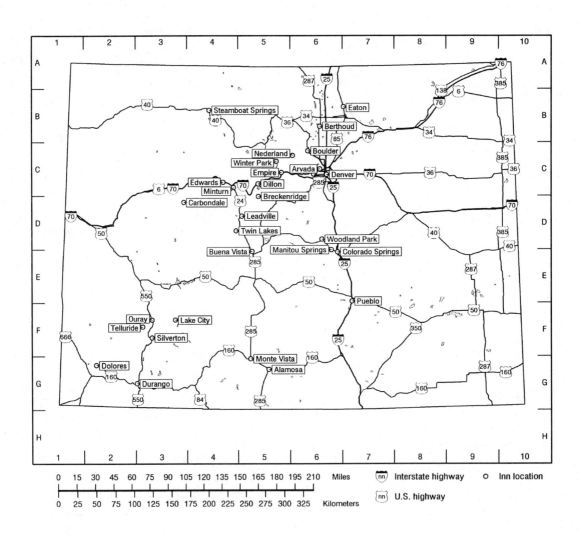

0   15 30 45 60 75 90 105 120 135 150 165 180 195 210   Miles

0   25 50 75 100 125 150 175 200 225 250 275 300 325   Kilometers

(nn) Interstate highway   ○ Inn location

(nn) U.S. highway

Alamosa   G5

Cottonwood Inn
123 San Juan Ave
Alamosa, CO 81101-2547
(719)589-3882 (800)955-2623 Fax:(719)589-6437
E-mail: julie@cottonwoodinn.com

Circa 1908. This refurbished Colorado bungalow is filled with antiques and paintings by local artists. The Stickley dining room set once belonged to Billy Adams, a Colorado governor in the 1920s. Blue-corn blueberry pancakes and flaming Grand  Marnier omelets are the inn's specialties. A favorite day trip is riding the Cumbres-Toltec Scenic Railroad over the La Magna Pass, site of an Indiana Jones movie.

Innkeeper(s): Julie Mordecai & George Sellman. $48-85. MC VISA AX DS PC TC. 9 rooms, 7 with PB. 4 suites. Breakfast and evening snack included in rates. Types of meals: gourmet breakfast and early coffee/tea. Beds: KQTD. Cable TV, VCR, fax and copier on premises. Antiques, parks and downhill skiing nearby.

Location: Close to Great Sand Dunes National Monument.

Publicity: *Rocky Mountain News, Country Inns, Denver Post, Milwaukee Journal, Channel 4 Denver.*

"My husband wants to come over every morning for blueberry pancakes and strawberry rhubarb sauce."

Certificate may be used: Nov. 1-April 31, excluding Crane Festival weekend.

Arvada   C6

The Tree House
6650 Simms St
Arvada, CO 80004-2534
(303)431-6352 Fax:(303)456-1414
E-mail: thetreehou@aol.com

Circa 1940. Each of the guest rooms at this modern, chalet-style bed & breakfast offers something special. Four of the rooms have a wood-burning fireplace, and the fifth guest room includes a bay window and a king-size brass bed topped with cozy quilts. There are 10 acres to wander, including wooded trails, and after a refreshing walk, guests can return and enjoy a soak in the outdoor Jacuzzi or just relax on the deck. Denver is less than 30 minutes from the home.

Innkeeper(s): LeAnne & Todd Thomas. $59-99. MC VISA. 5 rooms with PB, 4 with FP. Breakfast and afternoon tea included in rates. Types

of meals: full breakfast and gourmet breakfast. Beds: KQT. Air conditioning in room. Fax and spa on premises. Amusement parks, antiques, fishing, parks, downhill skiing, cross-country skiing, sporting events and theater nearby.

Certificate may be used: Weeknights in January through April & October, Sunday-Thursday.

Berthoud   B6

Berthoud B&B
444 N 1st St
Berthoud, CO 80513-1317
(970)532-4566 Fax:(970)532-4566

Circa 1895. With the Rocky Mountains as a backdrop and complete with a two-story turret and sweeping veranda, this inn reminds guests of a pic-

ture-perfect Victorian dollhouse. Tucked away in the turret is the Madame Pompadour Suite where Louis XV furniture graces the sitting area. The room is given a French country garden feel with its sleeping alcove with lavender walls, violet floral wallpaper, curtains, bed cover and orchid carpet. A chandelier hangs from the turret ceiling above a huge, circular bed, and 11 windows offer a view of the yard and its tall evergreens.

Innkeeper(s): Janet & Gary. $95-135. MC VISA AX DS PC TC. 7 rooms with PB. 2 suites. 1 conference room. Breakfast included in rates. Types of meals: gourmet breakfast and early coffee/tea. Afternoon tea, dinner, evening snack, lunch, gourmet lunch, banquet service, catering service and room service available. Beds: KQ. Turndown service, ceiling fan, TV and VCR in room. Fax, copier, spa, bicycles, library and pet boarding on premises. Handicap access. Amusement parks, antiques, fishing, parks, shopping, downhill skiing, cross-country skiing, sporting events, theater and watersports nearby.

Certificate may be used: January through May, September through December, Sunday-Thursday.

Boulder C6

The Inn on Mapleton Hill

1001 Spruce St
Boulder, CO 80302-4028
(303)449-6528

Circa 1899. The Magpie Inn employed nine local interior designers to refurbish the mansion. Each room was given special and unique attention, with the focus being romance with a Victorian theme. The result is a collection of antiques, custom furniture and softly hued fabrics to elicit memories of an elegant home. Visual delights abound from marble fireplaces and fine paintings to old photographs and prints of Boulder.

Innkeeper(s): Jacque Traeger. $88-135. MC VISA. 7 rooms. 1 suite. Breakfast included in rates. Types of meals: continental breakfast and full breakfast. Cable TV on premises. Antiques, shopping, downhill skiing, cross-country skiing, sporting events and theater nearby.

Certificate may be used: September-April.

Breckenridge D5

Hunt Placer Inn

275 Ski Hill Rd, PO Box 4898
Breckenridge, CO 80424-4898
(970)453-7573 (800)472-1430 Fax:(970)453-2335
E-mail: hpi@colorado.net

Circa 1994. Set among woods in a historic, gold-mining town, this delightful mountain chalet is located on what was an actual mining claim. Guest rooms are decorated in a variety of styles, from Southwestern to European, each with an elegant flair. The room and suite names reflect the decor, such as the Bavaria Suite or the Gold Rush Room. The morning menu changes daily, offering items such as Swiss muesli, fresh fruit, pancakes topped with praline sauce, creme brulee and quiche. A free shuttle takes wintertime guests to the nearby ski slopes and alpine slide.

Innkeeper(s): Carl & Gwen Ray. $95-185. MC VISA AX DC CB DS PC TC. 8 rooms with PB, 3 with FP. 1 conference room. Breakfast and afternoon tea included in rates. Types of meals: full breakfast, gourmet breakfast and early coffee/tea. Beds: QT. Cable TV, VCR and fax on premises. Handicap access. Antiques, fishing, parks, shopping, downhill skiing, cross-country skiing, theater and watersports nearby.

Certificate may be used: April, September through November, Sunday through Thursday.

Breckenridge (Dillion) D5

Swan Mountain Inn

16172 HWY 9
Breckenridge (Dillion), CO 80424
(970)453-7903 (800)578-3687

Circa 1986. Less than seven miles from the outstanding ski areas of Keystone, Breckenridge and Copper Mountain, this log home is a cozy, warm place to enjoy a mountain getaway. After a day enjoying nature, guests can dine by candlelight at the inn's dining room or enjoy a drink at the fireside bar. Relax in the glassed-inn sun porches, the decks or on a comfortable hammock.

Innkeeper(s): Steve Gessner. $40-100. MC VISA DS PC TC. 4 rooms, 3 with PB. 1 suite. Breakfast and afternoon tea included in rates. Types of meals: full breakfast and gourmet breakfast. Dinner and gourmet lunch available. Restaurant on premises. TV and VCR in room. Spa on premises. Handicap access. Antiques, fishing, parks, shopping, downhill skiing, cross-country skiing and watersports nearby.

Certificate may be used: April 16-June 30, Sept. 15-Nov. 21, Sunday-Thursday.

Buena Vista E5

Adobe Inn

PO Box 1560, 303 N Hwy 24
Buena Vista, CO 81211-1560
(719)395-6340

Circa 1883. These five guest rooms are located in a 19th-century Southwestern farmhouse. The exterior is unassuming. The interior is rustic and inviting, with exposed dark wood beams, tile floors and kiva fireplaces. There is a relaxing, two-person Jacuzzi. In the mornings, croissants, fresh fruit, eggs and breakfast meats are accompanied by juice, coffee and perhaps Mexican hot chocolate. The former president of France was once a guest.

Innkeeper(s): Paul, Marjorie & Michael Knox. $59-89. MC VISA PC TC. 5 rooms with PB. Breakfast included in rates. Types of meals: full breakfast and gourmet breakfast. Beds: KQD. Ceiling fan and TV in room. Antiques, fishing, parks, shopping, downhill skiing, cross-country skiing and golf nearby.

Publicity: *Chaffee County Times, Denver Post.*

"This has been a sweet and restful experience."

Certificate may be used: November-March except Thanksgiving week, Christmas and New Year's weeks and spring breaks, Monday-Thursday.

Trout City Inn

PO Box 431
Buena Vista, CO 81211-0431
(719)495-0348

Guests at this unique inn can sleep in an elegant Victorian Pullman car or in the Drover's caboose. Located on 40 acres of the San Isabel National Forest, the inn's site is on the path of two famous mountain railroads. Although the historic narrow gauge train is stationary, the locomotive has been used for parades. The depot rooms are furnished in authentic Victorian style, but the berth mattresses are custom made—longer and a bit firmer than those of a hundred years ago.

Innkeeper(s): Juel Kjeldsen. $35-40. MC VISA. 4 rooms. 1 conference room. Breakfast included in rates. Type of meal: full breakfast. VCR on premises. Antiques, shopping, downhill skiing, cross-country skiing and theater nearby.

Certificate may be used: June 15-Sept. 15, weekends only (Friday, Saturday, Sunday evenings).

Carbondale   D3

Ambiance Inn

66 N 2nd St
Carbondale, CO 81623-2102
(970)963-3597 (800)350-1515 Fax:(970)963-3130

Circa 1976. This contemporary chalet-style home is located in the beautiful Crystal Valley between Aspen and Glenwood Springs. Year-round activities are numerous in the area, but ski buffs will be excited to know that Aspen and Snowmass are only a 30-minute drive away. Glenwood Springs and the world's largest hot springs are just 15 minutes away. Custom picnic baskets for outings are available with two days' advance notice. The New Orleans Library is adjacent to all three guest rooms on the second floor.

Innkeeper(s): Norma & Robert Morris. $60-100. MC DS PC. 4 rooms with PB. 1 suite. Breakfast included in rates. Types of meals: full breakfast, gourmet breakfast and early coffee/tea. Beds: Q. Ceiling fan and TV in room. VCR on premises. Antiques, fishing, parks, shopping, downhill skiing, cross-country skiing and sporting events nearby.

Certificate may be used: Excludes holidays and Christmas week and peak summer weekends.

Colorado Springs   E6

Black Forest B&B

11170 Black Forest Rd
Colorado Springs, CO 80908-3986
(719)495-4208 (800)809-9901 Fax:(719)495-0688

Circa 1984. Ponderosa pines, golden aspens and fragrant meadows surround this massive log home built on the highest point east of the Rocky

Mountains. This rustic mountain setting is complete with 20 acres of beautiful country to explore. If you want to fully experience mountain living, the innkeepers will be more than happy to share their chores with you, which range from cutting firewood to planting Christmas trees on their tree farm. A greenhouse holds an indoor lap pool, sauna, fitness center and honeymoon suite.

Innkeeper(s): Robert & Susan Putnam. $75-125. MC VISA AX DS PC TC. 4 rooms with PB, 1 with FP. 3 suites. 2 cottages. 1 conference room. Breakfast and evening snack included in rates. Types of meals: continental-plus breakfast and early coffee/tea. Beds: KQDT. Ceiling fan in room. VCR, fax and copier on premises. Handicap access. Antiques, parks, shopping, cross-country skiing, sporting events and theater nearby.

Certificate may be used: November through April, except Christmas and Thanksgiving.

Cheyenne Canon Inn

2030 W Cheyenne Blvd
Colorado Springs, CO 80906
(719)633-0625 (800)633-0625 Fax:(800)633-8826

Circa 1921. World travelers Barbara and John Starr have filled this rustic home with interesting finds from their many visits to foreign lands. The home was built by the wife of a Manitou Springs sheriff and originally served as an upscale casino, and more infamously, a bordello. During the home's heyday as an inn, guests included the Marx Brothers and Lon Cheney. The massive home features more than 100 windows, all boasting beautiful views, original stained glass and silver wall sconces. Each of the

seven guest rooms and two cottages captures an unique international flavor. The innkeepers recently added "Le Petit Chateau," a romantic cottage tucked beneath 50-foot tall pines trees. Spend the night tucked away in a room reminiscent of a Swiss chalet or enjoy the atmosphere of an Oriental tea room in another guest quarter. The second-floor hot tub affords a view of Cheyenne Mountain. The innkeepers have created a relaxing retreat, but also offer many amenities for the business traveler including in-room phones, TVs and modem outlets. Innkeeper(s): John, Barbara & Josh Starr. $75-175. MC VISA AX DS PC TC. 9 rooms, 8 with PB, 3 with FP. 3 suites. 1 cottage. 2 conference rooms. Types of meals: full breakfast and early coffee/tea. Beds: KQT. Air conditioning, turndown service, ceiling fan, TV and VCR in room. Fax, copier, spa and library on premises. Antiques, fishing, parks, shopping, downhill skiing, cross-country skiing, sporting events and theater nearby.

Publicity: *Denver Post, Colorado Source, Beacon, National Geographic Traveler.*

"*It truly was 'home away from home.' You have made it so welcoming and warm. Needless to say our breakfasts at home will never come close to the Cheyenne Canon Inn!!*"

Certificate may be used: Nov. 1 to April 30, Sunday-Thursday. Holidays excluded.

The Painted Lady

1318 W Colorado Ave
Colorado Springs, CO 80904-4023
(719)473-3165

Circa 1894. Once a popular restaurant in Old Colorado City, the Painted Lady has been remodeled into a bed & breakfast by its new owners. The

three-story Victorian is decorated in a warm, romantic manner with lace and floral fabrics. Antique iron and four-poster beds, clawfoot tubs and brass fixtures fill the guest rooms. Hearty breakfasts, served on the veranda in summer, might include seafood quiche or souffles and homemade breads. Afternoon refreshments can be enjoyed in the parlor or on one of the porches. Innkeeper(s): Valerie Maslowski. $70-150. MC VISA AX DS PC TC. 2 suites. Breakfast included in rates. Types of meals: full breakfast and

early coffee/tea. Beds: QDT. Air conditioning, ceiling fan and TV in room. VCR on premises. Antiques, fishing, parks, shopping, downhill skiing, cross-country skiing, sporting events, theater and watersports nearby.

Location: In historic Old Colorado City.

"*Calm, peaceful. Our first B&B, very memorable.*"

Certificate may be used: Nov. 1 to April 30, Sunday-Thursday, excluding holidays.

Denver C6

Haus Berlin B&B

1651 Emerson St
Denver, CO 80218-1411
(303)837-9527 (800)659-0253 Fax:(303)837-9527
E-mail: haus.berlin@worldnet.att.net

Circa 1892. This brick Victorian townhouse is a delightful place from which to enjoy Denver. The inn is listed in the National Register of Historic Places and located in a neighborhood filled with charming architecture. The cozy guest rooms are well-appointed and feature beds dressed in fine linens and topped with down comforters. The suite is the most luxurious, and it offers a view of downtown Denver, which is a 10-minute walk from the home. The breakfast menu varies, one morning it might be eggs Benedict, the next day could bring a traditional European breakfast with freshly baked rolls, scones with lemon curd and imported hams and cheeses. Innkeeper(s): Christiana & Dennis Brown. $90-135. MC VISA AX DC DS PC TC. 4 rooms, 3 with PB. 1 suite. Breakfast included in rates. Types of meals: full breakfast, gourmet breakfast and early coffee/tea. Beds: KQ. Air conditioning, ceiling fan and TV in room. VCR and fax on premises. Amusement parks, antiques, fishing, parks, shopping, downhill skiing, cross-country skiing, sporting events, golf, theater and watersports nearby.

Publicity: *Denver Post, Life on Capital Hill.*

"*What a beautiful oasis in a big city.*"

Certificate may be used: Nov. 1-April 1, Sunday-Thursday (suite only) $130 per night.

Dolores G2

Mountain View B&B

28050 County Rd P
Dolores, CO 81323
(970)882-7861 (800)228-4592

Circa 1984. This sprawling ranch-type home has a magnificent view of the Mesa Verde National Park, which is 12 miles to its entrance. Besides spending a day or two touring the museum and cliff dwellings in Mesa Verde, guests can step outside this inn to enjoy its 22 acres of trails, woods and a small canyon with creek. In each direction, a short drive will take you to mountains, desert, canyon lands, mesa, forest lakes and world famous archaeological settings.

Innkeeper(s): Brenda & Cecil Dunn. $49-59. MC VISA PC TC. 8 rooms with PB. 4 suites. 1 conference room. Breakfast and evening snack included in rates. Types of meals: continental-plus breakfast, full breakfast and early coffee/tea. Dinner available. Beds: QDT. Ceiling fan in room. Spa and library on premises. Handicap access. Fishing, parks, shopping, downhill skiing, cross-country skiing and watersports nearby.

Certificate may be used: Jan. 5-April 30.

Durango   G3

Leland House B&B Suites
721 East Second Ave
Durango, CO 81301-5435
(970)385-1920 (800)664-1920 Fax:(970)385-1967

Circa 1927. The rooms in this Craftsman-style brick building are named after historic figures associated with this former apartment house and Durango's early industrial growth. The decor features unique cowboy and period antiques designed for both comfort and fun. Gourmet breakfasts include homemade granola, cranberry scones, and a

variety of entrees like Southwest burritos and multigrain waffles. Located in the historic district downtown, guests can take walking tours, enjoy specialty shops, restaurants, galleries and museums nearby.

Innkeeper(s): Kirk & Diane Komick. $95-155. MC VISA AX DS PC TC. 10 rooms with PB. 6 suites. Breakfast and afternoon tea included in rates. Types of meals: full breakfast and gourmet breakfast. Picnic lunch and catering service available. Restaurant on premises. Beds: QD. Air conditioning, ceiling fan and TV in room. VCR, fax and copier on premises. Antiques, fishing, parks, shopping, downhill skiing, cross-country skiing, theater and watersports nearby.

"It is great! Charming and warm, friendly staff and superb food. Marvelous historic photo collection."

Certificate may be used: Oct. 15 through May 15, except holidays.

The Rochester Hotel
721 East Second Ave
Durango, CO 81301
(970)385-1920 (800)664-1920 Fax:(970)385-1967

Circa 1892. This Federal-style inn's decor is inspired by many Western movies filmed in and

around the town. The building is an authentically restored late-Victorian hotel with the charm and luxary of the Old West.

The inn is furnished in antiques from the period. The inn is situated on a beautifully landscaped setting that features a flower-filled courtyard. Just one block from historic Main Avenue downtown, the inn is close to all major attractions, museums, galleries, shops, restaurants, and outdoor activities.

Innkeeper(s): Kirk & Diane Komick. $125-185. MC VISA AX DS PC TC. 15 rooms with PB. 2 suites. 2 conference rooms. Breakfast included in rates. Types of meals: full breakfast and gourmet breakfast. Afternoon tea, picnic lunch and catering service available. Beds: KQ. Air conditioning, ceiling fan and TV in room. VCR, fax and copier on premises. Handicap access. Antiques, fishing, parks, shopping, downhill skiing, cross-country skiing, theater and watersports nearby.

Publicity: *Conde Nast Traveler.*

"In a word — exceptional! Far exceeded expectations in every way."

Certificate may be used: Oct. 15 through May 15, excluding holidays.

Eaton   B7

The Victorian Veranda
515 Cheyenne Ave
Eaton, CO 80615-3473
(970)454-3890

This Queen Anne Victorian boasts a view of the Rocky Mountains from the swings on its wraparound porch. The interior features a hand-carved oak staircase and century-old antiques. The innkeepers provide a tandem bicycle for guests who wish to partake in a tour of the town's historic areas. The West Room boasts a black marble fireplace. The East Room, which overlooks the lush grounds, includes an antique brass bed and whirlpool tub. During mild weather, breakfasts are served on the inn's veranda.

Innkeeper(s): Nadine White. $45-60. 3 rooms. Breakfast included in rates. Type of meal: full breakfast.

Certificate may be used: January to December, Monday through Thursday, excluding holidays.

Edwards   C4

The Lazy Ranch B&B
PO Box 404
Edwards, CO 81632-0404
(970)926-3876 (800)655-9343 Fax:(970)926-3876

Circa 1886. Enjoy a taste of the Old West at this working horse ranch. The Lazy Ranch is the only original homestead left in the Vail Valley. A variety of animals, including chickens, peacocks, Porkchop the pig, rabbits, dogs and cats create the authentic farm atmosphere. Hearty country breakfasts are served with farm-fresh eggs. The innkeepers offer bonfires, barbecues and barn dances to make your country vacation complete. Couples might enjoy moonlight horseback rides accompanied by a romantic dinner. Innkeeper Buddy Calhoun's "Cowboy" artwork is displayed in a converted bunk house, which now serves as an art studio.

Innkeeper(s): Buddy & Linda Calhoun. $60-125. MC VISA DS TC. 4 rooms, 1 with PB, 1 with FP. 1 suite. Breakfast included in rates. Types of meals: full breakfast and early coffee/tea. Picnic lunch, catering service and catered breakfast available. Beds: QD. Turndown service in room. Cable TV, VCR, fax, copier, stables and pet boarding on premises. Fishing, shopping, downhill skiing, cross-country skiing and watersports nearby.

"As weekends go, they just don't get any better than the one spent at Lazy Ranch. Thank you so much for the hospitality."

Certificate may be used: April 1-Nov. 1, excluding all holidays.

Empire   C5

Mad Creek B&B
PO Box 404
Empire, CO 80438-0404
(303)569-2003

Circa 1881. This mountain town cottage has just the right combination of Victorian decor with lace, flowers, antiques and gingerbread trim on the facade. Unique touches include door frames of old mineshaft wood, kerosene lamps, Eastlake antiques and complimentary cross-country ski gear and mountain bikes. Relax in front of the rock fireplace while watching a movie, peruse the library filled with local lore, or plan your next adventure with Colorado guides and maps. Empire, which was once a mining town, is conveniently located within 15 to 45 minutes of at least six major ski areas.

Innkeeper(s): Heather & Mike Lopez. $49-69. MC VISA TC. 3 rooms, 1 with PB. Breakfast, afternoon tea and evening snack included in rates. Types of meals: full breakfast and early coffee/tea. Beds: QD. Ceiling fan in room. Cable TV, VCR and bicycles on premises. Antiques, fishing, parks, shopping, downhill skiing, cross-country skiing, theater and watersports nearby.

Certificate may be used: Oct. 15-Nov. 20, Sunday-Thursday; April 16-May 20, Sunday-Thursday.

Lake City   F3

Crystal Lodge
PO Box 246
Lake City, CO 81235-0246
(303)944-2201 (800)984-1234 Fax:(303)944-2503

With the San Juan Mountains as its backdrop, this rustic, log lodge offers a variety of comfortable accommodations. Aside from the lodge's nine bedchambers, there are several apartments and cottages, which offer kitchens and sitting or living areas. An extensive country breakfast is available each morning in the lodge's restaurant. Lake City, which once was a booming mining town, boasts the state's largest collection of restored Victorians. Outdoor enthusiasts will have no trouble finding something to do, as Lake City is surrounded by 600,000 acres of public land, perfect for fishing, hiking, horseback riding and many other activities.

Innkeeper(s): Ann Udell. $45-95. MC VISA. 18 rooms. Breakfast included in rates.

Certificate may be used: Oct. 1-May 25.

Old Carson Inn
8401 County Rd 30, PO Box 144
Lake City, CO 81235
(970)944-2511 (800)294-0608

Circa 1990. Located at an elevation of 9,400 feet, this massive log house provides a secluded mountain

setting in a forest of aspens and spruce. The Bonanza King Mine Room features a cathedral ceiling and soaring windows overlooking an aspen grove. Native American artifacts and antiques are sprinkled throughout the inn.

Innkeeper(s): Don & Judy Berry. $55-105. MC VISA DS. 7 rooms with PB. Breakfast included in rates. Type of meal: full breakfast. Picnic lunch available. Beds: KQ. Ceiling fan in room. VCR and spa on premises. Antiques, fishing, shopping and cross-country skiing nearby.

"Words are inadequate to express how very much we delighted in our stay at your beautiful home."

Certificate may be used: Oct. 1-June 1 excluding holidays.

Leadville D5

The Ice Palace Inn Bed & Breakfast
813 Spruce St
Leadville, CO 80461-3555
(719)486-8272 (800)754-2840 Fax:(719)486-0345

Circa 1899. Innkeeper Kami Kolakowski was born in this historic Colorado town, and it was her dream to one day return and run a bed & breakfast. Now with husband Giles, she has created a restful retreat out of this turn-of-the-century home built with lumber from the famed Leadville Ice Palace. Giles and Kami have filled the home with antiques and pieces of history from the Ice Palace and the town. Guests are treated to a mouth-watering gourmet breakfast with treats such as stuffed French toast or German apple pancakes.

Innkeeper(s): Giles & Kami Kolakowski. $69-129. MC VISA AX DS PC TC. 6 rooms with PB. Breakfast, afternoon tea and evening snack included in rates. Types of meals: gourmet breakfast and early coffee/tea. Catering service and room service available. Beds: QDT. Turndown service and ceiling fan in room. Cable TV, VCR and library on premises. Antiques, fishing, parks, shopping, downhill skiing, cross-country skiing, theater and watersports nearby.

Certificate may be used: Anytime upon availability. No holidays.

Peri & Ed's Mountain Hide Away
201 W 8th St
Leadville, CO 80461-3529
(719)486-0716 (800)933-3715 Fax:(719)486-2181

Circa 1879. This former boarding house was built during the boom days of Leadville. Families can picnic on the large lawn sprinkled with wildflowers under soaring pines. Shoppers and history buffs can enjoy exploring historic Main Street, one block away. The surrounding mountains are a natural playground offering a wide variety of activities, and the innkeepers will be happy to let you know their favorite spots and help with directions. The sunny Augusta Tabor room features a sprawling king-size bed with a warm view of the rugged peaks.

Innkeeper(s): Peri & Ed Solder. $45-85. MC VISA AX DS PC TC. 9 rooms, 5 with PB, 2 with FP. 2 suites. 2 cottages. Breakfast included in rates. Type of meal: full breakfast. Beds: KQDT. Ceiling fan in room. Cable TV, VCR and library on premises. Antiques, fishing, parks, shopping, downhill skiing, cross-country skiing and theater nearby.

Certificate may be used: October-Dec. 15, April 15-June 30, Monday-Wednesday

Wood Haven Manor
PO Box 1291, 809 Spruce
Leadville, CO 80461-1291
(719)486-0109 (800)748-2570 Fax:(719)486-0210

Circa 1898. Located on the town's Banker's Row, this Victorian inn is located in a winter wonderland, with cross-country and downhill skiing nearby, snowmobiling and back-country outings. Gourmet breakfasts include freshly baked bread, sourdough pancakes or eggs Santa Fe, in-season fruits and cool fruit smoothies.

Innkeeper(s): Bobby & Jolene Wood. $59-129. MC VISA AX DS PC TC. 8 rooms with PB. 3 suites. Breakfast, afternoon tea and evening snack included in rates. Types of meals: full breakfast, gourmet breakfast and early coffee/tea. Beds: QDT. Cable TV, VCR, fax, copier and library on premises. Amusement parks, antiques, fishing, parks, shopping, downhill skiing, cross-country skiing, theater and watersports nearby.

Location: Historic "Bankers Row."

Publicity: *Country Traditional, Country Almanac, Country Decorating Ideas.*

"The room, the food and the hospitality were truly wonderful."

Certificate may be used: Sunday through Thursday, except holidays, excluding July, August, December and March.

Minturn C4

Eagle River Inn
PO Box 100
Minturn, CO 81645-0100
(970)827-5761 (800)344-1750 Fax:(970)827-4020
E-mail: eri@vail.net

Circa 1894. Earth red adobe walls, rambling riverside decks, mature willow trees and brilliant flowers enhance the secluded backyard of this Southwestern-style inn. Inside, the lobby features comfortable Santa Fe furniture, an authentic beehive fireplace and a ceiling of traditional latilas and vegas. Baskets, rugs and weavings add warmth. Guest rooms found on two floors have views of the river or mountains. The innkeepers hold a wine tasting with appetizers each evening. Minturn, which had its beginnings as a stop on the Rio Grande Railroad, is the home of increasingly popular restaurants, shops and galleries.

Innkeeper(s): Patty Bidez. $75-180. MC VISA AX PC TC. 12 rooms with PB. Breakfast and evening snack included in rates. Type of meal: full breakfast. Beds: KT. TV in room. Fax and bicycles on premises. Fishing, shopping, downhill skiing, cross-country skiing and sporting events nearby.

Location: Vail Valley.

Publicity: *Rocky Mount, National Geographic Traveler.*

"We love this place and have decided to make it a yearly tradition!"

Certificate may be used: May 25-June 30 and Oct. 1 to Dec. 18, Sunday-Thursday.

Monte Vista
G5

The Windmill B&B
4340 W Hwy 160
Monte Vista, CO 81144
(719)852-0438 (800)467-3441

Circa 1959. This Southwestern-style inn affords panoramic views of the surrounding Sangre De Cristo and San Juan mountain ranges. The 22-acre grounds still include the namesake windmill that once was used to irrigate water in the yard and garden. Now it stands guard over the hot tub. Each of the guest rooms is decorated in a different theme, with a few antiques placed here and there. The plentiful country breakfast are served in a dining room with mountain views.

Innkeeper(s): Sharon & Dennis Kay. $65-99. MC VISA PC. 4 rooms with PB. Breakfast and evening snack included in rates. Types of meals: full breakfast, gourmet breakfast and early coffee/tea. Beds: KQT. Turndown service in room. Antiques, fishing, parks, shopping, downhill skiing, cross-country skiing and theater nearby.

Certificate may be used: Sept. 15 to June 1, Sunday-Friday.

Nederland
C6

Goldminer Hotel
601 Klondike Ave
Nederland, CO 80466-9542
(303)258-7770 (800)422-4629 Fax:(303)258-3850

Circa 1897. This turn-of-the-century hotel is a highlight in the Eldora National Historic District. Suites and rooms are decorated with period antiques. The inn provides packages that include guided jeep, horseback, hiking and fishing tours in the summer and backcountry ski tours in the winter.

Innkeeper(s): Scott Bruntjen. $69-129. MC VISA AX TC. 8 rooms, 4 with PB, 1 with FP. 1 suite. 1 cottage. 1 conference room. Breakfast included in rates. Types of meals: full breakfast and early coffee/tea. Beds: KDT. Cable TV, VCR, fax, copier, computer, spa and library on premises. Antiques, fishing, parks, shopping, downhill skiing, cross-country skiing and sporting events nearby.

Location: Eldora National Historic District.

Publicity: *Daily Camera, Mountain Ear.*

Certificate may be used: All except Dec. 18-Jan. 10, May 10-20; Friday-Saturday, June-October.

Ouray
F3

Damn Yankee B&B Inn
100 Sixth Ave, PO Box 709
Ouray, CO 81427
(970)325-4219 (800)845-7512 Fax:(970)325-4339
E-mail: bigsmac@montrose.net

Circa 1991. Nestled at the foot of mountains, this rustic hideaway affords glorious views from its second-story balcony and sitting room. The parlor boasts a baby grand piano and wood-burning fireplace, and guests will always find something to snack on in the sitting room, which is stocked with fruit, drinks and other treats. Guests planning to hit the nearby slopes will appreciate the inn's expansive, gourmet breakfast, which is served each morning. The innkeepers provide free admission to the Ouray Hot Springs, one of the area's popular attractions.

Innkeeper(s): Matt & Julie Croce. $72-175. MC VISA AX PC. 10 rooms with PB. 3 suites. 1 cottage. Breakfast and afternoon tea included in rates. Types of meals: gourmet breakfast and early coffee/tea. Beds: KQ. Ceiling fan and TV in room. VCR, fax and copier on premises. Handicap access. Fishing, downhill skiing and golf nearby.

Certificate may be used: Weekdays April 1-May 15 and weekdays Nov. 1-Dec. 15.

Pueblo
E7

Abriendo Inn
300 W Abriendo Ave
Pueblo, CO 81004-1814
(719)544-2703 Fax:(719)542-6544
E-mail: abriendo@rmi.net

Circa 1906. This three-story, 7,000-square-foot four-square-style mansion is embellished with dentil designs and wide porches supported by Ionic columns. Elegantly paneled and carved oak walls and woodwork provide a gracious setting for king-size brass beds, antique armoires and Oriental rugs. Breakfast specialties include raspberry muffins, Italian strada and nut breads. Ask for the music room with its own fireplace and bay window.

Innkeeper(s): Kerrelyn Trent. $59-120. MC VISA AX DC PC TC. 10 rooms with PB. 1 suite. Breakfast included in rates. Types of meals:

continental breakfast, full breakfast, gourmet breakfast and early coffee/tea. Beds: KQ. Air conditioning, ceiling fan, TV and VCR in room. Fax and copier on premises. Antiques, fishing, parks, shopping, cross-country skiing, sporting events, golf and watersports nearby.

Publicity: *Pueblo Chieftain, Rocky Mountain News, Denver Post.*

"Thank you for warm hospitality, cozy environment and fine cuisine! Outstanding!"

Certificate may be used: Sunday & Monday only, November through March, holidays excluded.

Silverton   F3

The Wyman Hotel & Inn
1371 Greene St
Silverton, CO 81433
(970)387-5372 (800)609-7845 Fax:(970)387-5745

Circa 1902. Silverton, a Victorian-era mining town at the base of the San Juan Mountains, is the location for this National Register hotel. The hotel still maintains an original tin ceiling and an elevator. However, the elevator is now housed in one of the guest rooms, surrounding a Jacuzzi tub. Other unique features include a stone carving of a mule, created by the hotel's builder. The mule is displayed on the roof. Aside from the historic ambiance, the innkeepers offer plenty of amenities. Rooms include a TV and VCR and there are hundreds of movies guests can choose, all free of charge. A buffet breakfast is served, featuring fresh fruit, muffins, breads, cereals, special egg dishes and Silverton Spuds, potatoes baked with onions, peppers, tomatoes, broccoli and cheese.

Innkeeper(s): Lorraine Lewis. $50-109. MC VISA AX PC TC. 19 rooms, 17 with PB. 2 suites. Breakfast, afternoon tea and picnic lunch included in rates. Types of meals: full breakfast, gourmet breakfast and early coffee/tea. Beds: KQ. Ceiling fan, TV and VCR in room. Fax, copier and library on premises. Antiques, fishing, parks, shopping, downhill skiing, cross-country skiing, theater and watersports nearby.

Certificate may be used: October & December weekdays, excluding holidays, April, May & October

Steamboat Springs   B4

The Inn at Steamboat
PO Box 775084, 3070 Columbine Dr
Steamboat Springs, CO 80477-5084
(970)879-2600 (800)872-2601 Fax:(970)879-9270

Circa 1972. Whatever the season, this 33-room inn is near many activities. Skiing is just three blocks away, and in the warm months, guests can hike, bike, go white-water rafting or take a trip through the wilderness on horseback. Most of the guest rooms, which feature country decor, offer views of the ski slopes or surrounding Yampa Valley. In the spring, the grounds are covered with flowers.

Innkeeper(s): Tom & Roxane Miller-Freutel. $39-139. MC VISA AX DS PC TC. 33 rooms, 31 with PB. 1 suite. 1 cottage. 1 conference room. Breakfast and afternoon tea included in rates. Types of meals: continental-plus breakfast and early coffee/tea. Evening snack and catering service available. Beds: QT. TV in room. Fax, copier, spa, swimming, sauna, bicycles and child care on premises. Handicap access. Fishing, parks, shopping, downhill skiing, cross-country skiing, golf, theater and watersports nearby.

"We will treasure the memory of our long weekend at your inn."

Certificate may be used: April 1-May 31 and Oct. 1-Nov. 31 (full non-discounted rates apply, some restrictions apply).

Steamboat Valley Guest House
PO Box 773815
Steamboat Springs, CO 80477-3815
(970)870-9017 (800)530-3866 Fax:(970)879-0361

Circa 1957. Enjoy a sleigh ride across snow-covered hills or take in the mountain view from the hot tub at this rustic Colorado home. Logs from the town mill and bricks from an old flour mill were used to construct the home, which features rooms with

exposed wooden beams, high ceilings and country furnishings. Beds are covered with fluffy comforters, and several guest rooms afford magnificent views of this skiing resort town. The innkeepers prepare a varied breakfast menu with staples such as Irish oatmeal to the more gourmet, such as a puffy souffle. The home is located in the Steamboat Springs' historic Old Town area.

Innkeeper(s): George & Alice Lund. $73-148. MC VISA AX DC CB DS PC TC. 4 rooms with PB, 1 with FP. 1 suite. Breakfast and afternoon tea included in rates. Types of meals: full breakfast and early coffee/tea. Beds: Q. Cable TV, VCR, fax, copier, spa and library on premises. Fishing, parks, shopping, downhill skiing, cross-country skiing, theater and watersports nearby.

Certificate may be used: Monday-Thursday, year round. Excludes holidays.

Telluride F3

New Sheridan Hotel

231 W Colorado Ave, PO Box 980
Telluride, CO 81435
(970)728-4351 (800)200-1891 Fax:(970)728-5024

Circa 1895. This charming hotel reflects the Victorian ambiance of a historic mining town. The building was redecorated recently to its former glory and is the only remaining original Victorian hotel and bar in Telluride. Much of the bar's interior is original, including a cherrywood back bar with carved lions imported from Austria. The adjoining Sheridan Opera House hosted such stars as Sarah Bernhardt, Lillian Gish and William Jennings Bryan. Guests can relax in their cozy guests rooms or in the library or parlor. Fluffy terry robes, in-room ceiling fans, a fitness room, rooftop Jacuzzi and evening wine and hors d'oeuvres await to pamper you. The hotel, one of the Four Sisters Inns, is a five-minute walk from ski lifts.

Innkeeper(s): John Coyle. $65-200. MC VISA AX TC. 32 rooms, 24 with PB. 6 suites. Breakfast included in rates. Type of meal: full breakfast. Picnic lunch available. Restaurant on premises. Beds: KQ. Turndown service in room. Fax, copier and bicycles on premises. Handicap access. Antiques, fishing, parks, shopping, downhill skiing, cross-country skiing, theater and watersports nearby.

Publicity: *Bon Appetit, In Style, San Francisco Examiner, Sunset, Arizona Republic*

Certificate may be used: April-November, Sunday-Thursday, excluding holidays, special events and blackout dates, subject to availability

Twin Lakes D4

Twin Lakes Mountain Retreat

PO Box 175
Twin Lakes, CO 81251-0175
(719)486-2593

Circa 1886. Plenty of trees and wildlife surround this cozy, two-story Victorian farmhouse, which is decorated with country furnishings and antiques. Early morning coffee is served in the warm kitchen in front of an antique wood cook stove, which is still used to prepare meals. Floor-to-ceiling windows offer lake and mountain views. The innkeepers provide special bath salts and soaps for guests who wish to take a long soak after a day exploring the outdoors.

Innkeeper(s): Roger & Denny Miller. $69-73. MC VISA PC TC. 5 rooms, 3 with PB. 1 cottage. Breakfast, afternoon tea and evening snack included in rates. Types of meals: full breakfast and early coffee/tea. Dinner available. Beds: QD. Turndown service in room. Cable TV, VCR and library on premises. Antiques, fishing, shopping, downhill skiing, cross-country skiing, theater and watersports nearby.

Publicity: *Denver Post.*

"Your friendliness and hospitality were a pleasure."

Certificate may be used: Monday-Friday excluding holidays. May 1 through Oct. 15.

Winter Park C5

Alpen Rose

244 Forest Tr, PO Box 769
Winter Park, CO 80482
(970)726-5039 (800)531-1373 Fax:(970)726-0993

Circa 1960. The innkeepers of this European-style mountain B&B like to share their love of the mountains with guests. There is a superb view of the James and Perry Peaks from the large southern deck where

you can witness spectacular sunrises and evening alpen glows. The view is enhanced by lofty pines, wildflowers and quaking aspens. Each of the bedrooms is decorated with treasures brought over from Austria, including traditional featherbeds for the queen-size beds. The town of Winter Park is a small, friendly community located 68 miles west of Denver.

Innkeeper(s): Robin & Rupert Sommerauer. $65-125. MC VISA AX DS PC TC. 6 rooms with PB, 1 with FP. Breakfast and afternoon tea included in rates. Types of meals: gourmet breakfast and early coffee/tea. Beds: KQT. Cable TV, VCR, fax, copier and spa on premises. Antiques, fishing, parks, shopping, downhill skiing, cross-country skiing and watersports nearby.

Certificate may be used: June 1 to Dec. 15, Sunday-Friday.

The Bear Paw Inn

871 Bear Paw Dr, PO Box 334
Winter Park, CO 80482
(970)887-1351 (800)474-0091 Fax:(970)887-1351

Circa 1989. This hand-hewn log home is exactly the type of welcoming retreat one might hope to enjoy on a vacation in the Colorado wilderness, and the panoramic views of the Continental Divide and Rocky Mountain National Park are just one reason. The cozy interior is highlighted by wood beams, log walls and antiques. There are three guest rooms, including one with a Jacuzzi tub and a private deck with a swing. Guests can snuggle up in feather beds topped with down comforters. Winter Park is a

Mecca for skiers, and ski areas are just a few miles from the Bear Paw, as is ice skating, snow mobiling and other winter activities. For summer guests, there is whitewater rafting, golfing, horseback riding and bike trails.

Innkeeper(s): Rick & Sue Callahan. $95-145. MC VISA PC TC. 3 rooms, 2 with PB. 1 suite. Breakfast included in rates. Types of meals: gourmet breakfast and early coffee/tea. Beds: Q. Turndown service in room. Cable TV, VCR, fax and copier on premises. Antiques, fishing, shopping, downhill skiing, cross-country skiing, theater and watersports nearby.

Publicity: *Cape Cod Life, Boston Globe, Los Angeles Times.*

"Outstanding hospitality."

Certificate may be used: Sunday-Thursday, holidays excluded, Dec. 15-Jan. 4 excluded.

Beau West B&B

148 Fir Dr, PO Box 587
Winter Park, CO 80482
(970)726-5145 (800)473-5145 Fax:(970)726-8607
E-mail: beauwest@juno.com

Circa 1968. This bed & breakfast features a unique contemporary architecture that blends well with its wooded surroundings. Guests enjoy views of the Rockies and the Continental Divide. The interior is comfortable, and the rooms feature a variety of different decorating styles, from Southwestern to Victorian. The suite includes a feather bed and whirlpool tub. Ski areas are within walking distance. In fact, it's just 500 yards to the base of the Winter Park and Mary Jane slopes.

Innkeeper(s): Bobby Goins. $75-150. MC VISA PC. 5 rooms with PB, 2 with FP. 3 suites. Breakfast included in rates. Types of meals: continental-plus breakfast, full breakfast and early coffee/tea. Beds: QT. Ceiling fan and TV in room. Fax and spa on premises. Handicap access. Antiques, fishing, parks, shopping, downhill skiing, cross-country skiing, golf, theater and watersports nearby.

Publicity: *Denver Post.*

Certificate may be used: Sunday-Thursday except during ski season, based on availability.

Candlelight Mountain Inn

148 Fern Way, PO Box 600
Winter Park, CO 80482
(970)887-2877 (800)546-4846

Circa 1978. Stroll down a candlelit lane to reach this mountainside inn, surrounded by woods. Relax in a glider swing as you gaze at a campfire and mountain views, or soak in the hot tub and watch shooting stars. The innkeepers have created a relaxing environment at their comfortable inn, which includes a common area with a

recreation room, toy room, dining area and guest kitchen. The inn is a perfect place to relax after a busy day of skiing, skating, biking, golfing or hiking. Other popular area activities include white-water rafting, jeep tours and taking in the scenery from a hot air balloon. The Rocky Mountain National Park is just 30 minutes from the inn.

Innkeeper(s): Kim & Tim Onnen. $45-85. PC TC. 4 rooms, 2 with PB. Breakfast and evening snack included in rates. Type of meal: full breakfast. Beds: QDT. VCR and pet boarding on premises. Antiques, fishing, parks, shopping, downhill skiing, cross-country skiing and theater nearby.

Certificate may be used: April 15-June 15 and Sept. 1-Dec. 1. All weekends and holidays April 15-June 15 and Sept. 1-Dec. 1 are excluded.

Outpost B&B Inn

687 County Rd 517, PO Box 41
Winter Park, CO 80482
(970)726-5346 (800)430-4538 Fax:(970)726-5346

Circa 1970. Rocky mountain peaks, woods and rolling pastures surround this 40-acre spread, which affords views of the Continental Divide. Guests stay in an antique-filled lodge inn. The inn's atrium includes a hot tub. The innkeepers serve a huge, multi-course feast for breakfast. During the winter months, the innkeepers offer free shuttle service to Winter Park and Mary Jane ski areas.

Innkeeper(s): Ken & Barbara Parker. $100-115. MC VISA AX DC DS PC TC. 7 rooms with PB. Breakfast and evening snack included in rates. Type of meal: gourmet breakfast. Beds: KQDT. VCR, fax and spa on premises. Fishing, parks, shopping, downhill skiing, cross-country skiing, theater and watersports nearby.

Certificate may be used: June 1-Dec. 15, Sunday-Thursday; Jan. 5-Feb. 10, Sunday-Thursday; April 5-May 31, Sunday-Thursday.

Woodland Park
D6

Pikes Peak Paradise
236 Pinecrest Rd, PO Box 5760
Woodland Park, CO 80863-8432
(719)687-6656 (800)728-8282 Fax:(719)687-9008
E-mail: woodlandco@aol.com

Circa 1987. This three-story Georgian Colonial with stately white columns rises unexpectedly from the wooded hills west of Colorado Springs. The entire south wall of the inn is made of glass to enhance its splendid views of Pikes Peak. A sliding glass door opens from each room onto a patio. Eggs Benedict and Belgian waffles are favorite breakfast dishes.
Innkeeper(s): Priscilla, Martin & Tim. $95-195. MC VISA AX DS PC TC. 6 rooms, 2 with PB, 3 with FP. 4 suites. Breakfast included in rates. Type of meal: gourmet breakfast. Beds: KQ. Ceiling fan in room. VCR, fax and spa on premises. Handicap access. Amusement parks, antiques, fishing, parks, shopping, cross-country skiing, sporting events, theater and watersports nearby.
Location: West of Colorado Springs, 25 minutes.
Publicity: *Rocky Mountain News.*
Certificate may be used: Oct. 15 to May 15, Sunday-Thursday.

Connecticut

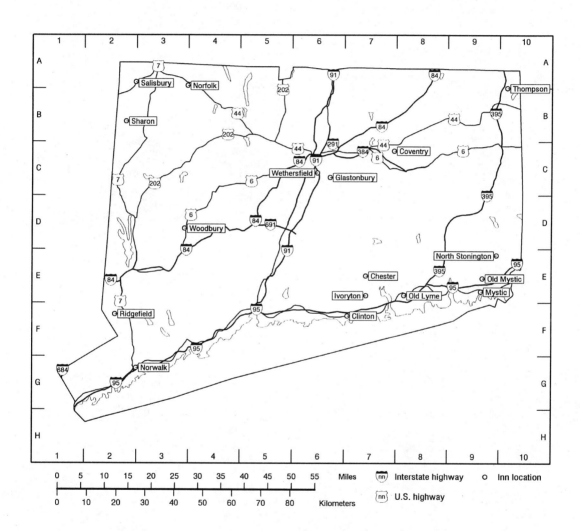

0 5 10 15 20 25 30 35 40 45 50 55 Miles

0 10 20 30 40 50 60 70 80 Kilometers

Interstate highway   Inn location

U.S. highway

Chester
E7

The Inn at Chester
318 W Main St
Chester, CT 06412-1026
(860)526-9541 (800)949-7829 Fax:(860)526-4387

Circa 1778. More than 200 years ago, Jeremiah Parmelee built a clapboard farmhouse along a winding road named the Killingworth Turnpike. The Parmelee Homestead stands as a reflection of the past and is an inspiration for the Inn at Chester. Each of the rooms is individually appointed with Eldred Wheeler Reproductions. The Lincoln Suite has a sitting room with a fireplace. Enjoy lively conversation or live music while imbibing your favorite drink at the inn's tavern, Dunk's Landing. Outside Dunk's Landing, a 30-foot fireplace soars into the rafters.

Innkeeper(s): Deborah Moore. $105-215. MC VISA AX DS. 42 rooms with PB, 2 with FP. 1 suite. 3 conference rooms. Breakfast and dinner included in rates. Type of meal: continental-plus breakfast. Lunch and banquet service available. Restaurant on premises. Beds: KQDT. Air conditioning and TV in room. VCR, fax, copier, sauna, bicycles, tennis, library and pet boarding on premises. Handicap access. Antiques, fishing, parks, shopping, downhill skiing, cross-country skiing, theater and watersports nearby.

Publicity: *New Haven Register, Hartford Courant, Pictorial Gazette, Discover Connecticut, New York Times.*

Certificate may be used: Nov. 1-April 1, Sunday-Thursday.

Clinton
F7

Captain Dibbell House
21 Commerce St
Clinton, CT 06413-2054
(860)669-1646 Fax:(860)669-1646

Circa 1866. Built by a sea captain, this graceful Victorian house is only two blocks from the harbor where innkeeper Ellis Adams used to sail his own vessel. A ledger of household accounts dating from the 1800s is on display, and there are fresh flowers in each guest room.

Innkeeper(s): Helen & Ellis Adams. $65-105. MC VISA PC TC. 4 rooms with PB. Breakfast included in rates. Type of meal: full breakfast. Beds: KQT. Air conditioning, turndown service and ceiling fan in room. Cable TV and bicycles on premises. Antiques, fishing, parks, shopping, theater and watersports nearby.

Location: Exit 63 & I-95, south on Rt. 81 to Rt. 1, east for 1 block, right on Commerce.

Publicity: *Clinton Recorder, New Haven Register, Hartford Courant.*

"This was our first experience with B&Bs and frankly, we didn't know what to expect. It was GREAT!"

Certificate may be used: Sunday through Thursday, holidays, special events weekends and month of October excluded.

Coventry
C7

Maple Hill Farm B&B
365 Goose Ln
Coventry, CT 06238-1215
(860)742-0635 (800)742-0635

Circa 1731. This historic farmhouse still possesses its original kitchen cupboards and a flour bin used for generations. Family heirlooms and the history of the former home owners are shared with guests.

There is a three-seat outhouse behind the inn. Visitors, of course, are provided with modern plumbing, as well as a screened porch and greenhouse in which to relax.

Innkeeper(s): Anthony Felice, Jr. & Marybeth Gorke-Felice. $55-75. MC VISA PC TC. 4 rooms, 1 with PB. Breakfast included in rates. Types of meals: full breakfast and early coffee/tea. Beds: DT. Turndown service in room. VCR, fax, copier, spa, swimming, stables, bicycles and library on premises. Antiques, fishing, parks, shopping, cross-country skiing, sporting events, theater and watersports nearby.

Location: A good stopping point between Boston and New York.

Publicity: *Journal Inquirer, Coventry Journal, Forbes, Hartford Courant, Yankee Traveler.*

"Comfortable rooms and delightful country ambiance."

Certificate may be used: Sunday-Thursday, except holidays, Valentine's Day

Glastonbury C6

Butternut Farm
1654 Main St
Glastonbury, CT 06033-2962
(860)633-7197 Fax:(860)659-1758

Circa 1720. This Colonial house sits on two acres of landscaped grounds amid trees and herb gardens. Prize-winning goats, pigeons, chickens, ducks, pigs and a llama are housed in the old barn on the property. Eighteenth-century Connecticut antiques, including a cherry highboy and cherry pencil-post canopy bed, are placed throughout the inn, enhancing the natural beauty of the pumpkin-pine floors and eight brick fireplaces.
Innkeeper(s): Don Reid. $70-90. AX PC TC. 4 rooms with PB, 3 with FP. 2 suites. Breakfast included in rates. Type of meal: full breakfast. Beds: DT. Air conditioning and VCR in room. Fax on premises. Antiques, fishing, parks, shopping, downhill skiing, cross-country skiing, sporting events and theater nearby.
Location: South of Glastonbury Center, 1.6 miles, 10 minutes to Hartford.
Publicity: *New York Times, House Beautiful, Yankee, Antiques.*
Certificate may be used: Sunday-Thursday, year-round, except holidays.

Ivoryton E7

The Copper Beech Inn
46 Main St
Ivoryton, CT 06442-1004
(860)767-0330 Fax:(860)767-7840

Circa 1887. The Copper Beech Inn was once the home of ivory importer A.W. Comstock, one of the early owners of the Comstock Cheney Company, which produced ivory combs and keyboards. The village took its name from the ivory trade centered here. An enormous copper beech tree shades the property. Each room in the renovated Carriage House boasts a whirlpool bath and French doors opening onto a deck. The wine list and French-country cuisine at the inn's restaurant have received numerous accolades.

Innkeeper(s): Eldon & Sally Senner. $118-196. MC VISA AX DC CB PC TC. 13 rooms with PB. 1 conference room. Breakfast included in rates. Type of meal: continental-plus breakfast. Banquet service available. Restaurant on premises. Beds: KQDT. Air conditioning and TV in room. Library on premises. Handicap access. Antiques, fishing, parks, shopping, theater and watersports nearby.
Location: Lower Connecticut River valley.
Publicity: *Los Angeles Times, Bon Appetit, Connecticut, Travel & Leisure, Discerning Traveler.*

"The grounds are beautiful ... just breathtaking ... accommodations are wonderful."

Certificate may be used: Nov. 1-May 15, Sunday-Thursday. Holidays excluded.

Mystic E9

The Whaler's Inn
20 E Main St
Mystic, CT 06355-2646
(860)536-1506 (800)243-2588 Fax:(860)572-1250

Circa 1901. This classical revival-style inn is built on the historical site of the Hoxie House, the Clinton House and the U.S. Hotel. Just as these famous 19th-century inns offered, the Whaler's Inn has the same charm and convenience for today's visitor to Mystic. Once a booming ship-building center, the town's connection to the sea is ongoing and the sailing schooners still pass beneath the Bascule Drawbridge in the center of town. The inn has indoor and outdoor dining available and more than 75 shops and restaurants are within walking distance.
Innkeeper(s): Richard Prisby. $69-135. MC VISA AX TC. 41 rooms with PB. 1 suite. 1 conference room. Type of meal: early coffee/tea. Dinner, lunch and gourmet lunch available. Restaurant on premises. Beds: KQD. Air conditioning and TV in room. Fax, copier and child care on premises. Handicap access. Antiques, fishing, parks, shopping and watersports nearby.
Certificate may be used: Nov. 26-March 28.

Norfolk A3

Manor House
69 Maple Ave
Norfolk, CT 06058-0447
(860)542-5690 Fax:(860)542-5690

Circa 1898. Charles Spofford, designer of London's subway, built this home with many gables, exquisite cherry paneling and grand staircase. There are Moorish arches and Tiffany windows. Guests can enjoy hot-mulled cider after a sleigh ride, hay ride, or horse and carriage drive along the country lanes nearby. The inn was named by "Discerning Traveler" as Connecticut's most romantic hideaway.

Innkeeper(s): Hank & Diane Tremblay. $85-190. MC VISA AX DS PC TC. 8 rooms with PB, 2 with FP. 1 suite. 1 conference room. Breakfast and afternoon tea included in rates. Types of meals: full breakfast, gourmet breakfast and early coffee/tea. Catering service, catered breakfast and room service available. Beds: KQDT. Ceiling fan in room. Cable TV, fax, computer and library on premises. Antiques, fishing, parks, shopping, downhill skiing, cross-country skiing, sporting events, theater and watersports nearby.

Location: Close to the Berkshires.

Publicity: *Boston Globe, Philadelphia Inquirer, Innsider, Rhode Island Monthly, Gourmet, National Geographic Traveler, Good Housekeeping.*

"Queen Victoria, eat your heart out."

Certificate may be used: Weekdays, excluding holidays and month of October.

North Stonington E9

Antiques & Accommodations

32 Main St
North Stonington, CT 06359-1709
(860)535-1736 (800)554-7829

Circa 1861. Set amongst the backdrop of an acre of herb, edible flower, perennial and cutting gardens, this Victorian treasure offers a romantic location for a weekend getaway. Rooms filled with antiques boast four-poster canopy beds and fresh flowers surrounded by a soft, pleasing decor. Honeymooners or couples celebrating an anniversary are presented with special amenities such as

balloons, champagne and heart-shaped waffles for breakfast. Candlelit breakfasts include unique items such as edible flowers along with the delicious entrees. Historic Mystic Seaport and Foxwood's Casino are just minutes from the inn.

Innkeeper(s): Ann & Tom Gray. $169-229. MC VISA. 5 rooms, 6 with PB. 2 suites. Breakfast included in rates. Type of meal: full breakfast. Beds: Q. Air conditioning, TV and VCR in room. Antiques and fishing nearby.

Publicity: *Country Inns, Woman's Day, New London Day*

"The building's old-fashioned welcome-all decor made us feel comfortable the moment we stepped in."

Certificate may be used: Sunday-Thursday.

Arbor House at Kruger's Old Maine Farm

75 Chester Maine Rd
North Stonington, CT 06359
(860)535-4221 Fax:(860)535-4221

Circa 1900. From this restored, turn-of-the-century farmhouse, guests enjoy a view of Connecticut's coastline and picturesque countryside. Spacious guest rooms are decorated in an uncluttered, country style. The farmhouse is surrounded by 37 acres, which includes a vineyard. The old barn has been converted into a winery. Three-course breakfasts are served each morning in the dining room.

Innkeeper(s): Allen & Michelle Kruger. $75-150. AP. MC VISA PC TC. 4 rooms, 2 with PB. 2 suites. Breakfast and afternoon tea included in rates. Types of meals: full breakfast and early coffee/tea. Beds: Q. Air conditioning, turndown service and TV in room. VCR, fax, stables and pet boarding on premises. Antiques, fishing, parks, shopping, cross-country skiing and watersports nearby.

Certificate may be used: Monday-Thursday, Jan. 15-April 15, Oct. 15-Nov. 7.

Norwalk G2

Silvermine Tavern

194 Perry Ave
Norwalk, CT 06850-1123
(203)847-4558 Fax:(203)847-9171

Circa 1790. The Silvermine consists of the Old Mill, the Country Store, the Coach House and the Tavern itself. Primitive paintings and furnishings, as well as family heirlooms, decorate the inn. Guest rooms and dining rooms overlook the Old Mill, the

waterfall and swans gliding across the millpond. Some guest rooms offer items such as canopy bed or private decks. In the summer, guests can dine al fresco and gaze at the mill pond.
Innkeeper(s): Frank Whitman, Jr. $90-110. MC VISA AX DC CB PC TC. 10 rooms with PB. Breakfast included in rates. Type of meal: continental breakfast. Dinner, lunch and banquet service available. Restaurant on premises. Beds: DT. Air conditioning in room. VCR, fax and copier on premises. Antiques, fishing, parks and shopping nearby.

Publicity: *Advocate, Greenwich Time.*

Certificate may be used: All year except October and no Friday arrivals.

Old Lyme
E8

Bee and Thistle Inn
100 Lyme St
Old Lyme, CT 06371-1426
(860)434-1667 (800)622-4946 Fax:(860)434-3402

Circa 1756. This stately inn is situated along the banks of the Lieutenant River. There are five and one-half acres of trees, lawns and a sunken English garden. The inn is furnished with Chippendale antiques and reproductions. A guitar duo plays in the parlor on Friday, and a harpist performs on Saturday evenings. Bee and Thistle was voted the most romantic inn in the state, the most romantic dinner spot, and for having the best restaurant in the state by readers of "Connecticut Magazine."
Innkeeper(s): Bob, Penny, Lori and Jeff Nelson. $75-215. EP. MC VISA AX DC PC TC. 11 rooms with PB, 1 with FP. 1 cottage. Type of meal: gourmet breakfast. Afternoon tea and lunch available. Restaurant on premises. Beds: KQDT. Air conditioning and ceiling fan in room. Antiques, fishing, parks, shopping, theater and watersports nearby.

Location: Historic district next to Florence Griswold Museum.

Publicity: *Countryside, Country Living, Money, New York, U.S. Air, New York Times, Country Traveler.*

Certificate may be used: Sunday-Thursday, except not Sunday on holiday weekends, excluding July, August, October

Old Mystic
E9

Red Brook Inn
2800 Gold Star Hwy, PO Box 237
Old Mystic, CT 06372-0237
(860)572-0349

Circa 1740. If there was no other reason to visit Old Mystic, a charming town brimming with activities, the Red Brook Inn would be reason enough. The Crary Homestead features two unique rooms, both with working fireplaces, while the Haley Tavern offers guest rooms with canopy beds and fireplaces. Innkeeper Ruth Keyes has selected a beautiful array of antiques to decorate her inn. Guests are sure to enjoy her wonderful authentic Colonial breakfasts. A special winter meal takes three days to complete and she prepares it over an open hearth. In addition to the full breakfasts, afternoon

and evening beverages are provided. The aquarium, Mystic Seaport Museum, a cider mill, casinos and many charming shops are only minutes away.
Innkeeper(s): Ruth Keyes. $95-189. MC VISA AX DS PC TC. 10 rooms with PB, 7 with FP. 3 conference rooms. Breakfast, afternoon tea and evening snack included in rates. Type of meal: full breakfast. Beds: QDT. Air conditioning in room. Cable TV, VCR and library on premises. Amusement parks, antiques, fishing, parks, shopping, sporting events, theater and watersports nearby.

Location: Off route 184 (Gold Star Highway).

Publicity: *Travel & Leisure, Yankee, New York, Country Decorating, Philadelphia Inquirer, National Geographic Traveler, Discerning Traveler.*

"The staff is wonderful. You made us feel at home. Thank you for your hospitality."

Certificate may be used: March 30-Jan. 15, not valid on weekends.

Ridgefield
F2

West Lane Inn
22 West Ln
Ridgefield, CT 06877-4914
(203)438-7323 Fax:(203)438-7325

Circa 1849. This National Register Victorian mansion on two acres features an enormous front veranda filled with white whicker chairs and tables overlooking a manicured lawn. A polished oak staircase rises to a third-floor landing and lounge. Chandeliers, wall sconces and floral wallpapers help to establish an intimate atmosphere. Although the

rooms do not have antiques, they feature amenities such as heated towel racks, extra-thick towels, air conditioning, remote control cable TVs and desks.
Innkeeper(s): Maureen Mayer & Deborah Prieger. $110-165. MC VISA AX DC CB. 20 rooms with PB, 2 with FP. Breakfast included in rates. Type of meal: continental breakfast. Evening snack and room service available. Beds: KQ. Air conditioning and ceiling fan in room. Handicap access. Antiques, fishing, shopping, cross-country skiing and theater nearby.
Publicity: *Stanford-Advocate, Greenwich Times, Home & Away Connecticut.*

"Thank you for the hospitality you showed us. The rooms are comfortable and quiet. I haven't slept this soundly in weeks."

Certificate may be used: Jan. 2-March 30, Sunday through Friday, except holidays.

Salisbury   A2

Under Mountain Inn
482 Under Mountain Rd
Salisbury, CT 06068-1104
(860)435-0242 Fax:(860)435-2379

Circa 1732. Situated on three acres, this was originally the home of iron magnate Jonathan Scoville. A thorned locust tree, believed to be the oldest in Connecticut, shades the inn. Paneling that now adorns the pub was discovered hidden between the ceiling and attic floorboards. The boards were probably placed there in violation of a Colonial law requiring all wide lumber to be given to the king of England. British-born Peter Higginson was happy to reclaim it in the name of the Crown.

*Under Mountain Inn
Salisbury, Connecticut*

Innkeeper(s): Peter & Marged Higginson. $160-195. 7 rooms with PB. Breakfast, afternoon tea and dinner included in rates. Restaurant on premises. Beds: KQD. Air conditioning in room. VCR and fax on premises.
Publicity: *Travel & Leisure, Country Inns, Yankee, Connecticut, Country Accents.*

"You're terrific!"

Certificate may be used: Nov. 30-April 30, Sunday-Thursday.

Sharon   B2

1890 Colonial B&B
Rt 41, PO Box 25
Sharon, CT 06069
(203)364-0436

Circa 1890. Summertime guests can find a cool place to sit on the screened porch of this center-hall Colonial home situated on five park-like acres. Guests visiting in the winter can warm up to any of the main floor fireplaces in the living room, dining room and den. Guest rooms are spacious and have high ceilings. A furnished apartment also is available with private entrance and kitchenette at special weekly rates.
Innkeeper(s): Carole "Kelly" Tangen. $85-109. 3 rooms with PB. 1 suite. Breakfast included in rates. Types of meals: full breakfast and early coffee/tea. Beds: QT. Turndown service, ceiling fan and TV in room. VCR on premises. Antiques, fishing, parks, shopping, downhill skiing, cross-country skiing, theater and watersports nearby.

Certificate may be used: Sunday to Friday, all year, except May-June & September-October and holidays.

Thompson   A10

Hickory Ridge Lakefront B&B
1084 Quaddick Town Farm Rd
Thompson, CT 06277-2929
(203)928-9530

Circa 1990. Enjoy three wooded acres in the private rural setting of this spacious post-and-beam home. The inn's property includes a chunk of the Quaddick Lake shoreline and canoes are available for guests. There's plenty of hiking to do with 17 private acres and access to miles of state lands. Quaddick State Park is within walking or bicycling distance. Breakfasts of baked goods and entrees are served at your convenience.
Innkeeper(s): Birdie Olson. $40-85. 3 rooms, 1 with PB, 1 with FP. 1 suite. Breakfast included in rates. Types of meals: full breakfast and early coffee/tea. Picnic lunch available. Beds: DT. Turndown service in

room. Cable TV, VCR and child care on premises. Antiques, fishing, shopping, cross-country skiing and theater nearby.

Certificate may be used: Sunday through Thursday, July 1-Oct. 30 (except holidays). Anytime Nov. 1-June 30 (except holidays and graduations).

Wethersfield   C6

Chester Bulkley House B&B
184 Main St
Wethersfield, CT 06109-2340
(860)563-4236

Circa 1830. Wide pine floors, hand-carved wood-work, working fireplaces and period pieces enhance the ambiance of this Greek Revival structure. Nestled in the historic village of Old Wethersfield and minutes from downtown Hartford, the inn offers a uniquely comfortable haven for business and holiday travelers. While visiting Hartford, guests may want to take in a performance of the opera, the symphony, the ballet or a Broadway show.

Innkeeper(s): Frank & Sophia Bottaro. $65-85. MC VISA AX DS TC. 12 rooms, 3 with PB. 1 suite. Breakfast included in rates. Types of meals: full breakfast and early coffee/tea. Afternoon tea and room service available. Beds: KQDT. Air conditioning and ceiling fan in room. Cable TV and fax on premises. Antiques, fishing, parks, shopping, downhill skiing, sporting events and theater nearby.

Certificate may be used: Jan. 2-April 30 and Nov. 1-Dec. 30, excluding holidays.

Woodbury   D3

Merryvale B&B
1204 Main St S
Woodbury, CT 06798-3804
(203)266-0800 Fax:(203)263-4479

Circa 1789. Merryvale, an elegant Colonial inn, is situated in a picturesque New England Village, known as an antique capitol of Connecticut. Guests can enjoy complimentary tea, coffee and biscuits throughout the day. A grand living room invites travelers to relax by the fireplace and enjoy a book from the extensive collection of classics and mysteries. During the week, guests enjoy an ample breakfast buffet and on weekends, the innkeepers prepare a Federal-style breakfast using historic, 18th-century recipes.

Innkeeper(s): Gary & Pat Ubaldi Nurnberger. $80-130. MC VISA AX DC. 4 rooms with PB. 2 suites. Breakfast included in rates. Type of meal: full breakfast. Beds: KQT. Air conditioning and TV in room. Amusement parks, antiques, fishing, shopping, downhill skiing and cross-country skiing nearby.

Publicity: *Voices, Yankee Traveler, Hartford Courant, Newtown Bee.*

"Your hospitality will always be remembered."

Certificate may be used: Jan. 7-Feb. 28, Monday-Sunday.

Delaware

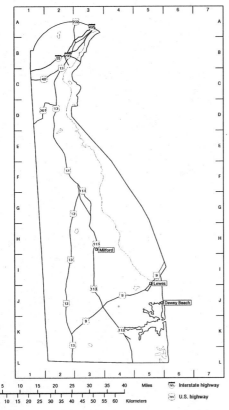

	Interstate highway
	U.S. highway

Dewey Beach   J5

Barry's Gull Cottage B&B
116 Chesapeake St
Dewey Beach, DE 19971
(302)227-7000 Fax:(302)227-7000

Circa 1962. It's only a block to the beach from this Nantucket-style home, which also affords views of a lake. Rooms feature antiques, beds covered in quilts, wicker furnishings and stained glass. The innkeepers pamper guests with treats throughout the day, beginning with a healthy breakfast. Afternoon tea is served, and the evening is topped off with sherry,
port wine, coffee and luscious chocolate cake. Relax in the hot tub illuminated by candlelight. The area offers plenty of shopping, from outlets to antiques, and good restaurants are close to this beach retreat. Innkeeper(s): Vivian & Bob Barry. $75-135. PC TC. 6 rooms. 1 suite. 1 cottage. Breakfast, afternoon tea and evening snack included in rates. Types of meals: full breakfast, gourmet breakfast and early coffee/tea. Beds: KQD. Air conditioning, turndown service, ceiling fan and TV in room. VCR, fax, copier, spa, bicycles and library on premises. Amusement parks, antiques, fishing, parks, shopping, theater and watersports nearby.

Certificate may be used: Monday-Thursday, May-June; after Sept. 15, October.

Lewes   I5

The Bay Moon B&B
128 Kings Hwy
Lewes, DE 19958-1418
(302)644-1802 (800)917-2307 Fax:(302)644-1802

Circa 1887. The exterior of this three-story, cedar Victorian is mysterious and unique. The front veranda is shrouded by the flowers and foliage that decorate the front walk. The custom-made, hand-crafted beds in the guest rooms are topped with feather pillows and down comforters. Cordials are placed in the room and there is a champagne turn-down service. During a nightly cocktail hour, appetizers and wine are served. The innkeeper offers plenty of amenities. Beach supplies and an outdoor shower are helpful for guests who want to enjoy the ocean, which is about one mile from the inn. Innkeeper(s): Laura Beth Kelly. $85-150. EP. MC VISA PC TC. 4 rooms with PB. 1 suite. Breakfast and evening snack included in rates. Types of meals: continental-plus breakfast and early coffee/tea. Beds: KQ. Turndown service, ceiling fan, TV and VCR in room. Fax, library and child care on premises. Handicap access. Antiques, fishing, parks, shopping, sporting events, theater and watersports nearby.

Certificate may be used: Sept. 15-June 15, weekdays Monday-Wednesday only, no holidays.

New Devon Inn
142 2nd St
Lewes, DE 19958-1324
(302)645-6466 (800)824-8754 Fax:(302)645-7196

Circa 1926. In the heart of the historic district, this inn has 24 individually decorated guest rooms. All rooms feature antique beds and turndown service. The inn, which prefers guests over the age of 16, also offers conference facilities, catering and convenient access to antiquing, beaches, dining and sightseeing. Two suites also are available. The shore is just a half-mile from the inn. Prime Hook National Wildlife Refuge and Cape Henlopen State Park are nearby.

Innkeeper(s): Suzanne Steele & Judith Henderson. $65-170. AP. MC VISA AX DC DS TC. 26 rooms with PB. 2 suites. 1 conference room. Type of meal: early coffee/tea. Restaurant on premises. Beds: QDT. Air conditioning and turndown service in room. Cable TV, fax and copier on premises. Handicap access. Antiques, fishing, parks, shopping and watersports nearby.

Publicity: *New York Times, Mid-Atlantic Country, National Geographic.*

Certificate may be used: Year-round, Sunday through Thursday, holidays excluded.

Wild Swan Inn
525 Kings Hwy
Lewes, DE 19958-1421
(302)645-8550 Fax:(302)645-8550

Circa 1900. This Queen Anne Victorian is a whimsical sight, painted in pink with white, green and burgundy trim. The interior is dotted with antiques and dressed in Victorian style. A full, gourmet breakfast and freshly ground coffee are served each morning. The innkeepers have placed many musical treasures in their inn, including an early Edison phonograph and a Victrola. Michael often serenades guests on a 1912 player piano during breakfast. Lewes, which was founded in 1631, is the first town in the first state. Wild Swan is within walking distance of downtown where several fine restaurants await you. Nearby Cape Henlopen State Park offers hiking and watersports, and the surrounding countryside is ideal for cycling and other outdoor activities.

Innkeeper(s): Michael & Hope Tyler. $85-120. PC TC. 3 rooms with PB. Breakfast and evening snack included in rates. Types of meals: gourmet breakfast and early coffee/tea. Beds: Q. Air conditioning and turndown service in room. Swimming, bicycles and library on premises. Antiques, fishing, parks, shopping, theater and watersports nearby.

Publicity: *Washington Post, Country Inns, Delaware Today, Country Collectible, Inn Spots & Special Places CNN Travel Guide.*

"The house is beautiful with lovely detailed pieces. Mike and Hope are gracious hosts. You'll sleep like a baby and wake up to a scrumptious breakfast and a great concert!"

Certificate may be used: Nov. 1-May 1, any day except holidays.

Milford H3

The Towers B&B
101 NW Front St
Milford, DE 19963-1022
(302)422-3814 (800)366-3814

Circa 1783. Once a simple colonial house, this ornate Steamboat Gothic fantasy features every imaginable Victorian architectural detail, all added in 1891. There are 10 distinct styles of gingerbread as well as towers, turrets, gables, porches and bays. Inside, chestnut and cherry woodwork, window seats and stained-glass windows are complemented with American and French antiques. The back garden boasts a gazebo, porch and swimming pool. Ask for the splendid Tower Room or Rapunzel Suite.

Innkeeper(s): Daniel & Rhonda Bond. $95-125. MC VISA. 6 rooms, 4 with PB. 2 suites. Breakfast included in rates. Beds: QD. Air conditioning and ceiling fan in room. Swimming on premises. Antiques, fishing, parks, shopping, theater and watersports nearby.

Location: In the historic district. A short drive to Delaware Bay & the Atlantic Ocean.

Publicity: *Washington Post, Baltimore Sun, Washingtonian, Mid-Atlantic Country.*

"I felt as if I were inside a beautiful Victorian Christmas card, surrounded by all the things Christmas should be."

Certificate may be used: Any night of the week throughout the year.

Florida

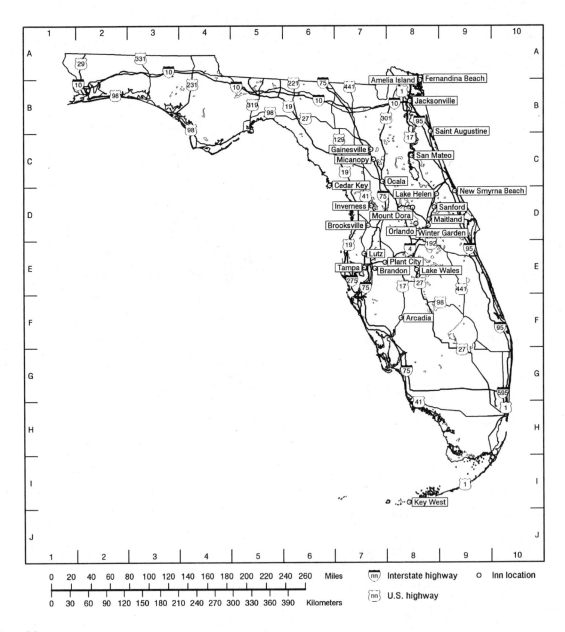

Map legend:
- (nn) Interstate highway
- (nn) U.S. highway
- o Inn location

Scale:
- 0 20 40 60 80 100 120 140 160 180 200 220 240 260 Miles
- 0 30 60 90 120 150 180 210 240 270 300 330 360 390 Kilometers

Amelia Island
B8

Florida House Inn
PO Box 688, 22 S 3rd St
Amelia Island, FL 32034-4207
(904)261-3300 (800)258-3301 Fax:(904)277-3831
E-mail: inkeepers@floridahouseinn.com

Circa 1857. Located in the heart of a 50-block historic National Register area, the Florida House Inn is thought to be the oldest continuously operating tourist hotel in Florida. Recently renovated, the inn features a small pub, a guest parlor, a library and a New Orleans-style courtyard in which guests may enjoy the shade of 200-year-old oaks. Rooms are decorated with country pine and oak antiques, cheerful handmade rugs and quilts. The Carnegies, Rockefellers and Ulysses S. Grant have been guests.
Innkeeper(s): Bob & Karen Warner. $70-130. MC VISA AX. 15 rooms with PB, 10 with FP. 1 suite. 1 conference room. Breakfast included in rates. Types of meals: full breakfast and early coffee/tea. Dinner, picnic lunch, lunch and catering service available. Restaurant on premises. Beds: KQT. Air conditioning, ceiling fan and TV in room. Fax and copier on premises. Handicap access. Antiques, fishing, sporting events and theater nearby.
Publicity: *Amelia Now, Tampa Tribune, Miami Herald, Toronto Star, Country Living, Ft. Lauderdale Sun Sentinel.*
Certificate may be used: Sunday through Thursday.

Arcadia
F8

Historic Parker House
427 W Hickory St
Arcadia, FL 34266-3703
(941)494-2499 (800)969-2499

Circa 1895. Period antiques, including a wonderful clock collection, grace the interior of this turn-of-the-century home, which was built by a local cattle baron. Along with two charming rooms and a bright, "yellow" suite, innkeepers Shelly and Bob Baumann added the spacious Blue Room, which offers a white iron and brass bed and clawfoot bath-

tub. An expanded continental breakfast with pastries, fresh fruits, cereals, muffins and a variety of beverages is offered each morning, and afternoon teas can be prepared on request.
Innkeeper(s): Bob & Shelly Baumann. $60-75. MC VISA AX TC. 4 rooms, 2 with PB, 2 with FP. 1 conference room. Breakfast and afternoon tea included in rates. Types of meals: continental-plus breakfast and early coffee/tea. Room service available. Beds: QDT. Air conditioning, ceiling fan and TV in room. Antiques, fishing, parks, shopping and watersports nearby.
Publicity: *Tampa Tribune, Desoto Sun Herald, Florida Travel & Life, Miami Herald (Palm Beach Edition), WINK-TV News.*

"Everything was first class and very comfortable."
Certificate may be used: May 1 to Dec. 15, Sunday-Friday.

Sandusky Manor B&B
606 E Oak St
Arcadia, FL 34266-4630
(941)494-7338 (800)348-5057 Fax:(941)494-2372
E-mail: d-ccoc@desoto.net

Circa 1913. This bungalow is named for its first resident, Carl Sandusky. The interior is comfortable and eclectic. There are collectibles, photographs, quilts, lanterns and old clocks throughout. Breakfasts with freshly baked biscuits, sweet rolls, fruit and egg dishes are served in the dining room or on the front porch. In the evenings, the innkeepers serve coffee, tea and dessert. Antique shops in historic downtown Arcadia, swamp buggy tours, golf and horseback riding are among the area attractions.
Innkeeper(s): Wayne & Judy Haligus. $65-75. AP. MC VISA AX DC DS TC. 5 rooms, 3 with PB. Breakfast and evening snack included in rates. Types of meals: full breakfast and early coffee/tea. Dinner, picnic lunch and lunch available. Beds: KQDT. Air conditioning, ceiling fan and VCR in room. Fax, bicycles and child care on premises. Antiques, fishing, shopping and golf nearby.

"The southern hospitality you provided was to die for!"
Certificate may be used: Sunday-Thursday, May through October.

Brandon
E7

Behind The Fence B&B Inn
1400 Viola Dr at Countryside
Brandon, FL 33511-7327
(813)685-8201 (800)448-2672

Circa 1976. Experience the charm of New England on Florida's west coast at this secluded country inn surrounded by tall pines and oaks. Although the frame of the home was built in the mid-1970s, the innkeepers searched Hillsborough County for 19th-century and turn-of-the-century artifacts, including old stairs, doors, windows, a pantry and the back porch. Guests can stay either in the main house or in a two-bedroom cottage. All rooms are filled with antique Amish-county furniture. The innkeepers

serve fresh popcorn on cool nights in front of the fireplace. Breakfast includes fresh fruit, cereals, juices, coffees and delicious Amish sweet rolls.
Innkeeper(s): Larry & Carolyn Yoss. $59-79. PC TC. 5 rooms, 3 with PB. 1 suite. 1 cottage. 1 conference room. Breakfast, afternoon tea and evening snack included in rates. Types of meals: continental-plus breakfast and early coffee/tea. Beds: DT. Air conditioning, TV and VCR in room. Swimming on premises. Amusement parks, antiques, fishing, parks, shopping, sporting events, theater and watersports nearby.
Publicity: *Brandon News, Travel Host, Country Living.*

"One of the best kept secrets in all of Tampa! Thanks again!"
Certificate may be used: August-November, Sunday-Thursday.

Brooksville D7

Verona House
201 S Main St
Brooksville, FL 34601-3337
(352)796-4001 (800)355-6717 Fax:(352)799-0612
E-mail: verona@niven.imsweb.net

Circa 1925. In the 1920s, the Verona was one of several styles of homes available to buyers through the Sears-Roebuck catalog. This inn arrived by train along with an instruction book. Obviously, its builder follow the directions, and now guests enjoy this charming Dutch Colonial. There are four rooms inside the house, and the innkeepers also offer a cottage with a kitchen and covered deck. Antique shopping and many outdoor activities are all nearby.
Innkeeper(s): Bob & Jan Boyd. $55-80. MC VISA AX DS PC TC. 4 rooms with PB. 1 cottage. Breakfast included in rates. Types of meals: continental breakfast, continental-plus breakfast, full breakfast and early coffee/tea. Room service available. Beds: QT. Air conditioning and ceiling fan in room. Cable TV, VCR, fax, copier and spa on premises. Handicap access. Antiques, fishing, parks, shopping, golf, theater and watersports nearby.
Certificate may be used: May 1-Sept. 30, Sunday-Thursday.

Cedar Key C6

Island Hotel
2nd & B St
Cedar Key, FL 32625
(352)543-5111

Circa 1859. The history of Island Hotel begins at about the same time as the history of Cedar Key, which was developed in the hopes that the Florida railroad would bring prosperity to the area. After the Civil War, this prosperity was realized for Cedar Key and the Island Hotel's builder Major John Parsons. Current innkeepers Dawn and Tony Cousins have worked to restore the home's traditional charm. Some rooms boast views of the Gulf or Back Bayou. All rooms include access to the inn's

balcony, an ideal spot for relaxation. A gourmet seafood restaurant is located on the premises promising a delightful array of local catch.
Innkeeper(s): Dawn & Tony Cousins. $75-105. MC VISA DS TC. 13 rooms, 11 with PB. Breakfast included in rates. Types of meals: full breakfast and gourmet breakfast. Restaurant on premises. Beds: KQD. Air conditioning and ceiling fan in room. Antiques, fishing, parks, sporting events and watersports nearby.

"A delight! Ernst Hemmingwayish or Humphery Bogartish - what atmosphere!"
Certificate may be used: June 30-Dec. 15, Sunday-Thursday, no holidays or festivals.

Fernandina Beach A8

The Taber House
PO Box 734
Fernandina Beach, FL 32035-0734
(904)261-6391

Circa 1857. This inn offers three suites, all authentic replicas of Victorian architecture, complete with gingerbread woodwork. Fernandina Beach, in

Florida's very northeast corner, boasts a charming historic district, of which the inn's cottages are at the geographic center. The innkeepers, veteran world travelers, have furnished each cottage with just the right touches. Each cottage features one or two queen beds and in-room phones.
Innkeeper(s): Frances Taber. $95-135. 3 suites. Breakfast included in rates. Type of meal: continental-plus breakfast. Beds: Q. Air conditioning, turndown service, TV and VCR in room. Pet boarding on premises. Antiques, fishing, shopping, sporting events, theater and watersports nearby.
Certificate may be used: Anytime.

Gainesville
C7

Magnolia Plantation
309 SE 7th St
Gainesville, FL 32601-6831
(352)375-6653 Fax:(352)338-0303

Circa 1885. This restored French Second Empire Victorian is in the National Register. Magnolia trees surround the house. Six guest rooms are filled with family heirlooms. All bathrooms feature clawfoot tubs and candles. Guests may enjoy the gardens, reflecting pool with waterfalls and gazebo. Bicycles are also available. Evening wine and snacks are included. The inn is two miles from the University of Florida.
Innkeeper(s): Joe & Cindy Montalto. $75-125. AP. MC VISA AX. 5 rooms with PB, 5 with FP. 1 cottage. Breakfast, afternoon tea and evening snack included in rates. Types of meals: full breakfast and early coffee/tea. Beds: Q. Air conditioning, turndown service and ceiling fan in room. Cable TV, VCR, fax, bicycles and library on premises. Antiques, parks, shopping, sporting events and theater nearby.

"This has been a charming, once-in-a-lifetime experience."

Certificate may be used: Sunday-Thursday or June, July, August last minute anytime.

Inverness
D7

Crown Hotel
109 N Seminole Ave
Inverness, FL 34450-4148
(352)344-5555 Fax:(352)726-4040

Circa 1890. This 19th-century inn began its life as a general store. In the 1980s, more than $2 million in renovations transformed it into an elegant hotel. An English ambiance permeates the interior, including replicas of the Crown Jewels, which are on display. Paintings of notable English royals and dignitaries follow guests up the grand staircase. The cozy bedchambers feature romantic Victorian touches, from the furnishings to the flowery wallpapers. There is an inviting pub, the Fox & Hounds, where guests can enjoy a bit of ale and steak and kidney pie. The hotel's restaurant, Churchill's, serves more formal fare. Outside, a double-decker bus provides added decoration. The inn offers a pool, tennis courts and golf courses are nearby. Orlando and Tampa are 20 miles away.

Innkeeper(s): Jill & Nigel Sumner. $70-85. MC VISA AX DC. 34 rooms with PB. 1 suite. 3 conference rooms. Breakfast included in rates. Type of meal: continental-plus breakfast. Afternoon tea, dinner, lunch and banquet service available. Restaurant on premises. Beds: QDT. Air conditioning and TV in room. Fax, copier and swimming on premises. Antiques, fishing, parks, golf and watersports nearby.
Publicity: *Southern Living, Country Inn, Miami Herald.*

Certificate may be used: Based on availability, year-round, not available holidays or Saturdays.

Key West
I8

Duval House
815 Duval St
Key West, FL 33040-7405
(305)294-1666 (800)223-8825 Fax:(305)292-1701

Circa 1890. The Duval House's seven Victorian houses surround a garden and a swimming pool. French doors open onto the tropical gardens. Guests may relax on the balconies. Continental Plus breakfast is served in the pool lounge. Rooms have wicker and antique furniture and Bahamian fans.
Innkeeper(s): Richard Kamradt. $80-260. MC VISA AX DC DS TC. 25 rooms. 4 suites. Breakfast included in rates. Beds: QD. Air conditioning and ceiling fan in room. Swimming on premises. Antiques, fishing, shopping and watersports nearby.
Publicity: *Newsday, Palm Beach Post, Cleveland Plain-Dealer, Roanoke Times, Brides, Vacations.*

"You certainly will see us again."

Certificate may be used: May 1-Dec. 14, Sunday through Thursday only, subject to availability.

Paradise Inn
819 Simonton St
Key West, FL 33040-7445
(305)293-8007 (800)888-9648 Fax:(305)293-0807
E-mail: ssegel3403@aol.com

Circa 1995. Although this inn was constructed recently, its Bahamian architecture is reminiscent of Key West's early days. Rooms are open and spacious, decorated with elegant, contemporary furnishings, such as king-size sleigh beds. Jacuzzi tubs and a bar with a refrigerator are a few of the in-room amenities. There is a fountain-fed pool, Jacuzzi and koi pond on the premises, too. In addition to the modern accommodations, guests also may stay in one of the historic cigar-makers' cottages. The cottages are ideal for families, and each has two bedrooms and two bathrooms. The inn is located in a Key West historic district and is close to the many shops, restaurants and nightclubs on Duval Street.

Innkeeper(s): Shel Segel. $160-495. MC VISA AX DC CB DS TC. 20 rooms with PB. 18 suites. 3 cottages. Breakfast included in rates. Type of meal: continental breakfast. Beds: K. Air conditioning, turndown service, ceiling fan, TV and VCR in room. Fax, copier, spa and swimming on premises. Handicap access. Antiques, fishing, parks, shopping, golf, theater and watersports nearby.

Publicity: *New York Times, Key West Citizen, New Mobility.*

"Your fresh rooms and lovely grounds are truly paradise."

Certificate may be used: June through September, Sunday through Thursday.

Lake Helen   D8

Clauser's B&B
201 E Kicklighter Rd
Lake Helen, FL 32744-3514
(904)228-0310 (800)220-0310 Fax:(904)228-2337
E-mail: clauserinn@totcon.com

Circa 1890. This three-story, turn-of-the-century vernacular Victorian inn is surrounded by a variety of trees in a quiet, country setting. The inn is listed in the national, state and local historic registers, and

offers eight guest rooms, all with private bath. Each room features a different type of country decor, such as Americana, English and prairie. Guests enjoy hot tubbing in the Victorian gazebo or relaxing on the inn's porches, which feature rockers, a swing and cozy wicker furniture. Borrow a bike to take a closer look at the historic district. Stetson University, fine dining and several state parks are nearby.

Innkeeper(s): Tom & Marge Clauser, Janet Watson. $65-120. MC VISA AX DS PC TC. 8 rooms with PB, 1 with FP. Breakfast and evening snack included in rates. Types of meals: full breakfast and early coffee/tea. Beds: KQ. Air conditioning and ceiling fan in room. Cable TV, VCR, fax,

copier, spa, bicycles and library on premises. Handicap access. Amusement parks, antiques, fishing, parks, sporting events, theater and watersports nearby.

Certificate may be used: April 1-Nov. 30, Sunday-Thursday.

Lake Wales   E8

Chalet Suzanne Country Inn & Restaurant
3800 Chalet Suzanne Dr
Lake Wales, FL 33853-7060
(941)676-6011 (800)433-6011 Fax:(941)676-1814

Circa 1924. Situated on 70 acres adjacent to Lake Suzanne, this country inn's architecture includes gabled roofs, balconies, spires and steeples. The superb restaurant has a glowing reputation, and

places of interest on the property include the Swiss Room, Wine Dungeon, Gift Boutique, Autograph Garden, Chapel Antiques, Ceramic Salon, Airstrip and the Soup Cannery. The inn has been transformed into a village of cottages and miniature chateaux, one connected to the other seemingly with no particular order.

Innkeeper(s): Carl & Vita Hinshaw. $139-195. MC VISA AX DC CB DS TC. 30 rooms with PB. Breakfast included in rates. Types of meals: full breakfast and early coffee/tea. Dinner, lunch and room service available. Restaurant on premises. Beds: KDT. Air conditioning, ceiling fan and TV in room. VCR, fax, copier, swimming and library on premises. Handicap access. Amusement parks, antiques, fishing, parks, shopping, sporting events, golf, theater and watersports nearby.

Location: Four miles north of Lake Wales. US Hwy 27 & Chalet Suzanne Rd.

Publicity: *Southern Living, Country Inns, National Geographic Traveler. Uncle Ben's 1992 award.*

"I now know why everyone always says, 'Wow!' when they come up from dinner. Please don't change a thing."

Certificate may be used: All year, Sunday through Thursday nights.

Maitland

D8

Thurston House

851 Lake Ave
Maitland, FL 32751-6306
(407)539-1911 (800)843-2721 Fax:(407)539-0365
E-mail: jball54@aol.com

Circa 1885. Just minutes from busy Orlando and the many attractions found nearby, this classic Queen Anne Victorian inn boasts a lakefront, countryside setting. Two of the inn's screened porches provide views of Lake Eulalia. Two parlors provide additional relaxing spots, and many guests like to stroll the grounds, which feature fruit trees and several bountiful gardens.

Innkeeper(s): Carole Ballard. $100-110. MC VISA AX. 4 rooms with PB. Breakfast and evening snack included in rates. Types of meals: continental-plus breakfast and early coffee/tea. Beds: Q. Air conditioning and ceiling fan in room. Cable TV, VCR, fax, copier and library on premises. Antiques, fishing, parks, shopping, sporting events and theater nearby.

Publicity: *Fort Lauderdale Sun Sentinel, Orlando Sentinel, Florida Living, Country Almanac.*

"Gracious hosts. What a jewel of a place. We couldn't have enjoyed ourselves more!"

Certificate may be used: June 1-Sept. 30, Sunday-Thursday.

Micanopy

C7

Herlong Mansion

402 NE Cholokka Blvd, PO Box 667
Micanopy, FL 32667
(352)466-3322 (800)437-5664 Fax:(352)466-3322

Circa 1845. This mid-Victorian mansion features four two-story carved-wood Roman Corinthian columns on its veranda. The mansion is surrounded by a garden with statuesque old oak and pecan trees. Herlong Mansion features leaded-glass windows, mahogany inlaid oak floors, 12-foot ceilings and floor-to-ceiling windows in the dining room. Guest rooms have fireplaces and are furnished with antiques.

Innkeeper(s): H.C. (Sonny) Howard, Jr. $50-170. MC VISA. 12 rooms with PB, 6 with FP. 4 suites. 2 cottages. 1 conference room. Breakfast and evening snack included in rates. Types of meals: full breakfast and early coffee/tea. Catering service available. Beds: KQD. Air conditioning and ceiling fan in room. Cable TV, VCR, fax, copier and bicycles on premises. Handicap access. Antiques, fishing, parks, sporting events and watersports nearby.

Publicity: *Country Inns, Travel & Leisure, National Geographic Traveler, Southern Living, Florida Living.*

Certificate may be used: May 1-Oct. 1, Sunday-Thursday, other than holidays.

Mount Dora

D8

Magnolia Inn

347 E 3rd Ave
Mount Dora, FL 32757-5654
(352)735-3800 (800)776-2112 Fax:(352)735-0258

Circa 1926. This Mediterranean-style inn in Central Florida offers elegant accommodations to its guests, who will experience the Florida Boom furnishings of the 1920s. Guests will enjoy the convenience of early coffee or tea before sitting down to the inn's full breakfasts. Guests can take a soak

in the inn's spa, relax in the hammock by the garden wall or swing beneath the magnolias. Lake Griffin State Recreational Area and Wekiwa Springs State Park are within easy driving distance. Just an hour from Disneyworld and the other Orlando major attractions, Mount Dora is the antique capital of Central Florida. Known as the Festival City, it is also recommended by "Money" Magazine as the best retirement location in Florida and is the site of Renninger's Winter Antique Extravaganzas. Romantic carriage rides and historic trolley tours of the downtown, two blocks from the inn, are available.

Innkeeper(s): Gerry & Lolita Johnson. $90-160. MC VISA AX PC TC. 4 rooms with PB. Breakfast included in rates. Types of meals: full breakfast and early coffee/tea. Beds: KQT. Air conditioning and ceiling fan in room. Cable TV, VCR, fax, copier and spa on premises. Amusement parks, antiques, fishing, parks, shopping, theater and watersports nearby.

Publicity: *Mount Dora Topic.*

"I love the way you pamper your guests."

Certificate may be used: Sunday through Thursday nights. Certificate good only on regular, full rates ($120).

New Smyrna Beach   D9

Night Swan Intracoastal B&B
512 S Riverside Dr
New Smyrna Beach, FL 32168-7345
(904)423-4940 (800)465-4261 Fax:(904)427-2814
E-mail: nightswanb@aol.com

Circa 1906. From the 140-foot dock at this water-side bed & breakfast, guests can gaze at stars, watch as ships pass or perhaps catch site of dolphins. The turn-of-the-century home is decorated with period furnishings, including an antique baby grand piano,

which guests are invited to use. Several guest rooms afford views of the Indian River, which is part of the Atlantic Intracoastal Waterway. The innkeepers have created several special packages, featuring catered gourmet dinners, boat tours or romantic baskets with chocolate, wine and flowers.
Innkeeper(s): Martha & Chuck Nighswonger. $65-129. MC VISA AX DS TC. 8 rooms with PB. 4 suites. 1 conference room. Breakfast and evening snack included in rates. Types of meals: full breakfast and early coffee/tea. Catering service available. Beds: KQ. Air conditioning, ceiling fan and TV in room. Fax and library on premises. Antiques, fishing, parks, shopping, theater and watersports nearby.
Certificate may be used: June 1-Jan. 30, Sunday-Thursday.

Ocala   C7

Seven Sisters Inn
820 SE Fort King St
Ocala, FL 34471-2320
(352)867-1170 Fax:(352)867-5266

Circa 1888. This highly acclaimed Queen Anne-style Victorian is located in the heart of the town's historic district. In 1986, the house was judged ìBest Restoration Projectî in the state by Florida Trust Historic Preservation Society. Guests may relax on the large covered porches or visit with other guests in the club room. A gourmet breakfast features a different entree daily, which include blueberry French

bread, three-cheese stuffed French toast, egg pesto and raspberry-oatmeal pancakes.
Innkeeper(s): Ken Oden & Bonnie Morehardt. $105-135. 8 rooms with PB, 3 with FP. 4 suites. 1 conference room. Breakfast, afternoon tea and evening snack included in rates. Types of meals: full breakfast, gourmet breakfast and early coffee/tea. Dinner and picnic lunch available. Beds: KQT. Air conditioning, turndown service, ceiling fan and TV in room. Fax and copier on premises. Amusement parks, antiques, fishing, parks, shopping, sporting events, theater and watersports nearby.
Publicity: *Southern Living Feature, Glamour, Conde Nast Traveler, Country Inns (one of twelve best).*
Certificate may be used: Sunday-Thursday, no holidays or weekends.

Orlando   D8

The Courtyard at Lake Lucerne
211 N Lucerne Circle E
Orlando, FL 32801-3721
(407)648-5188 (800)444-5289 Fax:(407)246-1368

Circa 1885. Three different styles of homes comprise this award-winning inn. The Norment-Parry Inn, built in 1885, is Orlando's oldest house and is restored as a Victorian inn complete with American and English antiques. The Wellborn is an example of Art Deco architecture, dates to the 1940s and offers one-bedroom suites including living rooms and kitchenettes. The I. W. Phillips House is an antebellum-style manor house and has three large rooms on the second floor, which overlook the courtyard and fountains below.
Innkeeper(s): Eleanor & Sam Meiner. $75-165. MC VISA AX DC. 24 rooms with PB, 2 with FP. 1 conference room. Breakfast included in

rates. Type of meal: continental-plus breakfast. Beds: KQD. Air conditioning, ceiling fan and TV in room. Copier and computer on premises. Amusement parks, antiques, fishing, shopping, sporting events, theater and watersports nearby.

Publicity: *Florida Historic Homes, Country Inns, Miami Herald, Southern Living, Country Victorian.*

"Best-kept secret in Orlando."

Certificate may be used: June, July, August, subject to availability.

Orlando (Winter Garden)
D8

Meadow Marsh B&B
940 Tildenville School Rd
Orlando (Winter Garden), FL 34787
(407)656-2064 (888)656-2064

Circa 1877. Meadow Marsh is located on 12 acres just outside the quiet village of Winter Garden, an Orlando suburb. One of the town's settlers built the Victorian manor, which is highlighted by verandas

on the first and second stories. The home remained in the original family until the 1980s. Today, guest rooms appear much as they probably did in the 19th century, filled with country Victorian pieces. However, there have been some pleasant additions, including whirlpool tubs in each of the two suites. A three-course breakfast is served, as is afternoon tea. The innkeeper moved her gift shop and tea room to Meadow Marsh in late 1996. The tea room serves luncheons by reservation Wednesday through Saturday.

Innkeeper(s): Cavelle & John Pawlack. $95-199. MC VISA TC. 5 rooms, 2 with PB, 1 with FP. 2 suites. 1 cottage. Breakfast, afternoon tea and evening snack included in rates. Dinner, picnic lunch, lunch and catering service available. Beds: QD. Air conditioning, turndown service and ceiling fan in room. Cable TV, VCR, fax, copier and library on premises. Amusement parks, antiques, parks, sporting events, theater and watersports nearby.

"What a beautiful home with such warm, gracious Southern hospitality."

Certificate may be used: Tuesday, Wednesday, Thursday during June 1-Sept. 30 in either Daisy's Country Corner or Lillian's Victorian Rooms, subject to availability, holidays excluded.

Saint Augustine
B8

Casa de la Paz Bayfront Inn
22 Avenida Menendez
Saint Augustine, FL 32084-3644
(904)829-2915 (800)929-2915

Circa 1915. Overlooking Matanzas Bay, Casa de la Paz was built after the devastating 1914 fire leveled much of the old city. An ornate stucco Mediterranean Revival house, it features clay barrel tile roofing, bracketed eaves, verandas and a lush

walled courtyard. The home is listed in the National Register of Historic Places. Guest rooms offer ceiling fans, central air, hardwood floors, antiques, a decanter of sherry, chocolates and complimentary beverages and snacks.

Innkeeper(s): Bob & Donna Mariott. $79-179. MC VISA AX PC TC. 6 rooms with PB, 1 with FP. Breakfast and afternoon tea included in rates. Types of meals: full breakfast and early coffee/tea. Beds: Q. Air conditioning, ceiling fan and TV in room. Antiques, fishing, parks, shopping, sporting events, theater and watersports nearby.

Publicity: *Innsider, US Air Magazine.*

"We will always recommend your beautifully restored, elegant home."

Certificate may be used: Sunday-Thursday, (holidays and special events excluded) all year, subject to availability.

Castle Garden B&B
15 Shenandoah St
Saint Augustine, FL 32084-2817
(904)829-3839

Circa 1860. This newly-restored Moorish Revival-style inn was the carriage house to Warden Castle. Among the seven guest rooms are three bridal suites with in-room Jacuzzi tubs and sunken bedrooms with cathedral ceilings. The innkeepers offer packages including carriage rides, picnic lunches, gift baskets and other enticing possibilities. Guests enjoy a homemade full, country breakfast each morning.

Innkeeper(s): Bruce & Kimmy Kloeckner. $75-150. MC VISA AX DS. 7 rooms with PB. 3 suites. Breakfast included in rates. Types of meals: full breakfast and early coffee/tea. Picnic lunch available. Beds: KQT. Air conditioning and ceiling fan in room. Cable TV on premises. Antiques, fishing, shopping, golf, theater and watersports nearby.

Certificate may be used: Monday through Thursday. Other times if available.

Old City House Inn & Restaurant
115 Cordova St
Saint Augustine, FL 32084-4413
(904)826-0113 Fax:(904)829-3798

Circa 1873. Saint Augustine is a treasure bed of history and this inn is strategically located in the center. A red-tile roof covers this former stable, and a veranda and courtyard add to the Spanish atmosphere. Gourmet breakfasts are prepared by innkeeper

John Compton, whose recipes have been printed in Food Arts magazine. Inn guests are privy to the expansive breakfasts, but can join others for lunch and dinner in the restaurant. Appetizers include baked brie and Alligator Fritters. For lunch, unique salads, fresh fish and chicken create the menu, while dinner choices include gourmet standards such as Filet Mignon or a more unusual Seafood Strudel.

Innkeeper(s): John & Darcy Compton. $75-150. MC VISA AX DC CB DS. 7 rooms with PB. Breakfast included in rates. Types of meals: full breakfast and early coffee/tea. Dinner and catering service available. Restaurant on premises. Beds: Q. Air conditioning, ceiling fan and TV in room. VCR, fax, copier and bicycles on premises. Handicap access. Antiques, fishing, shopping, theater and watersports nearby.

Location: In the heart of Saint Augustine, within walking distance of all the sights.

Publicity: *Florida Times Union, Florida Trend, Ft. Lauderdale Sun Sentinal.*

Certificate may be used: Sunday-Thursday.

Segui Inn
47 San Marco Ave
Saint Augustine, FL 32084-3276
(904)825-2811 Fax:(904)824-3967

This inn is located on the edge of Saint Augustine's historic district. Marcie's Room features a king bed with handmade wedding-ring quilt, clawfoot tub, Victorian couch and private balcony. Martha Lee's Room boasts a queen bed and daybed in a separate sitting area. The full breakfasts feature homemade bread and jams, and may include George's pancakes or waffles. Be sure to inquire about discounts for senior citizens, members of the military and parents of Flagler College students.

Innkeeper(s): Nikki Lent. $65-110. MC VISA. 4 rooms. 1 suite. Breakfast included in rates. Types of meals: full breakfast and early coffee/tea. Air conditioning and ceiling fan in room. Cable TV and VCR on premises. Antiques, shopping, sporting events and theater nearby.

Certificate may be used: Sunday through Thursday, excluding all holidays.

St. Francis Inn
279 Saint George St
Saint Augustine, FL 32084-5031
(904)824-6068 (800)824-6062 Fax:(904)810-5525
E-mail: innceasd@aug.com

Circa 1791. Long noted for its hospitality, the St. Francis Inn is nearly the oldest house in town. A classic example of Old World architecture, it was built by Gaspar Garcia who received a Spanish grant to the plot of land. Coquina was the main building material. A buffet breakfast is served. Some rooms have whirlpool tubs and fireplaces. The city of Saint Augustine was founded in 1565.

Innkeeper(s): Joseph Finnegan, Jr. $75-175. MC VISA AX PC. 14 rooms, 8 with PB, 4 with FP. 6 suites. 1 cottage. 2 conference rooms. Breakfast included in rates. Type of meal: early coffee/tea. Beds: KQDT. Air conditioning, ceiling fan and TV in room. Fax, copier, swimming and bicycles on premises. Antiques, fishing, parks, shopping, sporting events and watersports nearby.

Location: In the Saint Augustine Historic District, the nation's oldest city.

Publicity: *Orlando Sentinel.*

"We have stayed at many nice hotels but nothing like this. We are really enjoying it."

Certificate may be used: Sunday through Thursday, September through May (excluding holiday periods).

Victorian House B&B
11 Cadiz St
Saint Augustine, FL 32084-4431
(904)824-5214

Circa 1894. Enjoy the historic ambiance of Saint Augustine at this turn-of-the-century Victorian, decorated to reflect the grandeur of that gentile era. The heart-of-pine floors are topped with hand-hooked rugs, stenciling highlights the walls, and the innkeepers have filled the guest rooms with canopy beds and period furnishings. The expanded continental breakfast includes homemade granola, fruit and variety of freshly made breads and muffins.
Innkeeper(s): Daisy Morden. $80-115. MC VISA AX TC. 8 rooms with PB. 2 suites. Breakfast included in rates. Type of meal: continental-plus breakfast. Beds: KQTD. Air conditioning and ceiling fan in room. Cable TV on premises. Antiques, parks, shopping and theater nearby.

Certificate may be used: May-June, Monday-Thursday, except holidays, September-October, Monday-Thursday.

San Mateo   C8

Ferncourt B&B
150 Central Ave, PO Box 758
San Mateo, FL 32187
(904)329-9755

Circa 1889. This Victorian "painted lady," is one of the few remaining relics from San Mateo's heyday in the early 1900s. Teddy Roosevelt once visited the elegant home. The current innkeepers have restored the Victorian atmosphere with rooms decorated with bright, floral prints and gracious furnishings. Awake to the smells of brewing coffee and the sound of a rooster crowing before settling down to a full gourmet breakfast. Historic Saint Augustine is a quick, 25-mile drive.

Innkeeper(s): Jack & Dee Morgan. $55-75. MC VISA PC TC. 6 rooms, 5 with PB. Breakfast included in rates. Types of meals: gourmet breakfast and early coffee/tea. Beds: KQD. Air conditioning and ceiling fan in room. Cable TV, bicycles and library on premises. Handicap access.

Antiques, fishing, parks, shopping, golf and theater nearby.

"First class operation! A beautiful house with an impressive history and restoration. Great company and fine food."

Certificate may be used: Anytime as available, except holiday periods.

Sanford   D8

The Higgins House
420 S Oak Ave
Sanford, FL 32771-1826
(407)324-9238 (800)584-0014 Fax:(407)324-5060

Circa 1894. This inviting blue Queen Anne-style home features cross gables with patterned wood shingles, bay windows and a charming round window on the second floor. Pine floors, paddle fans and a piano in the parlor, which guests are encouraged to play, create Victorian ambiance. The second-story balcony affords views not only of a charming park and Sanford's oldest church, but of Space Shuttle launches from nearby Cape Canaveral. The Queen Anne room looks out over a Victorian box garden, while the Wicker Room features a bay window sitting area. The  Country Victorian room boasts a 19th-century brass bed. Guests also can opt to stay in Cochran's Cottage, which features two bedrooms and baths, a living room, kitchen and porch. Nature lovers will enjoy close access to Blue Spring State Park, Ocala National Forest, Lake Monroe and the Cape Canaveral National Seashore. And of course, Walt Disney World, Seaworld and Universal Studios aren't far away.
Innkeeper(s): Walter & Roberta Padgett. $85-165. MC VISA AX DS PC TC. 3 rooms. 1 cottage. Breakfast and evening snack included in rates. Types of meals: continental-plus breakfast and early coffee/tea. Picnic lunch available. Beds: QD. Air conditioning, turndown service and ceiling fan in room. Cable TV, VCR, spa and bicycles on premises. Antiques, fishing, parks, shopping and watersports nearby.
Location: In the historic district.
Publicity: *Southern Living, Sanford Herald, Connecticut Traveler, LifeTimes, Orlando Sentinel, Southern Accents, Country Inns, Florida Living.*

"The Higgins House is warm and friendly, filled with such pleasant sounds, and if you love beauty and nature, you're certain to enjoy the grounds."

Certificate may be used: Sunday-Thursday.

Tampa E7

Gram's Place
3109 N Ola Ave
Tampa, FL 33603-5744
(813)221-0596 Fax:(813)221-0596

Circa 1945. These two cottages offer a variety of amenities, including lush grounds with a Jacuzzi, waterfall, sundeck and courtyard. The innkeepers named their relaxing home after singer Gram Parsons. The home and comfortable guest rooms feature a mix of European and modern decor with a few simple, country touches. The home is just a few miles from downtown Tampa.

Innkeeper(s): Mark Holland. $55-75. MC VISA AX TC. 7 rooms, 4 with PB. Breakfast included in rates. Types of meals: continental breakfast and continental-plus breakfast. Beds: QF. Air conditioning, ceiling fan, TV and VCR in room. Fax and spa on premises. Amusement parks, antiques, fishing, parks, shopping, sporting events, theater and watersports nearby.

Certificate may be used: Monday-Wednesday, June to August.

Georgia

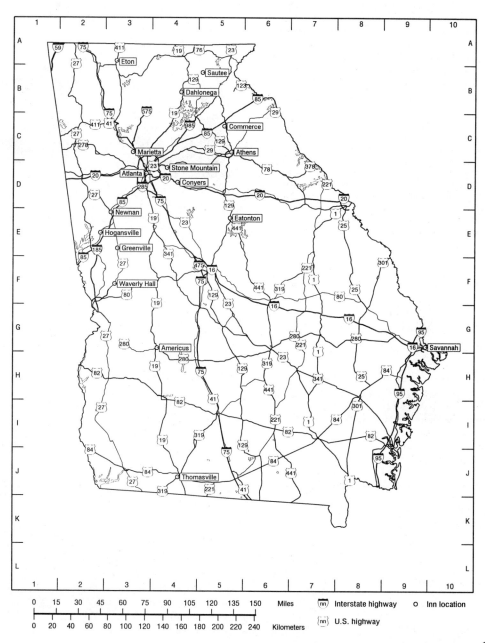

	Miles			○ Inn location

0 15 30 45 60 75 90 105 120 135 150   Miles

0 20 40 60 80 100 120 140 160 180 200 220 240   Kilometers

(nn) Interstate highway   ○ Inn location

{nn} U.S. highway

101

Americus
G4

1906 Pathway Inn B&B

501 S Lee St
Americus, GA 31709-3919
(912)928-2078 (800)889-1466 Fax:(912)928-2078

Circa 1906. This turn-of-the-century inn is located along the Andersonville Trail and not far from the city of Andersonville, a Civil War village. The gracious, wraparound porch is a perfect spot for relaxation. The innkeepers plan the breakfast times around their guests' schedules, serving up a country breakfast with freshly baked breads. The guest rooms offer romantic amenities such as whirlpools and snug down comforters. Two of the rooms are named in honor of Jimmy and Rosalynn Carter, whose hometown is just a short distance down the road. Late afternoons are reserved for wine and refreshments.
Innkeeper(s): Sheila & David Judah. $70-117. MC VISA AX DS PC TC. 5 rooms with PB, 2 with FP. Breakfast included in rates. Types of meals: gourmet breakfast and early coffee/tea. Evening snack and room service available. Beds: KQ. Air conditioning, turndown service, ceiling fan, TV and VCR in room. Fax and copier on premises. Antiques, parks and theater nearby.
Certificate may be used: Dec. 1-Jan. 20, Sunday-Saturday; March 1-31, Sunday-Saturday; Year-round Sunday-Friday, special event dates exempt.

Athens
C5

The Nicholson House

6295 Jefferson Rd
Athens, GA 30607-1714
(706)353-2200

This unique home was built as a two-story log dwelling in the early 19th century, and it served as a stagecoach stop on Old Federal Road. In 1947, an extensive restoration by J.P. Nicholson altered the home into a Colonial Revival manor built around the log structure. The six-acre grounds boasts natural springs and a nature walk, and the innkeepers offer a rocking chair porch for relaxation.
Innkeeper(s): Stuart Kelley. $75-105. MC VISA AX DS. 5 rooms. Breakfast included in rates. Type of meal: continental-plus breakfast.
Certificate may be used: All periods except peak times i.e. event weekends, football home games, and bike races.

Atlanta
D3

Beverly Hills Inn

65 Sheridan Dr NE
Atlanta, GA 30305-3121
(404)233-8520 (800)331-8520 Fax:(404)233-8659
E-mail: mit-bhi@mindspring.com

Circa 1929. Period furniture and polished-wood floors decorate this inn located in the Buckhead

neighborhood. There are private balconies, kitchens and a library with a collection of newspapers and books. The governor's mansion, Neiman-Marcus, Saks and Lord & Taylor are five minutes away.
Innkeeper(s): Mit Amin. $90-160. MC VISA AX DC DS PC TC. 18 suites. Breakfast included in rates. Type of meal: continental-plus breakfast. Beds: QD. Air conditioning and TV in room. Antiques, parks and shopping nearby.
Location: North on Peachtree 15 minutes then one-half block off Peachtree.
Publicity: *Country Inns, Southern Living, Time.*

"Our only regret is that we had so little time. Next stay we will plan to be here longer."

Certificate may be used: Anytime, subject to availability.

The Gaslight Inn B&B

1001 St Charles Ave NE
Atlanta, GA 30306-4221
(404)875-1001 Fax:(404)876-1001
E-mail: innkeeper@gaslightinn.com

Circa 1913. Flickering gas lanterns outside, original gas lighting inside and five working fireplaces add to the unique quality of this inn. Beautifully appointed
guest rooms offer
individual decor.
The Ivy Cottage is a
romantic bungalow
with a living room
and kitchen. The
regal English Suite
boasts a four-poster
bed covered in rich

blue hues and a private deck. The Rose Room features a fireplace and four-poster bed covered with lace. Located in the Virginia Highlands neighborhood, the inn is approximately five minutes from downtown and is served by Atlanta's public transportation system.

Innkeeper(s): Jim Moss, Shannon DeLaney. $95-195. MC VISA AX DS PC TC. 6 rooms with PB, 3 with FP. 3 suites. 2 cottages. 1 conference room. Breakfast included in rates. Types of meals: continental-plus breakfast and early coffee/tea. Beds: KQ. Air conditioning, ceiling fan, TV and VCR in room. Fax, copier, spa, sauna and library on premises. Handicap access. Amusement parks, antiques, parks, shopping, sporting events and theater nearby.

Publicity: *Travel Channel.*

"Best B&B I've ever stayed in."

Certificate may be used: Jan. 1-Feb. 1, Monday-Thursday.

King-Keith House B&B

889 Edgewood Ave NE
Atlanta, GA 30307

(404)688-7330 Fax:(404)584-0730

Circa 1890. This beautifully restored and preserved Queen Anne Victorian features many wonderful elements, including a whimsical chimney that vividly declares "1890," the year the home was built. Inside, the hardwood floors and intricate woodwork glisten. Walls are painted in deep, rich hues and antiques fill the rooms. Marble-topped tables and delicate love seats decorate the parlor. Each guest room is special, and beds are topped with luxury linens. One room is lit by a colorful stained-glass window, another features a Victorian dollhouse. The opulent home is located in an Atlanta historic district listed in the National Register. It's just two blocks from the subway station.

Innkeeper(s): Jan & Windell Keith. $50-125. MC VISA AX PC TC. 5 rooms, 2 with PB, 1 with FP. 1 suite. Breakfast included in rates. Types of meals: full breakfast, gourmet breakfast and early coffee/tea. Afternoon tea, catering service and room service available. Beds: KQDT. Air conditioning, ceiling fan and TV in room. Fax and child care on premises. Amusement parks, antiques, parks, shopping, sporting events, golf and theater nearby.

Certificate may be used: Sunday through Thursday (five days), all year.

Oakwood House B&B Inn

951 Edgewood Ave Ne
Atlanta, GA 30307-2582

(404)521-9320 Fax:(404)688-6034

E-mail: oakwoodbnb@aol.com

Circa 1911. This post-Victorian house has seen duty as a boarding house, travel agency and psychologists' offices. The inviting interior includes original moldings, stained glass, exposed brick and traditional furnishings. A mantel, which once graced an old-style movie theater, now makes its home at the inn. Bookworms will appreciate the innkeepers' large collection of books. The inn, located in Atlanta's charming Inman Park Historic District, is full of beautiful old homes. Guests are only a few minutes from the World Congress Center, stadiums, Underground Atlanta and shopping in exclusive Buckhead. The Jimmy Carter Library and Martin Luther King Jr. Tomb also are nearby. A subway station is only one a one half blocks away.

Innkeeper(s): Judy & Robert Hotchkiss. $75-175. MC VISA AX DS PC TC. 5 rooms with PB, 1 with FP. 1 suite. 2 conference rooms. Breakfast included in rates. Types of meals: continental-plus breakfast and early coffee/tea. Beds: KQT. Air conditioning, turndown service and ceiling fan in room. Fax, copier and library on premises. Handicap access. Amusement parks, antiques, parks, shopping, sporting events and theater nearby.

Location: Two miles east of downtown.

Publicity: *CBS, Style, Inn Times, Los Angeles Times, Men's Journal, Women's Health & Fitness, Style, Inn Times*

"Thanks for such a wonderful time! It was a delight to be in a neighborhood instead of a downtown conference hotel. MARTA access made it possible"

Certificate may be used: Sunday-Thursday if available; some holidays and special events excluded.

Commerce   C5

The Pittman House B&B

81 Homer Rd
Commerce, GA 30529-1806

(706)335-3823

Circa 1890. An hour's drive from Atlanta is this four-square Colonial inn, found in the rolling hills of Northeast Georgia. The inn has four guest rooms, furnished in antiques. The surrounding area offers many activities, including Lake Lanier, Lake

Hartwell, Hurricane Shoals, Crawford W. Long Museum, an outlet mall, a winery and a championship golf course. Innkeeper Tom Tomberlin, a woodcarver, has items for sale in an antique shop next to the inn.

Innkeeper(s): Tom & Dot Tomberlin. $55-65. MC VISA PC TC. 4 rooms, 2 with PB. Breakfast included in rates. Types of meals: full breakfast and early coffee/tea. Beds: D. Air conditioning and ceiling fan in room. Cable TV and VCR on premises. Antiques, fishing, parks, shopping, sporting events and watersports nearby.

Certificate may be used: Sunday through Thursday.

Conyers   D4

The Haynes Ridge Inn
2280 Costley Mill Rd
Conyers, GA 30013
(770)922-9151 Fax:(770)922-9236
E-mail: raw@520.com

Circa 1987. This comfortable ranch house offers four guest rooms, each decorated in country style. The home is surrounded by 16 acres, and in season, guests have use of the swimming pool. On the weekends, the innkeepers serve a hearty country breakfast with items such as baked French toast, fresh fruit and homemade muffins. The inn is near a golf course, the Georgia International Horse Park, and historic sites.

Innkeeper(s): Georgianna Wilk. $95. MAP. MC VISA PC TC. 4 rooms with PB. Breakfast, afternoon tea and evening snack included in rates. Types of meals: full breakfast and early coffee/tea. Beds: Q. Air conditioning, turndown service and ceiling fan in room. VCR, fax, swimming, library and child care on premises. Amusement parks, fishing, parks, shopping, sporting events and golf nearby.

"Haven't relaxed like this in ages! Your home and hospitality were delightful."

Certificate may be used: Year-round, based on availability.

Dahlonega   B4

Cavender Castle Winery
Hwy19/60 at Crisson Gold Mine
Dahlonega, GA 30533
(706)864-4759

This gothic-inspired castle is also home to a winery, and offers easy access to the many attractions of North Georgia's mountain country, including the Dahlonega Gold Museum. The inn sits atop Gold Hill, overlooking nine vine-covered acres. The Chardonnay Room boasts a mountain view and queen bed. Guests are welcome to play croquet or horseshoes, relax in the library, sample a taste of the Cavender's wines or explore the vineyards and gardens. The gourmet breakfast is served by candlelight.

Innkeeper(s): Linda Phillips. $65-85. MC VISA. 4 rooms. Breakfast included in rates. Types of meals: full breakfast and early coffee/tea. Dinner, picnic lunch, catering service and room service available. Air conditioning and ceiling fan in room. Antiques, shopping and theater nearby.

Certificate may be used: November through April.

Worley Homestead Inn
168 Main St W
Dahlonega, GA 30533-1640
(707)864-7002

Circa 1845. Four blocks from the historic town square is this beautiful old Colonial Revival inn. Several guest rooms are equipped with fireplaces, adding to the romantic atmosphere and Victorian ambiance. All the rooms feature antique beds. A popular spot for honeymooners and couples celebrating anniversaries, many guests take advantage of Dahlonega's proximity to the lures of the Chattahoochee National Forest.

Innkeeper(s): Bill & Francis. $75-85. MC VISA. 8 rooms. Breakfast included in rates. Types of meals: full breakfast and early coffee/tea. Air conditioning and TV in room. Antiques and shopping nearby.

Certificate may be used: January through March, excluding holidays and special events.

Eatonton   E5

The Crockett House
671 Madison Rd
Eatonton, GA 31024-7830
(706)485-2248

Circa 1895. This 19th-century home is an alluring stop on the historic Antebellum Trail, which stretches from Athens to Macon. The sisters who built the home lived there without electricity or plumbing until the 1970s. Today, however, the home features these modern conveniences, but still maintains old-fashioned charm. Several guest rooms offer the added amenity of fireplaces. The balcony and wraparound porches are scenic places to relax.

Innkeeper(s): Christa & Peter Crockett. $65-95. MC VISA AX PC TC. 6 rooms with PB, 4 with FP. Breakfast included in rates. Types of meals: full breakfast, gourmet breakfast and early coffee/tea. Afternoon tea, dinner, picnic lunch, lunch, gourmet lunch, catering service and catered breakfast available. Beds: KQD. Air conditioning, ceiling fan and TV in room. VCR and library on premises. Antiques, fishing, parks, shopping, sporting events, theater and watersports nearby.

Certificate may be used: Sunday through Thursday, January, February, March, & August, excluding special events and based on availability.

Eton
A3

Ivy Inn B&B
245 Fifth Ave E
Eton, GA 30724
(912)517-0526 (800)201-5477 Fax:(912)517-0526

Circa 1908. Dr. S.A. Brown, an Eton town founder, built this country home, and the house has changed hands only four times in its near-century of existence. There are three guest rooms, each with its own personality. The Woodbine includes the home's rustic original beaded board walls and ceiling. Another room, the Needlepoint, is full of its namesake works and affords a view of Grassy Mountain. Regional dishes, such as grits and Southern tomato pie accompany fresh fruits, muffins and other treats on the breakfast table. The area offers a variety of activities, from horseback riding to hiking or shopping.

Innkeeper(s): Gene & Juanita Twiggs. $87. MC VISA AX PC. 3 rooms with PB. Breakfast and evening snack included in rates. Types of meals: full breakfast and early coffee/tea. Beds: TD. Air conditioning and TV in room. Fax, copier, bicycles and library on premises. Antiques, fishing, parks, golf, theater and watersports nearby.

Publicity: *Dalton Daily Citizen, Georgia Journal, Chattanooga Free Press.*

"The service was incredible and the stay was very pleasant. We love your inn and your gracious hospitality."

Certificate may be used: Nov. 15-March 31.

Greenville
E3

Samples Plantation
15380 Roosevelt Hwy
Greenville, GA 30222
(706)672-4765 Fax:(706)672-9966

Circa 1832. The romance of the South lives on at this Antebellum mansion. The manor originally was part of the Render Plantation, and among the Render family were a Georgia governor, a congressman and a Supreme Court justice. Each guest room has been individually decorated with antiques, lace, satin and romance in mind. Guests are pampered with a homemade plantation-style breakfast. Shopping and other attractions, including Franklin Roosevelt's Little White House, are nearby. Atlanta is 50 miles away, and Callaway Gardens are 17 miles away.

Innkeeper(s): Marjorie Samples. $149-289. MC VISA PC TC. 7 suites, 6 with FP. Breakfast, afternoon tea, evening snack and picnic lunch included in rates. Types of meals: full breakfast and early coffee/tea. Beds: KQDT. Air conditioning, turndown service and ceiling fan in room. Cable TV, VCR, fax, copier, bicycles and library on premises. Amusement parks, antiques, fishing, parks, shopping, sporting events, theater and watersports nearby.

Publicity: *Columbia Ledger, Atlanta Journal.*

Certificate may be used: Sunday through Wednesday, January through May 30.

Hogansville
E2

Fair Oaks Inn
703 E Main St
Hogansville, GA 30230-1509
(706)637-8828

Circa 1901. This turn-of-the-century Victorian home is on the site of an original 1835 plantation. Each bedroom has a fireplace with authentic period mantels. There are a series of formal gardens with a swimming pool, and gazebo, lattice-covered swings and eight converted New Orleans street lights. The master suite has two fireplaces, a sitting room, bedroom with private bath, steam room and Jacuzzi. Breakfast is served in the formal dining room or on the sun porch.

Innkeeper(s): Ken Hammock & Wayne Jones. $75-125. MC VISA AX DC CB DS TC. 6 rooms, 2 with PB, 6 with FP. 2 suites. Breakfast included in rates. Type of meal: gourmet breakfast. Beds: KQ. Air conditioning and ceiling fan in room. Cable TV, VCR and bicycles on premises. Antiques and fishing nearby.

Certificate may be used: Sept. 15-April 1, Sunday-Thursday.

Marietta
C3

Whitlock Inn
57 Whitlock Ave
Marietta, GA 30064-2343
(770)428-1495 Fax:(770)919-9620

Circa 1900. This cherished Victorian has been restored and is located in a National Register Historic District, one block from the Marietta Square. Amenities even the Ritz doesn't provide are in every room, and you can rock on the front verandas. An afternoon snack also is served. There is a ballroom grandly suitable for weddings and business meetings.

Innkeeper(s): Alexis Edwards. $100. MC VISA AX DS. 5 rooms with PB. 3 conference rooms. Breakfast included in rates. Type of meal: continental-plus breakfast. Beds: KQT. Air conditioning, ceiling fan and TV in room. Fax and copier on premises. Amusement parks, antiques, parks, shopping, sporting events and theater nearby.

Publicity: *Marietta Daily Journal.*

"This is the most beautiful inn in Georgia and I've seen nearly all of them."

Certificate may be used: All year, Sunday-Thursday, not available on weekends.

Newnan
E3

Parrott Camp Soucy Home & Gardens

155 Greenville St
Newnan, GA 30263-2630
(404)502-0676 Fax:(404)253-4846

Circa 1884. Victorian touches were added to this stunning Second Empire home completing its wonderful exterior by 1886. Current innkeepers Helen and Rick Cousins patterned the interior after the famed Biltmore House, with its elegant, yet comfortable furnishings. Each unique room is filled with bright patterns, luxurious canopied beds and period antiques. Dark woodwork and high ceilings accent the decor. Guest quarters boast special amenities such as fireplaces, sitting areas, terrycloth robes and soft fluffy towels for guests who wish to relax in the spa or pool. For those preferring a soak in the tub, the Cousins provide bathtub pillows and bath foams. The library, which features a columned fireplace, includes a collection of books, classical music and classic movies. A full breakfast is served either in the dining room or on the veranda, which overlooks the home's four acres of gardens.

Innkeeper(s): Helen & Rick Cousins. $95-165. MC VISA. 4 rooms with PB. Breakfast included in rates. Type of meal: full breakfast. Afternoon tea available. Beds: Q. Antiques and theater nearby.

Publicity: *Atlanta Constitution.*

"Our weekend was absolutely delightful. It was extremely enjoyable to be totally pampered by both of you. All the elegant touches throughout the house and the warm conversations with you were appreciated. We'll be back, we loved it."

Certificate may be used: January through April, Sunday - Thursday.

Southern Comfort B&B Inn

66 La Grange St
Newnan, GA 30263-2649
(770)254-9266 (800)818-0066

Circa 1880. Grand columns and a second-story portico grace the exterior of this Greek Revival home, as well as a wraparound veranda on the first story. The home was built by John Simms, who served in the state legislature and as a calvary captain during the Civil War. The four guest rooms are antique-filled and feature items such as clawfoot tub

or perhaps a canopy bed. In the morning, a hearty Southern breakfast is prepared. Guests can walk to shops and restaurants.

Innkeeper(s): Barbara Waldrop & Lawrence Opal. $75-90. MC VISA AX DS PC TC. 4 rooms, 2 with PB, 4 with FP. Breakfast and evening snack included in rates. Types of meals: full breakfast and early coffee/tea. Room service available. Beds: QD. Air conditioning, turndown service, ceiling fan and TV in room. VCR, fax and bicycles on premises. Handicap access. Antiques, parks, shopping, sporting events and watersports nearby.

"A beautiful home with a character of its own."

Certificate may be used: Feb. 1-June 1 and Aug. 10-Dec. 31, Sunday-Saturday (all week).

Sautee
B5

The Stovall House

1526 Hwy 255 N
Sautee, GA 30571
(706)878-3355

Circa 1837. This house, built by Moses Harshaw and restored in 1983 by Ham Schwartz, has received two state awards for its restoration. The handsome farmhouse has an extensive wraparound porch providing vistas of 28 acres of cow pastures, meadows

and creeks. High ceilings, polished walnut woodwork and decorative stenciling provide a pleasant backdrop for the inn's collection of antiques. Victorian bathroom fixtures include pull-chain toilets and pedestal sinks. The inn has its own restaurant.

Innkeeper(s): Ham Schwartz. $68-80. MC VISA PC TC. 5 rooms with PB. Breakfast included in rates. Type of meal: continental breakfast. Dinner and catering service available. Restaurant on premises. Beds: KQDT. Air conditioning and ceiling fan in room. Library on premises. Amusement parks, antiques, fishing, parks, shopping, theater and watersports nearby.

Publicity: *Atlanta Journal.*

"Great to be home again. Very nostalgic and hospitable."

Certificate may be used: November through September, Sunday through Thursday.

Savannah   G9

Broughton Street Bed & Breakfast
511 E Broughton St
Savannah, GA 31401-3501
(912)232-6633 Fax:(912)232-6633
E-mail: savbnb@aol.com

Circa 1883. This historic Victorian townhouse offers two guest rooms. Each is decorated with Victorian furnishings, antiques and contemporary artwork. One room includes a Jacuzzi tub and a fireplace. In the afternoons, the innkeepers serve hors d'oeuvres to their guests. Breakfasts feature such items as quiche, homemade Amish bread and fresh fruit.

Innkeeper(s): Tonya & JP Saleeby. $125-165. MC VISA AX DS PC TC. 2 rooms with PB, 1 with FP. Breakfast, afternoon tea and evening snack included in rates. Type of meal: continental-plus breakfast. Beds: Q. Air conditioning, turndown service, ceiling fan, TV and VCR in room. Fax, copier, bicycles and library on premises. Antiques, fishing, parks, shopping, sporting events, golf, theater and watersports nearby.

"Our stay was so romantic, we're rejuvenated and ready to take on the world!"

Certificate may be used: June 1-Aug. 30, Sunday-Thursday, Tanner Room only.

Stone Mountain   D4

The Village Inn B & B
992 Ridge Ave
Stone Mountain, GA 30083-3676
(770)469-3459 (800)214-8385 Fax:(770)469-1051

Circa 1850. This city historic site was built as hotel, but served as a Confederate hospital during the Civil War. Rooms are decorated with period antiques and in a nostalgic country style that will take guests back in time to the mid-19th century. Although the inn has a decidedly historic feel, two of the guest rooms offer a whirlpool tub. The spacious Ballroom Suite includes a refrigerator, coffee maker, TV and VCR. Southern-style breakfasts are served, popular regional fare such as cheese grits or freshly baked buttermilk biscuits are a staple. Ask any resident of Atlanta, and they are sure to place a visit to Stone Mountain at the top of the sightseeing list. There are shops to explore in this charming village, and guests can walk or ride a tram up to the top of the mountain for a memorable view. The many attractions of Atlanta are nearby, as well.

Innkeeper(s): Rob & Deandra Bailey. $75-125. MC VISA AX DS PC TC. 6 rooms, 5 with PB, 1 with FP. 1 suite. Breakfast and early coffee/tea. Types of meals: full breakfast and early coffee/tea. Beds: KQDT. Air conditioning, turndown service, ceiling fan, TV and VCR in room. Fax on premises. Handicap access. Amusement parks, antiques, fishing, parks, shopping, sporting events, golf and theater nearby.

Publicity: *Southern Living, Campus Live, Inn Route*
Certificate may be used: Nov. 1-March 31, Monday-Friday, subject to availability.

Thomasville   J4

Serendipity Cottage
339 E Jefferson St
Thomasville, GA 31792-5108
(912)226-8111 (800)383-7377 Fax:(912)226-2656

Circa 1906. A wealthy Northerner hand picked the lumber used to build this four-square house for his family. The home still maintains its original oak pocket doors and leaded-glass windows. The decor in guest rooms ranges from Victorian with antiques to rooms decorated with wicker furnishings. Honeymooners will find a bottle of champagne placed in the room. Breakfasts are hearty and made from scratch, including freshly baked breads and homemade jams. The home is located in a neighborhood of historic houses, and guests can take a walking or driving tour of the town's many historic sites.

Innkeeper(s): Kathy & Ed Middleton. $75. PC TC. 3 rooms with PB, 2 with FP. Breakfast included in rates. Types of meals: continental breakfast, full breakfast and early coffee/tea. Beds: QD. Air conditioning, turndown service, ceiling fan, TV and VCR in room. Bicycles on premises. Antiques, fishing, parks, shopping, sporting events and theater nearby.

"Thank you for the wonderful weekend at Serendipity Cottage. The house is absolutely stunning and the food delicious."

Certificate may be used: June 1-Sept. 30, Sunday-Friday.

Waverly Hall   F3

Raintree Farms of Waverly Hall
8060 Ga Hwy 208
Waverly Hall, GA 31831
(706)582-3227 (800)433-0627 Fax:(706)582-3227

Circa 1833. Although it now rests on three acres, this early 19th-century home was once part of a large plantation and was later moved to its present location. The grounds include a small lake and a garden. The home is decorated in traditional style with some antiques. In the mornings, items such as almond-orange French toast or eggs and bacon are served.

Innkeeper(s): Sandra R. Lee. $85-100. DS PC TC. 4 rooms, 3 with PB, 4 with FP. Breakfast and afternoon tea included in rates. Types of meals: full breakfast and gourmet breakfast. Beds: QDT. Air conditioning, turndown service and ceiling fan in room. Cable TV, VCR, fax and library on premises. Antiques, fishing, parks, shopping, sporting events, golf, theater and watersports nearby.

Certificate may be used: Anytime subject to availability.

Hawaii

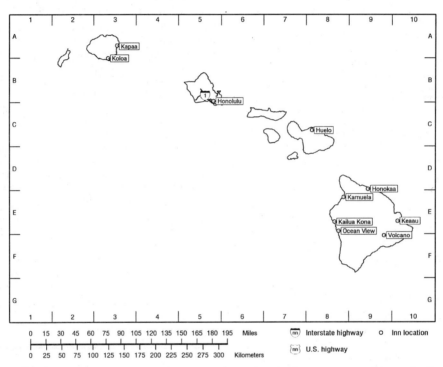

1	2	3	4	5	6	7	8	9	10	
A			Kapaa							A
			Koloa							
B					Honolulu					B
C							Huelo			C
D								Honokaa		D
E						Kamuela			E
						Kailua Kona	Keaau		
						Ocean View	Volcano		
F										F
G										G
	1	2	3	4	5	6	7	8	9	10

0 15 30 45 60 75 90 105 120 135 150 165 180 195 Miles   ⓝ Interstate highway   ○ Inn location

0 25 50 75 100 125 150 175 200 225 250 275 300 Kilometers   ⟨ⁿⁿ⟩ U.S. highway

Honokaa   D9

Hale Kukui
PO Box 5044
Honokaa, HI 96727-5044
(808)775-7130 (800)444-7130 Fax:(808)775-7130
Circa 1992. From the four-acre grounds that surround this snug cottage, guests can take in a 20-mile
view of spectacular Hawaii coastline. The grounds
feature a stream and a variety of tropical foliage,
including palms, plantains, bamboo and African
tulip trees. During the early months of the year,
humpback whales choose the waters below as a spot
to frolic. Half of the cottage is devoted to a two-
bedroom suite, which features a living room, kitchenette, bathroom and private lanai. The other section encompasses a studio unit, a compact version of
the suite. These rooms can be combined for larger

108

parties. As the nearest store is several miles away,
the hosts provide a variety of continental fare for
the first morning's stay.
Innkeeper(s): Bill & Sarah McCowatt. $85-125. PC TC. 2 suites. 1 cot-
tage. Beds: Q. Ceiling fan and VCR in room. Fax and swimming on
premises. Handicap access. Fishing, parks and watersports nearby.
Certificate may be used: March 15-Dec. 15, all week.

Honolulu   B5

The Manoa Valley Inn
2001 Vancouver Dr
Honolulu, HI 96822-2451
(808)947-6019 (800)535-0085 Fax:(808)946-6168
E-mail: marc@aloha.net
Circa 1915. This exquisite home offers the best of
two worlds, a beautiful, country home surrounded by
a tropical paradise. Each restored room features lavish
decor with ornate beds, ceiling fans and period furni-

ture. Little amenities such as the his and her robes create a romantic touch. Breakfasts with kona coffee, juices and fresh fruits are served, and after a day of sightseeing, evening wine and cheese are served. The inn's common rooms offer unique touches such as nickelodeon and antique Victrola. The Manoa Valley is a perfect location to enjoy Hawaii and is only blocks away from the University of Hawaii.

Innkeeper(s): Herb Fukushima. $99-199. MC VISA AX DC TC. 8 rooms, 3 with PB. 1 suite. 1 cottage. Breakfast and evening snack included in rates. Type of meal: continental breakfast. Beds: KQD. Ceiling fan in room. Cable TV, fax, copier and library on premises. Fishing, parks, shopping, sporting events, theater and watersports nearby.

Location: On the island of Oahu.

Publicity: *Travel & Leisure, LA Style.*

"A wonderful place!! Stepping back to a time of luxury!"

Certificate may be used: Year-round, based on availability, excluding holidays.

Huelo   C8

Hale Huelo
PO Box 1237, Door of Faith Church Rd
Huelo, HI 96708
(808)572-8669 Fax:(808)573-8403
E-mail: halehuel@maui.net

Circa 1997. This contemporary home boasts stunning views of the ocean and surrounding rainforest. The modern home features Asian influences in the design. The interior is definitely Hawaiian, bright tropical prints top the beds and the rooms are airy and bright. Guests can enjoy the view from their own balcony or perhaps while lounging by the pool. For breakfast, the innkeepers serve fruit fresh from the many trees on the property, as well as tropical juices, kona coffee and homemade breads. Hale Huelo is located on the island of Maui, and guests can spend the day hiking to a volcano, snorkeling, surfing or taking a helicopter tour of the scenic area.

Innkeeper(s): Doug Barrett & Seiji Kamijo. $85-125. PC TC. 3 rooms, 2 with PB. 1 suite. Breakfast included in rates. Types of meals: continental breakfast and continental-plus breakfast. Beds: Q. Ceiling fan, TV and VCR in room. Fax, copier, spa, swimming and library on premises. Antiques, fishing, parks, shopping, golf, theater and watersports nearby.

Certificate may be used: Anytime, subject to availability.

Kailua Kona   E8

Hale Maluhia B&B
76-770 Hualalai Rd
Kailua Kona, HI 96740-9776
(808)329-1123 (800)559-6627 Fax:(808)326-5487

Circa 1972. This one-acre estate was lovingly designed as a Hawaiian plantation-style home for many families to enjoy. The estate (House of Peace)

has a Victorian and wicker interior with overstuffed sofas, antiques and Oriental rugs. Banana, mango, papaya, breadfruit and banyan trees edge and shade the compound. The hillsides are terraced with flower and vegetable gardens. Beach and snorkeling equipment are available at no charge, and the beaches are within a 15-minute drive. Holualoa is a sleepy, old coffee town on a mountain side above Kailua-Kona.

Innkeeper(s): N.K. Smith. $55-225. MC VISA AX DS. 5 rooms, 3 with PB. 1 conference room. Breakfast included in rates. Types of meals: full breakfast and early coffee/tea. Beds: KQ D. TV in room. VCR and library on premises. Antiques, fishing, shopping, downhill skiing and theater nearby.

Publicity: *San Francisco Chronicle.*

"The most relaxing and enjoyable part of our vacation were the days we spent at Hale Maluhia."

Certificate may be used: July 15-Nov. 15.

Kamuela   E8

Kamuela's Mauna Kea View B&B
PO Box 6375
Kamuela, HI 96743-6375
(808)885-8425 Fax:(808)885-6514

Circa 1988. Guests opt either to stay in a private suite or in a little cottage at this bed & breakfast, which affords views of historic Parker Ranch and its namesake mountain, Mauna Kea. The suite and cottage both offer two bedrooms, a living room, fireplace, kitchenette and bathroom, all comfortably decorated. From the decks on both accommodations, guests enjoy mountain views. The bed & breakfast is located on the Big Island, where guests can enjoy plenty of ocean activities, historic sites, horseback riding and much more.

Innkeeper(s): Richard & Deb Mitchell. $65-75. MC VISA AX PC TC. 1 suite. 1 cottage. Breakfast included in rates. Type of meal: continental-plus breakfast. Beds: QDT. Ceiling fan and TV in room. Spa on premises. Antiques, fishing, parks, shopping, downhill skiing, golf, theater and watersports nearby.

Publicity: *Coffee Times.*

Certificate may be used: Cottage, Sunday-Wednesday, June and September.

Kapaa   A3

Rosewood
872 Kamalu Rd
Kapaa, HI 96746-9701
(808)822-5216 Fax:(808)822-5478

Circa 1900. For a truly Polynesian experience, guests can stay at this inn's rustic Thatched Cottage, which appears as a dream from "Robinson Crusoe." The cottage includes sleeping, living and dining areas as well as a small kitchen. There is also a Victorian Cottage with a kitchen, two bedrooms, dining area and laundry facilities. Inside the turn-of-the-century, plantation-style house, there are two guest rooms featuring country decor. For those on a budget, the innkeepers also offer accommodations in the Bunkhouse. Guests in the main house or cottages are treated to breakfasts of tropical fruits, homemade granola with macadamia nuts, Kona coffee and entrees such as Hawaiian sweet bread served as French toast. The acre grounds are lush with flowers, tropical plants, a variety of fruit trees and ponds with waterfalls.

Innkeeper(s): Norbert & Rosemary Smith. $65-115. PC TC. 5 rooms, 2 with PB. 2 cottages. Breakfast included in rates. Type of meal: continental-plus breakfast. Ceiling fan in room. Cable TV, VCR, fax, copier and child care on premises. Fishing and watersports nearby.

Certificate may be used: Anytime.

Keaau
E10

Rainforest Retreat
HCR 1, Box 5655, 16-1891 37th Ave
Keaau, HI 96749-9404
(808)982-9601 Fax:(808)966-6898
E-mail: orchids@khawaii.net

Circa 1988. The innkeepers at Rainforest Retreat offer two private, apartment-style accommodations, nestled on eight acres of grounds, which include an orchid nursery. Each is furnished comfortably with modern decor. The Ohia House offers views of Mauna Kea, a complete kitchen, a bathroom and king and double beds. The Garden Studio has a kitchenette, king-size bed and bathroom. The innkeepers keep items such as Kona coffee, beverages, breads and eggs in the guest refrigerators. The retreat is 45 minutes from Volcanoes National Park and snorkeling, tide pools and beaches are less than 30 minutes away.

Innkeeper(s): Lori Campbell. $65-110. MC VISA AX DS TC. 2 rooms, 1 with PB. 1 cottage. Breakfast included in rates. Type of meal: full breakfast. Beds: KQ. Copier, spa and bicycles on premises. Parks, shopping and watersports nearby.

Certificate may be used: May to August, Monday-Thursday.

Koloa
B3

Victoria Place B&B
3459 Lawailoa Ln
Koloa, HI 96756-9646
(808)332-9300 Fax:(808)332-9465

Circa 1970. Three guest rooms open out to a pool area surrounded by hibiscus, gardenia and bougainvillea. The light and cheerful rooms are tiny

but filled with native plants and flowers such as ginger and bird of paradise. For more spacious accommodations, request the apartment. Innkeeper Edee Seymour loves to share her island secrets with guests and can direct you to hidden beaches off the tourist track. (She has received an award for being the friendliest person on the island.)

Innkeeper(s): Edee Seymour. $60-111. PC TC. 3 rooms with PB. 1 suite. Breakfast included in rates. Type of meal: continental-plus breakfast. Beds: KQDT. Cable TV, VCR, fax, copier, swimming and library on premises. Handicap access. Parks, shopping, theater and watersports nearby.

Certificate may be used: When there is availability, Jan. 30-Dec. 1.

Ocean View
E8

Bougainvillea B&B
PO Box 6045
Ocean View, HI 96737-6045
(808)929-7089 (800)688-1763 Fax:(808)929-7089
E-mail: peaceful@interpac.net

Circa 1980. Visitors to this Hawaiian Plantation-style home will be treated to the expertise of an innkeeper who has an extensive background in travel as the owner of an agency and as a teacher. All ground arrangements can be made through her. While using the inn as your base, you can enjoy the Hawaii of old as well as all the diversity the Big Island has to offer. The inn is located in a historic area near Volcanoes National Park.

Innkeeper(s): Martie Jean & Don Nitsche. $59. MC VISA AX DC CB DS PC TC. 4 rooms with PB. Breakfast included in rates. Types of meals: continental-plus breakfast and gourmet breakfast. Beds: Q. Ceiling fan and VCR in room. Fax, copier, spa, swimming and bicycles on premises. Fishing, parks, theater and watersports nearby.

Certificate may be used: Jan. 10-Dec. 15, Sunday to Friday.

Volcano
F9

Volcano Inn
PO Box 963
Volcano, HI 96785-0963
(808)967-7773 (800)628-3876 Fax:(808)967-8067

Circa 1989. These six cedar cabins are located on a lush, three-acre spread adjacent to Volcanoes National Park. Three of the cabins include a fireplace or wood-burning stove, and four have a kitchen stocked with coffee and tea. As several cabins can sleep five to seven guests, families and groups are welcome.

Innkeeper(s): Ron Ober & Joan Prescott. $55-80. MC VISA PC TC. 6 cottages. Beds: KQDT. VCR in room. Fax on premises. Shopping and watersports nearby.

Certificate may be used: May 1-June 20, Aug. 25-Dec. 20, except over Thanksgiving holidays.

Idaho

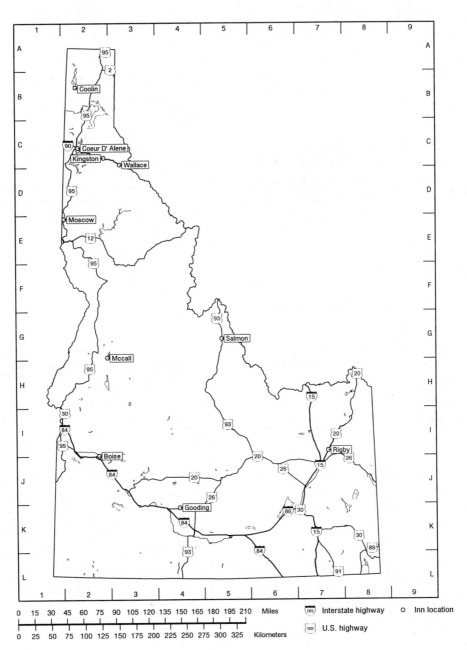

0   15   30   45   60   75   90   105 120 135 150 165 180 195 210   Miles

0   25   50   75   100 125 150 175 200 225 250 275 300 325   Kilometers

⬢ nn Interstate highway   ○ Inn location

⬡ nn U.S. highway

111

Boise
I2

B&B at Victoria's White House

10325 W Victory Rd
Boise, ID 83709-4079
(208)362-0507
E-mail: boisebandb@aol.com

Circa 1980. Although the inn is not historic, it's Colonial Revival-like architecture has incorporated many vintage components saved from local historic buildings, such as its banister, oak floors and fireplace mantels (gleaned from an old courthouse). Bogus Basin may be seen from the suite, which features a fireplace, large mirrored tub and parlor. In spring, more than a thousand tulips welcome the new season.

Innkeeper(s): Jeannette & Pablo Baldazo. $95. TC. 2 rooms with PB, 1 with FP. 1 suite. Breakfast included in rates. Beds: Q. Air conditioning, TV and VCR in room. Child care on premises. Fishing, shopping and golf nearby.

Certificate may be used: Throughout the year, based on availability and advance paid reservation.

Coeur d'Alene
C2

Country Ranch

1495 S Greenferry Rd
Coeur d'Alene, ID 83814-7606
(208)664-1189 Fax:(208)664-1189

Surrounded by almost 30 acres of woods and rolling hills, this serene retreat is an ideal spot to escape from life's hectic pace. Explore the hillside on a nature walk and guests are sure to find a variety of birds and other wildlife, perhaps deer and elk. Each of the guest suites is decorated with a queen-size poster bed. The Valley View Suite includes a sitting room with a mini-library. The Jacuzzi tub in the Mountain View Suite overlooks the ranch's orchard. The scent of freshly baked breads and gourmet coffee entices guests to the glass-enclosed morning room or formal dining room for a full, gourmet breakfast. In the evenings, hors d'oeuvres are served. There is a sports court on the premises. Spokane is 30 minutes away.

Innkeeper(s): Ann & Harry Holmberg. $95-125. MC VISA PC TC. 2 suites. Breakfast included in rates. Types of meals: full breakfast, gourmet breakfast and early coffee/tea. Evening snack available. Beds: Q. Air conditioning in room. VCR, fax and library on premises. Amusement parks, antiques, fishing, parks, shopping, downhill skiing, cross-country skiing, theater and watersports nearby.

Certificate may be used: May 1-Sept. 1, Sunday-Thursday.

The Roosevelt Inn

105 E Wallace Ave
Coeur d'Alene, ID 83814-2947
(208)765-5200 (800)290-3358 Fax:(208)664-4142

This turn-of-the-century, red brick home was named for President Theodore Roosevelt. As Roosevelt translates to Rosefield in Dutch, the innkeepers have kept a rosy theme running throughout the inn. Rooms feature turn-of-the-century furniture and some afford a lake view. Coeur d'Alene boasts many activities such as the world's longest floating boardwalk, and a variety of shops and restaurants are within walking distance of the inn. The natural surrounds offer hiking, boating, skiing and many other outdoor activities.

Innkeeper(s): John Marias. $70-125. MC VISA AX DS. 17 rooms. Breakfast included in rates. Type of meal: full breakfast.

Certificate may be used: October-April, Sunday-Thursday.

Wolf Lodge Creek B&B

715 N Wolf Lodge Creek Rd
Coeur d'Alene, ID 83814-9416
(208)667-5902 (800)919-9653 Fax:(208)667-1133

Circa 1994. Secluded on the edge of Coeur d'Alene National Forest, this natural wood home is surrounded by covered porches from which guests can enjoy a stunning view. There's an outdoor hot tub for guests to use after a day of hiking, golfing or skiing. There are four rooms and a suite, and each is individually decorated in a country style. All four rooms include a fireplace. The spacious suite includes an oversized tub, balcony and fireplace. Breakfasts are served buffet style, featuring the innkeeper's special granola, homemade breads, muffins, fresh fruit, yogurt, breakfast meats and entrees such as an oatmeal souffle or egg strata. Lake Coeur d'Alene is just a few minutes away, ski areas are within a half-hour drive, but guests can cross-country ski on the home's surrounding 27 acres.

Innkeeper(s): Tricia & David Freeman. $100-175. MC VISA DS PC TC. 5 rooms, 4 with PB, 5 with FP. 1 suite. 1 conference room. Breakfast included in rates. Types of meals: full breakfast and early coffee/tea. Picnic lunch available. Beds: KQ. Ceiling fan in room. Cable TV, VCR, fax, spa, stables and library on premises. Antiques, fishing, parks, downhill skiing, cross-country skiing, golf and watersports nearby.

Certificate may be used: All year, Sunday through Thursday nights.

Coolin   B2

Old Northern Inn
PO Box 177 Sherwood Beach Rd
Coolin, ID 83821-0177
(208)443-2426 Fax:(208)443-3856

Circa 1890. This historic inn was built to serve
guests riding the Great Northern rail line. Today,
travelers come to enjoy trout-filled Priest Lake and
all its offerings. The inn is located on the lake
shore, and guests enjoy use of a small marina and
private beach. There is also a volleyball court, but
guests are welcome to simply sit and relax on the
spacious deck. The natural surroundings are full of
wildlife, and it's not unusual to see deer, caribou and
even a moose. The hotel itself is a two-story log and
shingle structure, quite at home among the tall
cedars. The interior is warm and inviting. There is a
common area with a stone fireplace and country furnishings, as well as a view of mountains and the
lake. Rooms are decorated with turn-of-the-century
antiques, and the suites include a small sitting room.
Huckleberry pancakes have been a staple at the
inn's breakfast table since the 19th century. In the
afternoons, wine, cheese and fruit are served.
Innkeeper(s): Bob & Anita Martin. $85-130. MC VISA PC TC. 6 rooms,
4 with PB. 2 suites. Breakfast included in rates. Types of meals: full
breakfast and early coffee/tea. Beds: Q. Fax, copier and swimming on
premises. Handicap access. Antiques, fishing, shopping, cross-country
skiing, golf and watersports nearby.
Publicity: *Seattle Times.*

Certificate may be used: Monday through Thursday nights (Friday,
Saturday, Sunday nights excluded), valid from June 1-Oct. 15.

Gooding   K4

Gooding Hotel B&B
112 Main St
Gooding, ID 83330-1102
(208)934-4374

Circa 1906. An early Gooding settler, William B.
Kelly, built this historic hotel, which is the oldest
building in town. Each of the guest rooms is named
in honor of someone significant in the history of
Gooding or the hotel. A buffet breakfast is served
every morning in the William
Kelly Room. The area
offers many activi-
ties, from golfing and
fishing to exploring
ice caves or visit-
ing wineries and
museums.

Innkeeper(s): Dean & Judee Gooding. $45-60. MC VISA AX DS PC TC.
3 suites. Breakfast included in rates. Types of meals: continental breakfast, full breakfast and gourmet breakfast. Room service available.
Beds: QDT. Air conditioning and ceiling fan in room. Cable TV, copier
and bicycles on premises. Antiques, fishing, parks, shopping, downhill
skiing, cross-country skiing and golf nearby.
Certificate may be used: Year-round except Aug. 15-31.

Kingston   C2

Kingston 5 Ranch B&B
42297 Silver Valley Rd
Kingston, ID 83839-0130
(208)682-4862 (800)254-1852 Fax:(208)682-9445
E-mail: k5ranch@nidlink.com

Circa 1930. With the Coeur d'Alene Mountains as
its backdrop, this picturesque country farmhouse is a
wonderful place to escape and relax. Lazy mornings

begin as the scent of freshly ground coffee wafts
through the home. Then a hearty country breakfast
is served with cured ham, bacon, Belgian waffles
topped with fresh fruit, omelets and plenty of other
treats. Many of the ingredients are grown on the
farm. The original owners built a garage on the
property first and lived there until the Pennsylvania
Dutch barn and the farmhouse were built.
Innkeepers Walt and Pat Gentry have refurbished
the home completely, filling the guest rooms with
lace, down comforters and charming furnishings.
Rooms also offer romantic amenities such as an in-
room fireplace, mountain views, a four-poster bed,
private veranda, jetted tub and private decks with
an outdoor hot tub.
Innkeeper(s): Walter & Pat Gentry. $99-125. MC VISA PC TC. 2 rooms
with PB, 2 with FP. 1 suite. Breakfast included in rates. Types of meals:
full breakfast and early coffee/tea. Evening snack available. Beds: Q. Air
conditioning, turndown service, ceiling fan and TV in room. VCR, fax,
copier, spa, stables and bicycles on premises. Amusement parks,
antiques, fishing, parks, shopping, downhill skiing, cross-country skiing, theater and watersports nearby.

"The food was fabulous and so much!"

Certificate may be used: Sunday through Thursday, Jan. 2-May 14 &
Sept. 30-Nov. 23.

McCall G2

Northwest Passage

201 Rio Vista, PO Box 4208
McCall, ID 83638

(208)634-5349 (800)597-6658 Fax:(208)634-4977

Circa 1938. This mountain country inn rests on five acres and offers four guest rooms, two of them suites. Guests enjoy the inn's two sitting rooms, fireplace and full breakfasts. There are horse corrals on

the premises, and most pets can be accommodated when arrangements are made in advance. The inn is furnished in country decor and provides easy access to a myriad of recreational opportunities found in the area. Payette Lake is just a short distance from the inn, and the Brundage Mountain Ski Area and Ponderosa State Park are nearby.

Innkeeper(s): Steve Schott. $60-80. MC VISA DS. 6 rooms, 5 with PB, 1 with FP. 2 suites. 1 conference room. Breakfast included in rates. Type of meal: full breakfast. VCR and fax on premises. Antiques, fishing, shopping, downhill skiing, cross-country skiing and theater nearby.

Certificate may be used: Year-round except holiday weekends and during winter carnival (first week in February).

Moscow E2

Paradise Ridge B&B

3377 Blaine Rd
Moscow, ID 83843

(208)882-5292

Circa 1975. Four acres of woods surround this contemporary home, which affords views of buttes and mountains, as well as the town. The decor is a mix of styles, part traditional with a little bit of country. Innkeeper Solveig Miller was a caterer, so she prepares a wonderful breakfast. Huckleberry muffins, scones and oven-puff pancakes are among the homemade offerings.

Innkeeper(s): Jon R. & Solveig L. Miller. $65-85. PC TC. 3 rooms, 1 with PB. 1 suite. Breakfast included in rates. Types of meals: gourmet breakfast and early coffee/tea. Afternoon tea, gourmet lunch and banquet service available. Beds: KQ. Ceiling fan in room. Spa on premises. Antiques, fishing, parks, shopping, cross-country skiing, sporting events, golf, theater and watersports nearby.

"This certainly rates as one of the best, if not the best, B&B we have stayed in!"

Certificate may be used: Dec. 1-Jan. 30, any night.

Rigby I7

Blacksmith Inn

227 N 3900 East
Rigby, ID 83442

(208)745-6208 (888)745-6208 Fax:(208)745-0602

Circa 1996. This contemporary home features unusual architecture. The inn resembles two dome-shaped buildings connected together, and the home is built out of a dark, stained wood. The inn is new, so the innkeepers are constantly adding new items. They offer three guest rooms, but when complete, the inn will house six bedchambers, all with a private bath. Furnishings and decor are country in style, and quilt-topped beds are tucked beside walls painted with murals of mountains and woodland scenes. Breakfasts are served in a cheerful room with hardwood floors, a ceiling fan and plants. Scenery of forests and mountain peaks in the Rigby area is outstanding. Guests can ski, fish and hike, and Rigby also offers antique shops, museums and galleries.

Innkeeper(s): Mike & Karla Black. $60-75. MC VISA AX PC TC. 3 rooms with PB. Breakfast and evening snack included in rates. Types of meals: full breakfast and early coffee/tea. Beds: Q. Ceiling fan, TV and VCR in room. Fax, copier, stables and tennis on premises. Handicap access. Antiques, fishing, parks, shopping, downhill skiing, cross-country skiing, sporting events and theater nearby.

Certificate may be used: Oct. 1-March 30, Sunday through Saturday.

Salmon G5

Greyhouse Inn B&B

HC 61, Box 16
Salmon, ID 83467

(208)756-3968 (800)348-8097

Circa 1894. The scenery at Greyhouse is nothing short of wondrous. In the winter, when mountains are capped in white and the evergreens are shrouded in snow, this Victorian appears as a safe haven from the chilly weather. In the summer, the rocky peaks are a contrast to the whimsical house which looks like something out of an Old West town. The historic home is known around town as the old maternity hospital, but there is nothing medicinal about it now. The rooms are Victorian in style with antique furnishings. The parlor features deep red walls and carpeting, floral overstuffed sofas and a dressmaker's model garbed in a black Victorian gown. Outdoor enthusiasts will find no shortage of activities, from facing the rapids in nearby Salmon River to fishing to horseback riding. The town of Salmon is just 12 miles away.

Innkeeper(s): David & Sharon Osgood. $65-80. MC VISA PC TC. 4 rooms, 2 with PB. Breakfast included in rates. Types of meals: full breakfast and early coffee/tea. Afternoon tea and evening snack available. Beds: KQDT. Cable TV, VCR, bicycles, library and pet boarding on premises. Antiques, fishing, parks, shopping, downhill skiing, cross-country skiing, golf and watersports nearby.

"To come around the corner and find the Greyhouse, as we did, restores my faith! Such a miracle. We had a magical evening here, and we plan to return to stay for a few days. Thanks so much for your kindness and hospitality. We love idaho!"

Certificate may be used: Oct. 1-May 30.

Wallace   C3

21 Bank Street B&B
21 Bank St
Wallace, ID 83873-2149
(208)752-1292 (888)846-5051 Fax:(208)752-1291

Circa 1916. A former mayor built this home, which is a mixture of Mission and Victorian styles. It was used for several years as a convent. The home has an old-fashioned ambiance and features light Victorian decor. Guest rooms feature beds topped

with flowery prints and a canopy sash at the headboard. The town of Wallace is listed in the National Register and offers interesting mining sites, museums, antique shops and plenty of outdoor activities.

Innkeeper(s): Doug & Terri Austin. $65-75. MC VISA DS PC. 3 rooms. Breakfast included in rates. Types of meals: continental breakfast, full breakfast and early coffee/tea. Beds: Q. Turndown service in room. Cable TV, VCR, fax and library on premises. Antiques, fishing, shopping, downhill skiing and cross-country skiing nearby.

Certificate may be used: Dec. 1-May 31, Sunday-Thursday, subject to availability.

Illinois

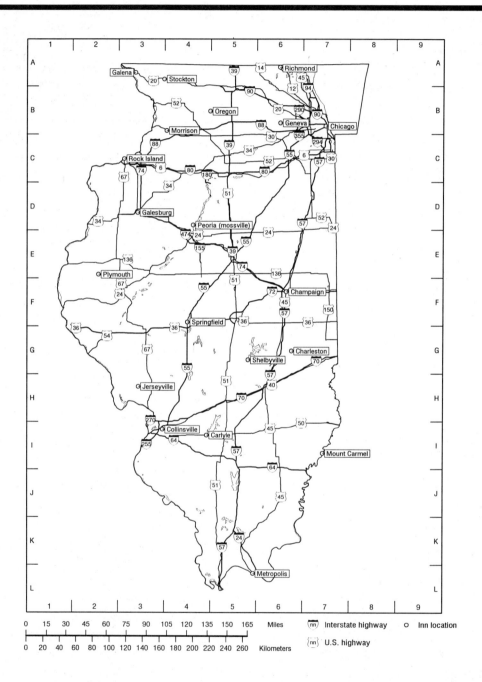

0 15 30 45 60 75 90 105 120 135 150 165   Miles

0 20 40 60 80 100 120 140 160 180 200 220 240 260   Kilometers

(nn) Interstate highway   o Inn location

(nn) U.S. highway

Carlyle
I4

Victorian Inn
1111 Franklin St
Carlyle, IL 62231-1835
(618)594-8506

This Clinton County historic landmark was built in Queen Anne style with stained-glass windows, a curving staircase, ornate woodwork, oak floors and pocket doors. Each of six fireplaces features unique tile. After arriving, guests are treated to tea for two in the Victorian parlor, which has a turn-of-the-century pump organ. Bedchambers are full of special amenities, such as fluffy robes and slippers. The innkeepers offer a special child's room, which features antique toys and playthings.

Innkeeper(s): Mary Mincks. $55-70. MC VISA. 2 rooms. Breakfast included in rates. Type of meal: full breakfast.

Certificate may be used: Sunday through Thursday, September through March.

Charleston
G6

Charleston B&B
2121 Cameron Pl
Charleston, IL 61920
(217)345-6463 (800)832-3366
E-mail: I-57 & Rt 16 East

Circa 1863. This Italianate home, built during the turmoil of the Civil War, was constructed by a Mexican War veteran and local brick mason. He created a sturdy home, with foot-thick walls made from clay taken from a local pond. The previous owner began the restoration process, using materials he salvaged during renovation of Charleston's Old Main. The oak banisters and wainscoting are some added items. The final restoration was completed by innkeepers Tom and Shirley Scism, who returned the home to its original luster. Rooms are filled with antiques and unique pieces from the Scism's world travels, including a remarkable collection of clocks. The one-acre grounds, sometimes referred to as Hickory Hills, are dotted with a variety of trees, highlighted by six massive hickories.

Innkeeper(s): Shirley & Tom Scism. $40-45. EP. MC VISA TC. 4 rooms, 1 with PB. 1 conference room. Breakfast included in rates. Types of meals: continental breakfast, continental-plus breakfast and early coffee/tea. Room service available. Beds: KQD. Air conditioning, turndown service, ceiling fan and TV in room. Fax and copier on premises. Antiques, fishing, parks, shopping, sporting events and theater nearby.

Certificate may be used: Except first two weeks in August, Christmas week, and one week in November (college homecoming).

Chicago
B7

Wooded Isle Suites & Apts
5750 S Stony Island Ave
Chicago, IL 60637-2051
(312)288-6305 (800)290-6844 Fax:(312)288-8972
E-mail: chavenswi@aol.com

Circa 1914. Although neither bed & breakfast nor country inn, this collection of two- and three-room apartment suites serves as a convenient, relaxing alternative to hotel travel. The suites are located in Chicago's Hyde Park area and are convenient to the many museums, shops, restaurants and attractions in the downtown area and Lake Michigan. The early 20th-century complex originally served as housing for employees of the Illinois Central Railroad Hospital. Each suite includes a long list of practical amenities, such as a kitchen stocked with pots, pans, dishes, coffee makers, coffee, tea bags and more. The decor is a pleasant, contemporary style.

Innkeeper(s): Charlie Havens & Sara Pitcher. $108-136. MC VISA AX DS PC. 13 suites. Beds: Q. Air conditioning, ceiling fan and TV in room. Fishing, parks, sporting events, theater and watersports nearby.

"We have all had very positive experiences at Wooded Isle. Everyone has been pleasant and tuned in to our joy."

Certificate may be used: Dec. 7-Jan. 8, Sunday-Thursday.

Collinsville
I3

Maggie's B&B
2102 N Keebler Ave
Collinsville, IL 62234-4713
(618)344-8283

Circa 1900. A rustic two-acre wooded area surrounds this friendly Victorian inn, once a boarding house. Rooms with 14-foot ceilings are furnished with exquisite antiques and art objects collected on worldwide travels. Downtown St. Louis, the Gateway Arch and the Mississippi riverfront are just 10 minutes away.

Innkeeper(s): Maggie Leyda. $40-85. PC TC. 5 rooms, 3 with PB, 2 with FP. 1 suite. 1 conference room. Breakfast included in rates. Types of meals: full breakfast and early coffee/tea. Beds: QDT. Air conditioning, turndown service, ceiling fan, TV and VCR in room. Spa and library on premises. Handicap access. Amusement parks, antiques, fishing, parks, shopping, sporting events and theater nearby.

Publicity: *Collinsville Herald Journal, Innsider, Belleville News, Democrat, Saint Louis Homes & Gardens, Cooking Light, USA Today.*

"We enjoyed a delightful stay. You've thought of everything. What fun!"

Certificate may be used: Sunday-Thursday, year-round except holidays.

Galena   A3

Cottage at Amber Creek
122 S Bench St
Galena, IL 61036
(815)777-9320 (800)781-9530 Fax:(815)777-9476

Circa 1840. This horse farm is set on 300 acres of woods, meadows and hilly countryside. There is a secluded cottage tucked in the woods. The cottage once served as the summer kitchen for the farm's main house, which was built in the 1840s. The cozy haven includes a small kitchen, fireplace, living room, bedroom and bathroom with a whirlpool tub. The antique four-poster bed is covered with down comforters and fluffy pillows. Firewood, towels and linens all are provided. For an extra charge, the hosts will provide flowers or champagne.

Innkeeper(s): Kate Freeman. $75-175. MC VISA AX DC DS PC TC. 1 room with PB. Breakfast included in rates. Type of meal: continental breakfast. Beds: Q. Air conditioning in room. Antiques, fishing, parks, shopping, downhill skiing, cross-country skiing and theater nearby.

Certificate may be used: Sunday through Thursday nights. All months except October.

Galesburg   D3

Seacord House
624 N Cherry St
Galesburg, IL 61401-2731
(309)342-4107

A former county sheriff and businessman built this Eastlake-style Victorian, which is located in the town's historic district. The home was named for its builder, William Seacord, a prominent local man whose family is mentioned in Carl Sandburg's autobiography. In keeping with the house's historical prominence, the innkeepers have tried to maintain its turn-of-the-century charm. Victorian wallpapers, lacy curtains and a collection of family antiques grace the guest rooms and living areas. The bedrooms, however, feature the modern amenity of waterbeds. For those celebrating romantic occasions,

the innkeepers provide heart-shaped muffins along with regular morning fare.

Innkeeper(s): Gwendolyn D. Johnson. $40. MC VISA. 3 rooms. Breakfast included in rates. Type of meal: continental-plus breakfast.

Certificate may be used: Any day between Nov. 1 and April 1.

Geneva   B6

The Oscar Swan Country Inn
1800 W State St
Geneva, IL 60134-1002
(630)232-0173

Circa 1902. This turn-of-the-century Colonial Revival house rests on seven acres of trees and lawns. Its 6,000 square feet are filled with homey touches. There is a historic barn on the property and a gazebo on the front lawn. A pillared breeze-

way connects the round garage to the house. The stone pool is round, as well. Nina is a retired home economics teacher and Hans speaks German and was a professor of business administration at Indiana University.

Innkeeper(s): Nina Heymann. $65-139. MC VISA AX. 8 rooms, 4 with PB. 3 conference rooms. Breakfast included in rates. Type of meal: full breakfast. Lunch and catering service available. Beds: KQD. Air conditioning and VCR in room. Antiques, shopping, cross-country skiing and theater nearby.

Publicity: *Chicago Tribune, Windmill News.*

"Thank you for making our wedding such a beautiful memory. The accommodations were wonderful, the food excellent."

Certificate may be used: January-July, November and December. Not Saturdays.

Jerseyville   H3

The Homeridge B&B
1470 N State St
Jerseyville, IL 62052-1127
(618)498-3442

Circa 1867. This red brick Italianate Victorian features ornate white trim, a stately front veranda and a cupola where guests often take in views of sunsets and the surrounding 18 acres. The home was constructed by Cornelius Fisher, just after the Civil War. In 1891, it was purchased by Senator Theodore Chapman and remained in his family until the 1960s. The innkeepers have filled the 14-room manor with traditional and Victorian furnish-

ings, enhancing the high ceilings and ornate woodwork typical of the era. Guests are invited to take a relaxing dip in the inn's swimming pool or relax with a refreshment on the veranda.

Innkeeper(s): Sue & Howard Landon. $66-75. MC VISA AX PC TC. 4 rooms with PB. Breakfast included in rates. Types of meals: full breakfast, early coffee/tea. Afternoon tea available. Beds: KDT. Air conditioning, ceiling fan in room. TV, VCR, copier, swimming, bicycles, library on premises. Amusement parks, antiques, fishing, parks, shopping, cross-country skiing, sporting events, theater and watersports nearby.

"A most beautiful, entertaining, snow-filled few days."

Certificate may be used: Nov. 1 through April 30.

Metropolis L5

Isle of View B&B
205 Metropolis St
Metropolis, IL 62960-2213
(618)524-5838 Fax:(618)524-2978

Circa 1889. Metropolis, billed as the "home of Superman," is not a bustling concrete city, but a quaint, country town tucked along the Ohio River. The Isle of View, a stunning Italianate manor, is just a short walk from shops, restaurants and the Players Riverboat Casino. Several rooms offer river views.

All the guest rooms are appointed in Victorian design with antiques. The Master Suite was originally the home's library and includes a unique coal-burning fireplace, canopy bed and two-person whirlpool tub.

Innkeeper(s): Kim & Gerald Offenburger. $55-115. MC VISA AX DC CB DS TC. 5 rooms with PB, 4 with FP. 1 conference room. Breakfast included in rates. Types of meals: gourmet breakfast and early coffee/tea. Banquet service and catering service available. Beds: KQD. Air conditioning, ceiling fan and TV in room. Antiques, fishing, parks, shopping, theater and watersports nearby.

"You may never want to leave."

Certificate may be used: November-March, Sunday-Friday.

Morrison B4

Hillendale B&B
600 W Lincolnway
Morrison, IL 61270-2058
(815)772-3454 (800)349-7702 Fax:(815)772-7023
E-mail: hillend@clinton.net

Circa 1891. Guests at Hillendale don't simply spend the night in the quaint town of Morrison, Ill., they spend the night in France, Italy, Hawaii or Africa. Each of the guests rooms in this Tudor manor reflects a different theme from around the world. Travelers and innkeepers Barb and Mike Winandy cleverly decorated each of the guest quarters. The Kimarrin room reflects Mayan culture with photographs of antiquities. The Outback, a private cottage, boasts a fireplace and whirlpool spa along with Australian decor. The Failte room includes a

rococo Victorian antique highback bed, fireplace and Irish-themed decor. And these are just a few of the possibilities. Barb creates wonderful breakfasts full of muffins, breads and special entrees. Stroll the two-acre grounds and you will encounter a three-tier water pond, which sits in front of a teahouse, built by the original owner after a trip to Japan. One of the tiers houses Japanese Koi and another a water garden. The area has riverboat gambling and plenty of outdoor activities. Carriage, hay and sleigh rides, and massages can be arranged.

Innkeeper(s): Barb & Mike Winandy. $55-150. MC VISA DC DS TC. 10 rooms with PB. Breakfast included in rates. Type of meal: full breakfast. Beds: KQ. Air conditioning, ceiling fan, TV and VCR in room. Fax and copier on premises. Antiques, fishing, parks, cross-country skiing and theater nearby.

Location: On the historic original Lincoln Highway.

Publicity: *New York Times, Sterling Gazette, Whiteside News Sentinel, Midwest Living, Home & Away.*

"We've never been any place else that made us feel so catered to and comfortable. Thank you for allowing us to stay in your beautiful home. We feel very privileged."

Certificate may be used: Sunday-Friday.

Mount Carmel   I7

Living Legacy Homestead
Box 146A, RR 2
Mount Carmel, IL 62863
(618)298-2476

Circa 1870. This turn-of-the-century German homestead features both farmhouse and log house settings. Antiques and period furniture abound, and visitors experience the unique sight of the log house's exposed interior walls and loft. The 10-acre grounds are home to flower, herb and vegetable gardens, and guests also are free to roam the meadows, barnyard and wildlife areas. Nearby are the Beall Woods State Natural Area and the Wabash River. A gift shop featuring antiques, crafts and collectibles is on the premises.

Innkeeper(s): Edna Schmidt Anderson. $50-70. TC. 4 rooms, 2 with PB. 1 cottage. 1 conference room. Breakfast included in rates. Types of meals: full breakfast and early coffee/tea. Dinner, evening snack, picnic lunch and lunch available. Beds: DT. Air conditioning and ceiling fan in room. Library on premises. Antiques, fishing and parks nearby.

Certificate may be used: April 1 to Nov. 30, Monday-Thursday.

The Poor Farm B&B
Poor Farm Rd
Mount Carmel, IL 62863-9803
(618)262-4663 (800)646-3276 Fax:(618)262-8199
E-mail: poorfarm@midwest.net

Circa 1915. This uniquely named inn served as a home for the homeless for more than a century. Today, the stately Federal-style structure hosts travelers and visitors to this area of Southeastern Illinois, offering a glimpse back in time to a gracious era. An antique player piano and VCRs add to guests' comfort, and the inn also has bicycles available for those wishing to explore the grounds. The Poor Farm B&B sits adjacent to a recreational park with a well-stocked lake and is within walking distance of an 18-hole golf course and driving range. Riverboat gambling is 45 minutes away in Evansville, Ind.

Innkeeper(s): Liz & John Stelzer. $45-85. MC VISA AX DS PC TC. 5 rooms with PB, 2 with FP. 2 suites. 2 conference rooms. Breakfast included in rates. Types of meals: full breakfast and early coffee/tea. Afternoon tea, dinner, evening snack, lunch, banquet service and catering service available. Restaurant on premises. Beds: QDT. Air conditioning, turndown service, ceiling fan and VCR in room. Fax, copier, bicycles and library on premises. Handicap access. Amusement parks, antiques, fishing, parks, shopping, cross-country skiing, sporting events, theater and watersports nearby.

"Delightful. Oatmeal supreme. Best in Illinois. Enjoyed every moment. Hi Yo Silver!"

Certificate may be used: Jan. 10-Nov. 15, Sunday-Thursday, holidays excluded.

Oregon   B4

Pinehill B&B
400 Mix St
Oregon, IL 61061-1113
(815)732-2061

Circa 1874. This Italianate country villa is listed in the National Register. Ornate touches include guest rooms with Italian marble fireplaces and French silk-screened mural wallpaper. Outside, guests may enjoy porches, swings and century-old pine trees. Seasonal events include daily chocolate tea parties featuring the inn's own exotic homemade fudge collection.

Innkeeper(s): Sharon Burdick. $65-195. PC TC. 5 rooms with PB, 3 with FP. 1 conference room. Breakfast and afternoon tea included in rates. Types of meals: gourmet breakfast and early coffee/tea. Beds: KQD. Air conditioning, turndown service and ceiling fan in room. Library on premises. Antiques, parks, shopping, sporting events and watersports nearby.

Publicity: *Fox Valley Living, Victorian Sampler, Freeport Journal.*

"We enjoyed our stay at Pine Hill, your gracious hospitality and the peacefulness. Our thanks to you for a delightful stay. We may have to come again, if just to get some fudge."

Certificate may be used: January, March, and April on Sunday, Monday, Tuesday, and Wednesday.

Peoria (Mossville)   D4

Old Church House Inn
1416 E Mossville Rd
Peoria (Mossville), IL 61552
(309)579-2300

Circa 1869. Once a church sanctuary, this restored Colonial-style home now features Victorian ambiance highlighted by the 18-foot wooden ceilings, arched windows and period furnishings. Each of the guest rooms offers something unique, such as an 1860s carved bedstead, featherbeds, handmade quilts and lacy curtains. Guests can enjoy a relaxing stroll through flower, herb and vegetable gardens, or sip afternoon tea.

Innkeeper(s): Dean & Holly Ramseyer. $75-105. MC VISA DS. 2 rooms, 1 with PB. Breakfast and afternoon tea included in rates. Types of meals: continental-plus breakfast and early coffee/tea. Picnic lunch and room service available. Beds: Q. Air conditioning and turndown service in room. Antiques, fishing, shopping, cross-country skiing, sporting events, theater and watersports nearby.

Location: Peoria's northside.

Publicity: *Chillicothe Bulletin, Journal Star.*

"Your hospitality, thoughtfulness, the cleanliness, beauty, I should just say everything was the best."

Certificate may be used: Monday-Thursday, all year on steeple rate only.

Plymouth   E2

Plymouth Rock Roost
201 W Summer St
Plymouth, IL 62367-1104
(309)458-6444 Fax:(309)837-4444

Circa 1904. A local banker built this Queen Anne Victorian, which boasts a wraparound veranda, gabled roof and an especially wide turret. The inn is decorated in light Victorian style, with an interesting mix of antiques. One guest room houses a desk that was original to the local post office, another features a huge pencil-post bed. The marble-appointed bathrooms feature oversized tubs and soft, fluffy decorator towels. The innkeepers also run an antique shop on the premises. Western Illinois University is nearby, as are historic sites, golfing and fishing.
Innkeeper(s): Ben Gentry & Joyce Steiner. $59. MC VISA PC TC. 3 rooms. Breakfast included in rates. Type of meal: full breakfast. Catering service available. Beds: KD. Air conditioning and TV in room. VCR, bicycles and library on premises. Antiques, fishing, parks, shopping, sporting events, golf and theater nearby.

Certificate may be used: Anytime rooms are available.

Richmond   A6

Gazebo House B&B
10314 East St
Richmond, IL 60071
(815)678-2505

Circa 1893. This intimate, homestay B&B is located in a charming "Painted Lady," whimsically painted and set on a fragrant five acres with gardens and trees. The well-designed interior has a hint of the Victorian era, with a few flowery touches, but mostly elegant and understated decor. One room offers a brass bed and a unique rocking horse, the other has a four-poster bed. The Richmond room also has a whirlpool tub. Guests can relax on the veranda, stroll the scenic grounds or relax with a good book. The innkeepers have more than 1,000 volumes on bookshelves around the home.
Innkeeper(s): Sandy & Jeff Heaney. $79-99. MC VISA DS PC. 2 rooms with PB, 1 with FP. Breakfast included in rates. Type of meal: continental-plus breakfast. Beds: Q. Air conditioning, ceiling fan and TV in room. VCR, fax, spa and library on premises. Antiques, fishing, parks, shopping, downhill skiing, cross-country skiing, golf, theater and watersports nearby.

Publicity: *Classic Cars Magazine, Chicago Tribune, NW Herald, Lakeland.*

"The quiet and calm atmosphere was just what I needed!"

Certificate may be used: Year-round, Sunday-Thursday.

Rock Island   C3

Victorian Inn
702 20th St
Rock Island, IL 61201-2638
(309)788-7068

Circa 1876. Built as a wedding present for the daughter of a Rock Island liquor baron, the inn's striking features include illuminated stained-glass tower windows. Other examples of the Victorian decor are the living room's beveled-plate-glass French doors and the dining room's Flemish Oak ceiling beams and paneling, crowned by turn-of-the-century tapestries. Standing within sight of three

other buildings listed in the National Register, the inn's wooded grounds are home to many songbirds from the area. A glassed-in Florida porch is perfect for relaxing during any season and a patio table in the gardens is a great place to enjoy a glass of pink lemonade on warm evenings.
Innkeeper(s): David & Barbara Parker. $65-120. MC VISA AX PC TC. 6 rooms with PB, 2 with FP. Breakfast and evening snack included in rates. Types of meals: continental breakfast, continental-plus breakfast, full breakfast, gourmet breakfast and early coffee/tea. Afternoon tea available. Beds: KQDT. Air conditioning and ceiling fan in room. Cable TV, copier and library on premises. Antiques, fishing, parks, cross-country skiing, sporting events, theater and watersports nearby.

Certificate may be used: Sunday-Thursday, subject to availability, year round.

Shelbyville   G5

The Shelby Historic House and Inn
816 W Main St
Shelbyville, IL 62565-1354
(217)774-3991 (800)342-9978 Fax:(217)774-2224

This Queen Anne Victorian inn is listed in the
National Register of Historic Places. The inn is
well known for its conference facilities, and is less
than a mile from Lake Shelbyville, one of the
state's most popular boating and fishing spots.
Guaranteed tee times are available at a neighboring
championship golf course. Three state parks are
nearby, and the Amish settlement near Arthur is
within easy driving distance.

Innkeeper(s): Ken Fry. $52-78. MC VISA AX DC CB DS TC. 38 rooms. 6
suites. 1 conference room. Type of meal: continental breakfast. Beds:
K. Air conditioning and TV in room. Fax on premises. Handicap access.
Antiques, fishing, parks, shopping, theater and watersports nearby.

Certificate may be used: Nov. 1 through May 15.

Springfield   F4

The Inn on Edwards B&B
810 E Edwards St
Springfield, IL 62703
(217)528-0420

Circa 1865. The cheerful blue Italianate Victorian
displays many original features, from its curving walnut staircase, fine woodwork and fireplace mantels
with faux marbling. The home was appointed by a
local interior design firm, and rooms feature

antiques. The home is adjacent to the Lincoln
Home National Historic Site, which includes
Abraham Lincoln's family home and several blocks
of Springfield.

Innkeeper(s): Charles Kirchner & Jay Jackson. $65-75. MC VISA PC. 4
rooms with PB. Breakfast included in rates. Type of meal: continental-
plus breakfast. Beds: QT. Air conditioning and ceiling fan in room.
Amusement parks, antiques, fishing, parks, shopping, sporting events,
golf, theater and watersports nearby.

Publicity: *State Journal Register.*

Certificate may be used: Jan. 30-Dec. 31, except June 26-29 and
Aug. 8-17.

Stockton   A3

Maple Lane Country Inn & Resort
3114 S Rush Creek Rd
Stockton, IL 61085-9039
(815)947-3773 Fax:(815)947-3773

Circa 1838. The expansive grounds of this large
Colonial Revival mansion, feature a guest house,
gazebo, and several farm buildings. The full
gourmet breakfasts will delight guests. Historic
Galena is within easy driving distance, as are several state parks.

Innkeeper(s): Rose & Bill Stout. $89-150. TC. 22 rooms with PB, 1 with
FP. 6 suites. 2 conference rooms. Breakfast included in rates. Types of
meals: full breakfast and gourmet breakfast. Banquet service and catering service available. Beds: QF. Air conditioning and VCR in room. Cable
TV, fax, copier, spa and sauna on premises. Antiques, fishing, parks,
shopping, downhill skiing, cross-country skiing, sporting events, theater and watersports nearby.

Certificate may be used: Sunday-Thursday, upon availability, except
holidays, hunting season and special events.

Indiana

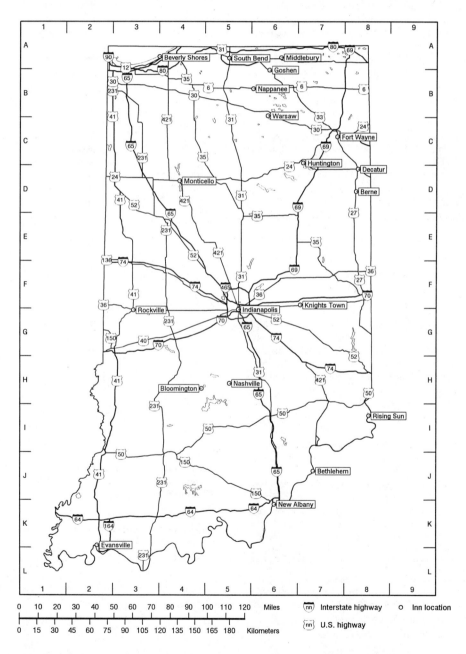

0 10 20 30 40 50 60 70 80 90 100 110 120 Miles

0 15 30 45 60 75 90 105 120 135 150 165 180 Kilometers

⌐nn⌐ Interstate highway   ○ Inn location

⌐nn⌐ U.S. highway

Berne   D8

Schug House Inn
706 W Main St
Berne, IN 46711-1328
(219)589-2303

Circa 1907. This Queen Anne home was built in 1907 by Emanuel Wanner. It was constructed for the Schug family, who occupied the home for 25 years, and whom the innkeepers chose the name of their inn. Victorian features decorate the home, including inlaid floors, pocket doors and a wraparound porch. Guest rooms boast walnut, cherry and oak furnishings. Fruit, cheeses and pastries are served on antique china each morning in the dining room. Horse-drawn carriages from the nearby Old Order Amish community often pass on the street outside.
Innkeeper(s): John Minch. $35-40. MC VISA. 9 rooms, 8 with PB. 1 conference room. Breakfast included in rates. Type of meal: continental breakfast. Beds: KQDT.
Certificate may be used: Jan. 4-June 15 and Oct. 1-Dec. 31.

Bethlehem   J7

The Inn at Bethlehem
101 Walnut St
Bethlehem, IN 47104
(812)293-3975

Circa 1830. This two-story, Federal-style inn sits atop a bluff overlooking the Ohio River. In its long history, it has seen uses as a grocery, jail and possibly a stop on the Underground Railroad. Rocking chairs and hammocks are ready for those who wish to relax, and there's 26 acres to explore. The inn is furnished with elegant pieces, including some period antiques. One of the innkeepers is an accomplished chef, so the breakfasts are a treat. Guests can make a reservation for a gourmet dinner in the inn's Rustic Lodge. Your menu might include saffron shrimp bisque, garden salad dressed with a balsamic vinaigrette, an appetizer of wild mushroom cream in a beggars purse, then bourbon pecan chicken or perhaps a beef tenderloin wrapped in smoky bacon and served with a Merlot sauce. Guests finish off the meal with a succulent dessert. Sunday brunch also is served.
Innkeeper(s): Lawrence & Debbie Llana. $30-150. MAP, AP. MC TC. 10 rooms with PB. 1 suite. 2 conference rooms. Breakfast included in rates. Types of meals: full breakfast, gourmet breakfast and early coffee/tea. Dinner, evening snack, picnic lunch, gourmet lunch and banquet service available. Restaurant on premises. Beds: KQDT. Air conditioning and ceiling fan in room. VCR, fax and bicycles on premises. Antiques, fishing, parks and shopping nearby.

"We love this place! It is now our little getaway."
Certificate may be used: Nov. 1-April 28, Sunday-Thursday.

Beverly Shores   A4

Dunes Shore Inn
33 Lakeshore County Rd, Box 807
Beverly Shores, IN 46301
(219)879-9029

Circa 1942. The Dunes Shore Inn started out as a summer hotel catering to Lithuanian folk, who were fond of the area because of its resemblance to the Baltic Sea region. It later became a boarding house for national park employees of the Indiana Dunes National Lakeshore. A concrete-block and frame building, the inn is located one block from Lake Michigan. Its rustic interior features an eclectic collection of furnishings. Guests gather in one of the upstairs lounges or around a Swedish tile stove in the knotty-pine lobby. The innkeepers have an apartment available May to October, which includes a private bath and kitchen.
Innkeeper(s): Rosemary & Fred Braun. $50-77. PC TC. 12 rooms. Breakfast included in rates. Types of meals: continental-plus breakfast and early coffee/tea. Beds: DT. Ceiling fan in room. VCR and library on premises. Amusement parks, antiques, fishing, parks, shopping, downhill skiing, cross-country skiing, sporting events, golf, theater and watersports nearby.
Publicity: *Milwaukee Journal, Chicago Sun-Times, Travel Holiday.*

"The setting was so perfect. Thank you."
Certificate may be used: May through October, Sunday-Thursday; November through April, available weekends (Friday-Saturday).

Bloomington   H4

The Bauer House B&B
4595 N Maple Grove Rd
Bloomington, IN 47404-9083
(812)336-4383

Circa 1864. This red brick farmhouse B&B features a double-tiered, columned porch welcoming guests to a peaceful stay. It is located three miles from downtown. A hearty Hoosier breakfast is served. Ask about the Hilly Hundred Bicycle Ride, Drum & Bugle competition and the Civil War reenactment days, all held nearby.
Innkeeper(s): Beverly Bauer. $45-55. 3 rooms, 2 with PB. Breakfast included in rates. Type of meal: continental-plus breakfast. Beds: D. Air conditioning in room. Antiques, shopping and sporting events nearby.
Location: Three miles from downtown.
Publicity: *Herald Times.*

"Your place is peaceful and quiet, a place to enjoy."
Certificate may be used: March through November, Sunday through Thursday.

Decatur
D8

Cragwood Inn B&B
303 N 2nd St
Decatur, IN 46733-1329
(219)728-2000

Circa 1900. This Queen Anne Victorian with four porches, gingerbread frosting, a turret and a graceful bay facade was built by a Decatur banker. Finely carved oak is magnificently displayed in the paneled ceilings, staircase and pillars of the parlor. Ornate tin ceilings, leaded-glass windows and a crystal chandelier are among other highlights. The wicker bed in the Garden Room looks out through a Palladian window. Two other rooms have their own fireplace. The innkeepers host weekend workshops for those interested in learning how to do fine needlework, including Battenburg lace and ribbon work. The also have chocolate lovers' weekends in March and October.

Innkeeper(s): George & Nancy Craig. $60-65. MC VISA PC TC. 4 rooms, 2 with PB, 2 with FP. 1 conference room. Breakfast and evening snack included in rates. Types of meals: full breakfast, gourmet breakfast and early coffee/tea. Beds: QDT. Air conditioning in room. VCR, bicycles and library on premises. Antiques and parks nearby.

Location: South of Fort Wayne.

Publicity: *Inside Chicago, Great Lakes Getaway, Christmas Victorian Craft.*

"Your wonderful hospitality, beautiful home and company made my trip that much more enjoyable."

Certificate may be used: Sunday-Thursday, anytime Jan. 1-April 1, when available.

Evansville
K2

Cool Breeze Estate B&B
1240 SE 2nd St
Evansville, IN 47713-1304
(812)422-9635

Circa 1906. This prairie school home is surrounded by more than an acre of grounds, ideal for those in search of peace and quiet. Truck and automobile maker Joseph Graham once lived here, as well as philanthropist Giltner Igleheart.  One room features the wallpaper mural, "Scenic America." The same mural was chosen by Jacqueline Kennedy to decorate the White House. The

sunny rooms have names such as Margaret Mitchell or Bronte. A zoo, art museum and riverboat casino are among the nearby attractions.

Innkeeper(s): Katelin & David Hills. $75. AX DC CB DS PC TC. 4 rooms with PB. 2 suites. 2 conference rooms. Breakfast included in rates. Type of meal: full breakfast. Beds: QD. Air conditioning in room. Cable TV, VCR and library on premises. Antiques, parks, shopping, sporting events, theater and watersports nearby.

Location: Old Ohio River city.

Publicity: *Evansville Courier, Midwest Living.*

"It was so much like discovering something wonderful from the past and disappearing into the warmth of childhood again."

Certificate may be used: Anytime; Sunday-Thursday.

Fort Wayne
C7

The Carole Lombard House B&B
704 Rockhill St
Fort Wayne, IN 46802-5918
(219)426-9896

Circa 1895. Jane Alice Peters, a.k.a. Carole Lombard, spent her first six years in this turn-of-the-century home located in Ft. Wayne's historic West-Central neighborhood. The innkeepers named two guest rooms in honor of Lombard and her second husband, Clark Gable. Each of these rooms features memorabilia from the Gable-Lombard romance. A video library with a collection of classic movies is available, including many of Lombard's films. The innkeepers provide bicycles for exploring Fort Wayne and also provide information for a self-guided architectural tour of the historic area.

Innkeeper(s): Bev Fiandt. $55-75. MC VISA DS PC TC. 4 rooms with PB. Breakfast included in rates. Types of meals: full breakfast and early coffee/tea. Beds: KQDT. Air conditioning and TV in room. VCR and bicycles on premises. Antiques, parks, sporting events and theater nearby.

Publicity: *Michigan Living.*

"The elegance and ambience are most appreciated."

Certificate may be used: Sunday-Thursday all year.

Goshen
B6

Waterford B&B
3004 S Main St
Goshen, IN 46526-5423
(219)533-6044

This Italianate inn, listed with the National Register, features all Midwest antiques in its furnishing schemes. The innkeeper, an avid antiquer, can provide tips on where to buy in the surrounding area. A full breakfast is served at the Waterford and guests also may relax in the sitting room or in front of the fireplace. The inn is a short distance from the state's chain of lakes, Amish country or famous South Bend, home of the University of Notre Dame. Innkeeper(s): Judith Forbes. $55-60. 4 rooms. Breakfast included in rates. Type of meal: full breakfast. Antiques and shopping nearby.

Certificate may be used: Jan. 1-March 31.

Huntington C7

Purviance House
326 S Jefferson St
Huntington, IN 46750-3327
(219)356-4218

Circa 1859. This Italianate-Greek Revival house is listed in the National Register of Historic Places. The inn features a winding cherry staircase, parquet floors, original interior shutters, tile fireplaces, ornate ceiling designs, antiques and period reproductions. The gold parlor offers well-stocked bookshelves.
Innkeeper(s): Bob & Jean Gernand. $45-55. MC VISA DS TC. 5 rooms, 2 with PB, 2 with FP. 2 conference rooms. Breakfast and evening snack included in rates. Types of meals: full breakfast and early coffee/tea. Banquet service and room service available. Beds: QDT. Air conditioning and ceiling fan in room. Library on premises. Antiques, fishing, parks, shopping and watersports nearby.

Location: One-half hour from Ft. Wayne.

Publicity: *Huntington County TAB, Purdue Alumnus, Richmond Palladium-Item.*

"A completely delightful experience!"

Certificate may be used: March 1-Dec. 20, Sunday-Friday.

Indianapolis G5

Renaissance Tower Historic Inn
230 E 9th St
Indianapolis, IN 46204-1151
(317)261-1652 (800)676-7786 Fax:(317)262-8648

Circa 1922. Nestled in the heart of the Historic St. Joseph District, this inn is listed in the National Register of Historic Places. The inn features distinctive construction details. Guest rooms have cherry four-poster beds, Queen Anne furniture, elegant sitting rooms and scenic bay windows. Each suite has a European-style fully equipped kitchen.
Innkeeper(s): Jeffrey Bowling. $75-85. MC VISA

AX PC TC. 80 suites. Beds: QD. Air conditioning and TV in room. Fax and copier on premises. Shopping, sporting events and theater nearby.
Publicity: *Indianapolis Business Journal, New York Times, Indianapolis Star, Muncie Star, TWA's Ambassador.*

"We were so pleased with your lovely decor in the rooms."

Certificate may be used: Nov. 1-March 1, rates subject to change, offer not valid with any other discounts, subject to availability.

Knightstown F7

Old Hoosier House
7601 S Greensboro Pike
Knightstown, IN 46148-9613
(765)345-2969 (800)775-5315

Circa 1840. The Old Hoosier House was owned by the Elisha Scovell family, who were friends of President Martin Van Buren, and the president stayed overnight in the home. Features of the Victorian house include tall, arched windows and a gabled entrance. Rooms are decorated with antiques and lace curtains. Hearty Hoosier breakfasts include such specialties as a breakfast pizza of egg, sausage and cheese, and Melt-Away Puff Pancakes. The inn's eight acres are wooded, and the deck overlooks a pond on the fourth hole of the adjacent golf course. Innkeeper(s): Jean & Tom Lewis. $60-70. PC. 4 rooms with PB, 1 with FP. 1 suite. Breakfast, afternoon tea and evening snack included in rates. Types of meals: full breakfast and early coffee/tea. Beds: KQT. Air conditioning and ceiling fan in room. Cable TV, VCR and library on premises. Handicap access. Antiques, fishing, parks, shopping, sporting events and theater nearby.

Location: Greensboro Pike & Rd. 750 S.

Publicity: *Indianapolis Star News, New Castle Courier-Times, Indianapolis Monthly.*

"We had such a wonderful time at your house. Very many thanks."

Certificate may be used: Anytime.

Middlebury A6

Bee Hive B&B
PO Box 1191
Middlebury, IN 46540-1191
(219)825-5023 Fax:(219)825-5023

Circa 1985. This comfortable home was built with native timber. Red oak beams and a special loft add ambiance and a homey feel. Rooms include country decor and snuggly quilts, which are handmade locally. Guests can spend the day relaxing or visit the nearby Amish communities. There are local craft shops and other attractions, which include flea markets and the Shipshewana auction. The bed & breakfast is only four miles from the oldest operating mill in Indiana.

Innkeeper(s): Herb & Treva Swarm. $52-68. MC VISA PC TC. 4 rooms, 1 with PB. 1 cottage. Breakfast and evening snack included in rates. Types of meals: full breakfast and early coffee/tea. Beds: QD. Air conditioning and ceiling fan in room. VCR, fax and copier on premises. Antiques, fishing, parks, shopping, downhill skiing, cross-country skiing, sporting events, theater and watersports nearby.

Location: In Amish Country.

"What a great place to rest the mind, body and soul."

Certificate may be used: Anytime.

Patchwork Quilt Country Inn

11748 CR 2
Middlebury, IN 46540
(219)825-2417 Fax:(219)825-5172
E-mail: rgminn@aol.com

Circa 1800. Located in the heart of Indiana's Amish country, this inn offers comfortable lodging and fine food. Some of the recipes are regionally famous, such as the award-winning Buttermilk Pecan Chicken. All guest rooms feature handsome quilts and country decor, and The Loft treats visitors to a whirlpool tub and kitchenette. Ask about the

four-hour guided tour of the surrounding Amish area. The alcohol- and smoke-free inn also is host to a gift shop.

Innkeeper(s): Ray & Rosetta Miller. $70-100. MC VISA PC TC. 15 rooms with PB. 2 suites. 2 conference rooms. Breakfast included in rates. Types of meals: full breakfast and early coffee/tea. Dinner, evening snack, lunch and banquet service available. Restaurant on premises. Beds: KQT. Air conditioning and TV in room. VCR, fax and copier on premises. Handicap access. Antiques, fishing, parks, shopping, downhill skiing, cross-country skiing, sporting events, golf and theater nearby.

Certificate may be used: November, Dec. 1-26, March and April

Monticello   D4

The Victoria

206 S Bluff St
Monticello, IN 47960-2309
(219)583-3440

This Queen Anne Victorian was built by innkeeper Karen McClintock's grandfather. Karen and husband, Steve, have filled the home with family antiques and collectibles, including a whimsical cow collection in the breakfast room. A grand, hand-carved oak staircase greets guests as they arrive.

Rooms are decorated in a Victorian country theme, setting off the high ceilings and polished wood floors. The grounds boast old magnolia and maple trees and perennials planted by Karen's grandparents.

Innkeeper(s): Karen McClintock. $50-60. 3 rooms. Breakfast included in rates. Type of meal: continental-plus breakfast.

Certificate may be used: October through April; Monday through Thursday.

Nappanee   B6

The Victorian Guest House

302 E Market St
Nappanee, IN 46550-2102
(217)773-4383

Circa 1887. Listed in the National Register, this three-story Queen Anne Victorian inn was built by Frank Coppes, one of America's first noted kitchen cabinet makers. Nappanee's location makes it an ideal stopping point for those exploring the heart of Amish country, or visiting the South Bend or chain of lakes areas. Visitors may choose from six guest rooms, including the Coppes Suite, with its original golden oak woodwork, antique tub and stained glass. Full breakfast is served at the antique 11-foot dining room table. Amish Acres is just one mile from the inn.

Innkeeper(s): Vickie Heinsberger. $75. MC VISA DS. 6 rooms with PB. Breakfast and afternoon tea included in rates. Types of meals: full breakfast and early coffee/tea. Evening snack, banquet service and catering service available. Beds: QDT. Air conditioning, turndown service, ceiling fan and TV in room. Antiques, shopping, sporting events, theater and watersports nearby.

Publicity: *Goshen News.*

Certificate may be used: Dec. 1-April 15, Monday-Thursday.

Nashville H5

Wraylyn Knoll B&B
PO Box 481
Nashville, IN 47448-0481
(812)988-0733

The village of Nashville offers more than 250 specialty shops and restaurants, but guests need not look far from the 12 acres that surround Wraylyn Knoll to find activity. Set on top of a hill and surrounded by woods, the grounds include a swimming pool, nature trails and a fishing pond. Guests can opt to stay in the main house or Dove Cottage, which includes two bedrooms. Weekend guests are treated to a full, country breakfast.

Innkeeper(s): Marcia Peters Wray. $50-80. MC VISA. 6 rooms. Breakfast included in rates. Type of meal: continental-plus breakfast.

Certificate may be used: Sunday through Thursday, March through September.

New Albany K6

Honeymoon Mansion B&B & Wedding Chapel
1014 E Main St
New Albany, IN 47150-5843
(812)945-0312 (800)759-7270
E-mail: honeymoonmansion.juno.com

Circa 1850. The innkeepers at Honeymoon Mansion can provide guests with the flowers, wedding chapel and honeymoon suite. All you need to bring is a bride or groom. An ordained minister is on the premises and guests can marry or renew their vows in the inn's Victorian wedding chapel. However, one need not be a newlywed to enjoy this bed & breakfast. Canopy beds, stained-glass windows and heart-shaped rugs are a few of the romantic touches. Several suites include marble Jacuzzis flanked on four sides with eight-foot-high marble columns, creating a dramatic and elegant effect. The home itself, a pre-Civil War Italianate-style home listed in the state and national historic registers, boasts many fine period features. Gingerbread trim, intricate molding and a grand staircase add to the Victorian ambiance. Guests are treated to an all-you-can-eat country breakfast with items such as homemade breads, biscuits and gravy, eggs, sausage and potatoes.

Innkeeper(s): J. Franklin & Beverly Dennis. $70-140. MC VISA PC TC. 6 suites. 2 conference rooms. Breakfast included in rates. Type of meal: full breakfast. Catering service available. Beds: Q. Air conditioning, ceiling fan, TV and VCR in room. Copier on premises. Handicap access. Amusement parks, antiques, fishing, parks, shopping, downhill skiing,

cross-country skiing, sporting events, theater and watersports nearby.
Location: On the Ohio Scenic Route in Southern Indiana.
Publicity: *Indianapolis Star, Courier-Journal, Evening News, Tribune.*

Certificate may be used: Sunday through Thursday, entire year except Derby week, New Year's and Valentine's Days, subject to availability.

Rising Sun I8

The Jelley House Country Inn
222 S Walnut St
Rising Sun, IN 47040-1142
(812)438-2319
E-mail: jmoore@seidata.com

Circa 1847. This pre-Civil War Colonial changed hands many times before current innkeepers Jeff and Jennifer Moore purchased the place. Antiques decorate the interior, as well as an old pump organ and a baby grand piano. The front porch is lined with comfortable chairs for those who wish to relax. The home is just two blocks from Riverfront Park and the Ohio River, and the innkeepers offer bikes for guests who wish to ride around and explore the area.

Innkeeper(s): Jeff & Jennifer Moore. $65-70. MC VISA PC TC. 5 rooms. 1 suite. Breakfast included in rates. Type of meal: continental-plus breakfast. Beds: QDT. Air conditioning, ceiling fan and TV in room. VCR and bicycles on premises. Antiques, fishing, parks, shopping, downhill skiing, sporting events, golf, theater and watersports nearby.
Publicity: *Recorded & News.*

"Beautifully decorated. You have preserved some of the old and new...enjoyed this home atmosphere."

Certificate may be used: Jan. 1-Dec. 31, Sunday through Thursday only.

Rockville G3

Billie Creek Inn
RR 2, Box 27, Billie Creek Village
Rockville, IN 47872
(765)569-3430 Fax:(765)569-3582

Circa 1996. Although this inn was built recently, it rests on the outskirts of historic Billie Creek Village. The village is a non-profit, turn-of-the-century living museum, complete with 30 historic buildings and three covered bridges. Guests can explore an 1830s cabin, a maple syrup camp, a general store and much more to experience how Americans lived in the 19th century. The innkeepers take part in the history, dressing in period costume. The inn is decorated in a comfortable, country style. The nine suites include the added amenity of a whirlpool tub. All inn guests receive complimentary admission to Billie Creek Village. Coffee and continental breakfast fare are available around the clock.

Innkeeper(s): Carol Gum & Doug Wetsheit. $49-99. MC VISA AX DS PC TC. 31 rooms with PB. 9 suites. 2 conference rooms. Breakfast included in rates. Type of meal: continental breakfast. Catering service available. Restaurant on premises. Beds: KD. Air conditioning and TV in room. VCR, fax, copier, swimming, stables and pet boarding on premises. Handicap access. Antiques, fishing, parks, shopping, sporting events, golf, theater and watersports nearby.

Certificate may be used: Year-round, Sunday through Thursday nights except during special events and the Parke County Covered Bridge festival.

Suits Us B&B
514 N College St
Rockville, IN 47872-1511
(765)569-5660 (888)478-4878

Circa 1883. Sixty miles west of Indianapolis is this stately Colonial Revival inn, where Woodrow Wilson, Annie Oakley and James Witcomb Riley were once guests of the Strause Family. The inn offers a fireplace and library, bicycles and an exercise room. Turkey Run State Park are nearby. The Ernie Pyle State Historic Site, Raccoon State Recreation Area and four golf courses are within easy driving distance.

Innkeeper(s): Marty & Bev Rose. $55-125. TC. 4 rooms with PB. 1 suite. Breakfast included in rates. Types of meals: full breakfast and early coffee/tea. Beds: KQD. Air conditioning, ceiling fan, TV and VCR in room. Bicycles on premises. Antiques, fishing, parks, shopping, golf and watersports nearby.

Publicity: *Touring America, Traces Historic Magazine.*

Certificate may be used: Sunday-Thursday (except special events), March 1-Nov. 30.

South Bend   A5

Oliver Inn
630 W Washington St
South Bend, IN 46601-1444
(219)232-4545 (888)697-4466 Fax:(219)288-9788

Circa 1886. This stately Queen Anne Victorian sits amid 30 towering maples and was once home to Josephine Oliver Ford, daughter of James Oliver, of

chilled plow fame. Located in South Bend's historic district, this inn offers a comfortable library and nine inviting guest rooms, some with built-in fireplaces or double Jacuzzis. The inn is within walking distance of downtown, and public transportation is available.

Innkeeper(s): Richard & Venera Monahan. $85-192. MC VISA AX DS PC TC. 9 rooms with PB, 2 with FP. 3 suites. 1 conference room. Breakfast and evening snack included in rates. Types of meals: continental-plus breakfast and early coffee/tea. Beds: KQ. Air conditioning, turndown service, ceiling fan and TV in room. Fax on premises. Handicap access. Antiques, fishing, parks, shopping, cross-country skiing, sporting events, theater and watersports nearby.

Certificate may be used: January-December, Sunday-Thursday. Not good on special event weekends, N.D. football, graduation, etc.

Warsaw   B6

Candlelight Inn
503 E Fort Wayne St
Warsaw, IN 46580-3338
(219)267-2906 (800)352-0640 Fax:(219)269-4646

Circa 1860. Canopy beds, pedestal sinks, clawfoot tubs and period antiques carry out the inn's "Gone With the Wind" theme. Scarlett's Chamber features rose wallpaper, a queen bed and mauve carpeting, while Rhett Butler's Chamber boasts navy walls, hardwood floors, a walnut canopy bed, burgundy velvet sofa and a Jacuzzi tub.

Innkeeper(s): Deborah Hambright. $74-129. MC VISA AX. 10 rooms with PB. Breakfast included in rates. Types of meals: full breakfast and early coffee/tea. Room service available. Air conditioning, turndown service, ceiling fan and TV in room. Fax on premises. Antiques, fishing, shopping and theater nearby.

Location: Two miles south on State Road 15 off Highway 30.

Certificate may be used: Anytime rooms available.

White Hill Manor
2513 E Center St
Warsaw, IN 46580-3819
(219)269-6933 Fax:(219)268-2260

Circa 1934. This elegantly crafted 4,500-square-foot English Tudor was constructed during the Depression when fine artisans were available at low cost. Handsome arched entryways and ceilings, crown molding and mullioned windows create a gracious intimate atmosphere. The mansion has been carefully renovated and decorated with a combination of traditional furnishings and contemporary English fabrics.

Innkeeper(s): Carm & Zoyla Henderson. $80-120. MC VISA AX DC DS. 8 rooms with PB. Breakfast included in rates. Type of meal: full breakfast. Beds: KQ. Handicap access. Fishing, downhill skiing and cross-country skiing nearby.

Publicity: *Indiana Business, USA Today.*

"It's the perfect place for an at-home getaway."

Certificate may be used: Nov. 1-Feb. 1, Sunday-Friday

Iowa

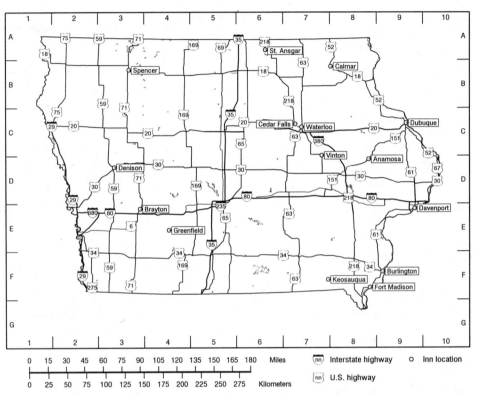

0	15	30	45	60	75	90	105	120	135	150	165	180	Miles
0	25	50	75	100	125	150	175	200	225	250	275	Kilometers

(nn) Interstate highway   ○ Inn location

(nn) U.S. highway

Anamosa

D8

The Shaw House
509 S Oak St
Anamosa, IA 52205-1537
(319)462-4485

Circa 1890. Framed by enormous old oak trees, this three-story Italianate mansion was built in the style of a Maine sea captain's house. Bordered by sweeping lawns and situated on a hillside on 45 acres, the inn provides views of graceful pastureland from the front porch swing and the tower. Polished oak, walnut and pine floors highlight the carved woodwork and antique furnishings. Guests can enjoy a short walk to downtown.

130

Innkeeper(s): Constance McKean. $70-85. 5 rooms, 2 with PB, 1 with FP. 1 suite. 1 conference room. Breakfast included in rates. Types of meals: full breakfast and early coffee/tea. Evening snack available. Beds: QDT. Air conditioning in room. Child care on premises. Antiques, fishing, shopping, downhill skiing, cross-country skiing, sporting events and theater nearby.

Publicity: *Cedar Rapids Gazette, Anamosa Journal-Eureka.*

"The views were fantastic as was the hospitality."

Certificate may be used: When room is available.

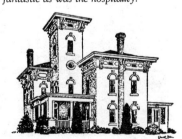

Brayton
E3

Hallock House B&B
PO Box 19, 3265 Jay Ave
Brayton, IA 50042-7524
(712)549-2449 (800)945-0663

Circa 1882. Innkeeper Ruth Barton's great-great Uncle, Isaac Hallock, built this Queen Anne Victorian. The home is an architectural gem, featuring high ceilings, ornate woodwork, carved pocket doors and a built-in china cupboard. And as is the Victorian tradition, several porches decorate the exterior. The home is across the street from the site of an old stagecoach stop, which bought an abundance of cattlemen into town, many of who stayed in the Hallock House. The innkeepers offer stable facilities and an exercise area for guests traveling with horses.

Innkeeper(s): Guy & Ruth Barton. $40. VISA TC. 2 rooms with PB. Breakfast included in rates. Type of meal: full breakfast. Beds: QD. Air conditioning and ceiling fan in room. VCR, bicycles and pet boarding on premises. Antiques, fishing, parks and shopping nearby.

Certificate may be used: Anytime except holidays, reservation required.

Burlington
F9

Schramm House B&B
616 Columbia St
Burlington, IA 52601
(319)754-0373 (800)683-7117 Fax:(319)754-0373

Circa 1866. "Colossal" would be an excellent word to describe this Queen Anne Victorian. The home is an impressive site in this Burlington historic district. The exterior is brick on the first story with clapboard on the second, and a third-story tower is one of the architectural highlights. Inside, the parquet floors and woodwork have been restored to their 19th-century grandeur. The home was built just after the Civil War ended by a local department store owner. Additions were made in the 1880s. Eventually, the home was converted into apartments, so the innkeepers took on quite a task refurbishing the place back to its original state. The Victorian is decorated with the innkeepers collection of antiques. One particularly appealing guest room includes an exposed brick wall and tin ceiling. Breakfast might begin with a baked pear topped with toasted almonds and a raspberry sauce. From there, freshly baked muffins arrive, followed by an entree, perhaps a frittata or French toast. All courses are served with fine china and crystal. The home is just six blocks from the Mississippi, and don't pass up a walk down historic Snake Alley.

Innkeeper(s): Sandy & Bruce Morrison. $75. MC VISA AX DS PC TC. 3 rooms with PB. Breakfast included in rates. Types of meals: full breakfast and early coffee/tea. Beds: QDT. Turndown service and ceiling fan in room. Cable TV, VCR, fax and library on premises. Antiques, fishing, parks, shopping and golf nearby.

Publicity: *Hawk Eye.*

"This historically interesting home has been restored to a charming B&B. I was raised in Burling, Iowa, and I am especially pleased to see this handsome old family home used in such a enjoyable way."

Certificate may be used: Sunday-Thursday, all year.

Calmar
B8

Calmar Guesthouse
103 W North St
Calmar, IA 52132-9801
(319)562-3851

Circa 1890. This beautifully restored Victorian home was built by John B. Kay, a lawyer and poet. Stained-glass windows, carved moldings, an oak-and-walnut staircase and gleaming woodwork highlight the gracious interior. A grandfather clock ticks in the living room. In the foyer, a friendship yellow rose is incorporated into the stained-glass window pane. Breakfast is served in the formal dining room. The Laura Ingalls Wilder Museum is nearby in Burr Oak. The Bily Brothers Clock Museum, Smallest Church, Luther College and Norweigian Museum are located nearby.

Innkeeper(s): Lucile Kruse. $45-50. MC VISA PC TC. 5 rooms, 1 with PB. Breakfast included in rates. Types of meals: full breakfast and early coffee/tea. Beds: Q. Air conditioning and TV in room. VCR, bicycles and library on premises. Antiques, fishing, parks, shopping, downhill skiing, cross-country skiing, sporting events, theater and watersports nearby.

Publicity: *Iowa Farmer Today, Calmar Courier, Minneapolis Star-Tribune, Home and Away, Iowan.*

"What a delight it was to stay here. No one could have made our stay more welcome or enjoyable."

Certificate may be used: Monday to Thursday, April to October only.

Cedar Falls
C7

The House by the Side of the Road
6804 Ranchero Rd
Cedar Falls, IA 50613-9689
(319)988-3691

Circa 1901. Located on 80 acres, this inn is a country-style farmhouse. Perfect for those seeking a retreat in the countryside, the rooms in the House by the Side of the Road feature ceiling fans and fireplaces. Corn and soybeans are raised on the property, located near Highway 20, a main link to

Dubuque and to the Cedar Rapids area. A dinner boat ride on Shell Rock River can be arranged, and an Amish community is nearby for quilt shopping and crafts.

Innkeeper(s): Harlan S. Hughes. $45. PC TC. 2 rooms. Breakfast included in rates. Types of meals: full breakfast and early coffee/tea. Beds: KD. Air conditioning in room. VCR on premises. Antiques, fishing, parks, shopping, sporting events, golf, theater and watersports nearby.

Publicity: *Waterloo-Cedar Falls Courier.*

Certificate may be used: August to December, open all year, certificate good if rooms are available.

Davenport   E9

Fulton's Landing Guest House
1206 E River Dr
Davenport, IA 52803-5742
(319)322-4069 Fax:(319)322-8186

Circa 1871. Enjoy views of the Mississippi River from the porches of this brick, Italianate home, which is listed in the National Register. The guest rooms are decorated with antiques, including ceiling fans. After enjoying the morning meal, guests have a variety of activities to choose. Riverboat gambling, shopping and downtown Davenport all are nearby.

Innkeeper(s): Pat & Bill Schmidt. $60-125. MC VISA AX. 5 rooms, 3 with PB. 1 suite. 2 conference rooms. Breakfast included in rates. Types of meals: full breakfast and gourmet breakfast. Banquet service, catering service and room service available. Beds: Q. Air conditioning, ceiling fan and TV in room. Fax, copier and bicycles on premises. Antiques, fishing, parks, shopping, cross-country skiing, sporting events, theater and watersports nearby.

Certificate may be used: Nov. 1 through April 30.

Denison   D3

Queen Belle Country Inn
1430 3rd Ave S
Denison, IA 51442
(712)263-6777

Circa 1889. The wide front veranda of this historic Victorian provides wicker chairs and other furnishings for those who wish to relax. The interior is decorated in country Victorian style with flowery wallpapers. The front parlor features an antique organ and piano. Guests will enjoy plenty of homemade food. The innkeepers provide breakfast, afternoon and evening snacks for guests. Gourmet dinner is also an option.

Innkeeper(s): Paul & Arleeta Lenz. $65-150. MC VISA PC TC. 4 rooms, 3 with PB, 1 with FP. 1 suite. 1 conference room. Breakfast, afternoon tea and evening snack included in rates. Types of meals: full breakfast, gourmet breakfast and early coffee/tea. Dinner and room service available. Beds: KQT. Air conditioning, turndown service, TV and VCR in

room. Fax, spa and library on premises. Handicap access. Antiques, fishing, parks, shopping, cross-country skiing, golf, theater and watersports nearby.

Certificate may be used: Year-round, Sunday-Thursday.

Dubuque   C9

The Mandolin Inn
199 Loras Blvd
Dubuque, IA 52001-4857
(319)556-0069 (800)524-7996 Fax:(319)556-0587

Circa 1908. This three-story brick Edwardian with Queen Anne wraparound veranda boasts a mosaic-tiled porch floor. Inside are in-laid mahogany and rosewood floors, bay windows and a turret that starts

in the parlor and ascends to the second-floor Holly Marie Room, decorated in a wedding motif. This room features a seven-piece French Walnut bedroom suite and a crystal chandelier. A three-course gourmet breakfast is served in the dining room with Italian tile depicting women's work at the turn-of-the-century. There is an herb garden outside the kitchen. A church is across the street and riverboat gambling is 12 blocks away.

Innkeeper(s): Jan Oswald. $75-135. MC VISA AX DS PC TC. 7 rooms, 5 with PB. 2 conference rooms. Breakfast included in rates. Types of meals: gourmet breakfast and early coffee/tea. Beds: KQD. Air conditioning, ceiling fan and TV in room. Fax on premises. Antiques, fishing, parks, shopping, downhill skiing, cross-country skiing, sporting events, theater and watersports nearby.

"From the moment we entered the Mandolin, we felt at home. I know we'll be back."

Certificate may be used: Sunday through Thursday. Year-round, except for holidays.

The Richards House
1492 Locust St
Dubuque, IA 52001-4714
(319)557-1492

Circa 1883. Owner David Stuart estimates that it will take several years to remove the concrete-based brown paint applied by a bridge painter in the '60s to cover the 7,000-square-foot, Stick-style Victorian house. The interior, however, only needed a tad of polish. The varnished cherry and bird's-eye maple

woodwork is set aglow under electrified gaslights. Ninety stained-glass windows, eight pocket doors with stained glass and a magnificent entryway reward those who pass through.

Innkeeper(s): Michelle A. Delaney. $40-95. MC VISA AX DC CB DS TC. 6 rooms, 3 with PB, 5 with FP. 1 suite. 1 conference room. Breakfast included in rates. Types of meals: full breakfast and early coffee/tea. Afternoon tea and evening snack available. Beds: Q. TV in room. VCR and fax on premises. Antiques, fishing, parks, shopping, downhill skiing, cross-country skiing, theater and watersports nearby.

Location: In the Jackson Park National Register Historic District.

Publicity: *Collectors Journal, Telegraph Herald.*

"Although the guide at the door had warned us that the interior was incredible, we were still flabbergasted when we stepped into the foyer of this house."

Certificate may be used: Sunday through Thursday, all year. Very limited availability on Fridays (call).

Fort Madison   F8

Kingsley Inn
707 Avenue H (Hwy 61)
Fort Madison, IA 52627
(319)372-7074 (800)441-2327 Fax:(319)372-7096

Circa 1858. Overlooking the Mississippi River, this century-old inn is located in downtown Fort Madison. Though furnished with antiques, all 14 rooms offer modern amenities and private baths (some with whirlpools) as well as river views. There also is a two-bedroom, two-bath suite. The suite includes a living room, dining area, kitchen and a whirlpool tub in one bathroom. A riverboat casino and a variety of shops are within a few blocks of the inn. There

is a restaurant, Alphas on the Riverfront, and a gift shop on the premises.

Innkeeper(s): Nannette Evans. $65-115. MC VISA AX DC DS. 14 rooms with PB. 1 suite. 1 conference room. Breakfast included in rates. Types of meals: continental-plus breakfast and early coffee/tea. Restaurant on premises. Beds: KQD. Air conditioning and TV in room. Fax on premises. Handicap access. Antiques, fishing, shopping and theater nearby.

Location: US Highway 61 in downtown Fort Madison.

Publicity: *Hawkeye.*

"Wow, how nice and relaxing, quiet atmosphere, great innkeeper, so personal, kind and friendly."

Certificate may be used: April-October, Monday-Thursday, weekends and holidays excluded. November through March, all days.

Greenfield   E4

The Brass Lantern
2446 State Hwy 92
Greenfield, IA 50849-9757
(515)743-2031 (888)743-2031 Fax:(515)343-7500
E-mail: info@brasslantern.com

Circa 1918. Located on 20 acres, this B&B is highlighted by an indoor pool complex with a curving 40-foot pool. Guest rooms are above this building and feature Southwestern, country and traditional themes. The innkeepers are happy to guide hunters to private hunting lands known for excellent pheasant and quail hunting. Madison Country and its famous bridges are within a 20-minute drive.

Innkeeper(s): Terry & Margie Moore. $85-145. PC TC. 3 rooms, 2 with PB. Breakfast included in rates. Types of meals: full breakfast and early coffee/tea. Evening snack available. Beds: Q. Air conditioning and TV in room. Fax, copier and child care on premises. Antiques, fishing, shopping and golf nearby.

Certificate may be used: Sunday-Thursday, Nov. 15-March 15.

Keosauqua   F7

Hotel Manning
100 Van Buren St
Keosauqua, IA 52565
(319)293-3232 (800)728-2718 Fax:(319)293-9960

Circa 1899. This historic riverfront inn offers a peek at bygone days. Its steamboat gothic exterior is joined by an interior that strives for historic authenticity. All bedrooms are furnished with antiques. Lacey-Keosauqua State Park and Lake Sugema are within easy driving distance. Inn guests enjoy a full breakfast. There is a 19-room, modern motel adjacent to the inn.

Innkeeper(s): Ron & Connie Davenport. $35-72. MC VISA DS PC. 18 rooms, 10 with PB. 2 suites. 1 conference room. Breakfast included in rates. Banquet service, catering service and catered breakfast available. Restaurant on premises. Beds: QD. Air conditioning and ceiling fan in

room. VCR, fax and copier on premises. Antiques, fishing, parks and shopping nearby.

Certificate may be used: Sunday-Thursday, May-October; anytime, November-April.

Mason House Inn of Bentonsport

RR 2, Box 237
Keosauqua, IA 52565
(319)592-3133

Circa 1846. A Murphy-style copper bathtub folds down out of the wall at this unusual inn built by Mormon craftsmen, who stayed in Bentonsport for one year on their trek to Utah. More than half of the furniture is original to the home, including a nine-foot walnut headboard and a nine-foot mirror.

This is the only operating pre-Civil War steamboat inn in Iowa. Guests can imagine the days when steamboats made their way up and down the Des Moines River, while taking in the scenery. A full breakfast is served, but if guests crave a mid-morning snack, each room is equipped with its own stocked cookie jar.

Innkeeper(s): William McDermet III. $39-74. MC VISA. 9 rooms, 5 with PB. 1 conference room. Breakfast included in rates. Types of meals: full breakfast and early coffee/tea. Dinner, picnic lunch and lunch available. Beds: KQ. Air conditioning and ceiling fan in room. Bicycles on premises. Handicap access. Antiques, shopping and cross-country skiing nearby.

Location: In the historic village of Bentonsport.

Publicity: *Des Moines Register, Fairfield Ledger, Friends.*

"The attention to detail was fantastic, food was wonderful and the setting was fascinating."

Certificate may be used: Sunday through Thursday, all year.

Spencer B3

The Hannah Marie Country Inn

4070 Highway 71
Spencer, IA 51301-2033
(712)262-1286 (800)972-1286 Fax:(712)262-3294

Circa 1907. Enjoy the romance of the country at Hannah Marie's, tucked on a rural highway in the midst of golden fields of corn. Feather beds topped with down comforters, in-room double whirlpool tubs, soften water and bubble bath are some of the

luxurious amenities. Each guest room has a special theme. Guests are given parasols for strolling along the grounds, which has herb, flower and vegetable gardens. The innkeepers host themed tea parties, children's etiquette lunches, herb workshops and afternoon tea. Guests can mingle with the Queen of Hearts or perhaps Queen Elizabeth at a garden party. A new butterfly garden also has been added. The full breakfasts are served by candlelight, or guests can opt for lighter fare delivered to their guest room door in a basket. Early evening refreshments also are included in the rates.

Innkeeper(s): Mary Nichols. $70-105. MC VISA DS PC TC. 6 rooms with PB. 1 conference room. Breakfast included in rates. Types of meals: continental breakfast, gourmet breakfast and early coffee/tea. Afternoon tea and gourmet lunch available. Beds: Q. Air conditioning and ceiling fan in room. Amusement parks, antiques, fishing, parks, shopping, theater and watersports nearby.

Location: Five miles south of Spencer.

Publicity: *Midwest Living, Partners, Des Moines Register, Sioux City Journal, Home and Away.*

"Best bed & breakfast in Iowa—Des Moines Register."

Certificate may be used: April, May, November, December.

St. Ansgar
A6

Blue Belle Inn B&B
PO Box 205, 513 W 4th St
St. Ansgar, IA 50472
(515)736-2225 Fax:(515)736-2225
E-mail: bluebelle@deskmedia.com/bluebelle

Circa 1896. This home was purchased from a Knoxville, Tenn., mail-order house. It's difficult to believe that stunning features, such as a tin ceiling, stained-glass windows, intricate woodwork and pocket doors could have come via the mail, but these original items are still here for guests to admire. Rooms are named after books special to the innkeeper. Four of the rooms include a Jacuzzi tub, and the Never Neverland room has a clawfoot tub. Other rooms offer a skylight, fireplace or perhaps a white iron bed. During the Christmas season, every

room has its own decorated tree. The innkeeper hosts a variety of themed luncheons, dinners and events, such as the April in Paris cooking workshop. Mother's Day brunches, the "Some Enchanted Evening" dinner or the posh "Pomp and Circumstance" dinner are some of the possibilities.
Innkeeper(s): Sherry Hansen. $40-130. MC VISA AX DS PC TC. 6 rooms, 5 with PB, 2 with FP. 2 suites. 2 conference rooms. Breakfast included in rates. Types of meals: continental breakfast, continental-plus breakfast, full breakfast, gourmet breakfast and early coffee/tea. Afternoon tea, dinner, evening snack, lunch, gourmet lunch, banquet service and room service available. Restaurant on premises. Beds: KQT. Air conditioning, TV and VCR in room. Fax and library on premises. Antiques, fishing, parks, shopping, golf and watersports nearby.
Publicity: *Minneapolis Star Tribune, Post-Bulletin, Midwest Living, Country, AAA Home & Away, Des Moines Register.*
Certificate may be used: Nov. 1-April 30, Monday-Thursday nights only, holidays excluded, subject to availability.

Vinton
C7

Lion & The Lamb B&B
913 2nd Ave
Vinton, IA 52349
(319)472-5086 (800)808-LAMB Fax:(319)472-5086
E-mail: lionlambbbb@aol.com
Circa 1892. This Queen Anne Victorian, a true

"Painted Lady," boasts a stunning exterior with intricate chimneys, gingerbread trim, gables and turrets. The home still maintains its original pocket doors and parquet flooring, and antiques add to the nostalgic flavor. One room boasts a 150-year-old bedroom set. Breakfasts, as any meal in such fine a house should, are served on china. Succulent French toast topped with powdered sugar and a rich strawberry sauce is a specialty. In the evenings, desserts are served.
Innkeeper(s): Richard & Rachel Waterbury. $65-85. MC VISA DS PC TC. 4 rooms, 2 with PB, 2 with FP. Breakfast included in rates. Types of meals: full breakfast and early coffee/tea. Catering service available. Beds: Q. Air conditioning and ceiling fan in room. VCR, fax and bicycles on premises. Antiques, fishing, parks, shopping, cross-country skiing, golf, theater and watersports nearby.
Publicity: *Cedar Valley Times, Waterloo Courier, Cedar Rapids Gazette.*

"It is a magical place!"

Certificate may be used: Jan. 5-April 30, Sunday-Thursday.

Waterloo
C7

The Daisy Wilton Inn
418 Walnut St
Waterloo, IA 50703-3817
(319)232-0801

Circa 1900. An extensive collection of Victorian furnishings decorate this historic Queen Anne home. Through the years, the Victorian had several owners and even served as a gambling hall at one time. The B&B is named for innkeeper Sue Brase's grandmother, and there are pictures of Daisy displayed in the home. Also in the home are family pieces, such as Daisy's writing desk. William Morris wallpapers, pre-Raphaelite artwork, fireplaces, antique clothing and Oriental rugs add to the authentic period ambiance. A full, gourmet breakfast is served, featuring items such as Grand Marnier French toast.
Innkeeper(s): Al & Sue Brase. $45-65. PC. 3 rooms, 1 with PB, 1 with FP. Breakfast and evening snack included in rates. Types of meals: continental-plus breakfast, full breakfast, gourmet breakfast and early coffee/tea. Beds: QD. Air conditioning in room. VCR, bicycles and library on premises. Antiques, fishing, parks, shopping, cross-country skiing, sporting events, golf, theater and watersports nearby.
Publicity: *Waterloo Courier.*

"I was amazed at the beauty of this house! I felt as if I were in a fairy tale. Every detail is perfect."

Certificate may be used: Jan. 30-Oct. 30, Sunday-Friday, subject to availability.

Kansas

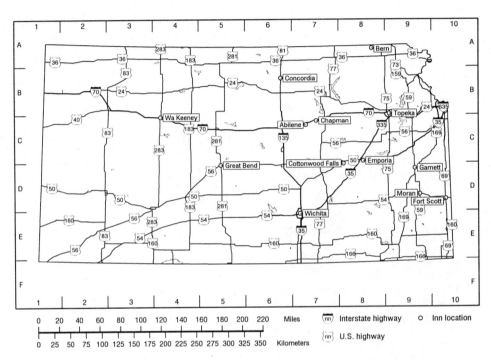

0 20 40 60 80 100 120 140 160 180 200 220   Miles

0 25 50 75 100 125 150 175 200 225 250 275 300 325 350   Kilometers

(nn) Interstate highway   o Inn location

(nn) U.S. highway

Abilene   C7

Ehrsam Place B&B
103 S Grant
Abilene, KS 67441
(785)263-8747 Fax:(785)263-8548

Circa 1879. In its early days, this home and the family who lived in it were the talk of the town. The family held an abundance of well-attended parties, and many rumors were spread about why the Ehrsam company safe was kept in the home's basement. Rumors aside, the home features a variety of architectural styles, leaning toward Georgian, with columns gracing the front entrance. The 20-acre grounds are fun to explore, offering a windmill, silo, stables, a carriage house and creek. The innkeepers encourage guests to explore the home as well, which rises three stories. The basement still houses the illusive safe. Rooms are decorated in a variety of styles, from Art Deco to Victorian. Guests can enjoy breakfast in bed if they choose. With advance notice, the innkeepers will prepare hors d'oeuvres, picnic lunches and dinners for their guests. Candlelight dinners for two also are available, and turn-down service is one of the romantic amenities.
Innkeeper(s): Mary & William Lambert. $55-85. MC VISA PC TC. 4 suites. 1 conference room. Breakfast, afternoon tea and evening snack included in rates. Types of meals: full breakfast and early coffee/tea. Dinner, picnic lunch, catering service and room service available. Beds: Q. Air conditioning, turndown service, ceiling fan and TV in room. VCR, fax and library on premises. Antiques, fishing, parks, shopping, sporting events, golf and theater nearby.

"Thank you for history, laughs and most all sharing your treasures with us."

Certificate may be used: All year, if on a weekend, stay must include a Thursday or Sunday night.

Kansas

Bern   A8

Lear Acres B&B
RR 1 Box 31
Bern, KS 66408-9715
(913)336-3903

Circa 1918. A working farm just south of the
Nebraska border, Lear Acres is exactly the down-
home setting it appears to be. The two-story farmhouse features three spacious guest rooms, all with
views of the surrounding countryside. Many of the
inn's furnishings are period pieces from the early
1900s. Guests will be greeted by a menagerie of farm
pets and animals, adding to the distinctly country
atmosphere. The full breakfast features food from
the innkeepers' farm and garden. Fall or winter
guests may ask for Grandma's cozy feather bed.
Innkeeper(s): Toby Lear. $35-38. 3 rooms. Breakfast included in rates.
Type of meal: full breakfast. Air conditioning, turndown service, ceiling
fan and VCR in room. Antiques nearby.

Certificate may be used: Any weekend, except Memorial Day with
minimum of 10-day advance reservation.

Chapman   C7

Windmill Inn B&B
1787 Rain Rd
Chapman, KS 67431-9317
(913)263-8755

Circa 1917. The Windmill Inn is a place of memories. Many were created by the innkeeper's grandparents, who built the home. Others are the happy
remembrances guests take home. The home is filled
with antiques, family heirlooms. Stained glass and a
window seat add to the charm. For an extra charge,
the innkeepers provide dinner or picnic lunches.
The wraparound porches offer a relaxing swing, and
on starry nights, the outdoor spa is the place to be.
Historic Abilene is just a few miles down the road,
offering a glimpse of an authentic Old West town,
located on the Chisolm Trail.
Innkeeper(s): Deb Sanders. $55-85. 4 rooms. Breakfast included in
rates. Type of meal: full breakfast.

Certificate may be used: Sunday through Thursday.

Concordia   B6

Crystle's B&B
508 W 7th St
Concordia, KS 66901-2708
(913)243-2192 (800)889-6373
Circa 1880. This Queen Anne Victorian inn has
been recognized by the city's historical society. The

home has been in the
owner's family for four
generations. Three of
the inn's five guest
rooms showcase
Crystle's impressive
plate collection.
The inn is filled
with charming
Victorian touches, and
a favorite feature is the
1916 Steinway grand piano in
the parlor. Guests may enjoy breakfast in their
room, the inn's dining room or, weather permitting,
on the sun-drenched front porch. Located in a
famous grain-production area of the state,
Concordia offers much of interest. Be sure to take in
the impressive Brown Grand Theatre.
Innkeeper(s): Betty Suther. $35-50. MC VISA. 5 rooms, 1 with PB. 1
conference room. Breakfast included in rates. Types of meals: full
breakfast and early coffee/tea. Beds: QD. Air conditioning in room.
Cable TV and VCR on premises. Antiques, parks, shopping and theater
nearby.
Publicity: *Blade Empire, Innsider.*

Certificate may be used: Off-season and during weekdays.

Cottonwood Falls   D8

1874 Stonehouse B&B on Mulberry Hill
Rt 1, Box 67A
Cottonwood Falls, KS 66845
(316)273-8481 Fax:(316)273-8481
E-mail: 5hmh1874@aol.com

Circa 1874. More than 100 acres surround this historic home, which is one of the state's oldest native
stone homes that is still in use. Each guest room
offers something special. The Rose Room includes a
sleigh bed, while the Blue Room and Yellow Room
offer views either of the quarry pond or the Flint
Hills. Explore the property and you'll see wildlife,
an old stone barn and corral ruins. The Cottonwood
River runs through the property at one point, offering fishing. The innkeepers can arrange for guests to
fish in a stocked pond, too.
Innkeeper(s): Dan & Carrie Riggs. $60-75. MC VISA TC. 3 rooms with
PB. Breakfast included in rates. Types of meals: continental breakfast,
full breakfast and gourmet breakfast. Beds: KQT. Air conditioning and
ceiling fan in room. VCR, fax, copier and library on premises. Antiques,
fishing, parks, shopping and watersports nearby.

*"I have never felt so pampered. Our walk around the
countryside was so peaceful and beautiful."*

Certificate may be used: Sunday-Thursday from Nov. 1-March 1, holiday excepted.

137

Emporia
C8

Plumb House B&B

628 Exchange St
Emporia, KS 66801-3008
(316)342-6881

Circa 1910. Named for former owners of this restored Victorian Shingle home, the Plumb House offers elegant touches of that period's finery throughout its attractive interior. Try the Rosalie Room, with its pink roses and white lace or the Horseless Carriage Room with old-fashioned tub

and rocking chair or the Loft, a suite with not only a view, but all the amenities of home, including TV, refrigerator and microwave. Be sure to inquire about the inn's two-hour Tea Party, available for that extra-special occasion.

Innkeeper(s): Barbara Stoecklin. $65-80. MC VISA AX PC TC. 5 rooms, 3 with PB, 1 with FP. 1 suite. 1 conference room. Breakfast, afternoon tea and evening snack included in rates. Types of meals: continental breakfast, full breakfast, gourmet breakfast and early coffee/tea. Room service available. Beds: KQDT. Air conditioning, turndown service and ceiling fan in room. Cable TV, VCR and spa on premises. Antiques, fishing, parks, shopping, sporting events and theater nearby.

Publicity: *Emporia Gazette, KSNW-TV, Wichita, Kansas.*

"This is the most elegant place I have ever had the pleasure to stay in. It's beautiful Victorian decor has refreshed my soul."

Certificate may be used: Anytime.

The White Rose Inn

901 Merchant St
Emporia, KS 66801-2813
(316)343-6336

Circa 1902. Emporia is a Midwest college town, and the White Rose Inn is a mere three blocks from Emporia State University. This Queen Anne Victorian home offers three private suites for its guests, all with a sitting room and queen beds. Each morning, guests will be treated to a different and delicious menu, and every afternoon, tea or espresso is served. Guests who so desire may have breakfast in bed, and the innkeepers will happily arrange for a

massage, manicure or pedicure. The inn also hosts weddings and family reunions.

Innkeeper(s): Samuel & Lisa Tosti. $50-75. MC VISA AX DC DS TC. 4 suites. Breakfast and afternoon tea included in rates. Types of meals: full breakfast, gourmet breakfast and early coffee/tea. Dinner, evening snack, picnic lunch, lunch, gourmet lunch, banquet service, catering service, catered breakfast and room service available. Beds: Q. Air conditioning, turndown service and TV in room. VCR on premises. Antiques, fishing, parks, sporting events and theater nearby.

Certificate may be used: Year-round based on availability.

Fort Scott
D10

The Chenault Mansion

820 S National Ave
Fort Scott, KS 66701-1321
(316)223-6800

Circa 1887. Curved-glass windows, stained glass, ornate woodwork, pocket doors and fireplaces have been refurbished in this gracious home to reflect its beginnings in the late 19th century. Antiques and a large china and glass collection add ambiance to the elegant rooms. Full breakfasts are served in the well-appointed dining room. The David P. & Mary Josephine Thomas Suite, located in the tower room, boasts a sitting room and wicker furnishings. Other rooms feature special pieces such as a hand-carved walnut bed, and two of the rooms have fireplaces.

Innkeeper(s): Robert Schafer. $65-80. MC VISA DS. 5 rooms. Breakfast included in rates. Type of meal: full breakfast.

Certificate may be used: All year - if stay is on weekend, Thursday or Sunday night must be included.

Lyons' House

742 S National Ave
Fort Scott, KS 66701-1319
(316)223-0779 (800)784-8378

Circa 1876. This four-story, landmark Italianate manor is one of the first mansions built on the prairie. The home features original chandeliers, which highlight the polished wood floors, family heirlooms and antiques. Innkeeper Pat Lyons serves up an abundant, Southern-style breakfast with treats such as biscuits and gravy or French toast with custard filling. Snacks are always available, and Pat keeps rooms stocked with tea and coffee service. Afternoon teas are served by request, and turndown service is one of the many romantic touches guests will enjoy. Pat has created several special packages for her guests, including her "Mystery in a Parlor" event, which combines gourmet meals with a murder-mystery game.

Innkeeper(s): Pat Lyons. $85-125. MC VISA AX. 4 rooms, 2 with PB. 1 suite. Breakfast included in rates. Type of meal: full breakfast.

Certificate may be used: Anytime Sunday-Thursday.

Garnett   D9

Kirk House
145 W 4th Ave
Garnett, KS 66032-1313
(913)448-5813 Fax:(913)448-6478

Circa 1913. Those interested in the arts will love
Kirk House. The innkeepers have backgrounds as
art dealers, and they count weaving and classical
music among their other interests. Guests receive
plenty of pampering at this inn, located in eastern

KIRK HOUSE·1913

Kansas, south of Ottawa. Food preparation and presentation are stressed here, with visitors enjoying
gourmet breakfasts, afternoon teas and evening
snacks. The inn also offers turndown service and a
sitting room and library for further relaxation.
Innkeeper(s): Robert Cugno & Robert Logan. $65-90. 5 rooms, 1 with
PB. Breakfast included in rates. Types of meals: full breakfast and
gourmet breakfast. Afternoon tea, evening snack and picnic lunch available. Beds: QDT. Turndown service in room. Cable TV and VCR on
premises. Antiques, fishing, shopping, sporting events, theater and
watersports nearby.
Publicity: *Metro News, Kansas, Topeka Capitol Journal, Wichita Eagle.*

*"What a nugget of class, beauty & culture in the middle of
Kansas! A feast for the eyes & mouth, too much to absorb
in one visit. Gracious, knowledgeable, sensitive innkeepers.
We can't rate this wonderful spot too highly."*
Certificate may be used: Sunday through Thursday, all year.

Great Bend   D5

Peaceful Acres B&B
RR 5 Box 153
Great Bend, KS 67530-9805
(316)793-7527

Circa 1899. A casual country setting greets guests
at Peaceful Acres, a comfortable farmhouse with
plenty of calves, chicken, dogs and cats to entertain
all visitors, especially children, who are more than
welcome here. Activities abound for the youngsters

and they also will enjoy the zoo in Great Bend, five
miles away. Cheyenne Bottoms and Pawnee Rock
are within easy driving distance.
Innkeeper(s): Dale & Doris Nitzel. $30. 2 rooms. 1 conference room.
Breakfast included in rates. Type of meal: full breakfast. Beds: QDT. Air
conditioning and ceiling fan in room. VCR and library on premises.
Antiques, fishing, parks and shopping nearby.

*"Thank you for the charming accommodations. The
food was very good and filling, and the place is peaceful,
just like the name. We enjoyed the company at breakfast! It felt like staying with family."*
Certificate may be used: Anytime available.

Moran   D9

Hedgeapple Acres B&B
4430 US 54 Hwy
Moran, KS 66755-9500
(316)237-4646

Circa 1974. Nestled on 80-acres of farmland, this
country home offers comfortable furnishings and
plenty of places to relax. One of the bedchambers
boasts a whirlpool tub, while another includes a fireplace. Guests not only enjoy a hearty country breakfast, but supper as well. Spend the day exploring the
area, which includes historic Fort Scott, or grab your
rod and reel and try out the farm's two stocked ponds.
Innkeeper(s): Jack & Ann Donaldson. $58-65. MC VISA AX DS PC TC.
6 rooms with PB, 1 with FP. 1 conference room. Breakfast, dinner and
evening snack included in rates. Types of meals: full breakfast and early
coffee/tea. Banquet service and catering service available. Restaurant
on premises. Beds: K. Air conditioning and ceiling fan in room. Cable
TV, VCR, fax and library on premises. Handicap access. Antiques, fishing, parks, shopping and theater nearby.
Certificate may be used: All year, Sunday through Thursday.

Topeka   B9

The Sunflower B&B
915 SW Munson Ave
Topeka, KS 66604-1129
(913)357-7509

Circa 1887. This National Register home is a
whimsical example of Queen Anne Victorian architecture with stained-glass windows, ornate plaster
moldings, medallions and reproductions of period
wallpapers. Antique Victorian furnishings and collectibles complete the look. The Giles Bedroom,
named for the home's original builder and a founding Topeka citizen, includes an Eastlake-style fireplace, bay window and carved walnut bed. The
Servants Quarters features a hand-painted bedroom
set and a fainting couch. The breakfast menu varies
from gourmet fare to homemade country goodies.

Innkeeper(s): Michael Stringer. $50-55. 2 rooms with PB. Breakfast included in rates. Types of meals: continental breakfast, full breakfast, gourmet breakfast and early coffee/tea. Evening snack available. Beds: D. Air conditioning, turndown service and ceiling fan in room. Cable TV, VCR and bicycles on premises. Antiques, fishing, parks, shopping, sporting events, theater and watersports nearby.

Certificate may be used: Oct. 15-May 15, Sunday through Thursday.

WaKeeney   C4

Thistle Hill B&B
RR 1 Box 93
WaKeeney, KS 67672-9736
(913)743-2644 (888)484-4785

Circa 1950. This modern cedar farmhouse has a unique, "older" feel, aided mainly by its porch, which is reminiscent of the Old West. The interior features an oak-floored dining room and views of the inn's gardens, farm and prairie. The second-story guest rooms include the Prairie Room, with a queen-size bed; the Sunflower Room, which boasts a handmade Kansas sunflower quilt and a view of the farm's working windmill; and the Oak Room, which offers a queen-size handmade fence-post bed and a hide-a-bed for extra family members. Guests may explore a 60-acre prairie-wildflower restoration, which attracts many species of birds.

Innkeeper(s): Dave & Mary Hendricks. $55-65. MC VISA PC TC. 3 rooms with PB. Breakfast and afternoon tea included in rates. Types of meals: full breakfast, gourmet breakfast and early coffee/tea. Beds: QD. Air conditioning and ceiling fan in room. Spa, stables and library on premises. Antiques, fishing, parks and shopping nearby.

Location: Halfway between Denver and Kansas City. Sternberg Museum, Cottonwood Ranch and Castle Rock nearby.

Publicity: *Kansas Weekend Guide, Kansas City Star, Country, Denver Post.*

Certificate may be used: Sept. 1-April 30 (except second weekend in November), Sunday-Thursday.

Wichita   E7

The Inn at The Park
3751 E Douglas Ave
Wichita, KS 67218-1002
(316)652-0500 (800)258-1951 Fax:(316)652-0610

Circa 1910. This popular three-story brick mansion offers many special touches, including unique furnishings in each of its 11 guest rooms, three of which are suites. Some of the rooms feature fireplaces, refrigerators or hot tubs. The inn's convenient location makes it ideal for business travelers or those interested in exploring Wichita at length. The inn's parkside setting provides additional opportunities for relaxation or recreation. Ask for information about shops and restaurants in Wichita's Old Town.

Innkeeper(s): Michelle Hickman. $85-145. MC VISA AX DS. 12 rooms with PB, 8 with FP. 3 suites. 1 conference room. Breakfast included in rates. Types of meals: continental-plus breakfast and early coffee/tea. Catering service available. Beds: KQ. Air conditioning, turndown service, TV and VCR in room. Fax, copier, computer and spa on premises. Antiques, shopping and theater nearby.

Publicity: *Wichita Business Journal.*

"This is truly a distinctive hotel. Your attention to detail is surpassed only by your devotion to excellent service."

Certificate may be used: All the time.

Kentucky

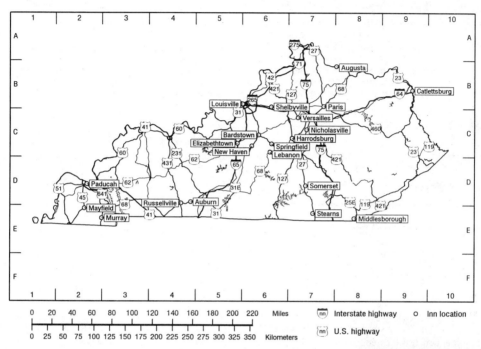

	1	2	3	4	5	6	7	8	9	10	
A											A
B											B
C											C
D											D
E											E
F											F
	1	2	3	4	5	6	7	8	9	10	

0 20 40 60 80 100 120 140 160 180 200 220   Miles

0 25 50 75 100 125 150 175 200 225 250 275 300 325 350   Kilometers

Ⓝ Interstate highway   ○ Inn location

Ⓝ U.S. highway

Auburn   D4

Auburn Guest House & Carriage House
421 W Main St
Auburn, KY 42206-5239
(502)542-6019

Circa 1938. This Southern Colonial mansion features mannequins dressed in vintage clothing. Guests may relax in the lounge, on the side porch or on the deck in the back of the house. The inn is furnished with antiques. The dressing room has an antique fainting couch. Guest rooms include the Primitive Room with chestnut pieces, the Maple Room, the Walnut Room, the Oak Room and the Cherry Room. The inn is listed in the National Register of Historic Places.

Innkeeper(s): David & Joy Williams. $55. 4 rooms, 2 with PB. Breakfast included in rates. Type of meal: full breakfast. Beds: D. Air conditioning and TV in room. Antiques and shopping nearby.

Location: On Highway 68 between Bowling Green and Russelville.

Publicity: *Logan County News.*

"I loved every second I spent in your beautiful home."

Certificate may be used: May 1-Dec. 1, Sunday-Friday.

Augusta
B8

Augusta Ayre
201 W 2nd St
Augusta, KY 41002-1004
(606)756-3228

Circa 1840. This Federal-style home was built by a freed slave and offers close access to the Ohio River and a city park. Each of the guest rooms includes a fireplace, and the sitting room is the perfect place to curl up and enjoy a book or old movie. Augusta offers many historic homes and antique shops to visit.
Innkeeper(s): Maynard Krum. $65-90. DS. 2 rooms, 2 with FP. Breakfast included in rates. Types of meals: full breakfast and early coffee/tea. Beds: D. Air conditioning and ceiling fan in room. Cable TV and VCR on premises. Antiques, fishing, parks and watersports nearby.

"Thank you for your generous hospitality and all the special touch surprises! A wonderful home away from home."

Certificate may be used: Sunday through Thursday, March to Aug. 30. Anytime, January & February, except holidays.

Bardstown
C6

Beautiful Dreamer B&B
440 E Stephen Foster Ave
Bardstown, KY 40004-2202
(502)348-4004 (800)811-8312

Circa 1995. From one of the porches at this Federal-style inn, guests can view My Old Kentucky Home, the actual house which inspired the famous Stephen Foster song. Civil War troops camped in the vicinity of the home, which is located in a historic district. The home was built in 1995, yet reflects a grandeur of an earlier era. Rooms are furnished elegantly with antiques and reproductions fashioned from cherry wood. One guest room includes a fireplace, others have either a four-poster or sleigh bed. Guests are encouraged to relax on a porch or in the upstairs sitting area, where refreshments and snacks are available. Coffee and tea are served in this area prior to breakfast. The morning meal is hearty and served family style. Fresh fruit is always available, and home-baked cinnamon or sweet rolls, baked French toast, biscuits and gravy, bacon, grits and egg dishes are among the special treats that change daily.
Innkeeper(s): Lynell Ginter. $79-99. MC VISA PC. 4 rooms with PB, 1 with FP. Breakfast and evening snack included in rates. Types of meals: full breakfast and early coffee/tea. Beds: QD. Air conditioning, ceiling fan and TV in room. Handicap access. Amusement parks, antiques, fishing, parks, shopping, theater and watersports nearby.

Certificate may be used: Jan. 1-May 1 & Sept. 1-Dec. 30, Sunday through Thursday. Not valid May 2-Aug. 31.

The Mansion Bed & Breakfast
1003 N 3rd St
Bardstown, KY 40004-2616
(502)348-2586 (800)399-2586 Fax:(502)349-6098

Circa 1851. The Confederate flag was raised for the first time in Kentucky on this property. The beautifully crafted Greek Revival mansion is in the National Register of Historic Places. Period antiques and hand-crocheted bedspreads, dust ruffles and shams are featured in the guest rooms. There are more than three acres of tall trees and gardens. The Courthouse in historic Bardstown is nine blocks away.
Innkeeper(s): Joseph & Charmaine Downs. $85-95. MC VISA DS. 8 rooms with PB. 1 conference room. Breakfast included in rates. Type of meal: continental-plus breakfast. Beds: KD. Air conditioning and ceiling fan in room. Cable TV and VCR on premises. Antiques, fishing, shopping and theater nearby.

Certificate may be used: All year on stays beginning on Sunday night through Wednesday.

Catlettsburg
B9

Levi Hampton House B&B
2206 Walnut St, US Rt 23
Catlettsburg, KY 41129
(606)739-8118 (888)538-4426 Fax:(606)739-6148
E-mail: bnb@ramlink.net

Circa 1847. Levi J. Hampton was one of the area's first settlers, and he built this pre-Civil War, Italianate-style home. Guest rooms are decorated with poster beds, candles and just a touch of lace. The innkeepers offer plenty of amenities for their business travelers, including computer jacks and fax or copier service. Guests enjoy early morning coffee or tea service in their rooms before joining the hosts for a full breakfast with treats such as homemade breads and perhaps a Southwestern-style quiche with tomatoes and salsa.
Innkeeper(s): Dennis & Kathy Stemen. $77-138. MC VISA. 5 rooms with PB, 3 with FP. 2 suites. 2 cottages. Breakfast and evening snack included in rates. Type of meal: full breakfast. Beds: QDT. Air conditioning and TV in room. VCR, fax and copier on premises. Amusement parks, antiques, fishing, parks, shopping, golf, theater and watersports nearby.
Publicity: *Ashland Daily Independent.*

"Having been in other B&Bs I know they all have their own unique qualities, but this one experience will be used to compare all others."

Certificate may be used: Sunday to Thursday, based on standard rates, no other discounts apply.

Elizabethtown C5

Olde Bethlehem Academy Inn
7051 Saint John Rd
Elizabethtown, KY 42701-8766
(502)862-9003 (800)662-5670

Circa 1818. Presidents and diplomats once were hosted at this Greek Revival mansion, originally the home of a Kentucky governor. The home later was used by the Sisters of Loretto as a chapel, school and home. The inn still includes the chapel, which is decorated by a large mural. The guest rooms are furnished with antiques and reproductions, and the innkeepers have won awards for their interior design, a mix of elegance and country styles. For guests in search of a relaxing spot, the covered veranda is lined with rockers and chairs.

Innkeeper(s): Michael Dooley. $75-85. MC VISA. 6 rooms with PB, 2 with FP. 1 conference room. Breakfast included in rates. Type of meal: full breakfast. Handicap access.

Location: Less than one hour from Mammoth Cave and Churchill Downs.

Certificate may be used: Subject to availability.

Harrodsburg C7

Canaan Land Farm B&B
700 Canaan Land Rd.
Harrodsburg, KY 40330-9220
(606)734-3984 (888)734-3984

Circa 1795. This National Register farmhouse, one of the oldest brick houses in Kentucky, is appointed with antiques, quilts and featherbeds. Your host is a shepherd/attorney and your hostess is a handspinner

artist. A large flock of sheep, goats and other assorted barnyard animals graze the pastures at this working farm. In 1995, the innkeepers reconstructed an 1815, historic log house on the grounds. The log house includes three guest rooms and two working fireplaces.

Innkeeper(s): Theo & Fred Bee. $75-125. PC TC. 7 rooms with PB, 2 with FP. Breakfast included in rates. Types of meals: full breakfast and early coffee/tea. Beds: DT. VCR, spa and swimming on premises. Antiques, fishing, parks, shopping, golf and watersports nearby.

Location: Two miles from Shakertown.

Publicity: *Danville Advocate, Lexington Herald Leader.*

"You truly have a gift for genuine hospitality."

Certificate may be used: Anytime of year, Sunday-Thursday.

Lebanon C6

Myrtledene B&B
370 N Spalding Ave
Lebanon, KY 40033-1563
(502)692-2223 (800)391-1721

Circa 1833. Once a Confederate general's headquarters at one point during the Civil War, this pink brick inn, located at a bend in the road, has greeted visitors entering Lebanon for more than 150 years.

When General John Hunt Morgan returned in 1863 to destroy the town, the white flag hoisted to signal a truce was flown at Myrtledene. A country breakfast usually features ham and biscuits as well as the innkeepers' specialty, peaches and cream French toast.

Innkeeper(s): James F. Spragens. $65. MC VISA PC TC. 4 rooms, 1 with FP. 1 conference room. Breakfast included in rates. Types of meals: full breakfast, gourmet breakfast and early coffee/tea. Afternoon tea available. Beds: DT. Air conditioning and turndown service in room. Cable TV, VCR and library on premises. Antiques, fishing, parks, shopping, theater and watersports nearby.

Publicity: *Lebanon Enterprise, Louisville Courier-Journal, Lebanon/Marion County Kentucky.*

"Our night in the Cabbage Rose Room was an experience of another time, another culture. Your skill in preparing and presenting breakfast was equally elegant! We'll be back!"

Certificate may be used: Anytime except Sept. 27-28.

Louisville B6

Ashton's Victorian Secret B&B
1132 S 1st St
Louisville, KY 40203-2804
(502)581-1914 (800)449-4691
E-mail: sroosa@ix.netcom.com

Circa 1883. This three-story Queen Anne Victorian has 11 fireplaces. Antiques and period furnishings are featured throughout the brick inn, located in Historic Old Louisville. Guest amenities include sundecks, washer-dryer facilities and a workout room with a bench press, rowing machine and stationary bicycle.

Innkeeper(s): Nan & Steve Roosa. $48-89. PC. 4 rooms, 1 with PB, 4 with FP. 1 suite. Breakfast included in rates. Type of meal: continental-plus breakfast. Beds: KQD. Air conditioning and ceiling fan in room. VCR on premises. Amusement parks, antiques, parks, shopping, downhill skiing, sporting events and theater nearby.

Certificate may be used: Jan. 2-Feb. 28.

The Inn at the Park
1332 S 4th St
Louisville, KY 40208-2314
(502)637-6930 (800)700-7275 Fax:(502)637-2796
E-mail: innatpark@aol.com

Circa 1886. An impressive sweeping staircase is one of many highlights at this handsome Richardsonian Romanesque inn, in the historic district of Old Louisville. Guests also will appreciate the hardwood floors, 14-foot ceilings and stone balconies on the second and third floors. The seven guest rooms offer a variety of amenities and a view of Central Park. Guests may enjoy breakfast in their rooms or in the well-appointed central dining area.
Innkeeper(s): John & Sandra Mullins. $79-149. MC VISA AX PC TC. 7 rooms with PB, 5 with FP. 3 suites. Breakfast included in rates. Types of meals: full breakfast and early coffee/tea. Beds: KQ. Air conditioning, ceiling fan and TV in room. VCR and fax on premises. Amusement parks, antiques, parks, shopping, sporting events and theater nearby.

Certificate may be used: Jan. 1-Dec. 31, Sunday-Thursday.

Rose Blossom
1353 S 4th St
Louisville, KY 40208-2349
(502)636-0295

This spacious Second Empire Victorian is listed in the National Register. Among its 18 rooms are seven guest rooms, three with private bath. Leaded glass in the entry hall and an oak stairwell add to the home's authentic old-time aura. Ten fireplaces are found, some with carved mantels and decorative tile. The first-floor bath boasts a whirlpool tub, and Mary has amassed an impressive collection of fine plates and china. The University of Louisville is within easy walking distance.
Innkeeper(s): Mary Ohlmann. $85-95. MC VISA AX DS. 7 rooms, 6 with PB. Breakfast included in rates. Types of meals: full breakfast and early coffee/tea. Catering service available. Air conditioning and turndown service in room. Cable TV on premises. Antiques, shopping, sporting events and theater nearby.

Certificate may be used: Most of the time, except Derby time (May), St. James Art Fair (October).

The Inn at Woodhaven
401 S Hubbard Lane
Louisville, KY 40208
(502)895-1011 (888)895-1011

Circa 1853. This Gothic Revival, painted in a cheerful shade of yellow, is still much the same as it was in the 1850s, when it served as the home on a prominent local farm. The rooms still feature the outstanding woodwork, and guest quarters are tastefully appointed with antiques. All seven guest rooms include a fireplace. Criss-cross window designs, winding staircases, decorative mantels and hardwood floors are other notable elements. The National Register home is close to all of Louisville's attractions.
Innkeeper(s): Marsha Burton. $70-90. MC VISA PC. 7 rooms with PB, 7 with FP. 2 suites. Breakfast included in rates. Types of meals: full breakfast and gourmet breakfast. Dinner and picnic lunch available. Beds: KQDT. Air conditioning, ceiling fan and TV in room. Fax, copier and library on premises. Handicap access. Amusement parks, antiques, parks, shopping, sporting events, golf, theater and watersports nearby.
Publicity: *Courier Journal.*

Certificate may be used: Monday-Thursday except Derby week.

Mayfield E2

Susan B. Seay's Magnolia Manor
401 S 7th St
Mayfield, KY 42066
(502)247-4108

Circa 1900. Doric columns and a second-story portico grace the exterior of this Greek Revival home. Brides often descend down the grand staircase, and the home is a popular site for weddings and receptions. Innkeeper Susan Seay has decorated the home with a variety of antiques. Beds are topped with quilts, and Oriental rugs and lacy curtains add ambiance. Three of the guest rooms have a shared bath.
Innkeeper(s): Susan B. Seay. $60-70. PC TC. 4 rooms, 1 with PB. 2 conference rooms. Breakfast and evening snack included in rates. Type of meal: continental-plus breakfast. Catering service available. Beds: TD. Air conditioning, ceiling fan and TV in room. VCR on premises. Antiques, fishing, parks, shopping, golf, theater and watersports nearby.
Publicity: *Country Inns.*

Certificate may be used: Upon availability. Anytime except April 15-30.

Middlesborough E8

The Ridge Runner B&B
208 Arthur Hts
Middlesborough, KY 40965-1728
(606)248-4299

Circa 1890. Bachelor buttons, lilacs and wildflowers line the white picket fence framing this 20-room brick Victorian mansion. Guests enjoy relaxing in its turn-of-the-century library and parlor filled with Victorian antiques. Ask for the President's Room and you'll enjoy the best view of the Cumberland Mountains. (The innkeeper's great, great-grandfather hosted Abe Lincoln the night before his Gettysburg address, and the inn boasts  some heirlooms from that home.) A family-style breakfast is provided and special diets can be accommodated if notified in advance. Cumberland Gap National Park is five miles away, and the inn is two miles from the twin tunnels that pass through the Cumberland Gap. Pine Mountain State Park is 12 miles away.

Innkeeper(s): Susan Richards & Irma Gall. $55-65. PC. 4 rooms, 2 with PB. Breakfast and evening snack included in rates. Type of meal: early coffee/tea. Beds: DT. Turndown service and ceiling fan in room. Antiques, parks and shopping nearby.

Publicity: *Lexington Herald Leader, Blue Ridge Country, Indianapolis Star, Daily News, Courier Journal, Country Inn.*

Certificate may be used: From Nov. 15-April 30, Sun.-Thurs., excluding holiday weekends (ex. Thanksgiving, Christmas, New Year's, etc.).

Murray
E2

The Diuguid House B&B
603 Main St
Murray, KY 42071-2034
(502)753-5470

Circa 1895. This Victorian house features eight-foot-wide hallways and a golden oak staircase with stained-glass window. There is a sitting area adjoining the portico. Guest rooms are generous in size.

Innkeeper(s): Karen & George Chapman. $40. MC VISA DC PC TC. 3 rooms. Breakfast included in rates. Types of meals: full breakfast and early coffee/tea.
Beds: QT. Air conditioning and turndown service in room. Cable TV on premises. Antiques, fishing, parks, theater, watersports nearby.
Location: Downtown Murray, near state university.
Publicity: *Murray State News.*

"We enjoyed our visit in your beautiful home, and your hospitality was outstanding."

Certificate may be used: Anytime except university graduation, homecoming, parents weekends and last weekend in April.

New Haven
C6

The Sherwood Inn
138 S Main St
New Haven, KY 40051-6355
(502)549-3386

Circa 1914. Since 1875, the Johnson family has owned the Sherwood Inn. A week after the original building burned in 1913, construction for the current building began. In the National Register, the inn catered to passengers of the nearby L & N (Louisville and Nashville) Railroad. Antiques and reproductions complement some  of the inn's original furnishings. The restaurant is open for dinner Wednesday through Saturday. The inn's slogan, first advertised in 1875 remains, "first class table and good accommodations."

Innkeeper(s): Cecilia Johnson. $45-65. MC VISA DS. 5 rooms, 3 with PB. Breakfast included in rates. Type of meal: full breakfast. Restaurant on premises. Beds: D. Air conditioning and ceiling fan in room. Cable TV on premises. Shopping nearby.
Location: Eleven miles south from Bardstown on US 31-E.
Publicity: *Kentucky Standard.*

"A memorable stop."

Certificate may be used: Upon availability.

Nicholasville
C7

Sandusky House & O'Neal Log Cabin B&B
1626 Delaney Ferry Rd
Nicholasville, KY 40356-8729
(606)223-4730
E-mail: humphlin@aol.com

Circa 1855. This Greek Revival inn rests in the tree-lined countryside, surrounded by horse farms and other small farms. Its tranquil setting offers a perfect getaway from busy nearby Lexington. The inn, which is listed on Kentucky's state register, boasts six porches, seven fireplaces and impressive brick columns. The three guest rooms feature desks, private baths and

turndown service. The innkeepers also offer lodging in a two-bedroom, 180-year-old log cabin. Although historic, the National Register cabin includes modern amenities such as a full kitchen and whirlpool tub. Area attractions include Asbury College, Keeneland Race Course, the Mary Todd Lincoln House and the University of Kentucky.

Innkeeper(s): Jim & Linda Humphrey. $75-95. MC VISA PC TC. 3 rooms with PB. 1 cottage. Breakfast included in rates. Types of meals: full breakfast and early coffee/tea. Beds: D. Air conditioning and turndown service in room. Cable TV and VCR on premises. Amusement parks, antiques, fishing, parks, shopping, sporting events, theater nearby.

Location: Eight miles from downtown Lexington.

Publicity: *Lexington Herald-Leader, Country Inns.*

Certificate may be used: Sunday-Thursday, April & October excluded.

Paducah   D2

The 1857's B&B

PO Box 7771
Paducah, KY 42001-0789
(502)444-3960 (800)264-5607 Fax:(502)444-6751

Circa 1857. Paducah's thriving, history-rich commercial district is home to this Folk Victorian inn, located in Market House Square. Guests choose from rooms such as the Master Bedroom, a suite featuring a king-size, four-poster bed or perhaps the Hunt Room, which includes a four-poster, queen-size canopy bed. The popular third-floor game room boasts an impressive mahogany billiard table. There is an outdoor hot tub on the deck. The Ohio River is an easy walk from the inn, and guests also will enjoy an evening stroll along the gas-lit brick sidewalks. The inn occupies the second and third floors of a former clothing store, with an Italian restaurant at street level.

Innkeeper(s): Deborah Bohnert. $65-95. MC VISA PC TC. 3 rooms. 1 suite. Breakfast included in rates. Types of meals: continental-plus breakfast and early coffee/tea. Room service available. Restaurant on premises. Beds: KQDT. Air conditioning, ceiling fan and TV in room. VCR, fax, copier and library on premises. Antiques, fishing, shopping, theater and watersports nearby.

Certificate may be used: January-March, October-November.

Paducah Harbor Plaza B&B

201 Broadway St
Paducah, KY 42001-0711
(502)442-2698 (800)719-7799

This striking, five-story brick structure was known as the Hotel Belvedere at the turn of the century. Guests now choose from four guest rooms on the second floor, where they also will find the arch-windowed Broadway Room, with its views of the Market House District and the Ohio River, just a block away. Breakfast is served in this room, which

also contains a 1911 player piano. The guest rooms all feature different color schemes and each is furnished with antique furniture and handmade quilts.

Innkeeper(s): Beverly McKinley. $55-75. MC VISA AX. 4 rooms. Breakfast included in rates. Type of meal: continental-plus breakfast. Air conditioning, ceiling fan and TV in room. VCR on premises. Antiques, shopping and theater nearby.

Certificate may be used: January, February, March, November, December.

Trinity Hills Farm

10455 Old Lovelaceville Rd
Paducah, KY 42001
(502)488-3999 (800)488-3998 Fax:(502)488-3997
E-mail: trinity8@apex.net

Circa 1995. This contemporary home is located at the edge of a lake among more than 17 acres of farmland. Guests can take a stroll down the walking trails and encounter peacocks, ducks, pygmy goats or the innkeeper's Arabian mare. Fishing and boating are other possibilities, or guests may simply relax and enjoy the view of the garden from the large deck. Guest rooms are elegantly furnished and are decorated with an interesting mix of collectibles. Each room has a small kitchenette, and the three suites include a whirlpool tub. Guests are treated to either country-style or gourmet fare in the mornings. In the evenings, a selection of desserts are served. The home is 12 miles west of Paducah.

Innkeeper(s): Mike & Ann Driver/Jim & Nancy Driver. $60-90. MC VISA DS PC TC. 5 rooms, 2 with PB, 1 with FP. 3 suites. Breakfast and evening snack included in rates. Types of meals: full breakfast, gourmet breakfast and early coffee/tea. Room service available. Beds: Q. Air conditioning, turndown service, ceiling fan, TV and VCR in room. Fax, spa, library and pet boarding on premises. Handicap access. Amusement parks, antiques, fishing, parks, shopping, sporting events, golf, theater and watersports nearby.

Publicity: *Paducah Life, Paducah Sun, Hartland B&B's*

"Trinity Hills is a very peaceful place to be alone with the one you love! We enjoyed our stay and the hot tub was great!"

Certificate may be used: Monday through Thursday except holidays.

Paris
B7

Pleasant Place B&B
515 Pleasant St
Paris, KY 40361
(606)987-4773 (800)890-5094 Fax:(606)987-8804

Circa 1889. Pleasant is an apt description for this Queen Anne Victorian, located in a historic Paris neighborhood. The innkeepers are just the third family to occupy this elegant home, which maintains many original architectural features, including a showpiece staircase. The three guest rooms each include a fireplace. Breakfasts feature Kentucky ham, homemade breads and gourmet casseroles. After a hearty breakfast, guests can explore Kentucky's famed horse country.

Innkeeper(s): Jeanine & Berkeley Scott. $55-75. MC VISA DS PC TC. 3 rooms, 2 with PB, 3 with FP. Breakfast included in rates. Types of meals: full breakfast, gourmet breakfast and early coffee/tea. Beds: KQ. Air conditioning and TV in room. VCR, fax and library on premises. Antiques, fishing, parks, shopping and golf nearby.

Publicity: *Bourbon Times.*

"Pleasant Place is beautiful and the food was wonderful."

Certificate may be used: Anytime except April and October, subject to availability.

Rosedale B&B
1917 Cypress St
Paris, KY 40361-1220
(606)987-1845 (800)644-1862

Circa 1862. Once the home of Civil War General John Croxton, this low-roofed Italianate inn was voted prettiest B&B in the Bluegrass area by the Lexington Herald-Leader in 1994. The four decorated guest rooms feature Colonial touches and are filled with antiques and paintings. Fresh flowers, down comforters and ceiling fans add to the rooms' comfort and charm. The Henry Clay Room, with its twin four-poster beds, is one option for visitors. Guests  may relax with a game of croquet, bocce, horseshoes, on benches found on the inn's three-acre lawn or on the screened porch. Duncan Tavern Historic Shrine is nearby, as well as beautiful horse farms.

Innkeeper(s): Katie & Jim Haag. $65-100. MC VISA PC TC. 4 rooms, 2 with PB. 2 suites. Breakfast and evening snack included in rates. Types of meals: full breakfast and early coffee/tea. Beds: DT. Air conditioning and ceiling fan in room. Cable TV, VCR and library on premises. Antiques, fishing, parks, shopping, sporting events and theater nearby.

"Your hospitality has been lovely and your home is a fine example of tradition and comfort."

Certificate may be used: January-December, Sunday-Thursday.

Russellville
D4

The Log House
2139 Franklin Rd
Russellville, KY 42276-9410
(502)726-8483 Fax:(502)726-2270
E-mail: 731333,647@compuserve.com

Circa 1976. This ideal log cabin retreat was built from hand-hewn logs from old cabins and barns in the area. Rooms are full of quilts, early American furnishings and folk art from around the world. The log walls and hardwood floors create an unparalleled atmosphere of country warmth. An impressive kitchen is decorated with an old-fashioned stove and crammed with knickknacks. Innkeeper Allison Dennis creates hand-woven garments and accessories in an adjacent studio. Nashville and Opryland are about an hour's drive, and the local area boasts a number of antique shops.

Innkeeper(s): Allison & Richard Dennis. $85-95. MC VISA AX DS PC TC. 4 rooms with PB, 2 with FP. Breakfast included in rates. Type of meal: gourmet breakfast. Room service available. Beds: QDT. Air conditioning in room. VCR, fax, copier, spa and library on premises. Amusement parks, antiques, fishing, parks, shopping, sporting events, theater and watersports nearby.

Certificate may be used: Anytime. Prior reservations are essential.

Shelbyville
B6

The Wallace House
613 Washington St
Shelbyville, KY 40065
(502)633-2006

Circa 1804. This Federal-style house, midway between Louisville and Frankfort, is listed in the National Register of Historic Places. Its four well-appointed guest suites all feature kitchenettes.

Innkeeper(s): Evelyn Laurent. $70-95. MC VISA AX. 7 rooms, 4 with PB. 4 suites. Breakfast included in rates. Type of meal: full breakfast. Beds: Q. Air conditioning and TV in room. Antiques, fishing, shopping and theater nearby.

Certificate may be used: Weekdays, excluding May 1-10.

Somerset
D7

Shadwick House
411 S Main St
Somerset, KY 42501-2062
(606)678-4675

This two-story home was built as a boarding house by the innkeeper's great-grandmother, Nellie Stringer Shadwick. Nellie opened her home to guests for many years, and after her death, daughter Marie Carmichael took over. John Dillinger was rumored to have been a guest at one time. Today, it's Marie's grandchildren who have continued the legacy of hospitality. The first floor has been transformed into a boutique with a variety of antiques and crafts, many fashioned by native Kentuckians. The rooms are decorated with antiques, some of which are original to the house.

Innkeeper(s): Ann Epperson. $40-50. MC VISA. 4 rooms. Breakfast included in rates. Type of meal: full breakfast.

Certificate may be used: Monday-Thursday, except holidays.

Springfield C6

Maple Hill Manor

2941 Perryville Rd
Springfield, KY 40069-9611
(606)336-3075 (800)886-7546

Circa 1851. This brick Revival home with Italianate detail is a Kentucky Landmark home and is listed in the National Register of Historic Places. It features 13-1/2-foot ceilings, 10-foot doors, nine-foot windows, a cherry spiral

staircase, stenciling in the foyer, a large parlor, period furnishings and a dining room with a fireplace. The library has floor-to-ceiling mahogany bookcases and the Honeymoon Room features a canopy bed and Jacuzzi. A large patio area is set among old maple trees.

Innkeeper(s): Kathleen Carroll. $50-90. MC VISA PC TC. 7 rooms with PB. 1 conference room. Breakfast included in rates. Types of meals: full breakfast and early coffee/tea. Evening snack available. Beds: QDT. Air conditioning and ceiling fan in room. VCR on premises. Antiques, fishing, shopping and theater nearby.

Publicity: *Danville's Advocate-Messenger, Springfield Sun, Eastside Weekend, Courier Journal.*

"Thank you again for your friendly and comfortable hospitality."

Certificate may be used: Sunday through Thursday.

Stearns E7

Marcum-Porter House

35 Hume St
Stearns, KY 42647-0369
(606)376-2242

Circa 1902. This two-story frame home once housed employees of the Stearns Coal & Lumber Company. Many guests like to wander the gardens of the historic inn. Golfers will enjoy a nearby nine-

hole course, believed to be the second-oldest course in the state. Be sure to take a ride on the Big South Fork Scenic Railway during your stay. Area attractions include Big South Fork National Recreation Area, Cumberland Falls State Park and Yahoo Falls.

Innkeeper(s): Patricia Porter Newton. $55-65. MC VISA PC TC. 4 rooms, 1 with PB. Breakfast, afternoon tea and evening snack included in rates. Types of meals: full breakfast, gourmet breakfast and early coffee/tea. Beds: D. Cable TV, VCR and library on premises. Antiques, fishing, parks, shopping and watersports nearby.

Certificate may be used: April 1-Nov. 1, excluding weekends & holidays. By reservation.

Versailles C7

Rose Hill Inn

233 Rose Hill
Versailles, KY 40383-1223
(606)873-5957 (800)307-0460
E-mail: rosehillbb@aol.com

Circa 1820. Both Confederate and Union troops used this manor during the Civil War. The home maintains many elegant features, including original woodwork, 14-foot ceilings and floors fashioned from timber on the property. The decor is comfortable, yet elegant. One guest room includes a copper bathtub, another includes a double marble Jacuzzi. The innkeepers restored the home's summer kitchen into a private cottage, which now includes a private porch, kitchen and two full-size beds. Three generations of the Amberg family live and work here, including friendly dogs. The Ambergs serve a hearty, full breakfast, and in the afternoon, appetizers are presented. Among the sites are a Shaker Village, antique shops, horse farms, Keeneland Race Track and a wildlife sanctuary.

Innkeeper(s): Sharon & Art Amberg. $59-99. MC VISA AX DS TC. 4 rooms with PB. 1 suite. 1 cottage. Breakfast and afternoon tea included in rates. Types of meals: full breakfast and early coffee/tea. Beds: KQDT. Air conditioning, turndown service, ceiling fan and TV in room. VCR, bicycles, library and child care on premises. Antiques, fishing, parks, shopping, sporting events and golf nearby.

"Everything was top-notch and we really enjoyed our stay in Miss Lucy's room."

Certificate may be used: Sunday-Thursday, Nov. 1-March 15 (except holidays).

Louisiana

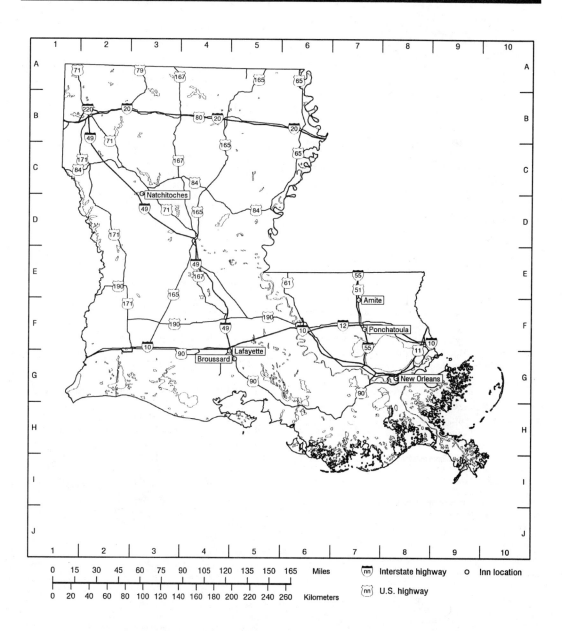

0   15   30   45   60   75   90   105 120 135 150 165   Miles

0   20   40   60   80   100 120 140 160 180 200 220 240 260   Kilometers

(nn) Interstate highway   o Inn location

(nn) U.S. highway

Amite
F7

Blythewood Plantation
PO Box 155, 400 Daniel St
Amite, LA 70422-2318
(504)345-6419

Circa 1885. The grounds surrounding this majestic plantation home were part of a Spanish land grant. The original home, a pre-Civil War manor, burned, but was rebuilt in the late 19th century. The grand rooms include a gas chandelier, leaded-glass doors and walnut mantels, all original features. In true Louisiana style, guests are served a refreshing mint julep upon arrival. Candlelight dinners can be arranged, as can special teas, parties and weddings.
Innkeeper(s): Maxine, Ann, Diane. $79-189. TC. 9 rooms. 2 conference rooms. Breakfast and dinner included in rates. Types of meals: full breakfast and gourmet breakfast. Evening snack, picnic lunch, lunch, gourmet lunch, banquet service and catered breakfast available. Beds: D. Air conditioning and TV in room. VCR on premises. Handicap access. Antiques, parks and watersports nearby.
Certificate may be used: Based on availability.

Elliott House
801 N Duncan Ave
Amite, LA 70422
(504)748-8553 (800)747-8553

Circa 1908. Innkeeper Flora Elliot Landwehr's grandfather, a State Court of Appeals judge, built this Neoclassical home. Flora and husband Joseph painstakingly restored the inheritance, which had deteriorated and was shrouded in overgrown brush. Now, the hardwood floors shine and rooms feature Victorian antiques. Three bedchambers have a fireplace. In the mornings, homemade granola, fresh fruit and Louisiana coffee accompany entrees such as eggs Benedict. Guests can spend the day relaxing at the inn and enjoying the four acres. The area offers plenty of outdoor activities, and New Orleans is an hour away.
Innkeeper(s): Joseph and Flora Landwehr. $70-80. MC VISA PC TC. 5 rooms, 4 with PB, 3 with FP. 1 suite. 1 conference room. Breakfast and afternoon tea included in rates. Types of meals: gourmet breakfast and early coffee/tea. Beds: KD. Air conditioning, ceiling fan, TV and VCR in room. Bicycles and library on premises. Antiques, fishing, parks, shopping, golf and watersports nearby.
Publicity: *Times Picayune.*

"What you are doing and the type of people you are, give folks a memory, not just a place to stay."
Certificate may be used: All seasons; Sunday through Thursday.

Broussard
G5

La Grande Maison
302 E Main St
Broussard, LA 70518
(318)837-4428 (800)837-5633 Fax:(318)837-5733

Circa 1911. This aptly named bed & breakfast boasts many Victorian architectural elements, including gables, gingerbread trim, a wide veranda and a turret that soars above the roofline. The National Register home is painted an inviting shade of pale blue and the grounds are dotted with flowers and old oak trees. Guest rooms feature Victorian furnishings and decor, such as a canopy bed topped with a floral comforter. The cozy turret room includes wicker furnishings and an iron bed. The full breakfast is served on well-appointed tables in the dining room, which is highlighted by a bay window with stained glass.
Innkeeper(s): Norman & Brenda Fakier. $85-195. MC VISA PC TC. 5 rooms with PB. Breakfast included in rates. Type of meal: full breakfast. Beds: KQD. Turndown service and ceiling fan in room. Cable TV, VCR and fax on premises. Handicap access.

"Highest standards and best in cajun hospitality."
Certificate may be used: June, July, August.

Lafayette
G4

Alida's, A B&B
2631 SE Evangeline Thruway
Lafayette, LA 70508-2168
(318)264-1191 (800)922-5867 Fax:(318)264-1415
E-mail: alidas@iamerica.net

Circa 1902. This home is named for teacher Alida Martin, who along with once owning this Queen Anne house, was responsible for educating many Lafayette citizens, including a few civic leaders.
Alida taught at the house until a one-room schoolhouse was constructed. The innkeepers named a room for Alida, decorated with a 19th-century walnut bed and matching  armoire. The bath still features the original clawfoot tub. Other rooms include special antiques, Bavarian collectibles and clawfoot tubs. After breakfast, guests can trek to nearby sites such as the Tabasco Plant and Live Oak Gardens on Jefferson Island.
Innkeeper(s): Tanya & Doug Greenwald. $75-125. MC VISA AX DS PC TC. 4 rooms with PB. 1 conference room. Breakfast and evening snack

included in rates. Types of meals: full breakfast and gourmet breakfast. Beds: QD. Air conditioning and ceiling fan in room. VCR, fax and copier on premises. Antiques, fishing, parks, shopping, sporting events nearby.

Certificate may be used: November-February.

Natchitoches C3

Fleur de Lis B&B
336 Second St
Natchitoches, LA 71457
(318)352-6621 (800)489-6621

Circa 1903. A prosperous lumberman built this Victorian so that his children could attend a nearby college. The home is located in a National Historic Landmark District, and it features original wood-

work and a pressed-tin ceiling. The guest rooms are decorated with period antiques. A full breakfast is served, perhaps French toast or Southern fare, such as grits and freshly made biscuits.
Innkeeper(s): Tom & Harriette Palmer. $65-80. MC VISA AX. 5 rooms with PB. 1 conference room. Breakfast included in rates. Types of meals: full breakfast, gourmet breakfast and early coffee/tea. Beds: KQ. Air conditioning and ceiling fan in room. Cable TV, VCR and bicycles on premises. Handicap access. Antiques, fishing, parks, shopping, sporting events, golf and watersports nearby.

"Each time I come, I feel more and more at home. It is a gift you have given me."

Certificate may be used: Sept. 1-April 30, Sunday-Thursday.

New Orleans G8

Fairchild House
1518 Prytania St
New Orleans, LA 70130-4416
(504)524-0154 (800)256-8096 Fax:(504)568-0063

Circa 1841. Situated in the oak-lined Lower Garden District of New Orleans, this Greek Revival home was built by architect L.H. Pilie. The inn

maintains its Victorian ambiance with elegantly appointed guest rooms. Wine and cheese is served upon guests' arrival. Excluding holidays and Sundays, afternoon tea can be served upon request. The inn, which is on the Mardi Gras parade route, is 17 blocks from the French Quarter and eight blocks from the convention center. Streetcars are nearby, as are many local attractions, including paddleboat cruises, Canal Place and Riverwalk shopping, an aquarium, zoo, the Charles Avenue mansions and Tulane and Loyola universities.
Innkeeper(s): Rita Olmo & Beatriz Aprigliano. $75-125. MC VISA AX TC. 7 rooms with PB. 1 suite. Breakfast included in rates. Type of meal: continental-plus breakfast. Beds: KQDT. Air conditioning and ceiling fan in room. Fax and copier on premises. Antiques, shopping and theater nearby.

Location: Lower garden district.

"Accommodations were great; staff was great...Hope to see ya'll soon!"

Certificate may be used: June 1-Aug. 31, please call during other seasons.

Garden District B&B
2418 Magazine St
New Orleans, LA 70130-5604
(504)895-4302 Fax:(504)895-4306

This restored Victorian home is nestled in New Orleans' Garden District and surrounded by gracious antebellum homes. The innkeepers have restored the pine floors and 12-foot ceilings to their original glory. Rooms include antiques, ceilings fans and Victorian decor. The patio is surrounded by a lush, tropical garden. Guests won't have to walk far to explore the hundreds of antique shops which line Magazine Street.
Innkeeper(s): Joseph Kinsella. $55-75. MC VISA. 6 rooms. Breakfast included in rates. Type of meal: continental breakfast.

Certificate may be used: June, July, August; other months on availability.

Lamothe House
621 Esplanade Ave
New Orleans, LA 70116-2018
(504)947-1161 (800)367-5858 Fax:(504)943-6536

Circa 1830. A carriageway that formerly cut through the center of many French Quarter buildings was enclosed at the Lamothe House in 1866, and it is now the foyer. Splendid Victorian furnishings enhance moldings, high ceilings and hand-turned mahogany stairway railings. Gilded opulence goes unchecked in the Mallard and Lafayette suites. Registration takes place in the second-story salon above the courtyard.
Innkeeper(s): Carol Chauppette. $75-250. MC VISA AX PC TC. 20 rooms with PB, 1 with FP. 9 suites. 2 cottages. 1 conference room. Breakfast included in rates. Type of meal: continental-plus breakfast. Afternoon tea available. Beds: QTD. Air conditioning, turndown service,

ceiling fan and TV in room. VCR, fax, copier, swimming and child care on premises. Amusement parks, antiques, fishing, parks, shopping, sporting events and theater nearby.

Publicity: *Houston Post, Travel & Leisure.*

Certificate may be used: All year anytime based on availability.

The Olivier Estate, A B&B

1839 Esplanada Ave
New Orleans, LA 70116-1744
(504)949-9600 (800)429-3240 Fax:(504)948-2219
E-mail: bnbolivier@aol.com

Circa 1855. The expansive parlor at this Spanish Colonial boasts a hand-crafted, marble-topped bar with a roulette wheel embedded in it, which was made for gangster Al Capone. This eclectic room also includes a mahogany, three-slate pool table with leather pockets, a handmade Italian gaming table and a 1950s vintage quarter slot machine. The spacious bedchambers include private entrances, and some offer working fireplaces and marble baths. During the week, a full breakfast is the morning fare, while on the weekends, the innkeepers offer a full, Creole-style brunch. An open bar, nightly turn-down service, airport transfers, and a 9 a.m. to 9 p.m. car service is offered daily. A hot tub, swimming pool and fresh flowers are just a few of the amenities guest will enjoy during their stay.

Innkeeper(s): Richard Saucier. $79-450. MC VISA AX. 5 rooms with PB. 4 suites. Breakfast included in rates. Type of meal: full breakfast. Beds: KQ. Antiques, fishing, theater and watersports nearby.

"The courtesy, hospitality and friendliness of the staff was incredible. We'll return again."

Certificate may be used: Non-special events.

The Prytania Park Hotel

1525 Prytania St
New Orleans, LA 70130-4415
(504)524-0427 (800)862-1984 Fax:(504)522-2977

Circa 1850. This hotel consists of a historic Greek Revival building and a new building, located in a National Historic Landmark District. Request the older rooms to enjoy the English Victorian repro-duction furnishings, garden chintz fabrics and 14-foot ceilings. Some of these rooms have fireplaces. Rooms in the new section feature refrigerators, microwaves and contemporary furnishings. Prytania Park, reminiscent of a small European hotel, is located on the historic St. Charles Avenue streetcar line. Free off-street parking is available.

Innkeeper(s): Edward Halpern. $99-229. MC VISA AX DC CB DS PC TC. 62 rooms with PB. 6 suites. Breakfast included in rates. Type of meal: continental-plus breakfast. Lunch available. Beds: KQDT. Air conditioning, ceiling fan and TV in room. Fax and copier on premises. Antiques, parks, shopping and sporting events nearby.

Location: Lower Garden District.

"A little jewel—Baton Rouge Advocate."

Certificate may be used: All year, based on space availability, not valid during special events, reservations required.

St. Peter Guest House Hotel

1005 Saint Peter St
New Orleans, LA 70116-3014
(504)524-9232 (800)535-7815 Fax:(504)523-5198

Circa 1800. The St. Peter House, which is ideally situated in the middle of the French Quarter, offers a delightful glance at New Orleans French heritage and 18th-century charm. From the lush courtyards to the gracious balconies, guests will enjoy the view of the busy quarter. Rooms are individually appoint-ed, some with period antiques.

Innkeeper(s): Brent Kovach. $49-225. MC VISA AX PC TC. 28 rooms with PB. 11 suites. Breakfast included in rates. Type of meal: continental-plus breakfast. Beds: KQDT. Air conditioning, turndown service, ceiling fan and TV in room. Fax on premises. Amusement parks, antiques, fishing, parks, shopping and theater nearby.

Certificate may be used: All year anytime based on availability.

Ponchatoula   F7

Bella Rose Mansion

225 N 8th St
Ponchatoula, LA 70454-3209
(504)386-3857 Fax:(504)386-3857

Circa 1942. This Georgian-style mansion boasts a three-story spiral staircase that rises up to a stained-glass dome. Master craftsmen detailed this luxurious manor with mahogany pan-eling, parquet floors, Waterford crystal chandeliers and a marble-walled solar-ium with a fountain.

The home once served as a monastery for Jesuit priests. The mansion includes an indoor terrazzo shuffleboard court and heated swimming pool. Gourmet breakfasts feature entrees such as eggs Benedict complemented with fresh fruits and juices. Ponchatoula's many antique shops have earned its nickname as Americaís Antique City.

Innkeeper(s): Rose James & Michael-Ray Britton. $125-225. MC VISA. 4 rooms with PB. 2 suites. Breakfast included in rates. Type of meal: gourmet breakfast. Beds: KQ. Air conditioning and ceiling fan in room. VCR, fax, copier, swimming, bicycles and library on premises. Antiques, fishing, parks, shopping, sporting events, theater and water-sports nearby.

Publicity: *Houston Chronicle, Sunday Star.*

"What a fabulous place! Your warmth is truly an asset. The peacefulness is just what we needed in our hectic lives."

Certificate may be used: Sunday through Thursday, excluding Mardi Gras and major holidays.

Maine

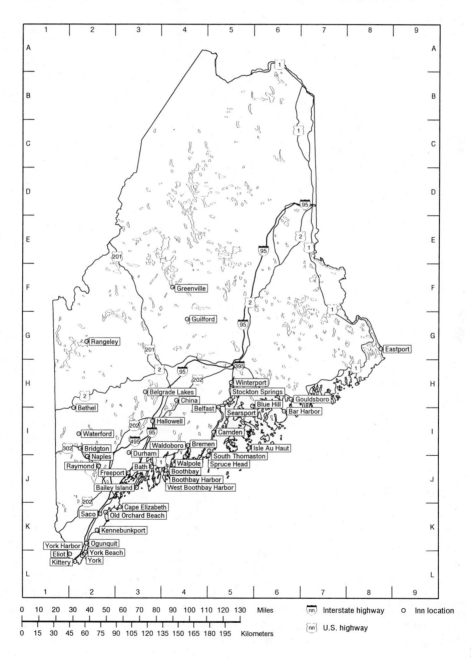

0 10 20 30 40 50 60 70 80 90 100 110 120 130   Miles

0 15 30 45 60 75 90 105 120 135 150 165 180 195   Kilometers

⌂nn⌂ Interstate highway   ○ Inn location

⌂nn⌂ U.S. highway

Bailey Island J3

Captain York House B&B
Route 24
Bailey Island, ME 04003
(207)833-6224
E-mail: 104502.1272@compuserve.com

Circa 1906. Bailey Island is the quaint fisherman's village of stories, poems and movies. Guests cross the world's only cribstone bridge to reach the island, where beautiful sunsets and dinners of
fresh Maine lobster
are the norm. This
shingled, turn-of-
the-century,
Mansard-style B&B
was the home of a
famous Maine sea

captain, Charles York. Now a homestay-style bed & breakfast, the innkeepers have restored the home to its former glory, filling it with many antiques. Guests at Captain York's enjoy water views from all the guest rooms. Wild Maine blueberries often find a significant place on the breakfast menu.
Innkeeper(s): Alan & Jean Thornton. $68-100. PC TC. 5 rooms, 3 with PB. Breakfast included in rates. Type of meal: full breakfast. Beds: QT. Cable TV and VCR on premises. Antiques, parks, shopping, sporting events, theater and watersports nearby.

"Bailey Island turned out to be the hidden treasure of our trip and we hope to return for your great hospitality again."
Certificate may be used: Jan. 5-March 31.

Log Cabin Lodging
PO Box 41
Bailey Island, ME 04003-0041
(207)833-5546 Fax:(207)833-7858
E-mail: logcab@ime.net

Circa 1950. This contemporary log structure houses six guest rooms, as well as the Log Cabin Restaurant. The rooms, three of which offer a kitchen, are simple and modern in style. Each guest room has a view of Casco Bay, the ocean or the White Mountains. The restaurant, warmed by the flames from the stone fireplace, boasts a variety of dishes featuring Maine lobster, as well as other seafood items, chowders, steaks, freshly baked breads and an array of tantalizing desserts.
Innkeeper(s): Sue & Neal Favreau. $89-175. MC VISA AX DS PC TC. 6 rooms, 5 with PB. 1 suite. Breakfast included in rates. Types of meals: full breakfast and early coffee/tea. Dinner and lunch available. Restaurant on premises. Beds: KQTD. TV and VCR in room. Fax and copier on premises. Handicap access. Antiques, fishing, parks, shopping, sporting events, golf, theater and watersports nearby.

Certificate may be used: Monday through Thursday, April, May & June.

Bar Harbor I6

Kedge
112 West St
Bar Harbor, ME 04609-1429
(207)288-5180 (800)597-8306

Circa 1870. Originally, this bed & breakfast was located at the edge of the harbor and served as a social club for gentlemen. In the 1880s, it was moved to its current location on West Street. The home rests on a portion of the street that is listed in the National Register of Historic Places. The interior is Victorian in style, flowered wallpapers brighten the rooms. One room has a whirlpool tub. The front porch is filled with hunter green wicker furnishings for those who wish to relax. For breakfast, innkeeper Margaret Roberts serves items such as baked peaches with Maine blueberries followed by gingerbread pancakes topped with marmalade syrup.
Innkeeper(s): Margaret Roberts. $55-160. MC VISA AX PC TC. 3 rooms with PB, 2 with FP. Breakfast included in rates. Types of meals: full breakfast and early coffee/tea. Beds: KQ. TV in room. Antiques, fishing, parks, shopping, cross-country skiing, golf, theater and watersports nearby.

Certificate may be used: Subject to availability, excluding holidays & summer weekends, Friday & Saturday, July1 through Oct. 15.

Manor House Inn
106 West St
Bar Harbor, ME 04609-1856
(207)288-3759 (800)437-0088 Fax:(207)288-2974

Circa 1887. Colonel James Foster built this 22-room Victorian mansion, now in the National Register. It is an example of the tradition of gracious summer living for
which Bar Harbor
was and is famous. In
addition to the main
house, there are sev-
eral charming cot-
tages situated in the
extensive gardens on
the property.

Innkeeper(s): Mac Noyes. $55-175. MC VISA. 14 rooms, 7 with PB, 6 with FP. 7 suites. Breakfast and afternoon tea included in rates. Types of meals: full breakfast and early coffee/tea. Beds: KQT. Ceiling fan in room. Cable TV, fax and copier on premises. Antiques, fishing, parks, shopping and watersports nearby.
Location: Close to Acadia National Park.
Publicity: *Discerning Traveler.*

"Wonderful honeymoon spot! Wonderful inn, elegant, delicious breakfasts, terrific innkeepers. We loved it all! It's our fourth time here and it's wonderful as always."
Certificate may be used: April through mid-June and Oct. 22 through mid-November. Sunday through Thursday.

The Maples Inn
16 Roberts Ave
Bar Harbor, ME 04609-1820
(207)288-3443 Fax:(207)288-0356

Circa 1903. This Victorian "summer cottage" once served wealthy summer visitors to Mt. Desert Island.

Located on a quiet residential street, away from Bar Harbor traffic, it has been tastefully restored and filled with Victorian furnishings. The inn is within walking distance of shops, boutiques and restaurants. Acadia National Park is five minutes away. Hiking, kayaking and cycling are among the nearby activities.

Innkeeper(s): Susan Sinclair. $60-150. MC VISA DS PC TC. 6 rooms with PB, 1 with FP. 1 suite. Breakfast and afternoon tea included in rates. Types of meals: gourmet breakfast and early coffee/tea. Beds: QT. Cable TV, fax and library on premises. Antiques, fishing, parks, shopping, cross-country skiing, sporting events, theater and watersports nearby.
Location: Within two blocks of the ocean.
Publicity: *San Diego Tribune, New York Times, Gourmet, Bon Appetit, Los Angeles Times.*

"What a wonderful place this is. Warm, comfortable, friendly, terrific breakfasts, great tips for adventure around the island. I could go on and on."
Certificate may be used: Jan. 1-April 30, holidays excluded.

Mira Monte Inn & Suites
69 Mount Desert St
Bar Harbor, ME 04609-1327
(207)288-4263 (800)553-5109 Fax:(207)288-3115
E-mail: mburns@acadia.net

Circa 1864. A gracious 18-room Victorian mansion, the Mira Monte has been newly renovated in the style of early Bar Harbor. It features period furnishings, pleasant common rooms, a library and wraparound porches. Situated on estate grounds, there are sweeping lawns, paved terraces and many gardens. The inn was one of the earliest of Bar Harbor's famous summer cottages. The two-room suites each feature canopy beds, two-person whirlpools, a parlor with a sleeper sofa, fireplace and kitchenette. The two-bedroom suite includes a full kitchen, dining area and parlor. The suites boast private decks with views of the gardens.
Innkeeper(s): Marian Burns. $95-180. MC VISA AX DC DS TC. 16 rooms, 15 with PB, 11 with FP. 3 suites. Breakfast and afternoon tea included in rates. Types of meals: full breakfast and early coffee/tea. Beds: KQT. Air conditioning, TV, VCR in room. Fax and library on premises. Handicap access. Antiques, fishing, parks, shopping, theater nearby.

Location: Five-minute walk from the waterfront, shops and restaurants.
Publicity: *Los Angeles Times.*

"On our third year at your wonderful inn in beautiful Bar Harbor. I think I enjoy it more each year. A perfect place to stay in a perfect environment."
Certificate may be used: May 1-June 10, holidays excluded & Oct. 18-31, holidays excluded.

The Ridgeway Inn
11 High St
Bar Harbor, ME 04609-1816
(207)288-9682

Circa 1890. Located on a quiet, tree-lined street, this Victorian B&B is a welcome sight for weary travelers. Each of the guest rooms is individually decorated and named after the cottages of the wealthy who made Bar Harbor their summer vacation spot. Many of these homes were destroyed in a 1947 fire, but the innkeepers have preserved their memory. Beds are covered with down comforters. One room includes a Jacuzzi tub, while another offers a private deck. The innkeepers serve an expansive, multi-course breakfast on fireside tables illuminated by candlelight. Freshly baked breads, scones and muffins are followed by a fruit recipe, which all precedes the daily entree.
Innkeeper(s): Lucie Rioux Hollfelder. $60-150. MC VISA PC TC. 5 rooms with PB. 2 suites. Breakfast and afternoon tea included in rates. Types of meals: full breakfast, gourmet breakfast and early coffee/tea. Beds: KQ. Amusement parks, antiques, fishing, parks, shopping, cross-country skiing, theater and watersports nearby.
Certificate may be used: May 1-June 15 (excluding Memorial Day weekend).

Town Motel & Guest House
12 Atlantic Ave
Bar Harbor, ME 04609-1704
(207)288-5548 (800)458-8644 Fax:(207)288-9406

Circa 1894. Although the innkeepers do offer simple, comfortable accommodations in their nine-room motel, they also offer a more historic experience in a late 19th-century Queen Anne Victorian. Bar Harbor has been a popular vacation spot for well over a century. This spacious house was built as a "cottage" for a wealthy family who spent their summers on Maine's scenic coast. The rooms are decorated with period furnishings, Oriental rugs, lacy curtains and flowery wallpapers. Each of eight rooms in the historic home has been decorated individually. Guests at the historic inn are treated to a continental-plus breakfast. Guests can walk to many attractions, and everything, from the harbor to Acadia National Park, is nearby.
Innkeeper(s): Joe, Paulette, Nicole, Christine. $75-140. MC VISA AX DS PC TC. 17 rooms with PB, 4 with FP. Breakfast included in rates. Types of meals: continental-plus breakfast and early coffee/tea. Beds: KQTD.

Air conditioning, ceiling fan and TV in room. VCR, fax and copier on premises. Antiques, fishing, parks, shopping, golf, theater and watersports nearby.

Certificate may be used: May through June, except Memorial Day weekend and after Labor Day weekend to Oct. 24.

Bath J3

Fairhaven Inn
RR 2 PO Box 85, N Bath Rd
Bath, ME 04530
(207)443-4391

Circa 1790. With its view of the Kennebec River, this site was so attractive that Pembleton Edgecomb built his Colonial house where a log cabin had previously stood. His descendants occupied it for the next 125 years. Antiques and country furniture fill the inn. Meadows and lawns, and woods of hemlock, birch and pine cover the inn's 16 acres.

Innkeeper(s): Susie & Dave Reed. $80-120. MC VISA DS PC TC. 8 rooms, 6 with PB. 1 suite. 1 cottage. 1 conference room. Breakfast included in rates. Types of meals: full breakfast and early coffee/tea. Beds: KQT. Cable TV, fax and library on premises. Antiques, parks, shopping, cross-country skiing, sporting events, theater and watersports nearby.

Publicity: *The State, Coastal Journal.*

"The Fairhaven is now marked in our book with a red star, definitely a place to remember and visit again."

Certificate may be used: Year-round, Sunday-Friday.

The Galen C. Moses House
1009 Washington St
Bath, ME 04530-2759
(207)442-8771

Circa 1874. This Victorian mansion is filled with beautiful architectural items, including stained-glass windows, wood-carved and marble fireplaces and a grand staircase. The innkeepers have filled the library, a study, morning room and the parlor with antiques. A corner fireplace warms the dining room, which overlooks the lawns and gardens. Tea is presented in the formal drawing room.

Innkeeper(s): James Haught, Larry Kieft. $65-95. MC VISA PC TC. 4 rooms with PB. Breakfast and afternoon tea included in rates. Types of meals: continental breakfast and gourmet breakfast. Beds: QDT. Turndown service in room. Cable TV, VCR and library on premises. Antiques, fishing, parks, shopping, cross-country skiing, theater and watersports nearby.

Publicity: *Philadelphia, Back Roads USA.*

"For our first try at B&B lodgings, we've probably started at the top, and nothing else will ever measure up to this. Wonderful food, wonderful home, grounds and wonderful hosts!"

Certificate may be used: Nov. 1-April 30.

Packard House
45 Pearl St
Bath, ME 04530-2746
(207)443-6069 (800)516-4578

Circa 1790. Shipbuilder Benjamin F. Packard restored this handsome home in 1870, and the inn still reflects the Victorian influence so prominent in Bath's busy ship-building years. The Packard family, who lived in the home for five generations, left many family mementos. Period furnishings, authentic colors and ship-building memorabilia recapture the romantic past of Bath. The Kennebec River is just a block away.

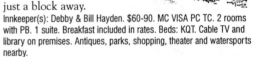

Innkeeper(s): Debby & Bill Hayden. $60-90. MC VISA PC TC. 2 rooms with PB. 1 suite. Breakfast included in rates. Beds: KQT. Cable TV and library on premises. Antiques, parks, shopping, theater and watersports nearby.

Location: Historic district.

Publicity: *Times Record, Maine Sunday Telegram, Coastal Journal.*

"Thanks for being wonderful hosts."

Certificate may be used: Nov. 1-April 30, Sunday-Thursday.

Belfast H5

The Jeweled Turret Inn
40 Pearl St
Belfast, ME 04915-1907
(207)338-2304 (800)696-2304

Circa 1898. This grand Victorian is named for the staircase that winds up the turret, lighted by stained- and leaded-glass panels and jewel-like embellishments. It was built for attorney James Harriman. Dark pine beams adorn the ceiling of the den, and the fireplace is constructed of bark and rocks from every state in the Union.

Elegant antiques furnish the guest rooms. Guests can relax in one of the inn's four parlors, which are furnished with period antiques, wallpapers, lace and boast fireplaces. The verandas feature wicker and iron bistro sets and views of the historic district. The inn is within walking distance of the town and its shops, restaurants and the harbor.

Innkeeper(s): Cathy & Carl Heffentrager. $75-95. MC VISA PC TC. 7 rooms with PB, 1 with FP. Breakfast and afternoon tea included in rates. Types of meals: gourmet breakfast and early coffee/tea. Beds: QDT. Ceiling fan in room. Antiques, fishing, shopping, downhill skiing, cross-country skiing, theater and watersports nearby.

Publicity: *Republican Journal, Waterville Sentinel, Los Angeles Times, Country Living, Victorian Homes.*

"The ambiance was so romantic that we felt like we were on our honeymoon."

Certificate may be used: April 1-June 30, September, Oct. 16-Nov. 30, (no holidays).

The Thomas Pitcher House B&B

19 Franklin St
Belfast, ME 04915-1105
(207)338-6454 (888)338-6454

Circa 1873. This richly appointed home was considered state-of-the-art back in 1873, for it was one of only a few homes offering central heat and hot or cold running water. Today, innkeepers have added plenty of modern amenities, but kept the ambiance of the Victorian era. Some vanities include original walnut and marble, while another bathroom includes tin ceilings and a step-down bath. Some rooms have cozy reading areas. Guests enjoy a full breakfast each morning with menus that feature specialties such as Maine blueberry buttermilk pancakes or a French toast puff made with homemade raisin bread.

Innkeeper(s): Fran & Ron Kresge. $65-85. MC VISA PC TC. 4 rooms with PB. Breakfast included in rates. Types of meals: gourmet breakfast and early coffee/tea. Beds: QD. Cable TV, VCR and library on premises. Antiques, fishing, parks, shopping, downhill skiing, cross-country skiing, theater and watersports nearby.

Publicity: *Boston Herald, Jackson Clarion-Ledger, Toronto Sunday Sun, Bride's, Knoxville News-Sentinel.*

"A home away from home."

Certificate may be used: Oct. 15-June 15 (Sunday through Saturday).

Belgrade Lakes H3

Wings Hill

PO Box 386
Belgrade Lakes, ME 04918-0386
(207)495-2400 (800)509-4647

Circa 1800. Antiques and original artwork grace the interior of this restored Cape-style farmhouse. The huge wraparound porch is screened in and an ideal place to relax. Many of the antiques and collectibles are available for sale. The innkeepers serve a country breakfast prepared in the quaint kitchen, an inviting room warmed by a woodburning stove. The innkeepers will help guests plan activities, including rentals for skiing, boating and snowmobiling.

Innkeeper(s): Dick Hofmann. $95. MC VISA. 8 rooms with PB. Breakfast included in rates. Types of meals: full breakfast and early coffee/tea. Afternoon tea available. Cable TV and VCR on premises. Antiques, fishing, shopping, downhill skiing, cross-country skiing, sporting events, theater and watersports nearby.

Certificate may be used: Sunday-Thursday, May-October.

Bethel I2

Abbott House

Rt 26
Bethel, ME 04217
(207)824-7600 (800)240-2377

Circa 1773. Guests at this 18th-century home are treated to a variety of soothing amenities. Innkeepers Joe Cardello and Penny Bohac-Cardello offer massage service, an outdoor hot tub and will set up goodies such as chocolates and flowers for guests celebrating a special occasion. Penny is an excellent baker and creates all the fresh breads for breakfast and afternoon tea. Her freshly baked treats, such as a succulent blueberry cake, complement Joe's array of breakfast fare. Joe serves up a hearty meal with meats, potatoes, egg dishes and fresh fruit, all garnished with edible flowers from the inn's garden. In warmer months, iced coffees and iced tea are served with the afternoon and evening refreshments.

Innkeeper(s): Joe Cardello, Penny Bohac-Cardello. $55-65. MC VISA AX. 5 rooms, 3 with PB. 1 suite. Breakfast, afternoon tea and evening snack included in rates. Types of meals: full breakfast and early coffee/tea. Dinner and catering service available. Beds: QDT. Cable TV and spa on premises. Antiques, fishing, parks, shopping, downhill skiing and cross-country skiing nearby.

Certificate may be used: All year, midweek (Sunday-Thursday), Spring-Summer-Fall, weekends.

L'Auberge Country Inn

Mill Hill Rd, PO Box 21
Bethel, ME 04217

(207)824-2774 (800)760-2774 Fax:(207)824-2774

In the foothills of the White Mountains, surrounded by five acres of gardens and woods, this former carriage house was converted to a guest house in the 1920s. Among its seven guest rooms are two spacious suites. The Theater Suite offers a four-poster queen bed and dressing room. The Family Suite can accommodate up to six guests. Mount Abrahms and Sunday River ski areas are just minutes away.
Innkeeper(s): Werner Kohlmeyer. $55-115. MC VISA AX DS. 6 rooms. 2 suites. 1 conference room. Breakfast included in rates. Types of meals: continental-plus breakfast and early coffee/tea. Banquet service and catering service available. Cable TV, VCR and child care on premises. Antiques, shopping, downhill skiing and cross-country skiing nearby.
Certificate may be used: Midweek, non-holiday.

Blue Hill   H5

Arcady Down East

HC 64 Box 370
Blue Hill, ME 04614-9603

(207)374-5576

Circa 1834. This attractive Victorian Shingle inn, listed in the National Register, offers many authentic touches, including period antiques and tin ceilings. The inn's seven guest rooms include the Celebration Suite, perfect for honeymooners with its cozy fireplace and sitting area. Another favorite with visitors is the Captain's Quarters, featuring a skylight to help highlight its unique furnishings. The impressive coastal beauty of Acadia National Park is a short drive from the inn.
Innkeeper(s): Gene & Bertha Wiseman. $85-110. MC VISA AX TC. 7 rooms, 5 with PB, 1 with FP. 1 suite. Breakfast included in rates. Types of meals: full breakfast and early coffee/tea. Beds: KQDT. Turndown service and ceiling fan in room. Bicycles and child care on premises. Antiques, fishing, parks, shopping, cross-country skiing, theater and watersports nearby.
Certificate may be used: Every night except month of August.

Boothbay   J4

Kenniston Hill Inn

Rt 27, PO Box 125
Boothbay, ME 04537-0125

(207)633-2159 (800)992-2915 Fax:(207)633-2159

Circa 1786. The elegant clapboard home is the oldest inn at Boothbay Harbor and was occupied by the Kenniston family for more than a century. Five of the antique-filled bedrooms have fireplaces. After a walk through the gardens or woods, warm up in the parlor next to the elegant, open-hearthed fire-

place. Boothbay Harbor offers something for everybody, including whale-watching excursions and dinner theaters.
Innkeeper(s): Susan & David Straight. $69-110. MC VISA DS PC TC. 10 rooms with PB, 5 with FP. Breakfast and afternoon tea included in rates. Types of meals: full breakfast and early coffee/tea.
Restaurant on premises. Beds: KQDT. Ceiling fan in room. Fax on premises. Antiques, fishing, parks, shopping, downhill skiing, cross-country skiing, theater and watersports nearby.
Publicity: *Boothbay Register.*

"England may be the home of the original bed & breakfast, but Kenniston Hill Inn is where it has been perfected!"
Certificate may be used: Jan. 1-May 31, Nov. 1-30 and December, excluding holiday weekends. Rate is $110 only.

Boothbay Harbor   J4

Harbour Towne Inn on the Waterfront

71 Townsend Ave
Boothbay Harbor, ME 04538-1158

(207)633-4300 (800)722-4240 Fax:(207)633-4300

Circa 1880. This waterfront Victorian inn boasts 11 guest rooms and one suite. Most rooms offer a private deck and the Penthouse has an outstanding view of the harbor. Breakfast is served in the inn's Sunroom, and guests also may relax in the parlor, which has a miniature antique library and a beautiful antique fire-

place. The inn's meticulous grounds include flower gardens and well-kept shrubs and trees. It's an easy walk to the village and its art galleries, restaurants and shops. Special off-season packages are available. Ft. William Henry and the Fisherman's Memorial are nearby.
Innkeeper(s): George Thomas. $69-275. MC VISA AX DS PC TC. 11 rooms with PB. 1 conference room. Breakfast included in rates. Type of meal: continental-plus breakfast. Beds: KQDT. TV in room. Fax and copier on premises. Handicap access. Antiques, fishing, parks, shopping, downhill skiing, cross-country skiing, theater and watersports nearby.
Certificate may be used: Off low season excluding Friday, Saturday nights; holiday, special events and the Penthouse.

Bremen J4

Roaring Brook B&B
Rt 32, 921 Waldoboro Rd
Bremen, ME 04551
(207)529-5467 (800)660-5467 Fax:(207)529-5467
E-mail: RoarBrook@aol.com

Circa 1940. Innkeepers Don and Lorelei Eckert have brought hospitality back to this New England Cape-style home, which served as a guest house in the 1950s. Aside from the guest rooms, enhanced by the country Colonial furnishings and decor, The innkeepers offer an efficiency apartment during the summer months. German pancakes, homemade breads and omelets are some of the delectables that might highlight the morning meal. The B&B is only a few miles from Round Pond, and lighthouses, antiquing and restaurants await guests in nearby villages.

Innkeeper(s): Don & Lorelei Eckert. $50-90. MC VISA TC. 4 rooms, 2 with PB, 1 with FP. 1 suite. Breakfast included in rates. Types of meals: full breakfast and early coffee/tea. Beds: QDT. Turndown service in room. Cable TV, VCR and fax on premises. Antiques, fishing, shopping, theater and watersports nearby.

Certificate may be used: Oct. 1-June 30, Sunday-Saturday.

Bridgton I2

Tarry-A-While Resort
Box A, Highland Ridge Rd
Bridgton, ME 04009
(207)647-2522 Fax:(207)647-5512

Circa 1897. Tarry-A-While offers a variety of comfortable accommodations, including a Victorian inn and cottages. There is also a social hall. The resort is located on a 25-acre hillside and there are plenty of outdoor activities. Tennis and boating are included in the rates, and sailing or waterskiing is available. An

18-hole golf course is a walk away. The inn's dining room, which overlooks Highland Lake and Pleasant Mountain, serves fine cuisine as you gaze at the sunset.

Innkeeper(s): Marc & Nancy Stretch. $70-130. MC VISA PC. 27 rooms, 22 with PB. Breakfast included in rates. Type of meal: continental breakfast. Beds: KQDT. Air conditioning in room. Bicycles and tennis on premises. Antiques, shopping and theater nearby.

"A definite return trip to romantic peaceful memories."

Certificate may be used: Anytime May 30-June 29 and Sept. 5-Oct. 5.

Camden I5

Blue Harbor House, A Village Inn
67 Elm St, Rt 1
Camden, ME 04843-1904
(207)236-3196 (800)248-3196 Fax:(207)236-6523
E-mail: MKKE83A@prodigy.com

Circa 1810. James Richards, Camden's first settler, built this Cape house on a 1768 homesite. (The King granted him the land as the first person to fulfill all the conditions of a settler.) An 1810 carriage house has been refurbished to offer private suites, some with whirlpool tubs. Breakfast is served on the sun porch overlooking the Camden Hills. Dinner, available by reservation, can be a gourmet affair or an authentic Maine  lobster bake on the lawn. The bustling harbor is a five-minute walk away.

Innkeeper(s): Jody Schmoll & Dennis Hayden. $85-135. MAP. MC VISA AX DS PC TC. 10 rooms with PB. 2 suites. 1 conference room. Breakfast and afternoon tea included in rates. Types of meals: gourmet breakfast and early coffee/tea. Beds: KQDT. Air conditioning, turndown service, TV and VCR in room. Fax, bicycles and library on premises. Antiques, fishing, parks, shopping, downhill skiing, cross-country skiing, theater and watersports nearby.

Location: Camden Village.

Publicity: *Dallas Morning News, Discerning Traveler, Country Living.*

"I don't know when I've enjoyed my stay in a country inn more."

Certificate may be used: Nov. 1-May 15, excludes Carriage House Suites.

Captain Swift Inn
72 Elm St
Camden, ME 04843-1907
(207)236-8113 (800)251-0865 Fax:(207)230-0464
E-mail: swiftinn@midcoast.com

Circa 1810. This Federal-style home remains much as it did in the 19th century. The innkeepers worked diligently to preserve the historic flavor, restoring the pine floors and moldings. The home's original five fireplaces and exposed beams add to the warm and cozy interior. The only addition to the home was a new section, which includes the innkeeper's

quarters, a kitchen and a guest room entirely accessible for guests with wheelchairs. The innkeepers prepare a gourmet, three-course breakfast with items that sound decadent, but are truly low in fat and cholesterol, such as an apple pancake souffle.

Innkeeper(s): Tom & Kathy Filip. $65-95. MC VISA PC TC. 4 rooms with PB. Breakfast and afternoon tea included in rates. Types of meals: full breakfast, gourmet breakfast and early coffee/tea. Beds: QT. Air conditioning in room. Cable TV, VCR, fax, copier and library on premises. Handicap access. Antiques, fishing, parks, shopping, downhill skiing, cross-country skiing, golf, theater and watersports nearby.

Publicity: *Maine Boats & Harbors, Boston Patriot Ledger, Teacups and Postcards, Secrets of Entertaining, Wake Up & Smell the Coffee.*

"We came intending to stay for one night and ended up staying for five. . .need we say more!"

Certificate may be used: Nov. 1-April 30, Sunday-Thursday.

Elms B&B

84 Elm St, Rt 1
Camden, ME 04843-1907
(207)236-6250 (800)755-3567 Fax:(207)236-7330

Circa 1806. Captain Calvin Curtis built this Colonial a few minutes' stroll from the picturesque harbor. Candlelight shimmers year round from the inn's windows. A sitting room, library and parlor are open for guests. Tastefully appointed bed chambers scattered with antiques are available in both the main house and the carriage house. A cottage garden can be seen beside the carriage house. A lighthouse theme permeates the decor, and there is a wide selection of lighthouse books, collectibles and artwork.

Innkeeper(s): Ted & Jo Panayotoff. $65-95. MC VISA TC. 6 rooms with PB, 1 with FP. Breakfast and afternoon tea included in rates. Types of meals: continental breakfast, full breakfast and early coffee/tea. Beds: QD. Handicap access. Antiques, fishing, parks, shopping, downhill skiing, cross-country skiing and theater nearby.

"If something is worth doing, it's worth doing first class, and your place is definitely first class."

Certificate may be used: Oct. 20-May 21 all days of the week.

Lord Camden Inn

24 Main St
Camden, ME 04843-1704
(207)236-4325 (800)336-4325 Fax:(207)236-7141
E-mail: lordcam@midcoast.com

Circa 1893. Lord Camden Inn, housed in a century-old brick building, offers the gentle warmth of a seaside inn with all the comforts and services of a modern downtown hotel. Located in the midst of Camden's fine shops and restaurants, the bustling waterfront and beautiful parks, Lord Camden Inn offers splendid views of the harbor, Camden Hill and the village. Amenities include private baths, cable TV, air conditioning, phones and elevator services.

Innkeeper(s): Stuart & Marianne Smith. $88-178. MC VISA PC. 31 rooms with PB. 4 suites. 2 conference rooms. Breakfast included in rates. Types of meals: continental-plus breakfast and early coffee/tea. Beds: KQD. Fax and copier on premises. Antiques, fishing, parks, shopping, skiing, theater and watersports nearby.

Certificate may be used: October through May.

Cape Elizabeth   K3

Inn By The Sea

40 Bowery Beach Rd
Cape Elizabeth, ME 04107-2514
(207)799-3134 (800)888-4287 Fax:(207)799-4779

Circa 1986. This cottage-style resort is like a modern version of the hotels and inns that dotted Maine's coast in its heyday as a summer spot. The inn has its own private boardwalk leading to Crescent Beach. Guests can enjoy swimming, tennis and shuffleboard without leaving the inn's grounds, which also offer a tea garden and gazebo. The well-appointed rooms are elegant, but not imposing, with Chippendale furnishings, wicker and floral chintz. Guests opting for one of the inn's cozy garden suites can grab a book from the inn's library and enjoy it from a rocker on their own private porch. Cuisine at the inn's gourmet Audubon Room is full of memorable items. In the summer months, the inn opens its outdoor West End Cafe and Pool Bar.

Innkeeper(s): Maureen McQuade. $100-390. EP. MC VISA AX DS TC. 43 suites, 6 with FP. 2 conference rooms. Type of meal: full breakfast. Dinner, picnic lunch, banquet service, catering service and room service available. Restaurant on premises. Beds: KQD. Turndown service, ceiling fan, TV and VCR in room. Fax, copier and bicycles on premises. Amusement parks, antiques, fishing, parks, shopping, downhill skiing, cross-country skiing, sporting events, theater and watersports nearby.

Certificate may be used: November-April, excluding holidays, Sunday-Friday.

China H4

Loons Call Inn
PO Box 342
China, ME 04926-0342
(207)968-2025 Fax:(207)968-2025

Circa 1974. Each year, a variety of birds return to this inn located by the banks of China Lake. The innkeepers, both members of the Audubon Society, enjoy keeping track of the eagles, blue herons, ospreys and, of course, the namesake loons that land on the shore. Guests staying in the semi-private library loft access the room via an oak spiral staircase. The bed is situated under a skylight, perfect for stargazing. The Executive Suite includes a reading area and whirlpool tub.

Innkeeper(s): Gary & Tera Coull. $75-99. MC VISA TC. 4 rooms, 3 with PB. 2 suites. Breakfast included in rates. Types of meals: continental breakfast, continental-plus breakfast, full breakfast, gourmet breakfast and early coffee/tea. Evening snack, lunch and banquet service available. Restaurant on premises. Beds: KQT. Cable TV, VCR, fax, copier, spa, bicycles and child care on premises. Antiques, fishing, parks, shopping, downhill skiing, cross-country skiing, sporting events, theater and watersports nearby.

Certificate may be used: All year with reservation 30 days in advance if available.

Durham I3

The Bagley House
1290 Royalsborough Rd
Durham, ME 04222-5225
(207)865-6566 (800)765-1772 Fax:(207)353-5878

Circa 1772. Six acres of fields and woods surround the Bagley House. Once an inn, a store and a schoolhouse, it is the oldest house in town. Guest rooms are decorated with colonial furnishings and hand-sewn Maine quilts. For breakfast, guests gather in the country kitchen in front of a huge brick fireplace and beehive oven.

Innkeeper(s): Suzanne O'Connor & Susan Backhouse. $70-125. MC VISA AX DS. 5 rooms with PB. 1 with FP. 1 conference room. Breakfast and afternoon tea included in rates. Types of meals: full breakfast and early coffee/tea. Evening snack and picnic lunch available. Beds: QDT. Fax on premises. Antiques, shopping, skiing, sporting events and theater nearby.

Location: Route 136, Durham.
Publicity: *Los Angeles Times, New England Getaways, Lewiston Sun, Springfield Register.*

"I had the good fortune to stumble on the Bagley House. The rooms are well-appointed and the innkeeper is as charming a host as you'll find."

Certificate may be used: November-June, Sunday-Thursday.

Eastport G8

The Milliken House
29 Washington St
Eastport, ME 04631-1324
(207)853-2955

Circa 1846. This inn is filled with beautiful furnishings and knickknacks, much of which belonged to the home's first owner, Benjamin Milliken. Ornately carved, marble-topped pieces and period decor take guests back in time to the Victorian era. Milliken maintained a wharf on Eastport's waterfront from which he serviced the tall trading ships that used the harbor as a  port of entry to the United States. An afternoon glass of port or sherry and chocolate turn-down service are among the amenities. Breakfasts are a gourmet treat, served in the dining room with its carved, antique furnishings.

Innkeeper(s): Joyce Weber. $40-60. MC VISA AX PC TC. 5 rooms. 1 conference room. Breakfast included in rates. Type of meal: full breakfast. Beds: QT.

"Your lovely place is so homey - fantastic breakfast!"

Certificate may be used: January-June, October-December. Any day.

Weston House
26 Boynton St
Eastport, ME 04631-1305
(207)853-2907 (800)853-2907

Circa 1810. Jonathan Weston, an 1802 Harvard graduate, built this Federal-style house on a hill overlooking Passamaquoddy Bay. John Audubon stayed here as a guest of the Westons while awaiting passage to Labrador in 1833. Each guest room is furnished with antiques and Oriental rugs. The Weston and Audubon rooms boast views of the bay and gardens. Breakfast menus vary, including such delectables as heavenly pancakes with hot apricot syrup or freshly baked muffins and coddled eggs. Seasonal brunches are served on weekends and holidays. The area is full of outdoor activities, including whale watching. Nearby Saint Andrews-by-the-Sea offers plenty of shops and restaurants.

Innkeeper(s): Jett & John Peterson. $55-75. PC TC. 5 rooms, 1 with FP. 1 suite. 1 conference room. Breakfast and afternoon tea included in rates. Type of meal: gourmet breakfast. Picnic lunch and catering service available. Beds: KQDT. TV in room. Fishing, shopping and theater nearby.

Publicity: *Downeast Magazine, Los Angeles Times, Boston Globe, Boston Magazine.*

"All parts of ourselves have been nourishes."

Certificate may be used: Subject to availability. All months with the exception of the month of August.

Eliot L2

High Meadows B&B

Rt 101
Eliot, ME 03903
(207)439-0590

Circa 1740. A ship's captain built this house, now filled with remembrances of colonial days. At one point, it was raised and a floor added underneath, so the upstairs is older than the downstairs. It is conveniently located to factory outlets in Kittery, Maine, and great dining and historic museums in Portsmouth, N.H. Smoking is permitted on the porch and terrace.

Innkeeper(s): Elaine & Ray. $60-80. MC VISA AX PC TC. 5 rooms, 4 with PB, 1 with FP. 1 conference room. Breakfast and afternoon tea included in rates. Types of meals: full breakfast and early coffee/tea. Beds: QDT. Turndown service in room. Cable TV on premises. Antiques, fishing, shopping and watersports nearby.

Publicity: *Portsmouth Herald, York County Focus.*

"High Meadows was the highlight of our trip."

Certificate may be used: Monday-Thursday; April, May, June.

Moses Paul Inn

270 Goodwin Rd
Eliot, ME 03903-1204
(207)439-1861 (800)552-6058

Circa 1780. This Colonial farmhouse is charming and hard to miss, with its barn-red exterior and white trim. The home is truly welcoming. Restored wood floors and woodwork gleam, and rooms, some with exposed beams, are decorated with treasures the innkeepers found at local auctions. Quilts, antiques and country furnishings are among the finds. The restored barn serves as an antique shop.

Be sure to ask the innkeepers about a French soldier who may still inhabit the halls in ghostly form. Kittery Outlet Malls and historic Portsmouth are just a few minutes away, as is the coastline.

Innkeeper(s): Joanne Weiss & Larry James. $55-75. MC VISA DS PC TC. 5 rooms, 2 with PB. Breakfast included in rates. Type of meal: full breakfast. Beds: QDT. Ceiling fan in room. Cable TV, VCR, fax and library on premises. Amusement parks, antiques, fishing, parks, shopping, downhill skiing, cross-country skiing, sporting events, theater and watersports nearby.

Certificate may be used: Anytime, subject to availability.

Freeport J3

The Isaac Randall House

5 Independence Dr
Freeport, ME 04032-1110
(207)865-9295 (800)865-9295 Fax:(207)865-9003
E-mail: ikesspot@aol.com

Circa 1823. Isaac Randall's Federal-style farmhouse was once a dairy farm and a stop on the Underground Railway for slaves escaping into Canada. Randall was a descendant of John Alden and Priscilla Mullins of the Mayflower. Longfellow

immortalized their romance in "The Courtship of Miles Standish." The inn is located on six wooded acres with a pond. Guest rooms are air-conditioned.

Innkeeper(s): Cindy Wellito. $65-125. MC VISA DS. 10 rooms with PB, 5 with FP. 1 conference room. Breakfast and evening snack included in rates. Type of meal: full breakfast. Beds: KQT. Air conditioning in room. Cable TV, VCR, fax, copier, spa, library and child care on premises. Antiques, fishing, parks, shopping, cross-country skiing, sporting events, golf, theater and watersports nearby.

Location: At the south edge of Freeport Village.

Publicity: *Toronto Star, Early American Life, Newsday.*

"Enchanted to find ourselves surrounded by all your charming antiques and beautiful furnishings."

Certificate may be used: Non-holiday, Sunday-Thursday, from Dec. 15-May 15.

Greenville
F4

Greenville Inn

Norris St, PO Box 1194
Greenville, ME 04441
(207)695-2206 (888)695-6000 Fax:(207)695-2206

Circa 1895. Lumber baron William Shaw built this inn, which sits on a hill overlooking Moosehead Lake and the Squaw Mountains. The inn includes many unique features. Ten years were needed to complete the embellishments on the cherry and mahogany paneling, which is found throughout the

inn. A spruce tree is painted on one of the leaded-glass windows on the stairway landing. The inn's six fireplaces are adorned with carved mantels, English tiles and mosaics. The inn's dining room is ideal for a romantic dinner. Fresh, seasonal ingredients fill the ever-changing menu, and the dining room also offers a variety of wine choices.

Innkeeper(s): Elfi, Michael and Susie Schnetzer. $85-195. MC VISA DS PC TC. 12 rooms, 5 with PB, 2 with FP. 1 suite. 6 cottages. Type of meal: continental-plus breakfast. Dinner available. Restaurant on premises. Beds: KQDT.

Location: Moosehead Lake, Greenville.

Publicity: *Maine Times, Portland Monthly, Bangor Daily News, Grays Sporting Journal.*

"The fanciest place in town. It is indeed a splendid place."

Certificate may be used: Nov. 1-April 30, subject to availability, not valid during holiday and winter vacation periods.

Guilford
G4

Trebor Inn

Golda Ct
Guilford, ME 04443
(207)876-4070 (888)4-TREBOR

Circa 1830. Seven guest rooms are available at this stately, turreted Victorian inn, which overlooks Guilford from high on a hill along the Moosehead Trail. Those who enjoy hunting bear, deer, partridge and pheasant should inquire about the inn's special rates for hunters. Meals are served family-style, and dinners are available on request. The family-oriented inn also accommodates business meetings, family reunions and weddings. Within five minutes of the

inn, visitors will find basketball courts, a nine-hole golf course and tennis courts. Peaks-Kenny State Park and Sebec Lake are nearby.

Innkeeper(s): Robert & Larraine Vernal. $50-65. MC VISA AX PC TC. 7 rooms, 2 with PB. Breakfast included in rates. Types of meals: full breakfast and early coffee/tea. Dinner available. Beds: DT. Cable TV and VCR on premises. Antiques, fishing, parks, shopping, downhill skiing, cross-country skiing, golf and watersports nearby.

Certificate may be used: Dec. 1-Oct. 28.

Hallowell (Augusta)

Maple Hill Farm B&B Inn

RR 1 Box 1145, Outlet Rd
Hallowell (Augusta), ME 04347-9721
(207)622-2708 (800)622-2708 Fax:(207)622-0655
E-mail: maple@mint.net

Circa 1890. Visitors to Maine's capitol city have the option of staying at this nearby inn, a peaceful farm setting adjacent to a 550-acre state wildlife management area that is available for canoeing, fishing, hiking and hunting. This Victorian Shingle-style inn was once a stagecoach stop and dairy farm. The inn's suite includes a double whirlpool tub. The inn, with its 62-acre grounds, easily accommodates conferences, parties and receptions. Guests are welcome to visit the many farm animals. Cobbossee

Lake is a five-minute drive from the inn. The center portion of Hallowell is listed as a National Historic District and offers antique shops and restaurants.

Innkeeper(s): Scott Cowger. $50-125. MC VISA AX DC CB DS. 7 rooms, 4 with PB. 1 suite. 1 conference room. Breakfast and afternoon tea included in rates. Types of meals: full breakfast and early coffee/tea. Evening snack, picnic lunch, banquet service and catering service available. Beds: QD. VCR on premises. Handicap access. Antiques, fishing, shopping, cross-country skiing, theater and watersports nearby.

Publicity: *Family Fun, An Explorer's Guide to Maine, The Forecaster, Portland Press Herald, Kennebec Journal, Maine Times.*

"You add many thoughtful touches to your service that set your B&B apart from others, and really make a difference."

Certificate may be used: May-October, Sunday-Wednesday; November-April, anytime, but not both Friday and Saturday.

Isle Au Haut I5

The Keeper's House

PO Box 26
Isle Au Haut, ME 04645-0026
(207)367-2261

Circa 1907. Designed and built by the U.S. Lighthouse Service, the handsome 48-foot-high Robinson Point Light guided vessels into this once-bustling island fishing village. Guests arrive on the mailboat. Innkeeper Judi Burke, whose father was a keeper at the Highland Lighthouse on Cape Cod,

provides picnic lunches so guests may explore the scenic island trails. Dinner is served in the keeper's dining room. The lighthouse is adjacent to the most remote section of Acadia National Park. It's not uncommon to hear the cry of an osprey, see deer approach the inn, or watch seals and porpoises cavorting off the point. Guest rooms are comfortable and serene, with stunning views of the island's ragged shore line, forests and Duck Harbor.

Innkeeper(s): Jeff & Judi Burke. $250-285. PC TC. 6 rooms. 1 cottage. Breakfast, dinner and picnic lunch included in rates. Types of meals: full breakfast, gourmet breakfast and early coffee/tea. Afternoon tea, lunch and gourmet lunch available. Beds: D. Swimming, bicycles and library on premises. Parks and shopping nearby.

Location: A small island six miles south of Stonington, reached by mailboat.

Publicity: *New York Times, USA Today, Los Angeles Times, Ladies Home Journal, Christian Science Monitor, Down East, New York Woman, Philadelphia Inquirer, McCalls, Country, Men's Journal, Travel & Leisure.*

"Simply one of the unique places on Earth."

Certificate may be used: May 1-June 15 and Oct. 16-31.

Kennebunkport K2

Cove House

11 S Maine St
Kennebunkport, ME 04046-6313
(207)967-3704

Circa 1793. This roomy Colonial Revival farmhouse overlooks Chick's Cove on the Kennebunk River. The inn's peaceful setting offers easy access to beaches, shops and the town. Three guest rooms serve visitors of this antique-filled home. Guests enjoy full breakfasts, which often include the inn's famous blueberry muffins, in the Flow Blue dining room. A popular gathering spot is the book-lined living room/library. Bicycles may be borrowed for a leisurely ride around the town. A cozy, secluded cottage with a screened front porch is another lodging option.

Innkeeper(s): Katherine Jones. $70-95. MC VISA PC TC. 3 rooms with PB. 1 cottage. Breakfast and afternoon tea included in rates. Types of meals: full breakfast and early coffee/tea. Beds: QT. Cable TV, VCR, bicycles and library on premises. Antiques, fishing, parks, shopping, cross-country skiing, theater and watersports nearby.

Certificate may be used: Nov. 1-May 15, excluding holiday weekends.

English Meadows Inn

141 Port Rd
Kennebunkport, ME 04043
(207)967-5766 (800)272-0698 Fax:(207)967-5766

Circa 1860. Bordered by century-old lilac bushes, this Queen Anne Victorian inn and attached carriage house offer 13 guest rooms. The inn's well-tended grounds, which include apple trees, gardens and lush lawns, invite bird-lovers or those who desire a relaxing stroll. Four-poster beds, afghans and handsewn quilts are found in many of the guest rooms. Visitors also will enjoy the talents of local artists, whose works are featured throughout the inn. Guests may eat breakfast in bed before heading out to explore Kennebunkport.

Innkeeper(s): Charles Doane. $85-115. MC VISA AX DS PC TC. 13 rooms with PB. 1 suite. 1 cottage. Breakfast and afternoon tea included in rates. Types of meals: full breakfast and early coffee/tea. Room service available. Beds: KQDT. Cable TV and fax on premises. Amusement parks, antiques, fishing, parks, shopping, cross-country skiing, theater and watersports nearby.

"Thanks for the memories! You have a warm Yankee hospitality here!"

Certificate may be used: November-May, Sunday through Thursday.

Kylemere House 1818

6 South St, PO Box 1333
Kennebunkport, ME 04046-1333
(207)967-2780

Circa 1818. Located in Maine's largest historic district, this Federal-style house was built by Daniel Walker, a descendant of an original Kennebunkport family. Later, Maine artist and architect Abbot

Graves purchased the property and named it "Crosstrees" for its maple trees. The inn features New England antiques and brilliant flower gardens in view of the formal dining room in spring and summer. A full breakfast is provided. Art galleries, beaches, antiquing and golf are nearby.
Innkeeper(s): Ruth Toohey. $90-150. MC VISA. 4 rooms with PB, 1 with FP. Breakfast included in rates. Types of meals: full breakfast and early coffee/tea. Beds: KQT. Antiques, fishing, shopping, theater nearby.
Publicity: *Boston Globe, Glamour, Regis and Kathie Lee Show.*

"Beautiful inn. Outstanding hospitality. Thanks for drying our sneakers, fixing our bikes. You are all a lot of fun!"

Certificate may be used: Sunday-Thursday, mid-May to mid-June and November.

Maine Stay Inn & Cottages

PO Box 500-A
Kennebunkport, ME 04046-6174
(207)967-2117 (800)950-2117 Fax:(207)967-8757
E-mail: innkeeper@mainestayinn.com

Circa 1860. In the National Register, this is a square-block Italianate contoured in a low hip-roof design. Later additions reflecting the Queen Anne period include a suspended spiral staircase, crystal windows, ornately carved mantels and moldings, bay windows and porches. A sea captain built the handsome cupola that became a favorite spot for making taffy. In the '20s, the cupola was a place from which to spot offshore rumrunners. Guests enjoy after-

noon tea with stories of the Maine Stay's heritage. One suite and one room in the main building and five of the cottage rooms have working fireplaces.
Innkeeper(s): Carol & Lindsay Copeland. $85-225. MC VISA AX PC TC. 17 rooms with PB, 7 with FP. 4 suites. 10 cottages. Breakfast and afternoon tea included in rates. Types of meals: full breakfast and early coffee/tea. Beds: KQDT. Air conditioning and TV in room. Fax, copier, computer and child care on premises. Amusement parks, antiques, fishing, shopping, cross-country skiing, theater and watersports nearby.
Location: In the Kennebunkport National Historic District.
Publicity: *Boston Globe, Discerning Traveler, Montreal Gazette, Innsider, Tourist News, Down East, Staten Island Advance, Birmingham News, Delaware County Times, Family Travel Times.*

"We have traveled the East Coast from Martha's Vineyard to Bar Harbor, and this is the only place we know we must return to."

Certificate may be used: Midweek, Monday through Thursday, late October through mid-June.

Kittery L2

Enchanted Nights B&B

29 Wentworth St Rt 103
Kittery, ME 03904
(207)439-1489

Circa 1890. The innkeepers bill this unique inn as a "Victorian fantasy for the romantic at heart." Each of the guest rooms is unique, from the spacious rooms with double whirlpool tubs to the cozy turret room. A whimsical combination of country French and Victorian decor permeates the interior. Wrought-iron beds and hand-painted furnishings add to the ambiance. Breakfasts, often with a vegetarian theme, are served with gourmet coffee in the morning room on antique floral china.
Innkeeper(s): Peter T. Lamandis. $47-145. MC VISA AX DS. 6 rooms with PB. Breakfast included in rates. Types of meals: full breakfast and gourmet breakfast. Beds: QD. Air conditioning, ceiling fan, TV and VCR in room. Bicycles and pet boarding on premises. Handicap access. Fishing, parks, shopping, theater and watersports nearby.

"The atmosphere was great. Your breakfast was elegant. The breakfast room made us feel we had gone back in time. All in all it was a very enjoyable stay."
Certificate may be used: Nov. 1-June 20, Sunday-Thursday.

Naples J2

Augustus Bove House

Corner Rts 302 & 114, Rr 1 Box 501
Naples, ME 04055
(207)693-6365 (800)693-6365

Circa 1830. A long front lawn nestles up against the stone foundation and veranda of this house, once known as the Hotel Naples, one of the area's summer hotels in the 1800s. The guest rooms are decorated in a Colonial style and modestly furnished with antiques. Many rooms provide a view of Long Lake. A fancy country breakfast is provided.

Innkeeper(s): David & Arlene Stetson. $49-135. MC VISA AX DS PC TC. 11 rooms, 7 with PB. 1 suite. Breakfast and afternoon tea included in rates. Types of meals: full breakfast and early coffee/tea. Beds: KQT. Air conditioning and TV in room. VCR, fax and spa on premises. Antiques, fishing, parks, shopping, downhill skiing, cross-country skiing, theater and watersports nearby.

Location: Corner of routes 302 & 114.

Publicity: *Brighton Times.*

"Beautiful place, rooms, and people."

Certificate may be used: Void July and August, holidays and first week of October.

Inn at Long Lake
Lake House Rd, PO Box 806
Naples, ME 04055
(207)693-6226 (800)437-0328

Circa 1906. Reopened in 1988, the inn housed the overflow guests from the Lake House resort about 90 years ago. Guests traveled to the resort via the Oxford-Cumberland Canal, and each room is named for a historic canal boat. The cozy rooms offer fluffy comforters and a warm, country decor in a romantic atmosphere. Warm up in front of a

crackling fire in the great room, or enjoy a cool Long Lake breeze on the veranda while watching horses in nearby pastures. Murder-mystery weekends offer a spooky alternative to your getaway plans.

Innkeeper(s): Maynard & Irene Hincks. $65-145. MC VISA DS PC TC. 16 rooms with PB. 2 suites. 1 conference room. Breakfast included in rates. Types of meals: continental-plus breakfast and early coffee/tea. Beds: QDT. Air conditioning in room. Library on premises. Antiques, fishing, parks, shopping, downhill skiing, cross-country skiing and watersports nearby.

Location: Sebago Lakes Region.

Publicity: *Bridgton News, Portland Press Herald.*

"Convenient location, tastefully done and the prettiest inn I've ever stayed in."

Certificate may be used: Oct. 16-May 14, Sunday-Thursday

Ogunquit K2

Scotch Hill Inn
PO Box 87, 175 Main St, US Rt 1
Ogunquit, ME 03907
(207)646-2890 Fax:(207)646-4324

Circa 1898. This Victorian is ideally situated just five blocks from the beach. Everything about the interior is bright and cheery. The parlor features yellow and white striped wallcoverings and a mix of traditional and Victorian furnishings. Head up the staircase, which is covered in rich hunter green carpeting and highlighted by yellow walls and a flowered border, to reach the guest rooms. Each is decorated differently. One might encounter a four-poster bed topped with a white comforter. In the mornings, a three-course breakfast begins with homemade scones. If weather permits, the meal is served on the inn's veranda. There are also two carriage houses on the premises, which are rented by the week. The homes are spacious with three to four bedrooms, living rooms and kitchens. The inn is open from April until mid-October.

Innkeeper(s): Donna & Dick Brown. $60-110. MC VISA TC. 8 rooms, 5 with PB, 1 with FP. 2 cottages. Breakfast and afternoon tea included in rates. Types of meals: full breakfast, gourmet breakfast and early coffee/tea. Beds: KQTD. Air conditioning in room. Cable TV, VCR and fax on premises. Amusement parks, antiques, fishing, parks, shopping, golf, theater and watersports nearby.

"What a beautiful stay for our first-year anniversary, thanks so much!"

Certificate may be used: April 1-Oct. 15, Sunday through Thursday.

Chestnut Tree Inn
PO Box 2201
Ogunquit, ME 03907-2201
(207)646-4529 (800)362-0757

Circa 1870. Gable roofs peak out from the top of this Victorian inn, which has greeted guests for more than a century. A smattering of antiques and Victorian decor creates a 19th-century atmosphere. Guests can relax on the porch or head out for a stroll on Marginal Way, a mile-long path set along Maine's scenic coastline. The beach, shops, Ogunquit Playhouse and a variety of restaurants are just a few minutes away.

Innkeeper(s): Cynthia Diana & Ronald St. Laurent. $35-125. MC VISA AX TC. 22 rooms, 15 with PB. 1 suite. Type of meal: continental-plus breakfast. Beds: QDT. Air conditioning and TV in room. Amusement parks, antiques, fishing, parks, shopping, downhill skiing, cross-country skiing, sporting events, theater and watersports nearby.

"Your inn was absolutely beautiful and peaceful. Your kindness will not be forgotten."

Certificate may be used: Monday-Thursday, May 15-June 15 and Sept. 15-Oct. 15.

Hartwell House

118 Shore Rd, PO Box 393
Ogunquit, ME 03907
(207)646-7210 (800)235-8883

Circa 1921. Hartwell House offers suites and guest rooms furnished with distinctive early American and English antiques. Many rooms are available with French doors opening to private balconies overlooking sculpted flower gardens. Breakfast may be enjoyed in the dining room or on the patio. Afternoon tea is served daily.

Innkeeper(s): William & Anne Mozingo. $80-175. MC VISA AX DS TC. 16 rooms with PB. 3 suites. 4 conference rooms. Breakfast and afternoon tea included in rates. Types of meals: gourmet breakfast and early coffee/tea. Catering service available. Beds: QT. Air conditioning and ceiling fan in room. Cable TV and fax on premises. Amusement parks, antiques, fishing, parks, shopping, cross-country skiing, sporting events, theater and watersports nearby.

Publicity: *Innsider.*

"This engaging country inn will be reserved for my special clients."

Certificate may be used: Nov. 6-April 26.

The Westhighland Inn

14 Shore Rd
Ogunquit, ME 03907
(207)646-2181

Circa 1895. This Dutch Colonial home features an enclosed front porch, decorated with wicker furnishings, flowers and plants. The interior is Victorian in decor with some elegant traditional touches. In the guest rooms, coordinating prints decorate the windows and the beds, and each room is different from the next. The innkeepers serve a plentiful buffet breakfast, as well as homemade treats in the afternoon. The inn is open from mid-May until mid-October. In addition to the inn rooms, the innkeepers offer three efficiency units.

Innkeeper(s): Steve & Linda Williams. $60-115. MC VISA PC TC. 12 rooms, 10 with PB. Breakfast included in rates. Types of meals: full breakfast and early coffee/tea. Beds: KQDT. Air conditioning and TV in room. VCR and pet boarding on premises. Amusement parks, antiques, fishing, parks, shopping, golf, theater and watersports nearby.

Certificate may be used: April 1-June 14, Sunday-Thursday; Sept. 10-Oct. 15, Sunday-Thursday.

Yardarm Village Inn

142 Shore Rd, PO Box 773
Ogunquit, ME 03907
(207)646-7006 (888)YARD-ARM Fax:(207)646-9034
E-mail: lcdrury@worldnet.att.net

Circa 1874. This three-story white inn is decorated with black shutters and features a wide covered front veranda lined with wicker rocking chairs for those who wish to enjoy the ocean view. Guest rooms are done in a Colonial-country style with comfortable furnishings. For an additional charge, the innkeepers will provide a light, continental breakfast. The innkeepers also offer two cottages. The inn houses a wine and cheese shop.

Innkeeper(s): L.C. & P.C. Drury. $59-99. PC TC. 8 rooms with PB. 3 suites. 2 cottages. Beds: KQDT. Air conditioning and TV in room. Fax and copier on premises. Amusement parks, fishing, parks, shopping, golf, theater and watersports nearby.

Certificate may be used: April 20-June 15, September after Labor Day to Columbus Day in October.

Old Orchard Beach   K2

Atlantic Birches Inn

20 Portland Ave Rt 98
Old Orchard Beach, ME 04064-2212
(207)934-5295 (888)934-5295
E-mail: dancyn@aol.com

Circa 1903. The front porch of this Shingle-style Victorian is shaded by white birch trees. Badminton and croquet are set up on the lawn. The house is a place for relaxation and enjoyment, an uncluttered, simple haven filled with comfortable furnishings. The guest rooms are decorated with a few antiques and pastel wallcoverings. Maine's coast offers an endless amount of activities, from boating to whale watching. It is a five-minute walk to the beach and the pier.

Innkeeper(s): Dan & Cyndi Bolduc. $49-89. EP. MC VISA AX DS TC. 8 rooms with PB. Breakfast included in rates. Type of meal: continental-plus breakfast. Beds: KQDT. Air conditioning and ceiling fan in room. Cable TV, VCR, copier, swimming and library on premises. Amusement parks, antiques, fishing, parks, shopping, sporting events and watersports nearby.

"Your home and family are just delightful! What a treat to stay in such a warm & loving home."

Certificate may be used: Nov. 1-May 1.

Rangeley   G2

Northwoods

PO Box 79
Rangeley, ME 04970-0079
(207)864-2440 (800)295-4968

Circa 1912. This immaculate Colonial Revival home, which has all the original woodwork intact, has a magnificent view of Rangeley Lake. Inside, guests can find a doll house museum filled with porcelain dolls and antiques. Still largely unspoiled, the sur-

rounding mountain and lake region offers a variety of activities, and moose can be seen grazing and walking through the area. The inn's formal and prominent character is part of the unique residential architecture of the town. Although centrally located in Rangeley Village, Northwoods has a peaceful and lofty quality.
Innkeeper(s): Janice Thorp. $70-90. MC VISA PC TC. 4 rooms, 3 with PB. Breakfast included in rates. Type of meal: full breakfast. Beds: QDT. Cable TV and VCR on premises. Antiques, fishing, downhill skiing, cross-country skiing, theater and watersports nearby.
Certificate may be used: Sunday-Thursday, 12 months.

Saco   K2

Crown 'n' Anchor Inn
121 North St, PO Box 228
Saco, ME 04072-0228
(207)282-3829 (800)561-8865 Fax:(207)282-7495

Circa 1827. This Greek Revival house, listed in the National Register, features both Victorian baroque and colonial antiques. A collection of British coronation memorabilia displayed throughout the inn includes 200 items.
Guests gather in the Victorian parlor or the formal library. The innkeepers, a college librarian and  an academic bookseller, lined the shelves with several thousand volumes, including extensive Civil War and British royal family collections and travel, theater and nautical books. Royal Dalton china, crystal and fresh flowers create a festive breakfast setting.
Innkeeper(s): John Barclay & Martha Forester. $60-95. MC VISA AX PC TC. 5 rooms with PB, 2 with FP. Breakfast included in rates. Meals: full breakfast, gourmet breakfast, early coffee/tea. Afternoon tea available. Beds: KQDT. TV in room. VCR, library on premises. Amusement parks, fishing, parks, skiing, sporting events, theater, watersports nearby.
Publicity: *Lincoln County News, Yankee, Saco, Biddeford, Old Orchard Beach Courier, Country, Portland Press Herald.*
Certificate may be used: Year-round, Sunday through Thursday with the exception of July and August.

Searsport   H5

Brass Lantern Inn
PO Box 407, 81 W Main St
Searsport, ME 04974-3501
(207)548-0150 (800)691-0150
E-mail: brasslan@brasslan.agate.net

Circa 1850. This Victorian inn is nestled at the edge of the woods on a rise overlooking Penobscot Bay. Showcased throughout the inn are many collectibles, antiques and family heirlooms, as well as artifacts from innkeeper Maggie Zieg's home in England. Enjoy breakfast by candlelight in the din-

ing room with its ornate tin ceiling, where you'll feast on Maine blueberry pancakes and other sumptuous treats. Centrally located between Camden and Bar Harbor, Searsport is known as the antique capital of Maine. There are many local attractions, including the Penobscot Marine Museum, fine shops and restaurants, as well as a public boat facility.
Innkeeper(s): Maggie & Dick Zieg. $65-90. MC VISA PC TC. 4 rooms with PB. Breakfast included in rates. Types of meals: full breakfast and early coffee/tea. Beds: DT. Cable TV and library on premises. Antiques, fishing, parks, shopping, cross-country skiing and theater nearby.
Publicity: *Country Living, Republication Journal, Travel Today, Down East.*
Certificate may be used: Monday-Thursday, Sept. to June, no holidays.

Thurston House B&B
PO Box 686, 8 Elm St
Searsport, ME 04974-3368
(207)548-2213 (800)240-2213
E-mail: thurston@acadia.net

Circa 1831. The innkeepers of this Colonial home proudly serve their "Forget About Lunch" breakfast, which consists of three courses, fresh prepared fruit, baked hot breads and then a sumptuous entree course. Special diets are happily accommodated as well. Stephen Thurston was the pastor of the first Congregational Church in Searsport for the heart of the 19th century. He was one of the town's most prominent citizens as well. In 1853, the 242-ton brig named after Thurston was launched.
Innkeeper(s): Carl Eppig. $45-65. MC VISA AX. 4 rooms, 2 with PB, 2 with FP. 1 suite. Breakfast included in rates. Types of meals: full breakfast and early coffee/tea. Afternoon tea available. Beds: DT. Antiques, fishing, shopping, sporting events, theater, watersports nearby.
Publicity: *Yankee, The Evening Times-Globe, The Clarion-Ledger*
Certificate may be used: November through May.

Searsport (Waldo County)

Watchtide
190 W Main St
Searsport (Waldo County), ME 04974
(207)548-6575 (800)698-6575
E-mail: watchtyd@agate.net

Circa 1795. Built for a sea captain, this New England Cape-style inn with its nearly four acres of lawns and gardens, has a spectacular view of Penobscot Bay. Breakfast is served on the wicker furnished porch, which overlooks the inn's bird sanctuary and the bay. An antique shop, with a large collection of angels made by the resident artist, is located in the adjacent barn. Guests can receive a discount at this shop.
Innkeeper(s): Nancy-Linn Nellis & Jack Elliott. $55-90. MC VISA DS PC TC. 4 rooms, 2 with PB. Breakfast and afternoon tea included in rates. Meals: gourmet breakfast and early coffee/tea. Beds: DT. Turndown service in room. TV and library on premises. Antiques, fishing, parks, shopping, skiing, sporting events, theater, watersports nearby.
Publicity: *Republican Journal, Daily Item, Courier Weekend, Bangor Daily News, Pilot Tribune, Clarion-Ledger, Patriot News, Herald-Times.*
Certificate may be used: Oct. 15-May 15, Sunday through Thursday.

South Thomaston I5

Weskeag at The Water
PO Box 213
South Thomaston, ME 04858-0213
(207)596-6676 (800)596-5576

Circa 1830. The backyard of this three-story house stretches to the edge of Weskeag River and Ballyhac Cove. Fifty yards from the house, there's reversing white-water rapids, created by the 10-foot tide that narrows into the estuary. Guests often sit by the water's edge to watch the birds and the lobster fishermen. Sea kayakers can launch at the inn and explore the nearby coves and then paddle on to the ocean. Innkeeper(s): Lynne Smith. $50-85. 9 rooms, 4 with PB. Breakfast included in rates. Meal: full breakfast. Beds: QD. Ceiling fan in room. TV, VCR on premises. Antiques, fishing, shopping, skiing , theater nearby.
Location: Overlooking the reversing white-water rapids that connect the salty Weskeag River to the bay.
Certificate may be used: Anytime Nov. 1-June 15 and Sunday through Thursday Sept. 15-Oct. 31.

Spruce Head J5

Craignair Inn
533 Clark Island Rd
Spruce Head, ME 04859
(207)594-7644 (800)320-9997 Fax:(207)596-7124

Circa 1930. Craignair originally was built to house stonecutters working in nearby granite quarries. Overlooking the docks of the Clark Island Quarry, where granite schooners once were loaded, this roomy, three-story inn is tastefully decorated with local antiques. Innkeeper(s): Theresa E. Smith. $74-102. MC VISA

AX PC TC. 24 rooms, 8 with PB. Breakfast included in rates. Types of meals: full breakfast and early coffee/tea. Banquet service, catering service and catered breakfast available. Restaurant on premises. Beds: KDT. Ceiling fan in room. Fax, copier and swimming on premises. Antiques, fishing, parks, shopping, skiing, theater, watersports nearby.
Location: Clark Island ocean view.
Publicity: *Boston Globe, Free Press, Tribune.*
Certificate may be used: Labor Day -June 30, excluding holiday weekends.

Stockton Springs H5

Whistlestop B&B
RR 1 Box 639
Stockton Springs, ME 04981-9801
(207)567-3727

Circa 1957. This traditional Cape Cod-style home, located on the edge of the village of Stockton Springs, overlooks quiet Stockton Harbor. Guests can relax on the patio or in the living room with grand piano, classical music and perhaps a fire in the hearth on cool evenings. Stockton Springs is located on Penobscot Bay, midway between Camden and Mount Desert Island. Guests taking a stroll down to one of the rocky beaches can find an abundance of wildlife and flowers along the shore. Innkeeper(s): Katherine Christie Wilson. $50-70. MC VISA PC TC. 2 rooms. Breakfast included in rates. Meals: full breakfast and early coffee/tea. Beds: KDT. TV, VCR and copier on premises. Antiques, fishing, parks, shopping, cross-country skiing, theater, watersports nearby.
Location: On Stockton Harbor (Penobscot Bay).
Certificate may be used: Anytime, except July, August and holiday weekends.

Waldoboro I4

Broad Bay Inn & Gallery
PO Box 607
Waldoboro, ME 04572-0607
(207)832-6668 (800)736-6769

Circa 1830. This Colonial inn lies in the heart of an unspoiled coastal village. You'll find Victorian furnishings throughout and some guest rooms have canopy beds. An established art gallery displays works by renowned artists, as well as limited-edition prints. Television, games and an art library are available in the common room. It's a short walk to restaurants, tennis, churches and the historic Waldo Theatre. Innkeeper(s): Libby Hopkins. $45-75. MC VISA. 5 rooms. Breakfast included in rates. Types of meals: full breakfast and early coffee/tea. Beds: DT. Cable TV, VCR and copier on premises. Antiques, fishing, parks, shopping, downhill skiing, cross-country skiing, theater and watersports nearby.
Publicity: *Boston Globe, Ford Times, Courier Gazette, Princeton Packet, Better Homes & Gardens Cookbook.*
Certificate may be used: Year-round, Sunday-Thursday.

Walpole J4

Brannon-Bunker Inn
349 S St Rt 129
Walpole, ME 04573
(207)563-5941 (800)563-9225

Circa 1820. This Cape-style house has been a home to many generations of Maine residents, one of whom was captain of a ship that sailed to the Arctic. During the '20s, the barn served as a dance hall. Later, it was converted into comfortable guest rooms. Victorian and American antiques are featured, and there are collections of military and political memorabilia. Innkeeper(s): Joe & Jeanne Hovance. $55-70. MC VISA AX PC TC. 8 rooms, 5 with PB. 1 suite. Breakfast included in rates. Type of meal: continental-plus breakfast. Beds: QDT. Cable TV, VCR, library and child care on premises. Handicap access. Antiques, fishing, parks, shopping, cross-country skiing, golf, theater and watersports nearby.

Publicity: *Times-Beacon Newspaper.*

"Wonderful beds, your gracious hospitality and the very best muffins anywhere made our stay a memorable one."

Certificate may be used: September through May, Sunday through Thursday, except holiday weekends.

Waterford   I2

Kedarburn Inn
Rt 35 Box 61
Waterford, ME 04088
(207)583-6182 Fax:(207)583-6424

Circa 1858. The innkeepers of this Victorian establishment invite guests to try a taste of olde English hospitality and cuisine at their inn, nestled in the foothills of the White Mountains in Western Maine. Located in a historic village, the inn sits beside the flowing Kedar Brook, which runs to the shores of Lake Keoka. Each of the spacious rooms is decorated with handmade quilts and dried flowers.
Explore the inn's shop and you'll discover a variety of quilts and crafts, all made by innkeeper Margaret Gibson. Ask about special quilting weekends. With prior reservation, the innkeepers will prepare an English afternoon tea.

Innkeeper(s): Margaret & Derek Gibson. $71-125. MC VISA AX DS PC TC. 7 rooms, 3 with PB. 1 suite. 1 conference room. Breakfast included in rates. Types of meals: full breakfast and early coffee/tea. Afternoon tea, dinner, evening snack, banquet service, catering service, catered breakfast and room service available. Restaurant on premises. Beds: KQDT. Air conditioning in room. TV, VCR, fax, pet boarding on premises. Antiques, fishing, shopping, skiing, theater, watersports nearby.

Location: In the White Mountains.

Publicity: *Maine Times.*

Certificate may be used: Jan. 1-Dec. 31.

West Boothbay Harbor J4

Lawnmeer Inn
PO Box 505
West Boothbay Harbor, ME 04575-0505
(207)633-2544 (800)633-7645 Fax:(207)633-2544

Circa 1899. This pleasant inn sits by the shoreline, providing a picturesque oceanfront setting. Located on a small, wooded island, it is accessed by a lift bridge. Family-oriented rooms are clean and homey, and there is a private honeymoon cottage in the Smoke House. The dining room is waterside and serves continental cuisine with an emphasis on seafood. Boothbay Harbor is two miles away.

Innkeeper(s): Lee & Jim Metzger. $50-170. MC VISA. 32 rooms with PB. 1 suite. 1 cottage. Types of meals: full breakfast and early coffee/tea. Dinner and banquet service available. Restaurant on premises. Beds: KQD. Computer on premises. Antiques, fishing, shopping, theater and watersports nearby.

Publicity: *Los Angeles Times, Getaways for Gourmets.*

"Your hospitality was warm and gracious and the food delectable."

Certificate may be used: Sunday through Thursday, May 19 to Columbus Day, when space available.

West Gouldsboro

Sunset House
Rt 186 HCR 60, Box 62
West Gouldsboro, ME 04607
(207)963-7156 (800)233-7156

Circa 1898. This coastal country farm inn is situated near Acadia National Park. Naturalists can observe rare birds and other wildlife in an unspoiled setting. Seven spacious bedrooms are spread over three floors. Four of the bedrooms have ocean views; a fifth overlooks a freshwater pond behind the house. During winter, guests can ice skate on the pond, while in summer it is used for swimming. The innkeepers have a resident cat and poodle, and  they also raise goats. Guests enjoy a full country breakfast cooked by Carl, who has been an executive chef for more than 20 years.

Innkeeper(s): Kathy & Carl Johnson. $69-79. MC VISA AX DC CB DS PC TC. 7 rooms, 3 with PB. Breakfast included in rates. Types of meals: full breakfast and early coffee/tea. Beds: KDT. VCR on premises. Antiques, fishing, parks, shopping and cross-country skiing nearby.

Location: Only 6.5 miles from the Schoodic Peninsula, which is the quiet side of Acadia National Park.

Certificate may be used: Excluding August, Jan. 1-Dec. 31.

Winterport   H5

Colonial Winterport Inn
114 Main St, PO Box 525
Winterport, ME 04496-0525
(207)223-5307
E-mail: fleetwood@innocent.com

Circa 1833. In the 1800s, visitors to Maine knew this Federal-style inn as the Frankfort Commercial House. Innkeepers Judie and Duncan Macnab are full of stories about the history of their pre-Civil War treasure, which offers a view of the Penobscot River.

The Macnabs have kept the decor simple with 19th-century antiques, and several rooms include fireplaces. Duncan, who handles the cooking, holds two degrees from the Cordon Bleu. He plans a different breakfast each day, accompanied by fresh fruits, breads and juices. Duncan also creates the five-course, gourmet dinners at the inn's restaurant.

Innkeeper(s): Duncan & Judie Macnab. $50-85. MC VISA AX DS TC. 6 rooms with PB, 3 with FP. 1 conference room. Breakfast included in rates. Types of meals: full breakfast and early coffee/tea. Dinner, picnic lunch, gourmet lunch, banquet service and catering service available. Restaurant on premises. Antiques, parks, shopping and theater nearby.

Certificate may be used: All year

York
L2

Dockside Guest Quarters
PO Box 205
York, ME 03909-0205
(207)363-2868 Fax:(207)363-1977
E-mail: info@docksidega.com

Circa 1900. This small resort provides a panoramic view of the Atlantic Ocean and harbor activities. Guest rooms are located in the classic, large New England home, which is the Maine House, and modern multi-unit cottages. Most rooms have private bal-conies or porches with unobstructed views of the water. Some suites have fireplaces. The resort is available for weddings. The on-premise restaurant is bi-level with floor to ceiling windows, affording each table a harbor view. Child care services are available.

Innkeeper(s): Lusty Family. $73-149. MC VISA DS PC. 21 rooms, 2 with FP. 6 suites. 1 conference room. Types of meals: continental-plus breakfast and early coffee/tea. Afternoon tea and lunch available. Restaurant on premises. Beds: KQDT. TV in room. Fax, bicycles, library and child care on premises. Amusement parks, antiques, fishing, parks, shopping, cross-country skiing, theater and watersports nearby.

Location: York Harbor, Maine Rt. 103.

Publicity: *Boston Globe.*

Certificate may be used: May 1-June 19, Oct. 9-May 1, excluding weekends and holidays.

York Beach
L2

Homestead Inn B&B
8 S Main St (Rt 1A), PO Box 15
York Beach, ME 03910
(207)363-8952

Circa 1905. This turn-of-the-century boarding house is next to Short Sands Beach. The original hard pine has been retained throughout. Bedrooms have a panoramic view of the ocean and hills. The house is kept cozy and warm by the heat of a woodstove and fireplace. Guests enjoy the sound of the surf and seagulls. Continental breakfast is offered on the sun deck or in the family dining room.

Innkeeper(s): Daniel Duffy. $49-69. 4 rooms. Breakfast included in rates. Type of meal: continental-plus breakfast. Afternoon tea and evening snack available. Beds: TD. Ceiling fan in room. Bicycles on premises. Amusement parks, antiques, fishing, shopping, sporting events and theater nearby.

Certificate may be used: April-June; September and October, Sunday-Thursday (not applicable July-August).

York Harbor
L2

York Harbor Inn
PO Box 573, Rt 1A
York Harbor, ME 03911-0573
(207)363-5119 (800)343-3869 Fax:(207)363-3545
E-mail: garyinkeep@aol.com

Circa 1800. The core building of the York Harbor Inn is a small log cabin constructed on the Isles of Shoals. Moved and reassembled at this dramatic location overlooking the entrance to York Harbor, the cabin is now a gathering room with a handsome stone fireplace. There is an English-style pub in the cellar, a large ballroom and five meeting rooms. The dining room and some guest rooms overlook the ocean. Several guest rooms have ocean view decks, working fireplaces and Jacuzzi spas. One three-room suite is available.

Innkeeper(s): Joseph & Garry Dominguez. $89-195. MAP. MC VISA AX DC CB PC TC. 33 rooms with PB, 4 with FP. 1 suite. 4 conference rooms. Breakfast included in rates. Types of meals: continental breakfast, continental-plus breakfast and early coffee/tea. Dinner, lunch, banquet service, catering service and room service available. Restaurant on premises. Beds: KQD. Air conditioning and TV in room. VCR, fax, copier, spa, swimming and child care on premises. Amusement parks, antiques, fishing, parks, shopping, cross-country skiing, theater and watersports nearby.

Location: York Harbor's historic district.

Publicity: *New York Times, Down East, Food & Wine.*

"It's hard to decide where to stay when you're paging through a book of country inns. This time we chose well."

Certificate may be used: Year-round, except Friday and Saturday in July and August, based on availability.

Maryland

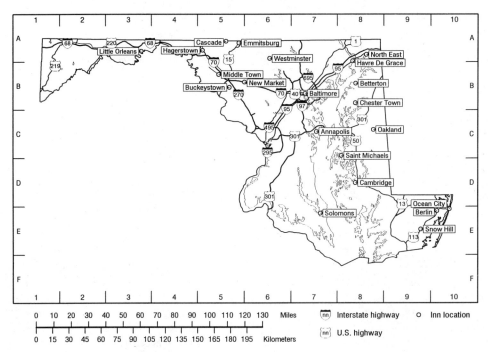

	1	2	3	4	5	6	7	8	9	10

Map legend:
- (nn) Interstate highway
- {nn} U.S. highway
- ○ Inn location

Miles: 0 10 20 30 40 50 60 70 80 90 100 110 120 130
Kilometers: 0 15 30 45 60 75 90 105 120 135 150 165 180 195

Annapolis   C7

Chesapeake Bay Lighthouse B&B
1423 Sharps Point Rd
Annapolis, MD 21401-6139
(410)757-0248

Circa 1923. Each of the guest rooms in this cottage-style working lighthouse boasts water views of scenic Chesapeake Bay. The innkeepers built their unique B&B from designs found in the National Archives. Grab a pair of binoculars and enjoy the sites of the Bay Bridge, Thomas Point Lighthouse or Annapolis harbor entrance and a 300-foot pier. The lighthouse is only six miles from Annapolis, which is full of historic attractions, shops and restaurants.
Innkeeper(s): Janice & Bill Costello. $95-149. MC VISA AX. 3 rooms. Breakfast included in rates. Type of meal: continental-plus breakfast. Air conditioning in room.
Certificate may be used: Jan. 1-March 31, Sunday through Thursday, holidays excluded.

Baltimore   B7

Betsy's B&B
1428 Park Ave
Baltimore, MD 21217-4230
(410)383-1274 (800)899-7533 Fax:(410)728-8957
E-mail: amandars@aol.com

Circa 1870. This four-story townhouse features a hallway floor laid with alternating strips of oak and walnut, ceiling medallions, large windows and marble mantels. Walls are decked with family heirlooms and other collectibles. Breakfast is served in the formal dining room, with a unique carved marble mantel. Each of the comfortably decorated guest rooms is spacious, with a private bath.
Innkeeper(s): Betsy Grater. $85-150. MC VISA AX DS PC TC. 3 rooms with PB. Breakfast included in rates. Type of meal: full breakfast. Beds: KQ. Air conditioning in room. Cable TV, VCR, fax, copier and computer on premises. Antiques, parks, shopping, sporting events, theater nearby.

172

Location: Inner Harbor, about 1.5 miles north.

Publicity: *Peabody Reflector, Nation's Business, Times Herald, Baltimore Sun, Working Woman, WJZ-TV.*

"What hotel room could ever compare to a large room in a 115-year-old house with 12-foot ceilings and a marble fireplace with hosts that could become dear longtime friends?"

Certificate may be used: Sunday through Thursday, except holiday weekends with Monday holiday.

Berlin
E10

Merry Sherwood Plantation
8909 Worcester Hwy
Berlin, MD 21811-3016
(410)641-0358 (800)660-0358 Fax:(410)641-3605

Circa 1859. This magnificent pre-Civil War mansion is a tribute to Southern plantation architecture. The inn features antique period furniture, handwoven, Victorian era rugs and a square grand piano. The ballroom, now a parlor for guests, boasts twin fireplaces and pier mirrors. (Ask to see the hidden cupboards behind the fireside bookcases in the

library.) Nineteen acres of grounds are beautifully landscaped and feature azaleas, boxwoods and 125 varieties of trees.

Innkeeper(s): Kirk Burbage. $95-175. MC VISA. 8 rooms, 6 with PB, 4 with FP. 1 suite. Breakfast included in rates. Type of meal: full breakfast. Afternoon tea available. Beds: QD. Air conditioning in room. Cable TV on premises. Amusement parks, antiques, fishing, shopping and watersports nearby.

Publicity: *Washington Post, Baltimore Sun, Southern Living.*

"Pure elegance and privacy at its finest."

Certificate may be used: Advance reservations required. Sunday through Thursday only, year-round and available at the discretion of innkeeper at all other times, including weekends. Notify innkeeper of promotion when making reservation. Other times based on availability.

Betterton
B8

Lantern Inn
115 Ericsson Ave, PO Box 29
Betterton, MD 21610-9746
(410)348-5809 (800)499-7265

Circa 1904. Framed by a picket fence and a wide front porch, this four-story country inn is located one block from the nettle-free public beach on Chesapeake Bay. Comfortable rooms are furnished with antiques and handmade quilts. The surrounding area is well-known for its wildlife preserves. Antique shops and restaurants are nearby. Kent County offers plenty of cycling possibilities, and there are detailed maps available at the inn for trips that start at the inn and go for 10 to 90 miles. Tennis courts are two blocks away.

Innkeeper(s): Ken & Ann Washburn. $70-90. MC VISA. 13 rooms, 4 with PB. Breakfast included in rates. Type of meal: continental-plus breakfast. Beds: KDT. Antiques and fishing nearby.

Location: On the Chesapeake Bay.

Publicity: *Richland Times-Dispatch, North Carolina Outdoorsman, Washingtonian, Mid-Atlantic Country.*

"Thanks for your warm hospitality."

Certificate may be used: Sunday through Thursday, Jan. 15-Dec. 15, holidays excluded.

Buckeystown
B5

Catoctin Inn & Antiques
3613 Buckeystown Pike
Buckeystown, MD 21717
(301)874-5555 (800)730-5550
E-mail: catoctin@fred.net

Circa 1780. The inn's four acres of dogwood, magnolias, maples and sweeping lawns overlook the village and the Catoctin Mountains range. Some special features of the inn include a library with marble fireplaces and a handsome wraparound veranda. A Victorian carriage house marks the site for weddings, showers and receptions for up to 150 guests. Twelve of the guest rooms include a fireplace and a whirlpool tub. Nearby villages to visit include Harper's Ferry, Antietam and New Market. Buckeystown's Monocacy River provides canoeing and fishing.

Innkeeper(s): Terry & Sarah MacGillivray. $85-150. MC VISA AX DS PC. 16 rooms with PB, 12 with FP. 8 suites. 3 cottages. 3 conference rooms. Breakfast and afternoon tea included in rates. Type of meal: full

breakfast. Catering service available. Beds: KQ. Air conditioning, turn-down service, TV and VCR in room. Library and child care on premises. Antiques, fishing, shopping, downhill skiing, cross-country skiing, sporting events and theater nearby.

Certificate may be used: January through April, Monday - Thursday.

Cambridge
D8

Glasgow B&B Inn
1500 Hambrooks Blvd
Cambridge, MD 21613
(410)228-0575

Circa 1760. Located along the Choptank River on seven acres, this brick colonial is reached by way of a long tree-lined driveway. The house was built by Dr. William Murray whose son was a friend to Thomas Jefferson and John Quincy Adams. (According to local legend, part of the U.S. Constitution was written here.) The inn is decorated with country colonial antiques and reproductions, enhanced by high ceilings, a mahogany staircase and deep-window seats.

Innkeeper(s): Martha Rayne. $85-125. MC VISA. 7 rooms, 3 with PB, 6 with FP. Breakfast included in rates. Type of meal: full breakfast. Beds: KQ.

Publicity: *Mid-Atlantic Country, Tidewater Times.*

Certificate may be used: Monday through Thursday.

Cascade
A5

Bluebird on The Mountain
14700 Eyler Ave
Cascade, MD 21719-1938
(301)241-4161 (800)362-9526

Circa 1900. In the mountain village of Cascade, this gracious shuttered Georgian manor is situated on two acres of trees and wildflowers. Three suites have double whirlpool tubs. There is an outdoor hot tub as

well. The Rose Garden Room and Mt. Magnolia suites have fireplaces and porches overlooking the back garden. The inn is appointed with antiques, lace and white linens, and white wicker. On Sundays, a full breakfast is served.

Innkeeper(s): Eda Smith-Eley. $105-125. MC VISA AX PC. 5 rooms with PB, 3 with FP. 2 suites. Breakfast included in rates. Types of meals: continental-plus breakfast, full breakfast, gourmet breakfast and early coffee/tea. Room service available. Beds: KQT. Air conditioning, turn-down service, ceiling fan, TV and VCR in room. Spa on premises. Antiques, fishing, parks, shopping, downhill skiing, sporting events, theater and watersports nearby.

Publicity: *Warm Welcomes, Baltimore Sun, Frederick News, Washington Post.*

"A wonderful balance of luxury and at-home comfort."

Certificate may be used: January-April, Monday-Thursday nights.

Chestertown
B8

Brampton Inn
25227 Chestertown Rd
Chestertown, MD 21620-3944
(410)778-1860 Fax:(410)778-1805
E-mail: brampton@friend.ly.net

Circa 1860. Situated on 35 acres of gardens, meadows and woodland on Maryland's Eastern Shore between the Chester River and Chesapeake Bay, Brampton is a graceful three-story brick, Greek Italianate Revival house. Swiss innkeeper Danielle Hanscom selected family antiques to furnish the parlor and dining room. A massive walnut staircase winds to the upstairs where spacious rooms feature canopied beds, antiques and reproductions. A full country breakfast is served.

Innkeeper(s): Michael & Danielle Hanscom. $95-155. MAP. MC VISA AX PC TC. 10 rooms, 8 with PB, 8 with FP. 2 suites. 2 cottages. Breakfast and afternoon tea included in rates. Types of meals: full breakfast, gourmet breakfast and early coffee/tea. Beds: KQDT. Air conditioning and ceiling fan in room. Fax, copier and library on premises. Handicap access. Antiques, shopping, theater and watersports nearby.

Publicity: *Washington Post, New York Times.*

"A stately beauty that exudes peace and tranquility."

Certificate may be used: All year, Sunday-Thursday.

Great Oak Manor
10568 Cliff Rd
Chestertown, MD 21620-4115
(410)778-5943 (800)504-3098 Fax:(410)778-5943

Circa 1938. This elegant Georgian mansion anchors vast lawns at the end of a long driveway. Situated directly on the Chesapeake Bay, it is a serene and picturesque country estate. A library with fireplace, den and formal parlors are available to guests. With its grand circular stairway, bayside gazebo, and nearby beach and marina, the Manor is a remarkable setting for events such as weddings and reunions. Chestertown is eight miles away.

Innkeeper(s): Don & Dianne Cantor. $76-145. MC VISA PC TC. 11 rooms with PB, 5 with FP. 1 suite. 2 conference rooms. Breakfast included in rates. Types of meals: continental-plus breakfast and early coffee/tea. Beds: KT. Air conditioning in room. VCR, fax, copier, bicycles and library on premises. Antiques, fishing, parks, shopping, sporting events, theater and watersports nearby.

Publicity: *Country Inns, Southern Living.*

"The charming setting, professional service and personal warmth we experienced at Great Oak will long be a pleasant memory. Thanks for everything!"

Certificate may be used: Dec. 1-April 1, Sunday - Thursday night.

The Inn at Mitchell House
8796 Maryland Pkwy
Chestertown, MD 21620-4209
(410)778-6500

Circa 1743. This pristine 18th-century manor house sits as a jewel on 12 acres overlooking Stoneybrook Pond. The guest rooms and the inn's several parlors are preserved and appointed in an authentic Colonial mood, heightened by handsome polished wide-board floors. Eastern Neck Island National Wildlife Refuge, Chesapeake Farms, St. Michaels, Annapolis and nearby Chestertown are all delightful to explore. The Inn at Mitchell House is a popular setting for romantic weddings and small corporate meetings.

Innkeeper(s): Tracy & Jim Stone. $75-110. MC VISA PC. 6 rooms, 5 with PB, 3 with FP. Breakfast included in rates. Types of meals: full breakfast and early coffee/tea. Restaurant on premises. Beds: KQD. Air conditioning, turndown service in room. VCR on premises. Antiques, fishing, shopping, sporting events, theater and watersports nearby.

Publicity: *Washingtonian, New York Magazine, Glamour, Philadelphia Inquirer, Baltimore Sun, Kent County News, Ten Best Inns in the Country, New York Times. Washington Post, National Geographic Traveler.*

Certificate may be used: Sunday - Thursday, excluding holidays.

Emmitsburg   A5

The Gallery Suites
304 E Main St
Emmitsburg, MD 21727
(301)447-3292 Fax:(301)447-2632

Circa 1912. This collection of suites is so named because the two are located on the second story of a building that houses an art gallery. Innkeeper Linda Postelle is an artist and her work is featured

throughout the suites, including murals on doors and walls. Antiques fill the whimsically decorated rooms. The suites are located in a historic building and were once used as apartments, so the rooms have been completely renovated and restored. Linda delivers breakfast to your door. The Gourmet Grill, a local eatery, also is on the premises.

Innkeeper(s): Linda Postelle. $95-120. MC VISA PC TC. 2 suites. Breakfast included in rates. Types of meals: continental breakfast, continental-plus breakfast, full breakfast, gourmet breakfast and early coffee/tea. Catered breakfast available. Restaurant on premises. Beds: Q. Air conditioning, ceiling fan, TV and VCR in room. Antiques, parks, downhill skiing, sporting events and golf nearby.

Publicity: *Frederick Gazette.*

Certificate may be used: All year except holidays and alumni and parent's weekends at local college.

Hagerstown   A5

Beaver Creek House B&B
20432 Beaver Creek Rd
Hagerstown, MD 21740-1514
(301)797-4764

Circa 1905. History buffs enjoy this turn-of-the-century inn located minutes away from Antietam and Harpers Ferry National Historical Parks. The surrounding villages house antique shops and some hold weekend auctions. The inn features a courtyard with a fountain and a country garden. Innkeepers

Don and Shirley Day furnished the home with family antiques and memorabilia. Guests can sip afternoon tea or complimentary sherry in the elegant parlor or just relax on the porch and take in the view of South Mountain.

Innkeeper(s): Donald & Shirley Day. $75-95. MC VISA AX PC TC. 5 rooms with PB. 1 conference room. Breakfast included in rates. Types of meals: full breakfast and gourmet breakfast. Beds: DT. Air conditioning and ceiling fan in room. Copier on premises. Amusement parks, antiques, fishing, parks, shopping, downhill skiing, cross-country skiing, sporting events, theater and watersports nearby.

Publicity: *Baltimore Sun, Hagerstown Journal, Herald Mail, Washington Post, Frederick.*

"Thanks so much for your hospitality. You're wonderful hosts and breakfast was delicious as usual. Don't change a thing."

Certificate may be used: Year-round, Monday through Thursday.

Sunday's B&B

39 Broadway
Hagerstown, MD 21740-4019
(301)797-4331 (800)221-4828

Circa 1890. This Queen Anne Victorian is appropriately appointed with period antiques. Fresh flowers and fruit baskets are provided and guests are pampered with a full breakfast, afternoon tea, evening wine and cheese and for late evening, bedside cordials and chocolates. Antietam, Harpers Ferry and the C&O Canal are nearby.

Innkeeper(s): Robert Ferrino. $75-115. MC VISA DC. 4 rooms, 3 with PB. Breakfast included in rates. Types of meals: full breakfast and early coffee/tea. Afternoon tea, dinner, picnic lunch and catering service available. Beds: QD. Air conditioning and TV in room. Antiques, fishing, parks, shopping, downhill skiing and theater nearby.

Location: Twenty minutes from Antietam Battlefields.

"A four star inn! Every detail perfect, decor and atmosphere astounding."

Certificate may be used: All year, Sunday-Thursday

Havre De Grace A8

Spencer Silver Mansion

200 S Union Ave
Havre De Grace, MD 21078-3224
(410)939-1097 (800)780-1485

Circa 1896. This elegant granite Victorian mansion is graced with bays, gables, balconies, a turret and a gazebo veranda. The Victorian decor, with antiques and Oriental rugs, complements the house's carved-oak woodwork, fireplace mantels and parquet floors. The Concord Point Lighthouse (oldest continuously operated lighthouse in America) is only a walk away. In addition to the four rooms in the main house, a romantic carriage house suite is available, featuring an in-room fireplace, TV, whirlpool bath and kitchenette.

Innkeeper(s): Carol Nemeth. $65-125. MC VISA AX DS PC TC. 5 rooms, 3 with PB, 1 with FP. 1 cottage. Breakfast included in rates. Types of meals: full breakfast and early coffee/tea. Beds: QDT. Air conditioning, turndown service and TV in room. Antiques, fishing, parks, shopping and watersports nearby.

Location: In the heart of the historic district, 2 blocks from the waterfront.

Publicity: *Mid-Atlantic Country, Maryland.*

"A fabulous find. Beautiful house, excellent hostess. I've stayed at a lot of B&Bs, but this house is the best."

Certificate may be used: Monday through Thursday, all year.

Middletown B5

Stone Manor Country Club

5820 Carroll Boyer Rd
Middletown, MD 21769-6315
(301)473-5454 Fax:(301)371-5622

Circa 1780. If you're searching for a romantic, secluded getaway and hope to be pampered with fine cuisine and elegant surroundings, head for this impressive stone estate house. Tucked between mountain ranges on 114 acres of picturesque farmland, the home often is the site of weddings and receptions. Despite the size of this manor home, the interior is intimate and inviting, filled with a variety of styles and furnishings. Each of the rooms, named for flowers, afford tranquil views of gardens, ponds or woods. A variety of drinks, fruit and cheese are placed in the guest rooms upon arrival. The inn hosts a variety of seminars, accompanied by gourmet buffets, with items such as chilled melon and lemon balm soup or pan roasted salmon with beurre blanc. The dinner menu is filled with equally impressive fare.

Innkeeper(s): Judith Harne. $125-250. MC VISA AX TC. 5 rooms with PB, 4 with FP. 4 suites. Breakfast included in rates. Meals: continental breakfast, continental-plus breakfast, full breakfast, gourmet breakfast, early coffee/tea. Afternoon tea, dinner, evening snack, picnic lunch, lunch, gourmet lunch, banquet service and catering service available. Restaurant on premises. Beds: Q. Air conditioning, turndown service, ceiling fan in room. VCR, fax, copier, child care on premises. Handicap access. Fishing, parks, skiing, sporting events, theater, watersports nearby.

Certificate may be used: January, February, March, July, August, November; Tuesday, Wednesday & Thursday evenings.

New Market B6

National Pike Inn

PO Box 299, 9 W Main St
New Market, MD 21774-0299
(301)865-5055

Circa 1796. This red shuttered brick Federal-style home is one of the few inns remaining on the National Pike, an old route that carried travelers from Baltimore to points west. The inn's Colonial decor includes wingback chairs, Oriental rugs and four-poster beds. Azalea gardens border a private courtyard and fountain. New Market, founded in 1793, offers more than 30 antique shops and other charming points of interest, including an old-fashioned general store and fine dining, all within walking distance of the inn.

Innkeeper(s): Tom & Terry Rimel. $75-125. MC VISA PC TC. 6 rooms, 4 with PB, 3 with FP. 1 suite. 1 conference room. Breakfast included in rates. Meal: full breakfast. Beds: QD. Air conditioning in room. TV and VCR on premises. Antiques, shopping, sporting events, theater nearby.

Location: Exit 62 off interstate 70, 6 miles east of Frederick, Maryland.

Publicity: *Mid-Atlantic Country, Country.*

Certificate may be used: Monday-Thursday, two-night minimum. Excludes special events.

North East
A8

The Mill House B&B
102 Mill Ln
North East, MD 21901-3924
(410)287-3532

Circa 1710. The Mill House is a combination of two houses: one the mill owners' house and the other the former kitchen and maid's quarters. In the Maryland Register of Historic Sites, the inn is filled with antiques such as an 18th-century tall case

clock, four-poster beds and Victorian slipper chairs. Wildflowers now grow on the property's five acres in the marsh between the mill ruins and the North East River. The village features antique and craft shops and the Upper Bay Museum. Ten minutes away is a factory outlet mall.

Innkeeper(s): Lucia & Nick Demond. $65-75. MC VISA DS PC TC. 2 rooms. Breakfast included in rates. Types of meals: full breakfast and early coffee/tea. Beds: D. Air conditioning in room. Antiques, fishing, parks, shopping, golf and watersports nearby.

Publicity: *Cecil Whig, Times of North East & Elkton, Aegis, Mid-Atlantic.*

"Our room was perfect, spacious and comfortable. The breakfasts were both delicious and plentiful."

Certificate may be used: March 1-Dec. 1, Sunday-Thursday.

Oakland
C8

Harley Farm B&B and Retreat Center
16766 Garrett Hwy
Oakland, MD 21550-4036
(301)387-9050 (888)231-FARM Fax:(301)387-9050
E-mail: kgillespie@harleyfarmbb.com

Circa 1990. From the drive, this B&B appears as an unassuming, albeit charming, farmhouse surrounded by acres of rolling hills. Inside, the innkeepers have added many elegant touches, transforming the home into a gracious retreat with Chinese carpets, tapestries and European furnishings. There is a luxury suite, which includes a heart-shaped Jacuzzi, king-size bed, kitchenette and a sitting room with a fireplace. The innkeepers host a variety of classes and workshops throughout the year, with subjects ranging from yoga, art, leadership and management. Guests can sign up for seasonal programs as well, one workshop teaches guests how to create their own Williamsburg Christmas, while another instructs how to prepare fresh apple and pumpkin butter. Croquet, badminton and volleyball courts are set up on the grounds, and summertime brings hay rides and barn dances.

Innkeeper(s): Wayne & Kam Gillespie. $70-100. MC VISA AX DS PC TC. 7 rooms with PB. 1 suite. Breakfast included in rates. Type of meal: full breakfast. Beds: QD. Air conditioning and ceiling fan in room. Cable TV, VCR, spa, bicycles and library on premises. Antiques, fishing, parks, shopping, skiing and watersports nearby.

Certificate may be used: Sunday-Thursday, not including holidays, all year.

Ocean City
E10

Atlantic House B&B
501 N Baltimore Ave
Ocean City, MD 21842-3926
(410)289-2333
E-mail: atlanticho@aol.com

Circa 1927. From the front porch of this bed & breakfast, guests can partake in ocean views. The rooms are decorated in antique oak and wicker complementing a relaxing beach stay. The morning breakfast buffet includes such items as freshly baked breads, fruit, egg casseroles, cereals and yogurt. In the afternoons, light refreshments also are served. The inn, nestled in the original Ocean City, is a short walk to the beach, boardwalk and shopping.

Innkeeper(s): Paul & Debi Cook. $55-145. MC VISA AX DS TC. 14 rooms, 8 with PB. 1 suite. Breakfast, afternoon tea and evening snack included in rates. Types of meals: full breakfast and early coffee/tea. Beds: QD. Air conditioning, ceiling fan and TV in room. Amusement parks, antiques, fishing, parks, shopping, sporting events, theater and watersports nearby.

"We were anxious to see if we made the right choice, we definitely did."

Certificate may be used: Labor Day to Memorial Day, Sunday-Thursday.

Saint Michaels
C8

Kemp House Inn
412 Talbot St, PO Box 638
Saint Michaels, MD 21663
(410)745-2243

Circa 1807. This two-story Georgian house was built by Colonel Joseph Kemp, a shipwright and one of the town forefathers. The inn is appointed in period furnishings accentuated by candlelight. Guest rooms include patchwork quilts, a collection of four-poster rope beds and old-fashioned nightshirts. There are several working fireplaces. Robert E. Lee is said to have been a guest.

Innkeeper(s): Diane M. Cooper. $70-110. MC VISA DS. 8 rooms, 6 with PB. 4 with FP. Breakfast included in rates. Types of meals: continental breakfast and early coffee/tea. Catered breakfast available. Beds: QDT. Air conditioning in room. Antiques, fishing, shopping and watersports nearby.

Location: Historic town on the eastern shore of the Chesapeake.

Publicity: *Gourmet, Philadelphia.*

"It was wonderful. We've stayed in many B&Bs, and this was one of the nicest!"

Certificate may be used: Sunday through Thursday nights, excluding holidays. Year-round.

Parsonage Inn

210 N Talbot St
Saint Michaels, MD 21663-2102
(410)745-5519 (800)394-5519

Circa 1883. A striking Victorian steeple rises next to the wide bay of this brick residence, once the home of Henry Clay Dodson, state senator, pharmacist and brickyard owner. The house features brick detail in a variety of patterns and inlays, perhaps a design statement for brick customers. Porches are decorated with filigree and spindled columns. Laura Ashley linens, late Victorian furnishings, fireplaces and decks add to the creature comforts. Four bikes await guests who wish to ride to Tilghman Island or to the ferry that goes to Oxford. Gourmet breakfast is served in the dining room.

Innkeeper(s): Will Workman. $80-160. MC VISA PC TC. 8 rooms with PB, 3 with FP. Breakfast included in rates. Type of meal: gourmet breakfast. Beds: KQD. Air conditioning and ceiling fan in room. Cable TV and bicycles on premises. Handicap access. Antiques, fishing, shopping and watersports nearby.

Location: In the historic district.

Publicity: *Wilmington, Delaware News Journal, Philadelphia Inquirer.*

"Striking, extensively renovated."

Certificate may be used: Sunday through Thursday, November until June.

The Inn at Perry Cabin

308 Watkins Ln
Saint Michaels, MD 21663-2114
(410)745-2200 (800)722-2949 Fax:(410)745-3348
E-mail: perrycbn@friend.ly.net

Circa 1812. Built around an early 19th-century farmhouse, this pristine waterside escape is one of the Laura Ashley Company's signature inns. A private boat dock, indoor swimming pool and excellent food service are all among the amenties that may be expected. Of course, fabulous fabrics and wall coverings are featured throughout.

Innkeeper(s): Stephen Creese. $150-575. MC VISA AX DC CB PC TC. 41 rooms with PB. 1 conference room. Breakfast and afternoon tea included in rates. Types of meals: continental breakfast, continental-plus breakfast, full breakfast, gourmet breakfast and early coffee/tea. Dinner, evening snack, picnic lunch, lunch, gourmet lunch, banquet service, catering service, catered breakfast and room service available. Restaurant on premises. Beds: KQDT. Air conditioning, turndown ser-

vice, TV and VCR in room. Fax, copier, spa, swimming, sauna, bicycles, tennis, library and child care on premises. Handicap access. Antiques, fishing, parks, shopping, sporting events, golf, theater and watersports nearby.

"The Inn at Perry Cabin is a little piece of heaven on earth."

Certificate may be used: Jan. 1-March 31, Monday-Thursday, on full rack rates only, subject to availability.

Snow Hill   E9

Chanceford Hall Inn

209 W Federal St
Snow Hill, MD 21863-1159
(410)632-2231

Circa 1759. This pre-Revolutionary War inn is listed in the National Register and Smithsonian's "Guide to Historic America." The home maintains many original features, including woodwork, floors

CIRCA 1759

and mantels. Rooms feature romantic, canopy beds and the home boasts 10 wood-burning fireplaces and Oriental rugs throughout. Wine and hors d'oeuvres are served after guests check in, and a full breakfast is served each morning in the inn's formal dining room. Spend the day exploring the Snow Hill area, or simply relax by the lap pool. The innkeepers offer bicycles for their guests.

Innkeeper(s): Michael & Thelma C. Driscoll. $115-135. PC TC. 5 rooms with PB, 4 with FP. 1 suite. Breakfast included in rates. Types of meals: full breakfast, gourmet breakfast and early coffee/tea. Beds: Q. Air conditioning in room. Cable TV, VCR, copier, swimming and bicycles on premises. Antiques, fishing, parks, shopping, sporting events and watersports nearby.

Certificate may be used: Monday through Thursday, December through May.

River House Inn

201 E Market St
Snow Hill, MD 21863-2000
(410)632-2722 Fax:(410)632-2866

Circa 1860. This picturesque Gothic Revival house rests on the banks of the Pocomoke River and boasts its own dock. Its two acres roll down to the river over long tree-studded lawns. Lawn furniture

and a hammock add to the invitation to relax as do the inn's porches. Some guest rooms feature marble fireplaces. The 17th-century village of Snow Hill boasts old brick sidewalks and historic homes. Canoes can be rented two doors from the inn or you may wish to take a river cruise on the innkeeper's pontoon boat.

Innkeeper(s): Larry & Susanne Knudsen. $100-160. MC VISA AX DS TC. 8 rooms with PB, 6 with FP. 1 suite. 1 cottage. Breakfast and evening snack included in rates. Types of meals: full breakfast and early coffee/tea. Beds: KQT. Air conditioning and ceiling fan in room. Cable TV, VCR, fax, copier, bicycles, library and child care on premises. Handicap access. Amusement parks, antiques, fishing, shopping and watersports nearby.

Publicity: *Daily Times*

Certificate may be used: November-March, except holiday weekend, April-October, Monday-Thursday, except holiday

Snow Hill Inn
104 E Market St
Snow Hill, MD 21863-1067
(410)632-2102 Fax:(410)632-3623

Circa 1790. Gables, chimneys and blue shutters highlight the exterior of this Victorian country home. Two of the guest rooms include working fireplaces, and all are decorated with period furnishings. Plan on taking a picnic, because the innkeepers will pack up a box or basket filled with gourmet goodies from the inn's restaurant. Walking tours of Snow Hill's historic district, which features more than 100 homes and churches, are popular.

Innkeeper(s): Jim & Kathy Washington. $75. MC VISA AX TC. 3 rooms with PB, 1 with FP. Breakfast included in rates. Type of meal: continental-plus breakfast. Dinner and lunch available. Restaurant on premises. Beds: QD. Air conditioning in room. Cable TV on premises. Antiques, fishing, parks, shopping and watersports nearby.

Certificate may be used: Sunday-Friday.

Solomons Island   E7

Solomons Victorian Inn
125 Charles Street
Solomons Island, MD 20688-0759
(410)326-4811 Fax:(410)326-0133

Circa 1906. The Davis family, renowned for their shipbuilding talents, constructed this elegant Queen Anne Victorian at the turn of the century. Each of

the inn's elegant common rooms and bedchambers boasts special touches such as antiques, Oriental rugs and lacy curtains. The inn's suite includes a whirlpool tub. The home affords views of Solomons Harbor and its entrance into the picturesque Chesapeake Bay. Guests are treated to an expansive breakfast in a dining room, which overlooks the harbor.

Innkeeper(s): Richard & Helen Bauer. $90-165. MC VISA PC. 6 rooms with PB. 1 suite. Breakfast and evening snack included in rates. Types of meals: full breakfast and early coffee/tea. Beds: KQ. Air conditioning in room. Cable TV, fax and library on premises. Antiques, fishing, parks, shopping, theater and watersports nearby.

"Instead of guests at a place of lodging, you made us feel like welcome friends in your home."

Certificate may be used: Oct. 15-March 31, Sunday-Thursday.

Westminster   A6

The Winchester Country Inn
111 Stoner Ave
Westminster, MD 21157-5451
(410)876-7373 (800)887-3950 Fax:(410)848-7409

Circa 1760. William Winchester, the founder of Westminster, built this unusual English-style house. It has a steeply slanted roof similar to those found in the Tidewater area. A central fireplace opens to both the parlor and the central hall. Colonial-period furnishings prevail, with some items loaned by  the local historic society. Community volunteers, historians, craftsmen and designers helped restore the inn. A non-profit agency provides some of the housekeeping and gardening staff from its developmentally disabled program.

Innkeeper(s): Sarah Martin. $40-75. AP. MC VISA AX DS. 5 rooms, 3 with PB. Breakfast included in rates. Type of meal: full breakfast. Catering service available. Beds: KQDT. Air conditioning, TV and VCR in room. Handicap access. Antiques, fishing, parks, shopping and theater nearby.

Publicity: *Country Living, Evening Sun, The Towson Flier, The Itinerary, Cracker Barrell, Carroll County Sun.*

"We give your inn an A+. Our stay was perfect."

Certificate may be used: Jan. 1-May 31, Sunday-Saturday; Oct. 1-Dec. 31, Sunday-Saturday.

Massachusetts

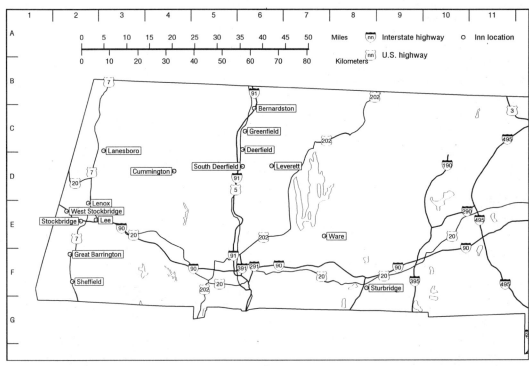

	1	2	3	4	5	6	7	8	9	10	11

A

Miles ⬡nn Interstate highway ○ Inn location

⬡nn U.S. highway Kilometers

B
7
91
202
Bernardston
3

C
Greenfield
202
Lanesboro
Deerfield
495

D
7
Cummington
South Deerfield
Leverett
190
20
91
5

E
Lenox
West Stockbridge
Stockbridge Lee
Ware
290
495
7
90
20
20
90

F
Great Barrington
90
91 291
90
20
90
20
90
495
Sheffield
391
395
202
20
Sturbridge

G

Barnstable   I17

Beechwood Inn
2839 Main St, Rt 6A
Barnstable, MA 02630-1017
(508)362-6618 (800)609-6618 Fax:(508)362-0298
E-mail: bwdinn@virtualcapecod.com

Circa 1853. Beechwood is a beautifully restored
Queen Anne Victorian offering period furnishings,
some rooms with fireplaces or ocean views. Its
warmth and elegance make it a favorite hideaway
for couples looking for a peaceful and romantic
return to the Victorian era. The inn is named for
rare old beech trees that shade the veranda.
Innkeeper(s): Debbie & Ken Traugot. $90-160. MC VISA AX PC TC. 6
rooms with PB, 2 with FP. Breakfast and afternoon tea included in rates.
Types of meals: full breakfast and early coffee/tea. Beds: KQD. Fax,

copier, bicycles and library on premises. Antiques, fishing, parks, shopping, sporting events, theater and watersports nearby.

Location: Cape Cod's historic North Shore.

Publicity: *National Trust Calendar, New England Weekends, Rhode
Island Monthly, Cape Cod Life.*

*"Your inn is pristine in every detail. We concluded that
the innkeepers, who are most hospitable, are the best
part of Beechwood."*

Certificate may be used: November through April, anytime except holiday weekends.

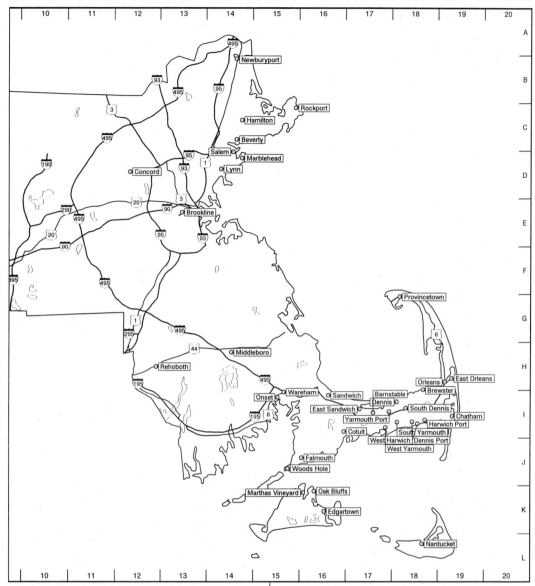

Map grid columns: 10 11 12 13 14 15 16 17 18 19 20
Map grid rows: A B C D E F G H I J K L

Map labels:
Newburyport
Rockport
Hamilton
Beverly
Salem
Marblehead
Lynn
Concord
Brookline
Provincetown
Middleboro
Rehoboth
Wareham
Onset
Sandwich
Barnstable
Dennis
East Sandwich
Yarmouth Port
Cotuit
West Harwich
South Yarmouth
West Yarmouth
Orleans
Brewster
East Orleans
South Dennis
Harwich Port
Dennis Port
Chatham
Falmouth
Woods Hole
Marthas Vineyard
Oak Bluffs
Edgartown
Nantucket

Bernardston C6

Falls River Inn

1 Brattleboro Rd
Bernardston, MA 01337-9532
(413)648-9904 Fax:(413)648-0538

Circa 1905. Guests have been welcomed to this site since the late 18th century. The first inn burned down in the 1800s, and the current Federal-style Victorian inn was built in its place. Guests will find various styles of antiques in their comfortable, country rooms, three of which include a fireplace. During the week, a continental breakfast is served, and on weekends, guests are treated to a full breakfast. The inn's restaurant is open Wednesday through Sunday, and features everything from chicken pot pie to pepper shrimp served on a bed of angel hair pasta and surrounded by an orange cream sauce. Don't forget to try the restaurant's signature "Vampire Chasers."

Innkeeper(s): Kerber Family. $66-85. MC VISA AX PC TC. 7 rooms with PB, 3 with FP. 1 conference room. Breakfast included in rates. Types of meals: gourmet breakfast and early coffee/tea. Dinner, lunch, banquet service, catering service and room service available. Restaurant on premises. Beds: KQDT. Ceiling fan in room. Cable TV, fax and copier on premises. Antiques, fishing, parks, shopping, downhill skiing, cross-country skiing, sporting events, golf, theater and watersports nearby.

Publicity: *Snow Country, America's Favorite Magazine, Franklin County Magazine.*

"The food was excellent, the rooms charming and clean, the whole atmosphere so relaxing."

Certificate may be used: March 1-May 1, Sunday-Saturday and July 1-September, Sunday-Friday.

Beverly   C14

Bunny's B&B
17 Kernwood Hgts
Beverly, MA 01915
(508)922-2392

Circa 1940. This Dutch Colonial inn is located on a scenic route along the state's northeastern coast. One room features a decorative fireplace and a handmade Oriental rug. Breakfasts in the formal dining room always feature homemade muffins and the innkeepers will make every effort to meet special dietary needs if notified in advance.

Innkeeper(s): Bunny & Joe Stacey. $55-85. TC. 4 rooms, 2 with PB. Breakfast included in rates. Type of meal: continental-plus breakfast. Beds: QDT. Antiques, parks, shopping and theater nearby.

Certificate may be used: Nov. 19-May 8, Sunday to Saturday.

Brewster   H18

Old Sea Pines Inn
2553 Main St, PO Box 1026
Brewster, MA 02631-1959
(508)896-6114 Fax:(508)896-8322

Circa 1900. This turn-of-the-century mansion on three-and-one-half acres of lawns and trees was formerly the Sea Pines School of Charm and Personality for Young Women, established in 1907. Recently renovated, the inn displays elegant wallpapers and a grand sweeping stairway. It is located near beaches and bike paths, as well as village shops and restaurants.

Innkeeper(s): Michele Rowan. $45-110. MC VISA AX DC DS. 21 rooms, 14 with PB, 3 with FP. 2 suites. 1 conference room. Breakfast and afternoon tea included in rates. Types of meals: full breakfast and early coffee/tea. Evening snack, picnic lunch, banquet service, catering service and room service available. Restaurant on premises. Beds: QDT. Air conditioning and TV in room. Handicap access. Antiques, fishing, shopping, theater and watersports nearby.

Location: Cape Cod.

Publicity: *New York Times, Cape Cod Oracle, For Women First, Home Office, Entrepreneur.*

"The loving care applied by Steve, Michele and staff is deeply appreciated."

Certificate may be used: Weekdays only March 31-May 31 and weekdays only Oct. 15-Dec. 21.

Brookline   E13

The Bertram Inn
92 Sewall Ave
Brookline, MA 02146-5327
(617)566-2234 (800)295-3822 Fax:(617)277-1887

Circa 1907. Antiques and authenticity are the rule at this turn-of-the-century Gothic Revival inn, found on a peaceful, tree-lined street two miles from central Boston. The Bertram Inn features old-English stylings and Victorian decor. Guests can enjoy breakfast or afternoon tea by the fire in the common room or, if weather permits, on the front porch overlooking the garden.  Boston College, Boston University, Fenway Park and the F.L. Olmstead National Historic Site all are nearby. Shops and restaurants are within walking distance, and the Boston area's many attractions are nearby. Parking is included in the rates.

Innkeeper(s): Bryan Austin. $69-174. MC VISA AX PC TC. 14 rooms, 11 with PB, 2 with FP. Breakfast included in rates. Type of meal: continental-plus breakfast. Afternoon tea available. Beds: KQDT. Air conditioning and TV in room. Fax on premises. Antiques, parks, shopping, sporting events and theater nearby.

"This B&B is just wonderful, I can't imagine a nicer place. Thank you for your warm generosity, a fine substitute for home."

Certificate may be used: Sunday-Thursday in December, January, February, March.

Cape Cod (Harwich Port)

Dunscroft By The Sea
Inn & Cottage
24 Pilgrim Rd
Cape Cod (Harwich Port), MA 02646
(508)432-0810 (800)432-4345 Fax:(508)432-5134

Circa 1920. The innkeepers at this Colonial Revival inn pride themselves on creating a quiet, romantic retreat for their guests. The Victorian

decor includes special touches such as romantic poetry books placed in the rooms, candles, chocolates and other surprises. Canopy and four-poster beds decorate the graciously appointed bedchambers. Rooms with a fireplace or double Jacuzzi tub also are available. In addition to the inn rooms, the King Suite is located in what was the chauffer's cottage and includes a fireplace. The inn grounds include a mile of private beach. Built as a private summer estate in 1920, the inn has been welcoming guests for nearly half a century. Innkeeper Alyce Cunningham prepares a sumptuous full, country breakfast on a lace-covered table set with elegant china. A short walk will take you to restaurants and shops.

Innkeeper(s): Alyce & Wally Cunningham. $95-225. MAP. MC VISA AX PC. 9 rooms with PB, 2 with FP. 1 suite. 1 cottage. 1 conference room. Breakfast included in rates. Type of meal: full breakfast. Catering service available. Beds: KQ. Air conditioning, ceiling fan and TV in room. Fax, copier, swimming, tennis and library on premises. Handicap access. Amusement parks, antiques, fishing, parks, shopping, cross-country skiing, sporting events, theater and watersports nearby.

Location: Ten miles east of Hyannis.

Publicity: *Cape Codder.*

"A quaint and delightful slice of New England. Your generous hospitality is greatly appreciated. Your place is beautiful."

Certificate may be used: Sept. 15-June 30 on an as available basis.

Chatham

Carriage House Inn
407 Old Harbor Rd
Chatham, MA 02633-2322
(508)945-4688 (800)355-8868 Fax:(508)945-4688
E-mail: patton@capecod.net

Circa 1890. This Colonial Revival inn is an easy find as it is located adjacent to Chatham's tallest flagpole. Antiques and family pieces decorate the interior. Chintzes and floral prints permeate the six guest rooms, and the three carriage house rooms each include a fireplace and an entrance to an outside sitting area. Breakfast items such as fresh fruit, juices, cereals, homemade muffins, scones and breads are presented on a sideboard buffet, and guests can enjoy the fare either in the dining room or on the sun porch. Borrow a bike for a tour of the area, or relax in front of the fireplace. Beach towels are furnished for trips to the shore, just a quarter mile away.

Innkeeper(s): Pam & Tom Patton. $125-175. MC VISA AX PC TC. 6 rooms with PB, 3 with FP. Breakfast and evening snack included in rates. Types of meals: continental-plus breakfast and early coffee/tea. Beds: Q. Air conditioning and ceiling fan in room. Cable TV, VCR, fax and bicycles on premises. Antiques, fishing, parks, shopping, theater and watersports nearby.

"This might well have been our best B&B experience ever. It was the hosts who made it so memorable."

Certificate may be used: November-April, Sunday-Thursday, excluding holidays. Subject to availability.

Cyrus Kent House
63 Cross St
Chatham, MA 02633-2207
(508)945-9104 (800)338-5368 Fax:(508)945-9104

Circa 1877. A former sea captain's home, the Cyrus Kent House was built in the Greek Revival style. The award-winning restoration retained many original features such as wide pine floorboards, ceiling rosettes, and marble fireplaces. Although furnished with antiques and reproductions, all modern ties are available. Most bedrooms have four-poster beds. Suites feature sitting rooms with fireplaces. Chatham's historic district is a short stroll away.

Innkeeper(s): Sharon Mitchell-Swan. $85-250. MC VISA. 10 rooms with PB. Breakfast and afternoon tea included in rates. Types of meals: continental-plus breakfast and early coffee/tea. Beds: QD. TV in room. Fax on premises. Antiques, fishing, shopping and watersports nearby.

Location: Located on a quiet side street within easy walking distance of the historic village of Chatham.

Publicity: *Country Inns.*

Certificate may be used: Nov. 1 through April 15.

Old Harbor Inn
22 Old Harbor Rd
Chatham, MA 02633-2315
(508)945-4434 (800)942-4434 Fax:(508)945-2492

Circa 1932. This pristine New England bed & breakfast was once the home of "Doc" Keene, a popular physician in the area. A meticulous renovation has created an elegant, beautifully appointed inn offering antique furnishings, designer linens and lavish amenities in an English country decor. A buffet breakfast, featuring Judy's homemade muffins, is served in the sunroom or on the deck. The beaches, boutiques and galleries are a walk away and there is an old grist mill, the Chatham Lighthouse, and a railroad museum. Band concerts are offered Friday nights in the summer at Kate Gould Park.

Innkeeper(s): Judy & Ray Braz. $105-195. MC VISA DC CB DS PC TC. 8 rooms with PB, 2 with FP. 1 conference room. Breakfast included in rates. Types of meals: continental-plus breakfast and early coffee/tea. Afternoon tea available. Beds: KQT. Air conditioning and ceiling fan in room. Antiques, fishing, parks, shopping, theater, watersports nearby.

Location: On the elbow of Cape Cod.

Publicity: *Cape Cod Life, Country Inns, Cape Cod Travel Guide, Yankee.*

Certificate may be used: Oct. 15-June 15, Sunday through Thursday.

Concord D12

Colonel Roger Brown House
1694 Main St
Concord, MA 01742-2831
(508)369-9119 (800)292-1369 Fax:(508)369-1305

Circa 1775. This house was the home of Minuteman Roger Brown, who fought the British at the Old North Bridge. The frame for this center-chimney Colonial was being raised on April 19, the day the battle took place. Some parts of the house were built as early as 1708. The adjacent Damon Mill houses a fitness club available to guests. Both buildings are in the National Register.

Innkeeper(s): Lauri Berlied. $75-100. MC VISA AX DC PC TC. 5 rooms with PB. 1 suite. Breakfast and afternoon tea included in rates. Type of meal: continental-plus breakfast. Beds: QDT. Air conditioning in room. Fax, copier, computer, spa, swimming, sauna and library on premises. Antiques, fishing, parks, shopping, downhill skiing, cross-country skiing, theater and watersports nearby.

Publicity: *Middlesex News, Concord Journal, Washingtonian.*

"The Colonel Roger Brown House makes coming to Concord even more of a treat! Many thanks for your warm hospitality."

Certificate may be used: Nov. 1-April 1, July 1-Aug. 31 on availability.

Hawthorne Inn
462 Lexington Rd
Concord, MA 01742-3729
(978)369-5610 Fax:(978)287-4949

Circa 1870. The Hawthorne Inn is situated on land that once belonged to Ralph Waldo Emerson, the Alcotts and Nathaniel Hawthorne. It was here that Bronson Alcott planted his fruit trees, made pathways to the Mill Brook, and erected his Bath House. Hawthorne purchased the land and repaired a path leading to his home with trees planted on either side. Two of these trees still stand. Across the road is Hawthorne's House, The Wayside. Next to it is the Alcott's Orchard House, and Grapevine

Cottage where the Concord grape was developed. Nearby is Sleepy Hollow Cemetery where Emerson, the Alcotts, the Thoreaus, and Hawthorne were laid to rest.

Innkeeper(s): Marilyn Mudry & Gregory Burch. $140-215. MC VISA AX DS PC TC. 7 rooms with PB. Breakfast and afternoon tea included in rates. Type of meal: continental-plus breakfast. Beds: QDT. Air conditioning in room. Fax and library on premises. Antiques, fishing, parks, shopping and cross-country skiing nearby.

Location: On the famed "Battle Road" of 1775. East of Town Green by eight-tenth of a mile.

Publicity: *New York Times, Boston Globe, Yankee.*

"Surely there couldn't be a better or more valuable location for a comfortable, old-fashioned country inn."

Certificate may be used: November-March, Saturday-Thursday (no Fridays).

Cotuit   I16

Salty Dog B&B Inn
451 Main St
Cotuit, MA 02635-3114
(508)428-5228

A 300-year-old oak rests in front of this seaside Victorian inn, which was owned originally by a sea captain. Guest rooms offer four-poster beds surrounded by country decor. The home features wide floor boards, antique moldings and Oriental rugs. Breakfasts of freshly baked muffins and breads are served in the fireplaced common room. Cotuit, known for its picturesque main street, as well as the surrounding Cape Cod, offers plenty of antiquing, shopping and restaurants.

Innkeeper(s): Gerald Goldstein. $65-105. MC VISA. 5 rooms. Breakfast included in rates. Type of meal: continental-plus breakfast.

Certificate may be used: April through December, Sunday through Thursday.

Cummington   D4

Cumworth Farm
472 W Cummington Rd
Cummington, MA 01026-9603
(413)634-5529

Circa 1780. Fresh raspberries and blueberries are harvested each season at this 200-year-old working farm. Innkeeper Ed McColgan produces 600 gallons of maple syrup each year in the farm's sugar house, and cattle and sheep also are raised. The farm house itself is decorated in colonial furnishings. Each guest room is filled with antiques and the cozy living room offers a wood stove for warming up on winter days. Cummington has a special fair each August

and nearby Worthington holds a balloon festival in the fall. Other local attractions include the Hill Gallery, which offers a variety of pottery and paintings by local artists.

Innkeeper(s): Edward McColgan. $75. PC. 6 rooms, 1 with FP. Breakfast included in rates. Type of meal: full breakfast. Beds: TD. Ceiling fan in room. Cable TV, copier and spa on premises. Amusement parks, antiques, parks, shopping, cross-country skiing, sporting events, golf, theater and watersports nearby.

Publicity: *Daily Hampshire Gazette, Bershire Eagle.*

"Quiet and calming."

Certificate may be used: May 1-Nov. 1, Tuesday, Wednesday, Thursday. No holiday or weekends.

Deerfield   C6

Deerfield Inn
81 Old Main St
Deerfield, MA 01342-0305
(413)774-5587 (800)926-3865 Fax:(413)773-8712

Circa 1884. The village of Deerfield was settled in 1670. Farmers in the area still unearth bones, ax and arrow heads from French/Indian massacre of 1704. Now 50 beautifully restored 18th and 19th century homes line mile-long main street, considered by many to be the loveliest street in New England. Fourteen of these houses are museums of Pioneer Valley decorative arts and are open year-round to the public. The Memorial Hall Museum,

open from May to November, is the oldest museum in New England and full of local antiquities. The inn is situated at the center of this peaceful village and for those who wish to truly experience New England's past, this is the place. The village has been designated a National Historic Landmark.

Innkeeper(s): Jane & Karl Sabo. $141-261. MC VISA AX. 23 rooms with PB. 1 conference room. Breakfast and afternoon tea included in rates. Type of meal: full breakfast. Dinner and lunch available. Restaurant on premises. Beds: QT. Fax and copier on premises. Handicap access. Antiques, fishing, cross-country skiing and theater nearby.

Location: Middle of historic village.

Publicity: *Travel Today, Country Accents, Colonial Homes, Country Living, Country Inns B&B, Yankee.*

"We've stayed at many New England inns, but the Deerfield Inn ranks among the best."

Certificate may be used: Sunday-Thursday, based on availability, excluding May, September, October.

Dennis I18

Isaiah Hall B&B Inn
152 Whig St
Dennis, MA 02638-1917
(508)385-9928 (800)736-0160 Fax:(508)385-5879

Circa 1857. Adjacent to the Cape's oldest cranberry bog is this Greek Revival farmhouse built by Isaiah Hall, a cooper. His brother was the first cultivator of

cranberries in America and Isaiah designed and patented the original barrel for shipping cranberries. In 1948, Dorothy Gripp, an artist, established the inn. Many examples of her artwork remain.
Innkeeper(s): Marie Brophy. $85-145. MC VISA AX TC. 9 rooms, 10 with PB, 1 with FP. 1 suite. Breakfast included in rates. Types of meals: continental-plus breakfast and early coffee/tea. Beds: QDT. Air conditioning in room. Cable TV and fax on premises. Antiques, fishing, parks, shopping, theater and watersports nearby.

Location: Cape Cod.

Publicity: *Cape Cod Life, New York Times, Golf, National Geographic Traveler.*

"Your place is so lovely and relaxing."

Certificate may be used: April & May, Sunday-Thursday, holidays excluded.

Dennisport I18

Rose Petal B&B
152 Sea St PO Box 974
Dennisport, MA 02639-2404
(508)398-8470

Circa 1872. This Cape Cod-style home was built for Almond Wixon, whose seafaring family was among the original settlers of Dennisport. In 1918, Wixon was lost at sea with all on board. The Wixon homestead was completely restored in 1986. Surrounded by a white picket fence and attractively landscaped yard, the Rose Petal is situated in the heart of Cape Cod, a short walk from the beach. Home-baked pastries highlight a full breakfast in the dining room.
Innkeeper(s): Gayle & Dan Kelly. $59-94. MC VISA AX. 3 rooms, 2 with PB. Breakfast included in rates. Types of meals: gourmet breakfast and

early coffee/tea. Beds: QT. Air conditioning in room. Cable TV on premises. Antiques, fishing, parks, shopping, theater and watersports nearby.

"Perfect. Every detail was appreciated."

Certificate may be used: January, February, March anytime; April, May, November, Monday, Tuesday, Wednesday, Thursday only.

East Orleans H19

Ship's Knees Inn
186 Beach Rd, PO Box 756
East Orleans, MA 02643
(508)255-1312 Fax:(508)240-1351

Circa 1820. This 175-year-old restored sea captain's home is a three-minute walk to the ocean. Rooms are decorated in a nautical style with antiques. Several rooms feature authentic ship's knees, hand-painted trunks, old clipper ship models and four-poster beds. Some rooms boast ocean views and the Master Suite has a working fireplace. The inn offers swimming and tennis facilities on the grounds. About three miles away, the innkeepers also offer a one-bedroom efficiency apartment and two heated cottages on the Cove. Head into town or spend the day basking in the beauty of Nauset Beach with its picturesque sand dunes.
Innkeeper(s): Jean & Ken Pitchford. $45-110. MC VISA. 11 rooms with PB, 3 with FP. Breakfast included in rates. Type of meal: continental breakfast. Beds: KQDT. Amusement parks, antiques, fishing, parks, shopping, theater and watersports nearby.

Location: One-and-a-half hours from Boston.

Publicity: *Boston Globe.*

"Warm, homey and very friendly atmosphere. Very impressed with the beamed ceilings."

Certificate may be used: All year, except July, August and holidays.

East Sandwich
I17

Wingscorton Farm Inn
Rt 6A, Olde Kings Hwy
East Sandwich, MA 02537
(508)888-0534

Circa 1763. Wingscorton is a working farm on seven acres of lawns, gardens and orchards. It adjoins a short walk to a private ocean beach. This Cape Cod manse, built by a Quaker family, is a historical landmark on what once was known as the King's Highway, the oldest historical district in the United States. All the rooms are furnished with antiques and working fireplaces (one with a secret compartment where runaway slaves hid). Breakfast features fresh produce with eggs, meats and vegetables from the farm's livestock and gardens. Pets and children welcome.

Innkeeper(s): Sheila Weyers & Richard Loring. $115-150. MC VISA AX PC TC. 7 rooms, 7 with FP. 4 suites. 2 cottages. Breakfast included in rates. Types of meals: full breakfast and gourmet breakfast. Beds: QDT. Swimming, library and child care on premises. Antiques, fishing, parks, shopping, downhill skiing, cross-country skiing, sporting events, theater and watersports nearby.

Location: North Side of Cape Cod, off Route 6A.

Publicity: *Boston Globe, New York Times.*

"Absolutely wonderful. We will always remember the wonderful time."

Certificate may be used: Nov. 1-May 1.

Edgartown
K16

Ashley Inn
129 Main St, PO Box 650
Edgartown, MA 02539
(508)627-9655 (800)477-9655

Circa 1860. A retired whaling captain built this gracious Georgian inn on Martha's Vineyard. Guest rooms are furnished in period antiques, brass and wicker. The inn is just four blocks from the beach, and its Main Street location offers easy access to Edgartown's many fine restaurants and shops. Breakfasts are served in the English tea room, and guests find the inn's grounds perfect for an after-meal stroll. Others like to relax in the hammock or in the comfortable sitting room. A special honeymoon package is available.

Innkeeper(s): Fred Hurley. $60-150. MC VISA AX. 8 rooms. 1 suite. Breakfast included in rates. Type of meal: continental breakfast. Air conditioning and TV in room. Antiques and shopping nearby.

Certificate may be used: Oct. 23-April 1, Nov. 1-Dec. 31.

Falmouth
J16

Village Green Inn
40 Main St
Falmouth, MA 02540-2667
(508)548-5621 (800)237-1119 Fax:(508)457-5051
E-mail: vgi40@aol.com

Circa 1804. The inn, listed in the National Register, originally was built in the Federal style for Braddock Dimmick, son of Revolutionary War General Joseph Dimmick. Later, "cranberry king"

John Crocker moved the house onto a granite slab foundation, remodeling it in the Victorian style. There are inlaid floors, large porches and gingerbread trim.

Innkeeper(s): Diane & Don Crosby. $85-145. MC VISA AX PC TC. 5 rooms with PB, 2 with FP. 1 suite. Breakfast and afternoon tea included in rates. Types of meals: full breakfast and early coffee/tea. Beds: Q. Air conditioning, ceiling fan and TV in room. Bicycles on premises. Antiques, fishing, parks, shopping, sporting events, theater and watersports nearby.

Location: Falmouth's historic village green.

Publicity: *Country Inns, Cape Cod Life, Yankee.*

"Tasteful, comfortable and the quintessential New England flavor ... You have turned us on to the B&B style of travel and we now have a standard to measure our future choices by."

Certificate may be used: January to mid-May, Sunday-Thursday

Great Barrington
F2

Seekonk Pines
142 Seekonk Cross Rd
Great Barrington, MA 01230-1571
(413)528-4192 (800)292-4192 Fax:(413)528-1076

Circa 1832. Known as the Crippen Farm from 1835-1879, Seekonk Pines Inn now includes both the original farmhouse and a Dutch Colonial wing. Green lawns, gardens and meadows surround the inn. The name "Seekonk" was the local Indian

name for the Canadian geese which migrate through this part of the Berkshires. The inn is an easy drive to Tanglewood.

Innkeeper(s): Bruce, Roberta & Rita Lefkowitz. $80-135. MC VISA AX. 6 rooms, 5 with PB. 1 suite. Breakfast included in rates. Type of meal: full breakfast. Beds: QDT. Air conditioning and ceiling fan in room. Cable TV, VCR, fax, copier, swimming, bicycles and library on premises. Antiques, fishing, shopping, downhill skiing, cross-country skiing, golf, theater and watersports nearby.

Location: Near Tanglewood.

Publicity: *Los Angeles Times, Boston Sunday Globe, Country Inns, The Boston Globe, New York Newsday*

"Of all the B&Bs we trekked through, yours was our first and most memorable! This has been our best ever Berkshire escape…thanks to your wonderful B&B."

Certificate may be used: Nov. 15-May 15, Sunday-Friday, not including holidays or holiday weeks.

Wainwright Inn

518 Main St
Great Barrington, MA 01230-2006
(413)528-2062

Circa 1766. This pre-Revolutionary War home opened for guests in 1766 as Tory Tavern and Inn, and during the war served as a fort and Colonial armory. The home was also used to lay the groundwork for the commercial use of AC current, when it was owned by Franklin Pope. Pope worked with Thomas Edison and General Electric founder William Stanley. If the history of this inn fails to impress, the rich interior should do the trick. Snuggle up in front of a roaring fire or relax on one of the wraparound porches. Muffins and fresh coffee are delivered to guests each morning. A full breakfast is served later in the fire-lit dining room. Each season brings new activity to the Great Barrington area, which is full of antique shops, orchards to visit, ski slopes and beautiful scenery. The nearby Hancock Shaker Village is a popular attraction.

Innkeeper(s): David Rolland. $50-125. MC VISA AX. 8 rooms. Breakfast included in rates. Type of meal: full breakfast.

Certificate may be used: November-June, Sunday-Thursday.

Windflower Inn

684 S Egremont Rd
Great Barrington, MA 01230-1932
(413)528-2720 (800)992-1993 Fax:(413)528-5147

Circa 1870. This country manor is situated on 10 acres shaded by giant oaks and maples. Early American and English antiques fill the spacious guest rooms. There is a piano room with shelves of books, and a clock collection is featured throughout. The inn's dinners have received excellent  reviews and feature herbs, vegetables and berries from the garden. Guests may cross the street for tennis and golf at the country club.

Innkeeper(s): Barbara & Gerald Liebert, Claudia & John Ryan. $110-160. MAP. AX PC TC. 13 rooms with PB, 6 with FP. Breakfast and afternoon tea included in rates. Types of meals: full breakfast and early coffee/tea. Beds: KQT. Air conditioning in room. Fax, copier, swimming and library on premises. Antiques, parks, shopping, downhill skiing, cross-country skiing, theater and watersports nearby.

Publicity: *Los Angeles Times, Boulevard, Redbook, Country Inns, Countryside, Road Best Traveled, Discerning Traveler.*

"Every creative comfort imaginable, great for heart, soul and stomach."

Certificate may be used: Nov. 1-June 30, Sunday-Thursday non-holiday. Monday-Wednesday, July 1-Oct. 31 non-holiday, non-fireplace September and October. B&B style only.

Greenfield   C6

The Brandt House

29 Highland Ave
Greenfield, MA 01301-3605
(413)774-3329 (800)235-3329 Fax:(413)772-2908
E-mail: brandt@crocker.com

Circa 1890. Three-and-a-half-acre lawns surround this impressive three-story Colonial Revival house, situated hilltop. The library and pool room are popular for lounging. A full breakfast often includes homemade scones. There is a clay tennis court, nature trails, badminton, horseshoes and in winter, lighted ice skating at a nearby pond. Historic Deerfield is within five minutes.

Innkeeper(s): Phoebe Compton. $90-165. MC VISA AX DS TC. 8 rooms, 6 with PB, 2 with FP. 1 suite. 1 conference room. Breakfast included in rates. Types of meals: continental-plus breakfast, full breakfast and early coffee/tea. Gourmet lunch available. Beds: KQT. Air conditioning, ceiling fan and TV in room. VCR, fax, copier, tennis and library on premises. Antiques, fishing, parks, shopping, downhill skiing, cross-country skiing, sporting events, theater and watersports nearby.

Harwich Port

"Ensconced deep in a featherbed under mounds of snow eiderdown, surrounded by a rich tapestry of childhood yesteryear, is like a foretaste of heaven."

Certificate may be used: November through April.

Hamilton — C14

Miles River Country Inn
823 Bay Rd, Box 149
Hamilton, MA 01936
(508)468-7206 Fax:(508)468-3999

Circa 1789. This rambling colonial inn sits on more than 30 acres of magnificent curving lawns bordered by trees and formal gardens that lead to the Miles River. There are meadows, woodlands and

wetlands surrounding the property and available for exploring. The river flows through the property, which is a haven for a wide variety of wildlife. Many of the inn's 12 fireplaces are in the guest rooms. Family heirloom antiques compliment the interior.
Innkeeper(s): Gretel & Peter Clark. $80-210. MC VISA AX PC TC. 8 rooms, 6 with PB, 4 with FP. 1 suite. 2 conference rooms. Breakfast and afternoon tea included in rates. Types of meals: full breakfast and early coffee/tea. Beds: QDT. Cable TV, VCR, fax, copier, bicycles and library on premises. Antiques, fishing, parks, shopping, downhill skiing, cross-country skiing, sporting events, theater and watersports nearby.
Publicity: *Boston Globe, Salem Evening News.*

Certificate may be used: Most weekdays, weekends November-April.

Augustus Snow House
528 Main St
Harwich Port, MA 02646-1842
(508)430-0528 (800)320-0528 Fax:(508)432-7995

Circa 1901. This gracious, Queen Anne Victorian is a turn-of-the-century gem, complete with a wide, wraparound veranda, gabled windows and a distinctive turret. Victorian wallpapers, stained glass and rich woodwork complement the interior, which is appropriately decorated in period style. Each of the romantic guest quarters offers something special. One room has a canopy bed and a fireplace, while another includes a relaxing clawfoot tub. Three rooms have Jacuzzi tubs. The king-size beds are dressed in fine linens. As is the Victorian way, afternoon refreshments are served each day. The breakfasts include delectables, such as banana chip muffins, baked pears in raspberry cream sauce or, possibly, baked French toast with layers of homemade cinnamon bread, bacon and cheese.
Innkeeper(s): Joyce & Steve Roth. $105-160. MC VISA AX DS PC TC. 5 rooms with PB, 1 with FP. Breakfast included in rates. Types of meals: gourmet breakfast and early coffee/tea. Afternoon tea available. Restaurant on premises. Beds: KQ. Air conditioning, ceiling fan and TV in room. Fax and copier on premises. Antiques, fishing, parks, shopping, golf and watersports nearby.

"Being able to walk to the beach early in the morning before breakfast was the perfect start to our stay. Breakfast was more than we ever thought we could eat."

Certificate may be used: Dec. 1-April 15, Sunday-Friday.

Captain's Quarters B&B Inn
85 Bank St
Harwich Port, MA 02646-1903
(508)432-1991 (800)992-6550

Circa 1850. This romantic Victorian inn features a classic wrap-around porch and a graceful, curving front stairway. Guest rooms include brass beds and charming decor. A continental breakfast is served each morning. The inn is a three-minute walk to the beach or the village.
Innkeeper(s): Ed Kenney. $85-95. MC VISA AX DS. 6 rooms with PB. Breakfast included in rates. Type of meal: continental-plus breakfast. Beds: QT. TV in room. Antiques and shopping nearby.
Location: One-and-a-half hours from Boston.

"A great romantic getaway with lovely rooms."

Certificate may be used: March through mid-June and mid-September through Oct. 31, excluding holidays.

Harbor Breeze

326 Lower County Rd
Harwich Port, MA 02646-1625
(508)432-0337 (800)272-4343 Fax:(508)432-1276
E-mail: dvangeld@capecod.net

Circa 1945. Ideally located across the street from picturesque Allens Harbor and only a short walk from the Brooks Road beach, this inn is a classic

Cape Cod home. A rambling connection of cedar shake additions, nestled in an attractive pine setting, surrounds a garden courtyard to form a guest wing. Flowered walkways lead to nine guest rooms, which are furnished in wicker, woods and country floral. There are restful sitting areas amid the pines and a swimming pool where you can enjoy the ocean breezes. A short walk down a shady tree-lined street brings you to a sandy beach on Nantucket Sound.

Innkeeper(s): Kathleen & David Van Gelder. $80-125. MC VISA AX DS PC TC. 9 rooms with PB, 1 with FP. Breakfast included in rates. Types of meals: continental-plus breakfast and early coffee/tea. Beds: KQT. TV in room. Swimming on premises. Antiques, fishing, parks, shopping, golf, theater and watersports nearby.

Certificate may be used: April 1-June 15 and Sept. 5-Oct. 31, Sunday through Friday. Not valid holidays or holiday weekends.

Lanesboro   C3

Whippletree B&B

10 Bailey Rd
Lanesboro, MA 01237-9600
(413)443-9874

Circa 1753. Decades before the first shots of the Revolutionary War were fired, this Federal Post & Beam farmhouse sat in its tranquil country setting. Today, after weathering the centuries, it still stands surrounded by five restful acres and offering views of the Berkshire Hills. Guest rooms are located either in the main house or in an adjacent renovated barn. There is a swimming pool on the premises, and guests are welcome to relax and enjoy the view from the inn's wraparound porch. The breakfasts are con-

tinental, but never ordinary, with items such as spicy mandarin muffins or carrot-pineapple squares.

Innkeeper(s): Chuck Lynch. $60-95. PC. 5 rooms, 2 with PB. 1 suite. Breakfast included in rates. Type of meal: continental-plus breakfast. Beds: Q. Air conditioning and TV in room. Swimming on premises. Amusement parks, antiques, fishing, parks, shopping, downhill skiing, cross-country skiing, sporting events, theater and watersports nearby.

Certificate may be used: Nov. 1-June 30, Sunday-Thursday.

Lee   E2

Devonfield

85 Stockbridge Rd
Lee, MA 01238-9308
(413)243-3298 (800)664-0880 Fax:(413)243-1360

Circa 1800. The original section of this Colonial inn was built by a Revolutionary War soldier. Guest rooms are spacious with charming furniture and patterned wallcoverings. Three of the rooms feature fireplaces. The one-bedroom cottage has both a fireplace and an efficiency kitchen. Guests are treated to a full breakfast. One need not wander far from the grounds to find something to do. The innkeepers offer a tennis court, swimming pool and bicycles

for guests, and a nine-hole golf course is just across the way. Inside, guests can relax in the living room with its fireplace and library or in the television room. The area is full of boutiques, antique shops and galleries to explore, as well as hiking, fishing and skiing. Tanglewood, summer home of the Boston Symphony, is close by.

Innkeeper(s): Sally & Ben Schenck. $70-260. MC VISA AX DS PC TC. 10 rooms with PB, 4 with FP. 4 suites. 1 cottage. Beds: KQT. Air conditioning in room. Cable TV, fax, copier, swimming, bicycles, tennis and library on premises.

Publicity: *Discerning Traveler.*

"*A special thank you for your warm and kind hospitality. We feel as though this is our home away from home.*"

Certificate may be used: Nov. 1-May 31, not including holidays.

Lenox

E2

Brook Farm Inn

15 Hawthorne St
Lenox, MA 01240-2404
(413)637-3013 (800)285-7638 Fax:(413)637-4751
E-mail: innkeeper@brookfarm.com.

Circa 1870. Brook Farm Inn is named after the original Brook Farm, a literary commune that sought to combine thinker and worker through a society of intelligent, cultivated members. In keeping with that theme, this gracious Victorian inn offers poetry and writing seminars and has a 650-volume poetry library. Canopy beds, Mozart and a swimming pool tend to the spirit.

Innkeeper(s): Joe & Anne Miller. $80-190. MC VISA DS PC TC. 12 rooms with PB, 6 with FP. Breakfast and afternoon tea included in rates. Types of meals: full breakfast and early coffee/tea. Beds: KQDT. Air conditioning and ceiling fan in room. Fax, copier and swimming on premises. Antiques, fishing, parks, shopping, downhill skiing, cross-country skiing, sporting events, theater and watersports nearby.

Location: In the heart of Berkshire County.

Publicity: *Berkshire Eagle, Country Inns, Travel & Leisure, Boston.*

"We've been traveling all our lives and never have we felt more at home."

Certificate may be used: Monday-Thursday, April 1-June 15.

The Gables Inn

81 Walker St, Rt 183
Lenox, MA 01240-2719
(413)637-3416 (800)382-9401

Circa 1885. At one time, this was the home of Pulitzer Prize-winning novelist, Edith Wharton. The Queen Anne-style Berkshire cottage features a handsome eight-sided library and Mrs. Wharton's own four-poster bed. An unusual indoor swimming pool with spa is available in warm weather.

Innkeeper(s): Mary & Frank Newton. $80-210. MC VISA DS PC TC. 18 rooms with PB, 15 with FP. 3 suites. Breakfast included in rates. Beds: Q. Air conditioning, TV and VCR in room. Fax, swimming and tennis on premises. Antiques, fishing, parks, shopping, downhill skiing, cross-

country skiing, sporting events, theater and watersports nearby.

Location: Within walking distance to Tanglewood, summer home of the Boston Symphony Orchestra.

Publicity: *P.M. Magazine, New York Times.*

"You made us feel like old friends and that good feeling enhanced our pleasure. In essence it was the best part of our trip."

Certificate may be used: Nov. 1 to May 20, Sunday - Thursday only.

The Kemble Inn

2 Kemble St
Lenox, MA 01240-2813
(413)637-4113 (800)353-4113

Circa 1881. Named for a famous 19th-century actress, Fanny Kemble, this three-story Georgian-style inn boasts an incredible view of the mountains in the Berkshires. The inn's 15 luxurious guest rooms are named for American authors, including

Nathaniel Hawthorne, Henry Wadsworth Longfellow, Herman Melville, Mark Twain and Edith Wharton. The impressive Fanny Kemble Room, which features mountain views, includes two fireplaces, a Jacuzzi tub and a king-size, four-poster bed. The inn is within minutes of five major ski areas, and Tanglewood is less than two miles away.

Innkeeper(s): J. Richard & Linda Reardon. $75-295. MC VISA DC CB DS PC TC. 15 rooms with PB, 6 with FP. Breakfast included in rates. Type of meal: continental breakfast. Air conditioning and TV in room. Handicap access. Antiques, fishing, parks, shopping, downhill skiing, cross-country skiing, theater and watersports nearby.

Publicity: *Country Inns.*

"Kemble Inn was a showcase B&B - just what we had hoped for."

Certificate may be used: Nov. 1-May 1, Sunday-Thursday, excludes holiday periods.

Lilac Inn

PO Box 2294, 33 Main St
Lenox, MA 01240-5294
(413)637-2172 Fax:(413)637-2172
E-mail: aliceatlilacinn@msn.com

Circa 1840. Aptly named for a flower, this Italian Revival inn features guest rooms that appear much like a garden. Flowery prints, wicker and antique furnishings and views of Lilac Park from the two porches enhance this cheerful atmosphere. Guests are treated to afternoon refreshments, with a proper mix of savory and sweet tidbits. Breakfasts are bountiful and delicious, yet surprisingly healthy with low-fat, vegetarian versions of treats such as banana nut bread, French toast, and vegetable quiche. The library is stocked with books and the living room, which has a fireplace, is a good place to curl up and relax. The innkeeper also offers a one-bedroom apartment with a kitchen.

Innkeeper(s): Alice Maleski. $100-199. PC. 5 rooms with PB, 1 with FP. Breakfast and afternoon tea included in rates. Types of meals: full breakfast, gourmet breakfast and early coffee/tea. Beds: KQT. Turndown service and ceiling fan in room. TV, VCR, fax, copier and library on premises. Handicap access. Antiques, fishing, parks, shopping, downhill skiing, cross-country skiing, golf, theater and watersports nearby.

"We are really looking forward to shamelessly overindulging in your breakfasts, and being carried away by the music, the time and the place."

Certificate may be used: Nov. 1-May 31, excluding weekends and holidays.

Seven Hills Country Inn

40 Plunkett St
Lenox, MA 01240-2704
(413)637-0060 (800)869-6518 Fax:(413)637-3651

Circa 1911. Descendants of those who sailed on the Mayflower built this rambling, Tudor-style mansion. The inn's 27 acres often serve as the site for weddings and receptions. The grounds include two tennis courts and a swimming pool. Guest rooms are elegantly appointed with antiques, and the mansion still maintains its hand-carved fireplaces and leaded glass windows. In addition to the original elements, some rooms contain the modern amenity of a whirlpool tub. The inn's chef, whose cuisine has been featured in Gourmet magazine, prepares creative, continental specialities. Seven Hills offers close access to many attractions in the Berkshires.

Innkeeper(s): Patricia & Jim Eder. $65-250. MAP. MC VISA AX DC CB DS PC TC. 52 rooms with PB, 5 with FP. 2 suites. 4 conference rooms. Breakfast included in rates. Type of meal: early coffee/tea. Beds: KQDT. Air conditioning in room. Cable TV, VCR, fax, copier, swimming, tennis, library and child care on premises. Handicap access. Antiques, fishing, parks, shopping, downhill skiing, cross-country skiing, theater and watersports nearby.

Certificate may be used: Jan. 1-April 30, all nights; May 1-June 30, Sunday-Friday; July 1-Aug. 31, Monday-Wednesday; Sept. 1-Oct. 26, Sunday-Friday; Oct. 27-Dec. 15, all nights; Dec. 16-31, Sunday-Friday.

Walker House

64 Walker St
Lenox, MA 01240-2718
(413)637-1271 (800)235-3098 Fax:(413)637-2387
E-mail: phoudek@vgernet.net

Circa 1804. This beautiful Federal-style house sits in the center of the village on three acres of graceful woods and restored gardens. Guest rooms have fireplaces and private baths. Each is named for a favorite composer  such as Beethoven, Mozart, or Handel. The innkeepers' musical backgrounds include associations with the San Francisco Opera, the New York City Opera, and the Los Angeles Philharmonic. Walker House concerts are scheduled from time to time. The innkeepers offer film and opera screenings nightly on a seven-foot screen. With prior approval, some pets may be allowed.

Innkeeper(s): Peggy & Richard Houdek. $70-190. PC. 8 rooms with PB, 5 with FP. 1 conference room. Breakfast and afternoon tea included in rates. Types of meals: continental-plus breakfast and early coffee/tea. Beds: QDT. Air conditioning in room. Cable TV, VCR, fax, copier and library on premises. Handicap access. Antiques, fishing, parks, shopping, downhill skiing, cross-country skiing, theater and watersports nearby.

Location: Route 183 & 7A.

Publicity: *Boston Globe, PBS, Los Angeles Times, New York Times, Dog Fancy.*

"We had a grand time staying with fellow music and opera lovers! Breakfasts were lovely."

Certificate may be used: November-May, Sunday through Thursday, excluding holidays.

Leverett   D6

Hannah Dudley House Inn

114 Dudleyville Rd
Leverett, MA 01054-9713
(413)367-2323

Circa 1797. Each season brings with it a new reason to visit this 18th-century Colonial, which is named for a member of the first family to inhabit this home. In autumn, the home's 110 acres explode in color. In winter, snow-capped pines add to the festive atmosphere, and guests snuggle up in front of a roaring fire. Two guest rooms include fireplaces, and the house offers four others. The guest room refrigerators are always stocked with drinks. At certain times of the year, dinner specials are available.

During warm months, guests enjoy use of a barbecue grill and swimming pool. Stroll the grounds and you'll find plenty of wildlife, including two ponds inhabited by ducks, goldfish, trout and bullfrogs. During the winter months, the pond transforms into the inn's skating rink.

Innkeeper(s): Erni & Daryl Johnson. $125-185. MC VISA PC TC. 4 rooms with PB, 2 with FP. 1 suite. Breakfast and evening snack included in rates. Types of meals: full breakfast and early coffee/tea. Dinner available. Beds: QD. Turndown service in room. Swimming and library on premises. Antiques, fishing, parks, shopping, downhill skiing, cross-country skiing, sporting events and theater nearby.

"Your generosity, hospitality, and friendliness made an already special time in our lives just that much more so. We look forward to our next visit to the welcome oasis you have created in Leverett."

Certificate may be used: Jan. 2-Aug. 31 and Nov. 1-Dec. 20, Monday-Thursday.

Lynn D14

Diamond District Breakfast Inn
142 Ocean St
Lynn, MA 01902-2007
(617)599-4470 (800)666-3076 Fax:(617)595-2200

Circa 1911. This 17-room Georgian house was built for shoe manufacturer P.J. Harney-Lynn. The Charles Pinkham family (son of Lydia Pinkham, a health tonic producer) later purchased it. Many of the original fixtures remain, and the inn is suitably furnished with Oriental rugs and antiques. The parlor features a collection of antique musical

instruments. There are several views of the ocean from the house, but the porch is the most popular spot for sea gazing. Breakfast is served in the dining room or on the porch. Fresh fruits, homemade breads and hot coffee, tea or cider start off the meal, followed by a special entree.

Innkeeper(s): Sandra & Jerry Caron. $80-195. MC VISA AX DC CB DS PC TC. 11 rooms, 7 with PB. 1 conference room. Breakfast included in rates. Type of meal: full breakfast. Beds: QDT. Air conditioning and ceiling fan in room. Fax, copier and computer on premises. Antiques, fishing, cross-country skiing and watersports nearby.

"The room was spectacular and breakfast was served beautifully. Bed and breakfast were both outstanding! Thanks so much for your hospitality."

Certificate may be used: Nov. 1-April, Monday-Thursday, excluding holidays.

Marblehead D14

The Nesting Place B&B
16 Village St
Marblehead, MA 01945-2213
(617)631-6655
E-mail: louiseltirqaol.com

Circa 1890. Conveniently located one-half hour away from Boston and Cape Ann, this turn-of-the-century house offers as much privacy as you require. Discover the world of the early clipper ships as you walk the narrow winding streets and the beaches of Marblehead's renowned harbor, only minutes away. There's a relaxing hot tub to top off a day of browsing through art galleries, antique shops and quaint boutiques. Massages and facials also are available.

Innkeeper(s): Louise Hirshberg. $65-75. MC VISA PC TC. 2 rooms. Breakfast included in rates. Types of meals: continental-plus breakfast and early coffee/tea. Beds: KQT. VCR and spa on premises. Antiques, fishing, parks, shopping, cross-country skiing, sporting events, theater and watersports nearby.

Certificate may be used: Nov. 1-May 15. May 16-July 15, weekdays only.

Spray Cliff on The Ocean
25 Spray Ave
Marblehead, MA 01945-2746
(617)631-6789 (800)626-1530 Fax:(617)639-4563

Circa 1910. Panoramic views stretch out in grand proportions from this romantic English Tudor mansion set high above the Atlantic. The inn provides a spacious and elegant atmosphere inside. The grounds of the inn include a brick terrace surrounded by lush flower gardens where eider ducks, black cormorants and seagulls gather. Spray Cliff is the only Marblehead B&B inn located directly on the ocean.

Innkeeper(s): Roger Plauche. $149-189. MC VISA AX. 7 rooms with PB, 3 with FP. Breakfast included in rates. Type of meal: continental-plus breakfast. Beds: KQ. Antiques, fishing, shopping, cross-country skiing, sporting events, theater and watersports nearby.

Location: Fifteen miles north of Boston.

Publicity: *New York Times, Glamour.*

"I prefer this atmosphere to a modern motel. It's more relaxed and love is everywhere!"

Certificate may be used: November through May (except holidays).

Martha's Vineyard   K16

Breakfast at Tiasquam
RR 1 Box 296
Martha's Vineyard, MA 02535-9705
(508)645-3685

Circa 1987. This unique farmhouse sits amid woodlands and rolling pastures. The multi-level decks look out to fields of wildflowers, oaks and evergreens. Relax in a hammock or in your comfortable

guest room. The sinks in the bathrooms were hand-thrown by potter Robert Parrott. The breakfast, as one might expect from the name, is delightful and varies season to season. Fresh corn-blueberry pancakes might be topped with Vermont maple syrup, or freshly caught fish may be found as part of the breakfast fare. Vacationers who just want to relax will appreciate the private, rural setting of this inn.

Innkeeper(s): Ron Crowe. $70-195. 8 rooms, 2 with PB, 1 with FP. Breakfast included in rates. Type of meal: full breakfast. Beds: KQTD. Ceiling fan in room. Cable TV, VCR and bicycles on premises. Handicap access. Antiques, fishing, shopping, theater and watersports nearby.

Location: Martha's Vineyard.

"Best breakfast on the island, the perfect B&B."

Certificate may be used: Oct. 15-May 20, Sunday-Thursday nights.

Captain Dexter House of Edgartown
35 Pease's Point Way, Box 2798
Martha's Vineyard, MA 02539
(508)627-7289 Fax:(508)627-3328

Circa 1843. Located just three blocks from Edgartown's harbor and historic district, this black-shuttered sea merchant's house has a graceful lawn and terraced flower gardens. A gentle Colonial atmosphere is enhanced by original wooden beams, exposed floorboards, working fireplaces, old-

fashioned dormers and a collection of period antiques. Luxurious canopy beds are featured, and some rooms include fireplaces.

Innkeeper(s): Rick Fenstemaker. $85-175. MC VISA AX PC TC. 8 rooms with PB, 2 with FP. 1 suite. Breakfast included in rates. Type of meal: continental-plus breakfast. Afternoon tea available. Beds: QD. Air conditioning and ceiling fan in room. Fax on premises. Antiques, fishing, parks, theater and watersports nearby.

Location: On a tree-lined residential street in downtown Edgartown on the island of Martha's Vineyard.

Publicity: *Island Getaways, Vineyard Gazette, Martha's Vineyard Times, Cape Cod Life.*

"Since we were on our honeymoon, we were hoping for a quiet, relaxing stay, and the Captain Dexter House was perfect!"

Certificate may be used: May 1-June 15; Sept. 5-Oct. 31; holidays and weekends excluded.

Captain Dexter House of Vineyard Haven
100 Main St, PO Box 2457
Martha's Vineyard, MA 02568
(508)627-7289 Fax:(508)627-3382

Circa 1840. Captain Dexter House was the home of sea captain Rodolphus Dexter. Authentic 18th-century antiques and reproductions are among the inn's appointments. There are Count Rumford fireplaces and hand-stencilled walls in several rooms.

Located on a street of historic homes, the inn is a short stroll to the beach, town and harbor. The innkeepers offer an evening aperitif and in the summer, lemonade is served.

Innkeeper(s): Rick Fenstemaker. $95-195. MC VISA AX PC TC. 11 rooms with PB, 4 with FP. Breakfast included in rates. Type of meal: continental-plus breakfast. Afternoon tea available. Beds: QD. Air conditioning and ceiling fan in room. Fax on premises. Antiques, fishing, parks, shopping, theater and watersports nearby.

Location: Martha's Vineyard.

Publicity: *Martha's Vineyard Times, Cape Cod Life.*

"The house is sensational. Your hospitality was all one could expect. You've made us permanent bed & breakfast fans."

Certificate may be used: May 1-June 15, Sept. 5-Oct. 31, holidays and weekends excluded.

Nancy's Auberge

98 Main St, PO Box 4433
Martha's Vineyard, MA 02568
(508)693-4434

Circa 1840. This 1840 Greek Revival home affords harbor views from its spot in a historic neighborhood once home to early settlers and whaling captains. Three of the antique-filled rooms include fireplaces, and one of the bedchambers boasts a harbor view. The inn is just a few blocks from the local ferry. Bicycle paths and beaches are nearby, as well as restaurants and a variety of shops.

Innkeeper(s): Nancy Hurd. $88-118. MC VISA. 3 rooms. Breakfast included in rates. Type of meal: continental-plus breakfast. VCR on premises. Antiques, shopping and theater nearby.

"It's so picturesque. It's like living on a postcard."

Certificate may be used: Monday through Thursday, November through April, holidays excluded

Twin Oaks Inn

8 Edgartown Rd, PO Box 1767
Martha's Vineyard, MA 02568
(508)693-8633 (800)696-8633 Fax:(508)693-5833

Circa 1906. Pastels and floral prints provide a relaxing atmosphere at this Dutch Colonial inn on Martha's Vineyard, which offers four guest rooms and an apartment with its own kitchen. The breakfast specialty is applecrisp, and guests also enjoy afternoon tea on the enclosed wraparound front porch.  The inn is within walking distance of the bicycle path, downtown businesses and the ferry, but its location off the main road affords a more relaxed and sedate feeling for visitors. The family-oriented inn accommodates family reunions, meetings and weddings, and its fireplace room is popular with honeymooners.

Innkeeper(s): Doris Clark. $55-180. MC VISA. 5 rooms, 3 with PB. 2 suites. 1 conference room. Breakfast included in rates. Types of meals: continental-plus breakfast and early coffee/tea. Afternoon tea available. Beds: QDT. Ceiling fan and TV in room. VCR on premises. Antiques, fishing, shopping, theater and watersports nearby.

Publicity: *Detroit Free Press.*

"We appreciated the wonderful welcome and kind hospitality shown us for our week's stay on your lovely island."

Certificate may be used: Jan. 1 through May 15.

Middleboro   H14

On Cranberry Pond B&B

43 Fuller St
Middleboro, MA 02346-1706
(508)946-0768 Fax:(508)947-8221
E-mail: ocpbandb@aol.com

Circa 1989. Nestled in the historic "cranberry capital of the world," this modern farmhouse rests on a working berry bog by the shores of its namesake tarn. There are two miles of trails to meander, and during berry picking season, guests can watch as buckets of the fruit are collected. The rooms are decorated with knickknacks and flowers, the Master Suite includes a working fireplace. Innkeeper Jeannine LaBossiere creates the breakfasts, which begin with fresh coffee, muffins, cookies and scones.

Innkeeper(s): Jeannine LaBossiere & Tim Dombrowski. $65-125. MC VISA AX DC CB PC TC. 6 rooms, 3 with PB, 2 with FP. 2 suites. 1 conference room. Breakfast and evening snack included in rates. Types of meals: full breakfast, gourmet breakfast and early coffee/tea. Afternoon tea and banquet service available. Beds: QDT. Air conditioning, turndown service, ceiling fan, TV and VCR in room. Fax, copier, stables, bicycles, library and pet boarding on premises. Amusement parks, antiques, fishing, parks, shopping, downhill skiing, theater and watersports nearby.

"Your dedication to making your guests comfortable is above and beyond. You are tops in your field."

Certificate may be used: All year

Nantucket   L18

House of The Seven Gables

32 Cliff Rd
Nantucket, MA 02554-3644
(508)228-4706

Circa 1865. Originally the annex of the Sea Cliff Inn, one of the island's oldest hotels, this three-story Queen Anne Victorian inn offers 10 guest rooms. Beaches, bike rentals, museums, restaurants, shops and tennis courts are all found nearby. The guest rooms are furnished with king or queen beds and period antiques. Breakfast is served each morning in the guest rooms, and often include homemade coffee cake, muffins or  Portuguese rolls.

Innkeeper(s): Sue Walton. $65-175. MC VISA AX. 10 rooms, 8 with PB. Breakfast included in rates. Type of meal: continental breakfast. Beds: KQF. Cable TV on premises. Antiques, fishing, shopping, theater and watersports nearby.

"You have a beautiful home and one that makes everyone feel relaxed and at home."

Certificate may be used: Sept. 9-June 11, Sunday-Thursday

Ivy Lodge

2 Chester St
Nantucket, MA 02554-3505
(508)228-7755 Fax:(508)228-0305

Circa 1790. This 18th-century Colonial has spent much of its life serving the needs of travelers. In the 1800s, the home was used both as an inn and a museum. Today, the home serves as a living museum of American history. The home still includes its classic, center chimney, pine floors and fireplaces. Guest rooms are decorated with antiques and beds topped with ornate bedspreads and lacy canopies. Vases filled with flowers add extra color. The Brant Point lighthouse is within walking distance of the inn, and the beach is nearby.

Innkeeper(s): Tuge Roseatra. $75-160. 6 rooms. Breakfast included in rates. Type of meal: continental-plus breakfast.

Certificate may be used: Nov. 1-April 30; Oct. 1-30 and May 1-June 15. Excluding holidays and all local festival days and weekends.

Seven Sea Street Inn

7 Sea St
Nantucket, MA 02554-3545
(508)228-3577 Fax:(508)228-3578
E-mail: seast7@nantucket.net

Circa 1987. Romance flourishes at this country inn located in the heart of Nantucket. Fishnet canopy beds, hardwood floors and Colonial furnishings create a cozy, elegant ambiance. Spend breakfast in bed enjoying home-baked breads and muffins with fresh juice and fruits. Relax in the Jacuzzi or take in the view of Nantucket from the innís widow walk deck. Enjoy a stroll down the cobblestone Main Street as you head to the wharf. The village is abound with galleries, boutiques and restaurants.

Innkeeper(s): Matthew & Mary Parker. $75-185. MC VISA AX DS PC TC. 11 rooms, 9 with PB. 2 suites. Breakfast included in rates. Type of meal: continental-plus breakfast. Beds: Q. Air conditioning, TV and VCR in room. Fax, spa and library on premises. Antiques, fishing, parks, shopping, cross-country skiing, sporting events, golf, theater and watersports nearby.

Publicity: *New York Times, First Magazine, Nantucket Journal.*

"We loved your inn and had the most restful and relaxed time on Nantucket."

Certificate may be used: November-March, Sunday-Thursday inclusive, excluding Thanksgiving week, based upon availability.

Stumble Inne

109 Orange St
Nantucket, MA 02554-3947
(508)228-4482 Fax:(508)228-4752

Circa 1704. This Nantucket Island inn is appointed with fine antiques. Six of the inn's rooms are across the street from the Stumble Inne at the Starbuck House, an early 19th-century Nantucket "half-house." Rooms feature wide pine floors, antique beds, ceiling fans and Laura Ashley decor.

Innkeeper(s): Mary Kay & Mal Condon. $45-190. MC VISA AX TC. 15 rooms, 10 with PB. 2 suites. Breakfast and afternoon tea included in rates. Types of meals: continental-plus breakfast, full breakfast and early coffee/tea. Beds: Q. Air conditioning, ceiling fan, TV and VCR in room. Fax on premises. Antiques, fishing, shopping, theater and watersports nearby.

Publicity: *Innsider.*

"We realize much of our happiness was due to the warm hospitality that was a part of every day."

Certificate may be used: Oct. 1-May 15, Sunday-Thursday, excluding holiday periods.

The White House

48 Center St
Nantucket, MA 02554-3664
(508)228-4677

Circa 1800. For more than 40 years a favorite hostelry of visitors to Nantucket, The White House is situated ideally in the heart of the historic district and a short walk to the beach and ferry terminal. The first floor houses an antique shop. Guests stay in rooms on the second floor or a housekeeping apartment. Afternoon wine and cheese is served in the garden.

Innkeeper(s): Nina Hellman. $70-120. MC VISA AX. 3 rooms with PB. 1 suite. Breakfast included in rates. Type of meal: continental breakfast. Beds: Q. Antiques, fishing, shopping, theater and watersports nearby.

Certificate may be used: Weekdays, mid-April to mid-June and mid-September to mid-October. Anytime mid-October through December. Excludes holidays and special island events.

The Woodbox Inn
29 Fair St
Nantucket, MA 02554-3798
(508)228-0587

Circa 1709. Nantucket's oldest inn was built by Captain George Bunker. In 1711, the captain constructed an adjoining house. Eventually, the two houses were made into one by cutting into the sides of both. Guest rooms are furnished with period antiques. The inn's gourmet dining room features an Early American atmosphere with low-beamed ceilings and pine-paneled walls. The restaurant received an award of excellence from Wine Spectator magazine.

Innkeeper(s): Dexter Tutein. $140-230. PC TC. 9 rooms with PB, 6 with FP. 6 suites. Type of meal: full breakfast. Restaurant on premises. Beds: KQDT. Antiques, fishing, parks, shopping, theater and watersports nearby.

Location: Historic district.

Publicity: *Wharton Alumni, Cape Cod Life, Boston Magazine.*

"Best breakfast on the island, Yesterday's Island."

Certificate may be used: Midweek, from mid-October to Jan. 1 and May 1 to Memorial Day, holidays excluded.

Newburyport
B14

Clark Currier Inn
45 Green St
Newburyport, MA 01950-2646
(508)465-8363 (800)360-6582

Circa 1803. Once the home of shipbuilder Thomas March Clark, this three-story Federal-style inn provides gracious accommodations to visitors in the Northeast Massachusetts area. Visitors will enjoy

the inn's details added by Samuel McEntire, one of the nation's most celebrated home builders and woodcarvers. Breakfast is served in the garden room, with an afternoon tea offered in the parlor. The inn's grounds also boast a picturesque garden and gazebo. Parker River National Wildlife Refuge and Maudslay State Park are nearby.

Innkeeper(s): Mary & Bob Nolan. $65-145. MC VISA AX DS PC TC. 8 rooms with PB. Breakfast and afternoon tea included in rates. Type of meal: continental breakfast. Beds: QDT. Air conditioning, TV and VCR in room. Bicycles, library and child care on premises. Handicap access. Amusement parks, antiques, fishing, parks, shopping, downhill skiing, cross-country skiing, sporting events, theater and watersports nearby.

"We had a lovely stay in your B&B! We appreciated your hospitality!"

Certificate may be used: Space available, January-May.

Oak Bluffs
K16

Admiral Benbow Inn
81 New York Ave, PO Box 2488
Oak Bluffs, MA 02557
(508)693-6825 Fax:(508)693-1131

Circa 1880. This Victorian inn was built by a sea captain, and its design is highlighted by a cupola on the roof. The inn is owned by the Black Dog Tavern Company, and the firm completely restored the historic home. There are six guest rooms, all decorated in Victorian style with period furnishings. The inn is within walking distance of shops, restaurants and other attractions.

Innkeeper(s): Joyce E. Dodge. $75-175. MC VISA AX DS PC TC. 6 rooms with PB. Breakfast included in rates. Types of meals: continental-plus breakfast and early coffee/tea. Afternoon tea available. Beds: QD. Ceiling fan in room. Cable TV, fax, copier and child care on premises. Antiques, fishing, shopping, golf, theater and watersports nearby.

"Full of beauty, charm and relaxation."

Certificate may be used: Oct. 1-Dec. 31; April 1-May 15; Sunday-Friday.

The Oak Bluffs Inn
Circuit and Pequot Ave
Oak Bluffs, MA 02557
(508)693-7171 (800)955-6235

Circa 1870. A widow's walk and gingerbread touches were added to this graceful home to enhance the Victorian atmosphere already prevalent throughout the inn. Rooms are decorated in Victorian style with antiques. Home-baked breads and fresh fruits start off the day. After enjoying the many activities Martha's Vineyard has to offer, return for a scrumptious afternoon tea with scones, tea sandwiches and pastries. Oak Bluffs originally was named Cottage City, and is full of quaint, gingerbread homes to view. Nearby Circuit Avenue offers shopping, ice cream parlors, eateries and the nation's oldest carousel.

Innkeeper(s): Maryann Mattera. $100-200. MC VISA AX DC DS. 9 rooms with PB. Breakfast included in rates. Type of meal: continental-plus breakfast. Beds: QD. Air conditioning and ceiling fan in room. Cable TV on premises. Antiques, fishing, parks, shopping, golf, theater and watersports nearby.

Certificate may be used: Weekdays: Oct.1-June 15. Anytime: Oct. 15-April 30.

The Tucker Inn
46 Massasoit Ave, PO Box 2680
Oak Bluffs, MA 02557
(508)693-1045

Circa 1872. Located on a quiet residential park within walking distance of retail establishments and the town beach, this two-story Victorian

Stick/Shingle inn offers visitors to Martha's Vineyard a choice of suites and guest rooms with shared and private baths. The former doctor's residence boasts an attractive veranda that is ideal for reading or relaxing after a busy day exploring the island's many attractions, or a trip to nearby Chappaquiddick. Public transportation and boat lines are a five-minute walk from the inn.

Innkeeper(s): William Reagan. $55-135. MC VISA. 8 rooms, 5 with PB. 2 suites. Breakfast included in rates. Type of meal: continental breakfast. Beds: QDT. Ceiling fan in room. Cable TV and VCR on premises. Antiques, fishing, shopping, theater and watersports nearby.

Certificate may be used: Oct. 1-June 15.

Onset   I15

Onset Pointe Inn
9 Eagle Way, PO Box 1450
Onset, MA 02558
(508)295-8442 (800)356-6738 Fax:(508)295-5241

Circa 1880. This restored Victorian mansion is surrounded by the ocean on a sandy part of Onset Point. Its casually elegant decor is enhanced by sea views, sunlight, bright colors and florals. Spacious verandas, an enclosed circular sun porch and a bayside gazebo are available to guests. Accommodations are divided among the main house and two cottages. A full breakfast is served in a waterfront dining room. The inn received the National Trust first prize for preservation in their B&B category.

Innkeeper(s): Debi & Joe Lopes. $45-150. MC VISA AX DS PC TC. 15 rooms with PB. 6 suites. 2 cottages. 1 conference room. Breakfast included in rates. Beds: QDT. Cable TV, fax, copier and swimming on premises. Handicap access. Antiques, fishing, parks, shopping, theater and watersports nearby.

Location: Village of Onset, at the gateway to Cape Cod.

"We've found the B&B we've been looking for!"

Certificate may be used: Anytime, October. 16 - April 30. Sunday-Thursday, May 1-October. 15 excluding July and August.

Orleans   H19

The Farmhouse at Nauset Beach
163 Beach Rd
Orleans, MA 02653-2732
(508)255-6654

Circa 1870. Feel the intimacy of Orleans and capture the flavor of Cape Cod at this quiet country inn resting in a seashore setting. Rooms in this Greek Revival-style inn are comfortably furnished to depict their 19th-century past. Some rooms offer ocean views, and one includes a decorated fireplace. Nauset Beach is a short walk away. Spend a day

charter fishing in Cape Cod Bay or the Atlantic. To make your stay complete, your itinerary can include antiquing, shopping, exploring quiet country lanes or a day at the beach. The inn is open year-round.

Innkeeper(s): Dorothy Standish. $42-105. MC VISA PC. 8 rooms with PB, 1 with FP. Breakfast included in rates. Type of meal: continental-plus breakfast. Beds: KQD. Ceiling fan and TV in room. Antiques, fishing, shopping, theater and watersports nearby.

Certificate may be used: October to April.

Provincetown   G18

Lamplighter Guest House
26 Bradford St
Provincetown, MA 02657-1321
(508)487-2529 (800)263-6574

Circa 1800. From the top of a hill, this former sea captain's home affords a panoramic view of Cape Cod Bay. Two suites offer views of the bay, and two other rooms boast harbor views. The innkeepers also offer accommodations in a small cottage adjacent to the main house. A concierge service is available, and guests also can be shuttled to and from the airport or nearby docks.

Innkeeper(s): Steve Vittum & Brent Lawyer. $45-149. MC VISA AX TC. 11 rooms, 6 with PB. 1 suite. Breakfast and evening snack included in rates. Types of meals: continental breakfast and early coffee/tea. Beds: KQD. Air conditioning, turndown service, ceiling fan and TV in room. Copier on premises. Antiques, fishing, parks, shopping, theater and watersports nearby.

Certificate may be used: Sept. 15 to June 30, holidays and special events excluded, space available basis only. Advanced reservations required.

Watership Inn
7 Winthrop St
Provincetown, MA 02657-2116
(508)487-0094 (800)330-9413 Fax:(508)487-2797

Circa 1820. This stately manor was built as a home port for a Provincetown sea captain. During the past 10 years, it has been renovated and the original beamed ceilings and polished plank floors provide a background for the inn's antiques and simple decor. Guests enjoy the inn's sun decks and large yard, which offers volleyball and croquet sets.

Innkeeper(s): Roger Haas. $36-154. MC VISA AX DS. 16 rooms, 14 with PB. Breakfast included in rates. Type of meal: continental-plus breakfast. Beds: QDT. Bicycles on premises. Antiques and parks nearby.
Location: One-half block from Provincetown Harbor.
Publicity: *Boston "In".*

"We found your hospitality and charming inn perfect for our brief yet wonderful escape from Boston."

Certificate may be used: Oct. 1 through April 30.

Rehoboth   H12

Gilbert's Tree Farm B&B
30 Spring St
Rehoboth, MA 02769-2408
(508)252-6416
E-mail: jeanneg47@aol.com

Circa 1835. This country farmhouse sits on 100 acres of woodland that includes an award-winning tree farm. Cross-country skiing, hiking, and pony-cart rides are found right outside the door. If they choose to, guests can even help with the farm chores, caring for horses and gardening. A swimming pool is open during summer. Three antique-filled bedrooms share a second-floor sitting room. The nearby town of Rehoboth is 350 years old.
Innkeeper(s): Jeanne & Martin Gilbert. $45-50. PC TC. 3 rooms. Breakfast, afternoon tea and evening snack included in rates. Types of meals: full breakfast and early coffee/tea. Beds: KDT. VCR, copier, swimming, stables, bicycles, library and pet boarding on premises. Antiques, fishing, parks, shopping, cross-country skiing, sporting events, theater and watersports nearby.

Location: Twelve miles east of Providence.
Publicity: *Attleboro Sun Chronicle, Country, Somerset Spectator, Country Gazette, Pawtucket Times.*

"This place has become my second home. Thank you for the family atmosphere of relaxation, fun, spontaneity and natural surroundings."

Certificate may be used: Nov. 1 through April 30, anytime.

Rockport   C15

Sally Webster Inn
34 Mount Pleasant St
Rockport, MA 01966-1713
(508)546-9251

Circa 1832. William Choate left this pre-Civil War home to be divided by his nine children. Sally Choate Webster, the ninth child, was to receive several first-floor rooms and the attic chamber, but ended up owning the entire home. Innkeepers Tiffany and David Muhlenberg have filled the gracious home with antiques and period reproductions, which complement the original pumpkin pine

floors, antique door moldings and six fireplaces. Shops, restaurants, the beach and the rocky coast are all within three blocks of the inn. Whale watching, kayaking, antique shop, music festivals, island tours and museums are among the myriad of nearby attractions. In addition to these, Salem is just 15 miles away, and Boston is a 35-mile drive.
Innkeeper(s): Tiffany Traynor-Muhlenberg. $55-94. MC VISA DS PC TC. 8 rooms with PB. Breakfast included in rates. Type of meal: continental-plus breakfast. Beds: DT. Air conditioning in room.

"All that a bed and breakfast should be."

Certificate may be used: Sunday-Friday, November-March

Tuck Inn
17 High St
Rockport, MA 01966-1644
(508)546-7260 (800)789-7260
E-mail: tuckinn@shore.net

Circa 1790. Two recent renovations have served to make this charming Colonial inn all the more enticing. Period antiques and paintings by local artists are featured throughout the spacious inn. A favorite gathering spot is the living room with its fireplace, wide pine floors, tasteful furnishings and a piano available for guest use.

Buffet breakfasts feature homemade breads, muffins, cakes and scones, granola accompanied by fresh fruit and yogurt. Guests may take a dip in the swimming pool or at local beaches. Within easy walking distance are the many art galleries, restaurants and shops of Bearskin Neck. A nearby train station offers convenient access to Boston.

Innkeeper(s): Liz & Scott Wood. $55-115. MC VISA PC TC. 11 rooms with PB. 1 suite. Breakfast included in rates. Types of meals: continental-plus breakfast and early coffee/tea. Afternoon tea available. Beds: KQDT. Air conditioning, ceiling fan and TV in room. VCR, swimming, bicycles and library on premises. Antiques, fishing, parks, shopping, downhill skiing, cross-country skiing, sporting events, theater and watersports nearby.

Publicity: *Fall River Herald News, North Shore News, Cape Ann Weekly.*

"Wonderful people, lovely scenery, and great food, all good for the soul! Your hospitality and service was wonderful and we look forward to returning very soon!"

Certificate may be used: Nov. 1-April 30, Sunday through Thursday.

Salem   D14

The Salem Inn

7 Summer St
Salem, MA 01970-3315
(508)741-0680 (800)446-2995 Fax:(508)744-8924

Circa 1834. This picturesque Federal-style inn is located in the heart of Salem's historic district, which features galleries, antiques, museums and the wharf and harbor. Many of the spacious guest rooms feature Jacuzzi tubs, fireplaces and canopy beds. Families will appreciate the two-room suites, which include kitchenettes. The dining area, with its brick walls and cozy atmosphere, is the perfect place to enjoy a light breakfast.

Innkeeper(s): Richard & Diane Pabich. $99-175. MC VISA AX DC CB DS TC. 33 rooms with PB, 15 with FP. 5 suites. 1 conference room. Breakfast included in rates. Type of meal: early coffee/tea. Restaurant on premises. Beds: KQT. Air conditioning and TV in room. Fax on premises. Antiques, fishing, parks, shopping, sporting events, theater and watersports nearby.

Location: Historic downtown.

Publicity: *New York Times, Boston Sunday Globe.*

"Delightful, charming. Our cup of tea."

Certificate may be used: Jan. 2-April 1, exclusive of holidays and special events

Sandwich   I16

Captain Ezra Nye House

152 Main St
Sandwich, MA 02563-2232
(508)888-6142 (800)388-2278 Fax:(508)833-2897
E-mail: captnye@aol.com

Circa 1829. Captain Ezra Nye built this house after a record-shattering Halifax to Boston run, and the stately Federal-style house reflects the opulence and romance of the clipper ship era. Hand-stenciled walls and museum-quality antiques decorate the

interior. Within walking distance are the Doll Museum, the Glass Museum, restaurants, shops, the famous Heritage Plantation, the beach and marina.

Innkeeper(s): Elaine & Harry Dickson. $85-110. MC VISA AX DS PC TC. 6 rooms with PB, 1 with FP. 1 suite. Breakfast included in rates. Types of meals: full breakfast, gourmet breakfast and early coffee/tea. Beds: QDT. Cable TV, VCR, fax and library on premises. Antiques, fishing, parks, shopping, theater and watersports nearby.

Location: In the heart of Sandwich Village, the oldest town on Cape Cod.

Publicity: *Glamour, Innsider, Cape Cod Life, Toronto Life, Yankee.*

"The prettiest room and most beautiful home we have been to. We had a wonderful time."

Certificate may be used: Sunday through Thursday, Nov. 1-April 30.

The Dunbar House

1 Water St
Sandwich, MA 02563-2303
(508)833-2485 Fax:(508)833-4713
E-mail: dunbar@capecod.net

Circa 1741. This Colonial-style house overlooks a pond in the charming setting of Cape Cod's oldest town. The three guest rooms are appointed in Colonial style, and all boast a view of the pond. The Ennerdale rooms has a four-poster bed. Each morning, guests are pampered with a homemade breakfast, and afternoon tea is served in the innkeeper's English tea shop. The inn is within walking distance to many historic sites and the beach.

Innkeeper(s): Nancy Iribarren & David Bell. $65-95. MC VISA PC TC. 3 rooms with PB, 3 with FP. Breakfast and afternoon tea included in rates. Types of meals: continental breakfast, continental-plus breakfast, full breakfast, gourmet breakfast and early coffee/tea. Lunch available. Restaurant on premises. Beds: QT. VCR, fax, copier, bicycles and library on premises. Antiques, fishing, parks, shopping, theater and watersports nearby.

Certificate may be used: Sunday-Thursday, Nov. 1-April 30.

The Summer House

158 Main St
Sandwich, MA 02563-2232
(508)888-4991 (800)241-3609

Circa 1835. The Summer House is a handsome Greek Revival in a setting of historic homes and public buildings. (Hiram Dillaway, one of the owners, was a famous mold maker for the Boston & Sandwich Glass Company.) The house is fully restored and decorated with antiques and hand-stitched quilts. Four of  the guest rooms have fireplaces. The breakfast room and parlor have black marble fireplaces. The sunporch overlooks an old-fashioned perennial garden, antique rose bushes, and a 70-year-old rhododendron hedge. The inn is open year-round.

Innkeeper(s): Marjorie & Kevin Huelsman. $65-95. MC VISA AX DS PC TC. 5 rooms with PB, 4 with FP. Breakfast and afternoon tea included in rates. Types of meals: full breakfast, gourmet breakfast and early coffee/tea. Beds: KQT. Library on premises. Antiques, fishing, parks, shopping, cross-country skiing, theater and watersports nearby.

Location: Center of village, Cape Cod.

Publicity: *Country Living, Boston, Cape Cod Times.*

"An absolutely gorgeous house and a super breakfast. I wish I could've stayed longer! Came for one night, stayed for three! Marvelous welcome."

Certificate may be used: Sunday-Thursday, November-March.

Sandwich (Cape Cod) *I16*

Isaiah Jones Homestead

165 Main St
Sandwich (Cape Cod), MA 02563-2283
(508)888-9115 (800)526-1625

Circa 1849. This fully restored Victorian homestead is situated on Main Street in the village. Eleven-foot ceilings and two bay windows are features of the Gathering Room. Guest rooms contain antique Victorian bedsteads such as the half-canopy bed of burled birch in the Deming Jarves Room,

where there is an over-sized whirlpool tub and a fireplace. Candlelight breakfasts are highlighted with the house speciality, freshly baked cornbread, inspired by nearby Sandwich Grist Mill.

Innkeeper(s): Jan & Doug Klapper. $75-155. MC VISA AX DS PC TC. 5 rooms with PB, 3 with FP. Breakfast and afternoon tea included in rates. Types of meals: full breakfast and early coffee/tea. Beds: QDT. Cable TV on premises. Antiques, fishing, parks, shopping, theater and watersports nearby.

Publicity: *Cape Cod Life, New England Travel, National Geographic Travel.*

"Excellent! The room was a delight, the food wonderful, the hospitality warm & friendly. One of the few times the reality exceeded the expectation."

Certificate may be used: Sunday-Thursday nights, Nov. 1-March 31.

Sheffield *F2*

Staveleigh House

59 Main St, PO 608
Sheffield, MA 01257
(413)229-2129

Circa 1821. The Reverend Bradford, minister of Old Parish Congregational Church, the oldest church in the Berkshires, built this home for his family. Afternoon tea is served and the inn is especially favored for its four-course breakfasts and gracious hospitality. Located next to the town green, the house is in a historic district in the midst of several fine antique shops. It is also near Tanglewood, skiing and all Berkshire attractions.

Innkeeper(s): Dorothy Marosy & Marion Whitman. $80-105. TC. 5 rooms, 2 with PB. Breakfast and afternoon tea included in rates. Types of meals: full breakfast and early coffee/tea. Beds: KQDT. Turndown service and ceiling fan in room. Handicap access. Antiques, fishing, parks, shopping, downhill skiing, cross-country skiing, theater and watersports nearby.

Publicity: *Los Angeles Times, Boston Globe.*

"Our annual needlework workshops are so much fun, we have a waiting list to join our group."

Certificate may be used: Sunday-Thursday, year-round; any day November-March, except holidays.

South Deerfield D6

Deerfield B&B - The Yellow Gabled House

111 N Main St
South Deerfield, MA 01373-1026
(413)665-4922

Circa 1800. Huge maple trees shade the yard of this historic house, four miles from historic Deerfield and one mile from Route 91. Decorated with antiques and old lace, two of the guest rooms have their own cozy sofa. The battle of Bloody Brook Massacre in 1675 occurred at this site, now landscaped with perennial English gardens.

Innkeeper(s): Edna Stahelek. $70-105. 3 rooms, 1 with PB. Breakfast included in rates. Types of meals: full breakfast, gourmet breakfast and early coffee/tea. Beds: QDT. Air conditioning, ceiling fan and TV in room. VCR on premises. Antiques, fishing, shopping, downhill skiing, cross-country skiing, sporting events and theater nearby.

Location: One mile from crossroads of I-91, Rt 116 & Rts 5 & 10.

Publicity: *Recorder, Boston Globe.*

"We are still speaking of that wonderful weekend and our good fortune in finding you."

Certificate may be used: December, January and February.

South Dennis I18

Captain Nickerson Inn

333 Main St
South Dennis, MA 02660-3643
(508)398-5966 (800)282-1619

Circa 1828. This Queen Anne Victorian inn is located in the mid-Cape area. Guests can relax on the front porch with white wicker rockers and tables. The guest rooms are decorated with period four-poster or white iron queen beds and hand-woven or Oriental-style rugs. The dining room has a fireplace and a stained-glass picture window. The Cape Cod bike Rail Trail, which is more than 20 miles long, is less than a mile away.

Innkeeper(s): Pat & Dave York. $65-95. MC VISA DS PC. 5 rooms, 3 with PB. Breakfast included in rates. Type of meal: full breakfast. Beds: QDT. Air conditioning and ceiling fan in room. Cable TV, VCR, fax and

bicycles on premises. Antiques, fishing, parks, shopping, theater and watersports nearby.

"Your inn is great!"

Certificate may be used: Nov. 15-May 20; midweek October and June.

South Yarmouth I18

Captain Farris House B&B

308 Main St
South Yarmouth, MA 02664-4530
(508)760-2818 (800)350-9477 Fax:(508)398-1262

Circa 1845. Listed in the National Register, this inn offers accommodations at both the Captain Allen Farris House and the adjacent Elisha Jenkins House. Eight rooms are found at the Captain's house, with two suites next door. The architectural stylings are Greek Revival and French Second Empire. Breakfasts are served either in the dining room, on the terrace or in the inn's courtyard. Be sure to inquire about picnic lunches, ideal for an afternoon of exploring the Cape's many attractions. Two blocks away is the Bass River.

Innkeeper(s): Scott Toney. $75-225. MC VISA AX. 10 rooms with PB. 4 suites. Breakfast included in rates. Type of meal: full breakfast. Afternoon tea, dinner, picnic lunch, lunch, gourmet lunch and catering service available. Beds: KQT. Turndown service and TV in room. Antiques, fishing, shopping, theater and watersports nearby.

Publicity: *Register.*

"As always, a wonderful, relaxing stay! Thanks for your warmth and hospitality."

Certificate may be used: Nov. 15-April 15. Holiday weekends with purchase of two nights. Limited number of rooms available.

Stockbridge E2

Arbor Rose B&B

8 Yale Hill, Box 114
Stockbridge, MA 01262
(413)298-4744

Circa 1810. This New England farmhouse overlooks an 1800s mill, pond and gardens with the mountains as a backdrop. During the winter months, guests often relax in front of the wood stove in the inn's cozy front parlor. Four-poster beds, antiques and rural-themed paintings decorate the rooms. The inn's 19th-century mill now houses guests. The mill was one of five in the vicinity and was still in operation as late as the 1930s. The Berkshire Theatre, open for the summer season, is across the street. The Norman Rockwell Museum, Tanglewood Music Festival, ski areas and antique, outlet and specialty shops are all within a seven-mile radius.

Innkeeper(s): Christina Alsop. $85-175. MC VISA AX PC TC. 5 rooms with PB. 1 conference room. Breakfast included in rates. Types of meals: full breakfast, gourmet breakfast and early coffee/tea. Beds: KQT. Air conditioning and ceiling fan in room. Antiques, parks, shopping, downhill skiing, cross-country skiing and theater nearby.

Location: One-half mile from center of Stockbridge.

Publicity: *Yankee Traveler.*

"If houses really do exude the spirit of events and feelings stored from their history, it explains why a visitor feels warmth and joy from the first turn up the driveway."

Certificate may be used: November-May, midweek.

The Inn at Stockbridge
PO Box 618
Stockbridge, MA 01262-0618
(413)298-3337 Fax:(413)298-3406

Circa 1906. Giant maples shade the drive leading to this Southern-style Georgian Colonial with its impressive pillared entrance. Located on 12 acres, the grounds include a reflecting pool, a fountain, meadows and woodland as well as wide vistas of the rolling hillsides. The guest rooms feature antiques and handsome 18th-century  reproductions. Breakfast is graciously presented with fine china, silver and linens.

Innkeeper(s): Alice & Lenny Schiller. $85-235. MC VISA AX PC TC. 8 rooms with PB. 2 suites. Breakfast and evening snack included in rates. Types of meals: full breakfast, gourmet breakfast and early coffee/tea. Beds: DT. Air conditioning in room. Cable TV, VCR, fax, copier, swimming and library on premises. Antiques, fishing, parks, shopping, downhill skiing, cross-country skiing, theater and watersports nearby.

Publicity: *Vogue, New York, New York Daily News, Country Inns Northeast, Arts & Antiques.*

"Classy & comfortable."

Certificate may be used: Sunday-Thursday, Nov. 1-May 15 excluding holidays.

Sturbridge   F8

Commonwealth Cottage
11 Summit Ave
Sturbridge, MA 01566-1225
(508)347-7708

Circa 1873. This 16-room Queen Anne Victorian house, on an acre near the Quinebaug River, is just a few minutes from Old Sturbridge Village. Both the dining room and parlor have fireplaces. The Baroque theme of the Sal Raciti room makes it one of the guest favorites and it features a queen mahogany bed. Breakfast may be offered on the

gazebo porch or in the formal dining room. It includes a variety of homemade specialties, such as freshly baked breads and cakes.

Innkeeper(s): Robert & Wiebke Gilbert. $85-145. PC TC. 5 rooms, 4 with PB. Types of meals: full breakfast and early coffee/tea. Evening snack available. Beds: QDT. Ceiling fan in room. Library on premises. Antiques, fishing, parks, shopping, theater and watersports nearby.

Publicity: *Long Island Newsday, Villager.*

"Your home is so warm and welcoming we feel as though we've stepped back in time. Our stay here has helped to make the wedding experience extra special!"

Certificate may be used: December-April, Sunday-Thursday, holiday weekends excluded.

Sturbridge Country Inn
PO Box 60, 530 Main St
Sturbridge, MA 01566-0060
(508)347-5503 Fax:(508)347-5319

Circa 1840. Shaded by an old silver maple, this classic Greek Revival house boasts a two-story columned entrance. The attached carriage house now serves as the lobby and displays the original post-and-beam construction and exposed rafters. All guest rooms have individual fireplaces and whirlpool tubs. They are appointed gracefully in reproduction colonial furnishings, including queen-size, four-posters. A patio and gazebo are favorite summertime retreats.

Innkeeper(s): Patricia Affenito. $59-159. MC VISA AX DS PC TC. 9 rooms with PB, 9 with FP. 1 suite. 1 conference room. Breakfast included in rates. Types of meals: continental breakfast and early coffee/tea. Room service available. Restaurant on premises. Beds: KQ. Air conditioning, ceiling fan, TV and VCR in room. Fax, copier and spa on premises. Antiques, fishing, parks, shopping, downhill skiing, cross-country skiing, theater and watersports nearby.

Location: Near Old Sturbridge Village.

Publicity: *Southbridge Evening News, Worcester Telegram & Gazette.*

"Best lodging I've ever seen."

Certificate may be used: November-August, Sunday-Thursday

Ware
E7

The Wildwood Inn
121 Church St
Ware, MA 01082-1203
(413)967-7798 (800)860-8098

Circa 1880. This yellow Victorian has a wrap-around porch and a beveled-glass front door. American primitive antiques include a collection of New England cradles and heirloom quilts, a saddle-

maker's bench, and a spinning wheel. The inn's two acres are dotted with maple, chestnut and apple trees. Through the woods you'll find a river.
Innkeeper(s): Fraidell Fenster & Richard Watson. $50-85. MC VISA AX DC PC TC. 9 rooms, 7 with PB. 1 suite. 2 conference rooms. Breakfast and afternoon tea included in rates. Types of meals: full breakfast and early coffee/tea. Banquet service, catering service and catered breakfast available. Beds: KQDT. Air conditioning, turndown service and ceiling fan in room. Bicycles, tennis and library on premises. Handicap access. Amusement parks, antiques, fishing, parks, shopping, downhill skiing, cross-country skiing, sporting events and theater nearby.
Publicity: *Boston Globe, National Geographic Traveler, Country, Worcester Telegram-Gazette.*

"Excellent accommodations, not only in rooms, but in the kind and thoughtful way you treat your guests. We'll be back!"
Certificate may be used: Nov. 1-June 30, excluding Brimfield Flea Market weeks. Sunday through Thursday.

Wareham
I15

The Cranberry Rose B&B
105 High St
Wareham, MA 02571-2053
(508)295-5665 (800)269-5665

Circa 1903. Innkeeper Chris Makepeace's family built this sturdy, New England home. The house eventually was sold to another family, but Chris and wife, Sue, bought the home several years ago and renovated it into a bed & breakfast. Chris and Sue

also have continued the Makepeace tradition as cranberry farmers. During the harvest, the two will prepare picnics and tours of their cranberry bogs. Sue has created several cranberry recipes, some of which she serves in the afternoon along with wine and sherry. Her recipe for Cranberry Bars was featured in Bon Appetit. The home is decorated in a cozy, country style with quilts, ceiling fans and antiques from an 18th-century boarding house.
Innkeeper(s): Sue & Chris Makepeace. $60-75. MC VISA PC TC. 3 rooms with PB. Breakfast and afternoon tea included in rates. Type of meal: early coffee/tea. Beds: KQDT. Air conditioning and ceiling fan in room. Cable TV, VCR, fax, copier and bicycles on premises. Antiques, fishing, parks, shopping, cross-country skiing, sporting events, theater and watersports nearby.

"My family found the Cranberry Rose to be the finest and very charming."
Certificate may be used: April 1-Dec. 31, Sunday-Friday.

Mulberry B&B
257 High St
Wareham, MA 02571-1407
(508)295-0684 Fax:(508)291-2909

Circa 1847. This former blacksmith's house is in the historic district of town and has been featured on the local garden club house tour. Frances, a former school teacher, has decorated the guest rooms in a country style with antiques. A deck, shaded by a tall mulberry tree, looks out to the back garden.

Innkeeper(s): Frances Murphy. $50-65. MC VISA AX DS PC TC. 3 rooms. Breakfast included in rates. Type of meal: full breakfast. Afternoon tea available. Beds: KDT. Air conditioning and turndown service in room. Cable TV and VCR on premises. Antiques, fishing, parks, shopping, cross-country skiing, sporting events, theater and watersports nearby.
Publicity: *Brockton Enterprise, Wareham Courier.*

"Thank you for your hospitality. The muffins were delicious."
Certificate may be used: Sunday through Thursday, May through October, anytime November through April.

West Harwich
I18

The Gingerbread House
141 Division St
West Harwich, MA 02671-1005
(508)432-1901 (800)788-1901

Circa 1883. This rambling Queen Anne Victorian is decked with ornate, gingerbread trim and gables. The innkeepers, of Polish descent, have added European flavor to their inn with a collection of Polish art, crystal and crafts. Aside from the scrumptious breakfasts, the innkeepers offer dinner service at the inn's restaurant. Proper afternoon teas are served in the Tea Room, which is located in the Carriage House. Sandwiches, freshly baked goods and scones are accompanied by Devon clotted cream and a selection of teas. The inn is near many of Cape Cod's shops and restaurants.
Innkeeper(s): Stacia & Les Kostecki. $45-105. MC VISA TC. 5 suites, 1 with FP. 1 conference room. Breakfast and afternoon tea included in rates. Types of meals: continental breakfast, continental-plus breakfast, full breakfast, gourmet breakfast and early coffee/tea. Dinner, evening snack, picnic lunch, gourmet lunch and room service available. Restaurant on premises. Beds: Q. Ceiling fan and TV in room. VCR and child care on premises. Handicap access. Antiques, fishing, parks, shopping and theater nearby.
Certificate may be used: Sept. 17-Dec. 10, Sunday-Saturday; May 1-Sept. 15, Sunday-Thursday, except for holidays.

West Stockbridge
E2

Card Lake Inn
PO Box 38
West Stockbridge, MA 01266-0038
(413)232-0272 Fax:(413)232-0272

Circa 1880. Located in the center of town, this Colonial Revival inn features a popular local restaurant on the premises. Norman Rockwell is said to have frequented its tavern. Stroll around historic West Stockbridge then enjoy the inn's deck cafe with its flower boxes and view of the sculpture garden of an art gallery across the street. Original lighting, hardwood floors and antiques are features of the inn. Chesterwood and Tanglewood are within easy driving distance.
Innkeeper(s): Ed & Lisa Robbins. $60-140. MC VISA AX DS. 8 rooms. Breakfast included in rates. Types of meals: continental breakfast and early coffee/tea. Restaurant on premises. Beds: KQ. Air conditioning and ceiling fan in room. Cable TV and VCR on premises. Amusement parks, antiques, shopping and sporting events nearby.
Certificate may be used: Anytime excluding weekends in June, July, August and October.

Marble Inn
4 Stockbridge Rd
West Stockbridge, MA 01266-0268
(413)232-7092

Circa 1835. This Georgian Colonial was built as the city's marble quarries and limestone works were expanding. Rooms are decorated with an impressive collection of antiques. The innkeepers have topped the restored wood floors with handmade rugs. The country-style guest rooms feature furnishings such as a pencil four-poster bed or an antique white iron bed. One room includes a bath with a clawfoot tub. As a night cap, guests are presented with sherry and cookies. Breakfasts include a wide variety of juices, homemade breads, fresh fruit and a selection of gourmet entrees. Guests might select a specialty omelet or perhaps eggnog French toast. With advance notice and for an extra charge, the

innkeepers will prepare a wonderful, gourmet picnic basket. The inn is close to museums, Tanglewood, the Shaker Village, antique shops and much more.
Innkeeper(s): Yvonne & Joe Kopper. $85-135. MC VISA AX DS PC TC. 4 rooms with PB, 1 with FP. Breakfast included in rates. Type of meal: gourmet breakfast. Picnic lunch available. Beds: QD. Air conditioning in room. Antiques, fishing, downhill skiing, cross-country skiing, theater and watersports nearby.
Certificate may be used: Nov. 1-May 25, not including holidays.

West Yarmouth
I17

Manor House
57 Maine Ave
West Yarmouth, MA 02673-5816
(508)771-3433 (800)962-6679

Circa 1920. This bed & breakfast is located on Cape Cod's south shore overlooking Lewis Bay. The beach and a boat ramp are within walking distance. The quiet neighborhood also is near whale watching, golf and fine dining. Take a ferry to one of the islands or just relax in the comfort of your own room. The fireplaced sitting room is a great place to finish a book.

Innkeeper(s): Rick & Liz Latshaw. $58-108. MC VISA AX PC TC. 6 rooms with PB. Breakfast and afternoon tea included in rates. Types of meals: continental-plus breakfast and early coffee/tea. Beds: QD. Air conditioning and turndown service in room. Cable TV, VCR and library on premises. Antiques, fishing, parks, shopping, theater and watersports nearby.

"An experience I am anxious to repeat."

Certificate may be used: Anytime between Nov. 1-May 14.

Woods Hole   J15

The Marlborough B&B
PO Box 238
Woods Hole, MA 02543-0238
(508)548-6218 (800)320-2322 Fax:(508)457-7519

Circa 1942. This is a faithful reproduction of a Cape-style cottage complete with picket fence and rambling roses. An English paddle-tennis court and swimming pool are popular spots in summer. In winter, breakfast is served beside a roaring fire. The inn is the closest bed & breakfast to the ferries to Martha's Vineyard and Nantucket.

Innkeeper(s): Al Hammond. $65-125. MC VISA AX PC. 5 rooms, 6 with PB. 1 cottage. Breakfast included in rates. Types of meals: gourmet breakfast and early coffee/tea. Beds: QD. Air conditioning in room. Cable TV, fax, swimming and tennis on premises. Antiques, fishing, shopping, theater and watersports nearby.

Location: Near Falmouth historic district.

Publicity: *Cape Cod Life.*

"Our stay at the Marlborough was a little bit of heaven."

Certificate may be used: Nov. 1-May 15, Sunday-Thursday.

Yarmouth Port   I17

Olde Captain's Inn on the Cape
101 Main St Rt 6A
Yarmouth Port, MA 02675-1709
(508)362-4496 (888)407-7161

Circa 1835. Located in the historic district and on Captain's Mile, this house is in the National Register. It is decorated in a traditional style, with coordinated wallpapers and carpets, and there are two suites that include kitchens and living rooms. Apple trees, blackberries and raspberries grow on the acre of grounds and often contribute to the breakfast menus. There is a summer veranda overlooking the property. Good restaurants are within walking distance.

Innkeeper(s): Sven Tilly. $40-100. 3 rooms, 1 with PB. 2 suites. Breakfast included in rates. Type of meal: continental-plus breakfast. Beds: KQD. TV in room. Antiques, fishing, shopping, sporting events, theater and watersports nearby.

Location: Cape Cod.

Certificate may be used: Anytime, Nov. 1-June 1. Sunday through Thursday, June 1-Nov. 1. Excludes holidays.

Michigan

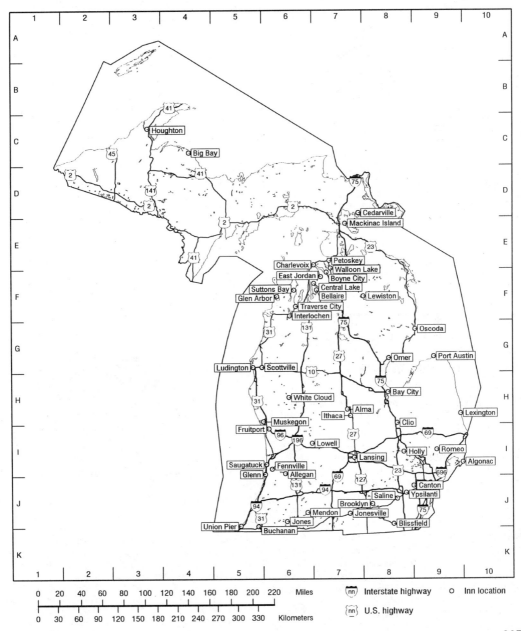

0 20 40 60 80 100 120 140 160 180 200 220 Miles

0 30 60 90 120 150 180 210 240 270 300 330 Kilometers

(nn) Interstate highway   ○ Inn location

(nn) U.S. highway

Algonac 19

Linda's Lighthouse Inn
5965 Pointe Tremble Rd Box 828
Algonac, MI 48001-4229
(810)794-2992 Fax:(810)794-2992

Circa 1909. Overlooking Dickerson Island, on the north branch of the St. Clair River, is this two-story Colonial inn, which once aided bootleggers who brought in liquor from Canada during Prohibition. Guests who arrive by boat and use the inn's 100 feet of dockage will have transportation to restaurants provided for them. Guests 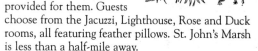 choose from the Jacuzzi, Lighthouse, Rose and Duck rooms, all featuring feather pillows. St. John's Marsh is less than a half-mile away.

Innkeeper(s): Ron & Linda (Russell) Yetsko. $75-125. MC VISA AX TC. 4 rooms with PB. Breakfast and evening snack included in rates. Types of meals: gourmet breakfast and early coffee/tea. Picnic lunch available. Beds: QD. Air conditioning, turndown service and ceiling fan in room. Cable TV, VCR, copier and bicycles on premises. Antiques, fishing, parks, shopping, cross-country skiing and watersports nearby.

Certificate may be used: From May 1-Oct. 31, Monday-Thursday, no holidays.

Allegan 16

Castle In The Country
340 M 40 S
Allegan, MI 49010-9609
(616)673-8054

Enjoy refreshing country views from every window at this three-story Victorian, which was built by a Civil War captain. Each of the guest quarters offers something special. The Bittersweet, which has a chandelier and private sitting area, boasts a view of Bittersweet Mountain. The Rose Gazebo is located in the home's turret. This unique, round room includes white, wicker furnishings and flowery linens. Each guest room is decorated with candles and fresh flowers. Homemade breads and pastries accompany the full, gourmet breakfasts, which can be enjoyed in the privacy of your bedchamber or in the formal dining room. The innkeepers host special events such as murder-mystery weekends and multi-day bicycle tours.

Innkeeper(s): Ruth Boren. $65-95. MC VISA. 4 rooms. Breakfast included in rates. Type of meal: full breakfast.

Certificate may be used: Sunday-Thursday, Nov. 1-April 20 (excluding holiday weekends).

Delano Inn
302 Cutler St
Allegan, MI 49010-1210
(616)673-2609

Circa 1863. This Italian Provincial mansion, surrounded by a wrought-iron fence, is listed in the National Register of Historic Places. The inn offers cozy sitting rooms and a summer porch. There are stenciled floors, lace curtains, marble fireplaces, crystal chandeliers, a spiral staircase, antique furnishings and European feather beds.

Innkeeper(s): Robert Ashley. $55-85. MC VISA. 5 rooms. 1 conference room. Breakfast included in rates. Type of meal: continental-plus breakfast. Beds: QDT. Air conditioning and ceiling fan in room. Cable TV and VCR on premises. Amusement parks, antiques, shopping, downhill skiing, cross-country skiing and theater nearby.

Publicity: *Allegan County News & Gazette.*

"The world would be a much more peaceful place if we all celebrated hospitality the way you folks do."

Certificate may be used: Jan. 2 through March 30.

Winchester Inn
524 Marshall St M-89
Allegan, MI 49010-1632
(616)673-3620 (800)582-5694

Circa 1864. This neo-Italian Renaissance mansion was built of double-layer brick and has been restored to its original beauty. Surrounded by a unique, hand-poured iron fence, the inn is decorated with period antiques, including antique toys and trains. The innkeeper's love for Christmas and other holidays is evident. Many christmas decorations, includ-

ing a 10-foot Victorian tree remain up throughout the year. The tree in the dining room is decorated for whatever holiday is near. For instance, around Halloween, pumpkins and gourds decorate the tree. Three guest rooms are decorated in a Christmas theme with trees, and another guest room's decor rotates in honor of the most current holiday.

Innkeeper(s): Denise & Dave Ferber. $70-90. MC VISA AX PC TC. 4 rooms with PB. Breakfast included in rates. Types of meals: continental-plus breakfast, full breakfast and early coffee/tea. Beds: KQD. Ceiling fan in room. Cable TV on premises. Antiques, fishing, parks, shopping, downhill skiing, cross-country skiing, sporting events, theater and watersports nearby.

Location: Near Grand Rapids, Kalamazoo, Holland, Saugatuck and Lake Michigan State Forest.

Publicity: *Architectural Digest, Home and Away, Midwest Living, Detroit Free Press, Cleveland Plain Dealer, Grand Rapids Press.*

"This is one of Michigan's loveliest country inns."

Certificate may be used: Sunday through Thursday, April through October. Any day November through March. Not during local festivals.

Alma   H7

Saravilla
633 N State St
Alma, MI 48801-1640
(517)463-4078

Circa 1894. This 11,000-square-foot Dutch Colonial home with its Queen Anne influences was built as a magnificent wedding gift for lumber baron Ammi W. Wright's only surviving child, Sara. Wright spared no expense building this mansion for his daughter, and the innkeepers have spared nothing in restoring the home to its former prominence. The foyer and dining room boast imported English oak woodwork. The foyer's hand-painted canvas wallcoverings and the ballroom's embossed wallpaper come from France. The home still features original leaded-glass windows, built-in bookcases, window seats and light fixtures. In 1993, the innkeepers added a sunroom with a hot tub that overlooks a formal garden. The full, formal breakfast includes such treats as homemade granola, freshly made coffeecakes, breads, muffins and a mix of entrees.

Innkeeper(s): Linda and Jon Darrow. $55-110. MC VISA DS PC TC. 7 rooms with PB, 3 with FP. Breakfast and afternoon tea included in rates. Type of meal: full breakfast. Room service available. Beds: KQDT. Antiques, fishing, cross-country skiing and theater nearby.

Location: Twenty minutes from Michigan's largest casino.

Publicity: *Morning Sun, Saginaw News, Sault Sunday.*

"I suggest we stay longer next time. We are looking forward to that visit."

Certificate may be used: Jan. 1-Dec. 31, Sunday-Friday.

Bay City   H8

Clements Inn
1712 Center Ave M-25
Bay City, MI 48708-6122
(517)894-4600 (800)442-4605 Fax:(517)895-8535

Circa 1886. The amber-paned windows and oak ceilings of this three-story Queen Anne Victorian inn are just a few of its impressive features. Built by William Clements, the home joined a number of other impressive estates on Center Avenue, most of which were owned by lumber barons. The inn's

well-appointed guest rooms are named for famous authors or fictional characters, continuing a strong tradition started by Clements, a collector of rare books. A winding staircase, original gas lighting fixtures and hand-carved woodwork have impressed many visitors.

Innkeeper(s): Brian & Karen Hepp. $70-175. MC VISA AX DC DS TC. 6 rooms with PB. 3 suites. Breakfast and evening snack included in rates. Types of meals: continental-plus breakfast and early coffee/tea. Beds: KQD. Air conditioning, TV and VCR in room. Fax on premises. Handicap access. Antiques, fishing, parks, shopping, downhill skiing, cross-country skiing and theater nearby.

Certificate may be used: Sunday-Thursday, Nov. 1-April 30.

Stonehedge Inn
924 Center Ave M-25
Bay City, MI 48708-6118
(517)894-4342

Circa 1889. An exquisite oak staircase greets guests as they enter this 19th-century Tudor-style home. Marble fireplaces and original brass light fixtures add an elegant flair to the common rooms. The home was built by a lumber baron and many of the original features are still in operation including speaking tubes and a dumb-waiter. Spend an afternoon cruising the riverwalk or take a look at the historic district and museum.

Innkeeper(s): Ruth Koerber. $75-85. MC VISA AX DS PC TC. 7 rooms. 1 conference room. Breakfast included in rates. Types of meals: continental breakfast, continental-plus breakfast, full breakfast and early coffee/tea. Beds: QDT. Air conditioning in room. Cable TV on premises. Antiques, fishing, parks, shopping, downhill skiing and theater nearby.

Location: Downtown.

Publicity: *Bay City Times, Midwest Living, Great Lakes Getaway, Michigan Tourist Monthly, Saginaw News.*

"Your facilities provided a unique and warm atmosphere, and your friendly hospitality added a very personal touch."

Certificate may be used: Nov. 1-May. 15

Bellaire   F7

Grand Victorian B&B Inn
402 N Bridge St
Bellaire, MI 49615-9591
(616)533-6111 (800)336-3860 Fax:(616)533-8197

Circa 1895. It's hard to believe that anything but joy has ever been associated with this beautiful Queen Anne Victorian inn, but its original owner, who built it in anticipation of his upcoming nuptials, left town broken-hearted when his wedding plans fell through. The eye-pleasing inn, with its gables, square corner towers, bays and overhangs, is listed in the National Register of Historic Places. There is much to do in this popular area of

Northern Michigan, with its famous nearby skiing and fishing spots, but the inn's impressive interior may entice guests to stay on the premises. Guest rooms are well-appointed with period antiques and lavish touches. Visitors may borrow a bicycle built for two for a relaxing tour of town.

Innkeeper(s): Jill Watson. $95-135. MC VISA AX. 4 rooms with PB. Breakfast and afternoon tea included in rates. Types of meals: full breakfast and early coffee/tea. Picnic lunch available. Beds: QD. Air conditioning in room. VCR on premises. Antiques, fishing, shopping, downhill skiing, cross-country skiing and watersports nearby.

Publicity: *Featured on Nabisco Crackers/Cookies Boxes Promotion, Midwest Living, Country Inns.*

"We certainly enjoyed our visit to the Grand Victorian. It has been our pleasure to stay in B&Bs in several countries, but never one more beautiful and almost never with such genial hosts."

Certificate may be used: Sunday through Thursday, Sept. 15-June 15.

Big Bay   C4

The Big Bay Point Lighthouse B&B
3 Lighthouse Rd
Big Bay, MI 49808
(906)345-9957
E-mail: Compuserve 72324,262

Circa 1896. With 4,500 feet of frontage on Lake Superior, this landmark lighthouse commands 534 acres of forests and a five-acre lawn. The interior of the lighthouse features a brick fireplace. Several guest rooms look out to the water. The tower room on the top floor offers truly unforgettable views.

Breakfast is light, so pack some extra food.

Innkeeper(s): Linda & Jeff Gamble. $85-155. PC TC. 7 rooms with PB. 2 suites. Breakfast and evening snack included in rates. Types of meals: full breakfast and early coffee/tea. Beds: QD. Ceiling fan in room. VCR, fax, copier and sauna on premises. Antiques, fishing, parks, shopping, downhill skiing, cross-country skiing, sporting events, theater and watersports nearby.

Location: Four miles northeast of Big Bay.

Publicity: *Los Angeles Times, USA Today.*

Certificate may be used: Nov. 1-May 15 excluding holidays & special promotions.

Blissfield   J8

Hiram D. Ellis Inn
415 W Adrian St US Hwy 223
Blissfield, MI 49228-1001
(517)486-3155

Circa 1883. This red brick Italianate house is in a village setting directly across from the 1851 Hathaway House, an elegant historic restaurant. Rooms at the Hiram D. Ellis Inn feature handsome antique bedsteads, armoires and floral wallpapers. Breakfast is served in the inn's common room, and the innkeeper receives rave reviews on her peach and apple dishes. (There are apple, peach and pear trees on the property.) Bicycles are available for riding around town, or you can walk to the train station and board the murder-mystery dinner train that runs on weekends.

Innkeeper(s): Christine Webster & Frank Seely. $75-95. MC VISA AX PC TC. 4 rooms with PB. Breakfast included in rates. Types of meals: continental-plus breakfast, full breakfast and early coffee/tea. Beds: QD. Air conditioning and TV in room. Bicycles on premises. Antiques, fishing, parks, shopping, cross-country skiing and theater nearby.

Publicity: *Ann Arbor News, Michigan Living.*

"I have now experienced what it is truly like to have been treated like a queen."

Certificate may be used: Sunday through Thursday.

Boyne City   F7

Deer Lake Bed & Breakfast
00631 E Deer Lake Rd
Boyne City, MI 49712-9614
(616)582-9039

Located in a comfortable, ranch-style home, this bed & breakfast offers guests water views and peaceful surroundings. Two rooms include private balconies overlooking the lake, and the other three guest quarters share a 40-foot balcony. The house is bright and airy with elegant, country furnishings, French doors and a few lacy touches. For those who enjoy the outdoors, the area offers golf, fishing, swimming, sailing, skiing and much more. For those more creatively inclined, the innkeepers, both former jewelers, offer ring-making classes.

Innkeeper(s): Glenn & Shirley Piepenburg. $80-95. MC VISA DS PC TC. 5 rooms with PB. Breakfast and evening snack included in rates. Types of meals: full breakfast and early coffee/tea. Beds: KQT. Air conditioning, turndown service and ceiling fan in room. Cable TV, VCR, swimming and bicycles on premises. Antiques, fishing, parks, shopping, downhill skiing, cross-country skiing and watersports nearby.

Certificate may be used: Jan. 4-Dec. 15, Sunday-Thursday, excluding holidays and special events.

Brooklyn   J8

Dewey Lake Manor
11811 Laird Rd
Brooklyn, MI 49230-9035
(517)467-7122

Circa 1868. This Italianate house overlooks Dewey Lake and is situated on 18 acres in the Irish Hills. The house is furnished in a country Victorian style with antiques. An enclosed porch is a favorite spot to relax and take in the views of the lake while having breakfast. Favorite pastimes include lakeside bonfires in the summertime and ice skating or cross-country skiing in the winter.

Innkeeper(s): Barb & Joe Phillips. $55-75. MC VISA AX. 5 rooms with

PB. 1 conference room. Breakfast included in rates. Types of meals: full breakfast and early coffee/tea. Evening snack and picnic lunch available. Beds: QDT. Air conditioning, ceiling fan and TV in room. VCR on premises. Antiques, fishing, shopping, cross-country skiing, sporting events, golf, theater and watersports nearby.

Location: In Irish Hills of southern Michigan.

Publicity: *Ann Arbor News.*

"I came back and brought my friends. It was wonderful."

Certificate may be used: November through April, holidays and special events excluded.

Buchanan   J5

The Primrose Path B&B
413 E Front St
Buchanan, MI 49107-1442
(616)695-6321 Fax:(616)695-6591
E-mail: primrose@qtm.net

Circa 1905. Both Tudor and Arts & Crafts influences are present in the design of this turn-of-the-century home. The interior boasts leaded-glass windows and a beautifully designed built-in china cabinet that is the centerpiece of the dining room. The four guest rooms feature romantic touches such as lacy curtains, decorated hats, antique wedding photos or perhaps a brass bed decorated with roses. Breakfast includes such delectable items as stuffed French toast topped with fresh blueberries or perhaps a flavorful quiche. The home is a short drive from South Bend, home of the University of Notre Dame. Shops, restaurants, wineries, antiquing and outdoor activities also are nearby.

Innkeeper(s): Kathy Barnett. $50-90. MC VISA PC TC. 4 rooms, 2 with PB. Breakfast included in rates. Type of meal: full breakfast. Beds: QD. Air conditioning and TV in room. VCR and fax on premises. Antiques, fishing, parks, sporting events, golf, theater and watersports nearby.

Certificate may be used: Jan. 30-May 1, Sunday through Thursday.

Canton   J9

Willow Brook Inn
44255 Warren Rd
Canton, MI 48187-2147
(313)454-0019 (888)454-1919

Circa 1929. Willow Brook winds its way through the backyard of this aptly named inn, situated on a lush, wooded acre. Innkeepers Bernadette and Michael Van Lenten filled their home with oak and pine country antiques and beds covered with soft quilts. They also added special toys and keepsakes from their own childhood to add a homey touch. After a peaceful rest, guests are invited to partake in the morning meal either in the "Teddy Bear" dining room, in the privacy of their rooms or in the sun room. Breakfasts consist of luscious treats such as homemade breads, scones topped with devon cream and a rich, egg dish.

Innkeeper(s): Bernadette & Michael Van Lenten. $85-115. MC VISA. 4 rooms with PB. 1 suite. Breakfast and evening snack included in rates. Types of meals: gourmet breakfast and early coffee/tea. Afternoon tea, picnic lunch and catering service available. Beds: KQDT. Turndown service, ceiling fan and VCR in room. Fax, copier, bicycles, pet boarding and child care on premises. Antiques, parks, shopping, cross-country skiing, sporting events, theater and watersports nearby.

Publicity: *Canton Observer, Canton Eagle, Detroit News.*

"We've stayed in B&B's in Europe, Australia and New Zealand, and we put yours at the top of the list for luxury, friendly care and delicious food (especially the scones). We're glad we found you. Thanks."

Certificate may be used: From Nov. 1-May 15, Sunday through Thursday, excluding Feb. 14.

Cedarville   D7

Island View Resort
PO Box 277
Cedarville, MI 49719-0277
(906)484-2252

These comfortable cottages offer a convenient, unique way to enjoy Michigan's scenic Les Cheneaux area. Each of the cottages includes a stocked kitchen and freshly made beds, but guests must provide their own towels and washcloths. All of the cottages sleep four comfortably. The water-front log cabin will sleep eight and boasts a fire-place. Several cottages afford lake views; the honeymoon cottage is a secluded, lakefront cabin with a private deck.
Innkeeper(s): Larry Smith. $59-89. MC VISA DS. 9 rooms. Breakfast included in rates.

Certificate may be used: May 1-June 15, Sunday-Thursday; Sept. 15-Oct. 31.

Central Lake   F7

Bridgewalk B&B
2287 S Main, PO Box 399
Central Lake, MI 49622-0399
(616)544-8122

Circa 1895. Secluded on a wooded acre, this three-story Victorian is accessible by crossing a foot bridge over a stream. Guest rooms are simply decorated with Victorian touches, floral prints and fresh flowers. The Garden Suite includes a clawfoot tub. Much of the home's Victorian elements have been restored, including pocket doors and the polished woodwork. Breakfasts begin with such items as a cold fruit soup, freshly baked muffins or scones accompanied with homemade jams and butters. A main dish, perhaps stuffed French toast, tops off the meal.
Innkeeper(s): Janet & Tom Meteer. $75-85. MC VISA PC TC. 5 rooms with PB. 1 suite. Breakfast included in rates. Types of meals: full breakfast and early coffee/tea. Beds: KQT. Ceiling fan in room. Antiques, fishing, parks, shopping, downhill skiing, cross-country skiing and watersports nearby.

Certificate may be used: Sunday through Thursday nights.

Torchlight Resort
PO Box 267
Central Lake, MI 49622-0267
(616)544-8263

Circa 1940. These one- and two-bedroom cottages are located on the edge of scenic Torch Lake. The cottages, which all boast lake views, include stocked kitchens and barbeque grills, but towels and linens

are not provided. The owners offer docking for private boats, and there is a beach and swimming area.
Innkeeper(s): Robert & Glenda Knott. $45-85. 6 rooms with PB. Breakfast included in rates. Beds: D. Fishing nearby.

Certificate may be used: First week of May through third week of June and last week of August through last week of October.

Charlevoix   E7

Belvedere Inn
306 Belvedere Ave
Charlevoix, MI 49720-1413
(616)547-2251 (800)280-4667 Fax:(616)547-2251

Circa 1887. Guests at this attractive two-story inn are just a short walk from a public beach. Visitors have their choice of seven rooms, including two suites. The Broqua Suite features a kitchen and private entrance, perfect for honeymooners or for those enjoying a longer-than-usual stay. All of the rooms

offer private baths and most have queen beds. Guests may opt to relax and enjoy the beautiful surroundings or take advantage of the many recreational activities available in the Charlevoix area, including Fisherman's Island State Park.
Innkeeper(s): Tom & Karen Watters. $60-115. MC VISA AX PC TC. 7 rooms, 5 with PB. 2 suites. Breakfast and evening snack included in rates. Type of meal: full breakfast. Beds: KQT. Ceiling fan in room. Cable TV, VCR, fax and bicycles on premises. Antiques, fishing, parks, shopping, downhill skiing, cross-country skiing and watersports nearby.

Certificate may be used: Oct. 1-May 24, anytime. Sunday-Thursday, June 1-30. Sunday-Thursday, Sept. 1-30.

MacDougall House B&B
109 Petoskey Ave
Charlevoix, MI 49720-1161
(616)547-5788

Circa 1896. This turn-of-the-century Victorian served guests for many years as the Northern Guest House. Today the home is still a warm, comfortable place for visitors. The Victorian decor and country furnishings are inviting. The front porch beckons guests who wish to simply relax and enjoy a good book while lounging in a rocking chair. As the inn's name suggests, there is a Scottish influence here, which is evident during the breakfast hour.

Innkeeper(s): Steven & Sandra Bennett. $58-98. MC VISA DS TC. 5 rooms with PB. Breakfast and afternoon tea included in rates. Types of meals: full breakfast and early coffee/tea. Beds: QD. Ceiling fan in room. Cable TV, VCR and child care on premises. Antiques, fishing, parks, shopping, downhill skiing, cross-country skiing and watersports nearby.

Certificate may be used: Sept. 1-March 1, reservation required.

Clio   H8

Cinnamon Stick B&B
12364 Genesee Rd
Clio, MI 48420-9142
(810)686-8391 Fax:(810)686-8094

Circa 1908. Guests enjoy a pastoral setting at this turn-of-the-century farmhouse, which is surrounded by 50 acres. The innkeepers have two Belgian Draft horses, which sometimes take guests on hay or sleigh rides on the scenic property. There are also walking trails and a stocked fishing pond to enjoy. Each of the five guest rooms is decorated in a different country style. The suite includes a sleigh bed and a whirlpool tub. The innkeepers prepare a homemade country breakfast each morning, with dishes such as Belgian waffles, smokey ham and freshly baked poppy seed muffins.

Innkeeper(s): Brian & Carol Powell. $60-125. MC VISA. 5 rooms, 4 with PB. 1 suite. 1 conference room. Breakfast, afternoon tea, dinner, evening snack and picnic lunch included in rates. Types of meals: full breakfast, gourmet breakfast and early coffee/tea. Lunch and gourmet lunch available. Beds: QD. Air conditioning and ceiling fan in room. Cable TV, VCR, fax, copier, spa, stables, bicycles, tennis, library, pet boarding and child care on premises. Amusement parks, antiques, fishing, parks, shopping, downhill skiing, cross-country skiing, sporting events, golf, theater and watersports nearby.

Publicity: *Grand Blanc Business Banner*

Certificate may be used: Jan. 1-June 1, Sunday-Friday, subject to availability.

East Jordan   F7

Easterly Inn
209 Easterly, PO Box 366
East Jordan, MI 49727
(616)536-3434

Circa 1906. Finely crafted woodwork of cherry, bird's-eye maple and oak are hints that this turn-of-the-century Victorian was built for a lumber merchant. Its three stories and 18 rooms have been carefully restored and furnished with fine antiques and period wallcoverings, which enhance its gleaming hardwood floors and leaded windows. Guest rooms include the Turret Room, which offers a tall, carved walnut and burl queen bed, and the Romantic Lace Room, with Victorian rose prints and a queen canopy bed. Breakfast is served in the semi-circular dining room.

Innkeeper(s): Joan Martin. $60-85. MC VISA PC. 4 rooms with PB. Breakfast included in rates. Type of meal: full breakfast. Beds: QD. Ceiling fan in room. Cable TV and library on premises. Antiques, fishing, parks, shopping, downhill skiing, cross-country skiing, golf and watersports nearby.

"A wonderful inn, full of history and romance. Thank you for sharing yourself with us."

Certificate may be used: May 1-June 20 and Sept. 2-Oct. 30, Monday-Thursday (excluding holiday periods and weekends).

Fennville   I6

The Kingsley House
626 W Main St
Fennville, MI 49408-9442
(616)561-6425 Fax:(616)561-2593
E-mail: garyking@accn.org

Circa 1886. Construction of this Queen Anne Victorian, with a three-story turret, was paid for in silver bricks by the Kingsley family. Mr. Kingsley is noted for having introduced the apple tree to the area. In recognition of him, guest rooms are named Dutchess, Golden Delicious, Granny Smith, McIntosh and Jonathan. The Northern Spy, complete with hot tub, is nestled in the third-floor suite. A winding oak staircase leads to the antique-filled guest chambers. Family heirlooms and other period pieces add to the inn's elegance.

Innkeeper(s): Gary & Kari King. $80-145. MC VISA AX DS PC TC. 8 rooms with PB, 3 with FP. 3 suites. Breakfast and evening snack included in rates. Types of meals: continental-plus breakfast, full breakfast and early coffee/tea. Picnic lunch available. Beds: KQD. Air conditioning, ceiling fan and TV in room. Fax, bicycles and library on premises. Antiques, fishing, parks, shopping, downhill skiing, cross-country skiing, sporting events, theater and watersports nearby.

Location: 196 South of Holland to Exit 34 then East 5 miles.

Publicity: *Innsider, Battle Creek Enquirer, Fennville Herald, Commercial Record, Glamour, Country, Country Victorian Decorating Ideas, National Geographic Traveler.*

"It was truly enjoyable. You have a lovely home and a gracious way of entertaining."

Certificate may be used: All year, Sunday-Thursday nights only.

Will O'Glenn Irish B&B
1286 64th St
Fennville, MI 49408
(616)227-3045 (888)237-3009 Fax:(616)227-3045
E-mail: egahan@accn.org

Circa 1920. With six stables and 17 acres of grounds, a stay at this farmhouse is bit like taking a trip to an Irish country farm. Innkeeper Ward Gahan hails from Ireland, and it is his heritage that is very much in evidence at Will O' Glenn. He and wife, Shelley, spent months restoring their historic, 4,500-square-foot home, the result is an elegant country decor. Guests enjoy a restful night's sleep under an Irish down comforter before awaking to enjoy a traditional Irish breakfast. The morning fare includes meats and coffee imported from Ward's native land, homemade Irish breads and local items such as fresh fruit and preserves. Lake Michigan is just minutes away, as are parks, wineries, shops and restaurants.

Innkeeper(s): Shelley & Ward Gahan. $75-129. MC VISA PC TC. 4 rooms with PB, 1 with FP. Breakfast included in rates. Types of meals: continental-plus breakfast, full breakfast and early coffee/tea. Beds: KQD. VCR, fax, copier, stables, bicycles and library on premises. Antiques, fishing, parks, shopping, downhill skiing, cross-country skiing, golf, theater and watersports nearby.

"You have mastered the art of running a true Irish B&B."

Certificate may be used: Nov. 1-May 1, Sunday-Sunday; May 1-Nov. 1, Sunday-Thursday.

Fruitport   I6

Village Park B&B
60 Park St
Fruitport, MI 49415-9668
(616)865-6289 (800)469-1118

Circa 1873. Located in the midst of Western Michigan's Tri-Cities area, this inn's small-town village location offers comfort and relaxation to those busy partaking of the many nearby activities. This farmhouse-style inn overlooks Spring Lake and a park where guests may picnic, play tennis, use a pedestrian/bike path and boat launch. There also is a hot tub and exercise room on the premises. The inn offers six guest rooms, all with private bath. A library is just across the street. P.J. Hoffmaster State Park, the Gillette Nature Sand Dune Center and Pleasure Island water park are nearby. Be sure to inquire about the inn's Wellness Weekends with massage.

Innkeeper(s): John Hewett. $60-95. MC VISA PC TC. 6 rooms with PB. Breakfast included in rates. Types of meals: continental breakfast, continental-plus breakfast, full breakfast and early coffee/tea. Beds: KDT. Air

conditioning in room. Cable TV, VCR, fax, spa, sauna and bicycles on premises. Amusement parks, antiques, fishing, parks, shopping, cross-country skiing, theater and watersports nearby.

Certificate may be used: Sunday through Thursday excluding June, July, August and holidays, subject to availability. Excludes corporate rates and packages.

Glen Arbor   F6

White Gull Inn
PO Box 351, 5926 SW Manitou Trl
Glen Arbor, MI 49636-9702
(616)334-4486 Fax:(616)334-3998

Circa 1900. One of Michigan's most scenic areas is home to the White Gull Inn. With the Sleeping Bear Dunes and alluring Glen Lake just minutes away, visitors will find no shortage of sightseeing or recreational activities during a stay here. The inn's farmhouse setting, country decor and five comfortable guest rooms offer a relaxing haven no matter what the season. Lake Michigan is a block away, and guests also will enjoy the area's fine dining and shopping opportunities.

Innkeeper(s): Bill & Dotti Thompson. $50-75. MC VISA AX DS TC. 6 rooms, 1 with FP. Breakfast included in rates. Type of meal: continental-plus breakfast. Beds: QDT. Air conditioning, TV and VCR in room. Antiques, fishing, parks, shopping, downhill skiing, cross-country skiing, theater and watersports nearby.

Certificate may be used: Nov. 1-May 1 except Dec. 21-27.

Holly   I8

Holly Crossing B&B
304 S Saginaw St
Holly, MI 48442-1614
(248)634-7075 (800)556-2262 Fax:(248)634-4481

Circa 1900. A unique wraparound veranda fashioned from stones decorates the exterior of this Queen Anne Victorian, which is surrounded by a white picket fence. The interior maintains original fireplace mantels and woodwork. Rooms are Victorian in style and comfortable, offering romantic items such as lacy curtains, silk flowers or perhaps even a double whirlpool tub. The spacious suite, named Tara, offers a whirlpool tub, fireplace and a private balcony. All guests enjoy a delicious full breakfast, but guests in the Tara, Oak and Fountain rooms have the meal delivered to their rooms and served with champagne. The inn is conveniently located within walking distance of shops and restaurant. Battle Alley, a quaint street filled with restored 19th-century buildings, offers many shops and is a popular local attraction. Holly is within 45 minutes of Detroit.

Innkeeper(s): Carl & Nicole Cooper. $49-169. MC VISA AX DS PC TC. 5 rooms with PB, 2 with FP. 1 suite. Breakfast included in rates. Type of meal: full breakfast. Room service available. Beds: QD. Air conditioning and ceiling fan in room. Fax, copier and library on premises. Antiques, parks, shopping, downhill skiing, cross-country skiing, golf and theater nearby.

Publicity: *Getaways Magazine, The Oakland Press*

"What a charming Bed & Breakfast! The Oak Room was delightful my husband and I enjoyed the old world charm mixed in with the modern necessities. This is the nicest B&B we have stayed in thus far."

Certificate may be used: Oct. 1-June 30, Sunday through Friday.

Houghton   C3

Charleston House B&B Inn

918 College Avenue
Houghton, MI 49931-2461
(906)482-7790 (800)482-7404 Fax:(906)482-7068

Circa 1900. Wide verandas on the first and second stories dominate the exterior of this impressive Colonial Revival-style home, which is painted in a light pink hue with white trim. There are ceiling fans and comfortable wicker furnishings on the verandas, and the second-story porch is a private haven for guests staying in the Daughter's Room. Most of the other bedchambers offer a view of the Portage Canal. Mother's Room makes up for its lack of a view by including a bay window, sitting area and clawfoot tub. The scents of brewing coffee and baking muffins will lure you out of your comfortable bed and down to a breakfast with homemade breads and granola, fresh fruit, yogurt and a special daily entree. The inn overlooks the canal, and Lake Superior is nearby, as is the MTU campus, skiing, shops, restaurants and the downtown area.
Innkeeper(s): John & Helen Sullivan. $78-140. MC VISA AX PC TC. 6 rooms with PB, 2 with FP. 1 suite. 2 conference rooms. Breakfast included in rates. Types of meals: full breakfast and early coffee/tea. Afternoon tea, banquet service, catering service and room service available. Beds: KQT. Air conditioning, turndown service, ceiling fan and TV in room. Fax, copier and library on premises. Amusement parks, antiques, fishing, parks, shopping, downhill skiing, cross-country skiing, sporting events, golf, theater and watersports nearby.

Publicity: *Michigan Explorer*

"Just a note to let you know that we enjoyed our stay at the Charleston Inn."

Certificate may be used: Nov. 1-May 1, Sunday-Friday.

Interlochen   F6

Between The Lakes B&B

4570 Case Blvd Box 280
Interlochen, MI 49643-9534
(616)276-7751 Fax:(616)276-7752

After more than two decades globetrotting as part of the foreign service, the owners of this bed & breakfast decided to become hosts instead of guests. Art, artifacts and furnishings from their world travels decorate the home. Two wooded acres offer privacy, and guests also may use the B&B's heated, indoor swimming pool. The home is within walking distance to Duck and Green lakes as well as the Interlochen Center for the Arts.
Innkeeper(s): Barbara & Gordon Evans. $65-75. MC VISA PC. 4 rooms with PB. Breakfast included in rates. Type of meal: continental-plus breakfast. Beds: KQT. VCR, fax and swimming on premises. Handicap access. Fishing, parks, shopping, cross-country skiing and watersports nearby.

Location: Within walking distance of Interlochen Center for the Arts.

Certificate may be used: Sunday through Thursday throughout the year, weekends from Sept. 30-May 31 or on space-available basis. One certificate holder per night.

Ithaca   H7

Bon Accord Farm B&B

532 E Polk Rd
Ithaca, MI 48847-9702
(517)875-3136

Circa 1872. This Italianate farmhouse is located on land that has been in the same family since 1854, and six generations of Allens have lived in the home. The front exterior is brick, but features fancy Victorian woodwork done in shades of green and burgundy. The wood siding on the rest of the house is striped with three rows of the dark green to every row of burgundy. The interior woodwork is impressive, as well, especially in the entry. Rooms are done in country style, beds are topped with colorful quilts. The innkeepers serve a hearty country breakfast with items such as banana-stuffed French toast, fried potatoes with homemade sausage and ice cream with freshly picked berries.
Innkeeper(s): Dick & JoAnn Allen. $48-78. MC VISA PC. 4 rooms, 2 with PB. Breakfast included in rates. Types of meals: full breakfast and gourmet breakfast. Beds: QD. Ceiling fan in room. VCR, bicycles and tennis on premises. Antiques, fishing, parks, shopping, cross-country skiing and golf nearby.

Certificate may be used: Jan. 1-July 15.

Chaffin Farms B&B

1245 W Washington Rd
Ithaca, MI 48847-9782
(517)875-3410

Circa 1892. Located in central Michigan between Mount Pleasant and Lansing, this inn was once a large dairy farm with 12 barns housing various farm animals. Guests will be impressed with the inn's colorful stone wall, built with rocks hauled in from the surrounding area. The inn is furnished with antiques, and visitors will marvel at the inn's impressive kitchen, which was featured in Country Woman magazine. Antiquing is popular in the area and Alma College is nearby.

Innkeeper(s): Susan Chaffin. $45-55. PC. 2 rooms, 1 with PB. Breakfast included in rates. Types of meals: continental-plus breakfast, full breakfast and early coffee/tea. Beds: QT. Air conditioning in room. Antiques, parks, shopping and sporting events nearby.

Certificate may be used: April 15 to Nov. 15.

Jones　　　　　　　　　　J6

The Sanctuary at Wildwood

58138 M-40
Jones, MI 49061-9713
(616)244-5910 (800)249-5910 Fax:(616)496-8403

Circa 1972. Travelers in search of relaxation and a little solitude will enjoy the serenity of this estate, surrounded by 95 forested acres. A stroll down the hiking trails introduces guests to a variety of wildlife, but even inside, guests are pampered by the inn's natural setting. One room, named Medicine Hawk, is adorned with a mural depicting a woodland scene. A mural of a pine forest graces the Quiet Solace room. The Keeper of the Wild Room includes a rustic birch headboard. Each of the rooms includes a fireplace, Jacuzzi and service bar. There also are three cottage suites, situated around a pond. From the dining and great rooms, guests can watch the abundant wildlife. The innkeeper offers a variety of interesting packages. A swimming pool is available during the summer months. Wineries are nearby, and the inn is a half hour from Notre Dame and Shipshewana.

Innkeeper(s): Dick & Dolly Buerkle. $139-179. MC VISA AX DS PC TC. 11 suites. 3 cottages. 1 conference room. Breakfast included in rates. Beds: Q. Air conditioning in room. Handicap access. Antiques, fishing, shopping, downhill skiing and cross-country skiing nearby.

Certificate may be used: Nov. 1-April 15, Sunday through Thursday only, excluding holidays periods.

Jonesville　　　　　　　　J7

Horse & Carriage B&B

7020 Brown Rd
Jonesville, MI 49250-9720
(517)849-2732 Fax:(517)849-2732

Circa 1898. Enjoy a peaceful old-fashioned day on the farm. Milk a cow, gather eggs and cuddle baby lambs. In the winter, families are treated to a horse-drawn sleigh ride at this early 18th-century home, which is surrounded by a 700-acre dairy farm. In the warmer months, horse-drawn carriage rides pass down an old country lane past Buck Lake. The innkeepers' family has lived on the property for more than 150 years. The home itself was built as a one-room schoolhouse. A mix of contemporary and country furnishings decorate the interior. The Rainbow Room, a perfect place for children, offers twin beds and a playroom. Guests are treated to hearty breakfasts made with farm-fresh eggs and cream from the farm's cows.

Innkeeper(s): Keith Brown & family. $50-75. PC. 3 rooms, 1 with PB. 1 suite. Breakfast and evening snack included in rates. Types of meals: continental breakfast, continental-plus breakfast, full breakfast, gourmet breakfast and early coffee/tea. Picnic lunch and catered breakfast available. Beds: QT. Air conditioning in room. Fax and copier on premises. Antiques, fishing, parks, shopping, cross-country skiing, sporting events, theater and watersports nearby.

Certificate may be used: Anytime subject to availability.

Munro House B&B

202 Maumee St
Jonesville, MI 49250-1247
(517)849-9292

Circa 1840. Ten fireplaces are found at the historic Munro House, named for George C. Munro, a Civil War brigadier general. The Greek Revival structure, Hillsdale County's first brick house, also served as a safe haven for slaves on the Underground Railroad. Visitors can still see a secret room, once used for hiding slaves. Many guests enjoy selecting one of the library's special-interest books and spend a quiet evening in front of a fireplace in their room. Five guest rooms include a fire-

A.M. Hill

place, and two rooms have a Jacuzzi tub. Breakfast is eaten overlooking the inn's gardens. Hillsdale College is just five miles away.

Innkeeper(s): Joyce Yarde. $47-150. MC VISA. 7 rooms with PB, 5 with FP. Breakfast included in rates. Type of meal: full breakfast. Evening snack available. Air conditioning, ceiling fan and TV in room. VCR on premises. Antiques, shopping, cross-country skiing, sporting events and theater nearby.

"What a delightful stay. Beautiful house, wonderful history and a delightful hostess. Felt like we knew her forever. We will tell all our friends."

Certificate may be used: Any Sunday through Friday.

Lansing   I7

Ask Me House

1027 Seymour Ave
Lansing, MI 48906-4836
(517)484-3127 (800)275-6341 Fax:(517)484-4193
E-mail: mekiener@aol.com

This early 20th-century home still includes its original hardwood floors and pocket doors. A hand-painted mural was added to the dining room in the 1940s. Guests can enjoy the unique art during the breakfasts, which are served on antique Limoges china and Depression glass. The innkeepers offer a quaint honeymoon cottage along with the guest rooms. The home is near a variety of museums, theaters, a historical village and Michigan State University.

Innkeeper(s): Mary Elaine Kiener & Alex Kruzel. $65-95. MC VISA PC TC. 4 rooms. 1 cottage. Breakfast included in rates. Types of meals: full breakfast, gourmet breakfast and early coffee/tea. Beds: DT. Ceiling fan in room. Cable TV, VCR and fax on premises. Antiques, parks, sporting events and theater nearby.

Certificate may be used: Anytime subject to availability.

Lewiston   F8

Gorton House

HCR 3 Box 3738, Wolflake Dr
Lewiston, MI 49756-8948
(517)786-2764 Fax:(517)786-2764

Wolf Lake sits beside this comfortable bed & breakfast. Rooms are filled with antiques and lace. The innkeepers offer a variety of activities including use of a fishing boat and putting green. The grounds boast a lakeside beach and hot tub under a gazebo. Inside, guests can relax near one of three fireplaces or take in a game of pool on the innkeepers' antique pool table. A hearty breakfast with entrees such as omelets or German pancakes is served along with fruits, juices and baked goods. In the summer, morn-

ing coffee can be enjoyed in the paddle boat. Freshly baked cookies are always available for a light snack. Antique shopping and golfing are some of the area's offerings.

Innkeeper(s): Lois Gorton. $55-75. 6 rooms. Breakfast included in rates. Type of meal: full breakfast.

Certificate may be used: Exclude all holidays.

Pine Ridge Lodge

Co Rd 489
Lewiston, MI 49756
(517)786-4789
E-mail: pineridg@northland.lib.mi.us

Circa 1948. This log lodge is right at home in its natural surroundings, secluded on 37 acres within the AuSable State Forest. Outdoor enthusiasts are frequent guests, and it's no wonder. The lodge has its own recreational director, as well as 20 miles of mountain biking trails and 10 kilometers of hiking and cross-country trails. Exposed log and wood walls add a rustic touch to the guest rooms and common areas. Each guest room also includes a log bed. Guests can play darts or shoot pool in the game room, which also has a fireplace. After a day of biking, hiking or skiing, come back and relax in the outdoor hot tub. Breakfasts are always hearty and homemade, a perfect start to a day full of activity.

Innkeeper(s): Doug Stiles & Suzan Anthony-Stiles. $65-85. MAP. PC TC. 7 rooms, 3 with PB. 1 cabin. Breakfast included in rates. Types of meals: full breakfast and early coffee/tea. Dinner, evening snack, picnic lunch, lunch and banquet service available. Beds: QTD. VCR, spa and library on premises. Antiques, fishing, parks, shopping, downhill skiing, cross-country skiing, golf and watersports nearby.

Publicity: *Ann Arbor News Bureau, The Montmorency County Tribune.*

Certificate may be used: Sunday through Thursday.

Lexington   H9

Governor's Inn

7277 Simons St
Lexington, MI 48450
(810)359-5770

Circa 1859. Former Michigan governor Albert Sleeper and his wife, Mary, made this Victorian their summer home. Mary's parents built the home, and she and Albert were married here. Wicker furnishings and antiques add to the Victorian charm. The wraparound porch is a wonderful place to relax. The dining room is warmed by a potbellied stove. An ornate, hand-carved staircase leads to the three guest rooms. One room includes an old chest that innkeeper Jim Boyda's grandparents brought with them when they sailed to America.

Innkeeper(s): Marlene & Jim Boyda. $55-65. MC VISA. 5 rooms, 3 with PB. Breakfast included in rates. Type of meal: continental-plus breakfast. Beds: D. Air conditioning in room. Antiques, fishing, parks, shopping, cross-country skiing, theater and watersports nearby.

Certificate may be used: Oct. 1-May 1, anyday.

Lowell   I6

McGee Homestead B&B
2534 Alden Nash NE
Lowell, MI 49331
(616)897-8142

Circa 1880. Just 18 miles from Grand Rapids, travelers will find the McGee Homestead B&B, an Italianate farmhouse with four antique-filled guest rooms. Surrounded by orchards, it is one of the largest farmhouses in the area. Breakfasts feature the inn's own fresh eggs. Guests may golf at an

adjacent course or enjoy nearby fishing and boating. Lowell is home to Michigan's largest antique mall, and many historic covered bridges are found in the surrounding countryside. Travelers who remain on the farm may relax in a hammock or visit a barnful of petting animals.

Innkeeper(s): Bill & Ardie Barber. $38-58. MC VISA AX DS PC TC. 4 rooms with PB. 1 conference room. Breakfast, afternoon tea and evening snack included in rates. Types of meals: full breakfast and early coffee/tea. Beds: KDT. Air conditioning, turndown service, ceiling fan and VCR in room. Library and child care on premises. Antiques, fishing, parks, shopping, downhill skiing and cross-country skiing nearby.

Certificate may be used: Sunday-Saturday, March-December. Anytime available.

Ludington   G5

The Doll House Inn
709 E Ludington Ave
Ludington, MI 49431-2224
(616)843-2286 (800)275-4616

Circa 1900. Antique dolls are among the special family heirlooms found throughout this Victorian inn. Seven rooms, decorated in lace curtains and brass or antique beds, include a bridal suite with a canopy bed and whirlpool tub for two. Guests can enjoy a full "heart-smart" breakfast on the wicker-filled porch. The beach is a short stroll from the inn.

Innkeeper(s): Barbara Gerovac. $65-110. MC VISA. 7 rooms, 5 with PB. 1 suite. Breakfast included in rates. Types of meals: full breakfast and early coffee/tea. Picnic lunch available. Beds: QTD. Air conditioning, turndown service and TV in room. VCR on premises. Antiques, shopping, downhill skiing, cross-country skiing, sporting events and theater nearby.

Location: Four blocks to business area and six blocks to Lake Michigan car ferry.

Certificate may be used: Closed January, no holidays, Sunday through Thursday (September through December), anytime February through April.

Lamplighter B&B
602 E Ludington Ave
Ludington, MI 49431-2223
(616)843-9792 (800)301-9792 Fax:(616)845-6070
E-mail: catsup@aol.com

Circa 1895. This Queen Anne home offers convenient access to Lake Michigan's beaches, the Badger Car Ferry to Wisconsin and Michigan state parks. A collection of European antiques and original paintings and lithographs by artists such as Chagall and Dali, decorate the inn. The home's centerpiece, a golden oak curved staircase, leads guests up to their rooms. The innkeepers have created a mix of hospitality and convenience that draws both vacationers and business travelers. A full, gourmet breakfast is served each morning. Freddy, the inn's resident cocker spaniel, is always available for a tour of the area. The innkeepers are fluent in German.

Innkeeper(s): Judy & Heinz Bertram. $89-129. MC VISA AX DS PC TC. 5 rooms with PB, 1 with FP. Breakfast included in rates. Types of meals: gourmet breakfast and early coffee/tea. Beds: QD. Air conditioning, turndown service and TV in room. VCR, fax, copier and bicycles on premises. Amusement parks, antiques, fishing, parks, shopping, cross-country skiing, golf and watersports nearby.

"For my husbands first bed and breakfast experience, it couldn't have been better."

Certificate may be used: November through April, holidays excluded.

The Inn at Ludington
701 E Ludington Ave
Ludington, MI 49431-2224
(616)845-7055 (800)845-9170

Circa 1890. This Queen Anne Victorian was built during the heyday of Ludington's lumbering era by a local pharmacist and doctor. Despite its elegant exterior with its three-story turret, the innkeepers stress relaxation at their inn. The rooms are filled with comfortable, vintage furnishings. Guests can

snuggle up with a book in front of a warming fireplace or enjoy a soak in a clawfoot tub. A hearty, buffet-style breakfast is served each morning. The innkeepers take great pride in their cuisine and are always happy to share some of their award-winning recipes with guests. After a day of beachcombing, antiquing, cross-country skiing or perhaps a bike ride, guests return to the inn to find a chocolate atop their pillow. Don't forget to ask about the innkeepers' murder-mystery weekends.

Innkeeper(s): Diane Shields & David Nemitz. $65-85. MC VISA AX PC TC. 6 rooms with PB, 2 with FP. 1 suite. Breakfast included in rates. Types of meals: full breakfast and early coffee/tea. Picnic lunch available. Beds: QD. Air conditioning, turndown service, ceiling fan and TV in room. Fax, copier and library on premises. Amusement parks, antiques, fishing, parks, shopping, downhill skiing, cross-country skiing, theater and watersports nearby.

Location: Near Lake Michigan.

Publicity: *Ludington Daily News, Detroit Free Press, Chicago Tribune, Country Accents.*

"Loved the room and everything else about the house."

Certificate may be used: November-April, anytime; May, June, September, October, weekdays (or weekends as available at last minute).

The Ludington House

501 E Ludington Ave
Ludington, MI 49431-2220
(616)845-7769

Enjoy the opulence of the Victorian era at this 19th-century home, which was built by a lumber baron. Grand rooms with high ceilings, stained glass and polished oak floors are enhanced by a country collection of period antiques. A showpiece carved, winding staircase and Italian mantels are other notable architectural features. An antique wedding gown decorates the Bridal Suite. The innkeepers will prepare a picnic lunch, and there are bicycles for guest use. The innkeepers also offer murder-mystery packages.

Innkeeper(s): Virginia Boegner. $80-90. MC VISA. 9 rooms. Breakfast included in rates. Type of meal: full breakfast.

Certificate may be used: Anytime except July and August and weekends in September and October. Bridal Suite with whirlpool and fireplace.

Welcome Home Inn

716 E Ludington Ave
Ludington, MI 49431-2225
(616)845-7699 (888)253-0982

Circa 1880. The owner of the local dry goods store built this Queen Anne Victorian. It has been restored to its 19th-century elegance. Among the furnishings are antiques such as the fanciful Victorian sofa in the parlor. Guest rooms are romantic. In one room, guests walk up two steps to reach a clawfoot tub located by the bay window. The Enchanted Cottage is the most idyllic with a black iron water bed with a canopy of black chiffon. The bed is draped with a pink comforter.

Innkeeper(s): Missy & Paula Price. $75-95. MC VISA PC TC. 4 rooms with PB. 1 suite. Breakfast and afternoon tea included in rates. Types of meals: full breakfast and gourmet breakfast. Beds: QT. Air conditioning, turndown service and ceiling fan in room. VCR and child care on premises. Antiques, fishing, parks, shopping, golf, theater and watersports nearby.

"Thank you so very much for your love and hospitality . . . your place is delightful, but most of all it is a reflection of both you and your precious spirit."

Certificate may be used: Nov. 1-May 31, any day of the week, Sunday-Saturday.

Mackinac Island E7

Harbour View Inn

PO Box 1207
Mackinac Island, MI 49757
(906)847-0101 Fax:(906)847-3998

Circa 1820. Harbour View was built as a private home in the early 19th century, and the inn features both Colonial and some Victorian architectural features. Guests can stay in the guest house, carriage house or in rooms in the main inn. All accommodations are decorated in an elegant Victorian style, some rooms offer harbor views and whirlpool tubs. The inn is open from May to October.

Innkeeper(s): David Zeilinger. $125-265. MC VISA AX DS PC TC. 65 rooms with PB, 4 with FP. 18 suites. 2 conference rooms. Breakfast included in rates. Type of meal: continental-plus breakfast. Beds: KQ. Air conditioning, ceiling fan and TV in room. VCR, fax, copier, spa and bicycles on premises. Handicap access.

Certificate may be used: Sunday-Thursday, May 10-June 11, Aug. 23-Oct. 22, not valid holidays or special events.

Mendon
J6

The Mendon Country Inn
PO Box 98
Mendon, MI 49072-9502
(616)496-8132 (800)304-3366 Fax:(616)496-8403
E-mail: wildwoodinns@voyager.net

Circa 1873. This two-story stagecoach inn was constructed with St. Joseph River clay bricks fired on the property. There are eight-foot windows, high ceilings and a walnut staircase. Country antiques are accentuated with woven rugs, collectibles and bright quilts. The nine suites include a fireplace and Jacuzzi tub. Depending on the season, guests may also borrow a tandem bike or arrange for a canoe trip. Special events are featured throughout the year. A rural Amish community and Shipshewana are nearby.

Innkeeper(s): Dick & Dolly Buerkle. $69-159. MC VISA AX DS PC TC. 18 rooms with PB, 14 with FP. 9 suites. 2 cottages. 2 conference rooms. Breakfast included in rates. Types of meals: continental-plus breakfast and early coffee/tea. Beds: QD. Air conditioning and ceiling fan in room. Fax, sauna, bicycles and library on premises. Handicap access. Antiques, fishing, shopping, downhill skiing and cross-country skiing nearby.

Location: Halfway between Chicago and Detroit.

Publicity: *Innsider, Country Home.*

"A great experience. Good food and great hosts. Thank you."

Certificate may be used: Nov. 1-April 15, Sunday-Thursday only, excluding holiday periods.

Muskegon
H6

Blue Country B&B
1415 Holton Rd
Muskegon, MI 49445-1446
(616)744-2555

Once known as the Brookside Tea House during Prohibition, this Craftsman home now is known for its family-oriented atmosphere and woodsy setting. Four guest rooms include the Blue Tea Rose Room, with a hand-carved sycamore bed and vanity, and the Whispering Woods Room, featuring wood furnishings and an attractive antique wall print. Guests will enjoy the teapot collection, and

they are welcome to try the electronic organ and hammered dulcimer. The inn is just 10 minutes from Lake Michigan. There are numerous area attractions, including Muskegon and Duck Lake state parks.

Innkeeper(s): Barbara Stevens. $61. 3 rooms. Breakfast included in rates. Types of meals: full breakfast and early coffee/tea. Evening snack and room service available. Air conditioning and turndown service in room. Cable TV, VCR and child care on premises. Amusement parks, antiques, shopping, cross-country skiing, sporting events and theater nearby.

Certificate may be used: All year, January-December, Sunday through Thursday.

Port City Victorian Inn
1259 Lakeshore Dr
Muskegon, MI 49441-1659
(616)759-0205 (800)274-3574 Fax:(616)759-0205

Circa 1877. Lumber baron and industrialist Alexander Rodgers, Sr. built this Queen Anne-style home. Among its impressive features are the grand entryway with a natural oak staircase and paneling, carved posts and spindles. The curved, leaded-glass windows in the inn's parlor offer a view of Muskegon Lake. Beveled-glass doors enclose the natural wood

fireplace in the sitting room, and high ceilings, intricate molding, polished oak floors and antiques further enhance the charm of this house. Guest rooms offer views of the lake, as well as double whirlpool tubs. The full breakfasts are served either on the sun porch, in the dining room or guests can enjoy the meal in the privacy of their room.

Innkeeper(s): Fred & Barbara Schossau. $65-125. MC VISA AX DS. 5 rooms, 3 with PB. 2 suites. Breakfast included in rates. Types of meals: full breakfast and early coffee/tea. Beds: QD. Air conditioning, turndown service and TV in room. VCR, fax, copier and bicycles on premises. Amusement parks, fishing, parks, shopping, cross-country skiing, theater and watersports nearby.

"The inn offers only comfort, good food and total peace of mind."

Certificate may be used: Oct. 1-April 30, Sunday-Thursday.

Omer
G8

Rifle River B&B
500 Center Ave
Omer, MI 48749
(517)653-2543

A gathering of maple trees shades this historic home, located in the heart of Omer. The town, which was founded just after the Civil War, has seen a multitude of disasters, and this sturdy home has stood through its fair share of floods, tornadoes and fires. The innkeepers offer four rooms decorated with antiques. Waterbeds and Jacuzzi tubs are relaxing amenities. The home, as its name might suggest, is only two blocks from the Rifle River, which offers fishing and canoeing.

Innkeeper(s): Joan Brock. $38-49. 4 rooms. Breakfast included in rates. Type of meal: continental breakfast.

Certificate may be used: September through April, anytime. May through August, Sunday through Thursday.

Oscoda
G9

Huron House
3124 N U.S.-23
Oscoda, MI 48750
(517)739-9255 Fax:(517)739-0195
E-mail: huronhouse@oscoda.com

This is a great place to take long walks on the sandy beaches of Lake Huron and follow-up with a relaxing soak in the hot tub, or if you book the Jacuzzi Suite, enjoy your own private whirlpool. Another favorite room overlooks the lake. Homemade Belgium waffles, crepes, muffins and quiche are some of the delicious breakfasts that await you, served in the privacy of your room, in the spacious second-floor breakfast room overlooking Lake Huron or on the outdoor decks. The inn is near the River Road National Forest Scenic Byway. The 22-mile route along the AuSable River provides some of the most breathtaking scenery in Michigan.

Innkeeper(s): Dennis & Martie Lorenz. $85-155. MC VISA PC. 12 rooms with PB, 5 with FP. 5 suites. Breakfast included in rates. Types of meals: continental-plus breakfast and early coffee/tea. Beds: KQ. Air conditioning, ceiling fan and TV in room. Fax and swimming on premises. Antiques, fishing, parks, cross-country skiing, golf and watersports nearby.

Certificate may be used: Nov. 1-April 30, Sunday through Thursday, subject to availability.

Petoskey (Bay View)
E7

Terrace Inn
1549 Glendale
Petoskey (Bay View), MI 49770
(616)347-2410 (800)530-9898 Fax:(616)347-2407
E-mail: terracei@freeway.net

Circa 1911. This late Victorian inn is located on what began as a Chautauqua summer resort, and more than 400 Victorian cottages have sprung up in this lakeside vacation spot. Terrace Inn was built in 1911, and most of its furnishings are original to the property. Guests will enjoy stunning views of Lake Michigan and Little Traverse Bay, and can enjoy the shore at the private Bay View beach. In keeping with the surrounding homes, the guest rooms are decorated in a romantic country cottage style. To take guests back in time, there are no televisions or telephones in the rooms. This historic resort town offers many attractions, from swimming and watersports to hiking to summer theater. During the summer season, the inn's restaurant is a great spot for dinner.

Innkeeper(s): Tom & Denise Erhart. $44-99. MC VISA AX. 44 rooms with PB. 1 conference room. Breakfast included in rates. Types of meals: continental-plus breakfast and early coffee/tea. Dinner, picnic lunch and banquet service available. Restaurant on premises. Beds: QDT. Air conditioning in room. Cable TV, VCR, copier, swimming, bicycles, tennis and child care on premises. Handicap access. Antiques, fishing, parks, shopping, downhill skiing, cross-country skiing, golf, theater and watersports nearby.

Publicity: *Oakland Press & Observer Eccentric, Michigan Magazine*

Certificate may be used: Sunday-Thursday, Nov. 1-May 1, Christmas, New Year's and other holiday periods excluded.

Port Austin
G9

Lake Street Manor
8569 Lake St
Port Austin, MI 48467
(517)738-7720

Circa 1875. As history has shown, the homes of lumber barons are often some of the most luxurious. This Victorian, with its peak roofs and gingerbread trim is no exception. The Culhane family, who made their fortune in the timber business, used this home as their summer retreat. In the 1930s, it was rented out as a summer guest house, and today innkeeper Carolyn Greenwood has once again opened the doors to visitors. The rooms have charming names: The Garden Basket Room, the Wedding Ring Room and the Raspberry Wine Room, to name a few. The Parlor Room, which includes a bay window, is accessed by double pocket doors, a characteristic feature in Victorian homes. The Bay Room, which is one of the inn's common rooms, includes a hot tub in front of a wood-burning stove.

Innkeeper(s): Carolyn Greenwood. $42-65. MC VISA DS. 5 rooms, 3 with PB. Breakfast included in rates. Type of meal: continental-plus breakfast. Room service available. Beds: D. Turndown service, ceiling fan, TV and VCR in room. Bicycles on premises. Antiques, fishing, parks, shopping, cross-country skiing, golf, theater and watersports nearby.

Certificate may be used: May 1-Oct. 31, Monday-Thursday.

Romeo   I9

Hess Manor B&B
186 S Main St
Romeo, MI 48065-5128
(810)752-4726 Fax:(810)752-6456

Circa 1854. This pre-Civil War home is located in a town listed in the National Register. The inn boasts a fireplace and Victorian decor. The innkeepers also renovated the inn's 110-year-old carriage house into an antique and gift shop. At night, guests are encouraged to enjoy the inn's Jacuzzi

under the stars. Much of Romeo's historic sites are within walking distance of Hess Manor, including galleries, antique shops, bookstores and restaurants. Frontier Town, a collection of Old West-style buildings, is a popular attraction.

Innkeeper(s): John & Ilene Hess. $54-70. MC VISA PC. 4 rooms, 2 with PB. Breakfast included in rates. Types of meals: gourmet breakfast and early coffee/tea. Beds: Q. Air conditioning in room. Cable TV, VCR and copier on premises. Antiques, fishing, parks, shopping, golf, theater and watersports nearby.

Certificate may be used: Nov. 1-April 30, all days.

Saline   J8

The Homestead B&B
9279 Macon Rd
Saline, MI 48176-9305
(313)429-9625

Circa 1851. The Homestead is a two-story brick farmhouse situated on 50 acres of fields, woods and river. The house has 15-inch-thick walls and is fur-

nished with Victorian antiques and family heirlooms. This was a favorite camping spot for Native Americans while they salted their fish, and many arrowheads have been found on the farm.

Activities include long walks through meadows of wildflowers and cross-country skiing in season. It is 40 minutes from Detroit and Toledo and 10 minutes from Ann Arbor.

Innkeeper(s): Shirley Grossman. $60-70. MC VISA AX DS TC. 5 rooms, 1 with PB. 1 conference room. Breakfast and evening snack included in rates. Types of meals: full breakfast and early coffee/tea. Beds: DT. Air conditioning in room. VCR on premises. Antiques, parks, shopping, cross-country skiing and sporting events nearby.

Location: Southeastern Michigan, within six miles of I-94 & US 23.

Publicity: *Ann Arbor News, Country Focus, Saline Reporter.*

"It is so nice to be back after three years and from 5,000 miles away!"

Certificate may be used: From Jan. 2-June 1, Sunday to Friday & Sept. 1-Dec. 30, Sunday to Friday.

Saugatuck   I6

Bayside Inn
618 Water St Box 1001
Saugatuck, MI 49453
(616)857-4321 Fax:(616)857-1870

Circa 1926. Located on the edge of the Kalamazoo River and across from the nature observation tower, this downtown inn was once a boathouse. The common room now has a fireplace and view of the water. Each guest room has its own deck. The inn is near several restaurants, shops and beaches. Fishing for salmon, perch and trout is popular.

Innkeeper(s): Kathy Wilson. $60-225. MC VISA AX DS. 10 rooms with PB, 4 with FP. 4 suites. 1 conference room. Breakfast included in rates. Type of meal: continental-plus breakfast. Beds: KQD. Air conditioning, TV and VCR in room. Fax, copier and spa on premises. Antiques, fishing, shopping, cross-country skiing, theater and watersports nearby.

Location: On the water in downtown Saugatuck.

"Our stay was wonderful, more pleasant than anticipated, we were so pleased. As for breakfast, it gets our A 1 rating."

Certificate may be used: November through March, Monday through Thursday excluding holidays.

The Red Dog B&B
132 Mason St
Saugatuck, MI 49453
(616)857-8851 (800)357-3250

Circa 1879. This comfortable, two-story farmhouse is located in the heart of downtown Saugatuck and is just a short walk away from shopping, restaurants and many of the town's seasonal activities. Rooms are furnished with a combination of traditional and antique furnishings. One room includes a fireplace and Jacuzzi tub for two. Guests can relax and enjoy views of the garden from the B&B's second-story porch, or warm up next to the fireplace in the living room. The full breakfast includes treats such as baked apple cinnamon French toast or a ham and cheese strata. The innkeepers offer special golf and off-season packages.

Innkeeper(s): Patrick & Kristine Clark. $60-110. MC VISA AX DC DS PC TC. 6 rooms with PB, 1 with FP. 1 suite. Breakfast included in rates. Types of meals: full breakfast and early coffee/tea. Beds: QD. Air conditioning, ceiling fan and TV in room. VCR, fax and copier on premises. Antiques, fishing, parks, shopping, cross-country skiing, theater and watersports nearby.

Publicity: *South Bend Trio, Michigan Cyclist, Restaurant and Institutions.*

Certificate may be used: November through April.

Twin Oaks Inn
PO Box 867, 227 Griffith St
Saugatuck, MI 49453-0867
(616)857-1600

Circa 1860. This large Queen Anne Victorian inn was a boarding house for lumbermen at the turn of the century. Now an old-English-style inn, it offers a variety of lodging choices, including three suites. One room has a Jacuzzi. Guests also may stay in the inn's cozy cottage, which boasts an outdoor hot tub. There are many diversions at Twin Oaks, including a collection of videotaped movies numbering more than 700. An English garden with a pond and fountain provides a relaxing setting, and guests also may borrow bicycles or play horseshoes on the inn's grounds.

Innkeeper(s): Jerry & Nancy Horney. $65-125. MC VISA DS TC. 7 rooms with PB. 3 suites. 1 conference room. Breakfast and evening snack included in rates. Types of meals: continental-plus breakfast, full breakfast and early coffee/tea. Beds: KQ. Air conditioning, TV and VCR in room. Antiques, fishing, parks, shopping, cross-country skiing, theater and watersports nearby.

Location: Downtown.

Publicity: *Home & Away, Cleveland Plain Dealer, South Bend Tribune, Shape, AAA Magazine.*

Certificate may be used: Nov. 1-April 30, Sunday-Thursday.

Saugatuck (Douglas) I6

Sherwood Forest B&B
938 Center St
Saugatuck (Douglas), MI 49453
(800)838-1246 Fax:(616)857-1996

Circa 1904. As the name suggests, this gracious Victorian is surrounded by woods and flanked with a large wraparound porch. Each guest room features antiques, one room offers a Jacuzzi and another an oak-manteled fireplace with a unique mural that transforms the room into a tree-top loft. A breakfast of delicious coffees or teas and homemade treats can be enjoyed either in the dining room or on the porch. The heated pool includes a mural of dolphins riding on ocean waves. White-sand beaches and the eastern shore of Lake Michigan are only a half block away.

Innkeeper(s): Keith & Susan Charak. $60-140. MC VISA DS PC. 4 rooms with PB, 1 with FP. 1 cottage. 1 conference room. Breakfast and afternoon tea included in rates. Types of meals: continental-plus breakfast and early coffee/tea. Catering service available. Beds: Q. Air conditioning and ceiling fan in room. Cable TV, VCR, fax, swimming and bicycles on premises. Antiques, fishing, parks, shopping, cross-country skiing, theater and watersports nearby.

Publicity: *Commercial Record, Chicago SunTimes, New York Times.*

"We enjoyed our weekend in the forest, the atmosphere was perfect, and your suggestions on where to eat and how to get around was very appreciated. Thanks for remembering our anniversary."

Certificate may be used: November-April, Sunday-Thursday.

Scottville
G5

Eden Hill B&B
1483 E Chauvez Rd
Scottville, MI 49454-9758
(616)757-2023

Descendants of John Adams have owned this home for more than 120 years, and a special family tree is available for viewing. This farmhouse is decorated in cheerful, country decor with comfortable furnishings and antiques. Each of the guest rooms is named after relatives who once resided in the house. The full country breakfasts offer a great start to a busy day exploring the Michigan countryside.

Innkeeper(s): Carla Craven. $60-77. MC VISA. 3 rooms. Breakfast included in rates. Type of meal: full breakfast.

Certificate may be used: All year, (summer, Sunday-Thursday only. Winter, fall and spring anytime). No holidays.

Suttons Bay
F6

Open Windows
PO Box 698, 613 St Marys Ave
Suttons Bay, MI 49682-0698
(616)271-4300 (800)520-3722

Circa 1893. The bay is just two blocks away for guests staying at this bed & breakfast, and those opting for the home's Rose Garden Room enjoy the water view from their quarters. The home's half-acre of grounds is dotted with flower gardens. Adirondack-style chairs, created by the innkeeper, line the front porch. Guests may borrow snowshoes in winter or use the home's grill and picnic table during the warmer months. Locally produced fresh fruits, entrees such as spinach and cheese crepes and homemade breads are among the breakfast fare, which is often served in a room with bay views.

Innkeeper(s): Don & Norma Blumenschine. $85-105. PC TC. 3 rooms with PB. Breakfast and evening snack included in rates. Types of meals: full breakfast, gourmet breakfast and early coffee/tea. Picnic lunch available. Beds: KQDT. Air conditioning and ceiling fan in room. Cable TV, VCR, bicycles and library on premises. Antiques, fishing, parks, shopping, downhill skiing, cross-country skiing, theater and watersports nearby.

Certificate may be used: Jan. 15-May 15, Sunday-Thursday.

Traverse City
F6

Victoriana 1898
622 Washington St
Traverse City, MI 49686-2646
(616)929-1009

Circa 1898. Egbert Ferris, a partner in the European Horse Hotel, built this Italianate Victorian manor and a two-story carriage house. Later, the bell tower

from the old Central School was moved onto the property and now serves as a handsome Greek Revival gazebo. The house has three parlors, all framed in fretwork. Etched and stained glass is found throughout. Guest rooms are furnished with family heirlooms. The house speciality is Belgian waffles topped with homemade cherry sauce.

Innkeeper(s): Flo & Bob Schermerhorn. $60-80. PC. 3 rooms with PB, 1 with FP. 1 suite. Breakfast and afternoon tea included in rates. Types of meals: gourmet breakfast and early coffee/tea. Beds: QD. Air conditioning and turndown service in room. Cable TV, VCR, fax and library on premises. Antiques, fishing, parks, shopping, downhill skiing, cross-country skiing, theater and watersports nearby.

Publicity: *Midwest Living, Oakland Press.*

"In all our B&B experiences, no one can compare with the Victoriana 1898. You're 100% in every category!"

Certificate may be used: Sunday - Thursday, November through April.

Union Pier
J5

Pine Garth B&B
15790 Lakeshore Rd
Union Pier, MI 49129-9340
(616)469-1642 Fax:(616)469-0418

Circa 1905. The seven rooms and five guest cottages at this charming bed & breakfast inn are decorated in a country style and each boasts something special. Some have a private deck and a wall of windows that look out to Lake Michigan. Other rooms feature items such as an unusual twig canopy bed, and several have whirlpool tubs. The deluxe cottages offer two queen-size beds, a wood-burning fireplace, VCR, cable TV and an outdoor tub on a private deck with a gas grill. Rates vary for the cottages. The inn has its own private beach and there are sand dunes, vineyards, forests and miles of beaches in the area.

Innkeeper(s): Paula & Russ Bulin. $115-170. MC VISA DS PC. 7 rooms with PB, 1 with FP. 5 cottages. 1 conference room. Breakfast included in rates. Types of meals: full breakfast and gourmet breakfast. Afternoon tea, evening snack and banquet service available. Beds: Q. Ceiling fan and VCR in room. Cable TV, fax, copier, swimming, bicycles and library on premises. Shopping nearby.

Location: On the shores of Lake Michigan with private beach.

Certificate may be used: Nov. 1-May 25, Sunday through Thursday, excluding holidays.

The Inn at Union Pier
9708 Berrien
Union Pier, MI 49129-0222
(616)469-4700 Fax:(616)469-4720

Circa 1920. Set on a shady acre across a country road from Lake Michigan, this inn features unique Swedish ceramic  fireplaces, a hot tub and sauna, a veranda ringing the house and a large common room with comfortable over-stuffed furniture and a grand piano.
Rooms offer such amenities as private balconies and porches, whirlpools, views of the English garden and furniture dating from the early 1900s. Breakfast includes fresh fruit and homemade jams made of fruit from surrounding farms.
Innkeeper(s): Joyce & Mark Pitts. $110-195. MC VISA DS PC TC. 16 rooms with PB, 12 with FP. 2 suites. 1 conference room. Breakfast and evening snack included in rates. Types of meals: continental breakfast, full breakfast, gourmet breakfast and early coffee/tea. Catering service available. Beds: KQT. Air conditioning and ceiling fan in room. Cable TV, VCR, fax, copier, spa, swimming, sauna, bicycles and library on premises. Handicap access. Antiques, fishing, parks, cross-country skiing, sporting events and watersports nearby.
Publicity: *Chicago Tribune, Chicago, Midwest Living, Chicago Sun Times, Country Living, Romantic Inns, The Travel Channel.*

"The food, the atmosphere, the accommodations, and of course, the entire staff made this the most relaxing weekend ever."

Certificate may be used: Oct. 1-May 25, Sunday through Thursday only, no holidays.

Walloon Lake   E7

Masters House B&B
2253 N Shore Dr
Walloon Lake, MI 49796
(616)535-2944

Circa 1890. This bed & breakfast once served as the location for the town's first telephone company. There are six comfortably decorated rooms, two with private bath. The home is within walking distance of the beach and shops and restaurants in town.
Innkeeper(s): Joe Breidenstein. $40-90. MC VISA PC TC. 6 rooms, 2 with PB. 1 cottage. Breakfast included in rates. Type of meal: continental-plus breakfast. Beds: KQDT. Cable TV and VCR on premises. Antiques, fishing, downhill skiing, cross-country skiing, theater and watersports nearby.

Certificate may be used: Any time-subject to availability, midweek most likely.

White Cloud   H6

Crow's Nest B&B
1440 N Luce Ave
White Cloud, MI 49349-9712
(616)689-0088 (800)354-0850

Circa 1900. On the banks of the White River, under the shade of century-old beech and maple trees, the Crow's Nest is decorated in a gracious country decor with early 19th-century antiques. There is a formal dining room where full breakfasts are served. Pumpkin pancakes is a specialty. A glass-enclosed porch features floor-to-ceiling views. The inn is located on five acres with formal gardens and clumps of raspberries and blueberries. Inner tubing and trout fishing are popular activities in the summer.
Innkeeper(s): Joyce & Dick Billingsley. $45-65. PC TC. 3 rooms, 1 with PB. Breakfast and evening snack included in rates. Type of meal: full breakfast. Beds: Q. Ceiling fan in room. VCR on premises. Fishing and cross-country skiing nearby.

"Great view! Breakfast was a delight."

Certificate may be used: Sept. 1 through April 30.

Ypsilanti   J8

Parish House Inn
103 S Huron St
Ypsilanti, MI 48197-5421
(313)480-4800 (800)480-4866 Fax:(313)480-7472

Circa 1893. This Queen Anne Victorian was named in honor of its service as a parsonage for the First Congregational Church. The home remained a parsonage for more than 50 years after its construction and then served as a church office and Sunday school building. It was moved to its present site in Ypsilanti's historic district in the late 1980s. The rooms are individually decorated with Victorian-style wallpapers and antiques. One guest room includes a two-person Jacuzzi tub. Those in search of a late-night snack need only venture into the kitchen to find drinks and the cookie jar. For special occasions, the innkeepers can arrange trays with flowers, non-alcoholic champagne, chocolates, fruit or cheese. The terrace overlooks the Huron River.
Innkeeper(s): Mrs. Chris Mason. $85-115. MC VISA AX PC TC. 9 rooms with PB, 2 with FP. 1 conference room. Breakfast and evening snack included in rates. Types of meals: continental breakfast, full breakfast, gourmet breakfast and early coffee/tea. Afternoon tea, picnic lunch, catering service and catered breakfast available. Beds: QDT. Air conditioning, ceiling fan, TV and VCR in room. Fax and library on premises. Handicap access. Amusement parks, antiques, fishing, parks, shopping, cross-country skiing, sporting events, theater and watersports nearby.

Certificate may be used: December through May, Sunday - Thursday

Minnesota

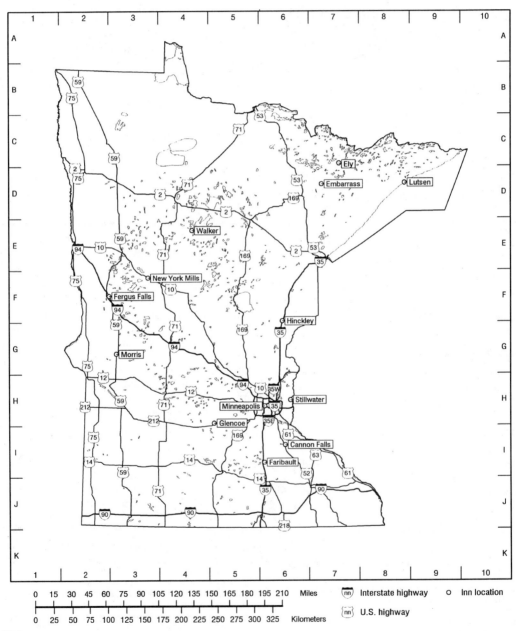

0 15 30 45 60 75 90 105 120 135 150 165 180 195 210 Miles

0   25 50 75 100 125 150 175 200 225 250 275 300 325 Kilometers

(nn) Interstate highway   o Inn location

(nn) U.S. highway

Cannon Falls   I6

Quill & Quilt
615 Hoffman St W
Cannon Falls, MN 55009-1923
(507)263-5507 (800)488-3849 Fax:(507)263-4599

Circa 1897. This three-story, gabled Colonial Revival house has six bay windows and several porches and decks. The inn features a well-stocked library, a front parlor with a fireplace, and handsomely decorated guest rooms. A favorite is the room with a double whirlpool tub, two bay windows, a king-size oak canopy bed and Victorian chairs.

Innkeeper(s): Staci Smith. $55-130. AP. MC VISA. 4 rooms with PB. 1 suite. Breakfast included in rates. Types of meals: continental breakfast and full breakfast. Beds: KQD. Spa on premises. Antiques, downhill skiing, cross-country skiing and watersports nearby.
Location: Forty-five miles from Minneapolis/St. Paul and Rochester.
Publicity: *Minneapolis Tribune, Country Quilts.*

"What a pleasure to find the charm and hospitality of an English country home while on holiday in the United States."
Certificate may be used: Sunday through Thursday, Nov. 1-April 30.

Ely   C7

Burntside Lodge
2755 Burntside Lodge Rd
Ely, MN 55731-8402
(218)365-3894

Circa 1913. "Staying here is like taking a vacation 60 years ago," states innkeeper Lou LaMontagne. Families have come here for more than 80 years to enjoy the waterfront and woodside setting. The lodge and its cabins are in the National Register and much of the original hand-carved furnishings remain from the jazz age. Fishing, listening to the cry of the loon and boating around the lake's 125 islands are popular activities. Breakfast and dinner are available in the waterside dining room.
Innkeeper(s): Lou & Lonnie LaMontagne. $90-165. MAP, EP. MC VISA AX DS PC TC. 24 cottages. Types of meals: full breakfast and early coffee/tea. Dinner and lunch available. Beds: KDT. VCR, fax, copier, swimming, sauna and library on premises. Antiques, fishing, parks, shopping and watersports nearby.
Location: Six miles southwest of Ely.
Certificate may be used: May 16-June 20, Aug. 22-Sept 26.

Embarrass   D7

Finnish Heritage Homestead
4776 Waisanen Rd
Embarrass, MN 55732-8347
(218)984-3318 (800)863-6545

Circa 1901. This turn-of-the-century Finnish-American log house offers outdoor recreation and family-style full breakfasts to visitors, who receive many personal touches, such as bath robes, slipper socks and turndown service. Guests also may utilize the inn's relaxing sauna and enjoy badminton, bocce ball, croquet and horseshoes on its spacious grounds. Terrific fishing and skiing are found nearby, and be sure to inquire about the availability of picnic lunches to take along. A gazebo and gift shop also are on the premises.
Innkeeper(s): Elaine Bragenton & Buzz Schultz. $50-58. PC TC. 4 rooms. Breakfast included in rates. Types of meals: full breakfast and early coffee/tea. Afternoon tea, evening snack, picnic lunch and room service available. Beds: QT. Turndown service and ceiling fan in room. VCR and sauna on premises. Antiques, fishing, parks, shopping, downhill skiing, cross-country skiing and watersports nearby.
Certificate may be used: Sunday to Thursday only.

Faribault   I6

Cherub Hill B&B Inn
105 1st Ave NW
Faribault, MN 55021-5102
(507)332-2024 (800)332-7254

Circa 1896. Midway between the Twin Cities and Albert Lea, this Queen Anne Victorian inn offers romantic accommodations to its guests, many of whom are honeymooners. Guests are treated to early coffee or tea before their full breakfasts are served. The three air-conditioned guest rooms, which all feature private baths and turndown service, also include one suite. Other available guest room amenities include a fireplace and whirlpool bath. The charming town features many historic buildings, fine restaurants and shops. Nerstrand-Big Woods and Sakatah Lake state parks are nearby.

Innkeeper(s): Jean Cummings. $80-95. MC VISA. 4 rooms, 3 with PB, 1 with FP. 1 suite. Breakfast included in rates. Types of meals: full breakfast and early coffee/tea. Beds: QD. Air conditioning, turndown service and ceiling fan in room. Antiques, fishing, shopping, cross-country skiing and sporting events nearby.

Certificate may be used: Sunday through Thursday, November-May.

Fergus Falls   F3

Bakketopp Hus
RR 2 Box 187A
Fergus Falls, MN 56537-9802
(218)739-2915 (800)739-2915

Circa 1976. From the decks of this wooded home, guests can enjoy the scenery of Long Lake and catch glimpses of wildlife. Antiques, handmade quilts and down comforters decorate the cozy guest rooms. One room includes a private spa and draped canopy bed. Another room includes a fireplace. A bounty of nearby outdoor activities are sure to please nature lovers, and antique shops and restaurants are nearby.

Innkeeper(s): Dennis & Judy Nims. $65-95. MC VISA DS PC TC. 3 rooms with PB. Breakfast, afternoon tea and evening snack included in rates. Types of meals: gourmet breakfast and early coffee/tea. Beds: Q. Air conditioning, ceiling fan and TV in room. VCR and swimming on premises. Amusement parks, antiques, fishing, parks, shopping, downhill skiing, cross-country skiing, theater and watersports nearby.

Publicity: *Minneapolis Tribune.*

Certificate may be used: Sunday through Thursday for months of March, November, December, January, February.

Glencoe   H5

Glencoe Castle B&B
831 13th St E
Glencoe, MN 55336-1503
(320)864-3043 (800)517-3334
E-mail: schoenr@hutchtel.net

Circa 1895. Glencoe Castle was built as a wedding promise to lure a bride from New York to Minnesota. She would move to Glencoe only if her husband built her a castle. This grand manor did the trick, with its carved woodwork, stained glass and ornate wood floors. The third floor originally was built as a ballroom. The home is decorated with antiques, Oriental and country pieces. Guests are treated to a lavish candlelight breakfast with such items as baked eggs in cream and Havarti cheese, Canadian bacon, blueberry French toast, homemade bread, pastries and fresh fruit. In the evenings, tea and dessert are served. There is a Victorian gift shop on the premises. For an extra charge, guests can arrange small meetings, parties, group teas, dinner or teas for two. The teas range from a light breakfast

tea to the more extravagant Victorian High Tea. Murder-Mystery events also can be arranged.

Innkeeper(s): Becky & Rick Schoeneck. $65-175. MC VISA AX DS PC. 4 rooms, 1 with PB, 1 with FP. Breakfast and evening snack included in rates. Type of meal: gourmet breakfast. Afternoon tea available. Beds: KD. Air conditioning in room. Cable TV, VCR, fax and copier on premises. Amusement parks, antiques, fishing, parks, shopping, downhill skiing, cross-country skiing, sporting events and theater nearby.

Certificate may be used: Nov. 1-March 31, Sunday-Thursday (except holiday weekends).

Hinckley   F6

Dakota Lodge B&B
Rt 3 Box 178
Hinckley, MN 55037-9418
(320)384-6052 Fax:(320)384-6052

Circa 1976. Although this inn is situated between Minneapolis and Duluth on six scenic acres, the innkeepers named their B&B in honor of their birthplace: North Dakota. The guest rooms are named after little known Dakota towns. The Medora and Kathryn rooms include whirlpools and fireplaces. Other rooms include lacy curtains, quilts and special furnishings. The country breakfasts are expansive with egg and meat dishes, fruit and a daily entree. Hinckley offers a variety of activities, including a 32-mile bike trail, a casino and antique shops.

Innkeeper(s): Mike Schmitz & Tad Hilborn. $58-135. MC VISA DS PC TC. 5 rooms with PB, 4 with FP. 1 cottage. Breakfast included in rates. Types of meals: full breakfast and early coffee/tea. Beds: KQ. Air conditioning and ceiling fan in room. VCR, fax, copier and library on premises. Antiques, fishing, parks, cross-country skiing and watersports nearby.

Certificate may be used: All year, Sunday-Thursday.

Lutsen   D8

Cascade Lodge
3719 W Hwy 61
Lutsen, MN 55612-9705
(218)387-1112 (800)322-9543 Fax:(218)387-1113
E-mail: cascade@cascadelodgemn.com

Circa 1938. A main lodge and 10 cabins (including log cabins), a four-unit motel and a nearby house, comprise Cascade Lodge, tucked away in the midst of Cascade River State Park, which overlooks Lake Superior. Cascade Creek meanders between the cabins toward the lake. The lodge has a natural-stone fireplace and the living room and restaurant areas are decorated with hunting trophies of moose, coyote, wolves and bear. Canoeing, hiking to Lookout Mountain, walking along Wild Flower Trail and watching the sunset from the lawn swing are favorite summer activities. The lodge is open all year.

Innkeeper(s): Gene & Laurene Glader. $35-170. MAP, EP, MC VISA AX DS PC TC. 11 cottages, 12 with PB, 9 with FP. 1 suite. 1 conference room. Type of meal: early coffee/tea. Restaurant on premises. Beds: QDT. VCR, fax, copier, computer, bicycles and library on premises. Antiques, fishing, parks, shopping, downhill skiing, cross-country skiing, golf, theater and watersports nearby.

Location: Overlooking Lake Superior on Highway 61.

Publicity: *Country Inns, Lake Superior.*

"We needed to get away and recharge ourselves. This was the perfect place."

Certificate may be used: March 30-May 15 and Oct. 19-Dec. 18, Sunday-Thursday.

Lindgren's B&B on Lake Superior
County Rd 35, PO Box 56
Lutsen, MN 55612-0056
(218)663-7450

Circa 1926. This '20s log home is in the Superior National Forest on the north shore of Lake Superior. The inn features massive stone fireplaces, a baby grand piano, wildlife decor and a Finnish-style sauna. The living room has tongue-and-groove, Western knotty cedar wood paneling and seven-foot windows offering a view of the lake. The innkeeper's homemade jams, freshly baked breads and entrees such as French Toast topped with homemade chokecherry syrup, eggs Benedict or Danish

pancakes get the day off to a pleasant start. In addition to horseshoes and a volleyball court, guests can gaze at the lake on a swinging love seat.

Innkeeper(s): Shirley Lindgren. $85-125. MC VISA PC. 4 rooms with PB, 1 with FP. Breakfast included in rates. Types of meals: full breakfast and early coffee/tea. Afternoon tea, evening snack and picnic lunch available. Beds: KDT. VCR, sauna and library on premises. Antiques, fishing, parks, shopping, downhill skiing, cross-country skiing, golf, theater and watersports nearby.

Location: On the Lake Superior Circle Tour.

Publicity: *Brainerd Daily Dispatch, Duluth News-Tribune, Tempo, Midwest Living, Minnesota Monthly, Lake Superior, Country, Minneapolis-St. Paul.*

"Your delectable dessert with anniversary cooler made a perfect end to a most memorable day for us."

Certificate may be used: Midweek (Monday-Thursday) April 1-June 1 and Nov. 1-Dec. 15, holidays excluded.

Minneapolis   H6

The LeBlanc House
302 University Ave NE
Minneapolis, MN 55413-2052
(612)379-2570

Circa 1896. Visitors to the University of Minnesota area should look no further than the LeBlanc House. The restored Queen Anne Victorian offers guests a historical perspective of life in the 1800s. The inn's convenient location also provides easy access to the Metrodome and downtown Minneapolis, while giving its guests a chance to

relax in style after exploring the area. Amelia's Room has a view of the city lights and visitors may be treated to gourmet specialties such as pistachio quiche or rum raisin French toast.

Innkeeper(s): Barb Zahasky & Bob Shulstad. $85-105. MC VISA AX PC. 3 rooms, 1 with PB. Breakfast included in rates. Type of meal: full breakfast. Beds: Q. Air conditioning, turndown service and ceiling fan in room. Amusement parks, antiques, fishing, parks, shopping, downhill skiing, cross-country skiing, sporting events, theater and watersports nearby.

Certificate may be used: Anytime Sunday through Thursday only.

Morris
G3

The American House
410 E 3rd St
Morris, MN 56267-1426
(320)589-4054

Circa 1900. One block from the Morris campus of the University of Minnesota, this is a two-story house with a wide veranda. It is decorated in a country style with original stencil designs, stained glass and family heirlooms. The Elizabeth Room holds a Jenny Lind bed with a hand-crocheted bedcover.
Innkeeper(s): Karen Berget. $35-50. MC VISA PC TC. 3 rooms. Breakfast included in rates. Type of meal: full breakfast. Beds: D. Air conditioning and ceiling fan in room. Cable TV and bicycles on premises. Fishing, shopping and cross-country skiing nearby.
Publicity: *Forum, Hancock Record.*

"It was most delightful!"

Certificate may be used: Anytime, subject to availability.

New York Mills
F3

Whistle Stop Inn B&B
RR 1 Box 85
New York Mills, MN 56567-9704
(218)385-2223 (800)328-6315

Circa 1903. A choo-choo theme permeates the atmosphere at this signature Victorian home. Antiques and railroad memorabilia decorate guest rooms with names such as Great Northern or Burlington Northern. The Northern Pacific room includes a bath with a clawfoot tub. For something unusual, try a night in the Cozy Caboose, which is exactly that, a restored 19th-century caboose. Despite the rustic nature, the caboose offers a double whirlpool tub. Freshly baked breads and seasonal fruit accompany the mouth-watering, homemade breakfasts.
Innkeeper(s): Roger & Jann Lee. $49-79. MC VISA AX DS PC. 4 rooms with PB. 1 suite. 1 cottage. 1 conference room. Breakfast included in rates. Types of meals: continental breakfast, full breakfast and early coffee/tea. Afternoon tea available. Beds: QD. Ceiling fan and TV in room. Bicycles on premises. Antiques, fishing, parks, shopping, cross-country skiing, golf and watersports nearby.
Certificate may be used: Year-round, Sunday-Thursday.

Stillwater
H6

Heirloom Inn B&B
1103 3rd St S
Stillwater, MN 55082-6253
(612)430-2289

Circa 1869. Within walking distance of historic downtown Stillwater, the Heirloom Inn is situated in a lovely residential area. The Victorian-Italianate home features a formal parlor with fireplace, a music room with grand piano, and a large screened porch with wicker rockers. Rooms are appointed with family heirlooms, quilts and hardwood floors with inlaid detail. Breakfast is served by candlelight in the dining room. A resident classical pianist performs for guests.
Innkeeper(s): Mark Brown. $89-95. PC. 3 rooms, 2 with PB. Breakfast and afternoon tea included in rates. Types of meals: continental breakfast, full breakfast, gourmet breakfast and early coffee/tea. Beds: D. Air conditioning and turndown service in room. Antiques, fishing, parks, shopping, downhill skiing, cross-country skiing, sporting events, golf and theater nearby.
Location: Historic Stillwater in the St. Croix River valley.

"The charming atmosphere provided us with much needed rest and relaxation."

Certificate may be used: Jan. 20-April 30, excluding holidays.

James A. Mulvey Residence Inn
622 W Churchill
Stillwater, MN 55082
(612)430-8008

Circa 1878. A charming river town is home to this Italianate-style inn, just a short distance from the Twin Cities, but far from the metro area in atmosphere. Visitors select from five guest rooms, including one suite. The rooms feature queen beds and

Victorian furnishings. The inn, just nine blocks from the St. Croix River, is a popular stop with couples celebrating anniversaries. Guests enjoy the inn's convenient early coffee or tea service that precedes the full breakfasts. Great antiquing, fishing and skiing are nearby, and there are many picnic spots in the area.

Innkeeper(s): Truett & Jill Lawson. $99-149. MC VISA PC TC. 5 rooms with PB, 3 with FP. 1 suite. Breakfast and afternoon tea included in rates. Types of meals: gourmet breakfast and early coffee/tea. Beds: QD. Air conditioning in room. Bicycles on premises. Antiques, fishing, parks, shopping, downhill skiing, cross-country skiing, theater and watersports nearby.

Certificate may be used: Monday-Thursday only

The William Sauntry Mansion
626 4th St N
Stillwater, MN 55082-4827
(612)430-2653 (800)828-2653 Fax:(612)351-7872
E-mail: halbardiers@worldnet.att.net

Circa 1890. This Queen Anne Victorian is stunning inside and out. Its exterior is that of a true "Painted Lady," done in shades of goldenrod and a deep green, with intricate trim. The palatial interior has been painstakingly restored, including the near dozen fireplaces, shining parquet floors and beautiful woodwork. Stained-glass windows add to the Victorian ambiance, as do the variety of fine antiques that fill the home. Each bedchamber has a fireplace, and some have whirlpool tubs. William Sauntry, a prominent lumber baron, built the 25-room manor, and it is listed in the National Register. With the many historic homes, Stillwater is a perfect town for those who wish to bask in all that is Victoriana. Minneapolis and the Mall of America are nearby.

Innkeeper(s): Art & Elaine Halbardier. $99-159. MC VISA. 7 rooms with PB, 7 with FP. Breakfast, afternoon tea and evening snack included in rates. Types of meals: gourmet breakfast and early coffee/tea. Beds: KQ. Air conditioning in room. Fax on premises. Fishing, parks, shopping, downhill skiing, sporting events, golf, theater and watersports nearby.

"The history here is intriguing, the rooms very nicely done and your cooking is superb."

Certificate may be used: Sunday through Thursday, November-May, excluding Christmas/New Year holidays, subject to availability. Not valid with any other discount or promotion.

Walker   E4

Peacecliff
HCR 73 Box 998d
Walker, MN 56484-9579
(218)547-2832

Circa 1957. Innkeepers Dave and Kathy Laursen are Minnesota natives, and after years away, returned to their home state and opened this serene, waterfront B&B. The English Tudor affords views of Lake Leech from most of its rooms, which are decorated with a mix of traditional and Victorian furnishings. The Laursens are nature lovers, having trekked across miles of mountain trails and scenic areas. They are happy to point out nearby recreation sites, including the North Country Trail, a 68-mile journey through Chippewa National Forest.

Innkeeper(s): Dave & Kathy Laursen. $58-95. MC VISA AX DS TC. 5 rooms, 1 with PB, 1 with FP. 1 suite. Breakfast included in rates. Types of meals: full breakfast, gourmet breakfast and early coffee/tea. Beds: QDT. Cable TV and VCR on premises. Amusement parks, antiques, fishing, parks, shopping, cross-country skiing, theater and watersports nearby.

Certificate may be used: Sunday-Thursday, except holidays

Tianna Farms B&B
PO Box 968
Walker, MN 56484-0968
(218)547-1306 (800)842-6620

Circa 1922. Overlooking beautiful Leech Lake, this former dairy farm was started by the grandfather of the current owner, as was the 18-hole golf course, now named Tianna Country Club. Guests receive 50 percent off green fees. The inn's lakefront resort area lures many visitors, who may choose from five rooms, ranging from the Garden and Hunting rooms, with two twin beds, to the Suite, with a king and two twin beds. The innkeepers also offer a cabin which sleeps six. The family-oriented Tianna Farms also can be reserved at whole-house rates for weekends or full weeks. There are tennis facilities and a trampoline on the premises. The area boasts hiking, biking and snowmobile trails.

Innkeeper(s): Linda Wenzel. $45-125. MC VISA DS TC. 5 rooms with PB. Breakfast and evening snack included in rates. Type of meal: full breakfast. Beds: KQT. Cable TV and VCR on premises. Antiques, fishing, parks, shopping, cross-country skiing and watersports nearby.

"What a wonderful place!"

Certificate may be used: Oct. 16-May 14.

Mississippi

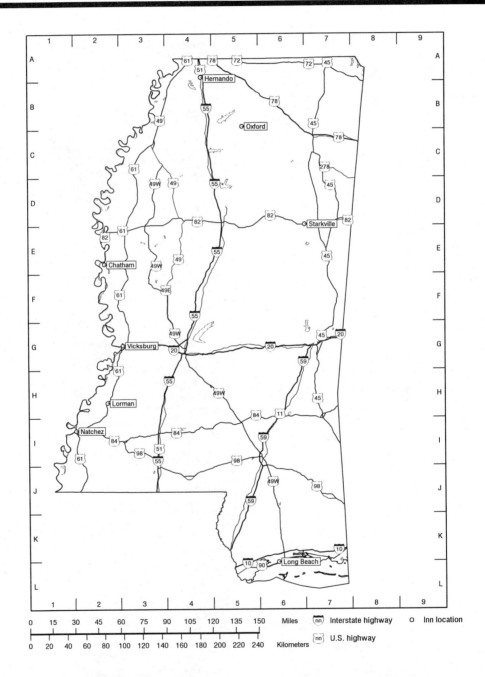

0 15 30 45 60 75 90 105 120 135 150   Miles

0 20 40 60 80 100 120 140 160 180 200 220 240   Kilometers

nn Interstate highway   o Inn location

nn U.S. highway

Chatham
E2

Mount Holly Plantation Inn
HC 63 Box 140
Chatham, MS 38731-9601
(601)827-2652 Fax:(601)827-5661

Circa 1855. This 20-room mansion, on six acres fronting Lake Washington, is in the Italianate style. It has 24-inch-thick walls of brick. Most of

the rooms are 25 by 25 feet. All bedrooms open off a large second-floor ballroom, including a room with a 12-foot-high canopy bed. Antique furnishings, bordered ceilings, and chandeliers decorate the interior.

Innkeeper(s): Ann Woods. $65-150. MC VISA DS PC TC. 7 rooms, 4 with PB, 4 with FP. 1 suite. 1 conference room. Breakfast included in rates. Types of meals: full breakfast and early coffee/tea. Beds: KQDT. Air conditioning and ceiling fan in room. Fax on premises. Antiques, fishing, parks and watersports nearby.

Location: On Lake Washington, close to Greenville.

Publicity: *Southern Living.*

Certificate may be used: July 1-Aug. 31 & Nov. 1-Feb. 28, excluding weekends and holidays.

Hernando
A4

Sassafras Inn
785 Hwy 51 S
Hernando, MS 38632-8149
(601)429-5864 (800)882-1897 Fax:(601)429-4591
E-mail: sassyinn@mem.net

Circa 1985. This modern inn offers guests to the state's Northwest corner a delightful respite from their travels or from the hustle and bustle of Memphis, 10 miles south. An impressive indoor swimming pool and spa are guest favorites and visitors also enjoy the cabana room for reading or lounging, or the recreation room with billiards, darts and ping pong. A romantic honeymoon cottage also is available. Arkabutla Lake is an easy drive from the inn.

Innkeeper(s): Dennis & Francee McClanahan. $80-175. MC VISA AX DS PC TC. 4 rooms, 3 with PB. 1 suite. 1 cottage. Breakfast, afternoon tea and evening snack included in rates. Types of meals: full breakfast and early coffee/tea. Beds: QD. Air conditioning, turndown service, ceiling

fan, TV and VCR in room. Fax, copier, spa, swimming and library on premises. Antiques, parks and watersports nearby.

Location: Near Graceland, 25 minutes from downtown Memphis.

Certificate may be used: All year, Sunday - Thursday, no holidays.

Long Beach
L6

Red Creek Inn, Vineyard & Racing Stables
7416 Red Creek Rd
Long Beach, MS 39560-8804
(601)452-3080 (800)729-9670 Fax:(601)452-4450

Circa 1899. This inn was built in the raised French cottage-style by a retired Italian sea captain, who wished to entice his bride to move from her parents' home in New Orleans. There are two swings on the 64-foot front porch and one swing that hangs from a 300-year-old oak tree. Magnolias and ancient live oaks, some registered with

the Live Oak Society of the Louisiana Garden Club, dot 11 acres. The inn features a parlor, six fireplaces, ceiling fans and antiques, including a Victorian organ, wooden radios and a Victrola. The inn's suite includes a Jacuzzi tub.

Innkeeper(s): Karl & "Toni" Mertz. $59-89. PC. 5 rooms, 3 with PB, 1 with FP. 1 suite. 1 conference room. Breakfast included in rates. Types of meals: continental-plus breakfast and early coffee/tea. Beds: DT. Air conditioning in room. Cable TV, VCR, fax, copier, stables and library on premises. Amusement parks, antiques, fishing, parks, shopping, theater and watersports nearby.

Publicity: *Jackson Daily News, Innviews, TV Channel 13, Mississippi ETV, Men's Journal.*

"We loved waking up here on these misty spring mornings. The Old South is here."

Certificate may be used: Sunday-Thursday, May-August and any time September-April (depending upon availability).

Lorman
H2

Canemont Plantation
Rt 2 Box 45
Lorman, MS 39096-9602
(601)877-3784 (800)423-0684 Fax:(601)877-2010

Circa 1855. Guests traveling down the famed Natchez Trace will want to reserve a stay at this 6,000-acre working plantation. Among the many treasures found on the inn grounds, guest will discover the former quarters of Ben Coleman, a slave who hid the plantation silver away from the Yankees during the Civil War. Windsor Plantation, considered to be one of the grandest antebellum manors east of the Mississippi, is found within the immense grounds. Plantation guests stay in one of three guest cottages, which are sprinkled by the main house, an Italianate Revival structure peaked with three chimneys. Each of the cottages includes a wood-burning fireplace or stove. The hosts offer guided tours of the grounds, where encounters with deer and birds aren't uncommon, and guests may fish in the stocked ponds.

Innkeeper(s): Ray & Rachel Forrest. $145-165. MAP. MC VISA. 3 suites, 3 with FP. 2 conference rooms. Breakfast, dinner and evening snack included in rates. Types of meals: full breakfast and gourmet breakfast. Picnic lunch, lunch, banquet service and catering service available. Restaurant on premises. Beds: KD. Air conditioning and ceiling fan in room. VCR, fax and copier on premises. Antiques, fishing, parks and shopping nearby.

Certificate may be used: June, July, August-Sunday through Thursday.

Rosswood Plantation

Hwy 552 East
Lorman, MS 39096
(601)437-4215 (800)533-5889 Fax:(601)437-6888
E-mail: whylander@aol.com

Circa 1857. Rosswood is a stately, columned mansion in an original plantation setting. Here, guests may find antiques, buried treasure, ghosts, history of a slave revolt, a Civil War battleground, the first owner's diary and genuine southern hospitality. Voted the "prettiest place in the country" by Farm & Ranch Living, the manor is a Mississippi Landmark and is in the National Register.

Innkeeper(s): Jean & Walt Hylander. $99-125. MC VISA AX DS PC TC. 4 rooms with PB, 4 with FP. Breakfast included in rates. Types of meals: gourmet breakfast and early coffee/tea. Beds: QDT. Air conditioning, ceiling fan and VCR in room. Fax, copier, spa, swimming and library on premises. Antiques, fishing, parks and shopping nearby.

Publicity: *Southern Living, The New York Times, Mississippi Magazine, Conde Nast Traveler, Inn Country USA.*

Certificate may be used: June, July, August, Sunday through Thursday.

Natchez   I2

Harper House

201 Arlington Ave
Natchez, MS 39120-3548
(601)445-5557

Circa 1892. Located in the Arlington Heights section of Natchez, this Queen Anne Victorian inn is a fine example of the city's popular Victorian-style homes. The inn's convenient location, midway between Baton Rouge and Vicksburg, makes it an ideal stop for those exploring this beautiful and his-

tory-rich region. Breakfast is served in a charming gazebo. Natchez-Under-the-Hill and the famous antebellum homes in the historic district are within easy walking distance. Natchez National Cemetery and Natchez State Park are nearby.

Innkeeper(s): Kay Warren. $90. MC VISA. 1 room. Breakfast included in rates. Types of meals: continental breakfast and full breakfast. Antiques, shopping and theater nearby.

Certificate may be used: November, December (excluding 23, 24, 25, 26). January-February.

Oxford   B5

Oliver-Britt House

512 Van Buren Ave
Oxford, MS 38655-3838
(601)234-8043

Circa 1905. White columns and a picturesque veranda highlight the exterior of this Greek Revival inn shaded by trees. English country comfort is the emphasis in the interior, which includes a collection of antiques. On weekends, guests are treated to a Southern-style breakfast with all the trimmings. A travel service is located on the premises.

Innkeeper(s): Glynn Oliver. $55-65. MC VISA AX DS TC. 5 rooms with PB. Breakfast included in rates. Types of meals: full breakfast and early coffee/tea. Banquet service and catering service available. Beds: KQ. Air conditioning, ceiling fan and TV in room. Antiques, parks, shopping and sporting events nearby.

Certificate may be used: Dec. 1-Feb. 28, Sunday-Thursday.

Starkville   D7

The Cedars B&B

2173 Oktoc Rd
Starkville, MS 39759-9251
(601)324-7569

Circa 1836. This historic plantation offers a glimpse of life in the 19th-century South. The late Colonial/Greek Revival structure was built primarily by slaves, with construction lasting two years. The inn's 183 acres boast fishing ponds, pasture and woods, and guests love to explore, hike and ride horses. Four guest rooms are available, two with private bath. Visitors enjoy the inn's collection of 19th- and early 20th-century horse and farm equip-

ment. Noxubee Wildlife Refuge and the Tombigbee National Forest are within easy driving distance.

Innkeeper(s): Erin Scanlon. $50-65. TC. 4 rooms, 2 with PB, 4 with FP. 2 conference rooms. Breakfast and evening snack included in rates. Types of meals: continental breakfast, continental-plus breakfast, full breakfast and early coffee/tea. Picnic lunch available. Beds: FT. Air conditioning in room. Antiques, fishing, parks, shopping, sporting events, theater and watersports nearby.

Certificate may be used: Anytime based on availability.

Vicksburg   G3

Balfour House
1002 Crawford St
Vicksburg, MS 39181-0781
(601)638-7113 (800)294-7113

Circa 1835. Writer and former resident Emma Balfour witnessed the Siege of Vicksburg from the window of this Greek Revival home. Until the Civil War, the home was the site of elegant balls attended by Southern belles in ornate gowns accompanied by Confederate beaus. Innkeepers Bob and Sharon Humble brought back these grand affairs during several re-enactment dances, in which guests dress up in period costume. The National Register home is a piece of history, with stunning architectural features, such as the showpiece, three-story elliptical spiral staircase. The home is an official site on the Civil War Discovery Trail, as well as a Vicksburg and Mississippi landmark.

Innkeeper(s): Bob & Sharon Humble. $85-150. MC VISA AX PC TC. 4 rooms with PB, 1 with FP. 1 conference room. Breakfast included in rates. Type of meal: gourmet breakfast. Catering service available. Beds: KQDT. Air conditioning and TV in room. Amusement parks, antiques, fishing, parks, shopping and theater nearby.

Certificate may be used: Jan. 30-Sept. 30, Sunday-Friday.

Belle of The Bends
508 Klein St
Vicksburg, MS 39180-4004
(601)634-0737 (800)844-2308

Circa 1876. Located in Vicksburg's Historic Garden District, this Victorian, Italianate mansion was built by Mississippi State Senator Murray F. Smith and his wife, Kate. It is nestled on a bluff overlooking the Mississippi River. The decor includes period antiques, Oriental rugs and memorabilia of the steamboats that plied the river waters in the 1880s

and early 1900s. Two bedrooms and the first- and second-story wraparound verandas provide views of the river. A plantation breakfast is served and a tour of the house and history of the steamboats owned by the Morrissey Line is given. A tour of the Victorian Gardens also is available to guests.

Innkeeper(s): Wallace & Josephine Pratt. $95-135. MC VISA AX DS. 4 rooms with PB. Breakfast and afternoon tea included in rates. Type of meal: full breakfast. Beds: KQDT. Air conditioning, TV and VCR in room. Antiques nearby.

Publicity: *Natchez Trace News Explorer, Victorian Style, Victoria.*

"Thank you for the personalized tour of the home and area. We greatly enjoyed our stay. This house got us into the spirit of the period."

Certificate may be used: January & February, except Valentine's Day, Sunday-Thursday.

Stained Glass Manor - Oak Hall
2430 Drummond St
Vicksburg, MS 39180
(601)638-8893 Fax:(601)636-3055
E-mail: vickbnb@magnolia.net

Circa 1902. Billed by the innkeepers as "Vicksburg's historic Vick inn," this restored, Mission-style manor boasts 38 stained-glass windows, original woodwork and light fixtures. Period furnishings create a Victorian flavor. George Washington Maher, who employed a young draftsman named Frank Lloyd Wright, probably designed the home, which was built from 1902 to 1908. Lewis J. Millet did the art for 36 of the stained-glass panels. The home's first owner, Fannie Vick Willis Johnson, was a descendent of the first Vick in Vicksburg. All but one guest room has a fireplace, and all are richly appointed with antiques, reproductions and Oriental rugs. "New Orleans" breakfasts begin with cafe au lait. Freshly baked breads, quiche and other treats follow.

Innkeeper(s): Bill & Shirley Smollen. $60-185. MC VISA DS TC. 6 rooms, 4 with PB, 10 with FP. 1 suite. 1 cottage. 3 conference rooms. Breakfast included in rates. Types of meals: continental-plus breakfast, gourmet breakfast and early coffee/tea. Beds: KQDT. Air conditioning and TV in room. VCR, fax and library on premises. Amusement parks, antiques, fishing, parks, shopping, theater and watersports nearby.

Certificate may be used: September 15-March 15, Sunday through Thursday. Holidays, weekends, Thanksgiving, Christmas, New Year's excluded

Missouri

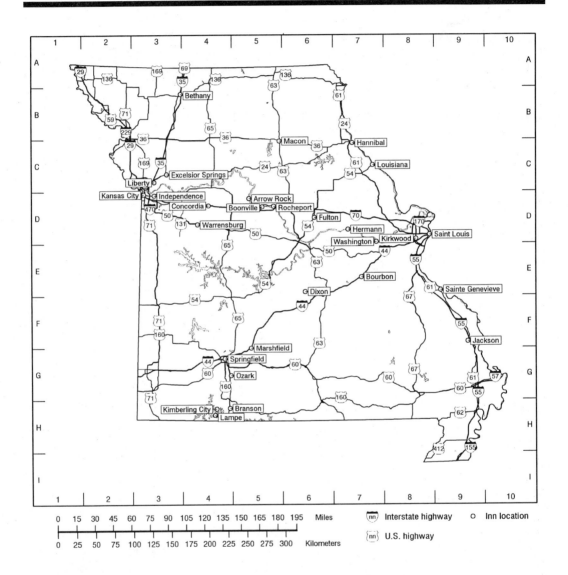

0 15 30 45 60 75 90 105 120 135 150 165 180 195 Miles

0 25 50 75 100 125 150 175 200 225 250 275 300 Kilometers

(nn) Interstate highway   o Inn location

(nn) U.S. highway

Arrow Rock   D5

Borgman's B&B
706 Van Buren St
Arrow Rock, MO 65320
(816)837-3350
E-mail: kborgman@vac1.rainis.net

Circa 1865. Borgman's B&B features a two-story porch and spacious guest rooms. Air conditioning and three new bathrooms have been added to this historic house. An old Victrola is available for

guests' use in the parlor, and Grandma's trunk offers local hand-crafted gift items. Historic Arrow Rock and its Old Tavern are a short walk away.
Innkeeper(s): Kathy & Helen Borgman. $50-55. PC TC. 4 rooms. Breakfast included in rates. Type of meal: continental-plus breakfast. Beds: D. Air conditioning in room. Antiques, fishing, parks, shopping and theater nearby.
Certificate may be used: Anytime September through May.

Bethany   B3

Unicorn Lodge B&B
119 S 15th St
Bethany, MO 64424-1925
(816)425-3676

Circa 1938. Midway between Kansas City and Des Moines, this Art Deco brick hotel offers a pleasant respite for Midwest travelers. Fifteen guest rooms are available, and most feature king or queen accommodations. Guests may watch TV in the inn's sitting room or take a relaxing stroll around the town square, just a few steps away. The innkeepers chose the Unicorn name for their establishment because it symbolizes graciousness and tranquility, and visitors will find its likeness throughout. There is a restaurant on the premises.
Innkeeper(s): Wynn Walter Pollock. $35-60. 15 rooms, 14 with PB. 1 suite. 1 conference room. Breakfast included in rates. Restaurant on premises. Beds: KQTD. Antiques, parks and shopping nearby.
Certificate may be used: Anytime.

Boonville   D5

Morgan Street Repose B&B
611 E Morgan St
Boonville, MO 65233-1221
(816)882-7195 (800)248-5061

Circa 1869. The historic Missouri River town of Boonville is home to this inn, comprised of two Italianate structures on the site of what once was a hotel that served travelers on the Santa Fe Trail. The inn is listed in the National Register of Historic Places. More than 400 antebellum and Victorian homes and buildings are found in town. Visitors enjoy their gourmet breakfasts in one of three dining rooms or in the Secret Garden. Several state parks are within easy driving distance, and the University of Missouri-Columbia is 20 miles to the east.
Innkeeper(s): Doris Shenk. $65-75. 3 rooms with PB. Breakfast and afternoon tea included in rates. Types of meals: full breakfast and early coffee/tea. Evening snack available. Beds: Q. Air conditioning and ceiling fan in room. Antiques and theater nearby.

"We had a wonderful, romantic, relaxing honeymoon in the Ashley Suite. The hospitality and atmosphere exceeded our expectations by far. The memory of our stay here will last a lifetime."

Certificate may be used: February through December, Sunday through Thursday.

Bourbon   E7

Meramec Farm Bed and Board
SR Box 50
Bourbon, MO 65441
(573)732-4765

Circa 1883. This farmhouse inn and cedar guest cabin are found on a working cattle operation, little more than an hour's drive from St. Louis. Seven generations have lived and worked the farm, which boasts 460 acres. Visitors stay in the 1880s farmhouse or the cabin, built from cedar cut on the

farm. The inn's proximity to the Meramec River and Vilander Bluffs provides excellent views and many outdoor activities. Spring visitors are treated to the sight of baby calves. Meramec Caverns and several state parks are nearby.

Innkeeper(s): Carol Springer. $70. 3 rooms, 1 with PB. 1 cottage. Breakfast included in rates. Types of meals: full breakfast and early coffee/tea. Picnic lunch available. Beds: QDT. Air conditioning and ceiling fan in room. Antiques and fishing nearby.

Location: Seventy-five miles southwest of St. Louis on scenic Meramec River.

Publicity: *Midwest Motorist, St. Louis Post-Dispatch, St. Louis.*

Certificate may be used: Sunday-Thursday, year-round.

Branson H4

The Inn at Fall Creek

391 Concord Ave
Branson, MO 65616-8642
(417)336-3422 (800)280-3422 Fax:(417)336-5950

Circa 1980. Surrounded by 60 wooded acres, this modern inn offers five guest rooms, two of them suites. Less than two miles from Branson's "strip," the inn is ideally located for those taking advantage of the area's many attractions, including nearby Silver Dollar City and Talking Rocks. Guests are treated to early coffee or tea and an evening snack in addition to a full breakfast. The inn's guest rooms are furnished in country decor. Rooms with fireplace, kitchenette or spa are available.

Innkeeper(s): J.C. McCracken. $70-95. MC VISA DS PC TC. 7 rooms, 4 with PB, 2 with FP. 2 suites. 1 conference room. Breakfast included in rates. Types of meals: full breakfast and early coffee/tea. Evening snack available. Beds: KQ. Air conditioning and ceiling fan in room. Fax and spa on premises. Amusement parks, antiques, fishing, shopping, theater and watersports nearby.

Certificate may be used: January-March.

Concordia D4

Fannie Lee B&B Inn

902 Main St
Concordia, MO 64020
(816)463-7395

The main house on this property was built by German immigrants, who added many wonderful elements to their house, including a double oak stairway and front entrance flanked by windows of beveled-plate glass. An iron fence surrounds the home, and European-style lampposts are a charming addition. The bed & breakfast boasts one of the largest private rose gardens in Missouri. Spring guests will be amazed by the thousands of blooms that brighten the grounds. Rooms are filled with

art collections and antiques, some of which date back 350 years.

Innkeeper(s): John Campbell. $65. MC VISA AX. 4 rooms. Breakfast included in rates. Type of meal: full breakfast.

Certificate may be used: Sunday through Thursday.

Dixon E6

Rock Eddy Bluff

HCR 62 Box 241
Dixon, MO 65459-8403
(314)759-6081 (800)335-5921

Circa 1991. This inn's rural, off-the-beaten-path location is ideal for those seeking a secluded, country retreat. Visitors choose from two guest rooms or the three-bedroom Turkey Ridge Cottage. The East and West rooms offer antique furnishings, queen beds and TVs, not to mention magnificent views. Amid a rolling river valley and wooded ridges, the inn's setting is a nature lover's delight, complete with canoeing, fishing and hiking. Canoes are provided, and the innkeepers will take guests on horse-drawn wagon excursions. More than 75 species of birds have been sighted here, including bald eagles and great blue herons.

Innkeeper(s): Kathy & Tom Corey. $59-97. MC VISA PC. 4 rooms, 1 with PB. 5 cottages. Breakfast and evening snack included in rates. Type of meal: full breakfast. Beds: QDT. Air conditioning, ceiling fan and VCR in room. Spa, swimming and stables on premises. Antiques, fishing, parks and watersports nearby.

Location: On a bluff above Gasconade River.

Certificate may be used: Sunday through Thursday, April 1-Dec. 1. All weeks December-April 1.

Excelsior Springs C3

Crescent Lake Manor

1261 Saint Louis Ave
Excelsior Springs, MO 64024-2938
(816)637-2958 (800)897-2958

Circa 1900. Surrounded by a moat, this three-story Georgian-style house is just a half-hour drive from Kansas City. The three guest rooms are decorated with country and traditional touches, and a swimming pool and tennis court are found on the 21-acre grounds. Golfers will find a challenge at Excelsior Springs Golf Course, and many guests enjoy visiting the nearby Hall of Waters for a relaxing mineral bath and massage.

Innkeeper(s): Mary Elizabeth Leake. $55-65. MAP. MC VISA. 4 rooms, 1 with PB. 1 suite. Breakfast included in rates. Types of meals: full breakfast and early coffee/tea. Beds: KQD. Air conditioning, ceiling fan, TV and VCR in room. Amusement parks, antiques, fishing, parks and shopping nearby.

Certificate may be used: Jan. 1-Nov. 1, Monday-Thursday.

Hannibal C7

Fifth Street Mansion B&B
213 S 5th St
Hannibal, MO 63401-4421
(573)221-0445 (800)874-5661 Fax:(573)221-3335

Circa 1858. This 20-room Italianate house listed in the National Register displays extended eaves and heavy brackets, tall windows and decorated lintels. A cupola affords a view of the town. Mark Twain was invited to dinner here by the Garth family and joined Laura Frazer (his Becky Thatcher) for the evening. An enormous stained-glass window lights the stairwell. The library features a stained-glass window with the family crest and is paneled with hand-grained walnut.

Innkeeper(s): Donalene & Mike Andreotti. $60-90. MC VISA AX DS TC. 7 rooms with PB. 1 conference room. Breakfast included in rates. Type of meal: full breakfast. Beds: Q. Air conditioning in room. Cable TV, VCR and fax on premises. Antiques, fishing and shopping nearby.
Location: North of St. Louis 100 miles.
Publicity: *Innsider, Country Inns.*

"We thoroughly enjoyed our visit. Terrific food and hospitality!"
Certificate may be used: Monday-Thursday - except holidays - October-March.

Garth Woodside Mansion
RR 3 Box 578
Hannibal, MO 63401-9634
(573)221-2789

Circa 1871. This Italian Renaissance mansion is set on 39 acres of meadow and woodland. Original Victorian antiques fill the house. An unusual flying staircase with no visible means of support vaults three stories. Best of all, is the Samuel Clemens Room where Mark Twain slept. Afternoon beverages are served, and there are nightshirts tucked away in your room.
Innkeeper(s): Irv & Diane Feinberg. $69-110. MC VISA. 8 rooms with PB, 4 with FP. Breakfast and afternoon tea included in rates. Types of meals: gourmet breakfast and early coffee/tea. Beds: QD. Air conditioning and turndown service in room. Amusement parks, antiques, fishing, parks and theater nearby.

Location: Along the Mississippi River just off highway 61.
Publicity: *Country Inns, Chicago Sun-Times, Glamour, Victorian Homes, Midwest Living, Innsider, Country Living, Conde Nast Traveler, Bon Appetit.*

"So beautiful and romantic and relaxing, we forgot we were here to work—Jeannie and Bob Ransom, Innsider."
Certificate may be used: Sunday-Thursday, November-April.

Hermann D7

Reiff House B&B
306 Market St
Hermann, MO 65041-1058
(573)486-2994 (800)482-2994 Fax:(573)486-8994
E-mail: sscheiter@ktcs.net

Circa 1871. Hermann, once a busy Missouri River port city, now is home to a beautiful National Historic District, where the inn is found. A three-story former hotel, now the inn holds the Hermann visitor center on the first floor. Guest rooms include the romantic Ivy Rose Suite. Breakfasts, which may feature freshly squeezed orange juice, German sausage, homemade muffins, quiche and sugar-free strawberry trifle, are enjoyed in the sitting room or courtyard, that turns into a German biergarten during Maifest and Oktoberfest weekends.
Innkeeper(s): Sue Scheiter. $70-100. MC VISA DS PC. 3 rooms with PB. Breakfast included in rates. Type of meal: full breakfast. Room service available. Beds: KQD. TV in room. VCR, fax, copier and spa on premises. Antiques, fishing, shopping, golf and theater nearby.
Certificate may be used: Year-round, Monday through Thursday.

Jackson   F9

Trisha's B&B
203 Bellevue
Jackson, MO 63755
(314)243-7427

Circa 1905. This inn offers a sitting room, library and spacious guest rooms. Some rooms have bay windows and are furnished with antiques and family heirlooms. Trisha provides fresh flowers and serves hand-picked fruits and homemade baked goods.

Innkeeper(s): Trisha Wischmann. $65-75. MC VISA AX. 4 rooms, 3 with PB. 1 conference room. Breakfast included in rates. Types of meals: full breakfast and gourmet breakfast. Beds: KQD. Fishing nearby.

Publicity: *Cash-Book Journal, Southeast Missourian.*

"You have created a beautiful home so naturally. Your B&B is filled with love and care—a really special place."

Certificate may be used: Year-round, Sunday-Thursday, January-December.

Kansas City   D3

Dome Ridge
14360 Walker Rd
Kansas City, MO 64163-1519
(816)532-4074

Circa 1985. The innkeeper custom-built this inn, a geodesic dome in a country setting just 10 minutes from the airport. One guest room boasts a king bed with a white iron and brass headboard, double spa and separate shower. In the inn's common areas, guests may enjoy a barbecue, CD player, fireplace, gazebo, library and pool table. The gourmet breakfasts, usually featuring Belgian waffles or California omelets, are served in the dining room, but guests are advised that the inn's kitchen is well worth checking out.

Innkeeper(s): Roberta Faust. $60-95. 4 rooms, 3 with PB. Breakfast included in rates. Types of meals: full breakfast and early coffee/tea. Beds: KQDT. Air conditioning in room. VCR on premises. Amusement parks, antiques, fishing, shopping, downhill skiing, sporting events and theater nearby.

Certificate may be used: Sunday through Thursday, all-year.

Kimberling City   H4

Cinnamon Hill B&B
24 Wildwood Ln
Kimberling City, MO 65686-9515
(417)739-5727 (800)925-1556

Circa 1984. Cinnamon Hill is a homey place for guests, and it is especially convenient for those heading to Branson, which is just a half-hour drive away. There are four guest rooms featuring a comfortable country decor, and each has a private entrance and access to the deck. Breakfast is a highlight, innkeeper Shirley DeVrient prepares an abundance of country fare. Guests feast on fresh fruit, eggs, bacon or sausage, biscuits & gravy, homemade breads and plenty of coffee, juice and tea.

Innkeeper(s): Shirley DeVrient. $55-65. MC VISA PC. 4 rooms with PB. Breakfast included in rates. Types of meals: full breakfast and early coffee/tea. Beds: QTD. Air conditioning, turndown service, ceiling fan and TV in room. Amusement parks, antiques, fishing, shopping, golf, theater and watersports nearby.

Publicity: *Ozark Mountain Visitor.*

"Thanks for the great place to stay! The room is lovely and the breakfasts were delicious!"

Certificate may be used: Anytime when there is a vacancy from January-May 31.

Kirkwood   D8

Fissy's Place
500 N Kirkwood Rd
Kirkwood, MO 63122-3914
(314)821-4494

Circa 1939. The innkeeper's past is just about as interesting as the history of this bed & breakfast. A former Miss Missouri, the innkeeper has acted in movies with the likes of Burt Reynolds and Robert Redford, and pictures of many movie stars decorate the home's interior. A trained interior designer, she also shares this talent in the cheerfully decorated guest rooms. Historic downtown Kirkwood is within walking distance to the home, which also offers close access to St. Louis.

Innkeeper(s): Fay Haas. $69-76. MC VISA PC TC. 3 rooms with PB. 1 conference room. Breakfast and evening snack included in rates. Types of meals: continental-plus breakfast, full breakfast and early coffee/tea. Catering service available. Beds: QDT. Air conditioning, turndown service, ceiling fan, TV and VCR in room. Copier on premises. Handicap access. Antiques, parks, shopping, sporting events and theater nearby.

Certificate may be used: Sunday-Thursday, January-April only

Lampe   H4

Grandpa's Farm B&B
HCR 1, PO Box 476
Lampe, MO 65681-0476
(417)779-5106 (800)280-5106

Circa 1891. This limestone farmhouse in the heart
of the Ozarks offers guests a chance to experience
country life in a relaxed farm setting. Midway
between Silver Dollar City and Eureka Springs,
Ark., and close to Branson, the inn boasts several
lodging options, including a duplex with suites and
a honeymoon suite. The innkeepers are known for
their substantial country breakfast and say guests
enjoy comparing how long the meal lasts before
they eat again. Although the inn's 186 acres are not
farmed extensively, domesticated farm animals are
on the premises.

Innkeeper(s): Keith & Pat Lamb. $65-85. MC VISA DS PC TC. 4 rooms
with PB. 3 suites. 1 conference room. Breakfast included in rates. Type of
meal: full breakfast. Beds: KD. Air conditioning and ceiling fan in room.
VCR, fax and spa on premises. Handicap access. Amusement parks,
antiques, fishing, parks, shopping, theater and watersports nearby.

Certificate may be used: All months except June, July, August,
October, no major holidays.

Louisiana   C7

Serando's House
918 Georgia St, PO Box 205
Louisiana, MO 63353-1812
(573)754-4067 (800)754-4067

Circa 1876. Southerners traveling up the Mississippi
River discovered this lush area in the early 19th century, founded it and named their little town Louisiana.
The town still features many of the earliest structures
in the downtown historic district. Serando's House
still showcases much of its original woodwork and
stained glass. The two guest rooms are comfortably
furnished, and one includes a balcony. Guests select
their breakfast from a variety of menu items.

Innkeeper(s): Tom & Jeannie Serandos. $65-85. MC VISA AX PC TC. 2
rooms, 1 with PB. Breakfast included in rates. Types of meals: full
breakfast and early coffee/tea. Dinner, picnic lunch and lunch available.
Beds: Q. Air conditioning, ceiling fan, TV and VCR in room. Spa on
premises. Antiques, fishing, parks, shopping and watersports nearby.
Publicity: *Discover Mid-America.*

Certificate may be used: Feb. 15-Nov. 20, weekdays, Monday through
Thursday.

Macon   C5

St. Agnes Hall B&B
706 Jackson St
Macon, MO 63552-5106
(816)385-2774 Fax:(816)385-4436

Circa 1846. During the late 19th century, this
home served a boarding house and day school for
young women. Rumor has it that a small room
located beneath the house, but not connected to
the basement, was used to hide slaves heading north
to freedom. The home is filled with unique collectibles and antiques, all surrounded by Victorian
decor. Breakfasts can be enjoyed in a variety of settings, on the veranda, in the garden, dining room or
in the privacy of your guest room.

Innkeeper(s): Scott & Carol Phillips. $60-75. MC VISA AX TC. 4 rooms,
3 with PB, 2 with FP. 1 suite. Breakfast included in rates. Types of
meals: full breakfast and early coffee/tea. Beds: KQ. Air conditioning,
ceiling fan and TV in room. VCR, fax and copier on premises. Antiques,
fishing, parks, shopping and watersports nearby.

Certificate may be used: Not honored for special events.

Marshfield   G5

Dickey House
331 S Clay St
Marshfield, MO 65706-2114
(417)468-3000 Fax:(417)859-5478

Circa 1913. This Greek Revival mansion is framed
by ancient oak trees and boasts eight massive two-
story Ionic columns. Burled woodwork, beveled glass

and polished hardwood floors accentuate the gracious rooms. Interior columns soar in the parlor, creating a suitably elegant setting for the innkeeper's outstanding collection of antiques. A queen-size canopy bed, fireplace and balcony are featured in the Heritage Room. Some rooms offer amenities such as Jacuzzi tubs, a fireplace and cable TV.

Innkeeper(s): William & Dorothy Buesgen. $60-105. MC VISA DS PC TC. 6 rooms with PB. 2 suites. 1 cottage. Breakfast included in rates. Types of meals: full breakfast and gourmet breakfast. Beds: KQD. Air conditioning, ceiling fan and VCR in room. Cable TV, fax, copier and library on premises. Handicap access.

"Thanks so much for all that you did to make our wedding special."

Certificate may be used: Anytime subject to availability, no holidays.

Ozark   G4

Dear's Rest Bed & Breakfast
1408 Cap Hill Ranch Rd
Ozark, MO 65721-6149
(417)581-3839 (800)588-2262 Fax:(417)581-3839
E-mail: info@dearsrest.com

Circa 1988. Amish craftsmen fashioned this cedar house in a beautiful, secluded wooded setting that is close to Southwest Missouri's many attractions. The B&B only accommodates one party at a time, providing guests extraordinary comfort and privacy. A fireplace and outdoor hot tub add to the allure. The surrounding area abounds with wildlife and many guests enjoy hiking along nearby Bull Creek in the Mark Twain National Forest. Branson and Springfield are 45 minutes away.

Innkeeper(s): Linda & Allan Schilter. $75-120. MC VISA DS PC. 2 rooms, 1 with FP. 1 suite. Breakfast and evening snack included in rates. Types of meals: full breakfast and early coffee/tea. Beds: DT. Air conditioning, ceiling fan and VCR in room. Fax, spa and swimming on premises. Amusement parks, antiques, fishing, shopping, golf, theater and watersports nearby.
Publicity: *Voice and View, Ozark Headliner.*

"You have a little bit of heaven here and to share it with others is very generous of you."
Certificate may be used: Nov. 1-April 30, Sunday-Thursday, no holidays.

Rocheport   D5

Roby River Run, A B&B
201 N Roby Farm Rd
Rocheport, MO 65279-9315
(573)698-2173 (888)762-9786

Circa 1854. Moses Payne, known as Boone County's "Millionaire Minister," chose these wooded, 10-acre grounds nestled near the banks of the Missouri River, on which to build his home. The Federal-style manor, which is listed in the National Register, offers three distinctive guest rooms. The Moses U. Payne room offers a cherry, Queen Anne

poster bed and a fireplace. The Sarah Payne room, named for Moses' second wife, boasts a rice bed and antique wash-stand. The Hattie McDaniel, named for the Academy Award-winning actress who portrayed Mammy in "Gone With the Wind," offers a peek at the inn's extensive collection of memorabilia from the movie. Homemade breakfasts include eggs, biscuits, country-cured ham and specialties such as marmalade-cream cheese stuffed French toast. Rocheport, a National Register town, offers several antique shops to explore, as well as the Katy Trail, a path for hikers and bikers that winds along the river. As the evening approaches, guests can head up to Les Bourgeois Vineyards and purchase a picnic basket, a bottle of Missouri wine and watch the sun set over the river.

Innkeeper(s): Gary Smith & Randall Kilgore. $80-90. MC VISA AX DS PC. 3 rooms, 1 with PB, 1 with FP. Type of meal: full breakfast. Beds: Q. Air conditioning and turndown service in room. VCR and stables on premises. Antiques nearby.

Certificate may be used: Monday-Thursday, Nov. 1-April 30.

School House B&B Inn
504 Third St
Rocheport, MO 65279
(573)698-2022

Circa 1914. This three-story brick building was once a schoolhouse. Now luxuriously appointed as a country inn, it features 13-foot-high ceilings, small

print wallpapers and a bridal suite with Victorian furnishings and a private spa. The basement houses an antique shop. Nearby is a winery and a trail along the river providing many scenic miles for cyclists and hikers.

Innkeeper(s): Vicki Ott & Penny Province. $85-155. MC VISA. 10 rooms with PB. 1 suite. 1 conference room. Breakfast and evening snack included in rates. Types of meals: continental breakfast, continental-plus breakfast, full breakfast and early coffee/tea. Afternoon tea available. Beds: KQDT. Air conditioning and ceiling fan in room. Cable TV, VCR, bicycles and library on premises. Antiques, fishing, parks, shopping, sporting events and theater nearby.

Publicity: *Midwest Motorist, Successful Farming, Hallmark Greeting Cards, Romance of Country Inns.*

"We are still talking about our great weekend in Rocheport. Thanks for the hospitality, the beautiful room and delicious breakfasts, they were really great."

Certificate may be used: January-April, June-September, November and December, Sunday through Thursday.

Saint Louis   D8

Doelling Haus
4817 Towne South Rd
Saint Louis, MO 63128-2817
(314)894-6796

Circa 1965. This suburban, two-story Dutch Colonial serves as a home away from home for St. Louis-area visitors. Guests choose from the Blue Danube, Bavarian or Black Forest rooms. Central air ensures year-round comfort, and guests are welcome to park in the garage. A patio and sitting room also are popular places to relax. The innkeepers sometimes can accommodate visitors' pets if prior agreement is reached. The inn offers convenient access to interstate highways, and the historic towns of Hermann, St. Charles and Ste. Genevieve are within easy driving distance.

Innkeeper(s): Carol & David Doelling. $65. AP. 2 rooms, 1 with PB. Breakfast and evening snack included in rates. Types of meals: continental-plus breakfast, full breakfast and early coffee/tea. Afternoon tea available. Beds: QD. Air conditioning and turndown service in room. Cable TV and VCR on premises. Amusement parks, antiques, fishing, parks, shopping, downhill skiing, sporting events, theater and watersports nearby.

Certificate may be used: Year-round, Sunday-Saturday.

The Eastlake Inn B&B
703 N Kirkwood Rd
Saint Louis, MO 63122-2719
(314)965-0066

Circa 1920. Just minutes from St. Louis, in the town of Kirkwood, this inn features the turn-of-the-century style of decor made popular by furniture designer Charles Eastlake. These period antiques add elegance and charm to the Colonial Revival inn. A collection of antique dolls and bears, and the dining room's 1,129-piece chandelier also receive attention. The full breakfasts sometimes are enjoyed

on the inn's sun porch. The Ulysses S. Grant National Historic Site, Hidden Valley Ski Area and Six Flags over Mid-America are nearby.

Innkeeper(s): Lori Ashdown. $62-72. MC VISA. 3 rooms with PB, 1 with FP. 1 conference room. Breakfast included in rates. Type of meal: full breakfast. Afternoon tea available. Beds: QD. Air conditioning, turndown service and ceiling fan in room. Cable TV and VCR on premises. Amusement parks, antiques, shopping, downhill skiing, sporting events and theater nearby.

Certificate may be used: Oct. 31-April 1.

Fleur-De-Lys Inn, Mansion at The Park
3500 Russell Blvd
Saint Louis, MO 63104
(314)773-3500 (888)969-3500 Fax:(314)773-6546

Circa 1912. The innkeepers at Fleur-de-Lys are ace decorators, creating bed chambers that are both warm and inviting, yet bright and cheerful at the same time. The Botanical Garden room features creamy yellow walls, a bed piled high with pillows and dressed with a puffy comforter and yellow gingham bed skirt. Another room, the Reservoir Park, is highlighted by a carved, four-poster plantation bed and masculine hues of burgundy and pale green. Other rooms include a king-size, antique iron and brass bed and a huge double bath, while another has a double Jacuzzi tub. Guests are pampered with amenities such as Turkish towels placed on heated towel racks, fresh flowers and a hot tub. There is a library, a cigar porch, a parlor and a gallery featuring works for sale by local artists. The inn is perfect for those seeking romance, but there are plenty of amenities for the business traveler. Fax, copying and printing services are available, as well as same-day dry cleaning, desks in each guest room and a selection of national and local papers available daily. Guests enjoy a gourmet breakfast, and in the evenings, hors d'oeuvres. Downtown St. Louis and many area attractions are five minutes away.

Innkeeper(s): Kathryn Leep. $85-175. MC VISA AX DC CB DS PC TC. 2 suites. 1 conference room. Breakfast and evening snack included in rates. Types of meals: gourmet breakfast and early coffee/tea. Dinner available. Beds: KQD. Air conditioning, turndown service, ceiling fan, TV and VCR in room. Fax, copier, spa and library on premises. Amusement parks, antiques, parks, shopping, sporting events and theater nearby.

Certificate may be used: Sept. 1-April 30, Sunday-Thursday.

Lafayette House
2156 Lafayette Ave
Saint Louis, MO 63104-2543
(314)772-4429 (800)641-8965 Fax:(314)664-2156

Circa 1876. Captain James Eads, designer and builder of the first trussed bridge across the Mississippi River, built this Queen Anne mansion as

a wedding present for his daughter Margaret. The rooms are furnished in antiques, and there is a suite with a kitchen on the third floor. The house overlooks Lafayette Park.

Innkeeper(s): Nancy Buhr, Anna Millet. $60-150. MC VISA AX DC CB DS PC TC. 6 rooms, 3 with PB. 1 suite. Breakfast included in rates. Types of meals: gourmet breakfast and early coffee/tea. Beds: QDT. Air conditioning and TV in room. VCR, fax and copier on premises. Antiques, parks, shopping, sporting events and theater nearby.

Location: In the center of St. Louis.

"We had a wonderful stay at your house and enjoyed the furnishings, delicious breakfasts and friendly pets."

Certificate may be used: Jan. 2-March 31, Sunday through Thursday.

Lehmann House B&B
10 Benton Pl
Saint Louis, MO 63104-2411
(314)231-6724

Circa 1893. This National Register manor's most prominent resident, former U.S. Solicitor General Frederick Lehmann, hosted Presidents Taft, Theodore Roosevelt and Coolidge at this gracious home. Several key turn-of-the-century literary figures also visited the Lehmann family. The inn's formal dining room, complete with oak paneling and a fireplace, is a stunning place to enjoy the formal breakfasts. Antiques and gracious furnishings dot the well-appointed guest rooms. The home is located in St. Louis' oldest historic district, Lafayette Square.

Innkeeper(s): Marie & Michael Davies. $65-80. MC VISA AX DC DS PC TC. 4 rooms, 2 with PB, 3 with FP. 3 conference rooms. Breakfast included in rates. Types of meals: full breakfast and early coffee/tea. Evening snack available. Beds: KQDT. Air conditioning and ceiling fan in room. Swimming, tennis and library on premises. Amusement parks, antiques, parks, shopping, sporting events and theater nearby.

"Wonderful mansion with great future ahead. Thanks for the wonderful hospitality."

Certificate may be used: Sunday-Thursday only, holidays and special events excluded.

Sainte Genevieve   E9

Inn St. Gemme Beauvais
78 N Main St
Sainte Genevieve, MO 63670-1336
(573)883-5744 (800)818-5744 Fax:(573)883-3899

Circa 1848. This three-story, Federal-style inn is an impressive site on Ste. Genevieve's Main Street. The town is one of the oldest west of the Mississippi River, and the St. Gemme Beauvais is the oldest operating Missouri bed & breakfast. The rooms are nicely appointed in period style, but there are modern amenities here, too. The Jacuzzi tubs in some guest rooms are one relaxing example. There is an outdoor hot tub as well. Guests are pampered with all sorts of cuisine, from full breakfasts to luncheons with sinfully rich desserts, and in the late afternoons, wine, hors d'oeuvres and refreshments are served.

Innkeeper(s): Janet Joggerst. $69-125. AP. MC VISA PC TC. 7 rooms with PB, 1 with FP. 5 suites. 2 conference rooms. Breakfast and afternoon tea included in rates. Types of meals: full breakfast, gourmet breakfast and early coffee/tea. Evening snack, picnic lunch, lunch, gourmet lunch, banquet service, catering service, catered breakfast and room service available. Restaurant on premises. Beds: QDT. Air conditioning, turndown service, ceiling fan and TV in room. VCR, fax, copier, spa and bicycles on premises. Antiques, parks and shopping nearby.

Certificate may be used: Every day but Saturdays & holidays; based on availability.

Main Street Inn

221 North Main St
Sainte Genevieve, MO 63670
(573)883-9199 (800)918-9199

Circa 1883. This exquisite inn is one of Missouri's finest bed & breakfast establishments. Built as the Meyer Hotel, the inn has welcomed guests for more than a century. Now completely renovated, each of the individually appointed rooms includes amenities such as bubble bath and flowers. Rooms are subtly decorated, and some have stencilled walls. Beds are topped with vintage quilts and tasteful linens. Two rooms include a whirlpool tub. The morning meal is prepared in a beautiful brick kitchen, which features an unusual blue cookstove, and is served in the elegant dining room. The menu changes from day to day, caramelized French toast is one of the inn's specialties.

Innkeeper(s): Ken & Karen Kulberg. $65-115. MC VISA AX DS PC TC. 7 rooms with PB. Breakfast and evening snack included in rates. Types of meals: gourmet breakfast and early coffee/tea. Beds: QDT. Air conditioning in room. Copier on premises. Antiques, parks and shopping nearby.

Certificate may be used: Jan. 15-Dec. 15, Sunday-Thursday.

Springfield   G4

Virginia Rose B&B

317 E Glenwood St
Springfield, MO 65807-3543
(417)883-0693 (800)345-1412

Circa 1906. Three generations of the Botts family lived in this home before it was sold to the current innkeepers, Virginia and Jackie Buck. The grounds still include the rustic red barn. Comfortable, country rooms are named after Buck family members and feature beds covered with quilts. The innkeepers also offer a two-bedroom suite, the Rambling Rose, which is decorated in a sportsman theme in honor of the nearby Bass Pro. Hearty breakfasts are served in the dining room, and the innkeepers will provide low-fat fare on request.

Innkeeper(s): Jackie & Virginia Buck. $50-90. MC VISA AX DS PC TC. 5 rooms, 3 with PB. 1 suite. Breakfast included in rates. Types of meals: full breakfast and early coffee/tea. Evening snack and picnic lunch available. Beds: QD. Air conditioning and turndown service in room. Cable TV, VCR and fax on premises. Amusement parks, antiques, fishing, parks, shopping, sporting events, theater and watersports nearby.

Publicity: *Auctions & Antiques, Springfield Business Journal, Today's Women Journal.*

"The accommodations are wonderful and the hospitality couldn't be warmer."

Certificate may be used: Any time, subject to availability.

Walnut Street Inn

900 E Walnut St
Springfield, MO 65806-2603
(417)864-6346 (800)593-6346 Fax:(417)864-6184
E-mail: walnutstinn@pcis.net

Circa 1894. This three-story Queen Anne gabled house has cast-iron Corinthian columns and a veranda. Polished wood floors and antiques are featured throughout. Upstairs you'll find the gathering room with a fireplace. Ask for the McCann guest room with two bay windows. A full breakfast is served, including items such as peach-stuffed French toast.

Innkeeper(s): Gary & Paula Blankenship. $69-139. MC VISA AX DC DS PC TC. 12 rooms with PB, 8 with FP. 5 suites. Breakfast included in rates. Types of meals: gourmet breakfast and early coffee/tea. Afternoon tea available. Beds: QD. Air conditioning, turndown service, ceiling fan, TV and VCR in room. Fax and copier on premises. Handicap access. Amusement parks, antiques, fishing, parks, shopping, sporting events, theater and watersports nearby.

Publicity: *Southern Living, Women's World, Midwest Living, Victoria, Country Inns, Innsider, Glamour, Midwest Motorist, Missouri, Saint Louis Post, Kansas City Star, USA Today.*

"Rest assured your establishment's qualities are unmatched and through your commitment to excellence you have won a life-long client."

Certificate may be used: Sunday-Thursday, excluding holidays and certain dates.

Warrensburg D4

Cedarcroft Farm B&B
431 SE County Rd Y
Warrensburg, MO 64093-8316
(816)747-5728 (800)368-4944
E-mail: bwayne@cedarcroft.com

Circa 1867. John Adams, a Union army veteran, and Sandra's great grandfather, built this house. There are 80 acres of woodlands, meadows and

creeks where deer, fox, coyotes and wild turkeys still roam. Two original barns remain. Guests stay in a private, two-bedroom suite, which can accommodate couples or families. Bill participates in Civil War reenactments and is happy to demonstrate clothing, weapons and customs of the era. Sandra cares for her quarter horses and provides the home-baked, full country breakfasts.

Innkeeper(s): Sandra & Bill Wayne. $75-90. MC VISA AX DS PC TC. 1 room. Breakfast and evening snack included in rates. Type of meal: full breakfast. Beds: D. Air conditioning in room. Cable TV and VCR on premises. Antiques, fishing, parks, shopping and theater nearby.

Location: About six miles southeast of Warrensburg, Mo., 60 miles from Kansas City.

Publicity: *Kansas City Star, Higginsville Advance, Midwest Motorist, KCTV, KMOS TV, Territorial Small Farm Today, Country America, Entrepreneur.*

"We enjoyed the nostalgia and peacefulness very much. Enjoyed your wonderful hospitality and great food."

Certificate may be used: Sept. 1-June 30, Sunday-Thursday.

Washington D7

Schwegmann House
438 W Front St
Washington, MO 63090-2103
(314)239-5025 (800)949-2262

Circa 1861. John F. Schwegmann, a native of Germany, built a flour mill on the Missouri riverfront. This stately three-story home was built to provide extra lodging for overnight customers who traveled long hours to the town. Today weary travelers enjoy the formal gardens and warm atmosphere of this restful home. Patios overlook the river, and the gracious rooms are decorated with antiques and handmade quilts. The new Miller Suite boasts a tub for two, and guests receive a bottle of Missouri wine and breakfast in bed. In the old summer kitchen, innkeepers have an old-time blacksmithing and wood-working shop. Guests enjoy full breakfasts complete with house specialties such as German apple pancakes or a three-cheese strata accompanied with homemade breads, meat, juice and fresh fruit. There are 11 wineries nearby, or guests can visit one of the many galleries, historic sites and antique shops in the area.

Innkeeper(s): Catherine & Bill Nagel. $65-150. MC VISA AX PC TC. 9 rooms with PB. 1 suite. Breakfast and evening snack included in rates. Types of meals: gourmet breakfast and early coffee/tea. Beds: QD. Air conditioning and ceiling fan in room. Cable TV and bicycles on premises. Antiques, fishing, parks, shopping and theater nearby.

Location: One hour west of St. Louis.

Publicity: *St. Louis Post-Dispatch, West County Journal, Midwest Living, Country Inns, Midwest Motorist, Ozark.*

"Like Grandma's house many years ago."

Certificate may be used: Sunday through Thursday. No Friday or Saturday to be included in stay. Not valid with any other specials.

Montana

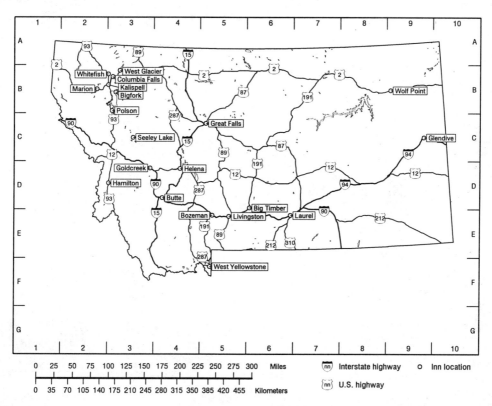

1	2	3	4	5	6	7	8	9	10

0 25 50 75 100 125 150 175 200 225 250 275 300 Miles

0 35 70 105 140 175 210 245 280 315 350 385 420 455 Kilometers

⬡nn Interstate highway   ○ Inn location

⬡nn U.S. highway

Bigfork   B3

Burggraf's Countrylane B&B
Rainbow Drive on Swan Lake
Bigfork, MT 59911
(406)837-4608 (800)525-3344 Fax:(406)837-2468

Circa 1984. This contemporary log home on Swan Lake, minutes from Flathead Lake in the Rockies, offers fine accommodations in one of America's most beautiful settings. Upon arrival, visitors enjoy hors d'oeuvres, chilled wine and fresh fruit. Ceiling fans, clock radios and turndown service are amenities. Picnic baskets are available and would be ideal for taking along on a paddle boat lake excursion.

Excellent skiing and snowmobiling opportunities await winter visitors, and all will enjoy the inn's seven scenic acres.

Innkeeper(s): Natalie & RJ Burggraf. $85-100. AP. MC VISA PC TC. 6 rooms with PB. Breakfast and evening snack included in rates. Types of meals: full breakfast, gourmet breakfast and early coffee/tea. Picnic lunch available. Beds: KQT. Ceiling fan, TV and VCR in room. Fax, copier, swimming, library and pet boarding on premises. Handicap access. Antiques, fishing, parks, shopping, downhill skiing, cross-country skiing, sporting events, theater and watersports nearby.

Certificate may be used: Any time, unrestricted.

Bozeman

E5

Lindley House
202 Lindley Pl
Bozeman, MT 59715-4833
(406)587-8403 (800)787-8404 Fax:(406)582-8112

Circa 1889. The beautiful Montana scenery is a perfect backdrop for this romantic bed & breakfast listed in the National Register. The pampering begins in the beautiful guest rooms, which offer plenty of soft, down comforters, feather pillows, fluffy robes and a collection of soaps and oils for a long soak in the tub. Each of the rooms is distinct and memorable. The Marie Antoinette Suite boasts a fireplace, sitting room, clawfoot tub and balcony. The Garden Room offers French Provencal decor with a private garden entrance. Other rooms

include items such
as wicker furnish-
ings, bay windows,
lacy curtains, a
French bistro table
or brass bed. The
gourmet breakfasts,
which feature spe-
cial treats such as
crepes, souffles and
a variety of breads,
yogurt and cereals,
are a perfect start
to the day.

Innkeeper(s): Stephanie Volz. $75-250. MC VISA. 5 rooms with PB. 2 suites. Breakfast and afternoon tea included in rates. Type of meal: full breakfast. Beds: KQT. Antiques, fishing, downhill skiing, cross-country skiing, theater and watersports nearby.

"Elegant, but comfortable. Beautifully restored, wonderful attention to detail."

Certificate may be used: Nov. 1-April 30, Monday through Thursday.

Torch & Toes B&B
309 S 3rd Ave
Bozeman, MT 59715-4636
(406)586-7285 (800)446-2138

Circa 1906. This Colonial Revival home, three blocks from the center of town, boasts an old-fashioned front porch with porch swing and a carriage house. Antique furnishings in the dining room feature a Victrola and a pillared and carved oak fireplace. Ron is a professor of architecture at nearby Montana State University and Judy is a weaver. Her loom and some of her colorful work are on display at this artisan's inn.

Innkeeper(s): Ron & Judy Hess. $80-90. MC VISA PC TC. 4 rooms with PB. Breakfast included in rates. Types of meals: full breakfast and

gourmet breakfast. Beds: KQT. Ceiling fan in room. Cable TV and VCR on premises. Antiques, fishing, parks, shopping, downhill skiing, cross-country skiing, sporting events, theater and watersports nearby.

Location: North of Yellowstone National Park.

Publicity: *Bozeman Chronicle, San Francisco Peninsula Parent, Northwest.*

"Thanks for your warm hospitality."

Certificate may be used: Anytime, subject to availability.

Voss Inn
319 S Willson Ave
Bozeman, MT 59715-4632
(406)587-0982 Fax:(406)585-2964

Circa 1883. The Voss Inn is a restored two-story house with a large front porch and a Victorian parlor. Old-fashioned furnishings include an upright piano and chandelier. Two of the inn's six rooms include air conditioning. A full breakfast is served, with fresh baked rolls kept in a unique warmer that's built into an ornate 1880s radiator.

Innkeeper(s): Bruce & Frankee Muller. $85-95. MC VISA AX PC TC. 6 rooms with PB. Breakfast and afternoon tea included in rates. Type of meal: gourmet breakfast. Picnic lunch available. Beds: KQ. Air conditioning in room. Cable TV and fax on premises. Antiques, fishing, parks, shopping, downhill skiing, cross-country skiing and watersports nearby.

Location: Four blocks south of downtown.

Publicity: *Sunset, Cosmopolitan, Gourmet, Countryside.*

"First class all the way."

Certificate may be used: January through June, October-Dec. 15. July-September excluded.

Butte
D4

Copper King Mansion
219 W Granite St
Butte, MT 59701-9235
(406)782-7580

Circa 1884. This turn-of-the-century marvel was built, as the name indicates, by W.A. Clark, one of the nation's leading copper barons. In the early 1900s, Clark made millions each month hauling copper out of Butte's vast mines. Stained-glass windows, gold leafing on the ceilings and elaborate woodwork are just a few of the opulent touches. Clark commissioned artisans brought in from Germany to carve the intricate staircase, which graces the front hall. The mansion is decked floor to ceiling in antiques collected by the innkeeper's mother and grandmother, who purchased the home from Clark's relatives. A three-room master suite includes two fireplaces, a lavish bedroom, a sitting room and a huge bathroom with a clawfoot tub.
Innkeeper(s): Maria Sigl. $55-95. MC VISA AX DS. 4 rooms. Breakfast included in rates. Type of meal: full breakfast.

Publicity: *Sunset Magazine.*

Certificate may be used: January, February, March, April, May, September, October, November, December.

Columbia Falls
B3

Plum Creek House
985 Vans Ave
Columbia Falls, MT 59912-3203
(406)892-1816 (800)682-1429 Fax:(406)892-1876

Incredible views of the Flathead Valley's forests and mountains greet guests at this contemporary riverfront ranch inn. The inn offers something for everyone, even family pets who may stay in the sheltered outdoor kennel. Outdoor recreational opportunities are boundless, but guests who wish to put their feet up and relax also will find this inn to their liking. A heated pool and outdoor spa lure many guests. Glacier National Park can be seen from the inn and is just a short drive away.
Innkeeper(s): Caroline Stevens. $60-105. MC VISA AX DC DS. 5 rooms. 1 suite. Breakfast included in rates. Types of meals: full breakfast and early coffee/tea. Evening snack, lunch, banquet service, catering service and room service available. Air conditioning, turndown service, ceiling fan, TV and VCR in room. Child care on premises. Antiques, shopping, downhill skiing, cross-country skiing and theater nearby.

Certificate may be used: Oct. 1-June 1 excluding holidays.

Glendive
C9

The Hostetler House B&B
113 N Douglas St
Glendive, MT 59330-1619
(406)365-4505 (800)965-8456 Fax:(406)365-8456

Circa 1912. Casual country decor mixed with handmade and heirloom furnishings are highlights at this two-story inn. The inn features many comforting touches, such as a romantic hot tub and gazebo, enclosed sun porch and sitting room filled

with books. The two guest rooms share a bath, and are furnished by Dea, an interior decorator. The full breakfasts may be enjoyed on Grandma's china in the dining room or on the sun porch. The Yellowstone River is one block from the inn, and downtown shopping is two blocks away. Makoshika State Park, home of numerous fossil finds, is nearby.
Innkeeper(s): Craig & Dea Hostetler. $50. MC VISA DS PC TC. 2 rooms. Breakfast included in rates. Types of meals: gourmet breakfast and early coffee/tea. Beds: D. Air conditioning and ceiling fan in room. Cable TV, VCR, fax, spa and library on premises. Antiques, fishing, parks, shopping, cross-country skiing, sporting events, theater and watersports nearby.

Publicity: *Ranger Review.*

"Warmth and loving care are evident throughout your exquisite home. Your attention to small details is uplifting. Thank you for a restful sojourn."

Certificate may be used: Anytime

Gold Creek
D3

LH Ranch B&B
471 Mullan Tr
Gold Creek, MT 59733
(406)288-3436

Circa 1851. Guests can take horseback riding lessons, pan for gold or roll up their sleeves and feed animals or bale hay at this 2,000-acre ranch. Relaxation is another option, and there are plenty of ideal spots. The home is furnished with a collection of family antiques. The LH Ranch is Montana's oldest operating bed & breakfast, open and run by the Lingenfelter family since 1955.

Innkeeper(s): Patti Lingenfelter-Hansen. $85. 2 rooms, 1 with FP. Breakfast included in rates. Types of meals: continental breakfast, continental-plus breakfast, full breakfast and early coffee/tea. Afternoon tea, dinner, evening snack, picnic lunch and lunch available. Beds: D. Amusement parks, antiques, fishing, parks, shopping, downhill skiing, cross-country skiing, theater and watersports nearby.

Certificate may be used: Jan. 1-Dec. 11.

Great Falls   C5

The Chalet B&B Inn
1204 4th Ave N
Great Falls, MT 59401-1414
(406)452-9001 (800)786-9002

Circa 1909. This simple stick-style Victorian chalet features handsomely decorated rooms highlighted by polished woodwork, French doors, beamed ceilings and leaded-glass windows. Marge is a noted San Francisco interior designer, now back in her hometown. David continues to carry on a family tradition as a violin maker. The C.M. Russell Museum is across the street on Old West Trail.

Innkeeper(s): Marge & David Anderson. $40-65. AX DS TC. 5 rooms, 3 with PB. 1 suite. Breakfast included in rates. Type of meal: early coffee/tea. Catered breakfast available. Beds: KQDT. Air conditioning and ceiling fan in room. Cable TV and VCR on premises. Antiques, fishing, parks, shopping, downhill skiing, cross-country skiing, theater and watersports nearby.

Publicity: *Great Falls Tribune.*

"Thanks for the royal treatment."

Certificate may be used: All year, based on availability.

Hamilton   D3

The Bavarian Farmhouse B&B
163 Bowman Rd
Hamilton, MT 59840-9638
(307)358-2033

Bavarian hospitality and flavor is found at this farmhouse inn, nestled amid a grove of large trees. Visitors are treated to a hearty German farm breakfast consisting of boiled eggs, breads, coffee, cereal, cheese, cold cuts, jam, juice, rolls and tea. The innkeepers, both experienced travelers, are happy to help arrange fishing, floating, horseback riding or hunting excursions if given advance notice. Efficiency cabins also are available. The Daly Mansion and Sleeping Child Hot Springs are within easy driving distance.

Innkeeper(s): Ann Reuthlinges. $45-55. 5 rooms.

Certificate may be used: Anytime other than over a Saturday night during July or August.

Deer Crossing B&B
396 Hayes Creek Rd
Hamilton, MT 59840-9744
(406)363-2232 (800)763-2232
E-mail: deercros@bitterroot.net

Circa 1980. This Western-style ranch bed & breakfast is located on 25 acres of woods and pastures. One suite includes a double Jacuzzi tub and another has a private balcony. After a day of horseback riding or hiking, guests can come back to the home and relax in the hot tub. In addition to the suites and guest rooms, travelers also can opt to stay in the bunkhouse, a historic homestead building with a wood-burning stove.

Innkeeper(s): Mary Lynch. $40-100. MC VISA AX. 6 rooms with PB, 1 with FP. 2 suites. Breakfast and evening snack included in rates. Types of meals: full breakfast and early coffee/tea. Dinner, picnic lunch and lunch available. Beds: QDT. Turndown service in room. VCR, bicycles and child care on premises. Handicap access. Antiques, parks, shopping, downhill skiing, cross-country skiing and watersports nearby.

Publicity: *Country Focus, Saline Reporter.*

"It is so nice to be back after three years and from 5,000 miles away!"

Certificate may be used: Oct. 1 to May 1 any day of the week.

Helena   D4

Appleton Inn B&B
1999 Euclid Ave, Hwy 12 West
Helena, MT 59601-1908
(406)449-7492 (800)956-1999 Fax:(406)449-1261
E-mail: appleton@ixi.net

Circa 1890. Montana's first resident dentist called this Victorian his home. It remained in his family until the 1970s when it was transformed into apartments. Fortunately, the innkeepers bought and restored the home, bringing back the original beauty. The innkeepers have their own furniture-making company and have created many of the pieces that decorate the guest rooms. Rooms range from the spacious Master Suite, with its oak, four-poster bed and bath with a clawfoot tub, to the quaint and cozy Attic Playroom. The inn is a convenient place to enjoy the Helena area, and there are mountain bikes on hand for those who wish to explore.

Innkeeper(s): Tom Woodall & Cheryl Boid. $60-125. AP. MC VISA AX DS PC TC. 5 rooms with PB. 1 suite. Breakfast included in rates. Afternoon tea and picnic lunch available. Beds: Q. Air conditioning in room. Cable TV, VCR, fax, copier and bicycles on premises. Antiques, fishing, parks, shopping, downhill skiing, cross-country skiing, sporting events, theater and watersports nearby.

"Cheryl and Tom have provided a perfect place to call home away from home. The surroundings are delightful - the rooms, the plants, the grounds - and the breakfast very tasty. And they provide lots of helpful information to help you enjoy touring the area. A truly delightful B&B."

Certificate may be used: Oct. 15-May 15, Sunday-Saturday.

Kalispell
B3

Switzer House Inn
205 5th Ave E
Kalispell, MT 59901-4544
(406)257-5837 (800)257-5837

Circa 1910. Originally built for a lumberman from Minnesota, this Queen Anne Victorian is found on Kalispell's historic east side. Guests enjoy relaxing on the wraparound porch or by taking a stroll to Woodland Park, two blocks away. Downtown galleries, museums, restaurants, shops and theaters are just five blocks from the

inn. Visitors select from the Queen Anne, Blanche's Corner, Lew's Retreat or Twin's rooms, all found on the inn's second floor. The gourmet breakfast is served buffet style and guests also may help themselves to hot chocolate or lemonade in the library.
Innkeeper(s): Heather Brigham. $65-85. MC VISA. 4 rooms. Breakfast and afternoon tea included in rates. Types of meals: full breakfast and early coffee/tea. Beds: QT. Turndown service in room. Cable TV and VCR on premises. Antiques, fishing, shopping, downhill skiing, cross-country skiing, theater and watersports nearby.

Publicity: *Daily Interlake.*

"Thanks so much for sharing such a beautiful place with us. You have created a very warm and welcoming atmosphere here."

Certificate may be used: Sept. 1-May 31, Monday through Sunday.

Laurel
E6

Riverside Bed & Breakfast
2231 Thiel Rd
Laurel, MT 59044-8841
(406)628-7890 (800)768-1580 Fax:(406)656-8306
E-mail: riversidebb@cwz.com

Circa 1970. This homestay is located in a contemporary home on an acre of grounds where the innkeepers' llamas roam. The Yellowstone River is just a few feet away for those who wish to fly fish, and the inn also offers a hot tub. The two cozy guest rooms are decorated in country style with soft floral comforters on the beds. The home is close to Billings, and it's less than an hour to skiing in the Old West town of Red Lodge.
Innkeeper(s): Lynn & Nancy Perey. $65. MC VISA TC. 2 rooms with PB. Breakfast and evening snack included in rates. Types of meals: full breakfast and early coffee/tea. Beds: QD. Cable TV, VCR, spa and bicycles on premises. Fishing, downhill skiing, cross-country skiing and golf nearby.

"What a pleasant surprise to meet new friends and have such a warm experience with our first b&b."

Certificate may be used: Oct. 1-April 30.

Livingston
E5

The River Inn on The Yellowstone
4950 Hwy 89 S
Livingston, MT 59047
(406)222-2429

Circa 1895. Crisp, airy rooms decorated with a Southwestern flavor are just part of the reason why this 100-year-old farmhouse is an ideal getaway. There are five acres to meander, including more than 500 feet of riverfront, and close access to a multitude of outdoor activities. Two rooms have decks boasting views of the river, and the third offers a canyon view. Guests also can stay in

251

Calamity Jane's, a rustic riverside cabin. For an unusual twist, summer guests can opt for Spangler's Wagon and experience life as it was on the range. This is a true, turn-of-the-century sheepherders' wagon and includes a double bed and woodstove. The innkeepers guide a variety of interesting hikes, bike and canoe trips in the summer and fall. The inn is close to many outdoor activities. Don't forget to check out Livingston, just a few miles away. The historic town has been used in several movies and maintains an authentic Old West spirit.

Innkeeper(s): Dee Dee VanZyl & Ursula Neese. $45-85. MC VISA. 3 rooms with PB. 1 cottage. Breakfast included in rates. Types of meals: full breakfast, gourmet breakfast and early coffee/tea. Picnic lunch available. Beds: QDT. VCR and bicycles on premises. Antiques, fishing, parks, shopping, downhill skiing, cross-country skiing, sporting events, theater and watersports nearby.

Certificate may be used: March 1-April 30, Oct. 1-31.

Marion
B2

Hargrave Ranch
300 Thompson River Rd
Marion, MT 59925-9710
(406)858-2284 (800)933-0696 Fax:(406)858-2284

Circa 1906. If you've ever wondered what it would be like to live on a working cattle ranch, a stay at this 86,000-acre spread will provide a glimpse into this Western lifestyle. Riding lessons, overnight camp-outs and lakeside picnics are just a few of the options available. Guests also may try their hand at cattle herding. Accommodations are unique and varied, and they include a log cabin (formerly a horse stable), the main house or two rustic cottages. The hosts prepare guests for their busy days with huge breakfasts with egg dishes, potatoes, yogurt, fruit, pancakes and other delectables. During the winter months, rates include cross-country skiing.

Innkeeper(s): Leo & Ellen Hargrave. $75-95. MC VISA TC. 10 rooms, 3 with PB, 2 with FP. 1 conference room. Breakfast, dinner, evening snack and picnic lunch included in rates. Types of meals: full breakfast and early coffee/tea. Lunch available. Beds: QDT. Ceiling fan in room. VCR, fax, copier, sauna and bicycles on premises. Antiques, fishing, parks, shopping, downhill skiing, cross-country skiing, theater and watersports nearby.

Certificate may be used: October-May 1.

Polson
B3

Hidden Pines
792 Lost Quartz Rd
Polson, MT 59860-9428
(406)849-5612 (800)505-5612

Circa 1976. Relax on the porch of this secluded, quiet home and the only sounds you'll hear are birds chirping and the breezes that blow across the wooded

grounds. Hidden Pines borders Flathead Lake, where guests will enjoy swimming and boating. The innkeepers offer picnic tables and lawn chairs for those who want to soak up the natural surroundings. The home's hot tub is a great place to end the day. The innkeepers prepare a hearty breakfast, but lighter fare is available. Each of the comfortable guest rooms features individual decor. The Deckside room has a private entrance onto the deck and hot tub area.

Innkeeper(s): Emy & Earl Atchley. $50-60. PC TC. 4 rooms, 2 with PB. Breakfast and picnic lunch included in rates. Types of meals: full breakfast and early coffee/tea. Beds: QD. Ceiling fan and VCR in room. Spa on premises. Antiques, fishing, parks, shopping, theater and watersports nearby.

Certificate may be used: June, July, August, Sunday through Thursday.

Seeley Lake
C3

The Emily A. B&B
Hwy 83, Box 350
Seeley Lake, MT 59868
(406)677-3474 (800)977-4639 Fax:(406)677-3474

Circa 1992. Nestled at the banks of the Columbia River, this rustic log home was fashioned from local timber. From the lodge, guests enjoy panoramic Rocky Mountain views. Stroll the inn's 158 acres and you'll find hiking trails, wildlife and plenty of places to fish. The home is named for innkeeper Marilyn Shope Peterson's grandmother, a remarkable woman who helped found Montana's Boulder School for the Deaf Mute. Despite being widowed at a young age, Emily managed to support herself and seven children by running a boarding house. Marilyn inherited her grandmother's hospitable skills and she, and husband Keith, pamper their guests. Rooms are decorated with Western furnishings, and beds are topped with feather duvets. There is a collection of Western art on hand, as well.

Innkeeper(s): Marilyn Shope Peterson. $95. MAP. MC VISA TC. 5 rooms, 2 with PB. 1 conference room. Types of meals: continental-plus breakfast, full breakfast and early coffee/tea. Afternoon tea, picnic lunch, banquet service and catered breakfast available. Beds: KQT. Cable TV, VCR, fax, copier, bicycles, pet boarding and child care on premises. Handicap access. Antiques, fishing, parks, shopping, downhill skiing, cross-country skiing, sporting events, theater and watersports nearby.

Certificate may be used: Oct. 1-May 1.

West Glacier
B3

Mountain Timbers Lodge
PO Box 94
West Glacier, MT 59936-0094
(406)387-5830 (800)841-3835 Fax:(406)387-5835

Circa 1973. With the wilderness of Glacier National Park as its backdrop, this rustic, log home is designed for nature lovers. The grounds include miles of professionally designed cross-country ski trails, and guests on a morning walk shouldn't be surprised if they encounter deer or elk sharing the countryside. The inviting interior complements the spectacular scenery. The huge living room is warmed by a rock and stone fireplace and decorated with Southwestern-style furnishings. For those who prefer to simply relax and curl up with a good book, the innkeepers offer a well-stocked library. Beds are topped with down comforters, and guests are further pampered with an outdoor hot tub.

Innkeeper(s): Karen Schweitzer. $55-125. MC VISA. 7 rooms, 4 with PB. 1 conference room. Breakfast included in rates. Type of meal: full breakfast. Beds: QDT. Fax, copier and spa on premises. Fishing nearby.

Location: One mile outside Glacier National Park.

Certificate may be used: Jan. 1-June 15 and Sept. 1-Dec. 23.

West Yellowstone   F5

Sportsman's High B&B
750 Deer St
West Yellowstone, MT 59758-9607
(406)646-7865 Fax:(406)646-9434

Circa 1984. Nature lovers will have a delightful time at this inn, a large contemporary home that blends Colonial, farm and rustic stylings. Four guest rooms and a log cabin are the lodging choices, all with private baths. Three resident collies enjoy showing visitors the inn's aspen- and pine-filled

grounds. Hiking trails, lakes and trout streams are found nearby and cross-country skiing and snowmobiling are enjoyed in winter. The innkeepers are avid birdwatchers, fly-fishers and fly-tiers, and a fly-tying bench is available. Bring a camera to record some of the inn's plentiful wildlife, ranging in size from hummingbirds to moose.

Innkeeper(s): Diana & Gary Baxter. $65-95. MC VISA AX TC. 5 rooms with PB. Breakfast included in rates. Types of meals: full breakfast, gourmet breakfast and early coffee/tea. Afternoon tea available. Beds: KQ. Ceiling fan in room. Cable TV, VCR, fax and spa on premises. Antiques, fishing, parks, downhill skiing, cross-country skiing, theater and watersports nearby.

Location: Eight miles from Yellowstone National Park.

Publicity: *Rocky Mountain Adventures, LA Times, West Yellowstone News.*

Certificate may be used: Oct. 1 to May 31.

Whitefish   B3

Crenshaw House
5465 Hwy 93 S
Whitefish, MT 59937-8410
(406)862-3496 (800)453-2863 Fax:(406)862-7640

Circa 1973. This contemporary farmhouse inn offers three guest rooms, all with private bath. Many amenities are found at the inn, including turndown service and a wake-up tray, which precedes the tasty gourmet breakfast prepared by innkeeper Anni Crenshaw-Rieker. Guests also enjoy afternoon tea and an evening snack. The inn also boasts a fireplace and spa, and child care can be arranged. Several state parks are found nearby.

Innkeeper(s): Anni Crenshaw-Rieker. $65-125. MAP. MC VISA AX DS PC TC. 3 rooms with PB. Breakfast included in rates. Types of meals: gourmet breakfast and early coffee/tea. Catering service available. Beds: KQDT. Turndown service in room. Cable TV, VCR, fax, copier, spa, library, pet boarding and child care on premises. Antiques, fishing, parks, shopping, downhill skiing, cross-country skiing, theater and watersports nearby.

Certificate may be used: Sept. 15-Dec. 15, Jan. 5-June 15, depending on availability. Not Christmas, New Year's.

Wolf Point   B9

Forsness Farm B&B
HCR 33 Box 5035
Wolf Point, MT 59201-9402
(406)653-2492

Circa 1926. A working farm/ranch is home to this Prairie-style inn, which was built by Indian traders and moved to its present location in 1975. Cattle, chickens, horses, milk cows, sheep and even a burro reside at the ranch, and guests are welcome to help with egg gathering or milking. Fishing for coho salmon, pike and prehistoric paddlefish is found in the Missouri River, less than two miles from the inn. Two upstairs guest rooms, one with king bed and the other with twin beds, share a bath with whirlpool tub. Summertime guests often enjoy Indian celebrations and the area also hosts an authentic Wild West rodeo.

Innkeeper(s): JoAnn & Dewey Forsness. $50. TC. 2 rooms. Breakfast and evening snack included in rates. Beds: KT. Fishing, shopping, theater and watersports nearby.

Certificate may be used: All year, Sunday-Friday.

Nebraska

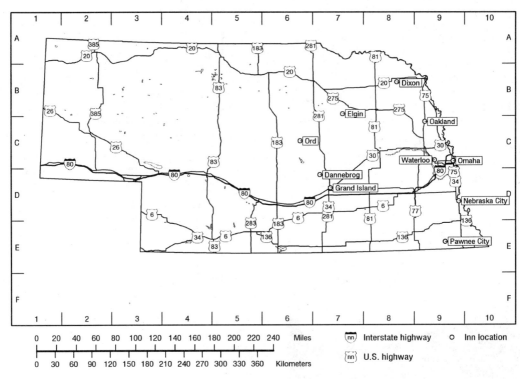

| 0 | 20 | 40 | 60 | 80 | 100 | 120 | 140 | 160 | 180 | 200 | 220 | 240 | Miles |

| 0 | 30 | 60 | 90 | 120 | 150 | 180 | 210 | 240 | 270 | 300 | 330 | 360 | Kilometers |

(nn) Interstate highway   ○ Inn location

(nn) U.S. highway

Dannebrog   **D7**

Nestle Inn
209 E Roger Welsch Ave
Dannebrog, NE 68831
(308)226-8252

Circa 1908. This small bed & breakfast features
two bedrooms. Each is decorated with whimsical
touches, such as sponge-painted walls, ivy stenciling and beds topped with bright quilts. The town
was founded by Danish immigrants, and a Danish
craftsman built this turn-of-the-century home.
Breakfast is included in the rates, but it is provided
at a restaurant that is one block away. The
innkeepers can provide a special catered dinner for
guests, served by candlelight. Guests can select
from 12 entree choices, including a variety of
Danish specialties.

Innkeeper(s): Gaylord & Judy Mickelsen. $50. PC. 2 rooms. Breakfast
included in rates. Type of meal: full breakfast. Catering service available. Beds: Q. Air conditioning in room. Library on premises. Antiques,
fishing, parks, shopping and golf nearby.

Publicity: *Grand Island Independent.*

*"You folks did a wonderful job restoring and decorating
the beautiful home! We had a lovely time and we will
highly recommend it to all! Especially our visiting
family."*

Certificate may be used: Subject to availability. Advance reservations
required. Not available first weekend June or second weekend in
December.

Dixon
B8

The George Farm
Rt 1, Box 50
Dixon, NE 68732-9728
(402)584-2625

Circa 1926. Two miles south of Highway 20, west of Sioux City, lies this air-conditioned farmhouse furnished in country decor. Although in a rural setting, the farm offers a wide array of activities within easy driving distance. Wayne State College is nearby, as are an abundance of local crafts and antique establishments. Marie, an avid antiquer, can provide help for those searching the area for special items. Relax with a stroll through the farm's 640 acres, or just enjoy some peace and quiet in the library. The inn accepts children and pets, with prior arrangement.
Innkeeper(s): Marie George. $40-45. PC. 5 rooms. Breakfast included in rates. Type of meal: full breakfast. Beds: QD. Air conditioning in room. VCR, fax and copier on premises.
Certificate may be used: Year-round except second weekend in July and first weekend of pheasant hunting season (usually first weekend of November).

Elgin
B7

Plantation House
401 Plantation St
Elgin, NE 68636-9301
(402)843-2287 Fax:(402)843-2287
E-mail: plantation@gpcom.net

Circa 1916. This historic mansion sits adjacent to Elgin City Park, and guests will marvel at its beauty and size. Once a small Victorian farmhouse, the Plantation House has evolved into a 20-room Greek Revival treasure. Visitors will be treated to a tour  and a large family-style breakfast, and may venture to the park to play tennis or horseshoes. The antique-filled guest rooms include the Stained Glass Room, with a queen bed and available twin-bed anteroom, and the Old Master Bedroom, with clawfoot tub and pedestal sink.
Innkeeper(s): Merland & Barbara Clark. $30-65. PC TC. 5 rooms, 2 with PB. 1 cottage. 2 conference rooms. Breakfast included in rates. Types of meals: full breakfast and early coffee/tea. Banquet service available. Beds: QT. Air conditioning, ceiling fan in room. TV, VCR, fax, copier, library on premises. Antiques, fishing, parks, shopping nearby.
Publicity: *Omaha World Herald, Norfolk Daily News, Home & Away, Midwest Living.*
"*Gorgeous house! Relaxing atmosphere. Just like going to Mom's house.*"
Certificate may be used: Sunday-Thursday, all year; anytime, Oct. 1-April 1 when available. Holidays excluded.

Grand Island
D7

Kirschke House B&B
1124 W 3rd St
Grand Island, NE 68801-5834
(308)381-6851 (800)381-6851

Circa 1902. A steeply sloping roofline and a two-story tower mark this distinctive, vine-covered brick Victorian house. Meticulously restored, there are polished wood floors, fresh wallpapers and carefully chosen antiques. The Roses Roses Room is a spacious accommodation with a lace canopy bed, wicker rocking chair and decorating accents of roses and vines. In the old brick wash house is a wooden hot tub. In winter  and spring, the area is popular for viewing the migration of sandhill cranes and whooping cranes.
Innkeeper(s): Lois Hank & Kiffani Smith. $55-145. MC VISA AX DS PC TC. 5 rooms, 2 with PB. 1 cottage. Breakfast included in rates. Meals: gourmet breakfast and early coffee/tea. Lunch and room service available. Beds: QDT. Air conditioning, ceiling fan in room. TV, VCR, spa, library on premises. Antiques, fishing, parks, shopping, watersports nearby.
Location: In the historic district near downtown.
Publicity: *Grand Island Daily Independent.*
Certificate may be used: Anytime.

Nebraska City
D9

Whispering Pines
RR 2
Nebraska City, NE 68410-9802
(402)873-5850

Circa 1892. An easy getaway from Kansas City, Lincoln or Omaha, Nebraska City's Whispering Pines offers visitors a relaxing alternative from big-city life. Fresh flowers in each bedroom greet guests at this two-story brick Italianate, furnished with Victorian and country decor. Situated on more than six acres of trees, flowers and ponds, the inn is a birdwatcher's delight. Breakfast is served formally in the dining room, or guests may opt to eat on the deck with its view of the garden and pines. The inn is within easy walking distance to Arbor Lodge, home of the founder of Arbor Day.
Innkeeper(s): W.B. Smulling. $50-75. MC VISA DS. 5 rooms, 2 with PB. Breakfast included in rates. Type of meal: gourmet breakfast.
Certificate may be used: All year, Sunday through Thursday.

Oakland C9

Benson B&B
402 N Oakland Ave
Oakland, NE 68045-1135
(402)685-6051

Circa 1905. This inn is on the second floor of the Benson Building, a sturdy, turreted brick structure built of walls nearly 12 inches thick. Decorated throughout in mauve, blue and cream, the Benson B&B features three comfortable guest rooms, and a restful, small-town atmosphere. Guests may visit the

Swedish Heritage Center and a nearby city park. An 18-hole golf course is a five-minute drive away. Check out the craft and gift store on the building's lower level, the inn's collection of soft drink memorabilia, and be sure to ask about the Troll Stroll.
Innkeeper(s): Stan & Norma Anderson. $47-55. PC TC. 3 rooms. Breakfast and evening snack included in rates. Types of meals: full breakfast and early coffee/tea. Beds: QD. Cable TV, VCR, spa and library on premises. Antiques, parks, shopping and sporting events nearby.
Certificate may be used: Jan. 2-May 15, any night.

Omaha C9

Offutt House
140 N 39th St
Omaha, NE 68131-2307
(402)553-0951

Circa 1894. This two-and-a-half-story, 14-room house is built like a chateau with a steep roof and tall windows. During the 1913 tornado, although almost every house in the neighborhood was leveled, the Offutt house stood firm. It is said that a decanter of sherry was blown from the dining room to the living room without anything spilling. The large parlor features a handsome fireplace, a wall of books and an inviting sofa. A bridal suite is tucked

under the gables of the third floor. A continental-plus breakfast is served during the week and a full breakfast is offered on the weekends.
Innkeeper(s): Janet & Paul Koenig. $65-105. MC VISA AX DS. 6 rooms with PB. 2 suites. Breakfast included in rates. Types of meals: continental-plus breakfast and full breakfast. Beds: KQD. Antiques, golf and theater nearby.
Location: Central Omaha.
Publicity: Midwest Living, Innsider, Bon Appetit, Innovations.

"Hospitable, comfortable, lovely. A wonderful place to stay and great central location."
Certificate may be used: January-April, excluding holidays and Saturdays.

Ord C6

The Shepherd's Inn
Rt 3, Box 108A
Ord, NE 68837
(308)728-3306

Circa 1917. Innkeeper Don Vancura was born in this house, and his grandparents built the early 20th-century farmhouse. The little bed & breakfast offers three guest bedrooms, decorated with antiques that are a mix of family pieces and items innkeeper Doris Vancura selected at local auctions. Children will especially love this inn, as there is a petting zoo on the grounds featuring goats, sheep and exotic birds. In the mornings, guests enjoy items such as waffles, French toast or breakfast casseroles.
Innkeeper(s): Don & Doris Vancura. $50-65. MC VISA AX DS PC TC. 3 rooms, 1 with PB. Breakfast and evening snack included in rates. Type of meal: full breakfast. Beds: QD. Air conditioning, turndown service and ceiling fan in room. VCR and spa on premises. Antiques, fishing, parks, shopping, cross-country skiing, golf and watersports nearby.

"We drive hours out of our way just to stay here for a reason—it's home and it's wonderful."
Certificate may be used: Dec. 1-April 1, Sunday-Friday.

Pawnee City E9

My Blue Heaven B&B
1041 5th St
Pawnee City, NE 68420-2532
(402)852-3131

Circa 1920. Not many travelers know that just a shade north of the Kansas state line, in Nebraska's Southeast corner, they may find heaven, as in My Blue Heaven B&B. Legend says that Pawnee City, the county seat, once was the area's largest Pawnee Indian village. The hosts pride themselves on hospitality and the small-town feel of their history-laden community, which also features a barbed wire museum of 800 varieties. The inn's two guest rooms, one of which is known as the Blue Berry Hill Room, are filled with antiques.

Innkeeper(s): Duane & Yvonne Dalluge. $30-35. MC VISA. 2 rooms. Breakfast included in rates. Type of meal: full breakfast. Beds: D. Air conditioning and ceiling fan in room. Cable TV and VCR on premises. Antiques, fishing, parks, shopping and golf nearby.

Certificate may be used: Nov. 1-April 1.

Waterloo C9

J.C. Robinson House B&B
102 E Lincoln Ave, PO Box 190
Waterloo, NE 68069-2004
(402)779-2704

Circa 1905. A short drive from Omaha, the Journey's End is an elegant, Neoclassical Greek Revival home boasting two impressive Ionic

columns. The inn, surrounded by large trees, is listed in the national and state historic registers. Antiques, including a stunning clock collection, are found throughout the attractive interior, and the Gone With the Wind Room offers a garden and orchard view. The home, built by seed company founder J.C. Robinson, also features a guest room in his name. Fishing and canoeing are a short walk away or guests may decide to soak up the village's relaxed atmosphere.

Innkeeper(s): John Clark. $50-75. 4 rooms. 1 conference room. Breakfast included in rates. Types of meals: full breakfast and early coffee/tea. Dinner, evening snack, gourmet lunch and banquet service available.

Certificate may be used: Oct. 1-April 30.

Nevada

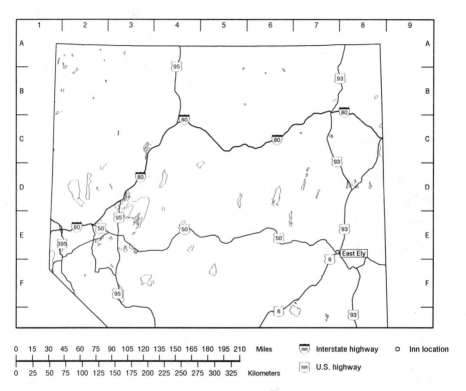

0   15 30 45 60 75 90 105 120 135 150 165 180 195 210   Miles

0   25 50 75 100 125 150 175 200 225 250 275 300 325   Kilometers

{nn} Interstate highway   o   Inn location

{nn} U.S. highway

East Ely   E7

Steptoe Valley Inn

220 E 11th St
East Ely, NV 89315-1110
(702)289-8687

Circa 1907. Originally a grocery store at the turn of
the century, this inn has been lovingly reconstructed and resembles a fancy, Old West-style store. The
interior is decorated
in Victorian coun-
try-cottage style.
Five uniquely deco-
rated guest rooms
are named for local

pioneers. The rooms also have views of the inn's
scenic surroundings, and three of them feature
queen beds. A nearby railroad museum offers train
rides and Great Basin National Park is 70 miles
away. This inn is open from June to October.
During the off-season, guests may inquire about the
inn at (702) 435-1196.

Innkeeper(s): Jane & Norman Lindley. $84-95. MC VISA AX PC TC. 5
rooms with PB. 1 conference room. Breakfast and evening snack
included in rates. Type of meal: full breakfast. Beds: QT. Air conditioning, ceiling fan and TV in room. VCR and library on premises. Fishing
and parks nearby.

Publicity: *Las Vegas Review Journal, Great Getaways, Yellow Brick Road.*

"Everything was so clean and first-rate."

Certificate may be used: Any time June through September, except 4th
of July weekend, Labor Day weekend, Arts in the Park Week (1st weekend in August) & horse race weekends (usually last 2 weeks in
August).

New Hampshire

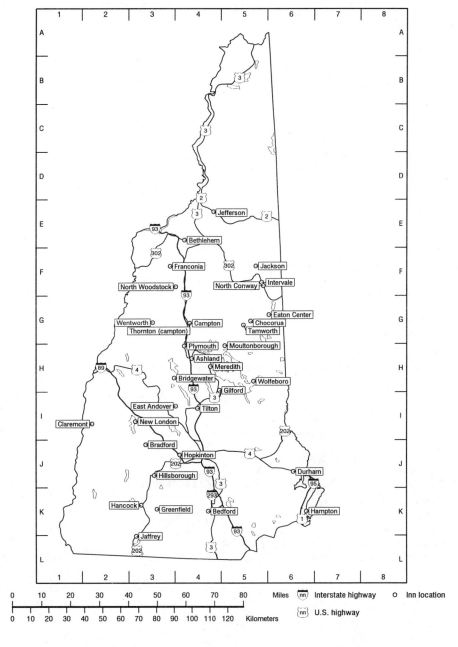

1	2	3	4	5	6	7	8

Jefferson

Bethlehem

Franconia

Jackson

North Woodstock

North Conway

Intervale

Eaton Center

Wentworth

Campton

Chocorua

Thornton (campton)

Tamworth

Plymouth

Moultonborough

Ashland

Meredith

Bridgewater

Wolfeboro

Gilford

East Andover

Tilton

Claremont

New London

Bradford

Hopkinton

Durham

Hillsborough

Hancock

Greenfield

Bedford

Hampton

Jaffrey

0	10	20	30	40	50	60	70	80	Miles

0	10	20	30	40	50	60	70	80	90	100	110	120	Kilometers

Interstate highway

Inn location

U.S. highway

Bedford   K4

Wayfarer Inn
121 South River Rd
Bedford, NH 03110
(603)622-3766 (800)843-8272 Fax:(603)623-5796

Circa 1744. The grounds at Wayfarer Inn are especially romantic. A covered bridge crosses over one of the two waterfalls, and the six acres also include woods and a millpond. The original portion of the hotel dates to mid-1700s, and it served as a working mill for more than two centuries. The modern hotel was added in 1962 and features nearly 200 guest rooms. The rooms are comfortable and pleasant. Meals are not included in the rates, but the hotel's Wayfarer Restaurant serves breakfast, lunch and dinner. There is a fitness center and both indoor and outdoor pools.

Innkeeper(s): Beth Roberts. $89-125. EP. MC VISA AX DC CB DS PC TC. 194 rooms, 188 with PB. 6 suites. 10 conference rooms. Restaurant on premises. Beds: KQD. Air conditioning, turndown service and TV in room. VCR, fax, copier, swimming and sauna on premises. Handicap access. Amusement parks, antiques, fishing, parks, shopping, downhill skiing, cross-country skiing, sporting events, golf, theater and watersports nearby.

Certificate may be used: Year-round, based upon availability, Monday-Sunday.

Bethlehem   E4

The Mulburn Inn
2370 Main St, Rt 302
Bethlehem, NH 03574
(603)869-3389 (800)457-9440 Fax:(603)869-5633
E-mail: the.mulburn.inn@connriver.net

Circa 1908. This summer cottage was known as the Ivie Estate, and many of the Ivie and Woolworth (as in the famed five and dime store) family members vacationed here in summer. Cary Grant and Barbara Hutton spent their honeymoon at the mansion. Polished oak staircases and stained-glass windows add to the atmosphere.

Innkeeper(s): The Skeels Family. $60-90. MC VISA AX DS PC TC. 7 rooms with PB. Breakfast and afternoon tea included in rates. Types of meals: full breakfast and early coffee/tea. Catered breakfast available. Beds: KQDT. Cable TV, VCR, fax, copier and library on premises. Amusement parks, antiques, fishing, parks, shopping, downhill skiing, cross-country skiing and golf nearby.

Publicity: *The Record, Yankee, Boston Globe.*

"You have put a lot of thought, charm, beauty and warmth into the inn. Your breakfasts were oh, so delicious!!"

Certificate may be used: Nov. 1-May 15.

Bradford   J3

Candlelite Inn
5 Greenhouse Ln
Bradford, NH 03221-3505
(603)938-5571

Nestled on more than three acres of countryside in the valley of the Lake Sunapee region, this Victorian inn has a gazebo porch perfect for sipping lemonade on a summer day. On winter days, keep warm by the parlor's fireplace while relaxing with a good book. All of the guest rooms have mountain views and are decorated with fresh flowers and plants. Quilts on the beds and walls, cross stitch pillows and pictures, and tole painting that includes plaques to table-top decorations are the innkeeper's creations.

Innkeeper(s): Marilyn Gordon. $65-75. MC VISA DS. 6 rooms. 1 suite. Breakfast included in rates. Types of meals: full breakfast and early coffee/tea. Evening snack available. Antiques, shopping, downhill skiing, cross-country skiing, sporting events and theater nearby.

Certificate may be used: Nov. 1-April 30.

The Rosewood Country Inn
67 Pleasant View Rd
Bradford, NH 03221-9109
(603)938-5253 Fax:(603)938-5253

Circa 1850. This three-story country Victorian inn in the Sunapee Region treats its guests to a candle-light and crystal breakfast and elegant accommodations that manage to avoid being stuffy. The inn prides itself on special touches. The innkeepers like to keep things interesting with ideas such as theme weekends and special breakfast fare, including cinnamon apple pancakes with cider sauce. Mount Sunapee Ski Area and Lake Sunapee are less than eight minutes away.

Innkeeper(s): Lesley & Dick Marquis. $79-140. MC VISA PC TC. 7 rooms with PB. 1 suite. 1 conference room. Breakfast included in rates. Types of meals: gourmet breakfast and early coffee/tea. Beds: QDT. Cable TV and fax on premises. Handicap access. Antiques, fishing, shopping, skiing, sporting events, theater and watersports nearby.

Certificate may be used: January through June, September, November and December; Sunday through Thursday.

Bridgewater   H3

The Inn on Newfound Lake
1030 Mayhew Tpke
Bridgewater, NH 03222-5108
(603)744-9111 (800)745-7990 Fax:(603)744-3894

Circa 1840. This inn was the mid-way stop on the stage coach route from Boston to Montreal and formerly was known as the Pasquaney Inn. A full

veranda overlooks the lake with its spectacular sunsets. Located in the foothills of the White Mountains, the inn is situated on more than seven acres of New Hampshire countryside.

Innkeeper(s): Phelps C. Boyce II. $55-105. MAP, AP. MC VISA AX DS. 31 rooms, 23 with PB. 2 suites. Breakfast included in rates. Type of meal: continental breakfast. Dinner available. Beds: QT. Antiques, fishing, downhill skiing, cross-country skiing and watersports nearby.

Publicity: *The Record Enterprise.*

"The rooms were quaint and cozy with just the right personal touches, and always immaculate. The bed and pillows were so comfortable, it was better than sleeping at home! The inn itself is magnificent, elegance never felt so warm and homey."

Certificate may be used: Oct. 15-May 15.

Campton   G4

Campton Inn

RR 2 Box 12, Main & Owl Sts
Campton, NH 03223-9411
(603)726-4449 Fax:(603)536-5610
E-mail: evtnh@ix.netcom.com

Circa 1836. Three steep gables mark the roof line of this historic country farmhouse. Simply but comfortably furnished rooms include a game room, a

large common room and a screened porch. A full breakfast is served, a good time to tap into the innkeepers' extensive knowledge of the area.

Innkeeper(s): Robbin & Peter Adams. $55-75. 6 rooms, 1 with PB. Breakfast included in rates. Type of meal: full breakfast. Beds: QDT. Antiques, fishing, parks, shopping, downhill skiing, cross-country skiing, sporting events, theater and watersports nearby.

Location: Heart of the White Mountain National Forest.

"What a great week. Excellent service!"

Certificate may be used: April 1-July 31 and Oct. 15-Dec. 23.

Mountain-Fare Inn

Mad River Rd, PO Box 553
Campton, NH 03223
(603)726-4283

Circa 1830. This white farmhouse is surrounded by flower gardens in the summer and unparalleled foliage during the fall. This early 19th-century village inn is an ideal spot from which to enjoy New Hampshire's many offerings. Each season brings with it different activities, from skiing to biking

and hiking or simply taking in the beautiful scenery. Downhill and cross-country skiers will enjoy the inn's lodge atmosphere during the winter, as well as the close access to ski areas. The inn is appointed in a charming New Hampshire style with country-cottage decor. The hearty breakfast is a favorite of returning guests.

Innkeeper(s): Susan & Nick Preston. $65-95. MAP, EP. 10 rooms, 8 with PB. Breakfast and afternoon tea included in rates. Type of meal: full breakfast. Beds: QDT. Cable TV, VCR and child care on premises. Antiques, fishing, parks, downhill skiing, cross-country skiing, sporting events, theater and watersports nearby.

Location: Two hours north of Boston in the White Mountains.

Publicity: *Ski, Skiing, Snow Country.*

"Thank you for your unusually caring attitude toward your guests."

Certificate may be used: Sunday through Thursday nights except Dec. 15-Jan. 2 and Sept. 15-Oct 20.

Chocorua   G5

Staffords-In-The-Field
PO Box 270
Chocorua, NH 03817-0270
(603)323-7766 Fax:(603)323-7531

Circa 1778. The main building of Stafford's, home
to a prosperous farm family for over 150 years, is
Federal style. It became a guest house in the 1890s.
An old apple orchard and sugar house remain, and
there's a kitchen garden and a nine-hole golf course
on the inn's 12 acres. A rocky brook still winds
through the rolling fields, and in the adjacent
woods, there's a natural swimming hole. Guest
rooms are furnished in antiques. A canoe on nearby
Lake Chocorua is available to guests.
Innkeeper(s): Ramona Stafford. $70-170. MAP. MC VISA. 14 rooms, 6
with PB, 1 with FP. Breakfast included in rates. Types of meals: full
breakfast and gourmet breakfast. Restaurant on premises. Beds: KQDT.
Location: White Mountains.
Publicity: *Esquire, Boston Globe, Seattle Times, Los Angeles Times.*
"Delicious food, delightful humor!"
Certificate may be used: Jan. 15 to Sept. 15 and November, subject to
availability.

Claremont   I2

Goddard Mansion B&B
25 Hillstead Rd
Claremont, NH 03743-3399
(603)543-0603 (800)736-0603 Fax:(603)543-0001

Circa 1905. This English-style manor house and
adjacent garden tea house is surrounded by seven
acres of lawns and gardens. Each of the guest rooms
is decorated in a different style. One features French
Country decor, another sports a Victorian look. The
living room with its fireplace, window seats and

baby grand piano is a perfect place to relax.
Homemade breakfasts, made using natural ingredients and fresh produce, include items such as souffles, pancakes, freshly baked muffins and fruit. The
hearty meals are served in the wood paneled dining
room highlighted by an antique Wurlitzer jukebox.
Innkeeper(s): Debbie Albee. $65-125. MC VISA AX DC CB DS PC TC.
10 rooms, 3 with PB. 1 suite. 2 conference rooms. Breakfast included
in rates. Types of meals: continental-plus breakfast, full breakfast and

gourmet breakfast. Beds: QDT. Air conditioning and turndown service in
room. Cable TV, VCR, fax, bicycles and library on premises. Antiques,
fishing, parks, shopping, skiing and theater nearby.
Publicity: *Eagle Times.*
*"Our trip would not have been as enjoyable without
having stayed at your inn."*
Certificate may be used: All year, excepting holidays and foliage season. Sunday through Thursday (one weekend night upon availability).

Durham   J6

University Guest House
47 Mill Rd
Durham, NH 03824-3006
(603)868-2728 Fax:(603)868-2744

Circa 1935. For the parents of college students, this
B&B is a perfect choice, located within walking distance of the University of New Hampshire. But
location isn't the only draw for guests at this Dutch
Colonial home. The secluded grounds are covered
with trees and foliage, creating a peaceful, natural
environment. The rooms are decorated like a country cottage. Walls are covered in bright, cheerful
prints, and the comfortable furnishings are highlighted with a few antiques and collectibles.
Innkeeper(s): Elizabeth Fischer. $50-90. 4 rooms. Breakfast included in
rates. Types of meals: continental-plus breakfast and early coffee/tea.
Beds: QT. Antiques, fishing, parks, shopping, cross-country skiing,
sporting events, theater and watersports nearby.
Certificate may be used: As space is available.

East Andover   I4

Highland Lake Inn B&B
Maple St
East Andover, NH 03231-0164
(603)735-6426 Fax:(603)735-5355

Circa 1767. This early Victorian inn overlooks three
mountains, and all the rooms have views of either
the lake or the mountains. Many guest rooms feature
handmade quilts and some have four-poster beds.
Guests may relax with a book from the inn's library
in front of the sitting room fireplace or walk the 12-
acre grounds and enjoy old apple and maple trees, as
well as the shoreline. Adjacent to a 21-acre nature
conservancy, there are scenic trails and a stream to
explore. Highland Lake is stocked with bass and also
has trout. Fresh fruit salads, hot entrees, and homemade breads are featured at breakfast.
Innkeeper(s): Mary Petras. $85-125. MC VISA AX. 10 rooms with PB.
Breakfast included in rates. Type of meal: full breakfast. Beds: KQT.
Ceiling fan in room. Cable TV and VCR on premises. Amusement parks,
antiques, fishing, shopping, downhill skiing, cross-country skiing,
sporting events, theater and watersports nearby.
Publicity: *Andover Beacon.*
"Place is very close to heaven."
Certificate may be used: Nov. 1-May 1.

Eaton Center G6

Rockhouse Mountain Farm Inn
PO Box 90
Eaton Center, NH 03832-0090
(603)447-2880

Circa 1900. This handsome old house is framed by maple trees on 450 acres of forests, streams, fields and wildflowers. Milking cows, pigs, geese, peacocks and llamas provide entertainment for city youngsters of all ages. Three generations of the Edges have operated this inn and some guests have been com-

ing since 1946, the year it opened. A 250-year-old barn bulges at times with new-mown hay, and there is a nearby beach with swimming and boating for the exclusive use of guests.

Innkeeper(s): Johnny & Alana Edge. $50-60. MAP. PC TC. 18 rooms, 8 with PB, 1 with FP. 2 cottages. Breakfast and dinner included in rates. Type of meal: full breakfast. Restaurant on premises. Beds: DT. Swimming, sauna, stables and library on premises. Handicap access. Antiques, fishing, parks, shopping, golf, theater and watersports nearby.

Location: Near the White Mountains.

Publicity: *New York Times, Family Circle, Woman's Day, Boston Globe, Country Vacations.*

"We have seen many lovely places, but Rockhouse remains the real high spot, the one to which we most want to return."

Certificate may be used: Rate is MAP. June 15-July 15, Labor Day to Sept. 25, Oct. 15-Nov. 1.

Franconia F3

Bungay Jar
PO Box 15, Easton Valley Rd
Franconia, NH 03580-0015
(603)823-7775 Fax:(603)444-0110

Circa 1967. An 18th-century barn was taken down and moved piece by piece to Easton Valley, six miles from Franconia. A post-and-beam, barn-style-home

JANE STAUFFER

was constructed on 12 wooded acres with a stream nearby and the White Mountains in view. The two-story living room, reminiscent of a hay loft, is decorated with antique country furnishings, as are all the guest rooms. Your host, a landscape architect, has planted herb and perennial gardens, featured in national magazines. Rates are higher during foliage.

Innkeeper(s): Kate Kerivan. $70-150. MC VISA AX DS PC TC. 7 rooms, 5 with PB, 2 with FP. 3 suites. 1 cottage. Breakfast and afternoon tea included in rates. Beds: KQDT. Sauna on premises. Antiques, fishing, parks, shopping, downhill skiing, cross-country skiing, theater and watersports nearby.

Publicity: *Country Accents, Discerning Traveler, Yankee, Birds & Bloom, Brides, American Homestyle.*

"Such a perfect spot with such a great view."

Certificate may be used: November through June; Monday through Thursday.

The Inn at Forest Hills
Rt 142, PO Box 783
Franconia, NH 03580
(603)823-9550 (800)280-9550 Fax:(603)823-8701
E-mail: innfhills@connriver.net

Circa 1890. This Tudor-style inn in the White Mountains offers a solarium, a living room with fireplace and a large common room with fireplace and cathedral ceilings. Breakfast is served with a quiet background of classical music in the dining room, where in the winter there's a blazing fireplace, and

in summer the French doors open to the scenery. Guest rooms feature a casual country decor with quilts, flowered wall coverings and some four-poster beds. Cross-country ski for free on the inn's property and at the local touring center. Downhill facilities are found at Bretton Woods, Cannon or Loon Mountain. Nearby Franconia Notch Park and the White Mountains feature trails designed for cycling and hiking. The innkeeper is a justice of the peace, and will do weddings or a renewal of vows.

Innkeeper(s): Gordon & Joanne Haym. $85-145. MC VISA AX DC PC TC. 7 rooms with PB. Breakfast included in rates. Type of meal: full breakfast. Evening snack available. Beds: KQ. Cable TV, VCR, fax, tennis and library on premises. Antiques, fishing, parks, shopping, downhill skiing, cross-country skiing and watersports nearby.

"What a delightful inn! I loved the casual country elegance of your B&B and can understand why you are so popular with brides and grooms."

Certificate may be used: Sunday through Thursday, Nov. 1-April 30, except President, Christmas and New Years' weekends.

Franconia Inn
1300 Easton Rd
Franconia, NH 03580-4921
(603)823-5542 (800)473-5299 Fax:(603)823-8078
E-mail: info@franconiainn.com

Circa 1934. Beautifully situated on 117 acres below the White Mountain's famous Franconia Notch, this white clapboard inn is three stories high. An oak-paneled library, parlor, rathskeller lounge and two verandas offer relaxing retreats. The inn's rooms

are simply decorated in a pleasing style and there is a special honeymoon suite with private Jacuzzi. Bach, classic wines and an elegant American cuisine are featured in the inn's unpretentious dining room. There's no shortage of activity here. The inn offers four clay tennis courts, horseback riding, a heated swimming pool, croquet, fishing, cross-country ski trails and glider rides among its outdoor amenities.

Innkeeper(s): Alec Morris. $75-135. MAP. EP. MC VISA AX. 34 rooms, 29 with PB, 3 with FP. 4 suites. 1 conference room. Breakfast included in rates. Types of meals: gourmet breakfast and early coffee/tea. Dinner, picnic lunch and catering service available. Restaurant on premises. Beds: KQDT. VCR, copier, spa, swimming, bicycles, tennis and child care on premises. Amusement parks, antiques, fishing, parks, shopping, skiing, sporting events and theater nearby.

Location: Exit 38 off I-93, two-and-a-half miles south on Route 116.
Publicity: *Philadelphia Inquirer, Boston Globe, Travel & Leisure, Powder.*

"The piece de resistance of the Franconia Notch is the Franconia Inn—Philadelphia Inquirer."

Certificate may be used: Midweek (Sunday-Thursday), non-holiday, from May 20-June 22. Midweek Sept. 5-Sept. 21; any time from Oct. 29-Dec. 21; Midweek, non-holiday Jan. 1-April 1.

Gilford   H4

Cartway House Inn
83 Old Lake Shore Rd
Gilford, NH 03246-6529
(603)528-1172

Circa 1791. Overlooking mountains and meadows, this clapboard colonial was built by shipbuilders and is one of 10 historic homes in Gilford. This is a popular area for bike tours, cross-country skiing, horseback riding and golf. The innkeepers speak several languages.

Innkeeper(s): Gretchen & Tony Shortway. $45-74. MC VISA AX PC. 7 rooms, 1 with PB. Breakfast and afternoon tea included in rates. Types of meals: full breakfast and gourmet breakfast. Beds: TD. Air conditioning and TV in room. Bicycles on premises. Amusement parks, antiques, fishing, parks, shopping, downhill skiing, cross-country skiing, sporting events, golf, theater and watersports nearby.

"Gretchen really knows how to make you feel welcome."

Certificate may be used: Monday through Friday, excluding holiday and event weekends.

Greenfield   K3

The Greenfield Inn
Forest Rd at Rts 31 N & 136
Greenfield, NH 03047
(603)547-6245 Fax:(603)547-2418
E-mail: bnbreakfast@aol.com

Circa 1817. In the 1850s this inn was purchased by Henry Dunklee, innkeeper of the old Mayfield Inn across the street. When there was an overflow of guests at his tavern, Mr. Dunklee accommodated them here. This totally renovated Victorian mansion features veranda views of Crotched, Temple and Monadnock Mountains. The gracious innkeepers and comfortable interiors have been enjoyed by many well-traveled guests, including Dolores and Bob Hope.

Innkeeper(s): Barbara & Vic Mangini. $49-119. MC VISA AX PC TC. 11 rooms, 8 with PB. 2 suites. 1 cottage. 1 conference room. Breakfast included in rates. Type of meal: full breakfast. Beds: KQDT. Air conditioning, ceiling fan and VCR in room. Fax, copier and library on premises. Antiques, fishing, parks, shopping, downhill skiing, cross-country skiing, theater and watersports nearby.

Location: Southern New Hampshire, 90 minutes from Boston.
Publicity: *Manchester Union Leader, Innsider.*

"I'm coming back for more of this New Hampshire therapy—Bob Hope."

Certificate may be used: Sunday night through Thursday night, Nov. 1-April 30, but not Thanksgiving, Christmas or New Year's weeks.

Hampton

K6

The Inn at Elmwood Corners
252 Winnacunnet Rd
Hampton, NH 03842-2726
(603)929-0443 (800)253-5691

Circa 1870. This old sea captain's house boasts a wide wraparound porch, filled with wicker in the summer. The inn is decorated with stenciled walls, braided rugs and col-lections such as thimbles and dolls. Mary has stitched the quilts that top the beds. The library is jammed and guests may borrow a book and finish reading it at home. A favorite breakfast is John's poached brook trout or Eggs Benedict.

Innkeeper(s): John & Mary Hornberger. $65-85. MC VISA TC. 7 rooms, 2 with PB. 2 suites. Breakfast included in rates. Beds: QT. Air conditioning in room. Cable TV and library on premises. Amusement parks, antiques, fishing, parks, shopping, cross-country skiing, theater and watersports nearby.

Location: Three miles east of I-95, one mile west of the ocean.

Publicity: *Portsmouth Herald, Hampton Union, Boston Globe, Country.*

"Very hospitable, can't think of a thing you need to add."

Certificate may be used: Not valid weekends from Memorial Day through October.

Victoria Inn
430 High St
Hampton, NH 03842-2311
(603)929-1437

Circa 1865. Elegance and style are featured at this Queen Anne Victorian inn just a half-mile from the ocean. A romantic gazebo, spacious guest rooms and Victorian furnishings throughout the inn add to its considerable charm. The Honeymoon Suite and Victoria Room are popular with those seeking privacy and luxury. Guests may borrow the inn's bicycles for a relaxing ride or read a book in its deluxe morning room. Common areas include the living room and the sitting room, with its cozy fireplace.

Innkeeper(s): Bill & Ruth Muzzey. $75-95. MC VISA PC TC. 6 rooms, 3 with PB. Breakfast included in rates. Types of meals: full breakfast and early coffee/tea. Beds: KQDT. Air conditioning, turndown service, ceiling fan and TV in room. VCR and library on premises. Antiques, fishing, parks, shopping, downhill skiing, cross-country skiing, sporting events, theater and watersports nearby.

Certificate may be used: Nov. 1-April 30.

Hancock

K3

The Hancock Inn
33 Main St
Hancock, NH 03449
(603)525-3318 (800)525-1789 Fax:(603)525-9301

Circa 1789. Travelers have enjoyed this old inn, now in the National Register of Historic Places, since the days it served as a stagecoach stop more than 200 years ago. Canopied beds are found in some rooms and there are hooked rugs, wing-back chairs and rock-

ers. The Mural Room boasts a pastoral mural painted in 1825. All rooms have hand-sewn quilts and antique appointments. The fireplaced common room has comfortable chairs and couches with a small bar.

Innkeeper(s): Linda & Joe Johnston. $98-150. MAP, AP, EP. MC VISA AX DC CB DS PC TC. 11 rooms with PB. Breakfast included in rates. Types of meals: full breakfast and early coffee/tea. Afternoon tea, dinner, picnic lunch and banquet service available. Beds: QDT. Air conditioning in room. Cable TV, fax and library on premises. Antiques, fishing, parks, shopping, downhill skiing, cross-country skiing, theater and watersports nearby.

Publicity: *Country Inns, Boston Globe, Keene Sentinel, Yankee Homes.*

"The warmth you extended was the most meaningful part of our visit."

Certificate may be used: November-July, not including holidays or holiday weekends.

Hillsborough

J3

The Inn at Maplewood Farm
447 Center Rd PO Box 1478
Hillsborough, NH 03244-4825
(603)464-4242 (800)644-6695 Fax:(603)464-5401

Circa 1794. Antique-lovers will enjoy this historic inn, which not only features attractive American and European pieces, but a location in the heart of antique and auction country. An 1880s barn has been renovated to include guest rooms, and the inn's gift shop is located in the original 1794 tavern

room. The innkeepers rebroadcast vintage radio programs, such as "Inner Sanctum," to the antique radios found in guest rooms. The inn borders scenic Fox State Forest and historic Hillsborough Center is just up the road.

Innkeeper(s): Laura & Jayme Simoes. $75-125. EP. MC VISA AX DS PC TC. 4 suites. 1 conference room. Breakfast included in rates. Types of meals: full breakfast and early coffee/tea. Picnic lunch available. Beds: KQDT. Air conditioning, turndown service and ceiling fan in room. VCR, fax and library on premises. Antiques, fishing, parks, shopping, downhill skiing, cross-country skiing and watersports nearby.

Publicity: *New York Times, Boston Globe, Chicago Tribune, Yankee, Boston Herald, Baltimore Sun.*

"*Your house is charming and you are both very hospitable.*"

Certificate may be used: Off-season, Nov. 1-April 30, midweek only (Sunday-Thursday).

Hopkinton   J4

The Country Porch B&B
281 Moran Rd
Hopkinton, NH 03229
(603)746-6391 Fax:(603)746-6391

Circa 1978. This farmhouse does in fact sport a large covered porch where guests are often found relaxing and enjoying the peaceful 15-acre grounds. The home was built in the late 1970s, but is a replica of an 18th-century Colonial. There are three guest rooms, decorated in Colonial style. One room has a fireplace, another includes a canopy bed. Whatever the season, guests will find something to do in the Hopkinton area. Guests can visit a restored Shaker Village, shop for antiques, fish, pick berries, ski and much more.

Innkeeper(s): Tom & Wendy Solomon. $60-75. MC VISA PC TC. 3 rooms with PB, 1 with FP. 1 conference room. Breakfast included in rates. Types of meals: full breakfast and early coffee/tea. Beds: KT. Ceiling fan in room. Cable TV, VCR, fax, copier and swimming on premises. Antiques, fishing, parks, shopping, downhill skiing, cross-country skiing, sporting events, golf, theater and watersports nearby.

"*A highlight of our trip and will be forever a treasured memory.*"

Certificate may be used: Nov. 1-April 30, Sunday-Saturday.

Intervale   F5

The Forest - A Country Inn
PO Box 37
Intervale, NH 03845-0037
(603)356-9772 (800)448-3534 Fax:(603)356-5652
E-mail: forest@moose.ncia.net

Circa 1830. This spacious Second Empire Victorian offers easy access to the many attractions of the Mt. Washington Valley. The inn's guest rooms are

uniquely decorated with country antique furnishings. Honeymooners often enjoy the privacy of the inn's turn-of-the-century stone cottage. A stream runs through the inn's 25 wooded acres, and guests may cross-country ski right on the property. The inn also boasts a built-in swimming pool. Breakfast fare could include apple pancakes, cinnamon French toast or spiced Belgian waffles. Heritage New Hampshire and Story Land are nearby.

Innkeeper(s): Bill & Lisa Guppy. $60-169. MC VISA AX DS PC TC. 12 rooms, 10 with PB, 5 with FP. 2 suites. 3 cottages. Breakfast and evening snack included in rates. Type of meal: full breakfast. Beds: QDT. Ceiling fan in room. Cable TV, fax and swimming on premises. Amusement parks, antiques, fishing, parks, shopping, downhill skiing, cross-country skiing, sporting events, theater and watersports nearby.

Certificate may be used: Anytime April, May, June, November-Dec. 20, holidays excluded.

Jackson   F5

Dana Place Inn
Rt 16, Pinkham Notch Rd
Jackson, NH 03846
(603)383-6822 (800)537-9276 Fax:(603)383-6022
E-mail: dpi@ncia.net

Circa 1860. The original owners received this Colonial farmhouse as a wedding present. The warm, cozy atmosphere of the inn is surpassed only by the spectacular mountain views. During autumn, the fall leaves explode with color, and guests can

enjoy the surroundings while taking a hike or bike ride through the area. The beautiful Ellis River is the perfect place for an afternoon of fly-fishing or a picnic. After a scrumptious country breakfast, winter guests can step out the door and into skis for a day of cross-country skiing.

Innkeeper(s): The Levine Family. $75-155. MAP. MC VISA AX DC CB DS PC TC. 33 rooms, 29 with PB. 4 suites. Breakfast and afternoon tea included in rates. Type of meal: full breakfast. Dinner, picnic lunch, banquet service and room service available. Restaurant on premises. Beds: KQDT. Air conditioning, ceiling fan and TV in room. VCR, fax, copier, spa, swimming, tennis and library on premises. Amusement parks, antiques, fishing, parks, shopping, downhill skiing, cross-country skiing, golf, theater and watersports nearby.

Location: At the base of Mt. Washington, White Mountain National Forest.

Publicity: *Travel & Leisure, Inn Spots, Bon Appetit, Country Journal.*

"We had such a delightful time at Dana Place Inn. We will recommend you to everyone."

Certificate may be used: Midweek, year-round, excluding February; August; Sept. 20-Oct. 20 & holiday periods.

Ellis River House

Rt 16, Box 656
Jackson, NH 03846
(603)383-9339 (800)233-8309 Fax:(603)383-4142
E-mail: 76073,1435@compuserve.com

Circa 1893. Andrew Harriman built this farmhouse, as well as the village town hall and three-room schoolhouse where the innkeepers' children attended school. Classic antiques and Laura Ashley prints decorate the guest rooms and riverfront "hon-

eymoon" cottage, and each window reveals views of magnificent mountains, the vineyard or spectacular Ellis River. In 1993, the innkeepers added 18 rooms, 13 of which feature fireplaces and three offer two-person Jacuzzis. They also added four family suites, a heated, outdoor pool, an indoor Jacuzzi and a sauna.

Innkeeper(s): Barry & Barbara Lubao. $79-229. MAP. MC VISA AX DC CB DS PC TC. 20 rooms with PB, 13 with FP. 4 suites. 1 cottage. 1 conference room. Breakfast included in rates. Types of meals: full breakfast and early coffee/tea. Afternoon tea, dinner and picnic lunch available. Beds: KQDT. Air conditioning and TV in room. Fax, spa, swimming and sauna on premises. Handicap access. Amusement parks, antiques, fishing, parks, shopping, downhill skiing, cross-country skiing, sporting events, theater and watersports nearby.

Location: White Mountain area.

Publicity: *Philadelphia Inquirer.*

"We have stayed at many B&Bs all over the world and are in agreement that the beauty and hospitality of Ellis River House is that of a world-class bed & breakfast."

Certificate may be used: Midweek, Sunday through Thursday, months of January, March, April, May, June, November, excluding holidays.

Paisley & Parsley B&B

Five Mile Circuit Rd
Jackson, NH 03846
(603)383-0859 Fax:(603)383-6973

Circa 1989. The two acres at this contemporary home boast wonderful gardens and grounds encompassed by woods. Rooms are decorated in Colonial style. One room features a canopy bed, another has its own sitting area. The Parsley, Sage, Rosemary & Thyme room is especially whimsical. The bed is painted a rich coral shade and topped with a light pink comforter. A pink and white quilt serves as a backdrop for the bed, and the walls are painted yellow. Breakfasts are a treat, gourmet entrees are served on fine china decorated with fern leaves. Kona coffee and special blended juices accompany the meal. In the afternoons, guests enjoy homemade scones and tea.

Innkeeper(s): Beatrice & Charles Stone. $85-135. MC VISA PC TC. 3 rooms with PB. 1 suite. Breakfast and afternoon tea included in rates. Types of meals: full breakfast, gourmet breakfast and early coffee/tea. Beds: KQDT. Ceiling fan, TV and VCR in room. Swimming, bicycles, library and child care on premises. Handicap access. Amusement parks, antiques, fishing, parks, shopping, downhill skiing, cross-country skiing, golf, theater and watersports nearby.

Publicity: *Boston Globe.*

"We have never had better breakfasts anywhere!"

Certificate may be used: Jan. 2-July 15, Sunday to Thursday; Oct. 25-Dec. 15, Sunday to Thursday.

Whitneys' Inn

Rt 16B, PO Box 822
Jackson, NH 03846
(603)383-8916 (800)677-5737 Fax:(603)383-6886

Circa 1842. This country inn offers romance, family recreation and a lovely setting at the base of the Black Mountain Ski Area. The inn specializes in recreation, as guests enjoy cookouts, cross-country and downhill skiing, hiking, lawn games, skating, sledding, sleigh rides, swimming and tennis. Popular nearby activities include trying out Jackson's two golf courses and picnicking at Jackson Falls.

Innkeeper(s): David Linne. $76-170. MAP. MC VISA AX DS PC TC. 29 rooms with PB, 3 with FP. 9 suites. 2 cottages. 1 conference room. Breakfast and dinner included in rates. Type of meal: full breakfast. Afternoon tea, picnic lunch and banquet service available. Restaurant on premises. Beds: KQDT. Cable TV, VCR, swimming, tennis and library on premises. Amusement parks, antiques, fishing, parks, downhill skiing, cross-country skiing, theater and watersports nearby.

Certificate may be used: Oct. 20-Nov. 20, Nov. 20-Dec. 20, all nights; Jan. 2-Feb. 10, March 16-Sept. 15, Sunday-Thursday.

Jaffrey L3

The Benjamin Prescott Inn
Rt 124 E, 433 Turnpike Rd
Jaffrey, NH 03452
(603)532-6637 Fax:(603)532-6637

Circa 1853. Colonel Prescott arrived on foot in Jaffrey in 1775 with an ax in his hand and a bag of beans on his back. The family built this classic Greek Revival many years later. Now, candles light the win-

dows, seen from the stonewall-lined lane adjacent to the inn. Each room bears the name of a Prescott family member and is furnished with antiques.
Innkeeper(s): Jan & Barry Miller. $65-140. EP. MC VISA AX PC TC. 9 rooms with PB. 2 suites. 1 conference room. Breakfast included in rates. Type of meal: full breakfast. Beds: KQDT. Ceiling fan in room. VCR, fax and library on premises. Antiques, fishing, parks, shopping, downhill skiing, cross-country skiing, sporting events, theater and watersports nearby.

"The coffee and breakfasts were delicious and the hospitality overwhelming."

Certificate may be used: Jan. 2-March 31, excluding holidays.

Jefferson E4

Applebrook B&B
Rt 115A, PO Box 178
Jefferson, NH 03583-0178
(603)586-7713 (800)545-6504
E-mail: applebrk@aol.com

Circa 1797. Panoramic views surround this large Victorian farmhouse nestled in the middle of New Hampshire's White Mountains. Guests can awake to the smell of freshly baked muffins made with locally picked berries. A comfortable, fire-lit sitting room

boasts stained glass, a goldfish pool and a beautiful view of Mt. Washington. Test your golfing skills at the nearby 18-hole championship course, or spend the day antique hunting. A trout stream and spring-fed rock pool are nearby. Wintertime guests can ice skate or race through the powder at nearby ski resorts or by way of snowmobile, finish off the day with a moonlight toboggan ride. After a full day, guests can enjoy a soak in the hot tub under the stars, where they might see shooting stars or the Northern Lights.
Innkeeper(s): Sandra Conley & Martin Kelly. $40-75. MC VISA AX PC TC. 14 rooms, 7 with PB. 1 conference room. Breakfast included in rates. Types of meals: full breakfast and early coffee/tea. Beds: KQDT. Ceiling fan in room. Spa and library on premises. Amusement parks, antiques, fishing, parks, shopping, downhill skiing, cross-country skiing, theater and watersports nearby.

Publicity: *PriceCostco Connection, New Hampshire Outdoor Companion, Outdoor.*

"We came for a night and stayed for a week."

Certificate may be used: Anytime except weekends July 1-Oct. 15 or Dec. 15-March 15.

Meredith H4

The Tuckernuck Inn
25 Red Gate Ln
Meredith, NH 03253-9804
(603)279-5521

Circa 1921. Lake Winnipesaukee is just a few minutes from Tuckernuck Inn, and there guests can go swimming, boating and fishing. The inn is decorated in early American style, with country furnishings, handmade quilts, stenciled walls and hardwood floors. Breakfast might include French toast made from homemade bread or perhaps strawberries and cream. In addition to the lake activities, guests can enjoy skiing, sleigh rides, antique and craft shops, country roads with covered bridges and beautiful fall foliage.
Innkeeper(s): Ken & Mel Ritzen. $60-75. PC TC. 5 rooms, 3 with PB. Breakfast included in rates. Types of meals: full breakfast and early coffee/tea. Beds: D. Cable TV, VCR and library on premises. Antiques, fishing, shopping, skiing, golf, theater and watersports nearby.

"Your home is so beautiful and so cozy."

Certificate may be used: Nov. 1-May 31, Sunday-Saturday.

Moultonborough H5

Olde Orchard Inn
RR 1 Box 256, Lee Rd & Lees Mill
Moultonborough, NH 03254-9502
(603)476-5004 (800)598-5845 Fax:(603)476-5419
E-mail: innkeep1@aol.com

Circa 1790. This farmhouse rests next to a mountain brook and pond in the midst of an apple orchard. Nine guest rooms are available, all with private baths. Three rooms have a Jacuzzi tub. After enjoying a large country breakfast, guests may borrow a bicycle for a ride to Lake Winnipesaukee, just a mile away. The inn is within an hour's drive of five downhill skiing areas, and guests also may cross-country ski nearby. The Castle in the Clouds and the Audubon Loon Center are nearby.

Innkeeper(s): Jim & Mary Senner. $70-125. MC VISA PC TC. 9 rooms with PB, 3 with FP. 1 cottage. Breakfast included in rates. Type of meal: full breakfast. Beds: QDT. Air conditioning in room. Cable TV, VCR, fax and child care on premises. Antiques, fishing, parks, shopping, downhill skiing, cross-country skiing, theater and watersports nearby.

Certificate may be used: Nov. 1-May 15, Friday and Saturday excluded.

New London   I3

Colonial Farm Inn
Rt 11, PO Box 1053
New London, NH 03257
(603)526-6121 (800)805-8504 Fax:(603)641-0314

Circa 1836. The village of New London holds what should be the world's most popular festival, the Chocolate Fest. The innkeepers at Colonial Farm won the award for top confection, a tangy chocolate-almond pate. The historic home, an example of a center-chimney Colonial, is decorated in a tasteful, period style with a mix of antiques and pieces such as four-poster beds. A memorable breakfast is served, and guests would be wise to save at least one night for dinner at the inn. The dining rooms, with exposed beams and plank floorboards, are cozy and romantic, and the food has drawn many compliments. Specialties include crostini with chicken liver pate and prosciutto, roasted red and green peppers with goat cheese, tenderloin of beef with a burgundy-shallot sauce or, perhaps, chicken stuffed with homemade boursin cheese and walnuts.

Innkeeper(s): Robert & Kathryn Joseph. $85-95. MC VISA AX PC TC. 5 rooms with PB. 1 conference room. Breakfast included in rates. Type of meal: full breakfast. Restaurant on premises. Beds: QDT. Air conditioning in room. Cable TV, VCR, bicycles and library on premises. Handicap access. Antiques, fishing, parks, shopping, downhill skiing, cross-country skiing, sporting events, theater and watersports nearby.

Certificate may be used: Jan. 1-Dec. 31 except weekends in the summer.

North Conway   F5

The 1785 Inn
3582 White Mountain Hwy
North Conway, NH 03860-1785
(603)356-9025 (800)421-1785 Fax:(603)356-6081
E-mail: the1785inn@aol.com

Circa 1785. The main section of this center-chimney house was built by Captain Elijah Dinsmore of the New Hampshire Rangers. He was granted the land for service in the American Revolution. Original hand-hewn beams, corner posts, fireplaces, and a brick oven are still visible and operating. The inn is located at the historical marker popularized by the White Mountain School of Art in the 19th century.

Innkeeper(s): Becky & Charles Mallar. $69-169. MC VISA AX DC CB DS PC TC. 17 rooms, 12 with PB. 1 suite. 2 conference rooms. Breakfast included in rates. Types of meals: full breakfast, gourmet breakfast and early coffee/tea. Dinner, evening snack, banquet service and room service available. Restaurant on premises. Beds: KQD. Air conditioning in room. Cable TV, VCR, fax, copier, swimming, library and child care on premises. Amusement parks, antiques, fishing, parks, shopping, downhill skiing, cross-country skiing, theater and watersports nearby.

Location: At the Scenic Vista Overlook two miles north of North Conway in the White Mountains.

Publicity: *Bon Appetit, Ski, Travel Holiday, Connecticut, Country.*

"*Occasionally in our lifetimes is a moment so unexpectedly perfect that we use it as our measure for our unforgettable moments. We just had such an experience at The 1785 Inn.*"

Certificate may be used: January, March-June, November-December, excluding holidays.

Cranmore Mt Lodge
859 Kearsarge Rd, PO Box 1194
North Conway, NH 03860-1194
(603)356-2044 (800)356-3596 Fax:(603)356-8963
E-mail: helfandd@nxi.com

Circa 1860. Babe Ruth was a frequent guest at this old New England farmhouse when his daughter was the owner. There are many rare Babe Ruth photos displayed in the inn and one guest room is still decorated with his furnishings. The barn on the property is held together with wooden pegs and contains dorm rooms.

Innkeeper(s): Judy & Dennis Helfand. $69-125. MC VISA AX DC DS PC TC. 21 rooms, 15 with PB. 1 suite. Breakfast included in rates. Types of meals: full breakfast and early coffee/tea. Beds: KQDT. Air conditioning, ceiling fan and TV in room. VCR, fax, copier, spa, swimming and tennis on premises. Amusement parks, antiques, fishing, parks, shopping, downhill skiing, cross-country skiing, theater and watersports nearby.

Location: Village of Kearsarge.

Publicity: *Ski Magazine, Snow Country, Montreal Gazette, Newsday.*

"*Your accommodations are lovely, your breakfasts delicious.*"

Certificate may be used: April 1-Sept. 15.

Victorian Harvest Inn
28 Locust Ln, Box 1763
North Conway, NH 03860
(603)356-3548 (800)642-0749 Fax:(603)356-8450

Circa 1853. Perched atop a hill in the Mt. Washington Valley, this Folk Victorian inn features comfortable surroundings and attention to detail. The country Victorian furnishings are highlighted by homemade quilts and teddy bears that visitors may adopt during their stay. The Victoria Station Room boasts its own carousel horse, and the Nook &

Cranny Room offers a view of the entire Moat Range. Cotswald Hideaway offers a skylight and gas fireplace. Guests

also enjoy strolling the grounds, which include a footbridge, gardens and a Victorian decorated pool.
Innkeeper(s): Linda & Robert Dahlberg. $70-120. MC VISA AX DS TC. 6 rooms, 4 with PB. Breakfast and afternoon tea included in rates. Type of meal: full breakfast. Air conditioning and ceiling fan in room. Cable TV, VCR, fax and copier on premises. Antiques, fishing, parks, shopping, skiing, theater and watersports nearby.
Certificate may be used: Sunday-Thursday, November-June, no holiday weeks.

North Woodstock   F4

Wilderness Inn
RFD 1, Box 69, Rts 3 & 112
North Woodstock, NH 03262-9710
(603)745-3890

Circa 1912. Surrounded by the White Mountain National Forest, this charming shingled home offers a picturesque getaway for every season. Guest rooms are furnished with antiques and Oriental rugs, and the innkeepers also offer family suites and a private cottage with a fireplace and a view of Lost River. Breakfast is a delightful affair with choices ranging from fresh muffins to brie cheese omelets, French toast topped with homemade apple syrup, crepes or specialty pancakes. For the children, the innkeepers create teddy bear pancakes or French toast. If you have room, an afternoon tea also is prepared.
Innkeeper(s): Michael Yarnell. $40-105. MAP. MC VISA AX PC TC. 7 rooms, 5 with PB. 1 cottage. Breakfast included in rates. Type of meal: gourmet breakfast. Beds: QDT.
"The stay at your inn, attempting and completing the 3D jig-jaw puzzle, combined with those unforgettable breakfasts, and your combined friendliness, makes the Wilderness Inn a place for special memories."
Certificate may be used: All midweek except holidays and July-October.

Plymouth   H4

Colonel Spencer Inn
RR 1, Box 206
Plymouth, NH 03264
(603)536-3438

Circa 1764. This pre-Revolutionary Colonial boasts Indian shutters, gleaming plank floors and a secret hiding place. Joseph Spencer, one of the home's early owners, fought at Bunker Hill and with General Washington. Within view of the river and the mountains, the inn is now a cozy retreat with warm Colonial decor. A suite with a kitchen is also available.

Innkeeper(s): Carolyn & Alan Hill. $45-65. PC TC. 7 rooms with PB. 1 suite. Breakfast and evening snack included in rates. Type of meal: full breakfast. Beds: D. Antiques, fishing, parks, shopping, downhill skiing, cross-country skiing, sporting events, theater and watersports nearby.
Location: Near lake and mountain district.

"You have something very special here and we very much enjoyed a little piece of it!"
Certificate may be used: November through July.

Crab Apple Inn B&B
PO Box 188
Plymouth, NH 03264-0188
(603)536-4476

Circa 1835. Behind an immaculate, white picket fence is a brick Federal house beside a small brook at the foot of Tenney Mountain. Rooms are appointed with antiques. The two-room suite includes an antique clawfoot tub and a canopy bed. The grounds have gardens and, of course, many crab apple trees.
Innkeeper(s): Christine DeCamp. $70-105. MC VISA PC TC. 5 rooms, 3 with PB. Breakfast and afternoon tea included in rates. Types of meals: gourmet breakfast and early coffee/tea. Beds: QDT. Air conditioning in room. Amusement parks, antiques, fishing, parks, shopping, skiing, sporting events, theater and watersports nearby.
Location: Gateway to White Mountains in the Baker River Valley.

"We are still excited about our trip. The Crab Apple Inn was the unanimous choice for our favorite place to stay."
Certificate may be used: May 1-Sept. 15, midweek only (Tuesday and Wednesday or Wednesday and Thursday).

Tamworth   G5

Whispering Pines B&B
Rt 113A & Hemenway Road
Tamworth, NH 03886
(603)323-7337

Circa 1901. Bordered on one edge by Hemenway State Forest, Whispering Pines is set upon 22 acres of woods. The guest rooms are decorated with antiques, and each is individually appointed with themes such as Woodlands and Memories. Items such as baked apple puffs and homemade muffins accompany the morning's breakfast entree. Shops and restaurants are nearby. There is an abundance of seasonal activities in the area, including berry picking, hay rides, summer theater, nature trails, bicycling, a popular farm festival and plenty of antiquing.
Innkeeper(s): Karen & Kim Erickson. $65-80. MC VISA DS PC TC. 4 rooms, 1 with PB. Breakfast and evening snack included in rates. Types of meals: full breakfast and early coffee/tea. Beds: KQD. Library on premises. Antiques, fishing, parks, shopping, downhill skiing, cross-country skiing, theater and watersports nearby.
Certificate may be used: From July 1-Oct. 1, excluding Saturdays.

Thornton (Campton) G4

Amber Lights Inn B&B

Rt 3
Thornton (Campton), NH 03223
(603)726-4077

Circa 1815. A breakfast to remember will delight this inn's guests, who are served a six-course, home-made meal in the Hannah Adams dining room. The Colonial inn offers five antique-filled guest rooms, all with queen beds and handmade quilts. Guests enjoy the inn's copper collection, on display in its country kitchen. They also like to relax in the sunny garden room, or quiet library, where wintertime visitors can watch other guests as they cross-country ski on the inn's grounds. Be sure to inquire about the inn's murder-mystery weekend packages. Fine downhill skiing is found within easy driving distance of the inn.

Innkeeper(s): Paul Sears & Carola Warnsman. $60-75. MC VISA AX DS PC TC. 5 rooms, 1 with PB. 2 suites. Breakfast included in rates. Types of meals: continental breakfast, full breakfast and gourmet breakfast. Beds: QT. Turndown service in room. Library on premises. Antiques, fishing, shopping, skiing, sporting events, theater, watersports nearby.

Location: In the White Mountains.

Publicity: NY NEX Update for Retirees, Union Leader.

"Another wonderful stay at Amber Lights. The food is, without question, the best, the surroundings always lovely and comfortable, however, there are no words for the wonderful hospitality!"

Certificate may be used: Anytime, April 1-July 31, also Nov. 1-Dec. 24, and weekdays only from Dec. 26-March 30.

Tilton I4

Tilton Manor

40 Chestnut St
Tilton, NH 03276-5546
(603)286-3457 Fax:(603)286-3308

Circa 1884. This turn-of-the-century Folk Victorian inn is just two blocks from downtown Tilton. The inn's comfortable guest rooms are furnished with antiques and sport handmade afghans. Guests are treated to a hearty country breakfast featuring freshly baked muffins, and dinner is available with advance reservations. Visitors enjoy relaxing in the sitting room, where they may play games, read or watch TV after a busy day exploring the historic area.

Gunstock and Highland ski resorts are nearby and the Daniel Webster Birthplace and Shaker Village are within easy driving distance. Shoppers will enjoy Tilton's latest addition — an outlet center.

Innkeeper(s): Chip & Diane. $60-70. MC VISA AX DS PC TC. 4 rooms, 2 with PB, 1 with FP. 2 suites. Breakfast included in rates. Type of meal: full breakfast. Beds: KDT. Cable TV, library and child care on premises. Antiques, fishing, shopping, skiing and watersports nearby.

Certificate may be used: All days, except holidays.

Wentworth G3

Wentworth Inn & Art Gallery

Ellsworth Hill Rd, Off Rt 25
Wentworth, NH 03282
(603)764-9923

Circa 1800. This Federal Colonial-style inn is located on Baker Pond Brook in the foothills of the White Mountains. The guest rooms are elegantly decorated. A full country breakfast and afternoon snacks are offered. Gourmet candle-light dining is available in the evening. The New Hampshire Vacations Tourist Information is located on the property and there is an art gallery and gift shop. A double-tiered veranda overlooks Mount Stinson.

Innkeeper(s): James Moffat. $60-80. MC VISA AX. 7 rooms, 4 with PB. 1 suite. 1 conference room. Breakfast included in rates. Types of meals: full breakfast and gourmet breakfast. Dinner, picnic lunch and lunch available. Restaurant on premises. Beds: Q. Cable TV and copier on premises. Antiques, fishing, shopping, downhill skiing, cross-country skiing, sporting events, theater and watersports nearby.

Location: In the foothills of the White Mountains.

Publicity: Eagle-Tribune, Union Leader, Yankee, Manchester Union Leader, WMUR-TV.

Certificate may be used: Anytime Sunday through Saturday, two-night minimum stay.

Wolfeboro H5

Tuc' Me Inn B&B

118 N Main St, PO Box 657, Rt 109N
Wolfeboro, NH 03894-4310
(603)569-5702

Circa 1850. This Federal Colonial-style house features a music room, parlor and screen porches. Afternoon tea with home-baked scones is served in the Victorian garden room. Chocolate chip or strawberry pancakes are often presented for breakfast in the dining room. The inn is a short walk to the quaint village of Wolfeboro and the shores of Lake Winnipesaukee.

Innkeeper(s): Terrille Foutz. $55-85. MC VISA. 7 rooms, 3 with PB. Breakfast included in rates. Types of meals: full breakfast and early coffee/tea. Afternoon tea available. Beds: QT. Air conditioning, ceiling fan and VCR in room. Antiques, fishing, shopping, skiing, theater nearby. Publicity: Granite State News, Wolfeboro Times.

Certificate may be used: April 15-Oct. 20, Monday through Thursday; Oct. 21-April 14, anytime.

New Jersey

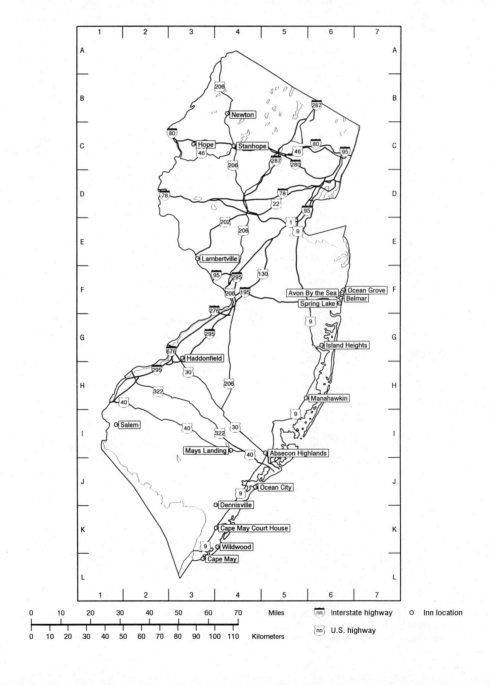

	Miles	Interstate highway	○ Inn location
0 10 20 30 40 50 60 70			
0 10 20 30 40 50 60 70 80 90 100 110	Kilometers	U.S. highway	

Absecon Highlands   I5

White Manor Inn

739 S 2nd Ave
Absecon Highlands, NJ 08201-9542
(609)748-3996 Fax:(609)652-0073

Circa 1932. This quiet country inn was built by the innkeeper's father and includes unique touches throughout, many created by innkeeper Howard Bensel himself, who became a master craftsman from his father's teachings and renovated the home extensively. Beautiful flowers and plants adorn both the lush

grounds and the interior of the home. Everything is comfortable and cozy at this charming B&B, a relaxing contrast to the glitz of nearby Atlantic City.
Innkeeper(s): Anna Mae & Howard R. Bensel Jr. $48-85. PC TC. 7 rooms, 5 with PB. 1 suite. 1 conference room. Breakfast and evening snack included in rates. Types of meals: continental breakfast, continental-plus breakfast and early coffee/tea. Beds: QDT. Air conditioning and ceiling fan in room. VCR on premises. Amusement parks, antiques, fishing, parks, shopping, sporting events, theater, watersports nearby.

"We felt more like relatives than total strangers. By far the most clean inn that I have seen — spotless!"

Certificate may be used: Monday through Thursday, Nov. 1-April 1.

Avon By The Sea   F6

The Avon Manor B&B Inn

109 Sylvania Ave
Avon By The Sea, NJ 07717-1338
(908)774-0110

Circa 1907. The Avon Manor was built as a private summer residence in the Colonial Revival style. The handsome facade is graced by a 100-foot wraparound veranda. Light, airy bedrooms are decorated with antiques, wicker and period pieces. Guests breakfast in a sunny dining room or on the veranda.

Innkeeper(s): Kathleen Curley. $80-110. 8 rooms, 6 with PB. Breakfast and afternoon tea included in rates. Type of meal: full breakfast. Beds: QDT. Air conditioning in room. Cable TV and child care on premises. Amusement parks, antiques, fishing, shopping, sporting events, theater and watersports nearby.

Location: A block from the beach.

Certificate may be used: Sunday to Thursday, June through September. Weekends, October through May. Not valid holidays, special event weekends or with other promotions.

Belmar   F6

The Seaflower B&B

110 9th Ave
Belmar, NJ 07719-2302
(908)681-6006

Circa 1907. This comfortable Dutch Colonial inn is a half-block from the beach and boardwalk. Guest rooms feature the sound of ocean waves and the scent of fresh flowers. Wallpapers set off an eclectic mixture of antiques, new four-poster and canopy beds, and an abundance of paintings. Guests enjoy the ocean views from the porch's teak Adirondack chairs. One of the major deep-sea fishing ports on the Northeast Coast is nearby at the mouth of the Shark River, and your hosts can help set up charters.
Innkeeper(s): Knute Iwaszko. $65-98. AX. 7 rooms, 6 with PB. 1 suite. Breakfast included in rates. Type of meal: full breakfast. Beds: QDT. Ceiling fan in room. Cable TV, VCR and pet boarding on premises. Amusement parks, antiques, fishing, shopping and theater nearby.

Location: One-half block from beach and boardwalk.

Publicity: *New Jersey Monthly.*

Certificate may be used: Anytime except July, August and weekends in June.

The Inn at The Shore

301 4th Ave
Belmar, NJ 07719-2104
(732)681-3762 Fax:(201)945-2944

Circa 1880. This country Victorian actually is near two different shores. Both the ocean and Silver Lake are within easy walking distance of the inn. From the inn's windows, guests can view swans on the lake or people perusing Belmar's boardwalk. The innkeepers decorated their Victorian home in period style. The inn's patio is set up for barbecues.
Innkeeper(s): Rosemary & Tom Volker. $50-115. MC VISA AX. 12 rooms, 3 with PB. 1 conference room. Breakfast included in rates. Type of meal: continental-plus breakfast. Air conditioning and TV in room. VCR and bicycles on premises. Amusement parks, antiques, fishing, parks, shopping, sporting events, theater and watersports nearby.

Certificate may be used: Sunday to Thursday, May 1-Sept. 30, Sunday to Saturday, Oct. 1-April 30, major holidays excluded.

Cape May L3

The Abbey Bed & Breakfast
34 Gurney St at Columbia Ave
Cape May, NJ 08204
(609)884-4506 Fax:(609)884-2379

Circa 1869. This inn consists of two buildings, one a Gothic Revival villa with a 60-foot tower, Gothic arched windows and shaded verandas. Furnishings include floor-to-ceiling mirrors, ornate gas chandeliers, marble-topped dressers and beds of carved walnut, wrought iron and brass. The cottage adjacent to the villa is a Second Empire-style home with a mansard roof. A full breakfast is served in the dining  room in spring and fall and on the veranda in the summer. Late afternoon refreshments and tea are served each day at 5 p.m. The beautiful inn is featured in the town's Grand Christmas Tour, and public tours and tea are offered three times a week in season.
Innkeeper(s): Jay & Marianne Schatz. $100-275. MC VISA DS TC. 14 rooms with PB. 2 suites. 2 conference rooms. Breakfast and afternoon tea included in rates. Types of meals: full breakfast, early coffee/tea. Beds: KQD. Antiques, fishing, parks, theater, watersports nearby.
Location: In the heart of Cape May's historic district.
Publicity: *Richmond Times-Dispatch, New York Times, Glamour, Philadelphia Inquirer, National Geographic Traveler.*
"Staying with you folks really makes the difference between a 'nice' vacation and a great one!"
Certificate may be used: Sunday or Monday through Thursday; April, May and October, except Victorian week.

Abigail Adams B&B By The Sea
12 Jackson St
Cape May, NJ 08204-1418
(609)884-1371

Circa 1888. This charming Victorian is only 100 feet from the beach which affords delightful sea breezes and ocean views. There is a free-standing circular staircase, as well as original fireplaces and woodwork through-  out. The decor is highlighted with flowered chintz and antiques, and the dining room is hand-stenciled.

284

Innkeeper(s): Kate Emerson. $75-185. MC VISA AX. 5 rooms, 3 with PB. Breakfast included in rates. Type of meal: full breakfast. Afternoon tea available. Beds: QD. Air conditioning and ceiling fan in room. Amusement parks, antiques, fishing, theater and watersports nearby.
Location: In the primary historic district, 100 feet from the beach and a half block from the mall.
"What a wonderful time. Comfortable & homey."
Certificate may be used: Oct. 15-May 15, Sunday-Thursday.

Captain Mey's B&B Inn
202 Ocean St
Cape May, NJ 08204-2322
(609)884-7793

Circa 1890. Named after Dutch explorer Capt. Cornelius J. Mey, who named the area, the inn displays its Dutch heritage with table-top Persian rugs, Delft china and imported Dutch lace curtains. The dining room features chestnut and oak Eastlake paneling and a fireplace. The charming exterior is painted in shades of lavender and cream. A hearty breakfast is served by candlelight, or on the wrap-around veranda in the summertime.

Innkeeper(s): George & Kathleen Blinn. $75-210. MC VISA AX PC TC. 7 rooms with PB. 1 suite. Breakfast and afternoon tea included in rates. Type of meal: full breakfast. Beds: QT. Air conditioning, ceiling fan and TV in room. Amusement parks, antiques, fishing, parks, shopping, theater and watersports nearby.
Publicity: *Atlantic City, Americana, Country Living, New Jersey Monthly, WKYW News (CBS) Philadelphia, WNJS (N.J. Network News Trenton.*
"The innkeepers pamper you so much you wish you could stay forever."
Certificate may be used: April to May & mid-October to Dec. 20, Sunday-Thursday, excluding weekends, holidays and special events.

The Carroll Villa B&B
19 Jackson St
Cape May, NJ 08204-1417
(609)884-9619 Fax:(609)884-0264

Circa 1882. This Victorian hotel is located one-half block from the ocean on the oldest street in the historic district of Cape May. Breakfast at the Villa is a memorable event, featuring dishes acclaimed by the New York Times and Frommer's. Homemade fruit breads, Italian omelets and Crab Eggs Benedict are a few specialties. Meals are served in the Mad Batter Restaurant on a European veranda, a secluded garden terrace or in the sky-lit Victorian dining room. The restaurant serves breakfast, lunch and dinner daily. The decor of this inn is decidedly Victorian with period antiques and wallpapers.

Innkeeper(s): Mark Kulkowitz & Pamela Ann Huber. $75-160. MC VISA AX DS PC. 22 rooms with PB. 2 conference rooms. Breakfast included in rates. Type of meal: early coffee/tea. Dinner, lunch, banquet service, catering service and catered breakfast available. Beds: QD. Air conditioning and ceiling fan in room. Cable TV, VCR, fax, copier and computer on premises. Amusement parks, antiques, fishing, parks, shopping and theater nearby.

Location: One-half block from the ocean.

Publicity: *Atlantic City Press, Asbury Press, Frommer's, New York Times, Washington Post.*

"Mr. Kulkowitz is a superb host. He strives to accommodate the diverse needs of guests."

Certificate may be used: Sept. 21-May 25, Sunday-Thursday, no holidays, weekends and Christmas week.

Fairthorne B&B

111 Ocean St
Cape May, NJ 08204-2319
(609)884-8791 (800)438-8742 Fax:(609)884-1902
E-mail: wehfair@aol.com

Circa 1892. Antiques abound in this three-story Colonial Revival. Lace curtains and a light color scheme complete the charming decor. The signature breakfasts include special daily entrees along with an assortment of home-baked breads and muffins. A light afternoon tea also is served with refreshments.

The proximity to the beach will be much appreciated by guests, and the innkeepers offer the use of beach towels, bicycles and sand chairs. The nearby historic district is full of fun shops and restaurants.

Innkeeper(s): Diane & Ed Hutchinson. $90-190. MC VISA AX DS TC. 7 rooms. 1 suite. Breakfast and afternoon tea included in rates. Types of meals: full breakfast and early coffee/tea. Beds: KQ. Air conditioning and ceiling fan in room. Fax on premises. Antiques, fishing, parks, shopping, theater and watersports nearby.

Publicity: *New Jersey Women's Magazine.*

"I feel as if I have come to stay with a dear old friend who has spared no expense to provide me with all that my heart can desire! ... I will savor the memory of your hospitality for years to come. Thanks so much."

Certificate may be used: Nov. 1-May 31, Sunday-Thursday, except holidays.

Gingerbread House

28 Gurney St
Cape May, NJ 08204
(609)884-0211

Circa 1869. The Gingerbread is one of eight original Stockton Row Cottages, summer retreats built for families from Philadelphia and Virginia. It is a half-block from the ocean and breezes waft over the wicker-filled porch. The inn is listed in the National Register. It has been meticulously restored and decorated with period antiques and a fine collection of paintings. The inn's woodwork is especially notable, guests enter through handmade teak double doors.

Innkeeper(s): Fred & Joan Echevarria. $90-200. MC VISA PC TC. 6 rooms, 2 with PB. 1 suite. Breakfast and afternoon tea included in rates. Type of meal: full breakfast. Beds: QD. Air conditioning in room. Antiques, fishing, parks, shopping, theater and watersports nearby.

Location: Historic District, one-half block from the beach.

Publicity: *Philadelphia Inquirer, New Jersey Monthly, Atlantic City Press.*

"The elegance, charm and authenticity of historic Cape May, but more than that, it appeals to us as `home'."

Certificate may be used: Monday through Thursday, Oct. 1-May 31.

John Wesley Inn

30 Gurney St
Cape May, NJ 08204
(609)884-1012

Circa 1869. The innkeepers of this graciously restored Carpenter Gothic home have won awards for their captivating exterior Christmas decorations, and holidays at the inn are a seasonal delight. The interior decor preserves the Victorian era so treasured in this seaside village. Antiques are set in rooms decorated with bright, patterned wallpapers and windows decked in lace. The innkeepers also offer a restored carriage house, featuring the same period decor, but the modern amenity of a stocked kitchen.

Innkeeper(s): John & Rita Tice. $75-165. PC TC. 6 rooms, 4 with PB. 2 cottages. 1 conference room. Breakfast included in rates. Type of meal: continental-plus breakfast. Beds: QD. Air conditioning and ceiling fan in room. Amusement parks, antiques, fishing, parks, shopping, theater and watersports nearby.

Certificate may be used: September to May, Sunday-Friday.

Mainstay Inn

635 Columbia Ave
Cape May, NJ 08204-2305
(609)884-8690

Circa 1872. This was once the elegant and exclusive Jackson's Clubhouse popular with gamblers. Many of the guest rooms and the grand parlor look much as they did in the 1870s. Fourteen-foot-high ceilings, elaborate chandeliers, a sweeping veranda and a cupola add to the atmosphere. Tom and Sue Carroll received the American Historic Inns award in 1988 for their preservation efforts, and have been making unforgettable memories for guests for 25 years. A writer for Conde Nast Traveler once wrote, "architecturally, no inn, anywhere, quite matches the Mainstay."

Innkeeper(s): Tom & Sue Carroll. $95-245. PC TC. 16 rooms with PB, 4 with FP. 7 suites. Breakfast and afternoon tea included in rates. Types of meals: continental breakfast, continental-plus breakfast, full breakfast, gourmet breakfast and early coffee/tea. Catered breakfast available. Beds: KQDT. Air conditioning, ceiling fan, TV and VCR in room. Library on premises. Handicap access. Amusement parks, antiques, fishing, parks, shopping, sporting events, theater, watersports nearby.
Location: Cape May National Landmark District.
Publicity: *Washington Post, Good Housekeeping, New York Times, Conde Nast Traveler, Smithsonian, Americana, Travel & Leisure, National Geographic Traveler.*

"By far the most lavishly and faithfully restored guesthouse...run by two arch-preservationists—Travel & Leisure."

Certificate may be used: Jan. 1-April 27 and Oct. 23-April 25. Sunday-Thursday only.

The Mason Cottage

625 Columbia Ave
Cape May, NJ 08204-2305
(609)884-3358 (800)716-2766

Circa 1871. Since 1946, this elegant seaside inn has been open to guests. The curved-mansard, wood-shingle roof was built by local shipyard carpenters. Much of the original furniture remains in the house, and it has endured both hurricanes and the 1878 Cape May fire. Two of the inn's suites include a fireplace and whirlpool tub.
Innkeeper(s): Dave & Joan Mason. $85-265. MC VISA AX TC. 9 rooms with PB, 2 with FP. 4 suites. 1 conference room. Breakfast and afternoon tea included in rates. Type of meal: full breakfast. Beds: QD. Air

conditioning and ceiling fan in room. Antiques, fishing, parks, shopping, theater and watersports nearby.
Location: In the historic district.

"We relaxed and enjoyed ourselves. You have a beautiful and elegant inn, and serve great breakfasts. We will be back on our next trip to Cape May."

Certificate may be used: April 1-June 15 and Sept. 21-Dec. 15, Monday-Thursday.

The Mission Inn

1117 New Jersey Ave
Cape May, NJ 08204-2638
(609)884-8380 (800)800-8380 Fax:(609)884-4191

Circa 1912. In a town filled with gingerbread trim and turrets, The Mission Inn is unusual. The Spanish Mission-style architecture and California decor are a departure from the town's notable Victorian flavor. Listed in the National Register, it is included among the 46 original historic structures of Cape May. In keeping with the more Western appearance, the innkeepers serve treats such as Santa Fe egg rolls for breakfast, along with fresh fruits and biscotti. The meal often is served on the veranda, where guests enjoy a view of the Jersey Shore. The innkeepers provide beach passes and can arrange trolley or house tours, carriage rides, boat cruises and more.
Innkeeper(s): Judith DeOrio & Diane Fischer. $105-175. MC VISA AX PC TC. 6 rooms with PB. 1 suite. 1 conference room. Breakfast and evening snack included in rates. Types of meals: full breakfast, gourmet breakfast and early coffee/tea. Beds: KQ. Air conditioning and ceiling fan in room. Cable TV, fax and copier on premises. Amusement parks, antiques, fishing, parks, shopping, theater and watersports nearby.
Certificate may be used: Monday through Thursday, May-June/September-October, holidays excluded.

Poor Richard's Inn

17 Jackson St
Cape May, NJ 08204-1417
(609)884-3536

Circa 1882. The unusual design of this Second-Empire house has been accentuated with five colors of paint. Arched gingerbread porches tie together the distinctive bays of the house's facade. The combination of exterior friezes, balustrades and fretwork has earned the inn an individual listing in the National Register.

Some rooms sport an eclectic country Victorian decor with patchwork quilts and pine furniture, while others tend toward a more traditional turn-of-the-century ambiance. An apartment suite is available.

Innkeeper(s): Richard Samuelson. $59-135. EP. MC VISA. 10 rooms with PB. 1 suite. Breakfast included in rates. Types of meals: continental-plus breakfast and early coffee/tea. Beds: QDT. Air conditioning and TV in room. Copier on premises. Amusement parks, antiques, fishing, parks, theater and watersports nearby.

Publicity: *Washington Post, New York Times, National Geographic Traveler, New Jersey.*

"Hold our spot on the porch. We'll be back before you know it."

Certificate may be used: Monday-Thursday, Sept. 20-June 15.

The Queen Victoria
102 Ocean St
Cape May, NJ 08204-2320
(609)884-8702

Circa 1881. Christmas is a special festival at these beautifully restored Victorians. Special tours, Charles Dickens' feasts and costumed carolers crowd the calendar. The rest of the year, well-stocked libraries, and long porches lined with antique rocking chairs provide for more sedate entertainment. "Victorian Homes" featured 23 color photographs of The Queen Victoria. Amenities include afternoon

tea and mixers, a fleet of bicycles, and evening turn-down service. The innkeepers also offer complimentary beach tags and towels for their summer guests. Suites feature a whirlpool tub, fireplace or private porch. Guest rooms are spread among three, adjacent Victorian homes, all beautifully appointed in Victorian country style.

Innkeeper(s): Joan & Dane Wells. $90-270. EP. PC. 23 rooms with PB, 2 with FP. 7 suites. 2 cottages. Breakfast and afternoon tea included in rates. Types of meals: full breakfast and early coffee/tea. Room service available. Beds: QD. Air conditioning, turndown service and ceiling fan in room. Cable TV, VCR, bicycles, library and child care on premises. Handicap access. Amusement parks, antiques, fishing, parks, shopping, theater and watersports nearby.

Location: In the heart of the historic district, one block from the beach.

Publicity: *Discerning Traveler, New York, Cover Girl, Washington Post, Victorian.*

"Especially impressed by the relaxed atmosphere and the excellent housekeeping."

Certificate may be used: Monday through Thursday, November through March, except Christmas week.

Rhythm of The Sea
1123 Beach Dr
Cape May, NJ 08204-2628
(609)884-7788

Circa 1915. The apt name of this oceanfront inn describes the soothing sounds of the sea that lull many a happy guest into a restful night's sleep. Many of the features of a Craftsman home are

incorporated in this seaside inn, which includes large, spacious rooms, adjoining dining and living areas with fireplaces and natural wood floors. Guests are given complimentary beach passes, towels and bicycles. From October through May, guests may enjoy private recitals performed by classical musicians who also stay at the inn. There is free parking available, and guests have use of bicycles.

Innkeeper(s): Richard & Carol Macaluso. $99-210. MC VISA AX DC PC. 7 rooms with PB, 1 with FP. Breakfast and afternoon tea included in rates. Type of meal: full breakfast. Beds: Q. Air conditioning in room. VCR, copier and bicycles on premises. Amusement parks, antiques, fishing, shopping, theater and watersports nearby.

Publicity: *Atlantic City Press, New Jersey Monthly, POV.*

"Your home is lovely, the atmosphere is soothing."

Certificate may be used: September-May, Sunday-Thursday, non-holiday periods.

Sea Holly B&B Inn
815 Stockton Ave
Cape May, NJ 08204-2446
(609)884-6294 Fax:(609)884-5157

Circa 1875. The home-baked cuisine at this three-story Gothic cottage is an absolute delight. Innkeeper Christy Igoe began her love for baking in childhood, and at age 12 she created her own chocolate chip cookie recipe and now has her own cookbook. Her goodies are served at breakfast and in the afternoons with tea and sherry. The home is decorated with authentic Renaissance Revival and

Eastlake antique pieces. Some rooms boast ocean views. The inn is a wonderful place for a special occasion, and honeymooners or those celebrating an anniversary receive complimentary champagne. In addi-

circa 1875

tion to the romantic amenities, the innkeeper provides practical extras such as hair dryers, irons and ironing boards in each room or suite. The suites also include a TV. Winter guests should be sure to ask about the inn's midweek winter specials.

Innkeeper(s): Christy Lacey-Igoe. $80-180. MC VISA AX TC. 8 rooms with PB. 2 suites. Breakfast and afternoon tea included in rates. Types of meals: full breakfast and early coffee/tea. Beds: KQ. Air conditioning and ceiling fan in room. Fax on premises. Amusement parks, antiques, fishing, parks, shopping, theater and watersports nearby.

Publicity: *Mid-Atlantic Newsletter, New Jersey Monthly, Fremans.*

"You have shown us what a real B&B is supposed to be like."

Certificate may be used: February, March, April, May, Sunday-Thursday; June, September, Monday-Thursday; October, November, December, Sunday-Thursday.

White Dove Cottage
619 Hughes St
Cape May, NJ 08204-2317
(609)884-0613 (800)321-3683

Circa 1866. The beautiful octagonal slate on the Mansard roof of this Second Empire house is just one of the inn's many handsome details. Bright sunny rooms are furnished in American and European antiques, period wallpapers, paintings, prints and handmade quilts. Rooms with fireplaces or Jacuzzi tub are available. Breakfast is served to the soft music of an antique music box and boasts heirloom crystal, fine china and lace. Located on a quiet, gas-lit street, the inn is two blocks from the beach, restaurants and shops. Ask about mystery weekends and the inn's Honeymoon and Romantic Escape packages.

Innkeeper(s): Frank & Sue Smith. $80-215. 4 rooms with PB. 2 suites. Breakfast and afternoon tea included in rates. Types of meals: full breakfast, gourmet breakfast and early coffee/tea. Beds: KQD. Antiques, fishing, shopping, theater and watersports nearby.

Location: Center of historic Cape May.

Certificate may be used: After Labor Day through June, Sunday-Thursday. Exclude Victorian week and Christmas week and holidays.

Cape May/Courthouse

Doctors Inn
2 N Main St
Cape May/Courthouse, NJ 08210-2118
(609)463-9330 Fax:(609)463-9650

Circa 1854. Several doctors have lived in this pre-Civil War home, including innkeeper Carolyn Crawford, a neonatologist. Each of the romantic guest rooms is named after a doctor and includes a working fireplace and whirlpool tub. There is an emphasis on health here, and the inn includes a spa with lap Jacuzzi and exercise equipment. The inn features a posh restaurant, Bradbury's, and serves a variety of gourmet fare; the seafood is especially noteworthy.

Innkeeper(s): Carolyn Crawford. $115-170. MC VISA AX DC DS TC. 6 rooms with PB, 6 with FP. 2 suites. 1 conference room. Breakfast and afternoon tea included in rates. Types of meals: full breakfast and early coffee/tea. Lunch, banquet service, catering service and room service available. Restaurant on premises. Beds: KQF. Air conditioning and TV in room. Spa and sauna on premises. Handicap access. Amusement parks, antiques, fishing, parks, shopping, theater, watersports nearby.

Certificate may be used: Jan. 15-April 30, Sunday-Thursday.

Dennisville   J4

Henry Ludlam Inn
1336 Rt 47
Dennisville, NJ 08214-3608
(609)861-5847

Circa 1804. This country inn borders picturesque Ludlam Lake. Canoeing, birding, biking and fishing are popular activities, and the innkeepers make sure you enjoy these at your peak by providing you with a full country breakfast. Some of the bedrooms have fireplaces, and all feature antique double and queen beds.

Innkeeper(s): Chuck & Pat DeArros. $85-125. MC VISA PC TC. 5 rooms with PB, 3 with FP. Breakfast included in rates. Types of meals: full breakfast, gourmet breakfast and early coffee/tea. Beds: QD. Air conditioning and ceiling fan in room. Antiques, fishing, parks, shopping, theater and watersports nearby.

Location: Cape May County.

Publicity: *Atlantic City Press, New Jersey Outdoors, Bright Side.*

"An unforgettable breakfast. Enjoy a piece of history!"

Certificate may be used: Sunday-Thursday, no weekends, no holidays.

Haddonfield   G3

Queen Anne Inn
44 W End Ave
Haddonfield, NJ 08033-2616
(609)428-2195 Fax:(609)354-1013

This National Trust home is located in historic Haddonfield, which has been praised as one of the top villages in the Delaware Valley. Historic homes, museums, antique shops and restaurants are just a short walk away from this Victorian treasure, which features a charming wraparound porch. Common rooms boast elegant decor and chandeliers, and bedchambers are decorated with antiques. The historic attractions of Philadelphia are less than 20 minutes away, and the train station is within walking distance of the inn.
Innkeeper(s): Nancy Lynn. $99-109. MC VISA AX DS. 7 rooms. Breakfast included in rates. Type of meal: continental-plus breakfast.

Certificate may be used: Sunday-Thursday, holidays excluded.

Hope   C3

The Inn at Millrace Pond
PO Box 359, Rt 59 at Millbrook Rd
Hope, NJ 07844-0359
(908)459-4884 (800)786-4673 Fax:(908)459-5276

Circa 1769. The former grist mill buildings house an authentically restored Colonial inn, set in the rolling hills of Northwestern New Jersey. Decorated in the Colonial period, many of the rooms feature original wide-board floors, antiques and Oriental rugs. Rooms in the limestone Grist Mill, a building listed in the National Register of Historic Places, boast hand-crafted American primitive reproductions and braided rugs. The inn's restaurant features the original millrace room, complete with running water. A former wheel chamber has a staircase that leads to the Tavern Room with its own walk-in fireplace and grain chute.
Innkeeper(s): Cordie & Charles Puttkammer. $85-165. MC VISA AX DC TC. 17 rooms with PB, 1 with FP. 1 suite. 1 conference room. Breakfast included in rates. Type of meal: continental-plus breakfast. Evening snack and banquet service available. Restaurant on premises. Beds: Q. Air conditioning and TV in room. Fax, copier and bicycles on premises. Handicap access. Amusement parks, antiques, fishing, parks, shopping and cross-country skiing nearby.

"The most interesting thing of all is the way these buildings have been restored."

Certificate may be used: All year, Sunday through Thursday.

Island Heights   G6

Studio of John F. Peto
102 Cedar Ave, PO Box 306
Island Heights, NJ 08732-0306
(908)270-6058

Circa 1889. This Victorian home is listed in the National Register of Historic Places and is of note because it was built by renowned artist John F. Peto. His granddaughter has opened the home for guests. Filled with artifacts, eclectic furnishings, memorabilia and reproductions of his art, the studio is decorated much as it was originally. There is a large screened porch with rocking chairs providing views down the hill to the river. A full breakfast is usually served.
Innkeeper(s): Joy Peto Smiley. $50-85. AX DS PC TC. 4 rooms. Breakfast included in rates. Type of meal: full breakfast. Beds: DT. Air conditioning and TV in room. Bicycles and library on premises. Amusement parks, antiques, fishing, parks, shopping and watersports nearby.

Location: Island Beach State Park.

Publicity: *House and Gardens Magazine, Observer Entertainer.*

"Breakfast is so great—we won't need any lunch."

Certificate may be used: Anytime except weekends in August.

Lambertville   E3

Chimney Hill B&B
207 Goat Hill Rd
Lambertville, NJ 08530
(609)397-1516 Fax:(609)397-9353

Circa 1820. Chimney Hill is a grand display of stonework, designed with both Federal and Greek Revival-style architecture. The inn's stone sunroom is particularly appealing, with its stone walls, fireplaces and windows looking out to the lush, eight-acre grounds. Five of the guest rooms include a fire-

place, and some have canopy beds. The innkeepers offer adventure, romance and special interest packages for their guests. There's plenty of seasonal activities nearby, from kayaking to skiing.
Innkeeper(s): Terry Ann & Richard Anderson. $75-190. MAP, AP. MC VISA AX PC TC. 8 rooms with PB, 4 with FP. 1 conference room. Breakfast and evening snack included in rates. Types of meals: continental-plus breakfast, full breakfast and early coffee/tea. Catering service available. Beds: KQD. Air conditioning in room. Copier and library on premises. Antiques, fishing, parks, shopping, downhill skiing, cross-country skiing, sporting events, theater and watersports nearby.

"We would be hard pressed to find a more perfect setting to begin our married life together."

Certificate may be used: Sunday through Thursday - all year round.

Manahawkin H5

Goose N. Berry Inn
190 N Main St
Manahawkin, NJ 08050-2932
(609)597-6350 Fax:(609)597-6918

Circa 1868. This Queen Anne Victorian, built by an English merchant, has been painstakingly restored and redecorated. Period antiques decorate the guest rooms, each of which has its own personal flair. The Capstan Room features a nautical Victorian theme with paintings in honor of the area's seafaring tradition. Another room is decorated with antique needlepoint samplers, some a century old. There are plenty of places to relax, including a library stocked with books. Guests enjoy a wide variety of items during the gourmet buffet breakfast, baked French toast, fresh fruit, homemade breads, egg dishes and gourmet coffee are among the options. The innkeepers have snacks available throughout the day. For those celebrating a special occasions, the innkeepers can prepare a tray with champagne, chocolates or perhaps wine and cheese.
Innkeeper(s): Tom & Donna Smith. $75-175. TC. 5 rooms with PB. 1 suite. 1 conference room. Breakfast, afternoon tea and evening snack included in rates. Types of meals: gourmet breakfast and early coffee/tea. Picnic lunch, gourmet lunch and catering service available. Beds: D. Air conditioning and turndown service in room. Bicycles on premises. Amusement parks, antiques, fishing, parks, shopping, theater and watersports nearby.

Certificate may be used: All year (except holidays), Sunday-Thursday.

Mays Landing I4

Abbott House
6056 Main St
Mays Landing, NJ 08330-1852
(609)625-4400

Guests at this Victorian-style mansion can relax on the bluff overlooking the Great Egg Harbor River, read on the second-floor veranda with its intricate

fretwork or take afternoon tea in the belvedere (cupola) with spectacular views of historic Mays Landing. The inn is within walking distance to Lake Lenape and its various summer attractions. Each room is individually decorated with antiques, wicker, handmade quilts and other special touches. The Victorian Parlor is a place for games, reading and conversation. Refreshments can be enjoyed on one of the many porches and verandas.
Innkeeper(s): Cliff Melder. $85-95. AX. 4 rooms. 1 suite. Breakfast included in rates. Type of meal: full breakfast. Air conditioning and turndown service in room. Antiques and shopping nearby.

Certificate may be used: January to June and October to December, anytime. July through September, Sunday to Thursday.

Newton B4

The Wooden Duck B&B
140 Goodale Rd, Andover Township
Newton, NJ 07860-2788
(201)300-0395 Fax:(201)300-0141

Circa 1978. Guests enjoy exploring the 17 acres of wooded grounds and fields that surround this country farmhouse. The innkeepers keep their home filled with things to do. Guests can watch movies, play games or enjoy a good book as they snuggle up next to the huge, double hearth fireplace in the inn's game room. During warm months, guest can use the outdoor pool. Rooms are comfortable and cozy, decorated in country style. The innkeepers display their unique collectibles throughout the home.
Innkeeper(s): Bob & Barbara Hadden. $90-110. MC VISA AX DS PC TC. 5 rooms with PB. Breakfast and evening snack included in rates. Type of meal: full breakfast. Beds: Q. Air conditioning, TV and VCR in room. Fax, copier, swimming and library on premises. Amusement parks, antiques, fishing, parks, shopping, downhill skiing, cross-country skiing, sporting events, theater and watersports nearby.

Certificate may be used: November through March, Sunday through Thursday.

Ocean City J4

Serendipity B&B
712 E 9th St
Ocean City, NJ 08226-3554
(609)399-1554 (800)842-8544 Fax:(609)399-1527

Circa 1912. The beach and boardwalk are less than half a block from this renovated inn. Healthy full breakfasts are served, and the innkeepers offer dinners by reservation with a mix of interesting, vegetarian items. In the summer, breakfasts

are served on a vine-shaded veranda. The guest rooms are decorated in pastels with wicker pieces. Innkeeper(s): Clara & Bill Plowfield. $70-129. MC VISA AX DS PC TC. 6 rooms, 4 with PB. Breakfast and evening snack included in rates. Type of meal: full breakfast. Dinner available. Beds: KQDT. Air conditioning, ceiling fan and TV in room. Library on premises. Amusement parks, antiques, fishing, parks, shopping, theater and watersports nearby.

"Serendipity is such a gift. For me it's a little like being adopted during vacation time by a caring sister and brother. Your home is a home away from home. You make it so."

Certificate may be used: Nov. 1-May 31, Sunday-Thursday.

Ocean Grove
F6

The Cordova
26 Webb Ave
Ocean Grove, NJ 07756-1334
(973)774-3084

Circa 1885. This Victorian community was founded as a Methodist retreat. Ocean-bathing and cars were not allowed until a few years ago, so there are no souvenir shops along the white sandy beach and wooden boardwalk. The inn has hosted Presidents Wilson, Cleveland and Roosevelt who were also speakers at the Great Auditorium with its 7,000

seats. The kitchen, lounge, picnic and barbecue areas make this a popular place for family reunions. Ask about the inn's murder-mystery and tai chi weekends. Two cottage apartments also are available. The inn is closed during the winter and early spring. For information during these times, call (212) 751-9577.
Innkeeper(s): Doris A. Chernik. $46-160. PC. 20 rooms, 5 with PB. 2 cottages. Breakfast included in rates. Type of meal: continental-plus breakfast. Beds: KQDT. VCR, bicycles and library on premises. Antiques and fishing nearby.
Publicity: *New Jersey, Asbury Park Press, St. Martin's Press, "O'New Jersey" by Robert Heide and John Gilman.*

"Warm, helpful and inviting, homey and lived-in atmosphere."

Certificate may be used: Memorial Day-October, Sunday-Thursday.

Pine Tree Inn
10 Main Ave
Ocean Grove, NJ 07756-1324
(732)775-3264

Circa 1870. This small Victorian inn is operated by a long-standing resident of the area and offers ocean views. Guest rooms are decorated in antiques and all the rooms are equipped with sinks. Bicycles and beach towels are available.
Innkeeper(s): Karen Mason. $55-110. MAP. MC VISA PC TC. 12 rooms, 4 with PB. 1 suite. Breakfast and afternoon tea included in rates. Types of meals: continental-plus breakfast and early coffee/tea. Beds: QD. Air conditioning, ceiling fan and TV in room. Bicycles on premises. Amusement parks, antiques, fishing, parks, shopping, theater and watersports nearby.
Publicity: *Country Living, USA Today.*
Certificate may be used: All year, Sunday-Thursday only, except on holiday weekends. Must show certificate.

Salem
I1

Brown's Historic Home B&B
41-43 Market St
Salem, NJ 08079
(609)935-8595 Fax:(609)935-8595

Circa 1738. Brown's Historic Home originally was built as a Colonial house. Around 1845, the house was modernized to the Victorian era. The inn is furnished with antiques and heirlooms, including a handmade chess set and quilt. The fireplaces are made of King of Prussia marble. The backyard garden features a lily pond, wildflowers and a waterfall. There is a ferry nearby offering transport  to Delaware. On Saturdays, guests can enjoy performances at the Cowtown Rodeo, eight miles away.
Innkeeper(s): William & Margaret Brown. $55-100. MC VISA AX DS TC. 3 rooms, 2 with PB, 1 with FP. Breakfast included in rates. Types of meals: full breakfast and early coffee/tea. Beds: DT. Air conditioning, ceiling fan and TV in room. Fax on premises. Antiques, fishing, parks, shopping, theater and watersports nearby.
Location: Fifteen minutes from Delaware Memorial Bridge.
Publicity: *Newsday, Mid-Atlantic Country, Early American Life, Today's Sunbeam.*

"Down-home-on-the-farm breakfasts with great hospitality."

Certificate may be used: Jan. 30-Nov. 21, Monday-Friday.

Spring Lake F6

Ashling Cottage
106 Sussex Ave
Spring Lake, NJ 07762-1248
(732)449-3553 (888)274-5464

Circa 1877. Surrounded by shady sycamores on a quiet residential street, this three-story Victorian residence features a mansard-and-gambrel roof with hooded gambrel dormers. One of the two porches has a square, pyramid-roofed pavilion, which has been glass-enclosed and screened. Guests can  watch the sun rise over the ocean one block away or set over Spring Lake. A full buffet breakfast can be enjoyed in the plant- and wicker-filled pavilion.
Innkeeper(s): Jack Stewart. $75-169. PC TC. 10 rooms, 8 with PB. Breakfast and afternoon tea included in rates. Types of meals: full breakfast and early coffee/tea. Beds: Q. Air conditioning and ceiling fan in room. Cable TV, VCR, bicycles and library on premises. Amusement parks, antiques, fishing, parks, shopping, sporting events, theater and watersports nearby.

Location: Six miles from exit 98.

Publicity: *New York Times, New Jersey Monthly, Town & Country, Country Living, New York, Harrods of London.*

Certificate may be used: May 1-June 15 and Sept. 22-Oct. 31.

Stanhope C4

Whistling Swan Inn
110 Main St
Stanhope, NJ 07874-2632
(201)347-6369 Fax:(201)347-3391
E-mail: wswan@worldnet.att.net

Circa 1905. This Queen Anne Victorian has a limestone wraparound veranda and a tall, steep-roofed turret. Family antiques fill the rooms and highlight the polished ornate woodwork, pocket doors and

winding staircase. It is a little more than a mile from Waterloo Village and the International Trade Zone.
Innkeeper(s): Joe Mulay & Paula Williams. $85-135. MC VISA AX DS PC TC. 10 rooms with PB. 1 suite. 1 conference room. Breakfast included in rates. Type of meal: full breakfast. Beds: Q. Air conditioning and ceiling fan in room. Cable TV, VCR, fax, copier and bicycles on premises. Antiques, fishing, parks, shopping, sporting events, theater and watersports nearby.

Location: East of the Pocono Mountains. Forty-five miles west of New York City in the scenic Skylands tourism region.

Publicity: *Sunday Herald, New York Times, New Jersey Monthly, Mid-Atlantic Country, Star Ledger, Daily Record, Philadelphia, Country, Chicago Sun Times.*

"Thank you for your outstanding hospitality. We had a delightful time while we were with you and will not hesitate to recommend the inn to our listening audience, friends and anyone else who will listen! — Joel H. Klein, Travel Editor, WOAI AM."

Certificate may be used: Sunday through Thursday, November through April.

Wildwood K4

Stuart's Once Upon A Time German B&B
2814 Atlantic Ave
Wildwood, NJ 08260-4902
(609)523-1101 (800)299-ONCE Fax:(609)523-1107

Circa 1905. In the early 20th century Dr. Henry Tomlin transformed his home into a sanitarium where patients with a "nervous condition" could come and relax. He believed his treatment, along with the home's ocean views and sea breezes would invigorate the patients. Today, guests still enjoy the views and sea air, as well as innkeepers Randall and Christa Stuart's hospitality and fine German cuisine. The spacious home includes seven guest rooms, each decorated with European antiques. In European style, most of the rooms share a bath. Breakfasts are served on individual tables and feature such items as fresh fruit, homemade breads, cold meats, cheeses, eggs and coffee imported from Germany. For an additional charge, the innkeepers will prepare a traditional German dinner, complete with soups, appetizers and a main course such as sauerbraten or a sauerkraut platter with bratwurst and mashed potatoes.
Innkeeper(s): Randall & Christa Stuart. $75-135. MC VISA TC. 7 rooms, 1 with PB, 1 with FP. Breakfast and afternoon tea included in rates. Type of meal: gourmet breakfast. Picnic lunch available. Beds: QDT. Air conditioning and ceiling fan in room. Cable TV and fax on premises. Amusement parks, antiques, fishing, parks, shopping, golf, theater and watersports nearby.

Publicity: *Herald News.*

"Superb, as always."

Certificate may be used: June 1-Sept. 30, Sunday-Friday; Oct. 1-May 31, anytime. Not to be combined with any other specials.

New Mexico

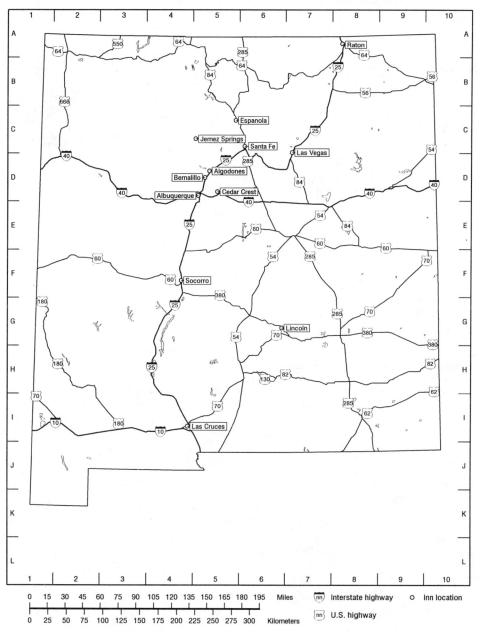

0 15 30 45 60 75 90 105 120 135 150 165 180 195   Miles

0 25 50 75 100 125 150 175 200 225 250 275 300   Kilometers

(nn) Interstate highway   o Inn location

(nn) U.S. highway

Albuquerque D5

Bottger Mansion B&B
110 San Felipe NW, Old Town
Albuquerque, NM 87104
(505)243-3639 Fax:(505)243-3639

Circa 1912. Just steps from the plaza in historic Old Town, this four-square Victorian mansion is a slight departure from the surrounding adobe archi-

tecture. The seven guest rooms feature brass, oak, cherry and mahogany four-poster beds. Evening wine and hors d'oeuvres are served. A soda fountain and coffee and tea bar are available at all times.

Innkeeper(s): Patsy Garcia. $89-139. MC VISA AX PC TC. 7 rooms with PB. 1 suite. Breakfast, afternoon tea and evening snack included in rates. Types of meals: continental breakfast, continental-plus breakfast, full breakfast, gourmet breakfast and early coffee/tea. Catered breakfast available. Beds: KQT. Air conditioning and ceiling fan in room. Cable TV, fax and copier on premises. Amusement parks, antiques, fishing, parks, shopping, downhill skiing, cross-country skiing, sporting events, theater and watersports nearby.

Location: In historic Old Town.
"Yours ranks with the best for ambiance and location."

Certificate may be used: January, February, June, November, December, Sunday through Friday, excludes Saturday nights.

Casa del Granjero
414 C De Baca Ln NW
Albuquerque, NM 87114-1600
(505)897-4144 (800)701-4144 Fax:(505)897-9788

Circa 1890. Innkeepers Victoria and Butch Farmer, who appropriately named their home Casa del Granjero, or "the farmer's house," have designed their bed & breakfast to reflect Southwestern style with a hint of old Spanish flair. The adobe's guest rooms all include a rustic, kiva fireplace. Cuarto Allegre is the largest suite, and includes a canopy bed covered in lace and French doors, which open onto a small porch. Cuarto del Rey affords a mountain view and includes Mexican furnishings and handmade quilts. Cuarto de Flores also has quilts, Mexican tile and French doors leading to a private porch. The innkeepers have a hot tub room for guest use in a special garden area. A variety of baked goods, New Mexican-style recipes and fresh fruit are served each morning in the dining room or on the portal. Several recipes have been featured in a cookbook.

Innkeeper(s): Victoria Farmer. $79-149. MC VISA. 8 rooms, 7 with PB. 4 suites. Breakfast included in rates. Type of meal: full breakfast. Picnic lunch, catering service and room service available. Beds: KQT. Antiques, fishing, skiing, theater and watersports nearby.

Publicity: *Hidden SW.*

"Wonderful place, wonderful people. Thanks so much."

Certificate may be used: January through August, Sunday through Thursday.

W.E. Mauger Estate
701 Roma Ave NW
Albuquerque, NM 87102-2038
(505)242-8755 Fax:(505)842-8835

Circa 1897. This former boarding house is now an elegantly restored Victorian in the National Register. Rooms are done in Victorian style with views of downtown Albuquerque and the Sandia

Mountains beyond. The second floor is decorated with antiques and lace. The inn is located six blocks from the convention center, which includes Civic Plaza, an aquarium, botanical garden, museum and free trolley service.

Innkeeper(s): Mark Brown & Keith Lewis. $89-149. MC VISA AX. 8 rooms with PB. 1 conference room. Breakfast included in rates. Types of meals: full breakfast and early coffee/tea. Evening snack available. Beds: KQDT. Air conditioning and ceiling fan in room. VCR on premises. Amusement parks, antiques, shopping and theater nearby.

Location: Central Albuquerque between downtown and old town.

Publicity: *Albuquerque Journal, Phoenix Home and Garden, Albuquerque Monthly, National Geographic Traveler, New Mexico Business Week, Golf Digest, Great Estates.*

"Because of your hospitality, kindness and warmth, we will always compare the quality of our experience by the W.E. Mauger Estate."

Certificate may be used: Reservations taken 10 days prior to stay, Nov. 15-March 1, except Thanksgiving, Christmas, New Year periods, Saturday night only upon availability.

The W.J. Marsh House Victorian B&B
301 Edith Blvd SE
Albuquerque, NM 87102-3532
(505)247-1001 (888)956-2774

Circa 1892. This three-story brick Queen Anne mansion is located in the Huning Highland Historic District. Original redwood doors and trim, porcelain fixtures and an ornate hand-carved fireplace are highlighted by high Victorian decor. A friendly ghost is said to inhabit the house, occasionally opening drawers and rearranging the furniture. The inn is listed in the National and State Historic Registers.

Innkeeper(s): Janice Lee Sperling, MD. $90-120. MC VISA TC. 6 rooms, 1 with FP. Breakfast included in rates. Type of meal: gourmet breakfast. Picnic lunch available. Beds: QDT. Air conditioning in room. Library on premises. Amusement parks, antiques, fishing, parks, shopping, downhill skiing, cross-country skiing, sporting events, theater and watersports nearby.

Location: In one of Albuquerque's four historic districts, Huning Highland.

Publicity: *Albuquerque Monthly.*

"We even have a ghost!"

Certificate may be used: Monday-Thursday except during Balloon Fiesta (first week in October) and major holidays. Certificate valid for Peach or Rose rooms only.

Bernalillo   D5

La Hacienda Grande
21 Baros Ln
Bernalillo, NM 87004
(505)867-1887 (800)353-1887 Fax:(505)867-4621
E-mail: lhg@swcp.com

Circa 1711. The rooms in this historic adobe inn surround a central courtyard. The first European trekked across the grounds as early as 1540. The land was part of a 1711 land grant from Spain, and owned by descendants of the original family until the innkeepers purchased it. The decor is Southwestern, and each bedchamber is filled with beautiful, rustic furnishings. One includes an iron high-poster bed and Jacuzzi tub, and others offer a kiva fireplace. Breakfasts are served in a dining room decorated with wood beams and a brick floor.
Innkeeper(s): Shoshana Zimmerman. $99-129. MC VISA AX DS TC. 6 rooms with PB, 5 with FP. 1 conference room. Breakfast included in rates. Types of meals: full breakfast and early coffee/tea. Beds: KQDT. Air conditioning in room. Cable TV, VCR, fax, copier and library on premises. Antiques, fishing, parks, shopping, downhill skiing, cross-country skiing, sporting events, theater and watersports nearby.

Certificate may be used: January-February, all seven days; remainder of year: Sunday-Thursday, based on availability.

Cedar Crest   D5

Elaine's, A B&B
PO Box 444, 72 Snowline Rd
Cedar Crest, NM 87008-0444
(505)281-2467 (800)821-3092

Circa 1979. This three-story log home is on four acres of evergreens in the forests of the Sandia Peaks. Rooms are furnished with European country antiques, and there are two fireplaces. Three varieties of hummingbirds visit the property. Guests enjoy views of the mountains from the inn's two balconies. Smoothies and raisin-cinnamon French toast are breakfast items.
Innkeeper(s): Elaine O'Neil. $85-99. MC VISA AX DS PC TC. 3 suites. Breakfast included in rates. Types of meals: full breakfast and gourmet breakfast. Beds: KQ. Amusement parks, antiques, parks, shopping, skiing, sporting events, golf and theater nearby.

Location: On four acres adjoining the Cibola National Forest in the Sandia Mountains.

Publicity: *Fodor's, New Mexico Magazine.*

"Fabulous! Mystical in the spring snow!"

Certificate may be used: Jan. 15-April 15, excluding holidays.

Espanola   C5

Casa del Rio
PO Box 92
Espanola, NM 87532-0092
(505)753-2035

This authentic, adobe guest house is filled with local handmade crafts, rugs, bed coverings and furniture. Bathrooms boast handmade Mexican tile, and rooms are decorated in traditional New Mexico style. The guest house also boasts a kiva fireplace.

The patio window affords a view of cliffs above the Rio Chama, which is just a short walk from the home. The innkeepers also breed Arabian horses and sheep on this working ranch. Casa del Rio is nearby many attractions, including Indian pueblos, Ghost Ranch Living Museum, galleries and an abundance of outdoor activities. The adobe is halfway between both Taos and Santa Fe.
Innkeeper(s): Eileen Sopanen-Vigil. $85-105. MC VISA. 2 rooms. Breakfast included in rates. Type of meal: full breakfast.

Certificate may be used: Sunday through Thursday, December through March.

Jemez Springs   C5

Jemez River B&B Inn
16445 Highway 4
Jemez Springs, NM 87025-9424
(505)829-3262 (800)809-3262

A little more than an hour outside of Albuquerque lies this rustic, adobe inn. For several years now, the home has been a welcoming haven for guests seeking a natural setting, and it also serves as a hummingbird sanctuary. The guest rooms surround the inn's courtyard, a striking outdoor garden with a flowing bird bath. The bath connects to a stream, which leads to the nearby Jemez River. Rooms are decorated in Southwestern style with artifacts honoring various Native American tribes. Beautiful pottery, baskets and many unique pieces decorate the guest rooms, which feature Mexican tile floors and wooden-beam ceilings. Each of the rooms is named for a different Native American nation. The inn, which affords views of the Jemez Mountains Virgin Mesa, also includes a gazebo, hot tub and exercise room.

Innkeeper(s): Larry Clutter. $70-159. MC VISA AX DC CB DS. 6 rooms. Breakfast included in rates. Type of meal: full breakfast.

Certificate may be used: Nov. 1-April 15, Sunday-Thursday

Las Cruces
I4

T.R.H. Smith Mansion B&B
909 N Alameda Blvd
Las Cruces, NM 88005-2124
(505)525-2525 (800)526-1914 Fax:(505)524-8227
E-mail: smithmansion@zianet.com

Circa 1914. This mansion is a colossal site, and it encompasses nearly 6,000 square feet, making it the largest residence in town. The home was built for a local banker, whose career ended in disgrace. Rumors are afloat that the home has buried treasure somewhere within its walls and possibly was used as a bordello. Although the latter is just speculation, what is true is that there are four well-appointed guest rooms, each vastly different in style. One room features Southwestern decor with patterned walls, a Mission-style bed and a drum that serves as a table, another room is done in a Polynesian style with a rattan bed decorated with mosquito netting.

Innkeeper(s): Marlene & Jay Tebo. $65-95. MC VISA AX DS PC TC. 4 rooms, 2 with PB, 1 with FP. Breakfast included in rates. Type of meal: gourmet breakfast. Beds: KQ. Air conditioning, turndown service and ceiling fan in room. Cable TV, VCR, fax and library on premises. Antiques, parks, shopping, sporting events, golf and theater nearby.

Publicity: *Las Cruces, N.M., News*

Certificate may be used: Jan. 1-Dec. 31, Sunday through Friday.

Las Vegas
C7

Plaza Hotel
230 Old Town Plaza
Las Vegas, NM 87701
(505)425-3591 (800)328-1882 Fax:(505)425-9659
Circa 1882. This brick Italianate Victorian hotel, once frequented by the likes of Doc Holliday, Big Nose Katy and members of the James Gang, was renovated in 1982. A stencil pattern found in the dining room inspired the selection of Victorian wallpaper borders in the guest rooms, decorated with a combination of contemporary and period furnishings. Guests are still drawn to the warm, dry air and the hot springs north of town.

Innkeeper(s): Wid & Kak Slick. $55-130. MC VISA AX DC DS TC. 37 rooms with PB. 4 suites. 1 conference room. Types of meals: continental breakfast, continental-plus breakfast, full breakfast and gourmet breakfast. Dinner, picnic lunch, lunch, gourmet lunch, banquet service,

catering service, catered breakfast and room service available. Restaurant on premises. Beds: KQDT. Air conditioning and TV in room. VCR and copier on premises. Handicap access. Antiques, fishing, parks, shopping, cross-country skiing and watersports nearby.

Certificate may be used: Sunday-Thursday, Sept. 1-May 1.

Lincoln
G6

Casa de Patron B&B Inn
PO Box 27, Hwy 380 E
Lincoln, NM 88338-0027
(505)653-4676 (800)524-5202 Fax:(505)653-4671
Circa 1860. This historic adobe once was used to imprison Billy the Kid and played an integral part in the colorful frontier days of Lincoln County. A shaded courtyard and walled garden add to the authentic Old West atmosphere, and the comfort-

able rooms are supplemented by two contemporary adobe casitas. Cleis plays the inn's pipe organ and arranges soapmaking workshops for guests. Salon evenings feature classical music and Old World cookery. Dinner is available by advance reservation.

Innkeeper(s): Jeremy & Cleis Jordan. $79-107. MC VISA PC. 7 rooms with PB, 2 with FP. 2 cottages. 1 conference room. Breakfast included in rates. Types of meals: continental-plus breakfast and full breakfast. Dinner and catering service available. Beds: KQDT. Ceiling fan in room. VCR, fax and copier on premises. Handicap access. Antiques, fishing, parks, shopping and downhill skiing nearby.

Location: In the foothills of the Sacramento and Capitan mountain ranges, southeastern New Mexico. Located 185 miles southeast of Albuquerque and 160 miles northeast of El Paso, TX.

Publicity: *Albuquerque Journal, Preservation News, Sunset, Travelin', Rocky Mountain News, Milwaukee Journal.*

Certificate may be used: All year (Sunday through Thursday) with blackout dates: Memorial Day weekend, July 4th weekend, Thanksgiving week and Christmas-New Year's week, first weekend in August.

Raton
A8

Red Violet Inn
344 N 2nd St
Raton, NM 87740-3807
(505)445-9778 (800)624-9778
Circa 1902. Innkeepers Ruth and John Hanrahan have decorated their turn-of-the-century Victorian with a sense of whimsy. The home was built along

the historic Santa Fe Trail for a minister and his wife. Rooms bear names such as The Yellow Hat or Handsome Jack. The furnishings are comfortable antiques surrounded by an eclectic mix of knick-knacks, including plate, pitcher and bowl collections. Breakfasts at the Red Violet are a treat, and the Hanrahans will provide a hearty lunch for an extra charge. Several of their tried-and-true recipes have been featured in a cookbook.

Innkeeper(s): Ruth & John Hanrahan. $50-75. MC VISA AX. 5 rooms, 3 with PB. Breakfast included in rates. Types of meals: full breakfast and gourmet breakfast. Afternoon tea and picnic lunch available. Beds: KQT. Ceiling fan in room. Cable TV, VCR, bicycles and pet boarding on premises. Antiques, fishing, parks, shopping, cross-country skiing and theater nearby.

Certificate may be used: October-January, all week, except holidays; March-May, all week.

Santa Fe   C6

Alexander's Inn
529 E Palace Ave
Santa Fe, NM 87501-2200
(505)986-1431 (888)321-5123 Fax:(505)982-8572
E-mail: alexandinn@aol.com

Circa 1903. Twin gables and a massive front porch are prominent features of this Craftsman-style brick and wood inn. French and American country decor, stained-glass windows and a selection of antiques create a light Victorian touch. The inn also features

beautiful gardens of roses and lilacs. Breakfast is often served in the backyard garden. Home-baked treats are offered to guests in the afternoon, and the innkeepers keep a few bicycles on hand for those who wish to explore the neighborhood.

Innkeeper(s): Carolyn Lee. $75-150. EP. MC VISA PC TC. 9 rooms, 7 with PB, 5 with FP. 1 suite. 3 cottages. Breakfast and afternoon tea included in rates. Types of meals: continental-plus breakfast, gourmet breakfast and early coffee/tea. Beds: KQT. TV and VCR in room. Fax, spa, bicycles, library and child care on premises. Antiques, fishing, parks, shopping, downhill skiing, cross-country skiing, theater and watersports nearby.

Publicity: *New Mexican, Glamour, Southwest Art, San Diego Union.*

"Thanks to the kindness and thoughtfulness of the staff, our three days in Santa Fe were magical."

Certificate may be used: November through February, Sunday through Thursday, no holidays.

Casa De La Cuma B&B
105 Paseo De La Cuma
Santa Fe, NM 87501-1213
(505)983-1717 (888)366-1717 Fax:(505)988-2883
E-mail: casacuma@swcp.com

Circa 1940. These two locations offer different types of travel experiences. The Chapelle Street Casitas has private suites with fully equipped and furnished kitchens, living rooms and bedrooms with hand-crafted Southwestern-style furniture. The Casitas is located in the heart of the historic district and is four blocks from the Plaza, which is the center of activity in Santa Fe. Casa De La Cuma B&B has three unique rooms decorated with Navajo textiles, original artwork and Southwestern-period furniture. The inn offers views of the Sangre De Cristo Mountains and is also within walking distance of the Plaza.

Innkeeper(s): Arthur & Donna Bailey. $65-145. MC VISA PC TC. 8 rooms, 6 with PB. 5 suites. Breakfast and evening snack included in rates. Type of meal: continental-plus breakfast. Afternoon tea available. Beds: KQT. Air conditioning, ceiling fan and TV in room. Fax on premises. Antiques, parks and downhill skiing nearby.

Publicity: *Denver Post.*

"Their pleasant nature, helpful hints for visitors and genuine hospitality were memorable and valuable to us."

Certificate may be used: Jan. 5-Feb. 28 & Nov. 1-Dec. 15 (Sunday-Thursday only).

Don Gaspar Compound
623 Don Gaspar Ave
Santa Fe, NM 87501-4427
(505)986-8664 (888)986-8664 Fax:(505)986-0696
E-mail: dongaspar@sfol.com

Circa 1912. This lush, peaceful hideaway is located within one of Santa Fe's first historic districts. Within the Compounds surrounding brick walls are brick pathways meandering through beautiful gardens, emerald lawns, trees and fountains. The elegant Southwestern decor is an idyllic match for the warmth and romance of the grounds. For those seeking privacy, the innkeepers offer the Main House, a historic Mission-style home perfect for a pair of romantics or a group as large as six. The house has two bedrooms, two bathrooms, a fully equipped kitchen and two woodburning fireplaces. In addition to the main house, there are three suites in a Territorial-style home with thick walls and polished wood floors. There also are two private casitas, each with a gas-burning fireplace. The Fountain Casita includes a fully equipped kitchen, while the Courtyard Casita offers a double whirlpool tub. All accommodations include a TV, telephone, microwave and refrigerators.

Innkeeper(s): Kim Van Deman. $85-220. MC VISA AX PC TC. 6 rooms with PB, 3 with FP. 5 suites. 1 cottage. Breakfast included in rates. Type of meal: continental-plus breakfast. Beds: KQ. Air conditioning, turn-down service and ceiling fan in room. Fax and copier on premises. Antiques, fishing, parks, shopping, downhill skiing, cross-country skiing, sporting events, theater and watersports nearby.

Location: Near the plaza in Santa Fe.

"Everything was simply perfect."

Certificate may be used: Dec. 1-May 31, Sunday-Thursday. Holidays, special events not included.

El Paradero

220 W Manhattan Ave
Santa Fe, NM 87501-2622
(505)988-1177
E-mail: elpara@trail.com

Circa 1820. This was originally a two-bedroom Spanish farmhouse that doubled in size to a Territorial style in 1860, was remodeled as a Victorian in 1912, and became a Pueblo Revival in 1920. All styles are present and provide a walk through many years of history. Innkeeper(s): Ouida MacGregor & Thomas Allen. $60-135. MC VISA. 14 rooms, 10 with PB, 5 with FP. 2 suites. 1 conference room. Breakfast and afternoon tea included in rates. Types of meals: gourmet breakfast and early coffee/tea. Beds: QT. Air conditioning in room. Cable TV on premises. Fishing, shopping, cross-country skiing and theater nearby.

Location: Downtown.

Publicity: *Innsider, Country Inns, Outside, Sunset, New York Times, Los Angeles Times, Travel & Leisure, America West, Travel & Holiday.*

"I'd like to LIVE here."

Certificate may be used: Sunday-Thursday, Nov. 28-Dec. 18; Jan. 6-Feb. 28.

Heart Seed B&B
Retreat Center and Spa

PO Box 6019
Santa Fe, NM 87502-6019
(505)471-7026

Circa 1991. Pinons and junipers cover the 100-acre grounds that surround this rustic retreat, which affords glorious mountain views. Pamper yourself at the center's spa with massages, herbal wraps and other decadent treats. The Desert Hearts Room is decorated in a '50s cowboy-cowgirl motif and includes two, queen-size beds. The Mountain-Sky Room boasts a wonderful view and a private deck.

Studio-apartment rooms are available for guests planning a long stay in Santa Fe. The studios offer fully equipped kitchenettes and can sleep up to four guests. All rooms have mountain views. The hosts have designed special discount packages for those who wish to enjoy the spa along with their stay. Innkeeper(s): Judith Polich. $79-89. VISA AX DS. 4 rooms with PB. 3 suites. 2 cottages. 1 conference room. Breakfast and evening snack included in rates. Types of meals: full breakfast, gourmet breakfast and early coffee/tea. Beds: Q. VCR, fax, copier, spa and library on premises. Antiques, fishing, shopping, downhill skiing, cross-country skiing, sporting events and theater nearby.

Certificate may be used: Monday-Thursday.

Preston House

106 E Faithway St
Santa Fe, NM 87501-2213
(505)982-3465 Fax:(505)982-3465

Circa 1886. This gracious 19th-century home is the only authentic example of Queen Anne architecture in Santa Fe. Owner Signe Bergman is also a well-known artist and designer. Her skills have created a wonderful Victorian atmosphere with period furnishings, bright wallpapers and beds covered with down quilts. Afternoon tea is a must, as Signe serves up a mouth-watering  array of cakes, pies, cookies and tarts. Signe offers seven additional rooms in a rustic, adobe home. Preston House, which is located in downtown Santa Fe, is within walking distance of the Plaza. Innkeeper(s): Ann Leighton. $48-160. MC VISA PC TC. 15 rooms, 13 with PB, 5 with FP. 1 suite. 2 cottages. 1 conference room. Breakfast and afternoon tea included in rates. Types of meals: continental-plus breakfast and early coffee/tea. Beds: KQDT. Air conditioning and ceiling fan in room. Fax and copier on premises. Handicap access. Fishing, parks, shopping, downhill skiing and theater nearby.

"We were extremely pleased — glad we found you. We shall return."

Certificate may be used: Sunday-Thursday, Nov. 1-May 1, no holidays.

Santa Fe (Algodones)

Hacienda Vargas

PO Box 307
Santa Fe (Algodones), NM 87001-0307
(505)867-9115 (800)261-0006 Fax:(505)867-1902
E-mail: hacvar@aol.com

Circa 1800. Nestled among the cottonwoods and mesas of the middle Rio Grande Valley, Hacienda Vargas has seen two centuries of Old West history.

It once served as a trading post for Native Americans as well as a 19th-century stagecoach stop between Santa Fe and Albuquerque. The grounds contain an adobe chapel, courtyard and gardens. The main house features five kiva fireplaces, Southwest antiques, Spanish tile, a library, art gallery and suites with private Jacuzzis.

Innkeeper(s): Paul & Jule De Vargas. $79-149. MC VISA PC TC. 7 rooms with PB, 7 with FP. 4 suites. Breakfast included in rates. Type of meal: full breakfast. Beds: QT. Air conditioning and ceiling fan in room. Fax and library on premises. Antiques, fishing, shopping, downhill skiing, sporting events, theater and watersports nearby.

Location: Twenty-two miles north of Albuquerque, 22 miles south of Santa Fe.

Publicity: *Vogue, San Francisco Chronicle, Albuquerque Journal.*

"This is the best! Breakfast was the best we've ever had!"

Certificate may be used: Monday through Wednesday except Balloon Fiesta (Oct. 1-15).

Socorro   F4

The Historic Eaton House
403 Eaton Ave
Socorro, NM 87801-4414
(505)835-1067 Fax:(505)835-3527

Circa 1881. Birdwatchers, prepare your binoculars. Within six miles of the Eaton House, bird-lovers might discover 345 species throughout the year. For those who prefer other activities, this home, which was built from native materials, offers guests plenty of other reasons to stay. Rooms are filled with antiques, artwork and furnishings built by local artisans. The Colonel Eaton Room features Victorian decor, flowered tile, lace, needlework and wood furnishings. The quaint Daughter's Room features push button switches, a clawfoot tub and twin beds designed for twin daughters 80 years ago. The innkeepers also offer two casitas during the year. Each of these rooms boasts fireplaces, high ceilings and unique decor. The innkeepers serve up gourmet breakfasts, which may include entrees such as blue-corn pancakes with walnuts or French toast marinated overnight in Grand Marinier. A special basket of goodies can be arranged for those wishing to bird-watch before breakfast is served.

Innkeeper(s): Anna Appleby. $85-135. MC VISA AX. 5 rooms with PB, 2 with FP. Breakfast included in rates. Types of meals: gourmet breakfast and early coffee/tea. Picnic lunch available. Beds: KQDT. Air conditioning and ceiling fan in room. Fax on premises. Handicap access. Antiques, fishing, parks, shopping and theater nearby.

Publicity: *American Way in Flight, Sunset, Atlanta Constitution, NY Times, Boston Globe, Portland Oregonian, Albuquerque*

Certificate may be used: June 1-Sept. 30, Sunday through Thursday.

New York

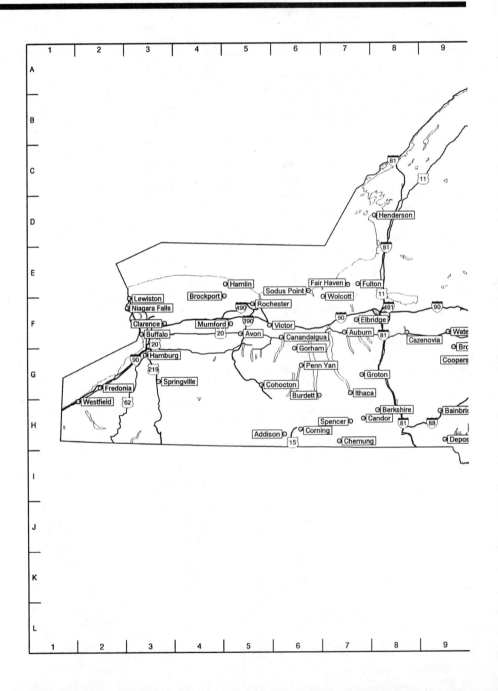

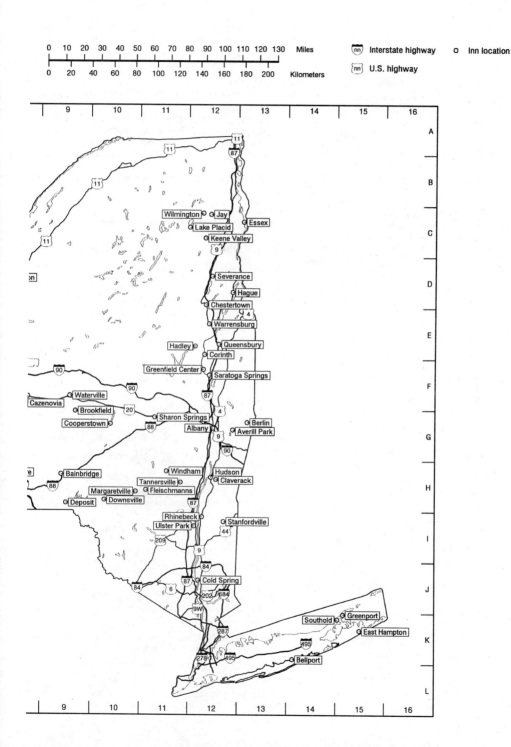

Miles

0 10 20 30 40 50 60 70 80 90 100 110 120 130

Kilometers

0 20 40 60 80 100 120 140 160 180 200

(nn) Interstate highway   o Inn location

{nn} U.S. highway

9   10   11   12   13   14   15   16

A

11

11   87

B

11

Wilmington o o Jay

11   Lake Placid o   o Essex

C

Keene Valley o

9

Severance

D

Hague

Chestertown

4

Warrensburg

E

Hadley o   o Queensbury

Corinth o

Greenfield Center o   o

Saratoga Springs

F

90

90   87

Waterville o

Cazenovia   20   4

Brookfield o   Sharon Springs o   Berlin

Cooperstown o   Albany o   Averill Park

88   9

90

G

Bainbridge o   o Windham   Hudson o

Tannersville o   o Claverack

88   Margaretville o   Fleischmanns o

Deposit o   o Downsville   87

H

Rhinebeck o

Ulster Park o   o Stanfordville

209   44

I

9

84

87 o   o Cold Spring

6   202   684

J

9W

287

Southold o   o Greenport

East Hampton

495

278   495

Bellport

K

L

9   10   11   12   13   14   15   16

291

Addison H6

Addison Rose B&B

37 Maple St
Addison, NY 14801-1009
(607)359-4650

Circa 1892. Located on a scenic highway south of the Finger Lakes, this Queen Anne Victorian "painted lady" inn is an easy getaway from Corning or Elmira. The inn, which is listed in the National Register, was built by a doctor for his bride and was presented to her on Christmas Eve, their wedding day. The three guest rooms offer authentic Victorian furnishings. Many fine examples of Victorian architecture exist in Addison. Pinnacle State Park is just east of town.

Innkeeper(s): William & Maryann Peters. $65-85. PC TC. 3 rooms with PB. Breakfast and afternoon tea included in rates. Types of meals: gourmet breakfast and early coffee/tea. Beds: DT. Ceiling fan in room. Library on premises. Antiques, fishing, parks, shopping and cross-country skiing nearby.

Certificate may be used: November-June, any day, subject to availability.

Albany G12

Mansion Hill Inn

115 Philip St
Albany, NY 12202-1731
(518)465-2038 Fax:(518)434-2313

Circa 1861. This Victorian houses guest rooms and apartment suites on the top two floors and a restaurant on the street level. Originally the home of brush maker Daniel Brown, it later served as a bulk grocery store. It is located in the historic district just around the corner from the Governor's Executive Mansion in the Mansion Neighborhood. It is a few minutes' walk to the State Capitol and the downtown Albany business district.

Innkeeper(s): Maryellen, Elizabeth & Stephen Stofelano Jr. $95-155. MC VISA AX DC CB DS PC TC. 8 rooms with PB. 1 conference room. Breakfast included in rates. Types of meals: continental-plus breakfast, full breakfast and gourmet breakfast. Dinner, gourmet lunch and room service available. Restaurant on premises. Beds: Q. Air conditioning and TV in room. VCR, fax, copier, pet boarding and child care on premises. Antiques, fishing, parks, shopping, sporting events and theater nearby.

"Rooms were beautiful and comfortable down to the shower curtain."

Certificate may be used: Available year-round on Fridays, Saturdays and Sundays; subject to availability and reservation.

Pine Haven B&B

531 Western Ave
Albany, NY 12203-1721
(518)482-1574

Circa 1896. This turn-of-the-century Victorian is located in Pine Hills, an Albany historic district. In keeping with this history, the innkeepers have tried to preserve the home's 19th-century charm. The rooms offer old-fashioned comfort with Victorian influences. The Capitol Building and other historic sites are nearby.

Innkeeper(s): Janice Tricarico. $64-79. PC TC. 5 rooms, 2 with PB. Breakfast included in rates. Types of meals: continental-plus breakfast and early coffee/tea. Beds: DT. Air conditioning in room. Antiques, parks, shopping, cross-country skiing, sporting events and theater nearby.

Certificate may be used: Anytime, depending only on availability.

Auburn F7

The Irish Rose - A Victorian B&B

102 South St
Auburn, NY 13021-4836
(315)255-0196 (800)255-0196 Fax:(315)255-0988

Circa 1872. A Victorian setting and Irish hospitality are blended at this National Register Queen Anne Victorian. The inn features cherry hardwood floors, cherry fireplace mantels and cherry doors. An uncluttered Victorian style includes some antiques. The innkeeper, once a head chef, provides a full gourmet buffet breakfast. On the grounds are a swimming pool and rose garden.

Innkeeper(s): Patricia Fitzpatrick. $65-105. MC VISA AX DS PC TC. 5 rooms, 3 with PB, 1 with FP. 1 suite. 1 conference room. Breakfast included in rates. Type of meal: gourmet breakfast. Picnic lunch, catering service and room service available. Beds: KQT. Air conditioning and ceiling fan in room. Cable TV, VCR, fax and copier on premises. Antiques, fishing, shopping, downhill skiing, cross-country skiing, sporting events, theater and watersports nearby.

Location: Fingerlakes Region.

Publicity: *Auburn Citizen, Syracuse News Times, Fingerlakes Magazine, Central New York Magazine, Echo Newspaper.*

"My first B&B experience, won't be my last. Romantic."

Certificate may be used: January-May, Sunday-Saturday. September-December, based on availability, seven days.

Averill Park G12

Ananas Hus B&B
148 South Rd
Averill Park, NY 12018-3414
(518)766-5035

Circa 1963. This ranch home in the mountains east of Albany offers stunning views of the Hudson River Valley. Visitors enjoy gourmet breakfasts and relaxing afternoon teas. There are 29 acres available to guests who wish to hike or play lawn games. The surrounding area offers antiquing, downhill skiing and shopping, and the inn's location provides convenient access to the recreation and sightseeing opportunities of three states. Cherry Plain State Park is nearby.

Innkeeper(s): Clyde & Thelma Olsen Tomlinson. $60. AX PC. 3 rooms. Breakfast included in rates. Types of meals: full breakfast, gourmet breakfast and early coffee/tea. Afternoon tea available. Beds: DT. VCR on premises. Antiques, fishing, downhill skiing, cross-country skiing, theater and watersports nearby.

Location: One mile off Rt. 43.
Publicity: *Discovery Press.*
Certificate may be used: Nov. 1-May 1, Monday through Thursday (excluding holidays).

The Gregory House Country Inn & Restaurant
Rt 43 PO Box 401
Averill Park, NY 12018-0401
(518)674-3774 Fax:(518)674-8916
E-mail: gregoryhse@aol.com

Circa 1830. This colonial house was built in the center of the village by stockbroker Elias Gregory. It became a restaurant in 1976. The historic section of the building now holds the restaurant, while a new portion accommodates overnight guests. It is decorated with Early American braided rugs and four-poster beds.

Innkeeper(s): Bette & Robert Jewell. $80-90. EP. MC VISA AX DC CB DS PC TC. 12 rooms with PB. 1 conference room. Breakfast included in rates. Type of meal: continental breakfast. Restaurant on premises. Beds: QDT. Air conditioning in room. Cable TV, VCR, fax, copier and swimming on premises. Amusement parks, antiques, fishing, parks, shopping, downhill skiing, cross-country skiing, sporting events, theater and watersports nearby.

Location: Minutes from Albany.
Publicity: *Hudson Valley, Albany Times Union, Schenectady Gazette, Courier, Sunday Record.*

"We experienced privacy and quiet, lovely surroundings indoors and out, excellent service, and as much friendliness as we were comfortable with, but no more."
Certificate may be used: Anytime Nov. 1-April 30.

Avon F5

Avon Inn
55 E Main St
Avon, NY 14414-1438
(716)226-8181 Fax:(716)226-8185

Circa 1820. This Greek Revival mansion, in both the state and national historic registers, has been providing lodging for more than a century. After 1866, the residence was turned into a health center that provided water cures from the local sulphur springs. The guest registry included the likes of Henry Ford, Thomas Edison and Eleanor Roosevelt. Though the inn is no longer a health spa, guests can still relax in the garden with its gazebo and fountain or on the Grecian-pillared front porch. A full-service restaurant and conference facilities are on the premises.

Innkeeper(s): Linda Reusch. $50-85. MC VISA AX DC CB DS TC. 15 rooms with PB. Breakfast included in rates. Types of meals: continental breakfast and early coffee/tea. Picnic lunch available. Restaurant on premises. Beds: KQD. Air conditioning in room. Cable TV, fax and copier on premises. Amusement parks, antiques, fishing, parks, shopping, downhill skiing and cross-country skiing nearby.

Location: Nestled in the village of Avon, 20 minutes south of Rochester.
Certificate may be used: Not valid Saturdays May 1-Oct. 31. Minimum stay is two nights.

Bainbridge H9

Berry Hill Farm B&B
PO Box 128
Bainbridge, NY 13733-0128
(607)967-8745 (800)497-8745 Fax:(607)967-8745

Circa 1820. Surrounded by flower and herb gardens, this farmhouse presides over 180 acres. Guest rooms are furnished in antiques and decorated with bunches of fresh and dried flowers. Organic gardens provide 100 varieties of annuals and perennials. There are tulips, poppies, lilacs, sweet peas and in May, the fruit trees are in bloom. A full country breakfast is served. By advance reservation you can arrange for a sleigh ride or horse-drawn wagon to take you through the woods and meadows of the Berry Hill Farm, or you may stroll through the gardens and woods on your own.

Innkeeper(s): Jean Fowler & Cecilia Rios. $60-70. MC VISA AX PC TC. 4 rooms. Breakfast included in rates. Types of meals: full breakfast and

early coffee/tea. Beds: QDT. Ceiling fan in room. VCR, fax, copier, swimming and library on premises. Antiques, fishing, parks, shopping, downhill skiing, cross-country skiing and sporting events nearby.

Publicity: *Tri-Town News, Daily Star.*

"The house is just wonderful and our rooms were exceptionally comfortable."

Certificate may be used: Jan. 2-April 30, anytime. May 1-Dec. 20, Sunday through Thursday only. Holidays and special events excluded.

Bellport   K14

Great South Bay Inn
160 S Country Rd
Bellport, NY 11713-2516
(516)286-8588 Fax:(516)286-2460

Circa 1890. Long Island's south shore is home to this Cape Cod-style inn filled with turn-of-the-century antiques. Six guest rooms are available, four with private baths and all featuring original wainscoting. Favorite relaxing spots include the garden room and parlor. The innkeepers are fluent in French and pride themselves on serving guests' individual needs, including pet accommodations or train station pick-ups. Fire Island National Seashore and the Wertheim National Wildlife Refuge are nearby.

Innkeeper(s): Michael Harvey & Judy Mortimer. $75-99. MC VISA TC. 6 rooms, 4 with PB, 1 with FP. 1 suite. Breakfast included in rates. Type of meal: full breakfast. Beds: QDT. Air conditioning, ceiling fan, TV and VCR in room. Fax, copier and bicycles on premises. Amusement parks, antiques, fishing, parks, shopping, golf, theater and watersports nearby.

Certificate may be used: Mid-January to mid-April, Rooms 5 & 6.

Berkshire   H8

Kinship B&B
12724 Rt 38
Berkshire, NY 13736
(607)657-4455 (800)493-2337

Circa 1809. An antique and collectible doll shop is found on the premises of this farmhouse-style inn. Post-and-beam construction, four fireplaces and plank floors reflect the inn's character. Kinship is centrally located for easy access to the Finger Lakes, upstate New York wineries and Ithaca, Cortland and Binghamton colleges. Four downhill ski areas and cross-country skiing are nearby. In the fall, visitors can enjoy the colors in Fillmore Glen, Treman and Watkins Glen.

Innkeeper(s): John & Carole Shipley. $45-85. TC. 4 rooms, 1 with FP. 1 suite. Breakfast and evening snack included in rates. Types of meals: full breakfast and gourmet breakfast. Picnic lunch available. Beds: KDT. Cable TV and VCR on premises. Antiques, fishing, parks, shopping, downhill skiing, cross-country skiing, sporting events, theater and watersports nearby.

Certificate may be used: April-December, Sunday-Saturday (excluding college weekends). Two-night minimum stay.

Berlin   G13

Sedgwick Inn
Rt 22, Box 250
Berlin, NY 12022
(518)658-2334 Fax:(518)658-3998

Circa 1791. The Sedgwick Inn sits on 12 acres in the Taconic Valley in the Berkshire Mountains. The main house features guest rooms, the low-ceilinged Coach Room Tavern and a glass-enclosed dining porch facing an English garden. A Colonial-style

motel behind the main house sits beside a rushing brook. A small antique shop, once a Civil War recruiting station, is designed in the Neoclassical style of the early 19th century. A converted carriage house with a hardwood dance floor and hand-hewn beams serves as a gift shop with prints, paintings, sculptures and a selection of unusual crafts and gourmet items.

Innkeeper(s): Edith Evans. $68-105. MC VISA AX DC CB DS TC. 11 rooms, 10 with PB. 1 suite. 1 conference room. Breakfast included in rates. Type of meal: full breakfast. Dinner, lunch and room service available. Restaurant on premises. Beds: KQD. Ceiling fan and TV in room. VCR and fax on premises. Antiques, fishing, parks, downhill skiing, cross-country skiing and theater nearby.

Location: Berkshire Mountains.

Publicity: *Berkshire Eagle, Hudson Valley Magazine, Albany Times Union, Good Housekeeping, USAir.*

"We were absolutely enchanted. We found this to be a charming place, a rare and wonderful treat."

Certificate may be used: Sunday-Thursday, no holiday Sundays.

Brockport   E5

The Portico B&B
3741 Lake Rd N
Brockport, NY 14420-1415
(716)637-0220

Named for its three porches, called porticos, this Greek Revival inn is situated amid blue spruce, maple and sycamore trees in a historic district. Tall columns and a cupola add to its charm. Three antique-filled guest rooms are available to visitors, who enjoy a full Victorian breakfast and kettledrum, also known as afternoon tea. The surrounding area offers many attractions, including the Cobblestone Museum, Darien Lake Amusement Park, George Eastman House and Strasenburgh Planetarium. Several colleges, golf courses and parks are nearby.

Innkeeper(s): Anne Klein. $60-70. 3 rooms. Breakfast included in rates. Types of meals: full breakfast and early coffee/tea. Turndown service in room. VCR on premises. Amusement parks, antiques, shopping, downhill skiing, cross-country skiing, sporting events and theater nearby.

Certificate may be used: Midweek, Monday through Thursday except October.

The Victorian B&B
320 S Main St
Brockport, NY 14420-2253
(716)637-7519 (800)836-1929 Fax:(716)637-2319

Circa 1890. Within walking distance of the historic Erie Canal, this Queen Anne Victorian inn is located on Brockport's Main Street. Visitors select from eight second-floor guest rooms, all with phones, private baths and TVs. Victorian furnishings are found throughout the inn.
A favorite spot is the solarium, with its three walls of windows, perfect for curling up with a book or magazine. Two first-floor sitting areas also pro-  vide relaxing havens for guests. Lake Ontario is just 10 miles away, and visitors will find much to explore in nearby Rochester.

Innkeeper(s): Sharon Kehoe. $59-98. PC TC. 8 rooms. Breakfast included in rates. Type of meal: full breakfast. Air conditioning in room. Cable TV and VCR on premises. Antiques, shopping, cross-country skiing, sporting events and theater nearby.

"As an unexpected guest, I was pleasantly surprised."

Certificate may be used: Nov. 15-April 30.

Brookfield   G9

Gates Hill Homestead
PO Box 96
Brookfield, NY 13314-0096
(315)899-5837

Circa 1976. This early American salt-box inn is found on 64 acres of forested farmland, and is home to a working farm and prize-winning Percheron horses. Early American furnishings highlight the inn's four guest rooms. The innkeepers also lead horse-drawn stagecoach tours of the history-rich area, complemented by a delicious, family-style din-

ner. Sleigh rides are available in winter, with or without dinner. Colgate University and the Upstate Auto Museum are within easy driving distance.

Innkeeper(s): Charlie & Donna Tanney. $64-79. VISA PC TC. 4 rooms, 2 with PB. Breakfast included in rates. Types of meals: full breakfast and early coffee/tea. Dinner available. Beds: DT. Air conditioning and ceiling fan in room. VCR and stables on premises. Antiques, cross-country skiing and theater nearby.

Certificate may be used: Monday through Thursday, inclusive April through November.

Buffalo   F3

Beau Fleuve B&B Inn
242 Linwood Ave
Buffalo, NY 14209-1802
(716)882-6116 (800)278-0245

Circa 1881. Each of the five rooms at this Victorian mini-mansion features a different style and celebrates the ethnic groups that settled in the Buffalo area. Artifacts accented by stunning stained-glass windows render homage to the Western New York Native American tribes in the Native American Common Area room. The 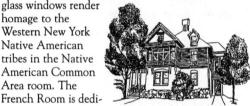 French Room is dedicated to the memory of French explorer LaSalle, credited as the first European to travel through the Niagara Frontier. Absolute comfort is complete with every touch, from the queen-size antique brass bed to the Louis XIV chairs and walls both covered in champagne damask. Other elegant rooms mark the contributions of the Irish, German, Italian and Polish immigrants. Set in the Linwood Historic District, this inn is in the middle of everything. Millionaires' Row is only one block away, in addition to nearby Niagara Falls, other historic neighborhoods, museums, art galleries, antique shops and a variety of restaurants. A friendly ambiance will remind guests why Buffalo is known as the "City of Good Neighbors."

Innkeeper(s): Ramona Pando Whitaker & Rik Whitaker. $67-80. MC VISA DS. 5 rooms, 1 with PB. Breakfast included in rates. Type of meal: full breakfast. Beds: QDT. Antiques, fishing, downhill skiing, cross-country skiing and theater nearby.

Publicity: *Buffalo News, WIVB-TV, New York Daily News, Preservation Coalition Tour House.*

"Relaxing, comfortable hospitality in beautiful surroundings."

Certificate may be used: From Nov. 1 to April 30, holidays excepted

Burdett
G6

The Red House Country Inn
4586 Picnic Area Rd
Burdett, NY 14818-9716
(607)546-8566

Circa 1844. Nestled within the 16,000-acre Finger Lakes National Forest, this old farmstead has an in-ground swimming pool, large veranda overlooking groomed lawns, flower gardens and picnic areas. Pet Samoyeds and goats share the seven acres. Next to the property are acres of wild blueberry patches and stocked fishing ponds. The Red House is near Seneca Lake, world-famous Glen Gorge, and Cornell University.

Innkeeper(s): Sandy Schmanke & Joan Martin. $59-89. MC VISA AX DS. 5 rooms, 1 with FP. Breakfast and afternoon tea included in rates. Types of meals: full breakfast and early coffee/tea. Beds: QDT. Antiques, fishing, parks, shopping, cross-country skiing, sporting events, theater and watersports nearby.

Location: Finger Lakes National Forest, near Watkins Glen.

Publicity: *New York Alive, Discerning Traveler, New York Magazine.*

"An Inn-credible delight. What a wonderful place to stay and a difficult place to leave. It doesn't get any better than this."

Certificate may be used: November-April, Sunday-Thursday.

Canandaigua
F6

The Acorn Inn
4508 Rt 64 S
Canandaigua, NY 14424
(716)229-2834 Fax:(716)229-5046

Circa 1795. Guests to this Federal Stagecoach inn can relax before the blazing fire of a large colonial fireplace equipped with antique crane and hanging iron pots. Guest rooms, two with fireplace, are furnished with period antiques, canopy beds, luxury

linens and bedding, and each has a comfortable sitting area. Books are provided in each guest room as well as in the libraries. After a day of visiting wineries, skiing, hiking in the Finger Lakes area and dinner at a local restaurant, guests can relax in an outdoor

Jacuzzi. Beds are turned down each night and a carafe of ice water and chocolates are placed in each room.
Innkeeper(s): Joan & Louis Clark. $53-165. MC VISA AX DS PC TC. 4 rooms with PB, 2 with FP. Breakfast and afternoon tea included in rates. Types of meals: gourmet breakfast and early coffee/tea. Beds: Q. Air conditioning, turndown service, TV and VCR in room. Fax, copier, spa and library on premises. Antiques, fishing, parks, shopping, downhill skiing, cross-country skiing, theater and watersports nearby.

Publicity: *New York, Mid-Atlantic.*

Certificate may be used: Monday-Thursday, Nov. 1-June 1, for Bristol and Hotchkiss rooms only; or other times by chance.

Enchanted Rose Inn B&B
7479 Rts 5 & 20, PO BOX 128
Canandaigua, NY 14424
(716)657-6003 Fax:(716)657-4405
E-mail: enchrose@servtech.com

Circa 1820. During the restoration of this early 19th-century home, the innkeepers uncovered the many original features, including the wood floors that now glimmer. The fireplace dates back to the 1790s, part of the original log home. The present structure was built onto the original in the 1820s. The innkeepers are only the fourth owners and have returned the home to its original glory. Freshly cut flowers from the inn's gardens are placed in the guest rooms, which feature antiques and romantic decor. The dining room table is set with beautiful china, a perfect accompaniment to the gourmet breakfasts. Afternoon tea is served in the rose garden or in an inviting fireplaced parlor.
Innkeeper(s): Jan & Howard Buhlmann. $95-125. MC VISA DS PC TC. 3 rooms, 2 with PB. 1 suite. Breakfast included in rates. Types of meals: full breakfast, gourmet breakfast and early coffee/tea. Evening snack available. Beds: Q. Air conditioning, turndown service, TV and VCR in room. Fax and library on premises. Antiques, fishing, parks, shopping, downhill skiing, cross-country skiing, sporting events, theater and watersports nearby.

Certificate may be used: Sunday-Thursday, November-April, no holidays.

Nottingham Lodge B&B
5741 Bristol Valley Rd, Rt 64
Canandaigua, NY 14424
(716)374-5355

Circa 1825. South of Canandaigua Lake in the heart of the Bristol Mountain Ski Center area, this Tudor-style inn offers stunning views of the nearby mountain from its valley setting. Visitors select from the Michelle Room, with its canopy bed; Valerie Room, four-poster; and Katheryn, iron and brass. The inn's full breakfast features fresh fruit and home-made baked goods, and it is served in the dining room with its breathtaking view of Bristol Mountain. Guests enjoy gathering around the cobblestone fireplace or hiking along the stream behind the inn.
Innkeeper(s): Bonnie Robinson. $60-65. MC VISA AX DS. 3 rooms. Breakfast included in rates. Type of meal: full breakfast. Antiques, shopping, downhill skiing, cross-country skiing and theater nearby.

Certificate may be used: Jan. 1-Sept. 30, Nov. 1-Dec. 24, anytime; Oct. 1-31, Sunday-Thursday.

Candor H7

The Edge of Thyme, A B&B Inn
6 Main St
Candor, NY 13743-1615
(607)659-5155 (800)722-7365 Fax:(607)659-5155

Circa 1840. Originally the summer home of John D. Rockefeller's secretary, this two-story Georgian-style inn offers gracious accommodations a short drive from Ithaca. The inn sports many interesting fea-

tures, including an impressive stairway, marble fireplaces, parquet floors, pergola (arbor) and windowed porch with leaded glass. Guests may relax in front of the inn's fireplace, catch up with reading in its library or watch television in the sitting room. An authentic turn-of-the-century full breakfast is served, and guests also may arrange for special high teas.
Innkeeper(s): Prof. Frank & Eva Mae Musgrave. $65-80. MC VISA AX TC. 5 rooms, 2 with PB. 2 suites. Breakfast included in rates. Types of meals: full breakfast, gourmet breakfast and early coffee/tea. Afternoon tea available. Beds: KQDT. Cable TV and VCR on premises. Antiques, fishing, parks, shopping, downhill skiing, cross-country skiing, sporting events and theater nearby.

Certificate may be used: Sunday through Thursday. Not valid in May.

Cazenovia F8

Brae Loch Inn
5 Albany St
Cazenovia, NY 13035-1403
(315)655-3431 Fax:(315)655-4844

Circa 1805. The innkeeper here wears a kilt to highlight the Brae Loch's Scottish theme. Four of the oldest rooms have fireplaces. There are Stickley furnishings, and the Princess Diana Room has a canopy of white eyelet. Guest rooms are on the second and third floors above the restaurant.
Innkeeper(s): Jim & Val Barr. $80-125. MC VISA AX TC. 14 rooms, 12 with PB. 1 conference room. Breakfast included in rates. Type of meal: continental breakfast. Banquet service, catering service and room service available. Restaurant on premises. Beds: KQDT. Air conditioning and TV in room. Fax, copier and swimming on premises. Antiques, fishing, parks, shopping, downhill skiing, cross-country skiing, sporting events, golf and watersports nearby.

Location: U.S. Route 20.
Publicity: *The Globe and Mail, Traveler Magazine, CNY.*

"Everything was just perfect. The Brae Loch and staff make you feel as if you were at home."
Certificate may be used: Jan. 1-May 1.

Chemung H7

Halcyon Place B&B
197 Washington St, PO Box 244
Chemung, NY 14825
(607)529-3544

Circa 1820. The innkeepers chose the name "halcyon" because it signifies tranquility and a healing richness. The historic Greek Revival inn and its grounds offer just that to guests, who will appreciate the fine period antiques, paneled doors, six-over-six windows of hand-blown glass and wide plank floors. An herb garden and screen porch also beckon visitors. Full breakfasts may include omelets with garden ingredients, raspberry muffins, rum sticky buns or waffles. The inn's three guest rooms feature double beds, and one boasts a romantic fireplace. Fine antiquing and golfing are found

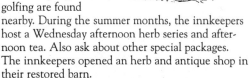

nearby. During the summer months, the innkeepers host a Wednesday afternoon herb series and afternoon tea. Also ask about other special packages. The innkeepers opened an herb and antique shop in their restored barn.
Innkeeper(s): Douglas & Yvonne Sloan. $55-70. PC TC. 3 rooms, 1 with PB, 1 with FP. Breakfast included in rates. Type of meal: gourmet breakfast. Afternoon tea available. Beds: D. Turndown service in room. Antiques, parks, shopping, cross-country skiing, sporting events, theater and watersports nearby.
Publicity: *Elmira Star Gazette, Chemung Valley Reporter, Evening Star.*
"We appreciate all the little touches you attend to, to make our stay special."
Certificate may be used: Sept. 1-May 31, anytime. Subject to availability.

Chestertown D12

The Friends Lake Inn
Friends Lake Rd
Chestertown, NY 12817
(518)494-4751 Fax:(518)494-4616

Circa 1860. Formerly a boardinghouse for tanners who worked in the area, this Mission-style inn now offers its guests elegant accommodations and fine dining. Overlooking Friends Lake, the inn provides easy access to many well-known skiing areas, including Gore Mountain. Guests are welcome to borrow a canoe for a lake outing and use the inn's private beach. Guest rooms

are well-appointed and most include four-poster beds. Many have breathtaking lake views or Jacuzzis. An outdoor hot tub is a favorite spot after a busy day of recreation. The 32 km Nordic Ski Center is on site with groomed wilderness trails, lessons and rentals. Trails are available for hiking, too. Innkeeper(s): Sharon & Greg Taylor. $175-325. MAP. MC VISA AX PC TC. 14 rooms with PB. Breakfast and dinner included in rates. Type of meal: full breakfast. Picnic lunch, catering service and room service available. Restaurant on premises. Beds: Q. Air conditioning and turndown service in room. Cable TV, VCR, fax, copier, swimming and library on premises. Handicap access. Amusement parks, antiques, fishing, parks, shopping, downhill skiing, cross-country skiing, sporting events, theater and watersports nearby.

"Everyone here is so pleasant, you end up feeling like family!"

Certificate may be used: Year round, Sunday-Thursday nights. Not valid on holidays or holiday weekends. Free lodging second night (dinner and breakfast extra charges).

Clarence   F3

Asa Ransom House
10529 Main St
Clarence, NY 14031-1624
(716)759-2315 Fax:(716)759-2791
E-mail: asaransom@aol.com

Circa 1853. Set on spacious lawns, behind a white picket fence, the Asa Ransom House rests on the site of the first grist mill built in Erie County. Silversmith Asa Ransom constructed an inn and grist mill here in response to the Holland Land Company's offering of free land to anyone who would start and operate a tavern. A specialty of the dining room is "Veal Perrott" and "Pistachio Banana Muffins."
Innkeeper(s): Robert & Judy Lenz. $85-145. MAP. EP. MC VISA DS PC TC. 9 rooms with PB, 7 with FP. 2 suites. 1 conference room. Breakfast

included in rates. Types of meals: full breakfast and early coffee/tea. Dinner available. Restaurant on premises. Beds: KQDT. Air conditioning and turndown service in room. Fax, copier and library on premises. Handicap access. Antiques, parks, shopping, cross-country skiing and theater nearby.

Publicity: *Country Living.*

"Popular spot keeps getting better."

Certificate may be used: February to May 31, Sept. 1-Dec. 15, Sunday-Thursday.

Claverack   H12

The Martindale B&B Inn
857 Rt-23
Claverack, NY 12513
(518)851-5405 Fax:(518)851-2568
E-mail: solterry@epix.net

Circa 1852. For more than 100 years, this farmhouse remained in the same family. Innkeepers Terry and Soll Berl purchased the home in 1986 and transformed into a small bed & breakfast. Although the exterior features Federal and Colonial architecture, the fancy trim is reminiscent of a Victorian home. The interior definitely favors the Victorian, including antiques, wicker and Oriental rugs. The vast grounds include a pond with a little dock and rowboat, as well as an enclosed gazebo.
Innkeeper(s): Terry & Soll Berl. $60-75. PC. 4 rooms, 2 with PB. Breakfast included in rates. Type of meal: full breakfast. Dinner available. Beds: DT. Ceiling fan in room. VCR, fax and tennis on premises. Antiques, fishing, parks, shopping, downhill skiing, cross-country skiing, golf and theater nearby.

Certificate may be used: Nov. 1-April 30, except holiday seasons.

Cohocton   G5

Button's Creekside Farm B&B
9705 CR 9
Cohocton, NY 14826-9453
(607)566-2406

Circa 1810. Families are welcomed and encouraged at this country farmhouse, which offers something for everyone. Children are invited to help with the farm chores, which might include gathering eggs or feeding a calf. Heartier guests can milk cows or bale hay if they wish, but relaxation is always an option. Innkeepers Arlan and Carol Button have owned and operated this 350-acre sheep and dairy farm for more than 20 years, and they are full of knowledge about the area. The Buttons serve traditional country fare with fresh fruit, pancakes, egg dishes, meats and potatoes. This is a comfortable family home decorated in a simple, Early American style with antiques.
Innkeeper(s): Arlan & Carol Button. $50. TC. 4 rooms, 1 with PB. 1 suite. Breakfast and evening snack included in rates. Type of meal: full breakfast. Beds: DT. Turndown service in room. Cable TV, VCR and

bicycles on premises. Antiques, fishing, parks, shopping, downhill skiing, cross-country skiing and sporting events nearby.

Certificate may be used: Jan. 1-Dec. 31, Sunday-Friday.

Cold Spring   J12

Pig Hill

73 Main St
Cold Spring, NY 10516-3014
(914)265-9247 Fax:(914)265-2155

Circa 1808. The antiques at this stately three-story inn can be purchased and range from Chippendale to chinoiserie style. Rooms feature formal English and Adirondack decor with special touches such as four-

poster or brass beds, painted rockers and, of course, pigs. The lawn features a tri-level garden. The delicious breakfasts can be shared with guests in the dining room or garden, or you can take it in the privacy of your room. The inn is about an hour out of New York City, and the train station is only two blocks away.

Innkeeper(s): Wendy O'Brien. $100-150. MC VISA AX. 8 rooms, 5 with PB, 6 with FP. 1 conference room. Breakfast included in rates. Type of meal: full breakfast. Afternoon tea and catering service available. Beds: QDT. Air conditioning and ceiling fan in room. Antiques, fishing, shopping, sporting events and theater nearby.

Publicity: *National Geographic, Woman's Home Journal, Country Inns, Getaways for Gourmets.*

"Some of our fondest memories of New York were at Pig Hill."

Certificate may be used: Monday-Thursday, excluding holidays, May and October.

Cooperstown   G10

Litco Farms B&B

PO Box 1048
Cooperstown, NY 13326-6048
(607)547-2501 Fax:(607)547-7079

The 70-acre grounds that surround this Greek Revival farmhouse include 18 acres of mapped wetlands. The natural setting includes trails lined with wildflowers and guests are sure to spot deer and a variety of birds. On cold days, guests can snuggle up to the wood-burning stove, and there are plenty of ideal spots for picnics during the warmer months. The scent of baking breads and fresh coffee entices guests to the morning meal of country fare.

Innkeeper(s): Jim & Margaret Wolff. $69-119. 4 rooms. Breakfast included in rates. Type of meal: full breakfast.

Certificate may be used: April 1-May 15 & Sept. 15-Oct. 30, Monday through Thursday.

Corning   H6

1865 White Birch B&B

69 E 1st St
Corning, NY 14830-2715
(607)962-6355

Circa 1865. This Victorian is a short walk from historic Market Street, the Corning Glass Museum and many restaurants. Guests will appreciate the detailed woodwork, hardwood floors, an impressive winding staircase and many antiques. The rooms are decorated in a cozy, country decor. Home-baked breakfasts provide the perfect start for a day of visiting wineries, antique shops or museums.

Innkeeper(s): Kathy Donahue. $50-70. MC VISA AX. 4 rooms, 2 with PB. Breakfast included in rates. Type of meal: full breakfast. Beds: QT. Cable TV on premises. Antiques, fishing, shopping, cross-country skiing, sporting events and theater nearby.

Location: In the heart of Finger Lakes.

"This is a beautiful home, decorated to make us feel warm and welcome."

Certificate may be used: January-March, November-December, Sunday through Thursday.

Delevan House

188 Delevan Ave
Corning, NY 14830-3224
(607)962-2347

Circa 1933. Visitors to the Corning area will find a touch of home at this comfortable Colonial Revival house on a hill overlooking town. The inn's screened porch offers the perfect spot for reading, relaxing or sipping a cool drink. A full breakfast is served before guests head out for a day of business, sightseeing or travel. The Finger Lakes are 30 miles away, and just two miles from the inn, visitors will find the city's historic district. The Mark Twain Home and Pinnacle State Park are nearby.

Innkeeper(s): Mary DePumpo. $60-85. TC. 8 rooms, 1 with PB. Breakfast included in rates. Types of meals: full breakfast, gourmet breakfast and early coffee/tea. Beds: D. TV in room. Antiques, fishing, parks, shopping, skiing, sporting events and watersports nearby.

Certificate may be used: Nov. 1-April 1, Monday-Sunday.

Cornith
E12

Agape Farm B&B
4894 Rt 9N
Cornith, NY 12822-1704
(518)654-7777

Circa 1870. Amid 33 acres of fields and woods, this Adirondack farmhouse is home to chickens and horses, as well as guests seeking a refreshing getaway. Visitors have their choice of six guest rooms, all with

ceiling fans, phones, private baths and views of the tranquil surroundings. The inn's wraparound porch lures many visitors, who often enjoy a glass of icy lemonade. Homemade breads, jams, jellies and muffins are part of the full breakfast served here, and guests are welcome to pick berries or gather a ripe tomato from the garden. A trout-filled stream on the grounds flows to the Hudson River, a mile away.
Innkeeper(s): Fred & Sigrid Koch. $60-125. MC VISA DS PC TC. 6 rooms with PB. 1 cottage. Breakfast, afternoon tea and evening snack included in rates. Types of meals: full breakfast and early coffee/tea. Beds: KQDT. Ceiling fan in room. Cable TV, VCR, library and child care on premises. Handicap access. Amusement parks, antiques, fishing, parks, shopping, downhill skiing, cross-country skiing, sporting events, theater and watersports nearby.
Location: Between Saratoga & Lake George attractions.

"Clean and impeccable, we were treated royally."

Certificate may be used: Sept. 15 to June 15.

Deposit
H9

The White Pillars Inn
82 2nd St
Deposit, NY 13754-1122
(607)467-4191 Fax:(607)467-2264

Circa 1820. Guests are greeted with freshly baked cookies at this exquisite Greek Revival inn. This is only the beginning of a food adventure to remember. After a restful night's sleep on a hand-carved, high-board bed, guests linger over a five-course breakfast, which might include an overstuffed omelette or a baked apple wrapped in pastry and topped with caramel sauce. Dinner is a gourmet's treat, and all meals are prepared by innkeeper Najla Aswad, whose

recipes have been recommended by Gourmet magazine. The inn is decorated with beautiful antiques, rich Persian carpets and colorful floral arrangements.
Innkeeper(s): Najla Aswad. $85-125. MC VISA AX DC CB DS. 5 rooms, 3 with PB. 1 suite. 1 conference room. Breakfast included in rates. Types of meals: full breakfast and gourmet breakfast. Catering service and room service available. Beds: KDT. Air conditioning, turndown service, TV and VCR in room. Fax and copier on premises. Antiques, fishing, shopping, downhill skiing, cross-country skiing and sporting events nearby.
Location: Foothills of the Catskills.
Publicity: *Gourmet.*

"The perfect place to do nothing but eat!"

Certificate may be used: November-April.

Downsville
H10

The Victoria Rose B&B
Main St, Box 542
Downsville, NY 13755
(607)363-7838 Fax:(516)928-1780
E-mail: nkeepr@aol.com

Circa 1897. A prominent local doctor built this Victorian home, which boasts original items such as stained-glass windows, a beautiful carved mantel and grand staircase. The home is decorated in Victorian style with period antiques and reproductions. Light, lacy curtains shade the windows, and rooms feature flowery wallpapers. There is a covered veranda on one side of the home, offering wicker furnishings for those who want to relax. In addition to breakfast, guests are pampered with afternoon tea. Those in search of outdoor activities will find fishing, hunting, golfing, several state parks and hiking trails all in the area.
Innkeeper(s): Bill & Debby Benzinger. $52-63. MC VISA PC. 4 rooms with PB. Breakfast, afternoon tea and evening snack included in rates. Types of meals: gourmet breakfast and early coffee/tea. Room service available. Beds: QD. Ceiling fan in room. Cable TV, VCR, bicycles and library on premises. Antiques, fishing, parks, shopping, cross-country skiing, sporting events, golf, theater and watersports nearby.
Certificate may be used: June 1-Dec. 31, Sunday-Friday.

East Hampton K15

Centennial House
13 Woods Ln
East Hampton, NY 11937-3247
(516)324-9414 Fax:(516)324-0493
E-mail: centhouse@hamptons.com

Circa 1876. For a spot of English country elegance, look no further than Centennial House, secluded on a acre of landscaped lawns and gardens on posh Long Island. Beds, whether four-poster or canopied, are dressed with fine linens and down comforters. A selection of designer soaps and bath amenities are provided along with soft towels and warm, comfortable robes. The innkeepers have decorated the inn with a variety of antiques. After breakfast, guests can lounge by the pool and enjoy the fragrance of flowers or take a stroll into the village, where shops and the beach await.
Innkeeper(s): Bernadette M. Meade. $150-375. MC VISA PC. 6 rooms with PB, 2 with FP. 1 cottage. Breakfast included in rates. Types of meals: full breakfast and early coffee/tea. Beds: KQD. Air conditioning, TV and VCR in room. Fax, copier and swimming on premises. Antiques, fishing, parks, shopping, cross-country skiing, golf, theater and watersports nearby.
Certificate may be used: Nov. 1-April 15, Sunday-Thursday.

Elbridge F7

Fox Ridge Farm B&B
4786 Foster Rd
Elbridge, NY 13060-9770
(315)673-4881 Fax:(315)673-3691
E-mail: foxridg@aol.com

Circa 1910. Guests shouldn't be surprised to encounter deer or other wildlife at this secluded country home surrounded by woods. The innkeepers have transformed the former farmhouse into a cozy inn with rooms boasting quilts, a four-poster bed and views of the woods or flower garden. Enjoy breakfasts in front of a fire in the large country kitchen. The innkeepers are happy to accommodate dietary needs. Snacks and refreshments are always available for hungry guests in the evening. Nearby Skaneateles Lake offers swimming, boating and other outdoor activities. Dinner cruises, touring wineries and antique shopping are other popular activities.
Innkeeper(s): Marge Sykes. $55-75. MC VISA AX DS PC TC. 3 rooms, 1 with PB. Breakfast and evening snack included in rates. Types of meals: continental-plus breakfast, full breakfast, gourmet breakfast and early coffee/tea. Beds: QD. VCR on premises. Antiques, fishing, parks, shopping, downhill skiing, cross-country skiing, sporting events, theater and watersports nearby.

"If I could, I would take Marge Sykes home to Seattle with us. We stayed 7 days for a family reunion. Great

company, marvelous hosts and the most delicious breakfasts everyday."
Certificate may be used: Anytime as available, except Fridays and Saturdays during July, August.

Essex C13

The Stone House
PO Box 43
Essex, NY 12936-0043
(518)963-7713 Fax:(518)963-7713

Circa 1826. Just a two-minute walk from the ferry that traverses Lake Champlain, this stately Georgian stonehouse offers a tranquil English country setting. Breakfast may be eaten in the elegant dining room or on the garden terrace, and guests also enjoy an evening snack and glass of wine by candlelight on the inn's porch. The charming hamlet of Essex, listed in the National Register, is waiting to be explored, and visitors may do so by borrowing one of the inn's bicycles. Antiquing, fine dining and shopping are found in town, and Lake Champlain and nearby Lake George provide many recreational activities.
Innkeeper(s): Sylvia Hobbs. $55-125. PC TC. 5 rooms, 2 with PB. 1 suite. Breakfast, afternoon tea and evening snack included in rates. Types of meals: continental-plus breakfast and early coffee/tea. Room service available. Beds: QDT. Air conditioning and turndown service in room. Cable TV, VCR, fax, copier, bicycles and library on premises. Antiques, fishing, parks, shopping, downhill skiing, cross-country skiing, golf, theater and watersports nearby.

"Without a doubt, the highlight of our trip!"
Certificate may be used: Mid-May to mid-October, mid-week only, Sunday through Thursday.

Fair Haven E7

Black Creek Farm B&B
PO Box 390
Fair Haven, NY 13064-0390
(315)947-5282

Circa 1888. Pines and towering birch trees frame this Victorian farmhouse inn, filled with an incredible assortment of authentic antiques. Set on 20 acres in the countryside west of Fair Haven, this inn offers a refreshing escape from big-city life. The inn's impressive furnishings come as no real surprise since there is an antique shop on the premises. Guests enjoy relaxing in a hammock, on the porch, or by taking a stroll along the peaceful country roads. The inn is two miles from Lake Ontario's shoreline and within easy reach of Fair Haven Beach State Park and Thorpe Vineyard.
Innkeeper(s): Bob & Kathy Sarber. $50-75. MC VISA DS PC. 3 rooms, 1 with PB. Breakfast and afternoon tea included in rates. Types of

meals: full breakfast and early coffee/tea. Evening snack available. Beds: DT. Air conditioning in room. VCR and bicycles on premises. Antiques, fishing, parks, cross-country skiing and watersports nearby.

Certificate may be used: Anytime except weekends (Friday-Sunday) in July and August.

Frost Haven B&B Inn
14380 West Bay Rd, PO Box 241
Fair Haven, NY 13064
(315)947-5331

This Federal-style inn near Lake Ontario offers a relaxing getaway for residents of nearby Rochester and Syracuse. Four guest rooms are available, all furnished with Victorian stylings and featuring bath robes and ceiling fans. Guests enjoy a full breakfast before beginning a busy day of antiquing, fishing, sightseeing, swimming or sunbathing. Fair Haven Beach State Park is nearby, and Fort Ontario is within easy driving distance.

Innkeeper(s): Brad & Chris Frost. $66. MC VISA AX. 7 rooms. Ceiling fan in room. VCR on premises. Antiques nearby.

Certificate may be used: Weekends July through Labor Day excluded.

Fleischmanns   H11

River Run
Main St, Box D4
Fleischmanns, NY 12430
(914)254-4884

Circa 1887. The backyard of this large three-story Victorian gently slopes to the river where the Bushkill and Little Red Kill trout streams meet. Inside, stained-glass windows surround the inn's common areas, shining on the oak-floored dining room and the book-filled parlor. The parlor also includes a fireplace and a piano. Adirondack chairs are situated comfortably on the front porch. Tennis courts, a pool, park, theater and restaurants are within walking distance, as is a country auction held each Saturday night. The inn is two and a half hours out of New York City, 35 minutes west of Woodstock, and accessible by public transportation.

Innkeeper(s): Larry Miller. $50-100. MC VISA PC. 10 rooms, 6 with PB. 1 suite. Breakfast and afternoon tea included in rates. Types of meals:

continental-plus breakfast and early coffee/tea. Beds: KQDT. Cable TV, VCR, bicycles and library on premises. Antiques, fishing, parks, shopping, downhill skiing, cross-country skiing, theater, watersports nearby.

Location: Country village in the high peaks of the Catskill Mountains.

Publicity: *Catskill Mountain News, Kingston Freeman, New York Times, New York Daily News, Philadelphia Inquirer, Inn Country USA.*

"We are really happy to know of a place that welcomes all of our family."

Certificate may be used: Weekends late March to mid-May and November-December; weekdays all year (all holiday periods excluded). Call for availability of other times.

Fredonia   G2

The White Inn
52 E Main St
Fredonia, NY 14063-1822
(716)672-2103 Fax:(716)672-2107

Circa 1868. This 23-room inn is situated in the center of Fredonia, a town reminiscent of George Bailey's New York home in "It's a Wonderful Life." Antiques and reproductions decorate the guest rooms and suites. Guests, as well as the general public, may enjoy gourmet meals at this inn, a charter member of the Duncan Hines "Family of Fine Restaurants." Cocktails and more casual fare are served in the lounge or on the 100-foot-long veranda. The nearby Chatauqua Institution presents a variety of lectures and concert performances during the summer. Wineries, golfing, state parks and shops are nearby.

Innkeeper(s): Robert Contiguglia & Kathleen Dennison. $79-169. EP. MC VISA AX DC DS PC TC. 23 rooms with PB, 2 with FP. 11 suites. 4 conference rooms. Breakfast included in rates. Type of meal: full breakfast. Dinner, lunch, banquet service and catering service available. Restaurant on premises. Beds: KQD. Air conditioning and TV in room. VCR, fax, copier and bicycles on premises. Handicap access. Antiques, parks, shopping, cross-country skiing and theater nearby.

Publicity: *Country Living, Innsider.*

"Thanks again for another wonderful stay."

Certificate may be used: November-April, Sunday-Thursday, excluding holiday weekends.

Fulton   E7

Battle Island Inn
2167 State Route 48 N
Fulton, NY 13069-4132
(315)593-3699 Fax:(315)592-5071
E-mail: hzgu49a@prodigy.com

Circa 1840. Topped with a gothic cupola, this family farmhouse overlooks the Oswego River and a golf course. There are three antique-filled parlors. Guest accommodations are furnished in a variety of styles including Victorian and Renaissance Revival. There are four wooded acres with lawns and gardens. Guests are often found relaxing on one of the inn's four porches and enjoying the views. The Honeymoon suite features a canopy bed, full bath and private jacuzzi.

Innkeeper(s): Richard & Joyce Rice. $60-125. AP. MC VISA AX DS PC TC. 5 rooms with PB. 1 suite. Breakfast included in rates. Types of meals: full breakfast, gourmet breakfast and early coffee/tea. Beds: QDT. Ceiling fan and TV in room. VCR, fax and copier on premises. Handicap access. Fishing, parks, shopping, cross-country skiing, theater and watersports nearby.

Location: Seven miles south of Oswego on Lake Ontario.

Publicity: *Lake Effect, Palladium Times, Travel, Journey, Oswego County Business, Valley News.*

"*We will certainly never forget our wonderful weeks at Battle Island Inn.*"

Certificate may be used: Sunday-Thursday.

Gorham   G6

The Gorham House
4752 E Swamp Rd
Gorham, NY 14461
(716)526-4402 Fax:(716)526-4402
E-mail: gorham.house@juno.com

Circa 1887. The Gorham House serves as a homey, country place to enjoy New York's Finger Lakes region. The five, secluded acres located between Canandaigua and Seneca lakes, include herb gardens, wildflowers and berry bushes. Part of the home dates back to the early 19th century, but it's the architecture of the 1887 expansion that accounts for the inn's Victorian touches. The interior is warm and cozy with comfortable, country furnishings. Some of the pieces are the innkeepers' family heirlooms. There are more than 50 wineries in the area, as well as a bounty of outdoor activities.
Innkeeper(s): Nancy & Al Rebmann. $65-90. PC TC. 3 rooms, 1 with PB. Breakfast included in rates. Types of meals: gourmet breakfast and early coffee/tea. Beds: QD. Air conditioning in room. Library on premises. Antiques, fishing, parks, shopping, downhill skiing, cross-country skiing, sporting events, theater and watersports nearby.
Certificate may be used: Jan. 1-Aug. 1, Sunday-Friday.

Greenfield Center   F12

The Wayside Inn
104 Wilton Rd
Greenfield Center, NY 12833-1705
(518)893-7249 Fax:(518)893-2884
Circa 1786. This Federal-style inn and arts center provides a unique atmosphere to visitors of the Saratoga Springs area. Situated on 10 acres amid a

brook, herb gardens, pond, wildflowers and willows, the inn originally served as a stagecoach tavern. Many interesting pieces, gathered during the innkeepers' 10 years living abroad, highlight the inn's interior. Visitors select from the Colonial American, European, Far East and Middle East rooms. Migrating birds are known to frequent the inn's picturesque pond.
Innkeeper(s): Karen & Dale Shook. $60-150. MC VISA DC DS. 3 rooms with PB. 1 suite. 2 conference rooms. Breakfast included in rates. Types of meals: full breakfast and early coffee/tea. Air conditioning and ceiling fan in room. Cable TV and VCR on premises. Amusement parks, antiques, shopping, downhill skiing, cross-country skiing, sporting events and theater nearby.
Certificate may be used: January-June, September, December; Sunday, Monday, Tuesday, Wednesday, Thursday. Space available.

Greenport   K15

The Bartlett House Inn
503 Front St
Greenport, NY 11944-1519
(516)477-0371
Circa 1908. A family residence for more than 60 years and then a convent for a nearby church, this large Victorian house became a bed & breakfast in 1982. Features include corinthian columns, stained-glass windows, two fireplaces and a large front porch. Period antiques complement the rich interior. The inn is within walking distance of shops, the harbor, the Shelter Island Ferry and train station.
Innkeeper(s): Bill & Diane May. $80-105. MC VISA PC TC. 10 rooms with PB, 1 with FP. 1 suite. 1 conference room. Breakfast included in rates. Meals: full breakfast and early coffee/tea. Beds: QDT. Air conditioning in room. Antiques, fishing, parks, shopping, watersports nearby.
Certificate may be used: Monday-Thursday, year-round, excluding holidays

Groton   G7

Gale House B&B
114 Williams St
Groton, NY 13073-1136
(607)898-4904
Circa 1890. Old-fashioned lace, crystal, elegant woodwork and antiques fill this beautiful Queen Anne Victorian inn. Each bedroom has its own

antique bed accentuated with beautiful blankets and pillows. During the week, guests are served continental-plus fare, and weekend guests are treated to a full breakfast with cereals, yogurt, fruit, freshly baked muffins, egg dishes and an entree such as waffles or French toast. Wineries, lake cruises and ski slopes are nearby. The inn is only 20 minutes from Cornell University, Ithaca College and SUNY Cortland. If road trips aren't your style, relax in the parlor or browse through the inn's antique shop.

Innkeeper(s): Barbara Ingraham. $85-105. MC VISA PC TC. 4 rooms, 2 with PB. Breakfast and evening snack included in rates. Types of meals: continental-plus breakfast and early coffee/tea. Afternoon tea and picnic lunch available. Beds: Q. Air conditioning, turndown service, ceiling fan and TV in room. Antiques, fishing, parks, shopping, downhill skiing, cross-country skiing, sporting events, theater and watersports nearby.

Location: Gateway to the eastern Finger Lakes.

"Everything about our stay was just perfect."

Certificate may be used: Monday through Thursday, year-round.

Hadley E12

Saratoga Rose
4274 Rockwell St
Hadley, NY 12835-0238
(518)696-2861 (800)942-5025 Fax:(518)696-5319

Circa 1885. This romantic Queen Anne Victorian offers a small, candlelit restaurant perfect for an evening for two. Breakfast specialties include Grand Marnier French toast and eggs Anthony. Rooms are

decorated in period style. The Queen Anne Room, decorated in blue, boasts a wood and tile fireplace and a quilt-covered bed. The Garden Room offers a private sunporch and an outside deck with a Jacuzzi spa. Each of the rooms features something special. Guests can take in the mountain view or relax on the veranda while sipping a cocktail.

Innkeeper(s): Nancy Merlino. $80-165. EP. MC VISA DS. 6 rooms with PB, 1 with FP. Breakfast included in rates. Types of meals: full breakfast and gourmet breakfast. Dinner, evening snack, picnic lunch, lunch, gourmet lunch, banquet service, catering service, catered breakfast and room service available. Beds: KD. Air conditioning and ceiling fan in room. Cable TV, VCR and spa on premises. Amusement parks, antiques, fishing, parks, shopping, downhill skiing, cross-country skiing, sporting events and theater nearby.

Publicity: *Getaways for Gourmets.*

"A must for the inn traveler."

Certificate may be used: November-May, Monday-Thursday, may exclude holidays, upon availability.

Hague D12

Trout House Village Resort
PO Box 510
Hague, NY 12836-0510
(518)543-6088 (800)368-6088

Circa 1934. On the shores of beautiful Lake George is this resort inn, offering accommodations in the lodge, authentic log cabins or cottages. Many of the guest rooms in the lodge boast lake views, while the log cabins offer jetted tubs and fireplaces. The guest quarters are furnished comfortably. The emphasis here is on the abundance of outdoor activities. Outstanding cross-country skiing, downhill skiing and snowmobiling are found nearby. The inn furnishes bicycles, canoes, kayaks, paddle boats, rowboats, sleds, shuffleboard, skis and toboggans. Summertime evenings offer games of capture-the-flag and soccer. Other activities include basketball, horseshoes, ping pong, a putting green and volleyball.

Innkeeper(s): Scott & Alice Patchett. $45-333. AP. MC VISA AX DS PC TC. 13 rooms, 11 with PB, 15 with FP. 1 suite. 15 cottages. 2 conference rooms. Type of meal: continental-plus breakfast. Banquet service available. Beds: QDT. TV and VCR in room. Swimming, bicycles, tennis, library and child care on premises. Handicap access. Amusement parks, antiques, fishing, parks, shopping, downhill skiing, cross-country skiing and watersports nearby.

"My wife and I felt the family warmth at this resort. There wasn't that coldness you get at larger resorts."

Certificate may be used: Sept. 15-June 1 weekdays, excluding holiday weeks.

Hamburg G3

Sharon's B&B Lake House
4862 Lake Shore Rd
Hamburg, NY 14075-5542
(716)627-7561

Circa 1935. This historic lakefront house is located 10 miles from Buffalo and 45 minutes from Niagara Falls. Overlooking Lake Erie, the West Lake Room and the Upper Lake Room provide spectacular views. The home's beautiful furnishings offer additional delights.

Innkeeper(s): Sharon & Vince Di Maria. $100-110. PC TC. 2 rooms, 1 with PB. Breakfast included in rates. Type of meal: gourmet breakfast. Afternoon tea available. Beds: D. Ceiling fan and TV in room. VCR and swimming on premises. Fishing, parks, shopping, downhill skiing, cross-country skiing, theater and watersports nearby.

Location: On the shore of Lake Erie.

"Spectacular view, exquisitely furnished."

Certificate may be used: Anytime, all year.

Hamlin
E5

Sandy Creek Manor House
1960 Redman Rd
Hamlin, NY 14464-9635
(716)964-7528 (800)594-0400

Circa 1910. Six acres of woods and perennial gardens provide the setting for this English Tudor house. Stained glass, polished woods and Amish quilts add warmth to the home. The innkeepers have placed many thoughtful amenities in each room, such as clock radios, fluffy robes, slippers and baskets of toiletries. Breakfast is served on the open porch in summer. Fisherman's Landing, on the banks of Sandy Creek, is a stroll away. Bullhead, trout and salmon are popular catches. There is a gift shop on premises. Ask about murder-mystery, sweetheart dinner and spa treatment packages.

Innkeeper(s): Shirley Hollink & James Krempasky. $50-70. MC VISA AX DS PC TC. 4 rooms, 1 with PB. Breakfast, afternoon tea and evening snack included in rates. Types of meals: continental breakfast, continental-plus breakfast, gourmet breakfast and early coffee/tea. Beds: KQDT. Air conditioning and TV in room. Antiques, fishing, parks, shopping, skiing, sporting events and watersports nearby.

Location: Four miles north of Rt 104; 25 miles northwest of Rochester; located near the Seaway Trail.

Publicity: *Rochester Times Union.*

"Delightful in every way."

Certificate may be used: Anytime.

Henderson
D8

Dobson House Bed & Breakfast
12035 County Route 123
Henderson, NY 13650-2098
(315)938-5901 (800)295-8905 Fax:(315)938-5901
E-mail: marksail@imcnet.net

Circa 1820. This historic treasure has been around longer than many of the century-old trees that dot its surrounding 26 acres. The early 18th-century home is built from limestone, which adds a bit of rustic charm to the elegant Federal-style architecture. The interior has been beautifully decorated in an elegant country style. Poster and white-iron beds are among the furnishings, and two rooms include small sitting areas. Breakfasts are sometimes served on the enclosed sun porch. The home is a mile from the harbor, which feeds into Lake Ontario. Skiing, hunting and lake activities are among the nearby attractions.

Innkeeper(s): Mark & Barbara Boyle. $65-75. MC VISA. 4 rooms, 2 with PB. Breakfast included in rates. Types of meals: full breakfast and early coffee/tea. Beds: KD. Turndown service in room. Amusement parks, antiques, fishing, parks, shopping, downhill skiing, cross-country skiing, sporting events, golf, theater and watersports nearby.

Publicity: *T.I. Guide, Seaway Trail Journey*

Certificate may be used: Sunday through Wednesday, May 1-Nov. 1.

Hudson
H12

The Inn at Blue Stores
2323 Rt 9
Hudson, NY 12534-0099
(518)537-4277

Circa 1908. A rural Hudson Valley setting may seem an unusual place for a Spanish-style inn, but this former gentlemen's farm now provides a unique setting for those seeking a relaxing getaway. Visitors will enjoy the inn's clay tile roof and stucco exterior,

along with its impressive interior, featuring black oak woodwork, leaded-glass entry and stained glass. Visitors are treated to full breakfasts and refreshing afternoon teas. The spacious porch and swimming pool are favorite spots for relaxing and socializing.

Innkeeper(s): Linda & Robert. $99-165. MC VISA. 5 rooms, 3 with PB. 1 suite. Breakfast included in rates. Types of meals: full breakfast and early coffee/tea. Afternoon tea available. Beds: KQT. Air conditioning and VCR in room. Fax and swimming on premises. Antiques, cross-country skiing, sporting events and theater nearby.

Certificate may be used: November-April, Monday-Thursday, except holidays.

Ithaca
G7

La Tourelle Country Inn
1150 Danby Rd, Rt 96b
Ithaca, NY 14850-9406
(607)273-2734 (800)765-1492 Fax:(607)273-4821

Circa 1986. This white stucco European-style country inn is located on 70 acres three miles from town, allowing for wildflower walks, cross-country skiing and all-season hiking. Adjacent Buttermilk Falls State  Park provides stone paths, waterfalls and streams. The inn is decorated with a hint of European decor and includes fireplace suites and tower suites. A continental breakfast arrives at your door in a basket, French Provincial style, and guests often tote it to the patio or gazebo to enjoy views of the rolling countryside. There is an indoor tennis court.

Innkeeper(s): Leslie Leonard. $75-125. EP. MC VISA AX TC. 34 rooms with PB, 1 with FP. 1 conference room. Breakfast included in rates. Types of meals: continental breakfast and early coffee/tea. Evening snack, banquet service and catering service available. Restaurant on premises. Beds: KQ. Air conditioning, TV and VCR in room. Copier and tennis on premises. Handicap access. Antiques, fishing, parks, shopping, skiing, sporting events, theater and watersports nearby.

Certificate may be used: Sunday through Thursday only.

Log Country Inn - B&B of Ithaca

PO Box 581
Ithaca, NY 14851-0581
(607)589-4771 (800)274-4771 Fax:(607)589-6151
E-mail: grunberg@logtv.com

Circa 1969. As the name indicates, this bed & breakfast is indeed fashioned from logs and rests in a picturesque country setting surrounded by 20 wooded acres. The cozy rooms are rustic with exposed beams and country furnishings. The decor is dotted with a European influence, as is the morning meal. Guests enjoy a full breakfast with blintzes or Russian pancakes.

Innkeeper(s): Wanda Grunberg. $45-75. MC VISA AX TC. 5 rooms, 3 with PB. 1 suite. Breakfast and afternoon tea included in rates. Type of meal: full breakfast. Beds: QDT. TV in room. VCR, fax and sauna on premises. Antiques, fishing, parks, shopping, cross-country skiing, sporting events and watersports nearby.

Certificate may be used: Jan. 15-May 1, Sunday-Thursday.

Rose Inn

Rt 34N, Box 6576
Ithaca, NY 14851-6576
(607)533-7905 Fax:(607)533-7908

Circa 1848. This classic Italianate mansion has long been famous for its circular staircase of Honduran mahogany. It is owned by Sherry Rosemann, a noted interior designer specializing in mid-19th-century architecture and furniture, and her husband Charles, a hotelier from Germany. On 20 landscaped acres, it is 10 minutes from Cornell University. The inn has been the recipient of many awards for its lodging and dining, including a four-star rating for seven years in a row.

Innkeeper(s): Charles & Sherry Rosemann. $100-275. MC VISA PC TC. 15 rooms, 10 with PB, 2 with FP. 5 suites. 1 conference room. Breakfast included in rates. Type of meal: full breakfast. Banquet service, catering service and catered breakfast available. Restaurant on premises. Beds: KQDT. Air conditioning, turndown service and ceiling fan in room. Cable TV, VCR, fax, copier and library on premises. Antiques, fishing, parks, shopping, downhill skiing, cross-country skiing, sporting events, theater and watersports nearby.

Publicity: *Country Inns, New York Times, Ithaca Times, New Woman, Toronto Globe & Mail, Newsday.*

"The blending of two outstanding talents, which when combined with your warmth, produce the ultimate experience in being away from home. Like staying with friends in their beautiful home."

Certificate may be used: Dec. 1-March 31, Sunday through Friday; April 1-Nov. 30, Monday through Thursday.

Ithaca (Spencer)

A Slice of Home B&B

178 N Main St
Ithaca (Spencer), NY 14883
(607)589-6073
E-mail: slice@lightlink.com

Circa 1850. This Italianate inn's location, approximately equidistant from Ithaca and Watkins Glen, offers a fine vantage point for exploring the Finger Lakes winery region. Although the area is well-known for its scenery, many recreational opportunities also are available. The innkeeper is happy to help guests

plan tours and has a special fondness for those traveling by bicycle. The inn offers five guest rooms, furnished in country decor. Guests may relax by taking a stroll on the inn's 10 acres, mountain hiking, biking or having a cookout in the inn's backyard. Guests can begin a cross-country ski excursion right from the back porch.

Innkeeper(s): Bea Brownell. $40-150. PC. 5 rooms with PB. 1 suite. Breakfast and evening snack included in rates. Types of meals: full breakfast and early coffee/tea. Picnic lunch available. Beds: KQD. Air conditioning and TV in room. VCR, copier and bicycles on premises. Antiques, fishing, parks, shopping, downhill skiing, cross-country skiing, sporting events, theater and watersports nearby.

Certificate may be used: All year, some weekends excepted.

Jay   C12

The Book & Blanket B&B

Rt 9N, PO Box 164
Jay, NY 12941-0164
(518)946-8323 Fax:(518)946-8323

Circa 1850. This Adirondack bed & breakfast served as the town's post office for many years and also as barracks for state troopers. Thankfully, however, it is now a restful bed & breakfast catering to the literary set. Guest rooms are named for authors and there are books in every nook and cranny of the house. Guests may even take one book home with them. Each of the guest rooms is comfortably furnished. From the inn's porch, guests can gaze at a covered bridge that crosses the nearby river.

Innkeeper(s): Kathy, Fred, Sam & Daisy the Basset Hound. $55-75. AX PC TC. 3 rooms, 1 with PB. Breakfast and evening snack included in rates. Types of meals: full breakfast and early coffee/tea. Afternoon tea available. Beds: QD. Cable TV, VCR, fax and library on premises. Antiques, fishing, shopping, skiing and watersports nearby.

Certificate may be used: Oct. 31-May 15, Sunday-Friday, excluding holidays.

Keene Valley C12

Trail's End Inn

Trail's End Rd, HC 01, Box 103
Keene Valley, NY 12943
(518)576-9860 Fax:(518)576-9235
E-mail: innkeeper@trailsendinn.com

Circa 1902. This charming mountain inn is in the heart of the Adirondack's High Peaks. Surrounded by woods and adjacent to a small pond, the inn offers spacious guest rooms with antique furnishings and country quilts. All-you-can-eat morning meals in the glassed-in breakfast room not only provide a lovely look at the countryside, but often a close-up view of various bird species. Fresh air and gorgeous views abound, and visitors enjoy invigorating hikes, trout fishing and fine cross-country skiing. Downhill skiers will love the challenge of nearby White Mountain, with the longest vertical drop in the East.
Innkeeper(s): Frank & Karen Kovacik. $49-125. MC VISA AX DS PC TC. 10 rooms, 3 with PB, 3 with FP. 2 suites. 1 cabin. Breakfast included in rates. Types of meals: full breakfast and early coffee/tea. Picnic lunch and catering service available. Beds: KQDT. Cable TV, VCR, fax, copier, library and child care on premises. Antiques, fishing, parks, shopping, downhill skiing, cross-country skiing, golf and watersports nearby.
Publicity: *Outside, Mid-Atlantic, Lake Placid News.*

"Thank you for a lovely stay."

Certificate may be used: Sunday through Thursday in April, May 1-15, June 1-15, Nov. 1-15 and Dec. 1-15, excluding holiday periods.

Lake Placid C12

Interlaken Inn

15 Interlaken Ave
Lake Placid, NY 12946-1142
(518)523-3180 (800)428-4369 Fax:(518)523-0117
Circa 1906. The five-course dinner at this Victorian inn is prepared by innkeeper Carol Johnson and her talented staff. The high-quality cuisine is rivaled only by the rich decor of this cozy inn. Walnut paneling covers the dining room walls, which are topped with a tin ceiling. Bedrooms are carefully decorated with wallpapers, fresh flowers and luxurious bed coverings. Spend the afternoon

gazing at the mountains and lakes that surround this Adirondack hideaway, or visit the Olympic venues.
Innkeeper(s): Carol & Roy Johnson. $120-180. MAP. MC VISA AX. 11 rooms with PB. 1 suite. Breakfast, afternoon tea and dinner included in rates. Types of meals: full breakfast and early coffee/tea. Restaurant on premises. Beds: KQD. Ceiling fan in room. Cable TV, VCR and fax on premises. Antiques, fishing, shopping, downhill skiing, cross-country skiing, sporting events, theater and watersports nearby.
Location: Quaint Olympic village.
Publicity: *Outside, Country Inns, Wine Trader.*
Certificate may be used: Jan. 1-June 31, Sunday to Thursday, Nov. 1-Dec. 23, anytime.

Lansing

The Federal House B&B

175 Ludlowville Rd
Lansing, NY 14882
(607)533-7362 (800)533-7362 Fax:(607)533-7899
Circa 1815. Salmon Creek Falls, a well-known fishing spot, is yards away from the inn. The rooms are furnished with antiques, which complement the original woodwork and hand-carved fireplace mantels. Each of the suites includes a television and a fireplace.
Innkeeper(s): Diane Carroll. $55-175. MC VISA AX DS PC TC. 4 rooms with PB, 2 with FP. 2 suites. Breakfast included in rates. Beds: KQDT. Air conditioning in room. Antiques, fishing, downhill skiing, cross-country skiing, theater and watersports nearby.
Publicity: *Ithaca Journal, Cortland Paper.*

"Your inn is so charming and your food was excellent."

Certificate may be used: Monday-Thursday, April & May, September & November.

Lewiston F3

The Cameo Inn

4710 Lower River Rd
Lewiston, NY 14092-1053
(716)745-3034
Circa 1875. This classic Queen Anne Victorian inn offers a breathtaking view of the lower Niagara River. Located on the Seaway Trail, the inn offers convenient access to sightseeing in this popular region. The inn's interior features family heirlooms and period antiques, and visitors choose from four guest rooms, including a three-room suite overlooking the river. Breakfast is served buffet-style, and the entrees, which change daily, may include German oven pancakes or Grand Marnier French toast. Area attractions include Old Fort Niagara, outlet malls and several state parks.
Innkeeper(s): Gregory Fisher. $65-115. 4 rooms, 2 with PB. 1 suite. Breakfast included in rates. Type of meal: full breakfast. Beds: QDT. Ceiling fan and TV in room. Amusement parks, antiques, fishing, shopping, skiing, sporting events, theater and watersports nearby.
Location: Five miles north of Niagara Falls.

Publicity: *Country Folk Art, Esquire, Journey, Seaway Trail, Waterways, Buffalo News.*

"I made the right choice when I selected Cameo."

Certificate may be used: Anytime Nov. 15-April 30; Sunday through Thursday May 1-Nov. 14. Holidays and special event periods excluded. All subject to availability.

The Little Blue House B&B
115 Center St
Lewiston, NY 14092-1537
(716)754-9425

Circa 1906. Located in the heart of the village's main street, this Colonial inn offers charming accommodations and convenient access to area activities. Three unique guest rooms are available, including a Chinese-themed room with a king bed and a Victorian-style room with a queen bed. The inn's decor includes antiques, collectibles and contemporary art. Ten minutes away are the American and Canadian Falls.

Innkeeper(s): Michael & Margot Kornfeld. $65-175. AX PC TC. 3 rooms, 1 with PB. 1 suite. Breakfast included in rates. Types of meals: continental-plus breakfast and gourmet breakfast. Beds: KQ. Air conditioning, ceiling fan and TV in room. VCR on premises. Amusement parks, antiques, fishing, parks, shopping, cross-country skiing, sporting events and theater nearby.

Certificate may be used: May through October-Sunday through Wednesday. November through April-seven days per week. Holidays and special events excluded.

Margaretville   H10

Margaretville Mountain Inn B&B
Margaretville Mountain Rd
Margaretville, NY 12455-9735
(914)586-3933

Circa 1886. Reminiscent of the Victorian era, this home rests on the site of the nation's first cauliflower farm. The owners have restored the slate roof, elaborate exterior woodwork and decorative interior woodwork. A full breakfast is served in the formal dining room on English china, or guests can enjoy the morning meal on the veranda, which overlooks the Catskill Mountains. The surrounding area offers a variety of activities including antique shopping, ice skating, golf, tennis, swimming, boating, fishing and hiking. The innkeepers offer ski packages.

Innkeeper(s): Carol Molnar. $50-85. MC VISA AX. 7 rooms, 4 with PB. Breakfast included in rates. Type of meal: gourmet breakfast. Beds: KQDT. Fax and computer on premises. Downhill skiing nearby.

Location: In the Catskill Mountains.

Publicity: *Spotlight, NY Wedding.*

"Truly a step back in time to all that was charming, elegant and wholesome—right here in the 20th century."

Certificate may be used: Sunday-Thursday, non-holidays. Weekends only in March and April.

Mumford   F5

Genesee Country Inn
948 George St
Mumford, NY 14511-0340
(716)538-2500 (800)697-8297 Fax:(716)538-4565

Circa 1833. This stone house with two-and-a-half-foot-thick limestone walls served as a plaster mill and later as a hub and wheel factory. Now, it is an inn set on six acres with views of streams, woodlands and ponds. There is a deck adjacent to a 16-foot waterfall. Ask for a garden room and enjoy a fireplace and your own balcony overlooking the mill ponds.

Innkeeper(s): Kim Rasmussen. $85-130. MC VISA DC DS. 9 rooms with PB, 3 with FP. Breakfast and afternoon tea included in rates. Type of meal: full breakfast. Beds: Q. Air conditioning in room. Fax and copier on premises. Amusement parks, antiques, parks, downhill skiing and watersports nearby.

"You may never want to leave."

Certificate may be used: Dec. 1-April 1, no holidays. No fireplace rooms eligible.

Niagara Falls   F3

The Cameo Manor North
3881 Lower River Rd
Niagara Falls, NY 14174
(716)745-3034

Circa 1860. This Colonial Revival inn offers a restful setting ideal for those seeking a peaceful getaway. The inn's three secluded acres add to its romantic setting, as does an interior that features several fireplaces. Visitors select from three suites, which feature private sun rooms, or two guest rooms that share a bath. Popular spots with guests include the library, outdoor deck and solarium. Fort Niagara and Wilson-Tuscarora state parks are nearby, and the American and Canadian Falls are within easy driving distance of the inn. The inn is actually located about six miles from Niagara Falls in the nearby village of Youngstown.

Innkeeper(s): Gregory Fisher. $75-175. 4 rooms. Breakfast included in rates. Type of meal: full breakfast.

Publicity: *Country Folk Art, Esquire, Journey, Seaway Trail, Waterways, Buffalo News.*

"I made the right choice when I selected Cameo."

Certificate may be used: Anytime Nov. 15-April 30, Sunday-Thursday; May 1-Nov. 14, holidays and special event periods excluded. All subject to availability.

Penn Yan   G6

The Wagener Estate B&B
351 Elm St
Penn Yan, NY 14527-1446
(315)536-4591

Circa 1794. Nestled in the Finger Lakes area on four shaded acres, this 16-room house features a wicker-furnished veranda where guests can relax in solitude or chat with others. Some of the early

hand-hewn framing and the original brick fireplace and oven can be seen in the Family Room at the north end of the house. Most of the land, which is known as Penn Yan, was once owned by the original occupants of the home, David Wagener and his wife, Rebecca. David died in 1799, leaving this property to his son, Squire Wagener, who is considered to be the founder of Penn Yan. Antiques, fishing, cross-country skiing, water sports and wineries nearby.

Innkeeper(s): Joanne & Scott Murray. $65-80. MC VISA AX DS. 6 rooms, 4 with PB. Breakfast included in rates. Type of meal: full breakfast. Beds: KQDT. Antiques, fishing, cross-country skiing and watersports nearby.

Publicity: *Finger Lakes Times, Chronicle Express, New York Times*

"Thanks so much for the wonderful hospitality and the magnificent culinary treats."

Certificate may be used: December through April, excluding holidays.

Queensbury   E12

The Crislip's B&B
693 Ridge Rd
Queensbury, NY 12804-6901
(518)793-6869

Circa 1802. This Federal-style house was built by Quakers and was once owned by the area's first doctor, who used it as a training center for young interns. There's an acre of lawns and annual gardens and a Victorian Italianate veranda overlooks the Green Mountains. The inn is furnished with 18th-century antiques and reproductions, including four-poster canopy beds and highboys. There's a keeping room with a huge fireplace. Historic stone walls flank the property.

Innkeeper(s): Ned & Joyce Crislip. $45-75. MC VISA TC. 3 rooms with PB. Breakfast included in rates. Types of meals: full breakfast and early coffee/tea. Beds: KD. Air conditioning in room. Cable TV on premises. Amusement parks, antiques, fishing, parks, shopping, downhill skiing, cross-country skiing, sporting events, theater and watersports nearby.

Location: Lake George, Saratoga area.

Certificate may be used: November through May, Sunday-Thursday.

Sanford's Ridge B&B
749 Ridge Rd
Queensbury, NY 12804-6903
(518)793-4923

Circa 1797. Visitors to the Adirondacks will find a bit of history and more than a little hospitality at this Federal-style inn, built by David Sanford after the Revolutionary War. The inn has retained its original elegance and added a few modern touches, such as an in-ground swimming pool and a sunny outdoor deck. Visitors select from the Haviland, Sanford and Webster rooms, all with private baths. Each room is

decorated in Colonial style with quilt-covered poster beds and antique furnishings. The full breakfasts include a special entree of the day and fruit grown on the premises. Lake George is a short drive away.

Innkeeper(s): Carolyn Rudolph. $65-95. MC VISA PC TC. 3 rooms with PB, 2 with FP. Breakfast included in rates. Type of meal: full breakfast. Beds: KQT. Air conditioning in room. Cable TV, swimming and library on premises. Amusement parks, antiques, fishing, parks, shopping, downhill skiing, cross-country skiing, theater and watersports nearby.

Certificate may be used: November-April 7, except holiday weekends or holiday periods. Any day of week or weekend.

Rhinebeck   I12

Mansakenning Carriage House
29 Ackert Hook Rd
Rhinebeck, NY 12572
(914)876-3500 Fax:(914)876-6179
E-mail: ajpease@sprynetm9.com

Circa 1895. Guests are sure to find this National Register Colonial a perfect country inn. Take a walk along the five acres, and you'll find hammocks strung between trees and chairs placed here and there for guests who wish to relax and enjoy the fragrant grounds. Step into any one of the seven guest rooms, and you'll instantly feel as though you've entered a cozy, romantic haven. Ralph Lauren linens dress the beds, which are topped with fluffy comforters. Exposed beams, fireplaces, wood floors and quilts add to the decor of the individually appointed guest rooms. Guests will find robes, specialty bath soaps, a coffee maker, refrigerator and a TV with VCR in their rooms. Innkeeper Michelle Dremann has had several recipes featured in cookbooks, and it is she who prepares the decadent morning feast. Rhinebeck is full of historic houses and buildings, as well guests can visit antique shops, galleries, wineries and restaurants.

Innkeeper(s): Michelle & John Dremann-Pease. $125-350. PC TC. 7 rooms with PB, 5 with FP. 5 suites. Breakfast included in rates. Type of meal: gourmet breakfast. Room service available. Beds: KQ. Air conditioning, ceiling fan, TV and VCR in room. Fax, copier and library on premises. Fishing, parks, shopping, downhill skiing, cross-country skiing, sporting events, golf, theater and watersports nearby.

Publicity: *New York Times, Bride's, Hudson Valley Magazine, New York Post, Poughkeepsie Journal, Wingspan, Time Out Magazine.*

Certificate may be used: January-June, weekdays.

Rochester F5

"428 Mt. Vernon" - A B&B Inn

428 Mount Vernon Ave
Rochester, NY 14620-2710
(716)271-0792 (800)836-3159

Circa 1917. Victorian furnishings and decor grace the interior of this stately Irish manor house. Set on two lush acres of shade trees and foliage, this secluded spot is perfect for guests in search of relaxation. Guests can create their morning meals from a varied breakfast menu. The inn is adjacent to Highland Park, a perfect spot for a picnic or birdwatching.

Innkeeper(s): Philip & Claire Lanzatella. $99. MC VISA AX TC. 7 rooms with PB, 3 with FP. 1 conference room. Breakfast included in rates. Types of meals: full breakfast, gourmet breakfast and early coffee/tea. Catering service and room service available. Beds: QDT. Air conditioning, turndown service, ceiling fan and TV in room. Amusement parks, antiques, parks, shopping, cross-country skiing and theater nearby.

"Everything was wonderful, they took care in every detail."

Certificate may be used: Jan. 15-April 1-Sunday-Thursday.

Dartmouth House B&B

215 Dartmouth St
Rochester, NY 14607-3202
(716)271-7872 Fax:(716)473-0778

Circa 1905. The lavish, four-course breakfasts served daily at this beautiful turn-of-the-century Edwardian home are unforgettable. Innkeeper and award-winning, gourmet cook Ellie Klein starts off the meal with special fresh juice, which is served in the parlor. From this point, guests are seated at the candlelit dining table to enjoy a series of delectable dishes, such as pears poached in port wine, a mouth-watering entree, a light, lemon ice and a rich dessert. And each of the courses is served on a separate pattern of Depression glass. If the breakfast isn't enough, Ellie and husband, Bill, have stocked the individually decorated guest rooms with flowers, fluffy towels, bathrobes and special bath amenities. Each of the bedchambers boasts antique collectibles, and guests can soak in inviting clawfoot tubs. Museums, colleges, restaurants and antique shops are among the many nearby attractions.

Innkeeper(s): Elinor & Bill Klein. $65-125. MC VISA AX DS PC TC. 4 rooms with PB. Breakfast included in rates. Types of meals: full breakfast and early coffee/tea. Beds: KQT. Air conditioning and ceiling fan in room. Cable TV, VCR, fax, bicycles and library on premises. Antiques, parks, shopping, theater and watersports nearby.

Publicity: *Democrat & Chronicle, DAKA, Genesee Country, Seaway Trail, Oneida News, Travelers News, Country Living.*

"The food was fabulous, the company fascinating, and the personal attention beyond comparison. You made me feel at home instantly."

Certificate may be used: Jan. 1-April 1, Monday through Thursday, excluding holidays and special events.

Strawberry Castle B&B

1883 Penfield Rd, Rt 441
Rochester, NY 14526
(716)385-3266

Circa 1875. A rosy brick Italianate villa, Strawberry Castle was once known for the grapes and strawberries grown on the property. Ornate plaster ceilings and original inside shutters are special features. There are six roof levels, carved ornamental brackets, and columned porches topped by a white cupola.

Innkeeper(s): Anne Felker. $60-95. MC VISA AX. 3 rooms with PB. 1 suite. 1 conference room. Breakfast included in rates. Type of meal: full breakfast. Beds: D. Air conditioning in room. Cable TV on premises. Amusement parks, antiques, fishing, shopping, downhill skiing, sporting events and theater nearby.

Location: East of Rochester on Route 441.
Publicity: *Upstate Magazine.*

"You have a most unusual place. We applaud your restoration efforts and are thankful you've made it available to travelers."

Certificate may be used: Sunday-Thursday, November through April.

Saratoga Springs   *F12*

Six Sisters B&B

149 Union Ave
Saratoga Springs, NY 12866-3518
(518)583-1173 Fax:(518)587-2470

Circa 1880. The unique architecture of this Victorian home features a large second-story bay window, a tiger oak front door decked with stained glass and a veranda accentuated with rocking chairs. Inside, the marble and hardwoods combine with antiques and Oriental rugs to create an elegant atmosphere. During racing season, guests can rise early and take a short walk to the local race track to watch the horses work out. Upon their return, guests are greeted with the aroma of a delicious, gourmet breakfast. Saratoga Springs' downtown area offers antique shops, boutiques and many restaurants.

Innkeeper(s): Kate Benton. $70-275. MC VISA AX DS PC TC. 4 rooms with PB. Breakfast included in rates. Types of meals: gourmet breakfast and early coffee/tea. Beds: KQ. Air conditioning, ceiling fan and TV in room. Fax on premises. Amusement parks, antiques, fishing, parks, shopping, skiing, sporting events, theater and watersports nearby.
Location: Thirty minutes north of Albany and thirty minutes south of Lake George.
Publicity: *Gourmet, Country Inns, Country Folk Art, Country Victorian, McCalls.*

"*The true definition of a bed & breakfast.*"
Certificate may be used: Sunday-Thursday except July, August and special events.

Westchester House B&B

102 Lincoln Ave
Saratoga Springs, NY 12866-4536
(518)587-7613 (800)581-7613

Circa 1885. This gracious Queen Anne Victorian has been welcoming vacationers for more than 100 years. Antiques from four generations of the Melvin's family grace the high-ceilinged rooms. Oriental rugs top gleaming wood floors, while antique clocks and lace curtains set a graceful tone. Guests gather on the wraparound porch, in the parlors or gardens for an afternoon refreshment of old-fashioned lemonade. Racing season rates are quoted separately.

Innkeeper(s): Bob & Stephanie Melvin. $90-250. MC VISA AX CB PC TC. 7 rooms with PB. 1 conference room. Breakfast and afternoon tea included in rates. Types of meals: continental-plus breakfast and early coffee/tea. Beds: KQT. Air conditioning and ceiling fan in room. Library on premises. Antiques, fishing, parks, shopping, cross-country skiing,

sporting events, theater and watersports nearby.
Location: Thirty miles north of Albany in the Adirondack foothills.
Publicity: *Getaways for Gourmets, Albany Times Union, Saratogian, Capital, Country Inns, New York Daily News, WNYT, Newsday, Hudson Valley.*

"*I adored your B&B and have raved about it to all. One of the most beautiful and welcoming places we've ever visited.*"
Certificate may be used: Sunday-Thursday, April-June 15, September, November, excluding holiday weekends.

Severance   *D12*

The Red House

PO Box 125
Severance, NY 12872-0125
(518)532-7734

Circa 1850. Twenty feet from the banks of Paradox Brook, on the West end of Paradox Lake, is this two-story farmhouse inn that boasts a multitude of recreational offerings for its guests, including swimming, tennis, boating and fishing. The inn features three guest rooms, one with private bath. The inn's full breakfasts include homemade breads and regional specialties. Be sure to plan a day trip to Fort Ticonderoga and ride the ferry across Lake Champlain to Vermont. Hiking and cross-country skiing are available within five miles of the inn.

Innkeeper(s): Helen Wildman. $55-85. PC. 3 rooms, 1 with PB. Breakfast included in rates. Type of meal: full breakfast. Beds: QDT. Swimming, tennis and library on premises. Antiques, fishing, parks, shopping, downhill skiing and cross-country skiing nearby.

"*Thanks for your wonderful hospitality.*"
Certificate may be used: Sunday through Thursday.

Sharon Springs   G11

Edgefield
Washington St, PO Box 152
Sharon Springs, NY 13459
(518)284-3339

Circa 1865. This home has seen many changes. It began as a farmhouse, a wing was added in the 1880s, and by the turn of the century, it sported an elegant Greek Revival facade. Edgefield is one of a collection of nearby homes used as a family compound for summer vacations. The rooms are decorated with traditional furnishings in a formal English-country style. In the English tradition, an afternoon tea is presented each day with scones, cookies and tea sandwiches. Sharon Springs includes many historic sites, and the town is listed in the National Register. Cooperstown and Albany are within 45 minutes of the home.
Innkeeper(s): Daniel Marshall Wood. $95-125. PC TC. 5 rooms with PB. Breakfast, afternoon tea and evening snack included in rates. Types of meals: full breakfast, gourmet breakfast and early coffee/tea. Beds: QT. Turndown service and ceiling fan in room. Cable TV, VCR and library on premises. Antiques, fishing, parks, shopping, golf, theater and watersports nearby.

"Truly what I always imagined the perfect B&B experience to be!"

Certificate may be used: Oct. 20-May 31, Sunday-Thursday.

Sodus Point   E6

Carriage House Inn
8375 Wickham Blvd
Sodus Point, NY 14555-9608
(315)483-2100 (800)292-2990

Circa 1870. The innkeeper at this inn offers accommodations in a historic Victorian home located on four acres in a residential area or in the stone carriage house on the shore of Lake Ontario. The carriage house overlooks the Sodus Point historic lighthouse. The inn offers beach access, and guests can walk to restaurants and charter boats.
Innkeeper(s): James Den Decker. $65. MC VISA. 8 rooms with PB. Breakfast and picnic lunch included in rates. Type of meal: full breakfast. Beds: KT. Antiques, fishing, golf and watersports nearby.
Publicity: *Finger Lakes Times, Democrat and Chronicle, WTVH.*

"My wife and I have been telling everyone about the beautiful room we had and your courtesy."

Certificate may be used: Dec. 1 through April 15.

Southold   K15

Goose Creek Guesthouse
1475 Waterview Dr, PO Box 377
Southold, NY 11971-2125
(516)765-3356

Circa 1860. Grover Pease left for the Civil War from this house, and after his death, his widow, Harriet, ran a summer boarding house here. The basement actually dates from the 1780s and is constructed of large rocks. The present house was moved here and put on the older foundation. Southold has

many historic homes and a guidebook is provided for visitors. The inn is close to the ferry to New London and the ferries to the South Shore via Shelter Island.
Innkeeper(s): Mary Mooney-Getoff. $55-85. PC TC. 4 rooms. Breakfast and afternoon tea included in rates. Types of meals: full breakfast, gourmet breakfast and early coffee/tea. Picnic lunch available. Beds: KQDT. Air conditioning in room. VCR and library on premises. Amusement parks, antiques, fishing, parks, shopping, theater and watersports nearby.
Location: One-and-one-half miles south of Rt 25 on the north fork of Long Island.
Publicity: *New York Times, Newsday.*

"We will be repeat guests. Count on it!!"

Certificate may be used: Anytime, subject to availability.

Springville   G3

The Franklin House
432 Franklin St
Springville, NY 14141-1130
(716)592-7877 Fax:(716)592-5388

Circa 1843. Once the home of a well-known area chicken farm, this Queen Anne Victorian inn now serves visitors to attraction-rich Western New York. An easy getaway from Buffalo, the inn offers three guest rooms, including a suite. Visitors will enjoy cross-country skiing on the inn's five acres or hot tubbing in the Hawaiian Room. An award-winning, homemade country-style breakfast is served before guests set out for their day's activities. Guests can hit the slopes at the Kissing Bridge Ski Area or visit Letchworth State Park, the Grand Canyon of the East.
Innkeeper(s): Paulette Timm. $60-110. MC VISA AX. 4 rooms. Breakfast included in rates. Types of meals: full breakfast and early cof-

fee/tea. Evening snack available. Air conditioning, turndown service, ceiling fan, TV and VCR in room. Antiques, shopping, downhill skiing, cross-country skiing and sporting events nearby.

Certificate may be used: Sunday-Thursday.

Stanfordville
I12

Lakehouse Inn on Golden Pond
Shelley Hill Rd
Stanfordville, NY 12581
(914)266-8093 (800)726-3323 Fax:(914)266-4051
Circa 1990. Romance abounds at this secluded contemporary home, which is surrounded by breathtaking vistas of woods and Golden Pond. Rest beneath a canopy flanked by lacy curtains as you gaze out the window. Enjoy a long, relaxing bath, or take a stroll around the 22-acre grounds. Each guest room includes a fireplace and whirlpool tub, and most include decks. The decor is a mix with a hint of Victorian, some Asian influences and modern touches that highlight the oak floors and vaulted pine ceilings. The innkeepers start off the day with a gourmet breakfast delivered to your room in a covered basket. Historic mansions and wineries are among the nearby attractions.
Innkeeper(s): Judy & Rich Kohler. $125-475. MC VISA PC. 9 rooms with PB, 7 with FP. 7 suites. 1 cottage. 1 conference room. Breakfast included in rates. Beds: KQ. Air conditioning, ceiling fan and VCR in room. Fax, copier and swimming on premises. Antiques, fishing, parks, shopping, cross-country skiing, sporting events, theater and watersports nearby.
Location: Ninety miles north of New York City.
Publicity: *Newsday, New York Post.*
Certificate may be used: Monday, Tuesday, Wednesday, excluding holidays.

Tannersville
H11

Kennedy House
PO Box 770
Tannersville, NY 12485-0770
(518)589-6082
Circa 1890. The Kennedy House was built in the 1920s as a temporary Red Cross hospital serving those scattered among the Catskill Mountains. Since 1987, the home has welcomed bed & breakfast guests who come for the comfortable surroundings and beautiful views of Cortina Valley, Rip Van Winkle Lake and the Hunter Mountain ski areas. Rooms afford wonderful views and are decorated with antiques. The innkeepers operated an antique and gift shop on the premises. The Catskills, a popular resort area since the early 19th century, offers a bounty of activities with each season.
Innkeeper(s): Donna Kennedy. $50-90. PC. 6 rooms, 4 with PB. Breakfast included in rates. Type of meal: continental-plus breakfast. Beds: QT. Ceiling fan in room. Cable TV and VCR on premises. Antiques, fishing, parks, shopping, skiing nearby.
Certificate may be used: Midweek, non-holiday.

Ulster Park
I12

Rennie's B&B
25 Ulster Ave
Ulster Park, NY 12487-5202
(914)331-5560 (800)447-8262 Fax:(914)298-2857
E-mail: renniesbb@aol.com
Circa 1928. From mail order, good things often come. This home, built from a kit purchased out of a Gordon-Van Tine catalog, was owned by the same family for 60 years, until the innkeepers purchased the home and transformed it into a bed & breakfast. The decor is light and airy with Arts & Crafts and Mission-style furnishings and Oriental rugs. Local produce and farm-fresh eggs fill the breakfast table, along with items such as homemade muffins, fresh fruit and crepes. The grounds, stretching out over more than two acres, include an apple orchard. Ulster Park is near many attractions, from historic sites to antique shops to hiking trails.
Innkeeper(s): Adele & Jonathan Wagman. $80-105. PC TC. 4 rooms with PB. Breakfast included in rates. Types of meals: full breakfast and early coffee/tea. Beds: QT. TV in room. Antiques, fishing, parks, shopping, cross-country skiing, golf and watersports nearby.
Publicity: *Ulster County News*

"Good food and good sleep. A place to stay longer!"

Certificate may be used: Nov. 1-April 30, Sunday through Thursday.

Victor
F5

Golden Rule B&B
6934 Rice Rd
Victor, NY 14564-9355
(716)924-0610
Circa 1865. Although the exterior of this bed & breakfast might invoke images of children trudging to school for a day of reading, writing and arithmetic, the interior is nothing short of elegant. The building still maintains its original sign and red front door. The original school bell is still housed in the belfry. But, inside, hardwood floors are covered with oriental rugs and elegant furnishings. Stenciled walls grace the bedrooms filled with antiques. One guest room boasts a canopied bed, and both include ceiling fans. The gourmet breakfasts are served by candlelight.
Innkeeper(s): Richard de Maurias. $55-80. PC. 2 rooms. Breakfast included in rates. Types of meals: continental-plus breakfast, gourmet breakfast and early coffee/tea. Afternoon tea available. Beds: QD. Air conditioning, turndown service and ceiling fan in room. Cable TV, VCR, fax and swimming on premises. Antiques, parks, shopping, downhill skiing and cross-country skiing nearby.

Certificate may be used: Weekdays, May to October; anytime, November to April.

Warrensburg   *E12*

Country Road Lodge B&B

HC 1 Box 227 Hickory Hill Rd
Warrensburg, NY 12885-9732
(518)623-2207 Fax:(518)623-4363
E-mail: parisibb@mail.netheaven.com

Circa 1929. This simple, rustic farmhouse lodge is situated on 35 acres along the Hudson River at the end of a country road. Rooms are clean and comfortable.

 A full breakfast is provided with homemade breads and muffins. The sitting room reveals panoramic views of the river and Sugarloaf Mountain.

Bird watching, hiking and skiing are popular activities. Groups often reserve all four guest rooms.

Innkeeper(s): Sandi & Steve Parisi. $55-58. PC. 4 rooms, 2 with PB. Breakfast included in rates. Types of meals: full breakfast and early coffee/tea. Beds: DT. Ceiling fan in room. Library on premises. Amusement parks, antiques, fishing, parks, skiing, theater, watersports nearby.

Location: Adirondack Mountains near Lake George.

Publicity: *North Jersey Herald & News.*

"Homey, casual atmosphere. We really had a wonderful time. You're both wonderful hosts and the Lodge is definitely our kind of B&B! We will always feel very special about this place and will always be back."

Certificate may be used: Year-round excluding January and February winter weekend packages.

House on The Hill B&B

Rt 28 Box 248
Warrensburg, NY 12885
(518)623-9390 (800)221-9390 Fax:(518)623-9396

Circa 1750. This historic Federal-style inn on a hill in the six million-acre Adirondack Park offers five guest rooms. After guests are treated to coffee and baked goods in their rooms, they enjoy the inn's full breakfasts in the sunroom, which offers wonderful views of the surrounding fields and woods from its many windows. Cross-country skiing, snowshoeing, biking and hiking may be enjoyed on the spacious grounds, covering 176 acres. Gore Mountain and Whiteface Olympic ski areas are close and Lake George is a 10-minute drive.

Innkeeper(s): Joe & Lynn Rubino. $99-149. MC VISA AX DC CB DS PC TC. 4 rooms, 3 with PB. Breakfast included in rates. Types of meals: continental breakfast, full breakfast and early coffee/tea. Beds: KQD. Air conditioning in room. Cable TV, VCR, fax and copier on premises. Handicap access. Amusement parks, antiques, fishing, parks, shopping, skiing, sporting events, theater and watersports nearby.

Publicity: *Chronicle, Post Star, G.F. Business Journal, Country Victorian.*

Certificate may be used: Sunday through Thursday, all year, subject to availability.

The Merrill Magee House

2 Hudson St PO Box 391
Warrensburg, NY 12885-0391
(518)623-2449

Circa 1839. This stately Greek Revival home offers beautiful antique fireplaces in every guest room. The Sage, Rosemary, Thyme and Coriander rooms feature sitting areas, and a family suite includes two bed-

rooms, a sitting room with a television, refrigerator and a bathroom with a clawfoot tub. The decor is romantic and distinctly Victorian. Romantic getaway packages include candlelight dinners. The local area hosts art and craft festivals, an antique car show, white-water rafting and Gore Mountain Oktoberfest. Tour the Adirondacks from the sky during September's balloon festival or browse through the world's largest garage sale in early October.

Innkeeper(s): Ken & Florence Carrington. $105-125. MAP. EP. MC VISA AX DS TC. 10 rooms with PB, 10 with FP. 1 cottage. 2 conference rooms. Breakfast included in rates. Types of meals: full breakfast and early coffee/tea. Dinner, lunch and banquet service available. Restaurant on premises. Beds: KQDT. Air conditioning and turndown service in room. Cable TV, spa, swimming and library on premises. Handicap access. Amusement parks, antiques, fishing, parks, shopping, skiing, sporting events, theater and watersports nearby.

Location: In Adirondack State Park.

"A really classy and friendly operation—a real joy."

Certificate may be used: Sunday through Thursday, non-holiday or special events.

Waterville   *F9*

B&B of Waterville

211 White St
Waterville, NY 13480-1149
(315)841-8295

Circa 1871. This two-story Victorian is in the Waterville Historic Triangle District, one block from Rt. 12 and 20 minutes away from Hamilton College and Colgate University. The hostess is an avid quilt maker and the house is filled with her handiwork. La Petite Maison, a fine French restaurant, is a few steps away. Thirty-five antique shops are within 10 miles.

Innkeeper(s): Stanley & Carol Sambora. $45-55. MC VISA PC TC. 3 rooms, 1 with PB. Breakfast included in rates. Type of meal: full breakfast. Beds: DT. Air conditioning in room. TV and VCR on premises. Amusement parks, antiques, fishing, parks, cross-country skiing nearby.

Location: Near Utica.

Publicity: *Observer Dispatch.*

"Don't change a thing ever. As a hopeless romantic, I felt that your B&B was just what we needed. We have come away renewed and refreshed. It's so lovely here, love to stay forever!"

Certificate may be used: As available, all year.

Westfield   H2

Westfield House
E Main Rd, PO Box 505, Rt 20
Westfield, NY 14787
(716)326-6262

Circa 1840. This brick home was built as a homestead on a large property of farmland and vineyards. The next owner constructed the impressive Greek Revival addition. The home also served guests as a tea room and later as a family-style eatery. Guests will enjoy the elegance of the past, which has been wonderfully preserved at Westfield House. Breakfasts are served on fine china and silver in the home's formal dining room. Wintertime guests enjoy their morning meal in front of a warm fire. Each of the rooms offers something special. The Ruth Thomas Room offers a four-poster bed, high ceilings, antique quilts and a fireplace, while the Rowan Place boasts beautiful furnishings and Gothic crystal windows that look out to maple trees.

Innkeeper(s): Betty & Jud Wilson. $60-85. MC VISA PC TC. 7 rooms, 6 with PB, 1 with FP. 1 suite. 2 conference rooms. Breakfast included in rates. Types of meals: full breakfast and early coffee/tea. Beds: KQD. Air conditioning and ceiling fan in room. Cable TV and VCR on premises. Handicap access. Antiques, fishing, parks, downhill skiing, cross-country skiing, golf, theater and watersports nearby.

Location: Southwestern New York state.

Publicity: *Canadian Leisure Ways, Seaway Trail.*

"Your accommodations and hospitality are wonderful! Simply outstanding. The living room changes its character by the hour."

Certificate may be used: Anytime all year (except July, August and October) when rooms are available.

The William Seward Inn
6645 S Portage Rd
Westfield, NY 14787-9602
(716)326-4151 (800)338-4151 Fax:(716)326-4163

Circa 1821. This two-story Greek Revival estate stands on a knoll overlooking Lake Erie. Seward was a Holland Land Company agent before becoming governor of New York. He later served as Lincoln's Secretary of State and is known for the Alaska Purchase. George Patterson bought Seward's home and also became governor of New York. Most of the mansion's furnishings are dated 1790 to 1870 from the Sheraton-Victorian period.

Innkeeper(s): James & Debbie Dahlberg. $85-165. MC VISA DS. 14 rooms with PB, 1 with FP. Breakfast included in rates. Type of meal: full breakfast. Beds: KQD. Air conditioning in room. Cable TV, fax and library on premises. Handicap access. Amusement parks, antiques, fishing, parks, shopping, downhill skiing, cross-country skiing and watersports nearby.

Location: Three hours from Cleveland, Pittsburgh and Toronto.

Publicity: *Intelligencer, Evening Observer, New York-Pennsylvania Collector, New York Times, Pittsburgh Post-Gazette, Toronto Globe & Mail.*

"The breakfasts are delicious. The solitude and your hospitality are what the doctor ordered."

Certificate may be used: Anytime, except Friday-Saturday, June 20 through October, some holiday weekends.

Wilmington   C12

Willkommen Hof
Rt 86, PO Box 240
Wilmington, NY 12997
(518)946-7669 (800)541-9119 Fax:(518)946-7626
E-mail: nybandb@aol.com

Circa 1925. This turn-of-the-century farmhouse served as an inn during the 1920s, but little else is known about its past. The innkeepers have created a cozy atmosphere, perfect for relaxation after a day exploring the Adirondack Mountain area. A large selection of books and a roaring fire greet guests who choose to settle down in the reading room. The innkeepers also offer a large selection of movies. Relax in the sauna or outdoor spa or simply enjoy the comfort of your bedchamber.

Innkeeper(s): Heike & Bert Yost. $30-105. MAP. MC VISA PC TC. 8 rooms, 3 with PB. 1 suite. Breakfast and afternoon tea included in rates. Type of meal: full breakfast. Restaurant on premises. Beds: KQDT. Ceiling fan in room. VCR, fax, spa, sauna, bicycles and pet boarding on premises. Antiques, fishing, parks, shopping, downhill skiing, cross-country skiing and watersports nearby.

"Vielen Dank! Alles war sehr schoen and the breakfasts were delicious."

Certificate may be used: Midweek, non-holiday, year-round.

Windham   H11

Albergo Allegria B&B
Rt 296, PO Box 267
Windham, NY 12496-0267
(518)734-5560 (800)625-2374 Fax:(518)734-5570

Circa 1876. Two former boarding houses were joined to create this luxurious, Victorian bed & breakfast whose name means "the inn of happiness." Guest quarters, laced with a Victorian theme, are decorated with period wallpapers and antique furnishings. One master suite includes an enormous Jacuzzi tub. There are plenty of relaxing options at Albergo Allegria, including a rustic lounge with a large fireplace and overstuffed couches. A second-story library, decorated with plants and wicker furnishings, is still another location to relax with a good book. Guests also can choose from more than 200 videos in the innkeeper's

movie collection. Located just a few feet behind the inn are the Carriage House Suites, each of which includes a double whirlpool tub, gas fireplaces, king-size beds and cathedral ceilings with skylights. The innkeepers came to the area to open LaGriglia, a deluxe, gourmet restaurant just across the way from the bed & breakfast. Their command of cuisine is evident each morning as guests feast on a variety home-baked muffins and pastries, gourmet omelets, waffles and other tempting treats. Albergo Allegria has been named a registered historic site.

Innkeeper(s): Vito & Lenore Radelich. $65-195. MC VISA DC DS TC. 21 rooms with PB, 7 with FP. 9 suites. Breakfast included in rates. Type of meal: gourmet breakfast. Afternoon tea available. Beds: KQT. Air conditioning, turndown service, ceiling fan, TV and VCR in room. Fax, copier and bicycles on premises. Handicap access. Amusement parks, antiques, fishing, parks, shopping, downhill skiing, cross-country skiing and watersports nearby.

Publicity: *Yankee.*

"A jewel of an inn! The ambiance was elegant, yet relaxed; beautiful, yet comfortable, reflecting the nurturance of two generations of skillful, generous innkeepers."

Certificate may be used: April 15-Nov. 15, Sunday-Thursday (non-holiday).

Country Suite B&B
Rt 23 W, PO Box 700
Windham, NY 12496
(518)734-4079
E-mail: ctrysuite@aol.com

This spacious country farmhouse in the Catskill Mountains offers easy access to the many scenic attractions of the region. Seven guest rooms, three with private baths, are available to visitors. The inn's country-style furnishings include antiques and family heirlooms. After a busy day of exploring the area, guests often gather in the inn's comfortable living room to relax. Ski Windham is just two miles from the inn and several other ski areas are within a 30-minute drive.

Innkeeper(s): Lorraine Seidel. $85-129. AX. 5 rooms. Breakfast included in rates. Type of meal: gourmet breakfast. Antiques and downhill skiing nearby.

"A beautifully restored place, a deliciously luxurious stay!"

Certificate may be used: Year-round except holidays. May not be used in conjunction with any other discount.

Danske Hus
361 South St
Windham, NY 12496
(518)734-6335

Circa 1865. Located just across the road from Ski Windham, and nestled between two golf courses, this farmhouse-style inn offers countryside and mountain views to its guests. Breakfast may be enjoyed in the heirloom-filled dining room or outside on a picturesque deck complete with the sounds of a babbling brook. Guests also enjoy a large living room, piano, woodburning fireplace and a sauna. The Catskills provide many other tourist attractions, including caverns, fairs and ethnic festivals, as well as shopping, antiquing and sporting activities. The innkeeper welcomes families with children, and with prior arrangement, dogs may be allowed.

Innkeeper(s): Barbara Jensen. $40-85. AX DS. 4 rooms, 3 with PB. Breakfast and afternoon tea included in rates. Meal: full breakfast. Beds: KQDT. TV, VCR, sauna, library, pet boarding, child care on premises. Amusement parks, antiques, fishing, parks, skiing, watersports nearby.

"Your warm and cozy home is surpassed only by your warm and friendly smile. Breakfast - Wow - it can't be beat!"

Certificate may be used: Anytime, except holidays, holiday weekends and Dec. 13-March 13.

Wolcott F7

Bonnie Castle Farm B&B
PO Box 188
Wolcott, NY 14590-0188
(315)587-2273 (800)587-4006 Fax:(315)587-4003

Circa 1887. This large, waterfront home is surrounded by expansive lawns and trees, which overlook the east side of Great Sodus Bay, a popular resort at the turn of the century. Accommodations include a suite and large guest rooms with water views. Other rooms feature wainscoting and cathedral ceilings. A full, gourmet breakfast includes a cereal bar, fresh fruit, juices and a variety of entrees such as Orange Blossom French toast,  sausages, a creamy potato casserole and fresh-baked pastries topped off with teas and Irish creme coffee.

Innkeeper(s): Eric & Georgia Pendleton. $75-132. MC VISA AX PC TC. 8 rooms with PB. 1 suite. Breakfast included in rates. Meals: full breakfast and gourmet breakfast. Beds: KQD. Air conditioning, ceiling fan, TV and VCR in room. Fax, copier, spa, swimming on premises. Antiques, fishing, parks, skiing, sporting events, theater, watersports nearby. Location: Halfway between Rochester & Syracuse on Sodus Bay.

"We love Bonnie Castle. You have a magnificent establishment. We are just crazy about your place. Hope to see you soon."

Certificate may be used: Anytime except Friday and Saturday in June, July and August.

North Carolina

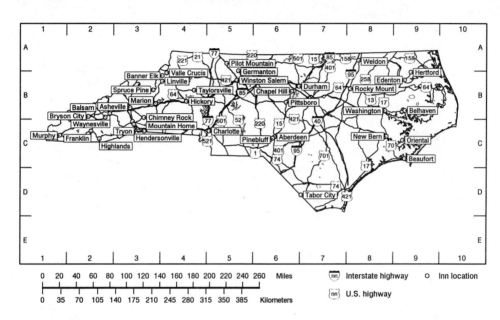

	Miles
0 20 40 60 80 100 120 140 160 180 200 220 240 260	
0 35 70 105 140 175 210 245 280 315 350 385	Kilometers

(nn) Interstate highway   ○ Inn location

(nn) U.S. highway

Aberdeen
C6

The Inn at Bryant House
214 N Poplar St
Aberdeen, NC 28315-2812
(910)944-3300 (800)453-4019 Fax:(910)944-8898
Circa 1913. This Colonial Revival inn has been restored to its original Southern splendor. Pastel colors flow through the entire house, and the sitting, dining and living rooms open to one another for easy access. Breakfast is served buffet-style in the dining or garden room. With advance notice, lunches and dinners can be served for small business meetings, wedding parties, family gatherings, club activities and weekend retreats. The Pinehurst area is known for rolling hills and more than 30 championship-quality golf courses.
Innkeeper(s): Abbie Gregory. $45-70. MC VISA AX DS. 8 rooms, 6 with PB. Breakfast included in rates. Type of meal: continental-plus breakfast. Beds: QDT. Air conditioning in room. Cable TV and VCR on premises. Antiques, shopping, sporting events and theater nearby.
"Excellent!! Bill & Abbie Gregory are just wonderful hosts. Superb continental breakfast."
Certificate may be used: Any time of the year, when available.

Page Manor House B&B
300 Page St
Aberdeen, NC 28315
(910)944-5970 Fax:(901)944-1172
Circa 1914. The only thing wrong with this bed & breakfast is that guests eventually have to leave, but they are sure to remember the beautiful decor, glorious cuisine and Southern hospitality. The decor is elegant, but not stuffy, and guests will feel right at home. Canopy beds, luxury linens and fluffy down pillows ensure a restful night sleep. Each guest room is individually decorated in a romantic style. Breakfast alone may be worth the trip. The multi-course fare changes daily, but a sample menu might include fresh strawberries topped with sweet vanilla cream, followed by a twist on the ordinary eggs Benedict with poached eggs on toasted Italian bread with a basil-pesto sauce and a dusting of freshly grated parmesan cheese. Golf courses, more than two dozen at last count, abound in the area. Antique shops, the zoo and the North Carolina Speedway are other possibilities.
Innkeeper(s): Sharon & Russ Cogan. $120-135. PC TC. 4 rooms with PB, 3 with FP. Breakfast included in rates. Types of meals: gourmet

breakfast and early coffee/tea. Beds: KQT. Air conditioning, ceiling fan, TV and VCR in room. Fax, copier, swimming and tennis on premises. Antiques, shopping, golf and theater nearby.

Publicity: *Fayetteville Observer, Pinehurst Magazine, Country Extra*

Certificate may be used: Dec. 1-Feb. 20 & June 1-Aug. 31, Monday, Tuesday, Wednesday.

Asheville   B3

Beaufort House Victorian B&B

61 N Liberty St
Asheville, NC 28801-1829
(704)254-9935

The Beaufort House is a stunning Queen Anne Victorian painted in a light salmon hue with coral and white trim. The sweeping wraparound porch, which boasts a covered gazebo, is especially appealing and a perfect spot for relaxation. There are 12 guest quarters, including rooms and suites in the main house and the Carriage House cottage. Most rooms and suites include a Jacuzzi tub, and two offer a clawfoot tub. The decor is Victorian, and each room is appointed in its own style. The cottage is a private haven with a loft bedroom, fireplace and its own deck. Because of its small kitchen, which is stocked with goodies, breakfast is not included in the Carriage House rates. The inn guests feast on a gourmet breakfast served with fancy table settings.

Innkeeper(s): Robert & Jacqueline Glasgow. $65-195. MC VISA PC TC. 12 rooms with PB. Breakfast and afternoon tea included in rates. Types of meals: gourmet breakfast, early coffee/tea, picnic lunch and afternoon tea. Beds: KQD. Air conditioning, ceiling fan TV and VCR in room. Bicycles and fax on premises. Antiques, parks, shopping, downhill skiing, golf and theater nearby.

Certificate may be used: Jan. 1-Feb. 28, Sunday-Thursday.

Carolina B&B

177 Cumberland Ave
Asheville, NC 28801-1736
(704)254-3608 (888)254-3608 Fax:(704)252-0640
E-mail: cesaul@aol.com

Circa 1900. Architect Richard Sharp Smith, whose credits include creating homes for such tycoons as George Vanderbilt, designed this home in Asheville's historic Montford district. Bay windows and porches decorate Carolina's exterior, as do innkeeper and landscape architect Sam Fain's well-attended grounds. Inside, rooms feature pine floors, high ceilings and many fireplaces. Guest rooms are furnished with antiques and unique collectibles, such as ice skates, lace collars and evening bags. The expansive breakfasts include fresh breads, fruits, egg dishes and breakfast meats.

Innkeeper(s): Connie Stahl. $75-150. AP. MC VISA DS PC TC. 7 rooms, 6 with PB, 5 with FP. 1 cottage. Breakfast and afternoon tea included in rates. Types of meals: gourmet breakfast and early coffee/tea. Catering service available. Beds: Q. Air conditioning, ceiling fan and TV in room. Fax, copier and spa on premises. Antiques, parks, shopping, downhill skiing, golf and theater nearby.

Publicity: *Orange County Register, Asheville Citizen-Times, Charlotte, Mid-Atlantic Country.*

"It was like a dream, exactly as we pictured the perfect honeymoon. Excellent host & hostess, very helpful and informative as to local area. Food was wonderful. Rated an A-plus."

Certificate may be used: Jan. 3-March 30, anytime except holidays; April 1-Sept. 30, Sunday-Wednesday except holidays.

Corner Oak Manor

53 Saint Dunstans Rd
Asheville, NC 28803-2620
(704)253-3525

Circa 1920. Surrounded by oak, maple and pine trees, this English Tudor inn is decorated with many fine oak antiques and handmade items. Innkeeper Karen Spradley has hand-stitched something special for each room, and the house features handmade items by local artisans. Breakfast delights include entrees such as Blueberry Ricotta Pancakes, Four Cheese and Herb Quiche and Orange French Toast. When you aren't enjoying local activities, you can sit on the shady deck, relax in the Jacuzzi, play a few songs on the piano or curl up with a good book.

Innkeeper(s): Karen & Andy Spradley. $90-150. MC VISA AX DS PC TC. 3 rooms with PB, 1 with FP. 1 cottage. Breakfast included in rates. Type

of meal: gourmet breakfast. Beds: Q. Air conditioning, ceiling fan in room. Antiques, fishing, parks, shopping, downhill skiing, theater nearby.

"Great food, comfortable bed, quiet, restful atmosphere, you provided it all and we enjoyed it all!"

Certificate may be used: January-March anytime except holidays, April through September & November, Sunday-Thursday only. No holidays, October & November excluded

Dogwood Cottage
40 Canterbury Rd N
Asheville, NC 28801-1560
(704)258-9725

Circa 1910. This Carolina mountain home is located a mile-and-a-half from downtown Asheville, on Sunset Mountain. The veranda, filled with white wicker and floral chintz prints, is the focal point of the inn during summer. It affords tree-top views of the Blue Ridge Mountains. Wing chairs and country pieces accent the inn's gleaming hardwood floors. Breakfast is served in the formal dining room or on the covered porch.

Innkeeper(s): Joan & Don Tracy. $95-105. MC VISA AX PC. 4 rooms with PB, 3 with FP. Breakfast included in rates. Types of meals: full breakfast, gourmet breakfast and early coffee/tea. Beds: Q. Air conditioning and ceiling fan in room. Cable TV, swimming and pet boarding on premises. Handicap access. Antiques, fishing, parks, shopping, downhill skiing, sporting events, theater and watersports nearby.

"Cozy, warm and gracious."

Certificate may be used: Sunday through Thursday only, not in October and December.

The Lion & The Rose
276 Montford Ave
Asheville, NC 28801-1660
(704)255-7673 (800)546-6988

Circa 1895. Asheville's Montford Historic District wouldn't be complete without this Queen Anne Victorian, listed in the National Register. Innkeepers Lisa and Rice Yordy preserve the history of this home with the Victorian decor and heavy English influences. The interior is gracious, showcasing the original leaded- and stained-glass windows and glossy woods. A wonderful afternoon tea is served each day, often on the inn's wraparound veranda. Lisa prepares the memorable breakfasts, which are served on English china with silver. Fresh flowers and chocolates welcome guests to their well-appointed rooms.

Innkeeper(s): Rice & Lisa Yordy. $115-175. MC VISA TC. 5 rooms with PB. 1 suite. Breakfast and afternoon tea included in rates. Type of meal: gourmet breakfast. Beds: QT. Air conditioning, turndown service, ceiling fan and TV in room. Antiques, fishing, parks, shopping, theater and watersports nearby.

Certificate may be used: Jan. 30-Sept. 30, Monday through Thursday.

The Inn on Montford
296 Montford Ave
Asheville, NC 28801-1660
(704)254-9569 (800)254-9569 Fax:(704)254-9518
E-mail: inninfo@aol.com

Circa 1900. This National Register home was one of a few Asheville homes designed by Richard Sharp Smith, who also served as the supervising architect for the lavish Biltmore Estate. The exterior is a simple and pleasing Arts & Crafts design flanked by a wide veranda, where guests can relax and enjoy the quiet neighborhood. There are four well-appointed guest rooms highlighted by beautiful antique beds. Three rooms include a whirlpool tub, and the fourth offers a clawfoot tub. All four have a fireplace. English and American antiques fill the elegant inn. Breakfasts include a special fruit dish, such as a baked banana souffle, freshly baked pastries or muffins and a special daily entree. Spend the day touring historic homes, take a trip to the Biltmore Estate or enjoy hiking and rafting in nearby wilderness areas.

Innkeeper(s): Ron and Lynn Carlson. $120-160. MC VISA AX DC DS PC TC. 4 rooms with PB, 4 with FP. Breakfast included in rates. Types of meals: full breakfast, gourmet breakfast and early coffee/tea. Beds: Q. Air conditioning in room. Cable TV, VCR, fax, copier and library on premises. Amusement parks, antiques, fishing, parks, shopping, downhill skiing, sporting events, golf, theater and watersports nearby.

Certificate may be used: Jan. 30-Sept. 30, Sunday-Thursday.

Balsam   B2

Balsam Mountain Inn
Balsam Mountain Inn Road
Balsam, NC 28707-0040
(704)456-9498 (800)224-9498 Fax:(704)456-9298

Circa 1905. This mountain inn with Neoclassical architecture overlooks the scenic hamlet of Balsam. The inn is listed in the National Register of Historic Places and is designated a Jackson County Historic Site. It features a mansard roof and wraparound porches with mountain views.

Innkeeper(s): Merrily Teasley. $90-150. MC VISA DS TC. 50 rooms with PB. 8 suites. Breakfast included in rates. Types of meals: full breakfast, gourmet breakfast and early coffee/tea. Dinner, picnic lunch, gourmet lunch, banquet service and room service available. Restaurant on premises. Beds: KD. Fax and copier on premises. Handicap access. Antiques, fishing, parks, shopping and downhill skiing nearby.

"What wonderful memories we have of this beautiful inn."

Certificate may be used: Sunday-Thursday, November-June & September, excluding holiday periods.

Banner Elk
B4

Beech Alpen Inn
700 Beech Mountain Pkwy
Banner Elk, NC 28604-8015
(704)387-2252 Fax:(704)387-2229

Circa 1968. This rustic inn is a Bavarian delight affording scenic vistas of the Blue Ridge Mountains. The innkeepers offer accommodations at Top of the Beech, a Swiss-style ski chalet with views of nearby slopes. The interiors of both properties are inviting. At the Beech Alpen, several guest rooms have stone fireplaces or French doors that open onto a balcony. Top of the Beech's great room is a wonderful place to relax, with a huge stone fireplace and comfortable furnishings. The Beech Alpen Restaurant serves a variety of dinner fare.

Innkeeper(s): Lisa & Taylor Rees. $44-135. MC VISA AX TC. 25 rooms with PB, 4 with FP. Breakfast included in rates. Types of meals: continental breakfast and early coffee/tea. Restaurant on premises. Beds: KQD. TV in room. Fax and copier on premises. Antiques, fishing, parks, shopping, downhill skiing, cross-country skiing, sporting events and theater nearby.

Certificate may be used: Sunday-Thursday, Jan. 3-Dec. 14.

Beaufort
C9

Pecan Tree Inn B&B
116 Queen St
Beaufort, NC 28516-2214
(919)728-6733

Circa 1866. Originally built as a Masonic lodge, this state historic landmark is in the heart of Beaufort's historic district. Gingerbread trim, Victorian porches, turrets and two-century-old pecan trees grace the exterior. Guests can relax in the parlor, on the

porches, or pay a visit to the flower and herb gardens. The Bridal Suite and "Wow" suite boast a king-size, canopied bed and two-person Jacuzzi.

Innkeeper(s): Susan & Joe Johnson. $65-125. MC VISA DS PC TC. 7 rooms with PB. 1 suite. Breakfast included in rates. Types of meals: continental-plus breakfast and early coffee/tea. Beds: KQ. Air conditioning and ceiling fan in room. Bicycles, library on premises. Amusement parks, antiques, fishing, parks, shopping and watersports nearby.

Location: In the heart of the historic district, one-half block from the waterfront.
Publicity: *Sunday Telegram, This Week, Conde Nast Traveler, State.*
"After visiting B&Bs far and wide I give Pecan Tree Inn a Five-Star rating in all respects."
Certificate may be used: October through April, Sunday through Thursday.

Belhaven
B9

River Forest Manor
600 E Main St
Belhaven, NC 27810-1622
(919)943-2151 (800)346-2151 Fax:(919)943-6628

Circa 1899. Both Twiggy and Walter Cronkite have passed through the two-story, pillared rotunda entrance of this white mansion located on the Atlantic Intracoastal Waterway. Ornate, carved ceilings, cut and leaded-glass windows and crystal chandeliers grace the inn. Antiques are found throughout. Each evening a smorgasbord buffet features more than 65 items from the inn's kitchen.

Innkeeper(s): Melba, Axson Jr. & Mark Smith. $65-85. MAP. MC VISA. 12 rooms with PB. Breakfast included in rates. Types of meals: continental breakfast and full breakfast. Dinner available. Restaurant on premises. Beds: KQD. Air conditioning and TV in room. VCR, fax and copier on premises. Antiques, fishing and watersports nearby.

Publicity: *Southern Living, National Geographic, North Carolina Accommodations, Country Inns, State, Historical Inns.*
"River Forest Manor is our favorite place in east North Carolina."
Certificate may be used: April 1-April 30, Sunday through Thursday.

Bryson City
B2

Randolph House
223 Fryemont Rd PO Box 816
Bryson City, NC 28713-0816
(704)488-3472 (800)480-3472

Circa 1895. Randolph House is a mountain estate tucked among pine trees and dogwoods, near the entrance of Great Smoky Mountain National Park. Antiques, some original to the house, fill this National Register home. Each guest room is appointed in a different color scheme. The house provides an unforgettable experience, not the least of which is the gourmet dining provided on the terrace or in the dining room.

Innkeeper(s): Bill & Ruth Randolph Adams. $110-160. MAP. MC VISA AX DS PC TC. 7 rooms, 3 with PB, 2 with FP. 2 suites. 1 cottage. 1 conference room. Breakfast and dinner included in rates. Meals: full breakfast and early coffee/tea. Restaurant on premises. Beds: KQDT. Air conditioning and TV in room. Library on premises. Handicap access. Antiques, fishing, parks, shopping and watersports nearby.

Publicity: *Tourist News, New York Times.*
"Very enjoyable, great food."
Certificate may be used: May-June and September, weekdays only. Breakfast only included, no dinner.

Chapel Hill   B6

The Inn at Bingham School
PO Box 267
Chapel Hill, NC 27514-0267
(919)563-5583 (800)566-5583 Fax:(919)563-9826

Circa 1790. This inn served as one of the locations of the famed Bingham School. This particular campus was the site of a liberal arts preparatory school for those aspiring to attend the University at Chapel Hill. The inn is listed as a National Trust property and has garnered awards for its restoration. The property still includes many historic structures including a 1790s log home, an 1801 addition, an 1835 Greek Revival home, the headmaster's office, which was built in 1845, and a well house, smokehouse and milk house. The dining rooms and living rooms include the original pine flooring, wainscoting and milk-based paint on the ceilings. Guests can opt to stay in the Log Room, located in the log cabin, with a tightwinder staircase and fireplace. Other possibilities include Rusty's Room with two antique rope beds. Some rooms feature special mantels, an antique clawfoot tub and one offers a bedroom glassed in on three sides. A mix of breakfasts are served, from a Southern style with grits and ham to French with quiche and souffles. Gourmet coffee and tea complement each meal.

Innkeeper(s): Francois & Christina Deprez. $75-120. MC VISA AX DS PC TC. 5 rooms with PB, 1 with FP. 1 suite. 1 cottage. 1 conference room. Breakfast and evening snack included in rates. Types of meals: full breakfast, gourmet breakfast and early coffee/tea. Picnic lunch available. Beds: QD. Air conditioning in room. Cable TV, VCR, fax and library on premises. Antiques, fishing, parks, shopping, sporting events, theater and watersports nearby.

Publicity: *Southern Inns, Mebane Enterprise, Burlington Times, Times News, Washington Post.*

"Our stay at the inn was like a dream, another time, another place. Francois & Christina were the most hospitable, friendly hosts we've ever met."

Certificate may be used: All year Sunday-Thursday (free night cannot fall on Friday or Saturday nights).

Charlotte   C5

The Homeplace B&B
5901 Sardis Rd
Charlotte, NC 28270-5369
(704)365-1936

Circa 1902. Situated on two-and-one-half wooded acres in Southeast Charlotte, this peaceful setting is an oasis in one of the South's fastest-growing cities. Bedrooms have 10-foot ceilings, heart-of-pine floors and blends of Country/Victorian decor. Special

touches include quilts, fine linens, handmade accessories, family antiques and original primitive paintings by innkeeper Peggy Dearien's father. Spend the afternoon or evening relaxing on the porches or walking the secluded gardens. While touring the grounds, you will see a 1930s log barn that was moved to the property in 1991.

Innkeeper(s): Margaret and Frank Dearien. $98-125. MC VISA AX. 4 rooms, 2 with PB. 1 suite. Breakfast included in rates. Meals: full breakfast and early coffee/tea. Beds: QT. Air conditioning, ceiling fan in room. TV, VCR on premises. Antiques, shopping, sporting events nearby.

Publicity: *Charlotte Observer, Birmingham News, Country, Southern Living's Weekend Vacations.*

"Everything was perfect. The room was superb, the food excellent!"

Certificate may be used: January, February, March, July, and August, Sunday through Thursday only.

Chimney Rock   B3

Esmeralda Inn
Hwy 74A PO Box 57
Chimney Rock, NC 28720
(704)625-9105

Circa 1890. Nestled in the Blue Ridge Mountains, this rustic country lodge served as home base for production of several silent movies, and notables such as Mary Pickford, Gloria Swanson, Douglas Fairbanks, Clark Gable and many others used the Esmeralda as a hideout. Lew Wallace, noted author, finished the script for "Ben Hur" in room No. 9. The lobby, constructed of natural trees and filled with local artifacts, is a favorite place for visitors to take refuge and relax.

Innkeeper(s): Ackie & Joanne Okpych. $48-75. MC VISA AX DS TC. 13 rooms, 7 with PB. 3 suites. 1 conference room. Breakfast and dinner included in rates. Picnic lunch and lunch available. Restaurant on premises. Beds: KQD. Ceiling fan in room. Library on premises. Antiques, fishing, parks, shopping and watersports nearby.

Certificate may be used: Sunday through Thursday, except October. Season is from March 17-Dec. 9.

Durham   B6

Blooming Garden Inn

513 Holloway St
Durham, NC 27701-3457
(919)687-0801 Fax:(919)688-1401

Circa 1890. Blooming Garden is an apt name for this bed & breakfast. Each guest room is artfully appointed with a different, colorful theme. For instance, the Tiffany Room is accentuated with stained-glass pieces. The Moroccan Room is dressed in dramatic hues of dark green, gold and red. Each room offers a special bed, as well. Most impressive is the mid-19th-century carved Rosewood bed. In addition to the colorful interior, the exterior is dotted with a bright mix of perennials and annuals. The inn's luxury suites include a double Jacuzzi tub. Homemade ginger waffles topped with a creamy lemon curd are among the specialties served for breakfast. For guests planning an extended stay in the area, the innkeepers offer accommodations in Holly House, a restored Victorian across the street from the inn. Extended-stay arrangements are possible across the street at Holly House, a nicely furnished, restored Victorian home. The home includes a suite and three guest rooms, common areas, access to a kitchen, phone, washer and dryer. The innkeepers offer special, economical rates for those planning an extended stay. The Durham area offers many fine restaurants.
Innkeeper(s): Dolly & Frank Pokrass. $95-185. MC VISA AX DC CB DS PC TC. 4 rooms with PB, 4 with FP. 2 suites. Breakfast included in rates. Types of meals: gourmet breakfast and early coffee/tea. Beds: DT. Air conditioning, ceiling fan and TV in room. VCR, fax, copier and library on premises. Antiques, parks, sporting events, theater nearby.

Certificate may be used: Jan. 30-Nov. 15, Sunday-Thursday only, excluding April, May & October, two-person Jacuzzi luxury suites.

Edenton   B9

The Lords Proprietors' Inn

300 N Broad St
Edenton, NC 27932-1905
(919)482-3641 (800)348-8933 Fax:(919)482-2432

Circa 1801. On Albemarle Sound, Edenton was one of the Colonial capitols of North Carolina. The inn consists of three houses, providing elegant accommodations in Edenton's Historic District. Breakfast and dinner are served in a separate dining room on a patio. A guided walking tour from the Visitor's Center provides an opportunity to see museum homes.

Innkeeper(s): Arch & Jane Edwards. $185-235. MAP. PC TC. 20 rooms with PB. 1 conference room. Breakfast and dinner included in rates. Types of meals: full breakfast and early coffee/tea. Beds: KQT. Air conditioning, ceiling fan, TV and VCR in room. Fax and child care on premises. Handicap access. Antiques, fishing and shopping nearby.

Location: Main street of town.

Publicity: *Southern Living, Mid-Atlantic Country, House Beautiful, Washington Post.*

"One of the friendliest and best-managed inns I have ever visited."

Certificate may be used: Anytime, except holidays and special weekends (i.e. April Pilgrimage). Dinner may be included in rate.

Trestle House Inn

RR 4, Box 370, 632 Soundside Rd
Edenton, NC 27932-9668
(919)482-2282 (800)645-8466 Fax:(919)482-7003
E-mail: thinn@coastalnet.com

Circa 1968. Trestle House is located on a six acres with a lake and a pond filled with largemouth bass. The interior is unique as it features beams that were actually trestles that once belonged to the Southern Railway Company. Rooms are named for different birds, such as the Osprey and Mallard rooms. Two rooms have a sleigh bed. The morning meal includes homemade breads, breakfast casseroles and fresh orange juice.
Innkeeper(s): Peter L. Bogus & Wendy S. Jewett. $80-100. MC VISA AX PC TC. 5 rooms with PB. 1 suite. Breakfast included in rates. Type of meal: gourmet breakfast. Beds: KQDT. Air conditioning and ceiling fan in room. Cable TV, VCR, fax, swimming, bicycles and library on premises. Antiques, fishing, parks, shopping, golf and watersports nearby.

"We have stayed at many B&B, but yours is special because it brings us close to nature. Your breakfast are wonderful and relaxing while eating and watching wildlife in their natural habitat!"

Certificate may be used: November 1-March 31, excluding holidays and holiday weekends.

Franklin
C2

Buttonwood Inn
50 Admiral Dr
Franklin, NC 28734-8474
(704)369-8985

Circa 1927. Trees surround this two-story batten board house located adjacent to the Franklin Golf Course. Local crafts and handmade family quilts accent the country decor. Wonderful breakfasts are served here—often Eggs Benedict, baked peaches and sausage and freshly baked scones with homemade lemon butter. On a sunny morning, enjoy breakfast on the deck and savor the Smoky Mountain vistas. Afterward, you'll be ready for white-water rafting, hiking and fishing.

Innkeeper(s): Liz Oehser. $60-90. PC TC. 4 rooms with PB. Breakfast and afternoon tea included in rates. Types of meals: full breakfast and early coffee/tea. Beds: KDT. Ceiling fan in room. Cable TV on premises. Antiques, fishing, parks and shopping nearby.

Certificate may be used: Sunday-Thursday, except October, no weekends or holidays.

Grandfather Mountain (Linville)

Linville Cottage Bed & Breakfast
PO Box 508
Grandfather Mountain
(Linville), NC 28646-0508
(704)733-6551

Circa 1910. Just two miles from North Carolina's Grandfather Mountain rests this Victorian cottage. The innkeepers emphasize country comfort, decorating their B&B with simple antiques and collectibles. English and herb gardens surround the inn. Visit the inn's shops or simply enjoy the mountain breezes from the front porch. The area is full of scenic sites, including the Blue Ridge Parkway and Linville Caverns.

Innkeeper(s): Fran Feely. $50-95. MC VISA PC TC. 4 rooms with PB. Breakfast and afternoon tea included in rates. Type of meal: continental-plus breakfast. Beds: QD. Cable TV, VCR and library on premises. Handicap access. Amusement parks, antiques, fishing, parks, shopping, downhill skiing, cross-country skiing, sporting events, theater and watersports nearby.

Certificate may be used: Monday to Thursday year-round, except on holidays or special local events.

Hendersonville
C3

Echo Mountain Inn
2849 Laurel Park Hwy
Hendersonville, NC 28739-8925
(704)692-4008 Fax:(704)697-2047

Circa 1896. Sitting on top of Davis Mountain, this large stone and wood inn has spectacular views, especially from the dining room and many of the guest rooms. Rooms are decorated with antiques and reproductions and many include a fireplace. The historic town of Hendersonville is three miles away. Gourmet dining includes an added touch of the city lights below. Guests may want to partake in refreshments of their choice served in the inn's fireside tavern.

Innkeeper(s): Karen Kovacik. $35-175. MC VISA AX DS. 31 rooms, 30 with PB. 2 suites. 1 conference room. Breakfast included in rates. Meals: continental breakfast and early coffee/tea. Dinner, picnic lunch, banquet service, room service available. Restaurant on premises. Beds: KQDT. Air conditioning, turndown service, TV, VCR in room. Child care on premises. Antiques, fishing, shopping, downhill skiing, theater nearby.

"It was quite fabulous and the food entirely too rich."

Certificate may be used: February-May, September, November-December, any day; June-August on Sunday-Thursday. Holidays and holiday weeks excluded, special events excluded.

The Waverly Inn
783 N Main St
Hendersonville, NC 28792-5079
(704)693-9193 (800)537-8195 Fax:(704)692-1010
E-mail: jsheiry@aol.com

Circa 1898. In the National Register, this three-story Victorian and Colonial Revival house has a two-tiered, sawn work trimmed porch and widow's walk. A beautifully carved Eastlake staircase and an original registration desk grace the inn. There are four-poster canopy beds and clawfoot tubs. Breakfast is served in the handsome dining room. The Waverly is the oldest surviving inn in Hendersonville.

Innkeeper(s): John & Diane Sheiry, Darla Olmstead. $89-139. MC VISA AX DS PC. 14 rooms with PB. 1 suite. Breakfast and evening snack included in rates. Type of meal: full breakfast. Picnic lunch available. Beds: KQDT. Air conditioning and ceiling fan in room. TV and fax on premises. Antiques, fishing, parks, shopping, cross-country skiing, theater nearby.

Location: Corner of 8th Ave & Main St (Rt 25 North)

Publicity: *New York Times, Country, Blue Ridge Country, Vogue, Southern Living, Travel South.*

"Our main topic of conversation while driving back was what a great time we had at your place."

Certificate may be used: January, February, March anytime. November, December, April, May, September, Sunday-Thursday.

Hertford
B9

1812 on The Perquimans B&B Inn

Rt 3, Box 10
Hertford, NC 27944
(919)426-1812

William and Sarah Fletcher were the first residents of this Federal-style plantation home, and the house is still in the family today. The Fletchers were Quakers and the first North Carolina residents to free their slaves, and also offered to pay the way for workers who wished to return to Africa. The farm rests along the banks of the Periquimans River, and the grounds retain many original outbuildings, including a brick dairy, smokehouse and a 19th-century frame barn. Inside, the mantels, marble and woodwork have been restored.

Innkeeper(s): Nancy D. Rascoe. $75-90. MC VISA. 5 rooms. Breakfast included in rates. Type of meal: full breakfast.

Certificate may be used: During the week.

Hickory
B4

The Hickory B&B

464 7th St SW
Hickory, NC 28602-2743
(704)324-0548 (800)654-2961

Circa 1908. Bedrooms in this Georgian-style inn are decorated with antiques, collectibles and fresh flowers. There's a parlor to sit in and chat and a library to enjoy a good book or play a game. Guests also can relax and enjoy songbirds from the inn's porches. The inn is located in a city that has evolved from a furniture and textile mill town of yesteryear into a cultural arts mecca of mountain communities. From mountains as well as to malls, Hickory satisfies the shopper as well as the sportsperson.

Innkeeper(s): Bob & Pat Lynch. $85-105. MC VISA PC. 4 rooms with PB. Breakfast included in rates. Types of meals: full breakfast and early coffee/tea. Afternoon tea available. Beds: Q. Air conditioning and ceiling fan in room. Cable TV, VCR, swimming and library on premises. Antiques, fishing, shopping, sporting events, golf and theater nearby.

Publicity: *Mid-Atlantic Country, Hickory Daily News, Charlotte Observer.*

"Now we know what Southern hospitality means. We had such a wonderful weekend with you."

Certificate may be used: Nov. 15-Aug. 31, holidays excluded, based upon availability and other promotions.

Highlands
C2

Morning Star Inn

480 Flat Mountain Estates Rd
Highlands, NC 28741-8325
(704)526-1009

Circa 1960. For anyone hoping to enjoy the serenity and scenery of North Carolina, this inn is an ideal place for that and more. Hammocks and rockers are found here and there on the two-acre grounds, dotted with gardens and fountains. There is a parlor with a stone fireplace and a wicker-filled sunporch. Rooms are decorated in a romantic and elegant style. Beds are dressed with fine linens and down comforters. To top off the amenities, one of the innkeepers is a culinary school graduate and prepares the mouthwatering cuisine guests enjoy at breakfast. On the weekends, afternoon refreshments are served. The innkeeper also is working on a cookbook, which will no doubt include tidbits such as Southwestern eggs and fresh fruit with amaretto cream sauce. For those interested in improving their culinary skills, cooking classes sometimes are available.

Innkeeper(s): Pat & Pat Allen. $115-145. MC VISA PC TC. 5 rooms with PB. 1 suite. Breakfast and evening snack included in rates. Type of meal: gourmet breakfast. Afternoon tea available. Beds: KQ. Air conditioning, turndown service, ceiling fan and TV in room. Fax and copier on premises. Antiques, fishing, shopping, downhill skiing, golf, theater and watersports nearby.

Publicity: *Victoria Magazine, Southern Living*

Certificate may be used: January-May, Sunday through Thursday.

Marion
B3

The Lodge at Blue Ridge

Rt 3, Box 295, US Hwy 221 N
Marion, NC 29752
(704)756-7001 Fax:(704)756-4267

Circa 1992. The scenery at this Blue Ridge Mountain getaway is spectacular. The lodge is part of a country club and nature preserve on the edge of Pisgah National Forest. Each room has a stone fireplace and a private porch. There is plenty for families to do. Children can take golf lessons, and the lodge has two swimming pools. Golf packages are available.

Innkeeper(s): Ed & Lorraine Meyer. $75-115. MC VISA AX DS PC TC. 12 rooms with PB, 12 with FP. 2 cottages. 1 conference room. Breakfast included in rates. Types of meals: continental breakfast, continental-plus breakfast and early coffee/tea. Banquet service, catering service and catered breakfast available. Restaurant on premises. Beds: KD. Air conditioning in room. Cable TV, fax, copier, swimming and child care on premises. Handicap access. Antiques, fishing, shopping, downhill skiing and golf nearby.

Publicity: *Citizen-Times, Summer in the High Country.*

"What a beautiful corner of the world."

Certificate may be used: Nov. 1-April 30, any day.

Mountain Home   C3

Mountain Home B&B
PO Box 234
Mountain Home, NC 28758-0234
(704)697-9090 (800)397-0066

Circa 1915. This home and its surrounding grounds have quite a history behind them. Although the inn itself was built in 1915, a plantation home once stood in this area, holding court over an enormous spread, which included a dairy, blacksmith shop, race track and stables. The plantation home was burnt at

the end of the Civil War, and it was not until the early 1900s that a hotel was built on a 640-acre parcel of the property. This, too, burnt, and in 1941, a local dentist built his family home out of the hotel's remains. Today, the guests once again travel to this picturesque spot to enjoy Southern hospitality. Rooms are romantically appointed with items such as a four-poster rice bed, a sleigh bed, skylights, fireplace or Jacuzzi tub. The front porch, with its rockers, is ready for those who wish to relax. Guests also are pampered with a hearty breakfast; raspberry stuffed French toast is a specialty. The innkeepers offer a variety of getaway packages.

Innkeeper(s): Blake & Tammie Levit, Judy Brown. $85-195. MC VISA PC. 7 rooms with PB, 1 with FP. 1 suite. 1 conference room. Breakfast and evening snack included in rates. Types of meals: full breakfast, gourmet breakfast and early coffee/tea. Banquet service available. Beds: KQD. Air conditioning and TV in room. Handicap access. Antiques, fishing, parks, shopping and theater nearby.

Publicity: *Arts & Entertainment.*

"Thanks for showing us what 'Southern hospitality' is like."

Certificate may be used: Sunday-Thursday, January-March.

Murphy   C1

Huntington Hall B&B
500 Valley River Ave
Murphy, NC 28906-2829
(704)837-9567 (800)824-6189 Fax:(704)837-2527
E-mail: hhallbnb@grove.net

Circa 1881. This two-story country Victorian home was built by J.H. Dillard, the town mayor and twice a member of the House of Representatives.

Clapboard siding and tall columns accent the large front porch. An English country theme is highlighted throughout. Afternoon refreshments and evening turndown service are included. Breakfast is served on the sun porch. Murder-mystery, summer-theater, and white-water-rafting packages are available.

Innkeeper(s): Kate & Bob DeLong. $65-95. MAP. MC VISA AX DC CB DS PC TC. 5 rooms with PB, 2 with FP. 1 conference room. Breakfast included in rates. Types of meals: full breakfast, gourmet breakfast and early coffee/tea. Beds: KQDT. Air conditioning, turndown service, ceiling fan and TV in room. VCR, fax, copier, tennis and library on premises. Antiques, fishing, parks, shopping, theater and watersports nearby.

Location: One block from downtown.

Publicity: *Atlanta Journal, Petersen's 4-Wheel, New York Times.*

"Your skill and attitude make it a pleasant experience to stay and rest at HH."

Certificate may be used: Sunday through Thursday any month.

New Bern   C8

Harmony House Inn
215 Pollock St
New Bern, NC 28560-4942
(919)636-3810 (800)636-3113 Fax:(919)636-3810
E-mail: harmony@nternet.net

Circa 1850. Long ago, this two-story Greek Revival was sawed in half and the west side moved nine feet to accommodate new hallways, additional rooms and a staircase. A wall was then built to divide the house into two sections. The rooms are decorated with antiques, the innkeeper's collection of handmade crafts and other collectibles. One of the suites includes a heart-shaped Jacuzzi tub. Offshore breezes sway blossoms in the lush garden. Cross the street to an excellent restaurant or take a picnic to the shore.

Innkeeper(s): Ed & Sooki Kirkpatrick. $99-130. MC VISA DS PC TC. 8 rooms, 9 with PB, 10 with FP. 2 suites. 2 conference rooms. Breakfast and evening snack included in rates. Types of meals: full breakfast and early coffee/tea. Beds: KQT. Air conditioning, ceiling fan and TV in room. Fax on premises. Antiques, parks, shopping and watersports nearby.

Location: In the historic district, four blocks to Tyron Palace.

Publicity: *Americana, Raleigh News and Observer.*

"We feel nourished even now, six months after our visit to Harmony House."

Certificate may be used: Year-round, Sunday through Thursday, based on availability.

The Magnolia House

315 George St
New Bern, NC 28562
(919)633-9488 (800)601-9488 Fax:(919)633-9488

Circa 1870. Magnolia House is an Italianate-style home painted a light pink hue with lilac shutters and white trim. The home is decorated with antiques, and there is a shop on the premises offering Victorian gifts, quilts, special teas and other interesting trinkets. Guest rooms are nicely appointed, and each is different. One room features a light blue floral wallpaper, lacy curtains and a sitting area with two antique chairs and marble-topped table. Another has an iron bed decorated with a bit of ivy. In the afternoons, a proper English tea with finger sandwiches and homemade breads, is served. In the mornings, guests can take breakfast on the veranda, in the home's parlor or in their rooms. Guests can borrow a bicycle for a tour of the town.

Innkeeper(s): Kim & John Trudo. $70-99. MAP. MC VISA AX DS PC TC. 3 rooms with PB. Breakfast and afternoon tea included in rates. Types of meals: full breakfast and early coffee/tea. Evening snack, picnic lunch and room service available. Beds: QD. Air conditioning, turndown service and TV in room. Fax, copier, bicycles and library on premises. Antiques, fishing, shopping, golf, theater and watersports nearby.

Publicity: *Southern Living, Mid-Atlantic Magazine, Chapel Hill News*

"Thank you both for a delightful home away from home. We were very comfortable and enjoyed your hospitality and your hospitality and your beautiful town."

Certificate may be used: Year-round, Sunday through Thursday, excluding holidays or local special events.

Oriental   C9

The Tar Heel Inn

508 Church St, Box 176
Oriental, NC 28571
(919)249-1078 Fax:(919)249-0005
E-mail: tarheel@pamlico-nc.com

Circa 1890. This inn is graciously appointed in English-country style, with four-poster and canopy beds dressed in fine linens. Fresh flowers, stenciling and Laura Ashley prints brighten the rooms. Before a day exploring the area, guests enjoy a gourmet breakfast. In the late afternoons, refreshments are served. Oriental, a village located at the junction of the Neuse River and Pamlico Sound, is known as a sailing capitol of the Carolinas.

Innkeeper(s): Shawna & Robert Hyde. $70-90. MC VISA PC. 8 rooms with PB. Breakfast and evening snack included in rates. Types of meals: full breakfast, gourmet breakfast and early coffee/tea. Beds: KQDT. Air conditioning and ceiling fan in room. Bicycles and library on premises. Antiques, fishing, parks, shopping, theater and watersports nearby.

Certificate may be used: March 1-May 31 and Oct. 1-Dec. 31, Sunday-Friday.

Pilot Mountain (Siloam)

The Blue Fawn B&B

3052 Siloam Rd
Pilot Mountain (Siloam), NC 27041
(910)374-2064 (800)948-7716

Circa 1892. This Greek Revival-style house, with its four two-story columns, is bordered by an old stone fence. Located 10 minutes from town, the Blue Fawn B&B offers a friendly stay in a small tobacco farming community. There are three porches, and one is off the second-story guest rooms, which are decorated comfortably with many quilts. Spinach  blue cheese strudel, Irish soda bread and fruit or homemade biscuits served with sausage gravy, fried potatoes and baked garlic cheese grits are some of the breakfast offerings. It's a tenth of a mile to the Yadkin River.

Innkeeper(s): Gino & Terri Cella. $55-85. MC VISA PC. 3 rooms with PB. 1 suite. Breakfast, afternoon tea and evening snack included in rates. Types of meals: full breakfast, gourmet breakfast and early coffee/tea. Picnic lunch, catering service and room service available. Beds: KQDT. Air conditioning, turndown service, ceiling fan and TV in room. VCR, bicycles and library on premises. Antiques, fishing, parks, shopping, theater and watersports nearby.

"Words could never express how welcome and at home you have made our family feel."

Certificate may be used: January-December.

Pinebluff   C6

Pine Cone Manor

450 E Philadelphia Ave
Pinebluff, NC 28375
(910)281-5307

Circa 1912. The family that built this home lived here for more than 60 years, finally selling it in the 1970s. Today the house is a comfortable B&B set on private, wooded acres that include a variety of the namesake pines. The front porch is an ideal place to relax, offering a collection of rockers and a swing. The area is full of interesting sites, NASCAR and horse racing tracks are just a few. There are dozens of golf courses and the World Golf Hall of Fame.

Innkeeper(s): Virginia H. Keith. $60-65. MC VISA PC TC. 3 rooms, 2 with PB, 1 with FP. 1 cottage. Breakfast included in rates. Types of meals: continental-plus breakfast and early coffee/tea. Beds: KQDT. Air conditioning, ceiling fan and TV in room. Library on premises. Antiques, parks, shopping and sporting events nearby.

Certificate may be used: Anytime subject to availability.

Rocky Mount
B8

Sunset Inn B&B
1210 Sunset Ave
Rocky Mount, NC 27804-5126
(919)446-9524 (800)786-7386

Circa 1920. This Georgian inn is an impressive site from its spot on Sunset Avenue. The innkeepers filled the home with antiques and vast collections of art. Each of the guest rooms is appointed with Victorian furnishings and decor. With advance notice, the innkeepers can accommodate pets.
Innkeeper(s): Dale & Herbert Fuerst. $60-100. MC VISA AX DS TC. 5 rooms with PB. 2 conference rooms. Breakfast included in rates. Types of meals: full breakfast and early coffee/tea. Catered breakfast available. Beds: KQT. Air conditioning and TV in room. Copier on premises. Amusement parks, antiques and parks nearby.
Certificate may be used: All year.

Spruce Pine
B3

Ansley Richmond Inn B&B
101 Pine Ave
Spruce Pine, NC 28777-2733
(704)765-6993

Circa 1939. The scent of freshly baked muffins and steaming coffee serves as a pleasing wake-up call for guests staying at this country mountain home. More than an acre of wooded grounds surround the inn, which overlooks the Toe River valley. Rooms are decorated with family heirlooms and antiques. Several guest chambers include four-poster beds. Crackling flames from the stone fireplace warm the living room, a perfect place to relax. The innkeepers keep a guest refrigerator in the butler's pantry.
Innkeeper(s): Bill Ansley & Lee Boucher. $45-70. MC VISA DS TC. 7 rooms with PB. Breakfast included in rates. Types of meals: full breakfast and early coffee/tea. Beds: QT. Ceiling fan in room. Cable TV, VCR and fax on premises. Antiques, parks, shopping, downhill skiing, cross-country skiing, golf and watersports nearby.
Certificate may be used: Sunday through Thursday, no holidays or special events. Nov. 1-Sept. 30 (not in October).

Tabor City
D7

Four Rooster Inn
403 Pireway Rd Rt 904
Tabor City, NC 28463-2519
(910)653-3878 (800)653-5008 Fax:(910)653-3878

Circa 1949. This inn is surrounded by more than an acre of lush grounds, featuring camellias and azaleas planted by the innkeeper's father. Antiques, fine linens and tables set with china and crystal await to pamper you. Afternoon tea is served in the parlor. The innkeepers place a tray with steaming

fresh coffee or tea and the newspaper beside your guest room door in the morning. After a good night's sleep and coffee, guests settle down to a lavish, gourmet Southern breakfast, served in the inn's formal dining room. Sherried fruit compote, yam bread and succulent French toast stuffed with cheese are just a few of the possible items guests might enjoy. Myrtle Beach offers golf courses galore, the first of which is just four miles from the inn.
Innkeeper(s): Gloria & Bob Rogers. $45-75. MAP. MC VISA AX DC DS PC TC. 4 rooms, 2 with PB. Breakfast, afternoon tea and evening snack included in rates. Types of meals: gourmet breakfast and early coffee/tea. Beds: QD. Air conditioning and turndown service in room. Cable TV and VCR on premises. Amusement parks, antiques, fishing, parks, shopping, sporting events, theater and watersports nearby.
Certificate may be used: Anytime, subject to availability.

Taylorsville
B4

Barkley House B&B
2522 NC Hwy 16 S
Taylorsville, NC 28681-8952
(704)632-9060

Circa 1896. This 19th-century home is decorated in a country Victorian motif with antiques and family heirlooms, including the wedding dress that belonged to the innkeeper's mother, which is on display in the parlor. Breakfast is a lavish, Southern affair. Guests are pampered with entrees such as breakfast casseroles or stuffed French toast served with hot chocolate or hot apple cider, biscuits and gravy, grits, juice and fresh fruit. The area offers galleries, historic mansions and the Emerald Hollow Gem Mine, where guests can dig for precious gems. Guests enjoy a personal brandy cabinet and there are brandy tastings around 5 p.m.
Innkeeper(s): Phyllis Barkley. $59. MC VISA AX DS PC TC. 4 rooms with PB, 1 with FP. Breakfast and evening snack included in rates. Types of meals: continental-plus breakfast, full breakfast, gourmet breakfast and early coffee/tea. Catered breakfast available. Beds: KQDT. Air conditioning, turndown service, ceiling fan and TV in room. VCR, spa and library on premises. Antiques, fishing, shopping and sporting events nearby.
Certificate may be used: January-December, Sunday-Thursday, no major holidays or Blue Grass festival.

Tryon
C3

Fox Trot Inn
PO Box 1561, 800 Lynn Rd
Tryon, NC 28782-2708
(704)859-9706

Circa 1915. Located on six acres in town, this turn-of-the-century home features mountain views and large guest rooms. There is a private guest cottage with its own kitchen and a hanging deck. The rooms are furnished with antiques. The Cherry Room in the main house has a four-poster, queen-size canopy

bed with a sitting area overlooking the inn's swimming pool. The Oak Suite includes a wood-paneled sitting room. A cozy fireplace warms the lobby.

Innkeeper(s): Wim Woody. $75-125. PC. 4 rooms with PB. 2 suites. 1 cottage. Breakfast included in rates. Type of meal: full breakfast. Beds: QDT. Air conditioning in room. Cable TV and swimming on premises. Antiques, fishing, parks, shopping and watersports nearby.

Certificate may be used: Year-round, subject to availability, excluding October. For inn only, not guest cottage.

Mimosa Inn
One Mimosa Inn Ln
Tryon, NC 28782
(704)859-7688

Circa 1903. The Mimosa is situated on the southern slope of the Blue Ridge Mountains. With its long rolling lawns and large columned veranda, the

inn has been a landmark and social gathering place for almost a century. Breakfasts are served either in the dining room or on the columned veranda.

Innkeeper(s): Jay & Sandi Franks. $65. MC VISA DS PC TC. 9 rooms with PB. 1 conference room. Breakfast included in rates. Types of meals: full breakfast and early coffee/tea. Beds: QT. Air conditioning in room. Cable TV and library on premises. Amusement parks, antiques, fishing, parks, shopping and theater nearby.

"Thanks for your hospitality. We could just feel that Southern charm."

Certificate may be used: January-March, Sunday-Thursday. April-December, Monday-Thursday.

Tryon Old South B&B
107 Markham Rd
Tryon, NC 28782-3054
(704)859-6965 (800)288-7966 Fax:(704)859-2756

Circa 1910. This Colonial Revival inn is located just two blocks from downtown and Trade Street's antique and gift shops. Located in the Thermal Belt, Tryon is known for its pleasant, mild weather. Guests

don't go away hungry from innkeeper Terry Cacioppo's large Southern-style breakfasts. Unique woodwork abounds in this inn and equally as impressive is a curving staircase. Behind the property is a large wooded area and several waterfalls are just a couple of miles away. The inn is close to Asheville attractions.

Innkeeper(s): Michael & Terry Cacioppo. $55-125. MC VISA DS PC TC. 6 rooms, 4 with PB. 2 cottages. Breakfast included in rates. Types of meals: full breakfast and early coffee/tea. Beds: QDT. Air conditioning in room. Cable TV, VCR, fax and copier on premises. Antiques, fishing, parks, shopping and theater nearby.

Certificate may be used: Weekdays, year-round.

Valle Crucis   B4

Mast Farm Inn
PO Box 704
Valle Crucis, NC 28691-0704
(704)963-5857 (888)963-5857 Fax:(704)963-6404
E-mail: stay@mastfarminn.com

Circa 1885. Listed in the National Register of Historic Places, this 18-acre farmstead includes a main house and seven outbuildings. The inn features a wraparound porch with rocking chairs, swings and a view of the mountain valley. Rooms are furnished with antiques, quilts and mountain crafts. In addition to the inn rooms, there are four cottages available, some with kitchens. Flowers and vegetables from the garden are specialties. Morning coffee can be delivered to your room. Dinners feature contemporary regional cuisine.

Innkeeper(s): Wanda Hinshaw & Kay Philipp. $90-175. MC VISA AX DS TC. 9 rooms with PB. 4 cottages. Breakfast included in rates. Type of meal: full breakfast. Restaurant on premises. Beds: KQD. Ceiling fan in room. Fax on premises. Handicap access. Antiques, downhill skiing, sporting events, theater and watersports nearby.

Publicity: *Blue Ridge Country, Southern Living.*

"We want to live here!"

Certificate may be used: Jan. 5-April 30, Sunday-Thursday, holiday weekends excluded.

Washington B8

Acadian House B&B
129 Van Norden St
Washington, NC 27889
(919)975-3967 (888)972-3393 Fax:(919)975-1148

Circa 1902. This turn-of-the-century Victorian is listed in the National Register of Historic Places and is located in a historic district. Rooms are simply and comfortably furnished with Victorian touches, such as an antique Singer sewing machine transformed into a table. The innkeepers both hail from Louisiana and serve New Orleans-style specialties for breakfast, including beignets and cafe au lait. Shops and restaurants are within walking distance, and the Pamlico River is just one block away.
Innkeeper(s): Johanna & Leonard Huber. $55-65. MC VISA AX PC TC. 4 rooms with PB, 3 with FP. 1 suite. Breakfast included in rates. Meals: full breakfast, gourmet breakfast and early coffee/tea. Beds: KQDT. Air conditioning, ceiling fan in room. Fax, bicycles and library on premises. Antiques, fishing, parks, shopping, sporting events, golf, theater nearby.

"We really enjoyed the comfortable atmosphere, the food was delectable."

Certificate may be used: Feb. 1-March 31, Sunday-Thursday; July, Sunday-Thursday; Nov. 1-Dec. 14, Sunday-Thursday.

Waynesville B2

Grandview Lodge
466 Lickstone Rd
Waynesville, NC 28786
(704)456-5212 (800)255-7826 Fax:(704)452-5432
E-mail: sarnold@haywood.main.nc.us

Circa 1890. Grandview Lodge is located on two-and-a-half acres in the Smoky Mountains. The land surrounding the lodge has an apple orchard, rhubarb patch, grape arbor  and vegetable garden for the inn's kitchen. Rooms are available in the main lodge and in a newer addition. The inn's dining room is known throughout the region and Linda, a home economist, has written "Recipes from Grandview Lodge."
Innkeeper(s): Stan & Linda Arnold. $100-120. MAP. PC TC. 11 rooms with PB, 3 with FP. 2 suites. Breakfast and dinner included in rates. Meals: full breakfast and early coffee/tea. Lunch available. Restaurant on premises. Beds: KQDT. Air conditioning, TV in room. VCR, fax, computer, library on premises. Amusement parks, antiques, fishing, parks, shopping, downhill skiing, sporting events, theater, watersports nearby.
Publicity: *Asheville Citizen, Winston-Salem Journal, Raleigh News & Observer.*

"It's easy to see why family and friends have been enjoying trips to Grandview."

Certificate may be used: November through May, anytime; June, July-September, Sunday through Thursday; not participating August and October. Rates include dinner.

Mountain Creek Inn
146 Chestnut Walk Dr.
Waynesville, NC 28786
(704)456-5509 Fax:(704)456-6728

Circa 1950. From its floor-to-ceiling windows, this hilltop lodge affords views of mountains and woods and is surrounded by more than five, peaceful acres. Meander through the gardens or take a leisurely stroll on a nature path. The innkeepers found their bed & breakfast while trekking through the Smoky Mountains on a tandem bicycle. If weather permits, the champagne continental breakfast is served on the deck. For an additional charge, picnic lunches and romantic getaway packages for two can be prepared.
Innkeeper(s): Guy & Hylah Smalley. $85-110. AP. MC VISA AX DS PC TC. 5 rooms with PB. Breakfast and afternoon tea included in rates. Types of meals: continental breakfast, full breakfast and early coffee/tea. Evening snack, picnic lunch and gourmet lunch available. Beds: KQ. Air conditioning and turndown service in room. Cable TV, VCR, spa, swimming and library on premises. Handicap access. Amusement parks, antiques, fishing, parks, shopping, downhill skiing, cross-country skiing, theater and watersports nearby.

Certificate may be used: Nov. 1-June 30, Sunday-Thursday.

Weldon A8

Weldon Place Inn
500 Washington Ave
Weldon, NC 27890-1644
(919)536-4582 (800)831-4470 Fax:(919)536-4708

Circa 1913. Sausage- and cheese-stuffed French toast is a pleasant way to start your morning at this Colonial Revival home. Located in a National Historic District, it is two miles from I-95. Wedding showers and other celebrations are popular here. There are beveled-glass windows, canopy beds and Italian fireplaces. Most of the inn's antiques are original to the house, including a horse-hair stuffed couch with its original upholstery. Select the Romantic Retreat package and you'll enjoy sweets, other treats, a gift bag, sparkling cider, a whirlpool tub and breakfast in bed.
Innkeeper(s): Angel & Andy Whitby. $65-89. MC VISA AX. 4 rooms with PB. Breakfast included in rates. Type of meal: full breakfast. Beds: D. Air conditioning and TV in room. VCR on premises. Antiques, fishing, shopping and theater nearby.

Certificate may be used: Anytime.

Winston-Salem   B5

Augustus T. Zevely Inn

803 S Main St
Winston-Salem, NC 27101-5332
(910)748-9299 (800)928-9299 Fax:(910)721-2211

Circa 1844. The Zevely Inn is the only lodging in Old Salem. Each of the rooms at this charming pre-Civil War inn have a view of historic Old Salem. Moravian furnishings and fixtures permeate the decor of each of the guest quarters, some of which boast working fireplaces and whirlpool/steam baths. The home's architecture is reminiscent of many structures built in Old Salem during the second quarter of the 19th century. The formal dining room and parlor, which can be used for weddings and parties, have woodburning fireplaces. The two-story porch offers visitors a view of the period gardens and a magnolia tree. A line of Old Salem furniture has been created by Lexington Furniture Industries, and several pieces were created especially for the Zevely Inn.

Innkeeper(s): Linda Anderson. $80-185. MC VISA AX PC TC. 12 rooms with PB, 3 with FP. 1 suite. Breakfast and evening snack included in rates. Beds: KQDT. Air conditioning and TV in room. Fax and copier on premises. Antiques, shopping, sporting events and theater nearby.
Publicity: Washington Post Travel, Salem Star, Winston-Salem Journal, Tasteful, Country Living, National Trust for Historic Preservation, Homes and Gardens, Homes Across America, Southern Living.
"Colonial charm with modern conveniences, great food. Very nice! Everything was superb."
Certificate may be used: November, December, January, February on Sundays, Mondays, excluding seasonal events.

Colonel Ludlow Inn

434 Summit at W 5th
Winston-Salem, NC 27101
(910)777-1887 (800)301-1887 Fax:(910)777-1890
E-mail: innkeeper@bbinn.com

Circa 1887. Located in a historic urban residential neighborhood, this inn is comprised of two adjacent Victorians. Both are listed in the National Register and boast such features as wraparound porches, gabled roofs, ornate entrances, beautiful windows and high ceilings. Guest rooms are decorated with Victorian antiques and each includes a double whirlpool tub. The innkeepers provide many thoughtful amenities, such as stocked mini-refrigerators, microwaves, coffee makers, stereos, TVs with VCRs and free movies, irons, bathrobes and hair dryers. There is a Nautilus exercise room, billiards room and a golf driving cage.

Innkeeper(s): Constance Creasman. $95-229. MC VISA AX DC DS PC TC. 10 rooms, 9 with PB, 5 with FP. Breakfast included in rates. Meals: full breakfast and early coffee/tea. Lunch, room service available. Beds: K. Air conditioning, ceiling fan, TV, VCR in room. Computer on premises. Antiques, fishing, parks, shopping, sporting events, theater nearby.
Location: Off Hwy I-40, near downtown.
Publicity: Winston-Salem Journal, Charlotte Observer, Mid-Atlantic Country, Southern Living, Southern Accents, USA Today, American Way.

"I have never seen anything like the meticulous and thorough attention to detail. — The Charlotte Observer"
Certificate may be used: Sunday-Monday.

Wachovia B&B

513 Wachovia St
Winston-Salem, NC 27101-5042
(910)777-0332

Circa 1907. This rose and white Victorian cottage with a wraparound porch is located on a quiet, tree-lined street. The inn is only a few blocks from the Winston-Salem city center and Old Salem Historic District. Guests may choose to eat their breakfast in the large dining room, in their rooms or on the porch. The innkeepers like to provide flexible check-in and check-out times and there is no rigid breakfast schedule. Within walking distance is the Stevens Center for performing arts, gourmet restaurants, antique and specialty shops and several exercise facilities and parks.

Innkeeper(s): Susan & Greg Pfaff. $55-65. MC VISA TC. 5 rooms, 2 with PB, 1 with FP. Breakfast included in rates. Types of meals: continental-plus breakfast, full breakfast and early coffee/tea. Beds: QDT. Air conditioning, turndown service and ceiling fan in room. Cable TV on premises. Antiques, parks, shopping, sporting events, theater nearby.
Publicity: Parentips, Winston-Salem.
Certificate may be used: All year subject to availability.

Winston-Salem (Germantown)

Meadowhaven B&B

PO Box 222
Winston-Salem (Germantown), NC 27019
(910)593-3996 Fax:(910)593-3138

Circa 1976. This contemporary chalet is located on 25 pastoral acres in the foothills of the Blue Ridge Mountains. There are guest rooms decorated in a romantic mix of contemporary and country styles, as well as a mountain-top cottage with two bedrooms and a log cabin that offers a mountain view. Overside tubs for two, fireplaces, a spa, heated indoor pool and a sauna are just some of the amenities awaiting guests. There is a game room on the premises, and guests also have use of pedal boats. Nearby attractions include Hanging Rock State Park and Dan River, perfect for canoeing or rafting. The inn is located 16 miles from Winston-Salem.

Germantown offers an art gallery and a winery.
Innkeeper(s): Samuel & Darlene Fain. $70-175. MC VISA AX DS PC TC. 6 rooms with PB, 2 with FP. 2 suites. 2 cottages. Breakfast and evening snack included in rates. Meals: full breakfast, early coffee/tea. Picnic lunch available. Beds: QD. Air conditioning, turndown service, ceiling fan, TV, VCR in room. Fax, copier, spa, swimming, sauna on premises. Antiques, fishing, parks, sporting events, theater, watersports nearby.
Certificate may be used: Sunday-Thursday except April, August, October and holidays.

North Dakota

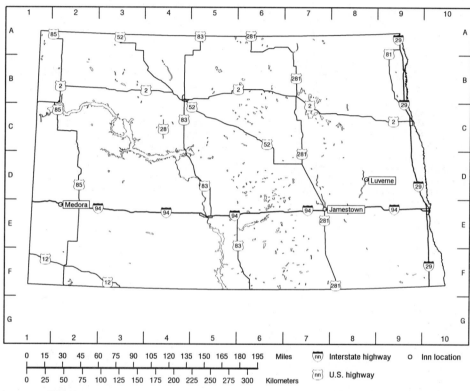

0   15   30   45   60   75   90   105 120 135 150 165 180 195   Miles
|—|—|—|—|—|—|—|—|—|—|—|—|—|—|

0   25   50   75   100 125 150 175 200 225 250 275 300   Kilometers
|—|—|—|—|—|—|—|—|—|—|—|—|—|

(nn) Interstate highway   O Inn location

[nn] U.S. highway

Jamestown   E7

Country Charm B&B
RR 3 Box 71
Jamestown, ND 58401
(701)251-1372 (800)331-1372

Circa 1897. Jamestown not only offers convenience — centrally located at the intersection of
the state's east-west interstate and main north-
south highway — it features the Country Charm, a
prairie farmhouse six miles from town and a short
hop from I-94. The inn's tranquil setting is accented by the surrounding pines and cottonwood trees.
The blue-dominated Patches and Lace Room features a multi-shaded patchwork quilt. Activities
and places of interest abound in the Jamestown
area, including Frontier Village and North Dakota's
oldest courthouse.

Innkeeper(s): Ethel Oxtoby. $42-53. 4 rooms. Breakfast included in
rates. Type of meal: full breakfast. Air conditioning and ceiling fan in
room. VCR on premises. Antiques, fishing, shopping, cross-country
skiing, sporting events and theater nearby.

Certificate may be used: Monday through Thursday, all year.

Luverne
D8

Volden Farm
RR 2, Box 50
Luverne, ND 58056
(701)769-2275

Circa 1885. Perennial gardens and a hedge of lilacs surround this redwood house with its newer addition. A favorite room is the North Room with a lace canopy bed, an old pie safe and a Texas Star quilt made by the host's grandmother. Guests enjoy soaking in the clawfoot tub while looking out to the apple and plum orchard. There is a library, music room and game room. The innkeepers also offer lodging in the Law Office, a separate little prairie house ideal for families. A stream, bordered by old oaks and formed by a natural spring, meanders through the property. The chickens here lay green and blue eggs. Supper is available by advanced arrangement.

Innkeeper(s): Jim & JoAnne Wold. $50-75. PC. 4 rooms. 1 suite. 1 cottage. Breakfast and evening snack included in rates. Types of meals: full breakfast, gourmet breakfast and early coffee/tea. Dinner, picnic lunch, lunch, gourmet lunch, catering service and room service available. Beds: KDT. VCR, bicycles and library on premises. Antiques, fishing, parks, shopping, downhill skiing, cross-country skiing and watersports nearby.

Location: 80 miles northwest of Fargo.

Publicity: *Fargo Forum, Horizons, Grand Forks Herald.*

"Very pleasant indeed! Jim & JoAnne make you feel good. There's so much to do, and the hospitality is amazing!"

Certificate may be used: Anytime, holidays excluded.

Medora
E2

The Rough Riders Hotel B&B
Medora, ND 58645
(701)623-4444 Fax:(701)623-4494

Circa 1865. This old hotel has the branding marks of Teddy Roosevelt's cattle ranch as well as other brands stamped into the rough-board facade out front. A wooden sidewalk helps to maintain the turn-of-the-century cow-town feeling. Rustic guest rooms are above the restaurant and are furnished with homesteader antiques original to the area. In the summer, an outdoor pageant is held complete with stagecoach and horses. In October, deer hunters are accommodated. The hotel, along with two motels, is managed by the non-profit Theodore Roosevelt Medora Foundation.

Innkeeper(s): Randy Hatzenbuhler. $55. MC VISA AX. 9 rooms with PB. Breakfast included in rates.

Certificate may be used: Oct. 1-May 1, excluding Friday and Saturday nights.

Ohio

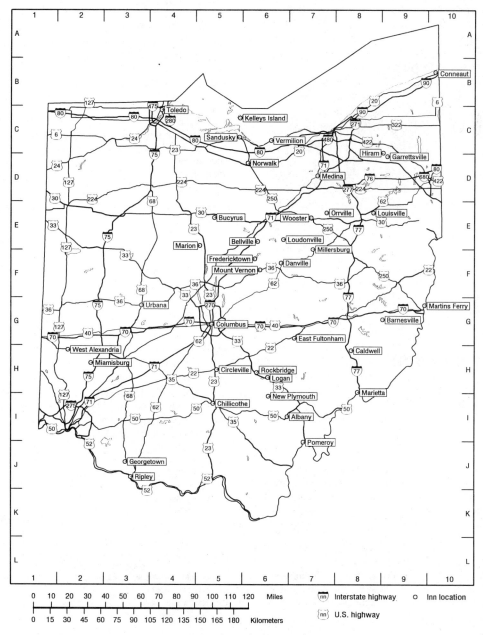

0 10 20 30 40 50 60 70 80 90 100 110 120 Miles

0 15 30 45 60 75 90 105 120 135 150 165 180 Kilometers

(nn) Interstate highway   o Inn location

(nn) U.S. highway

Albany
I6

Albany House
9 Clinton St
Albany, OH 45710
(614)698-6311 (800)600-4941

Circa 1860. Located seven miles from Ohio University in a quaint village setting, this inn is filled with antiques, quilts, Oriental rugs and collectibles. Because of four two-story columns, it is often referred

to as "Tara North." A new addition includes an indoor pool, showers and changing room.
Innkeeper(s): Sarah & Ted Hutchins. $65-100. MC VISA AX DS. 6 rooms, 2 with PB. 1 conference room. Breakfast and evening snack included in rates. Types of meals: continental-plus breakfast, gourmet breakfast and early coffee/tea. Beds: QDT. Antiques, fishing, parks, shopping, theater and watersports nearby.

Publicity: *Post.*

Certificate may be used: Weekdays, Sunday-Thursday; weekends if available.

Barnesville
G9

Georgian Pillars B&B
128 E Walnut St
Barnesville, OH 43713-1237
(614)425-3741 (800)525-3741

Victorian charm permeates this Georgian Revival home, which boasts ornate woodwork and stained-glass windows. The decidedly Victorian parlors offer a refreshing change of pace from the rush of modern times; one of the parlors has a fireplace. Posh breakfasts are served in the elegant dining room on Royal Doulton pieces. Teal and mauve hues abound in the guest rooms, which feature unique, Victorian furnishings with flowery prints. The bed & breakfast also houses a small gift shop with a signed, numbered set of "Barnesville Collection of Historic Miniature Houses."

Innkeeper(s): Janet Thompson. $45-55. MC VISA. 3 rooms. Breakfast included in rates. Type of meal: full breakfast.

Certificate may be used: Sunday through Thursday, June through Oct. 30; November through May, anytime.

Bellville
E6

Frederick Fitting House
72 Fitting Ave
Bellville, OH 44813-1043
(419)886-2863 Fax:(419)886-2863

This blue and white Italianate Victorian house commands a corner of the town of Bellville, 10 minutes from Ohio University. Rooms include the Colonial Room with a queen canopy bed and the Shaker Room with twin beds that can be converted to a king. Breakfast is served in the Victorian dining room or garden gazebo, but you may wish to carry it to the front porch or to the library where you can settle down during the winter in front of a roaring fire. Malabar Farms is nearby as is the Mohican River.
Innkeeper(s): Suzanne Wilson. $48-72. 3 rooms. Breakfast included in rates. Types of meals: full breakfast and early coffee/tea. Evening snack and picnic lunch available. Ceiling fan in room. Cable TV and VCR on premises. Antiques, shopping, downhill skiing, cross-country skiing and sporting events nearby.

Certificate may be used: Sunday-Thursday, May-October. Anyday, November-April.

Bucyrus
E5

Hide Away B&B
1601 SR 4
Bucyrus, OH 44820-9587
(419)562-3013 Fax:(419)562-3003

Circa 1938. This aptly named B&B sits on six acres, which afford views of the nearby Little Scioto River. The home was built by inventor S.H. Smith, who among his patents, was responsible for creating transistor radios used in World War II aircraft. Guest rooms are decorated in a comfortable country motif with special antiques and amenities such as a feathertick. The grounds include a swimming pool and relaxing Jacuzzi.
Innkeeper(s): Steve & Debbie Miller. $40-125. MC VISA AX DS TC. 4 rooms with PB. 2 conference rooms. Types of meals: continental breakfast, continental-plus breakfast, full breakfast, gourmet breakfast and early coffee/tea. Afternoon tea, dinner, evening snack, picnic lunch, lunch, gourmet lunch, banquet service, catering service and catered breakfast available. Beds: KQ. Air conditioning, turndown service and VCR in room. Fax, copier, spa, bicycles and child care on premises. Amusement parks, antiques, parks, shopping, downhill skiing, theater and watersports nearby.

Certificate may be used: Jan. 2-Dec. 31, Sunday-Thursday. Corporate rates not applicable.

Caldwell
H8

Harkins House Inn
715 West St
Caldwell, OH 43724
(614)732-7347

Circa 1905. Innkeeper Stacey Lucas' great-grandfather built this turn-of-the-century home, which features many Victorian elements. He was a founder of the town's First National Bank. High ceilings, intricate moldings and original woodwork remain, as does the grand staircase. The decor includes brightly painted walls and flowery wallpapers. The second-story hall features Victorian furnishings, rose walls with team stenciling and teal carpeting. Guests choose their own breakfast fare from a daily menu, which features items such as bacon, eggs, homemade muffins and coffee cake. State parks, antique shops and historic sites are nearby.

Innkeeper(s): Jeff & Stacey Lucas. $35-65. MC VISA AX PC TC. 2 rooms with PB. Breakfast included in rates. Types of meals: full breakfast and early coffee/tea. Beds: DT. Air conditioning in room. Cable TV, VCR, library and child care on premises. Antiques, fishing, parks, shopping, golf and theater nearby.

Publicity: *Journal-Leader.*

"Lucky for us we found your most interesting and beautiful home."

Certificate may be used: Jan. 5-April 30.

Chillicothe
I5

Chillicothe B&B
202 S Paint St
Chillicothe, OH 45601-3827
(614)772-6848

Circa 1867. This National Register home, which was constructed while the nation struggled with the Civil War, was built by the owner of the town's first paper mill. Innkeepers Katie and Jack Sullivan furnished the home with antiques and collectibles, including a collection of vintage clothing. Clothing is somewhat of a passion for Katie, who has created costumes for many local theatrical productions. Jack, an artist and photographer, will provide a tour of his studio to interested guests. Chillicothe, once the capital of Ohio, is full of many historic homes.

Innkeeper(s): Kathryn Sullivan. $35-50. MC VISA. 4 rooms. Breakfast included in rates. Type of meal: full breakfast.

Certificate may be used: Sunday through Thursday, year-round.

Circleville
H5

Penguin Crossing
3291 SR 56 W
Circleville, OH 43113-9622
(614)477-6222 (800)736-4846 Fax:(614)477-6222

Circa 1820. Once a stagecoach stop, now a romantic country getaway, this B&B offers amenities in the rooms such as a woodburning fireplace, clawfoot tub, brass bed or a heart-shaped Jacuzzi. As the name might suggest, the innkeepers have a collection of penguins on display. Breakfasts  include a selection of natural foods, and the innkeeper is happy to cater to special dietary needs.

Innkeeper(s): Ross & Tracey Irvin. $100-175. MC VISA DS PC TC. 4 rooms with PB, 1 with FP. Breakfast included in rates. Types of meals: gourmet breakfast and early coffee/tea. Beds: KQDT. Air conditioning and turndown service in room. VCR and fax on premises. Handicap access. Antiques, fishing, parks, shopping, theater and watersports nearby.

"If I had to describe this home in one word, it would be — enchanting."

Certificate may be used: All year, Monday-Thursday, all week January-April, except Valentine's Day or weekend.

Conneaut
B10

Campbell Braemar
390 State St
Conneaut, OH 44030-2510
(216)599-7362

Circa 1927. This little Colonial Revival house is decorated in a Scottish style, and a Scottish breakfast is provided. Guests are invited to use the  kitchen for light cooking as the hosts live next door. Wineries, golf, fishing, sandy beaches and hunting are nearby. The innkeepers also offer a fully furnished apartment with two large bedrooms, a living room, cable TV and a fully equipped kitchen.

Innkeeper(s): Mary & Andrew Campbell. $58-78. TC. 3 rooms. Breakfast and afternoon tea included in rates. Types of meals: continental breakfast, continental-plus breakfast, full breakfast and early coffee/tea. Beds: KQD. Air conditioning and TV in room. Antiques, fishing, parks and watersports nearby.

Certificate may be used: January-December, Sunday-Saturday.

Danville   F6

Red Fox Country Inn

26367 Danville Amity Rd
Danville, OH 43014-9769
(740)599-7369

Circa 1830. This inn, located on 15 scenic central Ohio acres, was built originally to house those traveling on the Danville-Amity Wagon Road and later became a farm home. Amish woven rag rugs and country antiques decorate the guest rooms. Some of the furnishings belonged to early owners, and some date to the 18th century. Three rooms include Amish-made oak beds and the fourth an 1880s brass and iron double bed. Breakfasts include fresh pastries, fruits, coffee and a variety of delectable entrees. Special dietary needs usually can be accommodated. Dinners are served by reservation. There are books and games available in the inn's sitting

room, and guests also are invited to relax on the front porch. An antique shop is housed in a renovated horse stable on the premises. Golfing, canoeing, fishing, horseback riding, hiking, biking, skiing and Mohican State Park are nearby, and the inn is 30 minutes from the largest Amish community in the United States.

Innkeeper(s): Ida & Mort Wolff. $65-85. MC VISA AX DS PC TC. 4 rooms with PB. Breakfast included in rates. Dinner, banquet service and catering service available. Beds: QD. Air conditioning in room. Library on premises.

Publicity: *Columbus Dispatch, Mount Vernon News, Cincinnati Enquirer, Cleveland.*

"Our dinner and breakfast were '5 star'. Thank you for the gracious hospitality and special kindness you showed us."

Certificate may be used: Weekdays all year round. Weekends Dec. 1-March 31. Excludes holidays and events at area colleges.

The White Oak Inn

29683 Walhonding Rd, SR 715
Danville, OH 43014-9681
(740)599-6107
E-mail: 74627.3717@compuserve.com

Circa 1915. Large oaks and ivy surround the wide front porch of this three-story farmhouse situated on

13 green acres. It is located on the former Indian trail and pioneer road that runs along the Kokosing River, and an Indian mound has been discovered on the property. The inn's woodwork is all original white oak, and guest rooms are furnished in antiques. Visitors often shop for maple syrup, cheese and handicrafts at nearby Amish farms. Three cozy fireplace rooms provide the perfect setting for romantic evenings.

Innkeeper(s): Yvonne & Ian Martin. $75-140. MAP. MC VISA AX DS PC TC. 10 rooms with PB, 3 with FP. 1 conference room. Breakfast and evening snack included in rates. Types of meals: full breakfast and early coffee/tea. Dinner and catering service available. Beds: QDT. Air conditioning and ceiling fan in room. Bicycles and library on premises. Antiques, fishing, parks, shopping and watersports nearby.

Location: Holmes County Amish area, north central Ohio.

Publicity: *Ladies Home Journal, Columbus Monthly, Cleveland Plain Dealer, Country, Glamour, Columbus Dispatch.*

"The dinner was just fabulous and we enjoyed playing the antique grand piano."

Certificate may be used: Sunday to Thursday nights all year-round.

East Fultonham   G7

Hill View Acres B&B

7320 Old Town Rd
East Fultonham, OH 43735
(614)849-2728

Circa 1905. Hill View Acres was an apt description for this relaxing country home, which is surrounded by more than 20 acres of rolling hills. The large deck is a wonderful place to sit and soak up the atmosphere. The grounds also include a swimming

pool and spa. Innkeeper Dawn Graham has won several local cooking contests and enjoys treating her guests to a hearty country breakfast each morning. Dawn and husband Jim work out the menu with guests the night before, taking in all dietary concerns. Dawn creates luscious items accompanied by homemade jams and jellies. The home is near many attractions, including wildlife preserves, museums, outlet shopping and the Ohio Ceramic Center.
Innkeeper(s): Jim & Dawn Graham. $45-70. MC VISA AX. 2 rooms. Breakfast included in rates. Types of meals: full breakfast and early coffee/tea. Dinner, evening snack, picnic lunch and lunch available. Beds: D. Air conditioning in room. Spa and swimming on premises. Antiques, fishing, parks and shopping nearby.

Certificate may be used: Jan. 1-Dec. 31, excluding Dec. 25.

Fredericktown   F6

Heartland Country Resort
2994 Township Rd 190
Fredericktown, OH 43019
(419)768-9300 (800)230-7030

Circa 1878. This remodeled farmhouse and luxury log cabin offer guests a serene country setting with hills, woods, pastures, fields, wooded trails, barns,

horse stables and riding arenas. The four suites include a fireplace and Jacuzzi tub. With full run of the huge house, guests also have their choice of a wide variety of recreation. Horseback riding is the recreation of choice for most visitors. Innkeeper Dorene Henschen tells guests not to miss the beauty of the woods as seen on the guided trail rides.
Innkeeper(s): Dorene Henschen. $80-155. MC VISA DS TC. 6 rooms with PB. 4 suites. Breakfast and afternoon tea included in rates. Type of meal: continental-plus breakfast. Dinner, picnic lunch and room service available. Beds: KQT. Antiques, fishing, downhill skiing, cross-country skiing and watersports nearby.
Publicity: *Columbus Dispatch, Country Extra, One Tank Trips, Getaways.*

"Warm hospitality . . . Beautiful surroundings and pure peace & quiet. What more could one want from a B&B in the country? Thank you for an excellent memory!"
Certificate may be used: Monday through Thursday.

Garrettsville   D9

Blueberry Hill B&B
11085 North St (RT 88)
Garrettsville, OH 44231
(216)527-5068

Although this restored Victorian is just minutes from downtown Garrettsville, the landscaped grounds create a secluded, pastoral setting. Relax in front of a woodburning fireplace or stroll through nearby woods. Rooms are decorated in Laura Ashley prints  with Victorian touches and the innkeepers own an impressive collection of artwork. The home is located on the outskirts of one of the largest Amish towns in the United States, and it is near both Hiram College and Kent State University.
Innkeeper(s): Deborah Darling. $60. 2 rooms. Breakfast included in rates. Type of meal: continental breakfast.

Certificate may be used: All year Monday through Thursday, except holidays.

Georgetown   J3

Bailey House
112 N Water St
Georgetown, OH 45121-1332
(937)378-3087

Circa 1830. The stately columns of this three-story Greek Revival house once greeted Ulysses S. Grant, a frequent visitor during his boyhood when he was sent to buy milk from the Bailey's. A story is told that Grant accidentally overheard that the Bailey boy was leaving West Point. Grant immediately ran

through the woods to the home of Congressman Thomas Hamer and petitioned an appointment in Bailey's place which he received, thus launching his military career. The inn has double parlors, pegged oak floors and Federal-style fireplace mantels. Antique washstands, chests and beds are found in the large guest rooms.

Innkeeper(s): Nancy Purdy & Jane Sininger. $55. PC. 4 rooms, 2 with FP. Breakfast and afternoon tea included in rates. Types of meals: full breakfast and early coffee/tea. Beds: QD. Air conditioning in room. Swimming and library on premises. Antiques, fishing, parks, shopping, golf and watersports nearby.

"Thank you for your warm hospitality, from the comfortable house to the delicious breakfast."

Certificate may be used: Oct. 1-May 30, Sunday-Thursday.

Hiram   C9

The Lily Ponds B&B
PO Box 322, 6720 Wakefield Rd
Hiram, OH 44234-0322
(330)569-3222 (800)325-5087 Fax:(330)569-3223

Circa 1940. This homestay is located on 20 acres of woodland dotted with rhododendron and mountain laurel. There are two large ponds and an old stone bridge. Your hostess works with a tour company and has traveled around the world. The inn's decor includes her collections of Eskimo art and artifacts and a variety of antiques. Pecan waffles served with locally harvested maple syrup are a favorite breakfast. Guests enjoy borrowing the canoe or hiking the inn's trails. Sea World is a 15-minute drive away.

Innkeeper(s): Marilane Spencer. $55-75. MC VISA. 3 rooms with PB. Breakfast included in rates. Types of meals: full breakfast and early coffee/tea. Beds: KQT. Air conditioning and TV in room. VCR, bicycles, library and child care on premises. Amusement parks, antiques, fishing, parks, shopping, downhill skiing, cross-country skiing and watersports nearby.

Location: 45 minutes from downtown Cleveland.

Publicity: *Record-Courier, Record-News.*

"We felt like we were staying with friends from the very start."

Certificate may be used: Any day, year-round, except Friday and Saturday, June through September.

Kelleys Island   C5

Fly Inn B&B
PO Box 471, Dwelle Ln
Kelleys Island, OH 43438-0471
(419)746-2525 (800)359-4661 Fax:(419)746-2525

Circa 1988. Kelleys Island, for those not familiar with Ohio, encompasses a 2,800-acre patch of land in Lake Erie, all designated a historic district in the National Register. One acre of this wooded island encircles this rustic B&B, adjacent to the airport. Guests can watch as light planes cruise by or visit the island's historic sites and winery. The guest rooms are comfortable and homey, with modern decor. During the summer, guests can dive into the inn's swimming pool, and the innkeepers offer bicycles for touring the area.

Innkeeper(s): Ken & Joann Neufer. $90-110. MC VISA DS. 4 rooms, 2 with PB. 1 conference room. Breakfast included in rates. Beds: KQ. Air conditioning in room. VCR, fax and bicycles on premises. Handicap access. Amusement parks, fishing, parks, shopping and watersports nearby.

Location: On Lake Erie.

Certificate may be used: Sunday through Thursday beginning Oct. 1 and ending April 30, no holidays included.

The Inn on Kelleys Island
PO Box 11
Kelleys Island, OH 43438-0011
(419)746-2258

Circa 1876. With a private deck on the shore of Lake Erie, this waterfront Victorian offers an acre of grounds. Built by the innkeeper's ancestor, Captain Frank Hamilton, the house features a black marble fireplace and a porch with a spectacular Lake Erie view. The Pilot House is a room with large windows looking out to the lake. The inn is close to the ferry and downtown with restaurants, taverns and shops.

Innkeeper(s): Lori Hayes. $65-85. 4 rooms. Breakfast included in rates. Types of meals: continental breakfast and early coffee/tea. Beds: D. Ceiling fan in room. VCR on premises. Amusement parks, antiques, fishing and shopping nearby.

Location: Lakefront on Kelleys Island.

Certificate may be used: Sunday-Thursday during months of April, May, September, October and November excluding holidays.

Logan   H6

The Inn at Cedar Falls
21190 SR 374
Logan, OH 43138
(614)385-7489 (800)653-2557 Fax:(614)385-0820

Circa 1987. This barn-style inn was constructed on 60 acres adjacent to Hocking State Park and one-half mile from the waterfalls. The kitchen and dining room is in a 19th-century log house with a wood-burning stove and 18-inch-wide plank floor. Accommodations in the new barn building are simple and comfortable, each furnished with antiques. There are also five, fully equipped log cabins available, each individually decorated. Verandas provide sweeping views of woodland and meadow. The grounds include organic gardens for the inn's gourmet dinners, and animals that have been spotted include bobcat, red fox, wild turkey and whitetail deer.

Innkeeper(s): Ellen Grinsfelder. $75-195. MC VISA PC. 14 rooms, 9 with PB, 5 with FP. 5 cottages. 1 conference room. Breakfast included in rates. Types of meals: full breakfast, gourmet breakfast and early coffee/tea. Dinner, picnic lunch, lunch and gourmet lunch available. Restaurant on premises. Beds: QT. Air conditioning in room. Fax, copier and library on premises. Handicap access. Antiques, fishing, parks, shopping, cross-country skiing and theater nearby.

Publicity: Post.

"*Very peaceful, relaxing and friendly. Couldn't be nicer.*"

Certificate may be used: Sunday through Thursday beginning Nov. 15 and ending April 15, no holidays included, rooms and cabins.

Louisville   E8

The Mainstay B&B
1320 E Main St
Louisville, OH 44641-1910
(216)875-1021

Circa 1886. Built by a Civil War veteran, this Victorian still has the original fish scale on its gables, and inside, it features carved-oak woodwork and oak doors. Guests are treated to a complimentary basket of fruit and cheese in their air-conditioned rooms. Outside are flower gardens with birdbaths and a water fountain. This is a great stop in the middle of a long trip because laundry facilities are available to guests. Nearby colleges are Malone, Walsh, Mount Union and Kent State University.

Innkeeper(s): Mary & Joe Shurilla. $50-60. AP. MC VISA PC. 3 rooms with PB. Breakfast and evening snack included in rates. Types of meals: full breakfast and early coffee/tea. Beds: QDT. Air conditioning in room. Cable TV and VCR on premises. Antiques, parks and downhill skiing nearby.

Certificate may be used: Sunday through Thursday, not holidays.

Marietta   H8

The Buckley House
332 Front St
Marietta, OH 45750-2913
(614)373-3080 Fax:(614)373-8000

Circa 1879. A double veranda accents this gable-front Greek Revival house and provides views of Muskingum Park and the river, as well as Lookout Point and the "Valley Gem," a traditional Mississippi river boat. Guests are served tea, evening aperitifs and breakfast from the inn's parlor, porches and dining room. Within a five-block area are museums, a mound cemetery, the W.P. Snyder Jr. Sternwheeler, boat rides, trolley tours and shops and restaurants.

Innkeeper(s): Dell & Alf Nicholas. $70-80. MC VISA DS PC TC. 3 rooms with PB, 1 with FP. 1 suite. Breakfast included in rates. Types of meals: full breakfast and early coffee/tea. Beds: KDT. Air conditioning and ceiling fan in room. Cable TV, VCR, fax, spa and library on premises. Antiques, fishing, parks, shopping, theater and watersports nearby.

Certificate may be used: Nov. 15-March 31, Monday-Thursday.

Marion   E5

Olde Towne Manor
245 Saint James St
Marion, OH 43302-5134
(614)382-2402 (800)341-6163

Circa 1920. This stone house, located in the heart of Marionís historic district, won Marionís most attractive building award in 1990. The home offers

bookworms the chance to browse through a 1,000-volume library. A gazebo or sauna are ideal settings for relaxation. The nearby home of President Warren G. Harding and the Harding Memorial will attract history buffs. In August, the town hosts the U.S. Open Drum and Bugle Corps National Championships, and the Marion Popcorn Festival is a unique attraction the weekend after Labor Day.

Innkeeper(s): Mary Louisa Rimbach. $55-65. MC VISA AX. 4 rooms with PB. Breakfast included in rates. Type of meal: full breakfast. Beds: QDT. Air conditioning in room. Cable TV, VCR and sauna on premises. Antiques, fishing, shopping and theater nearby.

Publicity: *Marion Star, News Life, Ohio Week.*

"Thanks for a warm and intimate home away from home! Lovely place with great hostess!"

Certificate may be used: Anytime, except Dec. 24 & 25.

Martins Ferry   G9

Mulberry Inn B&B
53 N 4th St
Martins Ferry, OH 43935-1523
(614)633-6058 (800)705-6171 Fax:(614)633-5923

Circa 1868. The Roosevelt Room in this Victorian inn once housed Eleanor Roosevelt during a "Bond Drive." Mrs. Blackford, goddaughter of Jefferson Davis, was the hostess during that time and was well-known for her hospitality during the Depression. The inn is decorated with country antiques and quilts.

Innkeeper(s): Charles & Shirley Probst. $45-60. MC VISA AX DS. 3 rooms, 1 with PB. Breakfast and evening snack included in rates. Types of meals: continental-plus breakfast and early coffee/tea. Beds: QD. Air conditioning, turndown service and ceiling fan in room. Cable TV on premises. Antiques, fishing, parks, shopping, downhill skiing, sporting events, theater and watersports nearby.

Location: Southeast Ohio along the Ohio River.

Publicity: *Times Leader, Herald Star, Akron Beacon Journal*

"This is my third stay and it's like coming home when I'm away on business. This beautiful home really softens my purpose for being here! As always, I enjoy your company, warmth, and great breakfast!"

Certificate may be used: Jan. 4-March 31, Sunday-Saturday.

Medina   D7

Livery Building
254 E Smith Rd
Medina, OH 44256-2623
(216)722-1332

This three-story Queen Anne, which once housed a local livery horse business, offers one immense suite featuring antique furnishings, small parlor and kitchenette with a wet bar. The wood-burning stove adds country charm. The innkeepers offer a full breakfast made from organic ingredients. The bed & breakfast is within walking distance of Medina's restored Victorian town square and historic district.

Innkeeper(s): Candace Hutton. $65. 1 room. Breakfast included in rates. Type of meal: full breakfast.

Certificate may be used: Anytime, June 1-Sept. 30.

Miamisburg   H2

English Manor B&B
505 E Linden Ave
Miamisburg, OH 45342-2850
(513)866-2288 (800)676-9456

This is a beautiful English Tudor mansion situated on a tree-lined street of Victorian homes. Well-chosen antiques combined with the innkeepers' personal heirlooms added to the inn's polished floors, sparkling leaded- and stained-glass windows and shining silver, make this an elegant retreat. Breakfast is served in the formal dining room or by the fireplace in your room, and in the afternoon, tea is served. Fine restaurants, a waterpark, baseball and theater are close by, as is The River Corridor bikeway on the banks of the Great Miami River.

Innkeeper(s): Ken Huelsman. $65-95. MC VISA AX DC CB DS. 5 rooms. 1 conference room. Breakfast included in rates. Type of meal: full breakfast. Air conditioning and turndown service in room. Cable TV and VCR on premises. Amusement parks, antiques, shopping, sporting events and theater nearby.

Certificate may be used: Sunday through Thursday.

Millersburg   F7

Bigham House
151 S Washington St
Millersburg, OH 44654-1315
(330)674-2337 (800)689-6950

Circa 1869. Bigham House is a two-story Victorian located in the world's largest Amish settlement. Antiques and Victorian reproductions decorate the rooms. Ask for Dr. Bigham's Room and you'll enjoy stained-glass windows, a fireplace and brass ceiling fan. Nearby activities include buggy rides and the restored Ohio Central Railway.

Innkeeper(s): John Henry Ellis. $70-80. MC VISA. 4 rooms, 3 with PB, 1 with FP. Breakfast included in rates. Types of meals: full breakfast and gourmet breakfast. Afternoon tea available. Beds: Q.

Location: In the heart of the largest Amish settlement in the world, Holmes County, Ohio.

Publicity: *Holmes County Traveler.*

Certificate may be used: November-April, Sunday-Thursday

Mount Vernon F6

Tuck'er Inn
12059 Tucker Rd
Mount Vernon, OH 43050
(614)392-5659

Circa 1969. There are 12 woodland acres to explore here. Guests can hike to ravines or enjoy the scenery around Granny Creek. There are two guest rooms in the main house, which was built in Colonial style. There is also a guest house in the woods with two bedrooms and a wood-burning stove. The guest house can sleep up to six people. The inn is within an hour of the sites of Amish country.
Innkeeper(s): Bill & Marian Cleland. $50-125. PC TC. 2 rooms with PB. 1 cottage. Breakfast included in rates. Type of meal: continental-plus breakfast. Beds: QD. Air conditioning in room. VCR, bicycles and library on premises. Antiques, fishing, parks, shopping, downhill skiing, cross-country skiing, sporting events and theater nearby.

"I had such a sweet night at your inn. Many, many thanks."

Certificate may be used: November-April, June, July; seven days subject to availability. Guesthouse $125.00 a night.

New Plymouth I6

Ravenwood Castle
65666 Bethel Rd
New Plymouth, OH 45654-9707
(614)596-2606 (800)477-1541 Fax:(614)596-5818

Circa 1995. Although this is a newer construction, the architect modeled the inn after a 12th-century, Norman-style castle, offering a glimpse back at Medieval England. A Great Hall with massive stone fireplace, dramatic rooms and suites with antique stained-glass windows and gas fireplaces make for a unique getaway. The castle, which overlooks Vinton County's Swan township, is surrounded by 50 acres of forest and large rock formations and is reached by a half-mile private road. There is a tea room and gift shop on the premises.
Innkeeper(s): Jim & Sue Maxwell. $85-165. MC VISA DS. 8 rooms with PB. 3 cottages. Breakfast included in rates. Types of meals: full breakfast and early coffee/tea. Afternoon tea, dinner, evening snack, picnic lunch and room service available. Restaurant on premises. Beds: KQD. Air conditioning and ceiling fan in room. VCR, fax and copier on premises. Handicap access. Antiques, fishing, shopping and watersports nearby.
Publicity: *Columbus Dispatch, Cincinnati Enquirer, Athens Messenger, Southeast Ohio Traveler, Vinton County Courier, Hocking Hills Travel News, A Taste for Columbus, Country Register, USA Today, Honeymoon.*

"The atmosphere is romantic, the food excellent, the hospitality super!"

Certificate may be used: Nov. 1-March 31, Sunday-Thursday, except holidays.

Norwalk D6

Boos Family Inn B&B
5054 SR 601
Norwalk, OH 44857-9729
(419)668-6257 Fax:(419)668-7722

Circa 1860. To see the modern additions to this former farm home, you would not at first realize that parts of this home date back to the mid-1800s. There are two acres of flowers, lawns and trees. Five minutes away is Thomas Edison's home, Ohio's largest outlet mall and Cedar Point.
Innkeeper(s): Don & Mary Boos. $45-85. MC VISA AX DS PC TC. 3 rooms with PB. 1 suite. Breakfast included in rates. Type of meal: continental breakfast. Beds: QD. Air conditioning and TV in room. Fax and copier on premises. Amusement parks, antiques, fishing, parks, shopping, downhill skiing, cross-country skiing, sporting events, theater and watersports nearby.
Certificate may be used: September through May, Monday through Thursday, June, July and August.

Orrville E7

Grandma's House B&B
5598 Chippewa Rd
Orrville, OH 44667-9750
(330)682-5112

Circa 1860. This home was built using bricks that were created and fired on the property. Innkeeper Dave Farver's family has lived here for half of the home's existence. Family heirlooms and antiques decorate the interior, as well as quilts handmade by innkeeper Marilyn Farver. Original chestnut woodwork and wainscoting remain, but there have been a few modern additions, such as a double whirlpool tub in Mae's Room. After one of Marilyn's memorable "from scratch" breakfasts, guests are free to explore the 16 wooded acres that surround the home.
Innkeeper(s): Marilyn & Dave Farver. $55-90. PC TC. 5 rooms, 3 with PB. Breakfast included in rates. Types of meals: continental-plus breakfast and early coffee/tea. Beds: QDT. Air conditioning and ceiling fan in room. Handicap access. Antiques, parks, shopping, cross-country skiing and theater nearby.
Publicity: *Wooster Daily Record, Northeast Ohio Avenues.*

"What a delight. We will definitely be back. Perfect."

Certificate may be used: Sunday through Thursday, all year. Anytime from November through April.

Pomeroy   J7

Holly Hill Inn
114 Butternut Ave
Pomeroy, OH 45769-1295
(614)992-5657 Fax:(614)992-2319

Circa 1836. This gracious clapboard inn with its
many shuttered windows is shaded by giant holly
trees. Original window panes of blown glass remain,
as well as wide-board floors, mantels and fireplaces.
The family's antique collection includes a crocheted
canopy bed in the Honeymoon Room overlooking a
working fireplace. Dozens of antique quilts are displayed and for sale. Guests are invited to borrow an
antique bike to ride through the countryside.
Innkeeper(s): John Fultz. $59-89. MC VISA DS. 4 rooms, 2 with FP. 1
conference room. Breakfast included in rates. Type of meal: full breakfast. Catering service available. Beds: DT. TV and VCR in room.
Antiques, shopping and sporting events nearby.

Publicity: *Sunday Times-Sentinel.*

*"Your inn is so beautiful, and it has so much historic
charm."*

Certificate may be used: Sunday through Thursday. Some weekends,
based on availability. Not special weekends and holidays.

Ripley   J3

Baird House B&B
201 N 2nd St
Ripley, OH 45167-1002
(513)392-4918

Circa 1825. A lacy wrought-iron porch and balcony decorate the front facade of this historic house,
while the second-floor porch at the rear offers views
of the Ohio River, 500 feet away. There are nine
marble fireplaces and an enormous chandelier in the
parlor. A full breakfast is served.
Innkeeper(s): Patricia Kittle. $75-95. 2 rooms, 1 with PB, 3 with FP.
Breakfast included in rates. Types of meals: full breakfast and early cof-
fee/tea. Afternoon tea and evening snack available. Beds: KDT. Air conditioning, turndown service and ceiling fan in room. Antiques, shopping
and sporting events nearby.

Location: Fifty miles east of Cincinnati.

Publicity: *Ohio Magazine*

"Anxious to return."

Certificate may be used: November through May, Monday through
Thursday or anytime available.

The Signal House
234 N Front St
Ripley, OH 45167-1015
(937)392-1640

Circa 1830. This Greek Italianate home is said to
have been used to aid the Underground Railroad. A
light in the attic told
Rev. John Rankin, a
dedicated abolition-
ist, that it was safe
to transport slaves
to freedom. Located
within a 55-acre
historical district,
guests can take a
glance back in
time, exploring
museums and

antique shops. Twelve-foot ceilings with ornate plas-
ter-work graces the parlor, and guests can sit on any
of three porches watching paddlewheelers traverse
the Ohio River.
Innkeeper(s): Vic & Betsy Billingsley. $65-75. MC VISA DS PC TC. 2
rooms, 2 with FP. Breakfast included in rates. Types of meals: full
breakfast and early coffee/tea. Beds: QD. Air conditioning and ceiling
fan in room. Cable TV, VCR, copier and library on premises. Antiques,
fishing, parks, shopping and watersports nearby.

Publicity: *Cincinnati Enquirer, Ohio Columbus Dispatch, Ohio Off the
Beaten Path, Dayton Daily News, Cincinnati Magazine.*

Certificate may be used: Monday-Thursday, no holidays.

Rockbridge   H6

Glenlaurel Inn
15042 Mount Olive Rd
Rockbridge, OH 43149-9738
(614)385-4070 (800)809-7378 Fax:(614)385-9669
E-mail: michael@glenlaurel.com

Circa 1994. Innkeeper Michael Daniels created
Glenlaurel to be like a Scottish country home. A
creek, with a waterfall, meanders through the 133-
acre grounds, which are covered with woods. There
are four rooms in the main house, two suites in the
nearby carriage, and guests also can select from four
different cottages tucked on the property. The guest
quarters are romantic and elegant done in a
European-country style. Bathrobes, luxurious
linens, soft comforters, down-filled pillows,
whirlpool tubs and fireplaces are among the possible amenities. The cottages are especially idyllic,
each includes a double-sided fireplace that warms
both the bedchamber and living room. Each night,
Saturdays excepted, a five-course dinner is an
option for guests. On Saturday night, a vast seven-
course meal is available.

Innkeeper(s): Michael Daniels. $110-240. MC VISA AX DC DS PC TC. 4 cottages with PB, 8 with FP. 2 suites. 1 conference room. Breakfast and afternoon tea included in rates. Types of meals: full breakfast and gourmet breakfast. Dinner and picnic lunch available. Restaurant on premises. Beds: Q. Air conditioning and ceiling fan in room. Cable TV, VCR, fax, copier, spa and library on premises. Handicap access. Antiques, fishing, parks, shopping, golf, theater and watersports nearby.

Publicity: *Lancaster Eagle-Gazette.*

"With a staff eager to help us and make us feel welcome, we leave today spoiled, satisfied and eager to return."

Certificate may be used: Sunday through Thursday, except during October.

Sandusky   C5

Wagner's 1844 Inn
230 E Washington St
Sandusky, OH 44870-2611
(419)626-1726 Fax:(419)626-8465

Circa 1844. This inn originally was constructed as a log cabin. Additions and renovations were made, and the house evolved into Italianate style accented with brackets under the eaves and black shutters on the second-story windows. A wrought-iron fence frames the house, and there are ornate wrought-iron porch rails. A billiard room and screened-in porch are available to guests. The ferry to Cedar Point and Lake Erie Island is within walking distance.

Innkeeper(s): Walt & Barb Wagner. $70-120. MC VISA DS. 3 rooms with PB, 2 with FP. Breakfast included in rates. Type of meal: continental breakfast. Beds: Q. Air conditioning in room. Cable TV and library on premises. Amusement parks, antiques, fishing, parks and shopping nearby.

Publicity: *Lorain Journal.*

"This B&B rates in our Top 10."

Certificate may be used: Nov. 1 to May 1.

Toledo   C4

The William Cummings House B&B
1022 N Superior St
Toledo, OH 43604-1961
(419)244-3219 Fax:(419)244-3219
E-mail: BnBToledo@aol.com

Circa 1857. This Second Empire Victorian, which is listed in the National Register, is located in the historic Vistula neighborhood. The inn's fine appointments, collected for several years, include period antiques, Victorian chandeliers, mirrors, wallcoverings and draperies. The hosts are classical musicians of renown. Sometimes the inn is the location for chamber music, poetry readings and other cultural events.

Innkeeper(s): Lowell Greer, Lorelei Crawford. $40-135. PC TC. 3 rooms. 1 suite. Breakfast and evening snack included in rates. Type of meal: continental-plus breakfast. Beds: KQDT. Air conditioning, ceiling fan and VCR in room. Fax, copier and library on premises. Amusement parks, antiques, fishing, parks, shopping, sporting events, theater and watersports nearby.

"We will never forget our wedding night at your B&B. We'll try to be in the area next anniversary."

Certificate may be used: October through May, Sunday through Thursday.

Urbana   G3

Northern Plantation B&B
3421 E RR 296
Urbana, OH 43078
(513)652-1782 (800)652-1782

Circa 1913. This Victorian farmhouse, located on 100 acres, is occupied by fourth-generation family members. (Marsha's father was born in the downstairs bedroom in 1914.) The Homestead Library is decorated traditionally and has a handsome fire-

place, while the dining room features a dining set and a china cabinet made by the innkeeper's great-grandfather. Most of the guest rooms have canopy beds. A large country breakfast is served. On the property is a fishing pond, corn fields, soybeans and woods with a creek. Nearby are Ohio Caverns and Indian Lake.

Innkeeper(s): Marsha J. Martin. $65-95. MC VISA DS. 4 rooms, 1 with PB. Breakfast included in rates. Types of meals: continental-plus breakfast and full breakfast. Evening snack available. Beds: KD. Air conditioning in room. Cable TV, VCR and library on premises. Antiques, parks, shopping and cross-country skiing nearby.

Certificate may be used: Any day, except holidays.

Vermilion   C6

Captain Gilchrist
5662 Huron St
Vermilion, OH 44089-1000
(216)967-1237

Captain J.C. Gilchrist, owner of the largest fleet of ships on the Great Lakes, built this charming 1885 Victorian, which is listed in the National Register. From the wraparound porch, guests can relax and enjoy the view. The grounds, nestled near Lake Erie's southern shore, are surrounded by gracious old buckeye trees. Guest rooms are filled with antiques. The innkeepers transformed the second-story ballroom into a comfortable common room filled with games and a TV. The large, continental breakfasts feature sweet rolls and muffins from Vermilion's century-old family bakery. The innkeepers also offer kitchen suites for those planning longer stays. The home is only 400 feet from city docks and the beach, and a two-block walk takes guests into the downtown area with its many shops and restaurants. A maritime museum and historic lighthouse are next door.

Innkeeper(s): Dan Roth. $65-89. MC VISA AX. 4 rooms. Breakfast included in rates. Type of meal: continental-plus breakfast.

Certificate may be used: Sunday through Thursday, September through May.

West Alexandria   H2

Twin Creek Country B&B
5353 Enterprise Rd
West Alexandria, OH 45381-9518
(513)787-3990

Circa 1835. This brick farmhouse is the oldest house in the township and the 170 acres surrounding the home were part of a land grant signed by Thomas Jefferson. Beautiful rich woodwork highlights the interior, which has an old-fashioned, country appeal. Innkeepers Mark and Carolyn Ulrich live in an adjacent home, providing their guests with extra privacy. The grounds offer more than 70 acres of woods to hike through. The innkeepers also own Twin Creek Townehouse B&B, an Italianate-style home that includes a tea room and catering business. The two upstairs guest rooms are decorated with local antiques. The tea room is an impressive feature, with a carved ceiling, marble fireplace and walls painted in a deep teal hue with rose trim.

Innkeeper(s): Dr. Mark & Carolyn Ulrich. $69-89. MC VISA AX DS PC TC. 2 rooms with PB. 1 suite. Breakfast and evening snack included in rates. Type of meal: full breakfast. Beds: DT. Air conditioning in room. Amusement parks, antiques, fishing, parks, shopping, sporting events, theater and watersports nearby.

Certificate may be used: No holidays; good Monday through Thursday, subject to availability.

Wooster   E7

Historic Overholt House B&B
1473 Beall Ave
Wooster, OH 44691-2303
(330)263-6300 (800)992-0643 Fax:(330)263-9378

Circa 1874. This burgundy Victorian with its peaked roofs and colorful trim literally was saved from the wrecking ball. Several concerned locals fought to have the home moved to another location rather than face demolition in order to make way for a parking lot. The current owners later purchased the historic home and furnished it with beautiful wall coverings, antiques and Victorian touches. The focal point of the interior is a magnificent walnut "flying staircase" that rises three stories. The innkeepers provide plenty of ways to spend a comfortable evening. The common room is stocked with games, a player piano and reading material. Autumn and winter guests are invited to snuggle up in front of a roaring fire while sipping a hot drink and munching on homemade cookies. Candlelight dinners can be arranged by reservation. The area boasts many craft, antique and gift shops, as well as Amish country sites and activities at the College of Wooster, which is adjacent to the Overholt House.

Innkeeper(s): Sandy Pohalski & Bobbie Walton. $63-70. MC VISA DS PC. 4 rooms with PB. 1 suite. Breakfast and evening snack included in rates. Types of meals: continental breakfast, continental-plus breakfast and early coffee/tea. Dinner available. Beds: QTFD. Air conditioning, ceiling fan, TV and VCR in room. Fax and spa on premises. Amusement parks, antiques, parks, shopping and theater nearby.

Publicity: *Exchange, Daily Record, Pathways, Akron Beacon Journal.*

"A real retreat. So quiet, clean and friendly. I feel pampered! An old penny always returns."

Certificate may be used: December to April, any time. Sunday through Thursday, all year.

Oklahoma

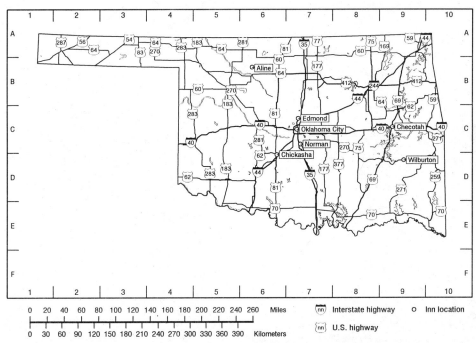

0   20   40   60   80 100 120 140 160 180 200 220 240 260   Miles
0   30   60   90 120 150 180 210 240 270 300 330 360 390   Kilometers

⬢ nn Interstate highway   ○ Inn location
⬢ nn U.S. highway

Aline   B6

Heritage Manor
RR 3 Box 33
Aline, OK 73716-9118
(405)463-2563 (800)295-2563

Circa 1903. A wonderful way to experience
Oklahoma history is to stay at the Heritage Manor,
two turn-of-the-century restored homes. One is an
American four-square house and the other, a glori-
fied Arts-and-Crafts-style home. Antiques were
gathered from area pioneer homes and include an
Edison Victrola Morning Glory Horn and a cathedral pump organ. Antique sofas and English leather
chairs fill the sitting room. Mannequins dressed in
pioneer clothing add to the decor. There are several
fireplaces, and a widow's walk tops the main house.
Innkeeper(s): A.J. & Carolyn Rexroat. $55-150. PC TC. 4 rooms. 2
suites. 2 conference rooms. Breakfast and evening snack included in
rates. Types of meals: full breakfast and early coffee/tea. Afternoon tea,
dinner, picnic lunch, lunch, gourmet lunch and banquet service available.
Restaurant on premises. Beds: D. Air conditioning and TV in room. VCR,
spa and library on premises. Handicap access. Antiques, fishing, parks,
shopping, sporting events, theater and watersports nearby.
Publicity: *Country, Enid Morning News, Daily Oklahoman.*
Certificate may be used: Year-round, Monday-Saturday.

Checotah   C9

Sharpe House
301 NW 2nd St
Checotah, OK 74426-2240
(918)473-2832

Circa 1911. Built on land originally bought from a
Creek Indian, this Southern plantation-style inn
was a teacherage—the rooming house for single
female teachers. It is furnished with heirlooms from
the innkeepers' families and hand-crafted accessories. The look of the house is antebellum, but the

specialty of the kitchen is Mexican cuisine. Family-style evening meals are available upon request. Checotah is located at the junction of I-40 and U.S. 69. This makes it the ideal base for your day trips of exploration or recreation in Green Country.

Innkeeper(s): Kay Kindt. $35-50. PC TC. 3 rooms, 2 with PB. 1 suite. Breakfast included in rates. Types of meals: continental breakfast, continental-plus breakfast, full breakfast and early coffee/tea. Catered breakfast available. Beds: D. Air conditioning, ceiling fan and TV in room. Library and child care on premises. Amusement parks, antiques, fishing, parks, shopping and watersports nearby.

Certificate may be used: Anytime, space available.

Chickasha   D6

Campbell-Richison House B&B
1428 Kansas
Chickasha, OK 73018
(405)222-1754

Circa 1909. Upon entering this prairie-style home, guests will notice a spacious entryway with a gracious stairway ascending to the second-floor guest rooms. The front parlor is a wonderful spot for relaxing, reading or just soaking up the history of the home. The dining room has a stained-glass window that gives off a kaleidoscope of beautiful colors when the morning sun shines through. A spacious yard encompasses one-quarter of a city block and has large shade trees that can be enjoyed from the wicker-lined porch.

Innkeeper(s): David Ratcliff. $39-59. 3 rooms, 1 with PB. Breakfast included in rates. Types of meals: continental-plus breakfast and early coffee/tea. Beds: D. Air conditioning in room. Cable TV and VCR on premises. Antiques, shopping and sporting events nearby.

Publicity: *Oklahoma Today, Chickasha Express, Cache Times Weekly, Chickasha Star.*

"We enjoyed our stay at your lovely B&B! It was just the getaway we needed to unwind from a stressful few weeks. Your hospitality fellowship and food were just wonderful."

Certificate may be used: Anytime, except December weekends and swap meet weekends.

Edmond   C7

The Arcadian Inn B&B
328 E 1st St
Edmond, OK 73034-4543
(405)348-6347 (800)299-6347 Fax:(405)348-6347

Circa 1908. Unwind in the garden spa of this Victorian inn or on the wraparound porch to enjoy the Oklahoma breeze. Breakfast may be served privately in your suite or in the dining room flooded with morning sunlight, beneath the ceiling paint-

c. 1908

ings of angels and Christ done by a local artisan. Located next to the University of Central Oklahoma, the inn is four blocks from downtown antique shopping. Guests will enjoy the private baths with Jacuzzis and clawfoot tubs.

Innkeeper(s): Martha & Gary Hall. $65-195. AP. MC VISA AX DS TC. 6 rooms with PB. 4 suites. Breakfast included in rates. Type of meal: full breakfast. Beds: KQ. Air conditioning, ceiling fan and TV in room. Fax and spa on premises. Amusement parks, antiques, fishing, parks, shopping, sporting events, theater and watersports nearby.

Publicity: *Daily Oklahoman, Antique Traveler.*

Certificate may be used: Sunday - Thursday, excluding holidays.

Norman   C7

Holmberg House B&B
766 Debarr Ave
Norman, OK 73069-4908
(405)321-6221 (800)646-6221 Fax:(405)321-6221

Circa 1914. Professor Fredrik Holmberg and his wife Signy built this Craftsman-style home across the street from the University of Oklahoma. Each of the antique-filled rooms has its own individual decor and style. For instance, the
Blue Danube Room is a romantic retreat filled with wicker, a wrought-iron bed and floral accents throughout. The Bed and Bath Room boasts an old-
fashioned tub next to a window seat. The parlor and front porch are perfect places to relax with friends, and the lush grounds include a cottage garden. Aside from close access to the university, Holmberg House is within walking distance to more than a dozen restaurants.

Innkeeper(s): MaryJo Meacham. $75-85. MC VISA AX DS PC TC. 4 rooms with PB. Breakfast included in rates. Types of meals: gourmet breakfast and early coffee/tea. Beds: QDT. Air conditioning, ceiling fan and TV in room. Fax, copier and library on premises. Antiques, parks, shopping, sporting events and theater nearby.

Publicity: *Metro Norman, Oklahoma City Journal Record, Norman Transcript, Country Inns.*

"Your hospitality and the delicious food were just super."

Certificate may be used: July 1-Sept. 31, Sunday-Friday

Oklahoma City
C7

The Grandison
1200 N Shartel Ave
Oklahoma City, OK 73103
(405)232-8778 (800)240-4667 Fax:(405)521-0011

Circa 1904. This brick and shingle three-story house is shaded by pecan, apple and fig trees. You'll find a pond and gazebo among the lawns and gardens. The building's original Belgian stained glass remains, and the decor is an airy country Victorian. The bridal suite includes a working fireplace, white-lace curtains and a clawfoot tub, with Jacuzzi.

Innkeeper(s): Claudia & Bob Wright. $75-150. MC VISA AX DS PC TC. 9 rooms with PB, 4 with FP. 3 suites. 1 conference room. Breakfast and evening snack included in rates. Types of meals: continental-plus breakfast, full breakfast and early coffee/tea. Banquet service, catering service and room service available. Beds: KQT. Air conditioning, ceiling fan, TV and VCR in room. Fax, copier, sauna and library on premises. Handicap access. Antiques, parks, sporting events and theater nearby.

Publicity: *Daily Oklahoman, Oklahoma Pride, Oklahoma Gazette, Discover Oklahoma.*

"Like going home to Grandma's!"

Certificate may be used: Anytime.

Wilburton
D9

The Dome House
315 E Main St
Wilburton, OK 74578-4411
(918)465-0092

Circa 1908. An area landmark since it was built, the Victorian inn's unique feature is its distinctive dome-topped, two-story turret. A sitting area in the turret and wide porches invite guests to relax and remember a simpler time. A parlor where guests can meet and enjoy conversation includes a fireplace. Situated in the heart of the beautiful Kiamichi Mountains, the inn is centrally located to a wide variety of outdoor activities. The Court House, Federal Building, post office and restaurants are all within walking distance.

Innkeeper(s): LaVerne McFerran. $45-75. DS PC TC. 5 rooms with PB. 3 suites. 1 cottage. Breakfast included in rates. Types of meals: continental-plus breakfast and early coffee/tea. Beds: QDT. Air conditioning, turndown service, ceiling fan and TV in room. VCR and library on premises. Fishing, parks, shopping and sporting events nearby.

Certificate may be used: Anytime during the week, Sunday through Thursday; when available on weekends.

Oregon

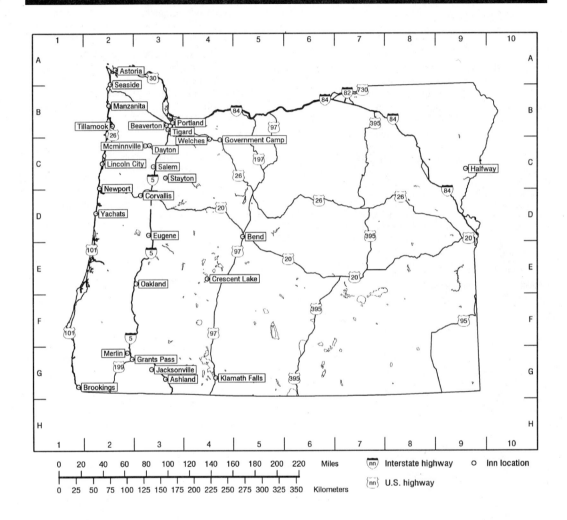

Astoria
Seaside
30
82 730
84
Manzanita
395 84
Tillamook
Portland
97
Beaverton
Tigard
26
Welches
Government Camp
Mcminnville
Dayton
197
Lincoln City
Salem
26
Halfway
5
Stayton
Newport
Corvallis
84
Yachats
20
20
Eugene
Bend
101
5
97
395
Oakland
20
Crescent Lake
20
395
95
97
395
Merlin
Grants Pass
199
Jacksonville
Ashland
Klamath Falls
395
Brookings

| 0 | 20 | 40 | 60 | 80 | 100 | 120 | 140 | 160 | 180 | 200 | 220 | Miles |

| 0 | 25 | 50 | 75 | 100 | 125 | 150 | 175 | 200 | 225 | 250 | 275 | 300 | 325 | 350 | Kilometers |

(nn) Interstate highway   ○ Inn location

(nn) U.S. highway

Ashland　　　G3

Chanticleer B&B Inn
120 Gresham St
Ashland, OR 97520-2807
(503)482-1919 (800)898-1950 Fax:(503)482-1919

Circa 1920. This gray clapboard, Craftsman-style house has been totally renovated and several rooms added. The inn is light and airy and decorated with antiques. Special features include the open hearth fireplace and bricked patio garden.
Innkeeper(s): Pebby Kuan. $90-160. MC VISA. 6 rooms with PB, 1 with FP. Breakfast included in rates. Types of meals: full breakfast, gourmet breakfast and early coffee/tea. Beds: QT. Air conditioning in room. Cable TV on premises. Antiques, shopping, downhill skiing, cross-country skiing, sporting events and theater nearby.
Publicity: *Country Home, Pacific Northwest.*

"Chanticleer has set the standard by which all others will be judged."

Certificate may be used: Nov. 1-March 31, excluding weekends and holidays.

Iris Inn
59 Manzanita St
Ashland, OR 97520-2615
(541)488-2286 (800)460-7650 Fax:(541)488-3709

Circa 1905. The Iris Inn is a restored Victorian set on a large flower-filled yard. It features simple American country antiques. The upstairs guest rooms have views of the valley and mountains. Evening sips of wine often are taken out on the large deck overlooking a rose garden. Breakfast boasts an elegant presentation with dishes such as buttermilk scones and Eggs Benedict.
Innkeeper(s): Vicki Lamb. $60-110. MC VISA. 5 rooms with PB. Breakfast included in rates. Type of meal: full breakfast. Beds: QDT. Air conditioning, turndown service and ceiling fan in room. Fax on premises. Antiques, fishing, shopping, downhill skiing, cross-country skiing, sporting events, theater and watersports nearby.
Location: Southern Oregon.
Publicity: *Sunset, Oregonian.*

"It's like returning to home to be at The Iris Inn."

Certificate may be used: October, Sunday-Thursday only; any night November-February; March-May, Sunday-Thursday, only. Discounts only with high season rate, not winter rate.

Mousetrap Inn
312 Helman St
Ashland, OR 97520-1138
(541)482-9228 (800)460-5453

Circa 1895. The century-old farmhouse is furnished with antiques and decorated with modern art and pottery created by the innkeepers. Breakfasts often feature organically grown foods and include treats

such as juice smoothies, fresh fruit, baked goods and frittatas. The grounds are dotted with gardens and there is a swing on the inn's porch. The inn is located in Ashland's historic Railroad District.
Innkeeper(s): Robert, Linda & Tessah Joseph. $70-95. MC VISA PC. 6 rooms with PB. Breakfast included in rates. Types of meals: full breakfast and early coffee/tea. Beds: Q. Air conditioning and ceiling fan in room. Fishing, parks, shopping, theater and watersports nearby.
Certificate may be used: April, May, October, any nights.

Mt. Ashland Inn
550 Mt Ashland Ski Rd
Ashland, OR 97520-9745
(541)482-8707 (800)830-8707 Fax:(541)482-8707

Circa 1987. Innkeepers Chuck and Laurel Biegert truly have mastered the art of innkeeping. It doesn't hurt that the two "keep" a spectacular mountain cedar log lodge surrounded by a pine forest. During chilly months, a fire crackles in the front room's magnificent stone fireplace. Guests trample in after a day on the slopes ready to enjoy a soak in the outdoor spa and sauna under a night sky sparkling with stars. Guest rooms and suites are appointed with elegant, yet comfortable furnishings. Quilts, antiques, double whirlpool tubs and wonderful views are just some of the surprises guests will discover. The Biegerts go all out during the holiday season, and from November to New Year's, the inn participates in the town's Festival of Lights. But winter isn't the only season to visit the inn, the area offers hiking, fishing, shopping, galleries, museums and more. No matter what time of year, guests are treated to a divine breakfast. The cuisine at Mount Ashland has been featured in several cookbooks, as well as Bon Appetit and Gourmet.
Innkeeper(s): Chuck & Laurel Biegert. $76-180. MC VISA AX DS PC. 5 rooms with PB, 3 with FP. 3 suites. 1 conference room. Breakfast included in rates. Type of meal: gourmet breakfast. Beds: KQT. Fax, copier, spa, sauna and bicycles on premises. Antiques, fishing, parks, shopping, downhill skiing, cross-country skiing, theater and watersports nearby.
Location: Fourteen miles from Ashland. Six miles west of I-5 on Mount Ashland Road.
Publicity: *Pacific Northwest, Edward Carter's Travels, Snow Country, Oregon, Glamour, Travel & Leisure, Country Living, Log Home Living.*

"I've wondered where my dreams go when I can't remember them. Now I know they come here, among the snow, trees, valley, dogs, wind, sun, and dance at night around the Lodge."

Certificate may be used: Sunday through Thursday, Oct. 15-May 31, excluding holiday periods.

Oak Hill Country B&B

2190 Siskiyou Blvd
Ashland, OR 97520-2531
(541)482-1554 (800)888-7434 Fax:(541)482-1378
E-mail: oakhill@mind.net

Circa 1910. Decorated with hints of French country, this Craftsman farmhouse has a fine front porch and expansive sunny deck in back creating relaxing areas for enjoying the less crowded south end of

town. A hearty country gourmet breakfast is served family style in the dining room. There are bicycles for exploring the area.

Innkeeper(s): Linda Johnson. $65-105. MC VISA. 6 rooms. Breakfast included in rates. Air conditioning and turndown service in room. Cable TV and VCR on premises. Antiques, fishing, shopping, downhill skiing, cross-country skiing and theater nearby.

Certificate may be used: November-May, Monday-Thursday, excluding holidays.

Pinehurst Inn at Jenny Creek

17250 Hwy 66
Ashland, OR 97520-9406
(503)488-1002

Circa 1923. This lodge, built from logs harvested on the property, once accommodated travelers along the new state highway 66, which was built to replace the Southern Oregon Wagon Road. As the name suggests, the inn is situated by the banks of Jenny Creek, and guest enjoy stunning canyon views from the upstairs sunroom. The lobby, with its huge stone fireplace, is a welcoming site. The inn also includes a full-service restaurant open for guests and the public. The inn is less than a half hour from Ashland, and Klamath Falls is 39 miles away.

Innkeeper(s): Mary Jo & Mike Moloney. $75-140. MC VISA DS. 6 rooms with PB. 2 suites. Breakfast and dinner included in rates. Types

of meals: full breakfast and early coffee/tea. Lunch available. Restaurant on premises. Beds: KQD. Ceiling fan in room. Antiques, fishing, shopping, downhill skiing, cross-country skiing and theater nearby.

Publicity: *Sunset, Travel & Leisure.*

"Romantic and peaceful. A favorite inn. Wonderful dinner and accommodations."

Certificate may be used: Feb. 14-Dec. 30, Wednesday-Friday.

The Woods House B&B

333 N Main St
Ashland, OR 97520-1703
(503)488-1598 (800)435-8260 Fax:(503)482-7912

Circa 1908. Built and occupied for almost 40 years by a prominent Ashland physician, each room of this Craftsman-style inn boasts special detail. Many guest rooms offer canopied beds and skylights. Full breakfasts are served either in the sunny dining room or in the garden under a spreading walnut

tree. After breakfast, take a stroll through the half-acre of terraced, English gardens. Located in the historic district, the inn is four blocks from Ashland's Shakespearean theaters.

Innkeeper(s): Francoise Roddy. $65-112. MC VISA. 6 rooms with PB. Breakfast included in rates. Types of meals: full breakfast and early coffee/tea. Room service available. Beds: KQT. Air conditioning in room. Cable TV, VCR, fax, copier and bicycles on premises. Antiques, shopping, downhill skiing, cross-country skiing and theater nearby.

Publicity: *The Times.*

"Within this house lies much hospitality, friendship and laughter. What more could a home ask to be?"

Certificate may be used: October-March, any nights.

Astoria A2

Benjamin Young Inn

3652 Duane St
Astoria, OR 97103
(503)325-6172 (800)201-1286
E-mail: benyoung@willapabay.org

Circa 1888. From this Queen Anne Victorian, guests can watch as ships and boats travel along the Columbia River. The home is listed in the National

Register of Historic Places, and many of its period elements have been preserved and restored. Guest rooms are decorated in a comfortable eclectic style with antiques, and all offer a river view. The spacious Fireplace Room includes a fireplace, Jacuzzi tub, king-size bed topped with a floral bedspread and a bay window with a river view. It also has an adjoining room with several more beds. Shops, museums and restaurants are just two miles away in Astoria.

Innkeeper(s): Carolyn & Ken Hammer. $75-135. MC VISA DC DS. 5 rooms, 2 with PB, 1 with FP. 3 suites. Breakfast and afternoon tea included in rates. Types of meals: gourmet breakfast and early coffee/tea. Catering service and catered breakfast available. Beds: KQT. TV and VCR in room. Tennis on premises. Antiques, fishing, parks, shopping, golf and theater nearby.

"Your home is absolutely gorgeous and the food and ambiance superb—so romantic, so wonderful!"

Certificate may be used: Sunday-Thursday, Nov. 15-March 15 except holidays.

Grandview B&B
1574 Grand Ave
Astoria, OR 97103-3733
(503)325-5555 (800)488-3250

Circa 1896. To fully enjoy its views of the Columbia River, this Victorian house has both a tower and a turret. Antiques and white wicker furnishings contribute to the inn's casual, homey feeling. The Meadow Room is particularly appealing to bird-lovers with its birdcage, bird books and bird wallpaper. Breakfast, served in the main-floor turret, frequently includes smoked salmon with bagels and cream cheese.

Innkeeper(s): Charleen Maxwell. $55-96. MC VISA DS. 9 rooms, 7 with PB, 3 with FP. 2 suites. Breakfast and evening snack included in rates. Type of meal: full breakfast. Beds: QT. Antiques, fishing, parks, shopping, theater and watersports nearby.

Publicity: *Pacific Northwest Magazine, Northwest Discoveries, Los Angeles Times, Oregonian, Daily Astorian.*

"We're still talking about our visit and the wonderful breakfast you served."

Certificate may be used: Nov. 1-May 17 holidays OK except two weekends in February may be excluded.

Inn-Chanted B&B
708 8th St
Astoria, OR 97103-4725
(503)325-5223 (800)455-7018

Circa 1883. This four-square Victorian was presented to Maude Hobson as wedding present from her father, John, an Astoria pioneer. Guest rooms afford views of the Columbia River. Silk brocade wallcoverings and crystal chandeliers are elegant touches to the interior of this home. Guests design their own breakfast, choosing from entrees such as puffed pancakes, almond creme crepes or quiches. Astoria is the oldest United States settlement west of the Mississippi River and offers a walking tour of historic homes and buildings.

Innkeeper(s): Richard & Dixie Swart. $50-110. EP. MC VISA AX DS TC. 3 rooms with PB, 1 with FP. 1 suite. Breakfast and afternoon tea included in rates. Types of meals: gourmet breakfast and early coffee/tea. Beds: QT. Ceiling fan, TV and VCR in room. Antiques, fishing, parks, theater and watersports nearby.

Certificate may be used: November-February.

Beaverton   B3

Yankee Tinker B&B
5480 SW 183rd Ave
Beaverton, OR 97007-3853
(503)649-0932 (800)846-5372 Fax:(503)649-0932
E-mail: yankeetb&b@aol.com

Circa 1969. This suburban ranch house is decorated with New England family heirlooms, antiques and country accents. Handmade quilts, flower gardens, and a large deck provide for a comfortable stay 10 miles from Portland, in Washington County's wine country. Peaches and cream French toast and herbed omelets are among the breakfast offerings.

Innkeeper(s): Jan & Ralph Wadleigh. $65-75. MC VISA AX DC DS PC TC. 3 rooms, 1 with PB. Breakfast and evening snack included in rates. Types of meals: full breakfast, gourmet breakfast and early coffee/tea. Beds: QT. Turndown service in room. VCR and fax on premises. Antiques, parks, shopping and golf nearby.

Publicity: *Hidden Pacific Northwest, Beaverton Business Advocate, The Times.*

Certificate may be used: Sunday through Thursday. Some festival dates excluded, not valid with other promotions.

Bend   D5

The Sather House B&B
7 NW Tumalo Ave
Bend, OR 97701
(541)388-1065

Circa 1911. This Craftsman-style home is listed in the local, county and national historic registers. One room includes a clawfoot tub that dates to

1910. Period furnishings are found in the nicely appointed guest rooms, which feature touches of Battenburg lace. The front porch is lined with wicker for those who wish to relax and enjoy the surroundings. For breakfast, innkeeper Robbie Giamboi serves items such as pancakes topped with her own homemade blackberry or apple syrup. Guests also enjoy afternoon tea.

Innkeeper(s): Robbie Giamboi. $80-97. MC VISA DS PC TC. 4 rooms, 2 with PB. Breakfast and afternoon tea included in rates. Types of meals: full breakfast, gourmet breakfast and early coffee/tea. Beds: KQDTR. Ceiling fan in room. Cable TV, VCR and library on premises. Antiques, fishing, parks, shopping, downhill skiing, cross-country skiing, sporting events, golf, theater and watersports nearby.

Publicity: *Bend Bulletin, Oregonian.*

Certificate may be used: Jan. 2-May 1, Sunday-Saturday.

Brookings   G1

South Coast Inn B&B
516 Redwood St
Brookings, OR 97415-9672
(541)469-5557 (800)525-9273 Fax:(541)469-6615
E-mail: scoastin@wave.net

Circa 1917. Enjoy panoramic views of the Pacific Ocean at this Craftsman-style inn built by renowned San Francisco architect Bernard Maybeck. All rooms are furnished with antiques, ceiling fans, VCRs and TVs. Two guest rooms afford panoramic views of the rugged coastline. A floor-to-ceiling stone fireplace and beamed ceilings make the parlor a great place to gather with friends. There are sun decks, a strolling garden and an indoor hot tub and sauna. The Brookings area offers something for everyone. Outdoor activities include hiking, boating, golfing, digging for clams or simply enjoying a stroll along the spectacular coastline. Concerts, galleries, museums, antiques, specialty shops and fine restaurants all can be found within the area.

Innkeeper(s): Ken Raith & Keith Pepper. $79-89. MC VISA AX DS PC TC. 3 rooms with PB. 1 cottage. Breakfast included in rates. Types of meals: full breakfast, gourmet breakfast and early coffee/tea. Beds: Q. Ceiling fan, TV and VCR in room. Fax, spa, sauna and library on premises. Antiques, fishing, parks, shopping, theater and watersports nearby.

"Thank you for your special brand of magic. What a place!"

Certificate may be used: November-April.

Corvallis   D3

Harrison House
2310 NW Harrison Blvd
Corvallis, OR 97330-5402
(541)752-6248 (800)233-6842
E-mail: harrisonhouse@proaxis.com

Circa 1939. This Dutch-Colonial-style house, adjacent to Oregon State University, was built by the Allison family who lived here until 1990. Upon its conversion to a bed & breakfast, it was graciously restored. The rooms are large and comfortable, dec-

orated and furnished in Williamsburg-style family antiques. The favorite guest room overlooks a side yard with beds of flowers and fruit trees. The full breakfast begins with a fruit course and features either eggs Benedict, various stuffed crepes or other regional fare. Antiques, fishing, hiking, shopping, skiing, sporting events and theater are nearby.

Innkeeper(s): Maria Tomlinson. $50-80. MC VISA AX DS. 4 rooms, 2 with PB. Type of meal: early coffee/tea. Evening snack available. Beds: KQD. TV in room. VCR, bicycles and pet boarding on premises. Amusement parks, antiques, fishing, shopping, downhill skiing, cross-country skiing, sporting events and theater nearby.

"What an exceptional weekend!"

Certificate may be used: Dec. 1 to Feb. 28, Sunday-Thursday.

Crescent Lake   E4

Willamette Pass Inn
PO Box 35
Crescent Lake, OR 97425-0035
(541)433-2211 (800)301-2218 Fax:(541)433-2855

Circa 1984. Each of the guest rooms at this rustic, comfortable lodge includes a fireplace and pine furnishings. Beds are topped with flannel sheets. Turndown service is a real treat, guests return from dinner to find cookies and muffins waiting. The inn is located in a national forest, ancient Indian grounds and more than one dozen lakes are nearby.

Innkeeper(s): George & Alicia Prigmore. $44-58. MC VISA DS PC TC. 12 rooms with PB, 10 with FP. Evening snack included in rates. Beds: Q. Turndown service, TV and VCR in room. Fax and library on premises. Handicap access. Antiques, fishing, parks, shopping, downhill skiing, cross-country skiing and watersports nearby.

Certificate may be used: All year, except holidays and Saturday nights.

Dayton   C3

Wine Country Farm
6855 NE Breyman Orchards Rd
Dayton, OR 97114-7220
(503)864-3446 (800)261-3446 Fax:(503)864-3446

Circa 1910. Surrounded by vineyards and orchards, Wine Country Farm is an eclectic French house sitting on a hill overlooking the Cascade Mountain Range. Arabian horses are raised here, and five varieties of grapes are grown. Request the master bedroom and you'll enjoy a fireplace. The innkeepers can arrange for a horse-drawn buggy ride and picnic. There are outdoor wedding facilities and a new wine tasting room. Downtown Portland and the Oregon coast are each an hour away.

Innkeeper(s): Joan Davenport. $75-125. MC VISA PC. 5 rooms with PB, 2 with FP. 1 suite. 1 conference room. Breakfast included in rates. Types of meals: full breakfast, gourmet breakfast and early coffee/tea. Picnic lunch, banquet service, catering service and room service available. Beds: KQDT. Air conditioning, ceiling fan and VCR in room. Fax, copier, stables, library and pet boarding on premises. Antiques, fishing, parks, shopping, downhill skiing, cross-country skiing, sporting events, theater and watersports nearby.

Publicity: *Wine Spectator.*

Certificate may be used: January through April, Monday-Thursday.

Eugene   D3

Campbell House, A City Inn
252 Pearl St
Eugene, OR 97401-2366
(541)343-1119 (800)264-2519 Fax:(541)343-2258
E-mail: campbellhouse@campbellhouse.com

Circa 1892. An acre of grounds surrounds this Victorian inn, built by a local timber owner and gold miner. The guest quarters range from a ground-level room featuring fly-fishing paraphernalia and knotty-pine paneling to an elegant two-room honeymoon suite on the second floor, complete with fireplace, jetted bathtub for two and a view of the mountains. The Campbell House, located in Eugene's

historic Skinner Butte District, is within walking distance of restaurants, the Hult Center for the Performing Arts, the 5th Street Public Market and antique shops. Outdoor activities include jogging or biking along riverside paths.

Innkeeper(s): Myra Plant. $72-235. MC VISA AX DS TC. 14 rooms with PB, 3 with FP. 1 suite. 3 conference rooms. Breakfast included in rates. Types of meals: full breakfast and early coffee/tea. Picnic lunch and room service available. Beds: KQDT. Air conditioning, turndown service, ceiling fan, TV and VCR in room. Fax, copier and library on premises. Handicap access. Antiques, fishing, parks, shopping, sporting events, theater and watersports nearby.

Publicity: *KVAL & KAUW News, Eugene Register Guard, Country Inns, Oregonian, Sunset*

"I guess we've never felt so pampered! Thank you so much. The room is beautiful! We had a wonderful getaway."

Certificate may be used: January through March, Sunday-Thursday (not valid during events, holidays or conferences).

Kjaer's House In Woods
814 Lorane Hwy
Eugene, OR 97405-2321
(541)343-3234 (800)437-4501

Circa 1910. This handsome Craftsman house on two landscaped acres was built by a Minnesota lawyer. It was originally accessible by streetcar.

Antiques include a square grand piano of rosewood and a collection of antique wedding photos. The house is attractively furnished and surrounded by flower gardens.

Innkeeper(s): George & Eunice Kjaer. $55-75. PC TC. 2 rooms with PB. 1 conference room. Breakfast included in rates. Types of meals: continental breakfast, full breakfast, gourmet breakfast and early coffee/tea. Beds: Q. Turndown service in room. Cable TV, VCR and library on premises. Antiques, fishing, parks, shopping, sporting events and theater nearby.

Publicity: *Register-Guard, Oregonian.*

"Lovely ambiance and greatest sleep ever. Delicious and beautiful food presentation."

Certificate may be used: Nov. 1-May 10.

The Oval Door

988 Lawrence St
Eugene, OR 97401-2827
(541)683-3160 (800)882-3160

Circa 1990. This is a New England farm-style house, complete with wraparound porch. It is located in a residential neighborhood 15 blocks from the University of Oregon. Guest rooms feature ceiling fans and antiques. There is a whirlpool room, library and parlor. Breakfast can be catered to your dietary needs.

Innkeeper(s): Judith McLane. $70-93. MC VISA AX. 4 rooms with PB. Beds: QT. Turndown service and ceiling fan in room. Cable TV, VCR, fax and library on premises.

Certificate may be used: Anytime except special event weekends.

Pookie's B&B on College Hill

2013 Charnelton St
Eugene, OR 97405-2819
(541)343-0383 (800)558-0383 Fax:(541)343-0383

Circa 1918. Pookie's is a charming Craftsman house with an English influence. Surrounded by maple and fir trees, the B&B is located in the College Hill neighborhood. Mahogany and oak

antiques decorate the rooms. The innkeeper worked for many years in the area as a concierge and can offer you expert help with excursion planning or business needs.

Innkeeper(s): Pookie & Doug Walling. $65-90. AP. PC TC. 3 rooms, 2 with PB. 1 suite. Breakfast included in rates. Types of meals: continental breakfast, continental-plus breakfast, full breakfast and early coffee/tea. Beds: KQT. Ceiling fan and TV in room. VCR, fax and copier on premises. Antiques, fishing, parks, shopping, sporting events, theater and watersports nearby.

Publicity: *Oregon Wine.*

"I love the attention to detail. The welcoming touches: flowers, the 'convenience basket' of necessary items . . . I'm happy to have discovered your lovely home."

Certificate may be used: November-April, Sunday-Wednesday nights; suite only.

Government Camp (Mt. Hood area)   C4

Falcon's Crest Inn

87287 Government Camp Loop Hwy
Government Camp, OR 97028
(503)272-3403 (800)624-7384 Fax:(503)272-3454

Circa 1983. This chalet-style home is located in an old growth forest in the scenic Mt. Hood area. Skiers enjoy close access to local slopes, and there is plenty of space to store equipment. Guests enjoy a view of the ski mountain from the Great Room, which includes a wood-burning stove. There are two other common areas for guests to use in this 6,500-square-foot home, which is somewhat like staying in an intimate mountain lodge. Guest rooms feature unique themes. The Cat Ballou Room is done in an Old West country style with an iron bed and an exposed cedar wall. The Safari Suite, complete with palm tree, is reminiscent of the jungle, with a large rattan chair and a bamboo bed draped with netting. One suite is dedicated to the innkeepers' grandmother, and others are done in French-country or Southwestern style. A family-style breakfast is included in the rates, but guests also can reserve a six-course gourmet dinner. The Saltimbocca, veal with prosciutto and mozzarella, is a specialty. The inn is located just off what was the Oregon Trail.

Innkeeper(s): BJ & Melody Johnson. $95-179. MC VISA AX DS PC TC. 5 rooms, 3 with PB. 2 suites. 1 conference room. Breakfast included in rates. Types of meals: continental-plus breakfast, full breakfast and early coffee/tea. Afternoon tea, banquet service, catering service and room service available. Restaurant on premises. Beds: KQT. Turndown service in room. VCR, fax, copier and bicycles on premises. Antiques, fishing, parks, shopping, downhill skiing, cross-country skiing, golf, theater and watersports nearby.

Publicity: *Sunset Magazine.*

Certificate may be used: Sunday through Thursday except holiday periods, subject to availability. (Not valid with any other discount card, coupon or certificate.)

Grants Pass   G2

Martha's House

764 NW 4th St
Grants Pass, OR 97526-1517
(503)476-4330 (800)261-0167

Circa 1910. If you pass by this inn in the morning, you may hear the happy chatter of guests on the veranda enjoying a breakfast of freshly baked breads, farm fresh eggs and local produce. And Felix the cat may be nearby. This Victorian farmhouse is close to

the center of town. Antique toys are a feature in Rachel's Room, which also harbors a Jacuzzi tub, queen brass bed and antiques. Enjoy the area's river rafting and nearby Shakespearean Festival.

Innkeeper(s): Evelyn & Glenn Hawkins. $50-85. EP. MC VISA. 3 rooms with PB. Breakfast and evening snack included in rates. Types of meals: full breakfast and early coffee/tea. Afternoon tea available. Beds: KQ. Air conditioning, turndown service, ceiling fan and TV in room. Fax on premises. Antiques, fishing, parks, shopping, theater and watersports nearby.

Certificate may be used: Sunday through Thursday.

Grants Pass (Merlin) G2

Pine Meadow Inn
1000 Crow Rd
Grants Pass (Merlin), OR 97532
(541)471-6277 (800)554-0806 Fax:(541)471-6277
E-mail: pmi@cpros.com

Circa 1991. Built on a wooded knoll, this handsome yellow farmhouse looks out on a four-acre meadow, which the innkeepers call their front yard. Five acres of private forest feature walking paths, gardens and private sitting areas. The home's wraparound porch offers wicker furniture, and there is a large deck and hot tub under towering pines. There also is a koi pond and waterfall where one can relax and contemplate. The inn is easily accessible from I-5, yet it feels worlds away.

Innkeeper(s): Nancy & Maloy Murdock. $80-110. PC. 4 rooms with PB. Breakfast included in rates. Types of meals: gourmet breakfast and early coffee/tea. Beds: Q. Air conditioning, turndown service and ceiling fan in room. Fax, copier, spa and library on premises. Antiques, fishing, parks, shopping, theater and watersports nearby.

Certificate may be used: Oct. 1-April 30, two consecutive nights.

Halfway C9

Birch Leaf Farm
Rt 1, Box 91
Halfway, OR 97834-9704
(503)742-2990

Circa 1905. Nestled in the middle of a 42-acre farm near the Oregon Trail and halfway between the Eagle Cap Wilderness and Hells Canyon, this National Register farmhouse boasts original woodwork and hardwood floors. Each guest room has a view of the Wallowa Mountains. A country-style breakfast is served complete with locally made jams and honey. Nearby activities include white-water rafting, jet-boat trips, pack trips and skiing through local mountains.

Innkeeper(s): Maryellen Olson. $65-70. VISA. 4 rooms, 1 with PB. 1 conference room. Breakfast included in rates. Types of meals: full breakfast and early coffee/tea. Afternoon tea and catering service available. Beds: KQDT. Antiques, fishing, shopping, downhill skiing and cross-country skiing nearby.

Location: Wallowa-Eagle Camp Wilderness & NRA-Hells Canyon area.
Publicity: *Hells Canyon Journal.*

"I will always remember the warmth and quiet comfort of your place."

Certificate may be used: Anytime, except holidays.

Jacksonville G3

Touvelle House
455 N Oregon St
Jacksonville, OR 97530-1891
(503)899-8938 (800)846-8422 Fax:(503)899-3992

Circa 1916. This Craftsman inn is two blocks away from the main street of this old Gold Rush town. The common areas of this Craftsman inn include The Library, which has a TV and VCR; The Great Room, featuring a large-stoned fireplace; The Sunroom, which consists of many windows; and The Dining Room, featuring an intricate built-in buffet. Guests can relax on either of two spacious covered verandas.

Innkeeper(s): Carolee Casey. $80-95. 6 rooms with PB. 1 suite. Breakfast included in rates. Type of meal: full breakfast. Beds: QDT. Antiques, fishing, downhill skiing, cross-country skiing, theater and watersports nearby.
Publicity: *Mail Tribune.*

"The accommodations are beautiful, the atmosphere superb, the breakfast and other goodies delightful, but it is the warmth and caring of the host and hostess that will make the difference in this B&B!! Thank you, special people for adding a place in our world."

Certificate may be used: Sunday-Thursday (except holidays) November-April.

Klamath Falls   G4

Thompsons' B&B
1420 Wild Plum Ct
Klamath Falls, OR 97601-1983
(541)882-7938
E-mail: tompohll@aol.com

Circa 1987. The huge picture windows in this comfortable retreat look out to a spectacular view of Klamath Lake and nearby mountains. Popular Moore Park is practically next door, providing a day of hiking, picnicking or relaxing at the marina. The inn is a perfect site to just relax and enjoy the view. Bird watching is a must, as the inn is home to pelicans, snow geese and many varieties of wild ducks. Innkeeper(s): Mary & Bill Pohll. $55-75. PC. 4 rooms with PB. Breakfast included in rates. Types of meals: full breakfast and early coffee/tea. Air conditioning and TV in room. Antiques, parks and watersports nearby.

"Hospitality as glorious as your surroundings."

Certificate may be used: December through February, Monday through Thursday.

Lincoln City   C2

The Enchanted Cottage
4507 SW Coast Ave
Lincoln City, OR 97367
(541)996-4101 Fax:(541)996-2682
E-mail: daythia@wcn.net

Circa 1940. This 4,000-square-foot house is 300 feet from the beach and a short walk from Siletz Bay with its herd of sea lions. Victoria's Secret is a favorite romantic guest room that features a queen canopy bed, antique furnishings and, best of all, the sounds of the Pacific surf. Ask for Sir Arthur's View if you must see and hear the ocean. This two-room suite also has a private deck and a living room with a fireplace and wet bar. Homemade breakfast casseroles are a specialty during the morning meal, which is served either in the dining room or on the deck overlooking the Pacific. Pets are allowed with some restrictions.
Innkeeper(s): David & Cynthia Gale Fitton, Robert M. Hill. $100-175. MC VISA PC TC. 3 rooms with PB, 1 with FP. 1 suite. Breakfast and

evening snack included in rates. Types of meals: full breakfast, gourmet breakfast and early coffee/tea. Dinner, catering service and room service available. Beds: KQ. Turndown service and TV in room. VCR, fax, copier and library on premises. Handicap access. Amusement parks, antiques, fishing, parks, shopping, golf, theater and watersports nearby.
Publicity: *Oregonian.*

Certificate may be used: October through April, except Saturday night. May and September, except Friday and Saturday night.

Manzanita   B2

The Arbors at Manzanita
78 Idaho Ave, PO Box 68
Manzanita, OR 97130
(503)368-7566

Circa 1920. This old-English-style cottage is a half block from the wide sandy beaches that the area is known for. The Neakahnie Mountains are in view as well as the panoramic stretches of the Pacific coastline. Ask for the Waves View room to enjoy the largest view. Enjoy the library, garden and the innkeeper's evening snacks.
Innkeeper(s): H.L. Burrow. $90-105. 2 rooms. Breakfast included in rates. Types of meals: full breakfast and gourmet breakfast. Beds: QT. Cable TV and VCR on premises. Antiques, fishing and shopping nearby.
Location: Two hundred feet from Pacific Ocean.

Certificate may be used: October through June 15, Sunday through Thursday.

McMinnville   C3

Baker Street B&B
129 S Baker St
McMinnville, OR 97128
(503)472-5575 (800)870-5575

Circa 1914. The natural wood that graces the interior of this Craftsman inn has been restored to its original luster. Vintage Victorian antiques and memorabilia decorate the rooms. Several guest rooms include clawfoot tubs, each features a different color scheme. Couples traveling together or those planning longer visits, might consider the Carnation Cottage, which includes two bedrooms, a bathroom, living room, kitchen and laundry facilities. The breakfast table is set with china and silver. The B&B is one hour from Portland and the coast, and there are gourmet restaurants and 40 wineries nearby.
Innkeeper(s): John & Cheryl Collins. $75-125. MC VISA AX DS PC TC. 4 rooms with PB. 1 cottage. Type of meal: full breakfast. Beds: KQDT. Air conditioning and VCR in room. Cable TV on premises. Antiques, parks and shopping nearby.

Certificate may be used: All year.

Oakland
E3

The Beckley House

PO Box 198
Oakland, OR 97462-0198
(503)459-9320

Local merchant Charles Beckley built this two-story home, a historic example of late 19th-century Classic Revival architecture. Rooms are furnished in Victorian style with period antiques, including a rare Victrola. One of the guest rooms boasts a white, iron bed. Fresh flowers brighten the rooms and add to the home's garden setting. Breakfasts are a treat, featuring entrees such as apple dumpings with cheese or Grand Marinier French toast. Enjoy a glass of wine or iced tea on the canopied swing or on the plant-filled patio. Walking tours of the historic town are available, as are romantic carriage rides.

Innkeeper(s): Karene Biedermann. $63-80. 2 rooms. Breakfast included in rates. Type of meal: continental breakfast.

Certificate may be used: October-April.

Portland
B3

Terwilliger Vista B&B

515 SW Westwood Dr
Portland, OR 97201-2791
(503)244-0602 (888)244-0602

Circa 1940. Bay windows accentuate the exterior of this stately Georgian Colonial home. A mix of modern and Art Deco furnishings decorate the interior. The home has an airy, uncluttered feel with its polished floors topped with Oriental rugs and muted tones. There is a canopy bed and fireplace in the spacious Garden Suite, and the Rose Suite overlooks the Willamette Valley. Other rooms offer garden views, bay windows or wicker furnishings. The house is located in what will be the Historical Terwilliger Boulevard Preserve.

Innkeeper(s): Dick & Jan Vatert. $75-125. MC VISA PC TC. 5 rooms with PB, 1 with FP. 2 suites. Breakfast and afternoon tea included in rates. Types of meals: continental breakfast, continental-plus breakfast, full breakfast, gourmet breakfast and early coffee/tea. Beds: KQT. Air conditioning and TV in room. Library on premises. Antiques, parks, shopping, sporting events and theater nearby.

"Like staying in House Beautiful."

Certificate may be used: Jan. 2-March 30, Sunday - Thursday nights.

Salem
C3

State House B&B

2146 State St
Salem, OR 97301-4350
(503)588-1340 (800)800-6712

Circa 1920. This three-story house sits on the banks of Mill Creek where ducks and geese meander past a huge old red maple down to the water. (A baby was abandoned here because the house looked "just right" and "surely had nice people there." The 12-year-old boy who found the baby on the side porch grew up to become a judge and legal counsel to Governor Mark Hatfield.) The inn is close to everything in Salem.

Innkeeper(s): Judy Uselman & Mike Winsett. $50-75. MC VISA DS. 4 rooms, 2 with PB. Breakfast included in rates. Type of meal: full breakfast. Beds: QD. Fax and copier on premises.

Location: One mile from the I-5 Santiam turn-off.

Publicity: *Statesman-Journal.*

"You do a wonderful job making people feel welcome and relaxed."

Certificate may be used: Sept. 15-May 15.

Seaside
A2

10th Avenue Inn Bed & Breakfast

125 10th Ave
Seaside, OR 97138-6203
(530)738-0643 (800)569-1114

Circa 1908. This bed & breakfast is just a few steps from the seashore, so guests enjoy close beach access and an ocean view. The interior is comfortable, the four guest rooms are modern and pleasant, and some of the furnishings are antiques. The innkeepers serve a variety of breakfast entrees, such as crepes Benedict or perhaps an apple puff pancake with sausage. After breakfast, guests can stroll to downtown Seaside or spend the day enjoying the ocean.

Innkeeper(s): Francie & Vern Starkey. $75-85. MC VISA DS PC TC. 4 rooms with PB. 1 cottage. Breakfast included in rates. Types of meals: full breakfast and early coffee/tea. Afternoon tea available. Beds: KQD. Turndown service and TV in room. VCR, fax and copier on premises. Amusement parks, antiques, fishing, parks, shopping, golf, theater and watersports nearby.

"Very clean, cozy house comfortable bed. Pleasing ocean view, convenient parking, convenient us of the common area."

Certificate may be used: Sunday through Thursday, February through April 30 and October through Dec. 20, no holidays.

Custer House B&B

811 1st Ave

Seaside, OR 97138-6803

(503)738-7825 (800)738-7852 Fax:(503)738-4324

E-mail: custerbb@seasurf.com

Circa 1900. Wicker furnishings and a clawfoot tub are features of one of the rooms in this farmhouse-style B&B. It is located four blocks from the ocean and two blocks from the Seaside Convention Center. Your host is retired from the Air Force. Enjoy exploring the area's historic forts and beaches. Innkeeper(s): Skip & Helen Custer. $55-75. MC VISA AX DC CB DS TC. 3 rooms, 1 with PB. 1 conference room. Breakfast included in rates. Type of meal: full breakfast. Beds: QT. Cable TV, VCR and bicycles on premises. Antiques, fishing, parks, shopping, theater and watersports nearby.

Publicity: *Oregon Adventures.*

Certificate may be used: Sunday through Thursday, Oct. 15-May 15.

The Guest House B&B

486 Necanicum Dr

Seaside, OR 97138-6039

(503)717-0495 (800)340-8150

Lewis and Clark once treaded the soil near this inn, and Indians once called the banks of the adjacent Necanicum River home. The Chateau affords mountain and river views, and guests will enjoy watching as the abundant water fowl pass by. Individually decorated rooms include special features such as four-poster beds, hand-crafted quilts, private decks, antique brass beds or lacy curtains. Innkeeper Barbara Kennedy serves a lavish breakfast with fresh fruit, juices, coffee and a daily entree in the Great Blue Heron Room on a family heirloom dining table. Guests are treated to breakfast as well as a panoramic view. The beach is just a few minutes away, as are the sites and sounds of charming Seaside.
Innkeeper(s): Barbara Kennedy. $65-95. MC VISA. 4 rooms. Breakfast included in rates. Type of meal: full breakfast.

Certificate may be used: October 15 through May 15. All days of week

Sand Dollar B&B

606 N Holladay Dr

Seaside, OR 97138-6926

(503)738-3491 (800)738-3491

Circa 1920. This Craftsman-style home looks a bit like a seashell, painted in light pink with dark pink trim. In fact, one of the guest rooms bears the name Sea Shell, filled with bright quilts and wicker. The Driftwood Room can be used as a two-bedroom suite for families. As the room names suggest, the house is decorated in a beach theme, graced by innkeeper Nita Hempfling's stained glasswork. Before breakfast is served, coffee or tea is delivered to the rooms.

Innkeeper(s): Robert & Nita Hempfling. $55-100. MC VISA AX DS TC. 3 rooms, 2 with PB. 1 suite. Breakfast and evening snack included in rates. Beds: KQT. Ceiling fan, TV and VCR in room. Bicycles on premises. Antiques, fishing, parks, shopping and watersports nearby.

Certificate may be used: Sept. 15-May 15, Sunday-Thursday.

Stayton   C3

The Inn at Gardner House Bed & Breakfast

633 N 3rd Ave

Stayton, OR 97383-1731

(503)769-6331

Circa 1893. A former Stayton postmaster and city councilman built this home, which features a wraparound veranda. Accommodations include a suite with a small kitchen and dining room. Each guest room is comfortably furnished, with some antiques. The innkeeper prepares creative breakfasts with homemade breads, fresh fruit and entrees such as asparagus quiche or breakfast burritos topped with salsa.
Innkeeper(s): Dick Jungwirth. $55-65. MC VISA AX DC CB DS PC TC. 4 rooms, 2 with PB. 1 suite. Breakfast included in rates. Types of meals: full breakfast, gourmet breakfast and early coffee/tea. Afternoon tea, dinner, evening snack, picnic lunch, lunch and gourmet lunch available. Restaurant on premises. Beds: QT. Air conditioning, TV and VCR in room. Copier and library on premises. Antiques, fishing, parks, shopping, downhill skiing, cross-country skiing, sporting events, theater and watersports nearby.

Certificate may be used: Jan. 1 to Dec. 31.

Tigard   B3

The Woven Glass Inn

14645 SW Beef Bend Rd

Tigard, OR 97224

(503)590-6040

Circa 1938. This comfortable farmhouse is surrounded by more than an acre of grounds, including a sunken garden. Guests staying in the suite enjoy a view of the garden. Beds in both guest rooms include fluffy down pillows and fine linens. The homestay is 20 minutes from Portland, and the area offers a variety of wineries to visit.

Innkeeper(s): Paul & Renee Giroux. $60-70. MC VISA AX DS PC TC. 2 rooms with PB. 1 suite. Breakfast included in rates. Type of meal: full breakfast. Beds: KQ. Turndown service in room. Cable TV and library on premises. Amusement parks, antiques, fishing, parks, shopping, downhill skiing, cross-country skiing, sporting events, golf, theater and watersports nearby.

"We needed a little rest and relaxation and we found it here. We loved everything."

Certificate may be used: Oct. 1-April 30, Monday-Sunday.

Tillamook
B2

Blue Haven Inn
3025 Gienger Rd
Tillamook, OR 97141-8258
(503)842-2265 Fax:(503)842-2265

Circa 1916. This Craftsman-style home has been refurbished and filled with antiques and collectibles. Guest rooms feature limited-edition plate series as themes. Tall evergreens, lawns and flower gardens add to the setting.

Innkeeper(s): Joy Still. $60-75. PC TC. 3 rooms, 1 with PB. Breakfast included in rates. Types of meals: full breakfast, gourmet breakfast and early coffee/tea. Beds: QD. Cable TV, VCR, fax, bicycles and library on premises. Antiques, fishing, parks, shopping and watersports nearby.

Publicity: *Oakland Tribune.*

"Your home is like a present to the eyes."

Certificate may be used: Sunday-Thursday, November-June.

Welches
C4

Old Welches Inn B&B
26401 E Welches Rd
Welches, OR 97067
(503)622-3754 Fax:(503)622-5370

Circa 1890. This cozy inn, which sports a blue tin roof, has a long history of hospitality. The building first opened its doors to guests in 1890, serving as a summer resort. Innkeepers Judi and Ted Mondun undertook a major task restoring their inn, which included peeling off almost a dozen layers of paint off walls in one room, exposing the original wallpaper. The inn has four guest rooms, each named for a variety of flower. The Sweet Briar is a rustic retreat with exposed cedar walls and a white iron bed. Other rooms feature items such as a sleigh bed. Two rooms offer mountain views, and one affords a vista

of Salmon River. The innkeepers also offer a two-bedroom cottage within walking distance of the river. The cottage also includes a river rock fireplace and fully equipped kitchen.

Innkeeper(s): Judith & Ted Mondun. $75-130. MC VISA AX DS PC TC. 4 rooms. 1 cottage. Breakfast and early coffee/tea. Beds: QD. Turndown service in room. Cable TV, VCR, fax and pet boarding on premises. Antiques, fishing, parks, shopping, downhill skiing, cross-country skiing, sporting events and golf nearby.

Publicity: *Oregonian, Sunset.*

"Breakfast was scrumptious, fit for a king (and all of his army)."

Certificate may be used: Jan. 31-May 15 and Oct. 1-Nov. 15; Sunday through Thursday.

Yachats
D2

Sea Quest
95354 Hwy 101 S
Yachats, OR 97498-9713
(541)547-3782 (800)341-4878 Fax:(541)547-3719

Circa 1990. This 6,000-square-foot cedar and glass house is only 100 feet from the ocean, located on two-and-one-half acres. Each guest room has a Jacuzzi tub and outside entrance. The second-floor breakfast room is distinguished by wide views of the

ocean, forest and Ten Mile Creek. Guests are often found relaxing in front of the home's floor-to-ceiling brick fireplace. More adventuresome guests may enjoy the Oregon coast and nearby aquariums.

Innkeeper(s): George & Elaine. $125-245. MC VISA DS PC. 5 rooms with PB. Breakfast included in rates. Types of meals: full breakfast and early coffee/tea. Beds: Q. Fax, spa, sauna and library on premises. Antiques, fishing, parks, shopping and watersports nearby.

Location: One hundred feet from the water, where the forest meets the sea.

Certificate may be used: Jan. 5-May 15, Sunday to Thursday only, no holidays.

Pennsylvania

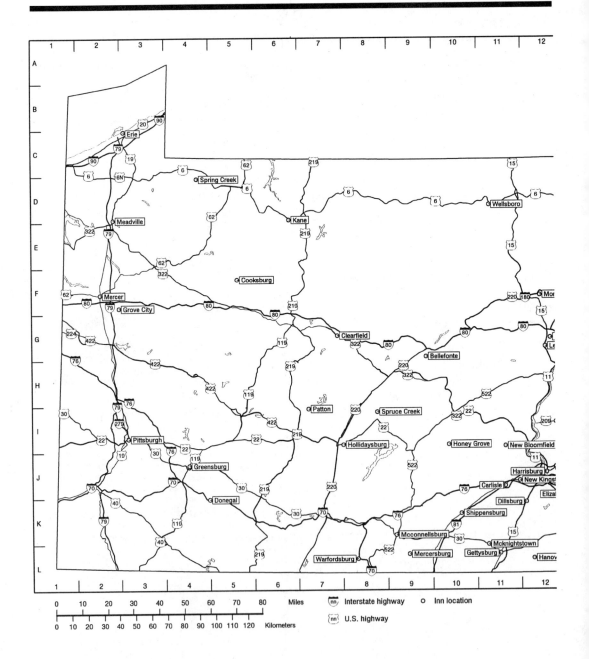

	Miles		Interstate highway	o	Inn location
0	10	20	30	40	50	60	70	80		Miles			U.S. highway
0	10	20	30	40	50	60	70	80	90	100	110	120	Kilometers

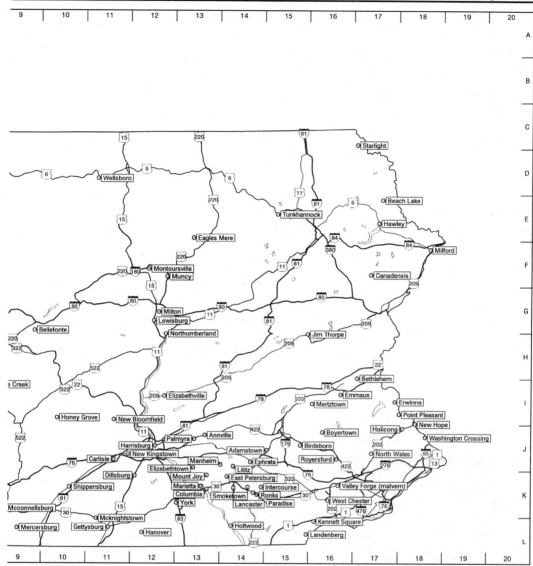

| | 9 | 10 | 11 | 12 | 13 | 14 | 15 | 16 | 17 | 18 | 19 | 20 |

Starlight

Wellsboro

Beach Lake

Tunkhannock
Hawley

Eagles Mere
Milford

Montoursville
Muncy
Canadensis

Milton
Lewisburg
Northumberland
Jim Thorpe

Bellefonte

Elizabethville
Bethlehem

Honey Grove
New Bloomfield
Emmaus
Mertztown
Erwinna

Point Pleasant
New Hope
Boyertown
Holicong
Washington Crossing

Harrisburg
Palmyra
Annville
North Wales
New Kingstown
Adamstown
Birdsboro
Carlisle
Manheim
Ephrata
Royersford
Elizabethtown
Lititz
Dillsburg
Mount Joy
East Petersburg
Shippensburg
Marietta
Intercourse
Valley Forge (malvern)
Columbia
Smoketown
Ronks
West Chester
Mcconnellsburg
York
Lancaster
Paradise
Mcknightstown
Kennett Square
Mercersburg
Gettysburg
Hanover
Holtwood
Landenberg

Adamstown   J15

Adamstown Inn
62 W Main St
Adamstown, PA 19501
(717)484-0800 (800)594-4808

Circa 1830. This square brick house, with its 1850s
pump organ found in the large parlor and other
local folk art, fits right into this community known
as one of the antique capitols of America (2,500
antique dealers). Other decorations include family
heirlooms, Victorian wallpaper, handmade quilts
and lace curtains. Before breakfast, coffee, tea or hot

361

chocolate is brought to your room. For outlet mall fans, Adamstown is 10 miles from Reading, which offers a vast assortment of top-quality merchandise. Innkeeper(s): Tom & Wanda Berman. $65-115. MC VISA DS PC TC. 4 rooms with PB, 2 with FP. 1 suite. Breakfast, afternoon tea and evening snack included in rates. Types of meals: continental-plus breakfast and early coffee/tea. Beds: KQD. Air conditioning and ceiling fan in room. Cable TV, copier and library on premises. Amusement parks, antiques, fishing, parks, shopping and theater nearby.

Publicity: *Lancaster Intelligencer, Reading Eagle, Travel & Leisure, Country Almanac.*

"Your warm hospitality and lovely home left us with such pleasant memories."

Certificate may be used: Sunday through Thursday, Nov. 1-March 31.

Annville J13

Swatara Creek Inn
Box 692, Rd 2
Annville, PA 17003
(717)865-3259

Circa 1860. A former boys' home, this bed & breakfast now boasts canopy beds and lacy curtains. The first floor of this Victorian mansion provides a sitting room, dining room and gift shop. A full breakfast is served in the dining room, but honeymooners can request their meal in the comfort of their rooms. For

chocolate lovers, nearby Hershey is a treat. Several shopping outlets are about an hour away or visit the Mount Hope Estate and Winery. For an unusual day trip, tour the Seltzer and Weaver Bologna plant in Lebanon. Each September, the town hosts a popular bologna festival. Nearby Lancaster County is the home of Amish communities.
Innkeeper(s): Jeanette Hess. $45-80. MC VISA AX DC DS. 10 rooms with PB. 1 suite. Breakfast included in rates. Types of meals: full breakfast and early coffee/tea. Beds: QT. Air conditioning in room. Handicap access. Amusement parks, antiques, fishing, parks, shopping, sporting events and theater nearby.

Publicity: *Daily News, Patriot-News.*

Certificate may be used: Sunday through Thursday, all year.

Beach Lake E17

East Shore House B&B
PO Box 250
Beach Lake, PA 18405-0250
(717)729-8523 Fax:(717)729-8080

Circa 1901. This Victorian-style home boasts a wraparound porch perfect for rest and relaxation. The gazebo, which sits on top of a bubbling brook, offers another enchanting rest spot. Rooms feature decor typical of turn-of-the-century boardinghouse rooms. Each season brings a host of new activities. In warm months, enjoy canoeing and hiking at nearby Delaware River. The "Fall Foliage Express" takes tourists on a train excursion through the local countryside. In winter, guests can snuggle up by the woodstove after a day of skiing or ice skating.
Innkeeper(s): Amy Wood. $45-65. MC VISA. 6 rooms, 4 with PB. Breakfast included in rates. Type of meal: full breakfast. Beds: D. Ceiling fan in room. Amusement parks, antiques, fishing, shopping and downhill skiing nearby.

Certificate may be used: Sunday through Thursday, year-round.

Bellefonte G9

Reynolds Mansion B&B
101 W Linn St
Bellefonte, PA 16823-1622
(814)353-8407 (800)899-3929
E-mail: jheidt@boole.com

Circa 1885. Bellefonte is a town with many impressive, historic homes, and this exquisite stone mansion is no exception. The home, a combination of late Victorian and Gothic styles, features extraordinary, hand-crafted woodwork and intricately laid wood floors, as well as eight fireplaces. Two guest rooms include a fireplace and some include a Jacuzzi tub. All enjoy a romantic atmosphere, heightened

by candles, fresh flowers and the poshest of furnishings and decor. Baked, stuffed French toast served with bacon or sausage is among the breakfast specialties, accompany by muffins, juices, cereals and a fruit compote created with more than a half dozen different fresh fruits. For a fun lunch or dinner, the innkeepers suggest the nearby Gamble Mill Tavern, a 200-year-old mill listed in the National Register.
Innkeeper(s): Joseph & Charlotte Heidt. $85-135. MC VISA PC TC. 3 suites, 2 with FP. 1 conference room. Breakfast included in rates. Types of meals: continental-plus breakfast, full breakfast, gourmet breakfast and early coffee/tea. Beds: KQ. Cable TV, VCR, fax, copier and library on premises. Antiques, fishing, parks, shopping, downhill skiing, cross-country skiing, sporting events, golf, theater and watersports nearby.

"Your bed & breakfast is such an inspiration to us."

Certificate may be used: Monday-Thursday, garden room.

Bethlehem   H17

Wydnor Hall
3612 Old Philadelphia Pike
Bethlehem, PA 18015-5320
(610)867-6851 (800)839-0020 Fax:(610)866-2062
Circa 1810. On the Old Philadelphia Pike, this Georgian fieldstone mansion is close to Lehigh University and the historic district. Tall trees shade the acre of grounds. Meticulously restored, the house is appointed with an English decor.

Amenities include pressed linens, down comforters and terry cloth robes. The breakfast table is set with fine china and silver. Homemade pastries, breads and cakes are served at tea time.
Innkeeper(s): Kristina & Charles Taylor. $110-140. MC VISA AX DC CB DS PC TC. 5 rooms with PB. 2 suites. 1 conference room. Breakfast included in rates. Type of meal: early coffee/tea. Afternoon tea available. Beds: KQD. Air conditioning, turndown service, ceiling fan and TV in room. Fax on premises. Amusement parks, antiques and sporting events nearby.
Publicity: *Express Times, Morning Call.*

"Wydnor Hall is warm, clean, charming, and comfortable. Your staff is cheerful, delightful and makes your guests feel graciously welcomed."

Certificate may be used: Weekends, January, February & March.

Birdsboro   J15

Brooke Mansion Victorian Inn
Washington St
Birdsboro, PA 19508
(610)582-9775 (800)544-1094
Circa 1888. Brooke Mansion, a stunning Victorian, is one of those exquisite homes you might pass by and wish you could see inside. The home is a fanciful display of Victorian architecture, the first owner built it as a wedding gift for his bride. Ornate stained glass, hand-carved woodwork, a circular library and a grand staircase are among the gems guests will marvel at in this 42-room manor. The interior includes fine antiques, some of which are family heirlooms. The area offers much to do, from antiquing to exploring Amish country. The inn is an hour's drive from Philadelphia.
Innkeeper(s): Marci & Pete Xenias. $99-135. PC TC. 4 rooms, 3 with PB. 1 suite. Breakfast included in rates. Types of meals: full breakfast and early coffee/tea. Beds: K. Air conditioning and ceiling fan in room. Library on premises. Antiques, parks, shopping, golf and theater nearby.
Publicity: *News of Southern Berks.*

Certificate may be used: January through March and July and August, Sunday through Thursday.

Boyertown   J16

The Enchanted Cottage
22 Deer Run Rd, Rd 4
Boyertown, PA 19512-8312
(610)845-8845
Circa 1984. This thatch and stone cottage looks much like one might imagine the woodcutter's tiny house in the fairy tale "Hansel and Gretel." Ivy covers the front of the cottage, which guests reach via a little stone path. Inside, exposed wood beams, a window seat and a wood stove create a cozy, romantic ambiance in the living room. The first floor also includes a kitchenette. Upstairs, guests will find a quilt-topped bed and a bathroom with a clawfoot tub. The innkeepers live in an adjacent home that rests about 100 yards away, and it is in their home that breakfasts are served. The cottage is near many attractions, including historic sites such as the Daniel Boone Home, Dupont Estate, Longwood Gardens, museums, Amish farms and a restored mining village.
Innkeeper(s): Peg & Richard Groff. $85-90. PC TC. 1 cottage. Breakfast included in rates. Types of meals: full breakfast and gourmet breakfast. Beds: D. Air conditioning and ceiling fan in room. Amusement parks, antiques, parks, downhill skiing and golf nearby.
Publicity: *Boyertown Area Times, Allentown News, Pittstown Mercury, Reading Times, Boyertown News.*

"The Enchanted Cottage is a place you've seen in dreams."

Certificate may be used: April 1-Sept. 30, Monday-Thursday.

Canadensis F17

Brookview Manor B&B Inn

RR 1 Box 365
Canadensis, PA 18325-9740
(717)595-2451 (800)585-7974 Fax:(717)595-2065

Circa 1911. By the side of the road, hanging from a tall evergreen, is the welcoming sign to this forest retreat. There are brightly dec-orated common rooms and four fireplaces. The carriage house has three bed-rooms and is suitable for small groups. The innkeepers like to share a "secret waterfall" within a 30-minute walk from the inn.

Innkeeper(s): Mary Anne Buckley. $100-150. MC VISA AX DS PC TC. 10 rooms, 9 with PB, 1 with FP. 1 suite. Breakfast and afternoon tea included in rates. Types of meals: full breakfast and early coffee/tea. Picnic lunch available. Beds: QD. Air conditioning in room. Cable TV, fax and copier on premises. Amusement parks, antiques, fishing, parks, shopping, downhill skiing, cross-country skiing, theater and water-sports nearby.

Location: On Rt 447, Pocono Mountains.

Publicity: *Mid-Atlantic Country, Bridal Guide.*

"Thanks for a great wedding weekend. Everything was perfect."

Certificate may be used: Year-round weekdays only, Sunday-Thursday evenings.

The Merry Inn

PO Box 757, Rt 390
Canadensis, PA 18325-0757
(717)595-2011 (800)858-4182

Circa 1942. Set in the picturesque Pocono Mountains, this inn is a 90-minute drive from the metropolitan New York and Philadelphia areas. The turn-of-the-century, mountainside home was built by two sisters and at one time was used as a board-ing house. Current owners and innkeepers Meredyth and Chris Huggard have decorated their B&B using an eclectic mix of styles. Each guest room is individually appointed, with styles ranging from Victorian to country. Guests enjoy use of an outdoor Jacuzzi set into the mountainside. Bedrooms are set up to accommodate families, and children are welcome here.

Innkeeper(s): Meredyth & Christopher Huggard. $65-95. MC VISA PC TC. 6 rooms. Breakfast included in rates. Type of meal: full breakfast. Beds: KQDT. VCR on premises. Antiques, fishing, parks, shopping, downhill skiing, cross-country skiing, theater and watersports nearby.

Certificate may be used: Anytime midweek, weekends November - April 15.

Carlisle J11

Line Limousin Farmhouse B&B

2070 Ritner Hwy
Carlisle, PA 17013-9303
(717)243-1281

Circa 1864. The grandchildren of Bob and Joan are the ninth generation of Lines to enjoy this 200-year-old homestead. A stone and brick exterior accents the farmhouse's graceful style, while inside, family heirlooms attest to the home's longevity. This is a breeding stock farm of 110 acres and the cattle raised here, Limousin, originate from the Limoges area of France. Giant maples shade the lawn and there are woods and stone fences.

Innkeeper(s): Bob & Joan Line. $65-75. PC. 4 rooms, 2 with PB. Breakfast included in rates. Type of meal: full breakfast. Beds: KQTL. Air conditioning and TV in room. VCR and library on premises. Amusement parks, antiques, fishing, parks, shopping, cross-country skiing, sporting events and theater nearby.

Certificate may be used: Monday through Thursday, except special events. Non-smokers only.

Pheasant Field B&B

150 Hickorytown Rd
Carlisle, PA 17013-9732
(717)258-0717 Fax:(717)258-0717
E-mail: pheasant@pa.net

Circa 1800. Located on eight acres of central Pennsylvania farmland, this brick, two-story Federal-style farmhouse features wooden shutters and a covered front porch. An early 19th-century stone barn is on the property, and horse boarding often is available. The Appalachian Trail is less than a mile away. Fly-fishing is popular at Yellow Breeches and Letort Spring. Dickinson College and Carlisle Fairgrounds are other points of interest.

Innkeeper(s): Denise Fegan. $65-95. MC VISA AX. 4 rooms, 2 with PB. Breakfast included in rates. Types of meals: full breakfast and early cof-fee/tea. Beds: KQ. Air conditioning and turndown service in room. Cable TV and VCR on premises. Amusement parks, antiques, fishing, downhill skiing, cross-country skiing and theater nearby.

Publicity: *Outdoor Traveler, Harrisburg Magazine.*

"You have an outstanding, charming and warm house. I felt for the first time as being home."

Certificate may be used: November through March.

Clearfield G7

Christopher Kratzer House

101 E Cherry St
Clearfield, PA 16830-2315
(814)765-5024 (888)252-2632

Circa 1840. This inn is the oldest home in town, built by a carpenter and architect who also started Clearfield's first newspaper. The innkeepers keep a book of history about the house and town for interested guests. The interior is a mix of antiques from different eras, many are family pieces. There are collections of art and musical instruments. Several guest rooms afford views of the Susquehanna River. Refreshments and a glass of wine are served in the afternoons. The inn's Bridal Suite Special includes complimentary champagne, fruit and snacks, and breakfast is served in the privacy of your room.
Innkeeper(s): Bruce & Ginny Baggett. $55-70. MC VISA DS PC TC. 4 rooms, 1 with PB. Breakfast, afternoon tea and evening snack included in rates. Types of meals: gourmet breakfast and early coffee/tea. Beds: KQT. Ceiling fan and TV in room. Library on premises. Antiques, fishing, parks, shopping, downhill skiing, cross-country skiing, sporting events and theater nearby.

Certificate may be used: Nov. 30-Aug. 31, Sunday-Saturday.

Victorian Loft B&B

216 S Front St
Clearfield, PA 16830-2218
(814)765-4805 (800)798-0456 Fax:(814)765-9596
E-mail: 70724,146@compuserve.com

Circa 1894. Accommodations at this bed & breakfast are available in either a historic Victorian home on the riverfront or in a private, three-bedroom cabin. The white brick home is dressed with colorful, gingerbread trim, and inside, a grand staircase, stained glass and antique furnishings add to the Victorian charm. The suite is ideal for families as it contains two bedrooms, a living room, dining room, kitchen and a bath with a whirlpool tub. The cabin, Cedarwood Lodge, sleeps six and is located on eight, wooded acres near Elliot State Park. This is a favorite setting for small groups.
Innkeeper(s): Tim & Peggy Durant. $45-100. MC VISA AX DS PC TC. 3 rooms, 1 with PB. 1 suite. 1 cottage. Breakfast included in rates. Types of meals: full breakfast and early coffee/tea. Beds: QD. Cable TV and VCR on premises. Antiques, fishing, parks, shopping, cross-country skiing, sporting events, theater and watersports nearby.

"A feeling of old-fashioned beauty. The elegance of roses and lace. All wrapped up into a romantic moment."
Certificate may be used: Sunday-Thursday nights based on availability.

Columbia K13

The Columbian

360 Chestnut St
Columbia, PA 17512-1156
(717)684-5869 (800)422-5869
E-mail: bedandb@aol.com

Circa 1897. This stately three-story mansion is a fine example of Colonial Revival architecture. Antique beds, a stained-glass window and home-baked breads are among its charms. Guests may relax on the wraparound sun porches.

C. BERNTHEIZEL '94

Innkeeper(s): Chris & Becky Will. $65-99. MC VISA PC TC. 5 rooms with PB, 2 with FP. 1 suite. Breakfast included in rates. Type of meal: full breakfast. Beds: QT. Air conditioning, ceiling fan and TV in room. Amusement parks, antiques, fishing, parks, shopping, downhill skiing, cross-country skiing, sporting events, theater and watersports nearby.

Publicity: *Philadelphia Inquirer, Lancaster Intelligencer Journal, Columbia News, Washington Post, Potomac, Allentown Morning Call.*

"In a word, extraordinary! Truly a home away from home. First B&B experience but will definitely not be my last."

Certificate may be used: Sunday - Thursday, December through April.

Cooksburg F5

Clarion River Lodge

HC 1 Box 22D
Cooksburg, PA 16217-9704
(814)744-8171 (800)648-6743 Fax:(814)744-8553

Circa 1964. This lodge is a rustic retreat above the Clarion River and surrounded by Cook Forest. Its pegged-oak flooring, oak beams, pine ceiling, wild cherry and butternut paneling and fieldstone fireplace add to the lodge's natural character. A distinctive glassed-in breezeway leads from the main building to the guest wing. Rooms are decorated with modern Scandinavian decor. Dinner and continental breakfast packages available.

Innkeeper(s): Ellen O'Day. $72-129. MC VISA AX TC. 20 rooms with PB. 1 conference room. Breakfast included in rates. Type of meal: continental breakfast. Beds: KQ. Air conditioning and TV in room. VCR and fax on premises. Antiques, fishing, parks, shopping and theater nearby.

Location: Adjacent to Cook Forest State Park and on the Clarion River.

Publicity: *Pittsburgh Press, Pittsburgh Women's Journal.*

"If your idea of Paradise is a secluded rustic retreat surrounded by the most beautiful country this side of the Rockies, search no more."

Certificate may be used: November-April, Sunday-Thursday, no holidays.

Dillsburg K12

The Peter Wolford House
440 Franklin Church Rd
Dillsburg, PA 17019-9766
(717)432-0757

Circa 1800. A Federal farmhouse in the National Register, the Peter Wolford House was constructed of Flemish Bond brick by a prominent grist mill operator. His brick-patterned bank barn, a unique

Pennsylvania and Maryland barn style, still stands. There are pine floors and many fireplaces, including a 10-foot-wide, walk-in fireplace used for cooking. Antiques and handmade quilts fill the guest rooms. Outside on the 10 acres are meadows, an herb garden and perennial borders accented by a handmade picket fence. State gamelands are adjacent to the inn.

Innkeeper(s): Ted & Loretta Pesano. $60-65. PC. 3 rooms, 2 with FP. Breakfast and evening snack included in rates. Types of meals: full breakfast and early coffee/tea. Beds: QD. Air conditioning and ceiling fan in room. Library on premises. Amusement parks, antiques, fishing, shopping, downhill skiing, sporting events, golf and theater nearby.

Publicity: *Pennsylvania Magazine.*

"Thank you for a splendid getaway."

Certificate may be used: January-March, Sunday-Friday and June-August, Sunday-Friday.

Donegal K4

Mountain View B&B & Antiques
Mountain View Rd
Donegal, PA 15628
(412)593-6349

Circa 1855. Six wooded acres surround this Georgian-style farmhouse, a county historic landmark. The innkeepers own Donegal antiques and have selected many fine 18th- and 19th-century

pieces to furnish the inn. There is a large barn on the property. Guests enjoy the rural setting for its outstanding views of the Laurel Mountains. Fallingwater, a famous Frank Lloyd Wright house, is 20 minutes away.

Innkeeper(s): Lesley O'Leary. $95-150. MC VISA AX DC DS. 7 rooms, 3 with PB. Breakfast included in rates. Types of meals: full breakfast and early coffee/tea. Evening snack available. Beds: QD. Air conditioning in room. Amusement parks, antiques, fishing, shopping, downhill skiing, cross-country skiing and theater nearby.

Certificate may be used: Anytime except holiday weekends and month of October.

Eagles Mere E13

Crestmont Inn
Crestmont Dr
Eagles Mere, PA 17731
(717)525-3519 (800)522-8767

Eagles Mere has been a vacation site since the late 19th century and still abounds with Victorian charm. The Crestmont Inn is no exception. The rooms are tastefully decorated with Oriental rugs, flowers and elegant furnishings. A hearty country breakfast is served each morning, and guests also are treated to a five-course dinner in the candlelit dining room. Savor a variety of mouth-watering entrees and finish off the evening with scrumptious desserts such as fresh fruit pies, English trifle or Orange Charlotte. The cocktail lounge is a perfect place to mingle and

enjoy hors d'oeuvres, wines and spirits. The inn grounds offer a large swimming pool, tennis and shuffleboard courts. The Wyoming State Forest borders the property, and golfing is just minutes away.
Innkeeper(s): Karen Oliver. $89-148. MC VISA. 16 rooms. Breakfast included in rates. Type of meal: full breakfast.

Certificate may be used: Sunday through Thursday, year-round

Shady Lane B&B
Allegheny Ave, PO Box 314
Eagles Mere, PA 17731
(717)525-3394 (800)524-1248

Circa 1947. This ranch-style house rests on two mountaintop acres. Eagles Mere is a Victorian town with gaslights and old-fashioned village shops. Crystal clear Eagles Mere Lake is surrounded by Laurel Path, a popular scenic walk. The Endless Mountains provide cross-country skiing, fishing and hiking. Tobogganing is popular on the Eagles Mere Toboggan Slide.
Innkeeper(s): Pat & Dennis Dougherty. $75. TC. 8 rooms, 7 with PB. 1 suite. Breakfast and afternoon tea included in rates. Types of meals: full breakfast and gourmet breakfast. Beds: KQDT. Ceiling fan in room. Cable TV on premises. Antiques, fishing, parks, shopping and cross-country skiing nearby.

Certificate may be used: Sunday through Thursday from Sept. 1-June 30 (not in July or August).

East Petersburg (Lancaster County)   *K14*

The George Zahm House
6070 Main St
East Petersburg, PA 17520-1266
(717)569-6026

Circa 1856. The bright red exterior of this Federal-style inn is a landmark in this village. The home is named for its builder and first resident, who constructed his sturdy dwelling with 18-inch-thick brick walls. Innkeeping is a family affair for owners Robyn Kemple-Keeports and husband, Jeff Keeports, who run the inn along with Robyn's mother, Daneen. The rooms are inviting and comfortable, yet elegant. Beautiful drapery, rich wallpapers and a collection of antique furniture combine to give the house an opulent feel. Many of the pieces are family heirlooms. Breakfasts with homemade specialty cakes, breads,

Belgian waffles and fresh fruits are served in the dining room on a table set with Blue Willow china.
Innkeeper(s): Robyn & Jeff Keeports. $65-85. MC VISA TC. 4 rooms, 3 with PB. 1 suite. Breakfast, afternoon tea and evening snack included in rates. Types of meals: continental-plus breakfast and early coffee/tea. Beds: KQDT. Air conditioning and ceiling fan in room. Handicap access. Amusement parks, antiques, parks, shopping, sporting events and theater nearby.

"An oasis - truly a wonderful place. Most charming."

Certificate may be used: Year-round, Sunday-Thursday.

Elizabethtown   *J13*

Apples Abound Inn B&B
518 S Market St
Elizabethtown, PA 17022-2530
(717)367-3018 Fax:(717)367-9788

Circa 1907. As the name suggests, apples do abound at this early 20th-century home, which features a unique apple collection. In the local historic register, this three-story, brick Victorian has a turret and a wide, wraparound veranda. Other features

include cranberry-colored glass transoms, bay windows, a stained-glass window, chestnut wood trim and doors and built-in china cabinets. Rooms are decorated with antiques and a traditional country decor. Lancaster, Harrisburg and Hershey are nearby.
Innkeeper(s): Jennifer & Jon Sheppard. $70-95. MC VISA PC TC. 5 rooms with PB. Breakfast included in rates. Types of meals: full breakfast and early coffee/tea. Beds: QD. Air conditioning, turndown service and ceiling fan in room. Amusement parks, antiques, fishing, parks, shopping, downhill skiing, cross-country skiing and sporting events nearby.

Certificate may be used: Jan. 1-March 31, Sunday-Saturday.

West Ridge Guest House
1285 W Ridge Rd
Elizabethtown, PA 17022-9739
(717)367-7783 Fax:(717)367-8468

Circa 1890. Guests at this country home have many choices. They may opt to relax and enjoy the view from the gazebo, or perhaps work out in the inn's exercise room. The hot tub provides yet another soothing possibility. Ask about rooms with whirlpool tubs. The 20-acre grounds also include two fishing ponds. The innkeepers pass out a breakfast menu to their guests, allowing them to choose the time they prefer to eat and a choice of entrees. Along with the traditional fruit, muffins or coffeecake and meats, guests choose items such as omelets, waffles or pancakes.

Innkeeper(s): Alice P. Heisey. $60-120. MC VISA AX. 9 rooms with PB, 3 with FP. 2 suites. Breakfast included in rates. Type of meal: full breakfast. Beds: KQ. Air conditioning, ceiling fan, TV and VCR in room. Fax, copier and spa on premises. Antiques, fishing, parks and shopping nearby.

Certificate may be used: All year, Sunday-Thursday, no holidays.

Elizabethville   I12

The Inn at Elizabethville
30 W Main St, Box V
Elizabethville, PA 17023
(717)362-3476 Fax:(717)362-4571

Circa 1883. This comfortable, two-story house was owned by a Civil War veteran and founder of a local wagon company. The innkeepers decided to buy and fix up the house to help support their other business, renovating old houses. The conference room features an unusual fireplace with cabinets and painted decorations. Rooms are filled with antiques and Mission oak-style furniture. County auctions, local craft fairs and outdoor activities entice guests. Comfortable living rooms, porches and a sun parlor are available for relaxation.

Innkeeper(s): Penny & Art Bell. $49-65. AP. MC VISA AX TC. 7 rooms with PB. 1 suite. 1 conference room. Breakfast included in rates. Type of meal: continental breakfast. Beds: DT. Air conditioning and ceiling fan in room. Cable TV, VCR, fax and copier on premises. Antiques, fishing, parks, shopping and watersports nearby.

Publicity: *Harrisburg Patriot-News, Upper Dauphin Sentinel.*

Certificate may be used: Anytime with prior notice.

Emmaus   I16

Leibert Gap Manor
4502 S Mountain Dr, PO Box 623
Emmaus, PA 18049-4503
(215)967-1242 (800)964-1242

This three-story Williamsburg-style house is on 17 acres. Random-width pine floors, open-beam ceilings and a Colonial fireplace are on the main floor. Primitive and cottage pieces, along with canopy beds and antiques, are found in the guest rooms. A solarium overlooks the Leibert Gap flyway and you may watch hawks and other birds pass by. In the

afternoon, enjoy tea and scones on the long brick porch. Nearby are 10 colleges as well as many antique shops and factory outlets.

Innkeeper(s): Pauline & Wayne Sheffer. $75-125. MC VISA AX DC CB. 4 rooms. 2 suites. 1 conference room. Breakfast included in rates. Type of meal: full breakfast. Catering service available. Air conditioning, turndown service and VCR in room. Cable TV on premises. Amusement parks, antiques, shopping, downhill skiing, sporting events and theater nearby.

Certificate may be used: Sunday through Thursday, January through March, space available. August-December excluded. April, May and June, space available.

Ephrata   J14

The 1777 House at Doneckers
301 W Main St
Ephrata, PA 17522-1713
(717)738-9502 Fax:(717)738-9552

Circa 1777. Jacob Gorgas, a devout member of the Ephrata Cloister and a clock maker, noted for crafting 150 eight-day Gorgas grandfather clocks, built this stately Dutch Colonial-style home. Guests can opt to stay in one of four antique-filled homes. The 1777 House, which includes 12 rooms, features hand-stenciled walls, suites with whirlpool baths, fireplaces, original stone masonry and an antique tiled floor. The home served as a tavern in the 1800s and an elegant inn in the early 1900s.

The Homestead includes four suites all with fireplaces and amenities such as Jacuzzis, sitting areas and four-poster beds. The Guesthouse features a variety of beautifully decorated rooms each named and themed in honor of local landmarks or significant citizens. The Gerhart House memorializes prominent innkeepers or hotel owners in Ephrata's history. All guests enjoy an expansive breakfast with freshly squeezed juice, fruits, breakfast cheeses, sausage, fresh pastries and other delicacies. The homes are part of the Donecker Community, which features upscale fashion stores, art galleries and a restaurant within walking distance of the 1777 House.

Innkeeper(s): Jill Brown. $89-185. MC VISA AX DC CB DS. 40 rooms, 12 with PB, 4 with FP. 6 suites. 1 conference room. Breakfast included in rates. Types of meals: continental-plus breakfast and gourmet breakfast. Restaurant on premises. Beds: KQDT. Air conditioning in room. Cable TV, fax, copier and spa on premises. Antiques, shopping and theater nearby.

Location: Junction of Routes 222 & 322 in Lancaster County.

Publicity: *Daily News, Country Inns.*

"A peaceful refuge."

Certificate may be used: Year-round, Sunday-Thursday, except holidays.

Erie

C3

Spencer House B&B

519 W 6th St
Erie, PA 16507-1128
(814)454-5984 (800)890-7263 Fax:(814)456-5091

Circa 1876. Still under renovation, this three-story Victorian Stick house features gabled windows and a wraparound porch. Original woodwork, much of it carved with scrolls and scripture, is one of the inn's most outstanding features. Twelve-foot ceilings, interior folding shutters and a well-stocked library with black walnut bookshelves are other highlights. The Tree Top Room offers a ceiling-to-floor canopy and a reading nook.

Innkeeper(s): Pat & Keith Hagenbuch. $65-95. MC VISA AX DS TC. 5 rooms with PB, 5 with FP. 1 suite. Breakfast and afternoon tea included in rates. Types of meals: continental breakfast, continental-plus breakfast, full breakfast and early coffee/tea. Dinner and picnic lunch available. Beds: Q. Air conditioning, ceiling fan, TV and VCR in room. Fax and copier on premises. Amusement parks, antiques, fishing, parks, shopping, downhill skiing, cross-country skiing, sporting events, theater and watersports nearby.

Certificate may be used: Sept. 30-April 30, Sunday-Thursday.

Erwinna (Bucks County)

I17

Evermay-On-The-Delaware

River Rd, PO Box 60
Erwinna (Bucks County), PA 18920
(610)294-9100 Fax:(610)294-8249

Circa 1700. Twenty-five acres of Bucks County at its best — rolling green meadows, lawns, stately maples and the silvery Delaware River, surround this three-story manor. Serving as an inn since 1871, it has hosted such guests as the Barrymore family. Rich walnut wainscoting, a grandfather clock and twin fireplaces warm the parlor, scented by vases of roses or gladiolus. Antique-filled guest rooms overlook the river or gardens.

Innkeeper(s): Bill & Danielle Moffly. $95-175. MC VISA PC TC. 16 rooms with PB. 1 suite. 2 cottages. 2 conference rooms. Breakfast and afternoon tea included in rates. Type of meal: continental-plus breakfast. Dinner and picnic lunch available. Restaurant on premises. Beds: QD. Air conditioning and turndown service in room. VCR, fax, copier, computer and library on premises. Handicap access. Antiques, fishing, parks, shopping, cross-country skiing, sporting events, theater and watersports nearby.

Publicity: *New York Times, Philadelphia, Travel & Leisure, Food and Wine, Child.*

"It was pure perfection. Everything from the flowers to the wonderful food."

Certificate may be used: Sunday through Thursday, excluding holidays.

Gettysburg

L11

Keystone Inn B&B

231 Hanover St
Gettysburg, PA 17325-1913
(717)337-3888

Circa 1913. Furniture maker Clayton Reaser constructed this three-story brick Victorian with a wide-columned porch hugging the north and west sides. Cut stone graces every door and window sill, each with a keystone. A chestnut staircase ascends the full three stories, and the interior is decorated with comfortable furnishings, ruffles and lace.

Innkeeper(s): Wilmer & Doris Martin. $59-109. MC VISA DS. 5 rooms with PB. 1 suite. Breakfast and afternoon tea included in rates. Types of meals: full breakfast and early coffee/tea. Beds: KQDT. Air conditioning in room. Library on premises. Amusement parks, antiques, fishing, parks, shopping, downhill skiing, cross-country skiing and theater nearby.

Location: Route 116 - East Gettysburg.

Publicity: *Gettysburg Times, Hanover Sun, York Sunday News, Pennsylvania, Lancaster Sunday News, Los Angeles Times.*

"We slept like lambs. This home has a warmth that is soothing."

Certificate may be used: November-April, Monday-Thursday.

The Old Appleford Inn

218 Carlisle St
Gettysburg, PA 17325-1305
(717)337-1711 (800)275-3373 Fax:(717)334-6228

Circa 1867. Located in the historic district, this Italianate-style brick mansion offers a taste of 19th-century charm and comfort. Among its inviting features are a plant-filled sunroom and a parlor with refurbished, 1918 grand piano. The innkeepers also display fine, linen needlework samplers and a collection of antique musical instruments. As the inn was built just following the Civil War, the innkeepers

have tried to keep a sense of turbulent history present. Most of the guest rooms are named for Civil War generals, another for Abraham Lincoln. Breakfasts are a fashionable affair served on fine china in the inn's Victorian dining room.

Innkeeper(s): John & Jane Wiley. $80-150. MC VISA AX DS PC TC. 10 rooms with PB, 2 with FP. 1 suite. Breakfast and afternoon tea included in rates. Types of meals: full breakfast and early coffee/tea. Catering service available. Beds: QD. Air conditioning in room. Fax and library on premises. Amusement parks, antiques, parks, shopping, downhill skiing and theater nearby.

Location: Two blocks from downtown, near battlefield and historic attractions.

Publicity: *Innsider, Gettysburg Times, Baltimore Sun, Philadelphia Magazine.*

"Everything in your place invites us back."

Certificate may be used: Sunday-Thursday, except July and August, excluding holidays or special events.

Gettysburg (McKnightstown)   L11

Country Escape
275 Old Rt 30, PO Box 195
Gettysburg (McKnightstown), PA 17343
(717)338-0611 Fax:(717)334-5227

Circa 1868. This country Victorian, a brick structure featuring a porch decked in gingerbread trim, rests on the route that Confederate soldiers took on their way to nearby Gettysburg. The home itself was built just a few years after the Civil War. There are three comfortable guest rooms, decorated in country style. For an extra fee, business travelers can use the inn's typing, copying, faxing or desktop publishing services. All guests can enjoy the outdoor hot tub. There is also a children's play area outside. A traditional American breakfast is served, with such hearty items as eggs, pancakes, bacon and sausage. The inn offers close access to the famous battlefield, as well as other historic sites.

Innkeeper(s): Merry Bush & Ross Hetrick. $50-75. MC VISA AX DS PC TC. 3 rooms, 1 with PB. Breakfast included in rates. Type of meal: full breakfast. Beds: Q. Air conditioning in room. Cable TV, VCR, fax, copier and spa on premises. Antiques, parks, shopping, downhill skiing, theater and watersports nearby.

Certificate may be used: Dec. 1-March 31, anyday.

Greensburg   J4

Huntland Farm B&B
Road 9, Box 21
Greensburg, PA 15601-9232
(412)834-8483 Fax:(412)838-8253

Circa 1848. Porches and flower gardens surround the three-story, columned, brick Georgian manor that presides over the inn's 100 acres. Corner bedrooms are furnished with English antiques. Fallingwater, the Frank Lloyd Wright house, is nearby. Other attractions include Hidden Valley, Ohiopyle water rafting, Bushy Run and Fort Ligonier.

Innkeeper(s): Robert & Elizabeth Weidlein. $75-85. AX PC TC. 4 rooms, 2 with FP. Breakfast included in rates. Type of meal: full breakfast. Beds: KQDT. Ceiling fan in room. Cable TV, VCR, fax, copier and library on premises. Antiques, parks, shopping and theater nearby.

Certificate may be used: All year. Nov. 1-May 1, any day; May 1-Oct. 31, weekdays only.

Grove City   F2

Snow Goose Inn
112 E Main St
Grove City, PA 16127
(412)458-4644 (800)317-4644

Circa 1895. This home was built as a residence for young women attending Grove City College. It was later used as a family home and offices for a local doctor. Eventually, it was transformed into an intimate bed & breakfast, offering four homey guest rooms. The interior is comfortable, decorated in country style with stenciling, collectibles and a few of the signature geese on display. Museums, shops, Amish farms and several state parks are in the vicinity, offering many activities.

Innkeeper(s): Orvil & Dorothy McMillen. $65. MC VISA. 4 rooms with PB. Breakfast and evening snack included in rates. Types of meals: continental breakfast, continental-plus breakfast, full breakfast, gourmet breakfast and early coffee/tea. Beds: QD. Air conditioning, TV and VCR in room. Amusement parks, antiques, fishing, parks, shopping, downhill skiing, cross-country skiing, sporting events, golf, theater and watersports nearby.

Publicity: *Allied News.*

"Your thoughtful touches and homey atmosphere were a balm to our chaotic lives."

Certificate may be used: All year.

Hanover L12

Beechmont B&B Inn

315 Broadway
Hanover, PA 17331-2505
(717)632-3013 (800)553-7009

Circa 1834. This gracious Georgian inn was a witness to the Civil War's first major battle on free soil, the Battle of Hanover. Decorated in Federal-period antiques, several guest rooms are named for the battle's commanders. The romantic Diller  Suite contains a marble fireplace and queen canopy bed. The inn is noted for elegant breakfasts.
Innkeeper(s): William & Susan Day. $80-135. MC VISA AX DS PC TC. 7 rooms with PB, 3 with FP. 3 suites. 1 conference room. Breakfast, afternoon tea and evening snack included in rates. Types of meals: full breakfast, gourmet breakfast and early coffee/tea. Picnic lunch and room service available. Beds: QD. Air conditioning, ceiling fan and TV in room. Copier and library on premises. Amusement parks, antiques, fishing, parks, shopping, downhill skiing, cross-country skiing, sporting events, theater and watersports nearby.

Location: Three miles from Lake Marburg.

Publicity: *Evening Sun, York Daily Record.*

"I had a marvelous time at your charming, lovely inn."

Certificate may be used: Sunday-Thursday, except holidays.

Harrisburg J12

Abide With Me B&B

2601 Walnut St
Harrisburg, PA 17103-1952
(717)236-5873

Circa 1870. A city historical site, this B&B is a brick Second Empire Victorian. There are three stories with shuttered windows, a large bay and a rounded front veranda. Oak, parquet and wideplank floors and fireplaces add to the interest inside. Modestly furnished, the B&B offers some antiques and country pieces. The Harrisburg State Capital is a mile-and-a-half away.
Innkeeper(s): Don & Joyce Adams. $56. PC. 3 rooms. Breakfast included in rates. Types of meals: gourmet breakfast and early coffee/tea. Beds: QDT. Air conditioning in room. Cable TV and VCR on premises. Amusement parks, antiques, fishing, parks, shopping, sporting events, theater and watersports nearby.

Certificate may be used: Upon availability, excluding first week of October.

Hawley E17

Academy Street B&B

528 Academy St
Hawley, PA 18428-1434
(717)226-3430 Fax:(717)226-1910

Circa 1863. This restored Civil War Victorian home boasts a mahogany front door with the original glass paneling, two large fireplaces (one in mosaic, the other in fine polished marble) and a living room with oak sideboard, polished marble mantel and yellow pine floor. The airy guest rooms have canopied

brass beds. Guests are welcome to afternoon tea, which includes an array of cakes and pastries. Full, gourmet breakfasts are served on weekends.
Innkeeper(s): Judith Lazan. $65-80. MC VISA. 7 rooms, 4 with PB. Breakfast and afternoon tea included in rates. Type of meal: early coffee/tea. Beds: QDT. Air conditioning, ceiling fan and TV in room. VCR on premises. Amusement parks, antiques, fishing, parks, shopping, theater and watersports nearby.

Publicity: *Wayne Independent, Citizens' Voice.*

"Truly wonderful everything!"

Certificate may be used: Monday through Friday.

Holicong J18

Barley Sheaf Farm

5281 York Rd, Rt 202 Box 10
Holicong, PA 18928
(215)794-5104 Fax:(215)794-5332

Circa 1740. Situated on part of the original William Penn land grant, this beautiful stone house with white shuttered windows and mansard roof is set on 30 acres of farmland. Once owned by noted playwright George Kaufman, it was the gathering place for the Marx Brothers, Lillian Hellman and S. J. Perlman. The bank barn, pond and majestic old trees round out a beautiful setting.
Innkeeper(s): Peter Suess. $105-235. MC VISA AX PC TC. 12 rooms with PB, 3 with FP. 4 suites. 3 conference rooms. Breakfast and afternoon tea included in rates. Types of meals: full breakfast and early coffee/tea. Catering service available. Beds: KQD. Air conditioning in room. Cable TV, VCR, fax, copier and swimming on premises. Handicap access. Amusement parks, antiques, fishing, parks, shopping, downhill skiing, cross-country skiing, theater and watersports nearby.

Location: Fifty miles north of Philadelphia in Bucks County.

Publicity: *Country Living, Romantic Inns of America, CNC Business Channel.*

Certificate may be used: Sunday through Thursday, no holidays.

Hollidaysburg   I8

Hoenstine's B&B

418 N Montgomery St
Hollidaysburg, PA 16648-1432
(814)695-0632 Fax:(814)696-7310

Circa 1839. This inn is an antique-lover's dream, as it boasts many pieces of original furniture. Stained-glass windows and the 10-foot-high ceilings add to the atmosphere. Breakfast is served in the home's formal dining room. Guests will sleep well in the comfortable and beautifully decorated rooms, espe-

cially knowing that the house is being protected by innkeeper Barbara Hoenstine's black standard poodle, Dickens, who is a happy guide and escort around the canal-era town. The B&B is within walking distance of shops, restaurants and the downtown historic district.

Innkeeper(s): Barbara Hoenstine. $50-80. MC VISA. 4 rooms, 1 with PB. Breakfast included in rates. Type of meal: full breakfast. Beds: QDT. Ceiling fan, TV and VCR in room. Copier on premises. Amusement parks, antiques, fishing, parks, shopping, downhill skiing, cross-country skiing and theater nearby.

"Thank you for a truly calm and quiet week. This was our first B&B experience and it won't be our last."

Certificate may be used: Nov. 1-March 30, Sunday-Thursday.

Parris House B&B

RR 2 Box 650
Hollidaysburg, PA 16648
(814)696-2849 Fax:(814)695-0044

Circa 1795. This stone Colonial was built at the turn of the 18th century, and it maintains much of its historic ambiance. The 200-year-old home was

built by a canal master. One particularly rustic and cozy bedchamber features the arched ceilings of the roof, an exposed stone wall and a clawfoot tub. The interior is somewhat Colonial in style; the restored wood floors shine, and furnishings include antiques. Innkeeper Stacey Parris prepares a hearty breakfast with entrees such as oatmeal pancakes with maple syrup and bacon. She also offers special packages for honeymooners or those seeking a romantic getaway.

Innkeeper(s): Stacy Parris. $75-85. MC VISA PC TC. 5 rooms with PB. Breakfast included in rates. Type of meal: full breakfast. Beds: DT. Air conditioning, turndown service and ceiling fan in room. Cable TV, VCR, fax and library on premises. Amusement parks, antiques, fishing, parks, shopping, downhill skiing, cross-country skiing, sporting events, golf, theater and watersports nearby.

Publicity: *Altoona Mirror.*

"Thank you for a beautiful atmosphere delicious food & great conversation. We'll be back."

Certificate may be used: Year-round, Sunday-Thursdays.

Holtwood   L14

Country Cottage

163 Magnolia Dr
Holtwood, PA 17532-9773
(717)284-2559 (800)560-3801

This simple brick cottage is adjacent to a main house where the innkeepers live. There are two comfortably furnished bedrooms, a dining room, small kitchen and a family room with a large stone fireplace. Two stained-glass windows flank the front door. Guests have use of an outdoor deck and spa. The innkeepers offer homemade muffins and coffee cake in the mornings. The cottage is close to many Pennsylvania Dutch country attractions.

Innkeeper(s): Donald & Jo Davis. $95. PC. 2 rooms, 1 with PB, 1 with FP. 1 cottage. Breakfast included in rates. Type of meal: continental breakfast. Beds: QD. Air conditioning, ceiling fan and VCR in room. Cable TV and spa on premises. Amusement parks, antiques, fishing, parks, shopping, downhill skiing, cross-country skiing, sporting events, golf, theater and watersports nearby.

Certificate may be used: Sunday-Friday, all year except Thanksgiving & Christmas holidays.

Honey Grove   I10

The Inn at McCullochs Mills

RR 1, Box 194
Honey Grove, PA 17035-9801
(717)734-3628 (800)377-5106

Circa 1890. Innkeepers Verne and Christine Penner spent several years restoring their inn, once home to a local millmaster. The original home burnt, and this charming 1882 Victorian was built in its place. The Penners offer a multitude of romantic amenities and extras that will make any getaway memorable. Carriage rides, moonlight sleigh rides, massages are among the choices. One getaway package includes limousine service to a local dinner theater. Guests are pampered with gourmet breakfasts served by candlelight, afternoon tea, chocolates, fresh flowers and more. Some rooms include clawfoot or Jacuzzi tubs.

Innkeeper(s): Verne & Christine Penner. $49-79. MC VISA DS PC. 5 rooms with PB. Breakfast, afternoon tea and evening snack included in rates. Types of meals: full breakfast, gourmet breakfast and early coffee/tea. Catering service available. Beds: QD. Air conditioning, turndown service and ceiling fan in room. Antiques, fishing, shopping, cross-country skiing, sporting events, golf and theater nearby.

Publicity: *Pennsylvania Magazine.*

"The house is a gem and has been restored to a top standard. We were so lucky to find you."

Certificate may be used: Any weekday, Monday-Thursday.

Intercourse   K14

Carriage Corner
3705 E Newport Rd, PO Box 371
Intercourse, PA 17534-0371
(717)768-3059

Circa 1981. Located on two acres, this is a two-story, white Colonial house. The inn is decorated with folk art and country furnishings. Homemade breads and hot cereals are served in the dining room. Walk five minutes to the village and explore shops displaying local crafts, pottery and handmade furniture. The inn is located near many Amish farms.

Innkeeper(s): Gordon & Gwen Schuit. $48-68. MC VISA PC. 5 rooms with PB. Breakfast included in rates. Type of meal: full breakfast. Beds: QD. Air conditioning and TV in room. Amusement parks, antiques, parks, shopping and theater nearby.

Location: Amish farmland and tourist area.

Certificate may be used: December-February, excluding holiday weekends.

Jim Thorpe   H15

Harry Packer Mansion
Packer Hill, PO Box 458
Jim Thorpe, PA 18229
(717)325-8566

Circa 1874. This extravagant Second Empire mansion was used as the model for the haunted mansion in Disney World. It was constructed of New England sandstone, and local brick and stone trimmed in cast iron. Past ornately carved columns on the front veranda, guests enter 400-pound, solid walnut doors. The opulent interior includes marble mantels, hand-painted ceilings and elegant antiques. Murder-mystery weekends are a mansion specialty, and Victorian Balls are held in June and December.

Innkeeper(s): Robert & Patricia Handwerk. $75-390. MC VISA TC. 13 rooms, 11 with PB. 3 suites. 3 conference rooms. Breakfast included in rates. Types of meals: full breakfast, gourmet breakfast and early coffee/tea. Beds: QD. Air conditioning, turndown service and ceiling fan in room. Cable TV and VCR on premises. Antiques, fishing, parks, shopping, downhill skiing, cross-country skiing and watersports nearby.

Location: Six miles south of Exit 34.

Publicity: *Philadelphia Inquirer, New York, Victorian Homes, Washington Post.*

"What a beautiful place and your hospitality was wonderful. We will see you again soon."

Certificate may be used: Sunday through Thursday night except for holidays.

The Inn at Jim Thorpe
24 Broadway
Jim Thorpe, PA 18229-2028
(717)325-2599 (800)329-2599 Fax:(717)325-9145
E-mail: innjt@ptd.net

Circa 1848. This massive New Orleans-style structure, now restored, hosted some colorful 19th-century guests, including Thomas Edison, John D. Rockefeller and Buffalo Bill. All rooms are appointed with Victorian furnishings and have private baths with pedestal sinks and

marble floors. Also on the premises are a Victorian dining room, Irish pub and a conference center. The inn is situated in the heart of Jim Thorpe, a quaint Victorian town that was known at the turn of the century as the "Switzerland of America." Historic mansion tours, museums and art galleries are nearby, and mountain biking and white-water rafting are among the outdoor activities.

Innkeeper(s): David Drury. $65-250. MAP. MC VISA AX DC DS TC. 24 rooms with PB, 3 with FP. 5 suites. 2 conference rooms. Breakfast included in rates. Type of meal: continental-plus breakfast. Dinner, lunch and room service available. Restaurant on premises. Beds: KQD. Air conditioning and TV in room. Fax and copier on premises. Handicap access. Antiques, fishing, parks, shopping, downhill skiing, cross-country skiing, theater and watersports nearby.

Location: In the western part of the Pocono Mountains.

Publicity: *Philadelphia Inquirer, Pennsylvania, Allentown Morning Call.*

"Thank you for having provided us a relaxing getaway."

Certificate may be used: Sunday-Thursday nights, excluding holidays.

Victoria Ann's B&B

68 Broadway
Jim Thorpe, PA 18229-2022
(717)325-8107 Fax:(717)325-8107

Circa 1860. Historic Millionaire's Row is the site of this Victorian, which is painted a deep red hue with blue trim. Innkeeper Louise Ogilvie preserves the 19th-century ambiance throughout the home, decorating the place with Victorian furnishings and bright wallpapers. Most rooms are European in style and share a bath. The two suites include a private bath. The grounds include a garden. Louise's history is as fascinating as the historic home's past. She was an actress and cabaret singer in New York and was proprietor of a renown nightclub in San Juan, Puerto Rico.

Innkeeper(s): Louise Ogilvie. $55-85. MC VISA AX DS TC. 8 rooms, 2 with PB. 2 suites. 1 conference room. Breakfast included in rates. Type of meal: full breakfast. Beds: KQDT. Air conditioning, turndown service, ceiling fan and TV in room. VCR, fax, copier and library on premises. Antiques, fishing, parks, shopping, downhill skiing, cross-country skiing, golf and watersports nearby.

Publicity: *Times News*

"We never thought our weekend would turn out to be such a wonderful adventure. Thank you for opening your inn to us."

Certificate may be used: Dec. 15-Jan 30, March-April 30, Sunday-Friday, May-midweek, Sunday-Friday, November-Dec.1.

Kane   D6

Kane Manor Country Inn

230 Clay St
Kane, PA 16735-1410
(814)837-6522 Fax:(814)837-6664
E-mail: kanemanor@aol.com

Circa 1896. This Georgian Revival inn, on 250 acres of woods and trails, was built for Dr. Elizabeth Kane, the first female doctor to practice in the area. Many of the family's possessions dating back to the American Revolution and the Civil War remain.

(Ask to see the attic.) Decor is a mixture of old family items in an unpretentious country style. There is a pub, popular with locals, on the premises. The building is in the National Register.

Innkeeper(s): Helen Johnson & Joyce Benek. $89-99. MC VISA AX DS PC TC. 10 rooms, 7 with PB. Breakfast and afternoon tea included in rates. Types of meals: continental breakfast, continental-plus breakfast, full breakfast and early coffee/tea. Beds: DT. TV in room. VCR, fax, copier and library on premises. Handicap access. Amusement parks, antiques, fishing, parks, shopping, downhill skiing, cross-country skiing and watersports nearby.

Publicity: *Pittsburgh Press, News Herald, Cleveland Plain Dealer, Youngstown Indicator.*

"It's a place I want to return to often, for rest and relaxation."

Certificate may be used: Jan. 1-Sept. 15 and Dec. 1-29.

Kennett Square   L16

Scarlett House

503 W State St
Kennett Square, PA 19348-3028
(610)444-9592 (800)820-9592

Circa 1910. This stone American four-square home features an extensive wraparound porch, a front door surrounded by leaded-glass windows and magnificent chestnut woodwork. Beyond the foyer are two downstairs parlors, while a second-floor parlor provides a sunny setting for afternoon tea. Rooms are furnished in romantic Victorian decor with period antiques. Beds are turned down with a flower and chocolate at night. An elegant gourmet breakfast is served with fine china, silver, crystal and lace linens. Mushroom-shaped chocolate chip scones are a novel breakfast specialty at the inn—a reminder that this is the acclaimed mushroom capital of the world.

Innkeeper(s): Jane & Sam Snyder. $75-125. MC VISA AX DS TC. 4 rooms, 2 with PB. 1 suite. 1 conference room. Breakfast, afternoon tea and evening snack included in rates. Types of meals: gourmet breakfast and early coffee/tea. Beds: QD. Ceiling fan in room. Cable TV on premises. Antiques, fishing, parks, shopping, theater and watersports nearby.

Location: Located in the heart of Brandywine Valley in the town of Kennett Square. Just 15 minutes to Wilmington, Del., and 30 minutes to the Philadelphia Airport.

"Truly an enchanting place."

Certificate may be used: Jan. 1-March 31, Sunday-Saturday; July 1-Aug. 31, Sunday-Thursday; Nov. 1-Dec. 31, Sunday-Saturday. No holidays or holiday weekends.

Lancaster   K14

Flowers & Thyme B&B
238 Strasburg Pike
Lancaster, PA 17602-1326
(717)393-1460
E-mail: Padutchbnb@aol.com

Circa 1941. This home was built by an Amishman for a Mennonite minister and his family. The innkeepers grew up among Amish and Mennonite

communities and are full of knowledge about the area and its history. Fresh flowers from the inn's beautiful gardens are placed in the guest rooms in season. A country breakfast is served in the breakfast room overlooking the herb garden. The inn is only minutes away from outlet stores and plenty of outdoor activities.

Innkeeper(s): Don & Ruth Harnish. $80-100. PC TC. 3 rooms with PB. 1 suite. Breakfast included in rates. Types of meals: full breakfast and gourmet breakfast. Beds: QD. Air conditioning and ceiling fan in room. Cable TV and library on premises. Amusement parks, antiques, parks, shopping, sporting events, theater and watersports nearby.

Publicity: *Lancaster newspapers*

"Your home is beautiful, perfectly decorated, warm and inviting and we felt so welcome. Your breakfast was delicious and served so elegantly."

Certificate may be used: Anytime, December through March; Sunday through Thursday, April through November.

The King's Cottage, A B&B Inn
1049 E King St
Lancaster, PA 17602-3231
(717)397-1017 (800)747-8717 Fax:(717)397-3447

Circa 1913. This Mission Revival house features a red-tile roof and stucco walls, common in many stately turn-of-the-century houses in California and New Mexico. Its elegant interiors include a sweep-

ing staircase, a library with marble fireplace, stained-glass windows and a solarium. The inn is appointed with Oriental rugs and antiques and fine 18th-century English reproductions. The formal dining room provides the location for gourmet morning meals.

Innkeeper(s): Karen Owens. $100-175. MC VISA DC DS. 9 rooms with PB. 1 conference room. Breakfast and afternoon tea included in rates. Type of meal: full breakfast. Beds: KQ. Turndown service in room. Cable TV on premises. Amusement parks, antiques, fishing, shopping, cross-country skiing, sporting events and theater nearby.

Location: Pennsylvania Dutch country.

Publicity: *Country, USA Weekend, Bon Appetit, Intelligencer Journal, Times.*

"I appreciate your attention to all our needs and look forward to recommending your inn to friends."

Certificate may be used: November-March, Monday-Thursday.

New Life Homestead B&B
1400 E King St, Rt 462
Lancaster, PA 17602-3240
(717)396-8928

Circa 1912. This two-and-a-half story brick home is situated within one mile of Amish Farms, and it's less than two miles from the City of Lancaster. Innkeepers Carol and Bill Giersch, both Mennonites, host evening discussions about the culture and history of Amish and Mennonite people. Carol's homemade breakfasts are made with local produce.

Innkeeper(s): Carol Giersch. $60-80. 3 rooms, 2 with PB. 1 suite. Breakfast included in rates. Type of meal: full breakfast. Evening snack available. Beds: QDT. Amusement parks, antiques, fishing, shopping, sporting events and theater nearby.

Location: In the heart of Pennsylvania Dutch country.

Publicity: *Keystone Gazette, Pennsylvania Dutch Traveler.*

"Reminded me of my childhood at home."

Certificate may be used: December to March, Monday to Thursday.

O'Flaherty's Dingeldein House B&B

1105 E King St
Lancaster, PA 17602-3233
(717)293-1723 (800)779-7765 Fax:(717)293-1947

Circa 1910. This Dutch Colonial home was once residence to the Armstrong family, who acquired fame and fortune in the tile floor industry. Springtime guests will brighten at the sight of this home's beautiful flowers. During winter months, innkeepers Jack and Sue Flatley deck the halls with plenty of seasonal decorations. The hearty country breakfast might include fresh-baked muffins, fruits, the innkeepers' special blend of coffee and mouthwatering omelets, pancakes or French toast. Cozy rooms include comfortable furnishings and cheery wall coverings. The innkeepers can arrange for guests to enjoy dinner at the home of one of their Amish friends.

Innkeeper(s): Jack & Sue Flatley. $80-100. MC VISA DS PC TC. 4 rooms with PB. 1 suite. Breakfast included in rates. Types of meals: full breakfast, gourmet breakfast and early coffee/tea. Beds: KQDT. Air conditioning and ceiling fan in room. Cable TV, VCR, fax, copier and library on premises. Amusement parks, antiques, fishing, parks, shopping, sporting events and theater nearby.

Location: 1 mile from downtown, 10 minutes from heart of Amish Country.

Publicity: *Gourmet.*

"You made our visit here very pleasant, your hospitality is what makes the stay here so wonderful."

Certificate may be used: January through April & December, Sunday through Saturday. June-November, Sunday-Thursday.

Witmer's Tavern - Historic 1725 Inn

2014 Old Philadelphia Pike
Lancaster, PA 17602-3413
(717)299-5305

Circa 1725. This pre-Revolutionary War inn is the sole survivor of 62 inns that once lined the old Lancaster-to-Philadelphia turnpike. Immigrant Conestoga wagon trains were made up here for the Western and Southern journeys to wilderness homesteads. Designated as a National Landmark, the property is restored to its original, rustic pioneer style. There are wide-board floors and antiques with original finish. History buffs will enjoy seeing the Indian escape tunnel entrance and knowing presidents Washington, Jefferson and Adams once stayed

here, as well as Lafayette and Benjamin Franklin. Guest rooms feature antiques, fresh flowers, antique quilts and original woodburning fireplaces.

Innkeeper(s): Brant Hartung. $60-90. PC. 7 rooms, 2 with PB, 7 with FP. Breakfast included in rates. Type of meal: continental-plus breakfast. Beds: D. Air conditioning in room. Amusement parks, antiques, fishing, parks, shopping, downhill skiing, cross-country skiing, sporting events, theater and watersports nearby.

Location: One mile east of Lancaster on Route 340.

Publicity: *Stuart News, Pennsylvania, Antique, Travel & Leisure, Mid-Atlantic, Country Living, Early American Life, Colonial Homes, USA Today.*

"Your personal attention and enthusiastic knowledge of the area and Witmer's history made it come alive and gave us the good feelings we came looking for."

Certificate may be used: December-April, Sunday through Thursday only, excluding all holidays.

Landenberg   L15

Cornerstone B&B Inn

300 Buttonwood Rd
Landenberg, PA 19350-9398
(610)274-2143 Fax:(610)274-0734

Circa 1704. The Cornerstone is a fine 18th-century country manor house filled with antique furnishings. Two fireplaces make the parlor inviting. Wing chairs, fresh flowers and working fireplaces add enjoyment to the guest rooms. Perennial gardens, a water garden and swimming pool with hot tub are additional amenities.

Innkeeper(s): Linda Chamberlin & Marty Mulligan. $75-150. MC VISA DS PC TC. 7 rooms with PB, 5 with FP. 1 suite. 6 cottages. Breakfast included in rates. Types of meals: full breakfast and early coffee/tea. Beds: KQT. Air conditioning and TV in room. VCR, fax, spa and swimming on premises. Amusement parks, antiques, parks, shopping, sporting events and theater nearby.

Certificate may be used: Sunday-Thursday, Jan. 2-Dec. 15.

Lewisburg
G12

Brookpark Farm B&B
100 Reitz Rd
Lewisburg, PA 17837-9653
(717)523-0220

Circa 1914. Twenty-five acres surround this three-story brick house. The innkeepers operate the Pennsylvania House Gallery in their enormous barn on the property. The inn, therefore, includes traditional, transitional and country designs from these furniture collections including cherry, pine and mahogany woods.

Innkeeper(s): Crystale & Todd Moyer. $63-68. MC VISA. 7 rooms. 3 suites. 2 conference rooms. Breakfast and afternoon tea included in rates. Types of meals: full breakfast, gourmet breakfast and early coffee/tea. Lunch and banquet service available. Restaurant on premises. Beds: Q. Air conditioning in room. Cable TV on premises. Amusement parks, antiques, fishing, parks, shopping, sporting events and theater nearby.

Certificate may be used: No restrictions, year-round.

Lititz
J14

The Alden House
62 E Main St
Lititz, PA 17543-1947
(717)627-3363 (800)584-0753
E-mail: aldenbb@ptdprolog.net

Circa 1850. For more than 200 years, breezes have carried the sound of church bells to the stately brick homes lining Main Street. The Alden House is a brick Victorian in the center of this historic district and within walking distance of the Pretzel House (first in the country) and the chocolate factory. A favorite room is the suite with a loft dressing room and private bath. A full breakfast is served, often carried to one of the inn's three porches.

Innkeeper(s): Fletcher & Joy Coleman. $85-120. MC VISA PC. 5 rooms with PB, 1 with FP. 3 suites. Breakfast included in rates. Type of meal: full breakfast. Beds: QD. Air conditioning, ceiling fan and TV in room. Amusement parks, antiques, fishing, parks, shopping and theater nearby.

Location: Seven miles North of Lancaster.

Publicity: *Connecticut Post, Pittsburgh Post-Gazette, Travel Holiday, Rockland Journal News, Penn Dutch Traveler, Now in Lancaster County, Philadelphia Inquirer.*

"Truly represents what bed & breakfast hospitality is all about. You are special innkeepers. Thanks for caring so much about your guests. It's like being home."

Certificate may be used: Sunday-Thursday, excluding holidays and special events.

Manheim
J14

Herr Farmhouse Inn
2256 Huber Dr
Manheim, PA 17545-9130
(717)653-9852 (800)584-0743

Circa 1750. This pre-Revolutionary War stone farmhouse is one of the oldest buildings in Lancaster County. The woodwork, including the moldings, cabinets and doors is original. Early American antiques and reproductions set the scene for a truly Colonial vacation. Two rooms include fireplaces. The kitchen, where a hearty continental breakfast is served, boasts a walk-in fireplace. Antique shopping, historic attractions and Amish dining are nearby.

Innkeeper(s): Barry Herr. $75-95. MC VISA PC TC. 4 rooms, 2 with PB, 2 with FP. 1 suite. Breakfast included in rates. Types of meals: full breakfast and early coffee/tea. Beds: KQDT. Air conditioning, turndown service and ceiling fan in room. Copier and library on premises. Amusement parks, antiques, fishing, parks, shopping and sporting events nearby.

Location: Nine miles west of Lancaster off Route 283 (Mt. Joy 230 exit).

Publicity: *Country Inns.*

"Your home is lovely. You've done a beautiful job of restoring and remodeling."

Certificate may be used: Monday through Thursday, holidays and special events excluded.

Jonde Lane Farm
1103 Auction Rd
Manheim, PA 17545
(717)665-4231

Circa 1859. Cattle graze and chickens cackle on this 100-acre working dairy and poultry farm. The farmhouse has been in the innkeepers' family since its construction in the mid-19th century. Guests can pitch in and help with the chores or just relax and enjoy the serene countryside. Children are welcome, and there's plenty for them to do, from bottle feeding a baby goat to helping feed chickens. The rooms feature a comfortable, country decor, and all bathrooms are shared. The innkeepers are Mennonite and begin each morning with special prayer, songs and then a hearty full breakfast. On Sundays, homemade continental fare is provided, and guests have the option of attending church with the family. The farm is close to Lancaster and other Pennsylvania Dutch country sites.

Innkeeper(s): John & Elaine Nissley. $45. MC VISA PC TC. 4 rooms. Breakfast included in rates. Types of meals: full breakfast and early coffee/tea. Beds: QDT. Air conditioning in room. Amusement parks, antiques, fishing, parks, shopping, golf and theater nearby.

Publicity: *In Pittsburgh*

"We all agreed, our stay with you was the highlight of our trip."

Certificate may be used: Nov. 1-March 30, Monday-Thursday, excluding holiday weekends.

Rose Manor B&B and Herbal Gift Shop
124 S Linden St
Manheim, PA 17545
(717)664-4932 (800)666-4932 Fax:(717)664-1611

Circa 1905. A local mill owner built this Spanish-style home, and it still maintains original light fixtures, woodwork and some wallcoverings. The grounds are decorated with roses and herb gardens. An herb theme is played out in the guest rooms, which feature names such as the Parsley, Sage, Rosemary and Thyme rooms. The fifth room is named the Basil, and its spacious quarters encompass the third story and feature the roof's angled ceiling. The decor is a comfortable Victorian style with some antiques. The innkeepers host many tea parties, and there is a gift shop on the premises. The inn's location provides close access to many Pennsylvania Dutch country attractions.

Innkeeper(s): Susan & Anne Jenal. $70-115. MC VISA PC. 5 rooms, 3 with PB. Breakfast included in rates. Type of meal: full breakfast. Afternoon tea and picnic lunch available. Beds: QTD. Air conditioning, ceiling fan and TV in room. Fax, copier and library on premises. Amusement parks, antiques, fishing, parks, shopping and theater nearby.

Publicity: *Lancaster County.*

"The atmosphere was so restful, the room was lovely and the hospitality was warm & generous. The table setting and breakfast was delicious to look at as well as consume."

Certificate may be used: Jan. 1-May 31; Nov. 1-Nov. 30; Sunday-Thursday.

Marietta   K13

The Noble House
113 W Market St
Marietta, PA 17547-1411
(717)426-4389

Circa 1810. A 12-foot-high ceiling and stenciled front hallway greet guests at this restored Federal-style brick home. A collection of antiques and knickknacks fills each of the rooms. Carved fireplaces, flower arrangements and candles add to the charm. One of the guest rooms features a unique

collection of dolls, another offers a four-poster brass bed. Guest rooms are individually decorated, one includes the theme of a 1950s railroad sleeper car. Breakfasts are served in the candlelit dining room with a combination of fruits, fresh breads, egg dishes, French toast and potatoes. The living room with its fireplace and piano is a wonderful location to relax with a good book.

Innkeeper(s): Elissa Noble. $75-95. 3 rooms with PB. 2 suites. Breakfast included in rates. Type of meal: full breakfast. Picnic lunch, catering service and room service available. Beds: KQDT.

Publicity: *Early American Life, Pennsylvania Dutch Hollydays, Elizabethtown Mount Joy Merchandiser.*

"Thank you for your hospitality. We felt like royalty, and enjoyed the detail in your beautiful home."

Certificate may be used: November-March, Sunday-Thursday.

Railroad House Restaurant B&B
280 W Front St
Marietta, PA 17547-1405
(717)426-4141

Circa 1820. The Railroad House, a sprawling old hotel, conjures up memories of the days when riding the rail was the way to travel. The house was built as a refuge for weary men who were working along the Susquehanna River. When the railroad finally made its way through Marietta, the rail station's waiting room and ticket office were located in what's now known as the Railroad House. The restored rooms feature antiques, Oriental rugs, Victorian decor and rustic touches such as exposed brick walls. The chefs at the inn's restaurant create a menu of American and continental dishes using spices and produce from the beautifully restored gardens. The innovative recipes have been featured in Bon Appetit. The innkeepers also host a variety of special events and weekends, including murder mysteries and clambakes serenaded by jazz bands. Carriage rides and special walking tours of Marietta can be arranged.

Innkeeper(s): Richard & Donna Chambers. $79-99. MC VISA TC. 10 rooms, 8 with PB. 1 cottage. 1 conference room. Breakfast included in rates. Types of meals: full breakfast, gourmet breakfast and early coffee/tea. Afternoon tea, dinner, evening snack, picnic lunch, lunch, gourmet lunch, banquet service, catering service and catered breakfast available. Restaurant on premises. Beds: QDT. Air conditioning in room. Copier and bicycles on premises. Amusement parks, antiques, fishing, parks, shopping, downhill skiing, sporting events, theater and watersports nearby.

Certificate may be used: Anytime.

River Inn

258 W Front St
Marietta, PA 17547-1405
(717)426-2290 (888)824-6622 Fax:(717)426-2966

Circa 1790. This Colonial has more than 200 years of history within its walls. The home is listed in the National Register and located in Marietta's historic district. Herb and flower gardens decorate the grounds. Relaxing in front of a fireplace is an easy task since the inn offers six, one of which resides in a guest room. Colonial decor and antiques permeate the interior. The inn is within walking distance to the Susquehanna River.

Innkeeper(s): Joyce & Bob Heiserman. $60-80. MC VISA DC CB DS PC TC. 3 rooms with PB, 1 with FP. Breakfast included in rates. Types of meals: full breakfast and early coffee/tea. Picnic lunch available. Beds: QT. Air conditioning in room. Cable TV, bicycles and library on premises. Amusement parks, antiques, fishing, parks, shopping, theater and watersports nearby.

Certificate may be used: Year-round, Sunday-Friday.

Vogt Farm B&B

1225 Colebrook Rd
Marietta, PA 17547-9101
(717)653-4810 (800)854-0399

Circa 1868. Twenty-eight acres surround this farmhouse. There are three porches from which to enjoy the pastoral scene of cattle and sheep. Keith offers a walking tour of the farm, including the grain elevator. The innkeepers have hosted guests for 20 years and have created a comfortable setting for overnight stays. Desks, private phones and a copier are available to business travelers.

Innkeeper(s): Keith & Kathy Vogt. $60-100. MC VISA AX DC DS PC TC. 3 rooms. 1 suite. Breakfast and evening snack included in rates. Types of meals: full breakfast and early coffee/tea. Beds: KQT. Air conditioning in room. Cable TV, VCR, copier and library on premises. Amusement parks, antiques, fishing, parks, shopping, sporting events and theater nearby.

"Thank you for your hospitality. Your warmth and friendliness made our stay pleasant. You have a lovely place."

Certificate may be used: Dec. 31-March 31; Sunday-Thursday, April 1-June 30, September & November.

McConnellsburg · K9

Market Street Inn

131 W Market St
McConnellsburg, PA 17233-1007
(717)485-5495

Circa 1903. This turn-of-the-century home exemplifies American four-square design. The home was built by a retired Union officer of the Civil War. The three guest rooms include four-poster, canopy beds and lace curtains. Locally smoked hickory sausage, homemade apple butter, lemon poppy seed muffins, herbed potatoes and a ham and egg roll topped with cheddar dill sauce are among the breakfast specialties. Cowans Gap State Park and Buchanan State Forest are nearby, as is Whitetail Ski Resort.

Innkeeper(s): Tim & Margie Taylor. $60. MC VISA AX PC TC. 3 rooms with PB. Breakfast included in rates. Type of meal: gourmet breakfast. Beds: QD. Air conditioning and TV in room. Fax, copier and library on premises. Antiques, fishing, parks, downhill skiing, cross-country skiing and watersports nearby.

Certificate may be used: March through August, Sunday - Thursday.

Meadville · D2

Fountainside B&B

628 Highland Ave
Meadville, PA 16335-1938
(814)337-7447

Circa 1855. A long front porch extends across the front of this farmhouse-style B&B. A full breakfast is served on the weekends, a continental breakfast during the week. Both Victorian and modern pieces are combined to furnish the rooms. Allegheny College is next door.

Innkeeper(s): Maureen Boyle. $50-65. MC VISA AX DS. 5 rooms. 1 conference room. Breakfast included in rates. Types of meals: continental breakfast, full breakfast and early coffee/tea. Evening snack and room service available. Turndown service and ceiling fan in room. Cable TV on premises. Amusement parks, antiques, shopping, cross-country skiing, sporting events and theater nearby.

Certificate may be used: Anytime room is available.

Mercer · F2

The Magoffin Inn

129 S Pitt St
Mercer, PA 16137-1211
(412)662-4611 (800)841-0824

Circa 1884. Dr. Magoffin built this house for his Pittsburgh bride, Henrietta Bouvard. The Queen Anne style is characterized by patterned brick masonry, gable detailing, bay windows and a wrap-around porch. The technique of marbleizing was used on six of the nine fireplaces. Magoffin Muffins are featured each morning. Dinner is available Friday and Saturday.

Innkeeper(s): Jacque McClelland. $115-125. MC VISA AX PC TC. 6 rooms, 5 with PB, 5 with FP. 1 suite. Breakfast and evening snack included in rates. Types of meals: full breakfast and early coffee/tea. Dinner available. Restaurant on premises. Beds: QD. Air conditioning and TV in room. Antiques, parks and shopping nearby.

Location: Near I-79 and I-80.

Publicity: *Western Reserve, Youngstown Vindicator.*

"While in Arizona we met a family from Africa who had stopped at the Magoffin House. After crossing the United States they said the Magoffin House was quite the nicest place they had stayed."

Certificate may be used: Sunday through Thursday nights.

Mercersburg L9

The Mercersburg Inn
405 S Main St
Mercersburg, PA 17236-9517
(717)328-5231 Fax:(717)328-3403

Circa 1909. Situated on a hill overlooking the Tuscorora Mountains, the valley and village, this 20,000-square-foot Georgian Revival mansion was built for industrialist Harry Byron. Six massive columns mark the entrance, which opens to a majestic hall featuring chestnut wainscoting and an elegant double stairway and rare scagliola (marbleized) columns. All the rooms are furnished with antiques and reproductions. A local craftsman built the inn's four-poster, canopied king-size beds. Many of the rooms have their own balconies and a few have fireplaces. During the weekends, the inn's chef prepares noteworthy, elegant five-course dinners, which feature an array of seasonal specialties.

Innkeeper(s): Walt & Sandy Filkowski. $110-210. MC VISA DS. 15 rooms with PB, 2 with FP. 1 conference room. Breakfast included in rates. Types of meals: full breakfast and gourmet breakfast. Picnic lunch and banquet service available. Restaurant on premises. Beds: KQT. Air conditioning in room. Cable TV, VCR and bicycles on premises. Antiques, fishing, shopping, downhill skiing, cross-country skiing, golf, theater and watersports nearby.

Publicity: *Mid-Atlantic Country, Washington Post, The Herald-Mail, Richmond News Leader, Washingtonian, Philadelphia Inquirer, Pittsburgh.*

"Elegance personified! Outstanding ambiance and warm hospitality."

Certificate may be used: Sunday-Thursday, non-holidays.

Mertztown I16

Longswamp B&B
1605 State St
Mertztown, PA 19539-8912
(610)682-6197 Fax:(610)682-4854

Circa 1789. Country gentleman Colonel Trexler added a mansard roof to this stately Federal mansion in 1860. Inside is a magnificent walnut staircase and pegged wood floors. As the story goes, the colonel discovered his unmarried daughter having an affair and shot her lover. He escaped hanging, but it was said that after his death his ghost could be seen in the upstairs bedroom watching the road. In 1905, an exorcism was reported to have sent his spirit to a nearby mountaintop.

Innkeeper(s): Elsa Dimick. $78-83. MC VISA AX. 10 rooms, 6 with PB, 2 with FP. 2 suites. Breakfast and afternoon tea included in rates. Types of meals: full breakfast, gourmet breakfast and early coffee/tea. Picnic lunch and catering service available. Beds: QT. Air conditioning and ceiling fan in room. Cable TV, VCR and bicycles on premises. Antiques, fishing, shopping, cross-country skiing and sporting events nearby.

Publicity: *Washingtonian, Weekend Travel, The Sun.*

"The warm country atmosphere turns strangers into friends."

Certificate may be used: November-April.

Milford F18

Cliff Park Inn & Golf Course
RR 4 Box 7200
Milford, PA 18337-9708
(717)296-6491 (800)225-6535 Fax:(717)296-3982

Circa 1820. This historic country inn is located on a 600-acre family estate, bordering the Delaware River. It has been in the Buchanan family since 1820. Rooms are spacious with individual climate control, telephone and Victorian-style furnishings. Cliff Park features both a full-service restaurant and golf school. The inn's golf course, established in 1913, is one of the oldest in the United States. Cliff Park's picturesque setting is popular for country weddings and private business conferences. Both B&B or MAP plans are offered.

Innkeeper(s): Harry W. Buchanan III. $93-160. MAP, AP, EP. MC VISA AX DC CB DS. 18 rooms with PB. 1 conference room. Breakfast included in rates. Type of meal: full breakfast. Dinner, picnic lunch and lunch available. Restaurant on premises. Beds: KQDT. Fax on premises. Handicap access. Cross-country skiing and watersports nearby.

Location: In the foothills of the Pocono Mountains on the Delaware River.

"Cliff Park Inn is the sort of inn I look for in the English countryside. It has that authentic charm that comes from History."

Certificate may be used: Nov. 1-May 20, Sunday-Thursday.

Milton   G12

Pau-Lyn's Country B&B
RR 3 Box 676
Milton, PA 17847-9506
(717)742-4110

Circa 1850. Recently renovated, this three-story Victorian brick home offers a formal dining room with a fireplace and antique musical instruments. A porch and patio overlook the large lawn. Nearby are working farms and dairies, covered bridges, mountains, hills and valleys.

Innkeeper(s): Evelyn Landis. $45-55. 7 rooms. 2 suites. Breakfast included in rates. Type of meal: full breakfast. Air conditioning in room. Cable TV on premises. Amusement parks, antiques, shopping, downhill skiing, cross-country skiing, sporting events and theater nearby.

Certificate may be used: Year-round, Sunday through Thursday, some weekends. All depend on availability.

Teneriff Farm B&B
Rd 1 Box 314
Milton, PA 17847-9402
(717)742-9061

Acres of farmland create a relaxing, natural environment at this turn-of-the-century Victorian. The home includes the detailed woodwork, French pocket doors and carved staircase one might expect from Victorian-era design, and these wonderful elements are complements to the comfortable, country decor. Although a working farm, this is a place for relaxing. Stroll the grounds or simply sip a cup of tea on the veranda. Breakfasts are created to fit the guests' needs.

Innkeeper(s): Christa Haseloff. $40-45. 3 rooms. Breakfast included in rates. Types of meals: continental breakfast, continental-plus breakfast and full breakfast.

Certificate may be used: Subject to availability.

Tomlinson Manor B&B
250 Broadway St
Milton, PA 17847-1706
(717)742-3657

Circa 1927. In the Georgian style, this appealing three-story stone manor was designed by Dr. Charles Tomlinson, a local physician and amateur architect. Shutters border the small-paned windows, and there are gardens all around. All the rooms, including the library, are furnished with antiques. Next door to the B&B is a dinner theater.

Innkeeper(s): Nancy Slease. $55. MC VISA. 3 rooms. Breakfast included in rates. Type of meal: full breakfast. Air conditioning in room. Cable TV and VCR on premises. Antiques, shopping, sporting events and theater nearby.

Certificate may be used: Anytime except college weekends.

Montoursville   F12

The Carriage House at Stonegate
RR 1 Box 11A
Montoursville, PA 17754-9801
(717)433-4340 Fax:(717)433-4653

Circa 1850. President Herbert Hoover was a descendant of the original settlers of this old homestead in the Loyalsock Creek Valley. Indians burned the original house, but the present farmhouse and numerous outbuildings date from the early 1800s. The Carriage House is set next to a brook.

Innkeeper(s): Harold & Dena Mesaris. $50-70. PC. 2 rooms. Breakfast included in rates. Type of meal: continental-plus breakfast. Beds: QD. TV in room. Fax, library, pet boarding and child care on premises. Amusement parks, antiques, fishing, parks, shopping, downhill skiing, cross-country skiing, sporting events, theater and watersports nearby.

Location: Six miles off I-180, north of Montoursville.

"A very fine B&B — the best that can be found. Gracious hosts."

Certificate may be used: Monday through Thursday nights, all months.

Mount Joy   K13

Cedar Hill Farm
305 Longenecker Rd
Mount Joy, PA 17552-8404
(717)653-4655

Circa 1817. Situated on 51 acres overlooking Chiques Creek, this stone farmhouse boasts a two-tiered front veranda affording pastoral views of the surrounding fields. The host was born in the house and is the third generation to have lived here since the Swarr family first purchased it in 1878. Family

heirlooms and antiques include an elaborately carved walnut bedstead, a marble-topped washstand and a "tumbling block" quilt. In the kitchen, a copper kettle, bread paddle and baskets of dried herbs accentuate the walk-in fireplace, where guests often linger over breakfast. Cedar Hill is a working poultry and grain farm.

Innkeeper(s): Russel & Gladys Swarr. $65-80. MC VISA AX DS TC. 5 rooms with PB. Breakfast included in rates. Types of meals: continental-plus breakfast and early coffee/tea. Beds: KQDT. Air conditioning in room. VCR and computer on premises. Amusement parks, antiques, fishing, parks, shopping, cross-country skiing, sporting events, theater and watersports nearby.

Location: Midway between Lancaster and Hershey.

Publicity: *Women's World, Lancaster Farming, Philadelphia, New York Times, Ladies Home Journal.*

"Dorothy can have Kansas, Scarlett can take Tara, Rick can keep Paris — I've stayed at Cedar Hill Farm."

Certificate may be used: Nov. 1-April 1, Sunday through Thursday, holidays excluded.

Hillside Farm B&B
607 Eby Chiques Rd
Mount Joy, PA 17552-8819
(717)653-6697 Fax:(717)653-5233

Circa 1863. This comfortable farm has a relaxing homey feel to it. Rooms are simply decorated and special extras such as handmade quilts and antiques add an elegant country touch. The home is a true monument to the cow. Dairy antiques, cow knickknacks and antique milk bottles abound.  Some of the bottles were found during the renovation of the home and its grounds. Spend the day hunting for bargains in nearby antique shops, malls and factory outlets, or tour local Amish and Pennsylvania Dutch attractions. The farm is a good vacation spot for families with children above the age of 10.

Innkeeper(s): Gary & Deborah Lintner. $55-70. MC VISA PC TC. 5 rooms, 3 with PB. Breakfast and evening snack included in rates. Types of meals: full breakfast and early coffee/tea. Afternoon tea available. Beds: KQDT. Air conditioning and ceiling fan in room. VCR, spa and library on premises. Amusement parks, antiques, fishing, parks, shopping, downhill skiing, cross-country skiing, theater and watersports nearby.

Location: In the heart of Dutch/Amish country.

"Warm, friendly, comfortable . . . feels like home."

Certificate may be used: Anytime except Friday and Saturday in September and October.

The Olde Square Inn
127 E Main St
Mount Joy, PA 17552-1513
(717)653-4525 (800)742-3533 Fax:(717)653-0976

Circa 1917. Located on the town square, this Neoclassical house features handsome columned fireplaces and leaded-glass windows. The innkeeper starts off the day with breakfast items such as baked

oatmeal, cherry cobbler, homemade breads and pancakes with a side of sausage. Amish farms and marketplaces are nearby. The town of Mount Joy offers restaurants, shops and parks all accessible with a short walk.

Innkeeper(s): Fran & Dave Hand. $65-105. MC VISA PC TC. 4 rooms with PB. Breakfast included in rates. Types of meals: full breakfast and early coffee/tea. Beds: KQDT. Air conditioning, TV and VCR in room. Fax on premises. Amusement parks, antiques, fishing, parks, shopping, sporting events and theater nearby.

Certificate may be used: Anytime, except weekends in September and October. Last minute if available.

Muncy F12

The Bodine House B&B
307 S Main St
Muncy, PA 17756-1507
(717)546-8949 Fax:(717)546-8949

Circa 1805. This Federal-style townhouse, framed by a white picket fence, is in the National Register. Antique and reproduction furnishings highlight the inn's four fireplaces, the parlor, study and library. A favorite guest room features a walnut canopy bed, hand-stenciled and bordered walls, and a framed sampler by the innkeeper's great-great-great-grandmother. Candlelight breakfasts are served beside the fireplace in a gracious Colonial dining room. Also available is a guest cottage with kitchenette.

Innkeeper(s): David & Marie Louise Smith. $50-125. MC VISA AX DS PC TC. 5 rooms with PB, 1 with FP. 1 cottage. Breakfast included in rates. Types of meals: full breakfast and early coffee/tea. Afternoon tea available. Beds: QDT. Air conditioning, turndown service and TV in room. VCR, fax, bicycles and library on premises. Antiques, fishing, parks, shopping, cross-country skiing and sporting events nearby.

Publicity: *Colonial Homes, Philadelphia Inquirer.*

"What an experience, made special by your wonderful hospitality."

Certificate may be used: Sunday through Thursday, year-round, subject to availability.

New Bloomfield   I11

Tressler House B&B
PO Box 38, 41 W Main St
New Bloomfield, PA 17068-0038
(717)582-2914

Circa 1830. A white picket fence frames the acre of lawn surrounding this Federal-period home. A spider web window transom marks the front entrance. Oriental rugs, coordinated fabrics and wallcoverings fill the 22 rooms. Old mill stones, collected by the former owner, are woven into the brick patio and sidewalk. There is a covered porch filled with antique wicker, and a walled duck pond. Smoked turkey sausages and blueberry pancakes often are featured at breakfast.

Innkeeper(s): David & Carol Ulsh. $55-65. 4 rooms, 2 with PB. Types of meals: full breakfast and early coffee/tea. Beds: DT. Air conditioning and TV in room.

Publicity: Perry County Times, Perry County Shopper, Antiques & Auction News.

Certificate may be used: Sunday-Thursday, upon availability, all year.

New Hope   I18

Hollileif B&B
677 Durham Rd (Rt 413)
New Hope, PA 18940
(215)598-3100

Circa 1700. This handsome former farmhouse sits on more than five rolling acres of scenic Bucks County countryside. The name "hollileif," which means "beloved tree," refers to the 40-foot holly trees that grace the entrance. Bedrooms are appointed with lace and fresh flowers. Afternoon refreshments in the parlor or patio are provided, as well as evening turndown service.

Innkeeper(s): Ellen & Richard Butkus. $85-155. MC VISA AX DS PC TC. 5 rooms with PB, 2 with FP. Breakfast and afternoon tea included in rates. Types of meals: gourmet breakfast and early coffee/tea. Beds: QD. Air conditioning, turndown service and ceiling fan in room. VCR,

fax, copier and library on premises. Antiques, fishing, parks, shopping, downhill skiing, cross-country skiing, theater and watersports nearby.

Location: Midway between Newtown and Buckingham.

Publicity: Trentonian, Bucks County Courier Times.

"The accommodations were lovely and the breakfasts delicious and unusual, but it is really the graciousness of our hosts that made the weekend memorable."

Certificate may be used: Sunday through Thursday except (1) during month of October, (2) holidays and holiday periods, (3) Dec. 26-31.

The Whitehall Inn
1370 Pineville Rd
New Hope, PA 18938-9495
(215)598-7945

Circa 1794. This white-plastered stone farmhouse is located on 13 country acres studded with stately maple and chestnut trees. Inside, a winding walnut staircase leads to antique-furnished guest rooms that offer wide pine floors, wavy-glass windows, high ceilings and some fireplaces. An antique clock collection, Oriental rugs and late Victorian furnishings are found throughout. Afternoon tea, evening chocolates and candlelight breakfasts served with heirloom china and sterling reflect the inn's many amenities. There are stables on the property and horseback riding may be arranged.

Innkeeper(s): Mike Wass. $140-190. MC VISA AX DC CB DS. 6 rooms. Breakfast included in rates. Types of meals: full breakfast and early coffee/tea. Air conditioning and turndown service in room. Amusement parks, antiques, shopping, cross-country skiing and theater nearby.

Certificate may be used: January through September, Monday through Thursday.

New Kingstown   J11

Kanaga House B&B
US Rt 11/Carlisle Pike
New Kingstown, PA 17072-0092
(717)697-2714

Circa 1775. This gracious three-story German stonehouse is built of limestone. The innkeepers have gathered historic information that links the builder of the home, Joseph Junkin, with the Revolutionary War, the Puritans and the first Covenater's Communion. A Joseph Junkin letter to his son, commander of the Battle of Brandywine, is in the parlor. The Elizabeth Junkin Room features a hope chest dated 1796, while the Eleanor Junkin Room offers a canopy bed with rose and blue bed hangings. Outside, an enormous gazebo creates a focal point for garden weddings.

Innkeeper(s): Mary Jane Kretzing. $60-85. MC VISA. 5 rooms with PB, 1 with FP. 1 conference room. Breakfast included in rates. Types of meals: full breakfast and early coffee/tea. Afternoon tea and picnic lunch available. Beds: Q. Air conditioning in room. Cable TV, VCR and copier on premises. Amusement parks, antiques, shopping, downhill skiing and theater nearby.

Location: Dutch Country.

Certificate may be used: Sunday through Thursday, all year.

North Wales J17

Joseph Ambler Inn
1005 Horsham Rd
North Wales, PA 19454-1413
(215)362-7500 Fax:(215)362-7500

Circa 1734. This fieldstone and wood house was built over a period of three centuries. Originally, it was part of a grant that Joseph Ambler, a Quaker wheelwright, obtained from William Penn in 1688. A large stone bank barn and tenant cottage on 12 acres constitute the remainder of the property. Guests enjoy the cherry wainscoting and walk-in fireplace in the schoolroom.

Innkeeper(s): Terry & Steve Kratz. $90-200. MC VISA AX DC CB DS. 28 rooms with PB. 2 suites. 1 conference room. Breakfast included in rates. Type of meal: full breakfast. Dinner and banquet service available. Restaurant on premises. Beds: QD. Air conditioning and TV in room. Handicap access. Antiques, shopping, downhill skiing, cross-country skiing, sporting events and theater nearby.

Publicity: *Colonial Homes, Country Living.*

"What a wonderful night my husband and I spent. We are already planning to come back to your wonderful getaway."

Certificate may be used: Anytime.

Northumberland H12

Campbell's B&B
707 Duke St
Northumberland, PA 17857-1709
(717)473-3276

Circa 1859. This old farmhouse has three stories and there are porches overlooking the well-planted grounds and rose gardens. A few antiques and reproductions add to the country decor. Lake Augusta is a mile away for fishing and boating.

Innkeeper(s): Bob & Millie Campbell. $55-65. 3 rooms, 2 with PB. 1 suite. 1 conference room. Breakfast, afternoon tea and evening snack included in rates. Types of meals: full breakfast and early coffee/tea. Beds: QT. Air conditioning, turndown service, ceiling fan and TV in room. VCR and swimming on premises. Amusement parks, antiques, fishing, parks, shopping, cross-country skiing, theater and watersports nearby.

Certificate may be used: Anytime except local college weekends. Monday through Thursday.

Palmyra J13

The Hen-Apple B&B
409 S Lingle Ave
Palmyra, PA 17078-9321
(717)838-8282

Circa 1825. Located at the edge of town, this Georgian farmhouse is surrounded by an acre of lawns and gardens. There are antiques and country pieces throughout. Breakfast is served to guests in the dining room or on the screened veranda. Hershey is two miles away, Lancaster and Gettysburg are nearby.

Innkeeper(s): Flo & Harold Eckert. $55-75. MC VISA AX TC. 6 rooms with PB. Breakfast included in rates. Type of meal: full breakfast. Beds: QDT. Air conditioning and ceiling fan in room. Cable TV on premises. Amusement parks, antiques, fishing, parks, shopping, sporting events, theater and watersports nearby.

Certificate may be used: Jan. 9-April 30, Friday, Saturday, Sunday; Sunday-Thursday, year-round excluding holidays and first week in Oct.

Paradise K14

Creekside Inn
44 Leacock Rd
Paradise, PA 17562-0435
(717)687-0333

Circa 1781. This 18th-century Georgian home was built by David Witmer, a prominent citizen and member of one of the first families to settle in the area. The stone exterior features a gable roof with

five bay windows. Relaxing guest quarters feature special amenities such as four-poster or Windsor beds. The Cameo and Creekside rooms boast fireplaces. A hearty, full breakfast is served each morning. Antique and outlet shopping, as well as a variety of sporting activities are nearby.

Innkeeper(s): Catherine & Dennis Zimmermann. $70-105. MC VISA. 5 rooms with PB. Breakfast included in rates. Types of meals: full breakfast and gourmet breakfast. Afternoon tea available. Beds: QDT. Antiques, fishing and theater nearby.

Certificate may be used: November - March; Sunday - Thursday, excluding holidays.

Pittsburgh I3

The Priory
614 Pressley St
Pittsburgh, PA 15212-5616
(412)231-3338 Fax:(412)231-4838

Circa 1888. The Priory, now a European-style hotel, was built to provide lodging for Benedictine priests traveling through Pittsburgh. It is adjacent to Pittsburgh's Grand Hall at the Priory in historic East Allegheny. The inn's design and maze of rooms and corridors give it a distinctly Old World flavor. All rooms are decorated with Victorian furnishings.
Innkeeper(s): Joanie Weldon, Ed & Mary Ann Graf. $100-150. MC VISA AX DC DS. 24 rooms with PB. 3 suites. 1 conference room. Breakfast included in rates. Type of meal: continental-plus breakfast. Beds: QDT. Handicap access. Theater nearby.

Publicity: *Pittsburgh Press, US Air, Country Inns, Innsider, Youngstown Vindicator, Travel & Leisure, Gourmet, Mid-Atlantic Country.*

"Although we had been told that the place was elegant, we were hardly prepared for the richness of detail. We felt as though we were guests in a manor."

Certificate may be used: December-March, excludes New Year's Eve and Valentine's Day.

Point Pleasant I18

Tattersall Inn
16 Cafferty Rd, PO Box 569
Point Pleasant, PA 18950
(215)297-8233 (800)297-4988
E-mail: nrhg17a@prodigy.com

Circa 1740. This plastered fieldstone house with its broad porches and wainscoted entry hall was the home of local mill owners for 150 years. The walls are 18 inches thick. Breakfast is usually served in the dining room where a vintage phonograph col-

lection is on display. Breakfast can also be brought to your room. The Colonial-style common room features a beamed ceiling and walk-in fireplace. Guests gather here for apple cider, cheese and crackers and tea or coffee in the late afternoon.
Innkeeper(s): Herbert & Geraldine Moss. $70-130. MC VISA AX DS PC TC. 6 rooms with PB, 2 with FP. 2 suites. 1 conference room. Breakfast, afternoon tea and evening snack included in rates. Types of meals: full breakfast and early coffee/tea. Room service available. Beds: QT. Air conditioning in room. Fax, copier and library on premises. Antiques, fishing, parks, shopping, cross-country skiing, theater and watersports nearby.

Location: Bucks County, New Hope area.

Publicity: *Courier Times, Philadelphia, New York Times, WYOU.*

"Thank you for your hospitality and warm welcome. The inn is charming and has a wonderful ambiance."

Certificate may be used: All year, Sunday-Thursday, holidays excluded.

Ronks K14

Candlelight Inn B&B
2574 Lincoln Hwy E
Ronks, PA 17572-9771
(717)299-6005 (800)772-2635 Fax:(717)299-6397
E-mail: Candleinn@aol.com

Circa 1920. Located in the Pennsylvania Dutch area, this Federal-style house offers a side porch for enjoying the home's acre and a half of tall trees and surrounding Amish farmland. Guest rooms feature Victorian decor. The inn's gourmet breakfast, which might include a creme caramel French toast, is served by candlelight. The innkeepers are professional classical musicians. Lancaster is five miles to the east.

Innkeeper(s): Tim & Heidi Soberick. $65-105. MC VISA DS PC TC. 6 rooms, 4 with PB. 1 suite. Breakfast included in rates. Types of meals: full breakfast and gourmet breakfast. Beds: KQT. Air conditioning in room. Cable TV and fax on premises. Amusement parks, antiques, fishing, parks, shopping, downhill skiing, cross-country skiing, sporting events, theater and watersports nearby.

Certificate may be used: December through June, Sunday to Thursday.

Shippensburg K10

Field & Pine B&B
2155 Ritner Hwy
Shippensburg, PA 17257-9756
(717)776-7179

Circa 1790. Local limestone was used to build this stone house, located on the main wagon road to Baltimore and Washington. Originally, it was a tavern and weigh station. The house is surrounded by stately pines, and sheep graze on the inn's 80 acres.

The bedrooms are hand-stenciled and furnished with quilts and antiques.

Innkeeper(s): Mary Ellen & Allan Williams. $65-75. MC VISA PC TC. 3 rooms, 1 with PB, 1 with FP. 1 suite. Breakfast and evening snack included in rates. Types of meals: gourmet breakfast and early coffee/tea. Beds: QDT. Air conditioning and turndown service in room. VCR on premises. Antiques, fishing, parks and shopping nearby.

Location: Twelve miles south of Carlisle, on US Rte 11.

Publicity: *Valley Times-Star.*

"Our visit in this lovely country home has been most delightful. The ambiance of antiques and tasteful decorating exemplifies real country living."

Certificate may be used: Sunday through Thursday, year-round.

McLean House B&B
80 W King St
Shippensburg, PA 17257-1212
(717)530-1390 (800)610-0330 Fax:(717)530-1390

Circa 1798. This inn is filled with an eclectic collection of furnishings, gathered from the innkeepers'

30 years of moves while in the army. Located in the historic district, the house is a combination of Victorian Stick style and Victorian Shingle style. Trout-filled Branch Creek borders the property and attracts mallard ducks, often seen from the dining area during breakfast. The innkeepers will advise you on visiting the dozens of antique and flea markets in the area. If you'd like, they also will arrange to escort you to your first auction.

Innkeeper(s): Bob & Jan Rose. $45. PC. 3 rooms, 1 with PB. Breakfast included in rates. Type of meal: full breakfast. Catered breakfast available. Beds: D. Air conditioning and ceiling fan in room. Cable TV, VCR, fax and swimming on premises. Antiques, fishing, parks and shopping nearby.

Certificate may be used: Sunday through Thursday, all year, subject to availability.

Smoketown K14

Homestead Lodging
184 Eastbrook Rd
Smoketown, PA 17576-9701
(717)393-6927 Fax:(717)393-1424

Circa 1984. An Amish farm rests adjacent to this newer brick Colonial, and from this bed & breakfast, guests can enjoy Pennsylvania Dutch country. Farmer's markets, antique shops, museums and restaurants all are nearby. Wood-paneled guest rooms are simply furnished and each includes a refrigerator and cable TV. Children are welcome.

Innkeeper(s): Robert & Lori Kepiro. $39-61. MC VISA AX DS. 5 rooms with PB. Breakfast included in rates. Type of meal: continental breakfast. Beds: QD. Air conditioning, ceiling fan and TV in room. Swimming and tennis on premises. Amusement parks, antiques, parks, shopping, golf, theater and watersports nearby.

"Your hospitality and immaculate lodge stay with us long after we leave."

Certificate may be used: November-April, Sunday-Wednesday, excluding holidays and holiday weekends.

Spring Creek D4

Spring Valley B&B
RR Box 117
Spring Creek, PA 16436-9507
(814)489-3000 (800)382-1324 Fax:(814)489-7333
E-mail: springvalley@penn.com

Circa 1820. Although located on Pennsylvania's Allegheny Plateau, this 105-acre spread feels more like a Western-style ranch. Deer and other wildlife roam the grounds, and there are hiking and cross-country ski trails on the premises. The land is adjacent to more than 8,000 acres of state game lands. There are two suites available in the main house as well as a log and cedar cottage. The cottage sleeps six and includes a fireplace and deck overlooking the woods. Four guests can stay comfortably in the Parlor Suite, which includes a corn-burning stove and clawfoot tub. For an additional fee, guests can enjoy guided, horseback trail rides.

Innkeeper(s): Jim Bird & Debora Regis. $75-130. MC VISA DS PC TC. 3 rooms. 2 cottages. Breakfast included in rates. Types of meals: continental breakfast, continental-plus breakfast, full breakfast, gourmet breakfast and early coffee/tea. Evening snack, picnic lunch, lunch, gourmet lunch, catering service, catered breakfast and room service available. Beds: QD. Ceiling fan and TV in room. VCR, fax, copier, stables, bicycles, library and child care on premises. Handicap access. Antiques, fishing, parks, shopping, downhill skiing, cross-country skiing, theater and watersports nearby.

Certificate may be used: Weekdays only, except holiday weekends, upon availability and excluding first two weeks in October.

Spruce Creek   I8

The Dell's B&B at Cedar Hill Farm
HC-01 Box 26 Rt 45
Spruce Creek, PA 16683-9707
(814)632-8319

Circa 1810. The original stone section of this house is joined by a later addition. The area overlooks Spruce Creek, famous for fly-fishing. Ask for the room with the brass bed and fireplace.

If you have children, you'll want to bring them in the spring when the newborn calves, pigs, chickens and beagle dogs arrive. Vegetables, pumpkins, corn and hay are grown on the farm's 100 acres. Nearby, a working dairy farm allows visitors during milking hours. A hearty Pennsylvania Dutch breakfast is served.

Innkeeper(s): Sharon Dell. $35-50. MC VISA AX DC DS. 4 rooms, 1 with FP. Breakfast included in rates. Type of meal: full breakfast. Beds: DT. Ceiling fan in room. Cable TV and VCR on premises. Amusement parks, antiques, shopping, downhill skiing and sporting events nearby.

"Lovely surroundings, delightful hosts."

Certificate may be used: December until May.

Starlight   C17

The Inn at Starlight Lake
PO Box 27
Starlight, PA 18461-0027
(717)798-2519 (800)248-2519 Fax:(717)798-2672

Circa 1909. Acres of woodland and meadow surround the last surviving railroad inn on the New

York, Ontario and Western lines. Originally a boarding house, the inn had its own store, church, school, blacksmith shop and creamery. Platforms, first erected to accommodate tents for the summer season, were later replaced by individual cottages. The inn is situated on the 45-acre, spring-fed Starlight Lake, providing summertime canoeing, swimming, fishing and sailing. (No motorboats are allowed on the lake.)

Innkeeper(s): Jack & Judy McMahon. $110-154. MAP, EP. MC VISA. 26 rooms, 20 with PB, 1 with FP. 1 suite. 1 conference room. Breakfast and dinner included in rates. Types of meals: full breakfast, gourmet breakfast and early coffee/tea. Evening snack, picnic lunch, lunch and banquet service available. Restaurant on premises. Beds: KQDT. Copier and bicycles on premises. Antiques, fishing, shopping, downhill skiing, cross-country skiing and watersports nearby.

Publicity: *New York Times, Philadelphia Inquirer, Newsday, Discerning Traveler, Freeman.*

"So great to be back to our home away from home."

Certificate may be used: September 15-June 15, Sunday-Friday, except when Sunday is part of a holiday weekend. Discount on room rate only.

Tunkhannock   E15

The Weeping Willow Inn
308 N Eaton Rd
Tunkhannock, PA 18657
(717)836-7257

Circa 1836. This Colonial, set on 22 acres, is filled with beautiful antiques and an elegant traditional decor. The home's original pine floor is topped with Oriental rugs. Breakfasts, with a fresh fruit parfait and perhaps apple-cinnamon French toast, are served by candlelight. The nearby Susquehanna River and mountains provide ample activities, from hiking to fishing and canoeing. Antique and craft shops also are plentiful in the area.

Innkeeper(s): Patty & Randy Ehrenzeller. $70-80. PC TC. 3 rooms with PB. Breakfast included in rates. Type of meal: full breakfast. Beds: QD. Air conditioning and turndown service in room. Antiques, fishing, parks, shopping, downhill skiing, cross-country skiing, golf and watersports nearby.

Certificate may be used: Sunday through Thursday, no holidays, Jan 3.-Dec. 20.

Valley Forge (Linfield) K16

Shearer Elegance
154 Main St
Valley Forge (Linfield), PA 19468-1139
(610)495-7429 (800)861-0308 Fax:(610)495-7814
E-mail: shearerc@aol.com

Circa 1897. This stone Queen Anne mansion is the height of Victorian opulence and style. Peaked roofs, intricate trim and a stenciled wraparound porch grace the exterior. Guests enter the home via a marble entry, which boasts a three-story staircase. Stained-glass windows and carved mantels are other notable features. The Victorian furnishings and decor complement the ornate workmanship, and lacy curtains are a romantic touch. The bedrooms feature hand-carved, built-in wardrobes. The grounds are dotted with gardens. The inn is located in the village of Linfield, about 15 minutes from Valley Forge.

Innkeeper(s): Shirley & Michael Shearer & Beth Smith. $75-140. AX PC TC. 7 rooms with PB. 2 suites. 3 conference rooms. Types of meals: full breakfast and early coffee/tea. Banquet service and catering service available. Beds: KQD. Air conditioning, ceiling fan, TV and VCR in room. Fax, copier and library on premises. Amusement parks, antiques, fishing, parks, shopping, downhill skiing, sporting events, golf and theater nearby.

Certificate may be used: Anytime, excluding holidays.

Valley Forge (Malvern) K16

The Great Valley House of Valley Forge
110 Swedesford Rd, Rd 3
Valley Forge (Malvern), PA 19355
(610)644-6759 Fax:(610)644-7019
E-mail: jeffbenson@unn.unisys.com

Circa 1691. This 300-year-old Colonial stone farmhouse sits on four acres just two miles from Valley Forge Park. Boxwoods line the walkway and ancient trees surround the house. Each of the three guest rooms is hand-stenciled and features a canopied or brass bed topped with handmade quilts. Guests enjoy a full breakfast before a 14-foot fireplace in the "summer kitchen," the oldest part of the house. On the grounds are a swimming pool, walking and hiking trails, and the home's original smokehouse.

Innkeeper(s): Pattye Benson. $75-90. AP. MC VISA DS PC TC. 3 rooms, 2 with PB. Breakfast included in rates. Types of meals: gourmet break-

fast and early coffee/tea. Picnic lunch available. Beds: QDT. Air conditioning, turndown service and TV in room. Fax and swimming on premises. Antiques, fishing, parks, shopping, cross-country skiing, sporting events, theater and watersports nearby.

Location: Two miles from Valley Forge National Park.

Publicity: *Main Line Philadelphia, Philadelphia Inquirer, Washington Post, New York Times, Suburban Newspaper, Phoenixville Sun.*

"As a business traveler, Patty's enthusiasm and warm welcome makes you feel just like you're home."

Certificate may be used: Year-round, Sunday-Thursday.

Warfordsburg L8

Buck Valley Ranch
Rt 2 Box 1170
Warfordsburg, PA 17267-9667
(717)294-3759 (800)294-3759 Fax:(717)294-3759

Circa 1930. Trail riding is a popular activity on the ranch's 64 acres in the Appalachian Mountains of South Central Pennsylvania. State game lands and forests border the ranch. The guest house, decorated in a ranch/cowboy style, is a private farmhouse that can accommodate eight people. Meals are prepared using homegrown vegetables and locally raised meats. Rates also include horseback riding.

Innkeeper(s): Nadine & Leon Fox. $60. MC VISA DS PC TC. 4 rooms. Breakfast, dinner, evening snack and picnic lunch included in rates. Types of meals: full breakfast, gourmet breakfast and early coffee/tea. Lunch and gourmet lunch available. Beds: DT. Air conditioning in room. Fax, copier, swimming, sauna and stables on premises. Amusement parks, antiques, fishing, parks, shopping, downhill skiing, cross-country skiing and watersports nearby.

Certificate may be used: March 1-Nov. 30, Sunday-Thursday (no weekends).

Washington Crossing J18

Inn to The Woods
150 Glenwood Dr
Washington Crossing, PA 18977-1518
(215)493-1974 (800)982-7619 Fax:(215)493-7592

Circa 1978. Located on 10 forested acres, this chalet offers seclusion and trails for hiking. Victorian furnishings and framed art add to the pleasingly appointed guest rooms. There is an indoor garden and fishpond. The chalet has beamed ceilings and parquet floors. On weekdays a continental breakfast is served, while on Saturday a full breakfast is provided. The fare for Sunday is a champagne brunch.

Innkeeper(s): Barry & Rosemary Rein. $85-175. MC VISA AX PC TC. 6 rooms with PB. 1 suite. 1 conference room. Breakfast, afternoon tea and evening snack included in rates. Types of meals: continental breakfast, continental-plus breakfast, full breakfast, gourmet breakfast and early coffee/tea. Dinner, picnic lunch, lunch, gourmet lunch, banquet service, catered breakfast and room service available. Beds: KQD. Air conditioning, ceiling fan and TV in room. VCR, fax, copier, bicycles and library on premises. Amusement parks, antiques, fishing, parks, shopping, cross-country skiing, theater and watersports nearby.

Certificate may be used: January-December, Sunday-Thursday, holidays excluded.

Wellsboro D11

Waln Street B&B
54 Waln St
Wellsboro, PA 16901-1936
(717)724-3543

Circa 1886. This three-story Dutch Colonial Revival Home is decorated with lace and walnut period pieces. Guests are invited to rock away the afternoon on a sweeping wraparound porch.

Evenings often are spent enjoying the sounds from a Grand piano in the drawing room. Soft beds are flanked with overstuffed pillows, and after a restful night's sleep, guests enjoy a lavish breakfast served on fine china and crystal. The bed & breakfast is located only two blocks from the quaint gaslights that decorate Wellsboro's main street.

Innkeeper(s): Catherine Casiello. $50-70. MC VISA. 4 rooms, 1 with PB. Breakfast included in rates. Type of meal: full breakfast. Beds: QD. Antiques, fishing, downhill skiing, cross-country skiing, theater and watersports nearby.

Publicity: *Wellsboro Gazette, Williamsport Sun Gazette.*

"You have a beautiful presentation. Splendid."

Certificate may be used: Winter, spring, summer, anytime. Fall weekdays.

West Chester K16

Bankhouse B&B
875 Hillsdale Rd
West Chester, PA 19382-1975
(610)344-7388

Circa 1765. Built into the bank of a quiet country road, this 18th-century house overlooks a 10-acre horse farm and pond. The interior is decorated with

country antiques, stenciling and folk art. Guests have a private entrance and porch. Two bedrooms share a common sitting room library. Hearty country breakfasts include German apple souffle pancakes, custard French toast and nearly 100 other recipes. West Chester and the Brandywine Valley attractions are conveniently close.

Innkeeper(s): Diana & Michael Bove. $65-90. TC. 2 rooms. 1 suite. Breakfast and evening snack included in rates. Types of meals: full breakfast, gourmet breakfast and early coffee/tea. Beds: DT. Air conditioning in room. Antiques, parks, shopping, cross-country skiing, sporting events and theater nearby.

Location: In Brandywine Valley.

Publicity: *Philadelphia Inquirer, Mercury, Bucks County Town & Country Living, Chester County Living, Washington Post.*

"Everything was so warm and inviting. One of my favorite places to keep coming back to."

Certificate may be used: Nov. 1-April 30, Sunday-Thursday.

York K13

Friendship House B&B
728 E Philadelphia St
York, PA 17403-1609
(717)843-8299

Circa 1897. A walk down East Philadelphia Street takes visitors past an unassuming row of 19th-century townhouses. The Friendship House is a welcoming site with its light blue shutters and pink trim. Innkeepers Becky Detwiler and Karen Maust have added a shot of Victorian influence to their charming townhouse B&B, decorating with wallcoverings and lacy curtains. A country feast is prepared some mornings with choices ranging from quiche to French toast accompanied with items such as baked apples, smoked sausage and homemade breads. Most items are selected carefully from a nearby farmer's market. Becky and Karen make sure guests never leave their friendly home empty-handed, offering a bottle of Pennsylvania's finest maple syrup upon departure.

Innkeeper(s): Becky Detwiler & Karen Maust. $50-65. 3 rooms, 2 with PB. 1 suite. Breakfast and evening snack included in rates. Types of meals: continental-plus breakfast and full breakfast. Beds: Q. Air conditioning in room. VCR on premises. Antiques, fishing, parks, shopping and theater nearby.

Certificate may be used: November-March.

Smyser-Bair House

30 S Beaver St
York, PA 17401-1301
(717)854-3411

Circa 1880. This four-story, red brick house stands on a corner in downtown York. Its green shutters and Italianate styling add a welcoming touch. The house is decorated in cheerful colors, highlighting finely carved moldings, a walnut staircase, high ceilings and parquet floors. It is appointed with crystal chandeliers, floor-to-ceiling gold leaf pier mirrors and Victorian antiques.

Innkeeper(s): Dianne Hartman. $60-80. MC VISA. 3 rooms, 3 with FP. 1 suite. Breakfast included in rates. Types of meals: continental breakfast, full breakfast and early coffee/tea. Afternoon tea available. Beds: QDT. Air conditioning in room. Amusement parks, antiques, fishing, parks, shopping, downhill skiing, golf and theater nearby.

Location: Between Lancaster and Gettysburg.

Publicity: *York Daily Record.*

"We really enjoyed the warmth and hospitality of the innkeepers. They really care about their guests."

Certificate may be used: Subject to availability.

Rhode Island

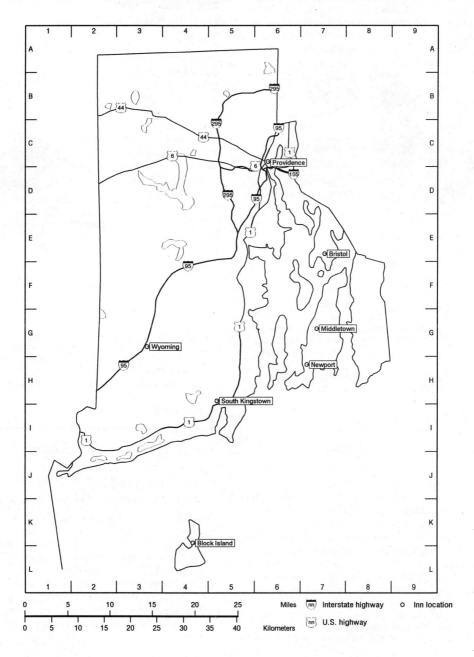

Miles   Interstate highway   o Inn location

U.S. highway

Block Island K4

The Bellevue House
PO Box 1198, High St
Block Island, RI 02807-1198
(401)466-2912

Offering a hilltop perch, meadow-like setting and ocean views, this Colonial Revival farmhouse inn in the Block Island Historic District has served guests for more than a century. A variety of accommodations includes five guest rooms with shared bath, five suites and two cottages. The Old Harbor Ferry,

restaurants and shops are just a five-minute walk from the inn. Guests may use ferries from New London, Conn., Montauk Point, N.Y., and Newport, Point Judith and Providence, R.I., to reach the island. Beaches, Block Island National Wildlife Reserve and Rodmans Hollow Nature Area are nearby. Children are welcome.

Innkeeper(s): Neva Flaherty. $70-160. MC VISA PC TC. 5 rooms. 2 cottages. Breakfast included in rates. Type of meal: continental breakfast. Beds: KQD. Library on premises. Fishing, parks, shopping and watersports nearby.

Certificate may be used: Sunday through Thursday, May 14-June 22, Sept. 10-Oct. 5. B&B rooms available for this offer.

Blue Dory Inn
PO Box 488, Dodge St
Block Island, RI 02807-0488
(401)466-5891 (800)992-7290 Fax:(401)466-9910

Circa 1887. This Shingle Victorian inn on Crescent Beach offers many guest rooms with ocean views. The Cottage, The Doll House and The Tea House are separate structures for those desiring more room or privacy. Antiques and Victorian touches are featured throughout. Year-round car ferry service, taking approximately one hour, is found at Point Judith, R.I. The island also may be reached by air on New England Airlines or by charter. Mohegan Bluffs Scenic Natural Area is nearby.

Innkeeper(s): Ann Loedy. $65-195. MC VISA AX DS PC TC. 14 rooms with PB. 3 suites. 4 cottages. 1 conference room. Breakfast and afternoon tea included in rates. Types of meals: continental-plus breakfast

and early coffee/tea. Catered breakfast available. Beds: KQDT. Cable TV, VCR, fax, copier, swimming and child care on premises. Antiques, fishing, parks, shopping, theater and watersports nearby.

"The Blue Dory is a wonderful place to stay. The room was lovely, the view spectacular and the sound of surf was both restful and tranquil."

Certificate may be used: Midweek Sept. 15-June 15, Sunday through Thursday.

Sheffield House
High St, Box C-2
Block Island, RI 02807
(401)466-2494 Fax:(401)466-5067

Circa 1888. Step off the ferry and step into a bygone era at this Queen Anne Victorian, which overlooks the Old Harbor district and scenic ocean vistas. Relax on the front porch or enjoy the fragrance as you stroll through the private garden. The cookie jar is always full of home-baked treats. Breakfasts are served in the quaint day room, which features a collection of milk bottles from around the world. Guests also can enjoy the morning meal in the garden surrounded by beautiful flowers and herbs. Guest rooms feature international touches, antiques and family pieces.

Innkeeper(s): Steve & Claire McQueeny. $50-165. MC VISA AX PC. 7 rooms, 5 with PB. Breakfast, afternoon tea and evening snack included in rates. Types of meals: continental-plus breakfast and early coffee/tea. Beds: Q. Ceiling fan in room. Antiques, fishing, parks, shopping and watersports nearby.

Certificate may be used: Oct. 15-May 15, Sunday-Thursday.

Bristol E7

The Joseph Reynolds House
956 Hope St
Bristol, RI 02809-1113
(401)254-0230 (800)754-0230 Fax:(401)254-2610

Circa 1684. The Joseph Reynolds House is a National Historic Landmark and the oldest known 17th-century, three-story wooden structure in New England. It was the military headquarters of General Lafayette in 1778. Gradually being restored to its original elegance, guest rooms are on the second and third floors. Most of the common rooms have high ceilings and were painted to look like marble. There is a Jacobean staircase, a keeping room and a great room.

Innkeeper(s): Wendy & Richard Anderson. $49-95. PC TC. 5 rooms. 2 suites. Breakfast and afternoon tea included in rates. Type of meal: gourmet breakfast. Beds: KQDT. Cable TV, VCR, fax, copier and library on premises. Antiques, fishing, parks, shopping, sporting events and theater nearby.

Location: Twenty-five minutes from Newport.

Publicity: *American Design, New England Colonial, New York Travel, Providence Journal, New England Magazine.*

"Wonderful, restful week after chaos."

Certificate may be used: November to April (not on holiday weeks); midweek year-round, subject to availability.

William's Grant Inn
154 High St
Bristol, RI 02809-2123
(401)253-4222 (800)596-4222

Circa 1808. This handsome Federal Colonial home was built by Governor William Bradford for his grandson. There are two beehive ovens and seven fireplaces as well as original wide-board pine floors and paired interior chimneys. Antique furnishings and folk art make the guest rooms inviting. The backyard is an ideal spot for relaxation with its patios, water garden and quaint stone walls.

Innkeeper(s): Michael Rose. $65-105. MC VISA AX DS PC TC. 5 rooms, 3 with PB, 5 with FP. Breakfast included in rates. Types of meals: full breakfast and gourmet breakfast. Afternoon tea available. Beds: QD. Turndown service and ceiling fan in room. Bicycles on premises. Antiques, fishing, parks, shopping, sporting events and watersports nearby.

Location: Located in the heart of Bristol's historic waterfront district.

Publicity: *New York Times, Sun Sentinal, Providence Journal, Bristol Phoenix.*

"We felt better than at home with the wonderful treats (the breakfasts were fabulous), the lovely rooms, the inn is full of inspiration and innovation . . ."

Certificate may be used: November-May, Sunday-Thursday, based on availability.

Middletown
G7

Lindsey's Guest House
6 James St
Middletown, RI 02842-5932
(401)846-9386
E-mail: 103611,2760@compuserve.com

Circa 1955. This contemporary split-level home in a residential area features three guest rooms, including one on the ground level that boasts a private entrance and is handicap-accessible. Breakfast is served in the dining room and usually includes cereal, coffee cake, fruit, juice, muffins and jam, and coffee or beverage of choice. The innkeeper has worked in the hospitality industry for more than 30 years and is happy to offer sightseeing tips. The Norman Bird Sanctuary and Sachuest Point National Wildlife Reserve are nearby.

Innkeeper(s): Anne T. Lindsey. $40-75. MC VISA AX PC TC. 2 rooms with PB. Breakfast included in rates. Type of meal: continental-plus breakfast. Beds: KD. Ceiling fan in room. VCR on premises. Handicap access. Antiques, fishing, parks, shopping, theater and watersports nearby.

Certificate may be used: Oct. 15-April 15 (all nights).

The Inn at Shadow Lawn
120 Miantonomi Ave
Middletown, RI 02842-5450
(401)847-0902 (800)352-3750 Fax:(401)848-6529

Circa 1855. This elegant, three-story Stick Victorian inn, listed in the National Register, offers a glimpse of fine living in an earlier age. The innkeepers' attention to detail is evident throughout, with French crystal chandeliers, stained-glass windows and parquet floors in the library as a few of the highlights. Parlors are found on each of the inn's floors. Newport's many attractions, including the Art Museum, sailing and the world famous Newport mansions are just a short drive from the inn.

Innkeeper(s): Randy & Selma Fabricant. $55-155. MC VISA AX TC. 8 rooms with PB, 8 with FP. 2 conference rooms. Breakfast included in rates. Type of meal: full breakfast. Beds: KQT. Air conditioning in room. Fax, copier and library on premises. Antiques nearby.

"A dream come true! Thanks for everything! We'll be back."
Certificate may be used: Jan. 11- April 1, Monday-Sunday, excluding holidays.

Newport   H7

Halidon Hill Guest House
Halidon Ave
Newport, RI 02840
(401)847-8318 (800)227-2130

Circa 1969. This contemporary, two-story Georgian-style inn offers a convenient location and comfortable accommodations for those exploring the Newport area. The two spacious suites both boast kitchenettes. The inn is just a 10-minute walk to Hammersmith Farm and provides easy access to the area's mansions, restaurants and shopping. Guests will enjoy lounging on the roomy deck near the in-ground pool, or in front of the fireplace in cooler weather. Newport Harbor and the Tennis Hall of Fame are nearby.
Innkeeper(s): Helen & Paul Burke. $75-200. AX DC DS PC TC. 2 suites. Breakfast included in rates. Types of meals: full breakfast and early coffee/tea. Beds: KQDT. Air conditioning, ceiling fan and TV in room. VCR and swimming on premises. Handicap access. Antiques, fishing, parks, shopping, sporting events, golf, theater and watersports nearby.
Certificate may be used: Weekdays May through October. Anytime November through April.

Hammett House Inn
505 Thames St
Newport, RI 02840-6723
(401)848-0593 (800)548-9417 Fax:(401)848-2258
E-mail: CIS 76470,3440

Circa 1758. This three-story Georgian Federal-style home has watched the nation grow and prosper from its little nook on Thames Street. The rooms are decorated with romance in mind. Especially picturesque are the Rose and Windward rooms, which afford views of Newport's harbor. The Pewter Room includes a unique metal canopy bed. The inn is a short walk from shops, restaurants and the waterfront.
Innkeeper(s): Marianne Spaziano. $95-195. MC VISA AX DS TC. 5 rooms with PB. Breakfast included in rates. Type of meal: continental-plus breakfast. Restaurant on premises. Beds: Q. Air conditioning and TV in room. Fax on premises. Antiques, fishing, parks, shopping, downhill skiing, theater and watersports nearby.
Certificate may be used: Anytime Nov. 16-April 1; April-June, Tuesday-Thursday only.

Hydrangea House Inn
16 Bellevue Ave
Newport, RI 02840-3206
(401)846-4435 (800)945-4667 Fax:(401)846-6602
E-mail: bandbinn@ids.net
The scent of fresh flowers welcomes guests into their cheery rooms at this B&B, which once housed a school of music. After abdicating his throne, King Edward was a guest at this home. Romance is emphasized by the decor in each of the individually appointed guest rooms, which feature wicker and antique furnishings. Breakfasts are served on the veranda, with its view of the gardens. In cooler weather, the breakfast buffet is set up in the art gallery, which features many original works.
Innkeeper(s): Grant Edmondson. $75-280. MC VISA. 6 rooms. Breakfast included in rates. Type of meal: full breakfast.
Certificate may be used: Nov. 1-April 30, Sunday-Wednesday.

Inntowne Inn
6 Mary St
Newport, RI 02840-3028
(401)846-9200 (800)457-7803 Fax:(401)846-1534

Circa 1935. This Colonial-style inn is an elegant spot from which to enjoy the seaside town of Newport. Waverly and Laura Ashley prints decorate the individually appointed guest rooms, some of which have four-poster or canopy beds. The innkeeper serves an expanded continental breakfast with items such as fresh fruit, quiche and ham and cheese croissants. Afternoon tea also is served. A day in Newport offers many activities, including touring the Tennis Hall of Fame, taking a cruise through the harbor, shopping for antiques or perhaps taking a trek down Cliff Walk, a one-and-a-half-mile path offering the ocean on one side and historic mansions on the other.
Innkeeper(s): Carmella Gardner. $95-189. MC VISA AX. 26 rooms with PB. 1 suite. Afternoon tea included in rates. Type of meal: continental-plus breakfast. Beds: KQDT. Air conditioning in room. Cable TV, VCR, fax, copier and library on premises. Antiques, parks and shopping nearby.

"Thank you for your excellent service with a smile."
Certificate may be used: Nov. 1-Feb. 28, Sunday through Thursday.

The Melville House
39 Clarke St
Newport, RI 02840-3023
(401)847-0640 Fax:(401)847-0956
E-mail: innkeepri@aol.com

Circa 1750. This attractive, National Register two-story Colonial inn once housed aides to General Rochambeau during the American Revolution. Early American furnishings decorate the interior. There is also an unusual collection of old appli-

ances, including a cherry-pitter, mincer and dough maker. A full breakfast includes Portuguese Quiche, Jonnycakes, homemade bread and Portuguese egg sandwiches. The inn is a pleasant walk from the waterfront and historic sites.

Innkeeper(s): Vincent DeRico & David Horan. $85-165. MC VISA AX DS PC TC. 7 rooms, 5 with PB, 1 with FP. 1 suite. Breakfast and afternoon tea included in rates. Types of meals: full breakfast, gourmet breakfast and early coffee/tea. Picnic lunch available. Beds: KDT. Air conditioning in room. Fax and bicycles on premises. Antiques, fishing, parks, shopping, theater and watersports nearby.

Location: In the heart of Newport's Historic Hill.

Publicity: *Country Inns, "Lodging Pick" for Newport, Good Housekeeping.*

"Comfortable with a quiet elegance."

Certificate may be used: November-April; Sunday-Thursday.

Willows of Newport-Romantic Inn & Garden
8-10 Willow St, Historic Point
Newport, RI 02840-1927
(401)846-5486 Fax:(401)849-8215

Circa 1740. There's little wonder why this charming inn is known as The Romantic Inn. The spectacular secret garden, with its abundance of foliage, colorful blooms and a heart-shaped fish pond, is a popular stop on Newport's Secret Garden Tour. The inn is a three-time recipient of the Newport Best Garden Award. The French Quarter room and Canopy Room both boast views of the gardens, and guests awake to the fragrances of the many flowers. The romantic Victorian Wedding Room, decorated in pastel greens and rose, offers a brass canopy bed, hand-painted furniture and a fireplace. The Colonial Wedding Room features lace accents, a

brass cannonball bed and an original 1740s fireplace. A continental breakfast is delivered to your room on bone china with silver services. Innkeeper Pattie Murphy, aside from her gardening and decorating skills, is a native Newporter and is full of information about the city.

Innkeeper(s): Patricia 'Pattie' Murphy. $98-198. PC TC. 8 rooms with PB. Breakfast and evening snack included in rates. Type of meal: continental-plus breakfast. Picnic lunch and room service available. Beds: KQD. Air conditioning in room. Antiques, fishing, parks, shopping and watersports nearby.

Publicity: *Newport Daily News, Bostonia, New Woman, PM Magazine*

"We enjoyed our getaway in your inn for its peace, elegance and emphasis on romance."

Certificate may be used: Year-round, Monday, Tuesday, Wednesday, Thursday.

Providence
C6

State House Inn
43 Jewett St
Providence, RI 02908-4904
(401)351-6111 Fax:(401)351-4261

Circa 1889. Shaker and Colonial furniture fill this turn-of-the-century home, located in the midst of a quaint and peaceful Providence neighborhood. The rooms provide amenities that will please any business traveler and have the country comfort and elegance

of days gone by. The common room contains a small library for guest use. A famed historic district, featuring restored homes and buildings, is three blocks away, and the capitol is a five-minute walk.

Innkeeper(s): Frank & Monica Hopton. $79-119. EP. MC VISA AX PC TC. 10 rooms with PB, 2 with FP. Breakfast included in rates. Type of meal: full breakfast. Afternoon tea available. Beds: KQ. Air conditioning and TV in room. Fax, copier and computer on premises. Antiques and parks nearby.

Location: Forty minutes from Newport.

Publicity: *Providence Magazine.*

"Thank you again for the warm, comfortable and very attractive accommodations."

Certificate may be used: Weekdays, year-round. Weekends in November-April.

South Kingstown H5

Admiral Dewey Inn
668 Matunuck Beach Rd
South Kingstown, RI 02879-7021
(401)783-2090 (800)457-2090 Fax:(401)783-0680

Circa 1898. Although the prices have risen a bit since this inn's days as a boarding house (the rate was 50 cents per night), this Stick-style home still offers hospitality and comfort. The National Register inn is within walking distance of Matunuck Beach. Guests can enjoy the sea breeze from the inn's wraparound porch. Period antiques decorate the guest rooms, some of which offer ocean views.

Innkeeper(s): Joan Lebel. $40-120. MC VISA PC. 10 rooms, 8 with PB. Breakfast included in rates. Types of meals: continental-plus breakfast and early coffee/tea. Picnic lunch available. Beds: QDT. Cable TV, VCR, fax, copier and swimming on premises. Antiques, fishing, parks, shopping, theater and watersports nearby.

Publicity: *Yankee Traveler, Rhode Island Monthly.*

Certificate may be used: Oct. 15-May 15, Sunday to Friday.

Wyoming G3

The Cookie Jar B&B
64 Kingstown Rd, Rt 138
Wyoming, RI 02898-1103
(401)539-2680 (800)767-4262

Circa 1732. The living room of this historic farmhouse inn once served as a blacksmith shop. The inn's original stone walls and wood ceiling remain, along with a granite fireplace built by a Native American stonemason. Years later, as rooms were added, the building became the Cookie Jar tea room, a name the innkeepers judged worth keeping. Visitors select their full breakfast fare from a menu provided the night before. The inn's grounds boast more than 60 fruit trees, a flower garden and a barn. Those who love the beach or fishing will find both fresh and salt water within a 20-minute drive.

Innkeeper(s): Charles Sohl. $75. PC TC. 3 suites. Breakfast included in rates. Type of meal: full breakfast. Beds: KQDT. Air conditioning and TV in room. VCR on premises. Amusement parks, antiques, fishing, shopping, downhill skiing, cross-country skiing, sporting events, theater and watersports nearby.

Location: Boston is slightly more than an hour from the inn.

"Our accommodations were so comfortable and the breakfasts delicious!"

Certificate may be used: Anytime except Friday and Saturday during months of May through October. Not valid on holidays or special events.

South Carolina

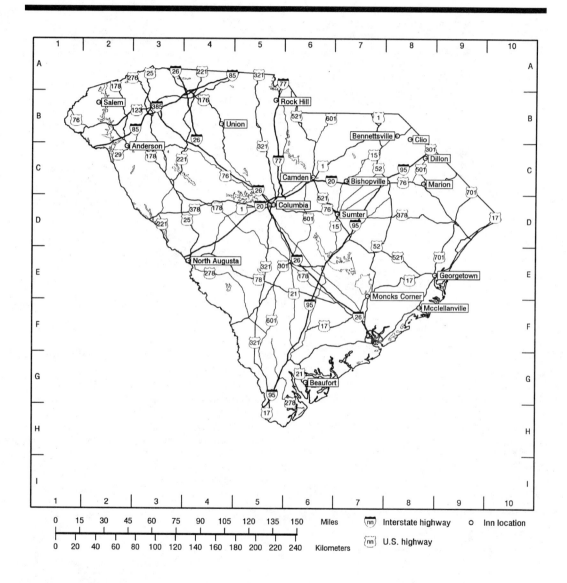

	Miles	0 15 30 45 60 75 90 105 120 135 150							
	Kilometers	0 20 40 60 80 100 120 140 160 180 200 220 240							

Interstate highway   o   Inn location
U.S. highway

Anderson   C2

Evergreen Inn
1103 S Main St
Anderson, SC 29624-2349
(803)225-1109

Circa 1834. This gracious Greek Revival house features tall columns rising to the third-story pediment and a wraparound veranda. It is located on two-and-a-half acres, next to another fine National Register mansion, which houses the inn's restaurant. Scarlet's Room features a tall four-poster bed and burgundy velvet drapes. Another guest room boasts an exotic navy satin canopy bed. Antique shops and the downtown area are within walking distance.

Innkeeper(s): Myrna Ryter. $56-70. MC VISA AX DC. 7 rooms, 6 with PB. 2 suites. 1 conference room. Breakfast included in rates. Types of meals: continental breakfast and gourmet breakfast. Dinner available. Restaurant on premises. Beds: KQ. Handicap access. Antiques nearby.

Location: Historical district.

Publicity: *Travel Host Magazine, Greenville News.*

"Fantastic! Very imaginative & fun."

Certificate may be used: All times.

River Inn
PO Box 2093, 612 E River St
Anderson, SC 29622-2093
(864)226-1431 Fax:(864)231-9847

Circa 1914. This three-story, dormered Georgian Plantation house borders the historic district of Anderson. Leaded glass, 10-foot beamed ceilings and working coal fireplaces mark this country manor. An eclectic collection of antiques include a mahogany dining set and leaded china cabinets. Each room has its own fireplace and bath. Mounds of azaleas, 70-year-old fragrant camellia sasanqua trees, roses and crepe myrtles add grace to the inn's five acres.

Innkeeper(s): Patricia Clark. $60-85. 4 rooms with PB, 4 with FP. 1 conference room. Breakfast and evening snack included in rates. Type of meal: full breakfast. Beds: KQDT. Air conditioning, ceiling fan and TV in room. VCR and spa on premises. Antiques, fishing, parks, shopping, sporting events, theater and watersports nearby.

Certificate may be used: January through July.

Beaufort   G6

The Beaufort Inn
809 Port Republic St
Beaufort, SC 29901-1257
(803)521-9000 Fax:(803)521-9500

Circa 1907. Every inch of this breathtaking inn offers something special. The interior is decorated to the hilt with lovely furnishings, plants, beautiful rugs and warm, inviting tones. Rooms include four-poster and canopy beds combined with the modern amenities such as two-person Jacuzzi tubs, fireplaces, wet bars and stocked refrigerators. Enjoy a complimentary full breakfast at the inn's gourmet restaurant. The chef offers everything

from a light breakfast of fresh fruit, cereal and a bagel to heartier treats such as whole grain French toast stuffed with Brie and sun-dried peaches served with fresh fruit and crisp bacon.

Innkeeper(s): Russell & Debbie Fielden. $125-185. MC VISA AX DS PC TC. 13 rooms with PB, 4 with FP. 1 suite. 1 conference room. Breakfast and afternoon tea included in rates. Types of meals: full breakfast, gourmet breakfast and early coffee/tea. Dinner, picnic lunch, gourmet lunch, banquet service, catering service and room service available. Restaurant on premises. Beds: KQ. Air conditioning, turndown service, ceiling fan and TV in room. VCR, fax, copier and bicycles on premises. Handicap access. Antiques, fishing, parks, shopping, theater and watersports nearby.

Publicity: *Beaufort, Southern Living, Country Inns, Carolina Style, US Air.*

Certificate may be used: December, January and February, Sunday through Wednesday night only. Good only for 4 rooms which have a rate of $175.

The Cuthbert House Inn B&B
1203 Bay St
Beaufort, SC 29902
(803)521-1315 (800)327-9275 Fax:(803)521-1314
E-mail: cuthbert@hargray.com

Circa 1790. This 18th-century Antebellum mansion, listed in the National Register, boasts a veranda overlooking Beaufort Bay. The home was built during Washington's presidency, and General W.T. Sherman was once a guest here. The home has been lovingly restored to its original grandeur. Rich painted walls are highlighted by fine molding. Hardwood floors are topped with Oriental rugs and elegant 19th-century furnishings. The morning meal is served in a breakfast room that overlooks the water. The surrounding area offers plenty of activities in every season, and for those celebrating a new marriage, a honeymoon package is available.

Innkeeper(s): Gary & Sharon Groves. $115-185.

MC VISA AX DS PC TC. 6 rooms with PB. 3 suites. 2 conference rooms. Breakfast included in rates. Types of meals: continental breakfast, full breakfast and early coffee/tea. Beds: KQDT. Air conditioning, turndown service and TV in room. VCR, fax and library on premises. Antiques, fishing, parks and watersports nearby.

Publicity: *Atlanta Journal.*

Certificate may be used: Jan. 10-Feb. 28, June, August, Sunday-Thursday.

The Rhett House Inn
1009 Craven St
Beaufort, SC 29902-5577
(803)524-9030 Fax:(803)524-1310

Circa 1820. Most people cannot pass this stunning two-story clapboard house without wanting to step up to the long veranda and try the hammock. Guest rooms are furnished in antiques, with quilts and fresh

flowers. Many guest rooms have fireplaces. Handsome gardens feature a fountain and are often the site for romantic weddings. Bicycles are available.

Innkeeper(s): Stephen Harrison. $125-175. MC VISA AX. 17 rooms with PB, 8 with FP. 1 suite. 1 conference room. Breakfast and afternoon tea included in rates. Types of meals: full breakfast and early coffee/tea. Dinner, evening snack, picnic lunch, catering service and room service available. Restaurant on premises. Beds: KQ. Air conditioning, turndown service, ceiling fan and TV in room. Fax on premises. Handicap access. Antiques, fishing, theater and watersports nearby.

Location: In historic downtown.

Publicity: *New York Times, Vogue, Elle, Conde Nast Traveler, Travel & Leisure, Self, Brides, Martha Stewart.*

"A dream come true!"

Certificate may be used: January, February, June through September and December, Sunday through Thursday.

Bennettsville   B8

The Breeden Inn & Carriage House
404 E Main St
Bennettsville, SC 29512-3112
(803)479-3665

Circa 1886. One especially bountiful cotton crop paid for the construction of this mansion, which local attorney Thomas Bouchier presented to his bride as a wedding gift. The exterior is graced with more than two dozen columns and the interior boasts a carved oak archway in the center hall.

Stained and beveled glass are found throughout the home, along with original light fixtures. Breakfasts can be served in the formal dining room or on the veranda. The innkeepers also offer accommodations in a restored guest house, which includes a gathering room, kitchen and front porch lined with rocking chairs and swings.

Innkeeper(s): Wesley & Bonnie Park. $55-65. MC VISA PC TC. 7 rooms with PB, 6 with FP. 1 suite. 1 cottage. 1 conference room. Breakfast and afternoon tea included in rates. Types of meals: full breakfast and early coffee/tea. Beds: DT. Air conditioning, ceiling fan and TV in room. VCR, fax, copier and swimming on premises. Antiques, fishing and theater nearby.

"We have so much enjoyed our stay here in your charming and comfortable inn."

Certificate may be used: Year-round. Not honored on special event dates or holidays.

Bishopville   C7

The Foxfire B&B
416 N Main St
Bishopville, SC 29010-1442
(803)484-5643

Circa 1922. A cotton broker built this unusual home, tinged with Spanish influences, such as its tile roof. The home is fashioned from bricks and the front exterior is decorated with a wraparound porch with tile floors and ceiling fans. Guests often choose this location to relax, and it's lined with rockers, chairs and a porch swing. The three rooms are comfortable, with pieces collected from around the world. There's plenty for children to do, the innkeepers have games and swings. For breakfast, the innkeepers serve Swedish coffee, homemade muffins, fresh fruit and special items such as flannel cakes or stuffed French toast.

Innkeeper(s): Harry & Jean Woodmansee. $60-75. PC. 3 rooms, 2 with FP. Breakfast included in rates. Types of meals: continental breakfast, full breakfast and early coffee/tea. Beds: QT. Air conditioning, ceiling fan and TV in room. VCR, bicycles and library on premises. Antiques, fishing, parks and golf nearby.

Publicity: *Lee County Observer.*

"We felt like two pampered kittens."

Certificate may be used: Jan. 25-Nov. 13, Sunday-Thursday.

Camden   C6

A Camden, SC Bed & Breakfast
127 Union St
Camden, SC 29020-2700
(803)432-2366
E-mail: jaerickson@city-online.com

Circa 1920. This Federal-style home is built on what was a battlefield during the Revolutionary and

Civil wars. The home originally served as the residence for a local judge. Rooms are decorated in a country style with many antiques. Guest will find poster beds topped with antique quilts, as well as quilts decorating the walls. Guests can stay in one of the rooms in the main house or in the adjacent cottage, which served as the judge's law library. Homemade breads and jam, savory egg dishes and fresh fruit are presented in the mornings on a breakfast table set with fine linens.

Innkeeper(s): Janie Erickson. $85-125. MC VISA AX DC CB DS PC TC. 3 rooms, 1 with PB, 3 with FP. 1 cottage. Breakfast included in rates. Types of meals: continental breakfast, continental-plus breakfast, full breakfast, gourmet breakfast and early coffee/tea. Evening snack and room service available. Beds: QT. Air conditioning and turndown service in room. Cable TV and fax on premises. Antiques, fishing, parks, shopping, golf, theater and watersports nearby.

"It was great being pampered by you."

Certificate may be used: July 1-Aug. 30, Sunday-Thursday.

Candlelight Inn
1904 Broad St
Camden, SC 29020-2606
(803)424-1057

Circa 1933. Two acres of camellias, azaleas and oak trees surround this Cape Cod-style home. As per the name, the innkeepers keep a candle in each window, welcoming guests to this homey bed & breakfast. The decor is a delightful and tasteful mix of country, with quilts, hand-crafted samplers, poster beds, family antiques and traditional furnishings. Each of the rooms is named for someone significant in the innkeeper's life, and a picture of the special person decorates each room. Guests will enjoy the hearty breakfast, which changes daily. Several of innkeeper Jo Ann Celani's recipes have been featured in a cookbook, and one recipe won a blue ribbon at the Michigan State Fair.

Innkeeper(s): Jo Ann & George Celani. $75-125. MC VISA DS PC TC. 3 rooms, 2 with PB. 1 suite. Breakfast and evening snack included in rates. Types of meals: full breakfast and early coffee/tea. Beds: QT. Air conditioning and turndown service in room. Library on premises. Antiques, fishing, parks, shopping, golf and theater nearby.

Publicity: *Chronicle-Independent, Sandlapper, Southern Inns and B&Bs*

"You have captured the true spirit of a bed & breakfast."

Certificate may be used: Based on availability excluding race weekends.

Clio   B8

Henry Bennett House
301 Red Bluff St
Clio, SC 29525-3009
(803)586-2701

A huge veranda, decorated with whimsical gingerbread trim, rambles around the exterior of this Victorian, which was built by a cotton farmer. A

turret and widow's walk also grace the home. Clawfoot tubs and working fireplaces are some of the amenities found in the comfortable guest rooms. The area offers several golf courses and antiquing.

Innkeeper(s): Connie Hodgkinson. $50. MC VISA. 3 rooms. Breakfast included in rates. Type of meal: full breakfast.

Certificate may be used: March-December.

Columbia   D5

Chesnut Cottage B&B
1718 Hampton St
Columbia, SC 29201-3420
(803)256-1718

Circa 1850. This inn was originally the home of Confederate General James Chesnut and his wife, writer Mary Boykin Miller Chesnut. She authored "A Diary From Dixie," written during the Civil War but published posthumously in 1905. The white frame one-and-a-half-story house has a central dormer with an arched window above the main entrance. The small porch has four octagonal columns and an ironwork balustrade. Hearty breakfasts are served in the privacy of your room, on the porch or in the main dining room. The innkeepers can provide you with sightseeing information, make advance dinner reservations, as well as cater to any other special interests you might have.

Innkeeper(s): Diane & Gale Garrett. $65-150. MC VISA AX DC DS TC. 4 rooms with PB. 1 suite. Breakfast and evening snack included in rates. Types of meals: continental breakfast, full breakfast, gourmet breakfast and early coffee/tea. Picnic lunch and room service available. Beds: KQ. Air conditioning, turndown service, ceiling fan and VCR in room. Fax and bicycles on premises. Antiques, fishing, parks, shopping, sporting events, theater and watersports nearby.

Publicity: *TV show "Breakfast with Christie," Sandlapper, London Financial Times.*

"You really know how to pamper and spoil. Chestnut Cottage is a great place to stay."

Certificate may be used: Jan. 1-May 1, July 1-Aug. 31, Sunday through Thursday.

Dillon   C8

Magnolia Inn B&B
601 E Main St - Hwy 9
Dillon, SC 29536
(803)774-0679

Circa 1903. This handsome Southern Colonial-style home was built by a prominent local family who used long-leaf, heart-pine wood among other fine materials in the construction. Stately columns flank the entry. On the ground floor is a library, parlor and dining room where breakfast is served. The upstairs guest rooms feature handsome four-poster, white iron and oak beds.

Innkeeper(s): Alan & Eileen Kemp. $55-65. MC VISA. 4 rooms with PB, 4 with FP. Breakfast included in rates. Type of meal: full breakfast. Beds: QD. Air conditioning and ceiling fan in room. Cable TV on premises. Antiques, fishing, parks and sporting events nearby.

Location: Easy, quick access from Interstate 95.

Publicity: *Sandlapper.*

"Your home is beautiful and our first bed & breakfast experience has won us over to do it again and again."

Certificate may be used: Sunday through Thursday.

Georgetown   E8

1790 House B&B Inn
630 Highmarket St
Georgetown, SC 29440-3652
(803)546-4821 (800)890-7432

Circa 1790. Located in the heart of a historic district, this beautifully restored West Indies Colonial just celebrated its 200th birthday. The spacious rooms feature 11-foot ceilings and seven fireplaces,

three in the guest bedrooms. The inn's decor reflects the plantations of a bygone era. Guests can stay in former slave quarters, renovated to include a queen bedroom and sitting area. Each of the romantic rooms features special touches, such as the Rice Planters' Room with its four-poster, canopy bed and window seat. The Dependency Cottage is a perfect honeymoon hideaway with a Jacuzzi tub and a private entrance enhanced with gardens and a patio. The inn is located one hour north of Charleston and 45 minutes south of Myrtle Beach.

Innkeeper(s): John & Patricia Wiley. $80-130. MC VISA AX DS PC TC. 6 rooms with PB, 1 with FP. 1 cottage. Breakfast and evening snack included in rates. Type of meal: gourmet breakfast. Picnic lunch available. Beds: KQT. Air conditioning, ceiling fan and TV in room. VCR and bicycles on premises. Antiques, fishing, parks, shopping, theater nearby.

Publicity: *Georgetown Times, Sun News, Charlotte Observer, Southern Living. USAir, Augusta, Pee Dee, Sandlapper.*

"The 1790 House always amazes me with its beauty. A warm welcome in a lovingly maintained home. Breakfasts were a joy to the palate."

Certificate may be used: Anytime in December-February. Sunday-Thursday for March-November.

Ashfield Manor
3030 S Island Rd
Georgetown, SC 29440-4422
(803)546-0464

Circa 1960. Breakfast with many homemade items is served in guests' rooms, the parlor or on the inn's long, screened porch. Georgetown is conveniently located 30 miles from Myrtle Beach and 60 miles from Charleston. A beautiful public beach is 15 minutes away at Pawleys Island. Located on Winyah Bay, the town's seaport offers area restaurants with abundant fresh seafood. Many homes and churches date back to the 1700s and can be seen on a walking tour or by carriage or tour train. Also available are harbor tours that allow you to see Georgetown and its plantations from the water.

Innkeeper(s): Carol Ashenfelder. $50-65. MC VISA AX DC CB DS. 4 rooms. Breakfast included in rates. Type of meal: continental breakfast. Beds: Q. Air conditioning, ceiling fan and TV in room. Amusement parks, antiques, fishing, shopping and theater nearby.

Certificate may be used: Based upon availability.

Du Pre House
921 Prince St
Georgetown, SC 29442-3549
(803)546-0298 (800)921-3877 Fax:(803)520-0771

Circa 1740. The lot upon which this pre-Revolutionary War gem stands was partitioned off in 1734, and the home built six years later. Three guest rooms have fireplaces, and all are decorated with a poster bed. A full breakfast is prepared featuring such items as French toast, a variety of quiche, fresh fruit and home-baked muffins. For those who love history, Georgetown, South Carolina's third oldest city, offers more than 60 registered National Historic Landmarks.

Innkeeper(s): Marshall Wile. $75-115. MC VISA PC TC. 5 rooms with PB. Breakfast, afternoon tea and evening snack included in rates. Types of meals: continental-plus breakfast, full breakfast and early coffee/tea. Picnic lunch available. Beds: Q. Air conditioning, turndown service and ceiling fan in room. Cable TV, fax, copier, spa, swimming and library on premises. Amusement parks, antiques, fishing, parks, shopping, theater and watersports nearby.

Certificate may be used: Nov. 15-May 15, Sunday-Thursday.

King's Inn at Georgetown
230 Broad St
Georgetown, SC 29440-3604
(803)527-6937 (800)251-8805 Fax:(803)527-6937

Circa 1825. Enjoy the height of elegance, as well as basking in history at this Federal-style mansion. Union troops seized the house and used it as headquarters during the Civil War. The home boasts features such as magnificent moldings, crystal chandeliers, beautifully restored original floors and three, antique-filled parlors. Individually decorated guest rooms include luxurious items such as canopy beds, private piazzas or perhaps an in-room double Jacuzzi. In 1995, Country Inns magazine named King's Inn as one of the year's Top 12. Gourmet breakfasts are served in the garden breakfast room, which overlooks the lap pool. Tables are set with fine linens, china, silver and crystal. The beach and Brookgreen, one of the world's largest outdoor sculpture gardens, are nearby.

Innkeeper(s): Marilyn & Jerry Burkhardt. $85-125. MC VISA AX. 7 rooms with PB. Breakfast and afternoon tea included in rates. Types of meals: full breakfast and early coffee/tea. Picnic lunch available. Beds: KQDT. Cable TV, VCR, bicycles and child care on premises. Antiques, fishing, parks, shopping, sporting events and theater nearby.

"Wonderful effect in every room with the brilliant use of color."

Certificate may be used: Sunday-Friday, all year.

The Shaw House B&B

613 Cypress Ct
Georgetown, SC 29440-3349
(803)546-9663

Circa 1985. Near Georgetown's historical district is the Shaw House. It features a beautiful view of the Willowbank marsh, which stretches out for more than 100 acres. Sometimes giant turtles come up

and lay eggs on the lawn. Guests enjoy rocking on the inn's front and back porches and identifying the large variety of birds that live here. A Southern home-cooked breakfast often includes grits, quiche and Mary's heart-shaped biscuits.

Innkeeper(s): Mary & Joe Shaw. $55-70. PC TC. 3 rooms with PB. Breakfast included in rates. Types of meals: full breakfast and early coffee/tea. Evening snack available. Beds: KQT. Air conditioning, turndown service, ceiling fan and TV in room. Bicycles and library on premises. Amusement parks, antiques, fishing, parks, shopping, theater and watersports nearby.

Publicity: *Charlotte Observer, Country.*

"Your home speaks of abundance and comfort and joy."

Certificate may be used: Sunday-Friday, any time available. $65-$70.

Winyah Bay B&B

403 Helena St
Georgetown, SC 29440-4404
(803)546-9051 (800)681-6176

Circa 1984. Enjoy the breezes from the bay as you stroll down the longest private dock in South Carolina. A small private island is on the premises, as well. The innkeepers have decorated the rooms in bold, vibrant colors, and each room boasts a view overlooking the bay and a bathroom with skylights. The cupboards are stocked with breakfast goodies, and guests have access to a refrigerator, microwave and coffeemaker.

Innkeeper(s): Peggy Wheeler. $50-65. MC VISA TC. 2 suites. 1 cottage. Breakfast and evening snack included in rates. Type of meal: continental-plus breakfast. Picnic lunch available. Beds: KD. Air conditioning, ceiling fan, TV and VCR in room. Amusement parks, antiques, fishing, shopping and theater nearby.

Certificate may be used: January, February and March.

Marion   C8

Montgomery's Grove

408 Harlee St
Marion, SC 29571-3144
(803)423-5220 Fax:(803)423-5220

Circa 1893. The stunning rooms of this majestic Eastlake-style manor are adorned in Victorian tradition with Oriental rugs, polished hardwood floors, chandeliers and gracious furnishings. High ceilings and fireplaces in each room complete the elegant look. Guest rooms are filled with antiques and magazines or books from the 1890s. Hearty full breakfasts are served each day on the wraparound porches, and candlelight dinner packages can be arranged. Guests will appreciate this inn's five acres of century-old trees and gardens. The inn is about a half-hour drive to famous Myrtle Beach.

Innkeeper(s): Coreen & Richard Roberts. $70-100. 5 rooms, 3 with PB. 1 suite. Breakfast included in rates. Type of meal: full breakfast. Afternoon tea, dinner, picnic lunch, lunch and catering service available. Beds: KQ. Antiques, fishing, theater and watersports nearby.

Publicity: *Pee Dee Magazine, Sandlapper, Marion Star, Palmetto Places TV.*

Certificate may be used: Anytime.

McClellanville
F8

Laurel Hill Plantation
8913 N Hwy 17
McClellanville, SC 29458-9423
(803)887-3708 (888)887-3708

From the large wraparound porch of this plantation house is a view of salt marshes, islands and the Atlantic Ocean. A nearby creek is the perfect loca-

tion for crabbing, and there is a fresh-water pond for fishing. The home was destroyed by Hurricane Hugo, but has been totally reconstructed in its original Low Country style. It is furnished with antiques, local crafts and folk art. The inn has a gift shop that features books, antiques and decorative items.

Innkeeper(s): Jackie & Lee Morrison. $85-95. MC VISA AX DC DS PC TC. 4 rooms with PB. Types of meals: full breakfast and early coffee/tea. Beds: QT. Air conditioning and ceiling fan in room. Antiques, fishing, parks, shopping and watersports nearby.

Location: Thirty minutes north of Charleston on Hwy. 17, one hour south of Myrtle Beach.

Publicity: *Country Living, Seabreeze, Pee Dee, State.*

"We came in search of authentic Southern Living and we received more than we had dreamed."

Certificate may be used: November, December, January, February; Monday-Thursday.

Moncks Corner
E7

Rice Hope Plantation Inn
206 Rice Hope Dr
Moncks Corner, SC 29461-9781
(803)761-4832 (800)569-4038 Fax:(803)884-0223

Circa 1840. Resting on 11 acres of natural beauty, the inn is set among live oaks on a bluff overlooking the Cooper River. On the property are formal gardens that boast 200-year-old camellias and many old varieties of azaleas and other trees and plants. Nearby attractions include the Trappist Monastery at Mepkin Plantation, Francis Marion National Forest, Cypress Gardens and historic Charleston. Outdoor occasions are great because of the inn's formal gardens and the Cooper River backdrop.

Innkeeper(s): Doris Kasprak. $60-85. MC VISA AX. 5 rooms, 3 with PB. 1 conference room. Breakfast included in rates. Types of meals: continental-plus breakfast, full breakfast and early coffee/tea. Afternoon tea, lunch, gourmet lunch, banquet service and catering service available. Restaurant on premises. Beds: QD. Air conditioning and ceiling fan in room. Antiques and fishing nearby.

Location: Forty-five miles from Historic Charleston.

Certificate may be used: Monday-Thursday, all year, when rooms available.

North Augusta
E4

Rosemary & Lookaway Halls
804 Carolina Ave
North Augusta, SC 29841-3436
(803)278-6222 (800)531-5578 Fax:(803)278-4877

Circa 1902. These historic homes are gracious examples of Southern elegance and charm. Manicured lawns adorn the exterior of both homes, which appear almost as a vision out of "Gone With the Wind." The Rosemary Hall boasts a spectacular heart-of-pine staircase. The homes stand as living museums, filled to the brim with beautiful furnishings and elegant decor, all highlighted by stained-glass windows, chandeliers and lacy touches. Some guest rooms include Jacuzzis, while others offer verandas. A proper afternoon tea is served each afternoon at Rosemary Hall. The Southern hospitality begins during the morning meal. The opulent gourmet fare might include baked orange-pecan English muffins served with Canadian bacon or, perhaps, a Southern strata with cheese and bacon. The catering menu is even more tasteful, and many weddings, showers and parties are hosted at these inns.

Innkeeper(s): Renee Sharrock & Geneva Robinson. $125-250. MC VISA AX DC CB DS PC TC. 23 rooms with PB. 2 conference rooms. Breakfast and evening snack included in rates. Types of meals: continental-plus breakfast, full breakfast and early coffee/tea. Beds: KQDT. Air conditioning, turndown service and TV in room. Fax and copier on premises. Handicap access. Antiques, fishing, parks, shopping, sporting events and watersports nearby.

Certificate may be used: Jan. 3-April 1, April 20-Sept. 1, Sunday-Tuesday.

Rock Hill
B5

East Main Guest House
600 E Main St
Rock Hill, SC 29730-5325
(803)366-1161

Circa 1919. Although this Craftsman-style home was built at the turn of the century, its second floor remained unfurnished until the innkeepers acquired the home in 1990. Today, the upstairs offers three individually decorated guest quarters, including the

Bridal Suite, which boasts a canopy bed and whirlpool garden tub. The East Bedroom offers a fireplace, and the Garden Room affords a view of the back garden. The innkeepers serve a bounty of freshly baked breads and muffins for breakfast, and wine and cheese is offered in the evenings. The home is within walking distance of downtown Rock Hill.

Innkeeper(s): Jerry Peterson. $59-79. MC VISA. 3 rooms with PB, 2 with FP. Breakfast included in rates. Type of meal: continental-plus breakfast. Fax and copier on premises. Fishing nearby.

Certificate may be used: Sunday through Thursday (not Friday or Saturday nights).

Salem   B2

Sunrise Farm B&B
325 Sunrise Dr
Salem, SC 29676-0164
(864)944-0121

Circa 1890. Situated on the remaining part of a 1,000-acre cotton plantation, this country Victorian features large porches with rockers and wicker. Guest rooms are furnished with period antiques, thick comforters, extra pillows and family heirlooms. The "corn crib" cottage is located in the original farm structure used for storing corn. It has a fully equipped kitchen, sitting area and bedroom with tub and shower. The June Rose Garden Cottage includes a river rock fireplace and full kitchen, as well as views of pastoral and mountain views.

Innkeeper(s): Barbara Laughter. $75-100. MC VISA PC TC. 4 rooms. 2 cottages. Breakfast and evening snack included in rates. Types of meals: continental-plus breakfast and full breakfast. Picnic lunch available. Beds: Q. Air conditioning, ceiling fan, TV and VCR in room. Antiques, fishing, parks, sporting events and watersports nearby.

"Saying thank you doesn't do our gratitude justice."

Certificate may be used: Jan. 1-Dec. 31, Sunday-Thursday.

Sumter   D7

Magnolia House
230 Church St
Sumter, SC 29150-4256
(803)775-6694 (888)666-0296
E-mail: magnoliahouse@sumter.net

Circa 1907. Each room of this Greek Revival home with its five fireplaces is decorated in antiques from a different era. Also gracing the inn are inlaid oak floors and stained-glass windows. Sumter's historic district includes neighborhood heroes such as George Franklin Haynesworth, who fired the first shot of The War Between the States. Guests may enjoy an afternoon refreshment in the formal backyard garden. Breakfast is served in the large dining room with massive French antiques.

Innkeeper(s): Carol & Buck Rogers. $75. MC VISA AX PC TC. 5 rooms, 3 with PB. 1 suite. Breakfast included in rates. Types of meals: full breakfast, gourmet breakfast and early coffee/tea. Beds: QDT. Air conditioning, turndown service and ceiling fan in room. Cable TV, VCR and bicycles on premises. Antiques, fishing, parks, shopping, golf and theater nearby.

Certificate may be used: Anytime.

Union   B4

The Inn at Merridun
100 Merridun Pl
Union, SC 29379-2200
(864)427-7052 (888)892-6020 Fax:(864)429-0373
E-mail: merridun@worldnet.att.net

Circa 1855. Nestled on nine acres of wooded ground, this Greek Revival inn is in a small Southern college town. During spring, see the South in its colorful splendor with blooming azaleas, magnolias and wisteria. Sip an iced drink on the inn's

marble verandas and relive memories of a bygone era. Soft strains of Mozart and Beethoven, as well as the smell of freshly baked cookies and country suppers, fill the air of this antebellum country inn.

Innkeeper(s): Jim & Peggy Waller. $85-125. MC VISA AX DS PC TC. 5 rooms with PB. 3 conference rooms. Breakfast included in rates. Types of meals: gourmet breakfast and early coffee/tea. Afternoon tea, dinner, picnic lunch, lunch, gourmet lunch, banquet service, catering service, catered breakfast and room service available. Beds: KQT. Air conditioning, ceiling fan and TV in room. VCR, fax, copier and library on premises. Amusement parks, antiques, fishing, parks, shopping, sporting events and watersports nearby.

Certificate may be used: Jan. 15-Nov. 15, Sunday-Friday.

South Dakota

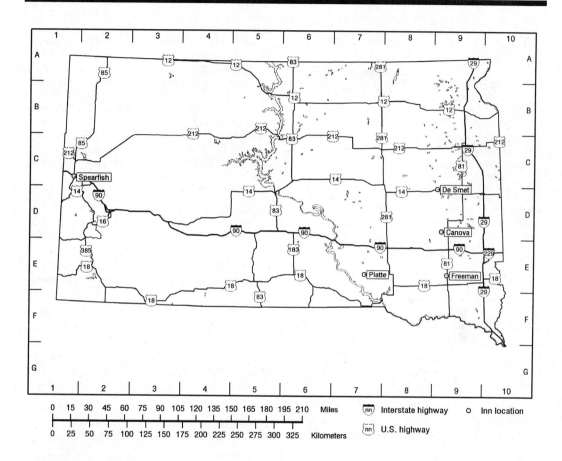

0 15 30 45 60 75 90 105 120 135 150 165 180 195 210   **Miles**

0 25 50 75 100 125 150 175 200 225 250 275 300 325   **Kilometers**

nn Interstate highway	o Inn location
nn U.S. highway	

Canova D9

B&B at Skoglund Farm

Rt 1 Box 45
Canova, SD 57321-9726
(605)247-3445

Circa 1917. This is a working farm on the South Dakota prairie. Peacocks stroll around the farm along with cattle, chickens, emu and other fowl. Guests can enjoy an evening meal with the family. The innkeepers offer special rates for families with children. The farm's rates are $30 per adult, $25 per teenager and $20 per child.

Innkeeper(s): Alden & Delores Skoglund.
$60. PC. 4 rooms. Breakfast and dinner included in rates. Types of meals: full breakfast and early coffee/tea. Evening snack available. Beds: QDT. VCR and library on premises. Antiques, fishing, parks, shopping, sporting events and watersports nearby.

Location: Southeast South Dakota.

"Thanks for the down-home hospitality and good food."

Certificate may be used: Anytime.

DeSmet D9

Prairie House Manor B&B

209 Pointsett Ave
DeSmet, SD 57231-9428
(605)854-9131 (800)297-2416 Fax:(605)854-9001

Circa 1894. Laura Ingalls Wilder wrote about the first owner of this house in her novel, "The Long Winter." The homey, country bed & breakfast offers rooms with items such as white iron beds, pedestal sinks and hardwood floors topped with rag rugs. In addition to the six rooms in the main house, the innkeepers also offer a cottage. Wilder was a resident of DeSmet, and the town features a church her father helped to build, as well as a schoolhouse where the author once taught.

Innkeeper(s): Larry & Connie Cheney. $59-79. MC VISA PC TC. 6 rooms with PB. 1 cottage. Breakfast included in rates. Types of meals: continental breakfast, full breakfast and early coffee/tea. Dinner and lunch available. Beds: KQDT. Air conditioning, ceiling fan, TV and VCR in room. Fax, bicycles and library on premises. Antiques, fishing, parks, shopping, cross-country skiing, golf, theater and watersports nearby.

Publicity: *Plainsman.*

"It was so much fun to stay in the prettiest house on the prairie."

Certificate may be used: May and September (all month); June, July, August-Sunday through Thursday only.

Platte E7

Grandma's House B&B

RR 1, Box 54, 721 E 7th St
Platte, SD 57369
(605)337-3589

Circa 1906. This Victorian farmhouse will stir memories of visits to Grandma. The interior is homey, done in a simple country style with antiques. The turn-of-the-century home maintains its original woodwork and a fireplace. The Prairie Queen room features a teal-blue satin bedspread with matching curtains of satin and white lace; an old sewing machine has been transformed into a sink. The Country Blue and Southern Rose rooms share a bath with a clawfoot tub. Breakfast menus feature items such as pancakes or French toast with eggs and bacon. Parks and a swimming pool are nearby, and guests can fish at the Missouri River, which is a 20-minute drive from the home.

Innkeeper(s): Delores & Albert Kuipers. $35-45. PC. 3 rooms, 1 with PB. Breakfast included in rates. Types of meals: full breakfast and early coffee/tea. Beds: QD. Air conditioning and ceiling fan in room. Cable TV and VCR on premises. Fishing, shopping, golf and watersports nearby.

Certificate may be used: Jan. 1-Oct. 10, Sunday - Thursday nights.

Spearfish C1

Eighth Street Inn

735 N 8th St
Spearfish, SD 57783-2147
(605)642-9812 (800)642-9812

Circa 1900. A mix of country furnishings and antiques, some of which are family heirlooms, create the warm, welcoming environment prevalent at this National Register home. Beds are covered with quilts, and rooms showcase the innkeepers' old family photos. Guest rooms are named in  honor of the innkeepers' grandparents. Breakfast are hearty, but include healthy offerings such as lean meats, fresh fruits and homemade breads.

Innkeeper(s): Brad & Sandy Young. $55-85. MC VISA TC. 5 rooms, 1 with PB. 1 suite. Breakfast included in rates. Type of meal: full breakfast. Beds: QD. VCR and spa on premises. Amusement parks, antiques, fishing, parks, shopping, downhill skiing, cross-country skiing, theater and watersports nearby.

Certificate may be used: Oct. 1-May 25, Sunday-Saturday.

Tennessee

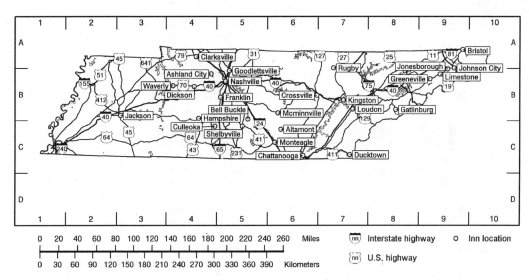

| 0 | 20 | 40 | 60 | 80 | 100 | 120 | 140 | 160 | 180 | 200 | 220 | 240 | 260 | Miles |

| 0 | 30 | 60 | 90 | 120 | 150 | 180 | 210 | 240 | 270 | 300 | 330 | 360 | 390 | Kilometers |

(nn) Interstate highway   o   Inn location

(nn) U.S. highway

Ashland City
B4

Bird Song Lodge
1306 Hwy 49 E
Ashland City, TN 37015-2848
(615)792-7928 Fax:(615)792-4005

Circa 1910. This rambling lodge-style house, in the National Register of Historic Places, was built with cedar logs by the Cheek family of Maxwell House coffee fame. Handsome furnishings and an art collection set off the chinked walls and beamed ceilings. The inn boasts a screened-in front porch, English gardens and green lawns. Hammocks swing underneath walnut and cedar trees, and there are

peach and pear trees on the 10 acres. Hike or picnic along Sycamore Creek, visit the barn or soak in the heated spa.

Innkeeper(s): Myrna & Jim Elmer. $90-100. MC VISA AX DS PC TC. 4 rooms, 3 with PB. 1 suite. Breakfast included in rates. Types of meals: full breakfast, gourmet breakfast and early coffee/tea. Evening snack, picnic lunch and catering service available. Beds: QD. Air conditioning and ceiling fan in room. Cable TV, VCR, fax, copier, spa and stables on premises. Antiques, fishing, parks, shopping and watersports nearby.

"Hands down, the best B&B we have ever stayed in! Wish we could come back every weekend."

Certificate may be used: Year-round except for holidays and weekends (Friday/Saturday) on a space available basis.

Bell Buckle
B5

Spindle House B&B
201 Hinkle Hill
Bell Buckle, TN 37020-0243
(615)389-6766

Circa 1920. This country home was built as a boarding house, and the innkeepers have hosted several of the former boarders as guests. Guests are encouraged to relax at this comfortable house. From the front porch, guests can rock away the hours and watch as rail cars pass. Each of the rooms has a different theme. The Sewing Room contains a dress form, while the Western Room commemorates the Native American and Cowboy traditions.

Innkeeper(s): Sue Thelen. $55-65. AX. 4 rooms. Breakfast included in rates. Types of meals: full breakfast and gourmet breakfast. Afternoon tea available. Beds: QDT. Fishing nearby.

Publicity: *Tullahoma News and Guardian.*

Certificate may be used: All months except August.

Bristol   A9

New Hope B&B
822 Georgia Ave
Bristol, TN 37620-4024
(423)989-3343 (888)989-3343

Circa 1892. Abram Reynolds, older brother of R.J. Reynolds, once owned the property that surrounds this inn, and one of the guest rooms is named in his honor. Each of the rooms has been creatively decorated with bright prints and cheerful wallcoverings, emphasizing the high ceilings and wood floors. Clawfoot tubs, transoms over the doors and distinctive woodwork are some of the period elements featured in this late Victorian home. Bristol is known as a birthplace for country music, and the innkeepers pay homage to the history with the whimsically decorated Tennessee Ernie Ford hallway. Ford got his start in Bristol, and pictures, record jackets, books and wallpaper fashioned from sheet music bedeck the hallway. The home is located in the historic Fairmont area, and a guided walking tour begins at New Hope. Half of the town of Bristol is located in Tennessee and the other half in Virginia.

Innkeeper(s): Tom & Tonda Fluke. $70-130. MC VISA PC TC. 4 rooms with PB, 1 with FP. Breakfast and evening snack included in rates. Types of meals: full breakfast, gourmet breakfast and early coffee/tea. Afternoon tea and room service available. Beds: KQT. Air conditioning, turndown service, ceiling fan and TV in room. VCR, bicycles and library on premises. Antiques, fishing, parks, shopping, downhill skiing, golf and theater nearby.

Publicity: *Tennessee Getaways.*

"It was like a second home in such a short time."

Certificate may be used: Jan. 15-March 30, Sunday-Thursday.

Clarksville   A4

Hachland Hill Inn
1601 Madison St
Clarksville, TN 37043-4980
(615)647-4084 Fax:(615)552-3454

Circa 1795. This log cabin contains a dining room and, in a stone-walled chamber, a place where pioneers sought refuge during Indian attacks. Three of

Clarksville's oldest log houses have been reconstructed in the garden where old-fashioned barbeque suppers and square dances are held. Newly built rooms are available in the brick building, so request the log cabin if you want authentic historic atmosphere.

Innkeeper(s): Phila Hach. $65. MC VISA AX. 20 rooms, 10 with PB, 3 with FP. 1 conference room. Type of meal: full breakfast. Beds: D. Fax on premises. Handicap access.

Location: Near Nashville.

Certificate may be used: Anytime if rooms available.

Crossville   B6

An-Jen Inn
RR 1 Box 594
Crossville, TN 38555-9700
(615)456-0515

Circa 1910. Innkeeper Sandra Monk-Goldston's family has lived on this 25-acre spread for seven generations. She was born in the turn-of-the-century house that now serves as a six-room bed & breakfast. She named her inn after two nieces, Andrea and Jennifer, and they each have a room named after them, as well. The inn is decorated in a nostalgic Victorian theme, with antiques and family pieces. In addition to the inn, Sandra operates the Fantasy Wedding Chapel in a adjacent building that resembles a tiny country church.

Innkeeper(s): Sandra & Ron Goldston. $60. PC. 6 rooms. Breakfast included in rates. Types of meals: full breakfast and early coffee/tea. Dinner, lunch and banquet service available. Beds: D. Air conditioning, turndown service, ceiling fan, TV and VCR in room. Spa and swimming on premises. Amusement parks, antiques, fishing, parks, shopping, sporting events, golf, theater and watersports nearby.

Publicity: *Tennessee Living.*

Certificate may be used: Anytime.

Culleoka (Columbia)   C4

Sweetwater Inn B&B
2436 Campbells Station Rd
Culleoka (Columbia), TN 38451-2304
(615)987-3077 (800)335-3077 Fax:(615)987-2525

Circa 1900. Surround yourself with the stunning Tennessee countryside at this rustic cedar ranch-style inn, which is right at home on 50 wooded acres, adjacent to the South Harpeth Creek. The guest rooms have been decorated masterfully by innkeeper Patsy Bruce. The decor is a sort of elegant country, comfortable yet sophisticated. Brightly patterned, antique quilts top the beds. Several guest rooms feature painted wood floors that resemble a checkerboard. Antiques, including a beautifully presented collection of handkerchiefs, are found throughout the inn. There is a western-style saloon at the inn, displaying items from Patsy's other career as a songwriter. She penned the famous tune, "Mamma, Don't Let Your Babies Grow Up to Be Cowboys." Nashville is nearby, but there is plenty to do in Franklin, which boasts specialty shops, restaurants and a myriad of antique shops.

Innkeeper(s): Sandy Shotwell. $100-135. MC VISA DS PC TC. 4 rooms with PB. 2 suites. Breakfast, afternoon tea and evening snack included in rates. Types of meals: full breakfast and gourmet breakfast. Picnic lunch, banquet service and catering service available. Beds: Q. Air conditioning, turndown service and ceiling fan in room. VCR, fax, copier and bicycles on premises. Antiques, fishing, parks, shopping, golf and theater nearby.

"Exceptional, beautiful, and so worthy of praise! It seemed a magical beginning to awaken in such a timeless place."

Certificate may be used: Sunday through Thursday, April 1-Sept. 30; Oct. 1-March 30, anytime.

Dickson   B4

The Inn on Main Street
112 S Main St
Dickson, TN 37055
(615)441-6879
E-mail: blashlee@worldnet.att.net

Circa 1900. Chimneys decorate both sides of this turn-of-the-century home, which offers verandas on both the first and second stories. Rooms are decorated with antiques. The Walker Suite is the grandest, and it's named for the home's first owners. The suite features a fireplace with the original carved mantel and mirror. The walls are painted a deep shade of red and the walnut bed is topped with a flowery country comforter. The bathroom includes a clawfoot tub. Among Dickson's attractions are the Ruskin and Jewel caves and antique malls. Nashville is within an hour of the home.

Innkeeper(s): Brett & Misha Lashlee. $55-85. MC VISA PC TC. 5 rooms, 4 with PB. 1 suite. Breakfast included in rates. Types of meals: continental-plus breakfast, gourmet breakfast and early coffee/tea. Afternoon tea available. Beds: KQDT. Air conditioning, ceiling fan, TV and VCR in room. Fax, library and pet boarding on premises. Handicap access. Amusement parks, antiques, fishing, parks, shopping, sporting events, golf and watersports nearby.

Publicity: *Dickson Herald*

"I can't think of a single thing you've missed. We enjoyed every minute of our stay here."

Certificate may be used: January-March, Sunday-Thursday only.

Ducktown   C7

The White House B&B
104 Main St, PO Box 668
Ducktown, TN 37326
(423)496-4166 (800)775-4166 Fax:(423)496-9778

Circa 1898. This Queen Anne Victorian boasts a wraparound porch with a swing. Rooms are decorated in traditional style with family antiques. Innkeepers pamper their guests with Tennessee hospitality, a hearty country breakfast and a mouthwatering sundae bar in the evenings. The innkeepers also help guests plan daily activities, and the area is bursting with possibilities. Hiking, horseback riding, panning for gold and driving tours are only a few choices. The Ocoee River is the perfect place for a river float trip or take on the challenge of roaring rapids. The river was selected as the site of the 1996 Summer Olympic Whitewater Slalom events.

Innkeeper(s): Dan & Mardee Kauffman. $60-70. MC VISA DS PC TC. 3 rooms, 1 with PB. Breakfast, afternoon tea and evening snack included in rates. Types of meals: full breakfast and early coffee/tea. Catering service and catered breakfast available. Beds: QT. Air conditioning and ceiling fan in room. Cable TV, VCR, fax and library on premises. Antiques, fishing, parks, shopping and watersports nearby.

Publicity: *Southern Living*

"We wanted a relaxing couple of days in the mountains and that's what we got. Thank you."

Certificate may be used: Sunday through Thursday, April-November. Everyday, December through March. Holidays and special events excluded.

Franklin   B5

Magnolia House B&B
1317 Columbia Ave
Franklin, TN 37064-3620
(615)794-8178

In summer, a blooming Magnolia tree shades the wicker-filled front porch of this gabled Craftsman cottage. The land is where the Battle of Franklin was fought. Furnishings range from 19th-century Victorian and Empire pieces to an Eastlake bedroom suite. The most popular breakfast here is Tennessee country ham, biscuits, cheese grits casserole and fresh fruit. An English flower garden and herb garden are in the back. Walk five blocks through a

maple shaded neighborhood of historic houses to downtown Franklin, 15 blocks of which are in the National Register of Historic Places.

Innkeeper(s): Betty Blankenship. $60-70. 3 rooms. Breakfast included in rates. Types of meals: full breakfast and early coffee/tea. Air conditioning, turndown service and ceiling fan in room. Cable TV and VCR on premises. Amusement parks, antiques, shopping and theater nearby.

Certificate may be used: Sunday through Thursday.

Namaste Acres Barn B&B

5436 Leipers Creek Rd
Franklin, TN 37064-9208
(615)791-0333

This handsome Dutch Colonial is directly across the street from the original Natchez Trace. As the B&B is within walking distance of miles of hiking and horseback riding trails, the innkeepers offer free horse boarding for their guests. Each of the suites includes private entrances and features individual themes. One room boasts rustic, cowboy decor with a claw-foot tub, hand-crafted furnishings, log and rope beds, and rough sawn lumber walls. The Franklin Quarters offers a sitting area where guests can settle down with a book from the large collection of historical material. The innkeepers chose the name Namaste from an Indian word, and carry an Indian theme in one of the guest rooms. Each of the quarters sleeps four comfortably. Namaste Acres is just 12 miles outside of historic Franklin, which offers plenty of shops, a self-guided walking tour, Civil War sites and the largest assortment of antique dealers in the United States.

Innkeeper(s): Lisa Winters. $65-80. MC VISA AX. 4 rooms. Breakfast included in rates. Type of meal: full breakfast.

Certificate may be used: Year-round, Sunday-Thursday.

Gatlinburg   B8

7th Heaven Log Inn on The Golf Resort

3944 Castle Rd
Gatlinburg, TN 37738-6321
(423)430-5000 (800)248-2923 Fax:(423)436-7748
E-mail: xg5f91a@prodigy.com

Circa 1991. Wake up to Eggs Benedict Mountain Style served on the deck among the tree tops and

you'll start to understand the inn's name. There are views of the golf course, dogwood trees, wild ducks and hummingbirds. Decks stretch for two stories all around the inn. Across the road is the Smoky Mountain National Park. Ride America's largest aerial tram, try the 1,800-foot Alpine Slide or hike and picnic in the Smoky Mountains.

Innkeeper(s): Cheryl & Donald Roese. $87-137. MC VISA PC TC. 5 rooms with PB. 1 suite. Breakfast and evening snack included in rates. Types of meals: full breakfast and early coffee/tea. Beds: KQD. Air conditioning and ceiling fan in room. Cable TV, VCR, fax, copier and sauna on premises. Amusement parks, antiques, fishing, parks, shopping, downhill skiing, sporting events, theater and watersports nearby.

Location: A short putt from the 7th green of Bent Creek Golf Resort.

"Five days was not enough. We'll be back."

Certificate may be used: Nov. 1-June 1, Sunday-Thursday, excluding holidays.

Goodlettsville   B5

Woodshire B&B

600 Woodshire Dr
Goodlettsville, TN 37072-2931
(615)859-7369

Circa 1850. A gentle gray and white salt-box house, the Woodshire also includes a reconstructed mid-19th-century log cabin. John's woodcrafts and Beverly's weavings and paintings add to the home's antiques to provide a warm and personal decor. Homemade breads and biscuits are offered at breakfast. Opryland is eight miles away.

Innkeeper(s): Beverly Grayson. $40-70. 3 rooms. Breakfast included in rates. Type of meal: continental breakfast. Air conditioning and TV in room. Amusement parks, antiques, shopping, sporting events and theater nearby.

Certificate may be used: Any Monday - Thursday nights, no weekends.

Greeneville   B9

Hilltop House B&B

6 Sanford Cir
Greeneville, TN 37743-4022
(423)639-8202

Circa 1920. Situated on a bluff overlooking the Nolichuckey River valley, this manor home boasts mountain views from each of the guest rooms. The Elizabeth Noel room, named for the original owner, includes among its treasures a canopy bed, sitting room and a private veranda, a perfect spot to watch the sunsets. After a hearty breakfast, take a stroll across the beautifully landscaped grounds. Innkeeper Denise Ashworth is a landscape architect and guests will marvel at her wonderful gardens. Ashworth sponsors several gardening workshops each year at the inn, covering topics such as flower arranging, Christmas decorations and landscaping your home grounds.

Innkeeper(s): Denise Ashworth. $75-80. MC VISA AX PC TC. 3 rooms with PB. Breakfast and afternoon tea included in rates. Types of meals: full breakfast, gourmet breakfast and early coffee/tea. Dinner, gourmet lunch and catering service available. Beds: KQD. Air conditioning, turn-down service, TV and VCR in room. Library on premises. Antiques, fishing, parks, shopping, golf, theater and watersports nearby.

Publicity: *Country Inns.*

"*Peaceful and comfortable, great change of pace.*"

Certificate may be used: January-April.

Hampshire B4

Ridgetop B&B
Hwy 412 W, PO Box 193
Hampshire, TN 38461-0193
(615)285-2777 (800)377-2770
E-mail: natcheztrace@worldnet.att.net

Circa 1979. This contemporary Western cedar house rests on 20 cleared acres along the top of the ridge. A quarter-mile below is a waterfall. Blueberries grow in abundance on the property and guests may pick them in summer. These provide the filling for luscious breakfast muffins, waffles and pancakes year-round. There are 170 acres in all, mostly wooded. Picture windows and a deck provide views of the trees and wildlife: flying squirrels, birds, raccoons and deer. The inn is handicap-accessible. The innkeepers will help guests plan excursions on the Natchez Trace, including biking trips.

Innkeeper(s): Bill & Kay Jones. $65-85. MC VISA PC TC. 1 room with PB, 1 with FP. 2 cottages. Breakfast included in rates. Types of meals: full breakfast and early coffee/tea. Beds: DT. Air conditioning and ceiling fan in room. Handicap access. Antiques, fishing, parks, shopping and watersports nearby.

Publicity: *Columbia Daily Herald.*

"*What a delightful visit! Thank you for creating such a peaceful, immaculate, interesting environment for us!*"

Certificate may be used: Nov. 15-March 15; July 6-Aug. 31.

Jackson B3

Highland Place B&B
519 N Highland Ave
Jackson, TN 38301
(901)427-1472

Circa 1911. This two-story house in the North Highland Historical District is five blocks from downtown. The inn is popular for bridal showers and dinners. There is a library and dining room where breakfast is served. The Hamilton Room features Chinese rugs and a wood-burning fireplace. The inn blends the old with the new, offering claw-foot tubs, tubs for two or a waterfall shower for two. Both the vacationer and corporate traveler will enjoy the amenities the inn offers. Corporate rates are available.

Innkeeper(s): Glenn & Janice Wall. Call for rates. 1 conference room. Antiques, shopping, sporting events and theater nearby.

Certificate may be used: Jan. 15-Dec. 15, Sunday-Saturday.

Johnson City A9

Hart House B&B
207 E Holston Ave
Johnson City, TN 37601-4612
(423)926-3147

Circa 1910. Antique shopping is a hobby of innkeepers Frank and Vanessa Gingras and this is evident in every nook and cranny of Hart House. The Dutch Colonial home is flanked by a wicker-filled porch complete with a swing, a perfect place to enjoy summer breezes. The cozy parlor and dining room each includes a fireplace, as does one of the guest rooms. Breakfast treats such as quiche, pecan pancakes or Belgian waffles are served up each morning along with a variety of fresh fruit and breads. Johnson City is near a variety of antique shops, an outlet mall and the Appalachian Trail.

Innkeeper(s): Francis Gingras. $60-65. MC VISA AX DS. 3 rooms with PB. Breakfast included in rates. Type of meal: full breakfast. Beds: Q. Antiques, fishing, downhill skiing, cross-country skiing, theater and watersports nearby.

Publicity: *Loafer.*

"*Impressive and charming throughout.*"

Certificate may be used: Anytime except first week in October.

Jonesborough B9

Aiken-Brow House
104 S 3rd Ave
Jonesborough, TN 37659-1006
(615)753-9440

Circa 1850. There's a beautiful gazebo on the grounds of this historic Greek Revival home, located a half-block from Main Street. There are porches for rocking and Victorian furnishings prevail. The inn is located in the Jonesborough Historic District.

Innkeeper(s): Calvin & Ann Brow. $65-100. TC. 3 rooms, 2 with PB. Breakfast included in rates. Types of meals: continental-plus breakfast, full breakfast and early coffee/tea. Beds: DT. Air conditioning in room. Cable TV on premises. Amusement parks, antiques, fishing, parks, shopping, downhill skiing, cross-country skiing, sporting events, theater and watersports nearby.

Publicity: *Blue Ridge, East Tennessee.*

Certificate may be used: All year, except Oct. 1-5, April 7-10, Aug. 25 & 26, Monday-Thursday.

Bowling Green Inn B&B

901 W College St

Jonesborough, TN 37659-5253

(423)753-6356

Circa 1772. Eleven acres surround this recently restored farmhouse that once was a stagecoach stop on the Old Stage Road between Bristol and Leesburg. Antique furnishings and country items decorate the inn. Jonesborough is Tennessee's oldest town and has retained its beautiful historic houses. Special events include a Civil War reenactment weekend with its Confederate Memorial Ball, quilting festivals, historic days and the National Storytelling Festival.

Innkeeper(s): Donna & Perry Cleveland. $50-60. MC VISA PC. 7 rooms, 1 with PB. 3 suites. Breakfast included in rates. Type of meal: full breakfast. Beds: QDT. Air conditioning, TV and VCR in room. Handicap access. Amusement parks, antiques, fishing, parks, shopping, sporting events, theater and watersports nearby.

Certificate may be used: Depending on availability, anytime except Aug. 25-26, Oct. 6-7, April 26-27.

Kingston   B7

Whitestone Country Inn

1200 Paint Rock Rd

Kingston, TN 37763-5843

(423)376-0113 (888)247-2464 Fax:(423)376-4454

E-mail: moreinfo@whitestones.com

Circa 1995. This regal farmhouse sits majestically on a hilltop overlooking miles of countryside and Watts Bar Lake. The inn is surrounded by 275 acres, some of which borders the scenic lake, where guests can enjoy fishing or simply communing with nature. There are four miles of hiking trails, and the many porches and decks are perfect places to relax. The inn's interior is as pleasing as the exterior surroundings. The guest rooms are elegantly appointed, and each includes a fireplace and whirlpool tub. Guests are treated to a hearty, country-style breakfast, and dinners are available by reservation. The inn is one hour from Chattanooga, Knoxville and the Great Smoky Mountains National Park.

Innkeeper(s): Paul & Jean Cowell. $85-125. EP. MC VISA PC TC. 12 rooms with PB, 12 with FP. 1 conference room. Breakfast included in rates. Type of meal: full breakfast. Dinner and picnic lunch available. Restaurant on premises. Beds: KQ. Air conditioning, turndown service, ceiling fan, TV and VCR in room. Fax, copier, spa, sauna and library on premises. Handicap access. Antiques, fishing, shopping, golf and watersports nearby.

"Not only have you built a place of beauty, you have

established a sanctuary of rest. An escape from the noise and hurry of everyday life."

Certificate may be used: Sunday through Thursday, Nov. 1-April 30, no discounts on weekends or from May 1-Nov. 1.

Limestone   B9

Snapp Inn B&B

1990 Davy Crockett Park Rd

Limestone, TN 37681-6026

(423)257-2482

Circa 1815. From the second-story porch of this brick Federal, guests enjoy views of local farmland as well as the sounds of Big Limestone Creek. The Smoky Mountains are seen from the back porch. Decorated with locally gathered antiques, the home is within walking distance of Davy  Crockett Birthplace State Park. A full country breakfast often includes Ruth's homemade biscuits.

Innkeeper(s): Ruth & Dan Dorgan. $65. MC VISA PC TC. 2 rooms with PB. Breakfast included in rates. Types of meals: full breakfast and early coffee/tea. Beds: QD. Air conditioning in room. Cable TV, VCR and library on premises. Antiques, fishing, parks, shopping, theater and watersports nearby.

Publicity: *Greenville Sun.*

Certificate may be used: Anytime, subject to availability.

Loudon   B7

The Mason Place B&B

600 Commerce St

Loudon, TN 37774-1101

(423)458-3921

Circa 1865. In the National Register, Mason Place received an award for its outstanding restoration. In the Greek Revival style, the inn has a red slate roof, graceful columns and a handsome double-tiered balcony overlooking three acres of lawns, trees and

gardens. There are 10 working fireplaces, a Grecian swimming pool, gazebo and wisteria-covered arbor. A grand entrance hall, fine antiques and tasteful furnishings make for an elegant decor, suitable for the mansion's 7,000 square feet.

Innkeeper(s): Bob & Donna Siewert. $96-120. PC TC. 5 rooms with PB, 5 with FP. Breakfast included in rates. Types of meals: gourmet breakfast and early coffee/tea. Afternoon tea and picnic lunch available. Beds: QD. Air conditioning in room. Cable TV, VCR, swimming, bicycles, tennis and library on premises. Amusement parks, antiques, fishing, parks, shopping, downhill skiing, cross-country skiing, sporting events, theater and watersports nearby.

Location: Smoky Mountains Cherokee National Forest.

Publicity: *Country Inn, Country Side, Country Travels, Tennessee Cross Roads, Antiquing in Tennessee, Knox-Chattanooga, Oak Ridge, Detroit Magazine.*

"*Absolutely wonderful in every way. You are in for a treat! The best getaway ever!*"

Certificate may be used: February-March, Monday-Thursday.

McMinnville B6

Historic Falcon Manor
2645 Faulkner Springs Rd
McMinnville, TN 37110-1193
(931)668-4444 Fax:(931)815-4444
E-mail: falconmanor@falconmanor.com

Circa 1896. Victorian glory is the theme at this restored manor, right down to the period clothing worn by the innkeepers during tours of their bed & breakfast. Museum-quality period furnishings fill each of the unique rooms, which are decorated in

traditional Victorian style. High ceilings, a sweeping staircase, chandeliers and white oak hardwood floors accent the decor. Relax on the wraparound porch with its comfortable rockers or learn of home's past from innkeepers George and Charlien McGlothin, who can tell a few ghost stories along with providing ample historical detail. Glorious full breakfasts are served each morning and evening refreshments and desserts are offered. The inn was the 1st prize winner of the National Trust for Historic Preservation's American Home Restoration Award in 1997.

Innkeeper(s): George & Charlien McGlothin. $75-105. MC VISA PC TC. 6 rooms, 4 with PB. Breakfast and evening snack included in rates. Types of meals: full breakfast and early coffee/tea. Banquet service and catering service available. Beds: KD. Air conditioning and ceiling fan in room. Cable TV, VCR, fax, copier and library on premises. Handicap access. Antiques, parks and watersports nearby.

Publicity: *Tennessee Magazine, Huntsville Times, Chattanooga Free Press, Country Extra, Preservation, Bob Villa's American Home, Mobile Register, PBS.*

"*Everything, from the absolutely beautiful rooms to the wonderful breakfast to the kindness and sincerity of the hosts, made our stay wonderful!*"

Certificate may be used: Sunday through Thursday year-round, subject to room availability.

Monteagle C6

Adams Edgeworth Inn
Monteagle Assembly
Monteagle, TN 37356
(931)924-4000 Fax:(931)924-3236

Circa 1896. This National Register Victorian inn recently has been refurbished in a country-chintz style. Original paintings, sculptures and fine antiques are found throughout. Wide verandas are

filled with wicker furnishings and breezy hammocks, and there's an award-winning chef who will prepare candlelit dinners. You can stroll through the 96-acre Victorian village that surrounds the inn and enjoy rolling hills, creeks and Victorian cottages. Waterfalls, natural caves and scenic overlooks are along the 150 miles of hiking trails of nearby South Cumberland State Park.

Innkeeper(s): Wendy Adams. $70-195. MAP, EP. MC VISA AX. 12 rooms with PB, 4 with FP. 1 suite. 1 conference room. Breakfast included in rates. Types of meals: continental breakfast and full breakfast. Dinner available. Beds: KQD. Air conditioning, ceiling fan and TV in room. VCR, fax and copier on premises. Handicap access. Antiques, fishing, parks, shopping, sporting events and theater nearby.

Location: On top of the Cumberland Mountains between Nashville & Chattanooga on I-24.

Publicity: *Country Inns, Chattanooga News Free Press, Tempo, Gourmet, Victorian Homes, Brides, Tennessean, Southern Living, PBS Crossroads, ABC TV, CBS TV, Inn Country, Travel Channel*

Certificate may be used: Jan., Feb. and March, Monday-Thursday.

Nashville   B5

The Hillsboro House
1933 20th Ave S
Nashville, TN 37212-3711
(615)292-5501

Circa 1904. The Hillsboro House is a cozy home base for guests wanting to experience the sites and sounds of Nashville. Vanderbilt University and famed Music Row are within walking distance from this Victorian home. After a dreamy night's sleep snuggled in a feather bed, guests are served a hearty homemade breakfast and head out for a day in Nashville, which offers a multitude of shops, outdoor activities and restaurants to explore.

Innkeeper(s): Andrea Beaudet. $95-105. MC VISA AX. 3 rooms with PB. Breakfast included in rates. Type of meal: full breakfast. Beds: Q. Antiques and theater nearby.

"This is the real thing, as fresh and welcoming as the ingredients in your fabulous breakfasts."

Certificate may be used: Sunday-Thursday, except during holidays and special events.

Rugby   A7

Newbury House at Historic Rugby
Hwy 52, PO Box 8
Rugby, TN 37733
(423)628-2430 Fax:(423)628-2266

Circa 1880. Mansard-roofed Newbury House first lodged visitors traveling to this English village when author and social reformer Thomas Hughes founded Rugby. Filled with authentic Victorian antiques, the inn includes some furnishings that are original to the colony. There are also several restored cottages on the property, and there is a two-room suite with a queen bed, two twin beds and a private bathroom.

Innkeeper(s): Historic Rugby. $62-84. MC VISA PC TC. 6 rooms, 4 with PB. 1 suite. 2 cottages. Breakfast included in rates. Types of meals: full breakfast and early coffee/tea. Afternoon tea, dinner, picnic lunch, lunch and banquet service available. Restaurant on premises. Beds: QTD. Air conditioning and ceiling fan in room. Library on premises. Antiques, fishing, parks, shopping and watersports nearby.

Publicity: *New York Times, Americana, USA Weekend, Tennessean, Southern Living, Atlanta Journal Constitution, Victorian Homes.*

"I love the peaceful atmosphere here and the beauty of nature surrounding Rugby."

Certificate may be used: Nov. 1-March 31, excluding Friday and Saturday nights.

Shelbyville   C5

Cinnamon Ridge B&B
799 Whitthorne St
Shelbyville, TN 37160-3501
(615)685-9200 Fax:(615)684-0978

Circa 1927. Tennessee offers many reasons to visit, not the least of which is this hospitable home. The light scent of cinnamon permeates the home, which is decorated with antiques in a mix of Colonial and Traditional styles. Innkeeper Pat Sherrill loves to pamper guests, especially with food. The full breakfasts are accompanied by candlelight and soft, soothing music. Pat serves afternoon teas and has created a few special events, including her Chocolate Lovers' Paradise, where guests enjoy a variety of cocoa-laden delicacies.

Innkeeper(s): Bill & Pat Sherrill. $55-65. MC VISA AX TC. 5 rooms with PB. 1 conference room. Breakfast, afternoon tea and evening snack included in rates. Types of meals: full breakfast and early coffee/tea. Beds: KQT. Air conditioning, ceiling fan and TV in room. VCR, fax and bicycles on premises. Amusement parks, antiques, fishing, parks, shopping, theater and watersports nearby.

Certificate may be used: Jan. 7-Nov. 13, Sunday through Wednesday.

Waverly   B4

Nolan House Inn
375 Hwy 13 N
Waverly, TN 37185
(615)296-2511

Circa 1870. This National Register home was built by prominent businessman James Nolan, who among his many occupations ran the Nolan House Hotel. The innkeepers have maintained Nolan's reputation for excellent hospitality at their Victorian-style inn, which features 19th-century furnishings throughout the home. The grounds boast walking trails, an old-fashioned stone fountain, gazebo and flower gardens.

Innkeeper(s): Linda & Patrick O'Lee. $60-75. PC TC. 3 rooms with PB, 3 with FP. 1 conference room. Breakfast included in rates. Types of meals: continental-plus breakfast and early coffee/tea. Afternoon tea available. Beds: QD. Air conditioning in room. Cable TV on premises. Antiques, parks and shopping nearby.

Certificate may be used: March through June.

Texas

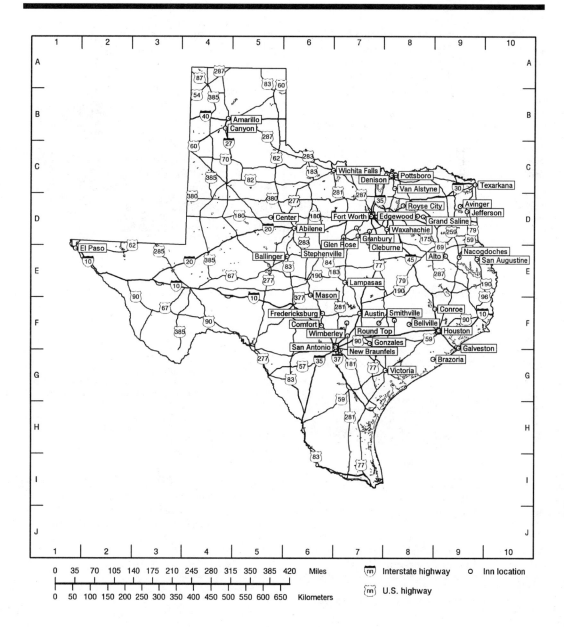

Miles
0 35 70 105 140 175 210 245 280 315 350 385 420

Kilometers
0 50 100 150 200 250 300 350 400 450 500 550 600 650

⟨nn⟩ Interstate highway   ○ Inn location

⟨nn⟩ U.S. highway

Abilene D6

Bolin's Prairie House B&B
508 Mulberry St
Abilene, TX 79601-4908
(915)675-5855 (800)673-5855

Circa 1902. This B&B was completely redesigned in 1920, omitting all references to the previous Victorian architecture and transforming into a prairie-style home. The home is filled with country antiques and knickknacks. Rooms bear the names Love, Joy, Peace and Patience, all clues to the relaxing, hospitable atmosphere. Peace includes a huge clawfoot tub.

Innkeeper(s): Sam & Ginny Bolin. $50-65. MC VISA AX TC. 4 rooms, 2 with PB. Breakfast included in rates. Type of meal: full breakfast. Beds: KQFT. Ceiling fan in room. Cable TV and VCR on premises. Antiques, fishing, parks, shopping, sporting events, theater and watersports nearby.

Certificate may be used: Sunday through Thursday.

Alto E9

Lincrest Lodge
Hwy 21 E, PO Box 799
Alto, TX 75925
(409)858-2223 Fax:(409)858-2232

The lush 16 acres surrounding this expansive Dutch Colonial Home overlook the Angelina River Valley. Many of the suites offer views of the beautiful valley. Hearty breakfasts are served each morning, and the porch cafe is a perfect place to enjoy the scenery

and a variety of deli treats. Box lunches can be prepared. The innkeepers serve an afternoon tea, which is followed on most nights by a country buffet dinner. The Alto area is an important historic area for Indian, Spanish and Texan colonization. Davy Crocket National Forest and Nacogdoches, the oldest town in Texas, are nearby attractions.

Innkeeper(s): Chester Woj. $75. MC VISA AX. 6 rooms. Breakfast included in rates. Type of meal: full breakfast.

Certificate may be used: All year, anytime, except Valentine weekend, Thanksgiving and Christmas weekends.

Amarillo B4

Parkview House B&B
1311 S Jefferson St
Amarillo, TX 79101-4029
(806)373-9464
E-mail: dia1311@aol.com

Circa 1908. Ionic columns support the wraparound wicker-filled front porch of this prairie Victorian. Herb and rose gardens, highlighted by a statuary and Victorian gazing ball, surround the property. Antique mahogany, walnut and oak pieces are found throughout. The French, Colonial, Dutch

and Victorian Rose rooms all feature draped bedsteads and romantic decor. Sticky buns, homemade granola and fruits are served in the kitchen or dining room. Guests can enjoy a soak under the stars in the inn's hot tub or borrow a bicycle for a tour of the historic neighborhood.

Innkeeper(s): Carol & Nabil Dia. $65-105. MC VISA AX PC TC. 5 rooms, 3 with PB. 1 suite. 1 cottage. Breakfast included in rates. Types of meals: continental breakfast, continental-plus breakfast, gourmet breakfast and early coffee/tea. Evening snack available. Beds: QD. Air conditioning in room. Cable TV, VCR, fax, computer and bicycles on premises. Amusement parks, antiques, parks, shopping, theater and watersports nearby.

Publicity: *Lubbock Avalanche, Amarillo Globe News, Accent West, Sunday Telegraph Review.*

"You are what give B&B's such a wonderful reputation. Thanks very much for the wonderful stay! The hospitality was warm and the ambiance incredible."

Certificate may be used: Anytime, excluding holidays or weekends, Christmas, New Year's, Valentine's, Memorial Day, Mother's and Father's Day, etc.

Austin F7

Carrington's Bluff

1900 David St
Austin, TX 78705-5312
(512)479-0638 (800)871-8908 Fax:(512)476-4769

Circa 1877. Situated on a tree-covered bluff in the heart of Austin, this inn sits next to a 500-year-old oak tree. The innkeepers, one a Texan, the other British, combine down-home hospitality with English charm. The house is filled with English and American antiques and handmade quilts. Rooms are carefully decorated with dried flowers, inviting colors and antique beds, such as the oak barley twist bed in the Martha Hill Carrington Room. After a hearty breakfast, relax on a 35-foot-long porch that overlooks the bluff. The Austin area is booming with things to do.

Innkeeper(s): Lisa & Edward Mugford. $69-99. MC VISA AX DC CB DS PC TC. 8 rooms, 6 with PB. 1 suite. 1 cottage. 1 conference room. Breakfast and evening snack included in rates. Types of meals: full breakfast, gourmet breakfast and early coffee/tea. Beds: KQDT. Air conditioning, ceiling fan and TV in room. VCR, fax, copier, library and child care on premises. Amusement parks, antiques, fishing, parks, shopping, sporting events, theater and watersports nearby.

Location: Downtown.

Publicity: *PBS Special.*

"Victorian writer's dream place."

Certificate may be used: Jan. 2-Dec. 24, Sunday-Thursday.

Governors' Inn

611 W 22nd St
Austin, TX 78705-5115
(512)479-0638 (800)871-8908 Fax:(512)476-4769

Circa 1897. This Neoclassical Victorian is just a few blocks from the University of Texas campus and three blocks from the State Capitol . Guests can enjoy the view of two acres of trees and foliage from the porches that decorate each story of the inn. The innkeepers have decorated the guest rooms with antiques and named them after former Texas governors. Several of the bathrooms include clawfoot tubs.

Innkeeper(s): Lisa & Edward Mugford. $69-99. MC VISA AX DC CB DS TC. 10 rooms with PB, 5 with FP. 1 conference room. Breakfast, afternoon tea and evening snack included in rates. Types of meals: full breakfast, gourmet breakfast and early coffee/tea. Picnic lunch, banquet service and catering service available. Beds: KQF. Air conditioning, turndown service, ceiling fan and TV in room. VCR, fax and copier on premises. Handicap access. Antiques, fishing, parks, shopping, sporting events, theater and watersports nearby.

Certificate may be used: Jan. 2-Dec. 24, Sunday-Thursday.

Woodburn House B&B

4401 Avenue D
Austin, TX 78751-3714
(512)458-4335 Fax:(512)458-4319
E-mail: woodburn@iamerica.net

Circa 1909. This stately home was named for Bettie Hamilton Woodburn, who bought the house in 1920. Hamilton's father was once the provisional governor of Texas and a friend of Abraham Lincoln. The home once was slated for demolition and saved in 1979 when George Boutwell bought the home for

$1, and moved it to its present location. A friendly dog greets guests, who will be taken immediately by the warmth of the home surrounded by old trees. The home is furnished with period antiques. Breakfasts are served formally in the dining room.

Innkeeper(s): Herb & Sandra Dickson. $79-89. MC VISA AX PC TC. 4 rooms with PB. Breakfast included in rates. Types of meals: gourmet breakfast and early coffee/tea. Beds: KQ. Air conditioning and ceiling fan in room. Cable TV, VCR and fax on premises. Antiques, fishing, parks, shopping, sporting events and theater nearby.

Publicity: *Austin Chronicle, Dallas Morning News.*

"The comfort, the breakfasts and the hospitality were excellent and greatly appreciated."

Certificate may be used: Sunday-Thursday, no holidays, excluding February, March, April, October & November.

Ballinger E6

Miz Virginia's B&B

107 S 6th St
Ballinger, TX 76821-5714
(915)365-2453 (800)344-0781

Circa 1886. Serving the community as a hotel and boarding house since before the turn of the century, this inn stands as one of the oldest buildings in town. An antique store and restaurant are now on the premises of the B&B. Guests can browse through collectibles. After getting a taste of shopping, there's more to be found in town with quaint shops of antiques, pottery, woodworking, arts and crafts. Courthouse Square hosts many festivities, including an annual Ethnic Festival and Christmas in Olde Ballinger.

Innkeeper(s): Juanita Chrisco. $45-65. MC VISA AX DS PC TC. 7 rooms, 2 with PB. 2 suites. Breakfast included in rates. Types of meals: full breakfast and early coffee/tea. Dinner available. Beds: D. Air conditioning in room. Cable TV, VCR and spa on premises. Amusement parks, antiques, parks, shopping, sporting events and watersports nearby.

Certificate may be used: Year-round.

Bellville   F8

High Cotton Inn
214 S Live Oak St
Bellville, TX 77418-2340
(409)865-9796 (800)321-9796 Fax:(409)865-5588

Use of the downstairs parlor, fenced swimming pool and bottomless cookie jar is encouraged at this Victorian B&B. Porch swings are strategically located on the balcony and front porch. There's a cozy upstairs sitting room for reading, television or conversation. Around 9 a.m. each morning, guests gather in the old family dining room for a full Southern-style breakfast. Innkeepers can provide information on excursions to Blue Bell Creamery, Winedale, Round Top and Festival Hill.

Innkeeper(s): Anna Horton. $50-60. 5 rooms. Breakfast included in rates. Type of meal: full breakfast. Air conditioning and ceiling fan in room. Cable TV on premises. Antiques nearby.

Certificate may be used: Sunday through Thursday.

Brazoria   G8

Roses and The River
7074 CR 506
Brazoria, TX 77422
(409)798-1070 (800)610-1070 Fax:(409)798-1070

Circa 1982. The San Bernard River provides the scenery at this farmhouse. Aside from the view on the home's wraparound veranda lined with rockers, a path leads to a riverside deck. A swing also hangs nearby from one of the many trees that grace the two acres. Bright, cheery rooms boast such names as New Dawn or Rise 'n' Shine, all rose varieties that grow in the area. Rainbow's End features window seats and a clawfooted, whirlpool tub. The breakfasts include anything from orange coolers to baked Alaska grapefruit to savory egg dishes. A historical museum, Varner-Hogg State Historical Park and a marine center all are nearby.

Innkeeper(s): Mary Jo & Dick Hosack. $94. MC VISA PC. 3 rooms with

PB. Breakfast and evening snack included in rates. Types of meals: full breakfast and early coffee/tea. Beds: Q. Air conditioning, turndown service, ceiling fan, TV and VCR in room. Fax and copier on premises. Antiques, fishing, parks, shopping, theater and watersports nearby.

Certificate may be used: Sunday through Thursday nights.

Canyon   B4

Country Home B&B
RR 1 Box 447
Canyon, TX 79015-9743
(806)655-7636 (800)664-7636

Circa 1989. This bed & breakfast is, as the title suggests, a quaint country home located on an acre of grounds that offer a restful porch swing and a gazebo. Each of the two guest rooms shares a bath with a clawfoot tub. Flowered prints, iron beds, candles, family heirlooms and antiques add to the country ambiance. Guests enjoy use of an outdoor hot tub. Homemade muffins, fresh fruit and specialties such as quiche often appear at the breakfast table.

Innkeeper(s): Tammy & Dennis Brooks. $70-85. MC VISA AX DS PC TC. 2 rooms. 1 cottage. Breakfast and evening snack included in rates. Types of meals: continental-plus breakfast, full breakfast and early coffee/tea. Beds: D. Air conditioning in room. VCR, spa and bicycles on premises. Amusement parks, antiques, parks, shopping and theater nearby.

Certificate may be used: October-April, Sunday-Thursday.

Historical Hudspeth House
1905 4th Ave
Canyon, TX 79015-4023
(806)655-9800 (800)655-9809 Fax:(806)655-7457
E-mail: hudspeth@juno.com

Circa 1909. Artist Georgia O'Keefe was once a guest at this three-story prairie home, which serves as a bed & breakfast. The home boasts many impressive architectural features, including an expansive entry with stained glass and a grandfather clock. The parlor boasts 12-foot ceilings and antiques, other rooms include chandeliers and huge fireplaces. Guests can arrange to have a candlelight dinner in their room.

Innkeeper(s): Mark & Mary Clark. $55-110. MC VISA AX DS PC TC. 8 rooms with PB, 5 with FP. 2 suites. 2 conference rooms. Breakfast included in rates. Type of meal: early coffee/tea. Beds: KQ. Air conditioning, ceiling fan and TV in room. Fax, copier and spa on premises. Amusement parks, antiques, parks, sporting events and theater nearby.

Certificate may be used: January, March, September, October, Sunday-Thursday only.

Center   D5

Pine Colony Inn
500 Shelbyville St
Center, TX 75935-3732
(409)598-7700

Circa 1940. This inn is a restored hotel with more than 8,000 square feet of antique-filled rooms. Artwork from local artist Woodrow Foster adorns the walls. These limited-edition prints are framed and sold by the innkeepers. The town is located between Toledo Bend, which has one of the largest man-made lakes in the United States, and Lake Pinkston, where the state record bass (just under 17 pounds) was caught in 1986. Ask the innkeepers about all the little-out-of-the-way places to see either by foot, bicycle or car.

Innkeeper(s): Marcille Hughes. $55-75. MC VISA. 10 rooms with PB. 4 suites. Breakfast included in rates. Types of meals: full breakfast and early coffee/tea. Air conditioning, turndown service, ceiling fan, TV and VCR in room. Amusement parks, antiques, fishing, parks, shopping, sporting events and watersports nearby.

Location: Near Louisiana border.

Certificate may be used: All days except Thanksgiving Day, Christmas Eve. All other days are acceptable.

Cleburne   D7

Anglin Queen Anne B&B
723 N Anglin St
Cleburne, TX 76031-3905
(817)645-5555

Circa 1892. This home, which was once owned by a cattle baron, is dominated by a three-story cupola set between two second-story porches. The first story includes a large round veranda with porch posts and gingerbread fretwork. The mansion's interior is embellished with wood paneling, molding and fancy carvings. Two main staircases have elaborate grillwork, paneling and stained glass. The dining rooms include a Northwind dining set, Oriental warlord's chair and a carved chair set from a European guest house.

Innkeeper(s): Billie Anne Leach. $49-149. 5 rooms. 1 suite. 1 conference room. Breakfast included in rates. Types of meals: continental-plus breakfast and early coffee/tea. Dinner, evening snack, picnic lunch, lunch, gourmet lunch, banquet service, catering service, catered breakfast and room service available. Air conditioning, ceiling fan and VCR in room. Amusement parks, antiques, shopping, sporting events and theater nearby.

Certificate may be used: Yearly.

Comfort   F6

Idlewilde
115 Hwy 473
Comfort, TX 78013
(210)995-3844

Circa 1902. This Western-style farmhouse and its cottages have come to be known as "Haven in the Hills." The home and surrounding grounds were a girls' summer camp for more than 60 years. The inn has no set check-in or check-out times. The innkeepers offer breakfast either in the main house

dining area or at your specified spot (which could be breakfast in bed). The large, unique hallways and center rooms are open and airy with lots of windows. Antiques and country French furniture decorate the entire lodge.

Innkeeper(s): Hank Engel & Connie Cazel. $77-93. MC VISA. 2 cottages, 1 with FP. 1 suite. 1 conference room. Breakfast included in rates. Type of meal: full breakfast. Picnic lunch available. Beds: Q. Amusement parks, antiques, fishing, shopping, sporting events and watersports nearby.

Location: Forty-five miles West of San Antonio.

Publicity: *Austin Chronicle, Hill Country Recorder.*

"Everyone should make a hobby of visiting B&Bs. Idlewilde should be at the top of their list."

Certificate may be used: Sunday through Thursday night, year-round, except holidays.

Conroe   F9

Heather's Glen . . . A B&B
200 E Phillips St
Conroe, TX 77301-2646
(409)441-6611 (800)66-JAMIE Fax:(409)441-6603

Circa 1900. This turn-of-the-century mansion still maintains many of its original features, such as heart-of-pine flooring, gracious staircases and antique glass windows. Verandas and covered porches decorate the exterior, creating ideal places to relax. Guest rooms are decorated in a romantic, country flavor. One room has a bed draped with a lacy canopy, and two rooms include double Jacuzzi tubs. Antique shops, an outlet mall and Lake

Conroe are nearby, and the home is within an hour of Houston.

Innkeeper(s): Ed & Jamie George. $65-95. MC VISA AX DS PC TC. 6 rooms, 5 with PB, 3 with FP. 1 suite. 3 conference rooms. Breakfast, afternoon tea and evening snack included in rates. Types of meals: full breakfast and early coffee/tea. Beds: QD. Air conditioning, turndown service, ceiling fan and TV in room. Fax, copier, sauna, library and pet boarding on premises. Handicap access. Amusement parks, antiques, fishing, parks, shopping, downhill skiing, sporting events, theater and watersports nearby.

Certificate may be used: Anytime except weekends and holidays.

Denison   C8

Ivy Blue B&B
1100 W Sears St
Denison, TX 75020-3326
(903)463-2479 (888)489-2583 Fax:(903)465-6773

Circa 1899. This Victorian charmer is set on a manicured lawn and shaded by several large trees. Guest rooms are named in honor of previous owners. Some of the furnishings and antiques that decorate the rooms are original to the home. Old newspaper clippings, antique dress patterns, historical documents and a time capsule are among the unique surprises guests might discover in their rooms. Fresh flowers, fragrant soaps and sachets add a touch of romance. Breakfasts are served on tables set with lace and antique china. Such items as banana almond waffles or bread pudding topped with berry sauce get the morning off to a great start. The inn's carriage house, which contains Lois' Cottage and the Feild Suite, is an ideal spot for children or for those who prefer a bit more privacy. Carriage house guests may opt to enjoy breakfast in their room.

Innkeeper(s): Lane & Tammy Segerstrom. $65-150. MC VISA AX DS PC TC. 6 rooms with PB. 3 suites. 3 cottages. Breakfast included in rates. Types of meals: gourmet breakfast and early coffee/tea. Evening snack and picnic lunch available. Air conditioning, ceiling fan and TV in room. VCR, fax, swimming and library on premises. Handicap access. Antiques, fishing, parks, shopping and watersports nearby.

Certificate may be used: Anytime except holidays

Edgewood   D8

Crooked Creek Farm
RR 1 Box 180
Edgewood, TX 75117-9709
(903)896-1284 (800)766-0790

Circa 1977. This traditional brick farmhouse, which is found in a rural community of 1,300, is nestled on the edge of the East Texas timberline. The farm covers more than 100 acres. Cattle are raised here and there are trees, creek, a nature trail, ponds and four fishing tanks on the property. A

hearty breakfast may feature country ham and bacon, eggs, biscuits and gravy and a fruit dish. In town, an ongoing bicentennial project includes a museum and 14 authentically restored and furnished structures representing rural life in 1900.

Innkeeper(s): Dorthy Thornton. $65-75. 6 rooms. Breakfast included in rates. Types of meals: full breakfast and early coffee/tea. Air conditioning and ceiling fan in room. Cable TV and VCR on premises. Antiques and shopping nearby.

Certificate may be used: All year, except "Canton Texas," first Monday weekend each month.

El Paso   E1

Sunset Heights B&B
717 W Yandell Dr
El Paso, TX 79902-3837
(915)544-1743 (800)767-8513 Fax:(915)544-5119

Circa 1905. This luxurious inn is accentuated by palm trees and Spanish-style arches. Inside, bedrooms are filled with antiques and boast brass and four-poster beds. Breakfast is a five- to eight-course feast prepared by innkeeper Richard Barnett. On any morning, a guest might awake to sample a breakfast with Southwestern flair, including Eggs Chillquillas and pit-smoked Machakas, a combination of smoked beef, avocado and onion. Juice, fresh

coffee, tea, dessert and fresh fruits top off the meal, which might begin with caviar and quiche. Enjoy the morning meal in the dining room or spend breakfast in bed.

Innkeeper(s): R. Barnett & Ms. R. Martinez, M.D. $75-200. MC VISA AX DS PC TC. 5 rooms with PB, 1 with FP. 1 suite. 1 cottage. 1 conference room. Breakfast included in rates. Types of meals: full breakfast and gourmet breakfast. Dinner and picnic lunch available. Beds: KQD. Air conditioning, turndown service, ceiling fan, TV and VCR in room. Fax, copier, spa and swimming on premises. Amusement parks, antiques, parks, shopping and sporting events nearby.

Location: Near downtown and the university.

Publicity: *Southwest Profile.*

Certificate may be used: Year-round, except holidays, Sun Bowl week, Christmas or New Year's week.

Fort Worth
D7

Miss Molly's Hotel
109 1/2 W Exchange Ave
Fort Worth, TX 76106-8508
(817)626-1522 (800)996-6559 Fax:(817)625-2723
Circa 1910. An Old West ambiance permeates
this hotel, which once was a house of ill repute.
Miss Josie's Room, named for the former madame,
is decked with elaborate wall and ceiling coverings
and carved oak furniture. The Gunslinger Room is
filled with pictures of famous and infamous gun-
fighters. Rodeo memorabilia decorates the Rodeo
Room, and twin iron beds and a pot belly stove
add flair to the Cowboy's Room. Telephones and
TV sets are the only things missing from the
rooms, as the innkeeper hopes to preserve the flavor of the past.
Innkeeper(s): Mark Hancock & Alice Williams. $75-170. MC VISA AX
DC CB DS PC TC. 8 rooms, 1 with PB. Breakfast included in rates.
Types of meals: continental-plus breakfast and early coffee/tea.
Restaurant on premises. Beds: TD. Air conditioning and ceiling fan in
room. Fax and copier on premises. Amusement parks, antiques, shop-
ping, sporting events and theater nearby.
Publicity: *British Bulldog, Arkansas Gazette, Dallas Morning News, Fort
Worth Star-Telegram, Continental Profiles.*
Certificate may be used: Year-round, Monday through Thursday,
excluding holidays and Stockyards annual special event dates.

Fredericksburg
F6

Allegani's Little Horse Inn
307 S Creek St
Fredericksburg, TX 78624-4652
(210)997-7448
Circa 1917. This historic ranch house is an ideal
way to travel with a family. The home offers two
bedrooms and a sleeping porch, as well as a fireplace
kitchen, living room and dining area. The front
porch includes a swing, and there's also a Jacuzzi
tub. Children and pets are welcome in this unit,
which is owned by Jani Schofield, the artist who
runs the Allegani's Sunday Haus. The Little Horse
Inn is just a few blocks from shops and restaurants.
Innkeeper(s): Jani Schofield. $85-150. 3 rooms. Breakfast included in
rates. Type of meal: continental breakfast.
Certificate may be used: Weekdays of January, February, May, August
and December, no event weekends.

Allegani's Sunday Haus
418 W Creek St
Fredericksburg, TX 78624-3114
(210)997-7448
Nearly a century ago, German ranchers and farmers
used a "Sunday house" as a place in town where
they could go and visit with their neighbors.
Allegani's Sunday Haus was used by Alfred Mohr
and his family, and the neighborhood is full of
German and Victorian flair. Innkeeper Jani
Schofield is a folk artist and created some of the furniture seen in the house. Lacy curtains, folk art,
antiques and hand-painted pieces add to the charming country decor.
Innkeeper(s): Jani Schofield. $65-95. 2 rooms. Breakfast included in
rates. Type of meal: continental breakfast.
Certificate may be used: January, February, May, August, September,
December. Not on event weekends.

Country Cottage Inn
249 E Main St
Fredericksburg, TX 78624-4114
(210)997-8549 Fax:(210)997-8549
Circa 1850. This beautifully preserved house was
built by blacksmith and cutler Frederick Kiehne.
With two-foot-thick walls, it was the first two-story
limestone house in town. The Country Cottage
holds a collection of Texas primitives and German
country antiques, accentuated by Laura Ashley
linens. Some of the baths include whirlpool tubs.
Full, regional-style breakfasts are left in each room.

Innkeeper(s): Mary Lou Rodriquez. $80-120. MC VISA PC. 4 rooms
with PB, 1 with FP. 2 suites. Breakfast included in rates. Type of meal:
full breakfast. Beds: KQD. Air conditioning, ceiling fan and TV in room.
Handicap access. Antiques, fishing, parks and watersports nearby.
Publicity: *Weekend Getaway, Dallas Morning News, Glamour, Texas
Highways.*

"A step back in time in 1850 style."

Certificate may be used: Year-round, Monday-Wednesday, excluding
holiday periods, spring breaks & local special events.

East of The Sun-West of The Moon
512 W Austin St
Fredericksburg, TX 78624-3210
(210)997-4981 (800)865-9668

Circa 1903. Having been recently remodeled to restore its charm and pioneer spirit, this yellow house has furnishings and decor that include an eclectic mix of Western, country antiques and a few contemporary pieces. Upon arrival, guests join the innkeepers for wine and cheese during a "get-acquainted time." Located one block north of Main Street, the inn is within walking distance of shopping, restaurants and entertainment. The living room has a wood-burning fireplace for cool, hill country evenings.

Innkeeper(s): Mark & Teresa Ray. $85. MC VISA TC. 2 rooms. Breakfast included in rates. Beds: QT. Air conditioning and ceiling fan in room. Cable TV on premises.

Certificate may be used: Sunday-Thursday, excluding holidays.

Fredericksburg (Luckenbach) *F6*

The Luckenbach Inn
HC 13, Box 9, Old Luckenbach Rd
Fredericksburg (Luckenbach),
TX 78624-9729
(830)997-2205 (800)997-1124 Fax:(830)997-1115
E-mail: theinn@luckenbachtx.com

Circa 1867. This rustic bed & breakfast inn actually is located about 10 minutes from Fredericksburg in the town of Luckenbach. The homestead originally belonged to Luckenbach's founding citizen, and his 1867 log cabin remains for guests to enjoy today. The cabin offers two bedrooms and a shared bath. Guests also can opt to stay in Old Smokehouse, another cottage. Other accommodations include two rooms and a suite. The suite has a full kitchen and private porch. The rooms offer a whirlpool tub, and one has a fireplace. Breakfasts are hearty and include items such as eggs Luckenbach, apple-smoked bacon, banana walnut pancakes, fresh fruit and other treats. The town is famous for its historic dance hall.

Innkeeper(s): Capt. Matt & Eva Marie Carinhas. $95-125. MC VISA AX DS PC TC. 6 rooms, 4 with PB, 2 with FP. 1 suite. 1 cottage. Breakfast included in rates. Types of meals: full breakfast and early coffee/tea. Beds: Q. Air conditioning and ceiling fan in room. Fax, copier and pet boarding on premises. Amusement parks, antiques, fishing, parks, shopping, golf and watersports nearby.

Publicity: *Dallas Morning News, San Antonio Express News, Southern Living Texas Vacation.*

"We had an excellent weekend at your inn."

Certificate may be used: Aug. 1-Sept. 30, Sunday-Thursday.

Galveston *F9*

Carousel Inn
712 Tenth St
Galveston, TX 77550-5116
(409)762-2166

Circa 1886. The Carousel Inn stands as a testament to Texas stamina. The home, located in a historic Galveston neighborhood, was one of a few left standing after a fierce storm ripped through the Gulf in 1900. The inn's namesake, a hand-carved carousel horse, decorates the parlor. The guest rooms are inviting with special touches such as leaf pine walls, a private porch swing or a roomy pineapple bed. The carriage house offers the added amenity of a sitting area, private entrance and antique walnut bed. The innkeepers offer a variety of home-baked treats each morning, served up in the cheerful breakfast room. The home is near many Galveston attractions including a rail museum, a tall ship and many shops and restaurants.

Innkeeper(s): Jim & Kathy Hughes. $80-95. MC VISA AX DS PC TC. 4 rooms with PB. 1 suite. Breakfast included in rates. Types of meals: continental-plus breakfast and early coffee/tea. Afternoon tea and picnic lunch available. Beds: KQD. Air conditioning and ceiling fan in room. Bicycles and library on premises. Amusement parks, antiques, fishing, shopping, theater and watersports nearby.

Certificate may be used: Sept. 15-April 15, subject to availability.

Michael's B&B
1715 35th St
Galveston, TX 77550-6717
(409)763-3760 (800)776-8302

Circa 1916. Built by Hans Guldman, Galveston's one-time vice-consul for Denmark, the massive red brick home sits on an acre of gardens that include Mrs. Guldman's greenhouse and fish pond. Guests can have breakfast in the formal dining room or in the sunroom overlooking the garden. The house holds a cache of family antiques with contemporary pieces and original art. Common rooms include a large dining room, parlor, sunroom and study. The home has been on Galveston's historic homes tour and garden tour.

Innkeeper(s): Mikey Isbell. $85. MC VISA. 4 rooms. Breakfast included in rates. Type of meal: full breakfast. Air conditioning and ceiling fan in room. Antiques and theater nearby.

Certificate may be used: Sunday-Thursday, anytime rooms are available April-September; anytime available during October-March.

Glen Rose
D7

Ye Ole' Maple Inn
PO Box 1141
Glen Rose, TX 76043-1141
(817)897-3456

Circa 1950. Pecan trees shade this comfortable home, which overlooks the Paluxy River. The interior is decorated with a variety of antiques, including a grandfather clock imported from Germany. The innkeepers also keep on display a Santa Claus collection. The fireplaced den offers a large selection of reading material. One of the bedrooms, decked in pink and gray hues, includes an iron and brass bed and wicker furnishings. The other features Victorian decor and a four-poster bed. Breakfasts include specialties such as oatmeal waffles with pecan sauce or an egg, sausage and apple casserole. Innkeeper Roberta Maple also serves up a mouth-watering selection of evening desserts such as peanut butter pie and Texas brownies.
Innkeeper(s): Roberta Maple. $65-80. MC VISA AX PC TC. 2 rooms with PB. Breakfast and evening snack included in rates. Type of meal: full breakfast. Beds: Q. Ceiling fan in room. Cable TV, VCR and library on premises. Handicap access. Antiques, fishing, shopping, theater and watersports nearby.

Certificate may be used: All year, Monday through Thursday; on weekends, January through March.

Gonzales
F7

St. James Inn
723 Saint James St
Gonzales, TX 78629-3411
(210)672-7066 Fax:(210)672-7787

Circa 1914. Ann and J.R. Covert spent three years restoring this massive Texas Hill Country mansion, once owned by a cattle baron. On the main floor is a tiled solarium, living room, reception hall, dining room, butler's pantry and kitchen. The second-floor guest rooms all have working

fireplaces and porches. The top-level room is a unique wind tunnel—a long crawl space with windows on either end—which provides natural air conditioning. Gourmet candlelight dinners are available in addition to the full breakfasts.
Innkeeper(s): Ann & J.R. Covert. $75-100. MC VISA AX PC TC. 5 rooms, 4 with PB, 5 with FP. 2 suites. 1 conference room. Breakfast and afternoon tea included in rates. Types of meals: full breakfast, gourmet breakfast and early coffee/tea. Dinner, picnic lunch, lunch, gourmet lunch and banquet service available. Beds: KQ. Air conditioning, turndown service, ceiling fan and TV in room. Antiques, fishing, parks, shopping, theater and watersports nearby.
Location: One hour east of San Antonio, one hour south of Austin.
Publicity: *Gonzales Inquirer, Houston Chronicle, Victoria Advocate, Austin American Statesman, San Antonio Express-News.*

"We had a wonderful weekend. It's a marvelous home and your hospitality is superb. We'll be back."

Certificate may be used: January-August.

Granbury
D7

Dabney House B&B
106 S Jones St
Granbury, TX 76048-1905
(817)579-1260 (800)566-1260 Fax:(817)579-0426

Circa 1907. Built during the Mission Period, this Craftsman-style country manor boasts original hard-

wood floors, stained-glass windows and some of the original light fixtures. The parlor and dining rooms have large, exposed, wooden beams and the ceilings throughout are 10-feet high. The Dabney Suite has a private entrance into an enclosed sun porch with rattan table and chairs that allow for a private breakfast. The bedroom of this suite is furnished with a four-post tester bed with drapes and an 1800 dresser.
Innkeeper(s): John & Gwen Hurley. $70-105. MC VISA AX PC TC. 4 rooms with PB. 1 suite. Breakfast and evening snack included in rates. Type of meal: full breakfast. Dinner available. Beds: Q. Air conditioning and ceiling fan in room. VCR, spa and library on premises. Antiques, fishing, parks, shopping, theater and watersports nearby.
Publicity: *Fort Worth Star Telegram, Dallas Morning News.*

"Very enjoyable and certainly up among the very best of the B&Bs you are likely to find in the United Kingdom. It reminded me of staying at grandma's house. Thanks for bringing back such warm memories."

Certificate may be used: Sunday through Thursday, all year, does not apply on major holidays or special events.

Pearl Street Inn B&B
319 W Pearl St
Granbury, TX 76048-2437
(817)579-7465 (888)732-7578

Circa 1912. Known historically as the B. M. Estes House, the inn is decorated with a mix of English, French and American antiques. The English Garden Suite is fashioned in a green, peach and ivy motif and features a king-size iron and brass bed,

English antique furniture, airy sitting room and full bath accented by a cast iron tub and 1912 wall sink. Other guest rooms include clawfoot tubs, crystal lamps and lace.

Innkeeper(s): Danette D. Hebda. $59-108. PC TC. 5 rooms with PB. 1 suite. Breakfast included in rates. Types of meals: full breakfast, gourmet breakfast and early coffee/tea. Beds: KD. Air conditioning and ceiling fan in room. VCR and copier on premises. Antiques, fishing, parks, shopping, theater and watersports nearby.
Publicity: *Dallas Morning News, New York Times, Fort Worth Star Telegram.*

"Needless to say, we want to stay forever! We had a grand time and highly enjoyed conversations and hospitality."

Certificate may be used: Sunday-Thursday, excluding special events.

Grand Saline   D8

BailiTeal Farm
RR 3, Box 379
Grand Saline, TX 75140-9803
(903)962-4475 (800)875-4874 Fax:(903)962-4475

Circa 1994. Although new, the two homes that comprise this bed & breakfast are replicas of an old Texas farmhouse and a barn. The barn house includes three rooms. The Wildflower Suite is the largest and can accommodate up to five guests. The suite includes a TV, VCR, antique tub and living

room. The two other rooms have access to a parlor with a wood-burning stove, piano and television. In the main house, there are two guest rooms, one with a clawfoot tub. These two rooms also share a small parlor. The decor is country, one room includes an iron bed, another features a bed topped with a fluffy blue and white flower comforter with matching wallpapers. There are 20 acres to explore, or one can enjoy the view of rolling farm on the inn's vast porches. Take a walk on a nature trail, enjoy a picnic or reel in a catfish from the inn's stocked pond.

Innkeeper(s): Judson & Dian Bailiff. $60-75. MC VISA AX PC. 7 rooms, 4 with PB. 1 suite. Breakfast included in rates. Types of meals: continental breakfast, full breakfast, gourmet breakfast and early coffee/tea. Dinner, evening snack, picnic lunch, lunch and gourmet lunch available. Beds: QDT. Air conditioning, turndown service, ceiling fan and VCR in room. Fax, copier and library on premises. Antiques, fishing, shopping, golf and theater nearby.

"The tour of the grounds with all the beauty of nature and the work you have done is outstanding."

Certificate may be used: Anytime except the Thursday-Saturday preceding the first Monday of each month.

Houston   F9

Angel Arbor B&B Inn
848 Heights Blvd
Houston, TX 77007-1507
(713)868-4654

Circa 1922. Each of the rooms at Angel Arbor has a heavenly name and elegant decor. The Angelique Room offers a cherry sleigh bed and a balcony overlooking the garden. Canopy or poster beds grace the other rooms and suite, named Gabriel, Raphael and Michael. The Georgian-style home is located in the historic Houston Heights neighborhood and was built by a prominent local family. The innkeeper, a cookbook author, prepares a mouthwatering homemade breakfast each morning. Ask about the innkeeper's special murder-mystery dinner parties.

Innkeeper(s): Marguerite Swanson. $100-119. MC VISA AX DS PC TC. 4 rooms with PB. 1 suite. 1 conference room. Breakfast included in rates. Types of meals: full breakfast, gourmet breakfast and early coffee/tea. Afternoon tea available. Beds: Q. Air conditioning, turndown service, ceiling fan, TV and VCR in room. Fax, copier and library on premises. Amusement parks, antiques, fishing, parks, shopping, sporting events, theater and watersports nearby.

Certificate may be used: Jan. 2-Dec. 15, Sunday-Friday.

Robin's Nest
4104 Greeley St
Houston, TX 77006-5609
(713)528-5821 (800)622-8343 Fax:(713)942-8297

Circa 1898. Legend denotes this former dairy farm as one of the oldest homes in Houston. The two-story wooden Queen Anne features original pine hardwoods, tall windows and fine fabrics. The beautifully landscaped grounds are another memorable feature. Guests will appreciate the inn's proximity to downtown Houston, theaters and gourmet restaurants. Located in the Montrose area of the city, the inn is less than an hour from popular attractions such as NASA and Galveston.

Innkeeper(s): Robin Smith. $65-110. MC VISA AX CB DS. 4 rooms with PB. 1 conference room. Breakfast included in rates. Type of meal: full breakfast. Beds: QDT. Air conditioning, ceiling fan and TV in room. Amusement parks, antiques, fishing, shopping, sporting events, theater and watersports nearby.

Location: Inside 610 Loop very near downtown, Brown Convention Center and Texas Medical Center. The inn is in the Museum and Arts District.

Publicity: *Houston Home and Garden, Houston Business Journal, Woman's Day, Houston Metropolitan, Houston Post, Southern Living, Texas Monthly, Houston Chronicle.*

"Fanciful and beautiful, comfortable and happy. We saw a whole new side of Houston, thanks to you."

Certificate may be used: Sunday-Thursday, all year.

Jefferson   D9

McKay House
306 E Delta St
Jefferson, TX 75657-2026
(903)665-7322 (800)468-2627

Circa 1851. Both Lady Bird Johnson and Alex Haley have enjoyed the gracious Southern hospitality offered at the McKay House. Accented by a Williamsburg-style picket fence, the Greek Revival cottage features a pillared front porch. Heart-of-pine floors, 14-foot ceilings and documented wallpapers complement antique furnishings. Orange and pecan French toast or home-baked muffins and shirred eggs are served on vintage china. Victorian nightshirts and gowns await guests in each of the bedchambers. A "gentleman's" style breakfast is served.

Innkeeper(s): Joseph & Alma Anne Parker. $80-145. MC VISA AX PC TC. 8 rooms, 7 with PB, 6 with FP. 3 suites. 1 cottage. 1 conference room. Breakfast included in rates. Types of meals: gourmet breakfast and early coffee/tea. Beds: QD. Air conditioning, ceiling fan and TV in room. Antiques, fishing, parks, shopping, theater and watersports nearby.

Publicity: *Southern Accents, Dallas Morning News, Country Home, Bride.*

"The facilities of the McKay House are exceeded only by the service and dedication of the owners."

Certificate may be used: Sunday through Thursday, not including Spring Break or festivals/holidays; space available, reserved one week in advance please.

Pride House
409 Broadway
Jefferson, TX 75657
(800)894-3526 Fax:(903)665-3901

Circa 1889. Mr. Brown, a sawmill owner, built this Victorian house using fine hardwoods, sometimes three layers deep. The windows are nine-feet tall on both the lower level and upstairs. The rooms include amenities such as fireplaces, balconies, canopy beds and private entrances. Most boasts original stained-glass windows. The West Room is decorated in crimson reds and features a gigantic clawfoot tub that has received an award from Houston Style Magazine for "best tub in Texas." A wide veranda stretches around two sides of the house.

Innkeeper(s): Carol Abernathy & Christel Frederick. $75-110. MC VISA PC TC. 10 rooms with PB, 3 with FP. 1 suite. 1 cottage. Breakfast and evening snack included in rates. Types of meals: gourmet breakfast and early coffee/tea. Beds: KQDT. Air conditioning and ceiling fan in room. Handicap access. Antiques, fishing and theater nearby.

Publicity: *Woman's Day, Country Home, Texas Highways, Texas Homes.*

"No five star hotel can compare to the hospitality of Pride House."

Certificate may be used: Sunday-Thursday & some Fridays, except local and national holidays.

Lake O' The Pines

McKenzie Manor
Woodland Shore, Hwy 729
Lake O' The Pines, TX 75630
(903)755-2240

Circa 1964. Nature trails with private ponds are right outside the door of this rustic, rock lodge set on the shore of Lake O' The Pines. Guests can sit on wide decks and watch eagles soar, beavers build dams and deer graze. Relax in the gazebo or by the large rock fireplace with a good book from the private library of innkeeper, historian and author Fred McKenzie. This four-generation family home is

designed with a large meeting room, vaulted ceilings and stained-glass windows. All rooms are adjacent to sitting areas and each room is decorated in its own unique style with antiques and family possessions. Innkeeper(s): Anne & Fred McKenzie. $65-95. MC VISA PC TC. 7 rooms, 5 with PB, 1 with FP. 1 suite. 1 conference room. Breakfast and afternoon tea included in rates. Types of meals: continental-plus breakfast, full breakfast and early coffee/tea. Catering service available. Beds: KQD. Air conditioning and ceiling fan in room. Cable TV, swimming and library on premises. Handicap access. Antiques, fishing, shopping, theater and watersports nearby.

Certificate may be used: Jan. 10 through Dec. 20.

Lampasas   E7

Historic Moses Hughes B&B

RR 2 Box 31

Lampasas, TX 76550-9601

(512)556-5923

Circa 1856. Nestled among ancient oaks in the heart of the Texas Hill Country, this native stone ranch house rests on 45 acres that include springs, a creek, wildlife and other natural beauty. The ranch

was built by Moses Hughes, the first white settler and founder of Lampasas. He and his wife decided to stay in the area after her health dramatically improved after visiting the springs. Guests can join the innkeepers on the stone patio or upstairs wooden porch for a taste of Texas Hill Country life. Innkeeper(s): Al & Beverly Solomon. $75-85. PC. 2 rooms with PB. Breakfast included in rates. Types of meals: full breakfast and gourmet breakfast. Beds: D. Air conditioning in room. VCR and library on premises. Antiques, fishing, parks and watersports nearby.

Publicity: *Dallas Morning News, Spiegel Catalog, Discover.*

"What a delightful respite! Thank you for sharing your very interesting philosophies and personalities with us at this very special B&B. We hate to leave."

Certificate may be used: Year-round, Sunday-Thursday, no holidays.

Mason   E6

Hasse House and Ranch

1221 Ischar St, PO Box 58

Mason, TX 76856

(888)414-2773

Circa 1883. Guests may explore the 320-acre Hasse ranch, which is a working ranch where deer, wild turkey, feral hogs and quail are common sights. After purchasing the land, Henry Hasse and his wife

lived in a log cabin on the property before building the sandstone home 23 years later. Three generations of Hasses have lived here, and today it is owned by a great-granddaughter who restored the home in 1980. The inn is located in the small German village of Art, Texas, which is located six miles east of Mason. The innkeepers rent the two-bedroom National Register home out to only one group or guest at a time, host free. The home is filled with period furniture and accessories, yet offers the modern convenience of an on-site washer and dryer and a fully stocked kitchen. The ranch grounds include a two-mile nature trail perfect for nature lovers. Innkeeper(s): Laverne Lee. $95. MC VISA PC TC. 2 rooms with PB. Breakfast included in rates. Type of meal: continental-plus breakfast. Beds: D. Air conditioning, ceiling fan and VCR in room. Library on premises. Handicap access. Antiques, fishing, parks, shopping and watersports nearby.

"We enjoyed every aspect of our stay; the atmosphere, sense of history, rustic setting with a touch of class. We would love to return the same time next year!"

Certificate may be used: Anytime except holidays.

Mason Square B&B

134 Ft McKavett, PO Box 298

Mason, TX 76856

(915)347-6398 (800)369-0405 Fax:(915)347-6398

Circa 1901. A fine collection of framed, historically significant maps of Texas and the Southwest that span centuries of discovery and settlement are throughout the guest rooms and hallway of this inn. Located on the second floor of a historic commercial building, the B&B has original pressed-tin ceilings, Victorian woodwork and doors, stained-glass transoms and oak floors. Guests can step outside for a stroll down memory lane as the inn is part of the courthouse square with buildings dating from 1879. Several antique shops, galleries and some local businesses have occupied the same buildings for generations.

Innkeeper(s): Brent Hinckley. $45-60. 3 rooms. Breakfast included in rates. Type of meal: continental-plus breakfast. Air conditioning and ceiling fan in room. VCR on premises. Antiques nearby.

Certificate may be used: All times, except holidays.

Nacogdoches   E9

Llano Grande Plantation
RR 4 Box 9400
Nacogdoches, TX 75964-9276
(409)569-1249
E-mail: 73717.2542@compuserv.com

Circa 1840. A collection of lodgings sit on this 600-acre property of creeks and pine forest. The accommodations are located on what was called the Llano Grande land grant, given to Pedro Jose Esparza in 1779. Among the buildings is the Tol Barret House, which dates to 1840, and is both a Texas Historic Landmark and listed in the National Register. This home includes a bedroom with four beds, as well as a kitchen and fireplace. The Sparks House, which dates to the mid-1800s, is another option. The Texas Landmark home has two bedrooms, fireplace, woodburning stove and sitting area. Also available is the Gate House, which is a Texas-style farmhouse with two bedrooms, kitchen and fireplace. There is also an Antebellum plantation home. In all of the homes, carefully chosen antiques resemble those of the original owners.

Innkeeper(s): Captain Charles & Ann Phillips. $60-95. PC TC. 3 suites, 3 with FP. Breakfast included in rates. Types of meals: continental-plus breakfast and full breakfast. Afternoon tea and catering service available. Air conditioning in room. Antiques, fishing, parks, shopping, sporting events, theater and watersports nearby.

Certificate may be used: April to Feb. 28, Sunday-Thursday, except local college (SFASU) events (homecoming, parents weekend, etc.).

New Braunfels   F7

The Rose Garden B&B
195 S Academy Ave
New Braunfels, TX 78130-5607
(210)629-3296

Circa 1930. In a town full of rich German heritage, this Colonial Revival inn features designer bedrooms, fluffy towels, scented soaps and potpourri-

filled rooms. Take a stroll along the cool, Comal Springs or browse antique shops, which are all within walking distance. Relax in the parlor by the fireplace or in the rose garden. Breakfast is served in the formal dining room, garden or brought to your room on a specially prepared tray. The inn is only one block from downtown.

Innkeeper(s): Dawn Mann. $75-105. 2 rooms with PB. Breakfast included in rates. Types of meals: full breakfast and early coffee/tea. Beds: Q. Turndown service and ceiling fan in room. Antiques, fishing, shopping, theater and watersports nearby.

Publicity: *Herald-Zeitung.*

"A getaway to a B&B like yours truly revitalizes the spirit and was just what we were looking for. The food was delicious and beautifully presented."

Certificate may be used: Monday-Thursday (year-round), excluding holidays and special events.

New Braunfels (Canyon Lake)   F7

Aunt Nora's B&B
120 Naked Indian Tr
New Braunfels (Canyon Lake), TX 78132
(210)905-3989 (800)687-2887

Circa 1983. Nestled on four acres, amid oak, cedar and Indian trees, this Texas country bed & breakfast has many nearby scenic areas that include a walk to the top of the hill to view Canyon Lake. The sitting room is a perfect place to relax among handmade furnishings, antiques, paintings, lacy crafts, a wood stove and natural wood floors. Enjoy the private collection of Pigtails & Lace hand-crafted dolls. The guest rooms are decorated with country curtains, natural woodwork, handmade maple and cherry wood furnishings, ceiling fans and quilts.

Innkeeper(s): I Haley. $75-150. 4 rooms with PB. Breakfast included in rates. Types of meals: continental breakfast and full breakfast. Air conditioning and ceiling fan in room. Spa on premises. Amusement parks, shopping and sporting events nearby.

Certificate may be used: November through March, Sunday through Thursday, excluding special events and holidays.

Pottsboro   C8

Yacht-O-Fun
PO Box 1480
Pottsboro, TX 75076-1480
(903)786-8188 Fax:(214)669-1550

Guests can stay in a nearby condo or in the cabin of this 51-foot yacht. Tours on Lake Texoma are included in this unusual bed & breakfast experience. Guests first embark on a moonlight cruise, then the

427

next morning brunch and another trip around the lake. The vessel includes two staterooms, and guests can relax and catch some rays on the sundeck or take in the view from the salon.

Innkeeper(s): Diana Greer. $225. 2 rooms. Breakfast included in rates. Type of meal: full breakfast.

Certificate may be used: April 1-Nov. 30. Rate includes two cruises.

Round Top F8

Heart of My Heart Ranch B&B
PO Box 106
Round Top, TX 78954-0106
(800)327-1242 Fax:(409)249-3171

Circa 1825. This log frontier home was built by Jared Groce, known as the father of Texas agriculture. Groce planted the state's first cotton, and built the first cotton gin in Texas. Well-appointed rooms feature antiques such as a cannonball or canopy bed. The Lone Star and Brookfield rooms boast fireplaces. The Lone Star has a unique staircase that leads up to the second-story Harwood Room. The innkeepers also offer accommodations in the charming carriage house, and a rustic setting in the 170-year-old log cabin. The cabin boasts a sleeping loft, stone fireplace, clawfoot tub and a complete kitchen. Rockers have been set up on the expansive front porch, perfect for relaxing. The lush grounds offer a swimming pool, Jacuzzi, fruit tree orchard and gardens. A hearty, country breakfast is served each morning, and for an extra charge, the innkeepers will prepare a picnic lunch.

Innkeeper(s): Frances Harris. $65-135. MC VISA AX DS. 17 rooms. Breakfast included in rates. Type of meal: full breakfast.

Certificate may be used: Sunday-Thursday.

Royce City D8

Country Lane B&B
RR 2 Box 94B
Royce City, TX 75189-9802
(214)636-2600 (800)240-8757 Fax:(214)635-2300

Circa 1992. Each of the guest rooms at this Texas-style farmhouse has a different movie theme, with names such as the Happy Trails suite. The Mae West room is a provocative place with lace and velvet touches. Some rooms have whirlpool tubs for two. Relax on the rocker-lined veranda and you'll enjoy views of the catfish pond, sunsets and starry skies. The breakfast table is set with china, crystal and linen napkins, and guests partake of gourmet coffees, freshly squeezed juice, homemade muffins, frittatas and fresh fruit.

Innkeeper(s): James & Annie Cornelius. $45-85. MC VISA AX. 5 rooms, 4 with PB. Breakfast included in rates. Types of meals: full breakfast and early coffee/tea. Evening snack, banquet service, catered breakfast and room service available. Beds: QDT. Air conditioning, ceiling fan and VCR in room. Fax and library on premises. Handicap access. Antiques, fishing, parks and watersports nearby.

Certificate may be used: Jan. 15-Oct. 31 Sunday-Thursday.

San Antonio F7

Noble Inns-Pancoast Carriage House
102 Turner
San Antonio, TX 78204-1329
(210)225-4045 (800)221-4045 Fax:(210)227-0877
E-mail: nobleinns@aol.com

Circa 1896. This two-story, Victorian carriage house is located in San Antonio's King William Historic District. Each of the three guest rooms is appointed in Victorian style with period antiques, a fireplace and a marble bath with clawfoot tub. The current innkeepers are the fifth generation of the Pancoast family to live on the property and are happy to share the town and family history. The kitchens are stocked with pastries, fresh fruit, cereal and beverages, so guests can prepare breakfast at their leisure. There is a swimming pool and heated spa on the premises.

Innkeeper(s): Don & Liesl Noble. $100-145. MC VISA AX DS PC TC. 3 suites, 3 with FP. Breakfast included in rates. Type of meal: continental-plus breakfast. Afternoon tea available. Beds: Q. Air conditioning, turndown service, ceiling fan and TV in room. Fax, spa and swimming on premises. Antiques, parks, shopping, sporting events and theater nearby.

"First impressions mean a lot, and we were delighted the moment we entered this suite."

Certificate may be used: Jan. 3-Feb. 12, Monday-Thursday & June 1-Aug. 28, Monday-Thursday; holidays excluded.

Noble Inns-The Jackson House
107 Madison
San Antonio, TX 78204
(210)225-4045 (800)221-4045 Fax:(210)227-0877
E-mail: nobleinns@aol.com

Circa 1894. This Victorian brick and limestone house is a sister bed & breakfast to the Pancoast Carriage House. The home, located in the King William Historic District, has been designated as a city historic structure. Rooms are decorated with Victorian antiques, fireplaces, marble baths and a clawfoot or whirlpool tub. The inn's unique gazebo, which encloses the spa, is surrounded by antique stained glass. Guests are pampered both with a full breakfast, as well as afternoon tea.

Innkeeper(s): Don & Liesl Noble. $95-155. MC VISA AX DS PC TC. 6 rooms with PB, 6 with FP. Breakfast and afternoon tea included in rates.

Type of meal: full breakfast. Beds: KQ. Air conditioning, turndown service, ceiling fan and TV in room. Fax, spa, swimming, bicycles and library on premises. Antiques, parks, shopping, sporting events and theater nearby.

"It couldn't have been better if we dreamed it! Thank you."

Certificate may be used: Jan. 3-Feb. 12, Monday-Thursday and June 1-Aug. 28, Monday-Thursday; holidays excluded.

San Augustine   E9

The Wade House
202 E Livingston St
San Augustine, TX 75972
(409)275-5489

Circa 1940. The Wade House is a Mount Vernon-style red brick house located two blocks from the old courthouse square. Guest rooms are decorated in a mixture of contemporary and antique furnishings and are cooled by both ceiling fans and air conditioning. The nearby Mission Park, under construction, commemorating the 1717 Spanish Mission Nuestra Senora de los Dolores de los Ais, will open in 1998.
Innkeeper(s): Nelsyn & Julia Wade. $50-90. MC VISA PC TC. 6 rooms, 4 with PB. 1 suite. 1 conference room. Breakfast included in rates. Types of meals: continental breakfast, continental-plus breakfast and early coffee/tea. Beds: KQDT. Air conditioning, ceiling fan and TV in room. Fishing and shopping nearby.
Location: Two blocks from the Central Courthouse Square.
Publicity: *San Augustine Tribune, Dallas Morning News.*

"The house is one of the most beautiful in the area. Each room is decorated to the utmost excellence."

Certificate may be used: Monday through Thursday, holidays excepted. Not during December, subject to availability.

Smithville   F7

The Katy House
201 Ramona St, PO Box 803
Smithville, TX 78957-0803
(512)237-4262 (800)843-5289 Fax:(512)237-2239
E-mail: thekatyh@onr.com

Circa 1909. The Italianate exterior is graced by an arched portico over the bay-windowed living room. The Georgian columns reflect the inn's turn-of-the-century origin. Long leaf pine floors, pocket doors and a graceful stairway accent the completely refurbished interior. The inn is decorated almost exclusively in American antique oak and railroad memorabilia. A leisurely 10-minute bicycle ride (innkeepers provide bikes) will take you to the banks of the Colorado River. Also available are maps that outline walking or biking tours with lists of some of the historical and interesting information of the area.

Innkeeper(s): Bruce & Sallie Blalock. $56-85. MC VISA PC TC. 4 rooms with PB. 1 suite. 2 cottages. Breakfast included in rates. Types of meals: full breakfast and early coffee/tea. Beds: Q. Air conditioning, ceiling fan and TV in room. VCR, fax, bicycles and pet boarding on premises. Antiques, fishing, parks, shopping and watersports nearby.
Certificate may be used: Sunday through Thursday.

Stephenville   D7

Oxford House
563 N Graham St
Stephenville, TX 76401-3548
(817)965-6885 Fax:(817)965-7555

Circa 1898. A $3,000 lawyer's fee provided funds for construction of The Oxford House, and the silver was brought to town in a buckboard by W. J. Oxford, Esq. The house was built of cypress with porches three-quarters of the way around. Hand-turned, gingerbread trim and a carved wooden ridgerow are special features.
Innkeeper(s): Bill & Paula Oxford. $65-75. MC VISA AX PC. 4 rooms with PB. Breakfast included in rates. Types of meals: full breakfast and early coffee/tea. Afternoon tea and catering service available. Beds: QD. Air conditioning in room. Amusement parks, antiques, parks and theater nearby.
Publicity: *Glamour, Dallas Morning News.*
Certificate may be used: All year.

Texarkana C9

Mansion on Main B&B

802 Main St

Texarkana, TX 75501-5104

(903)792-1835

Circa 1895. Spectacular two-story columns salvaged from the St. Louis World's Fair accent the exterior of this Neoclassical-style inn. Victorian nightgowns and sleepshirts are provided, and whether you are on a business trip or your honeymoon, expect to be pampered. Six bedchambers vary from the Butler's

Garret to the Governor's Suite and are all furnished with antiques and period appointments. Awake to the scent of dark roast cajun coffee, and then enjoy a full "gentleman's" breakfast in the parquet dining room. The inn is located in the downtown historic area. Enjoy a fireside cup of coffee or a lemonade on the veranda. The inn offers plenty of amenities for the business traveler, including fax machine, desks and modem connections.

Innkeeper(s): Lee & Inez Hayden. $60-109. MC VISA AX PC TC. 6 rooms with PB. 1 suite. Breakfast included in rates. Types of meals: full breakfast, gourmet breakfast and early coffee/tea. Afternoon tea available. Beds: QD. Air conditioning, ceiling fan and TV in room. Handicap access. Antiques, fishing, shopping and theater nearby.

"My first B&B in the United States and it compared to some of the great ones of Europe. The warmth, hospitality, excellent coffee and breakfast were a welcomed change from the cold harshness of a Holiday Inn. I'll be back."

Certificate may be used: Anytime, space available, reserved at least one week in advance.

Van Alstyne C8

Durning House B&B

205 W Stephens, PO Box 1173

Van Alstyne, TX 75495

(903)482-5188

Circa 1900. Decorated with American oak and antiques, the inn has been host to many events, including weddings, office parties, Christmas parties,

club meetings and murder-mystery dinners. Three life-size pigs grace the east garden. The innkeepers have published a cookbook titled "Hog Heaven" that includes more than 400 recipes featured at the inn. Your hosts also appear regularly on a TV show preparing recipes from "Hog Heaven."

Innkeeper(s): Brenda Hix & Sherry Heath. $75-95. MC VISA TC. 2 rooms. Type of meal: continental breakfast. Dinner available. Restaurant on premises. Beds: QD. Air conditioning and ceiling fan in room. Handicap access. Antiques, fishing, shopping, sporting events, theater and watersports nearby.

Certificate may be used: Year-round, Sunday-Friday.

Victoria G8

Friendly Oaks B&B

210 E Juan Linn St

Victoria, TX 77901-8145

(512)575-0000 Fax:(512)575-0000

E-mail: inn/sprbill@aol.com

Circa 1915. This Craftsman-style home is full of Texas country charm, and guests will find the place a comfortable spot for a getaway. The grounds are covered with the namesake oak trees. Each room has a different theme, one is decorated in a Scottish style, another has a cowboy flavor. Breakfasts, like everything else in Texas, are big. Guests start off with a variety of fruits, then might sample Texas-shaped scones and entrees such as pecan waffles or French toast. The inn is located in a historic neighborhood in downtown Victoria.

Innkeeper(s): Bill & CeeBee McLeod. $55-75. MC VISA AX DS PC TC. 4 rooms with PB. 1 conference room. Breakfast and afternoon tea included in rates. Types of meals: gourmet breakfast and early coffee/tea. Beds: QD. Air conditioning, turndown service and ceiling fan in room. Cable TV, VCR, fax and library on premises. Handicap access. Antiques, fishing, parks, shopping, golf, theater and watersports nearby.

Publicity: *Country Extra, Lifestyle.*

"Thanks so much for the great food, the tour of the town and the step back in history."

Certificate may be used: Sunday through Wednesday during January, February, July, August, September.

Wichita Falls C6

Harrison House B&B

2014 11th St

Wichita Falls, TX 76301-4905

(817)322-2299 (800)327-2299

This prairie-style inn features 10-foot ceilings, narrow-board oak floors, a hand-carved mantelpiece, gumwood paneling and detailed molding. The home was built by oilman, developer and philanthropist N.H. Martin. After the discovery of oil on the family

ranch in nearby Jolly, Martin and his partner went on to build the Country Club Estates. They donated the land on which Hardin Junior College (now Midwestern State University) was built. The inn also caters to special occasions and as many as 200 guests can be accommodated for a stand-up buffet.

Innkeeper(s): Suzanne Staha. $55-125. MC VISA AX. 4 rooms. 1 suite. Breakfast included in rates. Type of meal: full breakfast. Air conditioning and ceiling fan in room. Cable TV and VCR on premises. Antiques and shopping nearby.

Certificate may be used: Anytime with advance notice.

Wimberley   *F7*

Southwind
2701 FM 3237
Wimberley, TX 78676-5511
(512)847-5277 (800)508-5277

Circa 1985. Located three miles east of the quaint village of Wimberly, this early Texas-style inn sits on 25 wooded acres. Roam the unspoiled acres and discover deer crossing your path and armadillos, raccoons and foxes skittering just beyond your footsteps. During the wet season, enjoy clear natural springs with access to the swimming hole. There's a porch outside guest rooms and secluded cabins where one can sit in a rocking chair, feel gentle breezes and listen to birds sing. The parlor is a cool retreat in the summer and provides a warm fireplace in winter weather.

Innkeeper(s): Carrie Watson. $75-85. MC VISA AX DS PC TC. 5 rooms with PB, 3 with FP. 2 cottages. Breakfast included in rates. Types of meals: full breakfast and early coffee/tea. Beds: KQ. Air conditioning and ceiling fan in room. Library on premises. Handicap access. Amusement parks, antiques, fishing, parks, shopping, sporting events, theater and watersports nearby.

Certificate may be used: Sunday through Thursday nights only, except holidays and April, June and July.

Utah

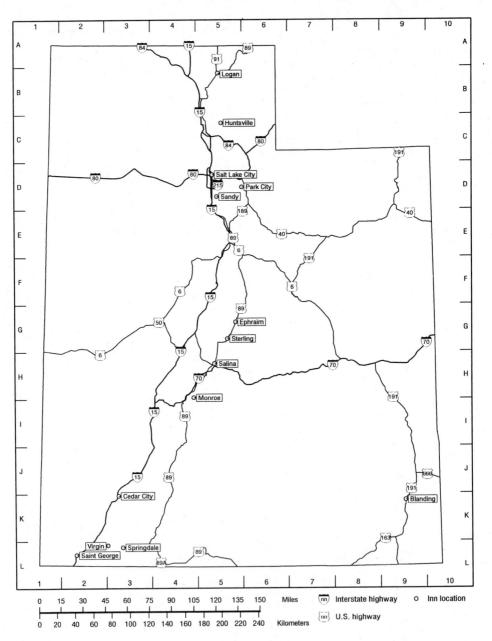

			Miles
0 15 30 45 60 75 90 105 120 135 150			
0 20 40 60 80 100 120 140 160 180 200 220 240			Kilometers

🔘 Interstate highway   ○ Inn location

🔘 U.S. highway

Blanding
K9

The Grayson Country Inn B&B
118 E 300 S
Blanding, UT 84511-2908
(801)678-2388 (800)365-0868

Circa 1908. Over the years, The Grayson Country Inn has served a number of purposes, including a small hotel and boarding house for Indian girls who

attended a local school. The inn is the perfect location to enjoy the many sites in the area, and is within walking distance from a pottery factory and gift shops. The area abounds with outdoor activities, as many national parks are nearby. Edge of the Cedars State Park is only a mile from the inn. A three-bedroom cottage is available for groups and/or families.
Innkeeper(s): Dennis & Lurlene Gutke. $42-67. MC VISA AX. 11 rooms with PB. 1 cottage. Breakfast included in rates. Type of meal: full breakfast. Beds: Q. Air conditioning, ceiling fan and TV in room. Library on premises. Fishing, parks, shopping and watersports nearby.
Publicity: *Salt Lake Tribune.*
Certificate may be used: All year

Cedar City
K3

Bard's Inn
150 S 100 W
Cedar City, UT 84720-3276
(801)586-6612

Circa 1910. This handsome bungalow features stained-glass windows, a wide front porch and a second-story porch. The Katharina Room has an antique, high-back queen bed and a twin-size walnut sleigh bed. Homemade pastries and fruit are served on the porch or in the formal dining room.
Innkeeper(s): Jack & Audrey Whipple. $75. MC VISA. 7 rooms, 5 with PB. Breakfast included in rates. Type of meal: continental-plus breakfast. Beds: QT. Air conditioning in room. Antiques, parks, shopping, downhill skiing, cross-country skiing, sporting events and theater nearby.
Certificate may be used: Anytime Oct. 1-May 31.

Paxman's House B&B
170 N 400 W
Cedar City, UT 84720-2421
(801)586-3755

Circa 1900. This steeply-gabled, turn-of-the-century Victorian offers a small veranda overlooking a residential street, two blocks from the Shakespearean Festival. Early Mormon pioneer pieces furnish the Pine Room, while walnut and marble Victorian furnishings fill the Master bedroom on the downstairs level. Breakfast includes fruit, cheese and homemade bread. Brian Head Ski Resort and Zion National Park are a short drive away.
Innkeeper(s): Karlene Paxman. $55-77. MC VISA. 3 rooms. Breakfast included in rates. Air conditioning in room. VCR on premises. Antiques, shopping, downhill skiing, cross-country skiing, sporting events and theater nearby.
Certificate may be used: Sept. 15-May 15, Sunday to Thursday.

Ephraim
G5

Ephraim Homestead
135 W 100 N (43-2)
Ephraim, UT 84627-1131
(801)283-6367

Circa 1880. Three buildings comprise this Mormon pioneer homestead. The Granary, circa 1860, is furnished in Mormon pioneer items and resembles a museum reproduction with its fireplace, cast-iron cookstove, rustic kitchen, antique beds and cradle. The barn offers two rustic rooms on the top floor, while the Victorian Gothic house, fashioned of adobe, is furnished in Eastlake antiques. It features Scandinavian/Victorian stencilings in its two tiny guest rooms located up steep stairs off the kitchen. Apple muffins and French toast are prepared on the wood stove for guests.
Innkeeper(s): Sherron Andreasen. $45-75. 3 suites. 1 cottage. Breakfast included in rates. Type of meal: full breakfast. Evening snack available. Air conditioning in room. Antiques, shopping, cross-country skiing, sporting events and theater nearby.
Certificate may be used: All year, excluding second and third weeks of July, Christmas, Thanksgiving eves and days.

Huntsville
C5

Jackson Fork Inn
7345 E 900 S
Huntsville, UT 84317-9778
(801)745-0051 (800)255-0672

Circa 1938. This former dairy barn was named after the hay fork that was used to transport hay into the barn. The romantic inn now includes eight guest rooms and a restaurant. Four rooms include two-person Jacuzzi tubs, and all are cozy and comfortable. A self-serve continental breakfast is prepared each day with muffins and fresh coffee. The inn is ideal for skiers and located near Powder Mountain, Nordic Valley and Snowbasin ski resorts.

Innkeeper(s): Vicki Petersen. $50-120. MC VISA AX DS PC TC. 8 rooms with PB. Breakfast included in rates. Lunch available. Beds: Q. Ceiling fan in room. Fishing, parks, shopping, downhill skiing, cross-country skiing and watersports nearby.

Certificate may be used: Monday - Thursday, excluding holidays.

Logan
B5

Center Street B&B
169 E Center St
Logan, UT 84321-4606
(801)752-3443

Circa 1879. Imagine wandering through a castle until you come to a room lit by the amber glow from the fireplace. A canopy bed awaits and above, Michelangelo's glorious works decorate the ceiling. If this doesn't spark your interest, pretend you've traveled back in time to the Old West in a suite with pine walls, a pool table, moose head and a pressed-brass ceiling. These are just two of the options at this most unusual bed & breakfast. Each of the rooms has its own theme, from the above mentioned Castle and Jesse James motifs to the bed-chambers with names such as Caribbean Sea Cave, Space Odyssey, Amazon Rainforest or perhaps the Arabian Nights Suite. Fireplaces and Jacuzzis (some heart-shaped) are among the amenities. Guests in three rooms each reserve a private time at the indoor pool, with walls adorned with murals of whales and sea creatures.

Innkeeper(s): Clyne & Ann Long Family. $57-180. MC VISA AX PC TC. 16 suites, 7 with FP. Breakfast included in rates. Type of meal: continental-plus breakfast. Beds: KQ. Air conditioning, TV and VCR in room. Spa and swimming on premises. Antiques, fishing, parks, shopping, downhill skiing, cross-country skiing, sporting events, golf, theater and watersports nearby.

Certificate may be used: Oct. 1-June 1, Sunday-Thursday except holidays and Dec. 20-Jan. 2. Subject to availability.

Monroe
H4

Peterson's B&B
PO Box 142
Monroe, UT 84754-0142
(801)527-4830

Circa 1895. Although it appears to be a modern ranch house, this home has sections more than 100 years old. For 20 years Mary Ann has hosted bed & breakfast guests here. A former cooking teacher, she offers breakfasts of Hawaiian French toast,

Pannokoken with applesauce and eggs Benedict. The fenced yard is shaded by an ancient apple tree. Carport parking is offered at this inn, which is open from April through October. Visit Fremont Indian State Park and discover petroglyphs and pictographs carved into the cliffs, as well as pit dwellings of the Fremonts. Hot springs, seven blocks away, are non-sulfurous. The B&B is near five national parks. Monroe is halfway between Denver and Los Angeles.

Innkeeper(s): Mary Ann Peterson. $70-75. 3 rooms, 2 with PB. Breakfast included in rates. Types of meals: gourmet breakfast and early coffee/tea. Beds: KDT. Air conditioning and turndown service in room. Cable TV and VCR on premises. Fishing, parks, shopping, cross-country skiing and theater nearby.

Certificate may be used: April 1-Oct. 31.

Park City
D6

The Imperial Hotel
221 Main St, PO Box 1628
Park City, UT 84060
(801)649-1904 (800)669-8824 Fax:(801)645-7421

Circa 1904. The Imperial, a historic turn-of-the-century hotel, is decorated to look like an Old West-style lodging complete with Victorian furnishings and antiques. Several guest rooms include amenities like clawfoot or Roman tubs and sitting areas. A few overlook Park City's historic Main Street. The inn's largest suite includes a bedroom and a spiral staircase leading up to a cozy loft area. Ski lockers, a Jacuzzi and transportation to area ski lifts are some of the amenities offered to guests.

Innkeeper(s): Paulette Anderson. $65-230. MC VISA AX DS TC. 10 rooms, 9 with PB. 1 suite. Breakfast included in rates. Types of meals: full breakfast and early coffee/tea. Evening snack available. Beds: KQT. TV in room. Fax and spa on premises. Antiques, fishing, parks, shopping, downhill skiing, cross-country skiing, sporting events, theater and watersports nearby.

Certificate may be used: April 15-June 15; Sept. 15-Nov. 15, space available.

The Old Miners' Lodge - A B&B Inn
615 Woodside Ave, PO Box 2639
Park City, UT 84060-2639
(801)645-8068 (800)648-8068 Fax:(801)645-7420

Circa 1889. This originally was established as a miners' boarding house by E. P. Ferry, owner of the Woodside-Norfolk silver mines. A two-story Victorian with Western flavor, the lodge is a significant structure in the Park City National Historic District. Just on the edge of the woods is a deck and a steaming hot tub.

Innkeeper(s): Susan Wynne & Liza Simpson. $60-255. MC VISA AX DC CB DS PC TC. 12 rooms with PB. 3 suites. 2 conference rooms. Breakfast and evening snack included in rates. Types of meals: full breakfast and early coffee/tea. Banquet service and catering service available. Beds: KQDT. Turndown service and ceiling fan in room. Fax, copier, spa and library on premises. Antiques, fishing, parks, shopping, downhill skiing, cross-country skiing and theater nearby.

Location: In the Park City Historic District.

Publicity: *Boston Herald, Los Angeles Times, Detroit Free Press, Washington Post, Ski, Bon Appetit.*

"This is the creme de la creme. The most wonderful place I have stayed at bar none, including ski country in the U.S. and Europe."

Certificate may be used: April 15-June 15, Sept. 15-Nov. 15, subject to availability.

Saint George
L2

Greene Gate Village Historic B&B Inn
76 W Tabernacle St
Saint George, UT 84770-3420
(801)628-6999 (800)350-6999 Fax:(801)628-6989
E-mail: greeneg8@inquo.net

Circa 1872. This is a cluster of six restored pioneer homes all located within one block. The Bentley House has comfortable Victorian decor, while the Supply Depot is decorated in a style reflective of its origin as a shop for wagoners on their way to California. The Orson  Pratt House and the Carriage House are other choices, all carefully restored. The fifth house contains three bedrooms each with private bath, a kitchen, living room and two fireplaces. One of the bedrooms has a large whirlpool tub.

Innkeeper(s): Barbara Greene. $55-125. MC VISA AX DS. 19 rooms, 16 with PB, 9 with FP. 6 suites. 1 conference room. Breakfast included in rates. Types of meals: full breakfast and early coffee/tea. Dinner, picnic lunch, catering service and room service available. Restaurant on premises. Beds: KQT. Air conditioning, TV and VCR in room. Handicap access. Antiques, fishing, shopping, downhill skiing, cross-country skiing, sporting events, theater and watersports nearby.

Publicity: *Deseret News, Spectrum, Better Homes & Garden, Sunset, Country.*

"You not only provided me with rest, comfort and wonderful food, but you fed my soul."

Certificate may be used: Sunday-Thursday.

Salina
H5

The Victorian Inn
190 W Main St
Salina, UT 84654-1153
(801)529-7342 (800)972-7183

A courtyard filled with a rose garden, stained-glass windows and fine wood floors and moldings set the tone for this Victorian experience. The inn has down comforters, king beds and antique clawfoot tubs. Abundant Grandmother-type servings are offered at breakfast.

The valley, surrounded by mountains as high as 12,000 feet, offers close spots for fishing, hunting and snowmobiling.

Innkeeper(s): Debbie Van Horn. $75-90. MC VISA. 3 rooms. Breakfast included in rates. Type of meal: full breakfast. Air conditioning in room. Cross-country skiing nearby.

Certificate may be used: Mid-June through mid-August, Sunday-Thursday only.

Salt Lake City   D5

The Anton Boxrud B&B
57 S 600 E
Salt Lake City, UT 84102-1006
(801)363-8035 (800)524-5511 Fax:(801)596-1316

Circa 1901. One of Salt Lake City's grand old homes, this Victorian home with eclectic style is on the register of the Salt Lake City Historical Society.

The interior is furnished with antiques from around the country and Old World details. In the sitting and dining rooms, guests will find chairs with intricate carvings, a table with carved swans for support, embossed brass door knobs and stained and beveled glass. The inn is located just a half-block south of the Utah Governor's Mansion.

Innkeeper(s): Mark Brown. $59-119. MC VISA AX DC CB DS. 7 rooms, 3 with PB. 1 suite. Breakfast included in rates. Types of meals: full breakfast and early coffee/tea. Evening snack available. Beds: KQT. Cable TV on premises. Amusement parks, antiques, fishing, shopping, downhill skiing, cross-country skiing, sporting events, theater and watersports nearby.

Publicity: *Salt Lake Tribune.*

Certificate may be used: Oct. 15 to Jan. 15.

Saltair B&B
164 S 900 E
Salt Lake City, UT 84102-4103
(801)533-8184 (800)733-8184 Fax:(801)595-0332

Circa 1903. The Saltair is the oldest continuously operating bed & breakfast in Utah and a offers a prime location to enjoy Salt Lake City. The simply decorated rooms include light, airy window dresses, charming furnishings and special touches. One room includes a wood-burning stove and exposed brick. Breakfasts, especially the delicious breads, are memorable. The inn is within walking distance to four historic districts and only one block from Temple Square and the Governor's Mansion. Day trips include treks to several national and state parks and the Wasatch Front ski areas.

Innkeeper(s): Nancy Saxton & Jan Bartlett. $75-129. MC VISA AX DC CB DS TC. 5 rooms, 2 with PB. Breakfast and evening snack included in rates. Types of meals: continental breakfast, continental-plus breakfast, full breakfast, gourmet breakfast and early coffee/tea. Beds: QT. Air conditioning in room. Cable TV, VCR, fax and spa on premises. Antiques, fishing, parks, shopping, downhill skiing, cross-country skiing, sporting events, theater and watersports nearby.

Location: Historic downtown district.

Publicity: *Mobil, Logan Sun.*

"Your swing and Saltair McMuffins were fabulous."

Certificate may be used: Oct. 1-30, Nov. 1-30, Dec. 1-15.

Wildflowers B&B
936 E 1700 S
Salt Lake City, UT 84105-3329
(801)466-0600 (800)569-0009 Fax:(801)484-7832

Circa 1891. Holding true to its name, the grounds surrounding this Victorian home are covered with all sorts of flowers ranging from wild geraniums to coreopsis to meadow rue. The outside beauty only serves to complement the magnificence on the inside of this historic residence. Hand-carved staircases, stained-glass windows, clawfoot bathtubs and original chandeliers make up just some of the touches that will make a stay here memorable. Situated in the heart of Salt Lake City, this home offers all the comfort one could ask for and the convenience of being just a few minutes away from skiing or a trip downtown. Like this classic residence, 10 nearby homes are also listed in the National Register of Historic Places.

Innkeeper(s): Jeri Parker & Cill Sparks. $70-125. MC VISA AX. 5 rooms with PB. 2 suites. 1 conference room. Breakfast included in rates. Type of meal: gourmet breakfast. Beds: KQD. Air conditioning, ceiling fan, TV and VCR in room. Fax, copier and bicycles on premises. Amusement parks, antiques, fishing, parks, shopping, downhill skiing, cross-country skiing, sporting events, theater and watersports nearby.

"Service above and beyond my expectations with people that I'll remember."

Certificate may be used: Not February, March, holidays. All other times depending on availability.

"Service above and beyond my expectations with people that I'll remember."

Certificate may be used: Not February, March, holidays. All other times depending on availability.

Sandy
D5

Mountain Hollow B&B Inn
10209 S Dimple Dell Rd
Sandy, UT 84092-4536
(801)942-3428 (800)757-3428 Fax:(801)943-7229
E-mail: kpl@aos.net

Circa 1973. Located just outside of Salt Lake City, this contemporary home is surrounded by the beautiful scenery of Little Cottonwood Canyon and the Watsatch Mountains. Ski areas are about 15 minutes away, and after a day on the slopes, guests can relax in their comfortable, country-style rooms; enjoy a soak in the outdoor hot tub; or take on a round of table tennis or pool in the game room. In warm weather, the breakfasts of fresh breads, fruit, cheese, hard-boiled eggs and other treats are served on the patio. In cool weather, the morning meal is presented fireside indoors.

Innkeeper(s): Kathy & Doug Larson. $75-150. MC VISA AX DS PC TC. 11 rooms, 4 with PB, 1 with FP. 1 suite. Breakfast and evening snack included in rates. Types of meals: continental-plus breakfast and full breakfast. Beds: KQDT. Air conditioning in room. VCR, fax, spa and library on premises. Amusement parks, antiques, fishing, parks, shopping, downhill skiing, cross-country skiing, sporting events, theater and watersports nearby.

"We couldn't have asked for a better place to enjoy our honeymoon."

Certificate may be used: May-October.

Springdale
L3

Harvest House B&B
29 Canyon View Dr
Springdale, UT 84767
(801)772-3880

Circa 1989. This home is located less than a mile from the entrance to spectacular Zion National Park. Day trips include scenic Bryce Canyon, Lake Powell

and the north rim of the Grand Canyon. The bedrooms are a perfect place for weary sightseers. Some rooms feature sun decks and sitting rooms.

Innkeeper(s): Roger & Leslie Coleman. $80-100. MC VISA DS PC TC. 4 rooms, 3 with PB. 1 suite. Breakfast included in rates. Type of meal: gourmet breakfast. Beds: Q. Air conditioning and ceiling fan in room. VCR, fax, spa and library on premises. Fishing, parks, shopping, downhill skiing, cross-country skiing, golf, theater and watersports nearby.
Location: One-half mile from Zion National Park.

"A winning combination — fantastic views, great food, genial hosts."

Certificate may be used: Monday-Thursday, Jan.2-February-March 31.

Sterling
G5

Cedar Crest Inn
819 Palisade Rd
Sterling, UT 84665
(801)835-6352

Circa 1903. Several structures comprise the Cedar Crest Inn, including the Swiss-style Lindenhaus, named for a giant linden tree adjacent to the home. The tree was brought to America from Germany as a seedling. Guests also can opt to stay in Linderhof, which offers three beautiful suites. The third structure on this 18-acre property is the popular Cedar Crest Restaurant, which serves a variety of gourmet entrees, including lobster, chicken Cordon Bleu and Filet Mignon. The grounds are beautiful, and on cold nights, guests can stay indoors and watch a favorite movie. The innkeepers have a selection of more than 300.

Innkeeper(s): Ron & Don Kelsch. $52-100. MC VISA AX DS. 12 rooms, 9 with PB. 2 suites. 1 conference room. Breakfast included in rates. Types of meals: full breakfast, gourmet breakfast and early coffee/tea. Banquet service and catered breakfast available. Restaurant on premises. Beds: KQD. Air conditioning, TV and VCR in room. Spa and bicycles on premises. Antiques, parks, shopping, cross-country skiing and watersports nearby.

Certificate may be used: August through December, holidays excluded.

Vermont

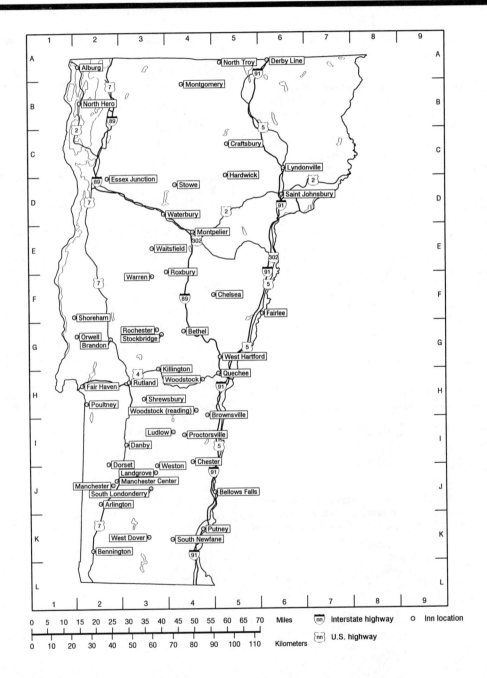

Miles: 0 5 10 15 20 25 30 35 40 45 50 55 60 65 70

Kilometers: 0 10 20 30 40 50 60 70 80 90 100 110

Interstate highway

U.S. highway

Inn location

Alburg
A2

Thomas Mott Homestead B&B
Blue Rock Rd, Rt 2 Box 149-B
Alburg, VT 05440-9620
(802)796-3736 (800)348-0843 Fax:(802)796-3736

Circa 1838. Each room in this restored farmhouse provides a special view of Lake Champlain, yet guests often may be found enjoying the view from the sitting room as they warm by the fireplace. There are also full views of Mt. Mansfield and nearby Jay Peak. Montreal Island is one hour away. Guests are sure to

enjoy the complimentary Ben & Jerry's ice cream. Patrick is a noted wine consultant and holds Master's Degrees in criminology, sociology and the classical arts. A boat dock, extending 75 feet onto the lake, recently has been added to the property.

Innkeeper(s): Patrick Schallert. $69-89. MC VISA AX DC CB DS PC TC. 5 rooms with PB, 1 with FP. 2 suites. 3 conference rooms. Breakfast and evening snack included in rates. Types of meals: gourmet breakfast and early coffee/tea. Beds: KQ. Turndown service and ceiling fan in room. Cable TV, fax, copier and library on premises. Amusement parks, antiques, fishing, parks, shopping, downhill skiing, cross-country skiing, sporting events, theater and watersports nearby.

Location: Northwest corner of Vermont.

Publicity: *Los Angeles Times, St. Alban's Messenger, Yankee Traveler, Boston Globe, Elle, Outside, Prime Time, Vermont Life.*

"Hospitality reigns. I loved the beautiful pressed maple leaf—it is perfect and so personal."

Certificate may be used: Nov. 1-April 30.

Arlington
J2

The Arlington Inn
Historic Rt 7A, PO Box 369
Arlington, VT 05250
(802)375-6532 (800)443-9442

Circa 1848. The Arlington Inn is one of Vermont's finest examples of Greek Revival architecture. Set on lushly landscaped grounds, the inn boasts elegantly appointed guest rooms filled with period antiques. Norman Rockwell once used the carriage house as a studio.

Innkeeper(s): Mark Gagnon. $70-160. MAP. MC VISA AX DC DS. 13 rooms with PB, 2 with FP. 5 suites. 1 conference room. Breakfast included in rates. Types of meals: full breakfast and gourmet breakfast.

Dinner and picnic lunch available. Beds: KQDT. Air conditioning in room. Cable TV, VCR, fax, copier and bicycles on premises. Antiques, fishing, shopping, downhill skiing, cross-country skiing, sporting events, theater and watersports nearby.

Location: Intersection of Route 313.

Publicity: *San Diego Times, Bon Appetit, Country Inns, Vermont Life, Gourmet, New York Magazine.*

"What a romantic place and such outrageous food!"

Certificate may be used: Weekdays, excluding Sept. 15-Oct. 23.

Arlington Manor House B&B
Buck Hill Rd, RR 2-420
Arlington, VT 05250
(802)375-6784

Circa 1908. A view of Mt. Equinox is enjoyed from the spacious terrace of this Dutch Colonial inn in the Battenkill River Valley. The inn also sports its own lighted tennis courts and is within easy walking distance of the Battenkill River, where canoeing, fishing and river tubing are popular activities. A variety of accommodations is offered, and two of the inn's guest rooms have romantic fireplaces. A bikers' workshop and bench stand are on the premises.

Innkeeper(s): Al & Kit McAllister. $50-130. MC VISA AX PC TC. 5 rooms, 4 with PB, 2 with FP. 1 suite. 2 conference rooms. Breakfast and afternoon tea included in rates. Types of meals: full breakfast, gourmet breakfast and early coffee/tea. Room service available. Beds: QDT. Air conditioning and turndown service in room. VCR, tennis and library on premises. Antiques, fishing, parks, shopping, downhill skiing, cross-country skiing, theater and watersports nearby.

Certificate may be used: November through June, except holiday periods

Hill Farm Inn
RR 2 Box 2015
Arlington, VT 05250-9311
(802)375-2269 (800)882-2545 Fax:(802)375-9918

Circa 1790. One of Vermont's original land grant farmsteads, Hill Farm Inn has welcomed guests since 1905 when the widow Mettie Hill opened her home to summer vacationers. The farm is surrounded by 50 peaceful acres that border the Battenkill River. Guests can relax and enjoy the simple life and 360-degree views of the mountains. Guest rooms are charming and cozy. Summer guests have the option of staying in one of four cabins. A large, country breakfast of homemade fare starts off each day.

Innkeeper(s): George & Joanne Hardy, Kelly Stork. $70-125. MC VISA AX DS. 15 rooms, 10 with PB. 2 suites. Breakfast and afternoon tea included in rates. Types of meals: full breakfast and early coffee/tea. Dinner available. Beds: KQTD. Cable TV, fax and copier on premises. Antiques, fishing, parks, shopping, downhill skiing and cross-country skiing nearby.

Location: One-half mile from Historic Route 7A.

Publicity: *Providence Journal, Boston Globe, Innsider, Country.*

"I have already taken the liberty of changing the meaning of relaxation in the dictionary to Hill Farm Inn. Thank you . . . It was great."

Certificate may be used: Nov. 1-Sept. 15, Sunday-Thursday; excluding holiday periods.

Ira Allen House
Rd 2, Box 2485
Arlington, VT 05250
(802)362-2284 Fax:(802)362-0928

Built by Ethan Allen's brother, this historic Colonial Revival inn is a state historic site. Hand-blown glass panes, hand-hewn beams, handmade bricks and wide-board floors provide evidence of the inn's longevity. Surrounded by farms and forest, the inn's

setting is perfect for those searching for some peace and quiet. Plenty of recreational activities also are found nearby, including fine trout fishing in the Battenkill River just across the street. Saturday-night dinners are available in winter, and guests are welcome to raid the living room fridge, where they will find complimentary soda and non-alcoholic beer.

Innkeeper(s): David Mardon. $55-70. MC VISA AX. 9 rooms. 2 suites. Breakfast included in rates. Type of meal: full breakfast. Dinner available. Ceiling fan in room. VCR on premises. Antiques, shopping, downhill skiing, cross-country skiing and theater nearby.

Certificate may be used: Year-round except foliage season (last week September-last week October) and holidays.

440

Bellows Falls   J5

River Mist B&B
7 Burt St
Bellows Falls, VT 05101-1401
(802)463-9023 Fax:(802)463-1571
E-mail: rmistbnb@vermontel.com

The scenic village of Bellows Falls is home to this turn-of-the-century Queen Anne Victorian inn, with its inviting wraparound porch and country

Victorian interior. Guests may relax in any of three sitting rooms or in front of the fireplace. Enjoy a day of antiquing, skiing or just wandering around the picturesque environs. Be sure to take a ride on the Green Mountain Flyer before leaving town.

Innkeeper(s): John & Linda Maresca. $35-75. 3 rooms. Breakfast included in rates. Type of meal: full breakfast. Cable TV on premises. Amusement parks, antiques, shopping, downhill skiing, cross-country skiing and theater nearby.

Certificate may be used: Anytime except foliage season weekends, Sept. 1-Oct. 31, and holiday weekends.

Bennington   K2

Molly Stark Inn
1067 Main St
Bennington, VT 05201-2635
(802)442-9631 (800)356-3076 Fax:(802)442-5224
E-mail: mollyinn@vermontel.com

Circa 1890. This attractive Queen Anne Victorian inn has been serving travelers for more than 50 years. Careful restoration has enabled it to retain its Victorian charm while offering the comforts today's guests have come to expect. Features include antique furnishings, clawfoot tubs, hardwood floors, handmade quilts and a woodstove. The inn's convenient Main Street location puts it within walking distance of many restaurants and shops, and just minutes from Historic Old Bennington. The Bennington Museum boasts paintings by Grandma Moses.

Innkeeper(s): Reed & Cammi Fendler. $65-145. MC VISA AX DS PC TC. 7 rooms with PB, 1 with FP. 1 cottage. Breakfast and evening snack included in rates. Types of meals: full breakfast and gourmet breakfast. Beds: KDT. Air conditioning, ceiling fan and TV in room. Bicycles on premises. Antiques, fishing, parks, shopping, downhill skiing, cross-country skiing, theater and watersports nearby.

Publicity: *Fodors, Yankee Traveler, Colonial Homes, Albany Times Union, Saratogian.*

"...like my grandma's house, only better."

Certificate may be used: Sunday-Thursday, Nov. 1-May 31.

Bethel G4

Greenhurst Inn

River St, Rd 2, Box 60
Bethel, VT 05032-9404
(802)234-9474 (800)510-2553

Circa 1890. In the National Register of Historic Places, Greenhurst is a gracious Victorian mansion built for the Harringtons of Philadelphia. Overlooking the White River, the inn's opulent interiors include etched windows once featured on the cover of Vermont Life. There are eight master-piece fireplaces and a north and south parlor.
Innkeeper(s): Lyle & Claire Wolf. $50-100. EP. MC VISA DS PC TC. 13 rooms, 7 with PB, 4 with FP. Breakfast included in rates. Types of meals: continental breakfast, continental-plus breakfast and early coffee/tea. Beds: QDT. Air conditioning in room. Cable TV, VCR and library on premises. Antiques, fishing, parks, shopping, downhill skiing, cross-country skiing, theater and watersports nearby.

Location: Midway between Boston and Montreal.

Publicity: *Los Angeles Times, Time, New York Times, Vermont Life.*

"The inn is magnificent! The hospitality unforgettable."

Certificate may be used: Sunday-Thursday, except Sept. 15-Oct. 15.

Brandon G2

The Gazebo Inn

On Rt 7 (25 Grove St)
Brandon, VT 05733
(802)247-3235 (888)858-3235
E-mail: gazebo@sover.net

Circa 1865. This National Register home is like a little museum with antique tools, toys, glass, bottles, musical instruments and other collectibles placed throughout the rooms. In the summer and fall months, the innkeepers open an antique shop on the premises, and the area is bursting with places to hunt for antiques and crafts. A variety of dishes, from traditional pancakes with locally produced maple syrup to huevos rancheros, are served each morning in the dining room. Guests are invited to simply sit and relax in the gazebo, on the porch or in front of a wood-burning stove.
Innkeeper(s): Janet & Joel Mondlak. $55-75. MC VISA AX DS TC. 4 rooms with PB. Breakfast included in rates. Type of meal: full breakfast. Beds: DT. Cable TV, copier and bicycles on premises. Antiques, fishing, parks, shopping, downhill skiing, cross-country skiing, sporting events, theater and watersports nearby.

"Thank you for your hospitality. We had a wonderful time. We will try to make this an annual event."

Certificate may be used: Always, except fall foliage and holiday weekends.

Hivue B&B Tree Farm

RR 1, Box 1023, High Pond Rd
Brandon, VT 05733-9704
(802)247-3042 (800)880-3042

Circa 1960. There are meadows and woods to mean-der through, and a stream stocked with trout winds its way through the 76-acre grounds at this raised ranch-style home. Accommodations are comfortable, a bit like an old country farmhouse. Guests enjoy views of the surrounding White Mountains. Brandon, a his-toric little village, is just a few miles down the road.
Innkeeper(s): William & Winifred Reuschle. $50. 3 rooms with PB. 1 conference room. Breakfast included in rates. Type of meal: full breakfast. Picnic lunch available. Beds: KD. Ceiling fan and VCR in room. Antiques, fishing, parks, shopping, downhill skiing, cross-country skiing and watersports nearby.

Certificate may be used: Jan. 1-May 23, Monday-Thursday; June 17-July 3, Monday-Wednesday; July 10-Aug. 30, Wednesday-Friday; Sept. 4-Sept. 24, Wednesday-Tuesday; Oct. 22-Dec. 23, Tuesday-Monday.

Moffett House

69 Park St
Brandon, VT 05733-1121
(802)247-3843 (800)752-5794

Circa 1856. This graceful French Second Empire house has a mansard roof and a Queen Anne Victorian veranda that was added in 1880. Widow

walks top the roof, and gingerbread trim adds to the streetside appeal of Moffett House. The inn was named after Hugh Moffett, Time-Life editor and Vermont legislator. A country breakfast is served in the dining room. The Kellington-Pico ski area is nearby.
Innkeeper(s): Mary Bowers, Doug Flanagan. $65-125. MAP, AP, EP. MC VISA. 7 rooms, 3 with PB. 1 suite. Breakfast included in rates. Types of meals: full breakfast and early coffee/tea. Dinner and picnic lunch available. Beds: KQTD. Ceiling fan and TV in room. Antiques, fishing, parks, shopping, skiing, theater and watersports nearby.
Publicity: *Rutland Business Journal.*

"My mother, aunt, cousin and I were all delighted with the lovely accommodations and the delicious breakfasts."
Certificate may be used: Sunday-Friday.

Rosebelle's Victorian Inn
PO Box 370, Rt 7
Brandon, VT 05733-0370
(802)247-0098 (888)767-3235
E-mail: rosebel@vermontel.com

Circa 1839. This elegant Second Empire Victorian inn with mansard roof is listed in the National Register of Historic Places. The home was part of the Underground Railroad. Impressive both inside and out, the inn and its six guest rooms have been

lovingly furnished with authentic Victorian pieces by the innkeepers. Favorite gathering spots include the comfortable common rooms and the wicker-filled porch. Guests also enjoy strolling the lush grounds where they often experience close encounters with butterflies and hummingbirds. The innkeepers, who speak French, offer gift certificates and special packages. The inn is near Middlebury College and minutes from major ski areas.
Innkeeper(s): Ginette & Norm Milot. $75-95. MC VISA AX PC TC. 6 rooms, 4 with PB. Breakfast included in rates. Type of meal: full breakfast. Beds: QDT. Ceiling fan in room. Cable TV and VCR on premises. Antiques, fishing, parks, shopping, downhill skiing, cross-country skiing, sporting events, theater and watersports nearby.
Location: Heart of Vermont and only a short drive to all of Vermont's special interests.

"You have captured a beautiful part of our history."
Certificate may be used: November-June, Sunday to Thursday, excluding holidays and special events. Call for possible weekend availability.

Brownsville   H4

Mill Brook B&B
PO Box 410
Brownsville, VT 05037-0410
(802)484-7283

Circa 1860. Once known as the House of Seven Gables, Mill Brook has been in constant use as a family home and for a while, a boarding house for mill loggers. Old German Fraktur paintings decorate the woodwork and there are three sitting rooms for guests. Antique furnishings are found throughout. Popular activities in the area include hang gliding, bike tours and canoeing.
Innkeeper(s): K. Carriere. $65-105. MC VISA. 5 rooms, 3 with PB. 3 suites. Breakfast included in rates. Types of meals: full breakfast and early coffee/tea. Evening snack and catering service available. Beds: QDT. Ceiling fan in room. VCR on premises. Antiques, shopping, downhill skiing, cross-country skiing, sporting events and theater nearby.
Location: Fourteen miles from Woodstock, seven from Windsor.

"Splendid hospitality. Your B&B was beyond our expectation."
Certificate may be used: Sunday-Thursday, Jan. 5-Sept. 10, Oct. 25-Nov. 20, Dec. 1-22. All times are subject to availability and cannot be used with any other discounts.

Chelsea   F5

Shire Inn
8 Main St, PO Box 37
Chelsea, VT 05038
(802)685-3031 (800)441-6908 Fax:(802)685-3871
E-mail: shireinn@sover.net

Circa 1832. Granite lintels over the windows and a sunburst light over the entry highlight this Adams-style brick home. The romantic inn, which is located in a 210-year-old historic village, has a grand spiral staircase ascending from wide-plank pumpkin pine floors in the entryway. Guest rooms include antique canopied beds, tall windows and 10-foot ceilings. Most have wood-burning fireplaces. Included on the

property's 23 acres are granite post fencing, perennial gardens dating from the 19th century, and a broad, rocky stream spanned by a farm bridge.
Innkeeper(s): Jay & Karen Keller. $86-210. MAP. MC VISA DS PC TC. 6 rooms with PB, 4 with FP. Breakfast and dinner included in rates. Types of meals: full breakfast and early coffee/tea. Afternoon tea available. Beds: KQD. Fax, copier, bicycles and library on premises. Antiques, fishing, parks, shopping, skiing, theater and watersports nearby.
Publicity: *Country Inn Review, Vermont Life.*

"What an inn should be! Absolutely delicious food - great hospitality! The rooms are filled with romance."
Certificate may be used: Anytime except Sept. 10-Oct. 20 and holidays.

Chester   I4

Chester Inn at Long Last
PO Box 589
Chester, VT 05143-0589
(802)875-2444 (888)243-7466 Fax:(802)875-6414
E-mail: chesinn@sover.net

Circa 1892. Located on the town green, this renovated inn reflects the personality of the owners Bill and Mary Ann Kearns. The inn was rebuilt in 1923 after being destroyed by fire. The home features fine cuisine and comfortable, friendly surroundings provided by the Kearns, their children and the staff. You may want to cuddle up with a book in the library, sit and rock on the front porch or play tennis on the inn's private courts.
Innkeeper(s): Mary Ann & Bill Kearns. $110-160. MAP, EP. MC VISA DS PC TC. 26 rooms with PB. 4 suites. 1 conference room. Breakfast and dinner included in rates. Types of meals: full breakfast and early coffee/tea. Banquet service available. Restaurant on premises. Beds: QD. Cable TV, VCR and copier on premises. Antiques, fishing, parks, shopping, downhill skiing, cross-country skiing and theater nearby.
Publicity: *New York Times, Philadelphia Inquirer, Gourmet.*

"An inn of character where character has real meaning."
Certificate may be used: Year-round, Sunday through Thursday, Jan. 3-Dec. 19, except during foliage season.

Hugging Bear Inn & Shoppe
Main St #32
Chester, VT 05143
(802)875-2412 (800)325-0519 Fax:(802)875-3823
E-mail: huggingbear@vbv-online.com

Circa 1850. Among the 4,000 teddy bear inhabitants of this white Victorian inn, several peek out from the third-story windows of the octagonal tower. There is a teddy bear shop on the premises and children and adults can borrow a bear to take to bed with them. Rooms are decorated with antiques and comfortable furniture. A bear puppet show is often staged during breakfast.
Innkeeper(s): Georgette Thomas. $55-95. MC VISA AX DS PC TC. 6 rooms with PB. Breakfast included in rates. Types of meals: full breakfast and early coffee/tea. Catered breakfast available. Beds: DT. Cable TV, VCR and library on premises. Antiques, fishing, parks, shopping,

downhill skiing and cross-country skiing nearby.
Publicity: *Rutland Daily Herald, Exxon Travel, Teddy Bear Review.*

"Thanks seems to be too small of a word to describe our greatest appreciation toward all of you for all of your warmth and hospitality."
Certificate may be used: Monday through Thursday, November through May except holiday weeks (Christmas, New Year's and Presidents' weeks).

Inn Victoria and Tea Pot Shoppe
On The Green, PO Box 788
Chester, VT 05143
(802)875-4288 (800)732-4288 Fax:(802)875-4323

Circa 1820. High tea is one of the highlights for guests, who can keep the memory alive by purchasing from the innkeeper's Tea Pot Shoppe. This Second Empire Victorian is among several historic houses and seven churches found in Chester's On the Green area. Many weekends include Victorian fairs and festivals. Overture to Christmas is a festive time for townspeople and visitors dressing Victorian and caroling door-to-door. Two summer theater groups are nearby.
Innkeeper(s): Tom & KC Lanagan. $75-125. MC VISA AX DC CB TC. 7 rooms with PB, 1 with FP. Breakfast and afternoon tea included in rates. Types of meals: full breakfast, gourmet breakfast and early coffee/tea. Beds: Q. Air conditioning, TV and VCR in room. Fax and spa on premises. Antiques, fishing, parks, shopping, downhill skiing, cross-country skiing, sporting events, theater and watersports nearby.
Certificate may be used: Sunday-Thursday, except Thanksgiving week, Sept. 20-Oct. 20, Dec. 22-Jan. 5

Craftsbury   C5

Craftsbury Inn
Main St, Box 36
Craftsbury, VT 05826-0036
(802)586-2848 (800)336-2848

Circa 1850. Bird's-eye maple woodwork and embossed tin ceilings testify to the history of this Greek Revival inn, which also features random-width floors with square nails. The foundation and porch steps were made of bull's-eye granite, quarried in town. The living room fireplace once graced the

first post office in Montpelier. Guest rooms sport country antiques and hand-made quilts. The dining room is open to the public by advance reservation and features four dinner seatings.

Innkeeper(s): Blake & Rebecca Gleason. $60-160. MAP, AP. MC VISA TC. 10 rooms, 6 with PB. 1 conference room. Breakfast included in rates. Meal: full breakfast. Dinner, picnic lunch, banquet service, catering service, catered breakfast available. Restaurant on premises. Beds: QDT. VCR on premises. Fishing, shopping, skiing, watersports nearby.

"Very comfortable - the dining was a special treat!"

Certificate may be used: Sunday through Thursday, January-December, except during foliage season.

Danby
I3

Quail's Nest B&B
PO Box 221
Danby, VT 05739-0221
(802)293-5099 Fax:(802)293-6300

Circa 1835. Located in the village, this Greek Revival inn features six guest rooms, and on each bed is found a handmade quilt. Full breakfasts are made to order by your innkeepers, who also provide early morning coffee or tea, afternoon tea and an evening snack. The Green Mountain National Forest is just to the east of the inn, providing many outstanding recreational opportunities. Outlet shopping is found just a few miles south in Manchester, and Alpine skiing is enjoyed at Bromley, Killington, Okemo, Pico and Stratton ski areas, all within easy driving distance.

Innkeeper(s): Greg & Nancy Diaz. $60-85. MC VISA AX PC TC. 6 rooms, 4 with PB. 1 conference room. Breakfast and afternoon tea included in rates. Meals: full breakfast and early coffee/tea. Beds: KDT. Turndown service in room. Cable TV and VCR on premises. Antiques, fishing, shopping, skiing, sporting events, theater, watersports nearby.

Certificate may be used: Sunday-Thursday; January-August, November, December, excluding our own special promotions.

Derby Line
A6

Derby Village Inn
46 Main St
Derby Line, VT 05830-9203
(802)873-3604

Circa 1900. This stately Victorian manor is more formal than whimsical, without the abundance of gingerbread trim common to the colorful "Painted Ladies."

The interior is elegant, boasting intricate wainscoting and original light fixtures. Antique-filled bedchambers are decorated with lovely wallpapers, Victorian sinks and vintage wall fixtures. The parlors are wonderful places to relax, one includes a baby grand piano and a fireplace. The inn's library also includes a fireplace. Innkeeper Phyllis Moreau's vast collection of Norman Rockwell plates decorates the high shelves that surround the kitchen. Phyllis also has designed many of the rugs and crafts found throughout the home.

Innkeeper(s): Tom & Phyllis Moreau. $60-70. MC VISA DS PC TC. 8 rooms, 5 with PB. Breakfast included in rates. Types of meals: full breakfast and early coffee/tea. Beds: QDT. Cable TV and library on premises. Antiques, fishing, parks, shopping, downhill skiing, cross-country skiing, theater and watersports nearby.

Certificate may be used: Anytime except Saturdays and Sept. 1-Oct. 31.

Dorset
I2

Marble West Inn
PO Box 847, Dorset West Rd
Dorset, VT 05251-0847
(802)867-4155 (800)453-7629

Circa 1840. This historic Greek Revival inn boasts many elegant touches, including stenciling in its entrance hallways done by one of the nation's top craftspeople. Guests also will enjoy Oriental rugs, handsome marble fireplaces and polished dark oak floors. Visitors delight at the many stunning views enjoyed at the inn, including Green Peak and Owl's Head mountains, flower-filled gardens and meadows and two trout-stocked ponds. Emerald Lake State Park is nearby.

Innkeeper(s): June & Wayne Erla. $90-135. MC VISA AX PC. 8 rooms with PB, 1 with FP. 1 suite. Breakfast and afternoon tea included in rates. Type of meal: full breakfast. Beds: KQDT. Turndown service in room. Library on premises. Antiques, fishing, parks, shopping, downhill skiing, cross-country skiing, theater and watersports nearby.

"A charming inn with wonderful hospitality. The room was comfortable, immaculate, and furnished with every imaginable need and comfort."

Certificate may be used: Anytime except fall foliage and holidays.

Essex Junction
D2

The Inn at Essex Junction
70 Essex Way
Essex Junction, VT 05452-3383
(802)878-1100 Fax:(802)878-0063
E-mail: innessex@together.net

Elegant furnishings and decor, each in a different style, grace the guest rooms at this luxurious Colonial inn, which carries a four-diamond rating. Several guest suites include whirlpool tubs, and 30 of the rooms include woodburning fireplaces. The

two restaurants are run by the New England Culinary Institute, one a gourmet bistro and the other a more casual cafe. The inn also includes a swimming pool, library, art gallery and a bakery.
Innkeeper(s): Jim Lamberti. $119-199. MC VISA AX DC CB DS. 97 rooms. Breakfast included in rates. Type of meal: continental breakfast.
Certificate may be used: November-July.

Fair Haven
H2

Maplewood Inn

Rt 22A S
Fair Haven, VT 05743
(802)265-8039 (800)253-7729 Fax:(802)265-8210
E-mail: maplewd@sover.net

Circa 1843. This beautifully restored Greek Revival house, which is on the National Register, was once the family home of the founder of Maplewood Dairy, Isaac Wood. Period antiques and reproductions grace the inn's spacious rooms and suites. Some rooms boast

fireplaces and all have sitting areas. A collection of antique spinning wheels and yarn winders is displayed. A porch wing, built around 1795, was a tavern formerly located down the road. Overlooking three acres of lawn, the inn offers an idyllic setting. The parlor's cordial bar and evening turndown service are among the many amenities offered by the innkeepers.
Innkeeper(s): Cindy & Doug Baird. $80-130. MC VISA AX DC CB DS PC TC. 5 rooms with PB, 4 with FP. 2 suites. 1 conference room. Breakfast, afternoon tea and evening snack included in rates. Beds: QD. Air conditioning, turndown service and TV in room. VCR, fax, copier and library on premises. Amusement parks, antiques, fishing, parks, shopping, skiing, sporting events, theater and watersports nearby.
Location: One mile south of Fair Haven village and 18 miles west of Rutland.
Publicity: *Country, Innsider, Americana, New England Getaways.*
"Your inn is perfection. Leaving under protest."
Certificate may be used: Jan. 2-June 30, anytime; July 1-Sept. 14, Sunday-Thursday; Nov. 1-Dec. 23, anytime.

Fairlee
F6

Silver Maple Lodge & Cottages

S Main St. RR 1, Box 8
Fairlee, VT 05045
(802)333-4326 (800)666-1946

Circa 1790. This old Cape farmhouse was expanded in the 1850s and became an inn in the '20s when Elmer & Della Batchelder opened their home

to guests. It became so successful that several cottages, built from lumber on the property, were added. For 60 years, the Batchelder family continued the operation. They misnamed the lodge, however, mistaking silver poplar trees on the property for what they thought were silver maples. Guest rooms are decorated with many of the inn's original furnishings, and the new innkeepers have carefully restored the rooms and added several bathrooms. A screened-in porch surrounds two sides of the house. Three of the cottages include working fireplaces and one is handicap accessible.
Innkeeper(s): Scott & Sharon Wright. $52-79. MC VISA AX DS PC TC. 16 rooms, 14 with PB, 3 with FP. 8 cottages. Breakfast included in rates. Type of meal: continental breakfast. Beds: KQDT. VCR, copier and bicycles on premises. Handicap access. Antiques, fishing, parks, shopping, downhill skiing, cross-country skiing, theater and watersports nearby.
Location: East central Vermont.
Publicity: *Boston Globe, Vermont Country Sampler, Travel Holiday, Travel America, New York Times.*
"Your gracious hospitality and attractive home all add up to a pleasant experience."
Certificate may be used: Sunday-Thursday, Nov. 1-Sept. 15.

Hardwick
C5

Carolyn's Victorian Inn

15 Church St, PO Box 1087
Hardwick, VT 05843-1087
(802)472-6338

Guests are treated to English tea and sweets upon arrival at this historic home, which boasts natural hardwood floors, original cherry woodwork and porches decorated with wicker. A cypress staircase leads up to the guest rooms, which have feather beds and quilts. The home's antiques are steeped in Vermont history. Carolyn serves up luscious breakfasts in the dining room on tables set with lacy tablecloths and fine linens. The special entrees include delectables such as banana-walnut pancakes, souffles or Yorkshire pudding with raspberry sauce.
Innkeeper(s): Carolyn Richter. $75-150. MC VISA. 5 rooms. Breakfast included in rates. Type of meal: full breakfast.
Certificate may be used: January, April, May, November, December.

Somerset House B&B
24 Highland Ave, PO Box 1098
Hardwick, VT 05843
(802)472-5484 (800)838-8074

Circa 1880. After having been away for two years in England, the innkeepers returned home to Vermont and settled in this gracious Victorian house to provide lodging for those visiting this beautiful part of the country. The home is located in the heart of the village and set amid lawns and flower gardens. Breakfast is served in the dining room.

Innkeeper(s): Ruth & David Gaillard. $65-80. EP. MC VISA PC TC. 4 rooms. Breakfast and afternoon tea included in rates. Types of meals: full breakfast and gourmet breakfast. Beds: QT. Library on premises. Antiques, fishing, shopping, downhill skiing, cross-country skiing, theater and watersports nearby.

"We found a treasure. C'est super fun."

Certificate may be used: Anytime except August-October and holidays.

Killington   G3

The Cascades Lodge & Restaurant
RR 1 Box 2848
Killington, VT 05751-9710
(802)422-3731 (800)345-0113 Fax:(802)422-3351

Circa 1980. Breathtaking views and modern amenities are found at this contemporary three-story country lodge in the heart of the Green Mountains. Guests enjoy an exercise area, indoor pool with sundeck, sauna and whirlpool. A bar and restaurant are on the premises, and the inn's amenities make it an ideal spot for meetings, reunions or weddings. Within walking distance is an 18-hole golf course and the Killington Summer Theater.

Innkeeper(s): Bob, Vickie & Andrew MacKenzie. $50-159. MAP. EP. MC VISA AX DS TC. 46 rooms, 45 with PB. 6 suites. Breakfast included in rates. Types of meals: full breakfast and early coffee/tea. Dinner, picnic lunch, catering service, room service available. Restaurant on premises. Beds: QD. TV in room. VCR, fax, copier, spa, sauna on premises. Handicap access. Antiques, fishing, parks, skiing, theater nearby.

Certificate may be used: May 15 to Oct. 15.

The Peak Chalet
PO Box 511, South View Path
Killington, VT 05751-0511
(802)422-4278

Circa 1978. This contemporary chalet-style inn is located in the heart of the Killington Ski Resort. That convenience is matched by the inn's elegant accom-

modations and attention to detail. Guest rooms feature either a four-poster, iron, panel or sleigh bed, all queen-size. The living room, with its impressive stone fireplace and view of the Green Mountains, is a favorite gathering spot for those not on the slopes.

Innkeeper(s): Greg & Diane Becker. $50-110. MC VISA AX DC PC TC. 4 rooms with PB. Breakfast and afternoon tea included in rates. Type of meal: continental-plus breakfast. Beds: QT. Cable TV and VCR on premises. Antiques, fishing, parks, shopping, downhill skiing, cross-country skiing, theater and watersports nearby.

Certificate may be used: Jan. 1-Sept. 21 and Oct. 15-Dec. 21, Sunday-Thursday, holidays excluded.

The Vermont Inn
Rt 4
Killington, VT 05751
(802)775-0708 (800)541-7795 Fax:(802)773-2440
E-mail: vtinn@aol.com

Circa 1840. Surrounded by mountain views, this rambling red and white farmhouse has provided lodging and superb cuisine for many years. Exposed

beams add to the atmosphere in the living and game rooms. The award-winning dining room provides candlelight tables beside a huge fieldstone fireplace.

Innkeeper(s): Megan & Greg Smith. $50-185. MAP. EP. MC VISA AX DC PC TC. 18 rooms with PB, 2 with FP. Breakfast and afternoon tea included in rates. Types of meals: full breakfast and early coffee/tea. Banquet service available. Beds: QDT. Air conditioning and ceiling fan in room. Cable TV, VCR, fax, copier, spa, swimming, sauna, tennis and library on premises. Handicap access. Antiques, fishing, parks, shopping, downhill skiing, cross-country skiing, theater, watersports nearby. Publicity: N.Y. Daily News, New Jersey Star Leader, Rutland Business Journal, Bridgeport Post Telegram, New York Times, Boston, Vermont.

"We had a wonderful time. The inn is breathtaking. Hope to be back."

Certificate may be used: Midweek, except during foliage season.

Landgrove   J3

Landgrove Inn
Rd Box 215, Landgrove Rd
Landgrove, VT 05148
(802)824-6673 (800)669-8466 Fax:(802)824-3055
E-mail: Vtinn@sover.net

Circa 1820. This rambling inn is located along a country lane in the valley of Landgrove in the Green Mountain National Forest. The Rafter Room is a lounge and pub with a fireside sofa for 12. Breakfast and dinner are served in the newly renovated and stenciled dining room. Evening sleigh or hay rides are often arranged. Rooms vary in style and bedding arrangements, including some newly decorated rooms with country decor, so inquire when making your reservation.

Innkeeper(s): Kathy & Jay Snyder. $85-125. MC VISA AX DS TC. 18 rooms, 16 with PB. 1 conference room. Breakfast included in rates. Type of meal: full breakfast. Afternoon tea and dinner available. Restaurant on premises. Beds: QD. Cable TV, VCR, fax, copier and spa on premises. Antiques, fishing, parks, shopping, downhill skiing, cross-country skiing and theater nearby.

"A true country inn with great food — we'll be back."

Certificate may be used: May 20-Sept. 20 and Dec. 20-April 1, Sunday through Thursday, non-holiday weeks.

Ludlow
I4

Echo Lake Inn
PO Box 154
Ludlow, VT 05149-0154
(802)228-8602 (800)356-6844 Fax:(802)228-3075
E-mail: echolkinn@aol.com

Circa 1840. Just minutes from Killington and Okemo ski areas, this New England country-style inn offers gourmet candlelight dining, a full country breakfast, library and parlor. Guests also may borrow canoes and

are allowed to pick wildflowers and berries in season. Guests will find golf, horseback riding, waterfalls and wineries within easy walking distance. The inn is located in Tyson, five miles north of Ludlow.

Innkeeper(s): John & Yvonne Pardieu, Chip Connelly. $99-219. MAP. MC VISA AX DS. 25 rooms, 10 with PB. 1 suite. Breakfast and dinner included in rates. Types of meals: full breakfast and early coffee/tea. Room service available. Restaurant on premises. Beds: QDT. Ceiling fan in room. Cable TV, fax, spa, swimming, sauna, tennis and library on premises. Antiques, fishing, shopping, downhill skiing, cross-country skiing, theater and watersports nearby.

Publicity: *Bon Appetit, Gourmet.*

"Very special! We've decided to make the Echo Lake Inn a yearly tradition for our family."

Certificate may be used: May 1-Sept. 20, Nov. 20-Dec. 23, Jan. 5-Feb. 12, Feb. 23-March 30, Sunday-Thursday, non holiday

Lyndonville
C6

Wheelock Inn B&B
RR 2 Box 160, Wheelock Rd
Lyndonville, VT 05851-9101
(802)626-8503 Fax:(802)626-3403

Circa 1809. This 19th-century farmhouse features handhewn beams and wide pine flooring. Renovations have added to the charm and attractiveness. Spacious grounds and a quiet setting make it ideal for both the outdoor enthusiast and those seeking an escape. A guest lounge provides a place for games or reading. Bean Pond and Branch Brook offer boating, fishing and swimming. The inn's gardens furnish flowers, fruit and vegetables. Burke Mountain is nearby.

Innkeeper(s): John Ayers. $45-75. MC VISA. 3 rooms. Breakfast included in rates. Types of meals: full breakfast and early coffee/tea. Evening snack and picnic lunch available. Cable TV and VCR on premises. Antiques, shopping, skiing and theater nearby.

Certificate may be used: Anytime except Sept. 15-Oct. 15 and President's Week (February).

Manchester
J2

The Battenkill Inn
PO Box 948
Manchester, VT 05254-0948
(802)362-4213 (800)441-1628 Fax:(802)362-0975

Circa 1840. There is something for everyone at this Victorian farmhouse inn. Guest rooms are filled with antiques, and four of them boast working fireplaces. Fine fishing is found in the Battenkill River on the inn's grounds, and guests also are welcome to stroll down to the pond to feed the ducks or play croquet on the lush lawns. Two sitting rooms with fireplaces are popular gathering areas. Dining and shopping experiences await visitors in Manchester Village and Emerald Lake State Park is a short drive from the inn.

Innkeeper(s): Laine & Yoshi Akiyama. $95-165. MC VISA AX TC. 11 rooms with PB, 4 with FP. Breakfast and evening snack included in rates. Types of meals: full breakfast and early coffee/tea. Beds: KQDT. Air conditioning, turndown service and ceiling fan in room. VCR, fax, copier and library on premises. Handicap access. Antiques, fishing, parks, shopping, skiing, theater and watersports nearby.

"The inn is beautiful and the atmosphere soothing."

Certificate may be used: November-June, Sunday-Thursday, no holidays.

Rose Apple Acres Farm

RR 2, Box 300, East Hill Rd
Manchester, VT 05859
(802)988-4300 Fax:(802)988-2309

Circa 1900. Surrounded by panoramic views, this 52-acre working farm is the perfect place for relaxing vacations. Rest on the porch and take in the view or tour the grounds, lush with gardens, woods and ponds. The innkeepers house sheep, goats, cows and Belgian horses on the farm. Homemade goodies abound on the breakfast table, and guests can purchase farm-made maple syrup, jams, jellies and honey. Home-spun yarn also is available. The surrounding area boasts a number of factories, including the Cabot Cheese Factory and Ben & Jerry's Ice Cream Factory. Tour the Bread and Puppet Museum or the Haskell Free Library and Opera House. In winter, skiing the slopes at Jay Peak is a must.

Innkeeper(s): Jay & Camilla Mead. $50-60. MC VISA. 3 rooms, 1 with PB. Breakfast included in rates. Type of meal: continental-plus breakfast. Beds: KTD. Cable TV, VCR, fax and swimming on premises. Antiques, fishing, shopping, downhill skiing, cross-country skiing, golf and watersports nearby.
Location: On the Canadian border.
Publicity: *Washington Times, Vermont Life, Montreal Gazette.*
"*So relaxing, non-stress here.*"

Certificate may be used: Sunday through Thursday, all year.

Village Country Inn

PO Box 408, Rt 7A
Manchester, VT 05254-0408
(802)362-1792 (800)370-0300 Fax:(802)362-7238

Circa 1889. Townsfolk refer to the Village Country Inn as the old summer house of the Kellogg cereal family. A Grecian-columned porch spans 100 feet across the front of the house and is filled with chintz-covered rockers and pots of flowers. Decorated in a French Country style, rooms feature French lace and antiques. Dinner is served in a garden dining room, which overlooks marble terraces and fountains.

Innkeeper(s): Anne Degen. $140-225. MAP. MC VISA AX DS. 31 rooms, 30 with PB. 12 suites. Breakfast and dinner included in rates. Types of meals: full breakfast, gourmet breakfast and early coffee/tea. Picnic

lunch available. Restaurant on premises. Beds: KQD. Air conditioning, turndown service, ceiling fan and TV in room. Fax on premises. Antiques, fishing, shopping, skiing and theater nearby.
Location: Historic route 7A.
Publicity: *Country Inns, Albany Times Union, Gourmet, Vacations, USA Today, ABC-TV, Country Decorating Ideas, Victorian.*

"*Absolutely charming. So much attention to detail. We loved it.*"

Certificate may be used: Sunday through Thursday, non-holiday, non-foliage, second night B&B only.

Wilburton Inn

PO Box 468
Manchester, VT 05254-0468
(802)362-2500 (800)648-4944 Fax:(802)362-1107

Circa 1902. Shaded by tall maples, this three-story brick mansion sits high on a hill overlooking the Battenkill Valley, which is set against a majestic mountain backdrop. In addition to the mansion, the inn offers four villas and a seven-bedroom reunion house. Carved moldings, mahogany paneling, Oriental carpets and leaded-glass windows are complemented by carefully chosen antiques. The inn's 20 acres provide three tennis courts, a pool, green lawns and sculpture gardens. The grounds are popular for country weddings. Gourmet dining is served in the billiard room with European ambiance. Two local country clubs provide the inn with golf privileges.

Innkeeper(s): Georgette Levis. $95-185. MAP. AP. MC VISA AX. 35 rooms, 6 with FP. 1 conference room. Breakfast included in rates. Type of meal: gourmet breakfast. Afternoon tea, dinner and room service available. Restaurant on premises. Beds: KQ. Fax, copier and computer on premises. Antiques, fishing, downhill skiing, cross-country skiing, golf, theater and watersports nearby.
Publicity: *Great Escapes TV, Travelhost, Getaways For Gourmets, Country Inns, Bed & Breakfast, Gourmet, Best Places to Stay In New England.*

"*Simply splendid! Peaceful, beautiful, elegant. Ambiance & ambiance!*"

Certificate may be used: April.

Manchester Center   J2

Manchester Highlands Inn

Highland Ave, Box 1754A
Manchester Center, VT 05255
(802)362-4565 (800)743-4565 Fax:(802)362-4028
E-mail: relax@highlandsinn.com

Circa 1898. This Queen Anne Victorian mansion sits proudly on the crest of a hill overlooking the village. From the three-story turret, guests can look out over Mt. Equinox, the Green Mountains and the valley below. Feather beds and down comforters adorn the beds in the guest rooms. A game room with billiards and a stone fireplace are popular in winter,

while summertime guests enjoy the outdoor pool, croquet lawn and veranda. Gourmet country breakfasts and home-baked afternoon snacks are served.

Innkeeper(s): Patricia & Robert Eichorn. $105-135. MC VISA AX PC TC. 15 rooms with PB. Breakfast and afternoon tea included in rates. Types of meals: full breakfast and gourmet breakfast. Beds: QDT. Cable TV, VCR, fax, swimming and library on premises. Antiques, fishing, parks, shopping, downhill skiing, cross-country skiing and theater nearby.

Publicity: *Toronto Sun, Vermont, Asbury Park Press, Vermont Weathervane, Yankee Traveler, Boston Globe.*

"We couldn't believe such a place existed. Now we can't wait to come again."

Certificate may be used: Monday through Thursday, Nov. 1-June 30, except holiday periods.

Montgomery   B4

Black Lantern Inn
Rt 118
Montgomery, VT 05470
(802)326-4507 (800)255-8661 Fax:(802)326-4077

Circa 1803. This brick inn and restaurant originally served as a stagecoach stop. There is a taproom with beamed ceilings and two downstairs lounges. A large three-bedroom suite has its own spa. Vermont antiques fill all the guest rooms. A few minutes from the inn, skiers (novice and expert) can ride the tramway to the top of Jay Peak.

Innkeeper(s): Rita & Allen Kalsmith. $60-125. MAP, EP. MC VISA AX DS PC TC. 16 rooms, 10 with PB. 6 suites. Breakfast included in rates. Type of meal: full breakfast. Restaurant on premises. Beds: KQDT. Ceiling fan and VCR in room. Fax on premises. Antiques, fishing, downhill skiing and cross-country skiing nearby.

Publicity: *Burlington Free Press, Los Angeles Times, Bon Appetit, Ottawa Citizen.*

"...one of the four or five great meals of your life—Jay Stone, Ottawa Citizen."

Certificate may be used: Anytime except holiday (Christmas) and fall foliage.

Montpelier   E4

Betsy's B&B
74 E State St
Montpelier, VT 05602-3112
(802)229-0466 Fax:(802)229-5412
E-mail: betsybb@plainfield.bypass.com

Circa 1895. Within walking distance of downtown and located in the state's largest historic preservation district, this Queen Anne Victorian with romantic turret and carriage house features lavish Victorian antiques throughout its interior. Bay windows, carved woodwork, high ceilings, lace curtains

and wood floors add to the authenticity. An exercise room, hot tub and porch tempt many visitors. The full breakfast varies in content but not quality, and guest favorites include sourdough banana pancakes.

Innkeeper(s): Jon & Betsy Anderson. $55-85. MC VISA AX DS PC TC. 10 rooms, 7 with PB. Breakfast included in rates. Type of meal: full breakfast. Beds: QDT. TV in room. VCR, fax and spa on premises. Antiques, fishing, parks, shopping, skiing, theater, watersports nearby.

Certificate may be used: Nov.1-April 30, holiday weekends excluded.

North Hero   B2

North Hero House
Rt 2 Box 106, Champlain Islands
North Hero, VT 05474
(802)372-8237

Circa 1891. This three-story inn stands on a slight rise overlooking Lake Champlain and Vermont's highest peak, Mt. Mansfield. Three other houses, including the Wadsworth store located at the City Dock, also provide accommodations for the inn's guests. Rooms hang over the water's edge and feature waterfront porches.

Innkeeper(s): Ann Marie Sherlock. $65-140. EP. MC VISA AX DS. 23 rooms, 21 with PB. Breakfast included in rates. Type of meal: continental-plus breakfast. Restaurant on premises. Beds: T. Sauna on premises. Handicap access.

Publicity: *Gourmet.*

"We have visited many inns and this house was by far the best, due mostly to the staff!"

Certificate may be used: All of May and June; Sunday, Monday, Tuesday, Wednesday - July, August, September and October.

Orwell
G2

Historic Brookside Farms
PO Box 36, Route 22A
Orwell, VT 05760-9615
(802)948-2727 Fax:(802)948-2015
E-mail: hbfinnvt@aol.com

Circa 1789. Nineteen stately Ionic columns grace the front of this Neoclassical Greek Revival farmhouse, which was designed by James Lamb. This is a working farm with Hereford cattle, Hampshire sheep, maple syrup production and poultry. There

are 300 acres of lush country landscape with several miles of cross-country skiing, plenty of places for hiking and a 26-acre pond for boating and fishing. Innkeeper Murray Korda is an orchestra leader/concert violinist and speaks nine languages. Downhill skiing, tennis and skating are nearby. The farm is family owned and operated.

Innkeeper(s): Joan & Murray Korda. $85-150. MAP, AP. 7 rooms, 2 with PB. 1 suite. 1 conference room. Breakfast and afternoon tea included in rates. Types of meals: gourmet breakfast and early coffee/tea. Dinner, evening snack, picnic lunch, lunch, gourmet lunch and banquet service available. Restaurant on premises. Beds: DT. VCR, fax, copier, computer and child care on premises. Handicap access. Antiques, fishing, downhill skiing, cross-country skiing, theater nearby.

Publicity: *New York Times, Burlington Free Press, Los Angeles Times, Preservation Magazine Antiques.*

"A wonderful piece of living history."

Certificate may be used: Jan. 1-May 15, June 1-Aug. 31, Nov. 1-Dec. 15.

Poultney
H2

Tower Hall B&B
2 Bentley Ave
Poultney, VT 05764-1134
(802)287-4004 (800)894-4004

Circa 1895. A three-story peaked turret lends the name to this Queen Anne inn located next to Green Mountain College. Stained glass, polished woodwork and original fireplace mantels add to the Victorian atmosphere, and the guest rooms are fur-

nished with antiques of the period. A sitting room adjacent to the guest rooms has its own fireplace. Kathy's cranberry nut and date nut breads are especially popular breakfast items.

Innkeeper(s): Kathy & Ed Kann. $55-75. MC VISA TC. 3 rooms, 1 with PB. Breakfast included in rates. Meals: continental-plus breakfast and early coffee/tea. Beds: D. TV in room. Bicycles on premises. Antiques, fishing, parks, shopping, cross-country skiing, watersports nearby.

Location: Adjacent to Green Mountain College, near lakes region.

Publicity: *Rutland Herald, Rutland Business Journal.*

"Your beautiful home was delightful and just the best place to stay!"

Certificate may be used: Nov. 1-April 30, Sunday-Saturday.

Proctorsville
I4

The Golden Stage Inn
Depot St, PO Box 218
Proctorsville, VT 05153
(802)226-7744 (800)253-8226 Fax:(802)226-7136

Circa 1780. The Golden Stage Inn was a stagecoach stop built shortly before Vermont's founding. It became a link in the Underground Railroad and the home of Cornelia Otis Skinner. Extensive gardens surround the wraparound porch as well as the swimming pool. The innkeepers offer a TTY number at (802) 226-7136 for those who are hearing impaired.

Innkeeper(s): Micki & Paul Smith-Darnauer. $145-170. MAP, MC VISA DS PC TC. 8 rooms with PB. 2 suites. Breakfast, dinner and evening snack included in rates. Types of meals: full breakfast and early coffee/tea. Beds: KQDT. Cable TV, VCR, fax, copier, swimming and library on premises. Antiques, fishing, shopping, downhill skiing, cross-country skiing, theater and watersports nearby.

Location: Near Ludlow.

Publicity: *Journal Inquirer, Gourmet, Los Angeles Times.*

"The essence of a country inn!"

Certificate may be used: Sunday through Thursday, Feb. 25-March 31 and May 1-Sept. 15, subject to availability, non-holidays; includes breakfasts but not dinners.

Putney
K4

Misty Meadows B&B
RR 1 Box 458
Putney, VT 05346-9601
(802)722-9517 (800)566-4789
E-mail: mistybnb@aol. com

Circa 1986. Herb and flower gardens and a gazebo overlooking a mountainous valley are two of the reasons why guests enjoy Misty Meadows. There are 10 acres to explore, dotted with wildflowers and a stream. Many guests are drawn to the living room, which offers a fireplace, books and games. The innkeepers' four, friendly cats often entertain guests as well. There is plenty to do in the area, including berry picking, historic tours, flea markets, canoeing and skiing.

Innkeeper(s): Jane & Dave Savage. $65-85. PC. 3 rooms with PB. Breakfast included in rates. Type of meal: full breakfast. Beds: KQD. Ceiling fan in room. Library on premises. Handicap access. Amusement parks, antiques, fishing, shopping, downhill skiing, cross-country skiing, theater and watersports nearby.

Certificate may be used: Jan. 1-Sept. 15, Nov. 1-December, no holiday weekends.

The Putney Inn
PO Box 181
Putney, VT 05346-0181
(802)387-5517 (800)653-5517 Fax:(802)387-5211

Circa 1790. The property surrounding this New England farmhouse was deeded to an English Army Captain by King George in 1790. The grounds' first home burned in a fire, and this inn was constructed on the original foundation. Eventually it became a Catholic seminary, and then an elegant country inn. Rooms are located in a 1960s building, adjacent to the main historic farmhouse. The rooms are decorated in a Colonial style with antiques. The inn's dining room, headed by renown chef Ann Cooper, features New England cuisine. The ingredients are fresh and locally produced, and might include appetizers such as smoked salmon on Johnnycakes with an apple cider vinaigrette. Entrees such as a mixed grill of local venison and game hen flavored by an apple-horseradish marinade follow. Craft and antique shops, hiking, skiing and biking are among the local activities.

Innkeeper(s): Randi Ziter. $78-158. MC VISA AX DS PC TC. 25 rooms with PB. 4 conference rooms. Breakfast included in rates. Types of meals: continental breakfast, continental-plus breakfast, full breakfast, gourmet breakfast and early coffee/tea. Afternoon tea, dinner, evening snack, picnic lunch, lunch, gourmet lunch, banquet service and catering service available. Restaurant on premises. Beds: Q. Air conditioning and TV in room. VCR, fax and copier on premises. Handicap access. Amusement parks, antiques, fishing, shopping, downhill skiing, cross-country skiing, golf, theater and watersports nearby.

Publicity: *Chicago Tribune, Boston Herald, Culinary Arts, US Air, Travel & Leisure, Vermont Life, Vermont Magazine.*

Certificate may be used: November through April. Holidays excluded. Based on availability.

Quechee   H5

Parker House Inn
16 Main St, Box 0780
Quechee, VT 05059
(802)295-6077
E-mail: parker-house-inn@valley.net

Circa 1857. State Sen. Joseph C. Parker built this riverside manor in 1857, and three of the guest rooms are named in honor of his family. Mornings at the inn begin with a delicious country breakfast served in the Parker House Restaurant's cozy dining rooms. The chefs are justifiably proud of their "comfort food" cuisine. Guests can stroll next door to watch the art of glass blowing, or take a walk along the Ottauquechee

River. The surroundings of this historic town provide hours of activity for nature-lovers and shutterbugs. Fall foliage, of course, is an autumnal delight.

Innkeeper(s): Barbara & Walt Forrester. $100-135. MAP. MC VISA AX PC TC. 7 rooms with PB. Breakfast included in rates. Types of meals: full breakfast and gourmet breakfast. Dinner and banquet service available. Restaurant on premises. Beds: KQ. Air conditioning and ceiling fan in room. Cable TV, VCR, fax and bicycles on premises. Antiques, fishing, downhill skiing, cross-country skiing, theater, watersports nearby.

Publicity: *Quechee Times.*

"The inn is lovely, the innkeepers are the greatest, excellent food and heavenly bed!"

Certificate may be used: Anytime, Nov. 1-April 30; Sunday through Thursday, May 1-July 30.

Rochester   G3

Liberty Hill Farm
RR 1 Box 158, Liberty Hill Rd
Rochester, VT 05767-9501
(802)767-3926
E-mail: libhilfarm@aol.com

Circa 1825. A working dairy farm with a herd of registered Holsteins, this farmhouse offers a country setting and easy access to recreational activities. The inn's location, between the White River and the Green Mountains, is ideal for outdoor enthusiasts and animal lovers. Barn cats, chickens, a dog, ducks, horses and turkeys are found on the grounds, not to mention the Holstein herd. Fishing, hiking, skiing and swimming are popular pastimes of guests, who are treated to a family-style dinner and full breakfast, both featuring many delicious homemade specialties.

Innkeeper(s): Robert & Beth Kennett. $120. MAP. PC TC. 7 rooms. Breakfast and dinner included in rates. Types of meals: full breakfast and early coffee/tea. Beds: QDT. VCR, fax, swimming, library and child care on premises. Antiques, fishing, parks, shopping, downhill skiing, cross-country skiing, sporting events, theater and watersports nearby.

Publicity: *New York Times, Boston Globe, Vermont Life, Family Circle, Family Fun, Woman's Day, Country Home.*

"We had a wonderful time exploring your farm and the countryside. The food was great."

Certificate may be used: January-May, except holidays, Sunday-Thursday nights only.

Roxbury   E4

The Inn at Johnnycake Flats
RR 1, Carrie Howe Rd
Roxbury, VT 05669
(802)485-8961

Circa 1806. The guest rooms in this registered historical site include family antiques, Shaker baskets and handmade quilts. The innkeepers can help you identify local wildflowers and birds. In winter, enjoy cross-country skiing and come home to sip hot cider beside the fire. Ask Debra and Jim about their hobby, cold climate gardening. A popular toboggan ride is down the lane in front of the inn. An old swimming hole, known to locals for many years, is popular.
Innkeeper(s): Debra & Jim Rogler. $65-75. DS PC TC. 4 rooms, 1 with PB. Breakfast and afternoon tea included in rates. Types of meals: continental breakfast, continental-plus breakfast, full breakfast and early coffee/tea. Beds: DT. Ceiling fan in room. VCR, bicycles and library on premises. Antiques, fishing, parks, shopping, downhill skiing, cross-country skiing, sporting events, theater and watersports nearby.

"You've nurtured a bit of paradise here, thanks for the lovely stay."

Certificate may be used: January-April, May (except first & second week), June, July (except second week), August, September (except third & fourth week), October (except first & second week), November and December, except holidays.

Rutland   H3

The Inn at Rutland
70 N Main St
Rutland, VT 05701-3249
(802)773-0575 (800)808-0575

Circa 1890. This distinctive Victorian mansion is filled with many period details, from high, plasterworked ceilings to leather wainscotting in the dining room. Leaded windows and interesting woodwork are found throughout. Guest rooms have been decorated to maintain Victorian charm without a loss of modern comforts. A wicker-filled porch and common rooms are available to guests. Located in

central Vermont, The Inn at Rutland is only 15 minutes from the Killington and Pico ski areas.
Innkeeper(s): Bob & Tanya Liberman. $49-195. MC VISA AX DC CB DS TC. 10 rooms with PB. 1 suite. 2 conference rooms. Breakfast included in rates. Types of meals: full breakfast and gourmet breakfast. Beds: KQD. Air conditioning, ceiling fan and TV in room. VCR, fax, copier and bicycles on premises. Antiques, fishing, parks, shopping, downhill skiing, cross-country skiing, sporting events, theater, watersports nearby.
Location: In central Vermont.

"A lovely page in the 'memory album' of our minds."

Certificate may be used: April 1-Aug. 31, Nov. 1-Dec. 15, Sunday-Thursday, excluding holidays,

Saint Johnsbury   D6

Looking Glass Inn
Rt 18 Box 199
Saint Johnsbury, VT 05819
(802)748-3052 (800)579-3644

Circa 1850. This historic Second Empire Victorian once served travelers in the early 19th century. Visitors today enjoy the same Northeast Vermont setting and old-time hospitality, including special romantic candlelight dinners that can be arranged by reservation. Visitors start their day with a large country breakfast served in the mauve-accented dining room. Later in the day, guests are welcome to relax with a cup of tea or glass of sherry. Idyllic country roads are found throughout the surrounding area, perfect for exploring year-round.
Innkeeper(s): Barbara & Perry Viles. $60-85. MC VISA PC TC. 6 rooms, 2 with PB. 1 conference room. Breakfast and afternoon tea included in rates. Types of meals: continental breakfast, continental-plus breakfast, full breakfast and early coffee/tea. Beds: DT. Library on premises. Antiques, fishing, parks, shopping, downhill skiing, cross-country skiing and watersports nearby.
Publicity: *Tampa Tribune.*
Certificate may be used: All year except holidays and period between Sept. 20 and Oct. 15.

Shoreham   F2

Shoreham Inn & Country Store
On The Green, Main St
Shoreham, VT 05770
(802)897-5081 (800)255-5081

Circa 1790. Located just five miles east of Fort Ticonderoga, this Federal-style inn is a favorite of nature-lovers. Fascinating antique shops and many covered bridges are found in the area. The inn's dining room, with its large open fire, is a popular gathering spot, and guests also are drawn to the restored 19th-century sitting rooms. Guest rooms are furnished with country antiques. A country store is on the premises.
Innkeeper(s): Julie & Jim Ortuno. $85. AP. MC VISA PC TC. 11 rooms. Breakfast included in rates. Types of meals: full breakfast and early cof-

Circa 1790

fee/tea. Dinner available. Copier, bicycles and library on premises. Antiques, fishing, parks, shopping, downhill skiing, cross-country skiing, sporting events, theater and watersports nearby.

Certificate may be used: Anytime on space available basis.

Shrewsbury H3

Crown Point Inn
Wiley Hill, PO Box 157
Shrewsbury, VT 05738
(802)492-3589 (800)492-8089

Circa 1850. During the Revolutionary War, the road that runs in front of this inn was used as the main supply route between Boston Harbor and Fort Ticonderoga. More than a century later, this Colonial inn was built. Its location is ideal, boasting views of mountains and surrounded by more than 100 acres. The guest rooms, decorated in an elegant country style, feature beds bedecked with Ralph Lauren linens and topped with down comforters. Breakfasts are healthy and hearty, often featuring low-fat and low-cholesterol fare. Homemade muffins, scones, entrees made from farm-fresh eggs, seasonal fruits and pancakes topped with Vermont maple syrup might appear on the breakfast table.
Innkeeper(s): Carol & B. Michael Calotta. $80-125. PC TC. 8 rooms, 6 with PB. 1 conference room. Breakfast and afternoon tea included in rates. Types of meals: full breakfast, gourmet breakfast and early coffee/tea. Picnic lunch and banquet service available. Beds: QT. Cable TV, VCR, swimming, bicycles, tennis and library on premises. Antiques, fishing, parks, shopping, downhill skiing, cross-country skiing, golf, theater and watersports nearby.
Publicity: *Country Inns.*
Certificate may be used: May 25-Sept. 20, Sunday-Thursday.

South Londonderry J3

Londonderry Inn
PO Box 301-931, Rt 100
South Londonderry, VT 05155
(802)824-5226 Fax:(802)824-3146
E-mail: londinn@sovernet.net

Circa 1826. For almost 100 years, the Melendy Homestead, overlooking the West River and the village, was a dairy farm. In 1940, it became an inn. A

tourist brochure promoting the area in 1881 said, "Are you overworked in the office, counting room or workshop and need invigorating influences? Come ramble over these hills and mountains and try the revivifying effects of Green Mountain oxygen." Dinner is available weekends and holiday periods, in season.
Innkeeper(s): Jim & Jean Cavanagh. $39-105. EP. 25 rooms, 20 with PB. 1 conference room. Breakfast included in rates. Dinner available. Restaurant on premises. Beds: KQDT. Cable TV, VCR, fax and copier on premises. Antiques, fishing, shopping, downhill skiing, cross-country skiing, sporting events, theater and watersports nearby.
Location: Route 100 between Manchester and Springfield.
Publicity: *New England Monthly, Ski, McCall's.*

"A weekend in a good country inn, such as the Londonderry, is on a par with a weekend on the ocean in Southern Maine, which is to say that it's as good as a full week nearly anyplace else — The Hornet."
Certificate may be used: All times subject to availability, excludes holiday periods, fall foliage, Christmas week, President's week and winter weekends.

South Newfane K4

The Inn at Inn at South Newfane
HCR 63, Box 57, Dover Rd
South Newfane, VT 05351-0057
(802)348-7191 Fax:(802)348-9325
E-mail: cullinn@sover.net

A wealthy Philadelphia family built this Colonial as their summer home. The inn is decorated in a comfortable style, with Oriental rugs and traditional furnishings. The front living room and entry are painted an inviting shade of yellow and offer an assortment of chairs to relax on, as well as reading material. Guest rooms are cozy and homey, and one might feature floral wallcoverings and a bed topped with quilts. Breakfasts are served in the morning room, which has a fireplace. The inn also has a restaurant, featuring a variety of gourmet fare. Guests might start off with a spinach and feta cheese tart or perhaps lobster bisque, then enjoy one of evening's entrees. From there, desserts such as warm apple crisp with homemade French vanilla ice cream, finish off the evening meal.
Innkeeper(s): Neville & Dawn Cullen. $95-115. MAP. MC VISA TC. 6 rooms with PB. Breakfast included in rates. Types of meals: continen-

tal-plus breakfast, full breakfast and gourmet breakfast. Evening snack, picnic lunch, lunch, banquet service, catering service and room service available. Restaurant on premises. Beds: KQT. Turndown service and ceiling fan in room. Swimming on premises. Antiques, fishing, parks, shopping, skiing, golf, theater and watersports nearby.

"Wonderfully calm and peaceful. Loved every minute."

Certificate may be used: Subject to availability, anytime except Sept. 19-Oct. 26.

Stockbridge G3

Stockbridge Inn B&B
PO Box 45
Stockbridge, VT 05772-0045
(802)746-8165 (800)588-8165

This Italianate inn has a history involving Justin Morgan, who was instrumental in developing the Morgan horse breed. The inn's location is in the countryside outside of Stockbridge and provides

easy access to the nearby White River, famed for its canoeing, trout fishing and white-water rafting. Killington Mountain skiing is within easy driving distance, and autumn colors in the surrounding area are hard to beat.

Innkeeper(s): Janice Hughes. $40-90. MC VISA. 6 rooms. Breakfast included in rates. Type of meal: full breakfast. Cable TV and VCR on premises. Antiques, shopping, downhill skiing, cross-country skiing and theater nearby.

Certificate may be used: Anytime except holiday weeks/weekends and fall foliage.

Stowe D4

Brass Lantern Inn
717 Maple St
Stowe, VT 05672-4250
(802)253-2229 (800)729-2980 Fax:(802)253-7425
E-mail: brasslntrn@aol.com

Circa 1810. This rambling farmhouse and carriage barn rests at the foot of Mt. Mansfield. A recent award-winning renovation has brought a new shine to the inn from the gleaming plank floors to the

polished woodwork and crackling fireplaces and soothing whirlpool tubs. Quilts and antiques fill the guest rooms and some, like the Honeymoon Room, have their own fireplace and mountain view. A complimentary afternoon and evening tea is provided along with a full Vermont-style breakfast. The inn is a three-time winner (1995-97) of the Golden Fork Award from the Gourmet Dinners Society of North America.

Innkeeper(s): Andy Aldrich. $75-225. MC VISA AX. 9 rooms with PB, 3 with FP. Breakfast and afternoon tea included in rates. Types of meals: full breakfast and early coffee/tea. Beds: QDT. Air conditioning in room. VCR, fax, copier and library on premises. Antiques, fishing, parks, shopping, downhill skiing, cross-country skiing, sporting events, theater and watersports nearby.
Location: One-half mile from village center.
Publicity: *Vermont, Vermont Life, Innsider, Discerning Traveler, Ski.*

"The little things made us glad we stopped."

Certificate may be used: Midweek and limited weekends during April, May and to mid-June; late October, November and to mid-December excluding holidays.

Plum Door
PO Box 606, School St
Stowe, VT 05672-0606
(802)253-9995 (800)258-7586

Circa 1890. The Plum Door is a relaxing place to enjoy a ski vacation. The innkeepers offer secure equipment lockers for each guest, and the inn is near many of Stowe's celebrated slopes. The cozy guest rooms include ceiling fans. The Dunbar and Spaulding rooms afford mountain views, and Dunbar also includes a fireplace. During the warmer months, the homemade continental breakfasts are served on the balcony. For an extra charge, guests enjoy privileges at a nearby athletic club.

Innkeeper(s): Herb & Fran Greenhalgh. $50-90. MC VISA TC. 3 rooms with PB, 1 with FP. Breakfast included in rates. Type of meal: continental-plus breakfast. Beds: Q. Ceiling fan in room. Cable TV and VCR on premises. Antiques, fishing, parks, shopping, skiing and theater nearby.

Certificate may be used: May 1-Sept. 15 & Oct. 15-Dec. 15, Sunday-Friday.

The Siebeness Inn
3681 Mountain Rd
Stowe, VT 05672-4764
(802)253-8942 (800)426-9001 Fax:(802)253-9232

Circa 1952. A multi-course full breakfast enjoyed with a view of majestic Mt. Mansfield is a highlight of this New England Colonial inn. The village of Stowe is just a few miles away, and a free trolley shuttle takes visitors there to partake of the town's many attractions. The inn offers bicycles, an exercise room, hot tub and pool for relaxing and recreation. A fireplace, library and television are available in the inn's common areas. Favorite guest activities include tours of Ben & Jerry's Ice Cream Factory, Green Mountain Chocolate Factory and the Shelburne Museum.

Innkeeper(s): Sue & Nils Andersen. $70-180. MAP. MC VISA AX DS PC TC. 12 rooms, 11 with PB. Breakfast included in rates. Types of meals: full breakfast and early coffee/tea. Afternoon tea and evening snack available. Restaurant on premises. Beds: KQDT. Air conditioning in room. Cable TV, VCR, fax, copier, spa, swimming, bicycles and library on premises. Antiques, fishing, parks, shopping, downhill skiing, cross-country skiing, sporting events, theater and watersports nearby.

Certificate may be used: January, April 1-June 30 (all days), Aug. 20-Sept. 15 (Sunday-Friday), Oct. 22-Dec. 15 (all days).

Ye Olde England Inne

433 Mountain Rd
Stowe, VT 05672-4628
(802)253-7558 (800)477-3771 Fax:(802)253-8944

Circa 1890. Originally a farmhouse, Ye Olde England Inne has acquired a Tudor facade, interior beams and stone work. Brass and copper pieces, Laura Ashley decor and English antiques add to the atmosphere. The inn sponsors polo events and fea-

tures a polo package. Gliding, golf and ski packages are also available. A popular honeymoon package includes champagne sleigh rides. Nightly entertainment is provided at Mr. Pickwick's Polo Pub and romantic dining is available at Copperfields.

Innkeeper(s): Christopher Francis. $98-375. MAP. MC VISA AX. 30 rooms, 20 with PB, 4 with FP. 12 suites. 1 conference room. Breakfast included in rates. Types of meals: full breakfast and gourmet breakfast. Afternoon tea and gourmet lunch available. Restaurant on premises. Beds: QDT. Air conditioning, ceiling fan and TV in room. Fax, copier and spa on premises. Antiques, parks, shopping, downhill skiing, cross-country skiing, sporting events and theater nearby.

Location: In the village.

Publicity: *National Geographic Traveler, Channel 5 TV in Boston.*

"Even more perfect than we anticipated."

Certificate may be used: Midweek, non-holiday, subject to advance reservations and availability.

Waitsfield

Lareau Farm Country Inn

PO Box 563, Rt 100
Waitsfield, VT 05673-0563
(802)496-4949 (800)833-0766

Circa 1794. This Greek Revival house was built by Simeon Stoddard, the town's first physician. Old-fashioned roses, lilacs, delphiniums, iris and peonies

fill the gardens. The inn sits in a wide meadow next to the crystal-clear Mad River. A canoe trip or a refreshing swim are possibilities here.

Innkeeper(s): Dan & Susan Easley. $60-125. MC VISA DS PC TC. 13 rooms, 11 with PB. 1 suite. 1 conference room. Breakfast included in rates. Types of meals: full breakfast, gourmet breakfast and early coffee/tea. Dinner available. Beds: QD. Swimming and library on premises. Antiques, fishing, shopping, downhill skiing, cross-country skiing and theater nearby.

Location: Central Vermont, Sugarbush Valley.

Publicity: *Pittsburgh Press, Philadelphia Inquirer, Los Angeles Times.*

"Hospitality is a gift. Thank you for sharing your gift so freely with us."

Certificate may be used: Dec. 15-April 1 and May 1-June 29, holiday weeks excluded.

Mad River Inn

Tremblay Rd, PO Box 75
Waitsfield, VT 05673
(802)496-7900 (800)832-8278 Fax:(802)496-5390

Circa 1860. Surrounded by the Green Mountains, this Queen Anne Victorian sits on seven scenic acres along the Mad River. The charming inn boasts attractive woodwork throughout, highlighted by ash, bird's-eye maple and cherry. Guest rooms feature European featherbeds and include the Hayden Breeze Room, with a king brass bed, large windows and sea relics, and the Abner Doubleday Room, with a queen ash bed and mementos of baseball's glory

days. The inn sports a billiard table, gazebo, organic gardens and a Jacuzzi overlooking the mountains. Guests can walk to a recreation path along the river. Innkeeper(s): Rita & Luc Maranda. $69-125. MC VISA AX. 10 rooms with PB. Breakfast and afternoon tea included in rates. Type of meal: gourmet breakfast. Beds: KQ. Turndown service and ceiling fan in room. Cable TV, VCR, fax, spa, stables and child care on premises. Antiques, fishing, shopping, downhill skiing, cross-country skiing, sporting events, theater and watersports nearby.

Publicity: *Innsider, Victorian Homes, Let's Live, Skiing, AAA Home & Away, Tea Time at the Inn, Travel & Leisure.*

"*Your hospitality was appreciated, beautiful house and accommodations, great food & friendly people, just to name a few things. We plan to return and we recommend the Mad River Inn to friends & family.*"

Certificate may be used: Sunday-Thursday, except Dec. 21-31, Sept. 21-Oct 15.

Millbrook Inn

Rfd Box 62
Waitsfield, VT 05673
(802)496-2405 (800)477-2809 Fax:(802)496-9735
E-mail: millbrkinn@aol.com

Circa 1855. Guests enter Millbrook through the warming room, where an antique Glenwood parlor stove usually is roaring. This classic Cape-style farmhouse is known for its individually stenciled guest rooms, Green Mountain views and one of the valley's best dining rooms. The inn's rates are listed for two people under the Modified American Plan. During the summer, the bed & breakfast rates are $68 for two people.

Innkeeper(s): Joan & Thom Gorman. $100-140. MAP. MC VISA AX. 7 rooms with PB. Breakfast and dinner included in rates. Type of meal: full breakfast. Restaurant on premises. Beds: QT. Ceiling fan in room. Bicycles on premises. Antiques, fishing, shopping, downhill skiing, cross-country skiing and golf nearby.

Publicity: *Daily News, L.A. Times, Boston Globe, Travel Today, Gourmet.*

"*A weekend at your place is just what the doctor had in mind.*"

Certificate may be used: Rate includes dinner also. Subject to availability winter weekdays-does not include Christmas week or February vacation week.

The Valley Inn

Rt 1 Box 8 Rt 100
Waitsfield, VT 05673
(802)496-3450 (800)638-8466

Circa 1949. This country inn offers guest rooms decorated with New England antiques, hand-stenciled walls and beds topped with quilts. The living room is a perfect place to relax, with a woodburning stove set into its grand stone fireplace. The inn's pub serves beverages and offers a variety of weekly specials. Dinner is served during ski season. For a true adventure, guests can learn how to fly a sailplane and soar over the Green Mountains with the host.

Innkeeper(s): Bill & Millie Stinson. $59-99. MAP. MC VISA AX TC. 20 rooms with PB. 1 conference room. Breakfast included in rates. Type of meal: full breakfast. Dinner available. Beds: QDT. Cable TV, VCR, copier, sauna and bicycles on premises. Handicap access. Antiques, fishing, parks, shopping, downhill skiing, cross-country skiing, theater and watersports nearby.

Certificate may be used: May 15-Sept. 15, Sunday-Friday; Jan. 2-Feb. 2, Sunday-Thursday. Dinner is included in the price in winter.

Waitsfield Inn

Rt 100, PO Box 969
Waitsfield, VT 05673
(802)496-3979 (800)758-3801

Circa 1825. This Federal-style home once served as a parsonage and was home to a state senator. Surrounded by a picket fence, the home's grounds boast a large garden. The old barn is now the common room and includes the original wood-planked flooring and a fireplace. Guest quarters are filled with period antiques. In the winter, freshly baked cookies and cider are served. As the inn is in the village of Waitsfield, all the town's sites are nearby. The area offers an abundance of outdoor activities throughout the year. Innkeeper(s): Ruth & Steve Lacey. $79-129. MC VISA AX DS PC TC. 14 rooms with PB. Breakfast included in rates. Type of meal: full breakfast. Beds: QDT. Antiques, fishing, shopping, downhill skiing, cross-country skiing and theater nearby.

Location: Near Sugarbush and Mad River Glen ski areas.

Certificate may be used: Sunday-Thursday, March, July, August, Sept.1-15. Anytime (excluding holidays) in January, April, May, June, November, December.

Warren F3

Beaver Pond Farm Inn

Rd Box 306, Golf Course Rd
Warren, VT 05674
(802)583-2861 Fax:(802)583-2860

Circa 1840. This Vermont farmhouse, formerly a working dairy and sheep farm, is situated in a meadow overlooking several beaver ponds. Present owners refurbished the home, decorating the tasteful rooms with antiques and Laura Ashley wallpapers. The innkeeper holds cooking classes here. For golf

lovers, the inn is located only 100 yards from the first tee of the Sugarbush Golf Course. The course is transformed into a cross-country ski center in the winter, offering miles of tracked and groomed trails. Downhill skiing is only one mile away.

Innkeeper(s): Robert & Elizabeth Hansen. $72-104. MC VISA AX PC. 6 rooms, 4 with PB. 1 conference room. Breakfast and evening snack included in rates. Types of meals: full breakfast and early coffee/tea. Dinner and picnic lunch available. Beds: KQT. Cable TV, VCR, fax and copier on premises. Handicap access. Antiques, fishing, shopping, skiing, sporting events, golf and theater nearby.

Location: Sugarbush Valley.

Publicity: *L.A. Times, New Woman, Innsider, Long Island Newsday.*

"The inn is simply magnificent. I have not been in a nicer one on three continents. Breakfast was outrageous."

Certificate may be used: June 1-Sept. 10, midweek only.

Waterbury   D3

The Inn at Blush Hill
Blush Hill Rd, Box 1266
Waterbury, VT 05676
(802)244-7529 (800)736-7522 Fax:(802)244-7314
E-mail: innatbh@aol.com

Circa 1790. This shingled Cape-style house was once a stagecoach stop en route to Stowe and is the oldest Inn in Waterbury. A 12-foot-long pine farmhand's table is set near the double fireplace and the

kitchen bay window, revealing views of the Worcester Mountains. A favorite summertime breakfast, served gardenside, is pancakes with fresh blueberries, topped with ice cream and maple syrup.

Innkeeper(s): Gary & Pam Gosselin. $69-130. MC VISA AX DS PC TC. 5 rooms with PB, 1 with FP. Breakfast, afternoon tea and evening snack included in rates. Types of meals: full breakfast, gourmet breakfast and early coffee/tea. Beds: QDT. Air conditioning, turndown service and ceiling fan in room. Cable TV, fax and library on premises. Antiques, fishing, parks, shopping, downhill skiing, cross-country skiing, theater and watersports nearby.

Location: Three-quarter mile off scenic Rte 100 at I-89.

Publicity: *Vermont, Charlotte Observer, Yankee, New York Times, Ski, New York Post, WCAX Television.*

"Our room was wonderful — especially the fireplace. Everything was so cozy and warm."

Certificate may be used: Sunday through Thursday, January to June; November-December (excluding holidays).

Waterbury   D3

Grunberg Haus B&B & Cabins
RR 2 Box 1595-No
Waterbury, VT 05676-9621
(802)244-7726 (800)800-7760
E-mail: grunhaus@aol.com

Circa 1972. This hillside Tyrolean chalet was hand-built by George and Irene Ballschneider. The Grunberg Haus captures the rustic charm of country guest homes in Austria with its wall of windows overlooking the Green Mountains, a massive fieldstone fireplace and a self-service Austrian pub. Rooms are decorated with antique furniture and cozy quilts. All rooms open onto the second-floor balcony that surrounds the chalet. Attractions in Stowe, the Mad River Valley, Montpelier and the Lake Champlain region are close at hand. Innkeepers regularly entertain their guests at the Steinway Grand piano.

Innkeeper(s): Chris Sellers & Mark Frohman. $55-125. MAP. MC VISA AX DS PC TC. 15 rooms, 10 with PB, 3 with FP. 1 suite. 4 cottages. 1 conference room. Breakfast and afternoon tea included in rates. Types of meals: full breakfast, gourmet breakfast and early coffee/tea. Beds: QDT. Spa, sauna, tennis and library on premises. Antiques, fishing, parks, shopping, skiing, theater and watersports nearby.

Location: South of Waterbury on scenic route 100, between Stowe and Waitsfield.

Publicity: *Hudson Dispatch, Innsider, Ski, Toronto Globe, Vermont, Washington Times, Yankee.*

"You made an ordinary overnight stay extraordinary."

Certificate may be used: March 20-June 20 (daily), Oct. 20-Dec. 20 (daily), January, February and March (Monday-Thursday).

Thatcher Brook Inn
PO Box 490, Rt 100 N
Waterbury, VT 05676-0490
(802)244-5911 (800)292-5911 Fax:(802)244-1294

Circa 1899. Listed in the Vermont Register of Historic Buildings, this restored Victorian mansion features a porch with twin gazebos. A covered walkway leads to the historic Wheeler House. Guest rooms are decorated in Laura Ashley-style. Six rooms have fireplaces, and some have whirlpool tubs. The inn's

restaurant, Victoria's Bar and Grill, is located on the property. Guests can dine fireside or by candlelight. Innkeeper(s): Kelly & Peter Varty. $75-185. MAP. MC VISA AX DC DS PC TC. 22 rooms with PB, 6 with FP. 1 suite. 1 conference room. Breakfast included in rates. Meal: full breakfast. Banquet service available. Restaurant on premises. Beds: KQDT. Ceiling fan in room. TV, VCR, fax, copier, library on premises. Handicap access. Antiques, fishing, parks, shopping, skiing, sporting events, theater, watersports nearby.

"I'd have to put on a black tie in Long Island to find food as good as this and best of all it's in a relaxed country atmosphere. Meals are underpriced."
Certificate may be used: Nov. through Aug., Sunday through Thursday.

West Dover
K3

Austin Hill Inn
Rt 100, Box 859
West Dover, VT 05356
(802)464-5281 (800)332-7352 Fax:(802)464-1229
E-mail: ahiinn@aol.com

Circa 1930. Situated outside the historic village of West Dover, at the edge of a mountain, this completely renovated inn has walls decorated with old barn board and floral Victorian wallpapers. Antiques and heirlooms include family photographs dating from 1845. Most rooms have balconies and four-poster or brass beds. A full country breakfast in the fireplaced dining room is offered, as well as afternoon tea, complimentary wine and cheese.
Innkeeper(s): Robbie Sweeney. $90-125. MC VISA AX DS. 12 rooms with PB. 1 conference room. Breakfast and afternoon tea included in rates. Type of meal: full breakfast. Catering service available. Beds: KQDT. Fax, copier and computer on premises. Antiques, fishing, parks, downhill skiing, cross-country skiing and theater nearby.
Location: Mount Snow Valley.
Publicity: *Garden City Life, Newsday, Greenwich Times.*
"Another repeat of perfection."
Certificate may be used: Sunday through Thursday, non-holidays excluding Sept. 15-Oct. 20.

West Hartford
G5

The Half Penney Inn B&B
PO Box 84
West Hartford, VT 05084-0084
(802)295-6082

Circa 1775. This brick Federal-style home was one of the first farms in Vermont and still features the original walk-in fireplace and bake ovens. Original wideboard floors, woodwork and window panes along with an assortment of antiques create a homey atmosphere. Guests enjoy roaming the 40 acres of meadows and woods. The Appalachian Trail is behind the inn and the White River is around the corner. Despite its secluded country location, the towns of Quechee, Woodstock and Hanover are close by. Golfing, horseback riding and hiking and skiing are in the area.

Innkeeper(s): Gretchen Fairweather, Bonny Hooper. $85-130. MC VISA AX. 5 rooms with PB, 1 with FP. Breakfast included in rates. Types of meals: full breakfast and early coffee/tea. Afternoon tea, picnic lunch and banquet service available. Beds: KQDT. Turndown service in room. Child care on premises. Antiques, fishing, parks, shopping, skiing, sporting events, theater and watersports nearby.
Publicity: *NBC-TV, BBC-TV, Valley News.*
"Wonderful breakfast. Your hospitality was warm and friendly, I felt right at home!"
Certificate may be used: Nov. 1-Sept. 15, Sunday-Thursday.

Weston
J3

Darling Family Inn
Rt 100
Weston, VT 05161
(802)824-3223

This two-story inn also features two cottages. Located in the Green Mountains, just minutes from Bromley, Okemo and Stratton ski areas, the inn provides a taste of life from the early Colonial days. Guest rooms feature handmade quilts crafted locally. The cottages include kitchenettes, and pets are welcome in the cottages if prior arrangements are made.
Innkeeper(s): Chapin Darling. $65-95. 7 rooms. 2 suites. Breakfast included in rates. Type of meal: full breakfast. Turndown service in room. VCR on premises. Antiques, shopping, skiing and theater nearby.
Certificate may be used: Sunday through Thursday, excluding Sundays of holiday weekends; January through June; Sept. 1-15; Oct. 15-Dec. 23.

Wilder Homestead Inn
25 Lawrence Hill Rd
Weston, VT 05161-5600
(802)824-8172 Fax:(802)824-5054

Circa 1827. Within walking distance of the Green Mountain National Forest, this inn with Federal and Greek Revival stylings features seven guest rooms, five with private baths and views. Five of the rooms have decorative fireplaces. Large country breakfasts may include fresh fruit, eggs, homemade biscuits with jam, hotcakes with genuine Vermont maple syrup, Lumberjack mush or sausage. Spring visitors enjoy wildflowers. A craft shop is on the premises.
Innkeeper(s): Roy & Peggy Varner. $65-110. MC VISA. 7 rooms, 5 with PB. Breakfast included in rates. Type of meal: full breakfast. Beds: KQDT. Ceiling fan in room. Cable TV and VCR on premises. Antiques, fishing, shopping, skiing, sporting events and theater nearby.
Publicity: *Gourmet, Country, Boston Globe, Sao Paulo, Brazil.*
Certificate may be used: Sunday through Thursday, non-holidays. January-March; May-July; November-December.

Woodstock   H4

Canterbury House

43 Pleasant St
Woodstock, VT 05091-1129
(802)457-3077 (800)390-3077

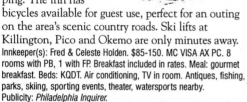

Circa 1880. National Geographic tabbed Woodstock as one of America's most beautiful villages, and this Victorian inn offers a lovely stopping place for those exploring the area. Visitors find themselves within easy walking distance of antique stores, art galleries, museums, restaurants and shopping. The inn has bicycles available for guest use, perfect for an outing on the area's scenic country roads. Ski lifts at Killington, Pico and Okemo are only minutes away.
Innkeeper(s): Fred & Celeste Holden. $85-150. MC VISA AX PC. 8 rooms with PB, 1 with FP. Breakfast included in rates. Meal: gourmet breakfast. Beds: KQDT. Air conditioning, TV in room. Antiques, fishing, parks, skiing, sporting events, theater, watersports nearby.
Publicity: *Philadelphia Inquirer.*
Certificate may be used: Jan. 2-June 15 or midweek (Monday-Thursday) June 16-Sept. 15, not on federal holidays

Carriage House of Woodstock

15 Rt 4 W
Woodstock, VT 05091-1253
(802)457-4322 Fax:(802)457-4322

Circa 1850. This century-old home features rooms filled with period antiques and individual decor. Those in search of relaxation will find plenty of possibilities, from a hammock tucked beneath a shade tree to a porch with a view of trees and fields. Antique shopping, the historic Billings Farm Museum and plenty of outdoor activities are found in the area. Fall and spring bring an explosion of color, and scenic drives take you under covered bridges.
Innkeeper(s): Dennis & Shirley Wagner. $95-135. MC VISA AX DS PC TC. 7 rooms with PB. Breakfast and afternoon tea included in rates. Types of meals: gourmet breakfast and early coffee/tea. Beds: QT. Air conditioning and turndown service in room. Cable TV, VCR, fax, copier, bicycles and library on premises. Antiques, fishing, parks, shopping, skiing, sporting events, theater and watersports nearby.
Certificate may be used: Sunday-Thursday, Nov. 1-Aug. 1, except holidays and holiday weekends.

Charleston House

21 Pleasant St
Woodstock, VT 05091-1131
(802)457-3843

Circa 1810. This authentically restored brick Greek Revival town house is furnished with antiques, an art collection and Oriental rugs. Most of the rooms boast four-poster beds. The Summer Kitchen room also offers a private entrance. A hearty full breakfast starts off the day, and the innkeepers serve afternoon refreshments as well.
Innkeeper(s): Bill Hough. $90-175. MC VISA AX. 9 rooms with PB. Breakfast included in rates. Type of meal: full breakfast. Antiques, fishing, downhill skiing, cross-country skiing, theater nearby.
Publicity: *Harbor News, Boston Business Journal, Weekend Getaway.*
"I felt like I was a king, elegant but extremely comfortable."
Certificate may be used: January-August anytime except holidays; November and December, except holidays.

Woodstocker B&B

61 River St
Woodstock, VT 05091-1227
(802)457-3896 Fax:(802)457-3897

Circa 1830. This early 19th-century, Cape-style inn is located at the base of Mt. Tom at the edge of the village of Woodstock. Hand-hewn wood beams create a rustic effect. The seven guest rooms and two suites are individually appointed. Buffet-style, full breakfasts get the day off to a great start. Guests can take a short walk across a covered bridge to shops and restaurants. Hikers will enjoy trails that wind up and around Mt. Tom. After a busy day, come back and enjoy a soak in the five-person whirlpool.
Innkeeper(s): Tom & Nancy Blackford. $85-145. MC VISA. 9 rooms with PB. 2 suites. Breakfast included in rates. Types of meals: full breakfast and early coffee/tea. Beds: QD. Air conditioning, ceiling fan and TV in room. VCR, fax and copier on premises. Antiques, fishing, shopping, skiing, sporting events, theater and watersports nearby.
Certificate may be used: Sunday through Thursday, except July 1-Oct. 20 and Dec. 20-Jan. 1.

Woodstock (Reading)   H4

Bailey's Mills B&B

PO Box 117, Bailey's Mills Rd
Woodstock (Reading), VT 05062
(802)484-7809 (800)639-3437

Circa 1820. This Federal-style inn features grand porches, 11 fireplaces, a "good-morning" staircase and a ballroom. Four generations of Baileys, as well as mill workers, lived in the home. There was once a country store on the premises. Guests can learn much about the home and the people who lived here through the innkeepers. Two of the guest rooms include a fireplace, and the suite has a private solarium. There's plenty to do here, from exploring the surrounding 48 acres to relaxing with a book on the porch swing or in a hammock. If you forgot your favorite novel, borrow a book from the inn's 2,200-volume library.
Innkeeper(s): Barbara Thaeder & Don Whitaker. $70-110. MC VISA PC TC. 3 rooms with PB, 2 with FP. 1 suite. Breakfast included in rates. Meals: continental-plus breakfast, early coffee/tea. Beds: KQ. Swimming, library on premises. Antiques, fishing, parks, skiing, theater nearby.
Certificate may be used: November-May, Sunday-Thursday or call anytime for last-minute openings.

Virginia

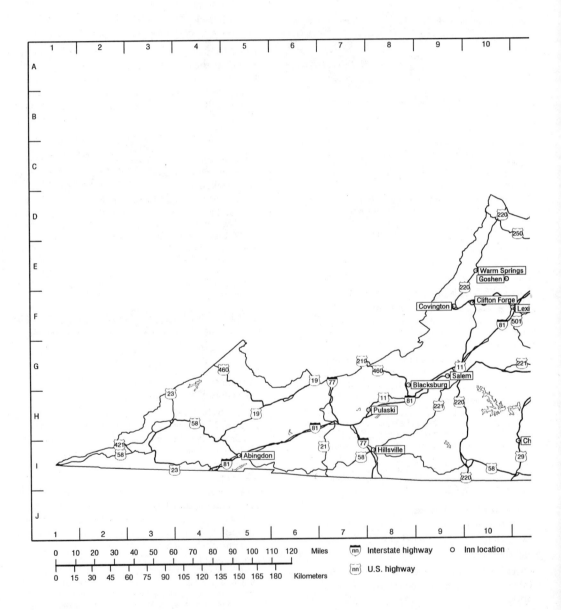

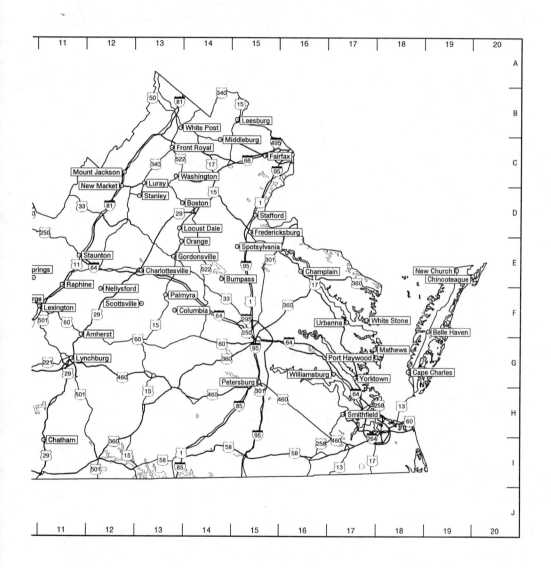

Abingdon I5

Maplewood Farm B&B
20004 Cleveland Rd
Abingdon, VA 24211-5836
(540)628-2640

Circa 1880. From the arched windows of this farm-house, an example of Virginia Vernacular design, guests can gaze out at the wooded countryside. This site is especially picturesque during the fall foliage season. There are more than 60 acres to wander, or guests can simply take in the view of trees and a lake from the deck. The decor is elegant, but not too posh, decorated with French influences. The home rests on a working horse farm, and guests can arrange to board their own horses on the property.
Innkeeper(s): Doris Placak. $75. TC. 3 rooms with PB. Breakfast and afternoon tea included in rates. Types of meals: full breakfast, gourmet breakfast and early coffee/tea. Evening snack and picnic lunch available. Beds: QDT. Child care on premises. Handicap access. Antiques, fishing, parks, shopping, downhill skiing, cross-country skiing, sporting events, theater and watersports nearby.
Certificate may be used: Year-round, except certain weekends in April, August and October.

White Birches
268 White Mills Rd
Abingdon, VA 24210
(540)676-2140 (800)247-2437

Circa 1910. This Cape Cod-style home, painted in creamy blue hues, is decorated with an assortment of English and American antiques. Oriental rugs decorate the floors. The covered porches, complete with plants, wicker and paddle fans, are an idyllic spot for the morning meal. A koi pond completes the lush look. The meal is a formal affair, served with silver, crystal and antique china. The innkeepers often choose this spot to serve afternoon refreshments. Outlet shopping, the popular Barter Theatre and a variety of restaurants are nearby.
Innkeeper(s): Michael & Paulette Wartella. $75. MC VISA AX PC. 3 rooms with PB. Breakfast and evening snack included in rates. Type of meal: full breakfast. Beds: Q. Air conditioning, turndown service, ceiling fan and TV in room. VCR on premises. Antiques, parks, shopping, downhill skiing and theater nearby.
Certificate may be used: Jan. 2 to March 15.

Amherst F11

Dulwich Manor B&B Inn
550 Richmond Hwy
Amherst, VA 24521-3962
(804)946-7207

Circa 1912. This red Flemish brick and white columned English Manor sits on five secluded acres at the end of a country lane and in the midst of 85 acres

of woodland and meadow. The Blue Ridge Mountains may be enjoyed from the veranda. The entry features a large center hall and a wide oak staircase. Walls are 14 inches thick. The 18 rooms include a 50-foot-long ballroom on the third floor. The inn is decorated with a mix of antiques, reproductions and modern art. Your host is a professional singer and actor, and your hostess was in public relations and a costumer for the theater.
Innkeeper(s): Bob & Judy Reilly. $69-89. PC TC. 6 rooms, 4 with PB, 2 with FP. Breakfast included in rates. Types of meals: full breakfast and early coffee/tea. Afternoon tea available. Beds: QD. Air conditioning and ceiling fan in room. Spa on premises. Antiques, fishing, parks, shopping, downhill skiing, sporting events, theater and watersports nearby.
Publicity: *Country Inn, Scene.*

"Our experience at Dulwich Manor surpassed all of our inn visits. A truly delightful stay!"

Certificate may be used: Sunday-Thursday, except May and October, holidays and holiday eves. Anytime, December-February, except holidays and holiday eves.

Belle Haven F19

Bay View Waterfront B&B
35350 Copes Dr
Belle Haven, VA 23306-1952
(804)442-6963 (800)442-6966

Circa 1800. This rambling inn stretches more than 100 feet across and has five roof levels. There are heart-pine floors, high ceilings and several fireplaces. The hillside location affords bay breezes and views of the Chesapeake, Occohannock Creek and the inn's surrounding 140 acres. The innkeepers are descendants of several generations who have owned and operated Bay View. If you come by water to the inn's deep water dock, look behind Channel Marker 16.

Innkeeper(s): Wayne & Mary Will Browning. $95. PC TC. 3 rooms, 1 with PB, 1 with FP. Breakfast included in rates. Meal: full breakfast. Beds: D. Air conditioning in room. VCR, swimming, bicycles, library on premises. Antiques, fishing, parks, theater, watersports nearby.

Publicity: *Rural Living, City.*

"We loved staying in your home, and especially in the room with a beautiful view of the bay. You have a lovely home and a beautiful location. Thank you so much for your hospitality."

Certificate may be used: Nov. 15-March 30, Sunday-Thursday, excluding holidays.

Blacksburg G8

Sycamore Tree B&B
PO Box 10937
Blacksburg, VA 24062-0937
(703)381-1597

Circa 1990. This inn sits on 126 acres at the foot of Hightop Mountain. Decorated in a traditional style, all the guest rooms have private baths. The innkeepers enjoy offering advice on local activities, such as nearby hiking on the Appalachian Trail and the walk to a 60-foot waterfall at the Cascades.

Innkeeper(s): Charles & Gilda Caines. $75-110. MC VISA. 6 rooms with PB. Breakfast included in rates. Types of meals: full breakfast and early coffee/tea. Beds: KQD. Air conditioning in room. VCR and fax on premises. Handicap access. Antiques, fishing, parks, shopping, sporting events, theater and watersports nearby.

Certificate may be used: Jan. 1-April 30, Sunday-Thursday. June 1-July 30, Sunday-Thursday.

Boston D13

Thistle Hill B&B
5541 Sperryville Pike
Boston, VA 22713
(703)987-9142 Fax:(703)987-9122

The inn, an antique shop and restaurant combine to create this restful bed & breakfast. The rambling home rests alongside a former military turnpike used during the Civil War. There are 10 acres of woods to stroll through, a stream, hot tub and a gazebo. Rooms are furnished with antiques and reproductions. The Little Thistle House, a romantic, cozy cottage, offers a sleigh bed, fireplace and sitting room for those seeking solitude. Breakfasts are huge—freshly baked muffins, fruit and coffee accompany the day's entree. Dinners are served by candlelight, and guests can arrange a private dinner for two.

Innkeeper(s): Marianne Topjian-Wilson. $95-145. MAP. MC VISA AX DS. 5 rooms, 4 with PB, 1 with FP. 1 conference room. Breakfast included in rates. Meals: full breakfast and gourmet breakfast. Afternoon tea available. Beds: Q. Fax and spa on premises. Handicap access. Publicity: *Washington Post.*

Certificate may be used: Sunday through Thursday, excluding holidays.

Bumpass E14

Rockland Farm Retreat
3609 Lewiston Rd
Bumpass, VA 23024-9659
(540)895-5098

Circa 1820. The 75 acres of Rockland Farm include pasture land, livestock, vineyard, crops and a farm pond for fishing. The grounds here are said to have spawned Alex Haley's "Roots." Guests can study documents and explore local cemeteries describing life under slavery in the area surrounding this historic home and 18th-century farmlands.

Innkeeper(s): Roy E. Mixon. $60-75. MAP. AX PC. 4 rooms, 3 with PB. 1 suite. 2 conference rooms. Breakfast included in rates. Type of meal: full breakfast. Dinner, lunch, banquet service and catering service available. Beds: DT. Air conditioning in room. VCR on premises. Amusement parks, antiques, fishing, parks, shopping and watersports nearby.

Location: Thirty minutes south of Fredericksburg, Rt 601 at Lake Anna.

Publicity: *Washington Post, Free Lance-Star.*

Certificate may be used: Jan. 1-Dec. 30, Sunday-Thursday. No holidays. No Friday & Saturday nights.

Cape Charles G18

Bay Avenue's Sunset B&B
108 Bay Ave
Cape Charles, VA 23310-3102
(804)331-2424 (888)422-9283 Fax:(804)331-4877

Circa 1915. Located on waterfront Chesapeake Bay property, this B&B offers delightful breezes from its Victorian porch. Newly renovated guest rooms include eclectic decor and Hunter fans. The Victoria Room offers a queen bed, fireplace and clawfoot tub. Awake to the scent of freshly brewed coffee. After  a hearty breakfast of fresh fruits, home-baked breads and delicious entrees, explore the uncrowded beach or take in a day of birdwatching, fishing or cycling.

Innkeeper(s): Albert Longo & Joyce Tribble. $75-95. MC VISA AX DS TC. 4 rooms with PB. Breakfast included in rates. Types of meals: full breakfast and early coffee/tea. Beds: Q. Air conditioning, ceiling fan, TV and VCR in room. Fax and bicycles on premises. Antiques, fishing, parks, theater and watersports nearby.

Publicity: *Port Folio, Southern Inns.*

"A charming room with a beautiful view! Saw the setting sun as well as the full moon shining on the water."

Certificate may be used: November through March, Sunday through Thursday.

Cape Charles House

645 Tazewell Ave
Cape Charles, VA 23310-3313
(757)331-4920 Fax:(757)331-4960

Circa 1912. A Cape Charles attorney built this Colonial Revival home on the site where the town's first schoolhouse was located. Each room is named for someone important to the house or the community. The Julia Wilkins Room is especially picturesque. Rich blue walls and white woodwork are accented by blue and white Dutch print curtains. There is a seamstress model with an antique dress, rocking chair and chaise. Other rooms are decorated with the same skill and style, with fine window dressings, artwork and a few carefully placed collectibles. Oriental rugs top the wood floors, and among the fine furnishings are family heirlooms. Breakfasts are gourmet and served either in the formal dining room or on the porch. Innkeeper Carol Evans prepares breakfast items such as chilled melon with a lime glaze and lemon yogurt topping, egg quesadillas, rosemary roasted potatoes and freshly baked muffins. From time to time, cooking classes and murder-mystery events are available. There are many attractions in the area, including wagon tours of Custis Working Farm, a historic walking tour of Cape Charles, antique shops, golfing and a nature conservancy.

Innkeeper(s): Bruce & Carol Evans. $68-105. MC VISA AX DS PC TC. 5 rooms with PB. Breakfast, afternoon tea and evening snack included in rates. Types of meals: gourmet breakfast and early coffee/tea. Gourmet lunch available. Beds: KQ. Air conditioning and ceiling fan in room. Cable TV, VCR, fax, copier and bicycles on premises. Antiques, fishing, parks, shopping, golf, theater and watersports nearby.

Publicity: *Southern Inns*

"Cape Charles House is first and foremost a home and we were made to feel at home."

Certificate may be used: Nov. 1-March 31 except holidays and special events, subject to availability, Sunday-Thursday in Alexander Cassatt Room.

Champlain   E16

Linden House B&B & Plantation

PO Box 23
Champlain, VA 22438-0023
(804)443-1170 (800)622-1202

Circa 1750. This restored planters home is designated a state landmark and listed in the National Register. The lush grounds boast walking trails, an English garden, gazebo, arbor and five porches. Each of the accommodations offers something special. The Carriage Suite features country decor, antiques, a private porch and a fireplace. The Robert E. Lee room has a high poster bed, fireplace and private bath. The Jefferson Davis room has a luxurious bath with a Jacuzzi and steam room. The fourth-floor

Linden Room affords a view of the countryside and features a queen-size bed and an alcove with a day bed adjoining the private bath. Other rooms also promise an enchanting experience. All rooms have their own television and refrigerator.

Innkeeper(s): Ken & Sandra Pounsberry. $85-135. MC VISA AX PC TC. 4 rooms with PB. 2 suites. Breakfast and afternoon tea included in rates. Types of meals: full breakfast and early coffee/tea. Evening snack, banquet service, catering service and catered breakfast available. Beds: Q. Air conditioning, turndown service, ceiling fan and VCR in room. Stables, bicycles and library on premises. Handicap access. Amusement parks, antiques, fishing, parks, shopping, theater and watersports nearby.

Certificate may be used: February through December, Sunday through Thursday.

Charlottesville   E13

The 1817 Antique Inn

1211 W Main St
Charlottesville, VA 22903-2823
(804)979-7353 (800)730-7443

Circa 1817. This historic bed & breakfast was built by Thomas Jefferson's own craftsman, James Dinsmore. The innkeeper is a published interior designer, a talent evident in each of the guest rooms

decked with bright colors and fashionable furnishings. Elegant rooms are appointed with a variety of unique antiques, and many of the beautiful pieces are available for purchase. The inn is within walking distance to the University of Virginia and a few blocks from the rotunda, restaurants and shops.

Innkeeper(s): Candace DeLoach Wilson. $89-199. MC VISA AX TC. 5 rooms with PB, 3 with FP. 2 suites. Breakfast and afternoon tea included in rates. Types of meals: continental-plus breakfast and early coffee/tea. Lunch, gourmet lunch, catering service and catered breakfast available. Restaurant on premises. Beds: KQD. Air conditioning, turndown service, ceiling fan and TV in room. VCR and bicycles on premises. Antiques, shopping, sporting events and theater nearby.

Publicity: *Charlottesville Observer, Cavalier Daily, Virginia Alumni News.*

"Felt right at home, slept like a baby, ate like a king, dreamed beautiful dreams, couldn't have been better!"

Certificate may be used: June & July, Sunday-Thursday; December & January, Sunday-Thursday; excluding holidays.

464

Clifton Country Inn
1296 Clifton Inn Dr
Charlottesville, VA 22911-3627
(804)971-1800 (888)971-1800 Fax:(804)971-7098
E-mail: reserve@cstone.net

Circa 1799. The first resident at Clifton was
Thomas Mann Randolph, who served as governor of
the state and was the son-in-law of Thomas
Jefferson. One of the gracious guest rooms boasts a
winter view of Jefferson's estate, Monticello.
Elegance and a careful attention to historical detail
has kept this remarkable country inn among the
best in the nation, garnering award upon award for
its accommodations and cuisine. In addition to the
main house, guests can opt to stay in Randolph's law
office, the livery or the carriage house. Aside from
the abundance of history at Clifton, the innkeepers

offer a variety of outdoor pursuits, including a tennis
court, swimming pool, lake and 40 acres of beautiful, wooded grounds. Breakfast at Clifton is a treat
with fresh fruits, lavish entrees, meat, juices and fine
coffees and teas. Afternoon tea is expansive with a
selection of delectable baked goods and gourmet
teas. Clifton also operates a gourmet restaurant featuring five- and six- course meals prepared by
innkeeper Craig Hartman, a Culinary Institute of
America graduate.

Innkeeper(s): Craig Hartman. $145-315. MC VISA PC. 14 rooms with
PB, 14 with FP. 7 suites. 7 cottages. 2 conference rooms. Breakfast and
afternoon tea included in rates. Types of meals: continental breakfast,
full breakfast, gourmet breakfast and early coffee/tea. Dinner, banquet
service, catering service and catered breakfast available. Restaurant on
premises. Beds: QD. Air conditioning and turndown service in room.
Fax, copier, spa, swimming, tennis, library and child care on premises.
Handicap access. Antiques, fishing, parks, shopping, downhill skiing,
cross-country skiing, sporting events and theater nearby.

Publicity: *International Living, Country Inns, Washington Post,
Baltimore Sun, Richmond Times Dispatch, Rural Retreats, New York
Times, Travel & Leisure.*

*"I've stayed at inns in 20 states and found this among
the best. This visit has been a lifetime dream come true."*

Certificate may be used: January, February, July, August; Tuesday and
Wednesday nights (holidays excluded, based on availability).

Charlottesville (Palmyra)

Palmer Country Manor
RR 2 Box 1390
Charlottesville (Palmyra), VA 22963-9801
(804)589-1300 (800)253-4306 Fax:(804)589-1300

Circa 1830. Each season brings a special beauty to
this farmhouse surrounded by 180 wooded acres. The
home and grounds originally belonged to a 2,500-acre
ranch, which was named Solitude, an apt title for this
secluded property. Guests can opt to stay in the historic house or in one of several little cottages. Each
cheery guest room is individually appointed and
includes a fireplace. The hearty country breakfasts are
served in a rustic room with exposed beams and brick
walls. Gourmet, candlelight dinners are another
romantic option available for guests. The area is full of
activities, including white-water rafting down the
James River or taking in the view on a balloon ride.

Innkeeper(s): Gregory & Kathleen Palmer. $85-125. MC VISA AX DC
DS. 12 rooms, 10 with PB, 10 with FP. Breakfast included in rates. Type
of meal: full breakfast. Afternoon tea, dinner, picnic lunch, lunch, catering service and room service available. Restaurant on premises. Beds:
KQ. Air conditioning in room. Bicycles on premises. Antiques, fishing,
parks, shopping, sporting events and watersports nearby.

Certificate may be used: All year, Monday through Thursday.

Chatham   I11

Eldon, The Inn at Chatham
SR 685, 1037 Chalk Level Rd
Chatham, VA 24531
(804)432-0935

Circa 1835. Beautiful gardens and white oaks surround this former tobacco plantation home set
among the backdrop of the Blue Ridge Mountains.
Stroll the grounds and discover sculptures and an
array of flowers and plants. Southern hospitality
reigns at this charming home filled with Empire
antiques. Guest rooms are light and airy and tastefully decorated with beautiful linens and traditional
knickknacks. Fresh flowers accentuate the bright,
cheerful rooms. A lavish, Southern-style breakfast is
served up each morning, and dinners at Eldon feature the gourmet creations of Chef Joel Wesley, a
graduate of the Culinary Institute of America. Eldon
is a popular location for weddings and parties.

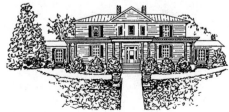

Innkeeper(s): Joy & Bob Lemm. $65-80. MC VISA PC TC. 4 rooms, 3 with PB. 1 suite. Breakfast included in rates. Types of meals: continental-plus breakfast, full breakfast, gourmet breakfast and early coffee/tea. Dinner available. Restaurant on premises. Beds: QDT. Air conditioning and turndown service in room. Swimming and library on premises. Handicap access. Antiques, parks, shopping and watersports nearby. Publicity: *Richmond Times, Chatham Star Tribune.*

"The food, the ambiance, your wonderful hospitality made for a most charming weekend."

Certificate may be used: January, February, March-anytime; April, May, June, July, August, Sunday-Thursday; Friday and Saturday as available.

Sims-Mitchell House B&B
PO Box 429
Chatham, VA 24531-0429
(804)432-0595 (800)967-2867 Fax:(804)432-0596
E-mail: foodhistory@juno.com

Circa 1870. This Italianate house has 11 fireplaces, original horsehair-based plaster, furnishings from several generations of Mitchells and original art by Southern artists. (Art created by your host also is displayed.) There is a two-bedroom suite and a separate two-bedroom cottage at the side yard offering pastoral views. Hargrave Military Academy and Chatham Hall are within a five-block walk. Henry operates the local planetarium, and Patricia is the author of several cookbooks and specializes in health-conscious Southern cuisine.
Innkeeper(s): Patricia & Henry Mitchell. $60-70. MC VISA AX PC TC. 2 suites. Breakfast included in rates. Type of meal: continental-plus breakfast. Air conditioning in room. Antiques nearby.
Certificate may be used: Monday through Thursday nights, except April-May and October-November.

Chincoteague   E20

The Watson House
4240 Main St
Chincoteague, VA 23336-2801
(757)336-1564 (800)336-6787 Fax:(757)336-5776

Circa 1898. Situated in town, this "painted lady" Victorian has a large front porch overlooking Main Street. The porch is a favorite spot of guests and often the location for afternoon tea and refreshments. Beach towels, chairs and bicycles are complimentary, and there is an outdoor shower for cleaning up after sunning.

Innkeeper(s): Tom & Jacque Derrickson, David & Jo Anne Snead. $65-115. MC VISA PC TC. 6 rooms with PB. 2 cottages. Breakfast and afternoon tea included in rates. Beds: QD. Air conditioning and ceiling fan in room. Fax and bicycles on premises. Antiques, fishing, parks, shopping and watersports nearby.
Certificate may be used: March, April and October, Monday through Thursday.

Chincoteague (New Church)

The Garden and The Sea Inn
PO Box 275
Chincoteague (New Church), VA 23415
(804)824-0672 (800)824-0672

Circa 1802. Gingerbread trim, a pair of brightly colored gables and two, adjacent verandas adorn the exterior of this Victorian. A warm, rich Victorian decor permeates the antique-filled guest rooms, an ideal setting for romance. Several rooms include whirlpool tubs. The inn's dining room serves gourmet dinners with an emphasis on fresh catches from the waters of the Eastern shore, but many continental items are featured as well.

Innkeeper(s): Tom & Sara Baker. $60-165. MC VISA AX DS PC TC. 6 rooms with PB. 1 conference room. Breakfast included in rates. Type of meal: continental-plus breakfast. Dinner, evening snack, picnic lunch, banquet service and catering service available. Restaurant on premises. Beds: Q. Air conditioning, ceiling fan and TV in room. VCR, fax, copier, library and pet boarding on premises. Handicap access. Antiques, fishing, parks, shopping and watersports nearby.
Certificate may be used: All dates, Sunday through Thursday. Not valid holidays or Pony Penning Week (usually last week in July).

Clifton Forge   F10

Longdale Inn
6209 Longdale Furnace Rd
Clifton Forge, VA 24422
(540)862-0892 (800)862-0386 Fax:(540)862-3554

Circa 1873. This Victorian was built by the ironmaster of the Longdale Furnace Company and is located in a state historic district named for the firm. The home boasts many unusual features, including a wraparound porch that includes a built-in gazebo. There are more than 12 acres to enjoy, as well as views of the surrounding Shenandoah Valley and the Allegheny Mountains. Rooms are cheerfully appointed in a Victorian style and include ceiling fans and fireplaces. Civil War sites, museums, plantations, zoos, shopping and outdoor activities are in the area.

Innkeeper(s): Bob Cormier. $85-130. MC VISA AX DS PC TC. 10 rooms, 5 with PB, 2 with FP. 1 suite. Breakfast included in rates. Types of meals: full breakfast and early coffee/tea. Afternoon tea available. Beds: KQDT. Ceiling fan in room. Cable TV, VCR, fax, copier, bicycles and library on premises. Antiques, fishing, parks, shopping, downhill skiing, cross-country skiing, golf, theater and watersports nearby.

"We've made our return reservation."

Certificate may be used: Jan. 2-April 30, all days.

Columbia   F13

Upper Byrd Farm B&B
6452 River Rd W
Columbia, VA 23038-2002
(804)842-2240

Circa 1890. This 26-acre farm rests on top of a hill overlooking the James River. The scenic location is dotted with trees and wildflowers. Innkeeper Ivona Kaz-Jepsen, a native of Lithuania, had her work cut out for her when she began renovation of the house, which was inhabited by college students. She transformed the home into an artist's retreat, filling it with antiques and her own artwork. The breakfast table is set with a beautiful mix of china, and the meal is served by candlelight.

Innkeeper(s): Ivona Kaz-Jepsen. $70. 3 rooms, 2 with FP. Breakfast included in rates. Types of meals: full breakfast, gourmet breakfast and early coffee/tea. Beds: KT. Air conditioning in room. VCR on premises. Antiques, fishing and watersports nearby.

Certificate may be used: June 15-Aug. 20.

Covington   F9

Milton Hall B&B Inn
207 Thorny Ln
Covington, VA 24426-5401
(540)965-0196

Circa 1874. This historic 44-acre estate adjoins the George Washington National Forest, and the inn appears as an exquisite English country manor with its buttressed porch towers, gables and Gothic trimmings. The home was built for the Viscountess of Milton, Maria Theresa Fitzwilliam, whose brother found the site while living in America and serving in the Union Army. Each spacious, romantic room boasts its own fireplace and is decorated in a different color scheme. The rooms reflect the styles of the late 1800s. A full English breakfast is served each morning and a proper afternoon tea also is offered.

Innkeeper(s): John & Vera Eckert. $75-140. MC VISA PC TC. 6 rooms with PB, 6 with FP. 1 suite. Breakfast included in rates. Picnic lunch available. Beds: Q. Air conditioning, turndown service, TV and VCR in room. Antiques, fishing, parks, downhill skiing and theater nearby.

Location: Adjoins George Washington National Forest.
Publicity: *Alleghany Highlander, Washington Post, Country Inns.*

"A lovely place, a relaxing atmosphere, delicious breakfasts, gracious hospitality. We thank you."

Certificate may be used: Anytime.

Fairfax   C15

Bailiwick Inn
4023 Chain Bridge Rd
Fairfax, VA 22030-4101
(703)691-2266 (800)366-7666 Fax:(703)934-2112

Circa 1800. Located across from the county courthouse where George Washington's will is filed, this three-story Federal brick house recently has been renovated. The first Civil War casualty occurred on what is now the inn's lawn. The elegant, early Virginia decor is reminiscent of the state's fine plantation mansions. Ask to stay in the Thomas Jefferson Room, a replica of Mr. Jefferson's bedroom at Monticello.

Innkeeper(s): Bob & Annette Bradley. $130-295. MC VISA AX. 14 rooms with PB, 4 with FP. 1 suite. 1 conference room. Breakfast and afternoon tea included in rates. Types of meals: full breakfast, gourmet breakfast and early coffee/tea. Restaurant on premises. Beds: KQT. Air conditioning and turndown service in room. VCR, fax and copier on premises. Antiques, parks, shopping, sporting events, theater nearby.

Publicity: *Washington Post, Journal, Fairfax Connection, Inn Times, Mid-Atlantic Country, Victoria, Country Inns.*

"A visit to your establishment clearly transcends any lodging experience that I can recall."

Certificate may be used: All year, Sunday-Thursday only.

Fredericksburg   D15

La Vista Plantation
4420 Guinea Station Rd
Fredericksburg, VA 22408-8850
(540)898-8444 (800)529-2823 Fax:(540)898-9414

Circa 1838. La Vista has a long and unusual past, rich in Civil War history. Both Confederate and Union armies camped here, and this is where the

Ninth Cavalry was sworn in. The house, a Classical Revival structure with high ceilings and pine floors, sits on 10 acres of pasture and woods. The grounds include a pond stocked with bass. Guest quarters include a spacious room with a king-size, four-poster bed and Empire furniture or a four-room apartment that can accommodate up to six guests and includes a fireplace. Breakfasts include homemade egg dishes from chickens raised on the property.

Innkeeper(s): Michele & Edward Schiesser. $95. MC VISA PC TC. 2 rooms with PB, 2 with FP. 1 suite. 1 conference room. Breakfast included in rates. Types of meals: full breakfast and early coffee/tea. Beds: KQDT. Air conditioning in room. Copier and library on premises. Amusement parks, antiques, fishing, parks, shopping, sporting events, theater and watersports nearby.
Location: Just outside historic Fredericksburg.
Publicity: *Free Lance Star, Mid-Atlantic Country.*
"*Coming here was an excellent choice. La Vista is charming, quiet and restful, all qualities we were seeking. Breakfast was delicious.*"
Certificate may be used: January and February, Monday-Thursday.

Front Royal   C13

Chester House Inn
43 Chester St
Front Royal, VA 22630-3368
(540)635-3937 (800)621-0441 Fax:(540)636-8695
E-mail: chesthse@rma.eda

Circa 1905. This stately Georgian-style estate rests on two acres of terraced gardens, which include vast plantings of boxwood, wisteria arbors, a fountain and brick walkways and walls. Elaborately carved marble mantels from London remain, and an original speaker tube extends from the second-floor bedroom to the kitchen. Just down the street is the renovated village commons, the Confederate Museum and the Belle Boyd Cottage.
Innkeeper(s): Bill & Ann Wilson. $65-180. MC VISA AX PC TC. 7 rooms, 5 with PB, 3 with FP. 1 suite. 1 cottage. Breakfast, afternoon tea and evening snack included in rates. Types of meals: continental-plus breakfast and early coffee/tea. Beds: KQDT. Air conditioning and turndown service in room. TV, VCR and fax on premises. Antiques, fishing, parks, shopping, cross-country skiing, theater and watersports nearby.
Publicity: *Winchester Star, Northern Virginia Daily, Blue Ridge Country.*

"*A home of greater charm would be hard to find.*"
Certificate may be used: Jan. 1-March 30 and June 1-Aug. 30, Sunday through Thursday.

Gordonsville   E13

Tivoli
9171 Tivoli Dr
Gordonsville, VA 22942-8115
(703)832-2225 (800)840-2225 Fax:(540)832-3691
E-mail: tivolibnb@aol.com

Circa 1903. Innkeeper Phil Audibert's family has owned this gracious mansion since the 1950s, but it wasn't until 1990 that he and wife Susie renovated the home and opened for guests. The commanding home, which is surrounded by a 235-acre cattle farm, affords views of the Blue Ridge Mountains. Tastefully decorated rooms are filled with antiques that span four centuries, and each guest room boasts a working fireplace. Phil and Susie offer champagne to guests upon arrival. The home is near plenty of historic attractions, including Montpelier, the home of James Madison, and several Civil War sites.
Innkeeper(s): Phil & Susie Audibert. $90-125. MC VISA PC TC. 4 rooms with PB, 4 with FP. 1 conference room. Breakfast included in rates. Types of meals: continental breakfast, continental-plus breakfast, full breakfast, gourmet breakfast and early coffee/tea. Beds: KQTD. Air conditioning and ceiling fan in room. Cable TV, VCR, fax and copier on premises. Antiques, fishing, parks, shopping, downhill skiing, cross-country skiing, sporting events, golf and theater nearby.
Certificate may be used: Anytime Feb. 16-March 31. Monday through Thursday, April through December.

Goshen   E10

The Hummingbird Inn
PO Box 147, 30 Wood Ln
Goshen, VA 24439-0147
(540)997-9065 (800)397-3214 Fax:(540)997-0289
E-mail: hmgbird@cfw.com

Circa 1853. This early Victorian villa is located in the Shenandoah Valley against the backdrop of the

Allegheny Mountains. Both the first and second floors offer wraparound verandas. Furnished with antiques, the inn features a library and sitting room with fireplaces. The rustic den and one guest room comprise the oldest portions of the inn, built around 1780. Four-course dinners, which include wine, are available by advance reservation. An old barn and babbling creek are on the grounds. Lexington, the Virginia Horse Center, Natural Bridge, the Blue Ridge Parkway and antiquing are all nearby.
Innkeeper(s): Diana & Jeremy Robinson. $75-125. MC VISA AX DS PC TC. 5 rooms with PB, 2 with FP. Breakfast included in rates. Types of meals: full breakfast and early coffee/tea. Beds: Q. Air conditioning and ceiling fan in room. VCR, fax, computer and library on premises. Handicap access. Antiques, fishing, shopping, downhill skiing, cross-country skiing and theater nearby.
Publicity: *Blue Ridge Country, Inn Spots and Special Places.*

"We enjoyed our stay so much that we returned two weeks later on our way back for a delicious home-cooked dinner, comfortable attractive atmosphere, and familiar faces to welcome us after a long journey."
Certificate may be used: Sunday-Thursday, November-May 15, holidays excluded.

Hillsville   I8

Bray's Manor B&B Inn
PO Box 385
Hillsville, VA 24343-0385
(703)728-7901 (800)753-2729

Circa 1991. This farmhouse was newly built to accommodate guests and now has private baths and a two-room apartment with its own Jacuzzi. The front porch overlooks the valley where Hereford cattle are usually found grazing. You can play croquet or badminton on the five acres or simply enjoy the view from the porch. Country breakfasts are served.
Innkeeper(s): Helen Bray. $69. MC VISA DS. 3 rooms. 1 suite. Breakfast included in rates. Types of meals: full breakfast and early coffee/tea. Air conditioning, turndown service and ceiling fan in room. VCR on premises. Antiques and shopping nearby.
Certificate may be used: March, April, May, June, July, November and December.

Leesburg   B15

The Norris House Inn
108 Loudoun St SW
Leesburg, VA 20175-2909
(703)777-1806 (800)644-1806 Fax:(703)771-8051
E-mail: jrtp01b@prodigy.com
Circa 1760. The Norris brothers, Northern Virginia's foremost architects and builders, purchased this building in 1850 and began extensive renovations several years later. They used the finest wood and brick available, remodeling the exterior

to an Eastlake style. Beautifully restored, the inn features built-in bookcases in the library and a cherry fireplace mantel. Evening libations are served.
Innkeeper(s): Pamela & Don McMurray. $90-135. MC VISA AX DC CB DS PC TC. 6 rooms, 3 with FP. 3 conference rooms. Breakfast included in rates. Types of meals: full breakfast and early coffee/tea. Afternoon tea available. Beds: QD. Air conditioning and turndown service in room. Fax, library on premises. Antiques, fishing, parks, watersports nearby. Location: In a historic district, less than one hour from Washington, D.C. Publicity: *N.Y. Times, Better Homes & Gardens, Washingtonian, Country Home.*

"Thank you for your gracious hospitality. We enjoyed everything about your lovely home, especially the extra little touches that really make the difference."
Certificate may be used: Sunday through Friday only.

Lexington   F11

Brierley Hill B&B Inn
RR 2 Box 21A
Lexington, VA 24450
(540)464-8421 (800)422-4925 Fax:(540)464-8925
Circa 1993. Visitors to this inn, which is set on eight acres, enjoy a spectacular view of the Shenandoah Valley and Blue Ridge Mountains. The natural setting aside, the interior is reason enough for a stay. The rooms are decorated in light, romantic colors, reminiscent of a field of wildflowers. Antiques and poster

beds blend with flowery prints, light wallpapers and knickknacks. Breakfasts, weather permitting, are served on the veranda, which offers a wonderful view.

Innkeeper(s): Barry & Carole Speton. $80-145. MC VISA TC. 6 rooms with PB, 2 with FP. 1 suite. Breakfast and afternoon tea included in rates. Types of meals: full breakfast and early coffee/tea. Beds: KQ. Air conditioning and ceiling fan in room. Cable TV, fax, copier and library on premises. Antiques, fishing, parks, shopping, downhill skiing, cross-country skiing, sporting events, theater and watersports nearby.

Certificate may be used: Nov. 1-March 31, Sunday-Thursday. Holidays not included.

Maple Hall

Rt 5, Box 223
Lexington, VA 24450-8842
(540)463-2044 Fax:(540)463-6693

Circa 1850. Maple Hall is one of the Historic Country Inns of Lexington, an elegant ensemble of some of Virginia's notable mansions and homes. The red brick manor, flanked by stately columns, remained in the original owner's family until the mid-1980s. Many of the rooms include working fireplaces and all are individually decorated with antiques. A restored

guest house, dating prior to the 1850 main house, includes three bedrooms, a kitchen and living room. Secluded accommodations also are available at Pond House, which includes four mini-suites and a back veranda with a view of the pond and surrounding countryside. The home rests on a 56-acre estate with boxwoods, walking trails, a fishing pond, swimming pool and tennis courts. Breakfast and evening wine is included. Gourmet dining, with specialties such as lobster bisque, prime rib or poached Alaskan salmon, is available at the inn's restaurant.

Innkeeper(s): Don Fredenburg. $95-160. MC VISA PC. 21 rooms with PB, 16 with FP. 5 suites. 2 cottages. 1 conference room. Breakfast included in rates. Type of meal: continental-plus breakfast. Banquet service available. Restaurant on premises. Beds: QDT. Air conditioning in room. VCR, fax, copier, swimming and tennis on premises. Antiques, fishing, parks, shopping, sporting events and theater nearby.

"The view from the back balcony was so peaceful and serene. What a perfect weekend!"

Certificate may be used: July and August, November and December (except first week), January-March.

Seven Hills Inn

408 S Main St
Lexington, VA 24450-2346
(540)463-4715 (888)845-3801 Fax:(540)463-6526

Circa 1929. This Colonial Revival house stands in the heart of the Shenandoah Valley. Carefully renovated, the inn's white columns and brick exterior are

reminiscent of a Southern plantation. The guest rooms, named after area homesteads, are furnished with antiques and reproductions, and the Fruit Hill room offers a Jacuzzi tub. Within a 10-minute walk is Washington and Lee University, the Virginia Military Institute and the Lexington Visitors Center.

Innkeeper(s): Shirley Ducommun. $75-125. MC VISA AX PC TC. 7 rooms, 6 with PB. 1 suite. Breakfast included in rates. Types of meals: full breakfast and early coffee/tea. Afternoon tea and catering service available. Beds: QDT. Cable TV, VCR, fax, copier and library on premises. Antiques, fishing, parks, shopping, sporting events, theater and watersports nearby.

"It's like visiting a favorite aunt."

Certificate may be used: February, March, April, June, July, August, September, November, December, January.

The Inn at Union Run

Union Run Rd
Lexington, VA 24450
(703)463-9715 (800)528-6466 Fax:(703)463-3526

Circa 1883. This inn was named for the spring-fed creek that meanders in front of this restored farmhouse. Union troops, specifically the 2nd and 4th Michigan Calvary, camped on the grounds during the Civil War. The home is surrounded by 10 acres with a fishing pond and brook. The innkeepers have traveled extensively throughout Europe and have brought the influence into their inn. The furnishings, many of which were fashioned out of oak, are a mix of American and Victorian styles.

Innkeeper(s): Roger & Jeanette Serens. $75-125. MAP. MC VISA AX TC. 8 rooms with PB, 1 with FP. 3 suites. 1 conference room. Breakfast and afternoon tea included in rates. Types of meals: full breakfast and early coffee/tea. Evening snack, picnic lunch, lunch, banquet service and room service available. Restaurant on premises. Beds: Q. Air conditioning, turndown service and ceiling fan in room. Fax, copier and pet boarding on premises. Handicap access. Antiques, fishing, parks, shopping, cross-country skiing, theater and watersports nearby.

Certificate may be used: January to December, excludes holidays, Sundays to Thursdays.

Locust Dale   D13

The Inn at Meander Plantation

HC 5, Box 460A
Locust Dale, VA 22948-9701
(540)672-4912 (800)385-4936 Fax:(540)672-0405
E-mail: inn@meander-plantation

Circa 1766. This elegant country estate was built by Henry Fry, close friend of Thomas Jefferson, who often stopped here on his way to Monticello. Ancient formal boxwood gardens, woodland and meadows are enjoyed by guests as well as views of the Blue Ridge Mountains from the rockers on the back porches.

The mansion is decorated serenely with elegant antiques and period reproductions, including queen-size, four-poster beds. The innkeeper is a food writer and will prepare special breakfasts for individual diets. Full dinner service and picnic baskets are available with advance reservations.

Innkeeper(s): Bob & Suzie Blanchard, Suzanne Thomas. $95-185. MC VISA PC TC. 8 rooms with PB, 5 with FP. 4 suites. 1 conference room. Breakfast included in rates. Types of meals: full breakfast and early coffee/tea. Afternoon tea, evening snack, picnic lunch and lunch available. Beds: KQD. Air conditioning in room. VCR, fax, stables, library, pet boarding and child care on premises. Antiques, fishing, parks, shopping, skiing, sporting events and theater nearby.

"Staying at the Inn at Meander Plantation feels like being immersed in another century while having the luxuries and amenities available today."

Certificate may be used: Year-round, Sunday through Thursday, excluding holidays.

Luray   C13

The Ruffner House
RR 4 Box 620
Luray, VA 22835-9704
(540)743-7855

Circa 1840. Situated on a farm nestled in the heart of the Shenandoah Valley, this stately manor was built by Peter Ruffner, the first settler of Page Valley and Luray. Ruffner family members discovered a cavern opposite the entrance to the Luray Caverns, which were found later. Purebred Arabian horses graze in the pasture on this 18-acre estate.

Innkeeper(s): Stephen Hand & John Gerace. $70-150. TC. 8 rooms, 6 with PB, 1 with FP. 2 suites. Breakfast included in rates. Types of meals: full breakfast and early coffee/tea. Evening snack and picnic lunch available. Beds: QD. Air conditioning and ceiling fan in room. Cable TV, VCR and spa on premises. Antiques, fishing, parks, shopping, downhill skiing, cross-country skiing, sporting events and watersports nearby.

Location: Shenandoah Valley, South of Hwys. 211 and 340.

Publicity: *Page News & Courier, Virginian Pilot.*

"This is the loveliest inn we have ever stayed in. We were made to feel very welcome and at ease."

Certificate may be used: Jan. 15-Sept. 15, Monday-Thursday. Nov. 1-Dec. 15, Monday-Thursday.

Spring Farm B&B
13 Wallace Ave
Luray, VA 22835-9067
(540)743-4701 (800)203-2814 Fax:(540)743-7851

Circa 1795. Spring Farm is on 10 acres two miles from Luray Caverns. Hite's Springs run through the land. The Greek Revival home has double front and back verandas. Rooms feature a mix of antique and new furnishings, and there is a fireplace in the living room. Ask for advice on shopping, dining and activities in the Shenandoah and they'll be happy to help you plan a getaway you'll long remember.

Innkeeper(s): Thelma Mayes & Susan Murphy. $75-150. MC VISA DC DS PC TC. 4 rooms, 2 with PB. 1 cottage. Breakfast, afternoon tea and evening snack included in rates. Types of meals: full breakfast and early coffee/tea. Picnic lunch available. Beds: QD. Air conditioning in room. Cable TV, VCR and fax on premises. Antiques, fishing, parks, shopping, downhill skiing and watersports nearby.

"Our first, but definitely not our last, visit."

Certificate may be used: Weekdays only during April through December (Tuesday-Thursday).

Lynchburg   G11

Lynchburg Mansion Inn B&B
405 Madison St
Lynchburg, VA 24504-2455
(804)528-5400 (800)352-1199

Circa 1914. This regal, Georgian mansion, with its majestic Greek Revival columns, is located on a brick-paved street in the Garland Hill Historic District. The grand hall showcases an oak and cherry staircase that leads up to the solarium. Breakfasts are served in the formal dining room on antique china. Romantic rooms feature inviting touches such as a four-poster beds, Laura Ashley and Ralph Lauren linens, Battenburg lace pillows and some

include fireplaces. The Veranda Suite, as the name suggests, opens onto a romantic circular veranda and a treetop sunroom. The Garden Suite, with its private garden entrance, includes an original claw-foot tub. There is a hot tub on the back porch, and the innkeepers have added gardens full of perennials, herbs, edible flowers and more, including a picturesque gazebo. Lynchburg offers many exciting activities, including the unique Community Market and plenty of galleries, antique shops and boutiques. Ski areas are about 45 minutes from the inn.

Innkeeper(s): Mauranna Sherman. $89-119. MC VISA AX DC. 5 rooms with PB, 2 with FP. 2 suites. 1 conference room. Breakfast included in rates. Types of meals: full breakfast, gourmet breakfast and early coffee/tea. Beds: KQ. Air conditioning, turndown service and TV in room. Handicap access. Antiques, shopping, downhill skiing, sporting events and theater nearby.

Location: Lynchburg is three hours from Washington, D.C.

Publicity: *News & Advance, Roanoker.*

"The Lynchburg Mansion Inn is the creme de la creme. You have earned all sorts of pats on the back for the restoration and hospitality you offer. It is truly elegant."

Certificate may be used: Year-round, excluding holidays, holiday eves and weekends around holidays; excludes weekends in April, May, June, August and October.

Mathews G17

Ravenswood Inn
PO Box 1430
Mathews, VA 23109-1430
(804)725-7272

Circa 1913. This intimate waterfront home is located on five acres along the banks of the East River, where passing boats still harvest crabs and oysters. A long screened porch captures river breezes. Most rooms feature a river view and are decorated in Victorian, country, nautical or wicker. Williamsburg, Jamestown and Yorktown are within an hour. Innkeeper(s): Ricky Durham. $70-120. TC. 5 rooms with PB. Breakfast included in rates. Types of meals: gourmet breakfast and early coffee/tea. Beds: KQT. Air conditioning and ceiling fan in room. Cable TV, VCR and spa on premises. Amusement parks, antiques, shopping, sporting events, theater and watersports nearby.

Publicity: *Virginian Pilot, Daily Press.*

"While Ravenswood is one of the most beautiful places we've ever been, it is your love, caring and friendship that has made it such a special place for us."

Certificate may be used: April-November, Sunday-Thursday.

Middleburg C14

Red Fox Inn & Mosby's Tavern
2 E Washington St
Middleburg, VA 22117-0385
(703)687-6301 (800)223-1728 Fax:(703)687-6187

Circa 1728. Originally Chinn's Ordinary, the inn was a popular stopping place for travelers between Winchester and Alexandria. During the Civil War, Colonel John Mosby and General Jeb Stuart met here. Guest rooms are furnished in 18th-century decor and most feature four-poster canopy beds. Innkeeper(s): F. Turner Reuter, Jr. $135-225. MC VISA AX DS TC. 24 rooms with PB, 3 with FP. 4 conference rooms. Breakfast included in rates. Types of meals: continental breakfast, continental-plus breakfast, full breakfast, gourmet breakfast and early coffee/tea. Afternoon tea, dinner, evening snack, picnic lunch, lunch, gourmet lunch, banquet service, catering service, catered breakfast and room service available. Restaurant on premises. Beds: KQ. Air conditioning, turndown service and TV in room. VCR, fax, copier, pet boarding and child care on premises. Handicap access. Antiques nearby.

Location: Thirty miles west of Washington on Route 50.

Publicity: *Washingtonian.*

Certificate may be used: Sunday-Thursday, all year.

Welbourne
22314 Welbourne Farm Ln
Middleburg, VA 20117
(540)687-3201

Circa 1775. This seventh-generation mansion once presided over 3,000 acres. With family members starting their own estates, Welbourne now stands at 600 acres. Furnishings and carpets were collected during world travels over the past 200 years and display a faded elegance of the past. Civil War stories fill the family history book, shared with guests. In the 1930s, F. Scott Fitzgerald and Thomas Wolfe and their literary friends used the house as a setting for their writings. Innkeeper(s): Nathaniel Morison III. $85-96. 7 rooms with PB, 7 with FP. 2 suites. 1 conference room. Breakfast included in rates. Type of meal: full breakfast. Beds: QT.

Location: Fifty miles west of Washington, D.C.

"Furnishings portray a house and home that's been around for a long, long time. And none of it is held back from guests. Life today at Welbourne is quiet and unobtrusive. It's genteel—Philip Hayward, Country Magazine."

Certificate may be used: All year (Sunday-Thursday).

Mount Jackson C12

Widow Kip's Country Inn
355 Orchard Dr
Mount Jackson, VA 22842-9753
(540)477-2400 (800)478-8714
E-mail: widodip@shentel.net

Circa 1830. This restored homestead with its sweeping view of the Massanutten Mountains is situated on seven acres. It's a stone's throw from a fork of the Shenandoah River. Locally crafted quilts enhance the four-poster, sleigh and hand-carved Victorian beds. Two restored cottages (the Silk Purse and Sow's Ear) create a Williamsburg-style courtyard. The inn offers a full country breakfast with homemade cakes and breads. Innkeeper(s): Betty & Bob Luse. $65-85. MC VISA PC TC. 5 rooms with PB, 5 with FP. 1 suite. 2 cottages. Breakfast included in rates. Types of meals: full breakfast and early coffee/tea. Beds: QD. Air conditioning, ceiling fan and TV in room. Swimming, bicycles and pet boarding on premises. Antiques, fishing, parks, shopping, downhill skiing, sporting events, theater and watersports nearby.

Location: I-81 to Mt. Jackson. Exit 273 to Route 11, south to 263W to Route 698.

Publicity: *Country Inns, Mid-Atlantic Country, Americana, Sojourner, Washington Post, Country.*

"You have set a standard of professional excellence, we will be back."

Certificate may be used: Jan. 1-March 30 and June 1-Aug. 30, Sunday through Thursday.

Nellysford F12

The Mark Addy
Rt 151 at Rt 613W, Box 375
Nellysford, VA 22958-9526
(804)361-1101 (800)278-2154

Circa 1837. It's not hard to understand why Dr. John Everett, the son of Thomas Jefferson's physician, chose this picturesque, Blue Mountain setting for his home. Everett expanded the simple, four-room farmhouse already present into a gracious manor. The well-appointed guest rooms feature double whirlpool baths, double showers or a clawfoot tub. Beds are covered with vintage linens, feather pillows and down comforters. There are plenty of relaxing possibilities, including five porches and a hammock among trees.
Innkeeper(s): John Storck Maddox & Saverio Anselmo. $90-125. EP. MC VISA PC TC. 9 rooms with PB. 1 suite. Types of meals: continental breakfast, full breakfast, gourmet breakfast and early coffee/tea. Afternoon tea, dinner, picnic lunch, lunch, gourmet lunch, banquet service, catering service and catered breakfast available. Beds: KQDT. Air conditioning and ceiling fan in room. Cable TV, VCR and library on premises. Handicap access. Antiques, fishing, parks, shopping, downhill skiing, sporting events and theater nearby.
Certificate may be used: January, March, June-September, December, Sunday to Thursday.

New Market C12

A Touch of Country B&B
9329 Congress St
New Market, VA 22844-9508
(540)740-8030

Circa 1870. This white clapboard Shenandoah Valley I-frame house has a second-story pediment centered above the veranda entrance. It was built by Captain William Rice, commander of the New Market Cavalry, and the house sits on what was once a battleground of the Civil War. Rice's unit was highly praised by General Lee. Guest chambers are in the main house and in the handsome carriage house.
Innkeeper(s): Jean Schoellig/Dawn Kasow. $60-75. MC VISA AX DS PC TC. 6 rooms with PB. Breakfast included in rates. Types of meals: full breakfast and early coffee/tea. Beds: QDT. Air conditioning in room. Cable TV and VCR on premises. Antiques, fishing, parks, shopping, skiing, sporting events and watersports nearby.
Publicity: *USA Today Weekend, Country.*

"*Every morning should start with sunshine, bird song and Dawn's strawberry pancakes.*"
Certificate may be used: Sunday through Thursday, April through November; anytime, December through March; no holiday weekends.

Cross Roads Inn B&B
9222 John Sevier Rd
New Market, VA 22844-9649
(540)740-4157

Circa 1925. This Victorian is full of Southern hospitality and European charm. The innkeepers serve imported Austrian coffee alongside the homemade breakfasts, and strudel is served as an afternoon refreshment. The home is decorated like an English garden, laced with antiques, some of which are family pieces. Four-poster and canopy beds are topped with fluffy, down comforters. The historic downtown area is within walking distance.
Innkeeper(s): Mary Lloyd & Roland Freisitzer. $55-95. MC VISA TC. 6 rooms with PB, 1 with FP. 1 conference room. Breakfast, afternoon tea and evening snack included in rates. Types of meals: full breakfast, gourmet breakfast and early coffee/tea. Beds: KQDT. Air conditioning and turndown service in room. Cable TV, VCR, fax and copier on premises. Handicap access. Antiques, fishing, parks, shopping, downhill skiing, sporting events, theater and watersports nearby.
Certificate may be used: November to September, Sunday-Thursday.

Red Shutter Farmhouse B&B
RR 1 Box 376
New Market, VA 22844-9306
(540)740-4281 Fax:(540)740-4661

Circa 1790. For generations, the veranda at the Red Shutter has been the location of choice during summer to view the valley and mountains. Located on 20 acres, the inn offers large rooms and suites and a library/conference room. Breakfast is in the dining room. Enjoy drives to the many area caverns, New Market Battlefield and Skyline Drive.
Innkeeper(s): Juanita Miller. $55-70. MC VISA PC TC. 5 rooms, 3 with PB, 3 with FP. 1 suite. 1 conference room. Breakfast included in rates. Types of meals: full breakfast and early coffee/tea. Beds: KQDT. Ceiling fan in room. VCR, fax and library on premises. Antiques, fishing, parks, shopping, downhill skiing, cross-country skiing and theater nearby.
Certificate may be used: Dec. 1-Feb. 29, anytime; March 1-Nov. 30, Monday through Thursday.

Orange E13

Hidden Inn
249 Caroline St
Orange, VA 22960-1529
(540)672-3625 Fax:(540)672-5029

Circa 1880. Acres of huge old trees can be seen from the wraparound veranda of this Victorian inn nestled in the Virginia countryside. Guests are pampered with afternoon tea, and a candlelight picnic can be ordered. Monticello, Montpelier, wineries, shopping and antiquing all are nearby, and after a day of exploring the area, guests can arrange a candlelight dinner at the inn.

Innkeeper(s): Barbara & Ray Lonick, Chrys Dermody. $99-169. MC VISA AX PC TC. 10 rooms with PB, 2 with FP. 2 cottages. Breakfast and afternoon tea included in rates. Types of meals: full breakfast and early coffee/tea. Beds: KQDT. Cable TV, VCR, fax, copier, computer and library on premises. Antiques, fishing, shopping, sporting events, theater and watersports nearby.

Location: Intersection of Rte 15 & Rte 20.

Publicity: *Forbes, Washington Post, Country Inns, Learning Channel, Inn Country USA.*

"It just doesn't get any better than this!"

Certificate may be used: Monday-Thursday, except May and October.

Willow Grove Inn
14079 Plantation Way
Orange, VA 22960
(703)672-5982 (800)349-1778 Fax:(703)672-3674

Circa 1778. The exterior of this inn is Classical Revival style, while the interior retains Federal simplicity. Located in Orange County, Virginia, the inn is listed in the National Register of Historic Places and has been designated a Virginia Historic Landmark. The mansion, nestled on 37 acres, has survived two wars. Generals Wayne and Muhlenberg camped here during the Revolution, and the mansion was under siege during the Civil War. Trenches and breastworks are visible near the manor house, and a cannonball was removed from the eaves not too long ago.

Innkeeper(s): Angela Malloy. $115-255. 7 rooms, 5 with PB. 2 suites. Breakfast included in rates. Type of meal: full breakfast. Picnic lunch available. Restaurant on premises. Beds: QDT. Antiques, fishing, theater and watersports nearby.

Publicity: *Southern Living, Country Inns, Victorian Homes, Countryside, Virginia, Washington Post, Washington Times, Country Accents, Baltimore Sun, Washingtonian.*

Certificate may be used: Tuesday, Wednesday, Thursday, MAP only, breakfast and dinner included. Four-course dinner off menu.

Petersburg   G15

The Owl & The Pussycat B&B
405 High St
Petersburg, VA 23803-3857
(804)733-0505 (888)733-0505 Fax:(804)862-0694
E-mail: owlcat@ctg.net

Circa 1895. Victorians have a way of standing out, and this Queen Anne is particularly unique, fashioned from creamy, yellow bricks. The innkeepers have decorated the home with Victorian antiques, such as the beds and dressers, and pieces from England. Among the impressive antiques is a carved walnut bed in the Pussycat Room and an Eastlake-style bed in the Owl Room. The home still has its

original gaslight fixtures and eight fireplaces, each decorated with different tiles and mantels. Midweek guests are served continental-plus fare, and weekend guests enjoy a full breakfast. English scones and Sally Lunn bread are specialties of the house. Civil War battlefields, museums, antique shops and restaurants are nearby.

Innkeeper(s): Juliette & John Swenson. $65-105. MC VISA PC TC. 6 rooms, 4 with PB. Breakfast included in rates. Types of meals: continental-plus breakfast and early coffee/tea. Picnic lunch available. Beds: KQT. Air conditioning in room. Cable TV, VCR and fax on premises. Antiques and parks nearby.

Certificate may be used: Nov. 10-March 30, any night.

Port Haywood   G18

Tabb's Creek Inn
PO Box 219 Rt 14 Matthews Co
Port Haywood, VA 23138-0219
(804)725-5136 Fax:(804)725-5136

Circa 1820. Surrounded by 30 acres of woods and located on the banks of Tabb's Creek, this post-Colonial farm features a detached guest cottage. There are maple, elm, magnolia trees and 150 rose bushes on the property. The suites and guest rooms feature fireplaces and antiques. Boats for rowing and canoeing, docks, a swimming pool, and private  waterview porches make this an especially attractive getaway for those seeking a dose of seclusion.

Innkeeper(s): Cabell & Catherine Venable. $125. PC TC. 4 rooms with PB, 1 with FP. 2 suites. Breakfast included in rates. Types of meals: full breakfast and early coffee/tea. Beds: KQD. Air conditioning, turndown service, ceiling fan and VCR in room. Cable TV, fax, copier, swimming, bicycles and library on premises. Antiques and fishing nearby.

Location: Mobjack Bay/Chesapeake Bay, near Yorktown/Williamsburg, Va.

"A spot of tea with a bit of heaven. Truly exceptional hosts. The best B&Bs I've happened across!"

Certificate may be used: All year.

Pulaski   H8

The Count Pulaski B&B and Garden
821 Jefferson Ave N
Pulaski, VA 24301-3609
(540)980-1163 (800)980-1163

Circa 1910. The innkeeper's many travels to Europe and Asia form the core of the inn's furnishings, which are combined with family antiques. The Colonial Revival house is located in the historic district on a half-acre of lawn and gardens. This inn

is located in a quiet, easy-to-find neighborhood and if time permits, the home offers close access to lakes, mountains, national and state parks, museums, art galleries and antique shops. Ask about the dinner cruise on the Pioneer Maid.

Innkeeper(s): Flo Stevenson. $95. MC VISA. 3 rooms with PB. 1 suite. Breakfast included in rates. Types of meals: full breakfast and early coffee/tea. Evening snack available. Beds: KQT. Air conditioning and ceiling fan in room. Cable TV on premises. Antiques, fishing, shopping and sporting events nearby.

Publicity: *Roanoke Times, Southwest Times.*

"I'm back again! Even better than my first visit. Thanks for making me feel so at home."

Certificate may be used: December, January, February, Monday through Thursday.

Raphine
E11

Oak Spring Farm B&B
5895 Borden Grant Tr
Raphine, VA 24472-9717
(540)377-2398 (800)841-8813

Circa 1826. A willow tree droops gracefully over a pond at Oak Spring Farm. Guests can take a stroll through the grounds with a perennial garden, lawn and orchard. The historic plantation house features porch views of the Blue Ridge Mountains and has been pristinely renovated. Guest rooms are decorated with family heirlooms, contemporary touches and fresh flowers. Friendly exotic animals belonging to the Natural Bridge Zoo live here.

Innkeeper(s): Celeste & John Wood. $85-95. MC VISA PC TC. 3 rooms with PB. 1 suite. Breakfast and afternoon tea included in rates. Types of meals: gourmet breakfast and early coffee/tea. Dinner available. Beds: Q. Air conditioning in room. Antiques, fishing, shopping, downhill skiing, sporting events and theater nearby.

Location: Halfway between historic Lexington and Staunton.

Publicity: *The News-Gazette, The News and County Press, Mid-Atlantic Country.*

"The good taste, the privacy, the decor and the hosts were unbeatable!"

Certificate may be used: Sunday-Thursday, Jan. 1-Dec. 1.

Salem
G9

The Inn at Burwell Place
601 W Main St
Salem, VA 24153-3515
(540)387-0250 (800)891-0250 Fax:(540)387-3279

Circa 1907. This mansion was built by a local industrialist, but the inn was named for Nathaniel Burwell, who owned the land prior to the home's construction. The home overlooks the Roanoke Valley and parts of Salem. Guest rooms feature antiques and beds dressed with down comforters and fine linens. Downtown Salem recently received a place in the National Register. The home, the site of many weddings, is a block from a restored 1890s duck pond and park.

Innkeeper(s): Cindi Lou MacMackin & Mark Bukowski. $80-120. MC VISA AX DS PC TC. 4 rooms with PB, 1 with FP. 2 suites. 2 conference rooms. Breakfast included in rates. Types of meals: continental breakfast, full breakfast and early coffee/tea. Banquet service, catering service and catered breakfast available. Beds: Q. Air conditioning, ceiling fan, TV in room. VCR, fax on premises. Amusement parks, antiques, fishing, parks, shopping, sporting events, theater, watersports nearby.

"It was truly elegant, a day I will always remember!"

Certificate may be used: All year, Sunday-Thursday nights, excludes holidays.

Scottsville
F13

High Meadows Vineyard & Mtn Sunset Inn
Rt 4 Box 6
Scottsville, VA 24590-9706
(804)286-2218 (800)232-1832 Fax:(804)286-2124
E-mail: peterhmi@aol.com

Circa 1832. Minutes from Charlottesville on the Constitution Highway (Route 20), High Meadows stands on 50 acres of gardens, forests, ponds, a creek and a vineyard. Listed in the National Register, it is actually two historic homes joined by a breezeway as well as a turn-of-the-century Queen Anne manor house. The inn is furnished in Federal and Victorian styles. Guests are treated to gracious Virginia hospitality in an elegant and peaceful setting with wine tasting and a romantic candlelight dinner every evening.

Innkeeper(s): Peter Sushka. $79-125. MAP. MC VISA. 14 rooms with PB, 12 with FP. 5 suites. 1 conference room. Breakfast included in rates. Types of meals: full breakfast and gourmet breakfast. Dinner available. Restaurant on premises. Beds: KQDT. Air conditioning, turndown service and ceiling fan in room. Handicap access. Antiques, fishing, shopping, skiing, sporting events, theater and watersports nearby.

Publicity: *Washington Times, Cavalier Daily, Daily Progress, Washington Post, Richmond Times Dispatch, Mid-Atlantic, Washingtonian.*

"We have rarely encountered such a smooth blend of hospitality and expertise in a totally relaxed environment."

Certificate may be used: All year, Sunday-Thursday, non-holidays; Sunday-Friday, Dec.1-March 1, non-holidays.

Smithfield   H17

Isle of Wight Inn
1607 S Church St
Smithfield, VA 23430-1831
(804)357-3176 (800)357-3245

Circa 1980. This Colonial inn is located in a historic seaside town, boasting more than 60 homes that date back to the mid-18th century. St. Luke's Church, the oldest in the United States, dating back to 1632, is located near the inn. Antiques and reproductions fill the rooms, the suites offer the added amenities of fireplaces and whirlpool tubs. The inn also houses a gift boutique and one of the area's finest antique shops, featuring old clocks and period furniture.

Innkeeper(s): Jackie Madrigel & Bob Hart. $59-119. MC VISA AX DS TC. 9 rooms with PB, 3 with FP. 2 suites. 1 conference room. Breakfast and evening snack included in rates. Types of meals: full breakfast and early coffee/tea. Beds: QDT. Air conditioning and TV in room. VCR and library on premises. Handicap access. Amusement parks, antiques, fishing, parks, shopping, theater and watersports nearby.

Certificate may be used: Sunday through Thursday, space available.

Spotsylvania   E15

Roxbury Mill B&B
6908 S Roxbury Mill Rd
Spotsylvania, VA 22553-2438
(540)582-6611

Circa 1723. Once a working mill for the Roxbury Plantation, this early 18th-century home has seen the formation of a nation and the wars that would follow. Civil War relics have been found on the property, which includes a dam and millpond. The innkeepers strive to maintain a sense of history at their B&B, keeping the decor in Colonial to pre-Civil War styles. The large master suite affords a view of the river from its private deck, and the bed is an 18th-century antique. Guest room offer a view, a private porch and antique furnishings. Traditional Southern-Colonial fare, from family recipes, fills the breakfast menu. Cornpone topped with slab bacon or country ham and biscuits are some of the appetizing choices. For late risers, the innkeepers also offer brunch.

Innkeeper(s): Joyce B. Ackerman. $75-150. MC VISA TC. 3 rooms, 2 with PB. 1 suite. Breakfast and afternoon tea included in rates. Types of meals: full breakfast, gourmet breakfast and early coffee/tea. Dinner and catering service available. Beds: QD. Air conditioning, turndown service, ceiling fan and TV in room. VCR on premises. Amusement parks, antiques, fishing, parks, shopping and watersports nearby.

Certificate may be used: Nov. 1-March 15, Sunday through Thursday.

Stafford   D15

Renaissance Manor B&B Inn & Art Gallery
2247 Courthouse Rd
Stafford, VA 22554-5508
(540)720-3785 (800)720-3784 Fax:(540)720-3785
E-mail: renbb@aol.com

Circa 1990. Although this elegant manor is a recent construction, it closely resembles Mount Vernon, the home of George Washington, which is just 20 miles away. Stroll the winding brick walkway and enjoy the site of gardens, a gazebo, fountain and rose arbors. Each of the rooms is named for a historical figure, including Martha's Retreat, in honor of America's original first lady. The room features a huge, four-poster bed and Jacuzzi tub. The breakfasts and afternoon tea are served on fine china, crystal and silver. The area offers several Civil War battlefields, national monuments and other historic sites.

Innkeeper(s): JoAnn Houser & Deneen Bernard. $55-150. MC VISA AX PC TC. 6 rooms, 4 with PB. 1 with FP. 2 suites. 1 conference room. Breakfast and afternoon tea included in rates. Types of meals: continental-plus breakfast and gourmet breakfast. Banquet service and catering service available. Beds: KQDT. Air conditioning, turndown service and ceiling fan in room. Cable TV, VCR, fax, copier and library on premises. Amusement parks, antiques, fishing, parks and shopping nearby.

Certificate may be used: Anytime.

Stanley   D13

Wisteria B&B
1126 Marksville Rd
Stanley, VA 22851
(540)778-3347

Circa 1895. This turn-of-the-century Victorian served as a post office, family home and a girl's school. The home has been restored and decorated with antiques. Guest rooms offer mountains views and feather beds topped with down comforters. The 15 acres include hiking trails and gardens. A five-course breakfast is served, and guests choose the time. The inn is six miles from Luray, and the Luray Caverns, rafting, canoeing, golf and horseback riding are among the nearby activities.

Innkeeper(s): Eric & Nicola Portch. $99-125. MC VISA DS PC TC. 4 rooms with PB. 2 cottages. Breakfast included in rates. Type of meal: gourmet breakfast. Picnic lunch and room service available. Beds: KQT. Air conditioning and ceiling fan in room. Cable TV, VCR, spa and library on premises. Antiques, fishing, parks, shopping and golf nearby.

Publicity: *Antique Traveler Magazine*

"The most relaxing and pleasant B&B I've ever stayed in! Virginia's best kept secret."

Certificate may be used: Jan. 2-April 30, Monday-Sunday, May 1-May 31, Sunday-Friday, June 1-Aug. 31, Monday-Sunday, September and October, Monday-Friday, November and December, Monday-Sunday.

Staunton   E11

Ashton Country House
1205 Middlebrook Ave
Staunton, VA 24401-4546
(540)885-7819 (800)296-7819

Circa 1860. This Greek Revival home is surrounded by 25 explorable acres where cows roam and birds frolic in the trees. A mix of traditional and Victorian antiques grace the interior. Four of the guest rooms include a fireplace, and each is appointed individually. The inn's porches, where afternoon tea often is served, are lined with chairs for those who seek relaxation and the scenery of rolling hills. Woodrow Wilson's birthplace is among the town's notable attractions.

Innkeeper(s): Dorie & Vince Di Stefano. $90-125. MC VISA PC TC. 5 rooms with PB. Breakfast, afternoon tea and evening snack included in rates. Picnic lunch available. Beds: QD. Air conditioning and ceiling fan in room. Cable TV and VCR on premises. Handicap access. Antiques, fishing, parks, shopping and watersports nearby.

Certificate may be used: Feb. 1-March 31, Monday-Thursday.

Frederick House
28 N New St
Staunton, VA 24401-4306
(540)885-4220 (800)334-5575

Circa 1810. Adjacent to Mary Baldwin College, this inn consists of six renovated town houses, the oldest of which is believed to be a copy of a home designed by Thomas Jefferson. A full breakfast is

served in Chumley's Tea Room. Guest rooms (some with fireplaces) are furnished with antiques and feature robes and ceiling fans. Original staircases and woodwork are highlighted throughout. Suites are available.

Innkeeper(s): Joe & Evy Harman. $65-150. MC VISA AX DC DS PC TC. 17 rooms with PB, 6 with FP. 8 suites. 1 conference room. Breakfast and picnic lunch included in rates. Types of meals: full breakfast, gourmet breakfast and early coffee/tea. Catering service available. Beds: KQDT. Air conditioning and TV in room. Library on premises. Antiques, fishing, parks, shopping, downhill skiing, cross-country skiing, sporting events, theater and watersports nearby.

Location: Downtown.

Publicity: *Richmond Times-Dispatch, News Journal, Washington Post, Blue Ridge Country.*

"Thanks for making the room so squeaky-clean and comfortable! I enjoyed the Virginia hospitality. The furnishings and decor are beautiful."

Certificate may be used: Weekdays, Sunday-Thursday, except May, August & October.

Thornrose House at Gypsy Hill
531 Thornrose Ave
Staunton, VA 24401-3161
(540)885-7026 (800)861-4338

Circa 1912. A columned veranda wraps around two sides of this gracious red brick Georgian-style house. Two sets of Greek pergolas grace the lawns and there are gardens of azalea, rhododendron and

hydrangea. The inn is furnished with a mix of antique oak and walnut period pieces and over-stuffed English country chairs. Bircher muesli, and hot-off-the-griddle whole grain banana pecan pancakes are popular breakfast items, served in the dining room (fireside on cool days). Across the street is a 300-acre park with lighted tennis courts, an 18-hole golf course and swimming pool.

Innkeeper(s): Otis & Suzy Huston. $55-80. 5 rooms with PB. Breakfast and afternoon tea included in rates. Type of meal: full breakfast. Beds: KQDT. Air conditioning, turndown service and ceiling fan in room. Cable TV on premises. Antiques, fishing, shopping, sporting events and theater nearby.

"We enjoyed ourselves beyond measure, the accommodations, the food, your helpfulness, but most of all your gracious spirits."

Certificate may be used: Dec. 1-March 31, Sunday through Thursday, no holidays.

Urbanna F17

Hewick Plantation
VSH 602/615, Box 82
Urbanna, VA 23175
(804)758-4214 Fax:(804)758-4080
E-mail: gzkq12a@prodigy.com and hewick1@aol.com
Circa 1678. A driveway lined with large oak trees
leads to this two-story brick Colonial located on 66
acres. There is an ancient family cemetery on the
grounds, and at the rear of the house is an archaeo-

logical dig conducted by the College of William and
Mary. A cross-stitch kit of Hewick Plantation, made
by the Heirloom Needlecraft company, is available
at the inn. The historic "Urbanna" coverlet is
another unique item on display. The innkeeper is a
10th-generation descendant of Christopher
Robinson, builder of Hewick Plantation and an
original trustee of the College of William and Mary.
Innkeeper(s): Helen & Ed Battleson. $95-150. MC VISA AX DS PC TC.
2 rooms with PB, 2 with FP. Breakfast included in rates. Type of meal:
continental-plus breakfast. Beds: QDT. Air conditioning and TV in room.
Fax and stables on premises. Amusement parks, antiques, fishing,
parks, shopping and watersports nearby.
Publicity: *Richmond Times Dispatch, Daily Press, Pleasant Living,
WRIC-TV, TV-Tokyo.*
Certificate may be used: November through June, Monday through
Thursday, no holidays.

Warm Springs E10

Three Hills Inn
PO Box 9
Warm Springs, VA 24484-0009
(540)839-5381 (888)234-4557 Fax:(540)839-5199
Circa 1913. Mary Johnston, who wrote the book
"To Have and to Hold," built this inn, which rests
on 38 mountainous acres. In 1917, Mary and her sisters opened the home to guests, earning a reputation
for the home's view of the Allegheny Mountains and
Warm Springs Gap. The innkeepers now offer lodging in the antique-filled main house or adjacent cottages. Some rooms include private decks, while oth-

ers have fireplaces or clawfoot tubs. Each of the cottages includes a kitchen; one has a working fireplace,
while another offers a woodburning stove.
Innkeeper(s): Julie & David Miller. $49-149. MC VISA DC PC TC. 12
rooms with PB, 3 with FP. 7 suites. 3 cottages. Breakfast and afternoon
tea included in rates. Types of meals: continental breakfast, gourmet
breakfast and early coffee/tea. Picnic lunch, banquet service and catering service available. Restaurant on premises. Beds: KQDT. TV in room.
VCR, fax, copier and child care on premises. Antiques, fishing, parks,
shopping, downhill skiing, cross-country skiing and theater nearby.
Certificate may be used: Anytime, except weekends in October and
major (legal) holidays.

Washington C13

Caledonia Farm - 1812
47 Dearing Rd (Flint Hill)
Washington, VA 22627
(540)675-3693 (800)262-1812 Fax:(540)675-3693
Circa 1812. This gracious Federal-style stone house
in the National Register is beautifully situated on 52
acres adjacent to Shenandoah National Park. It was
built by a Revolutionary War officer, and his musket
is displayed over a mantel. The house, a Virginia
Historic Landmark, has been restored with the original Colonial color scheme retained. All rooms have
working fireplaces and provide views of Skyline
Drive and the Blue Ridge Mountains. The innkeeper is a retired broadcaster.
Innkeeper(s): Phil Irwin. $80-140. MC VISA DS PC TC. 3 rooms, 2 with
PB, 3 with FP. 2 suites. 1 cottage. 1 conference room. Breakfast and
evening snack included in rates. Types of meals: gourmet breakfast and
early coffee/tea. Beds: D. Air conditioning, turndown service and VCR
in room. Fax, copier, spa, bicycles and library on premises. Antiques,
fishing, parks, shopping, downhill skiing, cross-country skiing, theater
and watersports nearby.
Location: Four miles north of Washington, Va.; 68 miles from
Washington, D.C.
Publicity: *Country, Country Almanac, Country Living, Blue Ridge
Country, Discovery, Washington Post, Baltimore Sun.*

*"We've stayed at many, many B&Bs. This is by far
the best!"*

Certificate may be used: Non-holiday, Sunday-Wednesday, Jan. 2-
Sept. 15.

Fairlea Farm Bed & Breakfast
636 Mt Salem Ave, PO Box 124
Washington, VA 22747
(540)675-3679 Fax:(540)675-1064

Circa 1960. View acres of rolling hills, farmland and the Blue Ridge Mountains from this fieldstone house. Rooms are decorated with crocheted canopies and four-poster beds. Plants and floral bedcovers add a homey feel. The stone terrace is set up for relaxing with chairs lined along the edge. As a young surveyor, George Washington inspected the boundaries of this historic village, which is just a short walk from Fairlea Farm, a working sheep and cattle farm.
Innkeeper(s): Susan & Walt Longyear. $75-125. PC TC. 3 rooms. 1 suite. Breakfast and afternoon tea included in rates. Types of meals: full breakfast, gourmet breakfast and early coffee/tea. Beds: QT. Air conditioning and turndown service in room. VCR, fax and copier on premises. Antiques, fishing, parks, shopping and theater nearby.

Certificate may be used: All year: Sunday through Thursday, except holidays.

Gay Street Inn
PO Box 237, Gay St
Washington, VA 22747
(540)675-3288

Circa 1855. After a day of Skyline Drive, Shenandoah National Park and the caverns of Luray and Front Royal, come home to this stucco, gabled farmhouse. If you've booked the fireplace room, a canopy bed will await you. Furnishings include period Shaker pieces. The innkeepers will be happy to steer you to the most interesting vineyards, "pick-your-own" fruit and vegetable farms and Made-In-Virginia food and craft shops. Five-star dining is within walking distance at The Inn at Little Washington.
Innkeeper(s): Robin & Donna Kevis. $95-135. MC VISA AX PC TC. 4 rooms with PB, 1 with FP. 1 suite. Breakfast and afternoon tea included in rates. Types of meals: continental-plus breakfast, full breakfast, gourmet breakfast and early coffee/tea. Picnic lunch available. Beds: Q. Air conditioning in room. Child care on premises. Handicap access. Antiques, fishing, parks, shopping, theater and watersports nearby.

"Thank you for a wonderful visit. Your hospitality was superb."

Certificate may be used: Any Sunday through Friday.

White Post   B13

L'Auberge Provencale
PO Box 119
White Post, VA 22663-0119
(540)837-1375 (800)638-1702 Fax:(540)837-2004

Circa 1753. This farmhouse was built with fieldstones gathered from the area. Hessian soldiers crafted the woodwork of the main house, Mt. Airy. As the name suggests, a French influence is prominent throughout the inn. Victorian and European antiques fill the elegant guest rooms, several of which include fireplaces. Innkeeper Alain Borel hails from a long line of master chefs, his expertise creates many happy culinary memories guests cherish. Many of the French-influenced items served at the inn's four-diamond restaurant, include ingredients from the inn's gardens, and Alain has been hailed by James Beard as a Great Country Inn Chef.
Innkeeper(s): Alain & Celeste Borel. $145-250. MC VISA AX DC DS PC TC. 11 rooms with PB, 6 with FP. 2 suites. 1 conference room. Breakfast included in rates. Type of meal: gourmet breakfast. Dinner, evening snack, picnic lunch, banquet service and room service available. Restaurant on premises. Beds: QD. Air conditioning, turndown service and ceiling fan in room. Fax and copier on premises. Handicap access. Antiques, fishing, parks, shopping and theater nearby.
Location: One mile south of Rt 50 on Rt 340.
Publicity: *Bon Appetit, Glamour, Washington Dossier, Washington Post, Baltimore, Richmond Times.*

"Peaceful view and atmosphere, extraordinary food and wines. Honeymoon and heaven all in one!"

Certificate may be used: Wednesday through Friday, no May or October or holidays.

White Stone   F17

Flowering Fields
RR 2 Box 160
White Stone, VA 22578-9722
(804)435-6238 Fax:(804)435-6238

Circa 1790. Guests will find plenty to do at this Victorian bed & breakfast. The game room is stocked with a pool table, games, darts and a fireplace. The grounds are shared by the innkeepers friendly dogs, cat and several horses. The parlor is a bit more formal, and the music room includes a baby grand piano. Guests are pampered with a selection of appetizers and beverages after check-in. Cookies and chocolates are available later in the evening, and the morning begins with a huge breakfast. Omelets, fried apples and unique items such as oyster frittatas are served, and the innkeepers will plan the meal around guests' dietary restrictions. Guest rooms include items such as a four-poster rice bed, antiques, Queen Anne chairs and Oriental rugs.
Innkeeper(s): Lloyd Niziol & Susan Moenssens. $75-120. PC TC. 5 rooms, 2 with PB. 1 suite. 1 conference room. Breakfast, afternoon tea and evening snack included in rates. Types of meals: full breakfast, gourmet breakfast and early coffee/tea. Beds: KQDT. Air conditioning and ceiling fan in room. Cable TV, VCR, fax, copier, bicycles and library on premises. Antiques, fishing, parks, shopping, watersports nearby.

Certificate may be used: Jan. 1-Dec. 31, Sunday-Saturday, excluding holiday weekends (Thanksgiving, Fourth of July, Memorial, Labor Day, Christmas).

Williamsburg   G17

Cedars
616 Jamestown Rd
Williamsburg, VA 23185-3945
(757)229-3591 (800)296-3591

Circa 1930. This three-story brick Georgian home is a short walk from Colonial Williamsburg and is located across from William and Mary College. Rooms are decorated with Traditional antiques, Colonial reproductions, fireplaces and four-poster or canopy beds. The bountiful breakfasts include a hearty entree, fresh fruits, breads, muffins and cereals.

Innkeeper(s): Carol, Jim & Brona Malecha. $76-165. MC VISA PC TC. 8 rooms with PB, 2 with FP. 2 suites. 1 cottage. Breakfast included in rates. Types of meals: full breakfast and early coffee/tea. Beds: KQT. Air conditioning and ceiling fan in room. Library on premises. Amusement parks, antiques, parks and shopping nearby.

Certificate may be used: Jan. 2-March 13, excluding holiday weekends.

Homestay B&B
517 Richmond Rd
Williamsburg, VA 23185-3537
(804)229-7468 (800)836-7468

Circa 1933. This Colonial Revival house is decorated with Victorian pieces inherited from the innkeeper's family. A screened back porch and fireplace in the living room are gathering spots. Collections of hand-crafted Noah's arks may be found throughout the house. The College of William and Mary is adjacent, and Colonial Williamsburg's is four blocks away.

Innkeeper(s): James Thomassen. $75-85. MC VISA. 3 rooms with PB. Breakfast included in rates. Type of meal: full breakfast. Beds: KT. Air conditioning and ceiling fan in room. Cable TV and VCR on premises. Amusement parks, antiques, sporting events and theater nearby.

"Our stay at your inn has been wonderful. Thank you so much for your warm and gracious welcome."

Certificate may be used: January and February, except holidays and holiday weekends. March, Sunday-Thursday only. Pre-payment by check only.

Williamsburg Manor B&B
600 Richmond Rd
Williamsburg, VA 23185-3540
(757)220-8011 (800)422-8011 Fax:(757)220-8011

Circa 1927. Built during the reconstruction of Colonial Williamsburg, this Georgian brick Colonial is just three blocks from the historic village. A grand staircase, culinary library, Waverly fabrics, Oriental rugs and antiques are featured. Breakfasts begin with fresh fruits and home-baked breads, followed by a special daily entree. Gourmet regional Virginia dinners also are available.

Innkeeper(s): Laura Sisane. $75-150. MC VISA PC TC. 5 rooms with PB. Breakfast included in rates. Types of meals: gourmet breakfast and early coffee/tea. Picnic lunch, lunch, gourmet lunch, catering service

and catered breakfast available. Beds: QT. Air conditioning, ceiling fan and TV in room. VCR and fax on premises. Amusement parks, antiques, fishing, parks, shopping, sporting events, theater and watersports nearby.

Location: Three blocks from colonial Williamsburg.

Publicity: *Williamsburg.*

"Lovely accommodations - scrumptious breakfast."

Certificate may be used: Jan. 5-March 15, July and August, Nov. 1-15. All midweek (Sunday-Thursday)

Yorktown   G17

York River Inn B&B
209 Ambler St
Yorktown, VA 23690-3702
(757)887-8800 (800)884-7003 Fax:(757)887-8800

Circa 1984. This inn is so-named because of its location overlooking the York River. Rooms are appointed in an elegant, Colonial style and are stocked with helpful amenities such as irons, ironing boards and hair dryers. Each of the three guest quarters include a sitting area with a TV, VCR and desk. The innkeeper, a native Virginia and former supervisor at Colonial Williamsburg, is full of historic knowledge. Yorktown, where the Revolutionary War ended, offers many historic sites.

Innkeeper(s): William W. Cole. $100-120. MC VISA PC. 3 rooms with PB. Breakfast, afternoon tea and evening snack included in rates. Types of meals: full breakfast, gourmet breakfast and early coffee/tea. Beds: Q. Air conditioning, TV and VCR in room. Fax, copier and library on premises. Antiques, fishing, parks, shopping, golf and watersports nearby.

Certificate may be used: Jan. 5-March 31, anytime.

Washington

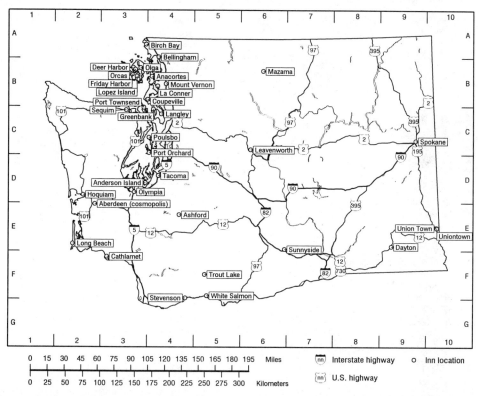

	1	2	3	4	5	6	7	8	9	10	
A				Birch Bay			97	395			A
				Bellingham							
B		Deer Harbor	Olga		Mazama						B
		Orcas	Anacortes								
		Friday Harbor	Mount Vernon								
		Lopez Island	La Conner					2			
		Port Townsend	Coupeville								
		Sequim	Langley				395				
C		Greenbank				97			Spokane		C
			Poulsbo		Leavenworth	2		195			
			Port Orchard				90				
D		Anderson Island	Tacoma			90					D
		Hoquiam	Olympia				395				
		Aberdeen (cosmopolis)				82					
E		Long Beach	Ashford	12			Union Town	Uniontown			E
		Cathlamet	5	12		Sunnyside	Dayton	12			
F		Stevenson	White Salmon	Trout Lake	97	82	730				F
G											G

| 0 15 30 45 60 75 90 105 120 135 150 165 180 195 | Miles | (nn) Interstate highway | o Inn location |
| 0 25 50 75 100 125 150 175 200 225 250 275 300 | Kilometers | (nn) U.S. highway | |

Aberdeen (Cosmopolis) *E2*

Cooney Mansion B&B
PO Box 54, 1705 Fifth St
Aberdeen (Cosmopolis), WA 98537-0054
(360)533-0602 (800)977-7823

Circa 1908. This former lumber magnate's home, in a wooded setting, boasts 37 rooms. In the National Register, it was built with a ballroom in the basement, nine bedrooms and eight bathrooms. There are soaking tubs in all of the rooms. Mission furnishings, original to the house, include the dining room set, sofas, desks and library tables. Weddings and corporate retreats are popular here.
Innkeeper(s): Judi & Jim Lohr. $65-165. MC VISA AX DC DS. 8 rooms, 5 with PB, 1 with FP. 1 suite. 1 conference room. Breakfast and after-

noon tea included in rates. Types of meals: full breakfast and early coffee/tea. Banquet service and catering service available. Beds: KQDT. Cable TV, VCR, fax, spa and sauna on premises. Antiques, fishing, parks, shopping, sporting events, theater and watersports nearby.
Publicity: *Sunset, Travel & Leisure, Country Inns.*
"*This is an exceptional inn because of the hosts, who really care about their guests.*"
Certificate may be used: Sept. 15-May 15, holidays excluded.

Anacortes
B4

Channel House
2902 Oakes Ave
Anacortes, WA 98221-1321
(360)293-9382 (800)238-4353 Fax:(360)299-9208

Circa 1902. Built by an Italian count, the Channel House is designated the Krebs House by the Historical Home Tour. Guest rooms view Puget

Sound and the San Juan Islands, and the ferry is minutes away. The inn has a Victorian flavor, with a library, three fireplaces, and a dining room with French doors leading out to the garden.
Innkeeper(s): Dennis & Pat McIntyre. $69-105. MC VISA AX DS PC TC. 6 rooms with PB, 2 with FP. 1 cottage. Breakfast and afternoon tea included in rates. Types of meals: full breakfast and early coffee/tea. Beds: KQ. Fax on premises. Antiques, fishing, parks, shopping, theater and watersports nearby.
Location: 85 miles north of Seattle.
Publicity: *Skagit Valley Herald.*
"The house is spectacular and your friendly thoughtfulness is the icing on the cake."
Certificate may be used: Oct . 1-April 30, Sunday through Thursday.

Old Brook Inn
530 Old Brook Ln
Anacortes, WA 98221-9657
(360)293-4768 (800)503-4768

Circa 1983. A traditional, New England decor complements this home's Cape Cod appearance. The three guest rooms are simply furnished in an uncluttered style. One includes a fireplace. The bed & breakfast is close to horseback riding facilities, and there is an orchard on the 10-acre grounds. The innkeeper gets the day off to a refreshing start with an ample breakfast of fruit, blueberry pancakes, baked egg dishes, potatoes and more.
Innkeeper(s): Richard M. Ash. $70-80. MC VISA DS PC TC. 3 rooms with PB. Breakfast included in rates. Types of meals: continental breakfast and continental-plus breakfast. Beds: QT. Turndown service in room. VCR, stables, library and pet boarding on premises. Antiques, fishing, parks and shopping nearby.
Certificate may be used: Jan. 1-March 30, April 15-June 15, Sept. 1-Dec. 31, Sunday-Thursday.

Anderson Island
D3

The Inn at Burg's Landing
8808 Villa Beach Rd
Anderson Island, WA 98303-9785
(206)884-9185 Fax:(206)488-8682

Circa 1987. A short ferry trip from Steilacoom and Tacoma, this log homestead boasts beautiful views of Mt. Rainier, Puget Sound and the Cascade Mountains. The master bedroom features a skylight and a private whirlpool bath. After a full breakfast, guests can spend the day at the inn's private beach. Golf, hiking and freshwater lakes are nearby, and the area has many seasonal activities, including Fourth of July fireworks, the Anderson Island fair and parade in September and a February Sweetheart Dance and Dinner.
Innkeeper(s): Ken & Annie Burg. $75-110. MC VISA PC TC. 4 rooms, 2 with PB. Breakfast included in rates. Meal: full breakfast. Beds: Q. VCR in room. Spa on premises. Fishing, parks, downhill skiing nearby.
Publicity: *Sunset, Tacoma News Tribune, Portland Oregonian.*
Certificate may be used: Sunday-Thursday, May 1-Sept. 30, Oct. 1-April 30, anytime.

Ashford
E4

Mountain Meadows Inn B&B
PO Box 291, 28912 SR 706 E
Ashford, WA 98304-9709
(360)569-2788

Circa 1910. Originally built for the superintendent of the Pacific National Lumber Company, the house boasts hanging baskets of fuschias which accentuate the veranda. Comfortable guest rooms feature a view of the woodland setting, occasionally visited by deer and elk. Breakfasts are prepared on an 1889 wood cooking stove.
Innkeeper(s): Harry & Michelle Latimer. $65-110. MC VISA PC TC. 6 rooms with PB. 1 conference room. Breakfast included in rates. Meal: full breakfast. Beds: KQDT. Turndown service. Library on premises. Antiques, fishing, parks, cross-country skiing, golf, watersports nearby.
Location: One-half mile west of Ashford.
Publicity: *Seattle Times, Pacific Northwest, Eastside Weekly, Prime Times.*
"Our stay here will be one of the nicest memories of our vacation."
Certificate may be used: Oct. 1 through May 31, Sunday-Thursday, excluding holidays.

Bellingham
A4

The Castle B&B
1103 15th St
Bellingham, WA 98225-6631
(360)676-0974

Circa 1889. All the guest rooms of this mauve Victorian mansion look out to Bellingham Bay and the San Juan Islands. Statuary, fountains and ponds accent the inn's gables, steeply pitched turret and bays. The Bayview Room, with its panoramic water view, is the inn's honeymoon suite, complete with private veranda and fireplace. Presented with the Mayor's Restoration Award, the inn's ornate castle-appropriate antiques mingle with your hosts' extensive lamp and clock collection sprinkled throughout the 21 rooms. There is also a waterfront cottage available and an antique shop on the premises.

Innkeeper(s): Gloria & Larry Harriman. $45-95. PC TC. 4 rooms, 3 with PB, 1 with FP. 2 suites. 1 conference room. Breakfast included in rates. Types of meals: continental-plus breakfast and early coffee/tea. Beds: KQDT. Cable TV and VCR on premises. Antiques, fishing, parks, shopping, downhill skiing, cross-country skiing, sporting events, theater and watersports nearby.

Location: Historic Fairhaven.

Publicity: *Sunset Magazine, Daughters of the Painted Ladies.*

"Never have I seen a B&B with so many museum-quality pieces of furniture."

Certificate may be used: Nov. 1-April 30, Wednesday & Thursday only.

Birch Bay A3

Birch Bay B&B
8068 Birch Bay Dr
Birch Bay, WA 98230-9017
(206)325-3500 Fax:(206)325-3500

This private, beachcomber cottage features a sun deck perfect for enjoying a summer day. The cottage offers comfortable, county decor and includes a bedroom, bathroom and kitchenette. The hosts keep the refrigerator stocked with juice, fresh eggs and bacon. During crabbing season, you'll find fresh crabmeat in the refrigerator. Guests are welcome to use the hosts' tandem bicycle, a perfect way to enjoy the scenic area. Birch Bay and nearby Semiahmoo offer plenty of restaurants, a dance hall and outlet shopping.

Innkeeper(s): Ronald Walken. $70. 1 room. Breakfast included in rates. Type of meal: continental breakfast.

Certificate may be used: Cottage, Monday through Thursday.

Cathlamet F3

The Gallery B&B at Little Cape Horn
4 Little Cape Horn Rd
Cathlamet, WA 98612-9544
(360)425-7395 Fax:(360)425-1351

Circa 1959. This unique modern home affords a view of the Columbia River and the surrounding valley. From the inn's redwood hot tub, guests can watch as ships traverse the river channel. The home is furnished with antiques, but the decor is contemporary, enhanced by a collection of artwork. Some of the guest rooms include Jacuzzi tubs. A gallery and gift shop are located on the premises.

Innkeeper(s): Eric & Carolyn Feasey. $80-135. 4 rooms, 3 with PB. 1 suite. 1 conference room. Breakfast included in rates. Types of meals:

continental breakfast, full breakfast, gourmet breakfast and early coffee/tea. Beds: QT. Air conditioning and ceiling fan in room. VCR, fax, copier and spa on premises. Fishing, parks, and watersports nearby.

Location: On the banks of the Lower Columbia River.

Publicity: *Portland Oregonian, Seattle Post Intelligencer.*

Certificate may be used: Jan. 1-Dec. 31, subject to availability.

Coupeville B4

Captain Whidbey Inn
2072 W Captain Whidbey Inn Rd
Coupeville, WA 98239
(360)678-4097 (800)366-4097 Fax:(360)678-4110

Circa 1907. Overlooking Whidbey Island's Penn Cove, this log inn has comfortable rooms featuring down comforters, feather beds and views of lagoons and gardens. The dining room also has a magnificent view and guests can enjoy their meals by the fireplace. The chef utilizes local catches such as steelhead, salmon, spot prawns and Penn Cove mussels. The proprietor is also a sailing captain, and guests can book an afternoon on his 52-foot ketch, Cutty Sark. The proprietor's family has run the inn for more than 30 years.

Innkeeper(s): Dennis A. Argent. $95-225. EP. MC VISA AX DC DS. 32 rooms, 20 with PB, 7 with FP. 1 conference room. Breakfast included in rates. Type of meal: full breakfast. Dinner, evening snack, picnic lunch and lunch available. Restaurant on premises. Beds: KQD. Fax and copier on premises. Antiques, shopping and theater nearby.

Location: Central Whidbey Island.

Publicity: *Gourmet Magazine, USA-Weekend.*

"I visit and stay here once a year and love it."

Certificate may be used: October-May, Sunday-Thursday, excluding special events/holidays.

Colonel Crockett Farm
1012 S Fort Casey Rd
Coupeville, WA 98239-9753
(360)678-3711

Circa 1855. In the National Register, this Victorian farmhouse presides over 40 island acres of lawns, meadows and country gardens. Sweeping views of Crockett Lake and Admiralty Inlet may be enjoyed from the inn and its grounds. The Crockett Room, a favorite of newlyweds, has a blue chintz canopied bed and fainting couch. Danny DeVito and Michael Douglas stayed at the inn during the Coupeville filming of War of the Roses.

Innkeeper(s): Beulah Whitlow. $65-95. MC VISA. 5 rooms with PB. Breakfast included in rates. Type of meal: full breakfast. Beds: KQD.

Antiques, shopping and theater nearby.

Location: On Whidbey Island near the Port Townsend ferry terminal at Keystone, near Fort Casey State Park.

Publicity: *Peninsula, Portland Oregonian, Country Inns, Glamour.*

"Everyone felt quite at home...such a beautiful spot."

Certificate may be used: October through April, Sunday (except on three-day holiday weekends) through Thursday (except Thanksgiving and Christmas).

The Inn at Penn Cove

702 N Main, PO Box 85
Coupeville, WA 98239
(360)678-8000 (800)688-2683

Circa 1887. Two restored historic houses, one a fanciful white and peach Italianate confection in the National Register, comprise the inn. Each house contains only three guest rooms affording a variety of small parlors for guests to enjoy. The most romantic accommodation is Desiree's Room with a fireplace, a whirlpool tub for two and mesmerizing views of Puget Sound and Mt. Baker.

Innkeeper(s): Gladys & Mitchell Howard. $75-125. MC VISA AX DS PC TC. 6 rooms, 4 with PB, 3 with FP. 1 conference room. Type of meal: full breakfast. Beds: KQ. Ceiling fan in room. Cable TV, VCR and computer on premises. Antiques and shopping nearby.

Publicity: *Whidbey News-Times, Country Inns, Glamour.*

"Our hosts were warm and friendly, but also gave us plenty of space and privacy - a good combination."

Certificate may be used: Oct. 15-March 15, Sunday-Friday; March 15-June 15, Sunday-Thursday.

The Victorian B&B

602 N Main
Coupeville, WA 98239-0761
(360)678-5305

Circa 1889. This graceful Italianate Victorian sits in the heart of one of the nation's few historic reserves. It was built for German immigrant Jacob Jenne, who became the proprietor of the Central Hotel on Front Street. Noted for having the first running water on the island, the house's old wooden water tower stands in the back garden. An old-fashioned storefront, once the local dentist's office, sits demurely behind a picket fence, now a private hideaway for guests.

Innkeeper(s): Alfred Sasso. $65-100. MC VISA. 3 rooms with PB. 1 suite. Breakfast included in rates. Type of meal: full breakfast. Beds: Q. TV and VCR on premises. Antiques, fishing, shopping, theater nearby.

Publicity: *Seattle Times, Country Inns.*

"If kindness and generosity are the precursors to success (and I certainly hope they are!), your success is assured."

Certificate may be used: October through May, Sunday through Friday.

Dayton E9

The Purple House

415 E Clay St
Dayton, WA 99328-1348
(509)382-3159 (800)486-2574

Circa 1882. History buffs will adore this aptly named bed & breakfast, colored in deep purple tones with white, gingerbread trim. The home, listed in the National Register, is the perfect place to enjoy Dayton, which boasts two historic districts and a multitude of preserved Victorian homes. Innkeeper Christine Williscroft has filled the home with

antiques and artwork. A highly praised cook, Christine prepares the European-style full breakfasts, as well as mouthwatering afternoon refreshments. Guests can relax in the richly appointed parlor or library, and the grounds also include a swimming pool.

Innkeeper(s): D. Christine Williscroft. $85-125. EP. MC VISA. 4 rooms, 2 with PB, 1 with FP. 1 suite. Breakfast and afternoon tea included in rates. Types of meals: full breakfast, gourmet breakfast and early coffee/tea. Dinner and picnic lunch available. Beds: QD. Air conditioning and ceiling fan in room. Cable TV, VCR, swimming, library and pet boarding on premises. Handicap access. Antiques, fishing, parks, shopping, downhill skiing, cross-country skiing, sporting events, theater and watersports nearby.

Publicity: *Sunset.*

"You have accomplished so very much with your bed & breakfast to make it a very special place to stay."

Certificate may be used: By arrangement only.

Weinhard Hotel

235 E Main St
Dayton, WA 99328-1352
(509)382-4032 Fax:(509)382-2640

Circa 1890. This luxurious Victorian hotel, tucked at the base of the scenic Blue Mountains, originally served up spirits as the Weinhard Saloon and Lodge Hall. Guests are transported back to the genteel Victorian era during their stay. After a restful sleep among period pieces, ornate carpeting and ceilings fans, guests might imagine the days when horses and buggies road through town. While the innkeepers have worked to preserve the history of the hotel, they didn't forget such modern luxuries as Jacuzzi tubs in each of the guest baths. The hotel boasts a beautiful Victorian roof garden, a perfect place to relax with a cup of tea or gourmet coffee. For a unique weekend, try the hotel's special Romantic Getaway package. Guests are presented with sparkling wine or champagne and a dozen roses. The package also includes a five-course meal served in the privacy of your own room.

Innkeeper(s): Virginia Butler. $65-115. MC VISA. 15 rooms with PB. Breakfast included in rates. Afternoon tea, dinner, lunch and catering service available. Restaurant on premises. Beds: Q.

Publicity: *Seattle, Daily Journal of Commerce, Sunset Magazine, Lewiston Morning Tribune, San Francisco Examiner, Spokesman Review.*

"It's spectacular! Thank you so much for all your kindness and caring hospitality."

Certificate may be used: Sunday-Thursday, year-round, except May 26-29, July 14-17, Sept.1-5, holidays.

Deer Harbor   B3

Deep Meadow Farm B&B
PO Box 321
Deer Harbor, WA 98243-0321
(360)376-5866

Circa 1939. Located on 40 acres, this homestead is one of the few family farms still remaining on Orcas Island. It served for many years as the local dairy farm. Now, with an added wing and new front porch it serves as a handsome B&B. Midwestern farm furniture and Civil War memorabilia furnish the inn, including a certificate from President Lincoln signed to the innkeeper's great-great-great Grandfather. There are two horses, a border collie and two cats. Kayaking and whale watching are popular pastimes.

Innkeeper(s): Anna Elisa Tejada-Boyle. $85-95. 2 rooms with PB. Breakfast and afternoon tea included in rates. Types of meals: full breakfast and early coffee/tea. Beds: D. VCR on premises. Antiques, fishing, shopping, theater and watersports nearby.

"Outstanding hospitality. The best of Orcas!"

Certificate may be used: Oct. 1 through April 30.

Friday Harbor   B3

San Juan Inn B&B
50 Spring St, Box 776
Friday Harbor, WA 98250-0776
(360)378-2070 (800)742-8210 Fax:(360)378-6437

Circa 1873. In the National Register, this old European-style hotel is filled with stained glass, old photographs and flowers picked from the inn's garden. A Victorian settee is situated under a cherry tree within sniffing distance of the lilacs and roses.

It's a half-block to the ferry landing. The innkeeper speaks Danish, German, Norwegian, French, Swedish and English.

Innkeeper(s): Annette & Skip Metzger. $70-175. MC VISA AX DS PC TC. 10 rooms, 4 with PB. 1 suite. Breakfast included in rates. Type of meal: continental-plus breakfast. Beds: KQDT. Ceiling fan, TV and VCR in room. Fax and spa on premises. Fishing, parks, shopping, theater and watersports nearby.

Certificate may be used: Oct. 1-April 30.

Tucker House B&B With Cottages
260 B St
Friday Harbor, WA 98250-8074
(360)378-2783 (800)965-0123 Fax:(360)378-6437

Circa 1898. Only two blocks from the ferry landing, the white picket fence bordering Tucker House is a welcome sight for guests. The spindled entrance leads to the parlor and the simply furnished five guest rooms in the house. A separate cottage next to the hot tub is popular with honeymooners.

Innkeeper(s): Skip & Annette Metzger. $75-135. MC VISA AX DS PC TC. 5 rooms, 3 with PB. 3 cottages. Breakfast included in rates. Types of meals: full breakfast and gourmet breakfast. Beds: QD. TV and VCR in room. Fax and spa on premises. Antiques, fishing, parks, shopping, theater and watersports nearby.

Location: San Juan Island.

Publicity: *Sunset, Pacific Northwest Magazine, Western Boatman.*

"A lovely place, the perfect getaway. We'll be back."

Certificate may be used: Oct. 16-April 1, excluding holidays or holiday periods.

Greenbank   C4

Guest House Cottages, A B&B Inn
3366 S Hwy 525, Whidbey Island
Greenbank, WA 98253-6400
(360)678-3115 Fax:(360)321-0631

Circa 1922. These storybook cottages and log home are nestled within a peaceful forest on 25 acres. The Hansel and Gretel cottage features stained-glass and criss-cross paned windows that give it the feel of a gingerbread house. Two of the cottages were built in 1922. Ask for the Lodge and you'll enjoy a private setting with a pond just beyond your deck. Inside is a Jacuzzi tub, stone fireplace, king bed, antiques and an intimate hunting lodge atmosphere.

Innkeeper(s): Don & Mary Jane Creger. $110-285. MC VISA AX DS PC TC. 1 suite. 6 cottages. Breakfast included in rates. Type of meal: full breakfast. Catered breakfast available. Beds: KQD. Air conditioning, turndown service, ceiling fan and VCR in room. Fax, copier, spa and swimming on premises. Antiques, fishing, parks, shopping, golf nearby.

Location: On Whidbey Island.

Publicity: *L.A. Times, Woman's Day, Sunset, Country Inns, Bride's.*

"The wonderful thing is to be by yourselves and rediscover what's important."

Certificate may be used: Nov. 15-March 15, Monday through Thursday, holidays and holiday weeks excluded.

Hoquiam   D2

Lytle House
509 Chenault Ave
Hoquiam, WA 98550-1821
(360)533-2320 (800)677-2320 Fax:(360)533-4025

Circa 1900. Set high on a hill overlooking the harbor, this massive three-story Queen Anne Victorian was built by a lumberman. There are graceful sun porches, arches and gingerbread trim. The Treehouse Room is shaded by a 100-foot copper beech tree, while the Rose Room offers a view of the harbor. Afternoon tea is available. The innkeepers will host a murder-mystery dinner party or elegant high tea by prior arrangement.

Innkeeper(s): Robert Bencala. $65-105. MC VISA AX. 8 rooms. 1 suite. Breakfast included in rates. Types of meals: full breakfast and early coffee/tea. Evening snack, banquet service and catering service available. Cable TV and VCR on premises. Antiques, shopping and theater nearby.

Certificate may be used: Sept. 15-May 1, excluding holidays. Some restrictions may apply.

La Conner   B4

Katy's Inn
503 S Third
La Conner, WA 98257-0869
(360)466-3366 (800)914-7767

Circa 1876. This pristinely renovated farmhouse is framed by flower gardens and graceful oak trees. Victorian wallpapers enhance a collection of antique furnishings. Each guest room opens to the veranda or balcony, providing a view of the countryside. Bicycles and boats can be rented from the village three blocks away.

Innkeeper(s): Bruce & Kathie Hubbard. $69-95. MC VISA AX DS. 4 rooms, 2 with PB. Breakfast and evening snack included in rates. Types of meals: full breakfast and early coffee/tea. Room service available. Beds: QD. Spa on premises. Antiques, fishing, parks, shopping and watersports nearby.

Location: Heart of town.

"The most charming and warmest of the B&Bs in which we stayed."

Certificate may be used: January & February, Sunday-Thursday.

The White Swan Guest House
1388 Moore Rd
La Conner, WA 98273-9249
(360)445-6805

Circa 1898. Guests will marvel at innkeeper Peter Goldfarb's beautiful gardens as they wind up the driveway to reach this charming, yellow Victorian farmhouse. Inside, guests are greeted with luscious home-baked chocolate chip cookies in the bright, cheery

kitchen. Guest rooms are filled with comfortable, Victorian furnishings, and there's even a cozy "Garden Cottage" to stay in, complete with its own kitchen and private sun deck. Each April, the area is host to the Skagit Valley Tulip festival. La Conner, a nearby fishing village, is full of shops and galleries to explore.

Innkeeper(s): Peter Goldfarb. $75-150. MC VISA PC TC. 4 rooms, 1 with PB. 1 cottage. Breakfast included in rates. Types of meals: continental-plus breakfast and early coffee/tea. Beds: KQD. Turndown service in room. Antiques, fishing, parks and shopping nearby.

"This has been a very pleasant interlude. What a beautiful, comfortable place you have here. We will be back."

Certificate may be used: October-March, Sunday-Friday in main house only.

Langley   C4

Island Tyme, Bed & Breakfast Inn
4940 S Bayview Rd
Langley, WA 98260-9778
(360)221-5078 (800)898-8963

Circa 1993. Located on Whidbey Island, this Victorian is a whimsical mix of colors topped with gingerbread trim and a turret. The inn's 10 acres ensure solitude, and romantic amenities abound. The Heirloom Suite boasts both a fireplace and a Jacuzzi

tub for two. The Turret room is tucked into the inn's tower and also offers a Jacuzzi tub for two. Quilts, antiques and collectibles are found throughout the guest rooms. The dining room, where the country breakfasts are served, is located in the inn's turret.
Innkeeper(s): Lyn & Phil Fauth. $90-140. MC VISA AX PC TC. 5 rooms with PB, 2 with FP. 1 suite. Breakfast and evening snack included in rates. Types of meals: gourmet breakfast and early coffee/tea. Beds: KQ. Turndown service, ceiling fan, TV and VCR in room. Library, pet boarding and child care on premises. Handicap access. Antiques, fishing, parks, shopping, theater and watersports nearby.
Certificate may be used: Oct. 15-April 30, except third weekend of Feb.

Saratoga Inn
PO Box 428
Langley, WA 98260
(800)698-2910 Fax:(360)221-5804

This romantic, island inn is located away from the hustle and bustle of Seattle. To reach the inn, guests hop aboard a ferry and take a 20-minute journey from the city to quiet Whidbey Island. The inn offers 15 elegantly appointed guest rooms, each with a fireplace. Each room also boasts a water view. Guests enjoy a full breakfast and afternoon with a variety of goodies. Guests can spend the day exploring the island, or hop aboard the ferry to visit the sites of Seattle. Saratoga Inn is a Four Sisters Inn.
Innkeeper(s): Jessica Anderegg. $110-225. 15 rooms with PB, 15 with FP. Breakfast and afternoon tea included in rates. Types of meals: full breakfast and early coffee/tea.
Certificate may be used: January-December, Sunday-Thursday only, holidays & special events not included. Subject to availability.

Twickenham House B&B Inn
5023 S Langley Rd
Langley, WA 98260-9609
(360)221-2334
E-mail: twiknham@whidbey.com

Circa 1990. If the beauty of Puget Sound isn't enough, this island inn will be sure to satisfy. The inn offers comfortable rooms with French Canadian and European pine furniture, and a gourmet, three-course breakfast is served each morning. The home has three living rooms with fireplaces and a British pub area. The inn shares the expansive 10-acre grounds with Northwest evergreens, ducks, sheep, hens and roosters. The island has many restaurants, boutiques and shops. Langley holds several seasonal events, including a country fair and a mystery weekend.
Innkeeper(s): Pat & Cece Egging. $85-120. MC VISA. 6 rooms, 4 with PB. 2 suites. 1 conference room. Breakfast included in rates. Types of meals: gourmet breakfast and early coffee/tea. Banquet service and catering service available. Beds: Q. VCR on premises. Antiques, fishing, shopping, theater and watersports nearby.
Location: The south end of Whidbey Island.
Publicity: *Sunset, Country Living, Oregonian, Odyssey.*
"Gracious and friendly hosts."
Certificate may be used: Monday-Thursday, excluding holiday periods.

Leavenworth   C6

Autumn Pond B&B
10388 Titus Rd
Leavenworth, WA 98826-9509
(509)548-4482 (800)222-9661 Fax:(509)548-7278
E-mail: info@autumnpond.com

Circa 1992. This modern ranch-style home is set at the base of the Cascade Mountains and offers stunning views, which one can enjoy from the outdoor hot tub. The interior is welcoming, with bright, flowery prints on the beds and country furnishings. Exposed beams add a rustic touch to the dining area and living room. Guests can feed the ducks at the pond or go for a paddleboat ride. After a homemade breakfast, head into Leavenworth and explore the shops and sites of this historic Bavarian town.
Innkeeper(s): Pam & Roger Kirkpatrick. $65-75. MC VISA PC. 6 rooms with PB. Breakfast included in rates. Types of meals: full breakfast and early coffee/tea. Beds: Q. Air conditioning in room. Fax, copier and spa on premises. Antiques, fishing, parks, shopping, downhill skiing, cross-country skiing, golf, theater and watersports nearby.

"This was a perfect way to celebrate our 36th anniversary. Everything has been wonderful."
Certificate may be used: Year-round, Sunday-Thursday, no festivals/holidays.

Haus Rohrbach Pension
12882 Ranger Rd
Leavenworth, WA 98826-9503
(509)548-7024 (800)548-4477 Fax:(509)548-5038

Circa 1975. This inn is located two minutes away from the village. Private fireplaces and whirlpools for two are features of each of three suites. Sourdough pancakes and cinnamon rolls are specialties of the house. Guests often take breakfast out to the deck to enjoy pastoral views that include grazing sheep and a pleasant pond. In the evening, return from whitewater rafting, tobagganning, skiing or sleigh rides to soak in the hot tub or indulge in the inn's complimentary desserts served in front of the wood stove.
Innkeeper(s): Kathryn Harrild. $75-160. MC VISA AX DS. 10 rooms, 8 with PB, 3 with FP. 3 suites. 2 conference rooms. Breakfast included in rates. Types of meals: full breakfast and early coffee/tea. Dinner, evening snack, picnic lunch, lunch, catering service and catered breakfast available. Beds: KQD. Air conditioning in room. Handicap access. Antiques, fishing, shopping, skiing nearby.
Location: Two minutes from the Bavarian village of Leavenworth.
Certificate may be used: March, April, November-all days. January, February, May, June, September, October-Sunday through Thursday.

Long Beach
E2

Boreas Bed & Breakfast
607 N Boulevard, PO Box 1344
Long Beach, WA 98631
(360)642-8069 (888)642-8069 Fax:(360)642-5353
E-mail: boreas@aone.com

Circa 1920. This inn started as a beach house and was remodeled eclectically with decks and a massive stone fireplace. There are two living rooms that offer views of the beach. Guest rooms all have ocean or mountain views (depending on the weather). Guests can enjoy the hot tub in the enclosed gazebo, take the path that winds through the dunes to the surf or walk to the boardwalk, restaurants and shopping. There is also a three-bedroom cottage available, and breakfast is not included in the cottage rates.
Innkeeper(s): Susie Goldsmith & Bill Verner. $75-120. MC VISA AX DC DS PC TC. 5 rooms. 3 suites. 1 cottage. Type of meal: full breakfast. Beds: KQDT. VCR, fax, spa, bicycles and library on premises. Antiques, fishing, parks, shopping and watersports nearby.
Certificate may be used: Sept. 15-May 15, Sunday-Thursday.

Scandinavian Gardens Inn
1610 S California St
Long Beach, WA 98631-9801
(360)642-8877 (800)988-9277 Fax:(360)642-8763
You are asked to honor a Scandinavian custom of removing your shoes upon entering this B&B. White wool carpeting and blond-wood pieces decorate the living room. A recreation room offers a hot tub and Finnish sauna. The Icelandic Room has an antique armoire and hand-painted cabinets, while the Swedish Suite features a two-person soaking tub tucked into a private nook. Breakfast items such as creamed rice, shrimp au gratin and Danish pastries are served smorgasbord-style with the hosts in costume.
Innkeeper(s): Marilyn Dakan. $75-125. MC VISA. 5 rooms. 1 suite. Breakfast included in rates. Type of meal: full breakfast. Turndown service in room. Antiques and shopping nearby.
Certificate may be used: Sunday-Thursday, holidays and festivals excluded

Lopez
B4

MacKaye Harbor Inn
RR 1 Box 1940
Lopez, WA 98261-9801
(360)468-2253 Fax:(360)468-2253
Circa 1927. This seaside home was the first house on the island to have electric lights as well as its first inn. Several guest rooms have views of the harbor or bay. The waterfront parlor is a perfect place to relax, and the eight-acre grounds include a quarter mile of beach. The innkeepers also offer accommodations in

two carriage house units. The studio unit includes a kitchenette and can sleep up to three people. Studio guests enjoy a full breakfast with the main house guests or can opt to have continental fare delivered to their door. The master unit includes a larger, stocked kitchen area and living room. The innkeepers also offer mountain bike and kayak rentals.
Innkeeper(s): Christy & Ingrid. $69-139. MC VISA PC TC. 5 rooms, 2 with PB, 1 with FP. 1 suite. 1 conference room. Breakfast included in rates. Types of meals: full breakfast, gourmet breakfast and early coffee/tea. Afternoon tea and picnic lunch available. Beds: KQDT. Turndown service in room. Fax, copier and bicycles on premises. Antiques, fishing, parks and watersports nearby.
Location: San Juan Islands.
Publicity: *Los Angeles Times, Sunset, Northwest.*
Certificate may be used: Oct. 20-March 30.

Mazama
B6

Mazama Country Inn
42 Lost River Rd, HCR 74 Box B-9
Mazama, WA 98833-9700
(509)996-2681 (800)843-7951 Fax:(509)996-2646
E-mail: mazama@methow.com

Circa 1985. With its log beams and cedar siding, this inn is a rustic retreat in an old mining town secluded in the beauty of the North Cascades. There are guest rooms in the inn and accommodations in cabins, a chalet and Phoenix House. Each of the latter three options is ideal for families, sleeping up to six or eight people. In the winter season, all three meals are included in the rates for inn guests. A hearty breakfast is served, and guests can pack their own lunch from a selection of items, then return to the lodge in the evening for a family-style dinner. On cold nights, the lounge's huge Russian fireplace is a perfect place to relax. Guests enjoy use of a sauna and hot tub, as well.
Innkeeper(s): George Turner. $70-175. MC VISA DS PC TC. 14 rooms with PB. 6 cottages. Breakfast included in rates. Types of meals: full breakfast and gourmet breakfast. Dinner, picnic lunch and lunch available. Restaurant on premises. Beds: QDT. VCR, fax, copier, spa, sauna and library on premises. Handicap access. Antiques, fishing, parks, shopping, cross-country skiing and golf nearby.
Publicity: *New York Times*
"Comfortable accommodations, great food, great staff — thanks!"
Certificate may be used: Oct. 15-Dec. 15 and March 15-May 15.

Olga
B3

Buck Bay Farm
SR Box 45
Olga, WA 98279
(360)376-2908
Before its reconstruction, this home was the spot for the town's community ball. The farmhouse is secluded on five acres and is decorated in country style. Down

pillows and comforters are a few homey touches. Homemade breakfasts include freshly baked muffins, scones and biscuits still steaming from the oven.

Innkeeper(s): Rick & Janet Bronkey. $70-95. MC VISA AX DS PC TC. 5 rooms, 3 with PB. 1 suite. Breakfast and evening snack included in rates. Types of meals: full breakfast and early coffee/tea. Beds: Q. Cable TV and spa on premises. Handicap access. Antiques, fishing, parks, shopping, theater and watersports nearby.

Publicity: *Island's Sounder*

Certificate may be used: Oct. 15-April 15, everyday except holiday weekends.

Olympia   D3

Puget View Guesthouse
7924 61st Ave NE
Olympia, WA 98516-9138
(360)413-9474

Circa 1933. This private, two-room log cottage is located on a lush property boasting views of Puget Sound. The innkeepers live on the property, but not in the cottage, so guests have the run of the little log hideaway. The country decor is simple and comfortable, and the cottage includes a microwave and a small refrigerator. For a small extra fee, the innkeepers will prepare a "Romantic Retreat" package.

Innkeeper(s): Dick & Barbara Yunker. $89. MC VISA PC TC. 1 cottage. Breakfast included in rates. Type of meal: continental-plus breakfast. Beds: QD. Parks and watersports nearby.

Publicity: *The Olympian.*

"Truly a beautiful place in the world."

Certificate may be used: Sunday-Thursday, subject to availability.

Orcas   B3

Chestnut Hill Inn B&B
PO Box 213
Orcas, WA 98280-0213
(360)376-5157 Fax:(360)376-5283
E-mail: chestnut@pacificrim.net

Circa 1970. Guests enjoying an early morning walk through the 16 acres of majestic countryside surrounding this inn are sure to see a variety of wildlife,

including frequent deer. Four-poster canopy feather beds create an inviting atmosphere in the bedchambers, all of which boast fireplaces. Homemade breads and muffins accompany the elegant morning entree, which changes from day to day. The grounds are a perfect place to enjoy a picnic, and the innkeepers will fix up a gourmet basket for those seeking a romantic outing. In the chilly months, a cup of afternoon tea is served alongside refreshments. The gazebo adds character to the inn's garden.

Innkeeper(s): Daniel & Marilyn Loewke. $105-195. MC VISA AX DS PC TC. 5 rooms, 4 with PB. 5 with FP. Breakfast included in rates. Types of meals: gourmet breakfast and early coffee/tea. Afternoon tea and picnic lunch available. Beds: Q. Ceiling fan in room. VCR, fax, stables and bicycles on premises. Parks, shopping, theater and watersports nearby.

Certificate may be used: Sunday-Thursday, Oct. 1-May 1, no holidays.

Port Orchard   C4

Northwest Interlude
3377 Sarann Ave E
Port Orchard, WA 98366-8109
(360)871-4676

Antiques such as Grandma's four-poster bed fill this contemporary Northwest home, overlooking Puget Sound and the Olympic Mountain range. Snacks are offered when you check in, and visitors enjoy evening turndown service and gourmet breakfasts. Pike Street Market in Seattle is a short ferry ride away.

Innkeeper(s): Barbara Cozad. $45-75. MC VISA. 3 rooms. Breakfast included in rates. Types of meals: full breakfast and early coffee/tea. Turndown service, TV and VCR in room. Antiques, shopping, cross-country skiing, sporting events and theater nearby.

"It was appropriate that we had a king-sized bed, since the moment we met Frances & Barbara we were treated royally."

Certificate may be used: October through March, except Thanksgiving and Christmas.

Port Townsend   C3

Ann Starrett Mansion
744 Clay St
Port Townsend, WA 98368-5808
(360)385-3205 (888)385-3205 Fax:(360)385-2976

Circa 1889. George Starrett came from Maine to Port Townsend and became the major residential builder. By 1889, he had constructed one house a week, totaling more than 350 houses. The Smithsonian believes the Ann Starrett's elaborate free-hung spiral staircase is the only one of its type in the United States. A frescoed dome atop the octagonal tower depicts four seasons and four virtues. On the first day of each season, the sun causes a ruby red light to point toward the appropriate painting. The mansion won a "Great American Home Award," from the National Trust for Historic Preservation.

Innkeeper(s): Bob & Edel Sokol. $75-225. MC VISA AX DS PC TC. 11 rooms with PB, 2 with FP. 2 suites. 2 cottages. 2 conference rooms. Breakfast included in rates. Type of meal: full breakfast. Afternoon tea available. Beds: KQDT. TV in room. VCR, fax, copier and spa on premises. Antiques, fishing, parks, shopping, cross-country skiing, theater and watersports nearby.
Location: Three blocks from the business district.
Publicity: *Peninsula, N.Y. Times, Vancouver Sun, S.F. Examiner, London Times, Colonial Homes, Elle, Leader, Japanese Travel, National Geographic Traveler, Victorian Magazine, Historic American Trails.*
"Staying here was like a dream come true."
Certificate may be used: November-March.

The English Inn
718 F St
Port Townsend, WA 98368-5211
(360)385-5302 (800)254-5302 Fax:(360)385-5302
E-mail: Nancy@Macaid.com

Circa 1885. This Italianate Victorian was built during Port Townsend's 19th-century heyday, when the town served the railroad and shipping industries. The home overlooks the Olympic Mountains, and several guest rooms offer mountain views. The rooms are named in honor of English poets. There is a

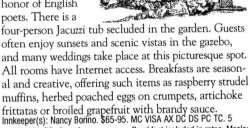

four-person Jacuzzi tub secluded in the garden. Guests often enjoy sunsets and scenic vistas in the gazebo, and many weddings take place at this picturesque spot. All rooms have Internet access. Breakfasts are seasonal and creative, offering such items as raspberry strudel muffins, herbed poached eggs on crumpets, artichoke frittatas or broiled grapefruit with brandy sauce.
Innkeeper(s): Nancy Borino. $65-95. MC VISA AX DC DS PC TC. 5 rooms with PB. 2 conference rooms. Breakfast included in rates. Meals: gourmet breakfast and early coffee/tea. Afternoon tea available. Beds: KQ. Ceiling fan in room. TV, VCR, fax, copier, spa, bicycles on premises. Antiques, fishing, parks, shopping, theater, watersports nearby.
Certificate may be used: Jan. 1-June 30 & Oct. 1-Dec. 31, Sunday-Friday.

Holly Hill House B&B
611 Polk St
Port Townsend, WA 98368-6531
(360)385-5619 (800)435-1454
E-mail: hollyhill@olympus.net

Circa 1872. A unique "upside-down" century-old Camperdown elm and several holly trees surround this aptly named bed & breakfast, built by Robert C. Hill, the co-founder of the First National Bank of Port Townsend. The cozy, romantic rooms are decorated with florals and lace. Billie's Room affords a view of Admiralty Inlet and Mt. Baker, while Lizette's Room offers Victorian decor and a view of the garden. The Skyview Room includes a wonderful skylight. The spacious Colonel's Room features a picture window with water and mountain views,

and the Morning Glory Room is a cozy retreat with lace-trimmed quilts. Expansive breakfasts are served in the dining room, and coffee and tea are always available. The inn's gardens are surrounded by a picket fence and nearly 200 rose bushes.
Innkeeper(s): Lynne Sterling. $78-145. 5 rooms with PB. 1 suite. Breakfast included in rates. Meals: full breakfast, early coffee/tea. Afternoon tea, evening snack, picnic lunch available. Beds: KQT. Turndown service. TV, library on premises. Antiques, fishing, parks, and theater nearby.
Location: Two miles from Fort Worden State Park and in the heart of historic district.
Certificate may be used: Oct. 31-April 30, Sunday to Thursday.

Lizzie's
731 Pierce St
Port Townsend, WA 98368-8042
(360)385-4168 (800)700-4168
E-mail: wickline@olympus.net

Circa 1887. Named for Lizzie Grant, a sea captain's wife, this Italianate Victorian is elegant and airy. In addition to the gracious interiors, some rooms command an outstanding view of Port Townsend Bay, Puget Sound, and the Olympic and Cascade mountain ranges. Each room is filled with antiques dating from 1840 to the turn of the century. The dog's house in the garden is a scale replica of the original house. Lizzie's is known for elaborate breakfasts, where guests are encouraged to help themselves to seconds.
Innkeeper(s): Patricia Wickline. $70-135. MC VISA DS PC TC. 7 rooms with PB. Breakfast included in rates. Meal: full breakfast. Beds: KQ.
Location: In uptown Historic District.
Publicity: *Travel & Leisure, Victorian Homes.*
"As they say in show biz, you're a hard act to follow."
Certificate may be used: October through May, Sunday thru Thursday.

Manresa Castle
PO Box 564, 7th & Sheridan
Port Townsend, WA 98368-0564
(360)385-5750 (800)732-1281 Fax:(360)385-5883

Circa 1892. When businessman Charles Eisenbeis built the largest private residence in Port Townsend, locals dubbed it "Eisenbeis Castle," because it resembled the castles in Eisenbeis' native Prussia. The home is truly a royal delight to behold, both inside and out. Luxurious European antiques and hand-painted wall coverings decorate the dining room and many of the castle's stately guest rooms. The turret suites are unique and many of the rooms have mountain and water views, but beware of the third floor. Rumors of ghosts in the upper floor have frightened some, but others seek out the "haunted" rooms for a spooky stay. Port Townsend offers a variety of galleries, gift shops and antiquing.
Innkeeper(s): Roger O'Connor. $68-175. MC VISA DS. 40 rooms with PB. 1 conference room. Breakfast included in rates. Type of meal: continental breakfast. Dinner, banquet service and catered breakfast avail-

able. Restaurant on premises. Beds: KQDT. TV in room. Antiques, fishing, shopping, theater and watersports nearby.

Publicity: *Island Independent, Leader News, Province Showcase, Sunset Magazine.*

Certificate may be used: Sunday through Friday, October through May.

Palace Hotel
1004 Water St
Port Townsend, WA 98368-6706
(360)946-5176 (800)962-0741 Fax:(360)385-0780

Circa 1889. This brick hotel has been restored and refurbished in a Victorian style. The Miss Rose Room has a six-foot Jacuzzi and is on the third floor. Some rooms have kitchenettes, such as Miss Kitty's Room, with its velvet settee, antique bed and wood stove.

Innkeeper(s): Michael & Spring Thomas. $65-129. MC VISA AX DS. 15 rooms. Breakfast included in rates. Type of meal: continental-plus breakfast. Restaurant on premises. Beds: KQD.

Certificate may be used: January to May, October to December, except Saturday nights.

Ravenscroft Inn
533 Quincy St
Port Townsend, WA 98368-5839
(360)385-2784 (800)782-2691 Fax:(360)385-6724

Circa 1987. A second suite has been added to this relaxing inn, which includes a fireplace and six-foot soaking tub. From the suite's large window seat, guests can enjoy the view of Mt. Baker. The room has an Impressionist touch, decorated in Monet colors. Other rooms are equally interesting, all individually decorated with Colonial influences. The inn is just three blocks from the water.

Innkeeper(s): Leah Hammer. $65-165. MC VISA AX DS PC TC. 8 rooms with PB, 2 suites. 1 conference room. Breakfast included in rates. Types of meals: full breakfast, gourmet breakfast and early coffee/tea. Afternoon tea and catering service available. Beds: KQT. Cable TV, VCR, fax and library on premises. Antiques, fishing, shopping, cross-country skiing, theater and watersports nearby.

Certificate may be used: Oct. 15-May 15, Sunday-Thursday, except holidays and special event dates

Poulsbo   C4

Foxbridge B&B
30680 Hwy 3 NE
Poulsbo, WA 98370
(360)598-5599 Fax:(360)598-3588

Circa 1993. The innkeepers at this Georgian-style home have taken the words bed & breakfast to heart. Each of the comfortable rooms has an individual

theme. The Country Garden room is a floral delight with a canopy bed. The Old World room includes a sleigh bed and down comforter. The Foxhunt room is done up in masculine hues with a four-poster bed. Antiques are placed throughout the home. As for the breakfast, each morning brings a new

menu. Heart-shaped waffles topped with blueberries and cream might be the fare one morning, while another could bring eggs Benedict or smoked-salmon quiche. All are served with cereals and a special starter, perhaps baked nectarines with cream Ambrose.

Innkeeper(s): Beverly & Chuck Higgins. $75-85. MC VISA PC. 3 rooms with PB, 3 with FP. Breakfast and afternoon tea included in rates. Types of meals: gourmet breakfast and early coffee/tea. Beds: Q. Turndown service in room. Fax and library on premises. Antiques, fishing, parks, shopping, cross-country skiing, theater and watersports nearby.

Certificate may be used: Nov. 1 to May 15.

Sequim   C3

Greywolf Inn
395 Keeler Rd
Sequim, WA 98382-9024
(360)683-5889 Fax:(360)683-1487

Built in a farmhouse style, this house is located on five acres. If you prefer a canopy bed, request the Pamela Room and enjoy Bavarian decor. Salmon and egg dishes are presented at breakfast. Decks surround the house, affording views of an occasional eagle, ducks in the pond and Mount Baker. A nature trail provides a pleasant walk through the fields, tall fir trees and over a small stream. Visit the buffalo that come up to the road at the Olympic Game Farm. Birdwatching and beachcombing are popular on the Dungeness Spit.

Innkeeper(s): Peggy Melang. $80-120. MC VISA AX. 5 rooms. 1 suite. Breakfast included in rates. Type of meal: full breakfast. Ceiling fan and VCR in room. Antiques, shopping, downhill skiing, cross-country skiing and theater nearby.

Certificate may be used: Anytime from Oct. 15-May 30. Offer limited to three rooms.

Spokane   C9

Fotheringham House
2128 W 2nd Ave
Spokane, WA 99204-0916
(509)838-1891 Fax:(509)838-1807

A vintage Victorian in the National Register, this inn was built by the first mayor of Spokane, David

Fotheringham. There are tin ceilings, a carved staircase, gabled porches and polished woodwork. Victorian furnishings and stained-glass pieces are featured.

Across the street is Coeur d'Alene Park and the Patsy Clark Mansion, a favorite Spokane restaurant. Walk two blocks to Elk Drug Store to enjoy the old-fashioned soda fountain.
Innkeeper(s): Jacquelin Johnson. $75-90. MC VISA. 4 rooms. Breakfast included in rates. Types of meals: full breakfast and early coffee/tea. Antiques, shopping, sporting events and theater nearby.
Certificate may be used: Consecutive nights Sunday through Thursday, November through April.

Marianna Stoltz House
427 E Indiana Ave
Spokane, WA 99207-2324
(509)483-4316 (800)978-6587 Fax:(509)483-6773

Circa 1908. Located on a tree-lined street, two miles from downtown Spokane, is this American four-square Victorian. It is in the local historic register and features a wraparound porch, high ceilings and leaded-glass windows. Furnishings include Oriental rugs and period pieces. Peach Melba Parfait and Stoltz House Strada are breakfast specialties.
Innkeeper(s): Phyllis & Jim Maguire. $65-85. MC VISA AX DC DS PC TC. 4 rooms, 2 with PB. 1 suite. Breakfast included in rates. Types of meals: full breakfast and early coffee/tea. Beds: KQT. Air conditioning and TV in room. Fax and copier on premises. Amusement parks, fishing, parks, shopping, downhill skiing, cross-country skiing, sporting events and theater nearby.
Certificate may be used: Nov. 1-March 31, holidays excluded.

Stevenson   F4

Sojourner Inn
142 Lyons Rd
Stevenson, WA 98648-6563
(509)427-7070 Fax:(509)427-4229

A contemporary tri-level cedar house, the Sojourner is set on a ridge with unparalleled views of the confluence of the Columbia and Wind Rivers. National forests surround the inn's four acres, and a pair of bald eagles reside on the property. In addition to the stunning river views, the inn offers an excellent library, back deck and patio. The innkeeper is a Cordon Bleu chef and can provide dinners and receptions for special occasions.

Innkeeper(s): Judith Yeckel. $40-115. MC VISA. 5 rooms. Breakfast included in rates. Types of meals: full breakfast and early coffee/tea. Dinner, evening snack, picnic lunch, gourmet lunch, catering service and room service available. Air conditioning in room. Cable TV and VCR on premises. Antiques, downhill skiing, cross-country skiing, sporting events and theater nearby.
Certificate may be used: Year-round, Sunday through Thursday nights.

Sunnyside   E6

Sunnyside Inn B&B
800 E Edison Ave
Sunnyside, WA 98944-2206
(509)839-5557 (800)221-4195

Circa 1919. This wine country inn offers spacious rooms, decorated in a comfortable, country style. Most of the rooms include baths with Jacuzzi tubs. The one bedroom without a Jacuzzi, includes the home's original early 20th-century fixtures. Two rooms offer fireplaces. Breakfasts are served in the inn's restaurant, which also offers dinner service.
Innkeeper(s): Jim & Geri Graves. $42-85. MC VISA AX DS TC. 10 rooms with PB, 2 with FP. Breakfast and evening snack included in rates. Types of meals: continental breakfast and full breakfast. Dinner and room service available. Beds: KQ. Air conditioning, ceiling fan and TV in room. Spa on premises. Antiques, fishing, parks, shopping, cross-country skiing and theater nearby.
Certificate may be used: Jan. 30-Nov. 10, Sunday-Thursday.

Tacoma   D4

Chinaberry Hill - An 1889 Victorian Inn
302 Tacoma Ave N
Tacoma, WA 98403
(253)272-1282 Fax:(253)272-1335
E-mail: chinaberry@wa.net

Circa 1889. In the 19th century, this Queen Anne was known as far away as China for its wondrous gardens, one of the earliest examples of landscape gardening in the Pacific Northwest. The home, a wedding present from a husband to his bride, is listed in the National Register. The innkeepers have selected a unique assortment of antiques and collectibles to decorate the manor. The house offers two Jacuzzi suites and a guest room, all eclectically decorated with items such as a four-poster rice bed or a canopy bed. There are two lodging options in the Catchpenny Cottage, a restored carriage house steps away from the manor. Guests can stay either in the romantic carriage suite or the Hay Loft, which includes a bedroom, sitting room, clawfoot tub and a unique hay chute. In the mornings, as the innkeepers say, guests enjoy "hearty breakfasts and serious coffee." Not a bad start to a day exploring Antique Row or Pt. Defiance, a 698-acre protected rainforest park with an aquarium, gardens, beaches and a zoo. Seattle is 30 minutes away.
Innkeeper(s): Cecil & Yarrow Wayman. $95-125. MC VISA AX DS PC TC. 5 rooms with PB, 1 with FP. 4 suites. 1 cottage. 2 conference

rooms. Breakfast and evening snack included in rates. Types of meals: continental-plus breakfast, gourmet breakfast and early coffee/tea. Beds: Q. Turndown service, ceiling fan, TV and VCR in room. Fax, copier and library on premises. Antiques, fishing, parks, shopping, sporting events, golf, theater and watersports nearby.
Publicity: *Seattle Magazine, Oregonian, Tacoma News Tribune, Tacoma Weekly, Olympian.*

". . . the highlight of our trip so far - wonderful . . .the company, the food, the accommodations, all the best."
Certificate may be used: November, January and February, Sunday through Thursday, excluding holiday periods, university events.

Commencement Bay B&B
3312 N Union Ave
Tacoma, WA 98407-6055
(253)752-8175 Fax:(253)759-4025
E-mail: greatviews@aol.com

Circa 1937. Watch boats sail across the bay while enjoying breakfast served with gourmet coffee at this Colonial Revival inn. Guest rooms feature bay or garden views and each is unique and individually decorated. The surrounding area includes historic sites, antique shops, waterfront restaurants, wooded nature trails and Pt. Defiance Zoo and Aquarium. Relax in a secluded hot tub and deck area or in the fireside room for reading and the romantic view. The B&B is 30 miles from both Seattle and Mt. Rainier park.
Innkeeper(s): Sharon & Bill Kaufmann. $75-115. AP. MC VISA AX DS PC TC. 3 rooms with PB. 3 conference rooms. Breakfast and evening snack included in rates. Types of meals: full breakfast and early coffee/tea. Beds: Q. TV and VCR in room. Fax, spa, bicycles and library on premises. Antiques, fishing, parks, shopping, sporting events, theater and watersports nearby.
Location: 30 miles to Seattle and Mount Rainier.
Publicity: *Tacoma Weekly, News Tribune, Tacoma Voice, Oregonian.*

"Perfect in every detail! The setting, breathtaking; the food, scrumptious and beautifully presented; the warmth and friendship here."
Certificate may be used: Nov. 1-March 31, Sunday-Thursday nights. April, May, September, October, Sunday-Tuesday nights

Trout Lake   F5

The Farm Bed & Breakfast
490 Sunnyside Rd
Trout Lake, WA 98650-9715
(509)395-2488

Circa 1890. Four acres surround this three-story yellow farmhouse, 25 miles north of the Columbia Gorge and Hood River. The old rail fence, meadow and forested foothills of Mount Adams create a pastoral scene appropriate for the inn's herd of Cashmere goats. A big farm breakfast is served. Inside, entertainment centers around the player piano, wood stove and satellite dish. Outdoors, take a flight from Trout Lake into Mount St. Helens, or gear up for huckleberry picking, trout fishing and hiking at nearby Gifford Pinchot National Forest. Ask the innkeepers about the fairs, rodeos and Saturday markets.

Innkeeper(s): Rosie & Dean Hostetter. $55-85. PC. 2 rooms. Breakfast included in rates. Types of meals: full breakfast and early coffee/tea. Lunch available. Beds: QD. Cable TV, VCR and bicycles on premises. Antiques, fishing, shopping, downhill skiing, cross-country skiing and watersports nearby.
Certificate may be used: Oct. 15-May 31.

Uniontown   E10

Churchyard Inn
206 Saint Boniface Street
Uniontown, WA 99179
(509)229-3200 Fax:(509)229-3200

Circa 1905. Not surprisingly, this historic inn is located adjacent to a church. From 1913 until the mid-1960s, the home served as a convent. The three-story brick home is adorned with a second-story portico supported by two columns. The innkeepers restored the home to its turn-of-the-century grace and also added modern heating, electrical and plumbing systems, as well as a new wing. The inn's restored red fir woodwork is a highlight. The seven guest rooms include a spacious third-floor suite with a kitchen and fireplace. The home is listed in the National Register of Historic Places.
Innkeeper(s): Marvin J. & Linda J. Entel. $55-135. MC VISA AX DS PC TC. 7 rooms with PB, 1 with FP. 1 suite. 1 conference room. Breakfast included in rates. Types of meals: continental breakfast, full breakfast and early coffee/tea. Beds: KQDT. Air conditioning, ceiling fan, TV and VCR in room. Fax on premises. Handicap access. Antiques, fishing, parks, shopping, sporting events, golf and watersports nearby.
Publicity: *Lewiston Tribune, Colfax Gazette, Moscow Daily News, Weekend Getaways.*

"Beautiful property, location and setting. I would recommend this wonderful B&B to anyone coming to the area."
Certificate may be used: Jan. 1-Dec. 30, Sunday-Thursday.

White Salmon   F5

Llama Ranch B&B
1980 Hwy 141
White Salmon, WA 98672-8032
(509)395-2786 (800)800-5262

Llamas abound at this unique, picturesque ranch, which affords views of Mt. Adams. Innkeepers Jerry and Rebeka Stone offer nature walks through the woods accompanied by some of their friendly llamas. The Stones also offer the unusual amenity of llama boarding. The White Salmon area, located in between the Mt. Adams Wilderness Area and Columbia Gorge, is full of interesting activities, including white-water rafting, horseback riding and berry picking.
Innkeeper(s): Jerry & Rebeka Stone. $55-75. MC VISA DS. 7 rooms. Breakfast included in rates. Type of meal: full breakfast.
Certificate may be used: Oct. 15-April 15.

Washington, D.C.

Adams Inn
1744 Lanier Pl NW
Washington, DC 20009-2118
(202)745-3600 (800)578-6807 Fax:(202)332-5867

Circa 1908. This restored town house has fireplaces, a library and parlor, all furnished home-style, as are the guest rooms. Former residents of this neighborhood include Tallulah Bankhead, Woodrow Wilson and Al Jolson. The Adams-Morgan area is home to diplomats, radio and television personalities and government workers. A notable firehouse across the street holds the record for the fastest response of a horse-drawn fire apparatus. Located in the restaurant area, 45 restaurants and shops are within walking distance.
Innkeeper(s): Gene & Nancy Thompson, Aime Owens. $55-70. MC VISA AX DC CB DS TC. 24 rooms, 12 with PB. Breakfast included in rates. Types of meals: continental-plus breakfast and early coffee/tea. Beds: DT. Air conditioning in room. Cable TV and library on premises. Antiques and parks nearby.
Location: 2 miles from White House, walking distance to major hotels.
Publicity: *Travel Host.*
"We enjoyed your friendly hospitality and the home-like atmosphere. Your suggestions on restaurants and help in planning our visit were appreciated."
Certificate may be used: Dec. 1-March 1, Sunday-Thursday.

The Embassy Inn
1627 16th St NW
Washington, DC 20009-3063
(202)234-7800 (800)423-9111 Fax:(202)234-3309

Circa 1910. This restored inn is furnished in a Federalist style. The comfortable lobby offers books and evening sherry. Conveniently located, the inn is seven blocks from the Adams Morgan area of ethnic restaurants. The Embassy's philosophy of innkeeping includes providing personal attention and cheerful hospitality. Concierge services are available.
Innkeeper(s): Jennifer Schroeder & Susan Stiles. $69-150. MC VISA AX DC CB TC. 38 rooms with PB. Breakfast included in rates. Type of meal: continental-plus breakfast. Beds: DT. Air conditioning and TV in room. Fax and copier on premises. Antiques, parks and theater nearby.
Location: Downtown D.C., 10 blocks north of the White House.
Publicity: *Los Angeles Times, Inn Times, Business Review.*
"When I return to D.C., I'll be back at the Embassy."
Certificate may be used: Year-round, based on availability. Monday-Sunday, except April Cherry Blossom.

Reeds B&B
PO Box 12011
Washington, DC 20005-0911
(202)328-3510 Fax:(202)332-3885

Circa 1887. This three-story Victorian townhouse was built by John Shipman, who owned one of the first construction companies in the city. The turn-of-the-century revitalization of Washington began in Logan Circle, considered to be the city's first truly residential area. During the house's restoration, flower gardens, terraces and fountains were added. Victorian antiques, original wood paneling, stained glass, chandeliers, as well as practical amenities, such as air conditioning and laundry facilities, make this a comfortable stay. There is a furnished apartment available, as well.
Innkeeper(s): Charles & Jackie Reed. $45-90. MC VISA AX DC TC. 6 rooms, 2 with FP. 1 suite. Breakfast included in rates. Meal: continental-plus breakfast. Beds: QD. Air conditioning, TV in room. Computer on premises. Antiques, parks, shopping, sporting events, theater nearby.
Location: Downtown, 10 blocks from White House.
Publicity: *Philadelphia Inquirer, Washington Gardner, Washington Post.*
"This home was the highlight of our stay in Washington! This was a superb home and location. The Reeds' treated us better than family."
Certificate may be used: January, February, March 1-15.

The Windsor Inn
1842 16th St NW
Washington, DC 20009-3316
(202)667-0300 (800)423-9111 Fax:(202)667-4503

Circa 1910. Recently renovated and situated in a neighborhood of renovated townhouses, the Windsor Inn is the sister property to the Embassy Inn. It is larger and offers suites and a small meeting room. The refurbished lobby is in an Art Deco style and a private club atmosphere prevails. It is five blocks to the Metro station at Dupont Circle. There are no elevators.
Innkeeper(s): Jennifer Schroeder & Susan Stiles. $69-125. MC VISA AX DC CB TC. 46 rooms with PB. 2 suites. 1 conference room. Breakfast included in rates. Meal: continental-plus breakfast. Beds: QDT. Air conditioning, TV in room. Fax, copier, library on premises. Parks, theater nearby.
Location: Twelve blocks north of the White House.
Publicity: *L.A. Times, Inn Times, Sunday Telegram.*
"Being here was like being home. Excellent service, would recommend."
Certificate may be used: Year-round, based on availability. Monday-Sunday, except April Cherry Blossom.

494

West Virginia

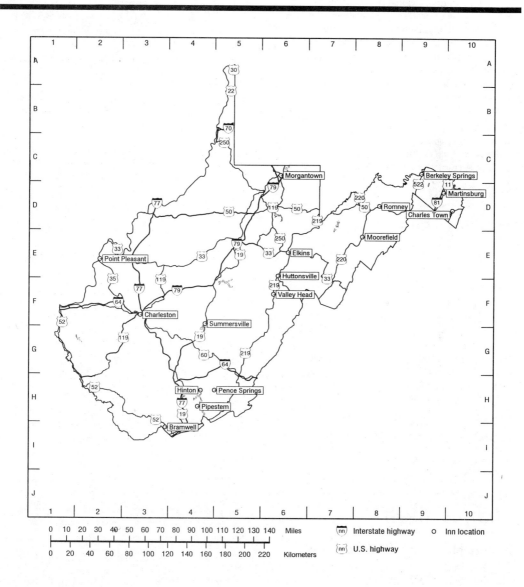

0 10 20 30 40 50 60 70 80 90 100 110 120 130 140   Miles

0 20 40 60 80 100 120 140 160 180 200 220   Kilometers

⬡ nn   Interstate highway   ○   Inn location

⬡ nn   U.S. highway

Berkeley Springs C9

The Manor Inn
415 Fairfax St
Berkeley Springs, WV 25411-1607
(304)258-1552 (800)225-5982

Circa 1878. In the National Register, this Second Empire Victorian features 12-foot ceilings, a mansard roof, large porch and French doors. The innkeeper is a quilter and collects antique quilts. George Washington is said to have bathed in the warm mineral springs in town where he owned a property a block from the Manor Inn. Roman and Turkish baths are featured in The Baths, a West Virginia State Park.
Innkeeper(s): Don & Dot Trask. $75-95. MC VISA PC TC. 4 rooms, 2 with PB. 1 suite. Breakfast included in rates. Types of meals: full breakfast, gourmet breakfast and early coffee/tea. Beds: QD. Air conditioning, ceiling fan and TV in room. VCR on premises. Antiques, fishing, parks, shopping, skiing, theater and watersports nearby.
Certificate may be used: Sunday through Thursday, non-holiday weeks

Bramwell I3

Perry House B&B
Main St, PO Box 248
Bramwell, WV 24715-0248
(304)248-8145 (800)328-0248 Fax:(304)248-8145
E-mail: perryhouse@netlinkcorp.com

Circa 1902. This brick Victorian was built by a bank cashier and remained in the family for 80 years, when the current innkeepers purchased it. The rooms are decorated in period style with antiques. The innkeepers offer a private cottage with three bedrooms, a kitchen, living room and laundry facilities. Although a small village, Bramwell once was home to more than a dozen millionaires, and some of these families' homes are located on the town walking tour. The inn is listed in the National Register.
Innkeeper(s): Charlie & Charlotte Sacre. $40-55. MC VISA PC TC. 4 rooms, 1 with PB. 1 cottage. Breakfast included in rates. Meals: continental breakfast and early coffee/tea. Beds: KDT. Air conditioning and ceiling fan in room. TV, fax, copier, library on premises. Antiques, fishing, parks, shopping, downhill skiing, theater, watersports nearby.
Certificate may be used: January-May, September-December, all days.

Charles Town D10

Gilbert House B&B of Middleway
PO Box 1104
Charles Town, WV 25414-7104
(304)725-0637

Circa 1760. A magnificent graystone of early Georgian design, the Gilbert House is located in one of the state's oldest European settlements. During restoration, graffiti found on the upstairs bedroom

walls included an 1832 drawing of the future President James Polk and a child's growth chart from the 1800s. Elegant appointments include fine Oriental rugs, tasteful art and antique furnishings. The inn is located in the 18th-century village of Middleway, which contains one of the country's most well-preserved collections  of log houses. The village had a mill site on the original settlers' trail into Shenandoah Valley ("Philadelphia Wagon Road" on Peter Jefferson's 1755 map of Virginia). Middleway was also the site of "wizard clip" hauntings during the last decade of the 1700s. The region was home to members of "Virginia Blues," commanded by Daniel Morgan during the American Revolutionary War.
Innkeeper(s): Bernard F. Heiler. $80-140. MC VISA AX PC TC. 3 rooms with PB, 2 with FP. 1 suite. Breakfast included in rates. Meals: full breakfast and gourmet breakfast. Beds: QT. Air conditioning in room. VCR, library on premises. Antiques, parks, shopping, theater nearby.
Location: Middleway historic district, 6 miles west of Charles Town.

"We have stayed at inns for fifteen years, and yours is at the top of the list as best ever!"
Certificate may be used: At base rate from Nov. 30 through August.

The Washington House Inn
216 S George St
Charles Town, WV 25414-1632
(304)725-7923 (800)297-6957 Fax:(304)728-5150
E-mail: mnvogel@intrepid.net

Circa 1899. This three-story brick Victorian was built by the descendants of President Washington's brothers, John Augustine and Samuel. Carved oak mantels, fireplaces, spacious guest rooms, antique furnishings and refreshments served on the wraparound porch make the inn memorable. Harpers Ferry National Historic Park, Antietam, and the Shenandoah and Potomac rivers are all within a 15-minute drive, as is Martinsburg outlet shopping.
Innkeeper(s): Mel & Nina Vogel. $70-125. MC VISA AX DS PC TC. 6 rooms with PB. 1 suite. 1 conference room. Breakfast, afternoon tea and evening snack included in rates. Meals: continental breakfast, continental-plus breakfast, full breakfast and early coffee/tea. Beds: QT. Air conditioning, turndown service, ceiling fan in room. TV, VCR, fax, copier and bicycles on premises. Antiques, fishing, parks, shopping, theater, watersports nearby.
Certificate may be used: Sunday-Thursday, Nov. 1-Aug. 31.

Charleston   F3

Benedict Haid Farm
8 Hale St
Charleston, WV 25301-2806
(304)346-1054

Circa 1869. Although no breakfast is served, we couldn't help including this farm on 350-mountain-top acres because it specializes in raising exotic animals that include llamas, guanacos and black mountain sheep, as well as donkeys and cows. There are two rustic cabins for those looking for an economical stay. Most will prefer the main German-built, hand-hewn log lodge, which features antique furnishings and a large screened-in deck with fireplace and hot tub. There is a stocked pond. Bring your own breakfast.
Innkeeper(s): Steve Jones. $100. MC VISA TC. 3 rooms. 1 cottage. Beds: D. Air conditioning in room. Cable TV, VCR and bicycles on premises. Fishing and cross-country skiing nearby.
Location: Twenty-three miles northeast of Charleston.
Publicity: *Television Travel Show, One Tank Trips.*

"Like stepping back in time."

Certificate may be used: Anytime, based on availability.

Elkins   E6

The Retreat
214 Harpertown Rd
Elkins, WV 26241
(304)636-2960 (888)636-2960 Fax:(304)637-6404
E-mail: retreat@neumedia.net

Circa 1903. This turn-of-the-century home is located near Davis and Elkins College, in the heart of West Virginia's beautiful Potomac Highland, gateway to the 840,000-acre Monongahela National Forest. Lounge in the sun or on shady porches and enjoy the warm days and cool nights of a mountain summer. Spectacular fall foliage on the hills surrounding the house, and spring-through-fall flowers are enjoyed by guests. Choose one of many activities in the area and let the innkeepers point you in the right direction with maps and a gourmet picnic.
Innkeeper(s): Leslie Henderson. $65. MC VISA PC. 6 rooms. 1 conference room. Breakfast included in rates. Type of meal: full breakfast. Cable TV and VCR on premises. Antiques, shopping, skiing, sporting events, golf, theater and watersports nearby.
Certificate may be used: Oct. 15-June 30, Sunday through Thursday.

Tunnel Mountain B&B
Rt 1, Box 59-1
Elkins, WV 26241-9711
(304)636-1684

Circa 1938. Nestled on five acres of wooded land, this three-story Fieldstone home offers privacy in a peaceful setting. Rooms are tastefully decorated with

antiques, collectibles and crafts. Each bedroom boasts a view of the surrounding mountains. The chestnut and knotty pine woodwork accentuate the decor. The fireplace in the large common room is a great place for warming up after a day of touring or skiing. The area is home to a number of interesting events, including a Dulcimer festival.
Innkeeper(s): Anne & Paul Beardslee. $65-75. PC TC. 3 rooms with PB, 1 with FP. Breakfast included in rates. Type of meal: full breakfast. Beds: QD. Air conditioning and TV in room. Antiques, fishing, parks, shopping, downhill skiing, cross-country skiing, theater and watersports nearby.
Publicity: *Blue Ridge Country.*
Certificate may be used: November to May, Sunday-Thursday.

Hinton   H4

Historic Hinton Manor
PO Box 1645
Hinton, WV 25951-1645
(304)466-3930

Local teacher, banker and salesman Joseph Roles drew up the blueprints for this manor, calling the place his dream home. The home was filled with fine furniture and decorated with woodwork imported from Bavaria. The current innkeepers found the home in disarray with a few furnishings and collectibles here and there. They polished up the woodwork, furnished the home with antiques and restored the original family's grand piano and other pieces. Several rooms showcase lace dresses worn by the Roles'  wife and sister. Breakfast is served by candlelight, and in the evenings, tea and dessert are served. The home is located in a National Historic District.
Innkeeper(s): Carla Leslie. $80. 2 rooms. Breakfast included in rates. Type of meal: continental breakfast.
Certificate may be used: April-December.

Huttonsville
E6

Hutton House
Rts 250/219, PO Box 88
Huttonsville, WV 26273
(304)335-6701

Circa 1898. This rambling Queen Anne Victorian in the National Register sits above the village, providing views of Tygart River Valley and the Laurel Mountains. Ornate windows, a three-story turret, pocket doors, wraparound porch and gingerbread trim are features. The inn is comfortably decorated with antiques and suitable Victorian touches. A full breakfast is served with antique Depression glass collected by the innkeeper.

Innkeeper(s): Loretta Murray. $60-70. MC VISA. 6 rooms. Breakfast included in rates. Type of meal: full breakfast. Evening snack available. Cable TV and VCR on premises. Shopping nearby.

Location: Near Snowshoe Ski Resort, Cass Railroad, City of Elkins, state and national parks.

Certificate may be used: Sunday-Thursday, all year, excluding festival or holiday (three-day) weekends, and Dec. 25-Jan. 1.

Martinsburg
D9

Aspen Hall Inn
405 Boyd Ave
Martinsburg, WV 25401-3417
(304)263-4385
E-mail: aspenhalo@ix.netcom.com

Circa 1745. This limestone Georgian manor, listed in the National Register, overlooks seven acres of lawns, gardens and a stream. The rooms are decorated in a Southern-plantation style, and there are double parlors, a library and dining room. Second-floor rooms feature canopy beds and are furnished with antiques.

Afternoon tea is served in the library or the garden gazebo. The property is mentioned in journals kept by George Washington, and he attended a wedding here. During the French and Indian War, Washington sent troops to protect the Quaker-owned building.

Innkeeper(s): Gordon & Lou Anne Claucherty. $95-125. MC VISA AX PC TC. 5 rooms with PB, 1 with FP. Breakfast, afternoon tea and

evening snack included in rates. Types of meals: full breakfast and early coffee/tea. Beds: QD. Air conditioning and TV in room. VCR, copier and library on premises. Antiques, fishing, parks, shopping, skiing, sporting events, golf, theater and watersports nearby.

Publicity: *Travel & Leisure, Mid-Atlantic Magazine, Country.*

"We are happy to pass out your brochures to our friends with hearty recommendation."

Certificate may be used: Feb. 16-Aug. 28, Sunday through Thursday, as space is available, advance reservations please.

Pulpit & Palette Inn
516 W John St
Martinsburg, WV 25401-2635
(304)263-7012

Circa 1870. Listed in the National Register, this Victorian inn is set off by a handsome iron fence. The interior is filled with a mix of American antiques, Tibetan rugs and art, setting off moldings and other architectural details in the library, drawing room and upstairs veranda. Your British-born innkeeper prepares afternoon tea for guests. The Blue Ridge Outlet Center is two blocks away.

Innkeeper(s): Bill & Janet Starr. $80. MC VISA TC. 2 rooms. Breakfast, afternoon tea and evening snack included in rates. Types of meals: full breakfast, gourmet breakfast and early coffee/tea. Beds: Q. Air conditioning and turndown service in room. Cable TV on premises. Antiques, parks, shopping and theater nearby.

Publicity: *Morning Herald, Antique Traveler, Journal.*

"You have set an ideal standard for comfort and company."

Certificate may be used: March 1 to May 31, Sunday-Thursday; Nov. 1 to Dec. 31, Sunday-Thursday.

Moorefield
E8

McMechen Inn
109 N Main St
Moorefield, WV 26836-1154
(304)538-7173 (800)298-2466 Fax:(304)538-7841

Circa 1853. This handsomely restored three-story brick Greek Revival townhouse is in the National Register. There are polished pine floors, a spectacular cherry staircase winding up to the third floor, walnut doors and woodwork, cranberry glass light fixtures and indoor folding shutters. Two parlors and a library add to the gracious dining room that houses the inn's restaurant. From May through September, guests can enjoy meals outdoors at the inn's Green Shutters Cafe. There is an antique, book and gift shop on the premises. The inn is often the site of weddings and receptions.

Innkeeper(s): Linda & Bob Curtis. $60-85. MC VISA AX DC PC TC. 7 rooms, 4 with PB. 1 suite. Breakfast, afternoon tea and evening snack included in rates. Types of meals: full breakfast and early coffee/tea. Dinner, lunch, banquet service, catering service, catered breakfast and room service available. Restaurant on premises. Beds: D. Air conditioning in room. VCR, fax, copier and library on premises. Antiques, fishing, parks, downhill skiing and theater nearby.

Certificate may be used: Jan. 30-Aug. 31, Sunday-Friday

Morgantown C6

Almost Heaven B&B
391 Scott Ave
Morgantown, WV 26505-8804
(304)296-4007 Fax:(304)296-4007
E-mail: vid@surfinusa.net

Circa 1990. A burgundy-colored door and steps add a hint of color to this white Federal-style house, which is set on two landscaped acres. Inside, guests will find Victorian decor and soft, feather beds. Innkeeper Cookie Coombs prepares a veritable feast for breakfast, with items such as biscuits and gravy, fried potatoes, apple dumplings, fresh fruit and pastries. The inn offers close access to West Virginia University.

Innkeeper(s): Cookie Coombs. $65-150. MC VISA AX DC CB DS PC TC. 5 rooms with PB. 1 suite. Breakfast included in rates. Type of meal: full breakfast. Beds: KQ. Air conditioning, ceiling fan, TV and VCR in room. Fax and library on premises. Antiques, fishing, parks, shopping, cross-country skiing, sporting events, golf, theater and watersports nearby.

Publicity: *Dominion Post.*

Certificate may be used: Jan. 1-March 15, Sunday-Friday.

Pence Springs H5

The Pence Springs Hotel
St Rts 3 & 12, PO Box 90
Pence Springs, WV 24962
(304)445-2606 (800)826-1829 Fax:(304)445-2204

Circa 1918. Listed in the National Register, this inn is known as one of the "historic springs of the Virginias." Mineral waters from Pence Springs captured a silver medal at the 1904 World's Fair. After the fair, the healing properties of the waters drew

many guests. From 1947 until the mid-1980s, the property was used as a state prison for women. A restoration effort began in 1986, and the inn once again welcomes guests. The inn's Art Deco-style furnishings and decor are reminiscent of the hotel's heyday in the 1920s when prominent and wealthy guests flocked to the hotel. Guests enjoy a full breakfast, and during the summer months, Sunday brunch is available. There are two restaurants in the hotel that serve dinner. The area boasts many outdoor activities, beautiful scenery and plenty of antique shopping.

Innkeeper(s): O. Ashby Berkley & Rosa Lee Berkley Miller. $70-100. MC VISA AX DC CB DS PC TC. 25 rooms, 15 with PB. 3 suites. 3 conference rooms. Breakfast included in rates. Types of meals: full breakfast and gourmet breakfast. Dinner, picnic lunch, banquet service, catering service and room service available. Restaurant on premises. Beds: KDT. Air conditioning in room. Cable TV, VCR, fax, copier, swimming, stables, bicycles and child care on premises. Handicap access. Antiques, fishing, parks, shopping, downhill skiing, theater, watersports nearby.

Publicity: *Southern Living, Mid-Atlantic Country, West Virginia Quarterly, MIT Press Journal, Goldenseal, Travel Host.*

"As always, I left your place rejuvenated. The property grows even more beautiful year after year."

Certificate may be used: April through December, Sunday through Thursday, non-holiday.

Pipestem H4

Walnut Grove Inn
HC 78 Box 260
Pipestem, WV 25979-9702
(304)466-6119 (800)701-1237

Circa 1850. Located on 38 acres, this red shingled country farmhouse has a century-old log barn and ancient cemetery with graves of Confederate soldiers and others prior to the Civil War. The farmhouse is decorated eclectically, and the front porch is furnished with rocking chairs and a swing. Swimming, basketball, badminton and horseshoes are available. A gourmet breakfast of biscuits and gravy, fresh eggs and homemade preserves is served in the dining room or screen room.

Innkeeper(s): Bonnie & Larry Graham. $65. MC VISA AX DS. 5 rooms with PB. Breakfast, afternoon tea and evening snack included in rates. Types of meals: continental-plus breakfast, gourmet breakfast and early coffee/tea. Beds: KQDT. Air conditioning in room. Cable TV and swimming on premises. Antiques, fishing, parks, shopping, downhill skiing, cross-country skiing, theater and watersports nearby.

Certificate may be used: Weekdays Monday through Thursday, all year; weekdays and weekends, Nov. 1-May 1.

Point Pleasant   E2

Stone Manor
12 Main St
Point Pleasant, WV 25550-1026
(304)675-3442

Circa 1887. This stone Victorian sits on the banks of the Kanawha River with a front porch that faces the river. Point Pleasant Battle Monument Park, adjacent to the inn, was built to commemorate the location of the first battle of the Revolutionary War. In the National Register, the inn was once the home of a family who ran a ferry boat crossing for the Ohio and Kanawha rivers. Now restored, the house is decorated with Victorian antiques and offers a pleasant garden with a Victorian fish pond and fountain.
Innkeeper(s): Janice & Tom Vance. $50. PC. 3 rooms, 3 with FP. Breakfast included in rates. Type of meal: full breakfast. Beds: QD. Air conditioning and VCR in room. Cable TV on premises.

Certificate may be used: Anytime except Oct. 12-15.

Romney   D8

Hampshire House 1884
165 N Grafton St
Romney, WV 26757-1616
(304)822-7171

Circa 1884. Located near the south branch of the Potomac River, the garden here has old boxwoods and walnut trees. The inn features ornate brickwork; tall, narrow windows; and fireplaces with handsome period mantels. A sitting room with a well-stocked library, a cozy patio and a music room with an antique pump organ are favorite places.
Innkeeper(s): Jane & Scott Simmons. $65-80. MC VISA AX DC DS PC TC. 5 rooms with PB, 3 with FP. 1 conference room. Breakfast included in rates. Types of meals: full breakfast and early coffee/tea. Evening snack available. Beds: QDT. Air conditioning, TV and VCR in room. Bicycles on premises. Antiques, fishing, shopping, watersports nearby.
Publicity: *Hampshire Review, Mid-Atlantic Country, Weekend Journal.*

"Your personal attention made us feel at home immediately."

Certificate may be used: November-May 1; weekdays only May 2-Sept. 30 (not honored in October).

Summersville   F4

Historic Brock House B&B Inn
1400 Webster Rd
Summersville, WV 26651-1524
(304)872-4887

Circa 1890. This Queen Anne farmhouse is the second venture into the bed & breakfast business for innkeepers Margie and Jim Martin. The exterior looks friendly and inviting, perhaps because of its long history of welcoming guests. The National Register inn originally served as a hotel and later as a boarding house. Margie has a degree in design, and her skills are evident in the cheerful, country rooms. Each of the guest rooms has a different color scheme and decor. One is decked in deep blue, another is appointed with flowery bedspreads and pastel curtains.
Innkeeper(s): Margie N. Martin. $70-90. MC VISA PC TC. 6 rooms, 4 with PB. 1 suite. 1 conference room. Breakfast, afternoon tea and evening snack included in rates. Types of meals: continental breakfast, full breakfast, gourmet breakfast and early coffee/tea. Catering service available. Beds: QT. Air conditioning and turndown service in room. Cable TV, VCR, fax and library on premises. Antiques, fishing, parks, shopping, theater and watersports nearby.

Certificate may be used: Jan. 30-Dec. 1 upon vacancy Sunday-Friday.

Valley Head   F6

Nakiska Chalet
HC 73 Box 24
Valley Head, WV 26294-9504
(304)339-6309 (800)225-5982

Circa 1982. On the way to this bed & breakfast, you'll be traveling the mountainous roads of West Virginia, and the hosts remind you to slow down and enjoy the scenery. Their A-frame house on 11 acres is surrounded by forests of sugar maples that display the best of foliage in autumn. Breakfast, served buffet-style, often includes local maple syrup atop blueberry pancakes. Wild turkey, deer, fox and grouse have been spotted from the deck.
Innkeeper(s): Joyce & Doug Cooper. $60-70. MC VISA DS PC. 4 rooms, 1 with PB. Breakfast and evening snack included in rates. Type of meal: full breakfast. Dinner available. Beds: KQT. Ceiling fan in room. Spa, sauna and library on premises. Fishing, downhill skiing and cross-country skiing nearby.

Certificate may be used: Sunday through Thursday nights, excluding holidays, subject to availability.

Wisconsin

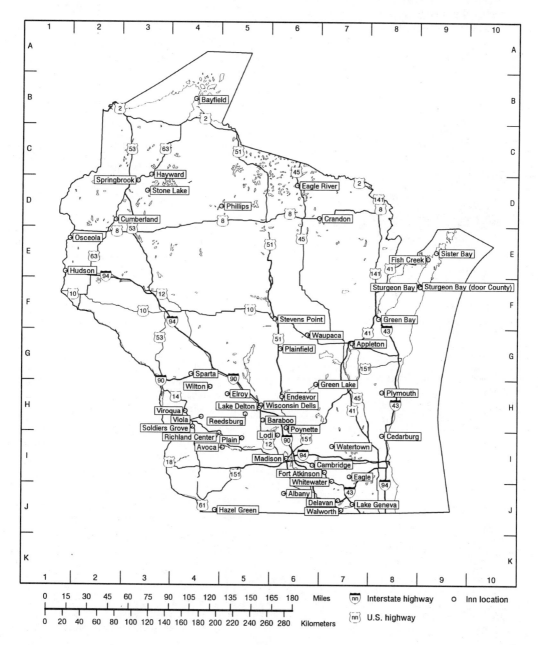

Grid coordinates: Columns 1–10 (top and bottom), Rows A–K (left and right).

- Bayfield
- 2
- 2
- 53
- 63
- 51
- 45
- Hayward
- Springbrook
- Stone Lake
- Eagle River
- 2
- Phillips
- 141
- 8
- 8
- 8
- Crandon
- Cumberland
- 53
- 51
- 45
- Osceola
- 8
- 63
- Fish Creek
- Sister Bay
- 141
- 41
- Hudson
- 94
- Sturgeon Bay
- Sturgeon Bay (door County)
- 10
- 12
- 10
- Stevens Point
- Green Bay
- 94
- Waupaca
- 41
- 43
- 53
- 51
- Plainfield
- Appleton
- 151
- Sparta
- 90
- 90
- Green Lake
- Plymouth
- Wilton
- 45
- 43
- 14
- Eilroy
- Endeavor
- 41
- Viroqua
- Lake Delton
- Wisconsin Dells
- Viola
- Reedsburg
- Baraboo
- Cedarburg
- Soldiers Grove
- Lodi
- Poynette
- Richland Center
- Plain
- 12
- 90
- 151
- Avoca
- Watertown
- 18
- Madison
- 94
- Cambridge
- Fort Atkinson
- Eagle
- 151
- Whitewater
- 94
- Albany
- 43
- Delavan
- Lake Geneva
- 61
- Hazel Green
- Walworth

Scale

```
0   15  30  45  60  75  90  105 120 135 150 165 180   Miles
0  20 40 60 80 100 120 140 160 180 200 220 240 260 280  Kilometers
```

Legend:
- (nn) Interstate highway   o Inn location
- (nn) U.S. highway

501

Albany J6

Albany Guest House
405 S Mill St
Albany, WI 53502-9502
(608)862-3636

Circa 1908. The brick walkway, red-tiled foyer, lace curtains and abundance of flowers set the comfortable tone for this three-story inn. An upright piano in the large foyer and fireplace in the living room also add to the pleasant atmosphere. The guest rooms have picture windows and hand-carved antiques. Outside, maple and black walnut trees and

various gardens grace the inn's eight-acre property. Guests can tour New Glarus, a village known as America's Little Switzerland, which is a short drive away. Also, not too far away is a cheese factory that is available for tours. Guests also can enjoy a bicycle ride on the nearby Sugar River Trail.
Innkeeper(s): Bob & Sally Braem. $55-75. MC VISA PC. 6 rooms, 4 with PB, 1 with FP. Breakfast included in rates. Types of meals: full breakfast and early coffee/tea. Beds: KQD. Air conditioning and ceiling fan in room. VCR and library on premises. Antiques, fishing, parks and cross-country skiing nearby.
Publicity: *Silent Sports, Madison, Monroe Evening Times.*
"Was even more than I expected."
Certificate may be used: Monday-Thursday, May-October. Anytime, November-April.

Oak Hill Manor
401 E Main St
Albany, WI 53502-9797
(608)862-1400 Fax:(608)862-1403

Circa 1908. The state's scenic Hidden Valley region is home to this American four-square inn, just 30 minutes south of Madison. Sylvia's Room boasts a five-foot iron and brass headboard on its queen bed, a view of the garden and a fireplace. The romantic Judith's Room features a heart-shaped queen canopy bed. Guests enjoy a three-course gourmet breakfast, including a sample of some of the area's outstanding cheeses. Nearby recreational activities include

canoeing the Sugar River, hiking the Ice Age Trail or riding the inn's bikes on the Sugar River Trail.
Innkeeper(s): Donna & Glen Rothe. $50-75. MC VISA PC TC. 4 rooms with PB, 1 with FP. Breakfast, afternoon tea and evening snack included in rates. Meals: gourmet breakfast, early coffee/tea. Beds: Q. Air conditioning in room. Cable TV, bicycles and library on premises. Antiques, fishing, parks, shopping, cross-country skiing and watersports nearby.
Certificate may be used: Sunday-Thursday, subject to availability.

Appleton G7

The Queen Anne B&B
837 E College Ave
Appleton, WI 54911-5619
(888)739-7966

Circa 1895. On a tree-lined street, The Queen Anne features polished oak, pine and maple floors, and beveled- and stained-glass windows. The dining area has bay windows. Furnishings include Victorian, Louis XV, Eastlake and Empire.
Innkeeper(s): Susan & Larry Bogenschutz. $65-105. 3 rooms, 1 with PB. 1 conference room. Type of meal: full breakfast. Beds: Q.
Publicity: *The Post Crescent, Valleysun.*
"The Queen Anne is an expression of your warmth & hospitality and a delightful place to be."
Certificate may be used: Monday-Thursday, January-March.

Avoca I5

Prairie Rose
107 S 2nd St
Avoca, WI 53506
(608)532-6878 (800)409-7673

Circa 1915. This comfortable home is filled with antiques and decorated in quaint, country style. The Rose Room boasts a fireplace, four-poster bed and private sitting area. The home is less than half an hour to many area sites, including the Wisconsin River, The House on the Rock and Frank Lloyd Wright's buildings.
Innkeeper(s): Barbara & Terry Struble. $45-55. PC TC. 3 rooms, 1 with PB, 1 with FP. Breakfast included in rates. Type of meal: full breakfast. Beds: D. Cable TV and VCR on premises. Antiques, fishing, parks, cross-country skiing and theater nearby.
Certificate may be used: Sunday through Thursday, all year.

Baraboo H5

Victorian Rose B&B
423 3rd Ave
Baraboo, WI 53913-2408
(608)356-7828

Circa 1893. Victorian charm can be found in this classic inn with its wraparound front porch, beveled mirror oak fireplace, sliding pocket doors and intricate woodwork. The decor includes period antiques and heirloom collectibles. The innkeepers are proud to show off their Wisconsin hospitality. The Queen Victoria room is ideal for enjoying honeymoons and anniversaries. The inn is within walking distance to historic downtown Baraboo, the Al Ringling Theater and Ochsner Park, with a zoo and picnic area overlooking the Baraboo River.

Innkeeper(s): Bob & Carolyn Stearns. $70-90. DS PC TC. 3 rooms with PB. 1 conference room. Breakfast and afternoon tea included in rates. Types of meals: gourmet breakfast and early coffee/tea. Beds: D. Air conditioning and ceiling fan in room. Cable TV, VCR and library on premises. Amusement parks, antiques, fishing, parks, shopping, downhill skiing, cross-country skiing, sporting events, watersports nearby.

Publicity: *Baraboo News Republic.*

"This has been so relaxing, stepping back in time. I always felt I was born too late. This period is the era I love."

Certificate may be used: All year, Sunday through Thursday (except holidays).

Bayfield   B4

Apple Tree Inn
Rt 1, Box 251, Hwy 135
Bayfield, WI 54814-9767
(715)779-5572 (800)400-6532

Circa 1911. The Apple Tree Inn is a fully restored farmhouse overlooking Lake Superior. It was once owned by a dairy farmer and landscape artist. A

hearty, country-style breakfast is served in the sunroom, which boasts a panoramic view of Madeline Island and Lake Superior. Guest rooms are furnished in early Americana style and three have lake views.

Innkeeper(s): Joanna Barningham. $49-84. MC VISA PC TC. 4 rooms with PB. Breakfast included in rates. Types of meals: full breakfast, gourmet breakfast and early coffee/tea. Picnic lunch available. Beds: KQD. Air conditioning and ceiling fan in room. Cable TV, VCR, pet boarding and child care on premises. Antiques, fishing, parks, shopping, downhill skiing, cross-country skiing, theater, watersports nearby.

Publicity: *Lake Superior.*

"You made us feel like old friends rather than guests."

Certificate may be used: Weekdays; Sunday-Thursday, Sept. 20-May 15.

Thimbleberry Inn B&B
15021 Pagent Rd, PO Box 1007
Bayfield, WI 54814
(715)779-5757

Circa 1992. The waters of Lake Superior sparkle beside the 400-foot shoreline adjacent to this natural wood home. The peaceful forest setting adds to the romance of the rooms, which include fireplaces. Innkeeper Sharon Locey writes a food column and currently is writing her first cookbook. Her culinary expertise makes breakfast a gourmet treat.  While enjoying your morning meal, watch for wildlife and bald eagles as they soar over the Loceys' 40 acres. The deck features a cedar hot tub perfect for relaxing after skiing, hiking or just spending the day by the lake's side.

Innkeeper(s): Sharon Locey. $75-115. 3 rooms with PB, 3 with FP. 1 suite. Breakfast included in rates. Types of meals: full breakfast and early coffee/tea. Beds: KQ. Antiques, fishing, shopping, skiing nearby.

Location: On Lake Superior looking at five of the Apostle Islands.

Certificate may be used: January-May 15, November-Dec. 15, Sunday-Thursday.

Cambridge   I6

The Night Heron B&B
315 E Water St
Cambridge, WI 53523
(608)423-4141

Circa 1866. This brick Italianate home is covered with ivy and the grounds are dotted with flowers. The home originally served as a tavern, dance hall and saloon. The Koshkonong River and a 300-acre nature park are across the way. Innkeeper Pamela Schorr is an interior designer and has decorated each of the three bedchambers with something unique. The Knotty Pine Room includes a skylight, ceiling and walls fashioned from pine, creating a cabin-like environment. The Rockdale Room features a metal ceiling, and the Indigo Bunting Room is full of artwork and includes a sitting area. Guests are presented with a bottle of champagne and enjoy use of a hot tub. The substantial breakfasts are served on the terrace under umbrella-covered tables.

Innkeeper(s): Pam Schorr & John Lehman. $70-75. TC. 3 rooms, 1 with PB. Breakfast included in rates. Types of meals: full breakfast and early coffee/tea. Beds: KQ. Air conditioning, ceiling fan, VCR in room. Fax, copier, spa, bicycles on premises. Antiques, fishing, parks, shopping, cross-country skiing, sporting events and theater nearby.

Certificate may be used: Jan. 1-June 1, Sunday-Thursday.

Cedarburg

I8

The Washington House Inn
W 62 N 573 Washington Ave
Cedarburg, WI 53012
(414)375-3550 (800)554-4717 Fax:(414)375-9422

Circa 1886. Completely renovated, this brick building is decorated in a light-hearted country Victorian style, featuring antiques, whirlpool baths and fireplaces. The original guest registry, more than 100 years old, is displayed proudly in the lobby.
Innkeeper(s): Wendy Porterfield. $59-189. MAP. MC VISA AX DC DS TC. 34 rooms with PB. 3 suites. 1 conference room. Breakfast included in rates. Meals: continental-plus breakfast, early coffee/tea. Beds: KQD. Air conditioning, ceiling fan, TV, VCR in room. Fax, copier, sauna on premises. Fishing, parks, cross-country skiing, sporting events, theater nearby. Location: In the heart of downtown Cedarburg.
Publicity: *Country Home, Chicago Sun-Times.*
"A piece of time lost to all but a fortunate few who will experience it. Please save it for my children."
Certificate may be used: Sunday through Thursday on $109-$189, no holidays.

Crandon

D6

Courthouse Square B&B
210 E Polk St
Crandon, WI 54520-1436
(715)478-2549

Circa 1905. Situated on the shores of Surprise Lake, this Victorian Shingle also manages to provide the conveniences of town with its location. The inn features antique and country furnishings, and each of its guest rooms offers a lake or park view. The area provides excellent antiquing and shopping opportunities, in addition to cross-country and downhill skiing. Visitors also enjoy borrowing a bike to explore the town, relaxing on the inn's porch or venturing across the street to a city park.
Innkeeper(s): Les & Bess Aho. $50-60. AX. 3 rooms, 1 with PB. Breakfast included in rates. Types of meals: gourmet breakfast and early coffee/tea. Afternoon tea and evening snack available. Beds: QDT. Ceiling fan in room. Cable TV and VCR on premises. Antiques, fishing, parks, shopping, skiing and watersports nearby.
Certificate may be used: Sunday to Thursday, except holidays & special events.

Cumberland

D2

The Rectory
1575 Second Ave, Box 1042
Cumberland, WI 54829
(715)822-3151

Circa 1905. This city's unique island setting makes it an ideal stopping point for those exploring the state's lake-rich Northwest. The German Gothic

inn, once home to the parish priest, features charming guest rooms, all filled with antiques, heirlooms and items of interest. The Mae Jenet Room, with its striking corner turret, features a doll collection and other unique toys. Breakfasts, served in the roomy parlor, often feature the inn's famous Breakfast Pie. A gaming casino is nearby, and 50 lakes are found within a 10-mile radius of Cumberland.
Innkeeper(s): Gerald & Ethel Anderson. $60-65. MC VISA. 4 rooms, 2 with PB. Ceiling fan in room. VCR on premises. Antiques, shopping, cross-country skiing and theater nearby.
Certificate may be used: Sunday-Thursday, excluding holidays and special events.

Delavan

J7

Lakeside Manor Inn
1809 S Shore Dr
Delavan, WI 53115-3618
(414)728-5354 Fax:(414)728-2043

Circa 1897. As the name suggests, this inn is located on the shores of Delavan lake. Relax and take in the view from the inn's wraparound veranda, fish off the inn's private pier or curl up with a good book in the fire-lit parlor. Guests can opt to stay in one of six rooms, a honeymoon suite or a waterfront guest house. The guest house includes two bedrooms, glass-enclosed sleeping porch, living room with fireplace and efficiency kitchen. Breakfast is not included in the guest house rates.
Innkeeper(s): Patricia K. McCauley. $79-189. MC VISA PC TC. 7 rooms, 4 with PB, 1 with FP. 1 suite. Breakfast included in rates. Types of meals: continental-plus breakfast, full breakfast and early coffee/tea. Beds: KQDT. Air conditioning, ceiling fan, TV and VCR in room. Fax and swimming on premises. Amusement parks, antiques, fishing, parks, shopping, downhill skiing, cross-country skiing, theater and watersports nearby.
Certificate may be used: Sunday through Thursday, four rooms included.

Eagle

I7

Novels Country Inn
PO Box 456, 229 E Main St
Eagle, WI 53119-0165
(414)594-3729 Fax:(414)962-2920

Circa 1896. The interior of this late 19th-century home boasts beautiful woodwork, from the carved staircase to the French doors that open into the living room. The interior features many Arts & Crafts-style pieces, as well as traditional furnishings. Homemade breads, fresh fruit, yogurt and egg dishes are among the breakfast fare. The area offers plenty of activities, such as cross-country skiing, horseback riding and shopping for antiques.
Innkeeper(s): Tom & Karrie Houlton. $65-95. MC VISA PC. 4 rooms, 1 with PB. Breakfast, evening snack and picnic lunch included in rates. Types of meals: continental breakfast, continental-plus breakfast, full

breakfast, gourmet breakfast and early coffee/tea. Gourmet lunch and catered breakfast available. Beds: KQ. Air conditioning in room. Bicycles and library on premises. Antiques, fishing, parks, shopping, cross-country skiing, golf and watersports nearby.

"Quiet, great breakfast. Will come back again soon."

Certificate may be used: January-March, Sunday-Thursday.

Eagle River
D6

Brennan Manor
1079 Everett Rd
Eagle River, WI 54521-8708
(715)479-7353

Circa 1928. This Tudor-style manor evokes images of a baronial hunting lodge with its 35-foot ceilings, timber rafters and suit of armor at the entry. Hand-carved woodwork, arched windows, and a 30-foot stone fireplace in the Great Room completes the Old World ambiance. On the grounds are two stone patios, expansive lawns leading to the lake, a private swimming beach, wet boat house and two piers. A lake-view guest house is available, as well as four lavishly decorated bedrooms that lead to an open balcony overlooking the Great Room.

Innkeeper(s): Robert Lawton. $69-99. MC VISA. 4 rooms with PB. Breakfast included in rates. Type of meal: full breakfast. Afternoon tea available. Beds: Q. VCR and bicycles on premises. Handicap access. Amusement parks, antiques, fishing, parks, shopping, downhill skiing, cross-country skiing, theater and watersports nearby.

Location: On the famed Eagle River Chain of Lakes.

Publicity: *Wisconsin Trails, Country Extra, Silent Sports, Northern Action, Best of the Northwoods.*

Certificate may be used: Sept. 15-June 15, except for special events, Sunday-Thursday.

Elroy
H5

East View B&B
33620 County P Rd
Elroy, WI 53929
(608)463-7564

Circa 1994. This comfortable ranch house offers splendid views of the countryside, with its rolling hills covered with woods. Autumn is a particularly scenic time for a visit, when the trees explode in color. The three guest rooms are simply furnished in a homey, country style with quilts topping the beds. Each room offers a pleasing view. Breakfast comes in several courses, with fresh fruit, homemade breads, a daily entree and finally a dessert. The area provides opportunities for hiking, biking, canoeing or browsing at local craft stores.

Innkeeper(s): Dom & Bev Puechner. $55-75. MC VISA. 3 rooms with PB. Breakfast included in rates. Meals: full breakfast, early coffee/tea. Beds: QD. Air conditioning, turndown service and ceiling fan in room. Amusement park, antiques, shopping, cross-country skiing, golf nearby. Publicity: *Country Inns*

"What a wonderful treat it was to stay at East View. The view was magnificent and the breakfasts superb."

Certificate may be used: Jan. -Dec. 31 except Holy Saturday, Easter Sunday, Thanksgiving, Christmas Eve, Christmas Day.

Endeavor
H6

Neenah Creek Inn & Pottery
W7956 Neenah Rd
Endeavor, WI 53930-9308
(608)587-2229 Fax:(608)587-2229

Circa 1900. Wildlife-lovers will enjoy the creekfront setting of this turn-of-the-century Portage brick farmhouse. The Circus Room honors nearby Baraboo and features a brass queen bed. Country furnishings are found throughout the inn. Guests enjoy relaxing in the common room, on the outdoor porch, in the solarium and in the spacious dining-living

room. The inn's 11 acres are filled with walking paths. Don't be shy about asking for a demonstration of the potter's wheel. Wisconsin Dells is an easy drive away.

Innkeeper(s): Pat & Doug Cook. $65-105. MC VISA DS TC. 4 rooms with PB. 1 suite. Breakfast and evening snack included in rates. Types of meals: full breakfast and gourmet breakfast. Beds: QT. Air conditioning in room. VCR, fax, copier and bicycles on premises. Amusement parks, antiques, fishing, parks, shopping, downhill skiing, cross-country skiing, golf and watersports nearby.

Certificate may be used: November through May, every day except Christmas and Valentine's Day weekends.

Fish Creek
E9

Thorp House Inn & Cottages
4135 Bluff Rd, PO Box 490
Fish Creek, WI 54212
(920)868-2444

Circa 1902. Freeman Thorp picked the site for this home because of its view of Green Bay and the village. Before his house was finished, however, he perished in the bay when the Erie L. Hackley sank. His wife completed it as a guest house. Each room is decorated with English or Victorian antiques. A stone fireplace is the focal point of the parlor, and four of the cottages on the property have fireplaces. Some cottages have whirlpools and all have kitchens, cable TVs and VCRs. Everything upon which the eye might rest must be "of the era." Breakfast is not included in the rates for cottage guests.

Innkeeper(s): Christine & Sverre Falck-Pedersen. $75-135. PC TC. 4 rooms with PB. 6 cottages. Breakfast included in rates. Meals: continental-plus breakfast, early coffee/tea. Beds: KQDT. Ceiling fans. Bikes on premises. Fishing, parks, cross-country skiing, theater, watersports nearby. Location: Heart of Door County, in the village of Fish Creek. Publicity: *Madison PM, Green Bay Press-Gazette, Milwaukee Journal/Sentinel, McCall's, Minnesota Monthly.*

"*Amazing attention to detail from restoration to the furnishings. A very first-class experience.*"

Certificate may be used: Sunday through Thursday nights, Nov. 6 through May, holidays excluded.

Fort Atkinson   I7

Lamp Post Inn
408 S Main St
Fort Atkinson, WI 53538-2231
(920)563-6561

Circa 1878. Prepare to enjoy an authentic Victorian experience at this charming, restored home. Innkeepers Debra and Mike Rusch get into the spirit of things by donning Victorian ware. Each of the guest rooms includes a working Victrola, which guests are encourage to use and enjoy. Debra and Mike pamper guests with fresh flowers and chocolates. Rooms are furnished completely with antiques. Breakfasts include specialties such as jelly-filled muffins, scones, Swedish puff pancakes and strawberry sorbet.
Innkeeper(s): Debra & Mike Rusch. $60-95. PC TC. 3 rooms, 2 with PB. Breakfast included in rates. Types of meals: gourmet breakfast and early coffee/tea. Afternoon tea, evening snack, picnic lunch and catering service available. Beds: D. Air conditioning and VCR in room.
Certificate may be used: Sunday through Thursday.

Green Bay   F8

The Astor House B&B
637 S Monroe Ave
Green Bay, WI 54301-3614
(414)432-3585 (888)303-6370
E-mail: astor@execpc.com

Circa 1888. Located in the Astor Historic District, the Astor House is completely surrounded by Victorian homes. Guests have their choice of five

rooms, each uniquely decorated for a range of ambiance, from the Vienna Balconies to the Marseilles Garden to the Hong Kong Retreat. The parlor, veranda and many suites feature a grand view of City Centre's lighted church towers. This home is also the first and only B&B in Green Bay and received the Mayor's Award for Remodeling and

Restoration. Business travelers should take notice of the private phone lines in each room, as well as the ability to hook up a modem.
Innkeeper(s): Doug Landwehr. $79-149. MC VISA AX DC DS. 5 rooms with PB, 4 with FP. 3 suites. Breakfast included in rates. Type of meal: continental-plus breakfast. Beds: KQDT. Air conditioning, TV and VCR in room. Amusement parks, antiques, fishing, parks, shopping, cross-country skiing, sporting events, theater and watersports nearby.
Certificate may be used: Monday-Thursday.

Green Lake   H6

McConnell Inn
497 S Lawson Dr
Green Lake, WI 54941
(414)294-6430

Circa 1901. This stately home features many of its original features, including leaded windows, woodwork, leather wainscoting and parquet floors. Each of the guest rooms includes beds covered with handmade quilts and clawfoot tubs. The grand, master suite comprises the entire third floor and boasts 14-foot vaulted beam ceilings, Victorian walnut furnishings, a Jacuzzi and six-foot oak buffet now converted into a unique bathroom vanity. Innkeeper Mary Jo Johnson, a pastry chef, creates the wonderful pastries that accompany an expansive breakfast with fresh fruit, granola and delectable entrees.
Innkeeper(s): Mary Jo Johnson. $80-130. MC VISA. 5 rooms. Breakfast included in rates. Type of meal: full breakfast.
Certificate may be used: November-April.

Hayward   C3

Lumberman's Mansion Inn
204 E Fourth St
Hayward, WI 54843-0885
(715)634-3012 Fax:(715)634-5724

Circa 1887. This Queen Anne Victorian, once the home of a local lumber baron, sits on a hill overlooking the city, park and pond. An oak staircase, maple floors, tiled fire-places, pocket doors and a carriage stoop are among the finely restored details. Antique furnishings blend with modern amenities such as whirlpool tubs and a video library. Wild rice pancakes, Wisconsin sausages and freshly squeezed cranberry juice are some of the regional specialties featured. The innkeepers host many seasonal events and evening lectures. Plays are sometimes performed on the front porch.

Innkeeper(s): Jan Blaedel. $70-100. MC VISA. 5 rooms with PB. 2 suites. 1 conference room. Breakfast and afternoon tea included in rates. Type of meal: full breakfast. Beds: Q. Spa and bicycles on premises. Antiques, fishing, downhill skiing, cross-country skiing and watersports nearby.

Location: One block from main street.

Publicity: *Sawyer County Record, Chicago Sun Times, Wisconsin Trails, Minneapolis Star Tribune, Wisconsin Country Life.*

"The food was excellent. And the extra personal touches (chocolate on the pillow, cookies & pie at night, muffins in the morning, etc.) were especially nice. This is definitely the best B&B we've ever been to."
Certificate may be used: Sunday-Thursday.

Mustard Seed
205 California, PO Box 262
Hayward, WI 54843
(715)634-2908

Circa 1895. Situated in a quiet neighborhood within easy walking distance of downtown Hayward, this inn offers guests a cozy mix of country antique and Scandinavian decor. The inn's enclosed yard helps afford privacy to guests, who may opt for the spacious Governor's Suite with its two-sided fireplace. (Wisconsin Governor Tommy Thompson was a recent visitor.) Breakfasts may be enjoyed in the formal dining area, country-style kitchen or on the patio in summer. Nearby attractions include Historyland, Telemark Ski Area and the National Fresh Water Fishing Hall of Fame.

Innkeeper(s): Mary Gervais. $45-85. MC VISA DS. 6 rooms, 4 with PB, 1 with FP. Breakfast included in rates. Meal: full breakfast. Beds: QDT.

Publicity: *Sawyer County Record.*

"We cannot believe our good fortune in finding you and your marvelous home."

Certificate may be used: Monday-Thursday, October through May, excluding last week in December and February.

Hazel Green   J4

De Winters of Hazel Green
2225 Main St, PO Box 384
Hazel Green, WI 53811
(608)854-2768

Circa 1847. This Federal and Greek Revival home dates back to pre-Civil War times. Innkeeper Don Simison was born in the home and his family heirlooms fill the house. A hearty homemade breakfast is served each morning. Explore Hazel Green or just relax at the inn. The city hosts some interesting attractions including a parade and open house of historic homes early in December.

Innkeeper(s): Don & Cari Simison. $45-75. TC. 3 rooms, 1 with PB. Breakfast included in rates. Type of meal: full breakfast. Beds: D. Air conditioning in room. Library on premises. Antiques, fishing, parks, shopping, downhill skiing and theater nearby.

"Good food and fun."

Certificate may be used: Any with reservation, only will take one certificate couple at a time on a busy weekend.

Wisconsin House Stagecoach Inn
2105 Main, PO Box 71
Hazel Green, WI 53811
(608)854-2233

Circa 1846. Located in southwest Wisconsin's historic lead mining region, this one-time stagecoach stop will delight antique-lovers. The innkeepers, who also deal in antiques, enjoy helping guests in their search for that special piece. The spacious two-story inn once hosted Ulysses S. Grant, whose home is just across the border in Illinois. One of the inn's guest rooms bears his name and features a walnut four-poster bed. Don't miss the chance to join the Dischs on a Friday or Saturday evening for one of their famous country inn dinners. The meals are served, by reservation only, at a handsome 16-foot-long dining table.

Innkeeper(s): Ken & Pat Disch. $55-110. MC VISA DS PC. 8 rooms, 6 with PB. 2 suites. Breakfast included in rates. Types of meals: full breakfast, gourmet breakfast and early coffee/tea. Dinner available. Beds: KQDT. Air conditioning in room. Cable TV, copier, bicycles and library on premises. Antiques, fishing, parks, downhill skiing, cross-country skiing and theater nearby.

Publicity: *Chicago Tribune, Milwaukee Journal, Country Living, Midwest Living.*

"Your ears should be burning because we are telling so many about you."

Certificate may be used: Anytime, except weekends Labor Day to Oct. 31.

Hudson
E1

Jefferson-Day House
1109 Third St
Hudson, WI 54016-1220
(715)386-7111

Circa 1857. Near the St. Croix River and 30 minutes from Mall of America, the Italianate Jefferson-Day House features guest rooms with both whirlpool tubs and gas fireplaces. Antique art and furnishings fill the rooms, and there is a formal dining room and library. Ask for the Captain's Room and you'll be rewarded with a cedar-lined bathroom, over-sized shower, antique brass bed, and a gas fireplace visible from the whirlpool tub for two. A four-course breakfast is served fireside on weekends, while continental-plus is the fare during the week.

Innkeeper(s): Tom & Sue Tyler. $99-179. MC VISA AX DS PC TC. 4 rooms with PB, 4 with FP. 1 suite. Breakfast and evening snack included in rates. Types of meals: full breakfast and gourmet breakfast. Beds: Q. Air conditioning in room. Cable TV, VCR, spa, bicycles and library on premises. Amusement parks, antiques, fishing, parks, shopping, downhill skiing, cross-country skiing, sporting events, theater and watersports nearby.

"Absolute perfection! That's the only way to describe our stay in the wonderful St. Croix suite!"

Certificate may be used: Any weekday of the year, Sunday-Thursday except holidays. Both days must be Sunday-Thursday.

Lake Delton
H5

The Swallow's Nest B&B
141 Sarrington, PO Box 418
Lake Delton, WI 53940
(608)254-6900

Circa 1988. This inn has a picturesque view of the Wisconsin Dells and Lake Delton. The Swallow's Nest features a two-story atrium with skylights, and cathedral windows and ceiling. Guests may relax on the screened deck, in the library by the fireplace or in the gazebo by the waterfall. The inn is furnished with English period furniture, rocking chairs, lace curtains, handmade quilts and goose-down comforters.

Innkeeper(s): Mary Ann Stemo. $65-70. MC VISA. 4 rooms with PB, 2 with FP. Breakfast included in rates. Type of meal: full breakfast. Beds: QDT. Air conditioning in room. Cable TV on premises. Amusement parks, antiques, shopping, downhill skiing, cross-country skiing, sporting events and theater nearby.

Publicity: *Milwaukee Journal, Wisconsin Trails.*

"Your home is beautiful, and the breakfasts were wonderful!"

Certificate may be used: Monday through Thursday, no holidays or holiday weekends.

Lake Geneva
J7

T.C. Smith Inn B&B
865 W Main St
Lake Geneva, WI 53147-1804
(414)248-1097 (800)423-0233 Fax:(414)248-1672

Circa 1845. Listed in the National Register of Historic Places, this High Victorian-style inn blends elements of Greek Revival and Italianate architecture. The inn has massive carved wooden doors, hand-painted moldings and woodwork, a high-ceilinged foyer, an original parquet floor, Oriental carpets, museum-quality period antiques and European oil paintings. Guests may enjoy tea in the Grand Parlor by a marble fireplace or enjoy breakfast on an open veranda overlooking Lake Geneva.

Innkeeper(s): The Marks Family. $95-350. MC VISA AX DC DS PC TC. 8 rooms with PB, 5 with FP. 2 suites. 1 conference room. Breakfast, afternoon tea and evening snack included in rates. Types of meals: full breakfast, gourmet breakfast and early coffee/tea. Room service available. Beds: KQD. Air conditioning, ceiling fan and VCR in room. Fax, copier, bicycles and child care on premises. Handicap access. Antiques, fishing, parks, downhill skiing, cross-country skiing, theater and watersports nearby.

Location: Forty miles from Milwaukee, seventy miles from Chicago.

Publicity: *Keystone Country Peddler, Pioneer Press Publication.*

"As much as we wanted to be on the beach, we found it impossible to leave the house. It's so beautiful and relaxing."

Certificate may be used: Nov. 15-May 15, no holidays, Sunday-Thursday.

Lodi
I6

Prairie Garden B&B
W13172 Hwy 188
Lodi, WI 53555
(608)592-5187 (800)380-8427
E-mail: prairiegarden@bigfoot.com

This 19th-century farmhouse offers four guest rooms, each decorated in a pleasant Victorian style. Innkeeper Todd Olson includes family pictures and his aunt's artwork within the decor. In the mornings, he or partner Dennis Stocks, deliver a delicious homemade breakfast to their guests' rooms. The B&B is closed to many attractions, including skiing, a nude beach, a casino, winery and Lake Wisconsin.

Innkeeper(s): Todd Olson & Dennis Stocks. $55-115. MC VISA DS PC. 4 rooms, 1 with PB. Breakfast and afternoon tea included in rates. Type of meal: full breakfast. Beds: D. Air conditioning, turndown service, ceiling fan and TV in room. VCR, fax, spa, stables and bicycles on premises. Handicap access. Amusement parks, antiques, fishing, parks, shopping, downhill skiing, cross-country skiing, sporting events, golf, theater and watersports nearby.

Publicity: *In Step Newsmagazine*

Certificate may be used: Nov. 1-April 30, Sunday through Thursday.

Victorian Treasure B&B Inn
115 Prairie St
Lodi, WI 53555-7147
(608)592-5199 (800)859-5199 Fax:(608)592-7147
E-mail: victorian@globaldialog.com

Circa 1893. Guests at Victorian Treasure stay in one of six guest rooms spread among two 19th-century Queen Anne Victorians. The interior boasts stained- and leaded-glass windows, pocket doors, rich restored woods and expansive porches. Four

suites include a whirlpool tub, fireplace and romantic decor with antiques. Full, gourmet breakfasts may include specialties such as eggs Florentine, an herb vegetable quiche or stuffed French toast topped with a seasonal fruit sauce.

Innkeeper(s): Todd & Kimberly Seidl. $79-169. MC VISA PC TC. 6 rooms with PB, 4 with FP. 4 suites. Breakfast and evening snack included in rates. Types of meals: gourmet breakfast and early coffee/tea. Beds: Q. Air conditioning in room. Fax, copier and library on premises. Antiques, parks, shopping, downhill skiing, cross-country skiing, sporting events, theater and watersports nearby.

Publicity: *Milwaukee Sentinel, Portage Daily Register, Baraboo News Republic, Chicago Sun-Times, Wisconsin Trails, State Journal.*

"Wow! We have stayed in B&Bs from Maine to Virginia to California. Who would have believed we would find the best so close to home?"

Certificate may be used: Sunday thru Thursday, Nov. 1-May 31; Monday-Thursday, June 1-Oct. 31, excluding holidays. Based on availability.

Madison

Arbor House, An Environmental Inn
3402 Monroe St
Madison, WI 53711-1702
(608)238-2981 Fax:(608)238-1175

Circa 1853. Nature-lovers not only will enjoy the inn's close access to a 1,280-acre nature preserve, they will appreciate the innkeepers' ecological theme. Organic sheets and towels are offered for guests as well as environmentally safe bath products. Arbor House is one of Madison's oldest existing homes and features plenty of historic features, such as romantic reading chairs and antiques, mixed with modern amenities and unique touches. Five rooms

include a whirlpool tub, four have a fireplace. The Annex guest rooms include private balconies. The innkeepers offer many amenities for business travelers, including value-added corporate rates. The award-winning inn has been recognized as a model of urban ecology. Lake Wingra is

within walking distance as are biking and nature trails, bird watching and a host of other outdoor activities. Guests enjoy complimentary canoeing and use of mountain bikes.

Innkeeper(s): John & Cathie Imes. $74-189. MC VISA AX PC TC. 8 rooms with PB, 2 with FP. 1 suite. 1 conference room. Breakfast included in rates. Types of meals: continental-plus breakfast and full breakfast. Beds: Q. Air conditioning, ceiling fan, TV and VCR in room. Fax and copier on premises. Handicap access. Antiques, fishing, parks, shopping, cross-country skiing, sporting events, watersports nearby.

Publicity: *E.*

"What a delightful treat in the middle of Madison. Absolutely, unquestionably, the best time I've spent in a hotel or otherwise. B&Bs are the only way to go! Thank you!"

Certificate may be used: January-March, Sunday-Thursday, excluding holidays.

Osceola

Pleasant Lake Inn
2238 60th Ave
Osceola, WI 54020-4509
(715)294-2545 (800)294-2545

Circa 1990. This country-style home commands a view of Pleasant Lake from its picturesque forest setting. All the rooms have their own sun room or private deck and two have double whirlpools. The original farm, a quarter of a mile from the inn, has been in the Berg family for more than 130 years. Maintained trails wind along the lake and through the woods, and an apple orchard is a favorite spot for picture-taking in the spring and apple-gathering in the fall. A full breakfast often includes Dutch pancakes made from freshly ground flour and served with honey from the innkeepers' beehives.

Innkeeper(s): Richard & Charlene Berg. $40-100. MC VISA DS. 4 rooms with PB. Breakfast and evening snack included in rates. Types of meals: full breakfast and early coffee/tea. Beds: Q. Air conditioning and ceiling fan in room. VCR on premises. Antiques, fishing, parks, shopping, skiing, theater and watersports nearby.

Location: Located just one hour from the Twin Cities and 10 minutes from Osceola.

Publicity: *Sun.*

"We enjoyed sharing our mornings with the hummingbirds and the evenings by the bonfire."

Certificate may be used: Monday-Thursday, Nov. 1-March 1, excluding holidays.

St. Croix River Inn
305 River St, PO Box 356
Osceola, WI 54020
(715)294-4248

Circa 1910. This stone house is poised on a bluff overlooking the St. Croix River. The sitting room overlooks the river. All guest rooms have whirlpool baths. Rooms feature such amenities as four-poster canopy beds, a tile fireplace, a Palladian window that stretches from floor to ceiling, sten-ciling, bull's-eye moldings and private balconies. Breakfast is served in bed.

Innkeeper(s): Bev Johnson. $85-200. MC VISA AX. 7 rooms with PB, 1 with FP. Breakfast included in rates. Type of meal: full breakfast. Beds: Q. Spa on premises. Fishing and parks nearby.
Location: St. Croix River Valley.
Publicity: *Chicago Sun-Times, Skyway News, St. Paul Pioneer Press.*
Certificate may be used: Sunday-Thursday, all year.

Phillips
D5

East Highland School House B&B
West 4342, Hwy D
Phillips, WI 54555
(715)339-3492

Guests are invited to ring the bell at this restored one-room schoolhouse. Additions were made to the build-ing in the 1920s, and rooms feature rustic exposed beams, brick walls and original light fixtures. Innkeepers Jeanne and Russ Kirchmeyer filled the home with family antiques and turn-of-the-century pieces. Lacy curtains, doilies and hand-hooked rugs lend to the romantic, country atmosphere. The kitchen, which once served as a stage for the school, is now where Jeanne prepares the expansive meals.

Innkeeper(s): Jeanne Kirchmeyer. $45-60. 4 rooms. Breakfast included in rates. Type of meal: full breakfast.
Certificate may be used: Year-round, weekends if available.

Plain
I5

Bettinger House B&B
855 Wachter Ave, Hwy 23
Plain, WI 53577
(608)546-2951 Fax:(608)546-2951

Circa 1904. This two-story brick inn once was home to the town's midwife, (and the innkeeper's grand-mother) who delivered more than 300 babies here. The current innkeepers are just as eager to bring new guests into their home. The Elizabeth Room, named for the midwife, boasts a round king-size bed and pri-

vate bath. Lavish country breakfasts often include potatoes dug from the innkeeper's off-site farm, sour cream cucumbers, breakfast pie with eggs and sausage, rhubarb coffeecake and sorbet. Area attrac-tions are plentiful, including the House on the Rock, St. Anne's Shrine and the Wisconsin River. Be sure to visit the nearby Cedar Grove Cheese Factory.

Innkeeper(s): Marie Neider. $50-65. MC VISA. 5 rooms, 3 with PB. Breakfast included in rates. Type of meal: full breakfast. Afternoon tea available. Beds: KQ. Air conditioning and ceiling fan in room. Cable TV, VCR, fax and copier on premises. Antiques, fishing, parks, shopping, cross-country skiing, theater and watersports nearby.
Certificate may be used: Sunday through Thursday, except holidays.

Plainfield
G6

Johnson Inn
231 W North St, Box 487
Plainfield, WI 54966-9704
(715)335-4383

Circa 1870. Located in a scenic region of Central Wisconsin known for its antiques, flea markets, lakes and hunting, this inn offers a fine stopping point for those exploring the area's attractions. Antiques, birch flooring, carved oak paneling and tall ceilings highlight the interior. The lacy Rathermel Room features a pink, blue and white color scheme, with wicker furnishings, queen bed and private bath, while the Sherman Safari Room boasts a unique jun-gle print decor and a queen bed. The innkeepers' well-tend-

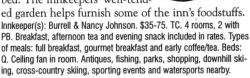

ed garden helps furnish some of the inn's foodstuffs.

Innkeeper(s): Burrell & Nancy Johnson. $35-75. TC. 4 rooms, 2 with PB. Breakfast, afternoon tea and evening snack included in rates. Types of meals: full breakfast, gourmet breakfast and early coffee/tea. Beds: Q. Ceiling fan in room. Antiques, fishing, parks, shopping, downhill ski-ing, cross-country skiing, sporting events and watersports nearby.
Certificate may be used: Year-round, Monday through Thursday, except first week in August.

Plymouth
H8

Hillwind Farm B&B
N 4922 Hillwind Rd
Plymouth, WI 53073
(920)892-2199

Circa 1856. Hillwind, a charming Victorian, is one of the oldest farmhouses in the county, built prior to the Civil War. The rooms are decorated in a roman-tic Victorian style with antiques, colorful wallpapers and luxurious linens. Three of the rooms offer a fireplace and double whirlpool tub. There are private porches for those who wish to relax and enjoy the pastoral setting. The breakfasts are sometimes served on the covered front veranda.

Innkeeper(s): Kim & Art Jasso. $140. MC VISA PC. 4 rooms with PB, 3 with FP. 1 suite. Breakfast included in rates. Beds: Q. Air conditioning, ceiling fan, TV and VCR in room. Antiques, fishing, parks, shopping, cross-country skiing, golf and watersports nearby.

"Thank you for a weekend we'll both never forget. We're engaged!"

Certificate may be used: Monday-Thursday, November through April, excludes month of February and holidays.

Yankee Hill Inn B&B
405 Collins St
Plymouth, WI 53073-2361
(414)892-2222

Circa 1870. Two outstanding examples of 19th-century architecture comprise this inn, one a striking Italianate Gothic listed in the National Register, and the other a Queen Anne Victorian with many cus-

tom touches. Between the two impressive structures, visitors will choose from 12 spacious guest rooms, all featuring antique furnishings and handmade quilts. Visitors can walk to downtown, where they will find an antique mall, shopping and fine dining.

Innkeeper(s): Peg Stahlman. $76-102. MC VISA. 12 rooms with PB. Breakfast included in rates. Types of meals: full breakfast and early coffee/tea. Beds: QD. VCR on premises. Antiques, fishing, shopping, cross-country skiing and theater nearby.

Publicity: *Wisconsin Country Life, Milwaukee Journal, Plymouth Review.*

"You have mastered the art of comfort. All the perfect little touches make this a dream come true. I only regret that we cannot stay forever."

Certificate may be used: Nov. 1-April 30, anytime except holidays or holiday weekends. May 1-Oct. 31, Monday through Thursday only.

Poynette   H6

Jamieson House
407 N Franklin St
Poynette, WI 53955-9490
(608)635-4100 Fax:(608)635-2292

Circa 1879. Victorian elegance and proximity to recreational activities and sightseeing attractions help bring enthusiastic guests to this inn, which consists of three different structures. A main house, guest house and schoolhouse are furnished with antiques gathered from the entire Midwest. Four of the rooms have whirlpool tubs, and the inn's breakfast fare is noteworthy. Water sports are just a few miles away on Lake Wisconsin, and Baraboo's Circus World Museum, Madison and the Wisconsin Dells are within easy driving distance.

Innkeeper(s): Heidemarie Hutchison. $65-130. MC VISA AX DS. 11 rooms with PB, 1 with FP. 1 conference room. Breakfast included in rates. Type of meal: full breakfast. Beds: KQDT.

Location: Between Madison & Wisconsin Dells.

Publicity: *Capital Times, North West News, Poynette Press.*

Certificate may be used: Sunday-Thursday, anytime.

Reedsburg   H5

Parkview B&B
211 N Park St
Reedsburg, WI 53959-1652
(608)524-4333

Circa 1895. Tantalizingly close to Baraboo and Wisconsin Dells, this central Wisconsin inn overlooks a city park in the historic district. The gracious innkeepers delight in tending to their guests' desires and offer wake-up coffee and a morning paper. The home's first owners were in the hardware business, so there are many original, unique fixtures, in addition to hardwood floors, intricate woodwork, leaded and etched windows and a suitors' window. The downtown business district is just a block away.

Innkeeper(s): Tom & Donna Hofmann. $60-80. MC VISA AX. 4 rooms, 2 with PB. Breakfast included in rates. Types of meals: gourmet breakfast and early coffee/tea. Evening snack available. Beds: QT. Air conditioning and ceiling fan in room. Cable TV on premises. Antiques, fishing, parks, shopping, downhill skiing and cross-country skiing nearby.

Publicity: *Reedsburg Times Press.*

"Your hospitality was great! You all made us feel right at home."

Certificate may be used: Sunday-Thursday, May 15-Oct. 15; anytime rest of the year.

Richland Center I4

Lambs Inn B&B
Rt 2, Box 144
Richland Center, WI 53581-9626
(608)585-4301

Circa 1800. An old-fashioned family farm in a scenic hidden valley is the setting for this inn, with four guest rooms and an adjacent cottage. Ann's Room, with its cream walls, lace curtains and rose carpet, is

highlighted by a quilt hand-pieced by Donna's grandmother. Marie's Room, with its yellow and blue tones, offers a stunning view of the valley. The country kitchen is a favorite gathering place. Breakfast fare sometimes features bread pudding or kringle.

Innkeeper(s): Donna & Dick Messerschmidt. $60-105. MC VISA. 6 rooms, 4 with PB. Breakfast and evening snack included in rates. Types of meals: continental-plus breakfast, full breakfast and early coffee/tea. Beds: KQT. Air conditioning and ceiling fan in room. VCR on premises. Antiques, fishing, parks, shopping, downhill skiing, cross-country skiing, theater and watersports nearby.

Certificate may be used: Jan. 1-Dec. 31.

Sister Bay E9

The Wooden Heart Inn
11086 Hwy 42
Sister Bay, WI 54234
(414)854-9097

This contemporary log home in the woods of beautiful Door County offers antique furnishings, ceiling fans and queen beds. An adjoining loft is available to read, relax or watch television. Guests also are welcome to join the innkeepers on the main floor to enjoy the fireplace and refreshments, which are served each evening. The full country breakfasts are served in the great room. A gift shop, specializing in Christmas, country and Scandinavian items, is on the premises.

Innkeeper(s): Mike Hagerman. $85-95. MC VISA. 3 rooms. Breakfast included in rates. Types of meals: full breakfast and early coffee/tea. Air conditioning and ceiling fan in room. TV, VCR on premises. Amusement parks, antiques, shopping, cross-country skiing and theater nearby.

Certificate may be used: Nov. 1-April 30, Sunday through Thursday.

Soldiers Grove H4

Old Oak Inn & Acorn Pub
Rt 1, Box 1500, Hwy 131 S
Soldiers Grove, WI 54655-9777
(608)624-5217

Circa 1900. Guests will find lodging and dining at this spacious Queen Anne Victorian turreted inn, a mile from town. Beautiful etched and stained glass and woodcarving dominate the interior, while the guest rooms boast antique-style furnishings and imported woodwork. The area is well-known for its antiquing, cross-country skiing and fishing, and many visitors just enjoy soaking up the abundant local scenery. The inn's facilities make it a natural location for meetings and receptions, and it also is popular with those celebrating anniversaries.

Innkeeper(s): Karen Norbert. $48-62. AP. MC VISA. 7 rooms. Types of meals: continental breakfast, continental-plus breakfast, full breakfast, gourmet breakfast and early coffee/tea. Afternoon tea, dinner, evening snack, picnic lunch, lunch, gourmet lunch, banquet service, catering service and catered breakfast available. Restaurant on premises. Beds: KDT. Air conditioning and TV in room. VCR on premises. Antiques, fishing, parks, shopping, skiing and watersports nearby.

Certificate may be used: Nov. 1-March 1, anytime; March 1-Oct. 31, Sunday through Thursday, with reservations.

Sparta G4

Briar Patch B&B
307 N Water St
Sparta, WI 54656-1742
(608)269-1026

This century-old home features original hardwood floors, country furnishings, antiques and collectibles. Early risers are offered coffee in the sun porch, which is decorated with wicker furnishings and a variety of plants. The aroma of freshly baked breads and other treats will lure even the deepest sleepers to the breakfast table where a hearty, country meal is served. Downtown Sparta and the popular Elroy-Sparta Bike Trail are nearby, along with antique shops and a bicycle/space museum.

Innkeeper(s): Nancy Holdeman. $75. MC VISA. 3 rooms. Breakfast included in rates. Type of meal: full breakfast.

Certificate may be used: November thru April, other major dates available according to availability and midweek vacancy. By reservation only.

The Franklin Victorian
220 E Franklin St
Sparta, WI 54656-1804
(608)269-3894 (800)845-8767

Circa 1800. Built for a banker when Sparta was the hub of social life, this house still boasts of such splendid woods as black ash, curly birch, quarter-cut white oak and red oak. Features include leaded windows in the library and dining room, many of the original filigreed brass light fixtures, and a magnificent sunset stained-glass window. Sparta is nestled among the hills of Wisconsin's Coulee Region. Area attractions include rivers, trout streams, 130 miles of bike trails, craft and antique shops.

Innkeeper(s): Lloyd & Jane Larson. $70-95. MC VISA. 4 rooms, 2 with PB, 1 with FP. 1 conference room. Breakfast included in rates. Types of meals: gourmet breakfast and early coffee/tea. Beds: KQ. Ceiling fan in room. Antiques, fishing, parks, shopping, downhill skiing, cross-country skiing and sporting events nearby.

Certificate may be used: Year-round, Sunday-Thursday.

Just-N-Trails Country Inn Nordic Ski Center
7452 Kathryn Ave
Sparta, WI 54656-9729
(608)269-4522 (800)488-4521 Fax:(608)269-3280

Circa 1920. Nestled in a scenic valley sits this 200-acre farm. Guests are encouraged to explore the hiking, snowshoe and cross-country ski trails. The innkeepers offer ski and snowshoe rentals for both adults and children. In addition to delightfully decorated rooms in the farmhouse, there are two Scandinavian log houses and a plush, restored granary for those desiring more privacy. Each of these cottages includes a whirlpool bath and a fireplace. There also is a suite in the farmhouse with a fireplace and whirlpool. The well-cared-for grounds and buildings reflect the innkeepers' pride in their home, which was built by Don's grandfather. Guests will find cats, kittens, rabbits, chickens and Peter, a pygmy goat, on the premises.

Innkeeper(s): Don & Donna Justin. $80-300. MC VISA AX DS PC TC. 7 rooms with PB, 5 with FP. 3 cottages. 1 conference room. Breakfast included in rates. Type of meal: full breakfast. Beds: KQDT. Air conditioning and ceiling fan in room. Antiques, fishing, parks, shopping, downhill skiing and cross-country skiing nearby.

Location: Elroy-Sparta bike trail.

Publicity: *Milwaukee Journal, Country, Wisconsin Woman, Wisconsin Trails, Travel America, Family Fun.*

Certificate may be used: Monday-Thursday except holidays.

Springbrook
D3

The Stout Trout B&B
Rt 1, Box 1630
Springbrook, WI 54875-9801
(715)466-2790

Circa 1900. Located on 40 acres of rolling, wooded countryside, The Stout Trout overlooks a lily-ringed bay on Gull Lake. The lake can be viewed from the living room, dining areas and second-floor guest rooms. The inn features wood-plank floors, folk art, classic prints and country-style furniture. Homemade jams and maple syrup are served.

Innkeeper(s): Kathleen Fredricks. $65. 4 rooms with PB. Breakfast included in rates. Type of meal: full breakfast. Beds: QD. Antiques, fishing, shopping, cross-country skiing and sporting events nearby.

Location: Northwest Wisconsin.

Publicity: *Chicago Tribune, Wisconsin West Magazine.*

"Thank you again for the comfortable setting, great food and gracious hospitality!"

Certificate may be used: Nov. 1-May 30, Sunday through Thursday.

Stevens Point
F6

A Dream of Yesteryear B&B
1100 Brawley St
Stevens Point, WI 54481-3536
(715)341-4525 Fax:(715)344-3047

Circa 1901. This elegant, three-story, 4,000-square-foot Queen Anne home is within walking distance of downtown, the Wisconsin River and the University of Wisconsin. The inn features golden oak woodwork, hardwood floors and leaded glass. Each guest room offers exquisite decor; the third-floor Ballroom Suite boasts a whirlpool. Gourmet breakfasts are served in the inn's formal  dining room. An excellent hiking trail is just a block from the inn.

Innkeeper(s): Bonnie & Bill Maher. $55-129. MC VISA AX DS PC TC. 6 rooms, 4 with PB. 2 suites. Breakfast, afternoon tea and evening snack included in rates. Types of meals: full breakfast, gourmet breakfast and early coffee/tea. Beds: KQDT. Air conditioning and TV in room. VCR, bicycles and library on premises. Amusement parks, antiques, fishing, parks, shopping, downhill skiing, cross-country skiing, sporting events, theater and watersports nearby.

Publicity: *Victorian Homes, Reach, Stevens Point Journal.*

"Something from a Hans Christian Anderson fairy tale."

Certificate may be used: Nov. 15-March 15, Monday-Thursday.

Stone Lake D3

Lake House

5793 Division (on the lake)
Stone Lake, WI 54876
(715)865-6803
E-mail: tweldon@win.bright.net

Circa 1917. This bed & breakfast is the oldest building in town and began its life as a hotel in Stone Lake's downtown area. Several years later, it was moved to its present lakeside location. Innkeepers Maxine Mashek and Terri Weldon renovated the homes interior, decorating it with antiques. There are plenty of places to relax, including common areas with fireplaces, a porch or on the deck overlooking the water. In addition to the B&B, there is an art gallery on the premises, featuring works of local artists.
Innkeeper(s): Maxine Mashek & Terri Weldon. $55-75. MC VISA PC TC. 4 rooms, 2 with PB, 1 with FP. Breakfast and afternoon tea included in rates. Types of meals: full breakfast, gourmet breakfast and early coffee/tea. Beds: QD. Air conditioning, ceiling fan and VCR in room. Cable TV, fax, swimming, bicycles and library on premises. Handicap access. Amusement parks, antiques, fishing, parks, shopping, downhill skiing, cross-country skiing, golf, theater and watersports nearby.
Publicity: *Four Seasons.*

Certificate may be used: March through June 30.

Sturgeon Bay F9

The Inn at Cedar Crossing

336 Louisiana St
Sturgeon Bay, WI 54235-2422
(414)743-4200 Fax:(414)743-4422

Circa 1884. This historic hotel, in the National Register, is a downtown two-story brick building that once housed street-level shops with second-floor apartments for the tailors, shopkeepers and pharmacists who worked below. The upstairs, now guest rooms, is decorated with rich fab-
rics and wallpapers
and fine antiques.
The Anniversary
Room has a
mahogany bed, fire-
place and double
whirlpool tub. The
Victorian-era dining
room and pub, both with fireplaces, are on the lower level. The waterfront is three blocks away.
Innkeeper(s): Terry Wulf. $90-150. MC VISA DS PC TC. 9 rooms with PB, 6 with FP. Breakfast and evening snack included in rates. Types of meals: continental-plus breakfast, full breakfast, gourmet breakfast and early coffee/tea. Dinner, picnic lunch, lunch, gourmet lunch, catering service, catered breakfast and room service available. Restaurant on premises. Beds: KQ. Air conditioning, TV and VCR in room. Fax, copier

and library on premises. Antiques, fishing, parks, shopping, downhill skiing, cross-country skiing, theater and watersports nearby.
Publicity: *New Month, Milwaukee Sentinel, Chicago Sun-Times, Country Inns, Bon Appetit, Gourmet, Green Bay Press Gazette, Midwest Living, Milwaukee Journal, Wisconsin Trails.*

"*The second-year stay at the inn was even better than the first. I couldn't have found a more romantic place.*"
Certificate may be used: Nov. 15-May 1, Sunday through Thursday (excludes holiday stays).

Scofield House B&B

908 Michigan St
Sturgeon Bay, WI 54235-1849
(414)743-7727 (888)463-0204 Fax:(414)743-7727

Circa 1902. Mayor Herbert Scofield, prominent locally in the lumber and hardware business, built this late-Victorian house with a sturdy square tower and inlaid floors that feature intricate borders patterned in cherry, birch, maple, walnut, and red and white oak. Oak moldings throughout the house boast raised designs of bows, ribbons, swags and flowers. Equally lavish decor is fea-
tured in the guest
rooms with fluffy
flowered comforters
and cabbage rose wall-
papers highlighting
romantic antique bed-
steads. Baked apple-
cinammon French toast is a house specialty. Modern amenities include many suites with fireplaces and double whirlpools. "Room at the Top" is a skylit 900-square-foot suite occupying the whole third floor and furnished with Victorian antiques.
Innkeeper(s): Bill & Fran Cecil. $93-196. PC TC. 6 rooms with PB, 5 with FP. 3 cottages. Breakfast and afternoon tea included in rates. Type of meal: gourmet breakfast. Beds: Q. Air conditioning, ceiling fan, TV and VCR in room. Fax and copier on premises. Amusement parks, antiques, fishing, parks, shopping, downhill skiing, cross-country skiing, sporting events, theater and watersports nearby.
Publicity: *Glamour, Country, Wisconsin Trails, Green Bay Press Gazette, Chicago Tribune, Milwaukee Sentinel-Journal, Midwest Living, Victorian Decorating & Lifestyle, Country Inns, National Geographic Traveler.*

"*You've introduced us to the fabulous world of B&Bs. I loved the porch swing and would have been content on it for the entire weekend.*"
Certificate may be used: Nov. 15-April 30, Monday thru Thursday only.

White Lace Inn

16 N 5th Ave
Sturgeon Bay, WI 54235-1714
(414)743-1105
E-mail: romance@whitelaceinn.com

Circa 1903. White Lace Inn is four Victorian houses, one an ornate Queen Anne. It is adjacent to two districts listed in the National Register. Often the site for romantic anniversary celebrations, a favorite suite has a two-sided fireplace, magnificent walnut Eastlake bed, English country fabrics and a two-person whirlpool tub. Enjoy the landscaped gardens and gazebo.

Innkeeper(s): Dennis & Bonnie Statz. $98-198. MC VISA AX DS. 18 rooms, 15 with PB. 5 suites. Breakfast included in rates. Type of meal: full breakfast. Beds: KQ. Spa on premises. Handicap access. Antiques, fishing, cross-country skiing, theater and watersports nearby.
Location: The inn is bordered by Door County, Lake Michigan on one side, Green Bay on the other.
Publicity: *Milwaukee Sentinel, Brides, National Geographic Traveler, Wisconsin Trails, Milwaukee, Country Home, Midwest Living.*

"*Each guest room is an overwhelming visual feast, a dazzling fusion of colors, textures and beautiful objects. It is one of these rare gems that established a tradition the day it opened — Wisconsin Trails.*"

Certificate may be used: November-April, Sunday through Thursday, holidays excluded.

Viola   H4

The Inn at Elk Run
S 4125 County Hwy SS
Viola, WI 54664
(608)625-2062 (800)729-7313 Fax:(608)625-4310

Circa 1905. This Dutch Colonial farmhouse in the scenic Mississippi River Valley region offers a relaxing getaway from city life. Visitors select from the Sarah, Simplicity or Sunrise rooms, all featuring ceiling fans, clock radios, desks, phone and turndown service. Guests are treated to full country breakfasts and afternoon teas. The area is well-known for its antiquing, apple orchards, bike trails and cross-country skiing. In addition, many guests enjoy exploring the local Amish settlement and shops or taking a canoe trip on the nearby Kickapoo River.

Innkeeper(s): Janet & Roger Hugg. $40-55. MC VISA. 3 rooms. Breakfast, afternoon tea and evening snack included in rates. Types of meals: full breakfast and early coffee/tea. Beds: QD. Fax and copier on premises. Antiques, fishing, shopping, downhill skiing, cross-country skiing and watersports nearby.
Certificate may be used: Dec. 1-April 30, any day of week.

Viroqua   H4

Viroqua Heritage Inn B&B's
217 & 220 E Jefferson St
Viroqua, WI 54665
(608)637-3306

Circa 1890. The three-story turret of this gabled Queen Anne mansion houses the sitting room of a guest chamber and the formal first-floor parlor. Columns, spindles and assorted gingerbread spice the exterior, while beveled glass, ornate fireplaces and crystal chandeliers grace the interior. An antique baby grand piano and Victrola reside in the music room. Breakfast is served on the original carved-oak buffet and dining table, on the balcony or front porch.

Innkeeper(s): Nancy Rhodes. $50-80. MC VISA DS PC TC. 9 rooms, 5 with PB, 1 with FP. 1 suite. Breakfast included in rates. Types of meals: full breakfast and early coffee/tea. Beds: KQD. Air conditioning in room. VCR, bicycles, library and child care on premises. Antiques, fishing, parks, shopping, downhill skiing, cross-country skiing, theater and watersports nearby.
Publicity: *Milwaukee Magazine.*

"*Wonderful house, great hosts.*"

Certificate may be used: Weekdays, all year, except September-October. All week, November-March, except holidays.

Walworth   J7

Arscott House B&B
PO Box 875, 241 S Main
Walworth, WI 53184-0875
(414)275-3233

Circa 1903. Built by a master carpenter at the turn of the century, this turreted Queen Anne Victorian has been lovingly restored to its original stylings. A new addition is the inn's Arizona Apartment, with Southwestern decor, a spacious sitting room, kitchen and a private, outside entrance. A roomy front porch and two outside decks are favorite relaxing spots, and a buffet breakfast is available to guests. The inn is just minutes from Lake Geneva's many attractions.

Innkeeper(s): Valerie C. Dudek. $45-145. MC VISA DS PC TC. 2 rooms. Breakfast and afternoon tea included in rates. Types of meals: full breakfast and early coffee/tea. Beds: QDT. Air conditioning, turndown service, ceiling fan, TV and VCR in room. Antiques, fishing, parks, shopping, skiing, theater and watersports nearby.

"*Enjoyed your gracious hospitality. Loved the breakfast. Loved your house. We'll be back again. Thank you for making our first anniversary such an enjoyable one.*"

Certificate may be used: Nov. 1-April 30, Sunday-Friday.

Watertown   I7

Brandt Quirk B&B
410 S 4th St
Watertown, WI 53094-4526
(414)261-7917

Circa 1875. This Greek Revival manor is named for its second owner, whose family owned the house for more than 70 years. Marble fireplaces and stained-glass windows add ambiance to the Victorian decor. Many of the antiques and crafts are also available for purchase. One suite includes a brass bed and Battenburg lace, while another features a pine cannonball bed set.

Innkeeper(s): Wayne & Elda Zuleger. $55-75. MC VISA TC. 5 rooms, 3 with PB. 3 suites. 1 conference room. Breakfast included in rates. Types of meals: full breakfast and early coffee/tea. Beds: Q. Air conditioning and TV in room. Antiques, fishing, parks, shopping, downhill skiing and cross-country skiing nearby.

Certificate may be used: Jan. 1-Feb. 29 (two-night minimum).

Waupaca
G6

Crystal River B&B
E1369 Rural Rd
Waupaca, WI 54981-9570
(715)258-5333

Circa 1853. The stately beauty of this historic Greek Revival farmhouse is rivaled only by its riverside setting. Each room features a view of the water, garden, woods or all three. A Victorian gazebo, down comforters and delicious breakfasts, with pecan sticky buns, a special favorite, add to guests' enjoyment. Exploring the village of Rural, which is in the National Register, will delight those interested in bygone days. Recreational activities abound, with the Chain O'Lakes and a state park nearby.

Innkeeper(s): Lois Sorenson. $55-95. MC VISA. 7 rooms, 2 with PB. Breakfast included in rates. Type of meal: full breakfast. Beds: Q. Air conditioning and ceiling fan in room. Cable TV on premises. Antiques, shopping, skiing and sporting events nearby.

Location: Historic district.

Publicity: *Resorter, Stevens Point Journal, Wisconsin Trail.*

"It was like being king for a day."

Certificate may be used: Sunday through Thursday, excluding Memorial and Labor Day weekends. Excludes June, July, August.

Thomas Pipe Inn
11032 Pipe Rd
Waupaca, WI 54981-8604
(715)824-3161

Circa 1854. A former stagecoach stop in the pre-railroad days, this historic Greek Revival inn offers four elegant guest rooms to visitors, many who have come to explore the Chain O'Lakes and its many attractions. Elizabeth's Room boasts a clawfoot tub and canopy bed, while the Florence Pipe Room features a brass bed loaded with pillows. The Thomas Pipe Room has a beautiful view of the woods, and Marjorie's Suite has an antique bed and sitting room with sleeper sofa and fireplace. Hartman's Creek State Park is a 10-minute drive from the inn.

Innkeeper(s): Marcella Windisch. $65-125. MC VISA. 4 rooms. 1 suite. Breakfast included in rates. Type of meal: full breakfast. Air conditioning in room. VCR on premises. Antiques, cross-country skiing nearby.

Certificate may be used: December through April, seven days a week.

Whitewater
I7

Victoria-On-Main B&B
622 W Main St
Whitewater, WI 53190-1855
(414)473-8400

Circa 1895. This Queen Anne Victorian is located in the heart of Whitewater National Historic District, adjacent to the University of Wisconsin. It was built for Edward Engebretson, mayor of Whitewater. Each guest room is named for a Wisconsin hardwood. The Red Oak Room, Cherry Room and Bird's Eye Maple Room all feature antiques, Laura Ashley prints and down comforters. A hearty breakfast is served, and there are kitchen facilities available for light meal preparation. Whitewater Lake and Kettle Moraine State Forest are five minutes away.

Innkeeper(s): Nancy Wendt. $65-75. MC VISA. 3 rooms, 1 with PB, 1 with FP. Breakfast included in rates. Types of meals: full breakfast and early coffee/tea. Beds: D. Ceiling fan in room. Cable TV on premises. Antiques, fishing, parks, shopping, cross-country skiing, theater and watersports nearby.

Location: Between Madison and Milwaukee.

"We loved it. Wonderful hospitality."

Certificate may be used: June through September and January, Sunday through Thursday.

Wilton
H4

Rice's Whispering Pines B&B
RR 2, Box 225
Wilton, WI 54670
(608)435-6531

Circa 1896. Guests will find this pleasant place for a getaway. There are 60 acres surrounding the main farmhouse, ensuring tranquility during one's stay. Tucked behind the century-old farmhouse are a bright red barn and grain elevators, adding to the rural setting. Although not a working farm, the property has chickens and horses. The comfortable home has been in the Rice family for three generations. There are three guest rooms, decorated in a homey country style. One room has a wilderness scene on the wall behind the white iron and brass bed. In another room, a swash of fabric, decorated with cream-colored tassels, is draped at the headboard of the bed, which rests on a backdrop of a tree. The third room offers two twin

beds, a queen-size bed and a day bed, all dressed in coordinating fabrics. The homestay is close to Amish communities and the Elroy-Sparta Bicycle Trail.
Innkeeper(s): Bill & Marilyn Rice. $60-70. PC TC. 3 rooms. Breakfast included in rates. Types of meals: full breakfast and early coffee/tea. Beds: QT. Air conditioning in room. Antiques, fishing, parks, shopping, downhill skiing and cross-country skiing nearby.

Publicity: *Summer Fun.*

"We loved the peace and quiet of Whispering Pines."
Certificate may be used: Nov. 1-March 30, Sunday-Monday, seven days a week.

Wisconsin Dells   H5

Hawk's View
E11344 Pocahontas Circle
Wisconsin Dells, WI 53965
(608)254-2979 Fax:(608)254-2979

Circa 1985. From the grounds at this chalet, guests can walk down to a private beach area. The home overlooks the Wisconsin River, and two of the guest rooms boast water views. Most rooms are quite spacious. The Yester Year is more intimate, but includes antiques and a brass bed. The Forest's Edge is particularly roomy, with more than 1,000 square feet to enjoy. This suite includes a fireplace, kitchen area and a private deck. Another room includes a whirlpool tub. The adjacent cottage includes two bedrooms, a sitting room and bathroom. Ski areas, a casino and circus museum are among the nearby attractions.
Innkeeper(s): Carol Moeller. $65-99. MC VISA PC TC. 3 rooms with PB, 1 with FP. 1 cottage. Breakfast included in rates. Types of meals: full breakfast and early coffee/tea. Beds: KQDT. Air conditioning, ceiling fan and VCR in room. Fax and copier on premises. Amusement parks, antiques, fishing, parks, shopping, downhill skiing, cross-country skiing, golf, theater and watersports nearby.

"What a perfect get-a-way!"
Certificate may be used: Sunday-Thursday, Nov. 1-April 30, excluding holidays.

Historic Bennett House
825 Oak St
Wisconsin Dells, WI 53965-1418
(608)254-2500

Circa 1863. This handsomely restored Greek Revival-style home, framed by a white picket fence, housed the Henry Bennetts, whose family still operates the Bennett photographic studio, the oldest continuously operating studio in the country. Noted for the first stop-action photography, Mr. Bennett's work is displayed in the Smithsonian. The National Register home is decorated in European and Victorian styles. The grounds are decorated with sun and shade gardens.
Innkeeper(s): Gail & Rich Obermeyer. $70-90. PC TC. 3 rooms, 1 with PB. 1 suite. Breakfast included in rates. Types of meals: gourmet breakfast and early coffee/tea. Beds: QD. Air conditioning, ceiling fan, TV and

VCR in room. Library on premises. Amusement parks, antiques, fishing, parks, shopping, downhill skiing, cross-country skiing, theater and watersports nearby.
Publicity: *Midwest Living, Travel & Leisure, Country Life.*

"We have told everyone of your little paradise and we hope to visit again very soon."
Certificate may be used: October through May, Sunday through Thursday.

Terrace Hill B&B
922 River Rd
Wisconsin Dells, WI 53965-1423
(608)253-9363

Circa 1900. With a park bordering one edge and the Wisconsin River just across the street, Terrace Hill guests are treated to pleasant surroundings both inside and out. The interior is a cheerful mix of Victorian and country decor. The Park View suite includes a canopy bed and a clawfoot tub, other rooms offer views and cozy surroundings. There are barbecue grills and picnic tables available for guest use. The inn is just a block and a half from downtown Wisconsin Dells.
Innkeeper(s): Len, Cookie, Lenard & Lynn Novak. $45-110. PC TC. 4 rooms, 3 with PB. 1 suite. Breakfast, afternoon tea and evening snack included in rates. Types of meals: full breakfast and early coffee/tea. Beds: Q. Air conditioning in room. Cable TV, VCR and library on premises. Amusement parks, antiques, fishing, parks, shopping, downhill skiing, cross-country skiing, theater and watersports nearby.
Certificate may be used: Sept. 20 to June 30.

Wisconsin Dells Thunder Valley B&B Inn
W15344 Waubeek Rd
Wisconsin Dells, WI 53965-9005
(608)254-4145

Circa 1870. As the area is full of both Scandinavian and Native American heritage, and the innkeeper of this country inn has tried to honor the traditions. Chief Yellow Thunder, for whom this inn is named, often camped out on the grounds and surrounding area. The inn's restaurant is highly acclaimed. Everything is fresh, including the wheat the innkeepers grind for the morning pancakes and rolls. There is a good selection of Wisconsin beer and wine, as well. Guests can stay in the farmhouse, which offers a microwave and refrigerator for guest use, or spend the night in one of two cottages. The Guest Hus features gable ceilings and a knotty pine interior. The Wee Hus is a smaller unit, and includes a refrigerator.
Innkeeper(s): Anita, Kari & Sigrid Nelson. $45-80. MC VISA. 10 rooms with PB. 1 cottage. Breakfast included in rates. Type of meal: full breakfast. Beds: KQD. Air conditioning in room. Handicap access.
Publicity: *Wisconsin Trails, Country Inns, Midwest Living, Chicago Sun-Times.*

"Thunder Valley is a favorite of Firstar Club members — delicious food served in a charming atmosphere with warm Scandinavian hospitality"
Certificate may be used: November through May on Sunday to Friday, upon availability.

Wyoming

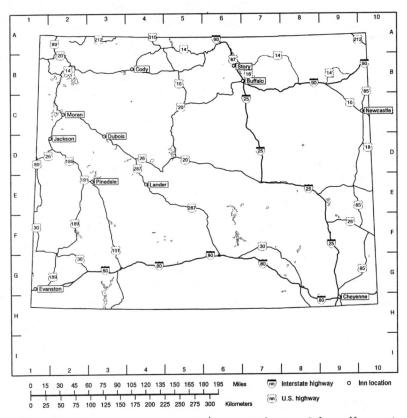

Buffalo
B7

Cloud Peak Inn
590 N Burritt Ave
Buffalo, WY 82834-1610
(307)684-5794 (800)715-5794 Fax:(307)684-7653

Circa 1906. Built at the turn of the century by a wealthy rancher, this inn features a graceful staircase, elegant parlor and spacious bedrooms. At the end of the day, guests can relax in front of the "fossilized" fireplace, soak in the Jacuzzi or unwind on the porch or balcony. Arrangements can be made for dinner although there are some excellent restaurants in the area. A fine golf course is only two blocks from the inn. The innkeepers will tell you about the secret fishing spots in the mountains that are sure bets. Geologic tours of the area can be arranged with prior notice.

Innkeeper(s): Rick & Kathy Brus. $45-75. MC VISA AX PC TC. 5 rooms, 3 with PB. 1 conference room. Breakfast, evening snack included in rates. Types of meals: full breakfast, gourmet breakfast, early coffee/tea. Banquet service, catering service available. Beds: KQDT. Ceiling fan in room. TV, VCR, fax, copier, spa, library on premises. Amusement parks, antiques, fishing, parks, shopping, skiing, watersports nearby.

Publicity: *Billings Gazette, Sheridan Press, Los Angeles Times.*

Certificate may be used: All year.

Cheyenne
H9

A. Drummonds Ranch B&B
399 Happy Jack Rd, Hwy 210
Cheyenne, WY 82007
(307)634-6042 Fax:(307)634-6042
E-mail: adrummond@juno.com

Circa 1990. With 120 acres of Wyoming wilderness and a nearby National Forest and State Park, this Old English-style farmhouse offers a quiet retreat. Private, outdoor Jacuzzis provide views of the sur-

rounding area and evening skies filled with stars. Some rooms include private entrances, window seats, a fireplace or a steam sauna. One unit is completely self-contained and includes a small kitchen. Homemade snacks, beverages and fresh fruit always are available for guests. Boarding is available for those traveling with horses and pets. A. Drummonds Ranch is located halfway between Cheyenne and Laramie. The University of Wyoming is nearby.

Innkeeper(s): Taydie Drummond. $60-150. MC VISA PC TC. 4 rooms, 2 with PB. 1 suite. Breakfast, afternoon tea and evening snack included in rates. Types of meals: full breakfast, gourmet breakfast and early coffee/tea. Dinner, picnic lunch and lunch available. Beds: QDT. Turndown service in room. VCR, fax, copier, sauna, bicycles, library, pet boarding and child care on premises. Fishing, parks, cross-country skiing, sporting events, theater and watersports nearby.

Certificate may be used: October-December, January-April, Monday nights through Thursday nights.

Adventurers' Country B&B
Raven Cry Ranch
3803 I-80 Service Rd
Cheyenne, WY 82001-9118
(307)632-4087 Fax:(307)635-6744

Circa 1985. Situated behind an adobe fence, this Southwestern-style inn rests on a knoll overlooking 102 acres of prairie. Guests enjoy the tree-lined adobe courtyard, flower gardens and a front veranda filled with rocking chairs and swings. The inn offers

murder-mystery weekends and a Western Adventure package. Weekly rodeos, a scenic rail excursion, and crystal and granite lakes are nearby.

Innkeeper(s): Fern White. $50-140. 5 rooms, 4 with PB, 1 with FP. 1 suite. Breakfast included in rates. Types of meals: full breakfast and early coffee/tea. Afternoon tea, dinner, evening snack, picnic lunch, lunch and room service available. Beds: KQ. Turndown service in room. Cable TV and VCR on premises. Antiques, parks, shopping, downhill skiing, cross-country skiing, sporting events and theater nearby.

"The service was superbly personalized with great attention to detail and a great down-home cowboy atmosphere."

Certificate may be used: All year, except July 18-31, based on availability; all months, any day of week.

Porch Swing
712 E 20th St
Cheyenne, WY 82001-3806
(307)778-7182 Fax:(307)778-7182
E-mail: porchswing@juno.com

At this Victorian inn, breakfast is served on the back porch in summer and by the dining room fire in cold weather. Guests can enjoy items like yeast waffles with maple syrup and fresh strawberries, orange pecan French toast and German pancakes with Swiss honey butter. All these recipes and more are found in the innkeepers' cookbook available for sale. The property's summer gardens are colorful and fragrant with a variety of perennials, aromatic and culinary herbs, wildflowers and annuals. The innkeepers would be happy to send you home with a cutting or seeds of something that's taken your fancy.

Innkeeper(s): Carole Eppler. $39-66. MC VISA. 3 rooms. Breakfast included in rates. Types of meals: full breakfast and early coffee/tea. Evening snack available. Cable TV and VCR on premises. Antiques, shopping, downhill skiing and sporting events nearby.

Certificate may be used: Anytime except last 10 days of July.

Cody
B4

Cody Guest Houses
1401 Rumsey Ave
Cody, WY 82414-3714
(307)587-6000 (800)587-6560 Fax:(307)587-8048

Circa 1906. As long as innkeepers Daren and Kathy Singer are in town, Cody's past will be preserved. This diligent couple have restored several historic local buildings, including the home of Cody's first mayor who later became a Wyoming governor. Extensive renovation was necessary on all of the guest houses, which include a 1906 Victorian home, two cottages and a brick home dating to 1926. The Mayor's Home, the Singer's latest addition, was purchased for $10 at auction and moved to its current location. It now includes three suites, each with a freshwater spa, and the first floor houses an antique shop, spa and cafe. Rooms are well-appointed in a variety of styles, from Victorian to Old West. Although breakfast is not included in the rates, guests are offered plenty of other amenities. Daily housekeeping, kitchens, laundry facilities, freshwater spas, fireplaces and in-room stereos, CD players and televisions are among the offerings.

Innkeeper(s): Kathy & Daren Singer. $50-250. MC VISA DS PC TC. 10 rooms with PB, 1 with FP. 8 suites. 3 cottages. 3 conference rooms. Catering service available. Beds: KQD. Air conditioning, ceiling fan, TV and VCR in room. Spa and library on premises. Antiques, fishing, parks, shopping, skiing, golf and watersports nearby.

Publicity: *Cody Enterprise.*

Certificate may be used: January-May and October-December.

The Lockhart B&B Inn

109 W Yellowstone Ave
Cody, WY 82414-8723
(307)587-6074 (800)377-7255 Fax:(307)587-8644

Circa 1890. Once the home of author and journalist Caroline Lockhart, this Victorian inn has beautiful mountain views from its veranda. The deck affords a view of the Shoshone River. Rooms are decorated with antiques, old-fashioned beds and a clawfoot tub. Breakfast is served on fine china at your private table in the dining room. Airport pick-up service is offered, as well as making reservations for dining, river rafting, golfing, rodeo events and more.

Innkeeper(s): Cindy Baldwin. $78-95. MC VISA DS. 7 rooms with PB. Breakfast included in rates. Type of meal: full breakfast. Picnic lunch available. Beds: QT. Air conditioning, ceiling fan, TV in room. Antiques, fishing, shopping, skiing, sporting events, theater, watersports nearby.

Publicity: *Glamour, AAA Today, National Geographic Traveler, Windsurf, New York Times, Houston Post, Los Angeles Times.*

"Just like going to grandma's house, like coming home to family — home away from home."

Certificate may be used: January-May, September-December.

Dubois
D3

Jakey's Fork Homestead

PO Box 635, 13 Fish Hatchery Rd
Dubois, WY 82513-0635
(307)455-2769

Circa 1896. Nestled on a hillside, this farmhouse-style inn overlooks the original turn-of-the-century log buildings and Jakey's Fork Creek, an unspoiled trout stream. This rustic home is heated by a wood stove and large brick fireplace. The rooms are decorated with mountain artwork and photography. Through the gardens and down the boardwalk are the original sod-covered homestead buildings. One of the buildings has been converted to a workshop where the innkeeper crafts unique handmade knives.

Innkeeper(s): Irene & Justin Bridges. $75-100. MC VISA PC TC. 3 rooms, 1 with PB. 1 cabin. Breakfast included in rates. Types of meals: full breakfast and early coffee/tea. Room service available. Beds: QDT. VCR, sauna and library on premises. Antiques, fishing, parks, shopping, downhill skiing, cross-country skiing and golf nearby.

"Our stay was beyond belief, our only complaint was that we had to leave."

Certificate may be used: Oct. 1-June 1, Monday-Friday.

Evanston
G1

Pine Gables Inn B&B

1049 Center St
Evanston, WY 82930-3432
(307)789-2069 (800)789-2069 Fax:(307)789-2787

Circa 1883. This Eastlake Victorian was built by A.V. Quinn, who ran the company store in town for the Union Pacific railroad. The rooms of this National Register home are filled with antiques, and the carved handmade beds are a highlight. The guest rooms are cheerful with romantic touches. One room features a beautiful antique bed decorated with a hint of ivy and bathroom with a pedestal sink and hand-stenciled walls. The inn's parlor is particularly inviting. Rich, rose-colored walls and white molding are enhanced by stenciling and an ornate ceiling. French doors lead out to the porch. In the mornings, guests feast on items such as waffles, omelets, quiche, fresh fruit and homemade muffins.

Innkeeper(s): Nephi & Ruby Jensen. $45-60. MC VISA AX DS PC TC. 4 rooms with PB, 1 with FP. Breakfast included in rates. Types of meals: full breakfast and early coffee/tea. Beds: QD. Ceiling fan and TV in room. Antiques, fishing, parks, shopping, cross-country skiing and golf nearby.

Certificate may be used: October to April.

Jackson
D2

H.C. Richards B&B

160 W Deloney
Jackson, WY 83001
(307)733-6704 Fax:(307)733-0930
E-mail: 102173.3657@compuserve.com

Circa 1969. Many afternoons at this ranch-style stone home are filled with the smells of baking scones, eccles cakes, crumpets or other special items from the large kitchen. Located just one-and-a-half

blocks west of the town square, the inn is within walking distance to many museums, art galleries, restaurants, theaters and shops. A tennis court, basketball court and park are just out the back door and skiing is a short six blocks away. The area is a paradise for outdoor enthusiasts, as the Grand Teton and Yellowstone national parks are nearby.
Innkeeper(s): Jackie Williams. $81-97. MC VISA PC TC. 3 rooms with PB. Breakfast and afternoon tea included in rates. Types of meals: full breakfast, gourmet breakfast and early coffee/tea. Room service available. Beds: QD. Turndown service and TV in room. VCR and fax on premises. Antiques, fishing, parks, shopping, downhill skiing, cross-country skiing, theater and watersports nearby.
Certificate may be used: April-May (excluding Memorial weekend), October and November.

Sassy Moose Inn
HC 362, Teton Village Rd
Jackson, WY 83001
(307)733-1277 (800)356-1277 Fax:(307)739-0793
E-mail: ckelley@wyoming.com

Circa 1992. All of the rooms at this log-house-style inn have spectacular Teton views. The Mountain Room has a rock fireplace, queen bed and mountain cabin decor. The River Room's decor is dominated by the colors of the Snake River and accented with antiques. The inn is five minutes from Teton Village and the Jackson Hole Ski Resort. Teton Pines Golf Course and Nordic Trails are just across the road. After a day of activities, enjoy sharing your experiences over tea or relaxing in the large hot tub.
Innkeeper(s): Polly Englant. $109-154. MC VISA AX DS. 5 rooms with PB, 4 with FP. 1 suite. Breakfast included in rates. Types of meals: full breakfast and early coffee/tea. Afternoon tea available. Beds: KQT. Cable TV, VCR, fax, copier, spa, pet boarding and child care on premises. Fishing, parks, shopping, downhill skiing, cross-country skiing, theater and watersports nearby.
Certificate may be used: Anytime except January-February and June-September.

Lander   E4

Piece of Cake B&B
PO Box 866, 2343 Baldwin Creek Rd
Lander, WY 82520-0866
(307)332-7608 (800)251-6080

Circa 1991. View roaming wildlife and the breathtaking Wind River Mountains from more than 1,000 square feet of deck attached to this lodge-style log home. Guest rooms include a Jacuzzi tub in a private bath. The inn is open year-round and winter guests can enjoy the Continental Divide Snowmobile Trail and the inn's 10,000 acres. In the summer, mountain bikes are available.
Innkeeper(s): Ed & Betty Lewis. $65-85. PC TC. 5 rooms with PB. 1 suite. 2 conference rooms. Breakfast and evening snack included in

rates. Types of meals: full breakfast, gourmet breakfast and early coffee/tea. Afternoon tea, dinner, picnic lunch, lunch, gourmet lunch, banquet service, catering service and room service available. Beds: QDT. Turndown service in room. VCR, fax, spa and pet boarding on premises. Antiques, fishing, parks, shopping, downhill skiing, cross-country skiing and watersports nearby.
Certificate may be used: March, April, October, November.

Moran   C2

The Inn at Buffalo Fork
18200 E Hwy 287, PO Box 311
Moran, WY 83013
(307)543-2010 (800)260-2010 Fax:(307)543-2010

This farmhouse with covered porch, shutters and gables has the incredible Teton Range as its backdrop. Herds of elk pass by and sandhill cranes visit this five-acre property, located in the heart of the Buffalo Valley ranch lands. Breakfast is served beside a rustic, river-rock hearth. The host has more than 25 years of experience guiding Snake River scenic tours and fishing expeditions. He is a lifelong resident, who is well-versed in the history and geography of the area, and also the grandson of one of the original Jackson Hole homesteaders.
Innkeeper(s): Jeannie Ferrin. $100-150. MC VISA AX. 5 rooms. 1 suite. Breakfast included in rates. Types of meals: full breakfast and early coffee/tea. Evening snack and picnic lunch available. Turndown service in room. Pet boarding and child care on premises. Downhill skiing, cross-country skiing and theater nearby.
Certificate may be used: Oct. 15-May 1, excluding holiday periods.

Diamond D Ranch-Outfitters
Buffalo Valley Rd, Box 211
Moran, WY 83013
(307)543-2479

Located on the scenic Buffalo Valley Road, this log house inn serves many purposes, including being an old hunting lodge, guest ranch, pack trip outfitter, cross-country skiing lodge, and snowmobile and base lodge for touring Yellowstone and Grand Teton national parks. There's a relaxed atmosphere with a flexible schedule. The main lodge has two units each with private baths, and the cabins have two units also with private baths. The staff teaches Western horsemanship and has horses for each guest's ability.
Innkeeper(s): Rod Doty. $99. 16 rooms. 2 suites. Breakfast included in rates. Type of meal: full breakfast. Dinner and lunch available. TV in room. Cross-country skiing nearby.
Certificate may be used: Oct. 31-May 15, Sunday through Thursday

Newcastle C10

EVA-Great Spirit Ranch B&B

1262 Beaver Creek Rd
Newcastle, WY 82701

(307)746-2537

E-mail: rspilln@trib.com

Circa 1985. Amidst spectacular scenery of mountains and woods, guests will find this modern log home. Although the home is new, it rests on what was an old stagecoach route. A century-old barn is located on the property, as well as ruins of a 19th-century bunkhouse. Although there are just two guest rooms, innkeeper Irene Spillane hopes to add several more. The interior features hardwood floors and high ceilings, and the guest rooms are comfortably furnished in a modern style. Irene offers fall hunting packages, where guests can search for deer, elk and turkey on the 525-acre property. The vast acreage borders Black Hills National Forest in South Dakota.
Innkeeper(s): Irene Spillane. $50-74. MC VISA PC TC. 2 rooms with PB. Breakfast included in rates. Type of meal: full breakfast. Beds: KQ. VCR, swimming, stables and library on premises. Handicap access. Antiques, fishing, parks, shopping, downhill skiing, cross-country skiing, golf and theater nearby.
Publicity: *News Letter Journal.*

"We enjoyed a very homely introduction to the wild west!"
Certificate may be used: Sept. 8-May 20 (Sunday-Saturday), discount does not apply to hunting.

Pinedale E3

Window on The Winds

10151 Hwy 191, PO Box 996
Pinedale, WY 82941

(307)367-2600 (888)367-1345 Fax:(307)367-2395

Circa 1968. At the base of the Wind River Mountains, this log house inn has lodgepole pine queen beds, down comforters and rustic furnishings. A grand room with a breathtaking view of the mountains offers a hearth for warmth and comfort. There is a sun room with a hot tub. Pinedale was the location for the Green River Rendezvous. In the early 1800s, trappers, traders, Indians and others in

the area would gather to trade goods. The Mountain Men and Indians of Pinedale re-enact the Rendezvous every year.
Innkeeper(s): Leanne McClain. $50-68. MC VISA PC TC. 4 rooms. 1 conference room. Breakfast and afternoon tea included in rates. Types of meals: full breakfast and early coffee/tea. Evening snack and picnic lunch available. Beds: QT. Cable TV, VCR, fax, copier, spa, stables and pet boarding on premises. Fishing, shopping, downhill skiing, cross-country skiing and watersports nearby.
Location: Wind River Mountains.
Certificate may be used: Sept. 1-May 31, all days of the week.

Story B6

Piney Creek Inn B&B

11 Skylark Ln, PO Box 456
Story, WY 82842

(307)683-2911

Circa 1956. There's an abundance of wildlife on the property of this secluded log-house-style inn nestled in the Big Horn Mountains. For the Old West buff, historic sites that are only minutes away include Fort Phil Kearny, Bozeman Trail, Little Big Horn Battlefield, numerous Indian battle sites and museums and galleries. Ranch experiences and trail ride packages are favorites. At the end of the day, relax

on the deck or in the common area, where visitors will find a television, books, magazines and games. Guests also can relax by the campfire for conversation and viewing the stars. Historical tours, ranch adventures and trail-ride packages are available.
Innkeeper(s): Vicky Hoff. $50-95. MAP. PC TC. 4 rooms, 2 with PB. 1 cottage. Breakfast and evening snack included in rates. Types of meals: continental breakfast, full breakfast and early coffee/tea. Dinner, picnic lunch and lunch available. Beds: KQDT. Ceiling fan in room. Cable TV, VCR, spa and library on premises. Handicap access. Antiques, fishing, shopping and theater nearby.
Certificate may be used: Nov. 1-April 30, excluding holidays.

Canada & U.S. Territories

PUERTO RICO — Ceiba

Ceiba Country Inn
PO Box 1067
Ceiba, PR 00735-1067
(809)885-0471 Fax:(809)885-0471
E-mail: prwilli@juno.com
Circa 1950. A large Spanish patio is available at this tropical country inn perched on rolling, green hills. Situated 500 feet above the valley floor, the

inn affords a view of the ocean with the isle of Culebra on the horizon. A continental buffet is served in the warm and sunny breakfast room. The inn is four miles from Puerto Del Rey, the largest marina in the Caribbean, and 10 miles from Luquillo Beach, which is a mile of white sand, dotted with coconut palms.
Innkeeper(s): Nicki Treat. $70. MC VISA AX DS TC. 9 rooms with PB. Breakfast included in rates. Type of meal: continental-plus breakfast. Beds: QT. Air conditioning in room. Cable TV, fax and library on premises. Handicap access. Fishing, shopping, golf and watersports nearby.
Certificate may be used: May-November.

VIRGIN ISLANDS — Saint Croix

Pink Fancy
27 Prince St
Saint Croix, VI 00820-5032
(809)773-8460 (800)524-2045 Fax:(809)773-6448
Circa 1780. Innkeepers George and Cindy Tyler strive to help guests enjoy their island visit. For those arriving in late afternoon or early evening, the Tylers can arrange to have a light snack or dinner waiting so guests can simply relax. Rental car pick-up and daily itineraries also can be arranged here. The inn was built in Dutch Colonial style and has been decorated in a tropical motif with ceiling fans. The rooms also include kitchenettes. There is a poolside happy hour each evening, and the innkeepers offer packages for honeymooners or those who wish to dive or snorkel.
Innkeeper(s): George & Cindy Tyler. $75-120. AP. MC VISA AX TC. 13 rooms with PB. Breakfast included in rates. Type of meal: continental-plus breakfast. Beds: KQT. Air conditioning, ceiling fan and TV in room. Fax and copier on premises. Antiques, fishing, parks, shopping and watersports nearby.
Certificate may be used: April 15 through Dec. 15.

BRITISH COLUMBIA — North Vancouver

Laburnum Cottage B&B
1388 Terrace Ave
North Vancouver, BC V7R 1B4
(604)988-4877 Fax:(604)988-4877
Set in one-half acre of beautifully kept English gardens, this country-style inn is surrounded by virgin forest, yet is only 15 minutes from downtown Vancouver. Afternoon tea is offered on the covered porch overlooking the award-winning gardens and meandering creek. In addition to the guest rooms, there are two self-contained cottages. Both cottages include a fireplace, kitchen facilities and a private bath. Check-in time is flexible and two major bus routes are only two blocks away.
Innkeeper(s): Delphine Masterton. $80-125. MC VISA. 6 rooms. 2 suites. Breakfast included in rates. Type of meal: full breakfast. Cable TV and VCR on premises. Shopping, skiing nearby.
Certificate may be used: November to April (low season) and non-legal holidays.

Peachland

Peach House B&B
4768A McLaughlan Pl
Peachland, BC V0H 1X0
(604)767-6546 (800)449-4133 Fax:(604)767-6546
Circa 1972. The Peach House is not just named so because of its Peachland location, but also the hue that decorates the exterior of the modern, ranch-style home. Each of the three guest rooms features an international theme, including English, Mexican and Egyptian. The breakfast menu varies and is always creative, with items such as whole wheat

peach pancakes or the unusual Chinese eggs. Guests also enjoy a lake view from the home, which is close to wineries, beaches, skiing and golf.

Innkeeper(s): Debra & Pauline Stepanow. $45-95. TC. 3 rooms with PB. 1 suite. Breakfast included in rates. Types of meals: full breakfast, gourmet breakfast and early coffee/tea. Beds: KQDT. Turndown service and ceiling fan in room. TV, VCR and fax on premises. Amusement parks, fishing, parks, shopping, skiing and watersports nearby.

"The best place ever. We will be back again! Thank you so much for an excellent two days."

Certificate may be used: Sept. 1-May 31, Sunday-Friday.

Sooke

Ocean Wilderness Country Inn
109 W Coast Rd, RR 2
Sooke, BC V0S 1N0
(250)646-2116 (800)323-2116 Fax:(250)646-2317

Circa 1940. The hot tub of this log house inn is in a Japanese gazebo overlooking the ocean. Reserve your time for a private soak, and terry bathrobes are supplied. The innkeepers are pleased to prepare picnic lunches and arrange fishing charters, nature walks and beachcombing.
Guests can enjoy
wonderful seafood
cookouts on Ocean
Wilderness beach.
Coffee is delivered
to your room a half
hour before break-
fast is served. Rooms
include antiques, sitting
areas and canopy beds. Two
of the rooms have hot tubs for two with spectacular ocean and Olympic Mountain views.

Innkeeper(s): Marion J. Rolston. $85-175. MC VISA AX TC. 9 rooms with PB. Breakfast included in rates. Types of meals: full breakfast and early coffee/tea. Picnic lunch and catered breakfast available. Beds: KQT. Fax and copier on premises. Handicap access. Amusement parks, antiques, fishing, parks, shopping and theater nearby.

Publicity: *Puget Sound Business Journal, Getaways from Vancouver.*

"Thank you for the most wonderful hospitality and accommodations of our entire vacation."

Certificate may be used: Oct. 1 to June 30.

Valemount

Rainbow Retreat B&B
PO Box 138
Valemount, BC V0E 2Z0
(604)566-9747

This authentically fashioned log cabin home rests beside an old fur-trader's route nestled in the Canadian Rockies and surrounded by woods. Guests are sure to see plenty of birds and wildlife, including

the occasional deer that march across the grounds. The innkeepers have kept the rustic touch, but added Victorian flair such as stained glass and a grand piano. Hearty breakfasts start off the day and gourmet dinners are made-to-order. The secluded retreat is just a few minutes from Mount Robson Provincial Park, and it's just a short walk to Fraser River, especially popular during the annual salmon spawning run.

Innkeeper(s): Keith Burchnall. $50-70. 2 rooms. Breakfast included in rates. Type of meal: full breakfast.

Certificate may be used: Anytime, except July and August.

Vancouver

The Manor Guest House
345 W 13th Ave
Vancouver, BC V5Y 1W2
(604)876-8494 Fax:(604)876-5763
E-mail: ManorGuestHouse@BC.sympatico.ca

Circa 1902. This turn-of-the-century Edwardian still features many original elements, including carved banisters, polished wood floors and ornate wainscoting. The home is one of the
city's oldest. The innkeeper
has decorated it with a collection of English
antiques. The penthouse
suite, which includes a
bedroom, loft, deck and
kitchen, boasts a view
of the city. Fresh
fruits, home-baked
breads and specialties
such as a cheese and
mushroom souffle or
blueberry cobbler
highlight the breakfast menu.

Innkeeper(s): Brenda Yablon. $65-125. MC VISA TC. 10 rooms, 6 with PB, 1 with FP. 1 suite. 1 conference room. Types of meals: full breakfast and gourmet breakfast. Beds: KQDT. TV in room. VCR, fax and copier on premises. Antiques, parks, shopping, downhill skiing, sporting events, theater and watersports nearby.

"We had a wonderful visit! I can't remember better breakfasts - truly memorable!"

Certificate may be used: Nov. 1-March 31, Sunday-Wednesday.

Vernon

Pleasant Valley B&B
4008 Pleasant Valley Rd
Vernon, BC V1T 4M2
(604)545-9504

Because of its central location, this Victorian inn is an ideal spot for outdoor enthusiasts to base their daily activities. The ski area of Silverstar Mountain is a 30-minute drive and two major lakes (Okanagan and Kalamalka) are 10 minutes from the inn. A fireplace in the living room brings warmth in the winter months, and an outdoor deck and hot tub are enjoyed year-round. The innkeeper can direct you to adventure travel packages and local wineries. Breakfasts can include a variety of quiche or stuffed French toast with peach sauce.

Innkeeper(s): Christine Somerville. $45-55. VISA. 3 rooms. Breakfast included in rates. Type of meal: full breakfast. Ceiling fan in room. Antiques, shopping, downhill skiing and cross-country skiing nearby.

Certificate may be used: Anytime, except for Canadian holiday weekends.

Victoria

Gregory's Guest House
5373 Patricia Bay Hwy
Victoria, BC V8Y 1S9
(250)658-8404 Fax:(250)658-4604

Circa 1919. The two acres of this historic hobby farm are just across the street from Elk Lake, six miles from Victoria near Butchart Gardens. All the rooms are decorated in antiques and duvets, and they feature garden and lake views. A traditional, full Canadian breakfast is served, and after the meal, guests can enjoy the hobby farm and animals or perhaps rent a boat at the lake.

Innkeeper(s): Paul & Elizabeth Gregory. $55-80. MC VISA PC TC. 3 rooms, 2 with PB. Breakfast included in rates. Type of meal: full breakfast. Beds: DT. Fax and library on premises. Antiques, fishing, parks, sporting events, theater and watersports nearby.

Location: On the east side of the highway, across from Elk Lake.

"Our family felt very welcome, loved the house and especially liked the super breakfasts."

Certificate may be used: Oct. 1-March 30. May not be used with other off-season specials.

Rose Cottage B&B
3059 Washington Ave
Victoria, BC V9A 1P7
(604)381-5985 Fax:(604)592-5221

The well-traveled hosts of this Folk-Victorian inn know the value their visitors place on a warm welcome. The innkeepers have plenty of inside information about Victoria to make your visit as adventurous or as relaxing as you want. The inn sits on a peaceful street close to downtown and a short distance from the Gorge Park Waterway. The decor includes large, high ceilings, period furniture, a guest parlor that boasts a nautical theme and a large dining room with library.

Innkeeper(s): Robert Bishop. $65-80. MC VISA. 3 rooms. Breakfast included in rates. Type of meal: full breakfast. Turndown service in room. Cable TV and VCR on premises. Antiques and shopping nearby.

Certificate may be used: Sept. 15 through May 31.

Whistler

Golden Dreams B&B
6412 Easy St
Whistler, BC V0N 1B6
(604)932-2667 (800)668-7055 Fax:(604)932-7055
E-mail: golden@whistler.net

Circa 1986. This private homestay boasts hearty vegetarian breakfasts that include homemade jam. The Victorian, Oriental and Aztec guest rooms feature duvets, sherry and slippers. Enjoy views of the mountains and the herb and flower gardens. There is a private Jacuzzi and a fireside family room, as well as a full guest kitchen. The home is a mile from ski lifts.

Innkeeper(s): Ann & Terry Spence. $65-105. MC VISA. 3 rooms, 1 with PB. 2 suites. Breakfast included in rates. Type of meal: gourmet breakfast. Catered breakfast available. Beds: QD. Ceiling fan in room. Cable TV, VCR, spa, bicycles, library and child care on premises. Fishing, parks, skiing, sporting events and watersports nearby.

"Great house, great food, terrific people."

Certificate may be used: April 15-June 15 and Sept. 15-Nov. 15, except holidays.

NEW BRUNSWICK — St. Andrews

Kingsbrae Arms
219 King St
St. Andrews, NB E0G 2X0
(506)529-1897 Fax:(506)529-1197
E-mail: kingbrae@nbnet.nb.ca

Circa 1897. A trip to this historic manor house is a bit like traveling to a welcoming English country estate. The five guest rooms and three suites have been decorated with the utmost of elegance. Each room has a fireplace, and beds are dressed with fine linens and puffy comforters. Guests might find a room with a canopy bed draped with velvet or perhaps a bath with a clawfoot tub, marble walls and a wood floor. For those who wish to relax, the library is a masculine retreat with a fireplace and dark, exposed wood beams. Guests also can take a swim in the outdoor, heated swimming pool. The innkeepers pamper you with a gourmet morning feast and tea in the afternoon. One also can arrange to enjoy a five-course dinner. The inn has a Canada Select five-star rating.

Innkeeper(s): Harry Chancey & David Oxford. $130-375. MC VISA PC. 8 rooms with PB, 8 with FP. 3 suites. 1 conference room. Breakfast, afternoon tea, evening snack included in rates. Types of meals: full breakfast, gourmet breakfast, early coffee/tea. Dinner, picnic lunch, lunch, gourmet lunch, banquet service, catered breakfast and room service available. Beds: KQ. Air conditioning, turndown service, ceiling fan, TV, VCR in room. Fax, copier, swimming, bicycles and library on premises. Antiques, fishing, parks, shopping, cross-country skiing, golf, watersports nearby.

Publicity: *Boston Globe, Atlantic Monthly, Canadian House & Home.*

Certificate may be used: All year, Monday-Thursday.

NOVA SCOTIA —
Liverpool

Lane's Privateer Inn & B&B
27-33 Bristol Ave, PO Box 509
Liverpool, NS B0T 1K0
(902)354-3456 (800)794-3332 Fax:(902)354-7220
Circa 1798. For more than 30 years, three generations of the Lane family have run this historic lodge
nestled among Nova Scotia's scenic coast and
forests. The inn is a participant in "A Taste of Nova
Scotia," which features a group of fine eateries that
meet strict government standards. Lane's hosts a
"Sip and Savour" series throughout the year, featuring wine tastings and gourmet meals. Breakfast at
the inn is a treat with specialty menus featuring
such items as haddock cakes and Eggs Benedict.
Nearby Kejimkujik National Park offers plenty of
outdoor activities, and beaches are only a few miles
away. Liverpool offers many fine shops and restaurants to enjoy.
Innkeeper(s): The Lane Family, Ron, Carol, Susan & Terry. $40-60. MC
VISA AX DC DS. 30 rooms, 27 with PB. Breakfast included in rates.
Afternoon tea, dinner, picnic lunch, lunch, catering service and room
service available. Restaurant on premises. Beds: QDT. Antiques, fishing,
cross-country skiing, theater and watersports nearby.
Publicity: *Encore Travel, Providence, Rhode Island News.*

"Warm and relaxed atmosphere!"
Certificate may be used: Oct. 15-May 15 (inclusive).

ONTARIO —
Alymer

Ye Olde Apple Yard B&B
RR 4
Alymer, ON N5H 2R2
(519)765-2708
This Italianate farmhouse is set on acres of secluded
countryside. Guests can stroll through the apple
orchard or simply relax with a picnic under the
trees. Romantic dinners for two can be arranged.
Guests can also enjoy the company of the resident
farm animals, or simply sit and relax by the fire-
place. The area offers many interesting shops and
Amish farms.
Innkeeper(s): Tino Smiaris. $60. 2 rooms. Breakfast included in rates.
Type of meal: full breakfast.
Certificate may be used: Monday to Thursday, Nov. 1-April 30.

Elora

Cedarbrook Farm B&B
RR 2
Elora, ON N0B 1S0
(519)843-3481
Circa 1876. A 100-acre working farm surrounds
this simple stone farmhouse where guests enjoy eat-
ing breakfast overlooking fields of cattle and
Arabian horses. A stream and trails on the property
may be explored or visit the nearby Mennonite
communities of Elmira and St. Jacobs. The town of
Elora and the Elora Gorge are a few minutes away.
Select a full or continental breakfast or choose a
vegetarian repast.
Innkeeper(s): M.I. Elste. $50. 2 rooms. Breakfast included in rates.
Types of meals: continental breakfast and full breakfast.

*"Very comfortable house, lovely countryside, thank you
for all of your hospitality."*
Certificate may be used: Nov. 1-April 30 all week; Sunday to
Wednesday balance of year.

Lakefield

Windmere
Selwyn, RR 3
Lakefield, ON K0L 2H0
(705)652-6292 (800)465-6327 Fax:(705)652-6949
Circa 1840. Windmere is a 100-acre working farm
set in the heart of the Kawartha Lakes. Joan and
Wally Wilkins' restored stone home, one of
Peterborough County's original homesteads, overlooks shaded grounds and a deep-water swimming
pond. Scottish stone
masons, brought to
Canada after the
War of 1812 to help
build the Rideau
Canal, built the
home. The
Wilkins' livestock
consists of Rob, the resident horse.
Innkeeper(s): Wallace Wilkins. $45-70. 3 rooms, 1 with PB. 1 suite.
Breakfast included in rates. Type of meal: full breakfast. Afternoon tea,
evening snack and picnic lunch available. Beds: DT. Air conditioning
and turndown service in room. Cable TV, VCR, fax and copier on
premises. Amusement parks, antiques, fishing, shopping, downhill skiing, cross-country skiing, theater and watersports nearby.

"Beautiful house and lovely people."
Certificate may be used: April-July, September-October, Monday to
Thursday.

Ottawa

Auberge McGee's Inn

185 Daly Ave
Ottawa, ON K1N 6E8
(613)237-6089 (800)262-4337 Fax:(613)237-6201
Circa 1886. The home was built for John McGee, Canada's first Clerk of Privy Council. The portico of this restored Victorian mansion is reminiscent of McGee's Irish roots featuring pillars that were common in Dublin architecture. Rooms are comfortable and decorated in soft, pleasing colors. Amenities such as mini-bars and mounted hair dryers add a touch of modern convenience. For extended stays, the inn provides the use of laundry facilities and a guest kitchenette. The innkeepers celebrate well over a decade of award-winning hospitality. Business travelers will appreciate items such as in-room phones with computer modem hook-ups and voice mail. There is no end to what guests can see and do in Ottawa. Visit the Byward Market, the many museums or the 230-store Rideau center.
Innkeeper(s): Anne Schutte & Mary Unger. $58-150. MC VISA. 14 rooms, 10 with PB, 3 with FP. 2 suites. 1 conference room. Breakfast included in rates. Type of meal: full breakfast. Beds: KQDT. Air conditioning and TV in room. Fax on premises. Antiques, parks, shopping, downhill skiing, cross-country skiing, sporting events, theater and watersports nearby.
Publicity: *Country Inns, Ottawa Citizen, LaPressee, Ottawa.*

"All we could ask for."

Certificate may be used: January, March, April, June, July, September to December; Monday-Thursday. Friday to Sunday, space permitting.

Rideau View Inn

177 Frank St
Ottawa, ON K2P 0X4
(613)236-9309 (800)658-3564 Fax:(613)237-6842
E-mail: rideau@istar.ca
Circa 1907. This large Edwardian home is located on a quiet residential street near the Rideau Canal. A hearty breakfast is served in the dining room. Guests are encouraged to relax in front of the fireplace in the living room.
Innkeeper(s): George Hartsgrove, Richard Brouse & Charles Young. $58-85. AP. MC VISA AX DC TC. 7 rooms, 2 with PB, 1 with FP. Breakfast included in rates. Type of meal: full breakfast. Beds: QDT. Air conditioning in room. Cable TV, VCR, fax and copier on premises. Antiques, parks, shopping, downhill skiing, cross-country skiing, sporting events and theater nearby.
Location: In the center of Ottawa.
Publicity: *Ottawa Citizen.*

Certificate may be used: Nov. 1-April 30, Sunday-Saturday.

Prince Edward Island — Charlottetown

Anne's Ocean View Haven B&B Inn

Box 2044, Kinloch Rd
Charlottetown, PE C1A 7N7
(902)569-4644 (800)665-4644 Fax:(902)569-4456
Circa 1986. Situated in a countryside setting with a panoramic view of Northumberland strait, this B&B offers quiet surroundings while being close to downtown. With both traditional and modern decor, the inn's guest rooms have sitting areas, refrigerators and four-piece baths. The island boasts beautiful, white sandy beaches and fertile red fields of potatoes. The beauty of the island attracts photographers from around the world and the many summer festivals provide much to do.
Innkeeper(s): R. Anne Olson. $70-120. 5 rooms with PB. 1 suite. Breakfast and picnic lunch included in rates. Type of meal: full breakfast. Dinner available. Beds: KQDT. Turndown service, TV and VCR in room. Fax, copier and child care on premises. Handicap access. Amusement parks, fishing, parks, shopping, cross-country skiing, sporting events, theater and watersports nearby.
Certificate may be used: Nov. 15-April 30.

Quebec — North Hatley

Cedar Gables

Box 355, 4080 Magog Rd
North Hatley, PQ J0B 2C0
(819)842-4120
Circa 1896. Bordering Lake Massiwippi, this gabled home boasts a wooded country setting. The inn's dock, canoes and rowboat are available to guests. Some bedrooms have lake views. Breakfast is served out on the veranda, weather permitting. The village is a five-minute walk from the inn.
Innkeeper(s): Ann & Don Fleischer. $80-104. MC VISA AX PC TC. 5 rooms with PB, 1 with FP. 1 suite. Breakfast and afternoon tea included in rates. Types of meals: continental-plus breakfast, gourmet breakfast and early coffee/tea. Catered breakfast available. Beds: K. TV and VCR in room. Swimming and library on premises. Handicap access. Antiques, fishing, parks, downhill skiing, cross-country skiing, sporting events, theater and watersports nearby.
Location: At lakeside on Lake Massiwippi in Quebec's eastern townships, 100 miles east of Montreal, 20 miles north of the Vermont-Quebec border.
Publicity: *Montreal Gazette.*

"We felt comfortable and at home the minute we stepped in the door."

Certificate may be used: Sunday-Thursday nights, generally mid-October through mid-May, with holiday exceptions.

Inns of Interest

African American History

Wingscorton Farm Inn . . .East Sandwich, Mass.
Munro House B&B . . . . .Jonesville, Mich.

Associated with Literary Figures

Ralph Waldo Emerson, Louisa May Alcott, Nathaniel Hawthorne
Hawthorne Inn . . . . .Concord, Mass..
F. Scott Fitzgerald, Thomas Wolfe
Welbourne . . . . .Middleburg, Va.
Jack London
Vichy Hot Springs Resort Inn . . . .Ukiah, Calif.
Becky Thatcher
Fifth Street Mansion B&B . . . . .Hannibal, Mo.
Mark Twain/Samuel Clemens
Vichy Hot Springs Resort & Inn . .Ukiah, Calif.
Fifth Street Mansion B&B . . . . .Hannibal, Mo.
Garth Woodside Mansion . . . . . .Hannibal, Mo.
Edith Wharton
The Gables Inn . . . . .Lenox, Mass.

Barns

Cornerstone B&B Inn . . . . . . .Landenberg, Pa.
Waitsfield Inn . . . . .Waitsfield, Vt.
Old Church House Inn . . . . . . .Mossville, Ill.

Civil War

The Mansion B&B . . . . .Bardstown, Ky.
La Vista Plantation . . . . . .Fredericksburg, Va..
The Sedgwick Inn . . . . .Berlin, N.Y.
Welbourne . . . . .Middleburg, Va.
A Touch of Country B&B . . .New Market, Va.

Cookbooks

Dairy Hollow House . . . . .Eureka Springs, Ark.
"Dairy Hollow House Cookbook"
"Dairy Hollow House Soup & Bread Cookbook"
The Old Yacht Club Inn . .Santa Barbara, Calif.
"The Old Yacht Club Inn Cookbook"
Sea Holly Inn . . . . .Cape May, N.J.
"Sea Holly Bed and Breakfast, A Sharing of Secrets"
Grandview Lodge . . . . .Waynesville, N.C.
"Recipes from Grandview Lodge"
The Durning House B&B and Tea Room
. . . . .Van Alstyne, Texas
"Hog Heaven"
Hill Farm Inn . . . . .Arlington, Vt.
"Recipes from the Kitchen of"
Sims-Mitchell House B&B . . . . .Chatham, Va.
"Waking Up Down South"
"Well Bless Your Heart,"Vols. I & II
"Butter'em While They're Hot"
Bombay House . . . . .Bainbridge Island, Wash.

"Breakfast with Bunny"
Ravenscroft Inn . . . . . .Port Townsend, Wash.
"Something's CookInn"

Farms and Orchards

Apple Blossom Inn B&B . . . .Ahwahnee, Calif.
Apple Lane Inn . . . . .Aptos, Calif.
Rockin' A B&B . . . . .Julian, Calif.
The Inn at Shallow Creek Farm . .Orland, Calif.
Living Spring Farm & Guest Ranch
. . . . .Platina, Calif.
Howard Creek Ranch . . . . . . .Westport, Calif.
Black Forest B&B . . . .Colorado Springs, Colo.
Maple Hill Farm . . . . .Coventry, Conn.
Kingston 5 Ranch B&B . . . . . . .Kingston, Id.
The Shaw House . . . . .Anamosa, Iowa
Lear Acres B&B . . . . .Bern, Kan.
Peaceful Acres B&B . . . . . . .Great Bend, Kan.
Canaan Land Farm B&B . . . .Harrodsburg, KY
Gilbert's B&B . . . . .Rehoboth, Mass.
Wingscorton Farm Inn . . . . .Sandwich, Mass.
Ellis River B&B . . . . .Jackson, N.H.
Vogt Farm B&B . . . . .Marietta, Pa.
Cedar Hill Farm . . . . .Mount Joy, Pa.
Field & Pine B&B . . . . .Shippensburg, Pa.
Dells B&B at Cedar Hill Farm
. . . . .Spruce Creek, Pa.
B&B at Skogland Farm . . . . . . .Canova, S.D.
Llano Grande Plantation . .Nacogdoches, Texas
Hill Farm Inn . . . . .Arlington, Vt.
Historic Brookside Farms . . . . . . .Orwell, Vt.
Liberty Hill Farm . . . . .Rochester, Vt.
Deep Meadow Farm B&B . .Deer Harbor, Wash.

Gold Mines & Gold Panning

Pearson's Pond Luxury Inn . . . .Juneau, Alaska.
Julian Gold Rush Hotel . . . . .Julian, Calif.
Dunbar House 1880 . . . . .Murphys, Calif.
Old Blewett Pass B&B . . . .Leavenworth, Wash.

Hot Springs

Vichy Hot Springs Resort & Inn . .Ukiah, Calif.

Inns Built Prior to 1799

1678 Hewick Plantation . . . . . . .Urbanna, Va.
1690 The Great Valley House of Valley Forge
. . . . .Malvern, Pa.
1700 Hacienda Vargas . . . . . .Algodones, N.M.
1700 Hollileif B&B . . . . .Newtown, Pa.
1704 Stumble Inne . . .Nantucket Island, Mass.
1709 The Woodbox Inn
. . . . .Nantucket Island, Mass.
1714 Hartwell House . . . . . . .Ogunquit, Maine
1720 Butternut Farm . . . . .Glastonbury, Conn.

1725 Witmer's Tavern - Historic 1725 Inn
. . . . .Lancaster, Pa.
1731 Maple Hill Farm B&B . .Coventry, Conn.
1732 The Cookie Jar B&B . . . .Wyoming, R.I.
1734 Joseph Ambler Inn . . . .North Wales, Pa.
1738 Brown's Historic Home B&B .Salem, N.J.
1738 Herr Farmhouse Inn . . . . .Manheim, Pa.
1739 The Ruffner House . . . . .Luray, Va.
1740 Red Brook Inn . . . . .Mystic, Conn.
1740 Henry Ludlam Inn . . . . . .Woodbine, N.J.
1740 Evermay-on-the-Delaware . . .Erwinna, Pa.
1740 Barley Sheaf Farm . . . . . .Holicong, Pa.
1743 The Inn at Mitchell House
. . . . .Chestertown, Mary.
1750 House on the Hill B&B
. . . .Lake George/Warrensburg, N.Y.
1750 Melville House . . . . .Newport, R.I.
1753 L'Auberge Provencale . . .White Post, Va.
1756 Bee and Thistle Inn . . .Old Lyme, Conn.
1759 Ira Allen House . . .Arlington, Vt.
1760 The Winchester Country Inn
. . . . .Westminster, Mary.
1760 Henry Ludlam Inn . . . . . .Woodbine, N.J.
1760 Gilbert House B&B of Middleburn
. . . . .Charles Town, W.V.
1763 Colonel Spencer Inn . . . .Plymouth, N.H.
1765 Bankhouse B&B . . . . .West Chester, Pa.
1767 Highland Lake Inn B&B
. . . . .East Andover, N.H.
1772 The Bagley House . . . . .Durham, Maine
1775 Colonel Roger Brown House
. . . . .Concord, Mass.
1775 Kanaga House B&B
. . . . . . .Harrisburg/N. Kingston, Pa.
1775 Welbourne . . . . .Middleburg, Va.
1776 The Inn at Chester . . . . .Chester, Conn.
1778 Staffords-in-the-Field . . .Chocorua, N.H.
1779 Miles River Country Inn .Hamilton, Mass.
1785 The 1785 Inn . . . .North Conway, N.H.
1786 Kenniston Hill Inn . . .Boothbay, Maine
1786 The Wayside Inn
. . . . .Greenfield Center, N.Y.
1787 The Lords Proprietors' Inn .Edenton, N.C.
1789 The Hancock Inn . . . . . .Hancock, N.H.
1789 Longswamp B&B . . . . . . .Mertztown, Pa.
1789 Historic Brookside Farms . . . .Orwell, Vt.
1790 Silvermine Tavern . . . . .Norwalk, Conn.
1790 Fairhaven Inn . . . . .Bath, Maine
1790 Crown 'N' Anchor . . . .Newcastle, Maine
1790 Tuck Inn . . . . .Rockport, Mass.
1790 Olde Orchard Inn . .Moultonboro, N.H.
1790 Pheasant Field B&B . . . . . . .Carlisle, Pa.
1790 Field & Pine B&B . . . .Shippensburg, Pa.

528

1790 1790 House . . . . .Georgetown, S.C.
1790 Hill Farm Inn . . . . .Arlington, Vt.
1790 Silver Maple Lodge & Cottages
. . . . .Fairlee, Vt.
1790 Shoreham Inn & Country Store
. . . . .Shoreham Village, Vt.
1790 Lareau Farm Country Inn .Waitsfield, Vt.
1790 Red Shutter Farmhouse B&B
. . . . .New Market, Va.
1791 St. Francis Inn . . . .Saint Augustine, Fla.
1791 The Sedgwick Inn . . . . . . .Berlin, N.Y.
1793 Cove House . . . . .Kennebunkport, Maine
1794 The Inn at Maplewood Farm
. . . . .Hillsboro, N.H.
1795 Canaan Land Farm B&B
. . . . .Harrodsburg, Ky.
1795 The Acorn Inn . . . . . .Canadaigua, N.Y.
1795 Maplewood Inn . . . . .Fair Haven, Vt.
1795 Spring Farm B&B . . . . .Luray, Va.
1796 National Pike Inn . . .New Market, Mary.
1797 Sanford's Ridge B&B . .Queensbury, N.Y.
1797 Bay View Waterfront B&B
. . . . .Belle Haven, Va.

Jail House

Casa de Patron . . . . .Lincoln, N.M.

Lighthouses

The Keeper's House . . . . .Isle Au Haut, Maine
Big Bay Point Lighthouse B&B
. . . . .Big Bay, Mich.

Llama Ranches

Canaan Land Farm B&B . . . .Harrodsburg, Ky.
Rockhouse Mountain Farm Inn
. . . . .Eaton Center, N.H.

Log Houses/Cabins

Ocean Wilderness Country Inn
. . . . .Sooke, British Columbia
Old Carson Inn . . . . .Lake City, Colo.
The Log House . . . . .Russellville, Ky.
Lindgren's B&B . . . . .Lutsen, Minn.
Trout House Village Resort . . . . . .Hague, N.Y.
Inn at Cedar Falls . . . . .Logan, Oh.
The Inn at Burg's Landing
. . . . .Anderson Island, Wash.

Old Mills

Lodge at Manuel Mill . . . . .Arnold, Calif.
Silvermine Tavern . . . . .Norwalk, Conn.
Arbor Rose B&B . . . . .Stockbridge, Mass.
Asa Ransom House . . . . .Clarence, N.Y.

Old Taverns

Red Brook Inn . . . . .Old Mystic, Conn.
Silvermine Tavern . . . . .Norwalk, Conn.
Witmer's Tavern-Historic 1725 Inn
. . . . .Lancaster, Pa.

Oldest Continuously Operated Inns

Historic National Hotel B&B
. . . . .Jamestown, Calif.

Julian Gold Rush Hotel . . . . .Julian, Calif.
Florida House Inn . . . . . .Amelia Island, Fla.
The Bellevue House . . . . . . .Block Island, R.I.

Ranches

Random Oaks Ranch . . . . .Julian, Calif.
Howard Creek Ranch . . . . . . .Westport, Calif.
The Lazy Ranch B&B . . . . . . .Edwards, Colo.
Pinehurst Inn at Jenny Creek . . . .Ashland, Ore.
Wine Country Farm . . . . .Dayton, Ore.

Revolutionary War

Colonel Roger Brown House . . .Concord, Mass.
Village Green Inn . . . . .Falmouth, Mass.
The Melville House . . . . .Newport, R.I.
Willow Grove Inn . . . . .Orange, Va.

Schoolhouses

The Bagley House . . . . .Durham, Maine
Old Sea Pines Inn . . . . .Brewster, Mass.
School House B&B . . . . .Rocheport, Mo.

Space Shuttle Launches

The Higgins House . . . . .Sanford, Fla.

Stagecoach Stops

Maple Hill Farm B&B Inn . . .Hallowell, Maine
The Inn at Bingham School . .Chapel Hill, N.C.
Mountain Home B&B . .Mountain Home, N.C.
Bowling Green Inn B&B . .Jonesborough, Tenn.
Inn at Blush Hill . . . . .Waterbury, Vt.

Still in the family

Crystle's B&B . . . . .Concordia, Kan.
The Sherwood Inn . . . . .New Haven, Vt.
Cedarcroft Farm B&B . . . . .Warrensburg, Mo.
Line Limousin Farmhouse B&B . . . .Carlisle, Pa.
Hasse House and Ranch . . . . . .Mason, Texas
Bay View Waterfront B&B . . .Belle Haven, Va.
Welbourne . . . . .Middleburg, Va.
Hewick Plantation . . . . .Urbanna, Va.

Three-seat Outhouse

Maple Hill Farm B&B . . . . . .Coventry, Conn.

Train Stations & Renovated Rail Cars

The Inn at Depot Hill
. . . . .Capitola-by-the-Sea, Calif.
Trout City Inn . . . . .Buena Vista, Colo.
Mountain Meadows Inn B&B . .Ashford, Wash.

Tunnels, Secret Passageways, Caves

Wingscorton Farm . . . . .East Sandwich, Mass.
Munro House B&B . . . . .Jonesville, Mich.
Colonel Spencer Inn . . . . . . .Plymouth, N.H.
Witmer's Tavern-Historic 1725 Inn
. . . . .Lancaster, Pa.
Lynchburg Mansion Inn . . . . .Lynchburg, Va.

Unusual Architecture

The Oscar Swan Country Inn . . . .Geneva, Ill.

Unusual Sleeping Places

In a winery
Cavender Castle Winery . . .Dahlonega, Georgia
50 yards from reversing whitewater rapids
The Weskeag Inn . . . . .South Tomaston, Maine
On or next to an archaelogical dig site
The White Oak Inn . . . . .Danville, Ohio
Hewick Plantation . . . . .Urbanna, Va.

Waterfalls

Sycamore Tree B&B . . . . .Blacksburg, Va.

Who Slept/Visited Here

John Adams
Witmer's Tavern-Historic 1725 Inn
. . . . .Lancaster, Pa.
John James Audubon
Weston House . . . . .Eastport, Maine
The Barrymore family
Evermay-on-the-Delaware . . . . . . .Erwinna, Pa.
Henry Bennett, photographer
Historic Bennett House . .Wisconsin Dells, Wis.
Sarah Bernhardt, Lillie Langtry
"An Elegant Victorian Mansion" .Eureka, Calif.
Billy the Kid
Casa de Patron . . . . .Lincoln, N.M.
Billy the Kid, Doc Holliday, Big Nose Katy
Plaza Hotel . . . . .Las Vegas, N.M.
Clark Gable, Carole Lombard
Gold Mountain Manor Historic B&B
. . . . .Big Bear, Calif.
Herbert Hoover
The Carriage House at Stonegate
. . . . .Montoursville, Pa.
Kellogg family
Village Country Inn . . .Manchester Village, Vt.
Jack London, Mark Twain, Theodore Roosevelt
Vichy Hot Springs Resort & Inn . .Ukiah, Calif.
Mary Pickford, Gloria Swanson, Douglas Fairbanks, Clark Gable
Esmeralda Inn . . . . .Chimney Rock, N.C.
Eleanor Roosevelt
Mulberry Inn B&B . . . . . .Martins Ferry, Ohio
Theodore Roosevelt
Vichy Hot Springs Resort & Inn . .Ukiah, Calif.
Lillian Russell
Bayview Hotel B&B Inn . . . . . . .Aptos, Calif.
Babe Ruth
Cranmore Mt. Lodge . . . .North Conway, N.H.
William Seward
The William Seward Inn . . . . . .Westfield, N.Y.
Martin Van Buren
Old Hoosier House . . . . . . .Knightstown, Ind.
Woodrow Wilson, Grover Cleveland
The Cordova . . . . .Ocean Grove, N.J.
Woolworth family, Barbara Hutton, Cary Grant
The Mulburn Inn . . . . .Bethlehem, N.H.

Publications From American Historic Inns

Bed & Breakfast and Country Inns, Ninth Edition

By Deborah Sakach

Imagine the thrill of receiving this unique book with its FREE night certificate as a gift. Now you can let someone else experience the magic of America's Country Inns with this unmatched offer. *Bed &*

Breakfasts and Country Inns is the most talked about guide among inngoers.

This fabulous guide features more than 1,600 Inns from across the United States and Canada. Best of all, no other "bookstore" guide offers a FREE night certificate.* This certificate can be used at any one of the Inns featured in the guide.

American Historic Inns, Inc. has been publishing books about Bed & Breakfasts since 1981. Its books and the FREE night offer have been recommended by many travel writers and editors, and featured in: *The New York Times, Washington Post, Boston Globe, Chicago Sun Times, USA Today, Good Housekeeping, Cosmopolitan, Consumer Reports* and more.

*With purchase of one night at the regular rate required. Subject to limitations.

539 pages, paperback, 500 illustrations. **Price $21.95**

The Official Guide to American Historic Inns
Completely Revised and Updated, Sixth Edition

By Deborah Sakach

Open the door to America's past with this fascinating guide to Historic Inns that reflect our colorful heritage. From Dutch Colonials to Queen Anne Victorians, these Bed & Breakfasts and Country Inns offer experiences of a lifetime.

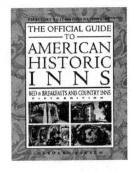

This special edition guide includes certified American Historic Inns that provide the utmost in hospitality, beauty, authentic restoration and preservation. Inns have been carefully selected so as to provide readers with the opportunity to visit genuine masterpieces.

With Inns dating back to as early as 1637, this guide is filled with treasures waiting to be discovered. Full descriptions, illustrations, guest comments and recommendations are all included to let you know what's in store for you before choosing to stay at America's Historic Inns.

528 pages, paperback, 800 illustrations. **Price $15.95**

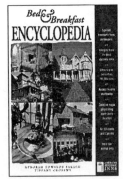

The Bed & Breakfast Encyclopedia

By Deborah Edwards Sakach & Tiffany Crosswy

Our latest creation! This massive guide is the most comprehensive guide on the market today. Packed with detailed listings to more than 2,000 bed & breakfasts and country inns, the Encyclopedia also includes an index to an additional 13,000 inns, detailed state maps and more than 900 illustrations. Recipes, helpful phone numbers, information about reservation services and informative articles about bed & breakfast hot spots, the best bed & breakfasts, inns of interest, how to start your own B&B and much, much more.

If you're planning a getaway, this all-inclusive guide is a must!

960 pages, paperback **Price $16.95**

the Road Best Traveled – Monthly Newsletter

Here's the only way to make sure you don't get left out of the latest Bed & Breakfast and Country Inn promotions. This travel newsletter is packed with information about more FREE night offers, huge discounts on lodgings and family vacation opportunities.

And that's not all! *The Road Best Traveled* is your one-stop travel shopping source to help you plan your next vacation. This outstanding publication includes the latest hotel bargains, methods to get the cheapest air fare, unbelievable cruise deals and affordable excursion packages to exotic and far off places.

Wait, there's more! As a special offer to readers of this book, you'll receive a special edition of *Bed & Breakfasts and Country Inns* FREE with your subscription. This book includes a FREE night certificate! A great gift for a friend or another FREE night for you!

One-year subscription (12 issues) (Reg. $48.00)   Special price $39.95
Special two-year subscription (Reg. $96.00)   Special price $69.95

Bed & Breakfast and Country Inn Travel Club Membership From American Historic Inns, Inc.

SAVE! SAVE! SAVE! We offer an exclusive discount club that lets you enjoy the excitement of Bed & Breakfast and Country Inn travel again and again. As a member of this once-in-a-lifetime offer you'll receive benefits that include savings of 25% to 50% off every night's stay!

Your membership card will entitle you to tremendous savings at some of the finest Inns in America. Members receive a guide with more than 1,100 Bed & Breakfasts and Country Inns to choose from. Plan affordable getaways to Inns nearby or visit an area of the country you've always wanted to experience.

The best part of being an American Historic Inns Travel Club Member is that the card can be used as many times as you like.

In addition to your card, you will get a FREE night's stay certificate—truly a club membership that's hard to pass up!

That's not all! Sign up for a charter membership now and receive a sample issue of *The Road Best Traveled*, the only monthly newsletter that keeps you up to date on all of the latest Bed & Breakfast and Country Inn promotions. Not only will you find out about saving on inn stays, but you will also find travel bargains on air fares, car rentals, cruises, vacation packages and more.

All travel club members receive:

- Travel club card entitling holder to 25% to 50% off lodging.
- FREE night's stay certificate.
- Guide to more than 1,100 participating Inns across America.
- Sample issue of *The Road Best Traveled*, a monthly newsletter with discount updates.

Membership is good for one year. Free night's stay with purchase of one night at the regular rate. Discount and certificate cannot be combined.

Introductory price with full benefits (Reg. $59.95) $49.95

How To Start & Run Your Own Bed & Breakfast Inn

By Ripley Hotch & Carl Glassman

In this book you'll discover the secrets of the best Inns. Learn how to decide whether owning or leasing an Inn is right for you. Find out what business strategies characterize a successful Inn and learn how to incorporate them in your own business.

If you've always dreamed of owning a Bed & Breakfast, then this book is for you!

182 pages, paperback.   Price $14.95

AMERICAN HISTORIC INNS INCORPORATED

PO Box 669
Dana Point
California
92629-0669
(714) 499-8070
Fax (714) 499-4022

Order Form

Date: _ _ / _ _ / _ _   Shipped: _ _ / _ _ / _ _

Name: _____

Street: _____

City/State/Zip: _____

Phone: (_ _ _) _ _ _ - _ _ _ _

QTY.	Prod. No.	Description	Amount	Total
_____	AHI9	Bed & Breakfasts and Country Inns	$21.95	_____
_____	AHIH6	The Official Guide to American Historic Inns	$15.95	_____
_____	AHIE1	Bed & Breakfasts Encyclopedia	$16.95	_____
_____	AHIN1	The Road Best Traveled Newsletter (one year; includes free-night guide and Shipping)	$39.95	_____
_____	AHIN2	The Road Best Traveled Newsletter (two years; includes free-night guide and Shipping)	$69.95	_____
_____	AHIC2	Bed & Breakfast and Country Inn Travel Club (Includes sample issue of The Road Best Traveled)	$49.95	_____
_____	CB03	How to Start Your Own B&B	$14.95	_____
		Subtotal		_____
		California buyers add 7.75% sales tax		_____
		Shipping and Handling on Book and Travel Club Orders 4th Class Book Rate (10-20 days): $2.25 for the first book. 75¢ each additional copy. Priority Mail (2-4 days): $3.75 for one copy. $5.50 – two copies. $6.50 – three copies.		_____
		TOTAL		_____

❏ Check/Money Order   ❏ Mastercard   ❏ Visa   ❏ American Express

Account Number _   Exp. Date _ _ / _ _

Name on card _____

Signature _____

INN EVALUATION FORM

Please copy and complete this form for each stay and mail to the address shown. Since 1981 we have maintained files that include thousands of evaluations from inngoers who have sent this form to us. This information helps us evaluate and update the inns listed in this guide.

Name of Inn: _____

City and State: _____

Date of Stay: _____

Your Name: _____

Address: _____

City/State/Zip: _____

Phone: (_ _ _) _ _ _ – _ _ _ _

Please use the following rating scale for the next items.
1: Outstanding.   2: Good.   3: Average.   4: Fair.   5: Poor.

Location	1	2	3	4	5
Cleanliness	1	2	3	4	5
Food Service	1	2	3	4	5
Privacy	1	2	3	4	5
Beds	1	2	3	4	5
Bathrooms	1	2	3	4	5
Parking	1	2	3	4	5
Handling of reservations	1	2	3	4	5
Attitude of staff	1	2	3	4	5
Overall rating	1	2	3	4	5

Comments on Above: _____

_____

_____

_____

_____

MAIL THE COMPLETED FORM TO:
American Historic Inns, Inc.
PO Box 669
Dana Point, CA 92629-0669
(714) 499-8070

Finally, a card for Bed & Breakfast and Country Inn travelers!

Take a good look at what the American Historic Inns™ MasterCard® card has to offer:

No Annual Fee

❖❖

A Buy-One-Night-Get-One-Night-Free Certificate worth up to $200 or more, valid when you stay at a participating Bed & Breakfast.

❖❖

A complimentary 96-page edition of *Bed & Breakfast and Country Inns*.

❖❖

A complimentary copy of *The Road Best Traveled*™, a monthly travel newsletter featuring the best Bed & Breakfast bargains, special events and packages.

❖❖

An option to join the American Historic Inn Bed & Breakfast and Country Inn Travel Club™ as a charter member at a discounted fee of only $20. (Annual travel club price is $59.95.) This club offers members up to 50% off at participating inns.

❖❖

Additional travel benefits through GoldPassage® Travel Service. ❖

❖❖

Issued through MBNA America Bank, N.A., the MasterCard is welcome at more than 11 million locations worldwide, including country inns, B&Bs, restaurants and retail shops.

Inn-dulge yourself, request the American Historic Inns MasterCard, today! To apply call MBNA at

1-800-847-7378
and mention code SAST.

*Certain restrictions apply to these and other benefits described in the Benefits Brochure and Guide to Coverage that are sent shortly after your account is opened.

GoldPassage Travel Services are the responsibility of and are provided to MBNA® Customers by an independently owned and operated travel agency.

American Historic Inns and *The Road Best Traveled* are trademarks of American Historic Inns, Inc.

MBNA America and GoldPassage are federally registered service marks of MBNA America Bank, N.A. MasterCard is a federally registered service mark of MasterCard International, Inc., used pursuant to license.

©1995 MBNA America Bank, N.A.